# *What they're saying about*

# Leggetts' Antiques Atlas™

*"Antique lovers should check out* **The Antiques Atlas,** *a listing of more than 15,000 shops in 48 states. The book includes reviews & travel maps."*

**Jerry Shriver, *USA Today***

*"This book certainly fills a void in the antique business."*

**Terry Kovel, *Kovels on Antiques & Collectibles***

*"**The Antiques Atlas** has it all - an exhaustive state-by-state guide to shops, lodging, and even entertainment along with excellent regional maps. How did we ever live without it?"*

***New England Antiques Journal***

*"It's the perfect gift for a friend who just can't say no to collecting."*

***Country Accents Magazine***

*"564 pages that you should spread out on the dining table when you're planning your road trip."*

***Maine Antique Digest* Staff**

*"**The Atlas** makes the entire antique-hunting effort an experience to savor and enjoy."*

**Anita Kerba, *Antique Trader Weekly***

*"This roundup of antiques shops all over the country will be popular with collectors always looking for a new shop to prowl around in."*

**Mark Marymont, *St. Louis News-Leader***

*"There's nothing worse than being somewhere unfamiliar and not knowing where all the antiques in town are. That's why **The Atlas** is so handy."*

**Nancy A. Ruhling, *Victorian Homes Magazine***

*"An ideal travel companion as you hit the road for antiques."*

**Ed Klimuska, *Lancaster, PA, New Era***

*"The bible of unusual and rare articles."*

**Fred Petrucelli, *Log Cabin Democrat***

*"It's a shopper's dream guide."*

**Ken Moore, *Naples Daily News***

*"**Antiques Atlas**: A treasure map, the most complete listing anywhere at this moment."*

**Barbara Hertenstein, *St. Louis Post-Dispatch***

*"**The Atlas**" makes life easy for antique hunters. You'll wonder how you ever did without it."*

**Ed Conrad, *Standard Speaker, PA***

*"The most comprehensive guide to antiquing in America."*

**Bob Milne, *Travelwriter Marketletter***

*"Even if you are not into antiques big time, this guide is still most interesting just to have around and look through."*

**Edith Smith, *The Valdosta Daily Times***

*"Up to now, we've had to depend on signs, area brochures and, if we're lucky, state and regional guides to point us toward antiques in unexplored territory. Now some enterprising dealers have come up with a book no collector should leave home without **"The Antiques Atlas**."*

**Peggy Welch Mershon, *About Antiques, Mansfield News Journal***

*"This isn't one **(The Antiques Atlas)** just to browse through at the bookstore, it's one to carry around everywhere you go."*

**Shanna Wiggens, *Argus Observer***

# *Leggetts' Antiques Atlas*™

*1999 Edition*

by Kim and David Leggett

Foreword by Ralph and Terry Kovel

THREE RIVERS PRESS
NEW YORK

Published by Three Rivers Press, a division of Crown Publishers, Inc., 201 East 50th Street, New York, New York 10022. Member of the Crown Publishing Group.

Random House, Inc. New York, Toronto, London, Sydney, Auckland
www.randomhouse.com



Printed in the United States of America

Library of Congress Cataloging-in-Publication Data
Leggetts' antiques atlas : 1999 edition / Kim and David Leggett ;
foreword by Ralph and Terry Kovel. – Rev. ed.
p. cm.
Originally published in different format by Rainy Day Pub. ,
c1997.

1. Antique dealers – United States – Directories. I. Leggett,
David. II. Title.
NK1127.L43 1999
745.1'025'73 – dc21 98-34759
CIP

ISBN 0-609-80394-8 (pbk.)

10 9 8 7 6 5 4 3 2 1

Revised Edition

# Dedication

This book is dedicated to a special person known only to us as "K." On November 30, 1996, we received the following message enclosed in a Christmas card. The return address offered no further indication as to the identity of this mysterious messenger.

It arrived on a particular day when we were extremely anxious over the outcome of *The Antique Atlas*, 1997 edition. Uncertain of its future and the impact in which it would have upon our lives, this message seemed to put everything into proper perspective.

## One Solitary Life

The first Christmas card of the season arrived today — early, and I am glad, for it reminds me of what the holidays ahead really mean. The message, "One Solitary Life" (author unknown) is a traditional greeting, but its words, like those of the Savior's birth, ring the bells of love.

"Here is a man who was born in an obscure village, the child of a peasant woman ... He worked in a carpenter shop ... and then He was an itinerant preacher. He never wrote a book ... held an office ... owned a home ... had a family ... went to college ... put His foot inside a big city ... traveled two hundred miles from the place where He was born. He had nothing to do with this world except for the power of His divine manhood. While still a young man, the tide of popular opinion turned against Him ... friends ran away ... one denied Him. He was turned over to His enemies ... went through the mockery of a trial ... was nailed upon a cross between two thieves.

"Nineteen wide centuries have come and gone and today He is the centerpiece of the human race and the leader of progress ... and all the navies that ever were built ... parliaments that ever sat ... kings that ever reigned, put together, have not affected the life of man upon this earth as powerfully as this One solitary life."

Jesus must have had "solitary" feelings, for surely He must have often been lonely. He was rebuked, doubted and denied. We know with Christian certainty that He is no longer lonely, having gone to join His Father; but we know also that there are others around us who feel rejected: in need of the peace and love Jesus offered to the world. I shall try to carry with me the message of joy and feelings of hope that were born within me again — with the arrival of a first Christmas card.

# Contents

# Foreword

Of course, we are always looking for that out-of-the-way shop filled with unrecognized treasures, that $1,000 vase priced $75. But when does it pay to leave the turnpike and go off into a small town to visit the shops? Local dealers often have brochures listing nearby antiques stores, the farm papers sometimes include a section on shopping for antiques, and the dealers are usually happy to lead us to the next area with stores. But we need more.

The *Leggetts' Antiques Atlas* is the first large national guide book that recognizes the problems of the out-of-state shopper searching for antiques. It has maps, places to stay, to eat, and a town-by-town guide to the shops and malls. We like to photocopy the pages about the states we plan to be in. That way we have some of the town history, detailed directions, and maps. There are also antique show schedules so we can try to arrive in a town when the big show is on.

Thank you, Kim and David, for writing this book that helped us out of a very scary night. We were driving in a rural area, no houses in sight, when the fog made it almost impossible to see. Once in a while a street sign was visible. The book listed a phone number for a nearby shop. We hoped the owner lived there and was awake as we called from the car phone to explain our problem. Antiques people are the best! The shop owner talked us along the road and through the fog telling us where to turn...Thirty minutes later we were at a motel.

We know it is impossible to ever do a complete listing of antiques shops. They open and close daily. The *Leggetts' Antiques Atlas* is as complete as any we have used.

Ralph and Terry Kovel
Authors
*Kovels' Antiques & Collectibles Price List*

# Introduction

Even as a child I loved to go "antiquing." Every Friday night my aunt and grandmother would take me along to a little country auction at "Peppermint Pond," where they often purchased incredible antiques at next to nothing prices. To this day my aunt still sleeps in a gorgeous six-foot-tall oak bed which she purchased for $20. Not one to be left out of a bargain-hunting, shopping excursion, I too purchased a fair amount of jumble and junk along with some "good stuff" (or so I thought). My room became the envy of cousins and friends who came to admire the long, sparkling strands of hippie beads, peace signs, strange-looking incense burners and other '60s memorabilia. Today, 30 years later, I prefer early American painted pieces over the "Partridge Family Does Dixie" look, but one thing has never changed-the intense desire to search and find "pieces of the past."

I was convinced that there were plenty of antique establishments all across America worth seeking out, but there was simply no handy way to find them. Because I could not find a book which provided such a listing, I resolved to research and write one myself. I am happy to say that most businesses were thrilled to be included in this book. Their personal stories are a testimony to their love and devotion to their business. Within these pages you will find a great mix of "antiquing" possibilities from the offerings of exclusive antique markets and group shops to the diverse selections of traditional antique and collectible shops and malls. All the antique shows listed in this book represent only the finest in antique furnishings and very early collectibles. Many of the bed and breakfast, country inns, and hotels are listed on the National Register of Historical Places and offer exceptional overnight accommodations. You'll also find information on historical towns and suggestions for some very interesting "in-town" side trips to add to your "antiquing" adventures. Should all this shopping make you hungry, I have thrown in a few select dining establishments as well.

The 1999 edition of *Leggetts' Antiques Atlas* promises to be even bigger and better. We have included more than 1,000 new bed-and-breakfast listings as well as reviews, along with hundreds of new antique shops and malls. Additionally, many of you called to request a listing of the largest malls in each state so we have added a "largest malls & shops" listing to the end of the book.

If in your travels you happen upon a shop/mall/market/show/auction, etc., that is not included, please call us. We would love to include them in our year 2000 edition. And most important, when visiting any of these businesses, please let them know you read about them in *Leggetts' Antiques Atlas*.

**Happy Hunting!**

**Call us any time — We would love to hear from you!**

**1-800-456-9326**

**Kim and David Leggett**

# How to Use This Book

1. The listings following the maps are in alphabetical order. Consequently, the numbers appearing on the maps will not be in numerical order.

2. The purpose of the maps is to direct you to a general location using major highways or interstates as references. Secondary highways and streets are intentionally omitted.

3. The directions in this book were submitted to *Leggetts' Antiques Atlas* by the listed business. Neither *Leggetts' Antiques Atlas* nor Crown Publishing Group accepts responsibility for incorrect directions.

4. At the time of publishing, the information in this book was verified to be correct. However, the publisher cannot be responsible for any inconvenience due to outdated or incorrect information.

**NOTE:** *At the time of printing, we were experiencing a large volume of area code changes. If you should reach a number which appears to be disconnected, call the operator to verify if there has been an area code change.*

# Alabama

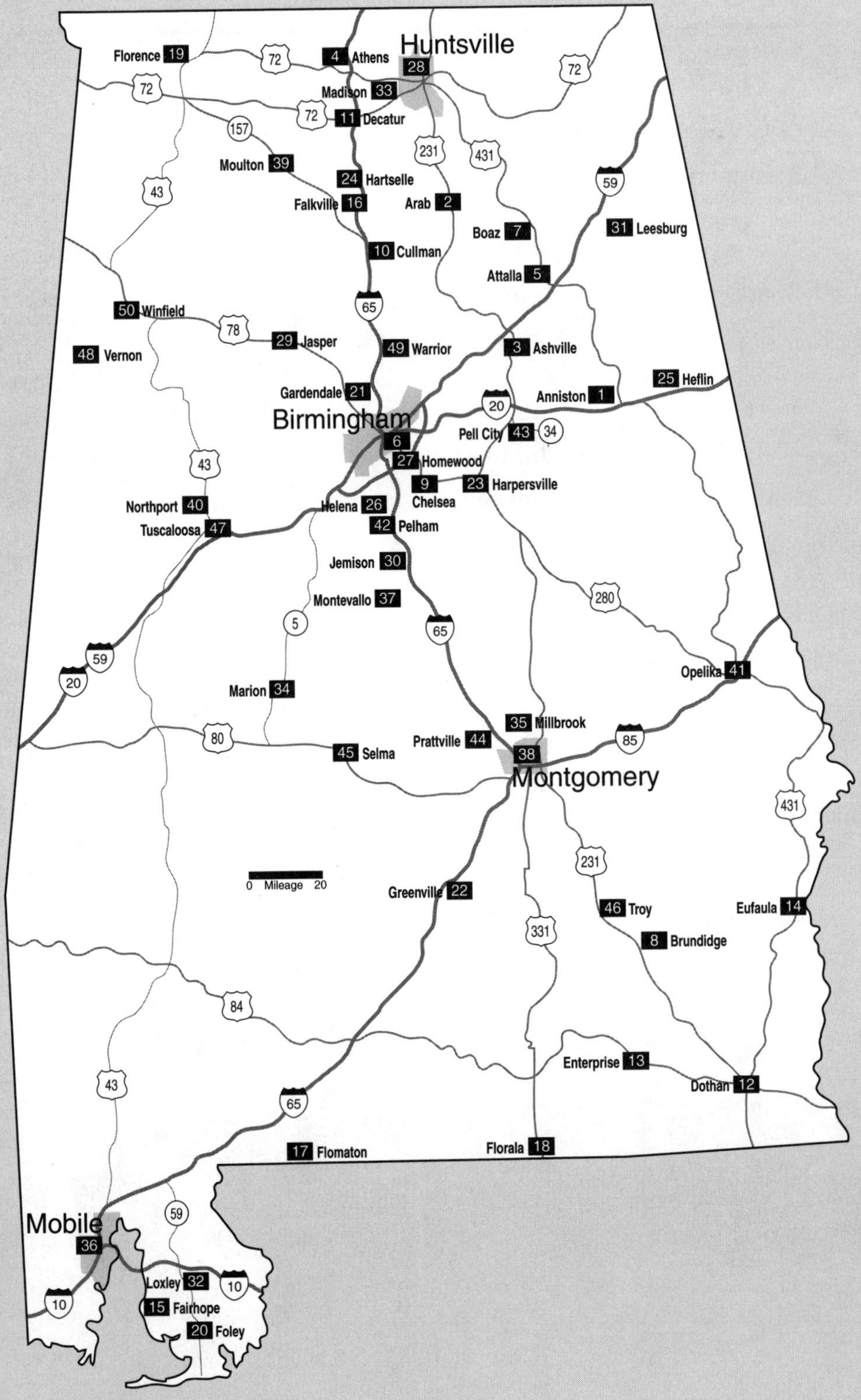

Florence 19
72
4 Athens
Huntsville
28
72
72
Madison 33
72
11 Decatur
157
231
431
Moulton 39
24 Hartselle
59
43
Falkville 16
Arab 2
Boaz 7
31 Leesburg
10 Cullman
Attalla 5
65
50 Winfield
78
29 Jasper
49 Warrior
3 Ashville
48 Vernon
25 Heflin
Gardendale 21
Anniston 1
20
Birmingham
6
Pell City 43
34
27 Homewood
43
9
23 Harpersville
Chelsea
Northport 40
Helena 26
Tuscaloosa 47
42 Pelham
Jemison 30
Montevallo 37
280
5
65
59
20
Opelika 41
Marion 34
35 Millbrook
Prattville 44
85
80
45 Selma
38
Montgomery
431
231
0 Mileage 20
Greenville 22
46 Troy
Eufaula 14
331
8 Brundidge
84
Enterprise 13
Dothan 12
43
65
17 Flomaton
Florala 18
59
Mobile
36
Loxley 32
10
10
15 Fairhope
20 Foley

# Riverchase Antique Gallery: Where the unique is the norm

The seasoned veteran, as well as the rookie, loves the thrill of the hunt. To an avid antiquer, the quest for that certain item, be it a Shaker cabinet or a Tiffany lamp, is often as exciting (and treasure-filled) as the find itself.

A fine spot to begin the hunt when traveling near Birmingham, Alabama, is Riverchase Antique Gallery. The 146 dealer gallery spans 36,000 square feet for your meandering pleasure. An abundance of furniture in styles such as French, English, Mission, Primitive and Shaker is displayed throughout the gallery. Riverchase Antique Gallery hosts an impressive inventory of bedroom and dining room suites, armoires and sideboards, in addition to many other pieces of fine furniture.

*Riverchase Dealers, left to right: Clarence Ballenger, Inez Symms, Bill Rippy, Elizabeth Rippy, Chris Fergin, Lilla Colburn, and Evel Colburn.*

At Riverchase Antique Gallery, the unusual is the norm. Dealers display juke boxes, refurbished telephones, lamps, glassware, china, paints, pottery, toys and collectibles. Is it any wonder Riverchase Antique Gallery was voted "The Best of Birmingham," ten years running?

*Riverchase Antique Gallery is located at 3454 Lorna Road in Birmingham. For days and hours of operation and directions see listing #6 (Birmingham).*

# Discover the tranquil gardens, intimacy and Southern charms of the delightful Jemison Inn

Old-time style in a small-town setting describes the Jemison Inn of Jemison, Alabama. The intimate inn provides three guest rooms, so reservations are a must to assure you a place to stay. The former family home, built in the 1930's has been refurbished and now boasts many heirloom antique furnishings. Southern charm and hospitality abound in this delightful inn. Fresh flowers grace each room. The full breakfast provided to lodgers is accompanied by fresh fruits in season. On fine spring and fall evenings, you can sit on the wrap-around porch enjoying an afternoon refreshment, compliments of the inn. A further touch of Southern style is punctuated by turned-down beds and mints on the pillows. The intimate, hospitable charm of the Jemison Inn makes it a great wind-down stop.

*The gardens at the Jemison Inn are a favorite spot of the guests.*

*The Jemison Inn is located at 212 Hwy. 191 in Jemison. For additional information on the Jemison Inn, please call the innkeepers at 205/688-2055. Rates $70.*

*Heirloom furnishings enhance the inviting sense of serenity at the Jemison Inn.*

*Sunlight floods the wrap-around porch where guests relax, and refreshments are served every afternoon at the Jemison Inn.*

## 1 ANNISTON

**Mulberry Corner Antiques**
1700 Al Highway 21 S.
205/835-3556

**B-Ring Exclusive Inc.**
1928 Cooper Ave.
205/237-8082

**Country Cabin**
7420 McClellan Blvd.
205/835-8174

**Anniston Galleries**
906 Noble St.
205/236-3741

**The Town Shop**
908 Noble St.
205/237-7356

**Petticoat's**
911 Noble Street
205/235-3944

**Jamie's Antique Village**
1429 Snow St.
205/831-2830

**Apple Barrel Antique Mall**
3320 Henry Road
205/237-0091

**Treasures & Keepsakes**
1900 Wilmer Ave.
205/235-2251

### *Great Places To Stay*

**The Victoria, A Country Inn**
1604 Quintard Ave.
1-800-260-8781

Queen Anne style built in 1888 - 48 guest rooms

## 2 ARAB

**Scott's Antiques, Gifts & Accessories**
117 N. Main St.
205/931-2006

**Where Memories Linger**
119 Main St.
205/931-2065

**Olde World Antique Gallery**
2330 N. Brindlee Mt. Pkwy.
205/586-2185

**Kelley's Gifts & Antiques**
220 Ruth Road
205/586-4169

**Jean's Antiques**
2893 Hwy. 231
205/586-5007

**Special Touchs**
Highway 231 N.
205/498-5504

## 3 ASHVILLE

**Ashville Antiques & Collectibles**
18 Court St. E.
205/594-5970

## 4 ATHENS

Have time to stop and explore a few days in Alabama? Grab your shovels and head for the hills. Rumor has it that an undetermined amount of gold and silver coins are buried in the quaint little Southern town of Athens, Alabama. Located in the rolling foothills of the Appalachian Mountains in northern Alabama, Athens is blessed with an abundance of historic homes and sites, many dating back to the mid-1800s. It is here, in this charming historic town, that the story of buried treasures unfolds.

As the Civil War was ending, soldiers loyal to the South collected a large amount of gold and silver coins. The plan was to take the treasure to Montgomery, but Union forces interfered. Near Athens, the wagon carrying the treasure sank in the murky Alabama clay, becoming immobile. While working to free it, the Confederate band was surprised by a small Union patrol. Believing the wagon contained weapons and ammunition, the Union sergeant ordered the wagon unloaded. A skirmish erupted between the two groups. Three of the Yankee soldiers were killed, along with two of the three Confederates. A wounded Union soldier escaped, leaving the Confederate leader - known only as Hansen - behind to defend the treasure. Dumping the treasure in the adjacent bog to conceal it from the Union armies, Hansen made his way to the home of a friend, where he reported his misfortune, along with the general location of the treasure. Hansen was killed shortly afterward by a Union soldier. His friend never recovered the coins.

**Sutton's Antiques**
1010 N. Jefferson St.
205/233-0235

**Athens Antique Mall**
309 S. Marion St.
205/230-0036

**Jinny's**
216 W. Market St.
205/233-1386

**Hickory House**
23101 U.S. Hwy. 72
205/232-9860

## 5 ATTALLA

**Days of Old**
418 4th St.
205/538-1950

**Col. John's Auction**
413 4th St. NW.
205/538-7884

**Memory Lane Antiques**
420 4th St. N.W.
205/538-8594

**Pembroke Antiques**
307 5th Ave.
205/570-0041

**Yesterday's Treasures Antiques**
426 4th St. N.W.
205/538-3111

**Courtyard Antiques**
318 5th Ave N.W.
205/538-3455

**Days Gone By**
328 5th Ave.
205/538-1920

**Gramling Antiques**
419 4th St. N.W.
205/538-2464

## 6 BIRMINGHAM

**Riverchase Antique Gallery**
3454 Lorna Road
205/823-6433
Mon.-Sat. 10-6, Sun. 1-6 (Closed Thanksgiving Day and Christmas Day)
*Directions: Located at I-459 and Lorna Road, across from the Galleria, only 10 minutes south of Birmingham.*

For specific information see review at the beginning of this section.

# Alabama

**Whistle Stop Treasure Shop**
1910 1st Ave. N.
205/951-5500

**Redmont Market Antiques**
2330 7th Ave. S.
205/320-0440

**Lakeview Antiques**
2427 7th Ave. S.
205/323-0888

**Alabama Auction Room Inc.**
2112 5th Ave. N.
205/252-4073

**Wardemond Galleries**
2808 18th St. S.
205/871-0433

**Interiors Market**
2817 2nd Ave. S.
205/323-2817

**Yester Year Antiques & Tea Shop**
587 Shades Crest Road
205/979-4742

**Architectural Heritage**
2807 2nd Ave. S.
205/322-3538

**Burch Antiques & Accessories**
5522 1st Ave. N.
205/591-3676

**Carriage Antique Village**
88 Green Springs Hwy.
205/942-8131

**Christopher House Antiques**
2949 18th St.
205/870-7106

**Denise Ginsburg Interlude**
2415 Canterbury Road
205/870-3376

**Edgewood Antiques**
731 Broadway St. (Rear)
205/870-3343

**Europa Antiques Inc.**
1820 29th Ave. S.
205/879-6222

**Kings House Antiques & Gifts**
2418 Montevallo Road
205/871-5787

**Little House Heirloom Gallery**
2915 Linden Ave.
205/879-4186

**Al's Antiques & Used Furniture**
7621 1st Ave. N.
205/836-2270

**Peck & Hill Antique Furniture**
2400 7th Ave. S.
205/252-3179

**Hanna Antiques Mall**
2424 7th Ave. S.
205/323-6036

**5th Avenue Antiques**
2410 5th Ave. S.
205/320-0500

**Christopher House Antiques**
2921 18th St. S.
205/870-7106

**Altadena Antiques by Wards**
4704 Cahaba River Road
205/967-8110

**Antique Art Exchange**
3199 Cahaba Heights Road
205/967-1700

**Bridges Antiques**
3949 Cypress Dr.
205/967-6233

**Cahaba Heights Antiques**
3131 Belwood Dr.
205/967-7915

**Christopher Glenn Inc.**
2713 19th St. S.
205/870-1236

**Cox Antiques**
88 Green Springs Hwy.
205/942-1887

**E. Earl's Antiques**
585 Shades Crest Rd.
205/978-7693

**Estate Sales Store**
4244 Cahaba Heights Ct.
205/969-0904

**Iron Art, Inc.**
2901 Cahaba Road
205/879-0529

**Levy's**
2116 2nd Ave. N.
205/251-3381

**Luke's Antiques & Collectibles**
237 Oxmoor Circle
205/942-9180

**Mary Adams Antiques**
1829 29th Ave. S.
205/871-7131

**Old World Market Place**
593 Shades Crest Rd.
205/823-9007

**Quilted Cat**
63 Church St.
205/871-4741

**Reed Books**
20th St. @ 1st Ave. S. #107
205/326-4460

**Summersfield Antiques**
3961 Crosshaven Dr.
205/969-0914

**On-A-Shoestring**
601 Shades Crest Rd.
205/822-8741

**Elegant Earth**
1907 Cahaba Rd.
205/870-3264

**Estate Antiques**
3253 Lorna Rd.
205/823-7303

**Oak Grove Antiques**
609 Oak Grove Rd.
205/945-7183

**Antique Mall East**
217 Oporto Madrid Blvd. N.
205/836-1097

**Birmingham Antique Mall**
2211 Magnolia Ave. S.
205/328-7761

**Vestavia Antiques & Interiors**
700 Montgomery Hwy.
205/979-8740

**Michael's Antiques**
1831 29th Ave. S.
205/871-2716

**Pump House Antiques**
3279 Cahaba Heights Rd.
205/967-2855

**Re Run Shop Antiques to Junk**
2209 3rd Ave. N.
205/328-3602

**Ruby Ansley Interiors Inc.**
2806 Petticoat Lane
205/871-8294

**Tricia's Treasures**
1433 Montgomery Hwy. #5
205/822-0004

**Attic Antiques**
5620 Cahaba Valley Rd.
205/991-6887

**Urban Farmer**
2809 18th St. S.
205/870-7118

**Lamb's Ears Ltd.**
3138 Cahaba Heights Road
205/969-3138

**Antiques & Dreams**
9184 Parkway E.
205/836-2411

**Maryon Allen Co.**
3215 Cliff Rd.
205/324-0479

**Chinaberry**
1 Hoyt Lane
205/879-5338

### *Favorite Places To Eat*

**Ollie's Barbeque**
515 University Blvd.
205/324-9485

Memphis, Tenn. has long been recognized as the home of the barbecued pig, but Ollie's Barbeque in Birmingham, Alabama, is sitting right on the doorstep.

Since 1926, the McClung family has been serving smoked meat not only to the hometown crowd, but to folks from as far away as Sacramento, California. Their original establishment on Birmingham's south side is gone, but their new pork place on University Boulevard displays a swanky pit built in the middle so customers can see just what it takes to make meat taste this good.

Sliced pork with crunchy edges is the most popular choice. On a plate or piled high in a sandwich, these tender wedges are topped with the McClung family recipe, a vinegar-tomato sauce. A choice of tossed salad, beans, french fries, or coleslaw comes with the meal. If you've saved room for dessert, you're in for a treat of homemade pies (chocolate, coconut, lemon and apple), a yummy end to a great meal!

### *Interesting Side Trips*

**Arlington**
331 Cotton Ave. S.W.
205/780-5656
Tues.-Sat., 10-4; Sun., 1-4 (closed Mon. and city holidays)
*Directions: Located 1 1/2 miles west of downtown Birmingham on 1st Ave. N. which becomes Cotton Ave. From I-65 South, take the 6th Ave. North exit; from I-65 North, take the 3rd Ave. North exit. Then follow the signs.*

In 1953, this many-times-renovated family home became the property of the City of Birmingham. Arlington is located in Elyton, one of the oldest sections of the city. Incorporated in 1821, Elyton was the first permanent county seat of Jefferson County.

Neither the exact date of Arlington's construction nor the builder's name are known, but construction of the present structure occurred sometime after purchase in 1842 by Judge William S. Mudd. The style of architecture is Greek Revival, easily identified by the central hallways upstairs and down, as well as the symmetry of rooms on either side of the hallways.

Today, the property has been restored to a grandeur reminiscent of its finest era. Arlington possesses an excellent collection of decorative arts, mostly 19th century American. Additional collections throughout the home have been made available through the generosity of local donors.

## 7 BOAZ

**Sana's Antiques on Main**
111 S. Main St.
205/593-8009

**Downtown Antique Gallery**
102 S. Main St.
205/593-0023

**Almost Antiques**
104 Thomas Ave.
205/593-1412

**Southern Heritage**
285-C U.S. Hwy 431 S.
205/593-1132

**Gazebo Antique Gallery**
106 Thomas Ave.
205/840-9444

**Boaz Antique Mall**
102 Thomas Ave.
205/593-1410

**Adams Antique Mall**
225 E. Mill Ave.
205/593-0406

**Past & Present Consignment Shop**
10306 Hwy. 168
205/593-0505

## 8 BRUNDIDGE

**City Antiques**
108 E. Troy St.
334/735-5164

**Rue's Antique Mall & Deli**
123 S. Main St.
334/735-3125

**Greens Antiques**
794 S. Main St.
334/735-2247

## 9 CHELSEA

**Chelsea Antique Mall**
14569 Hwy. 280
205/678-2151

## 10 CULLMAN

**Cullman Antique Alley**
500 County Road 1170
205/739-1900

**Yesterday's Antiques & Gifts**
105 2nd Ave. S.W.
205/739-3972

**South Wind Antiques**
301 3rd Ave. S.E.
205/737-9800

**Craig's Antiques & Gifts**
220 1st Ave. S.E.
205/734-2252

**Something Olde Something New**
214 2nd Ave. S.E.
205/734-3345

**Fireside Antiques**
1133 County Road 222
205/737-5135

**Magnolias & Lace**
1716 2nd Ave. N.W.
205/734-9639

**Southern Accents Arch Antiques**
308 2nd Ave. S.E.
205/737-0554

**Plantation Designs**
202 1st Ave. S.E.
205/734-0654

**Antiquities**
308 3rd St. S.E.
205/734-9953

**Golden Pond**
2045 County Road 222
205/739-0850

**Margo's Antiques & Gifts**
206 1st Ave. S.E.
205/734-1452

## 11 DECATUR

**London's**
114 Moulton St.
205/340-0900

**Sarah's Gifts & Antiques**
302 2nd Ave. S.E.
205/351-1451

**Hummingbird Antiques**
721 Bank St. N.E.
205/351-1451

**Antique Jungle**
219 E. 2nd Ave. S.E.
205/351-6278

**Rhodes Ferry**
502 Bank St. N.E.
205/308-0550

**Sykes Antiques**
726 NE Bank St.
205/355-2656

**Nebrig-Howell House Antiques**
722 Bank St. N.E.
205/351-1655

**Riverwalk Antique Mall**
818 Bank St. N.E.
205/340-0075

**Southland Collectibles, Ltd.**
3311 Old Moulton Road
205/350-7272

**C & W Trading Post**
14 Lee St. N.E.
205/350-9076

**Inglis House**
814 Bank St. N.E.
205/355-6118

**Country Cabin**
211 2nd Ave. S.E.
205/350-9744

**Weathervane**
206 2nd Ave. S.E.
205/350-1833

## 12 DOTHAN

**Miz Minnie's Antiques**
450 S. Oates St.
334/794-2061

**King's Clocks & Antiques**
1015 Headland Ave.
334/792-3964

**Wildot Inc.**
409 S. Oates St.
334/794-8372

**Ala. Antique Mall/Auction Center**
14341 S. U.S. 231 Ste. 2
334/702-0720

**Antique Attic**
5037 Fortner St.
334/792-5040

**Today**
107 S. Cherokee Ave.
334/702-7949

**Tadlock's Back Room**
1510 Montgomery Hwy.
334/793-5527

## 13 ENTERPRISE

**Country Matters & Antiques**
905 E. Park Ave.
334/347-4649

**Ronald Evans Antiques**
204 N. Main St.
334/347-4944

**Special Accents**
102 N. Main St.
334/347-0887

**Gaston's Antiques**
528 Glover Ave.
334/347-0285

**Country Matters & Antiques II**
1241 Shellfield Road
334/347-4649

## 14 EUFAULA

*Directions: From Montgomery, U.S. 82 southeast through Union Springs to Eufaula.*

Eufaula, Ala., is home to a little more than 13,000 citizens; however, this modest-sized city brags of being constructed of over 700 historic buildings. Situated along the banks of the Chattahoochee River, Eufaula was at one time a prosperous riverport town for planters throughout the states of Alabama, Georgia, and Florida. This town, blossoming in spring with dogwood and azaleas, is blessed with an abundance of antebellum homes characteristic of the deep South. The wealthy families of the 1840s and 1850s put their show of money into the exquisite and lavishly-presented homes, churches, and other buildings.

Unlike many of its sister cities whose beauty and grace were interrupted during the Civil War, Eufaula was fortunate that the Confederacy conceded before Union forces could occupy or destroy it. This resulted in the preservation of many hundreds of historic structures. In addition, during the post-war era, many other attractive homes and buildings rose in Eufaula. The tradition of admiration of fine craftsmanship and architecture set the stage for the preservation of these magnificent structures as well. Alabama is host to the finest 19th century small-town commercial district. Moreover, guests of the town discover the state's most luxurious and plentiful collection of domestic Italianate architecture. Seth Lore-Irwinton Historic District boasts many of the town's historic homes. Shorter Mansion (1884), Fendall Hall (1860), Holleman-Foy Home (1907), Hart-Milton House (1843) and Kendall Manor offer some of the best examples of Neoclassical and Italianate mansions. Waterford chandeliers, hand-stenciled walls and murals breathe the grace and style of times past within the walls of these homes. Broad Street possesses many of the historic commercial buildings. The Tavern, an inn in the 1830's, later a Confederate hospital, is presently a studio and private home listed on the National Register of Historic Places.

The Eufaula tourism council supplies brochures for walking and driving tours of the homes within the historic district. Although most homes are private, during Eufaula's Pilgrimage in April, many homeowners open their doors inviting visitors to enjoy the rooms and family heirlooms inside. The pilgrimage, furthermore, greets guests with open-air art exhibits, tea gardens and concerts. If not enough, one of the major antique shows in the state opens during the pilgrimage, occurring each year during the second weekend of April.

**Memory Lane**
106 S. Eufaula Ave.
334/616-0995

**Walker's Antiques**
149 S. Eufaula Ave.
334/687-5362

**Fagins Thieves Market**
317 S. Eufaula Ave.
334-687-4100

## 15 FAIRHOPE

**Bay Antiques & Collectibles**
328 De La Mare St.
334-928-2800

**Yester-Years Antiques**
56 S. Section St.
334/928-6933

**Antique Building Products**
17985 Hwy. 27
334/928-2880

**Bountiful Home**
203 Fairhope Ave.
334/990-8655

**Crown & Colony Antiques Etc.**
15 N. Section St.
334/928-4808

**Fairhope Antique Emporium**
52 S. Section St.
334/928-6290

**Interiors Mart**
122 Fairhope Ave.
334/928-1819

**Joy's Pation**
326 Fairhope Ave.
334/928-4640

**Past Pleasures Antiques**
19D N. Church St.
334/928-8484

**Silver Market**
19164 Scenic Hwy. 98
334/928-4657

## 16 FALKVILLE

**Interstate Antiques Mall**
I-65 at Exit 322
205/784-5302

## 17 FLOMATON

**Flomaton Antique Auction**
277 Old Hwy. 31
334/296-3059

## 18 FLORALA

**Stateline Mini Mall**
1517 W. Fifth Ave.
334/858-2741

**Florala Flea Market & Antique Mall**
1511 W. Fifth Ave. (Hwy. 331)
334/858-7000

## 19 FLORENCE

**Antiques on Court**
442 N. Court St.
205/766-4429

**Bellemeade Antique Mall**
Hwy. 72 E.
205/757-1050

**Estate Antique Mall**
3803 Florence Blvd.-Hwy. 72
205/757-9941

**Taylor's Treasures**
5136 Hwy. 17
205/764-7172

**Gifford's Antiques & Gifts**
1202 N. Wood Ave.
205/766-7340

**Trinkets & Antiques Shoppe**
533 E. Tuscaloosa St.
205/766-8781

**Collectibles Plus**
702 E. Mobile St.
205/767-6132

## 20 FOLEY

**Old Armory Mall**
812 N. McKenzie St.
334/943-7300

**Gas Works Antique Mall Inc.**
818 N. McKenzie St.
334/943-5555

**Southern Belle Antique Mall**
1000 S. McKenzie St.
334/943-8128

**Perdido Antiques Inc.**
323 S. Alston St.
334/943-5665

**Gift Horse Antique Stalls**
201 W. Laurel Ave.
334/943-7278

**Brown Mule Antique Mall**
8340 Hwy. 59 S.
334/943-4112

**Hollis "Ole Crush" Antique Mall**
200 S. McKenzie (Hwy. 59)
334/943-8154

## 21 GARDENDALE

**Gardendale Antique Mall**
2455 Decatur Hwy.
205/631-9044

**Baby Boomers Antiques**
753 Main St.
205/631-2781

## 22 GREENVILLE

**Gladys Seay Gallery**
142 Greenville Bypass
334/382-8110

## 23 HARPERSVILLE

**Hen/Son's Antique Mall**
917 U.S. 280 W.
205/672-7071

## 24 HARTSELLE

**Southern Antiques**
103 Railroad St S.W.
205/773-3923

**Jeanette's Jazzy Jk & Antiques**
115 Railroad St. S.W.
205/773-2299

**Jeff Sandlin's Antiques**
219 Main St. W.
205/773-4774

**Holladay Hill Antiques**
1807 Hwy. 32 N.W.
205/773-0116

**Hartselle Antique Mall**
209 Main St. W.
205/773-0081

**Heavenly Treasures & Gifts**
221 Main St. W.
205/773-4004

**Country Classic Antiques**
303 Main St. W.
205/773-9559

**Golden Oldies Antiques**
109 Main St. W.
205/773-1508

**Railroad Street Antique Mall**
113 Railroad St. SE.
205/773-2299

**Annie's Art & Antiques**
934 Hwy. 36 E.
205/773-5331

**Jim Norman Antiques & Auctions**
101 Main St.
205/773-6878

## 25 HEFLIN

### The Willoughby Street Mall
91-A Willoughby St.
205/463-5409
Mon.-Sat., 10-5; Sun, 1-5 (Closed New Year's Day, Easter, Mother's Day, Thanksgiving and Christmas Day)
*Directions: Traveling I-20, 70 miles from Atlanta, Ga. or Birmingham, Ala., exit 199. Turn north on Hwy. 9. Go 1 1/2 miles to Hwy. 78. Turn right on 78. Go approximately 3 blocks. Turn right on Coleman St. Go 1 block. Turn left on Willoughby St. Go 1/2 block. Old red brick high school building on right.*

Back in 1936, The Willoughby Street Mall was the Cleburne County High School of Heflin, Alabama. The red paint outside is original and the owners are restoring the building's interior to better represent its school days.

Today, this 35,000 square foot mall is filled with a collage of antiques and collectibles that includes pottery (Hull, Roseville, Shawnee), depression glass in a variety of patterns and colors, furnishings from Victorian to primitive and a list that goes on and on.

If you're in the market for Alabama art, be sure to visit the art gallery where local artist market their works.

**Colonial Cottage**
321 Ross St.
205/463-7149

## 26 HELENA

**Antique Monger**
5274 Helena Road
205/663-4977

**Our Place Antiques & Things**
Hwy. 261 Main St.
205/620-9361

## 27 HOMEWOOD

**Edgewood Antiques**
731 Rear Broadway St.
205/870-3343

**Little House Art Center**
2915 Linden Ave.
205/879-4186

**Michael's Antiques**
1831 29th Ave. S.
205/871-2716

**Europa Antiques Inc.**
1820 29th Ave.
205/879-6222

**Frankie Engel Antiques**
2949 18th St. S.
205/879-8331

**Carriage Antique Village**
88 Green Springs Hwy.
205/942-8131

## 28 HUNTSVILLE

**Cotton Pickin Antiques**
8402 Whitesburg Dr. S.
205/883-1010

**Madison Square Antiques**
1017 Old Monrovia Rd.
205/430-0909

**Hart Lex Antique Mall**
1030 Old Monrovia Rd.
205/830-4278

**Red Rooster Antique Mall**
12519 Memorial Pkwy. S.W.
205/881-6530

**Packard's Antiques**
11261 Memorial Pkwy. S.W.
205/881-1678

**Haysland Antique Mall**
11595 Memorial Pkwy.
205/883-0181

**Wilma's Antiques**
515 Pratt Ave.
205/536-7250

**Valerie Fursdon Inc.**
2212 Whitesburg Dr.
205/533-6768

**Railroad Station Antique Mall**
Natl. Historic Lombardo Bldg.
315 N. Jefferson St.
205/533-6550

**Pratt Avenue Antique Mall**
708 N.E. Pratt Ave.
205/536-3117

**Old Town Antique Mall**
820 Wellman Ave. N.E.
205/533-7002

**Kay's Kupboard**
515 Fountain Row
205/536-1415

**Golden Griffin**
104 Longwood Dr. S.E.
205/535-0882

**Gallery Antiques**
209 Russell St. N.E.
205/539-9118

**Darwin Antiques**
614 Lowe St.
205/539-9803

**Bulldog Antiques**
2338 Whitesburg Dr. S.
205/534-9893

**Ashton Place**
410 Governors Dr. S.W.
205/539-5464

**Antiques Etc.**
2801 Memorial Pkwy.
205/533-0330

**J. Jones Ltd.**
5000 Whitesburg Dr. S.
205/882-3043

**Jewel Shop**
117 Northside Square
205/534-7384

**Kurt Eklund Inc.**
806 Wellman Ave. N.E.
205/536-7314

**Walker House Antiques**
614 Madison St. S.E.
205/534-0320

## 29 JASPER

**The Antique Market**
5077 Hwy. 78 East
205/384-6997

## 30 JEMISON

**Touch of the Past**
120 Old Main
205/688-4938

**Jemison Antique Emporium**
106 Main St.
205/688-4711

**Valley View Antiques**
194 County Road 163
205/688-2518

**Petals From The Past**
16034 County Road 29
205/646-0069

**Jemison Trade Center Antique Mall**
Hwy. 44
205/688-9155

### *Great Places To Stay*

**The Jemison Inn**
212 Hwy. 191
205/688-2055
Open year round

For specific information see review at the beginning of this section.

## 31 LEESBURG

### *Great Places To Stay*

**the secret-Bed & Breakfast Lodge**
2356 Hwy. 68 W.
205/523-3825
Open year round
Reservations requested
*Directions: From I-59 take the Collinsville exit (exit 205). Follow Hwy. 68 east for 9 2/10 miles. Located on the left side of the street.*

"the secret" sits cozily among twelve acres of garden and wilderness atop Lookout Mountain. On a clear day you can see seven cities, including the skyline of Gadsden, the lights of Anniston and the industrial smokestacks of Rome, Georgia. It is perfectly situated on the edge of a mountain top so the sunrises and sunsets are spectacular.

Carl and Dianne Cruickshank, the owners and innkeepers, found "the secret" almost by accident. "We were looking at possible locations for a bed and breakfast," Diane said. "We had gone all through Etowah and Dekalb counties one Sunday, and we decided to take a look at this. It was love at first sight."

You might say Carl and Dianne rescued the house from despair. Originally built by People's Telephone Company owner Millard Weaver as a family home, the place had changed owners several times in the years following Weaver's death. It was then empty for a long time. The Cruickshanks came along at the right time while restoration was still possible. Carl performed most of the reconstruction himself.

Today, "the secret" provides a romantic atmosphere throughout the home with such amenities as an enormous central stone fireplace, a 22-foot vaulted living room/dining room ceiling and four spacious guest rooms. The home is furnished throughout with antiques, art, copper, brass, tile and rare woods. The 10-foot Lazy Susan table from which breakfast is served, has become quite a conversation piece among guests.

In addition to providing breath-taking scenery, the gardens and grounds are also home to two treasured peacocks.

## 32 LOXLEY

**Plunderosa Antiques**
Hwy. 59
334/964-5474

## 33 MADISON

**Purple Tree Antique Mall**
29730 U.S. Hwy. 72
205/233-5745

**Tally's Antique Mall**
7587 Hwy. 72 N.
205/722-7944

**West Station Antiques**
112 Main St.
205/772-0373

## 34 MARION

**Browsabout Antqs. & Things**
105 E. Jefferson St.
334/683-9856

**Pappy's Porch**
106 E. Green St.
334/683-9541

**Mary Bell Webb Odds & Ends**
311 Washington St.
334/683-0509

**Twink's Antiques & Gifts**
212 Washington St.
334/683-4770

**La Mason**
215 Washington St.
334/683-9131

**Old Victoria Antiques & Cafe**
216 Washington St.
334/683-2095

## 35 MILLBROOK

**Sisters Antique Mall**
1951 Market St.
334/285-5571

## 36 MOBILE

### Mobile Antique Gallery
1616 South Beltline Hwy.
334/666-6677
Mon.-Sat., 10-6; Sun, 1-6
*Directions: Located on the west side service road of I-65 at exit 1B. One mile north of I-10*

Voted "Best of Mobile" for three consecutive years, Mobile Antique Gallery presents an outstanding market of antiques and collectibles in a 21,000 square foot gallery. This bustling showplace houses the wares of well over 100 quality antique dealers offering exquisite furnishings, linens, silver, china, porcelains, depression-era glassware, antique toys and much, much more. A snack bar is located in the gallery.

**1848 Antiques**
356 Dauphin St.
334/432-1848

**Bentley's**
22S Florida St.
334/479-4015

**Cotton City Antique Mall**
2012 Airport Blvd.
334/479-9747

**Red Barn Antique Mall**
418 Dauphin Island Pkwy.
334/473-9227

**Gallery Old Shell**
1803 Old Shell Road
334/478-1822

**Antoinette's Antiques**
4401 Old Shell Road
334/344-7636

**Plantation Antique Galleries**
3750 Government Blvd.
334/666-7185

**Kearney Antiques**
1004 Government St.
334/438-9984

**Cobweb**
422 Dauphin Island Pkwy.
334/478-6202

**Dogwood Antiques**
2010 Airport Blvd.
334/479-9960

**E & J Galleries**
1421 Forest Hill
334/380-2072

**Mary's Corner**
2602 Old Shell Road
334/471-6060

**Antique Shop Inc.**
3510 Cottage Hill Road
334/661-1355

**Mobile Antique Gallery**
1616 S. Beltline Hwy.
334/666-6677

**Yellow House Antiques**
1902 Government St.
334/476-7382

**Criswell's Antiques**
4103 Moffat Road
334/344-4917

**Prichard Trading Post Inc.**
616 N. MLK Hwy.
334/452-3456

**Gemini Shop**
2006 Airport Blvd.
334/478-6695

**Dogwood Antiques**
2010 Airport Blvd.
334/479-9960

### *Interesting Side Trips*

**Oakleigh House Museum**
350 Oakleigh Place
334/432-1281
Mon.-Sat. 10-4 (closed legal holidays and Christmas week)
*Directions: 2 1/2 blocks South of Government St. between Roper St. and George St.*

Oakleigh Period House Museum and Historic Complex is operated by the Historic Mobile Preservation Society. The 3 1/2 landscaped acres consist of Oakleigh, the city's official ante-bellum period house museum, the Cox-Deasy House, and the Archives Building, which also houses the administrative offices of the Society.

Oakleigh, which was begun in 1833 by Mobile merchant James W. Roper, is included in the American Buildings Survey and the National Register of Historic Places. Mr. Roper was his own architect and incorporated unique and practical features into the design of his home. It is beautifully furnished with fine period collections of furniture, portraits, silver, china, jewelry, interesting kitchen implements and toys. The museum gift shop is on the ground floor of Oakleigh.

The Cox-Deasy House, circa 1850, is a contrast to Oakleigh. It is a raised Creole Cottage, typical of the modest middle-class city dwellers along the Gulf Coast. It is furnished in simple 19th-century antiques.

Guided tours of Oakleigh and the Cox-Deasy House are conducted by members of the Society.

## 37 MONTEVALLO

**Cedar Creek Antiques**
2979 Hwy. 119 S.
205/665-2446

**Montevallo Antiques**
615 Main St.
205/665-4142

**Arledge Antiques & Collectibles**
7611 Hwy. 22
205/665-7094

## 38 MONTGOMERY

**Nicole Maleine Antiques**
121 N. Goldwiate St.
334/834-8530

**Unique Treasures**
1712 Upper Wetumpka Road
334/834-0437

**Unicorn Shop Antiques**
1926 Mulberry St.
334/834-2550

**Bodiford's Antique Mall**
919 Hampton St.
334/265-4220

**Emily Dearman Antiques**
514 Cloverdale Road
334/269-5282

**Frances Edward's Antiques**
1010 E. Fairview Ave.
334/269-5100

**Louise Brooks Antiques**
1034 E. Fairview Ave.
334/265-8900

**Mulberry House Antiques**
2001 Mulberry St.
334/263-5131

**Old Cloverdale Antiques**
514 Cloverdale Road
334/262-6234

**May-Bell's Corner Antiques**
1429 Bell St.
334/265-3298

**Montgomery Antique Galleries**
1955 Eastern Blvd.
334/277-2490

**Windsor House**
423 Cloverdale Road
334/265-2104

**Yesteryear Antiques**
2908 McGehee Road, #A
334/288-1202

**Fantasy Land Flea Market**
3620 Atlanta Hwy.
334/272-8841

**Antiques In The Courtyard**
514 Cloverdale Road
334/262-1560

**Bell Street Brass**
1273 Bell St.
334/262-6345

**E. T's Antiques**
549 N. Eastern Blvd.
334/277-7288

**Elegant Junk & Antiques**
1800 W. 5th St.
334/272-8841

**Providence Antiques**
1717 Norman Bridge Road
334/264-1717

**Sara B's Flower & Antique Shop**
1807 W. 4th St.
334/262-6137

**Heirloom Jewelers & Collectibles**
6948 Vaughn Road
334/260-0066

**Sassafras Tea Room & Antiques**
532 Clay St.
334/265-7277

**Seven Sisters Antiques & Gifts**
546 Clay St.
334/262-2660

**Tresses N Treasures**
6565 Narrow Lane Road
334/284-0601

**SouthEast Antiques & Collectibles**
2530 East South Blvd.
334/284-5711

## 39 MOULTON

**The Shelton House Antiques**
2020 Morgan St.
205-974-1444

**Memories Antiques & Ideas**
716 Main St.
205/974-4301

**Blue Willow Antiques & Gifts**
607 County Road 217
205/974-3888

**Town Square Antique Mall**
734 Main St.
205/974-2345

## 40 NORTHPORT

**Anne Marie's Antiques**
5925 Hwy. 43
888/333-1398

## 41 OPELIKA

**Highway 280 Antique Mall**
4730 Alabama Hwy. 147 N.
334/821-8540

**Magnolia House**
807 Geneva St.
334/749-9648

**M. R. Brasher & Co.**
108 S. 8th St.
334/745-9394

**Olde Towne Antqs./Annie Maude's**
705 2nd Ave.
334/745-0580

**Blue Iris Antiques**
400 2nd Ave.
334/745-6756

## 42 PELHAM

**Antique The Co.**
200 Bearden Road
205/664-1864

**Joyce's Antiques**
2200 Commerce Circle
205/988-3535

**Emporium**
880 Oak Mountain Park Road
205/664-3691

**Colonial Galleries**
2000 Golf Course Road
205/338-7395

## 43 PELL CITY

**David Tims Wholesale Antiques**
Hwy. 34
205/338-7929

**Squirrel's Nest**
604 Hazelwood Dr.
205/338-2440

**Pell City Auction Company**
Hwy. 231 S.
205/525-4100

**Landi's Antique Mall**
Hwy. 231 N.
205/338-6255

## 44 PRATTVILLE

**Linda's Antique Mall**
1120 S. Memorial Dr.
334-361-9952

## 45 SELMA

**Selma Antique & Art Mall**
1410 Water Ave.
334/872-1663

**Hobson's Mercantile & Metal**
1207 Water Ave.
334/872-9928

**Gordon Antiques**
705 Dallas Ave.
334/875-2400

**Strothers & Golsons**
1001 Alabama Ave.
334/875-1008

## 46 TROY

**Denim Blues**
Pioneer Village, 4120 Hwy. 231 N.
334/566-1811

**Hillside Antiques**
4839 Hwy. 231 N.
334/735-5567

**Antique & Quilt Shop**
Pioneer Village, 4120 Hwy. 231 N.
334/566-9040

### *Great Places To Stay*

**Grace Hall B&B**
506 Lauderdale St.
334/875-5744
Antebellum mansion, circa 1857 - six guest rooms

## 47 TUSCALOOSA

**Hobby Horse Antique Mall**
5500 Old Montgomery Hwy.
205/752-1630

**Interiors By Shea**
501 Queen City Ave.
205/752-7432

**Eva's Antiques**
5210 University Blvd. E.
205/556-1922

**Boykin Antiques & Decorators**
1109 21st Ave.
205/759-5231

## 48 VERNON

**Falkner Antique Mall**
Courtsquare
205/695-9841

## 49 WARRIOR

**B. Cooper's Antiques & Collectibles**
133 Louisa St.
205/647-2272

**Ice House Antiques**
215 Louisa St.
205/647-0882

**Currier Antiques**
516 N. Main St.
205/647-8048

**Garden Gate Antiques**
516 N. Main St.
205/647-8048

## 50 WINFIELD

**Between A Rock & A Hard Place**
Hwy. 78 W.
205/487-2924

# Arizona

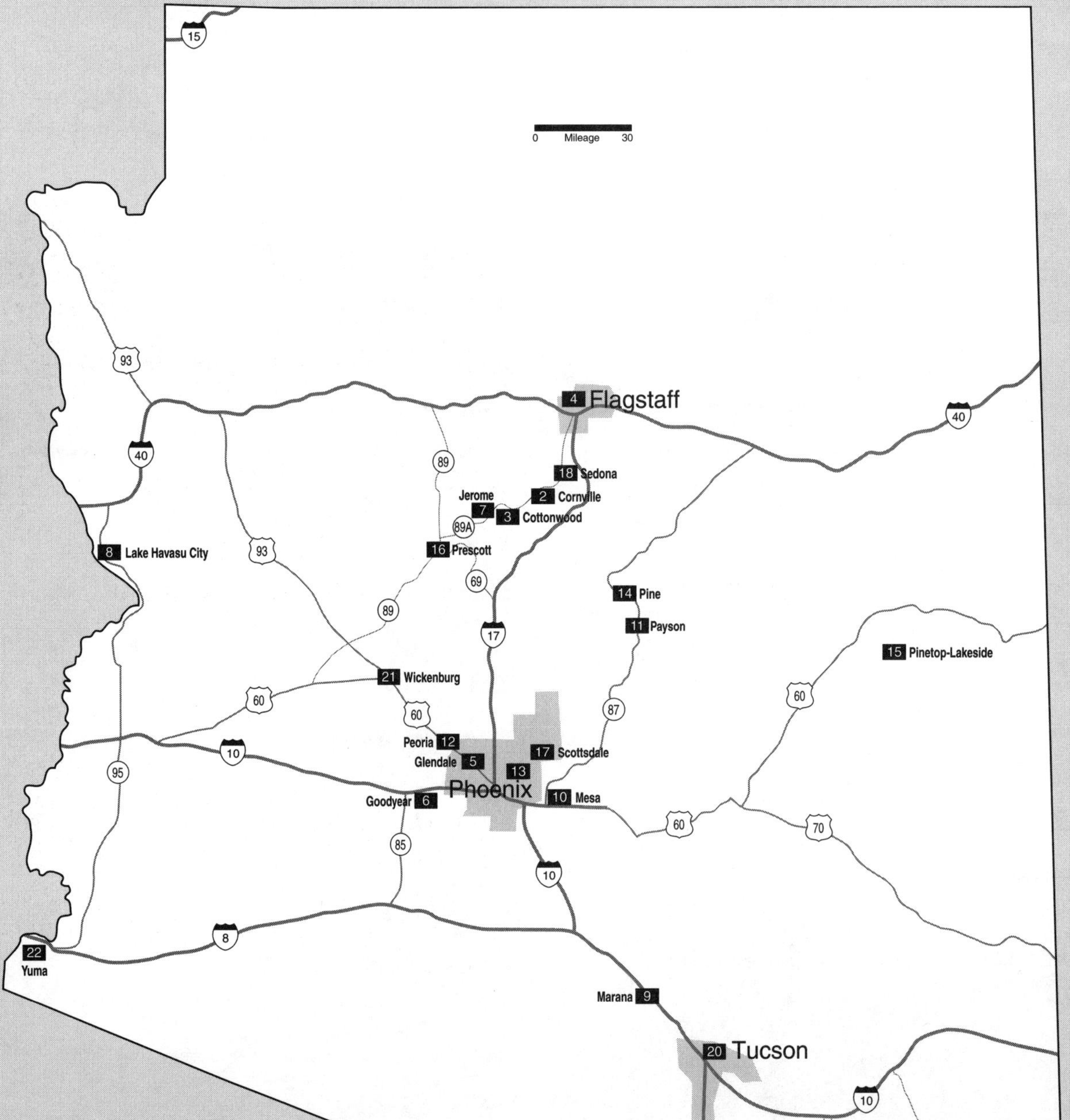

0 Mileage 30
15
93
40
89
93
89A
69
89
17
60
60
95
10
85
10
8
60
70
60
19
10
90
80
191
80
4 Flagstaff
18 Sedona
2 Cornville
Jerome
7
3 Cottonwood
16 Prescott
8 Lake Havasu City
14 Pine
11 Payson
15 Pinetop-Lakeside
21 Wickenburg
Peoria 12
Glendale 5
17 Scottsdale
13
Phoenix
10 Mesa
Goodyear 6
22
Yuma
Marana 9
20 Tucson
19 Tombstone
1 Bisbee

# Antiques Super-Mall, Antique Trove and Antique Centre: 600 dealers in a one-block area

Why drive all over town looking for unique antiques and collectibles when you can visit Arizona's premier "Antique Destinations" in Scottsdale. Always a favorite stop for the two of us, Antiques Super-Mall, Antique Trove and Antique Centre offer over 600 dealers within three large stores spanning a whopping 120,000 square feet! The best part is the malls are all located within a one block area and are open faithfully from 10 a.m. to 6 p.m. daily. If you are passing through late on Thursdays, all these fine stores are open until 8 p.m.

*For specific information on days and hours of operation and directions see listing #15 (Scottsdale).*

*What an abundance of antique riches! The sheer quantity of choices could never disappoint any eager seeker who's hot on the treasure-hunting trail at the Antiques Super-Mall, Antique Trove and Antique Centre in Scottsdale.*

# The Apple Tree: Early country and primitives

Located in the heart of Historic Downtown Glendale, The Apple Tree is 6,300 square feet of antiques and collectibles. Dealers offer quality merchandise including furniture, pottery, depression and elegant glass, toys, advertising, china, linens, quilts, lamps and much, much more. Owner Karen Hess-Landes specializes in early country and primitives, devoting more than half of the shop to this passion. Early pine cupboards, dry sinks, jelly cabinets, harvest tables, benches, chairs, pie safes, wooden bowls, crocks, redware, tin and iron, yellowware — if it's country, you'll find it at the Apple Tree. Merchandise is beautifully displayed and the staff is friendly, knowledgeable and willing to assist. Dealers and designers are always welcome and considerations are given. This is a full-service shop, accepting all major credit cards, checks, layaway, shipping and customer search service. Now in its seventh year, The Apple Tree was chosen Best Antiques Shop in the Phoenix metro Northwest Valley by readers of the *Arizona Republic*.

*A sideboard houses collectible pottery and cookware at The Apple Tree.*

*The Apple Tree has a very fine selection of high-quality rustic country furniture which is displayed with utmost attention to enhance the special characteristics of each individual piece.*

*The Apple Tree is located at 5811 W. Glendale Ave. For days and hours of operation and directions see listing #5 (Glendale).*

# Historic Downtown Glendale is Arizona's antique capital

Boasting the greatest concentration of antique shops in Arizona, this charming historic district is much more than just a lot of stores — it's an overall experience to all who visit. The more than 90 antique shops, specialty stores and unique restaurants are housed in old storefronts and century-old bungalows in a small-town atmosphere that is as American as apple pie. Nestled in a few blocks surrounding shady Murphy Park, 58th and Glendale Avenues, this wonderful pedestrian area features brick sidewalks, lined with trees, gas-style lamps and is dotted with comfortable benches that invite one to sit and soak up the ambience.

If you love to antique, are an avid collector, or just have the urge to "go back in time," downtown Glendale is the place for you. The shops are as varied as they are numerous. There are large multi-dealer malls, smaller shops and specialized dealers. This wide variety of establishments offers vintage sports and automobile memorabilia, nostalgic conversation pieces, captivating old books, yesterday's toys and dolls and thousands of other items of gone-by days. From one shop to another, you'll travel through time as you absorb the history of the 1800s, the Victorian era, the wild and roaring '20s, the simple and rustic charm of America's farms, the excitement and adventure of the old west, sports heros and yesterday's cars, and the quiet elegance and style of a previous generation.

The selection of quality merchandise, the convenience of parking and easy walking to shops, a small-town atmosphere in a picturesque setting, free rides on the town trolley, friendly shopkeepers, great food and hospitality, wonderful special events — these are just some of the reasons that Downtown Glendale was chosen as the "best place to antique in Arizona" by the *Arizona Republic* newspaper.

*Downtown Glendale is located at 59th and Glendale Avenues, just four miles west of I-17. Take the Glendale Ave. exit and drive approximately 20 minutes from downtown Phoenix, forty minutes from Scottsdale Road and Lincoln Dr., and 30 minutes from downtown Tempe.*

*Downtown Glendale boasts antique shops, unique restaurants, specialty dealers and much, much more.*

*Antiquers will find a delightful surprise — riding the courtesy Town Trolley which conveniently loops through the Historic and shopping districts of Downtown Glendale.*

# Bisbee: The center of it all

*Dotting Bisbee's narrow, winding streets are art galleries, antique and trinket shops, cafés, saloons and coffeehouses.*

Arizona's most interesting town — a place where you can read history in the ornate facades of turn-of-the-century buildings, or hear first hand from veterans of the copper mining days. It's a walker town with networks of tiny streets which remind one of a European village. Bisbee is jammed with antiques, boutiques, quaint inns, art galleries and live theatre. Be sure to tour the authentic copper mine. Bisbee boasts the best year-round climate on earth.

To stop in Bisbee is to stop in time. Nestled in the mile high Mule Mountains of southern Arizona, Bisbee has maintained an Old World charm seldom found anywhere in the United States. The fine collection of well-preserved turn-of-the-century Victorian structures are full of old west history and copper mining lore. Old miners' boarding houses have been refurbished into many charming small bed and breakfast establishments, of which no two are alike. Former saloons are now quaint shops, antique stores or art galleries, cafés and restaurants.

A popular activity is Bisbee's excellent self-guided fully-illustrated Walking Tour, which details each historic structure and guides the visitor with a map. Included in the Walking Tour is world-famous Brewery Gulch which in its heyday boasted upwards of 47 saloons and was considered the "liveliest spot between El Paso and San Francisco."

*To Bisbee: From Tucson, Take I-10 east to Arizona 80 and go south 50 miles. About four hours' drive from Phoenix.*

*For information on Bisbee shopping, lodging and sidetrips see listing #1 (Bisbee).*

*Great downtowns can't be forced. They just happen. Bisbee, the turn-of-the-century mining town turned artists' colony, is an outstanding example.*

## 1 BISBEE

Nestled in the Mule Mountains of Southeast Arizona, Bisbee takes you back to the turn of the century. A prominant mining center in the late 19th century, Bisbee preserves this atmosphere by offering a variety of lifestyles set in a matrix of the West's once extensive copper kingdom.

As you walk amidst the solid, stately brick buildings downtown, you can feel the wealth generated by the city's copper mines that were founded to answer the call of the Age of Electricity. As you drive the narrow, twisting streets, or walk endless flights of stairs, you will marvel at the early residents' ingenuity in adapting their lives to the steeply sloping canyons.

Don't leave town without a visit to the Bisbee Mining and Historical Museum, where you will see firsthand why Bisbee, once "Queen of the Copper Camps," is now a thriving community that draws tourists from around the world to experience turn-of-the-century life in an urban center on the frontier. Then go underground on the guided Queen Mine Tour, through what was once a working copper mine, and talk to former miners as they explain life in the dark underground shafts.

*For a look at the quaint, historic town of Bisbee see review at the beginning of this section.*

### On Consignment In Bisbee

100 Lowell Traffic Circle
520/432-4002
Tues.-Sat. 10:30-5:30 and 1st Sun. each month 12-5
*Directions: Located 1/4 mile south of the Lavender Pit Mine on the Traffic Circle (the only building right on the circle)*

Antiques and glass, tools and brass, vintage kitchenware, jewelry and lots of ???. On Consignment boasts of having something for every taste and budget. With over 600 consignors, the store has been described as "The Attic of Cochise County." Within its 12,000 sq. ft., this shopper's paradise is jam-packed with an amazing mix of old, new and the unusual. Strange things have been known to happen at On Consignment in Bisbee. A woman customer came in and recognized, high on the wall, a seascape painted by her husband's long-deceased great-aunt, who never left San Francisco. Like most of the great-aunt's paintings, it had been sold at a gallery. The family had only a few of her works and the woman was thrilled to find one for $25.

**Bisbee Antiques & Collectibles**
3 Main St.
520/432-4320

**Pentimento**
29 Main St.
520/432-2752

**Johnson's Antiques & Books**
45 Main St.
520/432-2736

**Flying Saucers Antqs. & Collectibles**
26A Brewery Ave.
520/432-4858

**Good Goods**
54 Brewery Gulch
520/432-2788

**Acorn Gift Shoppe & Antiques**
924 Hwy. 80, 1 Mile E. of Tunnel
520/432-7314

**Main Street Antiques**
67 Main St.
520/432-4104

**Horse Hotel Antiques**
69 Main St.
520/432-9050

**Crystal Moon**
76 Main St.
520/432-9088

**Timeless Treasures**
2 Copper Queen Plaza
520/432-5888

**Atalanta Music & Books**
38 Main St.
520/432-9976

**Cruceros**
23 Erie
520/432-1299

**Far Out Ranch**
78 Main St.
520/432-2912

**Johnson Gallery**
28 Main St.
520/432-2126

### *Great Places To Stay*

### Hotel La More/The Bisbee Inn

45 OK St.
1-888-432-5131 or 520/432-5131
Email Bisbeeinn@aol.com
Alfred & Elissa Strati, Proprietors
*Directions: For specific directions to The Bisbee Inn from your location, please call the Innkeepers.*

Originally built in 1917 as a miner's hotel, today the Inn is a certified historic restoration containing 20 guest rooms, most with private baths, original oak and period furnishings, and a charming dining room serving complimentary country breakfasts. It is located in the downtown historic district in close proximity to Brewery Gulch and other Bisbee points of interest.

### *Interesting Side Trips*

Bisbee boasts the oldest golf course in Arizona, live repertory theaters, numerous art galleries, pottery studios, jewelry, craftsmen and gem and mineral stores.

**Bisbee Mining and Historical Museum**
Located in downtown Historic Bisbee
Open 10-4, seven days, fee charged, senior discount
520/432-7071

**Queen Mine Tours**
Hwy. 80 interchange entering Old Bisbee
520/432-2071

## 2 CORNVILLE

### Eight Ball Antiques

1050 S. Page Springs Road
520/634-1479
Wed.-Sun. 10-5, Mon. & Tues. by chance
*Directions: Located 80 miles north of Phoenix or 45 miles south of Flagstaff. Take I-17 to McGuireville Exit #293. Travel west 9 miles on Cornville Road to Page Springs Road. Turn right on Page Springs Road. Go 1/4 mile, building is on left.*

"If you build it, they will come" - a commonly heard phrase originally coined by several "claim to fame" baseball teams. I borrowed it because it is so appropriate for Eight Ball Antiques. Nestled away in the sleepy little community of Cornville, Jim and his wife, Kristin, have successfully attracted collectors of the unusual from all over the U.S. You will understand this curious following the minute you enter the 4,500-square-foot building filled to the rafters with oddities such as service station memorabilia, wagon wheels, large games, peddle toys, Lincoln Log building sets, old tools, primitives and lots more. If one of the antique cars offered for sale won't fit into your trunk, you can opt for a scaled-down version. Jim has quite an assortment of collectible cars from which to choose.

Not your traditional antique "stop," I figured Jim must have some "highly guarded" sources for acquiring such offerings. He clarified my misconception by explaining that his forte for gathering this hodge-podge of gizmos and gadgets was a result of his 30 years of collecting. Looks like Jim and Kristin had one heck of a spring cleaning when they decided to open up shop!

## 3 COTTONWOOD

**Home Sweet Home**
303 S. Main St.
520/634-3304

**J & J Antiques & Things**
796 N. Main St.
520/639-1732

**Old Town Antiques**
712 N. Balboa St.
520/634-5461

## 4 FLAGSTAFF

**Carriage House Antique Mall**
413 N. San Francisco St.
520/774-1337

**Golden Memories**
101 S. Milton Road
520/774-5915

**Collection Connection**
901 N. Beaver
520/779-2943

**Incahoots**
9 E. Aspen Ave.
520/773-9447

**Mountain Christmas**
14 N. San Francisco St.
520/774-4054

**Old Highway Trading Post**
698 E. Route 66
520/774-0035

**Lightning Antiques**
1926 N. 4th St. #8
520/527-4444

***Great Places To Stay***

### The Inn at 410 Bed & Breakfast

410 North Leroux St.
520/774-0088

Turn of the century home - eight guest rooms with private baths.

## 5 GLENDALE

Known as Arizona's "Antique Capital," historic Glendale offers more than 80 antique and specialty shops, plus unique eateries and tea rooms in the Historic Downtown area.
*Directions: Downtown Glendale is located at 59th and Glendale Avenues, just 4 miles west of I-17. Take the Glendale Ave. exit and drive approximately 20 minutes from downtown Phoenix, 40 minutes from Scottsdale Road and Lincoln Dr. , and 30 minutes from downtown Tempe.*

For specific information see review at the beginning of this section.

### The Apple Tree

5811 W. Glendale Ave.
602/435-8486
Mon.-Sat. 10-5, Sun. 11-4
*Directions: (Phoenix Metro Area) From I-17, exit #205, Glendale Ave., go west 4 miles. From I-10, Exit #138. 59th Avenue, go North 5 miles to Glendale Ave., turn right (East) on Glendale Ave. Shop is on South Side of Glendale Ave. Between 59th and 58th Avenues.*

For specific information see review at the beginning of this section.

**Shaboom's**
5533 W. Glendale Ave.
602/842-8687

**Adventures Through Looking Glass**
5609 W. Glendale Ave.
602/930-7884

**Purple Elephant**
5734 W. Glendale Ave.
602/931-1991

**Nifties Antiques**
5745 W. Glendale Ave.
602/930-8407

**Ramblin Roads**
5747 W. Glendale Ave.
602/931-5084

**Lois Lovables Antiques**
5748 W. Glendale Ave.
602/934-8846

**Antique Arena**
5825 W. Glendale Ave.
602/930-7121

**Larry's Antiques**
7120 N. 55th Dr.
602/435-1133

**Strunk's Hollow**
6960 N. 57th Dr.
602/842-2842

**Old Mill Stream Antique & Cllbls.**
7021 N. 57th Dr.
602/939-2545

**Now Then & Always Inc.**
7021 N. 57th Dr.
602/931-1116

**Gatehouse Antiques**
7023 N. 57th Dr.
602/435-1919

**Antique Treasurers**
7025 N. 57th Dr.
602/931-8049

**Back To The Classic Antiques**
7031 N. 57th Dr.
602/939-5537

**Memories Past Antiques**
7138 N. 57th Dr.
602/435-9592

**Antique Emporium**
6835 N. 58th Dr.
602/842-3557

**Century House Antiques**
6835 N. 58th Ave.
602/939-1883

**Mr. Peabody's Antiques**
6835 N. 58th Ave.
602/842-0003

**Lamps by Shirley**
6835 N. 58th Ave.
602/842-3306

**Glendale Square Antiques**
7009 N. 58th Ave.
602/435-9952

**Grandma's House Antiques & Cllbls.**
7142 N. 58th Ave.
602/939-8874

**Sandy's Dream Dolls**
7154 N. 58th Ave.
602/931-1579

**Hometown Antiques**
5745 W. Palmaire Ave.
602/931-8790

**Second Debut**
5851 W. Palmaire Ave.
602/939-3922

**ABD/Murphy Park Place**
5809 W. Glendale Ave.
602/931-0235

**Casa De Lao**
5803 W. Glendale Ave.
602/937-9783

**Cooper Street Antiques**
5757 W. Glendale Ave.
602/939-7731

**Shady Nook Books & Antiques**
5751 W. Glendale Ave.
602/939-1462

**House of Gera**
7025 N. 58th Ave.
602/842-4631

**Arsenic & Old Lace**
7157 N. 59th Ave.
602/842-9611

**Remember That? Antiques**
5807 W. Myrtle Ave.
602/435-1179

**Antique Apparatus Exchange**
5802 W. Palmaire Ave.
602/435-1522

**Antique Etc.**
5753 W. Glendale Ave.
602/939-2732

## 6 GOODYEAR

**Your Hidden Treasures**
100 E. Western Ave.
602/932-9332

## 7 JEROME

Almost a mile high in the center of Arizona, the town of Jerome is a historic National Landmark. Once a roaring copper mining camp and a boom town of 15,000 people, Jerome was built on Cleopatra Hill above a vast deposit of copper. The mines, the workers and those who sought its wealth - miners and smelter workers, freighters and gamblers, bootleggers and saloon keepers, storekeepers and assorted Europeans, Latins and Asians, prostitutes and preachers, wives and children - all made Jerome, Ariz., what it was.

Prehistoric Native Americans were the first miners. The Spanish followed, seeking gold but finding copper. Anglos staked the first claims in the area in 1876, and United Verde Mining Operations began in 1883, followed by the Little Daisy chain. Americans, Mexicans, Croatians, Irish, Spaniards, Italians and Chinese added to the increasingly cosmopolitan mix that caused Jerome to grow rapidly from tent city to prosperous company town.

Billions of dollars of copper were extracted from the earth under Jerome. Changing times in the Arizona Territory saw pack burros, mule-drawn freight wagons and horses replaced by steam engines, autos and trucks. Fires ravaged the clapboard town again and again, but Jerome was always rebuilt. In 1918, underground mining was phased out after uncontrollable fires erupted in the 88 miles of tunnels under the town. Open pit mining brought dynamiting. The hills rattled and buildings cracked. The earth's surface began to shift and sections of the business district slid downward. Jerome's notorious "sliding jail" moved 225 feet and now rests across the road from its original site.

Dependent on the ups and downs of copper prices, labor unrest, depressions and wars, Jerome's mines finally closed in 1953. After the mines closed and "King Copper" left town, the population went from a peak of 15,000 in the 1920's to some 50 hardy souls in the late 1950's. The 1960's and 70's were the time of the counter culture, and Jerome offered a haven for artists, who renovated homes and opened abandoned shops to sell their wares. Soon newcomers and a few remaining Jerome old-timers were working together to bring Jerome back to life.

Today, Jerome is very much alive with writers, artists, artisans, musicians, historians, and families. The town is chock-full of shops and galleries, and about 95% of all the town's remaining buildings date from 1895 to the 1920s.

**Collector's Emporium**
301 N. Hull Ave.
520/639-3321

**Papillon**
410 Main St.
520/634-7626

### *Great Places To Stay*

**Ghost City Inn Bed and Breakfast**
541 N. Main St.
520/63GHOST (520/634-4678)
Open all year, rates $75-95, full breakfast included

Built in 1898, the historically registered Ghost City Inn Bed & Breakfast offers a veranda view from each guest room that scans the Verde Valley and the terraced red rocks of Sedona - a view that some say challenges the views of the Grand Canyon in magnificence. All five guest rooms contain an artful blend of Victorian and early American. A full-service breakfast and afternoon tea are provided, as well as a turn-down service with chocolates, and assistance with recreational plans.

## 8 LAKE HAVASU CITY

**Boulevard Mall**
2137 McCulloch Blvd. N.
520/855-7277

**Now & Then**
2104 McCulloch Blvd. N.
520/680-1700

**Remember When Antiques & Gifts**
2026 McCulloch Blvd. N.
520/453-9494

**Classic Golf & Collectibles**
2014 McCulloch Blvd.
520/453-2070

**Somewhere In Time Antiques**
1535 Marlboro Dr.
520/453-7778

**Whimsical Antiques**
1535 Marlboro Dr.
520/453-2112

## 9 MESA

### Carole & Maxine's Antiques

2353 E. Brown Road
602/964-6006
Email carole@azantique.com
Web site: www.azantique.com
Tues.-Sat. 11-5
*Directions: Traveling Hwy. 60 east of Phoenix, take Gilbert Road exit north to Brown Road. Turn east 1/2 mile on south side. Mesa is approximately 18 miles east of Phoenix. The shop is on E. Brown Road in Mesa.*

Ms. Augustin has been importing 18th and 19th century pine furniture and accessories from the U.K. for 37 years. The shop and the Augustin home is located on historical property. The farmhouse dates back to 1918 and the antique shop is situated in the two-story barn in back. Ms. Augustin was originally in business with her mother, but today she runs this elegant, "with the feel of country," upscale shop herself. Her knowledge of fine quality antiques is evident in the selections she has displayed throughout the shop. Along with the pine furnishings you'll find a delightful array of flow blue, as well as other fine blue and white pieces, Victorian glass, a sampling of decorative accessories, and "hard to find" exceptional copper and brass items.

**Stewart's Military Antiques**
108 W. Main St.
602/834-4004

**Country Attic**
1941 W. Guadalupe Road
602/838-0360

**Downtown Antiques**
202 W. Main St.
602/833-4838

**New Again Antiques**
212 W. Main St.
602/834-6189

**Glass Urn**
456 W. Main St. #G
602/833-2702

**Almost Anything**
3015 E. Main St. #101
602/924-6260

**Treasures From The Past Antiques**
106 E. McKellips Road
602/655-0090

**Beyond Expressions Antique**
3817 E. McKellips Road
602/854-7755

**Mesa Antique Mart**
1455 S. Stapley, Suite 12
602/813-1909

**Pam's Place**
1121 S. Country Club Dr.
602/827-9637

**Ron & Soph Antiques**
1060 W. Broadway
602/964-7437

**Antique Plaza**
114 W. Main St.
602/833-4844

***Interesting Side Trip***

### The Lost Dutchman

*Located in the Superstition Mountains just outside of Mesa*

There have been hundreds of reported claims to the Lost Dutchman treasure dating back as far as the 1870s. Perhaps the first recorded claim was made by The Dutchman, a man named Jacob Waltz who was actually of German descent. The gold is believed to be stashed away in the Superstition Mountains somewhere near the landmark known as Weaver's Needle. Additional clues published in the *Phoenix Gazette* during the late 1800s indicates that a lost cabin plays a significant part in the claim's location.

The question of whether this gold is, in fact, from a mine or the remains of some earlier expedition, is as much a mystery as the treasure itself. One of the many legends surrounding the Lost Dutchman indicates that in the 1840s a Mexican cartel unearthed the treasure from the mine. However, the miners were attacked by Apaches and never got out with the gold. Unaware of the importance of the yellow metal, the Indians ripped apart the sacks containing the gold, spreading it across the area.

If this story is true, then the Lost Dutchman isn't a mine at all. This would also mean Jacob Waltz wasn't digging; he was gathering the gold scattered by the Apaches. His claim was merely a cover for protection against other prospectors seeking the lavish bounty. According to Waltz, the same map used by the Mexican expedition led him and another German, Jacob Weiser, to discover the mine. Once again, their extraction of the gold was cut short by an Apache ambush similar to the one staged against the Mexicans in 1840. It is unclear whether Jacob Weiser survived, but Waltz made it out alive.

There is no indication that Waltz returned to collect his fortune prior to the earthquake on May 3, 1887. The gold, whether still in the mine or scattered on the ground, would have disappeared in the shifting of rock and earth. If, in fact, Waltz had located the Lost Dutchman, the identifiable landmarks which served as clues would have been dramatically altered by the quake. Nevertheless, Jacob Waltz definitely knew something about this mysterious lost treasure - too much of his life was consumed by its existence. On his deathbed on October 25, 1891, Waltz spoke one last time about the infamous Lost Dutchman. He told his caretaker, Mrs. Julia Thomas, the story of the fabulous mine he had discovered in the Superstition Mountains.

Given all the information reported by Jacob Waltz and countless others who have followed in his footsteps, it seems somewhat reasonable to believe the Lost Dutchman, in whatever form, exists.

## 10 PAYSON

**Country Corner**
111 E. State Hwy. 260
520/474-0014

**Granny's Attic**
800 E. State Hwy. 260
520/474-3962

**Star Valley USA Antiques**
55293 E. State Hwy. 260
520/472-7343

**The Teapot**
216 W. Main St.
520/474-0718

**Hopi House**
102 S. Beeline Hwy.
520/474-4000

**Payson Antique Mall**
1001 S. Beeline Hwy.
520/474-8988

**Hodge Podge Cottage**
204 S. Beeline Hwy.
520/472-7752

**Pioneer Village Trading Post**
1117 N. Beeline Hwy.
520/474-3911

## 11 PHOENIX

**Antique Gems**
2305 N. 7th St.
602/252-6288

**Spine**
1323 E. McDowell Road
602/252-4858

**Vintage Classics**
2301 N. 7th St.
602/252-7271

**Consignment Gallery**
330 E. Camelback Road
602/631-9630

**Mussallem Fine Arts Inc.**
5120 N. Central Ave.
602/277-5928

**Xavier Square Antiques**
4700 N. Central Ave.
602/248-8208

**Alcuin Books**
115 W. Camelback Road
602/279-3031

**Antique Gallery**
5037 N. Central Ave.
602/241-1174

**Central Antique Gallery**
36 E. Camelback Road
602/241-1636

**Pink Flamingo Antiques**
2241 N. 7th St.
602/261-7730

**Arizona Historical Cache Antiques**
5807 N. 7th St.
602/264-0629

**Bobbi's Antiques**
3838 N. 7th St.
602/264-1787

**Empire Antiques**
5003 N. 7th St.
602/240-2320

**Second Hand Rose**
1350 E. Indian School Road
602/266-5956

**Central Outpost**
9405 N. Central Ave.
602/997-2253

**Antique Gatherings**
3601 E. Indian School Road
602/956-8203

**Sweet Annie Doodle's**
5025 N. 7th St.
602/230-1058

**Travel Thru Time**
5115 N. 7th St.
602/274-0666

**Nook & Kranny**
4302 N. 7th St.
602/241-0228

**Wizard of Odz Antiques**
1643 E. Bell Road
602/788-1000

**Antiquary**
3044 N. 24th St.
602/955-8881

**Do Wah Diddy**
3642 E. Thomas Road
602/957-3874

**Antique Outpost**
10012 N. Cave Creek Road
602/943-9594

**Millie's Antiques, Gifts & Collectibles**
5102 N. Central Ave.
602/264-0294

**Nickelodeon**
110 W. Seldon Lane
602/943-3512

**Scott D Gram Arts & Antqs.**
1837 W. Thunderbird Road
602/548-3498

**Pzaz**
2528 E. Camelback Road
602/956-4402

**Antique Accents**
2515 E. Bell Road
601/493-1956

**Brass Armadillo**
12419 N. 28th Dr.
888/942-0030

**Sally's Attic Collectables**
24 E. Mohave St.
602/256-4536

**J & K Furniture**
2811 E. Bell Road
602/992-6990

**Labriola's Antique Gallery**
3311 N. 24th St.
602/956-5370

**Matlosz & Co. Antique Furniture**
2227 N. 24th St.
602/273-7974

**Eric's Antiques**
2539 W. Northern Ave.
602/995-2950

**Estate Gallery**
3157 E. Lincoln Dr.
602/956-8845

**Antique Market**
1601 N. 7th Ave.
602/255-0212

**Lamp Hospital**
1643 E. Bell Road
602/788-1000

**Stratford Court Antiques & Interiors**
4848 E. Cactus Road
602/788-6300

### *Interesting Side Trips*

### The Heard Museum

22 E. Monte Visa Road
One block east of Central Ave., and three blocks north of McDowell Road
602/252-8840 or 602/252-8848 (message)
Mon.-Sat. 9:30-5, Wed. 9:30-8, Sun. noon-5, closed on major holidays
Admission charges

Since first opening its doors in 1929, the Heard Museum has earned an international reputation for its outstanding representation of the culture and heritage of Native Americans in the Southwest, plus its unique exhibits and innovative programming. It is internationally recognized for its collections of artifacts and art documenting the history of native cultures, especially Southwestern Native Americans. The Heard Museum was founded in 1929 by Dwight B. and Maie Bartlett Heard, a prominent Phoenix couple who had moved to the Valley of the Sun in the mid-1880s from Chicago. The Heards were avid collectors of Native artifacts and art, especially those of Southwestern Native American cultures. The couple built the Heard Museum in order to share their collection. More than 250,000 people visit the Heard Museum each year - more than any other museum in Arizona. About 25,000 visitors are school children.

Located in central Phoenix, the Heard Museum is home to more than 35,000 objects, as well as an extensive 24,000-volume reference library. The variety of exhibits contain objects that run the gamut from 800 A.D.

to pieces made in the 1990s. The Spanish Colonial Revival building was especially designed on Heard property to house their renowned family collection. Today, visitors can enjoy the Heard's seven exhibit galleries and grounds. Frequently, Native American artists demonstrate beadworking, weaving or carving. Visitors have an opportunity to talk with the artists as they work.

## 12 PINE

**Gingerbread House**
Hwy. 87 & Randell Dr.
520/476-3504

**Apple Annie's**
Hardscrabble Road
520/476-4569

**Pineberry Antiques & Collectibles**
86 Hwy. 87
520/476-2219

## 13 PINETOP / LAKESIDE

**Harvest Moon Antiques**
392 W. Mountain Blvd.
520/367-6973

**Antiques & Stuff**
774 W. Woodland Lake Road
520/367-1732

**Billings Country Pine Antiques**
103 W. Yaeger Lane
520/367-1709

**White Mountain Antiques**
1691 W. White Mt. Blvd.
520/368-6266

**Pinecrest Lane Antiques**
50 E. Pinecrest Lane
520/367-0943

**Sweet Corn Antiques**
Hwy. 260
520/368-9090

**Sherry's Antiques Mall**
857 E. White Mountain Blvd.
520/367-5184

**Homestead Antiques & Collectibles**
Corner of Homestead/Mt. View
520/368-6592

**The Antique Mercantile Co.**
Hwy. 260
520/368-9090

**Wings of Faith Antiques**
1687 W. White Mountain Road
520/368-5772

**Orchard Antiques**
1664 W. White Mountain Blvd.
520/368-6563

## 14 PRESCOTT

Historic Prescott, established in 1864, is one of the oldest communities in Arizona. Located nearly a mile high on a pine-covered basin at the base of the Bradshaw Mountains, Prescott was the only United States territorial capital founded in a wilderness. It was spawned from gold fever after mountain man Joseph Reddeford Walker led the first prospectors to the site in 1863. What began as a ramshackle mining camp grew into the central Arizona territory's hub for trading and freighting. Miners, ranchers and cowboys found solace in the gambling halls and saloons that soon peppered the city's streets.

Prescott's first courthouse was built in 1867; its first hanging occurred in 1875 (the doomed man's innocence was proven 60 years later). Twice named territorial capital, it lost the honor first to Tucson in 1867, and finally to Phoenix in 1889. A devastating fire in 1900 all but leveled downtown, razing homes, hotels and businesses along the streets of Gurley, Montezuma and North Cortez. Undaunted, the citizens of Prescott rebuilt their lost structures in much finer fashion than those that had stood before.

Traces of Prescott's earlier days abound throughout the downtown area, from saloons boasting hand-carved mahogany bars to historic hotels, from the Hassayampa Inn to Sharlot Hall Museum. Take a turn up North Cortez, where an entire row of antique emporiums offer collections ranging from the distinctive to the whimsical. Step off the beaten path and you may discover that singular treasure of your dreams tucked inside one of the Alley shops.

**Book Nook**
324 W. Gurley St.
520/778-2130

**Collector's Mart**
133 N. Cortez
520/776-7969

**Lil Bit O'Everything**
136 S. Montezuma
520/445-6237

**Emporium on Cortez**
107 N. Cortez
520/778-3091

**Prescott Antiques & Crafts**
115 N. Cortez St.
520/445-7156

**Pennington's Antiques**
117 N. Cortez St.
520/445-3748

**131 North Cortez Antiques**
131 N. Cortez St.
520/445-6992

**Deja Vu**
134 N. Cortez St.
520/445-6732

**Merchandise Mart**
205 N. Cortez St.
520/776-1728

**Arizona Territory Antiques**
211 W. Aubrey St.
520/445-4656

**Young's Antiques & Collectibles**
115 W. Willis St.
520/717-1526

**A Hidden Treasure**
140 N. Cortez St.
520/776-4268

**Antique Bulldog**
711 Miller Valley Road
520/717-1484

**Atteberry's Antiques**
126 N. Cortez St.
520/778-6565

**Keystone Antiques**
127 N. Cortez St.
520/445-1757

**Old Firehouse Antiques**
334 S. Montezuma St.
520/778-2969

**Second Hand Man Inc.**
535 S. Montezuma St.
520/445-6007

### *Great Places To Stay*

**Mount Vernon Inn**
204 North Mount Vernon Ave.
520/778-0886

1900s Greek Revival, located in Arizona's largest Victorian neighborhood.

## 15 SCOTTSDALE

### The Song of the Balladeer

Back in the 1880s Chaplain Winfield Scott heard the siren song of the unexplored. The irresistible melody, which had already lured thousands to the California gold mines, called him to travel. Gazing at a vast stretch of undeveloped country, Scott proclaimed it "unequaled in greater fertility or richer promise." What would soon become an agricultural community, christened Scottsdale, recorded its first official historic moment.

That strong tie to a frontier past still exerts itself, with great charm and persistence, in modern Scottsdale. Cowboys, horses, a reverence for the land, and a respect for Western tradition are very much a part of the contemporary scene. Visitors come here today, as they did years ago, to explore the possibilities.

So what's the most direct way to experience the Old West? A guided horseback ride or jeep tour over desert trails, the snug fit of your cowboy hat's brim, the drowsy warmth of the sun, or the brilliant streaks of vermilion reddening the Western horizon, evoke a deeply nostalgic response. A mesquite campfire carrying the aroma of sizzling steaks, and the lonesome melodies of a cowboy balladeer will beckon you back in time and in spirit.

The ultimate immersion in life on the trail, however, is the dude ranch. Straying from authenticity just enough to keep guests happy, the ranch experience embraces the rowdy fun of haywagon rides, songfests, cookouts, trap and skeet shooting and of course, daily horseback excursions.

Most unusual, though, may be an overnight pack trip in the nearby Superstition Mountains. Here you can pan for gold and search like thousands of wild-eyed prospectors before you, for the legendary Lost Dutchman's Mine. (See #2 Mesa for more information on the Lost Dutchman's Mine.)

Scottsdale's truest, proudest passion, however, is reserved for the arts. This glorious environment inspired master architects Frank Lloyd Wright, Paolo Soleri and Bennie Gonzales, whose studios and works have helped to create the aesthetic appeal of the city.

With more than 120 galleries, studios and museums, Scottsdale shines as an internationally known art center. You'll want to plan an evening around the Scottsdale Art Walk held in downtown Scottsdale every Thursday night, year-round. The galleries stay open late, serve refreshments, and encourage you to meet their guests - artists, art critics, writers, musicians, dancers, and performers of all types.

**Antiques Super-Mall**
(formerly Arizona Antique Gallery)
1900 N. Scottsdale Road
602/874-2900
Mon.-Sun. 10-6, Thurs. 10-8

**Antique Centre**
2012 N. Scottsdale Road
602/675-9500

**Antique Trove**
2020 N. Scottsdale Road
602/947-6074

For specific information on the three shops listed above see review at the beginning of this section.

**Brown House Antiques**
7001 E. Main St., #4
602/423-0293

**J. H. Armer Co.**
6926 E. Main St.
602/947-2407

**Gray Goose Antiques**
7012 E. Main St.
602/423-5735

**Rose Tree Antiques**
7013 E. Main St.
602/949-1031

**Collectors' Finds Antiques Inc.**
7077 E. Main St.
602/946-9262

**Christopher's Galleries**
7056 E. Main St.
602/941-5501

**Music Box Shop Inc.**
7236 E. 1st Ave.
musicbox@getnet.com

**Bradbury's Antique Bazaar**
6166 B Scottsdale Road #603
602/998-1885

**Pewter & Wood Antiques**
10636 N. 71st Way
602/948-2060

**Impeccable Pig**
7042 E. Indian School Road
602/941-1141

**Ye Olde English Antiques Co.**
6522 E. Mescal St.
No Phone # Listed

**Estate Gallery**
7077 E. Main St., Suite 5
602/423-8023

**Carriage Trade Antiques Inc.**
7077 E. Main St.
602/970-6700

**J. Scott Antiques**
7001 E. Main St.
602/941-9260

**Richard II Antiques**
7004 Main St.
602/990-2320

**Irontiques**
7077 E. Main St., #4
602/947-9679

**Accents To The Max**
7140 E. 6th Ave.
602/947-3070

**Circa Galleries**
7056 E. Main St.
602/990-1121

**Mollard's**
7127 E. 6th Ave.
602/947-2203

**Gallery 10 Inc.**
34505 N. Scottsdale Road
602/945-3385

**Rustique Collections**
23417 N. Pima Road, Suite 165
602/473-7000

**John C. Hill Antique Indian Art**
6962 E. 1st Ave., Suite 104
602/946-2910

**Bishop Gallery**
7164 E. Main St.
602/949-9062

### *Great Places To Stay*

**The Phoenician Resort**
6000 E. Camelback Road
602/941-8200
1-800-888-8234 (U.S. and Canada)
(a property of the ITT Sheraton Luxury Collection)

An all-encompassing, international luxury resort harmoniously covering 250 acres at the base of Camelback Mountain. The Phoenician has only been in operation eight years, yet has garnered every possible award in all categories offered by national and international ratings surveys. An elegant vacation retreat, it offers an unparalleled combination of luxury accommodations, appointments, amenities and service.

## 16 SEDONA

**Greentree Stocks**
2756 W. Hwy. 89A
520/282-6547

**Compass Rose Gallery**
671 Hwy. 179
520/282-7904

**Claire's Sweet Antiques**
251 Hwy. 179
520/204-1340

**Claire's Sweet Antiques**
Basha's Center
520/204-1340

**Sedona Antique Mall**
6586 Hwy. 179
520/284-1125

## 17 TOMBSTONE

### How Tombstone Came To Be

Tombstone, Ariz., is one of the most recognizable names in American history. About 70 miles southeast of Tucson and 30 miles from the Mexican border in southeastern Arizona, Tombstone is one of the most famous of the silver boomtowns of the Old West. But it was actually named in ironic humor of a man's impending death!

With a prospector's outfit and $30, Edward Schieffelin headed for Apache country, east of Fort Huachuca, Arizona, to look for silver. When soldiers at the fort heard of his folly, they laughed and told him all he would find in those hills would be his tombstone...meaning that the Indians would surely get him. In late August, 1877, Schieffelin made his first of many silver strikes and named his rich vein "The Tombstone." He realized around $1 million from his claims in the early 1880s, and soon the town of Tombstone arose, the mightiest city between El Paso and San Francisco. Some reports go as far as to state that the population in the 1880s reached nearly 15,000 - larger than Los Angeles or San Francisco at the time! But the silver mines closed in 1889 and the population disappeared. Today about 1,600 people live in Tombstone, but hundreds of thousands of tourists visit each year.

On May 14, 1896, Schieffelin died in Oregon. In accordance with his wishes, he was buried in Tombstone, covered by a monument three miles west of town. On this monument is a marker inscribed, "This is my Tombstone."

### *Interesting Side Trips*

**The Bird Cage Theatre**
Downtown Tombstone, Arizona
Admission charged

The last of a bygone era of western history, the Bird Cage was the most famous honky-tonk in America between 1881 and 1889. The *New York Times* referred to it in 1882 as the wildest, wickedest night spot between Basin Street and the Barbary Coast! Tombstone was in its prime mining boom during the 1880s. At the same time, the Bird Cage was making a reputation for the town that would never be forgotten. In nine years this lusty den of iniquity never closed its doors 24 hours a day. Before its operation would end in 1898, it would be the sight of 16 gunfights. The 140 bullet holes that riddle the walls and the ceilings are mute evidence of these happenings.

The Bird Cage was named for the 14 bird cage crib compartments that are self-suspended from the ceiling overhanging the gambling casino and dance hall. It was in these compartments that the prostitutes (or ladies of the night, as they were called) plied their trade. The refrain from the song, *"She's Only A Bird In A Gilded Cage"* became one of the nation's most popular songs. These bird cages remain today with their original red velvet drapes and trimmings.

The entertainment on stage at the Bird Cage ranged from its nightly French circuit cancan dancers to risque performances for the male gender, to national headliners such as Eddie Foy, Lotta Crabtree and a host of others. The ladies of the town, and there were some, never entered the Bird Cage - or, for that matter, even walked on the same side of the street. The hand painted stage with its original curtain, retains its faded luster today, as in 1881.

Directly below the stage are the wine cellar, the dressing rooms and the poker room. Here the longest poker game in western history occurred. It was a house game and players had to buy a $1,000 minimum in chips for a seat in the game.The game ran continually for eight years, five months and three days! Today that poker table still stands as it was left, with its chairs on the dirt floor. Some of the most famous characters of western history came to the Bird Cage to gamble, drink and be entertained by its lovely ladies. Wyatt Earp met his third wife, Sadie Marcus, at the Bird Cage. Red-coated bartenders poured nothing but Tombstone's best at a custom-made cherrywood bar and back bar. The bar is flanked by a dumb-waiter that sent drinks upstairs to the ladies of the night and their men friends. Today it exists as Tombstone's only remaining bar of the 1880s in its original building.

When you look into the original French mirror of the back bar, you see the famous bar painting of Fatima, who has been hanging in the same location since 1882. She carries the scars of six bullet holes and stands nine feet high. When disaster struck Tombstone by the folding of the mines, the Bird Cage was sealed and boarded up with all its fixtures and furnishings intact. For almost 50 years it stood closed, its contents touched only by the passing of time. In 1934 the Bird Cage Theatre became a historic landmark of the American West, when it was opened for the public to visit. The Bird Cage stands today as an adolescent old maid in her infancy for all to see and to feel the nostalgia of the past. It is Tombstone's only historic landmark in its original state, preserved from its beginning in 1881, maintaining its lighting fixtures, chandeliers, drapes and gambling tables on the casino floor. Its massive grand piano is still in the orchestra pit. The coin operated juke box still plays today as in 1881. You also see Tombstone's most valuable individual antique - The Black Moriah. This original Boothill hearse is trimmed in 24K gold and sterling silver.

A big draw today for the Bird Cage is its ghosts - dozens, maybe even hundreds of them-that manifest themselves on a daily basis to just about everyone who comes to town. It seems that the paranormal is the "normal" order of modern Tombstone, complete with sights, sounds, smells, ghostly appearances, and objects that mysteriously and inexplicably appear and disappear. Bill Hunley (whose family built, owned and operated the Bird Cage), his family and friends, plus hundreds of tourists, have all documented these strange but (to Tombstone residents) normal occurrences. So have numerous parapsychologists, psychics and professional photographers. Some years ago, Duke University even sent a team of parapsychologists to conduct research at the Bird Cage where they counted 27 spirits and even took their photographs! So when people say that the past comes back to haunt us, they mean it literally in Tombstone!

**Third Street Antique Mall**
109 S. 3rd St.
520/457-9219

## 18 TUCSON

**American West Primitive Art**
363 S. Meyer Ave.
520/623-4091

**A Antiques Warehouse**
3450 E. 34th St.
520/326-9552

**Antiques & Old Things**
2549 E. Broadway Blvd.
520/325-4554

**Treasure Shop**
24 E. 15th St.
520/622-5070

**A Treasure Chest**
4041 E. Grant
520/327-9001

**Camille's**
2930 N. Swan Road #127
520/322-9163

**Saguard Moon Antiques Co-op**
45 S. 6th Ave.
520/623-5393

**Hammerblow Mining Museum**
1340 W. Glenn St.
520/882-7073

**Firehouse Antiques Center**
6522 E. 22nd St.
520/571-1775

**Christine's Curiosity Shop**
4940 E. Speedway Blvd.
520/323-0018

**Eisenhut Antiques**
2229 N. Country Club Road
520/327-9382

**Medicine Man Gallery**
7000 E. Tanque Verde Rd., Ste. 7
520/722-7798

**Antique Mini-Mall**
3408 E. Grant Road
520/326-6502

**Cat House Collectibles**
2924 E. Broadway Blvd.
520/795-2181

**Primitive Arts Gallery**
3026 E. Broadway Blvd.
520/326-4852

**Phyliss' Antiques**
1918 E. Prince Road
520/326-5712

**Country Emporium Antiques**
3431 N. Dodge Blvd.
520/327-7765

**Colonial Frontiers**
244 S. Park Ave.
520/327-7765

**Morning Star Antiques**
2000 E. Speedway Blvd.
520/881-3060

**Unique Antiques**
5000 E. Speedway Blvd.
520/323-0319

**Antq. Cntr. of Tucson/Unique Antqs.**
5000 E. Speedway Blvd.
520/323-0319

**Antique Mall**
3130 E. Grant Road
520/326-3070

**Arizona Mall**
3728 E. Grant Road
520/770-9840

**Country Trading Post**
2811 N. Country Club Road
520/325-7326

**Sunland Antiques Inc.**
2208 N. Country Club Road
520/323-1134

**Antique Presidio**
3024 E. Grant
520/323-1844

**B & T Antique Mall**
5602 E. 22nd St.
520/745-3849

**Elegant Junque Shop**
4932 E. Speedway Blvd.
520/881-8181

**Antique Center**
5000 E. Speedway Blvd.
520/323-0319

**Vintage Treasures & Antiques**
2351 N. Elvernon, Ste. J
520/795-7475

## 19 WICKENBURG

**An Antique Store**
272 E. Wickenburg Way
520/684-3357

**Treasures N Trashe**
1141 W. Wickenburg Way
520/684-7445

**Head-West Barber & Antique Shop**
605 W. Wickenburg Way (Hwy. 60)
520/684-3439

**Antique Village**
280 E. Wickenburg Way
520/684-5497

**Quarter-Horse Rancho Antiques**
30220 U.S. Hwy. 60 89
520/684-7445

## 20 YUMA

**Packrat's Den**
1360 S. 3rd Ave.
520/783-4071

**Bargain Spot**
385 S. Main St.
520/783-5889

**Gila Gallery Antiques**
195 S. Gila St.
520/783-6128

**Britain's Antiques**
4330 W. Riverside Dr.
520/783-4212

# Arkansas

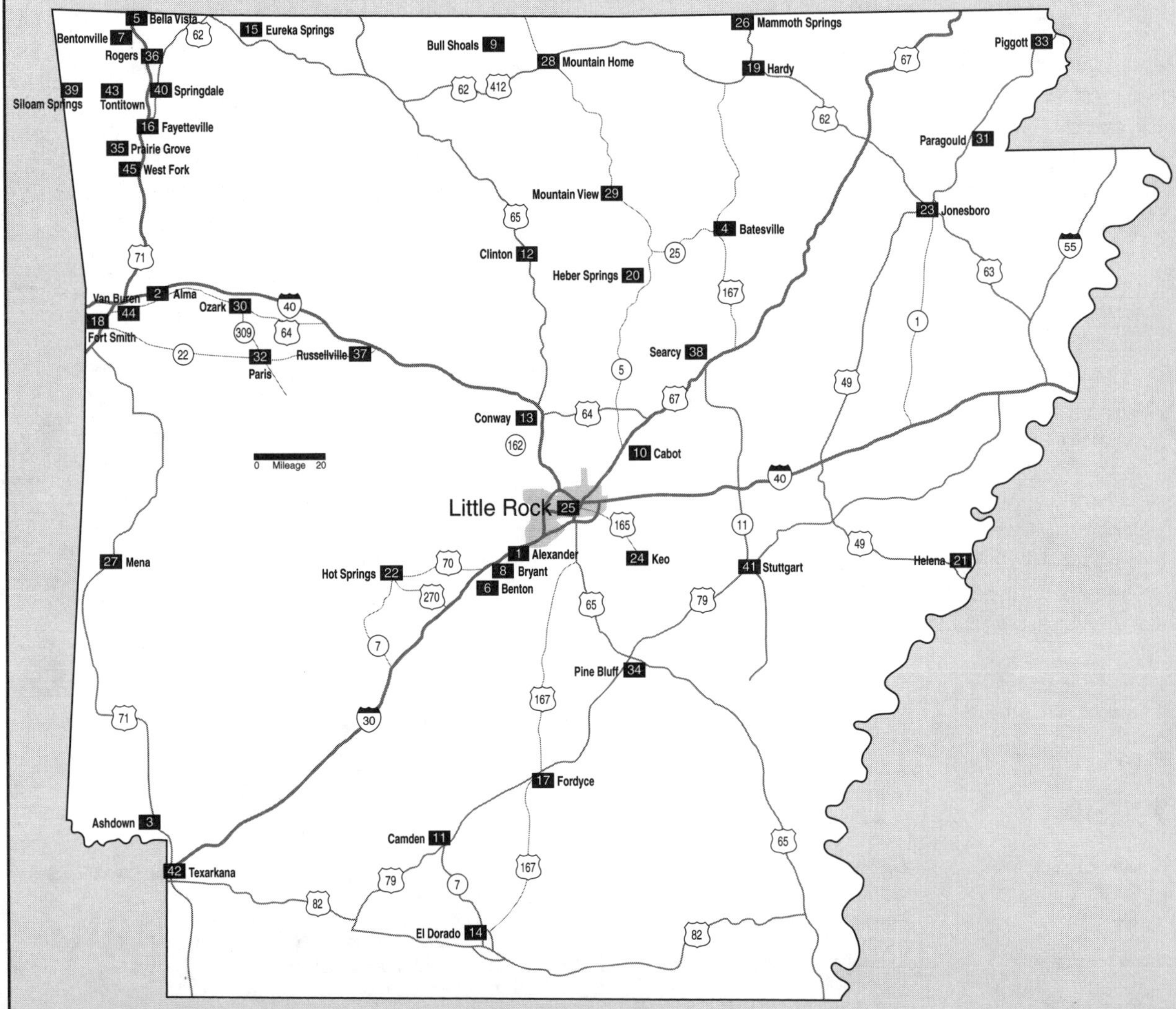

5 Bella Vista
Bentonville 7
Rogers 36
39 Siloam Springs
43 Tontitown
40 Springdale
16 Fayetteville
35 Prairie Grove
45 West Fork
15 Eureka Springs
Bull Shoals 9
28 Mountain Home
26 Mammoth Springs
19 Hardy
Piggott 33
Paragould 31
23 Jonesboro
Mountain View 29
4 Batesville
Clinton 12
Heber Springs 20
Van Buren
2 Alma
44
18
Fort Smith
Ozark 30
32 Paris
Russellville 37
Searcy 38
Conway 13
10 Cabot
0 Mileage 20
Little Rock 25
1 Alexander
8 Bryant
6 Benton
24 Keo
Hot Springs 22
27 Mena
41 Stuttgart
Helena 21
Pine Bluff 34
17 Fordyce
Ashdown 3
Camden 11
42 Texarkana
El Dorado 14
62
412
67
65
71
40
309
64
22
25
167
63
55
1
5
49
162
165
11
70
270
7
79
30
82

*Antiques on Park Avenue offers a general line of antiques, which include the most delightful finds.*

# Stuttgart: Rice and duck calling capital of the world

Although not a large city, the town of Stuttgart is bustling with activity. Probably best noted, by those living outside of town, as the home of The World's Championship Duck Calling Contest, Stuttgart has other attractions as well.

The Agricultural Museum provides its visitors with an understanding of the tools and methods of farming, as well as a glimpse of the lifestyle of days gone by; after all Stuttgart *is* the Rice Capital. A recent expansion documents the agricultural and transportation equipment that was used by local farmers in the past, and another addition records the history of duck hunting in the area. Stuttgart boasts an Art Center which provides year-round exhibits and related activities, such as classes. The duck calling contests draw visitors to the area several times a year, but Stuttgart also has a nationally-acclaimed miniature art show with representatives from more than a dozen states.

Stuttgart is also home to Antiques on Park Avenue. Earleen and Dwight were the first to open an antique mall in Stuttgart, which grew out of Earleen's love for collecting old things. After she had furnished two old homes with antiques, she found herself with lots of wonderful things, but nowhere to put them. That's when she convinced Dwight to renovate a portion of his truck repair shop to accommodate an antique mall. The entrance to the two-story shop is around and behind the building which houses the truck shop. She, along with several other dealers, carries a general line of antiques, but includes the unusual as well. The day I visited the shop I was delighted to find a stunning Victorian Renaissance baby cradle, hand-painted porcelains, estate jewelry, Stickley style and Art Nouveau furniture and one of my favorites, large copper pots.

Antiques on Park Avenue offers after hours showings by calling the mall at 870/673-1159 during open hours, or calling Dan at 870/673-1364 or Hotsey at 870/673-6640 after 5 p.m.

*Antiques on Park Avenue is located at 1703 S. Timber in Stuttgart. For additional information see listing #41 (Stuttgart).*

# Victorian elegance in the heart of Hot Springs

*The Gables Inn invites guests to enter the calming atmosphere of Victorian days, with special attention to every detail of comfort.*

Experience the romance and charm of this beautifully restored 1905 Victorian home, where turn-of-the-century quality of life comes alive with period decor and antiques. The Gables Inn Bed & Breakfast is the perfect setting for a wedding or romantic getaway. The inn is just blocks from Historical Downtown Hot Springs, Bathhouse Row, fine dining, antique shops, museums and entertainment.

The Gables offers four lovely rooms, each individually decorated and each with a private bath. A full breakfast is served on fine china and crystal.

*The Gables Inn is located at 318 Quapaw Ave. in Hot Springs. For additional information, call the innkeepers at 1-800-625-7576. Rates begin at $65.*

*Relax in comfort on the veranda, where cool breezes soothe the spirit.*

*The tea room is the setting for morning coffee; afterwards a delicious breakfast is served in the formal dining room of The Gables Inn.*

*Fine antiques add style; many special details original to the rooms have been restored to their elegant beauty.*

# Crescent Cottage Inn is one "Painted Lady" with colorful past, plenty of personality

*Crescent Cottage Inn is an important landmark of the "Silk Stocking District" of Eureka Springs. Its Victorian architecture has been featured in many national publications.*

Built in 1881 for Powell Clayton, the first governor of Arkansas after the Civil War, Crescent Cottage Inn is a famous historic landmark. This "Painted Lady" with three stories, turned posts, spindlework on front and back porches, a tower capped by a pointed hipped roof, curved topped tall windows, cut-out gable decorations and sunburst, is located at the residential beginning of the historic loop known in Governor Clayton's days as the "Silk Stocking District."It is the most historic and photographed house in town and appears in the famous book *American Painted Ladies.* Its photograph also graces the pages of *Victorian Express*. The house and guest rooms are filled with European antiques dating from 1770 to 1925. The living and dining rooms are separated by a great arch (the only one remaining by the English architect Bousell) and offers high coffered ceilings. A hand-pressed flower chandelier from 1882 hangs in the living room. There are four guest rooms, all with private baths, Jacuzzi, queen-size beds, TV, VCR and telephones.

Two of the guest rooms, Miss Adaline's Room and Charlotte's Room have double Jacuzzi spas, refrigerators and beautiful fireplaces along with unique hand-painted ceilings. The doors of the rooms open onto a porch with swings for enjoying the panoramic view while providing access to the lovely English gardens complete with a waterfall. The Sun Room, named from its origin as a sun porch, includes a Jacuzzi. The Cranberry Suite includes a sitting room and hand-painted ceilings. All guest rooms along with the two back verandas overlook a rare, larglely unobstructed view of a valley and totally forested mountain range.

A great full breakfast is served on the upper porch when possible (usually April through October), or in the dining room. Fresh local fruits, berries and melons, baked bananas, Belgian waffles, salsa souffle, oven-baked puff pancakes, smoked ham, bacon, sausages, juices, rich coffees, teas and hot chocolate are a part of the menu offered at the inn.

*The great arch is by the English architect Bousell; it lends historic importance and distinction to the interior of the Crescent Cottage Inn.*

Crescent Cottage Inn is a short walk to historic downtown attractions. A trolley stop is located across from the inn for those who prefer to tour the city by trolley. The area is known for two large lakes offering great swimming, boating and fishing, hiking trails, summer opera, art galleries, shops, restaurants, folk art and craft fairs and is home to The Great Passion Play. The town swells with tourists in the fall, mainly in October, for a glimpse of the beautifully colored leaves. Crowds gather again in spring for the wild flowering dogwood and redbud trees.

The inn, featured in *Country Living, Southern Living, Country Inns* and numerous newspapers throughout the U.S. has a three-diamond AAA rating, is Mobile quality rated and is also a member of and inspected by The Association of B&Bs of Arkansas. For more information on Crescent Cottage Inn, visit their web site at www.eureka-usa.com/crescott or call 501/253-6022 for a color brochure.

*Crescent Cottage Inn is located at 211 Spring St. in Eureka Springs. For additional information see listing #15 (Eureka Springs). Rates begin at $93.*

# Arkansas

## 1 ALEXANDER

**Blackwell Antiques**
23650 I-30
501/847-2191

**Partain's Antique Mall**
25014 I-30
501/847-4978

**Wornock's Antiques**
12590 I-30
501/847-8222

**Robeson's Antiques & Collectibles**
25608 I-30
501/847-4720

## 2 ALMA

**Days Gone By**
400 Heather Lane
501/632-0829
Jan. to 1st Mon. in Apr., Mon.-Sat. 9-6, Sun. 1-5.
1st Mon. in Apr. - Dec., Mon.-Sat. 9-9, Sun. 1-5

**"The" Flea Market**
1727 Hwy. 71 N.
501/632-2551

**Sisters 2 Too Antq. Mall, Flea Mkt.**
702 Hwy. 71 N.
501/632-2292

**Neva's Collectibles**
Jasmine Lane
501/632-5450

## 3 ASHDOWN

**The Castle**
120 Rankin St.
870/898-9080

**Country Store Antiques #1**
73 E. Main St.
870/898-5741

**Country Store Antiques #2**
330 Keller St.
870/898-5741

**Memories on Main**
69 E. Main St.
870/898-8112

**Memory Lane Antiques**
34 E. Commerce
870/898-8301

**Sandy's Collectibles**
370 Keller St.
870/898-5381

**Shades of Yesteryear**
42 E. Commerce
870/898-2295

## 4 BATESVILLE

**AARON's Antiques**
1382 Bates St.
870/793-7233

**Back In Time Antiques**
217 E. Main St.
870/793-6445

**Diamann's Antiques**
4401 Heber Springs Road
870/251-9151

**Ramsey Mt. Treasures**
553 Batesville Blvd.
870/793-5714

**Patterson Antique Shop**
535 White Dr.
870/793-1139

## 5 BELLA VISTA

**The Bella Vista Flea Market**
130 The Plaza - Hwy. 71
501/855-6999

**Treasures at Wishing Springs**
Wishing Springs Road
501/271-1991

## 6 BENTON

**Jerry Van Dyke's Den & Attic Antiques**
117 S. Market St.
501/860-5600

## 7 BENTONVILLE

**Sunshine Glassworks & Antiques**
206 Hwy. 72 E.
501/273-9218

**Oldies But Goodies Antiques**
305 N.W. 5th St.
501/273-6921

## 8 BRYANT

**Collector's Market**
22430 I-30
501/847-6899

**Galarena Antique Mall**
22430 I-30, Exit 123
501/847-6173

**Finders Keepers Flea Market**
23650 I-30
501/847-4647

**Blue Moon Antiques**
25608 Hwy. 30
501/847-7144

## 9 BULL SHOALS

### *Interesting Side Trip*

**Bull Shoals Caverns and Mountain Village 1890**
Located just off Hwy. 178 in Bull Shoals
501/445-7177 or 1-800-445-7177

In north central Arkansas you can see what life was like for turn-of-the-century settlers back to prehistoric man. Mountain Village 1890 is an authentically restored Ozark town that was retrieved from neglect and decay and completely resurrected as a living tribute to a hardy, resourceful and gentle people — the Ozark mountain folk. See life as it was over 100 years ago, then move to Bull Shoals Caverns, and visualize how prehistoric man, then indigenous Native Americans, and finally Ozark mountaineers lived in some of the world's oldest caverns. You'll see natural formations, an underground stream, underground rivers, a miniature lake and an underground waterfall, while learning how the caverns were formed.

## 10 CABOT

**Simpler Times Antiques**
114 Financial Dr.
501/941-1306

## 11 CAMDEN

**Downtown Antique Mall**
131 S. Adams St. S.E.
870/836-4244

## 12 CLINTON

**Antique Warehouse of Arkansas**
Hwy. 65 N. & 110
501/745-5842

## 13 CONWAY

**Antiques In The Red Barn**
IH-40 at Hwy. 64
501/329-9608

**Carmen's Antiques**
1017 Van Ronkle St.
501/327-6978

**Honey Hole Antiques**
382 Hwy. 65 N.
501/336-4046

**Sybella's**
286 Hwy. 65 N.
501/329-8847

**Conway Antique Mall**
925 Oak St.
501/450-3909

**Front Street Antiques**
910 Front St.
501/327-2185

**Bobbie's Antiques**
1015 Oak St.
501/327-7125

**Quattlebaum Antiques**
1010 Van Ronkle St.
501/329-8671

**Treasure Hunt**
5 D Gapview Road
501/329-6007

**Antiques Plus**
1014 Oak St.
501/450-7656

## 14 EL DORADO

**Peggy's Hobby House**
2908 Oak Lane
870/863-9553

**Marian's Downstairs Attic**
301 S. Madison Ave.
870/862-9580

**Blewster's Antiques & Gifts**
1603 W. Hillsboro St.
870/862-2903

**Blann's**
320 W. Main St.
870/863-9302

**Royal Gallery Antiques & Interiors**
114 E. Elm St.
870/862-8783

**Main St. Antique Mall**
209 E. Main St.
870/862-0028

**Friendship District**
800 E. Spring St.
870/863-3913

**Attic Treasures**
520 N. Jackson
870/862-6331

## 15 EUREKA SPRINGS

The Victorian era of the late 1800s and the Ozark Mountains in northern Arkansas have combined to create a beautifully unique town that has the distinction of having its entire downtown shopping district and residential area listed on the National Register of Historic Places. In Eureka Springs not only will you find hundreds of Victorian buildings, but there are narrow, winding mountain streets and lovely limestone walls built from Arkansas stone. Streets are sometimes hundreds of feet higher or lower than adjacent streets, and no streets cross at right angles. The town grew from belief in the legendary healing powers of its spring waters, as thousands of people traveled to the springs for their health. Today Eureka Springs is a world-famous Victorian resort town of native limestone buildings, gingerbread houses, shaded trails, springs and gazebos. The best way to explore this fascinating town is by trolley and on foot. Six trolley routes service most of the town's lodgings, each designated by a color displayed on a sign in the front window. Just west of town on U.S. 62 W. are two particularly fascinating attractions: the exquisitely beautiful Thorncrown Chapel, an architectural masterpiece, and the 33-acre Eureka Springs Botanical Gardens. Eureka Springs is also home to the nationally famous Passion Play, a spectacular outdoor drama depicting the life, death and resurrection of Christ. And from its roots as an artists' colony in the 1930s and 40s, the town is now one of the most respected fine arts centers for the Mid-South. The Eureka Springs and North Arkansas Railway offers a four-mile excursion (departing hourly) through the Ozarks. A more leisurely tour of the mountains is available by cruise boat on the scenic Beaver Lake.

**Old Sale Barn Antiques**
Hwy. 23 S. & 62 E.
501/253-5388

**Garrett's Antique Print**
125 Spring St.
501/253-9481

**Melinda's Memories**
49 Kingshighway
501/253-7023

**Mount Victoria**
28 Fairmount St.
501/253-7979

**Forgotten Treasures Antq. Dolls & Toys**
53 B Spring St.
501/253-9989

**Country Antiques**
Stadium Road
501/253-8731

**Springs Antiques**
6 S. Main St.
501/253-6025

**Bustopher Jones Antiques**
103 E. Van Buren
501/253-6946

**Mitchell's Folly Antiques**
130 Spring St.
501/253-7030

**Treasured Memories Antiques**
Hwy. 23 S.
501/253-4900

**Eureka Emporium**
Hwy. 187
501/253-9346

**Main St. Traders Gallery**
35 N. Main St.
501/253-6159

**Memories Past Antiques**
Hwy. 62 E.
501/253-5747

**Pump & Circumstance**
77 Mountain St.
501/253-6644

**Crystal Gardens Antiques**
190 Spring St.
501/253-9586

**Front Porch Antiques & Collectibles**
Hwy. 23 N.
501/253-6557

**Jack's Antiques**
R 1 Box 66 Hwy. 235
501/423-3725

**Yesteryears Antique Mall**
Hwy. 62/412 @ Rockhouse Road
501/253-5100

**Mr. Haney's Antiques & Collectibles**
Hwy. 62 W.
501/253-5752

*Great Places To Stay*

**Crescent Cottage Inn**
211 Spring St.
501/253-6022
Web site: www.eureka-usa.com/crescott
Rates: $93-130, includes breakfast
*Directions: For specific directions to Crescent Cottage Inn, please call the Innkeeper.*

For specific information see review at the beginning of this section.

## 16 FAYETTEVILLE

**Long Ago Antiques**
1934 E. Huntsville Road
501/443-3435

**Gift House**
525 Mission Blvd.
501/521-4334

**Long Ago Antiques**
304 W. Meadow
501/521-3459

**Sara Kathryn's**
600 Mission Blvd.
501/444-9991

**Hatfields Inc.**
123 N. College
501/521-3181

**Home Place**
701 North St.
501/443-4444

**Dickson Street Bookshop**
325 W. Dickson St.
501/442-8182

**Long Ago Antiques**
1934 Huntsville Road
501/443-3435

**Heritage House Antiques**
351 N. Highland Ave.
501/582-5653

**All My Treasures**
2932 E. Huntsville Road (Hwy. 16E.)
501/575-0250

**Feather Your Nest**
17 N. Block
501/443-3355

**Footprints**
4294 W. 6th
501/267-3951

## 17 FORDYCE

From a Civil War battleground and cemetery and vintage trains to antiques, Paul "Bear" Bryant, and a bakeshop/deli of national renown, Fordyce, Ark., is an intriguing little town in southern Arkansas. Although its present claim to fame is a vast pine forest, resources for Georgia-Pacific Industries, Fordyce has preserved a good portion of its colorful past. The town was named after Civil War Colonel Samuel Fordyce, who later built the Fordyce Bath House in Hot Springs. Even the first direct-dial long distance telephone call in the U.S. was made from Allied Telephone Company in Fordyce in 1960! There's a large historic district and a great many antique shops. The Dallas County Museum features the county's history and includes displays and memorabilia of one of its famous sons: the late, legendary Paul "Bear" Bryant, football coach for decades at the University of Alabama. The Wynne Phillips House Bed & Breakfast, a National Historic Register listing, is still owned and operated by one of the children whose parents bought the house in 1914. Hampton Springs Cemetery, near Carthage, is the only segregated burial site in the state, with graves dating back to 1916 and bearing primitive markings and accents of African heritage. And, of course, there's Klappenbach Bakery, offering a full menu of baked goods and a terrific sandwich shop next door. Then there's the annual Fordyce on the Cotton Belt Festival, a full week of fun in April with a parade, arts and crafts, food, antique cars and vintage trains on display.

**Main Street Antiques & Collectibles**
219 Main St.
870/352-7467

*Great Places To Stay*

**Wynne Phillips House Bed & Breakfast**
412 W. Fourth St.
870/352-7202
Rates: $55-60, including full breakfast

This rambling, pale apricot-colored clapboard home set in isolated splendor in the middle of an immaculately manicured lawn, is one of the most impressive bed & breakfasts you will encounter. It is surrounded by a complete walk-around porch, a veranda of incredible size and style. The second story is completely ringed with a balcony that follows the perimeter of the veranda, making the entire second story as accessible for strolling and sitting as the ground floor!

Built around 1904, this Colonial Revival style home was purchased in 1914 by Colonel Thomas Duncan Wynne, an attorney and three-time mayor, for his wife and the seven children who would be born there. The youngest of those seven children, Agnes Wynne Phillips, owns the house today with her husband, Colonel James H. Phillips, and operates it as a B & B. Agnes inherited the house in 1985 and turned it into a B & B because it was so large. It took her and Jim three years to restore the huge property. Drawing on the original house plans from archives in the Old State House in Little Rock, old photographs, newspaper clippings, and the memories of family and friends, Agnes and Jim have recreated the ambience of the home's earlier years.

There are five guest rooms with private baths, a glass-enclosed game room at the back of the house, and a 60-foot lap pool. The house is furnished from all different eras and styles, and includes antiques and family heirlooms. The downstairs boasts Chippendale chairs with needlepoint seats in the dining room, gas fireplaces in the parlor and a Mission-furnished library, with a scattering of Asian rugs and interesting pieces from the Phillips' travels (during Jim's army career they were posted in Pakistan and Germany, and moved 30 times). Upstairs each guest room is named after one of Agnes' siblings, and each is decorated with treasures from their childhood. Breakfast is prepared for guests by Walter, the house butler, who formerly was an army cook. Two types of grapes found only in the South are grown in the inn's arbor, and are offered in the inn's breakfast jelly.

## 18 FORT SMITH

**Coming Home**
809 S. Greenwood Ave.
501/782-4438

**Phoenix Village Antique Mall**
4600 Towson Ave.
501/648-9008

**Packrat's Antiques**
319 Rogers Ave.
501/783-3330

**Century Plaza**
3702 Century Dr.
501/646-8500

**Old Vogue Vintage Clothiers**
820 Garrison Ave.
501/783-1369

**Eva Gotlib Antique Galleries**
1110 Garrison Ave.
501/783-1711

**Now & Then Shoppe Inc.**
115 Lecta Ave.
501/783-8022

**Steve's Antiques**
4700 Towson Ave.
501/646-1121

### *Great Places To Stay*

**Beland Manor B&B**
1320 S. Albert Pike
501/782-3300

Colonial mansion - 8 guest rooms.

## 19 HARDY

**Old Hardy Town Mall**
710 E. Main St.
870/856-3575

**Rain Barrel Antiques**
Main St.
870/856-2242

**Steele's Antiques**
Main St.
870/856-3247

**Sugar Creek Antiques**
Shows/Mail Order
870/856-2909

**Donnie's Antiques**
4 Mi. East, Hwy. 62 & 63 E.
870/856-4358

**Victorian Lace**
703 Main St.
501/856-2902

**Memory Lane Mall**
621 Main St.
870/856-4044

## 20 HEBER SPRINGS

If you like beautiful lakes and rivers, scenic mountains, all kinds of water sports and outdoor activities, antiques, and general exploring, then Heber Springs, Ark., is tailor-made for you. The town hugs the eastern end of shimmering Greers Ferry Lake, a 40,000-acre U.S. Corps of Engineers facility. Just below the dam at Heber Springs is the Little Red River, one of America's best trout fishing streams. All around the lake and river are parks, resorts, accommodations and full-service marinas for all sorts of water-related activities.

The Heber Springs area is noted for its numerous antique, gift and collectibles shops, ranging from Depression glassware to 19th century European furniture. In addition to the antiques, there are Ozark crafts that represent an era when the Arkansas hill people had to produce the things necessary for survival in this isolated and primitive frontier. In October each year, Heber Springs hosts craftsmen from a wide geographical area for a three-day show and sale. Art is also an important aspect of the offering to tourists coming to this mountain community.

Heber Springs is also home to two nationally known producers of potpourri and fragrances, as well as another famous firm that sells framed prints of original paintings and decorative accessories. These companies supply gift shops all over the country and, to some extent, internationally. And there are festivals every year, from April through December. Nearby attractions to Heber Springs include the Ozark Folk Center in Mountain View, Blanchard Springs Caverns (just up the road from the Ozark Folk Center), Batesville (the state's oldest surviving town), and Little Rock.

**Antique Market Place Mall**
306 W. Main St.
501/362-2111

**Vintage Collection**
1105 S. 7th St.
501/362-7992

**Somewhere in Time**
304 W. Main St.
501/362-9429

**Virginia's Antiques & Collectibles**
Hwy. 25 N.
501-362-3282

**Browsing Post**
Hwy 25 S.
501/362-5560

## 21 HELENA

**Antique Mall of Helena**
428 Cherry St.
870/338-8612

**Sue Mathews Gifts & Antiques**
430 Cherry St.
870/338-6071

**Between Friends**
517 Cherry St.
501/338-3150

**On The Levee Antiques & Gifts**
107 Cherry St.
501/338-8500

**Magnolia Antiques**
322 Cherry St.
870/338-7991

**This Little Pig Antiques**
105 Cherry St.
870/338-3501

### *Great Places To Stay*

**Foxglove B&B**
229 Beech
870/338-9391

Stunning antiques abound in this nationally registered inn - 10 guest rooms.

## 22 HOT SPRINGS

**Seller's Showcase Antique Mall**
2138-E. Higdon Ferry Road
501/525-2098

**Antique & Collector's Showroom**
1100 Malvern Ave.
501/623-6278

**Three Sisters Antiques**
807 Airport Road Hwy. 70 W.
501/623-1909

**Kathern's Antiques**
2230 Malvern Ave., Suite E
501/624-4781

**Arkansas Minuteman**
821 Hobson Ave.
501/624-6420

**Shepard's Old Time Shop**
1 Carmona Center
501/922-3215

**Tillman's Antiques**
118 Central Ave.
501/624-4083

**Yum-Yum Antiques**
1313 Central Ave.
501/624-7046

**Morris Antique Mall**
1700 Central Ave.
501/623-4249

**Central Ave. Antiques**
2025 Central Ave.
501/623-9003

**Interior Spaces**
706 Central Ave.
501/623-7300

**Papa's Antiques**
308 Whittington Ave.
501/624-4211

**Bath House Row Antiques**
202 Spring St.
501/623-6888

**Oldies & Goodies**
2002 Higdon Ferry Road
501/525-5783

**Adele's Antiques & Yesteryear**
1704 Albert Pike
501/623-3573

**Country Cupboard Antiques**
1003 Park Ave.
501/623-8224

**Historic District Antiques**
514 Central Ave.
501/624-3370

**Shaw's Antiques**
1526 Central Ave.
501/624-0163

**Goodman Auctions & Watson Antqs.**
1819 Central Ave.
501/623-6061

**Anderson Antiques**
3400 Central Ave.
501/321-1252

**Quilt House Antiques**
5841 Central Ave.
501/525-1567

**Jay's Uniques**
309 Whittington Ave.
501/623-5911

**Old South Antique Mall**
5444 Central Ave.
501/525-6623

## *Great Places To Stay*

### The Gables Inn
318 Quapaw Ave.
1-800-625-7576, 501/623-7576

For specific information see review at the beginning of this section.

### Wildwood 1884 B&B
808 Park Ave.
501/624-4267

1884 Victorian - 5 guest rooms.

## *Favorite Places To Eat*

### Hamilton House
Hwy. 7 S. at Lake Hamilton
501/525-2727 or 501/525-1717
Open 5:30 daily, reservations recommended

If you truly love sumptuous, cosmopolitan dining, there's a place in Little Rock you don't want to miss! Hamilton House offers a menu that rivals many topnotch restaurants in the major metropolitan cities of the U.S. and Western Europe. Here they specialize in seafood, politically incorrect grain-fed and aged prime beef, poultry, and decadent desserts, heavy on the sinful chocolate dishes, with a wide selection of wines for dining and dessert. Worth a trip!

## *Interesting Side Trips*

### Hot Springs National Park

Hot Springs is America's favorite spa, a world-famous resort built around the thermal waters from the Ouachita Mountains. In this beautifully restored National Park area, you'll experience bathhouses, Victorian buildings, antique shops, art galleries, and interesting and educational museums and attractions.

Hot Springs has always been a special place. President Andrew Jackson made Hot Springs the first Federal Reservation in 1832, the first piece of America protected for future generations. Hot Springs was, in essence, America's first National Park.

### The Hot Springs Experience

Historic 1901 Short-Dodson House, 755 Park Avenue, 501/624-9555, was designed and built by Joseph G. Horn. This stunning Victorian mansion was placed on the Register of Historic Places in 1976. Here you'll see impressive and highly detailed oak and maple woodwork and flooring, along with stained glass. You can actually hold a piece of the Berlin Wall, read Dunham Short's love letter to Corala, stand face-to-face with Karla Parker's portrait of Moses and touch the world famous "Fainting Couch." Truly a "must see" in Hot Springs.

### The Witness: A Dramatic Musical Passion Play
501/623-9781

*The Witness* is the story of the birth, life, death and resurrection of Jesus Christ, as told and sung by the Apostle Peter. Everyone can see a little of themselves in this common fisherman, whose life was changed by the miraculous events he witnesses. You, too, will find yourself caught up in the struggles, human doubts and eventual great faith of the disciples, as each panoramic scene unfolds.

*The Witness* is performed outdoors in the Mid-America Amphitheatre, nestled in a beautiful wooded area of the Ouachita Mountains. Call for dates and times.

**Bathhouse Row**
(Located in the Heart of Hot Springs)

Visit the Fordyce Bathhouse Museum to experience the grandeur of the golden age of spas. Enjoy a luxurious bath for yourself in one of several bathhouses located on Bathhouse Row. You'll be relaxed and ready to "antique" in the many shops located adjacent to the bathhouses.

**Buckstaff Bathhouse**
Bathhouse Row
501/623-2308

Only in Hot Springs can you take a whirlpool bath and get a massage courtesy of the U.S. National Park Service! Buckstaff Bathhouse, a tradition on world-famous Bathhouse Row in Hot Springs, is operated under the regulation of the U.S. Dept. of the Interior, National Park Service. So relax and enjoy the ultimate bathing experience. Buckstaff has served bathers since 1912. A top-flight staff offers outstanding service, top facilities and famous Hot Springs thermal mineral water baths — an unbeatable combination for therapeutic bathing or just plain relaxing. Placed on the National Register of Historic Places in 1974, and declared a National Historic Landmark in 1987, Buckstaff offers massages, bathing packages, bathing supplies, separate men's and women's departments, and men's and women's sun decks.

## 23 JONESBORO

**Nettleton Antiques**
4920 E. Nettleton Ave.
870/932-8580

**Tymes Past Antiques**
305 S. Main St.
870/972-9444

**Forty Niner Antiques**
3105 Southwest Dr.
870/972-8536

**Collectors Corner**
4914 E. Nettleton Ave.
870/972-9659

## 24 KEO

**Morris Antiques**
306 Hwy. 232 W.
P. O. Box 127
501/842-3531 Fax: 501/842-2858
Mon.-Sat. 9-5, Sun. 12-5
*Directions: Take I-440 to Exit 7. Follow Hwy. 165 S. toward England. Go 13 miles to Keo. Turn right on Hwy. 232 at the flashing caution light. Go 3 blocks and turn right behind the Methodist Church.*

Known as "a place to look and look again", Morris Antiques offers 55,000 sq. ft. of antique paradise. With 8 buildings full of American, English, French, and Austrian furniture, you can easily spend a whole day browsing.

If you are interested in the very "big stuff" with lots of carvings and intricate inlays, this is the place to shop. Merchandise ranges from Victorian teester beds, massive sideboards, large ornate dining room sets, over 100 armoires, beautiful bedroom sets, to dainty parlor chairs, delicate end tables, practical halltrees, and durable oak pub tables.

Customers are welcome to wander through unusual things from the past such as old cars, farm implements, and a horse drawn hearse to name a few. There are even a variety of animals the children enjoy seeing, such as minature horses and a llama.

**Lemon's Antiques**
350 Main St.
501/842-2442

## 25 LITTLE ROCK, NORTH LITTLE ROCK

**Pasha Bass Antiques**
5811B Kavanaugh Blvd. (LR)
501/660-4245

**Dauphine**
5819 Kavanaugh Blvd. (LR)
501/664-6007

**Abingworth**
5823 Kavanaugh Blvd. (LR)
501/663-5554

**Cottage Collection**
701 N. Ash St. (@ Kavanaugh) (LR)
501/664-0883

**Crystal Hill Antique Mall**
5813 Crystal Hill Road (NLR)
501/753-3777

**New Town Antique Shoppes**
5913 Crystal Hill Road (NLR)
501/753-3460

**Marshall Clements Corp.**
1509 Rebsamen Park Road (LR)
501/663-1828

**Grand Finale**
1601 Rebsamen Park Road (LR)
501/661-9242

**Pflugrad Antiques**
5624 R St. (LR)
501/661-0188

**My Husband's Treasures**
4401 Camp Robinson Road (NLR)
501/791-3628

**Train Station Antiques**
1400 W. Markham (@ Victoria) (LR)
501/376-2010

**Fabulous Finds Antique Mall**
1521 Merrill Dr., Suite D175 (LR)
501/224-6622

**Lorenzen & Co. Booksellers**
7509 Cantrell Road (LR)
501/663-8811

**Hogan's Antique Furniture**
14600 Cantrell Road (LR)
501-868-9224

**Old Stuff Store**
4811 Jones Loop Road (LR)
501/821-3178

**Bowman Curve Antiques**
11600 Mara Lynn Road (LR)
501-228-4898

**Jordan's Antiques**
4705 Frazier Pike, College Station
501/490-1391

**General Store Antiques**
12227 Macarthur Dr. (NLR)
501/851-6202

**Collector's Haven Antiques**
12109 Macarthur Dr. (NLR)
501/851-2885

**Homestead Antiques**
4823 Rixie Road #B (NLR)
501/833-8676

**English Antiques Gallery**
5500 Landers Road (NLR)
501/945-6004

**I-40 Antique Mall**
Exit 142-13021 Long Fisher Road
501/851-0039

**Capital View Antiques**
3515 Old Cantrell Road (LR)
501/225-5171

**Antiques On The Wharf**
2312 Cantrell Road (LR)
501/376-6161

**Kavanaugh Antiques**
2622 Kavanaugh (LR)
501/661-0958

**LaVien Rose**
5800 R St., Suite 101 (LR)
501/661-1620

**Classic Collections**
301 N. Shackleford E-1 (LR)
501/219-2527

**Twin City Antique Mall**
5812 Crystal Hill Road (NLR)
501/812-0400

**Height of Fashion**
3625 Kavanaugh (LR)
501/664-0301

**Argenta Antique Mall**
201 E. Broadway (NLR)
501/372-7750

**Vagabonds**
5913 Kavanaugh (LR)
501/296-9696

**Private Treasures by Etta**
701 Parkdale Street (LR)
501/945-5314

**Needful Things**
21115 Arch St. (LR)
501/888-4882

**Lady I's Specialty Shoppe**
7706 Cantrell Road (LR)
501/228-4860

**Private Collections**
400 N. Bowman Road (LR)
501/228-0228

**Perdue's Antiques & Accents**
5711 Kavanaugh Blvd. (LR)
501/7663-4888

**Second Chance Collectables**
10 Office Park Dr. (LR)
501/224-5792

**Potential Treasures Antiques**
700 N. Van Buren St. (LR)
501/663-0608

**Mark's Nostalgia Land**
2719 Harold St. (NLR)
501/758-2086

**Z Gallery**
15607 Cantrell Road (LR)
501/868-6066

**Pike Plaza Antiques & Flea Market**
2657 Pike Ave. (NLR)
501/771-4877

### *Great Places To Stay*

**Dr. Witt's Quapaw Inn**
1868 Gaines
501/376-6873 or 1-800-732-5591
Check-in between 5-10, exceptions by prior arrangement
Reservations requested but not always necessary
*Directions: From I-30 take I-630 to the Broadway-Central Exit (IB). Follow the access road to Broadway. Turn left onto Broadway, go 8 blocks to 18 th St., go 2 blocks to Gaines, turn left onto Gaines. The inn is 1 1/2 blocks from where you turned onto Gaines - the big pink house on the right.*

Guests at Dr. Witt's Quapaw Inn not only get a good night's rest, but can also get the "inside scoop" on America's first family! Innkeeper Dottie Woodwind says that since Bill, Hillary and Chelsea were their neighbors during President Clinton's tenure as governor of Arkansas, the Woodwinds have dozens of Clinton family stories to tell, even some about Socks, the First Cat! Guests at Little Rock's original bed and breakfast can also get information on boarding the family horse, making theater and dinner reservations, and getting directions to the best places to visit. Breakfast at the inn is served to guests only.

## 26 MAMMOTH SPRING

**Country Store Antiques**
314 Main St.
870/625-3844

**Michael's Variety**
304 Main St.
870/625-3254

**Ozark Heritage**
301 Main St.
870/625-7303

**Cedar Jnct Craft & Flea Market**
Hwy. 63
870/625-3017

## 27 MENA

**Depot Antiques Mall**
519 Sherwood
501/394-1149

**Mena Street Antique Mall**
822 Mena St.
501/394-3231

**Bird's Nest Antiques & Crafts**
Hwy. 88 E.
501/394-3033

## 28 MOUNTAIN HOME

Located in north central Ark., Mountain Home is cradled in the gentle slopes of the Ozark Mountains.

With each moderate but distinct season, the Ozarks unfold to present a new panorama of color and beauty. Winter's light blanket of snow covers the forest floor during its brief hibernation. Although much of the plant life will temporarily succumb to winter's presence, the pines and cedars remain evergreen throughout the year. After a two to three month winter reprieve, the hills spring to life with pinks and whites of blossoming redbuds and dogwood trees and colorful wildflowers. Set against a new pale green cover, spring's blooms remind us of a water color palette of subtle, pastel colors.

Under a sky of intense blue, summer brings its own plethora of color to the forest - deep greens of the cedar glades compliment the various greens of the hardwoods. The cool temperatures of autumn drastically change the color scheme of the mountains, and the forest bursts into the fire-like colors of red, orange and gold.

The Ozarks offer miles of natural beauty any time of the year. You can wander the past while contemplating the present and dreaming of the future. It all combines to give you a wonderful time and place for "antiquing" in the picturesque setting of Mountain Home.

**The Farm House Antique & Craft Mall**
824 Club Blvd.
870/425-7211

**Earl's Antiques**
3348 Hwy. 62 W.
870/425-8578

**Dolls of Yesteryear**
6601 Hwy. 62 E.
870/492-4010

**Antique Mall of Mt. Home**
686 Hwy. 62 E.
870/424-2442

**Magnolia House Antiques**
6417 Hwy. 62 E.
870/492-6730

**Once Upon A Time Antiques**
625 Hwy. 62 E.
870/425-1722

**Ox Yoke Antiques**
4689 Hwy. 62 & 412 E.
870/492-5125

**Char's Place**
4588 Hwy. 62 E.
870/492-6644

**Remember When**
5655 Hwy. 62 E.
870/492-4551

**Back In Time**
Tracy Ferry County Road 53
870/425-7570

**Five South Antiques**
Hwy. 5 S.
870/425-3553

## 29 MOUNTAIN VIEW

**Dottie's Antiques**
Hwy. 66 W.
870/269-8427

**Mellon's Country Store**
Hwy. 9 N.
870/269-4005

**Sweet Caroline's Antiques**
Hwys. 5, 9 & 14
870/269-2621

### *Interesting Side Trips*

### The Ozark Folk Center

Spur 382 off AR Hwy. 5
501/269-3851 (information)
1-800-264-FOLK or 501/269-3871 (lodging and conference facilities)

Instead of buying antiques, here's the chance of a lifetime to see just how those antiques you love were crafted and to make some heirlooms yourself! A one-of-a-kind place, the Ozark Folk Center is America's only facility that works at preserving the heritage and way of life of the Ozark mountain people. There is such an incredible array of things to do, see, hear, and experience that visitors really should plan to spend at least a few days at the Center. Not only are there dozens of things going on at the Center from early mornings to very late at night, but you can also see the awesome Blanchard Springs Caverns just a few miles away, or go trout fishing in some of the best waters in the country, picnic and hike in the Ozarks, and then rest a day or two at Greers Ferry Lake before returning home.

The Center offers a full season of events, and hands-on activities, and Dry Creek Lodge offers comfortable rooms right at the facility. You can also design your own custom crafts workshops and enroll for private or group lessons in such old-time arts as: broom making, corn shuckery, natural dyes, spinning, weaving, herb gardening, blacksmithing, needlework, quilting, photography, pottery, hominy making, lye soap making, sorghum making, woodstove cookery, basket making, bowl carving, coopering, chair making, chair seat weaving, hickory bark peeling, shingle making, spoon carving, and woodcarving.

## 30 OZARK

Located in the picturesque mountain area known as the Ozarks and surrounded by beautiful lakes and countryside, the little town of Ozark was established in 1835. It got its name from French explorers who called this area "aux arc," meaning "big bend," a likely reference to the 19-mile bend in the Arkansas River on which this town is bordered.

A quaint little town, Ozark's history is rich with Civil War happenings. Originally built in the 1800s, the beautiful Franklin County Courthouse played host during the Civil War to Union troops who captured the courthouse, built gun ports in its walls and used it for supply storage. A Confederate raid destroyed its beauty and, in fact, when the last smoke cleared, all the houses in Ozark were burned except three. The structure was rebuilt in 1945 and is now listed on the Register of Historic Places.

There are several excursion possibilities in Ozark, a town which is a veritable "old attic" of discoveries for the collectibles and antiques enthusiast. Its charming square has shops to be explored and interesting spots to get a bite to eat. A "must see" is the old jail, built in 1914 out of locally quarried stone cut in random size blocks. Five public hangings, viewed by thousands, took place near this building - all hanged for murder.

**Coal Miner's Daughter Antiques**
300 Commercial
501/667-4542

## 31 PARAGOULD

**Faulkner County Place**
6205 W. Kingshighway
870/239-3301

**Paragould Antique Mall**
6312 W. Kingshighway
870/239-4485

**Williams Glass Barn**
330 Greene Road 796
870/236-3610

**Reba Mack's**
222 S. Pruett
870/236-6795

## 32 PARIS

**Miller's Antiques**
State Hwy. 22
501/963-2627

**Kountry Store**
State Hwy. 22 W.
501/635-2762

**Bullock's Antiques**
State Hwy. 22 W.
501/963-1300

**Red Barn Antiques**
State Hwy. 22 W.
501/934-4466

## 33 PIGGOTT

**Sugar Creek Antiques**
126 S. 2nd St.
870/598-3923

**Victorian Ribbons & Roses**
127 W. Main St.
870/598-2514

**Enchanted Forrest**
193 W. Main St.
870/598-3663

**Mother's Victorian Memories**
160 W. Main St.
870/598-5606

## 34 PINE BLUFF

**White House Antiques**
4005 Camden Road
870/879-1336

**Jo-Be's Antiques**
402 Portea Circle
870/534-1362

**Caroline's Victorian Country**
9404 Hwy. 270
870/247-4258

**Sissy's Log Cabin Inc.**
2319 Camden Road
870/879-3040

**Memories and More**
2603 S. Cherry St.
870/536-3116

**Amo's Antiques & Things**
1323 S. State St.
870/535-7500

**Chapel Plaza Antique Mall**
# 1 Chapel Plaza Hwy. 79 S.
870/879-4402

**Drake's Antiques & Jewelry**
3811 W. 4th Ave.
870/536-5321

## 35 PRAIRIE GROVE

**Country Charm Antiques**
16781 W. Hwy. 62
501/846-2689

**Antique Emporium**
107 E. Buchanan
501/846-4770

**Hidden Treasures**
116 N. Mock St.
501/846-4540

## 36 ROGERS

**The Rose Antique Mall**
2875 W. Walnut St.
501/631-8940

**Shelby Lane Mall**
719 W. Walnut St.
501/621-0111

**Clark's Depression Glass**
1003 N. 8th St.
501/636-4327

**Country House**
1007 N. 2nd St.
501/631-9200

**Yesteryears**
3704 Walnut St.
501/636-9273

**Vintage Antique Mall**
108 W. Walnut St.
501/631-3930

**Miss Judi's Passion**
103 W. Walnut St.
501/636-7758

**A & K Furniture**
1512 N. 2nd St.
501/636-0022

**McGregor's Antiques**
2143 W. Olive St.
501/636-6829

**Homestead Antique Mall**
3223 Hudson Road (Hwy. 102)
501/631-9003

## 37 RUSSELLVILLE

**Antique Mall**
1712 N. Arkansas Ave.
501/968-3449

**P J's Corner**
903 W. Main St.
501/968-1812

**Treasure House Antiques**
Hwy. 7
501/968-3652

**Emporium**
214 W. Main St.
501/968-1110

**This, That & Something Else Antqs.**
519 S. Arkansas Ave.
501/968-5356

**Antique Central Mall**
Hwy. 7, 4 mi. N. Of I-10
501/967-5855

**Sweet Memories Antique Mall**
212 W. Main St.
501/967-5354

**Dubois Antiques**
2614 W. Second Lane
501/968-8370

**Clopton's Antiques**
355 Humphrey Road (Dover)
501/331-2842

**All Our Treasures**
3018 N. Arkansas Ave.
501/968-7657

**Bradley's Antiques**
155 W. Gumlog Road (Hwy. 124)
501/967-2225

## 38 SEARCY

**Memory Lane Antiques**
1006 S. Main St.
501/268-2439

**Jessica Ray Antiques**
410 N. Oak St.
501/279-0611

**Searcy Emporium**
3015 E. Race Ave.
501/279-7025

**Family Memories**
1509 W. Pleasure
501/305-4380

**Bobs Antiques & Classic Car Parts**
3317 Hwy. 36 W.
501/268-3198

**Frances Antiques**
701 W. Race St.
501/268-2154

**Room Service Antique Mall**
2904 E. Race Ave.
501/279-0933

## 39 SILOAM SPRINGS

**Washington Street Antiques**
1001 S. Washington St.
501/524-9722

**Fantasy Land Flea Market**
1490 Hwy. 412 W.
501/524-6681

**Has Been Flea Market**
100 E. University
501/549-3315

**The French Hen**
120 S. Broadway
501/524-3788

**Classic Antique Mall**
Hwy. 412-W. Siloam Springs
918/422-5676

## 40 SPRINGDALE

**Famous Hardware Antique Mall**
113 W. Emma Ave.
501/756-6650

**Pat's Antiques**
2500 Melody Lane
501/751-6703

**Barker's Antiques**
Elm Springs & Oak Grove Roads
501/750-2305

**Magnolia House Flea Market Inc.**
312 S. Thompson
501/751-1787

**Discount Corner Flea Market Mall**
418 E. Emma Ave.
501/756-0764

**Best Yet Flea Market**
633 Sanders
501/751-4642

**Jennifer's Antique Mall & Flea Mkt.**
824 S. 48th St.
501/750-4646

## 41 STUTTGART

### Antiques on Park Avenue
1703 S. Timber
870/673-1179
Mon.-Sat. 10-5; Sun. 1-5
*Directions: From I-40 take the Hazen exit (#193). Travel south 2 to 3 miles on Hwy. 11 until the highway Ts into Hwy. 70. Take a left at the T, travel 2 miles to Hwy. 11 S., continue south on Hwy. 11 into Stuttgart. To get to Antiques On Park Avenue, turn left at the red light when you come into Stuttgart which is Hwy. 79. Go through the next light to the 2nd light which is 165 and Park. Take a right, travel approximately 3 miles, Antiques on Park Avenue is located on the right across from the car wash on the left.*

For specific information see review at the beginning of this section.

**Walt Krisell**
502 E. Second St.
870/673-3558

**Carol's Country Collectibles**
316 S. Main St.
870/673-6593

**Ponders Auction**
1504 S. Leslie St.
870/673-6551

## 42 TEXARKANA

**Sweet Temptations**
6707 E. Ninth St.
870/772-9687

**Yesterday's Rose**
6705 E. Ninth St.
870/772-2394

**Garden Gate Antiques**
6703 E. Ninth St.
870/773-1147

**M & M Antique Mall**
401 E. Broad St.
870/773-1871

## 43 TONITOWN

**Tonitown Flea Market & Antique Mall**
Hwy. 412 W.
501/361-9902

**Yesteryears Antique Mall**
Hwy. 412 W.
501/361-5747

**Historic Mercantile Flea Market**
136 Henri De Tonti Blvd.
501/361-2003

**The 412 Flea Market**
Hwy. 412 W.
501/361-9118

## 44 VAN BUREN

Just across the river from Ft. Smith, Ark., and right at the Oklahoma state line, Van Buren is an antique lover's dream. Its restored Victorian Main Street is a smorgasbord of tiny shops and warehouses filled with furniture, including the largest importer of European antique furniture in the Southwestern U.S. The shops are also filled with rare glass treasures, vintage hats and clothing, Coca-Cola and other trademark collectibles, antique toys, porcelain and china dolls, Victorian prints, and old tins and canisters. And since it's one of the original entryways to the Southwest, you can also shop for anything "southwestern," including turquoise and sterling silver jewelry, Navaho rugs and blankets, hand-thrown pottery, and western art of all kinds.

If you tire of shopping, you can take the "scenic route" and enjoy Ozark beauty from the Ozark Scenic Railway vintage train, or the Frontier Bell excursion river boat that travels along the Arkansas River. Top it all off with a couple of nights at the Old Van Buren Inn on Main Street, and you've got a great little vacation!

**Antique Mall Of Van Buren**
415 Main St.
501/474-7896

**Antique Warehouse & Mall**
402 Main St.
501/474-4808

**Bridgewater's Antiques**
616 Main St.
501/474-8616

**Grapevine Shoppe, Inc.**
615 Main St. #A
501/474-5800

**T J's Treasures & Bevie's**
715 Main St.
501/474-7678

**Whiteaker Ark. Oil Stone**
708 Main St.
501/474-6416

**Victorias Antiques**
514 Main St.
501/474-6299

**Carter's Trading Post**
412 Main St.
501/471-7182

***Great Places To Stay***

### Old Van Buren Inn
633 Main St., corner of 7th and Main
501/474-4202

Built in 1889, Victorian - outstanding restaurant - 3 guest rooms.

## 45 WEST FORK

**West Fork Antiques**
34 McGee Road
501/839-8202

# California

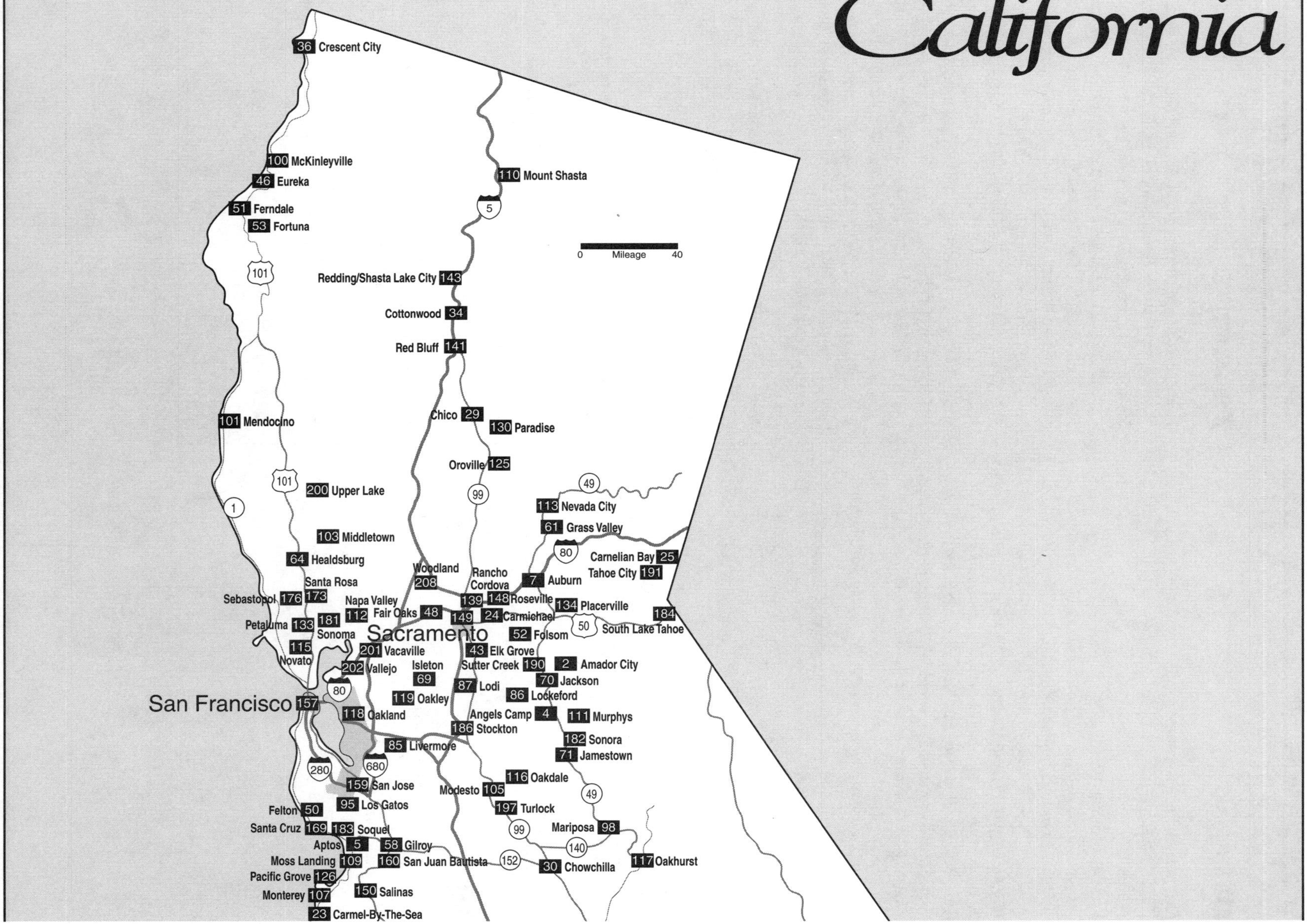

36 Crescent City
100 McKinleyville
46 Eureka
51 Ferndale
53 Fortuna
110 Mount Shasta
5
0 Mileage 40
101
Redding/Shasta Lake City 143
Cottonwood 34
Red Bluff 141
Chico 29
130 Paradise
101 Mendocino
Oroville 125
101
200 Upper Lake
99
1
49
113 Nevada City
61 Grass Valley
103 Middletown
80
Carnelian Bay 25
64 Healdsburg
Woodland 208
Rancho Cordova
7 Auburn
Tahoe City 191
Santa Rosa
Sebastopol 176 173
Napa Valley
139 148 Roseville
134 Placerville
112 Fair Oaks 48
149 24 Carmichael
184
Petaluma 133 181
Sonoma
Sacramento
52 Folsom
50
South Lake Tahoe
115
Novato
201 Vacaville
43 Elk Grove
202 Vallejo
Isleton 69
Sutter Creek 190
2 Amador City
80
87 Lodi
70 Jackson
119 Oakley
86 Lockeford
San Francisco 157
118 Oakland
Angels Camp 4
111 Murphys
186 Stockton
182 Sonora
85 Livermore
71 Jamestown
280
680
116 Oakdale
159 San Jose
Modesto 105
49
95 Los Gatos
197 Turlock
Felton 50
Santa Cruz 169
183 Soquel
99
Mariposa 98
Aptos 5
58 Gilroy
140
Moss Landing 109
160 San Juan Bautista
152
30 Chowchilla
117 Oakhurst
Pacific Grove 126
150 Salinas
Monterey 107
23 Carmel-By-The-Sea

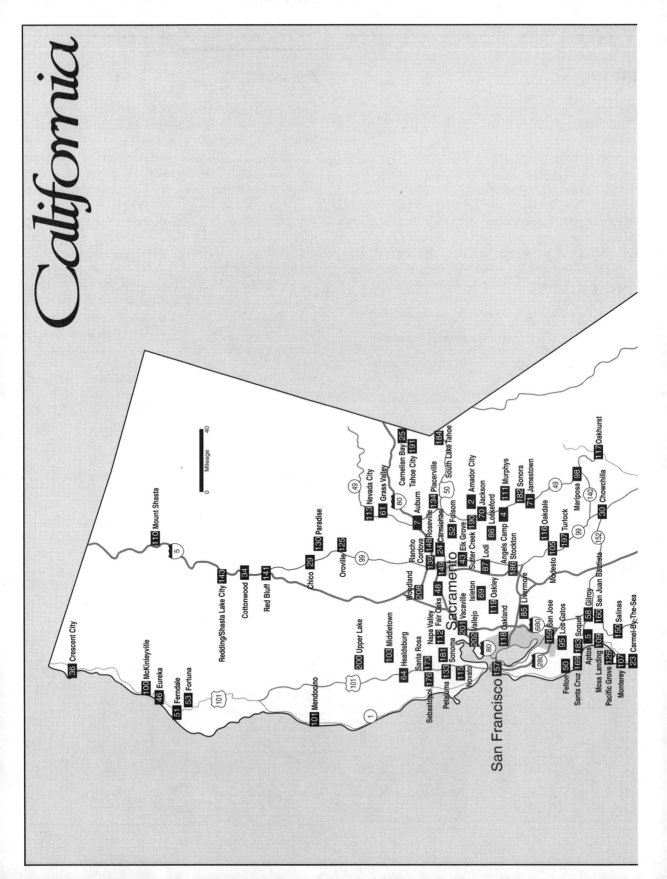

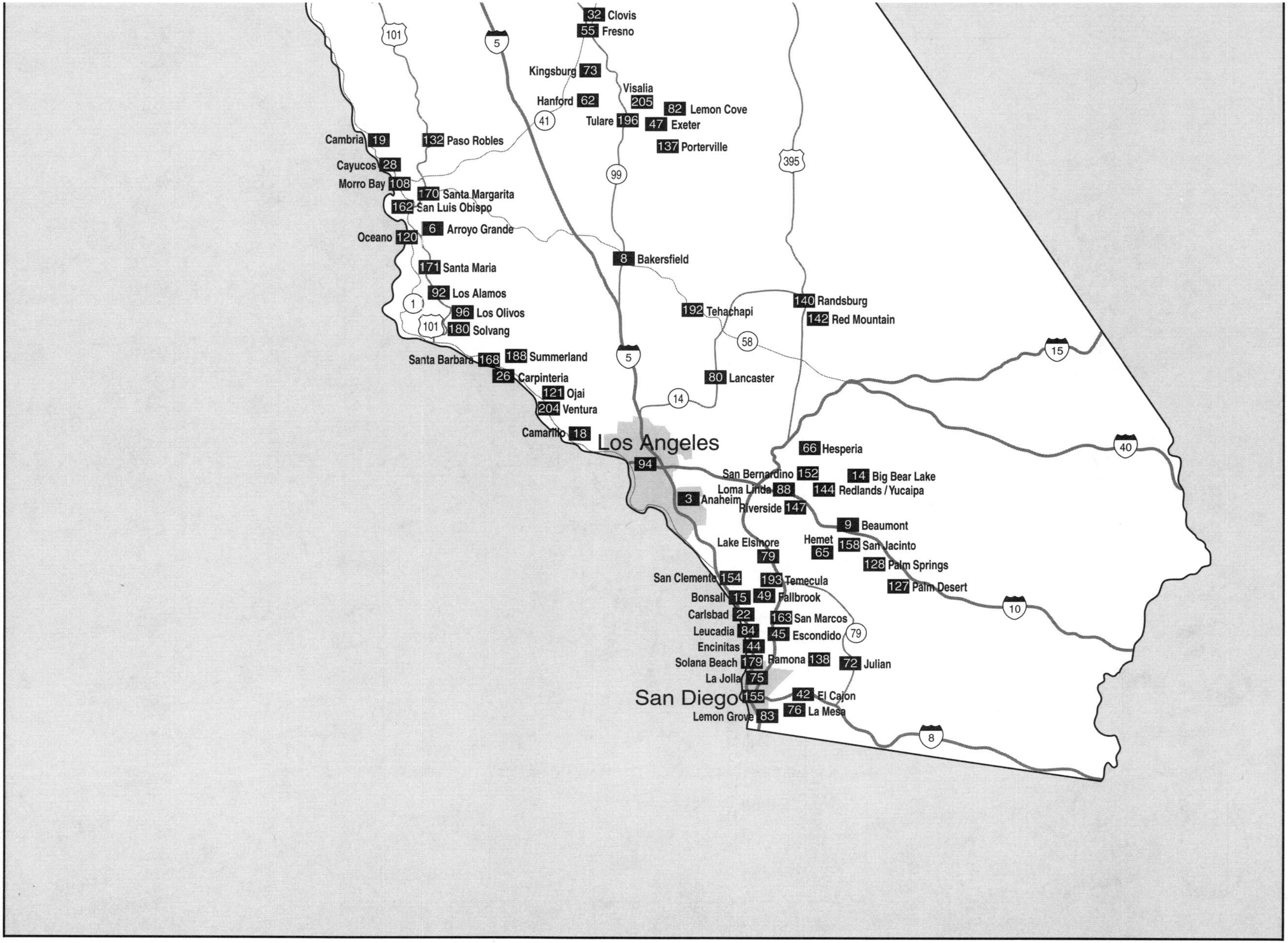
32 Clovis
55 Fresno
Kingsburg 73
Hanford 62
Visalia 205
82 Lemon Cove
Tulare 196
47 Exeter
137 Porterville
Cambria 19
132 Paso Robles
Cayucos 28
Morro Bay 108
170 Santa Margarita
162 San Luis Obispo
6 Arroyo Grande
Oceano 120
8 Bakersfield
171 Santa Maria
92 Los Alamos
96 Los Olivos
180 Solvang
192 Tehachapi
140 Randsburg
142 Red Mountain
Santa Barbara 168
188 Summerland
26 Carpinteria
80 Lancaster
121 Ojai
204 Ventura
Camarillo 18
Los Angeles
94
66 Hesperia
San Bernardino 152
14 Big Bear Lake
Loma Linda 88
144 Redlands / Yucaipa
3 Anaheim
Riverside 147
9 Beaumont
Lake Elsinore 79
Hemet 65
158 San Jacinto
128 Palm Springs
San Clemente 154
193 Temecula
127 Palm Desert
Bonsall 15
49 Fallbrook
Carlsbad 22
163 San Marcos
Leucadia 84
45 Escondido
Encinitas 44
Solana Beach 179
Ramona 138
72 Julian
La Jolla 75
San Diego 155
42 El Cajon
Lemon Grove 83
76 La Mesa
101
5
41
99
395
1
58
15
14
40
10
79
8

# California Los Angeles Area

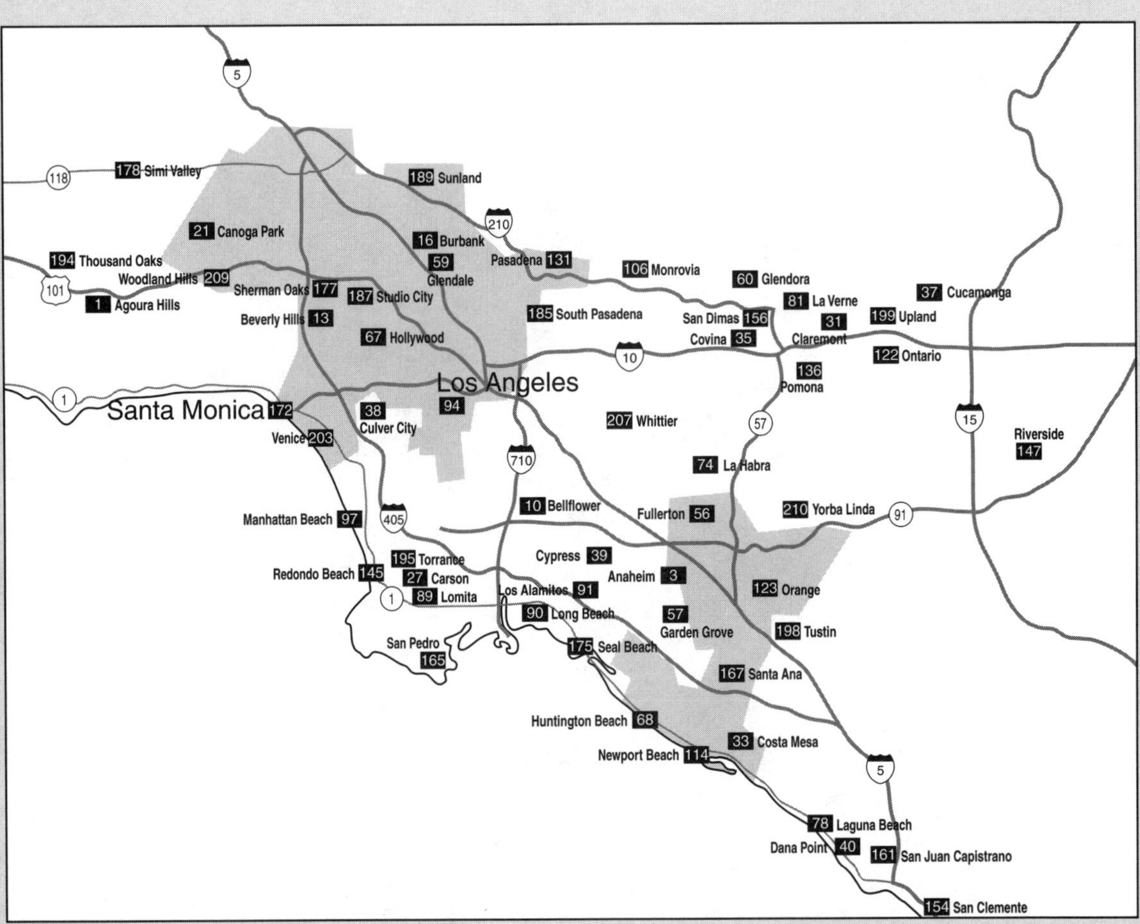

# California San Francisco Area

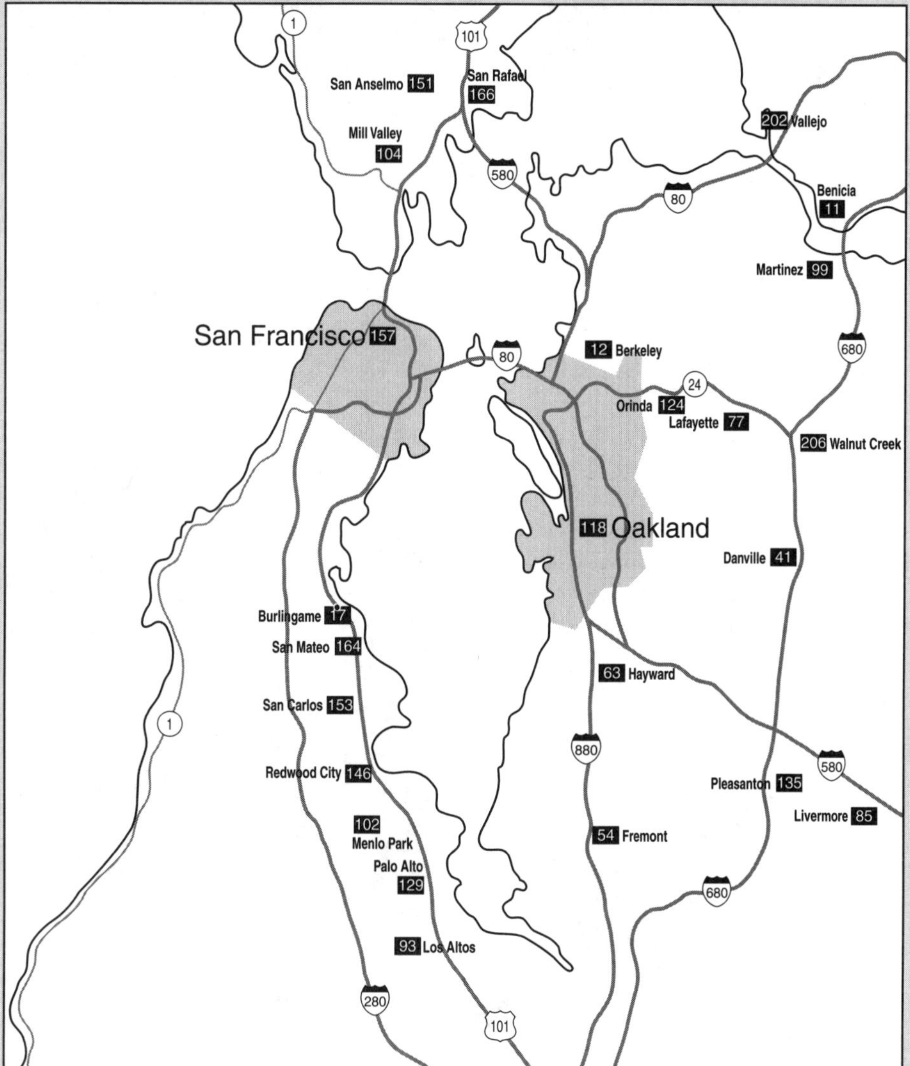

# Stories and Style

## Abigail's Elegant Victorian recalls gentler era

In a town full of historic buildings (nearly 1,600, in fact) this inn stands as one of the finest examples of Eastlake cottage-style architecture along the West Coast. Though it looks like a mansion, the structure is classified as a "cottage" because of its one-and-a-half stories, two flanking bay windows, and ornate barge boards that festoon the gables.

William S. Clark, twice the mayor of Eureka, lived here for over fifty years. Because his family figured prominently in Eureka's history (and literally owned half the town), Clark entertained many famous guests, such as Lily Langtry and Ulysses S. Grant, at his home during the turn of the century.

After one hundred years of private ownership, the home was recently turned into a bed and breakfast inn. Its name is derived from its 1888 newspaper description, "An elegant Victorian mansion." New owners, Doug and Lily Vieyra, a spirited couple, love playing their roles to the hilt. They also operate The Chalet of France, an unusual Swiss-style mountain retreat, complete with Tyrolean costumes. The motto for their new inn is, "Come to where history lives." Doug says, "We want to relive that exciting transition period from the horse to the automobile." They greet their guests in vintage costumes, and enjoy staging mystery weekends, classical concerts, and guided tours of Eureka in antique cars.

*Owners Doug and Lily Vieyra enjoy the roles of innkeepers.*

Elaborate ceilings, painted chandelier medallions, wall coverings by Bradbury & Bradbury, and carved fireplaces enhance the original splendor of the two parlors, dining room and library. An enclosed porch wraps around the back of the house, where a Finnish sauna is concealed. (Belgian-born Lily also offers Swedish massages.) A formal garden of over one-hundred roses beckons guests to step outside, and go back to a gentler era of croquet and afternoon tea.

*Decor that includes ornate ceilings, festooned with chandeliers, and antique furnishings, creates an elegant scene in the interior of Abigail's Elegant Victorian.*

*Abigail's Elegant Victorian is located at 1406 C Street in Eureka. For additional information call the innkeepers at 707/444-3144. Rates begin at $85.*

# Savor the selection at the Santa Monica Antique Market

Santa Monica Antique Market is located on Los Angeles' fashionable West Side and houses over 150 dealers and 20,000 square feet of merchandise. The inventory comes from all over the world and includes all types of furnishings and collectibles. Rediscover the Age of Romance with distinctive antique and custom-made decorative accessories from the Victorian through the Art Deco periods. You'll find exquisite lamps and chandeliers, signature jewelry, figurines, cherubs, pottery and assorted items of uncommon beauty reminiscent of Victorian times.

Create the pleasure of outdoor living in your garden room or terrace with gilded wooden columns, statues, fountains, handsomely crafted wrought iron pieces and neo-classical accents. If you enjoy and cherish America's textile arts, accessories and furnishings, then you're in for a treat. The Market offers lovely antique quilts dating from 1870-1940, stunning iron and brass beds, a 1910 white wicker chair, bird houses from 1920-1940, and many fine and unusual folk art pieces. You'll also find a superb representation of country primitives such as Shaker and Mennonite shutters, mantels, pie safes, windows and old watering cans.

The Market displays some wonderful American arts and crafts movement pieces. Furniture bearing the distinctive names of Stickley, Limberts, Lifetime and Harden can be found along with hand-hammered copper lighting and metalwork by Roycroft and Dirk Van Erp.

Travel through American Modernism to Italian Baroque with architectural fragments: pediments, finials and columns, Paladian mirrors, tin work, mercury glass, paintings, iron work and Latin American furniture.

One of the Market's greatest successes has been the ability to tailor services to the different needs of its diverse customer base. Santa Monica Antique Market offers a layaway plan, 48-hour at home trial period, delivery, international shipping, item searches, restoration and appraisal referrals, bridal registry, gift certificates, free gift wrapping and off-hours shopping, popular among celebrity clientele. Other bonuses include a book section, an espresso bar, and free valet parking.

*Santa Monica Antique Market is located at 1607 Lincoln Blvd. in Santa Monica. For additional information, call 310/314-4899 or see listing #172 (Santa Monica).*

*The Age of Romance is represented with an uncommon assortment of furnishings and accessories of rare beauty.*

*Whether it's the American Arts and Crafts movement from the turn of the century or Country primitives from all corners of the nation, the selection is outstanding at the Santa Monica Antique Market.*

*The 140 dealers in 15,000 square feet filled with treasures at The Cranberry House offer A to Z for your perusal.*

# Serious splendor at The Cranberry House

Designers, prop masters, serious collectors, flea market fanatics and avid antique perfectionists all declare The Cranberry House as their source for the best in treasure hunting. One hundred forty dealers in 15,000 square feet offer Americana, fine and costume jewelry, linens and quilts, smoking collectibles, vintage accessories and silver, toys and the best in furniture of domestic and European heritage from Roccoco to Modern. Still can't find it? Register for the "Wish List" and their friendly, knowledgeable staff will assist with a no obligation search and notify you when your "wish" arrives. Worldwide shipping, layaway, bridal registry, custom gift wrap, 24-hour approval program, and gift certificates are all a part of the excellent customer service.

*Prop masters know they'll find what they need here.*

Be sure to attend the annual Birthday Sale the third weekend in May with discounts up to 50%. Also not to be missed is the Holiday Open House the second weekend in December. The breathtaking holiday decor, free gourmet eats and 10% off everything sales create an unforgettable shopping experience. Get your personal invitation to both events by adding your name to the guest registry.

*The Cranberry House is located at 12318 Ventura Blvd. in Studio City. For additional information see listing #187 (Studio City).*

*The finest selection of furniture and vintage accessories from every period vie for your attention at The Cranberry House.*

# Solvang Antiques Center: Simply the finest

Solvang Antique Center is California's finest multiple-dealer gallery featuring an overwhelming selection of high quality antiques making for a unique resource for collectors, designers and dealers. The open floor plan with over 100 well-lit galleries and showcases creates a delightful museum-like shopping environment. Sixty-five quality dealers from around the world present European carved furniture, quality American oak, porcelain, sterling silver, cut glass, estate jewelry, paintings, sculpture, pianos, clocks, music boxes, watches, scales, tools and lighting. In addition, the gallery offers expert in-house restoration of antique furniture, clocks, watches, music boxes and scales. Solvang Antique Center provides worldwide delivery and a "hard to find items" locator service.

*Unique shops are housed in a European-style villa.*

*Solvang Antique Center is located at 486 First St. (Solvang), in the beautiful Santa Ynez Valley. This picturesque European-style villa features over 300 unique shops and restaurants attracting more than 2.5 million visitors each year. It is only 3 miles off Hwy. 101 between Los Angeles and San Francisco, just 35 miles north of Santa Barbara. For specific directions to Solvang Antique Center see listing #180 (Solvang).*

*Dealers from around the world present their finest merchandise for your consideration at the Solvang Antique Center.*

SOLVANG ANTIQUE CENTER

*From fine jewelry to antique tools, the selection is exquisite at the Solvang Antique Center*

*Bessie's Honeymoon Cottage is a private hideaway, the emphasis of the decor is meant to enhance romance during those special stays at the Old Owl Inn.*

# Bed, breakfast and antiquing

## The Old Owl Inn is joined with Cottontail Antiques to offer a complete experience

The Old Owl Inn, originally owned by Slim Riffle, was at one time a library in the town of Atolia. Slim moved it to Red Mountain in 1918. He then added on to the building and turned it into a bar, brothel and gambling salon.

The Owl witnessed many shoot-outs, bar-room brawls and two-fisted poker games. Legend has that the ladies of the evening along with illegal booze were hidden in tunnels below and out of sight of the watchful eye of the local sheriff.

Today, The Owl Cottages is a bed and breakfast decorated with antiques throughout. Guests can stay in Slim's Cottage, a spacious two-bedroom with kitchen, living room and old-fashioned bath, which was the private home of Slim Riffle. Bessie's Honeymoon Cottage is also available for that special romantic night or weekend, with kitchen and private bath.

*Take home a memento of your stay from Cottontail Antiques.*

The newly expanded Cottontail Antiques is located on the property, providing antiquers with treasures to take home as a memento of their stay at the Old Owl Inn, including Fenton, angels and needlework items.

*Cottontail Antiques and Old Owl Inn Bed & Breakfast is located at 701 Hwy. 395 in Red Mountain. For additional information see listing #142 (Red Mountain).*

*The organization of the AANTEEK AAVENUE MALL is as exceptional as the selection and the pricing. Truly no one need go home empty-handed.*

# AANTEEK AAVENUE MALL wins customers with outstanding value on exceptional selections

AANTEEK AAVENUE MALL is one of our favorite stops within a three-block walk of 22 antique stores in Carlsbad. The shop consists of 5,000 square feet of exceptionally organized antiques and collectibles.

*The AANTEEK AAVENUE MALL in Carlsbad.*

There are several reasons why this shop is among our favorites. The selections and the price ranges offer something for everyone. From $1.00 to $25,000, no one should leave empty-handed in this incredible shop. The owner is a jewel himself and particularly loves to work with dealers to offer the very best prices possible.

Dresden, flow blue, Roseville, Bauer, cut glass, sterling, art, Hummels, Royal Doulton, stained glass lamps, estate jewelry, California pottery, pens, Franciscan and exceptional furnishings are just a sampling of the selections you'll find at AANTEEK AVENUE MALL.

*AANTEEK AAVENUE MALL is located at 2832 State St. in Carlsbad. For additional information and directions to the mall see listing #22 (Carlsbad).*

*Fine furnishings abound within the 5,000 square feet of the AANTEEK AAVENUE MALL.*

## 1 AGOURA HILLS

**Agoura Antique Mart**
28863 Agoura Road
818/706-8366

**Showcase Antiques**
5021 Kanan Road
818/865-8268

**Sandy Lane Antique Mall**
28878 Roadside Dr.
818/991-0229

**Antique Mall**
28826 Roadside Dr.
818/991-8541

**Victoria's Antique Mall**
28912 Roadside Dr.
818/879-8626

## 2 AMADOR CITY

**Sherrill's Country Store**
14175 State Hwy. 49
209/267-5578

**Mac Clan Antiques**
14215 State Hwy. 49
209/267-1032

**Jensen's Antique Dolls Bears**
14227 State Hwy. 49
209/267-5639

**Roth Van Anda Antiques**
14461 W. School
209/267-5411

**Victorian Closet**
14170 State Hwy. 49
209/267-5250

**Country Living**
Hwy. 49
209/267-0874

**Miller's Antiques & Collectibles**
14183 State Hwy. 49
209/267-1582

## 3 ANAHEIM

**Len & Kathy's Collectible Toys**
1215 S. Beach Blvd., Suite E & F
714/995-4151

**Treasure Cliff**
1783 W. Lincoln Ave.
714/491-2830

**Lincoln Antique Mall**
1811 W. Lincoln Ave.
714/778-2522

**Antique Alley**
10351 Magnolia St.
714/821-1576

## 4 ANGELS CAMP

**Calaveras Coin & Collectibles**
1255 S. Main St.
209/736-2646

**Angels Camp Mercantile**
1267 S. Main St.
209/736-4100

**Grandmother's Antiques**
1273 S. Main St.
209/736-0863

**Orphan Annie's Emporium**
1284 Main St.
209/736-9086

**Nellie Lou's**
Main St.
209/836-6728

**Mystic Hollow**
1219A S. Main St.
209/736-0826

## 5 APTOS

**Village Fair**
417 Trout Gulch Road
408/688-9883

20 individual shops under one roof.

## 6 ARROYO GRANDE

**Rich Man-Poor Man Antiques**
106 W. Branch St.
805/489-8511

**Branch St. Antique Mall**
126 E. Branch St.
805/473-3276

**Village Antique Mart**
126 E. Branch St. #A
805/489-6528

**Glance At The Past**
410 E. Branch St.
805/489-5666

**Creekside Antiques**
122 E. Branch St.
805/473-2505

## 7 AUBURN

**Fine's Antique Mall & Gallery**
337 Commercial St.
916/888-7607

**Old West Trail Antiques**
343 Commercial St.
916/823-2784

**Sweet Sue Old & New**
345 Commercial St.
916/885-5537

**Antiques International**
4035 Grass Valley Hwy.
916/888-0324

**Betty Nelson Antiques**
1586 Lincoln Way
916/823-2519

**Mercantile Antiques**
875 Nevada St.
916/888-8740

**Serendipity**
135 Sacramento St.
916/885-1252

**As Time Goes By**
321 Commercial St.
916/823-7723

**Pauline's Antiques of Auburn**
301 Commercial St.
916/885-6828

**Oshay's Flowers & Antiques**
1280 Grass Valley Hwy.
916/823-1169

**Wild Horse Antiques**
923 Lincoln Way
916/823-7870

## 8 BAKERSFIELD

**Renaissance**
168 H St.
805/327-2902

**Cleo's Attic Antiques**
1888 S. Chester Ave.
805/832-8202

**Edison Antiques**
2227 Edison Hwy.
805/322-6174

**Collectorium**
2414 Edison Hwy.
805/322-4712

**Antique Loft**
6 H St.
805/325-2402

**Fond Memories**
151 H St.
805/322-9326

**Season's**
166 H St.
805/323-7673

**Childhood Memories Antiques**
1106 H St.
805/326-0346

**Betty's Barn of Antiques**
4811 Morro Dr.
805/366-5620

**Central Park Antique Mall**
701 19th St.
805/633-1143

**Somewhere In Time**
1312 19th St.
805/326-8562

**Five & Dime Antiques**
1400 19th St.
805/323-8048

**Johnny Crow's Garden**
5635 Taft Hwy.
805/836-9828

**Aatelier Antiques & Art**
612 18th St.
805/326-1922

**Bow-Tique Furniture & Accessories**
1420 19th St., Ste. A
805/322-8500

**Harvey's Antiques & Gifts**
230 Bernard St.
805/322-8676

**Cottage Gardens**
30 H St.
805/322-6254

**Golden West Antiques**
500 E. 18th St.
805/395-1174

**Good Brother's Antiques & Gifts**
332 Hwy. 43 (F St.)
805/758-2663

**Peabody's Books-Records**
2315 Edison Hwy.
805/322-8382

**Sam's**
2491 Edison Hwy.
805/323-3798

**Chris Vanderlei**
3031 H St.
805/323-0742

**Pidgeon Hill**
167 H St.
805/323-1226

**Grandma's Trunk**
1115 H St.
805/323-2730

**Great American Antiques**
625 19th St.
805/322-1776

**Nothin' New**
1310 19th St.
805/327-9664

**Timeless Treasures**
1320 19th St.
805/327-5052

**Curiosity Shop Antiques**
1607 19th St.
805/324-7112

**Old World Emporium**
731 16th St.
805/861-0940

**A-Plus Pak-Rats**
10711 Rosedale Hwy.
805/588-1212

**Consign It Stores, Inc.**
H Street at Brundage
805/325-2401

**Memory Lane Antique Mall**
1810 R St.
805/327-8232

**Estate of American Heritage**
1420 Ste. C 19th St.
805/325-3132

**Gone Junkin'**
1703 N. Chester
805/393-5251

**Goodies From The Past**
1610 19th St.
805/636-0368

**Peaches 'n' Cream**
159 H St.
805/634-9704

**Timeless Dreams**
316 State St.
805/746-6764

## 9 BEAUMONT

**Larry Nelson's Antiques**
136 E. 6th St.
909/769-1171

**Beaumont Antique Mall**
450 E. 6th St.
909/845-1397

**Browning's**
504 W. 6th St.
909/845-8608

**Legacy Antiques**
442 E. Sixth St.
909/845-5600

**Toys In The Attic**
200 E. 6th St.
909/769-0011

**R & R Antiques & Collectibles**
273 E. 6th St.
909/845-2787

**Nelson's Antique Mall**
630 California
909/769-1934

**Chatterbox**
350 E. 6th St.
909/769-1071

**Decorating Addict Antiques**
480 E. 6th St.
909/845-5856

**L & M Coins & Collectibles**
725 A Beaumont Ave.
909/769-2800

**Wholesale Antique Mall**
320 E. 6th St.
909/845-0155

**Parson's Cottage Antiques**
402 E. 6th St.
909/845-2523

**Jacqueline's Antique Mall**
626 Beaumont
909/769-0023

**Memories Antiques**
280 E. 6th St.
909/845-6255

## 10 BELLFLOWER

**Fischer Antiques**
17041 Lakewood Blvd.
310/633-6718

**Vic Clar Antiques Juke Boxes**
9313 Rose St.
562/866-7106

## 11 BENICIA

**This That N Whatever**
129 1st St.
707/745-8706

**Kindred Spirits**
632 1st St.
707/745-6533

**Consigntiques**
917 1st St.
707/746-6675

**Lottie Ballou Vintage Clothing**
130 W. E St.
707/747-9433

**Possessions of the Past**
435 1st St.
707/748-4487

**Benicia Antique Shop**
305 1st St.
707/745-0978

**Jeanie's**
727 1st St.
707/746-8464

**Lundin House of Antiques**
Corner 1st & J St.
707/745-1554

**Discover Yesterday**
364 1st St.
707/747-0726

**Golden Horseshoe Antiques**
415 1st St.
707/745-2255

## 12 BERKELEY

**Lorne Gay Antiques**
2990 Adeline St.
510/649-8550

**Jack's Antiques**
3021 Adeline St.
510/845-6221

**Betty Jane's Collectibles**
3192 Adeline St.
510/652-4586

**Military Artifacts & Collectibles**
1601 Ashby Ave.
510/841-2244

**Berkeley Collectibles Shop**
2280 Fulton
510/848-3199

**June Kadish Antiques**
1878 Solano Ave.
510/52802785

**It's Her Business Junque Funk**
2508 San Pablo Ave.
510/845-1663

**Laurent Bermudez Primitive Arts**
1859 Solano Ave. #B
510/527-1042

**Asiantique**
933 Parker St.
510/843-7515

**Behm-Powell Collection**
1347 Martin Luther King Jr. Way
510/526-7227

**Craftsman Home**
3048 Claremont Ave.
510/655-6503

**Fenton MacLaren**
1325 San Pablo Ave.
510/526-5377

**Lundberg Haberdashery**
396 Colusa Ave.
510/524-3003

**Eugene's Antiques**
2001 Milvia St.
510/548-5954

**Reliance Antiques**
830 Gilman St.
510/525-7003

**Von Homert Antiques**
1989 Ashby Ave.
510/548-1327

**Trout Farm Antiques**
2179 Bancroft Way
510/843-3565

**Louis A Capellino Antiques**
1987 Ashby Ave.
510/845-5590

**Grove Antiques (Sat. Only)**
1417 MLK Jr. Way #A
510/525-9120

**Brent's Unique Shop**
1824 San Pablo Ave.
510/841-9051

**Rosebud Gallery**
1857 Solano Ave.
510/525-6454

**Antiques by Tony**
3017 Adeline St.
510/649-9016

**Aura Jewelers**
2122 Vine St. #A
510/644-1487

**Continental Art Shop**
2490 Telegraph Ave.
510/843-2957

**Carol-Davis Antiques**
2808 Adeline St. #A
510/843-7582

**Laci's**
2982 Adeline St.
510/843-7290

**Moe's Books**
2476 Telegraph Ave.
510/849-2087

**Nomad's Gallery**
2548 Telegraph Ave.
510/841-5622

**People's Bazaar**
3258 Adeline St.
510/655-8008

**Zentrum Antiques**
1085 Ashby Ave.
510/841-1808

## 13 BEVERLY HILLS

**Sherwood's Spirit of America**
325 N. Beverly Dr.
310/274-6700

**Roth & Co.**
9511 Brighton Way
310/271-5485

**Auntie Barbara's Antiques**
238 S. Beverly Dr.
310/285-0873

**Barakat Antiques Gallery**
9876 Wilshire Blvd.
310/859-0676

**Royal-Athena Galleries**
9478 W. Olympic, Ste. 304
310/277-0133

**Krono's**
421 N. Rodeo Dr.
310/205-0766

**Chait Gallery Beverly Hills**
9330 Civic Center Dr.
310/828-8537

**Amphora Arts & Antiques**
308 N. Rodeo Dr.
310/273-4222

**Jake's Antiques**
8668 Wilshire Blvd.
310/360-0416

**Soltani Rugs & Antiques**
267 N. Canon Dr.
310/858-1770

## 14 BIG BEAR LAKE/BIG BEAR CITY

**M & B Antiques**
40143 Big Bear Blvd.
909/866-4200

**Weber's Thrift & Save**
39998 Big Bear Blvd.
909/866-2758

**Village Antiques**
40671 Village Dr.
909/866-6115

**Dinky's & Ruthy's**
40629 Lakeview Dr.
909/866-1729

**Boulevard Antiques**
41114 Big Bear Blvd.
909/866-4086

**Fox Farm Antique Mall**
42146 Fox Farm Road
909/866-0618

**A Sign of the Times**
525 W. Big Bear Blvd.
909/585-4208

**Way Out There**
1107 Baldwin Lake
909/585-5145

**Boulder Bay Antiques**
39209 Big Bear Blvd.
909/866-4293

**Big Bear Thrift & Treasures**
40074 Big Bear Blvd.
909/866-4336

**Harris House Antiques & Cllbls.**
579 Paine Road
909/866-0491

**Joanie's Attic**
40747 Lakeview Dr.
909/584-2468

**Myers Old & New Antiques**
41578 Big Bear Blvd.
909/866-4149

**Yours, Mine & Ours**
612 W. Big Bear Blvd.
909/584-2675

**Fowler's**
212 E. Big Bear Blvd.
909/585-7522

**Fox Den Antiques**
39434 N. Shore Dr.
909/866-3196

### *Great Places To Stay*

**Gold Mountain Manor Historic B&B**
1117 Anita
1-800-509-2604

Built in 1928, Gold Mountain Manor is Big Bear's only historic bed & breakfast. This 7000 sq. ft. historic log mansion sits on an acre of forested pine trees in a quiet residential area. The estate is within walking distance of the national forest and is a ten minute drive from all of Big Bear's recreational activities. It is a getaway for romance and relaxation! Decorated in antiques, the six rooms have queen-sized beds and wood burning fireplaces. Featured in the books, *Best Places to Kiss & Fifty Most Romantic Places in Southern California*.

## 15 BONSALL

**This Old House**
30158 Mission Road
760/631-2888

## 16 BURBANK

**Tower Trading Co.**
1314 W. Magnolia Blvd.
818/848-3950

**AARS**
2926 W. Magnolia Blvd.
818/558-1033

**Renaissance Antiques**
3317 W. Magnolia Blvd.
818/567-0935

**Madrid Antiques**
3416 W. Magnolia Blvd.
818/845-9028

**Victorian Rose Antiques**
3421 W. Magnolia Blvd.
818/842-3201

**White Elephant**
3422 W. Magnolia Blvd.
818/842-0721

**Antique Attic**
4005 W. Riverside Dr.
818/566-7155

**Magnolia House Antiques & Cllbls.**
3910 W. Magnolia Blvd.
818/843-8750

**Best of Times**
2918 1/2 W. Magnolia Blvd.
818-848-5851

**Five Sisters**
2524 W. Magnolia Blvd.
818/566-6897

**Napolean Gifts & Antiques**
2912 W. Burbank Blvd.
818-566-1958

## 17 BURLINGAME

**Burlingame Antiques**
915 Howard Ave.
650/344-4050

**Fat Cat Antiques**
247 California Dr.
650/348-1119

**Whistling Swan Antiques**
359 Primrose Road
650/343-1419

**Wood Duck Antiques**
363 Primrose Road
650/348-0542

**Heirloom's Antique Mall**
783 California Dr.
650/344-8800

**Kern's Fine Jewelry**
235 Park Road
650/348-7557

**Period Hardware**
1499 Bayshore Hwy. #104
650/697-4972

## 18 CAMARILLO

**Unique Antiques**
65 Palm Dr.
805/484-4100

**The Antique Mall of Camarillo**
58 Palm Dr.
805/484-7710

**Ingersoll's Antiques**
62 Palm Dr.
805/482-9936

**Augusta's Showroom**
2280 Ventura Blvd.
805/987-9883

**Abagail's Attic Antiques**
2633 Ventura Blvd.
805/388-0334

**Savannah West**
2235 Ventura Blvd.
805/383-6836

**The Yellow House Antiques**
2369 Ventura Blvd.
805/482-0330

**Antique Corner**
92 Palm Dr.
805/484-5913

**Window Box Antiques**
72 Palm Dr.
805/987-8191

## 19 CAMBRIA

**Morning Song**
4210 Branch St.
805/927-7101

**Once Upon A Time**
555 Main St.
805/927-5554

**Granny Had One Antiques**
712 Main St.
805/927-7047

**Fairey's Antiques**
715 Main St.
805/927-3665

**Urban Roots**
768 Main St.
805/927-7234

**Cambria Antique Center Mall**
2110 Main St.
805/927-2353

**Antiques on Main**
2338 Main St.
805/927-4292

**Country Collectibles**
2380 Main St. #A
805/927-0245

**Moonstone Antique Emporium**
5620 Moonstone Beach Dr.
805/927-5624

### *Great Places To Stay*

**Sylvia's Rigdon Hall Inn**
4022 Burton Dr.
805/927-5125

Burton Drive Inn (Sylvia's) is located on historical Burton Drive, in the heart of Cambria's original village, just six miles south of the famous Hearst Castle. The recently renovated Inn features eight elegant, quiet, spacious suites, individually decorated and impeccably maintained. Each of the deluxe suites includes a large sitting room with luxurious furnishings. Bedrooms feature a king-sized bed.

**The J. Patrick House**
2990 Burton Dr.
1-800-341-5258

The J. Patrick House is an authentic log cabin bed and breakfast nestled in the woods. There are eight spacious and romantic rooms, all with woodburning fireplaces and private baths. Each guest room is uniquely decorated in country charm. At 5:30 each day, enjoy the company of guests with hosts Barbara and Mel as you gather around the fireplace with your selection of wine or hor d'oeuvres.

## 20 CAMPBELL

**Donna's Antiques**
301 E. Campbell Ave.
408/866-1252

**Second Time Around**
327 E. Campbell Ave.
408/379-7240

**Woodworks Antiques**
841 Union Ave.
408/377-9778

**All Things Past & Present**
313 E. Campbell Ave.
408/378-3605

## 21 CANOGA PARK

**Collector's Eye**
21435 Sherman Way
818/347-9343

**Now & Then**
21501 Sherman Way
818/340-4007

**Antique Cottage**
21513 Sherman Way
818/347-8778

**Claudia's Collectibles**
21511 Sherman Way
818/702-6261

**Sadie's Corner Antiques**
21515 Sherman Way
818/704-7600

**Jeanne's Antiques & Collectibles**
21523 Sherman Way
818/702-9266

**Old Country Road**
21529 Sherman Way
818/340-3760

**Affordable Antiques**
21612 Sherman Way
818/348-2909

**Kingston Galleries, Inc.**
8573 Canoga Ave.
818-885-7694

**Turn of the Century Antiques**
21531 Sherman Way
818/704-7711

**West Hills Antique Center**
6633 Fallbrook Ave.
818/888-1362

**Zulia's Antiques**
21525 Sherman Way
818/888-6660

**Courtyard Antiques**
7207 Alabama
818/992-5189

## 22 CARLSBAD

**AANTEEK AAVENUE MALL**
2832 State St.
760/434-8742
Daily 11-5, closed major holidays only
*Directions: Take I-5 to Carlsbad Village Dr., then turn west and go 5 blocks to State St. Turn north (right) and go 1 full block, cross over Grand Ave., and count 6 stores on the right (east) side of State St.*

AANTEEK AAVENUE MALL is 5000 square feet of extra clean, well lighted, well stocked antiques and collectibles. Dresden, flow blue, Roseville, Bauer, cut glass, sterling, art, mirrors, steins, furniture, paper, books, Royal Doulton, Hummels, extensive selection of display aids and reference books, reproduction silk and stained glass lamp shades, lamps, windows, jewelry, California Pottery, flatware, china sets, rare Franciscan, cigarette lighters, lanterns, patches, pens, hood ornaments, toys, inkwells, book ends, perfumes, purses, paperweights, photos, figurines, collector plates, and much, much more. Very eclectic, you won't be sorry! Friendly and helpful staff who feel it is their pleasure to open cases for their customer.

**From Clara's Attic**
561 Carlsbad Village Dr.
760/720-9384

**Black Whale Lghting & Antiques**
562 Carlsbad Village Dr.
760/434-3113

**Carlsbad House of Antqs. & Doll House**
2752 State St.
760/720-1061

**Olde Ivy Antiques**
2928 State St.
760/729-8607

**De Witts Antiques**
2946 State St.
760/720-1175

**Roseboro House**
2971 State St.
760/729-3667

**Mulloy's Estate Jewelry**
2978 State St.
760/729-5774

**Backroads Antiques**
2988 State St.
760/729-3032

**Antiques Junction**
457 Carlsbad Village Dr.
760/434-2332

**Country Treasures**
4901 El Camino Real
760/730-7474

**Byrne's Antiques Restoration Co.**
2698 State St.
760/434-7800

**Postal's Antiques**
2825 State St.
760/729-7816

**U.S. Antiques**
2525 El Camino Real
760/720-5254

**Sunflower Cottage**
2525 El Camino Real
760/434-7643

**Antique Crossroads**
3021 State St.
760/434-3355

**Gallery of Miniatures**
2763 State St.
760/729-3231

**Hattie P's Treasures**
2921 Roosevelt St.
760/729-5010

**A&E Antiques & Estate Jewelry**
2802 State St.
760/434-6400

**Lisa's Miniatures, Collectibles, Gifts**
3077 State St.
760/434-1358

## 23 CARMEL/CARMEL VALLEY

Nestled in a pine forest above a spectacular white sand beach, the one-square-mile village of Carmel is reminiscent of European charm. There is no mail delivery: homes are known only by name and have no addresses. Winding streets, secluded alleyways, courtyards and arcades are highlighted by 70 art studios and galleries, numerous antique shops, specialty boutiques and small cafes.

Carmel is also the home of Mission Ranch Restaurant, owned by actor and two-term Carmel mayor, Clint Eastwood. Clint bought the historic Mission Ranch property in 1986. The ranch, built in the mid-1880s, was a dairy farm until the '20s. What is now the restaurant was once the dairy's creamery.

The dining room has a cozy ranch decor, complete with checkered tablecloths and a large stone fireplace. For views of the scenic pastoral grounds, one can eat outside on a wide deck with umbrella tables.

The basic menu is ranch-style: prime rib, steaks and BBQ ribs. If this doesn't arouse your tastebuds, Chef Craig Ling offers other house specialities from which to choose: loin of lamb, salmon, fresh seafood, roasted chicken, beef brochette and meatless lasagna for vegetarians. Dinners include soup or salad, twice-baked potatoes and fresh vegetables. The restaurant offers an appetizer, a la carte and a homemade dessert menu as well.

**Mission Ranch Restaurant**
26270 Dolores
408/625-9040
Hours:
Dinner, 4:30-10:00 - 7 days
Lunch, 11:30-3, Sat. only
Brunch, 9:30-2:30 - Sun.

**Anna Beck Antiques**
26358 Carmel Rancho Lane
408/624-3112

**Langer's Antiques**
Delores (Between Ocean & 7th)
408/624-2102

**Trappings**
W. Juniper between 5th & 6th
408/626-4500

**Robt Cordy Antiques**
Lincoln & 6th
408/625-5839

**Great Things Antiques**
Ocean Ave.
408/624-7178

**Antiques Francais**
3742 The Barnyard
408/624-7444

**Carmel Valley Antiques**
7151 Carmel Valley Road
408/624-3414

**Mid Valley Antiques**
312 W. Carmel Valley Road #320
408/624-0261

**Off The Wall**
Lincoln (Between 5th & 6th)
408/624-6165

**T. B. Scanlon Antiques**
Carmel Valley
408/659-4788

**Maxine Klaput Antiques**
Mission & 7th
408/624-8823

**Robertson's Antiques**
Delores & 7th
408/624-7517

**Anderle Gallery**
Lincoln, Ocean & 7th
408/624-4199

**Magpie Antiques**
Ocean Ave. & Lincoln
408/622-9341

**Hildegunn Hawley Antiques**
Delores (Between 5th & 6th)
408/626-3457

**Keller & Scott**
Delores near 5th St.
408/624-0465

**Luciano Antiques**
San Carlos St.
408/624-9396

**Laura's Antiques & Collectibles**
3724 The Barnyard
408/625-6480

**Sandy's Antiques**
1 Esquiline Road
408/659-2629

**Teeleet Antiques**
25 Pilot Road
408/625-2134

***Great Places To Stay***

**Candle Light Inn**
P. O. Box 1900
1-800-433-4732

This Tudor-style inn offers charm and warmth with a friendly staff who provides good old-fashioned service. Rooms have king beds, wood-burning fireplaces and full kitchens or standard rooms with one king bed and two double beds. Rates include a picnic basket breakfast and the morning newspaper delivered to your door. Located in the heart of the village, within walking distance to all the shops, galleries and restaurants.

**The Stonehouse Inn**
8th below Monte Verde
408/624-4569 or 1-800-748-6618
Open daily 10-9
Rates: $99-199
*Directions: Traveling Hwy. 1 south or north, take Ocean Ave. exit. Travel Ocean Ave. to Junipero, turn left, proceed to 8th, turn right, travel five blocks to Monte Verde. Located on the left side (south side) of block between Monte Verde and Casanova.*

This charming inn has a complete stone exterior, hand-shaped by local Indians when it was built in 1906. Through the years, Mrs. "Nana" Foster, the original owner, often invited notable artists and writers from the San Francisco Bay area to stay in her Carmel home. Sinclair Lewis, Jack London and Lotta Crabtree were among these guests. Rooms are named in their honor.

A glass enclosed front porch provides the entrance and sets the mood for the warmth and ambiance you are soon to experience.

Guests often gather in the living room in front of the large stone fireplace to enjoy not only the warmth of the fire, but the pleasure of meeting new friends from around the world.

The restful bedrooms are light and airy, some having a view of the ocean through the trees. Each room is decorated in soft colors and features antiques, cozy quilts, fresh flowers, fruit and special touches.

A generous breakfast is served each morning in the sunny dining room, the peaceful garden or before the fire.

**Tally Ho Inn**
Monte Verde & 6th
1-800-652-2632
Web site: www.tallyho-inn.com

Secluded and tranquil, the 1920 Tally Ho Inn offers a true English countryside atmosphere. Only half a block from the heart of Carmel, the Tally Ho is an idyllic retreat of flowers, gardens, fireplaces and a soothing view of the ocean. Take a short picturesque stroll to Carmel's famous white sandy beach and revel in the fabulous views of the Pacific Ocean, Pebble Beach and Point Lobos. Accommodates fourteen guests.

## 24 CARMICHAEL

**Queen Anne Cottage**
2633 El Camino Ave.
916/481-4944

**For Olde Tyme Sake**
6030 Fair Oak Blvd.
916/978-9818

**Antiques Unlimited**
6328 Fair Oaks Blvd.
916/482-6533

**Hovis Antiques**
7800 Fair Oaks Blvd.
916/944-4736

**The White House**
6210 Fair Oaks Blvd.
916/979-9742

**The Elegant Antique Barn**
6443 Fair Oaks Blvd.
916/973-8590

## 25 CARNELIAN BAY

**The Meadows Collection**
By Appointment Only
530/546-5516

## 26 CARPINTERIA

**Angels**
4846 Carpinteria Ave.
805/684-8148

**Magpie Collections**
961 Linden Ave.
805/684-6034

**Antique Delights**
771 Linden Ave.
805/684-2717

## 27 CARSON

**Memory Lane Antique Mall**
20740 S. Figueroa St.
301/538-4130

## 28 CAYUCOS

**Cayucos Antiques**
151 Cayucos Dr.
805/995-2206

**Cayucos Trading Post**
98 N. Ocean Ave.
805/995-3453

**Rich Man - Poor Man Antique Mall**
146 N. Ocean Ave.
805/995-3631

**Remember When**
152 N. Ocean Ave.
805/995-1232

**American Pie**
890 S. Ocean Ave.
805/995-0832

## 29 CHICO

**Country Squyres' Antiques**
164 E. 3rd St.
916/342-6764

**Trends & Traditions**
126 W. 3rd St.
916/891-5622

**American Antiques**
1355 Guill St.
916/345-0379

**Soot & Shine Shed Antiques**
11708 Butte Creek Island Rd.
916/342-8806

**8th & Main Antiques Center**
745 Main St.
916/893-5534

**Antique Annex**
1421 Carnaby St.
916/893-8823

**Hidden Treasure Antiques**
2234 Park Ave.
916/893-5773

**Voses Shopping Center**
9145 Cohasset Road
916/342-5214

## 30 CHOWCHILLA

While driving through Central California, look for the quaint agricultural town of Chowchilla, an easy and convenient exit off of State Freeway 99 and State Hwy. 152, where you and your family can park your R.V. and rest and relax in a palm shaded park. Adjacent is a cluster of seven antique shops within a four-block area located on the main street through town. Enjoy this low key pioneering atmosphere where you can take your time to shop and browse among friendly small town people. There are also numerous restaurants and sandwich shops with a variety of cuisines available.

Chowchilla has an unusual history in its development. This small city named after an Indian tribe, did not explode in population as did most early California settlements. However, it sits in the geographical center of the state and requires only a short drive west to the ocean front attractions and a short drive east to the high Sierra Nevada Mountains and to the entrance of the beautiful Yosemite Valley. (The Sierras offer many scenic routes that includes Redwood forests, mountain lakes, streams and camping.) It is located in the most productive agriculture area in the world. The Central Valley boasts the production of 250 agricultural commodities.

**The Parrott Shop**
535 Robertson Blvd.
209/665-4311
Open daily 10:30-5

Harvey & Geri Parrott, owners of The Parrott Shop, have been antique collectors for 25 years. Their shop on Robertson St. is filled with over 10,000 items within its 4,000 square feet. A large selection of prints, glassware (including carnival and depression), crystal, china, pottery such as Roseville, Weller, Hull, Bauer, Fiesta and McCoy can be found among this eclectic offering of antiques. Military items, costume jewelry, tools, kitchen ware, fishing items, books, cookie jars, decanters, bird cages, musical instruments, lighting, furnishings of several periods and styles are also available. They even have a section devoted to oriental pieces along with a special area for quilters.

**Frontier Towne**
521 Robertson Blvd.
209/665-3900
Open daily 10:30-5, closed Thurs.
Owner: Sandy Batey

Frontier Towne opened its doors in 1985 as one of the first collectives in the San Joaquin Valley. The interior resembles the main street of an old western town, complete with settings of an old general store, bank, saloon, boarding house and blacksmith shop. This 5,000 sq. ft. shop offers a huge variety of antiques and collectibles. Western collectibles are a speciality of the owner as she is a ranch raised cowgirl and still rides and competes in rodeos (in her spare time!). A very interesting stop on your antique trail.

**The 2nd Frontier**
529 Robertson Blvd.
209/665-3900
Open daily 10:30-5, closed Thurs.

The 2nd Frontier which opened in 1997 is the sister shop to Frontier Towne. Specializing in retro furniture and large items, the shop has a quickly changing inventory - mostly due to its exceptionally low prices.

**His & Hers Antiques**
527 Robertson Blvd.
209/665-1911
Open daily 11-5

Noted as one of the fun places to shop in Chowchilla, His & Hers Antiques offers something for everyone from primitive to formal. Twelve dealers from Fresno to San Francisco supply the wares which make up this eclectic inventory.

**Village Antiques**
510 Robertson Blvd.
209/665-1487
Thurs.-Mon. 9-5, Tues. 9-2

For the past ten years, Brigette Brooks has offered her customers a unique blend of antiques and collectibles. In addition to the usual and the unusual, she also carries old paper items.

**The Glasstique Shoppe**
331 Robertson Blvd.
209/665-5676
Daily 10-5, closed Wed.

This shoppe, which is 1700 square feet in size, specializes in flow blue porcelain, beautiful furniture, and a general line of antiques and collectibles.

The owners have been collecting antiques for thirty-five years and have operated The Glasstique Shoppe for ten years at this location.

**Gray Duck Antique Mall**
216 Robertson Blvd.
209/665-3305
Web site: grammy@madnet.net
Daily 10-5, closed Wed.

Gray Duck Antique Mall has established itself over the past fifteen years as a special place to shop. This 3,000 sq. ft. showcase mall specializes in advertising, war memorabilia, toys and western tack along with a general line of antiques and collectibles.

## 31 CLAREMONT

**Cat In The Window**
206 W. Bonita Ave.
909/399-0297

**Cambridge Row Antiques**
206 W. Bonita Ave.
909/625-1931

**Barbara Cheatley Antiques**
215 Yale Ave.
909/621-4161

## 32 CLOVIS

**Osterberg's Mercantile**
Fifth St.
209/298-4291

**Clovis Antique Mall 1&2**
530 & 532 Fifth St.
209/298-1090

**Old Town Antiques**
410 Clovis Ave.
209/325-1208

**Peacock Alley Antiques**
614 Fifth St.
209/299-1186

**Olde Time Antique Mall**
460 Clovis Ave.
209/299-2575

**Melton's Carousel World**
425 Pollasky Ave.
209/298-8930

**Treasured Memories**
460 Clovis Ave.
209/299-4266

**4th Street Antique Mall**
461 Pollasky Ave.
209/323-1636

**Donnie Lu's Gifts & Treasures**
320 Pollasky Ave.
209/299-5538

## 33 COSTA MESA

**Panier De Fleurs**
2915 S. Bristol
714/979-1819

**Castle Antiques**
112 E. 18th St.
714/722-6779

**Jack & Gloria's Antiques**
1304 Logan Ave., #E,F,G
714/546-5450

**Fanfare Tiffany Lamps**
1765 Newport Blvd.
714/642-6692

**Greenville Station**
1685 Tustin Ave.
714/642-0218

**Heirloom Galleries**
369 E. 17th St.
714/631-4633

**Cottage Company**
1686 Tustin Ave.
714/722-0777

**The Country Inn**
130 E. 17th St., Unit P
714/722-1177

**Musket & Sabre Antique Arms**
446 W. 19th St.
714/645-0036

**Old Stones**
Appointment Only
714/574-8033

**Richard Felch Antiques**
120 Virginia Place
714/642-8911

**Zazy Goona Antique Mall**
1770 Orange Ave.
714/646-4561

**Crofton Antiques**
670 W. 17th St.
714/642-4585

**Treasures on Consignment**
2220 Fairview Road
714/645-5477

**Consignment Gallery**
270 E. 17th St.
714/631-2622

**Stix & Stones**
333 E. 17th St., Unit B-12
714/646-7233

**Normandy Metal**
1603 Superior Ave.
714/631-5555

**Jack & Gloria's II**
2981 Fairview Road
714/751-3809

## 34 COTTONWOOD

**Country Lane Antiques**
20839 Front St.
916/347-5598

**Abbey Gayle's Fine Things**
20840 Front St.
916/347-9669

**Cottonwood Antiques**
3306 Main St.
916/347-0692

## 35 COVINA

**Signs of the Times Antiques**
110 N. Citrus Ave.
818/966-7101

**Nostalgia Nook Antiques**
112 N. Citrus Ave.
818/339-8699

**Collector's Alley**
225 N. Citrus Ave.
818/858-9964

**Vestige Antiques**
312 N. Citrus Ave.
818/967-8970

**Looking Back**
316 N. Citrus Ave.
818/966-8842

**Ivy & The Rose**
113 W. College St.
818/967-1171

**Old Covina Antique Emporium**
514 N. Citrus Ave.
818/859-9972

**G & L Collectibles**
332 N. Citrus Ave.
818/966-6829

## 36 CRESCENT CITY

**Antiques Etc.**
280 U.S. Hwy. 101 S.
707/464-9012

**Sunset House Antiques**
1060 Sunset Circle
707/464-6631

**Eclectic**
305 U.S. Hwy. 101 S.
707/464-7907

**Sylvia's Attic**
285 L St.
707/464-9466

**Shrader Antiques**
2025 U.S. Hwy. 199
707/458-3525

## 37 CUCAMONGA

**A's Antiques**
8078 Archibald
909/989-8017

## 38 CULVER CITY

**Beaded Bird**
3811 Bagley Ave.
310/204-3594

**Aunt Iris's Antiques**
10762 Washington Blvd.
310/838-5349

## 39 CYPRESS

**Cora & Mac's Glass Antiques**
5012 Ball Road
714/229-8325

**Anne Michael's**
5917 Cerritos Ave.
714/821-7990

## 40 DANA POINT

**The Landmark Antiques**
34241 Coast Hwy.
714/489-1793

**Traditions Tea Room**
34241 Pacific Coast Hwy. #101
714/248-7660

## 41 DANVILLE

**Antiques Du Coeur**
391 Hartz Ave.
510/837-5049

**Rue 137**
398 Hartz Ave.
510/837-1148

**Danville Antiques**
111 Town & Country Road
510/837-4784

**Menagerie Antiques**
105 Town and Country Dr.
510/837-3929

**Sweet Ivy**
3470 Blackhawk Plaza Circle
510/736-0949

**French Country**
398 Hartz Ave.
510/837-1148

## 42 EL CAJON

**Antique Mercantile Co.**
161 E. Main St.
619/441-8804

**Main Street Antique Mall**
237 E. Main St.
619/447-0800

**The Doll Den**
231 W. Douglas
619/44-2198

**Stuff Your Mom Throughout**
144 E. Main St.
619/440-2440

**Flinn Springs Country Store**
14860 Olde Hwy. 80
619/443-1842

**Magnolia Antique Mall**
456 N. Magnolia Ave.
619/444-0628

**Antique Blvd. Mall**
799 El Cajon
619/447-8057

**The Beehive**
1258 Broadway
619/444-4837

## 43 ELK GROVE

**Dalin Jewelers**
8765 Elk Grove Blvd.
916/685-6530

**Country Blend**
9084 Elk Grove Blvd.
916-686-8223

**Bells Cookie Jar**
9086 Elk Grove Blvd.
916/685-7810

**Country Grove Antiques**
9098 Elk Grove Blvd.
916/685-2082

**Remember When**
9116 Elk Grove Blvd.
916/685-6776

## 44 ENCINITAS

**Simply Nostalgia**
162 S. Rancho Sante Fe Road
619/943-1328

**Antique Crossroads**
765 S. Coast Hwy. 101
760/753-0292

**Paris Flea Market**
N. Coast Hwy. 101
760/633-1373

**Coastal Consignment Connection**
850 S. Coast Hwy. 101
760/943-1199

## 45 ESCONDIDO

**Victorian Garden Antiques**
115 W. Grand Ave.
760/737-9669

**121 Grand Antiques**
121 W. Grand Ave.
760/489-0338

**Escondido Antique Mall**
135 W. Grand Ave.
760/743-3210

**Memory Lane Antiques**
158 E. Grand Ave.
760/480-1215

**In The Cave**
227 E. Grand Ave.
760/739-9117

**Art's Antiques & Collectibles**
252 E. Grand Ave.
760/746-7104

**Cornucopia Antiques**
317 E. Grand Ave.
760/745-9792

**Hidden Valley Antique Empor**
333 E. Grand Ave.
760/737-0333

**Grab Bag Antiques**
150 E. Grand Ave.
760/480-1861

**Lionheart Consignment**
262 E. Grand Ave.
760/746-8636

## 46 EUREKA

### Antiques and Goodies
1128 3rd St.
707/442-0445
Mon.-Sat.10-5, Sun. during the summer.
*Directions: Traveling south on U.S. 101 turn right on M St., left on 3rd; shop is on the left. Traveling north on U.S. 101 turn left on L St., right on 3rd; shop is on the right.*

Located amongst the grand Victorian homes of Eureka, Antiques and Goodies will quickly become one of your favorite antiquing experiences. It's one of those nice places where quality is still affordable. The shop offers seven full rooms (5000 sq. ft.) of exceptional imported 19th century furnishings and smalls. The owners take great pride in their ability to find the best bargains which is evidenced in the hand selected inventory from Great Britain and throughout the continent.

The shop specializes in English, French and Japanese furniture, Victorian housewares, tools and clocks. You will also find a large selection of Quimper, Mottoware, Majolica and British commemoratives.

**Antique Annex**
208 F St.
707/443-9113

**Old Town Antiques**
318 F St.
707/442-3235

**Eureka Antique Mall**
533 F St.
707/445-8835

**Hexagram Antiques**
426 3rd St.
707/443-4334

**The Hose Company**
1401 3rd St.
707/445-4673

**Antique Bottles & Relics**
2235 Broadway St.
707/442-2667

**Empire Furniture Antiques**
111 5th St.
707/442-1871

**Antique Arcade**
501 3rd St.
707/442-3895

**Kit-N-Kaboodle**
527 3rd St.
707/442-5760

***Great Places To Stay***

### A Weaver's Inn
1440 B St.
Web site: www.humboldt1.com/~weavrinn
1-800-992-8119

A Weaver's Inn provides an atmosphere reflecting warmth and the elegance of the Victorian era. Your stay will be in a gracious Queen Anne home surrounded by a cottage-style, fenced garden and spacious lawn (for playing croquet or quiet contemplation). Three lovely guest rooms and the two-room Pamela Suite are furnished with many antiques, down comforters and fresh flowers from the garden. Each room reflects the genteel elegance of a by-gone era, including two with fireplaces. Located only ten blocks from historic Old Town. From the inn you can easily access a tour of the harbor or a carriage ride along the waterfront.

**Carter House Victorians**
301 L St.
Web site: www.carterhouse.com
1-800-404-1390

Welcoming travelers since 1981, The Carter House is an enclave of three magnificent Victorians perched alongside Humboldt Bay at the gateway to Eureka's historic district. Guest rooms feature antiques, private baths and luxuriant amenities to soothe the soul and delight the senses. Dinner at Restaurant 301 is truly a celebration of the senses. The gardens provide herbs and fresh vegetables for the chefs.

**Abigail's Elegant Victorian Bed & Breakfast**
1406 C St.
707/444-3144
Web site: www.bnbcity.com/inns/20016

For specific information see review at the beginning of this section.

## 47 EXETER

**Exeter Antiques**
216 E. Pine
209/594-4221

**Tumbleweeds**
400 Rock Hill Dr.
209/592-2565

**By The Water Tower**
141 S. B St.
209/594-4060

**Greenleave's Antiques**
277 E. Pine
209/592-1880

**Antique's & More**
275 E. Pine
209/592-5697

**Pine Street Relics**
201 E. Pine
209/592/4170

**Heritage Plaza**
196 E. Pine
209/592-8101

**Snazzy Antiques**
228 E. Pine
209/592-9606

**Olde Town Exchange**
117 E. Pine
209/592-5858

## 48 FAIR OAKS

**Mary Scott Antiques**
10211 Fair Oaks Blvd.
916/967-2493

**Blue Eagle Antiques**
10201 Fair Oaks Blvd.
916/966-4947

## 49 FALLBROOK

**Jewelry Connection**
113 N. Main St.
760/723-4629

**Millies Antique N Old Lace**
3137 S. Mission Road, #A
760/723-9206

**Country Elegance**
3137 S. Mission Road, #B
760/723-3417

**Ivy House Antiques**
3137 S. Mission Road, #B
760/728-7038

**Tin Barn Antiques**
3137 S. Mission Road, #D
760/723-1609

**Kirk's Antiques**
321 N. Orange Ave.
760/728-6333

**Thomas Antiques**
2809 S. Mission Road
760/728-5156

## 50 FELTON

**Carousel Gallery Antique Dolls**
6931 Hwy. 9
408/335-3076

**Huckleberry House**
Antiques By Appointment
408/335-1395

**OJ's American Antiques**
135 Valhalla Way
508/335-5590

## 51 FERNDALE

**Foggy Bottoms**
563 Main St.
707/786-9188
Mon.-Sat. 12-5, Sun. 12-4
*Directions: Take the Ferndale exit from Hwy. 101. Cross over Fernbridge Drive into Ferndale. Foggy Bottoms is in the first block of the business district on Main St. near Shaw Ave.*

Foggy Bottoms Antiques, named for the foggy veil which often descends upon this quaint valley town, is located in a State Historic Landmark town, on a National Historic Landmark street.

The shop, housed in a 1,000-square-foot turn-of-the-century building, may be small but is richly blessed with notable charm. "It's all I can handle," says Jacque Ramirez, who is both shopkeeper and owner of Foggy Bottoms. She is also co-owner (with her husband, Richard) of Grandmother's House Bed and Breakfast located just seconds away from the shop at 861 Howard St.

Foggy Bottom's "claim to fame" is its offering of many old radio program cassettes. The shop stocks a hodge-podge of unusual smalls; china, porcelains, a nice selection of salt and pepper shakers, early rolling pins, pottery and just about anything old that Jacque finds interesting.

For some unknown reason, Ferndale happens to be the home to many avid sweater knitters, and for that reason Foggy Bottoms offers an ample selection of yarns, patterns and accessories for the genteel looper.

After a long day of antiquing and sight-seeing in this "picture postcard" valley, you're always welcome to stay at Grandmother's House. Built in 1901, this bed and breakfast offers gracious accommodations with all the romance and charm of the turn of the century. The three guest rooms are decorated with antique furnishings, as is the rest of the house. The dining room provides a parlor with wood-burning fireplace.

Enjoy the peaceful back porch while watching buffalo graze in a nearby pasture. Located in a quiet residential neighborhood.

**Golden Gait Mercantile**
421 Main St.
707/786-4891

**Cream City Mall**
1400 Main St.
707/786-4997

**Aunt Jane's Collectibles**
Main St.
707/786-4903

### *Great Places To Stay*

**Gingerbread Mansion Inn**
400 Berding St.
707/786-4000
Rates: $100-205
Four-Diamond Rated

Located in a well-preserved Victorian Village, The Gingerbread Mansion Inn is one of northern California's most photographed homes. The inn is a striking display of superior Victorian architecture surrounded by immaculately groomed English gardens.

## 52 FOLSOM

**As Time Goes By Antiques**
306 Rile St.
916/985-6206

**Sheepish Grin Antique Market**
625 Sutter St.
916/885-0257

**Thistle & Rose Scottish Antiques**
722 Sutter St.
916/353-1936

**Dal Bello Antiques Collective**
727 Sutter St.
916/985-3772

**Williams Carriage House Antiques**
728 Sutter St.
916/985-7416

**Emily's Antique Corner**
732 Sutter St.
916/985-6222

**Curiosity Shoppe**
801 1/2 Sutter St.
916/985-0534

**Olde Towne Antiques**
809 Sutter St.
916/985-2853

**Colonies**
813 Sutter St.
916/985-3442

**Cottage In The Mall**
813 Sutter St.
916/985-0496

**Setnik's In Time Again**
815 Sutter St.
916/985-2390

**A-Arts Antiques**
707 Sutter St.
916/985-6429

**Folsum Mercantile Exchange**
726 Sutter St.
916/985-2169

## 53 FORTUNA

**Fernbridge Antique Mall**
597 Fernbridge Dr.
707/725-8820

**Rundells Antiques & Collectibles**
569 Main St.
707/725-9175

**Antique Depot**
1122 Main St.
707/725-5503

**Fortuna Art & Old Things**
1026 Main St.
707/725-3003

## 54 FREMONT

**Cherished Memories/Dodi's Dolls**
37390 Niles Blvd.
510/792-2559

**My Friends & I**
37521 Niles Blvd.
510/792-0118

**The Clock Man**
120 J St.
510/794-5928

**Antiques Junction**
37312 Niles Blvd.
510/793-3481

**With a Little Help My Friends**
37313 Niles Blvd.
510/797-2088

**Niles Blvd. Antique Center**
37825 Niles Blvd.
510/790-1221

**Morning Glory Antiques**
37372 Niles Blvd.
510/790-3374

**Woodhaven**
37396 Niles Blvd.
510/745-7666

**The Store**
37415 Niles Blvd.
510/797-8471

**Shades Of The Past**
37495 Niles Blvd.
510/791-2415

**Ma Mere Intl.**
37501 Niles Blvd.
510/793-8043

**Les Belles Antiques**
37549 Niles Blvd.
510/794-4773

**Bite & Browse**
37565 Niles Blvd.
510/796-4537

**Lost In The Attic**
37663 Niles Blvd.
510/791-2420

**Old and New**
37675 Niles Blvd.
510/792-4757

**East Bay Dolls & Bears**
37721 Niles Blvd.
510/792-2559

**Side Street Antiques**
37581 Niles Blvd.
510/795-9005

**Jean & Bea's Toys U-NU**
37769 Niles Blvd.
510/793-2848

**Timeless Treasures**
37769 Niles Blvd.
510/795-7755

**S & H Antiques**
130 J St.
510/792-7792

**Niles Antique Co-op**
37759 Niles Blvd.
510/744-1602

## 55 FRESNO

**Treasure of Sierra Madre**
463 E. Belmont Ave.
209/264-9343

**Dug 'O' Vic's European Antiques**
1310 N. Blackstone Ave.
209/442-8494

**Chesterfield Antiques**
5092 N. Blackstone Ave.
209/225-4736

**Bell Antiques**
3265 E. Belmont Ave.
209/485-8381

**Lina's Antiques**
1918 N. Echo Ave.
209/497-9767

**Alice's Palace**
22 E. Olive Ave.
209/485-4408

**Fulton's Folly Antique Mall**
920 E. Olive Ave.
209/268-3856

**Antiques & Favorite Things**
444 E. Olive Ave.
209/497-0217

**Collectique**
140 E. Olive Ave.
209/441-1252

**It's About Time**
1526 N. Van Ness Ave.
209/264-3529

**Valentino's Altern. Apprl.**
814 E. Olive Ave.
209/233-6900

**Fellini's**
836 N. Fulton St.
209/498-3321

**Marcel's Antiques**
834 N. Van Ness Ave.
209/266-3040

**Yosemite Coins & Antiques**
4568 N. 1st St.
209/229-5672

## 56 FULLERTON

**Krypton**
101 E. Commonwealth Ave., #C
714/446-0592

**George's Antiques**
201 W. Commonwealth Ave.
714/871-4347

**Doll Trunk**
531 W. Commonwealth Ave.
714/526-1467

**Susan Herpel Antique Quilts**
By appointment only
714/870-8989

**Amerage Avenue Antiques**
122 N. Harbor Blvd., Ste. 110
714/525-6383

**Antique Companion**
204 N. Harbor Blvd.
714/525-2756

**Harbor Antique Mall**
207 N. Harbor Blvd.
714/680-0532

**Ashley Rose Antique**
213 N. Harbor Blvd.
714/871-4656

**Eclectic Antiques**
108 E. Amerige Ave.
714/871-7373

**Antique Mine**
124 E. Commonwealth Ave.
714/526-2200

**Back Home Antiques**
509 W. Commonwealth Ave.
714/526-3553

**Jones Mercantile**
531 W. Commonwealth Ave.
714/879-3501

**Antique Gallery**
110 N. Harbor Blvd.
714/871-3850

**Kindred Co.**
202 N. Harbor Blvd.
714/879-2324

**Old Towne Fullerton Antiques**
206 N. Harbor Blvd.
714/447-9046

**Apropos Antiques**
112 E. Amerige Ave.
714/871-8920

**David's Antiques & Clocks**
201 N. Harbor Blvd.
714/447-4308

**Silver Lining**
122 N. Harbor Blvd. #109
714/871-8760

## 57 GARDEN GROVE

**Private Collections**
12931 Main St.
714/539-4419

**L C & Sally's Antiques**
12951 Main St.
714/530-3035

**Garden Grove Mercantile**
12941 Main St.
714/534-1857

**Sleepy Hollow Antique Mall**
12965 Main St.
714/539-9187

## 58 GILROY

**Final Frontier**
7411 Monterey St.
408/847-1050

**Monterey St. Antiques**
7511 Monterey St.
408/848-3788

**Garbos Antiques & Collectibles**
7517 Monterey St.
408/848-6722

**Littlejohn's Fine Jewelry**
8220 Monterey St.
408/842-1001

**Gilroy Antiques**
7445 Monterey St.
408/842-1776

**Serendipity**
7515 Monterey St.
408/842-0399

**Hampton Court Antiques**
7542 Monterey St.
408/847-2455

**Lindsey & Friends Antique Mall**
7888 Monterey St.
408/842-5586

## 59 GLENDALE

**Fiona's**
3463 N. Verdugo Road
818/249-6776

**About Antiques**
3533 Ocean View Blvd.
818/249-8587

## 60 GLENDORA

**Millie's Dolls**
140 N. Glendora Ave.
818/963-8311

**Country Village Antiques**
163 N. Glendora Ave.
818/914-6860

**Anything Goes Emporium**
218 N. Glendora Ave.
818/963-3939

**Old Packing House**
243 S. Vermont Ave.
818/963-8171

**Orange Tree Antiques**
216 N. Glendora Ave.
818/335-3376

## 61 GRASS VALLEY

**Grass Valley Antique Emporium**
150 Mill St.
916/272-7302

**Al's Attic Antiques**
11671 Maltman Dr.
916/272-1777

**The Rubaiyat**
151 Mill St.
916/272-4844

**Young's Olde Treasures**
101 S. Church St.
916/274-1917

**Duck Soup**
160 Mill St.
916/477-7891

**Auntie's Attic**
504 Whiting St.
916/273-1095

**Granny's Treasure Chest**
132 E. Main St.
916/272-5129

**The Palace Antiques & Collectibles**
138 E. Main St.
916/273-6043

### Great Places To Stay

**Elam Biggs Bed & Breakfast**
220 Colfax Ave.
530/477-0906

The Elam Biggs Home was built in 1892 by one of Grass Valley's foremost successful merchants. This beautiful Queen Anne Victorian is set amidst a large yard surrounded by tall old shade trees and a rose-covered picket fence. All this is just a short stroll to historic downtown. This grand home is a perfect setting for that special time away, or a steppingstone to the history of the Gold Rush Era. When Elam Biggs built this house for his family, it was said to be "the most modern and scientific of its time." Eight guest accommodations.

**Holbrooke Hotel & Purcell House**
212 W. Main St.
916/273-1353

The Holbrooke Hotel invites guests to indulge in the elegance of a bygone era. Established in 1851, the hotel is located in the heart of the scenic Sierra Nevada Motherlode, and is a California Registered Historical Landmark. The Hotel has hosted many luminaries from four of America's most famed presidents, Ulysses S. Grant, Benjamin Harris, James A. Garfield and Grover Cleveland to boxers Gentleman Jim Corbett and Bob Fitzsimmons.

**Murphys Inn**
318 Neal St.
916/273-6873

Built in 1866 by a gold mine owner for his new bride, Murphy's Inn is a beautifully restored Greek Revival home. All rooms are beautifully decorated with antiques. The 130-year sequoia tree overlooks a wonderful deck for relaxing and reading. All rooms have private baths. Some rooms have fireplaces. A full hot breakfast is served. Chocolate chip cookies and soft drinks are always available.

## 62 HANFORD

**Country Bazaar**
7090 N. Douty St.
209/584-8798

**Corner**
102 E. 6th St.
209/584-7097

**Livery Stable Shops**
113 S. Douty St.
209/582-0356

**Hanford Antique Emporium**
108 E. 8th St.
209/583-8202

## 63 HAYWARD

**Hayward Faire Antiques**
926 B St.
510/537-7823

**Jeannie's Antiques**
1013 B St.
510/582-1773

**Antique Connection**
1033 B St.
510/889-8608

**Creative Cottage**
938 B St.
510/728-7644

**Incurable Collector**
944 B St.
510/733-5122

**Ryan's Country Farm Antiques**
1028 B St.
510/881-7755

**B Street Antiques**
1025 B St.
510/889-8549

## 64 HEALDSBURG

**Antique Harvest**
225 Healdsburg Ave.
707/433-0223

**Vintage Antiques Etc.**
328 Healdsburg Ave.
707/433-7461

**Going Vintage Antiques & Collectibles**
44 Mill St.
707/433-4501

**Healdsburg Classic Antiques**
226 Healdsburg Ave.
707/433-4315

**Irish Cottage Antiques**
112 Matheson St.
707/433-4850

**Vintage Plaza Antiques**
44 Mill St.
707/433-8409

### Great Places To Stay

**Bergerie**
5325 Eastside Rd.

Bergerie is a romantic, private bed and breakfast in the heart of Sonoma County wine country in Northern California. Located on an estate of ten acres, nestled in a forest of redwood trees, there are hiking trails, a trout pond and lots of wildlife to enjoy.

**Camellia Inn**
211 North St.
Web site: www.camellia.com
1-800-727-8182

An 1869 Italianate Victorian townhouse on half acre grounds. Antiques fill nine spacious bedrooms, each with private bath. Double parlors with twin marble fireplaces and a dining room with a massive mahogany mantle return you to the elegance of yesteryear. Several rooms have double whirlpool tubs, gas fireplaces or private entrances. Afternoon refreshments are served in the parlor or by the swimming pool.

**George Alexander House**
423 Matheson St.
1-800-310-1358

The George Alexander House, built in 1905, is noted for its exuberant ornamental details and its many quatrefoil windows. As an inn, it is ideally situated a few blocks from Healdsburg's Plaza where visitors may taste wine, dine in wonderful restaurants, or browse in unique shops. The inn has four guest rooms, each with its own bath, two large parlors for guest use, many books, good art, and Oriental rugs.

## 65 HEMET

**Hermitage Antiques**
910 E. Florida Ave., #B2
909/925-1968

**Fond Memories**
123 N. Havard St.
909/652-2511

**Second Time Around**
699 N. San Jacinto St.
909/652-6798

**Charlotte's Antiques**
41171 Crest Dr.
909/658-4870

**Buyer's Inn**
123 Harvard Ave.
909/652-2727

**Jamie's Junque**
25760 New Chicago Ave.
909/927-7090

**Rusty Relics**
135 N. Harvard St.
909/766-7784

## 66 HESPERIA

**Carousel Faire**
15800 Main St.
760/244-2336

**Antiques By Janie**
15885 Main St., #220
760/244-9797

**Apple Pie Antiques**
15885 Main St.
760/947-4474

**Miss Jenny's**
15885 Main St., #170
760/947-4020

**Sonja's Treasures**
15885 Main St.
760/947-6642

**Eufemia's Antiquery**
11605 Mariposa Road
760/244-4828

**Silvia's Boutique**
15885 Main St.
760/244-0796

**Making Memories**
15885 Main St., #160
760/947-6259

**Cobblestone Square Antiques**
15885 Main St.
760/244-5301

**Miss Jenny's II**
15885 Main St., #260
760/947-2229

## 67 HOLLYWOOD/WEST HOLLYWOOD

**Rye Byers Antiques**
8424 Melrose Ave.
213/655-2095

**City Antiques**
8444 Melrose Ave.
213/658-6354

**Villa Medici**
8687 Melrose Ave.
310/659-9984

**Papillion Gallery**
8818 Melrose Ave.
310/659-9984

**W Antiques**
8925 Melrose Ave.
310/275-5099

**Antiques & Design**
610 N. Robertson Blvd.
310/659-0946

**Ashby's Antiques**
638 N. Robertson Blvd.
310/854-1006

**John Alan Antiques**
644 N. Robertson Blvd.
310/854-5438

**Gregory's Country Home**
8747 Sunset Blvd.
310/652-7288

**Last Moving Picture Co.**
6307 Hollywood Blvd.
213/467-0838

### *Great Places To Stay*

**Radisson Hollywood Roosevelt Hotel**
7000 Hollywood Blvd.
213/466-7000 or for reservations 1-800-833-3333

Situated right in the heart of Hollywood, The Radisson Hollywood Roosevelt Hotel is a stylish property built in 1927 as the centerpiece of the film world - a role it still fulfills. Always the place to see and be seen, it staged the first-ever Academy Awards ceremony in its Blossom Ballroom in 1929, and it has hosted a variety of major movie premieres and opening night galas during the following four decades.Today the hotel features 335 beautifully appointed rooms, including twenty luxury suites.

## 68 HUNTINGTON BEACH

**Way Back When**
8901 Atlanta Ave.
714/960-5335

**Country Cottage**
18211 Enterprise Lane, #B
714/842-5959

**Back In Tyme Antiques**
517 Walnut Ave.
714/536-2194

## 69 ISLETON

**Country Cupboard**
15 Main
916/777-6737

**Junk & Treasures**
112 2nd
916/777-4828

**Windmill Antiques Etc.**
15041 State Hwy. 160
916/777-6112

## 70 JACKSON

**Amador Antique Emporium**
12311 Martell Road
209/223-2030

**Water Street Antiques**
11101 State Hwy. 88
209/223-4189

**National Hotel Antiques**
2 Water St.
209/223-3447

**Specialty Shop**
5 Main St.
209/223-3036

**Sisters**
5 Main St.
209/223-2930

## 71 JAMESTOWN

**Main St. Mercantile**
18138 Main St.
209/984-6551

**Bear Essentials Antiques**
18145 Main St.
209/984-5315

**Butterfield House Country Gifts**
18158 Main St.
209/984-3068

**Over The Hill Antiques**
18205 Main St.
209/984-3237

**Crackel & Co.**
18210 Main St.
209/984-4080

**Pine Tree Peddlers**
18211 Main St.
209/984-3647

**Jamestown Mercantile Antiques**
18255 Main St.
209/984-5148

**Mostly Pennsylvania**
18278 Main St.
209/984-0533

**Daisy Tree II**
18280 Main St.
209/984-0661

**Now & Then Antiques**
17775 State Hwy. 108
209/984-4224

## 72 JULIAN

**Wynola Timeless Treasures**
4355 Hwy. 78, #C
760/765-3113

**Antique Boutique**
2626 Main St.
760/765-0541

**Applewood & Co.**
2804 Washington
760/765-1185

### *Great Places To Stay*

### Butterfield Bed and Breakfast
2284 Sunset Dr.
760/765-2179

An added treat to your visit to the tiny hamlet of Julian is a memorable stay at Butterfield Bed and Breakfast. Four guest rooms (French Bedroom, Country Rose, Feathernest, Apple Cellar Sweet) each with private bath and two with a fireplace and Rose Bud Cottage, all create a weekend to remember.

### Julian White House B&B Inn
3014 Blue Jay Dr.
1-800-948-4687

Recommended by K-ABC's Elmer Dill, 'The innkeepers, Alan & Mary Marvin, are the perfect hosts for your romantic escape to the past.' This petite Colonial Mansion is located in the mountainous countryside of Julian. Secret Garden of Roses lends itself to afternoon relaxation or evening star gazing. All guest rooms are appointed with authentic antiques, private baths and queen beds.

## 73 KINGSBURG

**Swedish Village Antiques**
1135 Draper St.
209/897-4419

**Apple Duplin Antiques**
1440 Draper St.
209/897-5936

**Granny's Attic**
1513 Draper St.
209-897-4203

## 74 LA HABRA

**Su Casa Antiques**
310 E. Whittier Blvd.
562/694-3108

**Ragtime Antiques**
901 W. Whittier Blvd.
562/694-5414

**Clockworks**
2204 W. Whittier Blvd.
562/694-5608

## 75 LA JOLLA

**McGee's Antiques of La Jolla**
7467 Cuvier St.
619/459-1256

**Renaissance Art & Antiques**
7715 Fay Ave.
619/454-3887

**Antiques of Europe**
7437 Girard Ave.
619/459-5886

**Glorius Antiques**
7645 Girard Ave.
619/459-2222

**Silver Store**
7909 Girard Ave.
619/459-3241

**Circa**
7861 Herschel Ave.
619/454-7962

**Bird Rock Antiques**
5623 La Jolla Blvd.
619/459-4091

**Angelique's**
1237 Prospect St., Ste. U
619/459-5769

**Alcala Gallery**
950 Silverado St.
619/454-6610

**Taylor Antique Gallery**
1000 Torrey Pines Road
619/456-1041

**La Jolla Consignment & Mall**
7509 Girard Ave.
619/456-0936

**Early American Numismatics**
P. O. Box 2442
619/459-4159

## 76 LA MESA

**Antique Elegance**
8363 Center Dr., #5B
619/697-8766

**Grossmont Antique Mart**
8379 Center Dr.
619/466-2040

**Country Loft**
8166 La Mesa Blvd.
619/466-5411

**Rocking Horse Antique Mall**
8223 La Mesa Blvd.
619/469-6191

**Time & Treasures**
8290 La Mesa Blvd.
619/460-8004

**Bloom 'n Antiques**
8360 La Mesa Blvd.
619/462-7100

**La Mesa Village Antiques**
8371 La Mesa Blvd.
619/461-7940

**Image Maker**
8219 La Mesa Blvd.
619/461-9490

**Boulevard Antiques**
8362 La Mesa Blvd.
619/698-8555

**Mesa Verde**
8295 La Mesa Blvd.
619/462-7630

**Norma Jean's Antiques**
8341 La Mesa Blvd.
619/466-6640

**Finders Keepers**
8371 La Mesa Blvd.
619/698-6777

## 77 LAFAYETTE

**Antiquary**
1020 Brown Ave.
510/284-5611

**Brown Ave Collective**
1030 Brown Ave.
510/284-7069

**Clocks Etc.**
3401 Mount Diablo Blvd.
510/284-4720

## 78 LAGUNA BEACH

**Laguna Antiques & Consignment**
330 N. Coast Hwy.
714/497-9744

**Gallery One of Laguna**
1220 N. Coast Hwy.
714/494-4444

**Ruins Antiques**
1231-33 N. Coast Hwy.
714/376-0025

**Melange**
1235 N. Coast Hwy.
714/497-4915

**Antiqua**
1290 N. Coast Hwy.
714/494-5860

**Antiques & Interiors**
448 S. Coast Hwy.
714/376-2005

**Family Jewels**
490 S. Coast Hwy.
714/494-2436

**Richard Yeakel Antiques**
1099 S. Coast Hwy.
714/494-5526

**Antique Boutique**
1432 S. Coast Hwy.
714/494-1571

**Iron Maiden**
1524 S. Coast Hwy.
714/497-0414

**Redfern Gallery**
1540 S. Coast Hwy.
714/497-3356

**Kaehler's Fine Arts**
332 Forest Ave.
714/494-3864

**Consignment Corner**
888 Glenneyre St.
714/497-1010

**Roberta Gauthey Antiques**
1166 Glenneyre St.
714/494-9925

**Jerry's Antiquities N Things**
1295 Glenneyre St.
714/494-0019

## 79 LAKE ELSINORE

**Antique Corner**
106 W. Graham Ave.
909/674-7989

**Chimes**
201 W. Graham Ave.
909/674-3456

**Grand Antique Mall**
18273 Grand Ave.
909/678-5095

**Antique Emporium**
101 S. Main St.
909/245-3977

**Enchanted Treasures**
169 N. Main St.
909/674-8336

## 80 LANCASTER

**Antiques & Things**
44625 Sierra Hwy.
805/945-0504

**Buffy's Antiques & Collectibles**
3606 E. Ave. I
805/946-0335

## 81 LA VERNE

**Generations**
2343 D St.
909/593-4936

**Yesterday's Antiques**
2320 D St.
909/593-4456

**Sweet Memories**
2336 D St.
909/596-2944

**Ken's Olden Oddities**
1910 White Ave.
909/593-1846

## 82 LEMON COVE

**Walker House Antiques**
33513 Sierra Dr., Hwy. 198
209/597-2361

### *Great Places To Stay*

**Mesa Verde Plantation Bed & Breakfast**
33038 Sierra Hwy. 198
209/597-2555 or 1-800-240-1466
Web site: www.psnw.com/~mvpbb
Email: mvpbb@psnw.com
Rates: $70-125
*Directions: Take Hwy. 99 to the town of Visalia. Go 23.5 miles east on Hwy. 198.*

Scott and Marie Munger operate their bed & breakfast at an old citrus plantation in the foothills of the Sierra Nevada Mountains. To carry out the plantation theme, Scott and Marie have named and decorated all eight guest rooms after characters from Gone With The Wind. There's the Melanie, the Scarlett O'Hara, the Belle Watling, the Rhett Butler, the Ashley Wilkes, Mammy's Room, Prissy's Room, and the Aunt Pitty Pat. From the descriptions of the rooms they sent us, they are right on the mark for matching decor to personalities!

The Mesa Verde also offers guests orange groves for meandering, a spa, heated pool, gazebo, hammocks under the trees, verandas and fireplaces. Guests can also enjoy a gourmet breakfast in the elegant dining room or outside in the courtyard garden, where you can dine with the hummingbirds.

## 83 LEMON GROVE

**Years of Yesterday Antiques**
7895 Broadway
619/464-3892

**Lemon Grove Antique Mall**
7919 Broadway
619/461-1361

**Broadway Antique Mall**
7945 Broadway
619/461-1399

**Vivian's**
7968-7970 Broadway
619/461-2728

## 84 LEUCADIA

**Collectors Cottage**
1786 N. Coast Hwy. 101
760/436-7937

**Grandpa's Antiques**
1240B N. Coast Hwy 101
760/942-5202

**Caldwell's Antiques**
1234 N. Coast Hwy. 101
760/753-2369

**ABC Trading Co.**
1240 N. Coast Hwy. 101
760/753-5160

**Acanthus Fine Antiques**
1010 N. Coast Hwy. 101
760/633-1515

**Antique Clock Shop**
1340 N. Coast Hwy. 101
760/753-8844

## 85 LIVERMORE

**Livermore Trading Post**
250 Church St.
510/443-2822

**Cleo's Memory Lane Antiques**
2041 1st St.
510/443-2536

**Adams Family Antiques**
2047 1st St.
510/443-9408

**Yesterday's**
2053 1st St.
510/373-1817

**Anne Marie's Antiques & Things**
2074 1st St.
510/454-9870

**Forget Me Not**
2187 1st St.
510/606-6330

**Bill's Antiques & Collectibles**
2339 1st St.
510/449-9002

**Blue Door Antiques**
321 N. L St.
510/449-2111

## 86 LOCKEFORD

**Foxglove Antiques**
13333 Hwy. 88
209/727-3008
Mon.-Sun. 10-5, closed Tues.
*Directions: Traveling south from Sacramento on Hwy. 99 to Lodi (or traveling north from Stockton on Hwy. 99), take Hwy. 12 east, travel approximately 6 miles to Hwy. 88, follow Hwy. 88 northeast to Lockeford. Located next to Post Office.*

It will come as no surprise that Foxglove Antiques offers a nice selection of Roseville pottery. The owner, Gloria Mollring, is the author of Roseville Pottery Collector's Price Guide. If pottery is not your fancy, Gloria and her husband, Jim, provide an eclectic selection for any curious shopper. Exceptional period pieces, jewelry, books, dolls, and paper collectibles are just a few of the many antiques available at this shop.

## 87 LODI

**Old Friends Antiques**
225 N. California St.
209/367-0607

**Grave's Country Antiques**
15 N. Cherokee Lane
209/368-5740

**Grand J D Antiques**
440 E. Kettleman Lane
209/334-1140

**Moehring's Antiques**
440 E. Kettleman Lane
209/369-1818

**Victoria – 1894 Victorian House**
861 E. Pine St.
209/333-1762

**Mickey's Antqs. & Collectibles Mall**
14 N. School St.
209/369-9112

## 88 LOMA LINDA

**Loma Linda Antique Mall**
24997 Redlands Blvd.
909/796-4776

## 89 LOMITA

**A & D Antiques**
2055 1/2 Pacific Coast Hwy.
310/326-2434

**Anna Vocka's Antiques**
1856 Pacific Coast Hwy.
310/325-2574

**Gloria's Antiques**
2032 Pacific Coast Hwy.
310/530-5060

## 90 LONG BEACH

**Quick's Antiques**
2545 E. Broadway
562/433-8038

**William J Hossack Antiques**
2720 E. Broadway
562/439-4195

**Outre' Antiques**
2747 E. Broadway
562/439-0339

**Kelly's Place**
412 Cherry Ave.
562/438-2537

**Antique Clock Gallery**
2122 E. 4th St.
562/438-5486

**Millie's Place**
144 Linden Ave.
562/435-8566

**Kathy's Antiques**
1340 E. Market St.
562/422-6987

**Long Beach Antique Mall**
3100 E. Pacific Coast Hwy.
562/494-2526

**Sleepy Hollow Antique Mall**
5689 Paramount Blvd.
562/634-8370

**Antiques & More**
327 Pine Ave.
562/432-1173

**Redondo House**
274 Redondo Ave.
562/434-5239

**Antique Adoption**
4160 N. Viking Way
562/420-1919

**Village Vault Antiques**
5423 E. Village Road
562/425-7455

**Julie's Antique Mall**
1133 E. Wardlow Road
562/989-7799

## 91 LOS ALAMITOS

**Whiskers & Co. Antiques**
10670 Los Alamitos Blvd.
562/493-4700

**Los Alamitos Antique Shop**
10702 Los Alamitos Blvd.
562/493-5911

**Estate Store**
10899 Los Alamitos Blvd.
562/430-8819

**Coliseum Antiques**
10909 Los Alamitos Blvd.
562/598-0811

## 92 LOS ALAMOS

**Gussied Up**
349 Bell St.
805/344-2504

**General Store Antiques**
458 Bell St.
805/344-2123

**Krall Antiques**
515 Bell St.
805/344-6311

**The Prop Shop**
Bell St.
805/344-3121

**Los Alamos Depot Mall**
515 Leslae
805/344-3315

## 93 LOS ALTOS

**Patrician Antiques**
197 1st St.
415/948-5218

**Oriental Corner**
280 Main St.
415/941-3207

**Maria's Antiques of Los Altos**
288 1st St.
415/948-1965

**Geranium House Antiques**
371 1st St.
415/941-2620

**Maria's Antiques of Los Altos**
393 Main St.
415/941-9682

## 94 LOS ANGELES

**Art Spectrum**
2151 Ave. of the Stars
310/788-0720

**Bus Stop**
5273 1/2 E. Beverly Blvd.
213/728-6720

**Fainting Couch**
7260 Beverly Blvd.
213/930-0106

**Houle Rare Books & Autographs**
7405 Beverly Blvd.
213/937-5858

**Futurama**
7956 Beverly Blvd.
213/651-5767

**Beverly Hills Antiquarian**
8840 Beverly Blvd., #32
310/278-0120

**Marc Navarro Antiques**
8840 Beverly Blvd.
310/285-9650

**918 Antique Gallery**
8840 Beverly Blvd.
310/271-0404

**Antiquarius Center**
8840 Beverly Blvd.
310/274-2363

**Angele Hobin**
8840 Beverly Blvd.
310/276-4449

**European Antiques**
8840 Beverly Blvd.
310/274-3089

**Excalibur Antique Jewelry**
8840 Beverly Blvd.
310/859-2320

**London Imports**
8840 Beverly Blvd.
310/858-7416

**Lief**
8922 Beverly Blvd.
310/550-8118

**Catchell Five**
1740 Colorado Ave.
213/256-0114

**Circa Antiques**
3608 Edenhurst Ave.
213/662-6600

**Farmer's Market Arts & Antiques**
140 S. Fairfax Ave., #N
213/931-4804

**Showcase Gallery**
140 S. Fairfax Ave.
213/939-7403

**Menyea's Decor**
3113 W. Florence Ave.
213/752-9326

**Penny Lane**
2820 Gilroy St.
213/667-1838

**Caravan Book Store**
550 S. Grand Ave.
213/626-9944

**La Maison Du Bal**
705 N. Harper Ave.
213/655-8215

**Rosetta Gallery**
1958 Hillhurst Ave.
213/913-0827

**Simply Unique Collectibles**
1903 Hyperion Ave.
213/661-5454

**Fat Chance**
162 N. La Brea Ave.
213/930-1960

**Repeat Performance**
318 N. La Brea Ave.
213/938-0609

**Iron N' Antique Accents**
342 N. La Brea Ave.
213/934-3953

**Retro Gallery**
524 1/2 N. La Brea Ave.
213/936-5261

**Virtue**
149 S. La Brea Ave.
213/932-1789

**Francesca Dona**
665 S. La Brea Ave.
213/933-0433

**Consignment Collections**
355 N. La Cienega Blvd.
310/657-2590

**Dagmar**
514 N. La Cienega Blvd.
310/652-1167

**Gregorius-Pineo**
653 N. La Cienega Blvd.
310/659-0588

**Blake's Antiques**
665 N. La Cienega Blvd.
310/289-0970

**Quatrian**
700 N. La Cienega Blvd.
310/652-0243

**Therien & Co.**
716 N. La Cienega Blvd.
310/657-4615

**Remains To Be Seen Antiques**
735 N. La Cienega Blvd.
310/659-3358

**Pat McGann Antiques**
748 N. La Cienega Blvd.
310/358-0977

**Blackman Cruz**
800 N. La Cienega Blvd.
310/657-9228

**Nina Schwimmer Antiques**
804 N. La Cienega Blvd.
310/657-4060

**Ralf's Antiques**
807 N. La Cienega Blvd.
310/659-1966

**Richard Gould Antiques**
808 N. La Cienega Blvd.
310/657-9416

**Abraham Larry Antiques**
810 N. La Cienega Blvd.
310/651-4834

**Christianne Carty Antiques**
814 N. La Cienega Blvd.
310/657-2630

**Chateau Allegre**
815 N. La Cienega Blvd.
310/657-7259

**Baldacchino Antiques**
919 N. La Cienega Blvd.
310/657-6810

**Antique Rug Co.**
928 N. La Cienega Blvd.
310/659-3847

**Lifetime Arts & Crafts Gallery**
7111 Melrose Ave.
213/939-7441

**Denny Burt Modern Antiques**
7208 Melrose Ave.
213/936-5269

**Pictorial Antiques**
7965 Melrose Ave.
213/951-1060

**Pine Mine**
7974 Melrose Ave.
213/852-1939

**Burke's Country Pine Inc.**
8080 Melrose Ave.
213/655-1114

**Thanks For The Memories**
8319 Melrose Ave.
213/852-9407

**Recollections II**
8377 W. Melrose Ave.
213/655-6221

**French Antiques**
8404 Melrose Ave.
213/653-5222

**Marshall Galleries**
8420 Melrose Ave.
213/852-1964

**Empire Gallery**
8442 Melrose Ave.
213/655-9404

**French Antique Clock**
8465 Melrose Ave.
213/651-3034

**Charles Gill, Inc.**
8475 Melrose Ave.
213/653-3434

**Dassin Gallery**
8687 Melrose Ave., #B131
310/652-0203

**Evans & Gerst Antiques**
910 N. La Cienega Blvd.
310/657-0112

**Smith & Houchins**
921 N. La Cienega Blvd.
310/652-0308

**Niakin Gallery**
935 N. La Cienega Blvd.
310/652-6586

**Circa 1910 Antiques**
7206 Melrose Ave.
213/965-1910

**Off The Wall Antiques**
7325 Melrose Ave.
213/930-1185

**Grumps Antiques & Collectibles**
7965 1/2 Melrose Ave.
213/655-3564

**Napolean Antiques**
8050 Melrose Ave.
213/658-7853

**Hays House of Wicker**
8253 Melrose Ave.
213/653-2999

**Archipelago**
8323 Melrose Ave.
213/653-7133

**Marshall Galleries**
8401 Melrose Ave.
213/852-6630

**J F Chen Antiques**
8414 Melrose Ave.
213/655-6310

**Blue House**
8440 Melrose Ave.
213/852-0747

**CBH Antiques**
8452 Melrose Ave.
213/653-3939

**J P Hemmings Antiques USA**
8471 Melrose Ave.
213/655-7823

**Cota's Antiques**
8573 Melrose Ave.
310/659-1822

**Deanna Yohanna Antiques**
8908 Melrose Ave.
310/550-0052

**Rosh Antique Galleries**
8400 Melrose Place
213/655-6969

**B Nagel Antiques**
8410 Melrose Place
213/655-0115

**La Maison Francaise Antiques**
8420 Melrose Place
213/653-6534

**Licorne Antiques**
8432 Melrose Place
213/852-4765

**R. Tallow Antiques**
8454 Melrose Place
213/653-2122

**Connoisseur Antiques**
8468 Melrose Place
213/658-8432

**Charles Pollack Antiques**
8478 Melrose Place
213/651-5852

**Recollections I**
140 S. Orlando Ave.
213/852-7123

**Blagg's**
2901 Rowena Ave.
213/661-9011

**Camille Chez Antiques**
513 N. Robertson Blvd.
310/276-2729

**Gazebo Antiques**
120 S. Robertson Blvd.
310/275-5650

**Acquisitions**
1020 S. Robertson Blvd.
310/289-0196

**Paladin Antiques**
7356 Santa Monica Blvd.
213/851-8222

**Ramon's Antique Store**
8250 Santa Monica Blvd.
213/848-2986

**Antiques Plus**
11914 1/2 Santa Monica Blvd.
310/826-1170

**Ragtime**
11715 San Vincente Blvd.
310/820-3599

**Mehran Antiques**
840 Melrose Place
213/658-8444

**Museum Antiques**
8417 Melrose Place
310/652-3023

**Karl The Twelfth Swedish Antiques**
8428 Melrose Place
213/852-0303

**Sabet Antiques**
8451 Melrose Place
213/651-5222

**Villa Medici**
8460 Melrose Place
213/951-9172

**Tent Antiques**
8469 Melrose Place
213/651-1234

**R M Barokh Antiques**
8481 Melrose Place
213/655-2771

**Other Times Books**
10617 W. Pico Blvd.
310/475-2547

**Hideaway House Antiques**
143 N. Robertson Blvd.
310/276-4319

**Chelsea Antiques**
117 S. Robertson Blvd.
310/859-3895

**Collection**
315 S. Robertson Blvd.
310/205-3840

**An Antique Affaire**
2600 S. Robertson Blvd.
310/838-2051

**Big White Elephant**
7974 Santa Monica Blvd.
213/654-1928

**Antique Way**
11729 Santa Monica Blvd.
310/477-3972

**Portabella**
11715 San Vincente Blvd
310/820-3599

**Family Tree**
8655 S. Sepulveda Blvd.
310/641-2122

**Westchester Faire**
8655 S Sepulveda Blvd.
310/670-4000

**London Bridge Antiques**
8655 S. Sepulveda Blvd.
310/216-7677

**Stephen Hilliger Antiques**
8655 S. Sepulveda Blvd.
310/670-9306

**Rose Antiques**
8655 Sepulveda Blvd.
310/641-6967

**Rubbish**
1627 Silver Lake Blvd.
213/661-5575

**Arthur Green**
2201 W. Sunset Blvd.
213/413-3427

**Minnette's Antiques Etcetera**
2209 W. Sunset Blvd.
213/413-5595

**Wells**
2209 Sunset Blvd.
213/413-0558

**Arts & Antiques**
2211 W. Sunset Blvd.
213/413-5964

**Peron Antiques & Collectibles**
2213 W. Sunset Blvd.
213/413-7051

**China House Funky Junk**
5652 W. 3rd St.
213/935-9555

**Giermo Antique Lighting**
8405 W. 3rd St.
213/653-3450

**Electica**
8745 W. 3rd St.
310/275-1004

**Harry Studio Antiques Warehouse**
8639 Venice Blvd.
310/559-7863

**High Noon**
9929 Venice Blvd.
310/202-9010

**Joe's Antiques**
3520 1/2 Washington Blvd.
213/737-4267

**Antique Guild**
3225 Helms Bakery Bldg.
310/838-3131

## 95 LOS GATOS

**Main Street Antiques**
150 W. Main St.
408/395-3035

**Maria's Antiques**
112 N. Santa Cruz Ave.
408/395-5933

**Curious Book Shoppe**
23 E. Main St.
408/354-5560

**Patterson's Antiques**
88 W. Main St.
408/354-1718

**Antiquarium**
98 W. Main St.
408/354-7878

**Jean Newhart Antiques**
110 W. Main St.
408/354-1646

**Main St Antiques**
150 W. Main St.
408/395-3035

**Les Poisson Antiques**
25 N. Santa Cruz Ave.
408/354-7937

## 96 LOS OLIVOS

**Linrich Antiques & Collectibles**
2879 Grand Ave.
805/686-0802

**Haywire**
2900 Grand Ave.
805/688-9911

**Maria Tatiana Gallery**
2920 Grand Ave.
805/688-9622

## 97 MANHATTAN BEACH

**Once Upon a Quilt**
312 Manhattan Beach Blvd.
310/379-1264

## 98 MARIPOSA

Downtown Mariposa offers a historic glimpse of the gold rush days. Many buildings evident of the era now house antiques, art galleries and fine dining establishments. Mariposa is the home of the oldest continuously operating courthouse west of the Rocky Mountains.

**Jailhouse Square Gifts/Antiques**
5018 Bullion St.
209/966-3998

**Chocolate Soup/Jailhouse Too**
Corner 6th & Bullion
209/966-5683

**Correia's Antiques**
5031 B Hwy. 140
209/966-5448

**Campbell's Antiques**
Corner 4th & Hwy. 140
209/966-4660

**Anita's Antiques**
Corner Hwy. 140 & 4th
209/966-2433

**Princeton Empor Antiques**
4976 Mt. Bullion Cutoff
209/966-2372

**Fabled Kottage**
5029 State Hwy., #C
209/742-7075

### *Great Places To Stay*

**Restful Nest Bed & Breakfast Resort**
4274 Buckeye Creek Road
209/742-7127
Web site: www.yosemite.net/mariposa/mhotels/restful/
*Directions: From Merced (37 miles); from Hwy. 99 take I-40 E. Make a right on Yaqui Gulch Road. Go about 3 1/2 miles, Yaqui Gulch turns into Buckeye Road. Follow Buckeye Road for approximately 1 mile. Make a left on Buckeye Creek Road. The Restful Nest is 3/10 mile on the right.*
*From Fresno & Oakhurst: From Fresno, take 41 N. to Oakhurst. From Oakhurst, take 49 N. Go 30 miles to Ben Hur. Make a left on Ben Hur. Follow Ben Hur to Buckeye Road. Make a right to Buckeye Creek Road. The Restful Nest is 3/10 mile on the right.*

Nestled in the beautiful foothills of the Sierra Nevada mountains in the heart of California Gold Country, the Restful Nest offers an experience of olden California hospitality with the flavor of Provence.

Three tastefully appointed guest rooms promise pleasant relaxation and refreshment. Each room has a private entrance, a private bath and fresh air windows, overlooking majestic oaks and rolling hills.

The aroma of freshly baked brioche and other breads (rated tops by visitors from France and Belgium) will lure you to the country dining room where, along with these delicious breads, you will enjoy homemade sausages, luscious California fruits, country jams, preserves, juice, freshly brewed coffee and a variety of teas.

## 99 MARTINEZ

**Antique Connection**
817 Arnold Dr.
510/372-8229

**Another Time**
911 Alhambra Ave.
510/229-5025

**Nature's Way Doll Center**
917 Alhambra, Ste. A
510/228-5263

**Cobweb Antiques**
735 Escobar St.
510-229-9038

**Ferry Street Antiques**
413 Ferry St.
510/370-9091

**Antique Corner**
500 Ferry St.
510/372-9330

**Olde Towne Antiques**
516 Ferry St.
510/370-8345

**Our Shoppe**
606 Ferry St.
510/228-9919

**Asilee's Victorian Antiques**
608 Ferry St.
510/229-0653

**Sheila a Grilli Bookseller**
610 Ferry St.
510/228-6422

**Crance's Antiques**
605 Main St.
510/229-2775

**Bill & Mike's Antiques**
609 Main St.
510/229-3664

**First Street Antiques**
613 Main St.
510/228-7560

**Lipary Sports Collectibles**
617 Main St.
510/370-6032

**Shannon's Olde & Goodies**
623 Main St.
510/372-6045

**The Military Store**
625 Main St.
510/372-5897

**B J's Antiques & Collectibles**
627 Main St.
510/228-1202

**Attic Child Antiques**
653 Main St.
510/228-3072

**Molly's Collectibles**
718 Main St.
510/370-7466

**Martinez Antiques & Collectibles**
724 Main St.
510/335-0939

**Bayol's Antiques & Collectibles**
728 Main St.
510/372-3398

**Plain & Fancy Antiques**
802 Main St.
510/229-4288

**Family Traditions**
810 Main St.
510/229-4331

**Annie's Unique Antiques**
814 Main St.
510/228-0394

## 100 MCKINLEYVILLE

**Almost All Antiques**
2764 Central Ave.
707/839-0456

## 101 MENDOCINO

**Golden Goose**
45094 Main St.
707/937-4655

**Primrose Lane**
44770 Larkin Road
707/937-2107

### *Great Places To Stay*

**Blackberry Inn**
44951 Larkin Road
707/937-5281

Blackberry Inn has adopted the theme of a western frontier town in order to tap the nostalgia of this myth. Each room is entirely different and represents a well-known establishment associated with a frontier town. There is the Sheriff, Livery Stable, General Store, Barber Shop, The Bank, and of course the town fancy house known as Belle's Place, which is truly one of the most beautiful rooms on all the Mendocino Coast. All rooms have separate, private entrances, and private baths.

**Joshua Grindle Inn**
44800 Little Lake Road
Web site: www.joshgrin.com
1-800-474-6353

New England charm in coastal California? Situated on two acres in the historic village, this lovely home was built in 1879 by Joshua Grindle, the town banker. The rooms (all private baths), are located in the Main House, the Cypress Cottage, and the Watertower and are furnished with Early American and Shaker antiques. Each room has comfortably arranged sitting areas, and some have ocean views, others have fireplaces. A full gourmet breakfast is served. AAA Three Diamond property.

**Stanford Inn By the Sea**
Coast Hwy. & Comptcheukiah Road
Web site: www.stanfordinn.com
1-800-331-8884

A rustic, yet elegant, inn with beautifully landscaped grounds on ten acres with swans, llamas, horses, and organic farm. The lodge sits atop a meadow overlooking the ocean and historic Mendocino. Guest rooms are furnished with antiques and four poster beds with designer comforters. Work from local artists, plants, woodburning fireplaces, books, and plush towels enhance the persona of this special coastal retreat. Country wines are provided daily as is the Stanford's special blend of locally roasted gourmet organic coffee for each room's drip maker. Breakfast is served in the inn's dining room featuring organic foods prepared to order.

## Whitegate Inn

P.O. Box 150
Web site: www.whitegateinn.com
1-800-531-7282

The Whitegate Inn, built in 1883, lies in the heart of Mendocino. An English garden sets off the pristine white exterior. Originally the home of the town's first doctor, today it remains an elegant Victorian lady offering six professionally decorated bedchambers filled with antiques and fresh flowers. A full breakfast is served in the sunny dining room on fine china and sterling silver.

## 102 MENLO PARK

**Millstreet Antiques**
1131 Chestnut St.
415/323-9010

**Mary J Rafferty Antiques**
1158 Chestnut St.
415/321-6878

**Conversation Piece**
889 Santa Cruz Ave.
415/327-9101

## 103 MIDDLETOWN

**Middletown Antiques Collective**
21207 Calistoga
707/987-2633

**Cobb Mountain Antiques**
17140 Hwy. 175
707/928-5972

**Dorothy's Antiques**
21304 Hwy. 175
707/987-0325

## 104 MILL VALLEY

**Luck Would Have It**
14 Locust Ave.
415/380-8625

**Nellus Antiques**
357 Miller Ave.
415/388-2277

**Via Diva Antiques**
27 Throckmorton Ave.
415/389-0911

**Capricorn Antiques**
100 Throckmorton Ave.
415/388-1720

**Dowds Barn**
157 Throckmorton Ave.
415/388-8110

## 105 MODESTO

**Chelsea Square Antiques**
305 Downey Ave.
209/578-5504

**Hatch Road Antique Mall**
2909 E. Hatch Road
209/538-0663

**Crow Trading Company**
707 I St.
209/579-2173

**The March Hare**
321 Downey Ave.
209/524-8336

**Retro Antiques**
502 Scenic Dr.
209/522-2959

**Looking Back Antiques**
1136 Tully Road
209/523-1443

**Antique Emporium**
1511 J St.
209/579-9730

**Antique Emporium**
1208 Ninth St.
209/527-6004

**M. L. & Co.**
2308 McHenry Ave.
209/491-0340

**McCoys Antiques**
503 Scenic Dr.
209/549-9827

**Austin Antiques**
204 Sylvan Ave.
209/526-2509

**And Another Thing**
317 Downey Ave.
No phone number

**Kay's Collectibles**
530 14th St.
209/522-6562

**Melrose Place**
1700 McHenry Ave.
209/525-8981

**Sarah Frances Antiques**
1208 J St.
209/523-4937

**Sticks & Stones Collection**
3338 Oakdale Road
209/551-9540

## 106 MONROVIA

**Patty's Antiques**
109 W. Foothill Blvd.
818/358-0344

**Monrovia West Antique Mall**
925 W. Foothill Blvd.
818/357-5235

**Kaleidoscope Antiques**
306 S. Myrtle Ave.
818/303-4042

**Through The Years**
401 1/2 S. Myrtle Ave.
818/305-5259

**Frills**
504 S. Myrtle Ave.
818/303-3201

## 107 MONTEREY

**Alicia's Antiques**
835 Cannery Row
408/372-1423

**Treasure Bay**
801 Lighthouse Ave.
408/656-9303

**Pieces of Olde**
868 Lighthouse
408/372-1521

**Cannery Row Antique Mall**
471 Wave St.
408/655-0264

### *Great Places To Stay*

## Victorian Inn

487 Foam St.

The Victorian Inn - Monterey's inviting hideaway. All guest rooms have marble fireplaces, honor bars and private patios, balconies or window seats. Guests can enjoy the outdoor garden hot tub, complimentary continental breakfast and afternoon wine and cheese served in the parlor. Walk to the Aquarium, Fisherman's Wharf and Cannery Row.

## 108 MORRO BAY

**Antiques Et Cetera**
1141 Main St.
805/772-2279

**Glass Basket**
245 Morro Bay Blvd.
805/772-4569

**Wit's End**
257 Morro Bay Blvd.
805/772-8669

**O Susanna**
325 Morro Bay Blvd.
805/772-4001

**Madam & The Cowboy**
333 Morro Bay Blvd.
805/772-2048

**Scruples Antiques**
450 Morro Bay Blvd.
805/772-9207

**Woody's Antiques**
870 Morro Bay Blvd.
805/772-8669

**Cindi's Antiques**
820 Morro Bay Blvd.
805/772-5948

## 109 MOSS LANDING

**Then & Now**
Moss Landing Road
408/633-4373

**Potter Palmer Antiques**
Moss Landing Road
408/633-5415

**Moss Landing Antique Co.**
Moss Landing Road
408/633-3988

**Life In The Past Lane**
Moss Landing Road
408/633-6100

**Harbor House Antiques**
7092 Moss Landing Road
408/633-8555

**Zyanya Collectibles**
7981 Moss Land Road, #A
408/633-4266

**Moss Landing Merc Antiques**
7981 Moss Landing Road
408/633-8520

**Up Your Alley**
8011 Moss Landing Road
408/633-5188

**Little Red Barn Antiques**
8045 Moss Landing Road
408/633-5583

**Paul Messer Antiques**
8461 Moss Landing Road
408/633-4361

**Waterfront Antiques**
7902F Sandholdt Road
408/633-1112

## 110 MOUNT SHASTA

**Mount Shasta Black Bear Gallery**
201 N. Mount Shasta Blvd.
916/926-2334

**Halfords Antiques**
407 N. Mount Shasta Blvd.
916/926-3901

**Antiques Etc.**
612 S. Mount Shasta Blvd.
916/926-2231

## 111 MURPHYS

### D.E.A. Bathroom Machineries

495 Main St.
209/728-2031
1-800-255-4426

Porcelain glistens from five showrooms in the former Odd Fellows Hall. You will find antique bathroom fixtures from soap dishes to sitz baths, bathroom scales to bathroom sinks, lighting fixtures, wash basins, clawfoot tubs, drinking fountains, brass hooks to brothel tokens. Showrooms are filled with spittoons, wooden toilet tanks, steam radiators, antique mail boxes, medicine cabinets, rib-cage showers (bigger than some bathrooms), and toilets. Toilets made back when toilet making was an art. Gorgeous toilets with sculptured tanks and bowls, gracefully and flowing bulbous, some hand-painted, some with raised ornamentation.

The most decorative bowl, called "The Deluge" is the rarest of the collection. Sorry, it's not for sale. It's an original, manufactured by Thomas Twyford, who worked in Victorian England for the most renowned toilet maker of them all, Thomas Crapper.

If you can't make it to the showroom, D.E.A. offers two mail order catalogues featuring their supply of the above plus much, much more in antique and reproduction fixtures and accessories. Video catalogues are also available to provide clients a better idea of their hundreds of antique products.

The company boasts a rather impressive client list: Ted Turner, Mark Harmon, Sally Jesse Raphael, Lloyd Bridges and Ralph Lauren have all purchased fixtures from D.E.A. Museums, bed and breakfasts, public and private restoration projects from all over the country have also looked to D.E.A. for their architectural needs.

The store has become quite a tourist attraction over the past 20 years. Sightseers have been known to wander into the store just for a peek at the unusual "stuff" offered there. And more unusual "stuff" is always on the way. The owner, Tom Schellar, travels across the United States looking for deals on all kinds of antiques. Anything interesting, he buys it — and in his delightful store, he'll probably sell it.

**All That Glitters**
434 Main St.
209/728-2700

**Sue's Antiques**
466 Main St.
209/728-9148

## 112 NAPA VALLEY

There are approximately 184 wineries dotting the picturesque countryside known as the Napa Valley. Many were established well over 100 years ago and are still operating today. Most offer samplings in the tasting rooms located in the elegant mansions once owned by the founding winemakers.

One such estate is the Beringer Vineyards. Established in 1876 by Jacob and Frederick Beringer, it is the oldest continuously operated winery in the Napa Valley. The tasting room is located in Frederick's mansion (The Rhine House) and is elegantly decorated with stained glass, carved oak wainscoating, slate roof and wood floors. The excellent guided tour of the St. Helena Winery leads you through the wine caves tunneled deep into the hillside where Beringer vintages age in oak cooperage.

California's first three-story stone gravity-flow winery, Far Niente, was completed in 1885 and the words "Far Niente" were carved into its stone face. A loose translation from the Italian phrase "In Dolce Far Niente" suggests "life without a care." The winery's operation ceased with prohibition and Far Niente lay sleeping for 60-odd years until it was purchased and renovated by the present owners.

Winemaking at Freemont Abby in St. Helena dates from the fall of 1886 when Josephine Tychson, the first woman to build a winery in California, began operating on the site. The present owners began their enterprise in 1967. The wines, Chardonny, Merlot, Cabernet Sauvignon, Cabernet Bosche and Johanniskerg Riesling, have won international acclaim. The tasting room is furnished with antiques and Oriental rugs.

It was in the stone cellar of St. Clement Vineyards' historic Rosenbaum House that the eighth Napa Valley winery was established before the turn of the century. It is in that same hundred-year-old cellar that St. Clement wines are aged today.

The Rosenbaum House, a landmark Victorian, has been meticulously restored and is now open to visitors for the first time since 1878. The parlor now serves as an intimate tasting room. The porch swing on the veranda, picnic tables on the shaded patio and the expansive gardens offer a nostalgic vantage from which to view the valley.

Established in 1890, Sutter Home has been owned since 1947 by the Trinchero family. It is renowned for its rich, robust Amador County Zinfandel and its pale pink White Zinfandel, the best-selling premium wine in America. Sutter Home also produces a full line of high-quality varietal wines sold under the Sutter Home Fre brand name.

The Sutter Home Victorian house and gardens are landmarks in Napa Valley-featuring over 800 varieties of plant life, including 100 varieties of roses, 50 different daylilies, a dazzling array of camellias, lupines, columbines, begonias, century-old palm and orange trees and an extensive herb garden. Sutter Home's Visitor's Center, housed in the original winery building, features special exhibits evoking 19th century Napa Valley, as well as complimentary tastings.

***NOTE:*** *For a complete listing of Napa Valley wineries and tour information, call Napa Valley Visitors Bureau at 1-800-651-8953.*

### *Antiquing in the Napa Valley*

#### *CALISTOGA*

**The Tin Barn Collective**
At the Gliderport
1510 Lincoln Ave.
707/942-0618
Open daily, 10-5

Offers a distinctive array of antiques and collectibles including china and crystal, vintage lighting, art pottery, prints and paintings, silver and linens, wicker and wrought iron, jewelry, arts and crafts, country primitives, French antiques, Orientalia, art deco and a new garden center.

#### *NAPA*

**Antiques Etc.**
3043 California Blvd. off Trancas
707/255-4545
"The Estate Shop" Open Tues.-Sat. 11-5 or by appointment

Thousands of collectibles, memorabilia, paintings, textiles, musical instruments, Indian baskets, rugs, art glass, cut glass, dolls, furniture, lamps, clocks, jewelry, pottery and more in a warehouse setting. Appraisal service.

**Gullwigg & Thacker Antiques**
1988A Wise Dr.
707/252-7038
Open daily 10-5

Not a "My grandmother had one of those" shop (unless, of course, she was 200 years old). Decidedly different. Varied in content. Compassionately priced, 17th, 18th, 19th, 20th century antiques.

**The Irish Pedlar**
1988A Wise Dr.
707/253-9091
Open daily 10-5

Offers an extensive selection of one-of-a-kind, old country pine and a large variety of accessories to accent the pine—linens, quimper, French wine related items, decoys.

**Napa Coin Gallery**
3053 Jefferson (Sam's Plaza)
707/255-7225
Tues.-Fri. 11-5, Sat. 11-4, closed Sun. and Mon.

"The One Stop Shop" for gold and silver coins and all supplies. Estate jewelry as well as coin jewelry items. Small antiques. Old postcards and other interesting historical items.

**Red Hen Antiques**
5091 St. Helena Hwy.
707/257-0822
Open daily 10-5

Situated in the vineyards on Hwy. 20 between Napa and Yountville, Red Hen Antiques houses more than 65 quality antique dealers. It features an extensive array of well-displayed collectibles, antiques and gifts. A landmark antique showplace.

**Riverfront Antique Center**
805 Soscol Ave. below 3rd St.
707/253-1966
Open daily 10-5:30

75+ dealers, 24,000 square feet. Napa's newest multi-dealer antiques mall offers a large selection of unique and affordable antiques and collectibles.

### *ST. HELENA*

**Elrod's Antiques**
3000 St. Helena Hwy.
707/963-1901
Open daily 11-5

**European Country Antiques**
1148 Main St.
707/963-4666
Mon.-Sat. 10-5, Sun. 12-4

Specializes in German pine wood antiques.

**St. Helena, St. Helena Antiques**
1231 Main St.
707/963-5878
Open daily 11-5 and by appointment

Rare and unusual antiques, antiquities and collectibles. Tools, rugs, corkscrews, quilts, primitives, garden appointments, ethnic objects, masks, furniture, clocks, china, decanters, guns, paintings. Buy and sell.

### *YOUNTVILLE*

**Antique Fair**
6412 Washington St
707/944-8440
Open daily 10-5
Web site: www.antiquefair.com

An impressive selection of French furniture and accessories.

## *BED AND BREAKFASTS IN THE NAPA VALLEY*

### *ANGWIN*

**Forest Manor**
415 Cold Springs Road
707/965-3538, 1-800-788-0364

Secluded 20-acre English Tudor estate tucked among forest and vineyards above St. Helena. Described as "one of the most romantic country inns ... a small exclusive resort," the three-story Manor features high vaulted ceilings, massive hand-carved beams, fireplaces, verandas. The romantic honeymoon suite has a fireplace and a private jacuzzi for two.

### *CALISTOGA*

**Brannan Cottage Inn**
109 Wapoo Ave.
707/942-4200

Delightful gardens surround this quiet 6-room gingerbread Victorian, winner of the 1985 Napa Landmarks Award for historic preservation in Napa County. Known for its original wild flower stencils, the inn offers a sunny courtyard & parlor with fireplace. Listed on the National Register of Historic Places, this is the only guest house left on its original site built for the "Calistoga Hot Springs Resort" in 1860.

**Calistoga Country Lodge**
2883 Foothill Blvd.
707/942-5555

Secluded lodge in the western foothills of Calistoga. Beautifully decorated with American antiques, bleached pine, lodgepole furniture and Indian artifacts.

**Calistoga Inn/Napa Valley Brewing Co.**
1250 Lincoln Ave.
707/942-4101

A landmark building built at the turn of the century, the Calistoga Inn is located on the main street of town. The inn features a fine restaurant, an outdoor patio-grill and beer wine garden, and an in-house pub brewery where Calistoga Lager is brewed and served fresh.

**Calistoga Wayside Inn**
1523 Foothill Blvd.
707/942-0645

A 1920s Spanish style home situated in a secluded park-like setting on half acre with decorative gardens. Relax in the hammock.

**Calistoga Wishing Well Inn**
2653 Foothill Blvd. (Hwy. 128)
707/942-5534

A three-story farmhouse, situated among vineyards on four acres with a breathtaking mountain view.

**Christopher's Inn**
1010 Foothill Blvd.
707/942-5755

Original 1930s cottages have been transformed into intimate rooms, interiors by Laura Ashley and antique furnishings, many with fireplaces. Some rooms have patio gardens.

**Culver's, a Country Inn**
1805 Foothill Blvd.
707/942-4535

This completely restored country Victorian home, circa 1875, is a registered historical landmark. Each of the bedrooms has period furniture, including a uniquely designed quilt. Living room with fireplace, porch with view of Mount St. Helena.

**The Elms**
1300 Cedar St.
707/942-9476, 1-800-235-4316

A three-story French Victorian built in 1871 and on the National Register of Historic Places, The Elms offers charm and elegance within walking distance of Calistoga. Located on a quiet street next to a park, it has antique filled rooms with fireplaces, feather beds, down comforters, and bathrobes. Complimentary wine and cheese and a large gourmet breakfast are served in the dining room.

**Falcons Nest**
471 Kortum Canyon Road
707/942-0758

A secluded hilltop estate nestled on 7 acres. Panoramic views overlooking the Napa Valley. Just minutes to the wineries and spas. All rooms have Country French decor with queen beds, and you can enjoy the spa under the stars. Breakfast is served on the balcony.

Fanny's
1206 Spring St.
1-888-942-9491

Built in 1915 as a comfortable family home, Fanny's has now been renovated and named for Robert Louis Stevenson's bride. The exterior of the house has a full length porch ready with rocking chairs and a swing. Inside, bedrooms feature plank floors, feather comforters and window seats that will take you back to grandma's attic. The living room and dining room are rich with charm. An old fireplace, numerous soft quilts, sofas and an array of nooks and crannies are perfect for hiding away or meeting new people.

**Foothill House**
3037 Foothill Blvd.
707/942-6933, 1-800-942-6933

Nestled among the western foothills just north of Calistoga, the Foothill House began as a simple farmhouse at the turn of the century. The cozy yet spacious rooms are individually decorated with country antiques, and a queen or king four poster bed. Gourmet breakfast, complimentary wine; hors d'oeuvres served in the evening.

**Hill Crest B&B**
3225 Lake County Hwy.
707/942-6334

Located near the base of Mt. St. Helena, this rambling country home is filled with cherished family heirlooms. Antique silver, china, oriental rugs, books and other furnishings are the legacy of the Tubbs and Reid families. There's a small lake for fishing, and you may hike on 36 hilly acres, take a dip in the pool or relax in the sun and take in the breathtaking view.

**Meadowlark Country House**
601 Petrified Forest Road
707/942-5651

Built in 1886 and situated on 20 forested acres, this two-story country home has been remodeled for modern comfort and retains its relaxed country atmosphere. Each room has queen bed and view of forest, gardens or meadows. California breakfast included.

**The Pink Mansion**
1415 Foothill Blvd.
707/942-0558

Painted pink in the 1930's by Aunt Alma, this 120-year-old Calistoga landmark offers a combination of Victorian elegance and modern luxury. The formal living room with fireplace, as well as the dining room and game room, are for guests' use. Each room has a postcard view of the hills and local landmarks, and downtown Calistoga is within walking distance. Full gourmet breakfast. Three acres of landscaped gardens and wooded escapes. For those who enjoy a late night swim, the indoor heated pool and jacuzzi are a must.

**Quail Mountain Bed & Breakfast**
4455 North St., Helena Hwy.
707/942-0316

A secluded, luxury romantic estate located on 26 acres, 300 ft. above Napa Valley on a heavily forested mountain range with a vineyard and orchard on the property. Full breakfast is served in the sunny solarium common room or formal dining room in winter months.

**Scarlett's Country Inn**
3918 Silverado Trail
707/942-6669

Three exquisitely appointed suites set in the quiet mood of green lawns and tall pines overlooking the vineyards. Breakfast under the apple trees or in your own sitting room. Close to wineries and spas.

**Scott Courtyard**
1443 2nd St.
707/942-0948

Just two blocks from downtown Calistoga, Scott Courtyard resembles a Mediterranean villa with latticed courtyard and private gardens. The large social room has been described as "tropical Art Deco" with a bistro kitchen where a full breakfast is served pool side.

**Silver Rose Inn**
351 Rosedale Road
707/942-9581

Located near the end of picturesque Silverado Trail at Rosedale Road, high on a rocky outcropping and surrounded by centuries-old live oak trees, this lovely retreat has a panoramic view of the upper Napa Valley with its spreading vineyards and the towering Palisade mountains. All nine tastefully decorated guest rooms have private baths and some have balconies, fireplaces and whirlpool tubs. The Silver Rose has recently added a new hot springs spa. For the exclusive use of guests staying at the inn, the new spa includes mud, seaweed, herbal baths, hydro massage, facials and massage services.

**Stephen's Wine Way Inn**
1019 Foothill Blvd.
707/942-0680, 1-800-572-0679

A restored 1915 home where the atmosphere is casual and the innkeepers are like old friends. You can enjoy a glass of wine on the spectacular multi-level deck or by the fire in the parlor. Enjoy a full gourmet breakfast from an ever-growing collection of recipes. Each room is individually decorated in antiques and quilts. A cottage offers privacy for those who prefer it.

**Trailside Inn**
4201 Silverado Trail
707/942-4106

This charming 1930 farmhouse in the country has three suites, each with private entrance, porch-deck, bedroom, kitchen, bath and living room with fireplace. Complimentary wine, mineral water, fresh baked bread and breakfast fixings provided.

**Triple S Ranch**
4600 Mt. Home Ranch Road
707/942-6730

Rustic cabins and a homey atmosphere make this mountain hideaway a pleasant place to relax and unwind. There's a swimming pool, restaurant and cocktail lounge and many scenic mountain trails to hike. Nearby are the Old Faithful Geyser of California and the Petrified Forest.

**Zinfandel House**
1253 Summit Dr.
707/942-0733

A private home located in a wooded setting above the valley floor between St. Helena and Calistoga. The 1,000-square-foot deck offers a spectacular view of the valley. Two tastefully decorated rooms. Wine is offered and a lovely breakfast is served in the morning.

*NAPA*

**Arbor Guest House**
1436 G St.
707/252-8144

This 1906 Colonial transition home and carriage house have been completely restored for the comfort of guests. Rooms are beautifully appointed with antiques. Two rooms have spa tubs. For guests seeking privacy and seclusion, the carriage house bed/sitting rooms, both with fireplaces, are most fitting. A charming garden motif is featured throughout the Inn, with the wallpaper, window coverings and the medley of period furniture in brass, iron, oak, mahogany, wicker and carved and beveled glass.

**Beazley House**
1910 First St.
1-800-559-1649

Napa's first bed and breakfast is located in central Napa in a fine old neighborhood. The shingle style/colonial revival mansion of over 4,400 square feet was built in 1902. It has six guest rooms, all with private baths. Behind the mansion the carriage house has been reproduced and has five rooms, all with private baths, fireplaces and private, two-person spas. A full breakfast of home-baked muffins, fresh fruit and crustless cheese quiche is served in the mansion's formal dining room. In the spacious living room, complimentary tea is available to guests each afternoon.

**The Blue Violet Mansion**
443 Brown St.
707/253-BLUE

A large, elegant 1886 Queen Anne Victorian, the mansion was built for Emanuel Manasse, an executive at the Sawyer Tannery. Lovingly restored, and winner of the 1993 Landmarks Award of Merit for historical restoration. Located in the historic district of Old Town Napa, it is within walking distance of downtown shops and restaurants. The home now offers large, cheerful rooms with queen or king beds, fireplaces, balconies, spas and private baths. Outside is a garden gazebo with a swing, a shaded deck and rose garden. Full country breakfast and afternoon and evening refreshments are included.

**Brookside Vineyard**
3194 Redwood Road
707/944-1661

This gracious country bed and breakfast is also a picturesque working vineyard. A tree shaded lane leads you to the serene creek setting of this comfortable California mission-style inn. The three spacious guest rooms each have adjoining baths, and are tastefully furnished with antiques and collectibles. One room has a private patio, fireplace and sauna. Guests enjoy complimentary afternoon wine on the deck with a glorious view, or in the living room next to the fireplace. After dinner cordials are available in the cozy library. A full breakfast is served in the gazebo overlooking a stand of Douglas fir and the natural beauty of a creek lined with oak and bay trees.

**The Candlelight Inn**
1045 Easum Dr.
707/257-3717

This English Tudor, built in 1929 on one park-like acre in the city of Napa, has nine romantic rooms, one with its own sauna. The elegant living room features high contoured ceilings and a fireplace, and the innkeepers serve an exquisite breakfast and provide an afternoon social hour in the dining room, where the view through the French doors into the garden will delight you.

**Cedar Gables Inn**
486 Coombs St.
707/224-7969

Built in 1892, Cedar Gables is styled after 16th Century English Country homes. Six beautifully appointed guest rooms are furnished with antiques - some have whirlpool tubs and fireplaces. All have private baths. Each evening, innkeepers Margaret and Craig Snasdell welcome you with a spread of fruit, cheeses and wine. A bountiful breakfast is served in the cheerful sunroom.

**Churchill Manor**
485 Brown St.
707/253-7733

An 1889 National Landmark, Churchill Manor is the largest home of its time in the Napa Valley. The mansion rests amid lush grounds and is surrounded by an expansive veranda with twenty-two gleaming white columns. Entering through leaded-glass doors, guests are surrounded by magnificent woodwork, fixtures, and antique furnishings. While lavish in appointments, Churchill Manor is also warm and inviting. Guests enjoy afternoon fresh-baked cookies and refreshments, and a two-hour wine and cheese reception in the evening, and gourmet breakfast in the marble-tiled solarium.

**Country Garden Inn**
1815 Silverado Trail
707/255-1197

Situated on one and a half acres of mature woodland riverside property, the inn was built in the 1850s as a coach house on the Silverado Trail. The building is surrounded by trees and flowers, brick and stone pathways, a garden terrace, and there's a circular rose garden with a lily pond, fountain and large aviary. Each spacious room is furnished with antiques. Several have private jacuzzis and fireplaces. Full breakfast, afternoon tea and evening hors d'oeuvres are included.

**Cross Roads Inn**
6380 Silverado Trail
707/944-0646

Offering unparalleled views and complete privacy from its 20-acre vantage point high in the eastern hills of the Napa Valley, Crossroads Inn has spacious, individually decorated suites with wine bars and jacuzzi spas. Breakfast can be served in your suite or on your private deck. Afternoon tea, wine and cocktails are served around the native stone fireplace, and brandies are offered before retiring.

**The Hennessey House**
1727 Main St.
707/226-3774

This Eastlake-style Queen Anne Victorian was once the residence and office of Dr. Edward Zack Hennessey, an early, prominent Napa County physician. The house is now listed on the Register of Historic Places. Rooms have private baths, and some have canopy or feather beds, fireplaces and whirlpool tubs. The house is furnished with English or Belgian antiques, and the dining room features a hand painted, stamped ceiling.

**Hillview Country Inn**
1205 Hillview Lane
707/224-5004

Enjoy the country life at Hillview Country Inn, a spectacular 100-year-old estate where you can stroll the beautifully manicured grounds amid fruit trees, herb garden, lavish lawns and the Old English Rose Garden. In the inn's gracious parlor, you can start your morning with a sumptuous country breakfast. Each guest suite is distinctly decorated, and includes a fruit and wine basket upon arrival and a sweeping view of the Napa Valley.

**Inn on Randolph**
411 Randolph St.
707/257-2886

A showcase for area artists, every room in this restored 1860 Gothic Revival has been embellished with original designs - from handpainted murals and faux finishes to a distinctive willow canopy bed. Each generously proportioned guest room offers a sitting area, private bath and robes. Some feature a double or deep soaking whirlpool tub, gas fireplace or private deck. Comfortable sitting areas have marble fireplaces. The one-half acre of landscaped grounds provides a sundeck, gazebo and hammock.

**La Belle Epoque**
1386 Calistoga Ave.
707/257-2161

A Queen Anne Majesty built in 1893, with its multi-gabled dormers and high-hipped roof, La Belle Epoque is one of the finest examples of Victorian architecture in the wine country. Decorative flat and molded carvings can be seen in the gables and bays, and the original stained glass windows remain in the transoms and semi-circular windows. Guest rooms are decorated with fine period furniture, and several have fireplaces. Generous gourmet breakfast. Complimentary wine and hors d'oeuvres served in wine tasting room.

**La Residence**
4066 St. Helena Hwy.
707/253-0337

A French barn and 1870 mansion in its own 2 acre park-like setting, beautifully restored and furnished. The spacious rooms and suites have private baths, fireplaces, French doors, verandas or patios, and are luxuriously appointed. A spa and heated pool are framed by heritage oaks and towering pines. Full breakfast in sun-filled dining room with classical piano and fireplace included, as are sunset wine and hors d'oeuvres.

**The Napa Inn**
1137 Warren
707/257-1444, 1-800-435-1144

A three-story Queen Anne Victorian located on a quiet tree-lined street in a historic section of the town of Napa, the inn is furnished with turn-of-the-century antiques in each of the six guest rooms, parlor and formal dining room.

**Oak Knoll Inn**
2200 E. Oak Knoll Ave.
707/255-2200

A romantic, elegant, all-stone French country inn secluded within an expansive vineyard preserve. Features pool and hot tub and rooms with Italian marble fireplaces, private baths, vaulted ceilings, king-size brass beds and separate French door entrances, providing views of Stag's Leap Palisades and the surrounding oak-studded hillsides. A full breakfast in the morning, and wine and hors d'oeuvres in the evening are served on the deck overlooking the vineyards, or in front of the fireplace in the dining room.

**The Old World Inn**
1301 Jefferson
707/257-0112

A unique and memorable Victorian, decorated in the bright Scandinavian colors of artist Carl Larsson. Afternoon tea and cookies, nightly hors d'oeuvres, and an evening gourmet dessert buffet are offered.

**Stahlecker House Bed & Breakfast, Country Inn & Gardens**
1042 Easum Dr.
707/257-1588

A secluded, quiet country inn, Stahlecker House is located just minutes from the wineries. Canopy beds, antique furnishings and a comfortable gathering room with fireplace, contribute to a relaxed, homey atmosphere. A quiet, restful deck overlooks lawns, gardens and shade trees. Complimentary lemonade, coffee, tea and cookies.

**Trubody Ranch**
5444 St. Helena Hwy.
707/255-5907

Built in 1872, Trubody Ranch is a Gothic Revival Victorian home with water tower. Surrounded by 120 acres of family-owned vineyard land, the ranch is located in the center of Napa Valley. Rooms are furnished in family antiques of the period. Guests enjoy garden and vineyard strolls. There are views from both rooms. Breakfast is freshly baked breads, home-grown fruit in season, fruit juice, tea and coffee.

***ST. HELENA***

**The Ambrose Bierce House**
1515 Main St.
707/963-3003

Ambrose Bierce, famous witty author of The Devil's Dictionary and many short stories, lived in this house on the main street of St. Helena until 1913, when he mysteriously vanished into Mexico. His former residence, now a luxurious bed and breakfast inn, was built in 1872. Like Bierce himself, the inn is an intriguing blend of ingredients—luxury, history and hospitality. Bedroom suites are furnished with antiques, including comfortable queen-sized brass beds and armoires. Bathrooms have brass fittings, clawfoot tubs and showers. Suites are named for the historical figures whose presence touched Bierce and the Napa Valley in the late 1800s: Ambrose Bierce himself; Lillie Lantry, the era's most scandalous woman; Edward Muybridge, acclaimed "father of the motion picture", and Lillie Hitchcock Coit, the legendary "Belle of San Francisco." Complimentary gourmet breakfast of coffee, juice, fruits and pastries.

**Asplund Conn Valley Inn**
726 Rossi Road
707/963-4614

Nestled in lush garden surroundings with views of the vineyards and rolling hills, the inn is truly in the country, yet just five minutes away from Main Street, St. Helena. Antique furnishings, garden views, library and fireplace. Complimentary fruit, cheese and wine and a full breakfast. Country roads for strolling. Fishing nearby.

**Bartels Ranch and Country Inn**
1200 Conn Valley Road
707/963-4001

Peaceful, romantic, 60-acre country estate with 10,000 acre views-amidst vineyards! Award-winning "3 star" accommodations feature 3 guest rooms and one champagne suite with spa, sauna, and fireplace. Private baths include robes. Full breakfast served til noon in choice view settings. Unique entertainment room offers fireside billiards, chess, piano and library. Evening social hour, dessert, tea, coffee & cookies served 24 hours.

**Bylund House Bed & Breakfast Inn**
2000 Howell Mtn. Road
707/963-9073

Secluded country estate in the tradition of the Northern Italian Villa just minutes from downtown St. Helena. Two very private rooms with private baths, balconies and custom appointments. Complimentary wine, hors d'oeuvres and lavish continental breakfast.

**Chestelson House**
1417 Kearney St.
707/963-2238

Victorian home in a quiet residential neighborhood away from the busy highways. Gracious hospitality, delicious full breakfast and afternoon social hour. View of the mountains from the wide veranda.

**The Cinnamon Bear**
1407 Kearney St.
707/963-4653

This charming bed & breakfast home is just a 2-block walk to St. Helena's Main St. shops and restaurants. Antiques, quilts and teddy bears fill the rooms. Afternoon refreshments and dessert in the evening are followed by a full gourmet breakfast. Read by the fireplace or relax on the spacious porch of this quaint place to stay.

**Creekside Inn**
945 Main St.
707/963-7244

Located in the heart of St. Helena, yet sheltered from the hustle and bustle of town by ancient oaks and by the murmurs of White Sulphur Creek rippling past its secluded rear garden patio, Creekside offers three guest rooms furnished in a Country French theme. There's a fireplace in the common room, and a full breakfast is served in the sunroom or on the creekside patio.

**Deer Run**
3995 Spring Mtn. Road
707/963-3794

A truly secluded, peaceful mountain, four-acre retreat, Deer Run is nestled in the forest on Spring Mountain above the valley vineyards, affording the quiet serenity of a private hideaway. All units have fireplaces and antique furnishings. And there's a heated swimming pool. A full breakfast is served in the dining area.

**Erika's Hillside**
285 Fawn Park
707/963-2887

This hillside chalet, just two miles from St. Helena, has a peaceful, wooded country setting and a view of vineyards and wineries. The grounds are nicely landscaped. The rooms are spacious, bright and airy with private entrances and bath, fireplace and hot tub. Continental breakfast is served in the solarium. The structure - more than 100 years old - has been remodeled and personally decorated by German-born innkeeper, Erika Cunningham.

**Glass Mountain Inn**
3100 Silverado Trail
707/963-3512

In the midst of the Napa Valley's vineyards, yet snuggled among century-old redwoods, pines and oaks, proudly stands the majestic Victorian Glass Mountain Inn. Towers, turrets and stained glass enhance the inn, where amenities include hand carved oak fireplaces, whirlpool and Roman soaking tubs. A full breakfast is served in a stone dining room viewing a candlelit wine cave built in the 1800's.

**Harvest Inn**
1 Main St.
707/963-9463

This elegant AAA Four Diamond English Tudor-style inn has spacious and secure cottages furnished with original antiques. Many cottages also include elaborate brick fireplaces, wet bars and vineyard views. Deluxe spa suites are available. 24-hour pool and Jacuzzi, wine bar and conference rooms with cobblestone fireplaces and stained glass windows are available.

**Hilltop House**
9550 St. Helena Road
707/963-8743

Just minutes from St. Helena, Hilltop House is a peaceful mountain hideaway on 135 acres of unspoiled wilderness on the Napa County line, which offers a hang glider's view of the historic Mayacama Mountains.

**Hotel St. Helena**
1309 Main St.
707/963-4388

Victorian hotel located on St. Helena's Main St. Offers richly furnished antique filled-rooms with private or shared baths. The Hotel is within walking distance of St. Helena's many fine restaurants and wineries.

**Ink House**
1575 St. Helena Hwy.
707/963-3890

A traditional Italianate Victorian built by Theron H. Ink in 1884. This historic valley home offers four charming guest bedrooms complete with era furnishings with private baths. In the parlor, guests are invited to read or play the antique pump organ. A glass-walled observatory features a 360-degree view of the vineyards.

**Judy's Ranch House**
701 Rossi Road
707/963-3081

At Judy's country-style bed and breakfast, surrounded by a 3-acre Merlot vineyard, you can enjoy the oak trees and seasonal creek that run through the seven acres, or take a walk down a peaceful country road.

**La Fleur B&B**
1475 Inglewood Ave.
707/963-0233

This Victorian, nestled among the vineyards, features three beautifully appointed rooms, all with fireplaces and private baths. A deluxe full breakfast is served in the solarium overlooking the surrounding vineyards. A private tour of Villa Helena Winery comes with your stay.

**Oliver House Bed & Breakfast**
2970 Silverado Trail
707/963-4089

A Swiss chalet nestled in the hills with a panoramic view of the Napa Valley. There are four bedrooms with antiques; one has a 115-year-old brass bed. Another bedroom has its own private fireplace.The focal point of the cozy living room parlor is a large stone fireplace. Breakfast of muffins, fruit and pastries is served. Visitors are welcome to stroll around the lovely grounds of the four-acre estate.

**Rustridge Ranch**
2910 Lower Chiles Valley Road
707/965-9353

A family-owned and operated estate where grapes and horses grow together, Rustridge Ranch and Winery is seven miles east of the Silverado Trail in the picturesque rolling hills of the Chiles Valley. Thoroughbred racehorses graze among the oak trees and along the hillsides, while vineyards envelop the valley. The rambling Southwestern ranch-style house has been remodeled and converted into a gracious, contemporary bed and breakfast inn.

**Shady Oaks Country Inn**
399 Zinfandel Lane
707/963-1190

Old-fashioned elegance and warm hospitality welcome you to this country inn. Secluded and romantic on 2 acres and nestled in the vineyards among some of the finest wineries and restaurants in the Napa Valley. The guest rooms and their country comforts are housed in a 1920s home and a winery built in the 1800s. The rooms are furnished with antiques, fine linens and private baths. A full champagne gourmet breakfast is served fireside, in bed or on the garden veranda. Wine and cheese are served each evening.

**Spanish Villa Inn**
474 Glass Mountain Road
707/963-7483

Nestled in a wooded valley on Glass Mountain Road, the villa is a short scenic drive from St. Helena and Calistoga. Each room includes a king-size bed, private bath and Tiffany lamps. Breakfast is served in the galleria. Neatly manicured grounds with ancient oak trees, palms and flower gardens surround the villa.

**Sutter Home Winery B&B**
277 S. St. Helena Hwy.
707/963-3104

Situated on the beautifully landscaped grounds of this historic old winery, Sutter Home's guest rooms offer Victorian elegance and a central location convenient for fine dining, shopping and relaxed wine country touring. Accommodations include antique furnishings, fireplaces, as well as, an expanded continental breakfast featuring freshly baked goods, fruit juices, cereals and coffee.

**Vigne Del Uomo Felice**
1871 Cabernet Lane
707/963-2376

Situated on the west side of Napa Valley surrounded by the peace and quiet of the vineyards, Vigne del Uomo Felice is, appropriately translated, Ranch of the Happy Man. The completely furnished stone cottage with bedroom, bath and studio offers guests the opportunity to shed their cares.

**Villa St. Helena**
2727 Sulphur Springs Ave.
707/963-2514

A grand Mediterranean-style villa located in the hills above St. Helena. This secluded 20-acre wooded estate combines quiet country elegance with panoramic views of beautiful Napa Valley. Built in 1941 to accommodate elaborate entertaining with its spacious courtyard and view-filled walking trails, the Villa has a comfortable interior featuring period-style furniture.

**White Sulphur Springs Resort**
3100 White Sulphur Springs Road
707/963-8588

California's first resort, established 1852, White Sulphur Springs has two small inns and nine cottages, outdoor sulphur soaking pool, massage, mud wraps and jacuzzi, and hiking trails. It is a rustic old-world retreat with 330 acres of redwood, fir and madrone forests—secluded, yet only 3 miles from St. Helena.

**Wine Country Inn**
1152 Lodi Lane
707/963-7077

Perched on a knoll overlooking manicured vineyards and nearby hills, this country inn offers 24 individually decorated guest rooms. The Smiths used local antiques and family-made quilts to create an atmosphere of warmth and comfort. Fireplaces and balconies add charm.

**Wine Country Victorian and Cottages**
707/963-0852

This classic Victorian beauty is situated amid majestic oaks, elms and pines. In the adjoining gardens the estate also offers Wine Country Cottage, originally guest quarters for the main residence, now a cozy self-contained unit. You'll find "country quiet" here, as well as many delightful surprises in Napa Valley's oldest bed & breakfast.

**Zinfandel Inn**
800 Zinfandel Lane
707/963-3512

**Burgundy House**
6711 Washington
707/944-0889

A stone two-story brandy distillery built in 1891 of local fieldstone and river rock now houses the country inn. Five comfortable and cozy rooms, each with private bath, welcome you, as does a decanter of local wine. Antique country furniture and period furnishings complement the rugged masonry. A full breakfast is served in the "distillery" or in the beautiful garden outside.

**Maison Fleurie**
6529 Yount St.
707/944-2056, 800/788-0369

The Maison Fleurie, Four Sisters Inns newest inn, is a luxurious haven of French country romance. Two-foot-thick brick walls, terra cotta tile and paned windows are reminiscent of a farmhouse in Provence. The inn has 13 beautifully decorated guest rooms, a swimming pool and outdoor spa, spacious landscaped grounds and a cozy dining room serving a gourmet breakfast to each guest. Wine tastings, dinner reservations, balloon rides, spa services and sightseeing itineraries are carefully planned by the inn's attentive staff. In the afternoon, wine and hor d'oeuvres are served, as well as cookies, fruit and beverages throughout the day.

**Napa Valley Railway Inn**
6503 Washington St.
707/944-2000

Rekindling the nostalgia evoked by names like Burlington Route, Great Northern RR and Southern Pacific, the inn consists of nine turn-of-the-century railroad cars — three cozy cabooses and six spacious railcars restored to their original glory. Interiors are furnished to suggest the opulence of the era, with the added comfort of contemporary amenities. Each suite has a brass bed, sitting room with a loveseat for relaxing, and a full bath. Adjacent to Vintage 1870, Yountville, with its restaurants, shops and galleries.

**Oleander House**
7433 St. Helena Hwy.
707/944-8315

Comfortable, elegant, sun-drenched and carefree, this Country French two-story B & B combines old-world design with modern amenities. Guests enjoy spacious rooms with queen-size beds, high ceilings, private bath, balcony, fireplace, antiques and Laura Ashley decor. Landscaped patio garden. A full gourmet breakfast is served. Knowledgeable innkeepers assist with advice on the valley's best attractions. Within walking distance of Mustards Restaurant.

**Vintage Inn, Napa Valley**
6541 Washington St.
707/944-1112

Created by California artist Kip Stewart, the inn features spacious, exquisitely appointed guest rooms, each with wood-burning fireplace, refrigerator, whirlpool bath spa, in-room brewed coffee and terry robes. An elaborate California Champagne breakfast is included, along with afternoon tea and nightly turn-down service. Recipient of AAA's prestigious Four Diamond Award. Walk to Vintage 1870 and many fine restaurants.

**The Webber Place**
6610 Webber St.
707/944-8384

Surrounded by a white picket fence, The Webber Place is a red farmhouse built in 1850. It is now a homey and affordable bed and breakfast inn decorated in Americana Folk Art style. Artist Diane Bartholomew bought the place seven years ago, and she has her studio next door. On sunny afternoons she serves sun tea and cookies on the front porch, and in the morning the farmhouse kitchen smells of coffee, biscuits and bacon as she sets to work making a real country breakfast. Guest rooms have ornate iron and brass beds covered with antique quilts. Two rooms share a deep old-fashioned tub with brass fixtures, and the other two rooms have tub alcoves right in the room. The Veranda suite is much larger, with a hammock on its own sheltered veranda and entrance.

### *Favorite Places To Eat*

**Spring Street**
1245 Spring St. – St. Helena
707/963-5578

This bungalow-turned-restaurant on Spring Street, St. Helena, was the home for nearly 50 years of opera singer Walter Martina and his wife, Dionisia, who moved to St. Helena in 1915 to manage the popular William Tell Hotel. The Martina's loved to entertain. Their guests gather for gourmet cooking, fine wine and music in the lush adjoining garden with its vine-covered trellis beside the oval fountain. Spring Street Restaurant carries on the tradition of good food and wines, serving Saturday and Sunday brunch that features fresh baked biscuits, sweet rolls, muffins, special omelettes and homemade preserves; weekday lunches featuring special sandwiches, salads and homemade desserts, and delicious, American fare dinners daily. Everything is available for takeout and may be ordered ahead by calling the restaurant.

**Trilogy**
1234 Main St.
707/963-5507

You enter this small, intimate restaurant through an iron gate and a courtyard off St. Helena's Hunt St. and find yourself in a quiet dining room with gracious furniture, elegant chandeliers, flowers on cloth-covered tables and classical stereo music. The California French cuisine of chef Diane Pariseau is delicious to the palate and delightful to the eye. Trilogy's wine list is exciting and cosmopolitan and goes far beyond the choices you find in many larger wine country restaurants. Local produce and fresh fish and poultry, never frozen, are featured and the sauces — French — are prepared in the restaurant's own kitchen. People watchers will enjoy watching the passing parade on St. Helena's quaint Main St. from the dining room, and those who enjoy outdoor dining will find the courtyard a pleasant place in fair weather.

**Triple S Ranch**
4600 Mt. Home Ranch Road – North of Calistoga
707/942-6730

A ranch and restaurant operated by the Schellenger family for more than 30 years, Triple S Ranch serves up nostalgia along with mouth-watering meals. Perched high in the Sonoma Mountains near the Petrified Forest, The Triple S Restaurant was converted from the ranch's original redwood barn built more than a century ago. Thick homemade soup or large salads with plenty of French bread accompany each dinner, and there's a choice of delicious country specialties. The portions are generous. Onion rings at Triple S are legendary, and the ranch has become famous for them. They also have french fried frog legs! After dinner, you might enjoy a game of bocci ball or horseshoes.

## 113 NEVADA CITY

**Nevada City Warehouse**
75 Bost Ave.
916/265-6000

**La Cache**
218 Broad St.
916/265-8104

**Assay Office Antiques**
130 Main St.
916/265-8126

**Shaws Antiques**
210 Main St.
916/265-2668

**Main Street Antique Shop**
214 1/2 Main St.
916/265-3108

**2nd Time Around**
548 Searls Ave.
916/265-8844

**Tinnery**
205 York St.
916/265-0599

### *Great Places To Stay*

**Emma Nevada House**
528 E. Broad St.
1-800-916-EMMA

Nineteenth Century Opera Star Emma Nevada would be proud of the inn bearing her name. This completely restored and decorated 1856 Victorian sparkles like a jew from an abundance of original, water-float glass windows, one of many marvelous architectural details. The six guest rooms are a mix of grand, high-ceilings, and cozy intimate settings, all with private baths (some jacuzzi tubs), queen beds, and fluffy down comforters.

**Flume's End Bed and Breakfast Inn**
317 S. Pine St.
1-800-991-8118

The Gold Country's most unique bed and breakfast, Flume's End rests on a picturesque hillside sloping down to the natural waterfalls of a famous creek meandering through three wooded acres of natural beauty. In the 1800s the historic flume beside the inn brought Sierra Mountain gold miners "waters of good fortune." The ambiance you will experience at Flume's End will make your visit equally bountiful.

## 114 NEWPORT BEACH

**Vallejo Gallery**
1610 W. Coast Hwy.
714/642-7945

**Jane's Antiques**
2811 Lafayette Road
714/673-5688

**Antiques 4 U**
312 N. Newport Blvd.
714/548-4123

**Old Newport Antiques**
477 N. Newport Blvd.
714/548-8713

**A Secret Affair**
3441 Via Lido, Ste. A & B
714/673-3717

**Grandma's Cottage**
400 Westminster Ave.
714/645-9258

**Jeffries Ltd.**
852 Production Place
714/642-4154

## 115 NOVATO

**Consignment Shop**
818 Grant Ave.
415/892-3496

**Now & Then**
902 Grant Ave.
415/892-0640

**Black Pt Antiques Collectibles & Gifts**
35 Harbor Dr.
415/892-5100

## 116 OAKDALE

**Past & Present Antiques**
219 E. F St.
209/847-1228

**Twice Treasured**
231 E. F St.
209/848-2750

**Two Gals Trading Post**
1725 E. F St.
209/847-3350

**Peddler's Attic**
223 S. Sierra Ave.
209/847-4710

## 117 OAKHURST

**Good Oldaze**
Hwy. 41 & 426
209/683-6161

**Oakhurst Frameworks**
49027 Road 426
209/683-7845

**Collectors Mall**
40982 N. State Hwy. 41
209/683-5006

## 118 OAKLAND

**Tim's Antiques & Collectibles**
5371 Bancroft Ave.
510/533-7493

**Williamsburg Antiques**
5375 Bancroft Ave.
510/532-1870

**Deerfield's Collectibles**
5383 Bancroft Ave.
510/534-6411

**Good The Bad & The Ugly**
5322 & 26 College Ave.
510/420-1740

**Rockridge Antiques**
5601 College Ave.
510/652-7115

**Avenue Antiques**
6007 College Ave.
510/652-7620

**Garcia's Antiques**
2278 E. 14th St.
510/535-1339

**Richard a Pecchi Antiques**
30 Jack London Square #110
510/465-9006

**Lost and Found Antiques**
4220 Piedmond Ave.
510/654-2007

## 119 OAKLEY

**Lena's Antiques**
3510 Main St.
510/625-4878

**Norcross Timeless Treasures**
3639 Main St.
510/625-0193

**Country Courthouse**
3663 Main St.
510/625-1099

## 120 OCEANO

**A Pier At The Past**
368 Pier Ave.
805/473-1521
(Open during summer 10-6 Wed.-Sun.)(during winter 11-5 Wed.-Sun.)-Mon. & Tues. by chance.
*Directions: From Hwy. 101 north: Take Los Barros Rd. exit to Oceano. From Hwy. 101 south: Take 4th St. exit to Grand, right to Hwy. 1, left to Pier Ave., right to the shop and the beach. a Pier At The Past is on State Hwy. #1, 3 miles south of Pismo Beach and 2 miles north of Nipomo.*

I don't know which you'll love the most - the antique shop or George Kiner himself. He is the epitome of the "laid back" California lifestyle. George set up shop on the beach at Oceano in 1994, but he has been in business in California for 35 years. Starting out in the 1960s, before the major rekindling of interest in antiques took hold, George was one of the early Union Street dealers. He owned several shops in various San Francisco locations - one of which was the ever-popular Varietorium. It was dubbed "the" place to shop for antiques, and George, with his myna bird Susie, became quite well known.

George opened two more shops in California, one in the San Fernando Valley and one in Studio City. Both were destroyed by earthquakes. These events prompted his move to Oceano, where he opened a fun little shop called A Pier At The Past.

It is, according to George, right at the entranceway for the tricycles and A.T.V.s heading for the Oceano Dunes, "the only place on the West Coast where you can drive down and find 1,000 campsites." There used to be a pier at the beach years ago, but it was lost in a storm. The gutted building that houses A Pier At The Past had been a building block restaurant. George rented it, put up temporary walls for his paintings, hung some lighting and was in business. He knows how temporary things can be, having weathered the earthquakes and lost stores over the years. George also lives in the shop, which visitors often don't realize as they browse. He keeps everything open. "You can walk through into the living room and on into the bedroom," says George. "If someone wants to buy my bed, I'll sell it and sleep on a futon until I find something I like."

Besides his bed, George carries lots of cups and saucers, paintings from all periods, costume jewelry and accessories, beaded purses, compacts and barber bottles, Indian pottery, unusual furniture pieces, lots of little tables, Oriental decorative items, English Bristol china, German Royal Bonn porcelain and kitchen items to the 1930s.

If you know you're going to stop by, you might want to call first - George is often out on the beach taking a walk.

**Central Coast Outdoor Antique & Collectible Market**
Oceano Airport
561 Air Park Dr.
805/481-9095 (Dealer Information)
2nd Saturday of each month
7 a.m.-2 p.m.
*Directions: Off Hwy. 1, south of Pismo Beach.*

On the second Saturday of every month, the Oceano Airport parking lot is transformed into an antique mecca. This open air market is only one and a half blocks from Pismo Beach and is part of the beautiful tourist area of San Luis Obispo County. The Market features free admission and parking.

**The Hangar Antiques & Collectibles**
Oceano Airport
561 Air Park Dr.
805/481-9095
Open Fri., Sat., & Sun. or by appointment

This unusual setting for antiques was once an old airplane hangar. Today, it is packed with quality antiques and collectibles ranging from gas and oil memorabilia, airplane related items, many big boy toys, as well as wonderful items for the ladies. Constantly changing inventory.

## 121 OJAI

**Gracie's Antique Mall**
238 E. Ojai Ave.
805/646-8879

**Antique Collection**
236 W. Ojai Ave.
805/646-6688

**Treasures of Ojai**
110 N. Signal St.
805/646-2852

## 122 ONTARIO

**Ontario Antiques Annex**
127 W. B St.
909/391-8628

**Ontario Antiques**
203 W. B St.
909/391-1200

**Inland Empire Antiques**
216 W. B St.
909/986-9779

**Martha's Antique Mall**
326 N. Euclid Ave.
909/984-5220

**Golden Web**
235 N. Euclid
909/986-6398

**Treasures 'N' Junk**
215 S. San Antonio
909/983-3300

## 123 ORANGE

**S & E Gallery**
227A E. Chapman Ave.
714/532-6787

**American Roots**
105 W. Chapman Ave.
714/639-3424

**Daisy's Antiques**
131 W. Chapman Ave.
714/633-6475

**Country Roads Antiques**
204 W. Chapman Ave.
714/532-3041

**Tony's Architectural & Garden**
123 N. Olive
714/538-1900

**Treasures From The Past**
611 W. Chapman Ave.
714/997-9702

**Mulherin & O Dell's Antiques**
106 N. Glassell St.
714/771-3390

**Anthony's Fine Antiques**
114 N. Glassell St.
714/538-1900

**George The Second**
117 N. Glassell St.
714/744-1870

**Rocking Chair Emporium**
123 N. Glassell St.
714/633-5206

**Happiness By The Bushel**
128 N. Glassell St.
714/538-3324

**It's About Time**
131 N. Glassell St.
714/538-7645

**Grand Avenue Antiques**
140 N. Glassell St.
714/538-3540

**Antique Place**
142 N. Glassell St.
714/538-4455

**Encore Presentations**
144 N. Glassell St.
714/744-4845

**Jim & Shirley's Antiques**
146 N. Glassell St.
714/639-9662

**Mr C's Rare Records**
148 N. Glassell St.
714/532-3835

**Antiques & Me**
149 N. Glassell St.
714/639-4084

**A & P Collectables**
151 N. Glassell St.
714/997-1370

**Attic Delights**
155 N. Glassell St.
714/639-8351

**Lucky Find Antiques**
160 N. Glassell St.
714/771-6364

**Antiques Antiques**
165 N. Glassell St.
714/639-4084

**Woody's Early Misc.**
169 & 173 N. Glassell St.
714/744-8199

**Le Chalet Antiques & Doll Shop**
277 N. Glassell St.
714/633-2650

**Rick Sloane Antiques**
2055 N. Glassell St.
714/637-1257

**Watch And Wares**
108 S. Glassell St.
714/633-2030

**Antique Annex**
109 S. Glassell St.
714/997-4320

**Partners Eclectic Antiques**
110 S. Glassell St.
714/744-4340

**Jewelry & Gift Mart**
110 1/2 S. Glassell St.
714/633-2325

**Dorothy & Friends Antiques**
114 1/2 Glassell St.
714/771-5087

**Orange Circle Antique Mall**
118 S. Glassell St.
714/538-8160

**Uncle Tom's Antiques**
119 S. Glassell St.
714/538-3826

**Someplace In Time**
132 S. Glassell St.
714/538-9411

**Muff's Antiques**
135 S. Glassell St.
714/997-0243

**Nick Schaner Antiques**
136 S. Glassell St.
714/744-0204

**Just For Fun**
140 S. Glassell St.
714/633-7405

**Plaza 42 Antiques**
141 S. Glassell St.
714/633-9090

**Summerhill Limited**
142 S. Glassell St.
714/771-7782

**Victoria Co.**
146 S. Glassell St.
714/538-7927

**Antique Station**
178 S. Glassell St.
714/633-3934

**Ruby's Antique Jewelry**
111 N. Olive St.
714/538-1762

**Old Towne Orange Antique Mall**
119 N. Olive St.
714/532-6255

**Willard Antiques**
143 S. Olive St.
714/771-7138

**Rothdale's Fine Antiques**
40 Plaza Square
714/289-6900

**J & J Antiques**
55 Plaza Square
714/288-9057

**Tea Leaf Cottage**
60 Plaza Square
714/771-7752

**China Terrace Antiques**
1192 N. Tustin Ave.
714/771-4555

## 124 ORINDA

**The Family Jewels**
572 Tahos Road
510/254-4422

**Karla's Antiques**
83 Orinda Way
510/254-0964

**Orinda Village Antiques**
107 Orinda Way
510/254-2206

## 125 OROVILLE

**Day Dreams**
1462 Myers St.
916/534-8624

**Old Town Emporium**
2034 Montgomery St.
916/533-7787

**Lock Stock & Barrell**
2061 Montgomery St.
916/534-7515

**Carousel Antiques**
2421 Montgomery St.
916/534-8433

**Miners Alley Collective**
1354 Myers St.
916/534-7871

## 126 PACIFIC GROVE

**Patrick's**
105 Central
408/372-3995

**Woodenickle**
529 Central
408/646-8050

**Antique Warehouse**
2707 David Ave.
408/375-1456

**Camden & Castleberry Antiques**
2711 David Ave.
408/375-0701

**Trotter's Antiques**
301-303 Forest Ave.
408/373-3505

**Antique Clock Shop**
489 Lighthouse Ave.
408/372-6435

**Front Row Center**
633 C Lighthouse Ave.
408/375-5625

### *Interesting Side Trips*

**Point Pinos Lighthouse**
Asilomar Ave. off Ocean View Blvd.
408/648-3116

Built in 1856, oldest continuously operating lighthouse on the West Coast.

## 127 PALM DESERT

**Treasure House**
73199 El Paseo, Ste. C & D
760/568-1461

## 128 PALM SPRINGS

**Palm Springs Art Gallery**
170 E. Arenas Road
760/778-6969

**Pars Gallery**
353 S. Palm Canyon, #A
760/322-7179

**Irene's Antiques**
457 N. Palm Canyon Dr.
760/320-6654

**Robert Kaplan Antiques**
469 N. Palm Canyon Dr.
760/323-7144

**Campbell's Estate Gallery**
886 N. Palm Canyon Dr.
760/323-6044

**Carlan Collection**
1556 N. Palm Canyon Dr.
760/322-8002

***Great Places To Stay***

**Casa Cody Bed & Breakfast Country Inn**
175 South Cahuilla Road
760/320-9346
Fax: 760/325-8610
Rates vary by season

A romantic, historic hideaway nestled against the spectacular San Jacinto Mountains in the heart of Palm Springs Village, Casa Cody is the oldest operating hotel in Palm Springs. It was founded in the 1920s by the beautiful Hollywood pioneer, Harriet Cody, cousin to the legendary Buffalo Bill. The inn has 23 single-story accommodations in five early California hacienda-style buildings, all decorated in Sante Fe decor, and surrounding bougainvillaea and citrus-filled courtyards. Guests have a choice of single or double rooms, studios, and one or two bedroom suites, each with private baths and entrances. There's a one-bedroom cottage and a historic two-bedroom adobe for those who desire even more seclusion. The inn also offers two pools and a tree-shaded whirlpool spa.

**Ingleside Inn & Melvyns Restaurant & Lounge**
200 W. Ramon Road
Web site: www.prinet.com/ingleside

Favorite Hideaway of the Biggest Names in Show Business, Industry and Politics. Featured 'One of the Ten Best'-Lifestyles of the Rich and Famous. Experience the beauty and old world charm that place the historic Ingleside Inn at the top of every Traveler's "Wish List". An oasis where quiet elegance reigns in a setting of unequaled serenity, sunshine and personalized service by European-trained staff. The world famous Melvyn's Restaurant is still a Palm Springs tradition.

## 129 PALO ALTO

**Antique Emporium**
4219 El Camino Real
415/494-2868

**Adele's Antiques**
231 Hamilton Ave.
415/322-7184

**Kimura Gallery**
482 Hamilton Ave.
415/322-3984

**Antiques Unlimited**
542 High St.
415/328-3748

**Hilary Thatz Inc.**
38 Stanford Shopping Center
415/323-4200

**Di Capi Ltd.**
10 Town & Country Village
415/327-1541

**Alan Jay Co.**
14 Town & Country Village
415/462-9900

**Cotton Works**
500 University Ave.
415/327-1800

## 130 PARADISE

**19th Century Antique Shop**
5447 Skyway
916/872-8723

**Time Was**
5610 Skyway
916/877-7844

**Penny Ante Antiques**
5701 Skyway
916/877-0047

**Patti's Snoop Shoppe**
7357 Skyway
916/872-4008

**Attic Treasures**
7409 Skyway
916/876-1541

**Deloris' Antiques - Collectibles**
7639 Skyway
916/872-2828

## 131 PASADENA

**Carol's Antiques**
1866 N. Allen
818/798-1072

**Chuck's Antiques**
23 N. Altadena
818/564-9582

**Jay's Antiques**
95B N. Arroyo Pkwy.
818/792-0485

**Jane Warren Antiques**
832 E. California Blvd.
818/584-9431

**Carlson-Powers Antiques**
1 W. California Blvd., Ste. 411
818/577-9589

**Dovetail Antiques**
1 W. California Blvd., Ste. 412
818/792-9410

**On The Twentieth Century**
910 E. Colorado Blvd.
818/795-0667

**Time Recyclers**
2552 E. Colorado Blvd.
818/440-1880

**Tiffany Tree**
498 Del Rosa Dr.
818/796-4406

**Antiques & Objects**
446 S. Fair Oaks Ave.
818/796-8224

**Georgene's Antiques**
448 S. Fair Oaks Ave.
818/440-9926

**Marc's Antiques**
460 S. Fair Oaks Ave.
818/795-3770

**Pasadena Antique Center**
480 S. Fair Oaks Ave.
818/449-7706

**Blackwelders Antiques & Fine Art**
696 E. Colorado Blvd.
818/584-0723

**Oliver's Antiques Fine Arts**
597 E. Green St.
818/449-3463

**Kelley Gallery**
770 E. Green St., #102
818/577-5657

**Green Dolphin St. Antiques**
985 E. Green St.
818/577-7087

**J & N Antiques**
989 E. Green St.
818/792-7366

**Pasadena Antique Mall**
44 E. Holly St.
818/304-9886

**Showcase Antiques**
60 N. Lake Ave.
818/577-9660

**Marco Polo Antique Shop**
62 N. Raymond Ave.
818/356-0835

**Design Center Antiques**
70 N. Raymond Ave.
213/681-6230

**A Matter of Taste**
328 S. Rosemead Blvd.
818/792-2735

**Novotny's Antique Gallery**
60 N. Lake Ave.
818/577-9660

## 132 PASO ROBLES

**Antique Emporium**
1307 Park St.
805/238-1078

**Great American Antiques**
1305 Spring St.
805/239-1203

**Homestead Antiques & Collectibles**
1320 Pine St.
805/238-9183

**Sentimental Journey**
1344 Pine St.
805/239-1001

**Heritage House Antique Gallery**
1345 Park St.
805/239-1386

## 133 PETALUMA

**R & L Antiques**
3690 Bodega Ave.
707/762-2494

**Kentucky Street Antiques**
127 Kentucky St.
707/765-1698

**Waddles-N-Hops**
145 Kentucky St.
707/778-3438

**Dolores Hitchinson Antiques**
146 Kentucky St.
707/763-8905

**Doris's Antiques**
152 Kentucky St.
707/765-0627

**Fraley's Antiques**
110 Petaluma Blvd. N., #A
707/763-4087

**Chanticleer Antiques**
145 Petaluma Blvd. N.
707/763-9177

**Chelsea Antiques**
148 Petaluma Blvd. N.
707/763-7686

**Antique Market Place**
304 Petaluma Blvd. N.
707/765-1155

**Antique Collector**
523 Petaluma Blvd. S.
707/763-7371

**Vintage Bank Antiques**
101 Petaluma Blvd.
707/769-3097

## 134 PLACERVILLE

**Jennings Way Antiques**
3182 Center St.
916/642-0446

**Treasure Tent Antiques**
376 Main St.
916/626-9364

**Empire Antiques**
420 Main St.
916/626-8931

**The Loft**
420 Main St.
916/626-8931

**Olde Dorado Antique Emporium**
435 Main St.
916/622-4792

**Placerville Antiques & Collectibles**
440 Main St.
916/626-3425

**Beever's Antiques & Books**
462-464 Main St.
916/626-3314

**Memory Lane Antiques**
460 Main St.
916/626-9207

## 135 PLEASANTON

**Olde Towne Antiques**
465 Main St.
510/484-2446

**B J Gardner Fine Period Furniture**
531 Main St.
510/484-5456

**Main St. Antiques & Collectibles**
641 Main St.
510/426-0279

**Cattelan's Antique Furn**
719 Main St.
510/485-1705

**Clutter Box**
99 W. Neal St.
510/462-8640

## 136 POMONA

### Swan Song
197 E. Second St. (Antique Row)
909/620-5767
562/433-1033 (Appt.)
Open by appointment

Swan Song is an exceptional, upscale antique shop with a unique setting. Primitives and country furnishings fill the basement of what once was the old department store. The main floor is reserved for oil paintings, art glass, silver, oriental, and fine china. The second story is filled (over 100 pieces) with Victorian furniture, vintage clothing, along with American and Indian pottery. The third and final floor of this shop features quilts, traditional antique furnishings along with designer pieces. If you're not in the market to purchase these exquisite items, you can rent them. Everything in the store is available for rental. Sounds like a great place to plan a wedding or party.

**Pfeiffer's Collectibles**
147 E. 2nd St.
909/629-8860

**Girl's Antiques**
151 E. 2nd St.
909/622-5773

**Jack's Antiques**
161 E. 2nd St.
909/633-5589

**Pomona Antique Center**
162 E. 2nd St.
909/620/7406

**My Way Antiques**
175 E. 2nd St.
909/620-6696

**Persnickity Antiquity**
180 E. 2nd St.
909/620-8996

**Ralph's Inland Empire Antiques**
185 E. 2nd St.
909/622-0451

**Robbins Antique Mall**
200 E. 2nd St.
909/623-9835

**Grandpa's Antiques**
205 E. 2nd St.
909/629-5854

**Grandma's Goodies**
211 E. 2nd St.
909/629-3906

**Collector's Choice**
104 S. Locust
909/865-7110

**Dragon Antiques**
216 E. 2nd St.
909/620-6660

**Kaiser Bill's Military Shop**
224 E. 2nd St.
909/622-5046

**Lila's Place**
233 E. 2nd St.
909/620-7270

**Empire House Antiques**
237 E. 2nd St.
909/622-9291

**Olde Towne Pomona Mall**
260 E. 2nd St.
909/622-1011

**McBeth's Antiques**
263 E. 2nd St.
909/622-0615

**Nothing Common Antiques**
265 E. 2nd St.
909/620-1229

**Harrie's General Store**
269 E. 2nd St.
909/629-1446

**Hobbs & Fried Mercantile**
275 E. 2nd St.
909/629-1112

**Sanders Antiques**
279 E. 2nd St.
909/620-8295

**China Closet**
290 E. 2nd St.
909/622-2922

**Southwest Antiques**
198 E. 2nd St.
909/620-8334

## 137 PORTERVILLE

**Now & Then Country Mall**
19230 Ave. 152
209/783-9313

**Jerico Antique Emporium**
134 N. Main St.
209/784-2211

**Sandie's**
32 W. Mill Ave.
209/781-6740

**Junk N Tique**
36 W. Mill Ave.
209/783-2448

**J. Fox Antiques**
40 W. Mill Ave.
209/784-1737

**Irene's Antiques**
33 W. Putnam Ave.
209/782-8245

**Downing Antiques**
1522 W. Putnam Ave.
209/784-1465

**Cotton Center Trading Post**
15366 Road 192
209/784-4012

## 138 RAMONA

**Ye Olde Curio Shoppe**
738 Main St.
760/789-6365

**Old Town Antiques**
760 Main St.
760/788-2670

**Ramona Antiques & Collectibles**
872 Main St.
760/789-7816

**Peterson's Antiques & Collectibles**
2405 Main St.
760/789-2027

## 139 RANCHO CORDOVA

**Antique Plaza**
11395 Folsom Blvd.
916/852-8517

## 140 RANDSBURG

**Cottage Hotel Bed & Breakfast & Antiques**
130 Butte Ave.
760/374-2285
Thurs.-Mon. 11-5, closed Tues.-Wed. (sometimes) and during Christmas/New Year.

This is the place to go to be pampered - a quiet getaway with an enclosed Jacuzzi for all-season use. Hidden away in the California High Desert in the historical gold mining town of Randsburg, the Cottage Hotel Bed & Breakfast began at the turn of the century with the gold boom in Randsburg. Today all the rooms have been restored to reflect that era, with period furnishings being the key. There are common areas for relaxing and viewing the desert, and even accommodations in the Housekeeping Cottage next door for families with small children. Located conveniently between Highways 14 and 395, the Cottage Hotel Bed & Breakfast is also listed in the Auto Club (AAA) tour book for California and Nevada, and the *Bed & Breakfast Guide Gateway To Death Valley*. According to innkeeper Brenda Ingram, Randsburg is called "The Living Ghost Town," but she assures us that all the ghosts are very friendly!

## 141 RED BLUFF

**Antiques N Things**
339 Ash St.
916/527-7098

**Great American Antiques**
613 Main St.
916/529-4340

**Stelle's Main St. Antiques**
623 Main St.
916/529-2238

**Kramer's Antiques**
644 Main St.
916/527-1701

**Hunt House Antiques**
718 Main St.
916/527-6104

**Kelco Antiques & Collectibles**
1445 Vista Way
916/529-3245

**Washington St. Antiques**
610 Washington St.
916/528-1701

## 142 RED MOUNTAIN

**Old Owl Inn Cottages a Bed & Breakfast**
**Cottontail Antiques, Collectibles & Gifts**
701 Hwy. 395
760/374-2235 or 1-888-653-6954 (toll free)
Antique shop open daily except Wed. from 10-5
Bed and Breakfast open daily
*Directions: 25 miles north of intersections Hwy. 395 and 58. Twenty miles south of Ridgecrest.*

For specific information see review at the beginning of this section.

## 143 REDDING/SHASTA LAKE CITY

**Absolutely Wonderful Antiques**
2948 Cascade Blvd.
916/275-4046

**Barabara's Antiques**
3266 Cascade Blvd.
916/275-6879

**Antiques & Accents**
3266 Cascade Blvd., #12
916/275-2619

**Hollibaugh Antiques**
3266 Cascade Blvd.
916/275-2990

**I-5 Antique Mall**
3270A Cascade Blvd.
916/275-6990

## 144 REDLANDS/YUCAIPA

### Ila's Antiques and Collectibles
215 East Redlands Blvd.
(located in the Packing House Mall, in "The Cellar")
909/793-8898
Mon.-Sun., 11-5:30
*Directions: Traveling I-10, exit at Orange St. and go south 3 blocks, turn left to 7th and Redlands Blvd.*

Ila's Antiques is located in "The Cellar" of the old Banner Packing House. In the early days of the 1900s, this historic building housed a citrus packing company which shipped sweet California oranges to markets all across the U.S.

To get to Ila's, you must first pass through the Packing House Mall (a separate business) which houses 80 dealers offering a wide variety of antiques and collectibles. Once inside, take the stairs to "the cellar," where you'll discover 3,000 square feet of the finest antiques in the area. This shop undoubtedly has one of the largest costume jewelry collections in the U.S. - over 5,000 pieces! In addition, you'll find silver, crystal, Czechoslovakian glass, china, antique dolls and some select furniture pieces.

**Laurel Jones China**
409 N. Orange
909/793-8611

**Emma's Trunk**
1701 Orange Tree Lane
909/798-7865

**Carriage Barn Antiques**
31181 Outer Hwy. 10 S.
909/794-3919

**Antique Exchange Mall**
31251 Outer Hwy. 10
909/794-9190

**Sandlin's Antiques**
31491 Outer Hwy. 10
909/794-4311

**Marion Side Door Antiques**
31567 Outer Hwy. 10
909/794-1320

**Fiddler's Cove**
31567 Outer Hwy. 10, #1
909/794-6102

**Cripe's Antiques**
31583 Outer Hwy. 10 S.
909/794-5355

**Raney's Freeway Antiques**
31597 Outer Hwy. 10
909/794-4851

**Out Back Antiques**
31599 Outer Hwy. 10
909/794-0530

**Antique Gallery**
31629 Outer Hwy. 10, Unit E
909/794-0244

**Ellen's Antiques**
31629 Outer Hwy. 10, Unit F
909/794-9340

**Cathy's Cottage Antiques**
31843 Outer Hwy. 10
909/389-9436

**Keepsake Antique Mall**
31933 Outer Hwy. 10
909/794-1076

**Last Stop Antique Shop**
32019 Outer Hwy. 10 S.
909/795-5612

**The Packing House**
215 E. Redlands Blvd.
909/792-9021

**Precious Times Antiques**
1740 W. Redlands Blvd.
909/792-7768

**Eclectic Art Gallery**
516 Texas St.
909/793-7016

**Paul Melzer Rare Books**
12 E. Vine St.
909/792-7299

**Gatherings**
330-a N. Third St.
909/792-1216

**The Blues**
114 E. State St.
909/798-8055

**C. B. Antiques**
316 E. Citrus Ave.
909/792-0017

**Antique Arcade**
31159 Outer Hwy. 10 S.
909/794-5919

**Vintage Clothing & Books**
31629 Outer Hwy. 10, B
909/794-1785

**Chandlers Cove**
Brookside Plaza – 1512 Barton Road
909/307-0622

**Olde Hollow Treet**
38480 Oak Glen Road
909/797-5032

**Memory Lane Antiques**
31773 Outer Hwy. 10 S.
909/794-3514

**Antiques Unlimited**
31567 Outer Hwy. 10 S.
909/794-4066

**Anne's Yesteryear's**
31663 Outer Hwy. 10 S.
909/795-5446

## 145 REDONDO BEACH

**Patina**
1815 1/2 S. Catalina Ave.
310/373-5587

**Antique Corral**
145 S. Pacific Coast Hwy.
310/374-0007

**Le Grange Country Furniture**
719 S. Pacific Coast Hwy.
310/540-7535

**Vicki's Antiques & Collectibles**
1221 S. Pacific Coast Hwy.
310/540-6363

**Antique Doll Closet**
1303 S. Pacific Coast Hwy.
310/540-8212

## 146 REDWOOD CITY

**Athena Antiques Inc.**
926 Broadway St.
415/363-0282

**Palace Market Antiques**
825 Main St.
415/364-4645

**Finders Keepers Antiques**
837 Main St.
415/365-1750

**Redwood Cafe & Spice Co.**
1020 Main St.
415/364-1288

**Eclectric Antiques**
1101 Main St.
415/364-1549

## 147 RIVERSIDE

### Abbey's Antiques
3671 Main St.
909/788-9725
Mon.-Sat.10-5:30, Sun. by chance.

Offering 2,000 square feet of fine antiques, vintage clothing, linens, jewelry, silver and more.

**Mission Antiques**
4308 Lime St.
909/684-5639

**Katy's Collectibles**
6062 Magnolia Ave.
909/369-9030

**Amazing Grace Antiques**
3541 Main St.
909/788-9729

**Darlene Nemer**
3596 Main St.
909/684-9010

**Seventh Heaven Antiques**
3605 Market St.
909/784-6528

**Beasley's Antiques**
3757 Mission Inn Ave.
909/682-8127

**The Gas Pump**
9637 Magnolia
909/689-7113

**Mr. Beasley's Auction**
3878 6th St.
909/682-4279

**Cinnamon Lane Antique Mall**
6056 Magnolia Ave.
909/781-6625

**Karen's Antiques**
9631 Magnolia Ave.
909/358-0304

**R R Antiques**
3583 Market St.
909/781-6350

**Mrs. Darling**
4267 Main St.
909/682-0425

**Petey's Place**
4212 Market St.
909/686-4520

**Crystal's Antique Mall**
4205 Main St.
909/781-9922

**Victorian Rose Antique Mall**
3784 Elizabeth St.
909/788-5510

## 148 ROSEVILLE

**Roseville Antique Mall**
106 Judah St.
916/773-4003

**Terri Andrus' Treasures**
1304 Buttercup Court – Section D #5
916/782-6158

**Pepper Tree**
223 Vernon St.
916/783-1979

**Home Passage Antiques**
229 Vernon St.
916/782-5111

**Antique Trove**
238 Vernon St.
916/786-2777

**Julie's Antique Mall**
625 Vernon St.
916/783-3006

**Around Again Antiques**
342 Lincoln St.
916/783-8542

**Tin Soldiers**
222 Vernon St.
916/786-6604

**Antique Store**
226 Vernon St.
916/774-0660

**Velvet Purse Antiques**
230 Vernon St.
916/784-3432

**This N That**
243 Vernon St.
916/786-7784

**Memories Past Antiques**
801 Vernon St.
916/786-2606

## 149 SACRAMENTO

### Historic Old Sacramento

The Old Sacramento historic area, a registered national landmark and state historic park, is a 28-acre site on the banks of the Sacramento River. It is a vital historic, business, residential, shopping, and dining district with a fascinating past and the greatest concentration of historic buildings in California.

John Sutter arrived in 1839 and founded the first permanent settlement in the area. After the gold discovery in 1848, businesses sprang up along the riverfront in what is now Old Sacramento. There were hotels, saloons, bathhouses, the first theatre in California, and a variety of shops where would-be miners could outfit themselves for the gold fields.

Transportation has always figured prominently in Sacramento's history. The city was the western terminus of the short-lived Pony Express and the transcontinental railroad. Today, Old Sacramento is home to the largest interpretive railroad museum in North America-the California State Railroad Museum. The 100,000-square-foot museum displays 21 meticulously restored locomotives and cars, and over 40 one-of-a-kind exhibits tell the fascinating story of railroad history from 1850 to the present. Historic equipment and exhibits on the transcontinental railroad and 19th century rail travel are housed in the reconstructed 1876 Central Pacific Railroad Passenger Station.

About one mile from the California State Railroad Museum, just on the edge of Old Sacramento, is another spectacular facility dedicated to transportation-the Towe Ford Museum. The world's most complete antique Ford automobile collection includes every year and model produced by Ford between 1903 and 1953. There are more than 150 cars and trucks, with many in excellent original condition and others that have been beautifully and authentically restored. The collection also includes an array of original and restored cars from the late '50s, '60s, and '70s.

Other museums include the California Military Museum, the Discovery Museum and the Crocker Art Museum. Explore historic Old Sacramento with a self-guided "Walking Tour," which is available from the Visitor Information Center at 2nd and K streets. One hundred unique shops and 20 eclectic restaurants will satisfy even the most discerning visitor. Numerous special events take place here year-round including the Sacramento Jazz Jubilee, Festival de la Familia, Pacific Rim Festival and a couple of collectors' fairs.

### Haulbaurs Timeless Treasures

3207 Marysville Blvd.
916/924-1371
Mon.-Sat. 10-5:30
*Directions: Traveling business 80 from San Francisco to Sacramento, take the Marconi exit, head west. Marconi becomes Arcade, Arcade takes you to Marysville Blvd. Located near the corner of Arcade and Marysville Blvd.*

Haulbaurs Timeless Treasures has been in operation for four years. It is amazing how that many treasures can be up for grabs in 1,700 square feet of space. The shop is literally filled to the brim with some of the most unusual collectibles west of the Mississippi.

Do you collect antique fishing gear? They have it—lots of it! What about old telephones? Yes, they have those, too. Cookie jars, bird cages, books, musical instruments, tools? - yes, all there. European army collectibles, European beer steins - (you won't be bored). Oh, and did I mention German pencil sharpeners and German toys? - Got Em! It's one of those, "It's no telling what you'll find in here" kind of shops.

**Anna's Collectibles**
1905 Capitol Ave.
916/441-1310

**Antique's Etc.**
4749 Folsom Blvd.
916/739-1483

**Closet**
1107 Front St.
916/442-3446

**Lovell's Antique Mall**
2114 P St.
916/442-4640

**Slater Antiques & Collectibles**
609 N. 10th St.
916/442-6183

**Wee Jumble Shop**
1221 19th St.
916/447-5643

**Grandpa's Antiques**
1423 28th St.
916/456-4594

**Discovery Antiques**
855 57th St.
916/739-1757

**Gravy Boat Antiques**
855 57th St.
916/457-1205

**Elaine's Jewel Box**
866 57th St.
916/451-6059

**Sullivan's Antiques**
866 57th St.
916/457-9183

**57th Street Antique Mall**
875 57th St. (off H St.)
916/451-3110

**Old World Antiques**
6313 Elvas Ave.
916/456-9131

**Memory Lane**
1025 Front St.
916/488-0981

**River City Antique Mall**
10117 Mills Road
916/362-7778

**Bookmine**
1015 2nd St.
916/441-4609

**Antique Tresors Legacy**
1512 16th St.
916/446-6960

**Swanberg's Antiques & Collectibles**
2673 21st St.
916/456-5300

**Chez Antique**
855 57th St.
916/455-7504

**Windmill Antiques**
855 57th St.
916/454-1487

**Every Era Antiques**
855 57th St.
916/456-1767

**Bagwell's Antiques**
866 57th St.
916/455-3409

**Fifty-Seventh St. Antiques**
875 57th St.
916/451-3110

## *Great Places To Stay*

### Amber House
1315 22nd St.
Web site: www.amberhouse.com
1-800-755-6526

Just eight blocks from the state capitol, Amber House offers a quiet sanctuary for a romantic interlude or a special hideaway for the business traveler. Each room has its own special appeal. Seven rooms have jacuzzi bath tubs for two. Included in the rates is a full gourmet breakfast, served in the guests room, dining room or on the veranda.

### Hartley House B&B Inn
700 22nd St.
1-800-831-5806

Hartley House is a stunning turn-of-the century mansion, built in 1906 and surrounded by the majestic elm trees and stately homes of historic Boulevard Park in midtown Sacramento. Exquisitely appointed rooms are conveniently located near the State Capitol, Old Sacramento, the Sacramento Community Convention Center, and the city's finest restaurants, coffee cafes and dessert shops. They even have a cookie jar filled with freshly baked cookies!

### Inn at Parkside
2116 Sixth St.
Web site: www.innatparkside.com
1-800-995-7275

This stunning Mediterranean Revival grand mansion is furnished with museum quality antiques and stained glass throughout. Neoclassic art adorns walls and ceilings, with faux painting and original murals. A full gourmet breakfast is served in the dining room, garden or guestroom. There is a ballroom and garden area for small weddings, receptions, meetings or other special events. Inn at Parkside is the winner of the 1996 Sacramento Old City Association award for best commerical historic renovation and the 1997 award for best front entry.

### Riverboat Delta King Hotel
1000 Front St. (on the Sacramento River)
Old Sacramento
916/444-5464

This magnificently restored dockside paddlewheeler has been entertaining guests since 1927. Spend the night in one of 44 elegant staterooms on the shores of the Sacramento River.

If murder and suspense intrigue you, you will enjoy the Suspects Murder Mystery Dinner Theatre on the Delta King Friday and Saturday evenings. Match wits with a master detective searching for clues and interrogating guests. Look out, you may be a suspect yourself!

***Interesting Side Trips***

**Exploring Gold Country**

Sacramento was the original jumping off point for the goldminers, and today it's the perfect base for exploring the Gold Country, an area so rich in lore that you may easily find yourself transported back to that era. Remnants of this exciting time in California history are still visible all around. To reach the northern mines, take Interstate 80 east from Sacramento toward the town of Auburn, a quaint gem with great antique stores and a variety of restaurants. From here head north on Hwy. 49 to the Empire State Mine in Grass Valley. From Auburn you may also head south on Hwy. 49 to Coloma, the original gold discovery site in 1848. Continue south on 49 through Placerville and stop at one of the many El Dorado or Amador County wineries for a taste. On to Calaveras County and Angels Camp, home to the Jumping Frog Jubilee during the third week in May. Other well-preserved Gold Rush era towns include Murphys, San Andreas, Mokelumne Hills and Copperopolis. Don't miss Calaveras Big Trees State Park with its giant sequoias. Have you every tried spelunking? Moaning, California and Mercer Caverns are just the places for it. There're dozens of eclectic art galleries, quaint antique shops and excellent eateries all around the area. Take an hour to ride the train in the breathtaking foothills scenery at Railtown State Park near Jamestown, or pan for gold in a clear mountain stream. Sonora, Columbia State Park and Groveland are other draws for Gold Country visitors.

Heading south on Hwy. 49 stop in Coulterville, one of the best-preserved Gold Rush towns in the Sierra foothills. Enjoy boating and fishing at Lakes McClure and McSwain, and visit the oldest continuously operating courthouse west of the Rocky Mountains in the quaint town of Mariposa. At the end of a long day relax in the pine-covered community of Fish Camp located at the southern entrance to Yosemite National Park.

## 150 SALINAS

**Echo Valley Antiques**
849 Echo Valley Road
408/663-4305

**Bonanza Antiques**
467 El Camino Real
408/422-7621

**Lily's Odds & Ends**
10 W. Gakilan St.
408/757-4562

**Hall Tree Antique Mall**
202 Main St.
408/757-6918

**Generation Gap**
338 Monterey St.
408/751-6148

**Country Peddler Antiques**
347 Monterey St.
408/424-2292

## 151 SAN ANSELMO

**Greenfield Antiques**
8 Bank St.
415/454-4614

**C Fetherston Antiques**
10 Bank St.
415/453-6607

**Center Market**
Center Blvd. & Saunders
415/454-3127

**Antique Habit**
10 Greenfield Ave.
415/457-1241

**Oveda Maurer Antiques**
34 Greenfield Ave.
415/454-6439

**Antique World**
216 Greenfield Ave.
415/454-2203

**Roger Barber Asian Antiques**
114 Pine St.
415/457-6844

**Modern I Gallery**
500 Red Hill Ave.
415/456-3960

**Michael Good Fine & Rare Books**
35 San Anselmo Ave.
415/452-6092

**Shadows**
429 San Anselmo Ave.
415/459-0574

**Vintage Flamingo**
528 San Anselmo Ave.
415/721-7275

**Yanni's Antiques**
538 San Anselmo Ave.
415/459-2996

**Second Hand Land**
703 San Anselmo Ave.
415/454-5057

**Dove Place Antiques**
160 Sir Francis Drake Blvd.
415/453-1490

**Legacy Antiques**
204 Sir Francis Drake Blvd.
415/457-7166

**Sanford's Antiques**
2 Tunstead Ave.
415/454-4731

**Aurora Gallery**
306 Sir Francis Drake Blvd.
415/459-6822

**Kisetsu & The French Garden**
310 Sir Francis Drake Blvd.
415/456-9070

**San Anselmo Country Store**
312 Sir Francis Drake Blvd.
415/258-0922

**Collective Antiques**
316 Sir Francis Drake Blvd.
415/453-6373

**Pavillion Antiques**
610 Sir Francis Drake Blvd.
415/459-2002

## 152 SAN BERNARDINO

**Mueller's Vintage Collectibles**
363 S. Arrowhead Ave.
909/384-8110

**Treasure Mart Antiques.**
293 E. Redlands Blvd.
909/825-7264

**Old Fashion Shop West**
1927 N. E St.
909/882-5819

**The Heritage Gallery**
1520A S. E St.
909/888-3377

**A Touch of Class**
214 W. Highland Ave.
909/883-1495

**AEL Antique Mall**
24735 Redlands Blvd.
909/796-0380

## 153 SAN CARLOS

**Antiques Trove**
1119 Industrial Road
650/593-1300

**Antique Collage Collective**
654 Laurel St.
650/595-1776

**Felicity's Collectibles**
600 Laurel St.
650/593-9559

**Laurel Street Antiques**
671 Laurel St.
650/593-1152

## 154 SAN CLEMENTE

**Plum Precious Antiques**
101 Avenida Miramar
714/361-0162

**San Clemente Antiques**
214 Avenida Del Mar
714/498-2992

**Three Centuries Antique Gallery**
408 N. El Camino Real
714/492-6609

**Patrice Antiques**
1602 N. El Camino Real
714/498-3230

**Garden Antiques**
109 S. El Camino Real
714/492-8344

**Antiques & Collectibles**
159 Avenida Del Mar
714/369-7321

**Forgotten Dreams**
1062 Call Del Cerro Bldg. #1226
714/361-0054

**Stanford Court Antiques**
106 Avenida Del Mar
714/366-6290

**Zachery's Crossing**
307 N. El Camino Real
714/498-1148

**Pacific Trader**
1407 N. El Camino Real
714/366-3049

**Victoria's Antiques**
101 N. El Camino Real
714/366-6232

**Penny N' Sues**
218 Avenida Del Mar
714/492-6027

**Blue Moon Antiques**
111 W. Avenida Palizada, #10A
714/498-4907

## 155 SAN DIEGO

### Adams Avenue Antique Row and Park Blvd.

**Adams Ave Consign**
2873 Adams Ave.
619/281-9663

**Alouette Antiques**
2936 Adams Ave.
619/284-9408

**Mary's Finest Collectibles**
3027 Adams Ave.
619/280-6802

**Hunter's Antiques**
2602 Adams Ave.
619/295-1994

**Resurrected Furniture**
2814 Adams Ave.
619/283-3318

**Country Cousins**
2889 Adams Ave.
619/284-3039

**Antique Seller**
2938 Adams Ave.
619/283-8467

**Gledhill's Vintage Furniture**
2610 Adams Ave.
619/296-8272

**Refindery**
3463 Adams Ave.
619/563-0655

**Virtu Garden & Home Antiques**
4416 Park Blvd.
619/543-9150

**TMH Antiques & Art**
4615 Park Blvd.
619/291-1730

**What Mama Had**
4215 Park Blvd.
619/296-7277

**Rocky's Antiques, Books, Collectibles**
4608 Park Blvd.
619/297-1639

**Alessandria**
2606 Adams Ave.
619/296-4662

**Miscellanea**
4610 Park Blvd.
619/295-6488

### Downtown-Gas Lamp Area

**Palace Antiques**
363 5th Ave., #104
619/234-4004

**5th & J Antique Mall**
501 J St.
619/338-9559

**Empire Enterprises**
704 J St.
619/239-9216

**Third Floor Antiques**
448 W. Market (Cracker Factory)
619/238-7339

**Unicorn Antiques**
704 J St.
619/232-1696

**Second Floor Antique Mall**
448 W. Market (Cracker Factory)
619/236-9484

**Burton's Antiques**
448 W. Market (Cracker Factory)
619/236-9484

**LaRosa Family Antiques Center**
445 8th Ave.
619/234-1970

**Gaslamp Books, Prints & Antiques**
413 Market
619/237-1492

**Memories Antiques**
448 W. Market (Cracker Factory)
619/231-9133

**Bobbie's Paper Dolls**
448 W. Market (Cracker Factory)
619/233-0055

**Elite Antiques**
448 W. Market (Cracker Factory)
619/238-1038

**Lincoln Roberts Gallery**
411 Market
619/702-5884

**Legacy's Antiques**
448 W. Market (Cracker Factory)
619/232-7236

**Bert's Antiques**
448 W. Market (Cracker Factory)
619/239-5531

### Ocean Beach Antique District

**Vignettes-Antiques**
4828 Newport Ave.
619/222-9244

**Mallory & Sons Antiques**
4926 Newport Ave.
619/226-8658

**Newport Avenue Antiques**
4836 Newport Ave.
619/224-1994

**Ocean Beach Antique Mall**
4878 Newport Ave.
619/222-1967

**Newport Ave. Antique Center**
4864 Newport Ave.
619/222-8686

**Cottage Antiques**
4882 Newport Ave.
619/222-1967

**Antiques & Stuff by Ruth**
4051 Voltaire, Ste. B
619/222-2232

### Old Town Area

**Circa a.d.**
3867 4th Ave.
619/293-3328

**Antique Alley Mall**
1911 San Diego Ave.
619/688-1911

**Country Craftsman**
2465 Heritage Park Row
619/294-4600

### Hillcrest Area

**Papyrus Antiques & Unusual Shop**
116 W. Washington St.
619/298-9291

**Mission Gallery**
320 W. Washington St.
619/692-3566

**House of Heirlooms**
801 University Ave.
619/298-0502

**The Private Collector**
800 W. Washington St.
619/296-5553

### North Park District

**St. Vincent De Paul Center Shoppe**
3137 El Cajon Blvd.
619/624-9701

### El Cortes District

**Paper Antiquities**
1552 5th Ave.
619/239-0656

### Additonal shops in San Diego

**Beverlee's Antiques**
1062 Garnet Ave.
619/274-1933

**Lost Your Marbles Too**
3933 30th St.
619/291-3061

**Whooping Crane Antiques**
1617 W. Lewis St.
619/291-9232

**Antique Castings**
8333 LaMesa, Ste. B
619/466-8665

**English Garden**
4140 Morena Blvd. #B
619/456-1793

**T & R Antiques Warehouse**
4630 Santa Fe St.
619/272-2500

***Great Places To Stay***

### Carole's Bed and Breakfast
3227 Grim Ave.
619/280-5258

Built in 1904 by Mayor Fray, this historic site has the handsome style and craftsmanship of its time. It has been restored by the present owners who live on site giving it constant loving care. The decor is of its period, with antiques and comfort as the focus. There are five guest accommodations. Amenities include a black bottom pool, spa and a rose garden. Location is within walking distance to Balboa Park, and many small shops and restaurants.

### Heritage Park Inn
2470 Heritage Park Row
Email: innkeeper@heritageparkinn.com
1-800-995-2470

Unique lodging for discriminating travelers...far from ordinary...yet central to everything. Nestled in a quiet Victorian park, lined with cobblestone walkways in the heart of historic Old Town. This award winning Queen Anne mansion is only minutes from the San Diego Zoo, shops, beaches and restaurants. Twelve guest accommodations.

## 156 SAN DIMAS

**Just Us Antiques**
120 W. Bonita Ave.
909/599-0568

**Old Towne Antique Mall**
125 W. Bonita Ave.
909/394-1836

**Jabberwocky Antiques**
138 W. Bonita Ave., #101A
909/394-0084

**Heart of the Village Antique**
155 W. Bonita Ave.
909/394-0628

**Annie's Antiques & Collectibles**
161 W. Bonita Ave.
909/592-2616

**Two Eager Beavers Antiques**
165 W. Bonita Ave.
909/592-3087

**Frontier Village Antiques**
115 N. Monte Vista Ave.
909/394-0628

## 157 SAN FRANCISCO

**Clyde & Eva's Antique Shop**
3942 Balboa St.
415/387-3902

**Antique Traders**
4300 California St.
415/668-4444

**Browsers Nook**
530 Castro St.
415/861-2216

**Brand X Antiques**
570 Castro St.
415/626-8908

**Lovejoy's Antiques & Tea Room**
1195 Church St.
415/648-5895

**Schlep Sisters**
4327 18th St.
415/626-0581

**Grand Central Station Antiques**
595 Castro St.
415/863-3604

**Homes of Charm**
1544 Church St.
415/647-4586

**Alley Cat Jewels**
1547 Church St.
415/285-3668

**Old Stuff**
2325 Clement St.
415/668-2220

**Garden Spot**
3029 Clement St.
415/751-8190

**Mureta's Antiques**
2418 Fillmore St.
415/922-5652

**Other Shop**
112 Gough St.
415/621-1590

**Deco to 50's**
149 Gough St.
415/553-4500

**Decodence**
149 Gough St.
415/553-4500

**Vintage Modern**
182 Gough St.
415/861-8162

**J C's Collectables**
564 Hayes St.
415/558-6904

**Jekyll's On Hyde**
1044 Hyde St.
415/775-3502

**Thomas Livingston Antiques**
414 Jackson St.
415/296-8150

**Lotus Collection**
434 Jackson St.
415/398-8115

**Dora Mauri Antichita**
455 Jackson St.
415/296-8500

**Challiss House**
463 Jackson St.
415/397-6999

**Sen's Antiques Inc.**
200 Kansas St.
415/487-3888

**D Carnegie Antiques**
601 Kansas St.
415/641-4704

**North Beach Antiques & Collectibles**
734 Lombard St.
415/346-2448

**Browsers Nook**
1592 Market St.
415/861-3801

**Isak Kindenauer Antiques**
4143 19th St.
415/552-6436

**Four Corners Antiques**
90 Parnassus Ave.
415/753-6111

**Russian Hill Antiques**
2200 Polk St.
415/441-5561

**Lupardo**
3232 Sacremento St.
415/928-8662

**Modern Era Decor**
149 Gough St.
415/431-8599

**Henry's Antiques & Art Gallery**
319 Grant Ave.
415/291-0319

**Foster-Gwin Antiques**
38 Hotaling Place
415/397-4986

**Hyde & Seek Antiques**
1913 Hyde St.
415/776-8865

**Louis D Fenton Antiques**
432 Jackson St.
415/398-3046

**Edward Marshall Antiques**
441 Jackson St.
415/399-0980

**Daniel Stein Antiques**
458 Jackson St.
415/956-5620

**Hunt Antiques**
478 Jackson St.
415/989-9531

**Antiques Antiques**
245 Kansas St.
415/252-7600

**Willmann Country Pine**
650 King St.
415/626-6547

**Golden Gate Antiques**
1564 Market St.
415/626-3377

**Grand Central Station Antiques**
1632 Market St., #A
415/252-8155

**In My Dreams**
1300 Pacific Ave.
415/885-6696

**La Belle Antiques**
2035 Polk St.
415/673-1181

**Alexander Collections**
309 W. Portal Ave.
415/661-5454

**Woodchuck Antiques**
3597 Sacramento St.
415/922-6416

**Every Era Antiques**
3599 Sacramento St.
415/346-0313

**Sixth Ave. Antiques**
189 6th Ave.
415/386-2500

**Biscuit Jar Antiques**
2134 Taraval St.
415/665-4520

**Tampico**
2147 Union St.
415/563-3785

**Upstairs/Downstairs**
890 Valencia St.
415/647-4211

**San Francisco Antique Design Mall**
701 Bayshore Blvd.
415/656-3530

**Harvey Antiques**
700 7th St., 2nd Floor
415/431-8888

**Quality First**
608 Taraval St.
415/665-6442

**Telegraph Hill Antiques**
580 Union St.
415/982-7055

**Collective Antiques**
212 Utah St.
415/621-3800

**Decorum**
1400 Vallejo St.
415/474-6886

### *Great Places To Stay*

**A Country Cottage**
#5 Dolores Terrace
415/479-1913

A cozy country style bed and breakfast in the heart of San Francisco. The four guest rooms are comfortably furnished in country antiques and brass beds. The house is located at the end of a quiet street away from the city noise.

**Archbishops Mansion**
1000 Fulton St.
1-800-543-5820

The Archbishop's Mansion, which opened as a bed and breakfast in 1982, was built in 1904 as the residence for the Catholic Archbishop of San Francisco. It is a beautifully restored 'Belle poque' mansion that is furnished throughout with European antiques. Each individually decorated guestroom has a private bath and many have a working fireplace. There are two romantic rooms with double jacuzzi tubs and five spacious suites. Guests enjoy a generous continental breakfast.

**Bock's Bed and Breakfast**
1448 Willard St.
415/664-6842

Opened in 1980 as a bed and breakfast, this lovely 1906 restored Edwardian residence is the family home of your host and her Scottish Terrier, Rosie. Two blocks from the Golden Gate Park and an easy walk to shops and restaurants.

**Subtleties: Carol's Cow Hollow Inn**
2821 Steiner St.
Web site: www.subtleties.com
1-800-400-8295

The former President of ABC wrote: "Without a doubt, this is the best B&B we have ever stayed in, and there have been many. Lots of space, good beds, great food, wonderful advise and computer printouts for visiting the city, and the cheerful, smiling and generous faces of Carol and Sacha. We are recommending it to all our friends."

Located in the heart of Pacific Heights/Cow Hollow, Carol's Cow Hollow Inn is within walking distance from delightful Union Street Victorian architecture, sidewalk cafes, fun boutiques, and delicious, inexpensive restaurants that locals prefer. Fisherman's Wharf, Chinatown, cable cars, and Golden Gate Park are easy to get to and you don't need a car. Each of the three rooms is spacious, decorated with original oil paintings and views of the bay make for a memorable stay.

**The Garden Studio**
1387 6th Ave.
415/753-3574

Tired of tourist hotels? Want to mingle with the natives and be minutes from all the famous San Francisco sights? Then we have the place for you. A quiet studio apartment opening onto your own private garden. The Inner Sunset is a safe, urban neighborhood filled with excellent restaurants. Two blocks from Golden Gate Park (the Arboretum and Aquarium), and twenty minutes to Chinatown, cable cars, Fisherman's Wharf, etc.

**The Spencer House**
1080 Haight St.
415/626-9205

The Spencer House is a splendid Queen Anne Victorian mansion built in 1887 that evokes the luxurious, classic mood of a fine European house. Its original graciousness meticulously restored, the home brims with European and Oriental antiques and fabrics, draperies and linens. There are six guest rooms, each with private bath, in this 8,000 square foot private home. Guests are offered feather beds and down duvets in an atmosphere enriched by oriental rugs and exquisite antiques.

**The Willows B&B Inn**
710 14th St.
415/431-4770

The Willows Inn is located within the Gay and Lesbian Castro neighborhood. The rustic country decor is a beautiful combination of handcrafted bentwood willow furnishings, antique dressers and armoires, plantation shutters, cozy comforters, and plants. Kimono bathrobes are provided along with fine English soaps and shampoo. A continental plus breakfast is served in bed with the morning newspaper and an evening port and chocolate bed turndown service is available. Twelve guest rooms are available.

**Victorian Inn On The Park**
301 Lyon St.
1-800-435-1967

Lisa and William Benau have been the innkeepers at this "truly" family owned business since it opened in 1981. Both Lisa and Willie love food and wine and know all the best restaurants and local food hangouts. They collect wine and cook as well so they can lead you to the best wine stores and specialty food shops. Willie is also a true sports fan and knows all the local sports arenas and game schedules. Everything from bookstores, clothing shops, antique shops to theater and nightclubs are interests of the Innkeepers. Lisa's mom, Shirley Weber, is responsible for most of the decorating and remodeling at the Inn. Lisa and Willie's two children, Cassandra and Zachary, often help guests as well. Many Saturday and Sunday mornings they are assisting in serving breakfast.

## 158 SAN JACINTO

**Country Heritage Antiques**
2385 S. San Jacinto Ave.
909/658-8468

**Corner Antiques**
2525 S. San Jacinto Ave.
909/925-1799

**Ann's Attic**
2547 S. San Jacinto Ave.
909/925-0272

**Yellow House Antiques**
410 E. Main St.
909/487-7879

## 159 SAN JOSE

**Time Tunnel Vintage Toys**
532 S. Bascom Ave.
408/298-1709

**William B. Huff Antiques**
999 Lincoln Ave.
408/287-8820

**Past & Presents**
1324 Lincoln Ave.
408/297-1822

**Willow Glen Collective**
1349 Lincoln Ave.
408/947-7222

**Gold Street Antiques**
2092 Lincoln Ave.
408/266-9999

**Ancora Ancora**
751 W. San Carlos St.
408/977-1429

**Antique Village**
1225 W. San Carlos St.
408/292-2667

**San Carlos St. Antiques**
1401 W. San Carlos St.
408/293-8105

**Laurelwood Antiques & Collectibles**
1824 W. San Carlos St.
408/287-1863

**Briarwood Antiques & Collectibles**
1885 W. San Carlos St.
408/292-1720

**Annette's Antiques**
1887 W. San Carlos St.
408/289-1929

**Antique Colony**
1915 W. San Carlos St.
408/293-9844

**Antique Dreams**
1916 W. San Carlos St.
408/998-2339

**Antique Memories & Collectibles**
2314 Steven Creek Blvd.
408/977-1758

**Antique Decor/A Treasure of Joy**
1957 W. San Carlos St.
408/298-5814

**Rosewood Antiques**
1897 W. San Carlos St.
408/292-1296

### *Interesting Side Trips*

**The Winchester Mystery House**
525 S. Winchester Blvd.
408/247-2000

Was widowed heiress, Sarah Winchester, a few bricks shy of a full load, believing she'd ward off the spirits of hostile Indians and others by the continuous thirty-eight-year construction of what eventually became her 160-room, $5.5 million mansion? Or was she merely a frustrated architectural genius, the first to discern the value of many late nineteenth-century innovations, who, rather than using a blueprint, sketched as the "spirits" moved her? Her home was among the first in the country to have elevators, wool insulation, gas lights and stove, an "annunciator" intercom with which she could page her many servants from anywhere in the house, and built-in scrub boards and soap holders, which she patented.

This is the puzzle posed to visitors of the Winchester Mystery House in San Jose, California, which was built and rebuilt from 1884 until practically the moment after Sarah Winchester's death in 1922. At 24,000 square feet, it has 10,000 windows, 2,000 doors, 52 skylights, 47 fireplaces (one of which is hand carved), 40 staircases and bedrooms, 13 bathrooms, six kitchens, three elevators, two basements, and one shower.

Only the best was used, and this Victorian home boasts parquet floors with multifaceted inlaid patterns of precious hardwoods; gold and silver chandeliers; exquisite art glass windows, and doors with hinges and designs of silver, bronze, and gold. Storerooms still contain tens of thousands of dollars worth of Tiffany doors and windows, as well as precious silks, satins, linens, and other fabrics. a glass-lined conservatory not only guaranteed sunlight but also had a metal sub-flooring that could be drained to the garden below whenever the servants watered the plants. An accoustically balanced ballroom that cost the then-outrageous sum of $9000 was put together using carpenter's glue and wooden pegs, with tiny nails used only in moldings and floorings.

But the mansion, which rambles over nearly six acres and is four stories (down from seven before the San Francisco earthquake), brims with oddities. Stairways lead to ceilings, and doors open into walls. Pillars on fireplaces are installed upside down, ostensibly to confuse evil spirits. One $1500 Tiffany window will never see the light of day because it's blocked off by a wall. Skylights shoot up from the floor, and a five-foot door, just right for the diminutive (four feet, ten inches, one hundred pounds) Sarah, stands next to a normal-sized one that leads nowhere. One cabinet opens up to one-half inch of storage space, while the closet across from it reveals the back thirty rooms of the home.

The number thirteen abounds. Several rooms have thirteen panels with the same number of windows, which, in turn, have "guess how many" panes. a baker's dozen can be found in the lights in the chandeliers, in the cupolas in the greenhouse, and in the palms that line the front driveway. Sarah's last will and testament consisted of thirteen parts and was signed thirteen times, and legend has it that when she dined, it was on a gold service set for herself and twelve invisible guests. To further encourage ghost busting, the house had only two mirrors.

In order to better understand the house, one needs to delve into the enigma that was Sarah Pardee Winchester. Born in 1839, in New Haven, Connecticut, she married William Winchester in 1862. He was the son of Oliver Winchester, inventor and manufacturer of the repeating rifle that allegedly won the West. According to several accounts, Sarah was an attractive, cultured musician who spoke four languages.

But her life was far from normal. Her only daughter, Anna, died in infancy, and a few years later in 1881 her husband succumbed to pulmonary tuberculosis. "Sarah had never fully recovered from the first loss, so this further intensified her anguish," states Shozo Kagoshima, director of marketing for the museum. Sarah was now incredibly wealthy, thanks to the invention that had the dubious honor of having killed more game, Indians, and U.S. soldiers than any other weapon in American history. She inherited $20 million and nearly 50 percent of the stock in the Winchester company, the latter of which gave her a tax-free (until 1913) stipend of about $1000 a day. So money was no object.

To ease her grief, Sarah went to a "seer" in Boston, who told her that "the spirits of all those the Winchester rifles had killed sought their revenge by taking the lives of her loved ones," relates Kagoshima. "Furthermore, they'd placed a curse on her and would haunt her forever." But Sarah could construct her own escape hatch, the medium said, by "moving West, buying a house, and continually building on it as the spirits directed." That way, she could escape the hostile ones (particularly Indians), while providing a comfortable respite for friendly ghosts (including perhaps Casper), and possibly guaranteeing eternal life.

So Sarah traveled to San Jose and plunked down nearly $13,000 in gold coins to buy an eight-room farmhouse from a Dr. Caldwell. Thus an exquisite behemoth was born.

Renovated in 1973, the rambling structure has 110 rooms open to the public, about 20 more than were in use when Sarah was alive. "The rest were damaged by the 1906 earthquake or are offices," explains Kagoshima. Other than normal restoration to maintain the status quo "the house is to remain the same as when she died."

"Sarah was an eccentric, although she had many good ideas about building and modern conveniences," sums up Kagoshima. The Winchester Mystery House may never be solved, but it—and everyone connected with it—has had a long, strange trip.

## 160 SAN JUAN BAUTISTA

**Lillian Johnson Antiques**
405 3rd St.
408/623-4381

**Gerrie's Collectibles Etc.**
406 3rd St.
408/623-1017

**Golden Wheel Antiques**
407 3rd St.
408/623-4767

## 161 SAN JUAN CAPISTRANO

### Old Mission San Juan Capistrano

There is one historic place in Southern California where visitors gather, only to return again and again. It is the famous old Spanish Mission at San Juan Capistrano, the quaint little town located above the shores of the Pacific, halfway between San Diego and Los Angeles along the old Camino Real.

Mission San Juan Capistrano is beautiful, old and romantic. You can hear the tolling of its centuries old bells and walk down its time worn paths. Its serenity and peace amid lush gardens and cool fountains, cloistered by old adobe walls, offers visitors seclusion from the sounds and sights of a busy world.

Founded over two centuries ago, the Mission is a monument to California's multi-cultural history, embracing its Spanish, Mexican, Native American and European heritage. Originally built as a self-sufficient community by Spanish padres and Indian laborers, the Mission was a center for agriculture, industry and education. The spiritual and cultural heritage of the Mission is owed to the legendary Fr. Junipero Serra, who founded over eight missions in California and earned heroic stature as the "Father of California", becoming its first citizen in July of 1769.

Today, you'll discover many areas of interest within the Mission walls, including the museum, founding documents, early soldiers barracks, friars quarters, an olive millstone, cemetery, and an aqueduct system. Then, continue with a walk through the renowned gardens to the majestic ruins of the great Stone Church, and along the path to beautiful little Serra Chapel, oldest building in California.

You can see the little adobe church, "Father Serra's Chapel", the oldest building still in use in California. Constructed in 1777, it houses a magnificent Baroque altar which is over 350 years old. The famous "Golden Altar" was shipped from Spain to California in 10 large crates containing 396 pieces. Originally intended for use in the Los Angeles Cathedral, the altar piece was given to the Mission in 1922. Crafted of Spanish cherry wood covered with gold leaf, the 22 feet high and 18 feet wide golden altar features 52 carved angels who watch over visitors today.

The setting is very spiritual. Light falls on it from a long narrow window above. Viewed through the hundred foot nave which is usually in semi-darkness, the shimming golden sight is one not easily forgotten.

There are many romantic legends about the Mission. The most popular are about the swallows of Capistrano. Swallow's Day is celebrated annually on March 19. Visitors from all over the world come to witness the return of the swallows to Capistrano. Legend says the swallows, seeking sanctuary from an innkeeper who destroyed their nests, took up residence at the old Mission. They return to the site each year to nest, knowing their young can be safe within the Mission walls.

You'll also learn about the legend of Magdalena, whose penance was to walk up and down the church aisle with a lighted candle to atone for disobeying her father, who had forbidden her from courting a man beneath her station in life. On her first day of penance, December 8, 1812, an earthquake destroyed the great Stone Church and buried her in the ruins. It is said that on certain nights in December her candlelight can still be seen shining out of the church ruins.

**General Information:** The Mission is open from 8:30 a.m. to 5:00 p.m. daily except on Thanksgiving, Christmas and Good Friday afternoon. Admission is $5 for adults and $4 for seniors and children. Members free. There is usually no extra charge for exhibitions or special events.

**Location:** The Mission is conveniently located one block from the Ortega exit off the 5 Freeway, at the corner of Camino Capistrano and Ortega Hwy.

**Visitors Center:** To book a guided tour or arrange a special event, call 714/248-2049. To write for information, please send inquiry to P.O. Box 697, San Juan Capistrano, CA 92693.

**Yesterday's Paper**
31815 Camino Capistrano, Suite C11
714/248-0945
Open daily 11-5 (7 days a week)
*Directions: From the I-5 exit (Ortega Hwy. 74) to west 2 blocks to Camino Capistrano St., turn left, shop is on right. Located in the Historic District.*

Yesterday's Paper provides over 25 years of experience and an extensive inventory in providing everything old made of paper to their customers. Whether for the collector, for the historian, or for the customer who wants a piece of nostalgia from their childhood; a tour through their 3 large rooms of wall and case displays plus neatly organized inventory bins allows you to find items quickly and easily.

The shop offers additions for your collection or decorating needs whether it's books, magazines, illustrations, maps, movie material, posters, documents, postcards, advertising cards, calendars, menus, photos, comics, sheet music, catalogs, labels, railroad paper, aviation paper, sports paper, stock certificates, checks, valentines, pin-ups and more.

Mail service is available both for in-store, call-in, or mail order customers as well.

**Majorca of San Juan**
31815 Camino Capistrano
714/496-7465

**Old Barn Mall**
31792 Camino Capistrano
714/493-9144

**Just Perfect Antiques**
31815 Camino Capistrano
714/240-8821

**Decorative Arts Villa**
31431 Camino Capistrano
714/488-9600

**Gifts For The Home International**
31681 Camino Capistrano
714/443-3913

**Grand Avenue Antiques**
33208 B Paseo Cerveza
714/661-1053

**Sentimental Journey West**
31843 Camino Capistrano
714/661-4560

**Durenberger & Friends**
31531 Camino Capistrano
714/240-5181

**Encore Antiques**
31815 Camino Capistrano
714/661-3483

**Curiosity Antiques**
31107 Rancho Viejo Road, #B2
714/240-1553

**Studio Five Design**
31511 Camino Capistrano
714/240-1474

**Ye Old Collector Shop**
31815 Camino Capistrano
714/496-6724

**Wild Goose Chase**
31521 Camino Capistrano, #A
714/487-2720

### *Favorite Places To Eat*

**Capistrano Depot**
26701 Verdugo St.-Amtrak Station
714/488-7600

**L'Hirondelle French Cuisine**
31661 Camino Capistrano-Mission Hacienda
714/661-0425

**Ramos House Cafe**
31752 Los Rios St.-Historic District
714/443-1342

**Sidewalk Cafe**
31882 Del Obispo-Plaza Del Obispo
714/443-0423

## 162 SAN LUIS OBISPO

**Treasure Island Antiques**
645 Higuera St
805/543-0532

**Showroom**
1531 Monterey St.
805/546-8266

### *Great Places To Stay*

**Apple Farm Inn**
2015 Monterey St.
1-800-255-2040

The comforts of a first-rate hotel and atmosphere of a turn-of-the-century bed and breakfast, blend to create the charming Apple Farm Inn. On a creekside setting surrounded by shady Sycamores and beautiful gardens, this country-Victorian inn is an elegant peaceful retreat. Rich decor, distinctive beds and a fireplace that conveys warmth and hospitality, give each room its own identity. Accomodates sixty-nine guest.

**Heritage Inn B&B**
978 Olive Street
805/544-7440

Heritage Inn is located at the crossroads of Hwy. 101 and Hwy. 1, midway between Los Angeles and San Francisco. This gorgeous turn-of-the-century Victorian home is within walking distance of quaint downtown and San Luis Obispo Mission. Just minutes from beautiful beaches for sunbathing and sport fishing, natural hot springs, horseback riding and of course, the famous Hearst Castle. Hiking, picnicing and very popular winery tours are a wonderful way to enjoy the wild flowered countryside. Each room has its own special touch, a cozy fireplace, old fashioned window seat, or a walk-out terrace with views of the mountain and creek. Peaceful creekside gardens abound with playful kitties and guests are often delighted to find ducks and deer sharing this natural area.

## 163 SAN MARCOS

**San Marcos Antique Village**
983 Grand Ave.
760/744-8718

**Burdock Victorian Lamp Co.**
757 N. Twin Oaks Valley Road #5
760/591-3911

**Vicki Harman, Antiques-Estates**
1440 Grand Ave.
760/591-4746

## 164 SAN MATEO

**Hoosier-Town Antiques**
726 S. Amphlett Blvd.
650/343-3673

**Camelot Antiques & Art**
714 S. B St.
650/343-7663

**Ellsworth Place Antiques**
115 S. Ellsworth Ave.
650/347-5906

**B Street Collective**
710 S. B St.
650/342-0993

**Come C Interiors**
807 S. B St.
650/344-5899

**Canterbury Antiques**
1705 Gum St.
650/570-7010

**Shawn's**
2218 Palm Ave.
650/574-2097

**Come C Antiques**
159 South Blvd.
650/344-5899

**Memory House Antiques**
74 E. 3rd Ave.
650/344-5600

**Albert's Antiques**
310 S. San Mateo Ave.
650/348-2369

**Look What I Found**
168 South Blvd.
650/573-7113

## 165 SAN PEDRO

**South Bay Antiques**
100 W. 1st St.
310/833-2578

## 166 SAN RAFAEL

**English Country Pine & Design**
2066 4th St.
415/485-3800

**Collier Lighting**
3100 Kerner Blvd.
415/454-6672

**Bargain Box Sunny Hills**
508 Irwin St.
415/459-2396

**Twenty Ross Common**
20 Ross St.
415/925-1482

## 167 SANTA ANA

**Steven-Thomas Antiques**
800 E. Dyer Rd.
714/957-6017

**Charles Wallace Antiques Inc.**
2929 S. Harbor Blvd.
714/556-9901

**Lyman Drake Antiques**
2901 S. Harbor Blvd.
714/979-2811

**Second Season**
2380 N. Tustin
714/835-0180

## 168 SANTA BARBARA

**Collector's Corner**
701 Anacapa St.
805/965-8915

**Awalk In The Woods**
15 E. Anapamu St.
805/966-1331

**Elders**
512 Brinkerhoff Ave.
805/962-0933

**Mary's On The Avenue**
529 Brinkerhoff Ave.
805/962-8047

**Corner Cottage**
536 Brinkerhoff Ave.
805/962-7010

**Main Antiques**
39 E. DeLa Guerra St.
805/962-7710

**Adobe Antiques**
707 Anacapa St.
805/966-2556

**Peregrine Galleries**
508 Brinkerhoff Ave.
805/963-3134

**Hightower & Russell**
528 Brinkerhoff Ave.
805/965-5687

**Robert Livernois Art**
533 Brinkerhoff Ave.
805/962-4247

**Peregrin**
1133 Coast Village Road
805/969-9671

**Moriarty's Lamps**
305 E. Haley St.
805/966-1124

**Mackey Anqs/Pine Trader**
410 E. Haley St.
805/962-0250

**Mingei**
736 State St.
805/963-3257

**Amphora Arts & Antiques**
1321 State St.
805/899-2122

**State St Antique Mall**
710 State St.
805/965-2575

**Indigo**
1323 State St.
805/962-6909

### *Great Places To Stay*

**Casa Del Mar Inn**
18 Bath St.
1-800-433-3097

A unique Mediterranean-style family inn with lush gardens year round, located one-half block from the beach. Walk to excellent shopping, fine restaurants, and all beach activities. A variety of room types offer accommodation options ranging from one or two-room bungalow-style family suites with full kitchens and fireplaces to cozy rooms with one king or queen size bed. All rooms feature private entrance and private bath. Amenities include a garden courtyard spa and sun deck.

**Cheshire Cat Inn**
36 W. Valerio St.
Web site: www.cheshire@chesirecat.com
805/569-1610

A 17-room inn, the Cheshire Cat comprises of two-100 year old Queen Ann side-by-side Victorians, three cottages and a coach house, surrounded by romantic flower gardens, a spa filled gazebo, brick patios, decks with private sitting areas and fountains. The guest rooms, which are decorated in a Laura Ashley - Alice in Wonderland theme, with English antiques all have phones and baths.

**Glenborough Inn Bed & Breakfast**
1327 Bath St.
1-800-962-0589

Private, Romantic, Intimate..The inn with its three homes, reflecting Victorian and California Craftsman eras, is surrounded by gardens on a quiet tree lined street just three blocks from downtown and fourteen blocks from the seashore. Luxuriate in the privately-reserved garden spa and pamper yourself with a hot breakfast served to your room or in the gardens. Relax around the parlor fireplace or in the gardens as you enjoy a refreshment or quiet moment. The inn is located in the heart of historic downtown Santa Barbara.

**Laguna Garden Inn**
909 Laguna St.
1-888-770-8880

A quiet, very private Victorian era cottage (c.1874). A peaceful getaway with old-fashioned front porch, spacious tree-shaded sunny deck with award-winning flower gardens and enchanting mountain views. Two blocks to popular downtown restaurants, quality shopping and theatres. Open-air tram to the beach and Stearn's Wharf from this central location.

**Montecito Inn**
1295 Coast Village Road
Web site: www.montecitoinn.com
1-800-843-2017

The Montecito Inn is unique among Santa Barbara landmarks. Located two blocks from the beach, the hotel is a product of Hollywood's Golden Era, built in 1928 by silent screen legend Charlie Chaplin as a haven for tinsel town celebrities. Today's red tile roof and white plaster walls pay homage to the original construction.

During its renovation, the wishing well that inspired composer Richard Rodgers to write his memorable love song, "There's a Small Hotel" (1936) was lost. A replica of that well now sits in the highly acclaimed Montecito Cafe. Magnificently restored, the inn's sixty rooms include seven one-bedroom luxery suites featuring spacious Italian marble bathrooms with jacuzzi tubs and custom fireplaces. Cinema buffs will delight in the inn's complete library of Chaplin films.

**Secret Garden Inn and Cottages**
1908 Bath St.
1-800-676-1622

The Secret Garden is one of Santa Barbara's oldest inns, formerly called the Blue Quail. The inn consists of a main house and four cottages set in a lush jasmine, jacaranda and camellia filled garden. The intertwined branches of the Persimmon, Avocado and Pecan trees combined with the high hedges and private lawns, add to the secrecy of the garden while Hummingbirds, Blue Jays and the trickling of fountains add peace and tranquility. All nine rooms and cottages have private bathrooms with showers.

**Simpson House Inn**
121 East Arrellaga St.
Web site: www.simpsonhouseinn.com
1-800-676-1280

North America's only 5 diamonds AAA B&B. Nestled in an acre of English gardens in downtown Santa Barbara, the Simpson House Inn offers fourteen luxurious guest accommodations. The original 1874 Eastlake-Victorian house contains six antique-filled guest rooms, along with a formal dining room, and elegant living room with fireplace. The renovated Barn features four suites, each with a king size bed, sitting area, fireplace, and wet bar. Three individual private cottages come with Jacuzzi spa-tubs, stone faced fireplaces, private garden patios and queen-size canopied featherbeds.

**The Tiffany Inn**
1323 De La Vina St.
1-800-999-5672

Classic antiques and period furnishings welcome you throughout this lovingly restored 1898 Victorian home. Guest rooms all have queen or king beds, garden or mountain views and most have fireplaces. The three suites also feature whirlpool spas. Tiffany is a short walk from exclusive downtown shops, restaurants, galleries, theaters and museums. A sumptuous breakfast is served on the garden veranda. Enjoy wine and cheese in front of the main fireplace in the afternoon.

## 169 SANTA CRUZ

The Santa Cruz area, a popular antique destination, has designed a way for visitors to preview the area's antique and collectible stores. Their on-line directory (www.santacruzantiques.com) contains a complete listing of the antique stores to visit.

The web site includes a master list of every store from the San Lorenzo Valley to Aptos. Each store's listing consists of their address and phone number along with a link to a map on which they appear. Some of the shops have an expanded listing of their merchandise and some have links to their own web pages.

A visitor to the site can also go directly to the maps page to locate all the stores in a different shopping area such as Soquel Village or San Lorenzo Valley. The maps can then be printed out and used for travel.

There is a resource page on the web site which also includes antique resources such as furniture refinishing and china repair services as well as links to various Santa Cruz sites.

There is also a calendar of events which lists Northern California and Central California antique shows for 1998. A special attraction to the site is a live spy cam positioned above the famous Santa Cruz Boardwalk so visitors can check the day's weather before they plan their trip. Look in the near future for a complete list of restaurants and lodging available.

By Jayne Skeff, Antique & Collectables

**Modern Life**
925 41st Ave.
408/475-1410

**Mr Goodie's**
1541 Pacific Ave.
408/427-9997

**Lovejoys**
2600 Soquel Ave.
408/479-4480

**Hall's Surrey House Antiques**
708 Water St.
408/423-2475

**Possibilities Unlimited**
1043 Water St.
408/427-1131

***Great Places To Stay***

**Chateau Victorian**
118 First St.
408/458-9458
Open daily
Rates: $110-140
*Directions: Hwy 17 drops onto Ocean St./Beaches. Go to the end of Ocean St. which forms a "T" at the light. Right on San Lorenzo to next light; left on Riverside, go over bridge through the light to the next stop sign; right on 2nd St., next stop sign left on Cliff St.; go one block; right on 1st St.; just past the first building on the left is parking. House is on the right.*
*From Hwy 1, coming from the north. Coming in on Mission St., go to 4th stop light; right on Bay St. to the end, forming a "T"; left on West Cliff Dr., which drops onto Beach St.; bottom of small hill is a stop sign; continue straight to next stop sign; left on Cliff St.; go one short block; left on First St.*
*From Hwy 1, coming from the south; ends in a fish hook and drops onto Ocean St./Beaches, and as above.*

Replete with decorative cornices, bay windows and gingerbread trim, Chateau Victorian was built around 1885. It was turned into an elegant bed & breakfast in 1983. The inn was originally a single-family residence for a family that obviously enjoyed the beach and the ocean. Within a block of Chateau Victorian is a beautiful beach, stretching for nearly a mile from the San Lorenzo River to beyond the wharf.

Wood-burning fireplaces adorn all seven rooms and each room offers its own special touch of Victorian-styled themes. The Garden Room contains an original Victorian bay window and a four-poster canopy bed. The Bay Side Room has a marble fireplace and a clawfoot tub. The Pleasure Point Room has a bay window seat overlooking a garden of flowers. Old-fashioned armoires, and private entrances to The Patio Room and Sunrise Room, provide an intimate "home away from home" atmosphere. There is a Lighthouse Room and a Natural Bridges Room with high ceilings and redwood crossbeams. From this room guests will also enjoy a small view of Loma Prieta Mountain.

A breakfast of fresh fruits, croissants, muffins, preserves, juices, coffee and teas are available from 9-10:30 a.m. in the lounge, on the secluded deck or the patio.

## 170 SANTA MARGARITA

**Gasoline Alley Antiques**
2200 El Camino Real
805/438-5322

**Kathy's Antiques**
2324 El Camino Real
805/438-3542

**Faded Glory Antiques**
2719 El Camino Real
805/438-3770

**Carriage House Antiques**
22302 El Camino Real
805/438-5062

**Little Store Antiques**
22705 El Camino Real
805/438-5347

## 171 SANTA MARIA

**Little Store Antiques**
22705 El Camino Real
805/438-5347

**Golden Retriever Antiques**
111 W. Main St.
805/349-1038

**Antique Mall**
1573 Stowell Center Plaza
805/922-6464

## 172 SANTA MONICA

**Santa Monica Antique Market**
1607 Lincoln Blvd.
310/314-4899
Mon.-Sat., 10-6, Sun., 12-5
Free valet parking

For specific information see review at the beginning of this section and in the editorial center.

**House of Yorke**
549 11th St.
310/395-2744

**Clifford Antiques**
1655 Lincoln Blvd.
310/452-7668

**Main Street Antiques**
2665 Main St.
310/392-4519

**Raintree Antiques**
2711 Main St.
310/392-7731

**British Collectibles Ltd.**
1727 Wilshire Blvd.
310/453-3322

**Quilt Gallery**
1025 Montana Ave.
310/393-1148

**Rosemarie McCaffrey**
1203 Montana Ave.
310/395-7711

**Brenda Cain Store**
1211 Montana Ave.
310/395-1559

**Montana Country**
1311 Montana Ave.
310/393-3324

**Prince of Wales**
1316 Montana Ave.
310/458-1566

**Country Pine & Design**
1318 Montana Ave.
310/451-0317

**Twigs**
1401 Montana Ave.
310/451-9934

**Blue House**
1402 Montana Ave.
310/451-2243

**Federico's**
1522 Montana Ave.
310/458-4134

**Caswell Antiques**
1322 2nd St.
310/394-3384

*Great Places To Stay*

**Channel Road Inn**
219 W. Channel Road
310/459-1920

Originally the home of Thomas McCall, a pioneering Santa Monica businessman, this house was moved from a hilltop site to its current location tucked in a hillside of Santa Monica Canyon, one block from the beach. With the help of the local historical society, innkeeper Susan Zolla saved the Colonial Revival building from demolition and turned it into a gracious inn, one of the only within view of the beach in Los Angeles County. The house is sheathed in blue shingles, a rarity in Los Angeles. Room rates are slightly lower Sunday through Thursday. The Inn accommodates fourteen guests.

## 173 SANTA ROSA

**Antiques Apples & Art**
105 3rd St.
707/578-1414

**Marianne Antiques**
111 3rd St.
707/579-5749

**Whistle Stop Antiques**
130 4th St.
707/542-9474

**Blue Goose Antiques**
60 W. 6th St.
707/527-8859

**C & H Antiques**
204 Wilson St.
707/527-7421

**Treasure House**
700 Wilson St.
707/523-1188

*Great Places To Stay*

**Pygmalion House**
331 Orange St.
707/526-3407
Open year round
*Directions: For specific directions from your location, please call the innkeepers.*

If you're looking for the perfect romantic getaway that won't cost you a fortune, you need look no further than Pygmalion House in Santa Rosa, California. Pygmalion House is nestled in a quiet neighborhood just a couple of blocks from Santa Rosa's Old Town. It is within walking distance to the various antique shops as well as some wonderful restaurants and coffee houses.

Pygmalion House, one of Santa Rosa's historical landmarks, is a fine example of Victorian Queen Anne architecture. This charming home was built in the 1800s on land owned by one of the city's leading developers, Mr. Thomas Ludwig. This house withstood the great earthquake and fire of 1906 which devastated much of Santa Rosa's heritage.

Pygmalion House derives its name from an ancient Greek myth, which was the basis for George Bernard Shaw's play 'Pygmalion' and the musical 'My Fair Lady.' The name reflects the transformation, brought about by painstaking renovation, from an old dilapidated house to the grand lady it is today.

You'll find this gracious bed and breakfast full of antiques from the collection of the famous stripper, Gypsy Rose Lee and the famous madam and past Sausalito mayor, Sally Stanford. Each of the guest rooms are quiet and nicely decorated, including private bath, and a queen or king-size bed. The main room, or "double parlor" includes a beautiful fireplace as well as an offset sitting area that looks out from octagon-shaped windows.

Each morning you'll feast on the full breakfast that is served from 8 a.m. to 9:30 a.m. Breakfast includes fresh fruit or melon, fresh baked muffins and croissants, and eggs with either ham, bacon, or sausage. Fresh squeezed orange juice is also served as well as Pygmalion House's fresh ground blend of five different kinds of coffee, including Kona coffee from Hawaii.

With all of these special touches that Pygmalion House offers you would think that a nights stay would be expensive. Well the best thing about this B&B is their prices. You can get a room with a queen-sized bed for only $75 per night and a king-sized bed for $85. Considering that B&B's can run a much as $100-200 a night, Pygmalion House offers it's guests true value for their money as well as a wonderful experience that is sure to bring you back time and time again.

## 174 SARATOGA

**Carol's Antique Gallery**
14455 Big Basin Way
408/867-7055

**M E Benson's Antiques**
14521 Big Basin Way
408/741-0314

**Bit O Country**
14527 Big Basin Way
408/867-9199

**McKenzie House Antiques**
14554 Big Basin Way
408/867-1341

**Front Window**
12378 Saratoga Sunnyvale Road
408/253-2980

**Blue Candlestick**
14320 Saratoga Sunnyvale Road
408/867-3658

## 175 SEAL BEACH

**Audrey's Antiques**
132 Main St.
562/430-7213

**Antique Gallery**
217 Main St.
562/594-4985

**Finders Keepers Unlimited**
406 Marina Dr.
562/493-4952

## 176 SEBASTOPOL

**Carol's Curios**
961 Gravenstein Hwy.
707/823-8334

**Country Cottage Antiques**
1235 Gravenstein Hwy.
707/823-4733

**Antique Society**
2661 Gravenstein Hwy.
707/829-1733

**Ed's Antiques**
2661 Gravenstein Hwy.
707/829-5363

**Willow Tree Antiques**
2701 Gravenstein Hwy.
707/823-3101

**Lone Pine Antiques**
3598 Gravenstein Hwy.
707/823-6768

**Llano House Antiques**
4353 Gravenstein Hwy.
707/829-9322

**Sebastopol Antique Mall**
755 Petaluma Ave.
707/829-9322

## 177 SHERMAN OAKS

**Outer Limits**
13542 Ventura Blvd.
818/906-8133

**Marilyn Hirsty Antiques**
13627 Ventura Blvd.
818/995-4128

**Piccolo Pete's**
13814 Ventura Blvd.
818/990-5421

**Sherman Oaks Antique Mall**
14034 Ventura Blvd.
818/906-0338

**Aunt Teeks**
4337 Woodman Ave.
818/784-3341

## 178 SIMI VALLEY

### A Collectors Paradise - Penny Pinchers
4265 Valley Fair St.
805/527-0056
Web site: www.city.411
Mon.-Sat. 10-5, Sun. 11-5
*Directions: From the 405 Freeway: Take Hwy. 118 west to the Tapo Cyn. exit, make a left to Cochran, make another left and go three blocks to Winifred, make a right and go about 10 blocks to Valley Fair. OR from Hwy. 101, take 23 North, which changes into the 118 East. Go to Tapo Cyn. exit, make a right, go to Cochran, make a left, go three blocks to Winifred, make a right and go about 10 blocks to Valley Fair.*

In business for 32 years, Penny Pinchers offers Empire furniture and depression glass, plus all types of nostalgic antiques and collectibles. They also offer the very hard, but not frequently found, services of furniture repair, jewelry repair and custom work, and appraisals. Also a full antique and collectible book library is available for the customers' use.

**Memories Antiques**
4325 Valley Fair St.
805/526-6308

**Pine Haven Antiques**
4371 Valley Fair St.
805/520-3801

**Antiques At Willie's**
4345 Valley Fair St.
805/584-2580

## 179 SOLANA BEACH

**Antique Warehouse**
212 S. Cedros Ave.
619/755-5156

**Appleby Intl. Art**
143 S. Cedros Ave.
619/259-0404

**Geissmann Rudolf Oriental Carpet**
143 S. Cedros Ave.
619/481-3489

## 180 SOLVANG

California is noted for having a little bit of everything in the state, but what about the title of "Danish Capital of America"? In the gently rolling Santa Ynez Valley, Solvang (which means sunny field in Danish) was founded in 1911 by Danes from the Midwest seeking to establish a West Coast Danish colony and folk school. Over the years the town began to look more and more Danish as the townspeople, perhaps encouraged by visits from Danish royalty, turned increasingly to Danish-style architecture. Today, visiting Danes say the town looks more like Denmark than the original country, with buildings of timber-framed white stucco, sloping green copper or wood shingle roofs, gables, dormer and towers, cobblestone sidewalks, outdoor cafes, and shops with leaded-glass windows. There are even four windmills - one still turns.

Specific Danish sites in Solvang include a half-scale replica of the Little Mermaid (the original sits in the Copenhagen harbor), and the Bethania Lutheran Church, a typical rural Danish church with hand-carved pulpits and a scale model of a Danish sailing ship hanging from the ceiling. The Elverhoy Museum preserves the history of Solvang with old photographs, crafts, period rooms, and other exhibits, and the Hans Christian Anderson Museum honors the life and work of the father and master of the modern fairy tale.

But Solvang's most historic site is, ironically, not Danish. It is the beautifully restored adobe Mission Santa Ines, established in 1804 as the 19th of the 21 missions built in California by Spanish Franciscan priests. The chapel, in continuous use since 1817, is decorated with murals by Indian artists and masterpieces of Moorish art and architecture.

But for the shopper, Solvang is Valhalla! There are 350 shops, noted for their antiques, paintings and Danish goods (pastries, music boxes, porcelain figurines, knotted sweaters, folk art, handmade lace, and Danish costumes.) After shopping, visitors can tour the town by carriage or on the Honen, a replica of a turn-of-the-century Copenhagen streetcar pulled by a pair of Belgian draft horses. And to tour the picturesque valley, hang gliders and bicycles are the only way to go!

**Solvang Antique Center**
486 First St.
805/686-2322
Open 7 days a week 10-6
Cafe/Bistro in same building, open daily 11-9
*Directions: From the south (Los Angeles, Santa Barbara): Hwy. 101 north to Buellton. Take Solvang Exit (Hwy. 246) east into Solvang (3 miles). Just past Solvang Park in the center of the village turn right onto First St. The Solvang Antique Center is on the left in the middle of the block.*
*or Hwy. 101 north to Santa Barbara. Take Hwy. 154 exit (San Marcos Pass) past Lake Cachuma. Take Solvang Exit (Hwy. 246) west into Solvang. Once in the Solvang village, go one block past the stop light at Alisal Road. The Solvang Antique Center is on the left in the middle of the block.*
*Both of the above routes are scenic. The first route is a divided highway. The second route is about 15 minutes shorter, but the road is a winding mountain road through the Los Padres National Forest.*
*From the north (San Francisco, Hearst Castle): Hwy. 101 south to Buellton. Take Solvang exit (Hwy. 246) east into Solvang (3 miles). Just past Solvang Park in the center of the village turn right onto First St. The Solvang Antique Center is on the left in the middle of the block.*

For specific information see review at the beginning of this section.

**Home Ranch**
444 Atterdag Road
805/686-0069

**Frogmore House Antiques**
1676 Oak St.
805/688-8985

## 181 SONOMA

**Buffy Antique**
414 1st St.
707/996-5626

**Antique Center of Sonoma**
120 W. Napa St.
707/996-9947

**D Tenenbaum Antiques**
128 W. Napa St.
707/935-7146

**Cat & The Fiddle**
153 W. Napa St.
707/996-5651

**Curry & I Antiques**
17000 Sonoma Hwy.
707/996-8226

## 182 SONORA

**Antique Passions**
8 S. Washington St.
209/532-8874

**Antiques Etcetera**
18 S. Washington St.
209/532-9544

**Carriage Trade Antiques**
36 S. Washington St.
209/532-0282

**Castagnola's Empor. Antiques**
93 S. Washington St.
209/533-8443

**Baer's 1851 Antiques**
105 S. Washington St.
209/533-2460

**Pine Tree Peddlers**
107 S. Washington St.
209/533-2356

## 183 SOQUEL

**Wayne's Antiques**
2940 S. Main St.
408/462-0616

**Crawford Antiques**
4401 Soquel Dr.
408/462-1528

**Frank's Antiques**
4900 Soquel Dr.
408/462-3953

**Country Garden Antiques**
4904 Soquel Dr.
408/462-5188

**After Effects**
4920 Soquel Dr.
408/475-5991

**Edward & Sons Antiques**
5025 Soquel Dr.
408/479-7122

**Vintage Textiles**
4631 Soquel Dr.
408/476-9007

**Trader's Emporium**
4940 Soquel Dr.
408/475-9201

**Tiffany's Antiques**
3010 Center St.
408/477-9808

**Baker & Co.**
5011 Soquel Dr.
408/479/4404

**Front Porch Antiques**
5320 Soquel Dr.
408/475-1108

**Wisteria Antiques and Design**
5870 Soquel Dr.
408/462-2900

## 184 SOUTH LAKE TAHOE

**Auntie Q's 2nd Hand Treasures**
800 Emerald Bay Road
916/542-2169

**Hanifin's Art & Antiques**
855 Emerald Bay Road
916/542-4663

**Hannifin's Antiques**
868 Emerald Bay Road
916/544-6769

**Sierra Bookshop**
3445 Lake Tahoe Blvd.
916/541-4222

## 185 SOUTH PASADENA

**Isn't It Romantic**
950 Mission St.
818/441-4824

**Yoko**
1011 Mission St.
818/441-4758

**Mission Antiques**
1018 Mission St., #3
818/799-1327

**And Etc.**
1110 Mission St.
818/799-6581

## 186 STOCKTON

**Buckeye Appliance**
714 W. Fremont St.
209/464-9643
*Directions: Going north on I-5 take the Pershing St. exit. Make a left at bottom of ramp. Go 2 blocks to stop light (Fremont St.), make a left. Store is approximately 10 blocks down on right side of street. Going south on I-5 take Oak St./Fremont exit. Make a left at bottom of ramp (Fremont St.). Go approximately 11 blocks.*

*Located on the right side of the street.*

A visit to Buckeye reminds you of Grandma's kitchen. Remember the heavy 50s stoves that had the deep well? You can find them here. The shop carries 50s chrome dinettes, porcelain top tables, Hoosier cabinets and tons of kitchen collectibles. Everything you need for a Retro kitchen.

**This shop specializes in the sales, service, parts and restoration of antique gas stoves.*

**Ivy**
209 Dorris Place
209/466-6652

**A & B Antiques**
216 W. Harding Way
209/946-4337

**Peckler's Antiques**
220 W. Harding Way
209/462-7992

**Lions Den Antiques**
230 W. Harding Way
209/547-0433

**House of Clocks**
311 Lincoln Center
209/951-1363

**Memory's Antiques & Collectibles**
2220 Pacific Ave.
209/462-5258

**Trotting Horse Antiques**
9177 Thornton Road
209/477-0549

**Mardel's Antique Annex**
917 N. Yosemite St.
209/546-0926

**Mardel's Antiques**
926 N. Yosemite St.
209/948-8948

## 187 STUDIO CITY

### The Cranberry House

12318 Ventura Blvd.
818/506-8945
Open daily 11-6
*Directions: Take Hwy. 405 north to Hwy. 101 east (to Los Angeles). Exit at Coldwater Canyon, turn right to Ventura Blvd., then turn left. Cranberry House is on the right about 2 miles. OR take Hwy. 5 north to Hwy. 134 West, take Hwy. 134 West to Hwy. 101 West, take Hwy. 101 west to Laurel Canyon, turn left onto Ventura Blvd., then right and go about 3 blocks. Cranberry House will be on the left. Look for the 100-foot cranberry awning on the front!*

For specific information see review at the beginning of this section.

**Ivy Cottage**
12206 Ventura Blvd.
818/762-9844

**Fables Antiques**
12300 Ventura Blvd.
818/506-2904

**Mother of Pearl & Sons**
12328 Ventura Blvd.
818/505-8057

**Ferret**
12334 Ventura Blvd.
818/769-2427

**Pearl River**
13031 Ventura Blvd.
818/986-5666

**Kings Cross**
13059 Ventura Blvd.
818/905-3382

## 188 SUMMERLAND

**Mary Suding Fine Antiques**
2173 Ortega Hill Road, 2nd Floor
805/969-4324

**Christian-Tevis Antiques**
2173 Ortega Hill Road
805/969-0966

**Summerland Antique Collective**
2194 Ortega Hill Road
805/565-3189

**Summerland Antique Annex**
2240 Lillie Ave.
805/565-5226

**Urban Hunter**
2272 Lillie Ave.
805/969-7987

**Antico II**
2280 Lillie Ave.
805/565-4899

**Summerhill Antiques**
2280 Lillie Ave.
805/969-3366

**Lillie Antiques & Accessories**
2560 Lillie Ave.
805/565-1271

**Heather House Antiques**
2448 Lillie Ave.
805/565-1561

**Gentlemen Antiquarians**
2560 Lillie Ave.
805/565-1271

## 189 SUNLAND

### Adventure In Postcards

8423 Foothill Blvd.
818/352-5663
Wed.-Sat. 10-5, unless out of town buying or selling
*Directions: Located just 1/2 mile east of the #210 Freeway at the Sunland Blvd. offramp (Sunland becomes Foothill one block east of the freeway).*

If you are looking for a very small, portable, inexpensive piece of Americana, Lee Brown's emporium in Sunland may have just what you need. The shop is truly an adventure in postcards.

With something like a quarter of a million postcards in stock, covering everything imaginable, most of Lee's cards are in the $1-5 range and are dated pre-World War I. Although some signed cards can pull $100 or so, and a few rare ones can fetch $1,000 at an art auction, thousands of the little pictures sell for just 20 cents, making postcards one of the most affordable and interesting collectibles available.

The Sunland shop stocks everything from depictions of natural disasters, like the 1906 San Francisco earthquake, to one-eyed cows and nudes reading books. Other paper ephemera and some miscellaneous smalls are also offered.

#### *Interesting Story*

It was three years ago that Brown discovered a very special holiday card that stood out among the thousands she was sorting. "I seldom read the backs of postcards, there's just not time; but I noticed some handwriting that I recognized," Brown said. "Then I spotted my grandmother's name, Mabel Holdefer, on a card dated 1908. She had sent it to a relative." Her grandmother raised her, so finding the card was a real treasure. I'm sure that's one postcard that will never be sold.

**Antiques Etc.**
7906 Foothill Blvd.
818/352-3197

**Cathy's Cottage**
8417 Foothill Blvd.
818/353-7807

## 190 SUTTER CREEK

**Klima's Antiques**
94 Boston Alley
209/267-5318

**Creekside Shops**
22 Main St.
209/267-5520

**Alicia's**
26 Main St.
209/267-0719

**Somewhere In Time**
34 Main St.
209/267-5789

**Columbian Lady**
61 Main St.
209/267-0059

**Old Hotel Antiques**
68 Main St.
209/267-5901

**Water Street Antiques**
78 Main St.
209/267-0585

**Arnolds Antiques**
80 Main St.
209/267-0603

**Cobweb Collection Antiques**
83 Main St.
209/267-0690

**O'Neill's Antiques**
84 Main St.
209/267-0450

**Jackson Antiques**
28 Main St.
209/223-0188

## 191 TAHOE CITY

**Girasole**
319 W. Lake Blvd.
916/581-4255

## 192 TEHACHAPI

### Mom & Apple Pie Antiques
798 Tucker Road, #2
805/822-8765
Tues.-Fri. 10-5, Sat. 10-5:30, Sun. 12-5, closed Mon.
Open late or open early if needed for you out-of-towners!

Mom & Apple Pie Antiques began business September 1, 1996. Courtney Kearnes, owner, decided to open up shop after the antique store she managed closed in July of 1996. With the help of husband Brent, son Jarred (3) and daughter Taylor (1), Mom got the store up and running in a month. The business is now a REAL family affair, as her moms and dads (2 of each) are involved in the business with her!

The 2000 square foot shop is home to 12 dealers from all around the area. Most of the dealers have 20+ years of experience in the business and deal in QUALITY, QUALITY, QUALITY merchandise. The shop specializes in vintage jewelry (Victorian through 60s), timepieces, vintage linens & lace, quilts, sewing implements, Victorian smalls of all kinds, country primitives including furniture, and so much more! They dabble in just about everything and will do mail order business on most items. Visit their website for a firsthand look.

The atmosphere is inviting, with fresh hot coffee or apple cider in the cool months, and refreshing iced tea in the summer. They offer special presentations for local clubs or groups on request. Come see it to believe it - Mom would love to show you some down home hospitality!

**Kathy's Mini Mall**
104 W. Tehachapi Blvd.
805/822-6691

**Apple Country Antiques**
114 W. Tehachapi Blvd.
805/822-7777

**Grace's Antiques**
20300 Valley Blvd., #E
805/822-5989

## 193 TEMECULA

**Across The River Antiques**
28418 Felix Valdez Ave.
909/699-9525

**Granny's Attic**
28450 Felix Valdez Ave., #C
909/699-9449

**Always Wanted Antiques**
28545 Felix Valdez Ave.
909/695-1136

**Chaparral Antique Mall**
28465 Front St.
909/676-0070

**A To Z Antiques**
28480 Front St.
909/699-3294

**Loft**
28480 Front St.
909/676-5179

**Old Town Antique Faire**
28601 Front St.
909/694-8786

**Mr R's Antiques**
28635 Front St.
909/676-2002

**Gramma Audrey's Antiques Too**
28636 Front St.
909/699-9338

**Shire Limited**
28656 Front St.
909/676-9233

**Nana's Antique Mall**
28677 Front St., #C
909/699-3839

**Country Seller & Friends Antiques**
42050 Main St.
909/676-2322

**Treasures You'll Cherish**
42012 Main St.
909/694-6990

**Timeless Treasures**
28475 Front St., Suite A
909/695-2926

**Nancy's Antique Mall**
42030 Main St., #BF
909/699-3889

**Packards Antiques**
42031 Main St., #C
909/693-9442

**Gramma Audrey's Antiques**
42031 Main St.
909/699-9139

**Morgan's Antiques**
42049 Main St.
909/676-2722

**Temecula Trading Post**
42081 Main St.
909/767-5759

**Juliet's Collectibles**
44060 Margarita Road
909/693-1410

## 194 THOUSAND OAKS

**2nd Edition**
368 E. Thousand Oaks Blvd.
805/497-9727

**Antique Suites Mall**
783 E. Thousand Oaks Blvd.
805/373-0366

**Maggie & Me Antiques**
783 E. Thousand Oaks Blvd.
805/496-1603

**Antiques of Tomorrow**
3075 E. Thousand Oaks Blvd.
805/494-4095

## 195 TORRANCE

**Kasden's Antiques**
24548 Hawthorne Blvd.
310/378-8132

**Dunk Antiques**
4164 Pacific Coast Hwy.
310/375-6175

**Janson & Son Antiques**
1325 Sartori Ave.
310/787-1670

**Collector's Gallery**
833 Torrance Blvd.
310/532-2166

**Pieces of the Past Antique Mall**
19032 S Vermont Ave.
310/324-6767

## 196 TULARE

**Old Town Emporium**
207 S. K St.
209/688-8483

## 197 TURLOCK

**Yesterday's Expressions**
116 S. Center St.
209/669-7003

**Trinkets To Treasures**
125 S. Center St.
209/667-4988

**J B's Antiques**
1237 N. Golden State Blvd.
209/632-8220

**Johnson's Flowers & Collectibles**
417 E. Main
209/634-4467

**Main Street Antiques**
208 E. Main
209/669-7000

## 198 TUSTIN

**Tustin Consignments**
474 El Camino Real
714/730-5037

**Angels Garden**
486 El Camino Real
714/669-1337

**Bruce Cole Noland Antiques**
500 El Camino Real
714/730-5502

**Step Back In Time**
528 El Camino Real
714/734-9093

**Not Just Antiques**
546 El Camino Real
714/731-8813

**Gerdas Antiques**
550 El Camino Real
714/832-4932

**Olde Town Tustin Antique Mall**
650 El Camino Real
714/838-1144

**Van Dorens Consignments**
17321 17th St.
714/505-3141

**Schafer's Antiques**
171 N. Tustin Ave.
714/541-5555

## 199 UPLAND

**Calico Reflections**
130 E. 9th St.
909/981-2135

**Collectors Cottage**
243 E. 9th St.
909/920-1136

**Antique Alley**
257 E. 9th St
909/985-5563

**Myra's Antiques**
139 N. 2nd Ave.
909/981-7002

**Carriage House Antiques**
152 N. 2nd Ave.
909/982-2543

**Kiosk Corner**
188 N. 2nd Ave.
909/981-2876

**Alphenaar's Antiques**
251 N. 2nd Ave.
909/949-7978

**Sideboard**
170 N. 2nd Ave.
909/981-7652

**Classic Collectibles**
136 E. 9th St.
909/985-9543

**The Art Room Antiques**
291 N. 2nd Ave.
909/946-8160

**Upland Ole ' Town**
270 N. 2nd Ave.
909/981-2408

## 200 UPPER LAKE

**Vintage Store**
375 N. Hwy. 2
707/275-0303

**First & Main**
9495 Main St.
707/275-3124

## 201 VACAVILLE

**Bygone Shoppe Antiques**
143 McClellan St.
707/449-3575

**Past & Presents**
333 Merchant St.
707/449-0384

**Vasquez Antiques & Collectibles**
357 Merchant St.
707/447-9434

## 202 VALLEJO

**Yesteryear's Marketplace**
433 Georgia St.
707/557-4671
Mon.-Sat., 10-5
Sun. afternoon by chance - knock if light is on.
*Directions: From I-80 take Georgia St. exit west to Old Town. 30 yards past Sonoma Blvd. (Hwy 29). Parking front and rear.*

With 9,500 square feet of almost everything in antiques and collectibles the shop is located in the Redman's Hall which housed the National Dollar store in the 1930s.

Since 1990 it has been the home of a wonderful shop filled to the brim with a wide variety of crystal, art glass, china, pottery, lamps, prints, paper goods, vintage small appliances, costume jewelry and furniture - ranging from kitsch to elegant.

### *Interesting Side Trips*

**St. Peter's Chapel at Mare Island**
328 Seawind Dr.
707-557-1538

Famous for its 29 stained glass windows, most designed by the Tiffany Studios of New York.

## 203 VENICE

**Revival**
1356 Abbot Kinney Blvd.
310/396-1360

**Neptina**
1329 1/2 Abbot Kinney Blvd.
310/396-1630

**Bountiful**
1335 Abbot Kinney Blvd.
310/450-3620

## 204 VENTURA

**Antique Alley**
263 S. Laurel St.
805/643-0708

**Antique Accents**
315 E. Main St.
805/643-4511

**Heirlooms Antique Mall**
327 E. Main St.
805/648-4833

**Attic Treasures**
337 E. Main St.
805/641-1039

**Antiques Etc. Mall**
369 E. Main St.
805/643-6983

**Main Street Antique Mall**
384 E. Main St.
805/648-3268

**Nicholby Antique Mall**
404 E. Main St.
805/653-1195

**My Last Hurrah/Attic Trunk**
451 E. Main St., #9
805/643-6510

**Times Remembered**
467 E. Main St.
805/643-3137

**Sevoy Antiques**
494 E. Main St.
805/641-1890

**Red House Antiques**
1234 E. Main St
805/643-6787

**Sherlock's Antique Lighting**
8672 N. Ventura Ave.
805/649-4683

**Garden Angel Collective**
1414 E. Main St.
805/643-1980

**Park Place Collectibles**
1416 E. Main St.
805/652-1761

**Bid Time Return**
1920 E. Main St.
805/641-2003

**Oak Street Antiques**
27 S. Oak St.
805/652-0053

**Curio Cottage**
64 S. Oak St.
805/648-5508

**Sevoy Antiques**
1501 Palma Dr.
805/642-8031

**America Antiques**
2459 Palma Dr.
805/650-6265

## 205 VISALIA

**Planning Mill Mall**
515 E. Center Ave.
209/625-8887

**Stuff N Such**
1214 E. Houston
209/734-4114

**Cottage**
15472 E. Mineral King
209/734-8996

**Carriage House Antiques**
15484 E. Mineral King
209/635-8818

**White's House Antiques**
4628 W. Mineral King
209/734-2128

**Spit 'n' Polish Antiques**
15361 Ave. 280
209/247-3558

**Antiques at the Works Showcase Mall**
26644 S. Mooney
209/685-1125

## 206 WALNUT CREEK

**Sundance Antiques**
2323 Boulevard Circle
510/930-6200

**Our Showroom Antiques**
2363 Boulevard Circle
510/947-6844

**Quail Country Antiques**
1581 Boulevard Way
510/944-0930

**Walnut Creek Antiques**
2050 N. Broadway
510/947-4900

## 207 WHITTIER

**Virginia's Antiques**
6536 Greenleaf Ave.
562/696-2810

**Treasure Chest Antiques**
6718 Greenleaf Ave.
562/696-6608

**Uptown Antiques**
6725 Greenleaf Ave.
562/698-1316

**Yesterdays Memories**
12310 Penn St.
562/696-6124

**Yellow Pipe Antiques**
13309 Philadelphia St.
562/945-2362

**Pepe's Antiques**
13310 Philadelphia St.
562/945-1676

**Elegant Elephant**
6751 Washington Ave.
562/698-7037

**King Richards Antique Mall**
12301 Whittier Blvd.
562/698-5974

**All The Kings Toys**
12323 Whittier Blvd.
562/696-3166

## 208 WOODLAND

**Bee's Antiques & Collectibles**
1021 Lincoln Ave.
916/662-3246

**Old Depot Antiques**
1021 Lincoln Ave.
916/662-1215

**Tinker's Antiques & Collectibles**
338 Main St.
916/662-3204

**House Dresser**
518 Main St.
916/661-9596

**Antiques on Main**
528 Main St.
916/668-1815

## 209 WOODLAND HILLS

**Affordable Antiques**
4870 Topanga Canyon Blvd.
818/888-2568

**Joseph Wahl Arts**
5305 Topanga Canyon Blvd.
818/340-9245

**Antique Frames & Furniture**
22845 Ventura Blvd.
818/224-4845

## 210 YORBA LINDA

**C.P. McGinnis & Co.**
4887 Main St.
714/777-8990

**Susan Tanner Antiques**
4884 Main St.
714/693-1913

**Dixie Lee's Antiques**
4900 Main St.
714/779-3905

**Gifts N Treasures**
4897 Main St.
714/777-8371

# Colorado

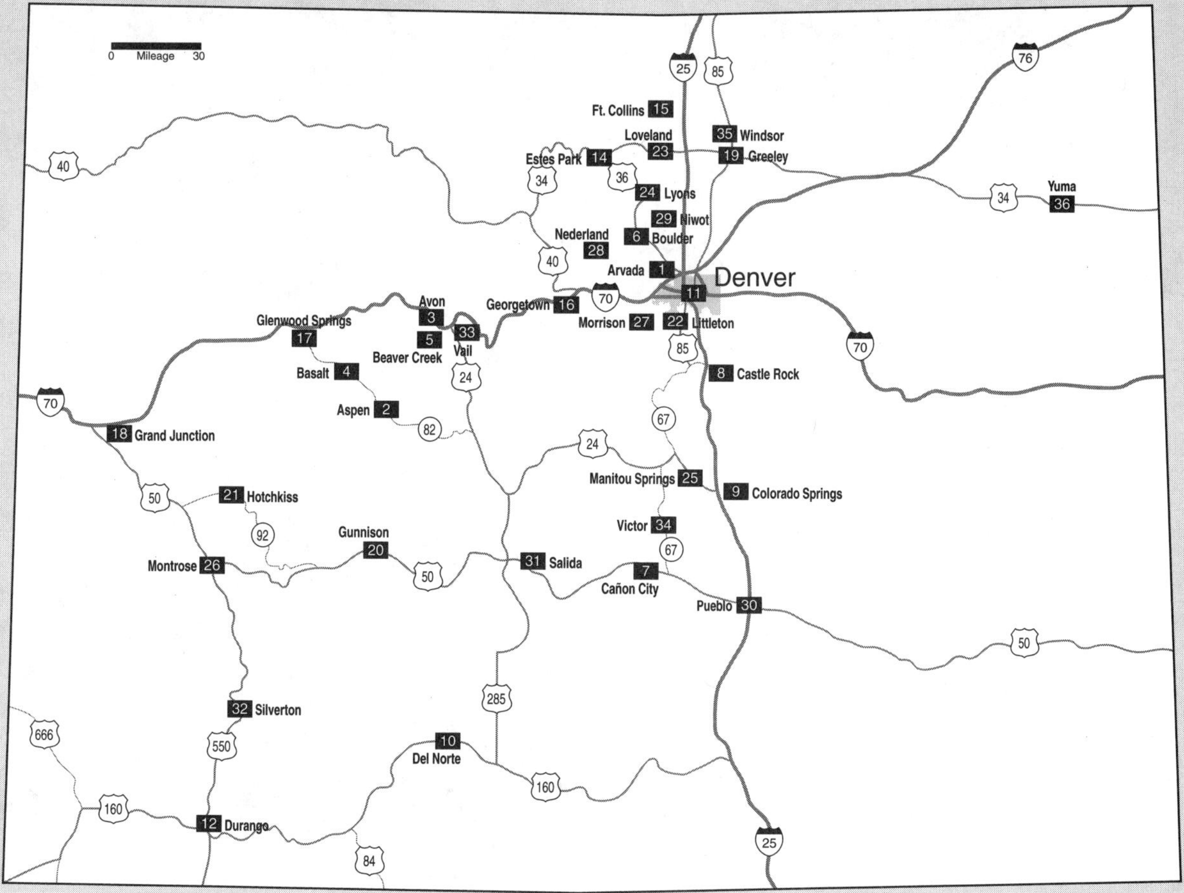
0 Mileage 30
Denver
Ft. Collins 15
Loveland 23
35 Windsor
19 Greeley
Estes Park 14
24 Lyons
29 Niwot
6 Boulder
Nederland 28
Arvada 1
11
Georgetown 16
Avon 3
5
33 Vail
Beaver Creek
Glenwood Springs 17
Morrison 27
22 Littleton
8 Castle Rock
Basalt 4
Aspen 2
18 Grand Junction
Manitou Springs 25
9 Colorado Springs
21 Hotchkiss
Victor 34
Gunnison 20
Montrose 26
31 Salida
7 Cañon City
Pueblo 30
32 Silverton
10 Del Norte
12 Durango
Yuma 36
25
85
76
40
34
36
70
24
82
67
50
92
285
666
550
160
84

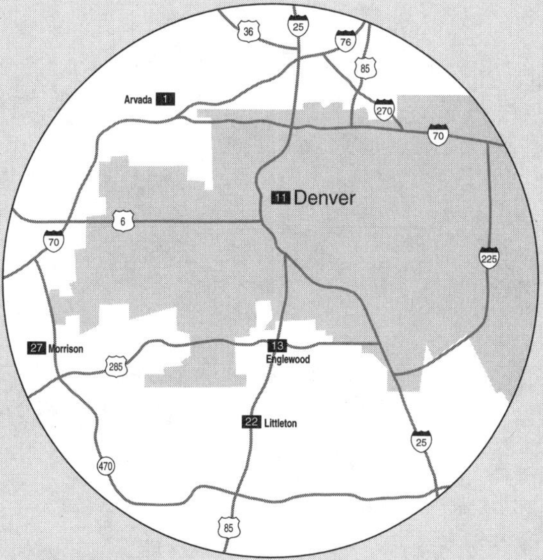
Arvada 1
11 Denver
27 Morrison
13 Englewood
22 Littleton
36
25
76
85
270
70
6
225
285
470

# Room at the Inn

## Graceful Queen Anne style tastefully augmented by modern touches of luxury

Ideally located in the historic center of Colorado Springs, Room at the Inn retains the charm, romance and gracious hospitality of the Victorian Era. A wealthy mine investor and his wife built the house in 1896 in classic Queen Anne style. The inn features original hand-painted murals, four Italian tiled fireplaces, fish scale siding, a wrap-around veranda and a three-story turret overlooking a wide tree-lined avenue. Room at the Inn has been carefully restored to its former elegance with the added luxury and comfort of modern amenities.

The five guest rooms in the Main House offer private baths, queen size beds, period antiques and oriental rugs. Each room has distinguishing characteristics such as fireplaces, whirlpool or soaking tubs for two and turret sitting areas.

The Carriage House has two guest rooms with private baths.

*Luxurious appointments include period antique furniture and oriental rugs. Individual rooms have unique features, a fireplace, whirlpool or a turret sitting area.*

*Room at the Inn is located at 618 N. Nevada Ave. in Colorado Springs. Call the innkeepers at 1-800-579-4621 for specific directions.*

*Handsome rooms reflect the care with which this home in the classic Queen Anne style has been restored. Interiors have been designed and furnished creating an atmosphere of great charm.*

# The state's largest: Colorado Antique Gallery

## Estate jewelry, fine china

The Colorado Antique Gallery located in Littleton, is Colorado's largest antiques mall with over 50,000 square feet and 200 of Colorado's best antique dealers. The variety of merchandise is unlimited — a great selection of fine china, depression glass, estate jewelry, RS Prussia, Royal Bayreuth, and much, much more. Since opening in 1992, the Gallery has become a favorite stop, not only for Colorado's antiques enthusiasts, but also for collectors from across the country. A combination of quality merchandise as well as friendly and helpful salespeople has earned the Colorado Antiques Gallery a reputation for being top notch.

*The Colorado Antique Gallery is located at 5501 S. Broadway in Littleton. For additional information see listing # 22 (Littleton).*

*A dazzling selection of merchandise awaits your inspection at the Colorado Antique Gallery. Seemingly every variety of collectible under the sun is gathered here, to make this a must-see for serious antiquers everywhere.*

*The selection of flow blue china rivals that seen anywhere in the country.*

*Van Dyke's Antiques is chock full of the most fascinating collection of high quality antiques from pickle casters to paintings.*

# Van Dyke's Antiques: Where to go for flow blue

## Magnificent selection piques the interest

For those interested in flow blue china, Van Dyke's Antiques has one of the largest selections to be found. In addition, the shop is filled with a magnificent selection of other quality antiques such as: Victorian glass, pocket watch holders, pickle casters, brides baskets, epergnes, scent bottles and lusters. You'll also find American and European furniture, silver, paintings, prints, perfume bottles, lighting, lamps, crystal and more.

*Van Dyke's Antiques is located at 3663 S. Broadway in Englewood. For days and hours of operation and directions or to visit their web site, see listing # 13 (Englewood).*

*Investigating the many treasure-filled nooks of the Antique Market and the Antique Guild can easily take a day.*

# Antique Market and Antique Guild

## Mainstays of Denver's Antique Row

The Antique Market and the Antique Guild offer the wares of over 250 vendors in one block at the top of Denver's Antique Row on South Broadway just two blocks south of Interstate 25. The Market at 1212 S. Broadway has the most entertaining inventory of antiques and collectibles in the region. Known for its eclectic mix of merchandise and its reasonable prices, the Market offers free off-street parking and a delightful café with home-cooked baked goods and sandwiches to make for a complete shopping experience. The mall specializes in oak and primitives as well as a large selection of '50s furniture. There is not much that the collector cannot find at the Antique Market from cowboy collectibles to fine china.

The Antique Guild, a cooperative of individual businesses a half a block down from the Market, shows off gorgeous antique furnishings. Specialists in rare books, glassware and old radios are a feature.

The Antique Market and the Antique Guild are the anchor stores for a four-block area known as Antique Row in Denver. This is the most extensive collection of antiques in the Rocky Mountain Region, one that should not be missed for the aficionado or the family looking for a fun afternoon of entertainment.

Antique Row is easily accessible from the interstate and Denver's Light Rail, originating near downtown hotels, arriving only two blocks from the Antique Market. Check Antique Row's web page at http://www.webolutions.com/antiquerow.

*The Antique Market is located at 1212 S. Broadway and the Antique Guild is located at 1298 S. Broadway in Denver. For additional information see listing #11 (Denver).*

# Colorado

## 1 ARVADA

**Penny's**
5713 Olde Wadsworth Blvd.
303/403-0290

**Arvada Antique Emporium**
7519 Grandview Ave.
303/422-6433

**Cabin Antiques**
7505 Grandview Ave.
303/467-7807

**Elegant Glass Antiques**
7501 Grandview Ave.
303/424-9330

**Foxhaven Farms Antiques**
7513 Grandview Ave.
303/420-2747

**House of Rees**
7509 Grandview Ave.
303/424-0663

**Olde Wadsworth Antiques**
7511 Grandview Ave.
303/424-8686

## 2 ASPEN

**Alderfer's Antiques**
309 E. Main St.
970/925-5051

**Country Flowers**
433 E. Cooper St.
970/925-6522

**MC Hugh Antiques**
431 E. Hyman Ave.
970/925-5751

**Katie Ingham Antique Quilts**
257 Glen Eagles Dr.
970/925-2595

**Fetzers**
308 S. Hunter
970/925-5447

**Morocco**
616 E. Hyman Ave.
970/925-9275

**Cooper St. Art & Antique**
316 S. Mill St.
970/925-1795

**Curious George**
426 E. Hyman Ave.
970-925-3315

## 3 AVON

**Shaggy Ram**
1160 W. Beaver Creek Blvd.
970/949-4377

**Grammy's Attic**
Hwy. 6 & 24
970/949-6099

## 4 BASALT

**Basalt Antiques**
132 Midland Ave. Mall
970/927-3326

**Double D Lazy T Trading Co.**
22826 Hwy. 82
970/927-9679

**Old Paint & Memories**
50 Sunset Dr.
970/927-8096

**Little Bear Antiques & Uniques**
402 C Park Ave.
970/927-8091

## 5 BEAVER CREEK

**Note: Below is a wonderful story submitted by the Vail Valley Tourism & Convention Bureau.*

A bear in Beaver Creek was yearning for a spa vacation. Earlier, he'd secretly watched vacationers soaking, enjoying wine and sharing stories of mountain hikes and river rafting adventures, Swedish massages and mud treatments. Long after they departed, he climbed atop the floating cover of a bubbling hot tub and swatted at the delicious-looking hummingbird feeders above.

Locals in the valley like to enjoy the good life, too, you know.

**Grammy's Attic**
41131 U.S. Hwy. 6 & 24
970/949-6099

**Shaggy Ram**
1060 W. Beaver Creek Blvd.
970/926-4663

## 6 BOULDER

**8th & Pearl Antiques**
740 Pearl St.
303/444-0699

**Classic Facets**
2010 10th St.
303/938-8851

**Indochine**
2525 Arapahoe Ave. E31
303/444-7734

**Sage Gallery Antiques**
5360 Arapahoe Ave.
303/449-6799

**Candy's Vintage Clothing**
4483 Broadway St.
303/442-6186

**Crystal Galleries Ltd.**
1302 Pearl St.
303/444-2277

**Rosetree Cottage**
2525 Arapahoe Ave. #E34
303/442-5794

**American Heritage Antiques**
1412 Sunshine Canyon Dr.
303/939-8890

**Bargain Store Antiques**
1949 Pearl St.
303/443-0671

### *Great Places To Stay*

**Inn on Mapleton Hill**
1001 Spruce St.
1-800-276-6528
Email: maphillinn@aol.com

The Inn on Mapleton Hill is a one hundred year old home welcoming visitors to Colorado in the tradition and warm hospitality of its early settlers. It all started in 1899 when Emma Clarke, a widowed dressmaker and daughter of a Canadian sea captain first opened the three story red brick building for boarders, many of which were school teachers. Situated in what is now known as the Mapleton Hill Historic District, it continues to serve as a haven of hospitality.

## 7 CAÑON CITY

**Sherrilyn Antiques**
202 Main St.
719/275-5849

**Greenhorn Enterprises**
1434 Pine St.
719/275-1444

**Lone Tree Antiques**
429 S. 9th St.
719/275-0712

## 8 CASTLE ROCK

**Auntie Lisa's Antiques**
1647 Park St.
303/688-7552

## 9 COLORADO SPRINGS

It was in 1870 that Civil War hero and retired army general, William Jackson Palmer, caught his first glimpse of what is now Colorado Springs. After the war, the rapidly growing railroad industry had captured his interest, and he had come to the Pikes Peak region to investigate the possibilities of expansion.

In 1871, enchanted by the beauty of the region, Palmer began laying out the city of his dreams. He fancied to build a tourist resort on the region's reputation as a healthful climate. He dubbed the town Colorado Springs, although the closest mineral springs were six miles away in Manitou Springs, several hours by buggy.

In the 1800s only the very wealthy could afford to tour, so Palmer saw to it that the finest hotels and private mansions were built. Attracting Europeans in droves, Colorado Springs earned the nickname "Little London."

In 1893, an eastern school teacher making her first visit to the young city was captivated, as General Palmer had been, by the area's grandeur. After a trip to the top of Pikes Peak, teacher and poet, Katharine Lee Bates, wrote what would become her most famous work. Later set to music, "America the Beautiful" has become perhaps the nation's most beloved patriotic anthem.

In the years that followed the founding of Colorado Springs, thousands of others have been inspired by the beauty of the region. From that inspiration the citizens of the Pikes Peak region have grown to appreciate their rich cultural heritage. Today the city boasts many fine historical homes, museums, a living history farm and some of the most spectacular views in the world.

**Antique Gallery**
21 N. Nevada Ave.
719/633-6070

**McIntosh Weller Antiques**
1013 S. Tejon St.
719/520-5316

**Jug & Basin Antiques**
1420 W. Colorado Ave.
719/633-9346

**Villagers Antiques & Collectibles**
2426 W. Colorado Ave.
719/632-1400

**Antique Legacy**
2624 W. Colorado Ave.
719/578-0637

**Antique Merchants**
14 S. Tejon St.
719/442-6928

**Kaya Gaya**
1015 S. Tejon St.
719/578-5858

**Dean & Co. Antiques**
2607 W. Colorado Ave.
719/635-3122

**Avenue Antiques & Collectibles**
2502 W. Colorado Ave.
719/520-9894

**Adobe Walls**
2808 W. Colorado Ave.
719/635-3394

**My Mother's Attic Antiques**
207 W. Rockrimmon Blvd. #F
719/528-2594

**NuNN Art & Antiques**
717 N. Union Blvd.
719/473-4746

**Antiques Unique on 8th Street**
1515 S. 8th St.
719/475-8633

**Iron Pump Antiques**
1024 S. Royer St.
719/636-3940

**Antique Mart**
829 N. Union Blvd.
719/633-6070

**Lace Chest**
101 S. 25th St.
719/632-1770

**Country Pines Antiques**
6005 Templeton Gap Road
719/596-4004

**Nevada Avenue Antiques**
405 S. Nevada Ave.
719/473-3351

**Legend Antiques**
2165 Broadway St.
719/448-9414

**Colorado Country Antique Mall**
2109 Broadway St.
719/520-5680

**Consignment of Collectables**
5681 N. Academy Blvd.
719/528-5922

**Korean Antique Gallery**
1788 S. 8th St. #A
719/386-0305

### *Great Places To Stay*

**Room at the Inn**
618 North Nevada Ave.
1-888-442-1896

For specific information see review at the beginning of this section.

### *Interesting Side Trips*

**Van Briggle Art Pottery**
600 South 21st St.
719/633-7729
Tours: Mon.-Sat. — call for times
*Directions: Five minutes west of downtown Colorado Springs at 21st St. and Hwy. 24.*

Van Briggle Art Pottery has been mixing clay, water and fire with the potter's magic since 1899. It is one of the oldest active art potteries remaining in the United States. The company was founded by acclaimed potter and sculptor Artus Van Briggle, together with his wife, Anne, who was also an accomplished artist. The Van Briggles designed their creations by incorporating flowing floral motifs, carefully patterned to enhance the graceful shapes of the pottery, and then finishing the pieces with the soft "matte" glazes which have come to represent the Van Briggle style. These beautiful glazes grace a variety of designs, from Art Nouveau to current Southwestern styles. You will also find figurines, distinctive lamp shades, bowls, vases and lamps made at the studio.

**Rock Ledge Ranch**
1805 30th St.
719/578-6777
Call for hours June-August

Located near the Gateway Rocks to the Gardens of the Gods, the Rock Ledge Ranch, formerly the White House Ranch, provides a living history of an early Colorado Springs ranch, with exhibits and demonstrations of old-time ranching.

**Ghost Town Museum**
Hwy. 24
719/634-0696
Open year round

Ghost Town Museum is an authentically reconstructed Old West town built from the very buildings abandoned after the Pikes Peak Region's gold mining era. Explore the boardwalk that connects the saloon, jail, blacksmith and merchants of "Main Street" to the livery (which houses stagecoaches, buggies, carriages of the day, and turn-of-the-century automobiles) and the Victorian Home. Each exhibit displays a fascinating array of valuable collectibles such as those actually used by our ancestors — your great-grandparents!

**North Pole**
Santa's Workshop
North Pole, Colo.
719/684-9432
Open mid-May through December
*Directions: Drive 10 miles west of Colorado Springs on Hwy. 24 to Cascade (Exit 141 from I-25) and follow the signs.*

Imagine a place where every day is Christmas. Where your children can meet and talk to Santa Claus himself. Where your family can ride a mountaintop ferris wheel, a swinging space shuttle, an antique carousel, an aerial tram through the treetops, a miniature train and more.

Where you can enjoy tasty foods and snacks, and picnic in an evergreen forest. Where your kids can feed live deer, create their own colorful candle, watch a magician perform and play in a game-packed arcade. Where you can mail cards postmarked "The North Pole".

You don't have to imagine such a place because it really exists...at the North Pole, home of Santa's Workshop...at the foot of Pikes Peak. Call for exact days and times.

### *Favorite Places To Eat*

**Giuseppe's Old Depot Restaurant**
10 S. Sierra Madre
719/635-3111
*Directions: Downtown, 1 block west of Antlers/Doubletree.*

On October 26, 1871, the first passenger train from Denver stopped at the site of the soon-to-be Denver & Rio Grande Western Railroad Station in the infant city of Colorado Springs. The history of Colorado can hardly be considered without the history of the railroad. Rich in timber and minerals, the new territory attracted adventurous souls filled with optimism as well as foresight.

Perhaps nothing reflects the courage and glamour of those times more than this Denver Rio Grande Western Railroad Station. Constructed of "glass stone" found near Castle Rock, Colorado, the Depot still shakes to the freight and coal trains of today. The last passenger train pulled out of the Depot in 1966, but the memories have been preserved in the many photographs and memorabilia gracing the walls of the station. The original oak doors still open wide to welcome today's guests. The floor of the main Dining Room still bears the original tiles that have been polished smooth by millions of feet since 1887. Colorado Spruce was used for the twenty- foot ceiling in the former passenger waiting room. The cherubim overlooking the north and south ends of this room have been preserved from a less fortunate structure, The Burns Theater.

The Depot has provided a whistle stop for former presidents, Theodore and Franklin Roosevelt, as well as Harry Truman during campaigns for the presidency.

Today the customers inside this 107-year-old historically restored station aren't passengers. They are diners feasting upon such specialties as stonebaked pizza and lasagna, savory ribs and steak, prime rib, spaghetti, or one of the many other scrumptious choices offered by Giuseppe's Old Depot Restaurant.

## 10 DEL NORTE

### *Great Places To Stay*

**La Garita Creek Ranch**
38145 County Road 39-E
719/754-2533
*Directions: 17 miles south of Sayuache or 18 miles north of Monte Vista on Hwy. 285 — turn west at La Garita sign (Road G). Continue approximately 6 miles past La Garita Store to fork in road. Take left fork. Continue approximately 4 miles to the next fork. You will see La Garita Creek Ranch sign. Take right fork for 1 mile. Turn right at sign onto the property.*

If you're feeling energetic after all that antique shopping, you've come to the right place. La Garita Creek Ranch offers plenty of activities for further explorations. You might try horseback riding along the scenic trails or fishing in a nearby creek. The true adventurists can test their skills in Penitente Canyon, the world renowned rock climbing area. Then end your perfect day in a quiet mountain cabin, complete with fireplace and hot tub. The ranch offers a full bar and restaurant.

## 11 DENVER

**Antique Market**
1212 S. Broadway
303/744-0281
Mon.-Sat. 10-5:30, Sun. 11-5

**Antique Guild**
1298 S. Broadway
303/722-3365, 303/744-0368 fax
Mon.-Sat. 10-5:30, Sun. 12-5
*Directions: Take I-25, Exit 207, 4 blocks south to the corner of Louisiana and S. Broadway*

For specific information see review at the beginning of this section.

**The Gallagher Collection**
Books and Antiques at the Antique Guild
1298 South Broadway
303/756-5821
24-hour FAX 303/736-7112
Email gallabks@dimensional.com
Mon.-Sat. 10-5:30, Sun. 12-5
*Directions: Take I-25, exit 207, 4 blocks south to the corner of Louisiana and South Broadway.*

Located in the old potato chip factory amidst Denver's Antique Row, The Gallagher Collection offers an outstanding array of unusual books in all fields. You'll find significant selections in Western, Americana, Children's, Illustrated, Leather and Decorative Bindings, History, Biography, Natural History, Birds, Hunting and Fishing, and Cookbooks, plus additional books in other fields. They even offer antiques for the library and a significant selection of original World War I and II posters.

In addition to authors to read, they offer authors to play. Remember when you used to play the Authors Card Game. Now you can play it again and share it with your children and grandchildren. Also available, and played the same way: Childrens Authors, Women Authors, American Authors, Civil War Series, and Baseball.

The Gallagher Collection also buys books and provides a book search service. As members of the Rocky Mountain Antiquarian Booksellers Association, they adhere to the highest standards of the book trade. You'll enjoy perusing the wonderful antique cast iron bookshelves for that special book in a friendly, comfortable setting.

**Architectural Salvage, Inc.**
1215 Delaware St.
303/615-5432
Open Mon.-Sat. 10-5, Sun. 12-5
*Directions: Traveling I-25, take exit 210 A (Colfax exit), east 1 mile, south on Delaware 2 1/2 blocks. (Delaware runs south only from Colfax between Rocky Mountain News Building and The Denver Mint.)*

No reproductions here. For 10 years, Architectural Salvage has provided customers with outstanding antique doors, lighting, windows, leaded glass, clawfoot tubs, shutters, gates, columns and more. Everything is neatly arranged indoors for your convenience.

**Maggie May's Sandbox**
212 S. Broadway
303/744-8656

**Antique Mercantile**
1229 S. Broadway
303/777-8842

**Antique Alcove**
1236 S. Broadway
303/722-4649

**Amsterdam Antiques**
1428 S. Broadway
303/722-9715

**Rosalie McDowell Antiques**
1400 S. Broadway
303/777-0601

**Hooked on Glass**
1407 S. Broadway
303/778-7845

**Al's Collectables & Antiques**
1438 S. Broadway
303/733-6502

**Stuart-Buchanan Antiques**
1530 15th St.
303/825-1222

**Aspen Antiques**
1464 S. Broadway
303/733-6463

**Glass Roots Antiques**
27 E. Dakota
303/778-8693

**Wazee Deco**
1730 Wazee St.
303/293-2144

**Foxy's Antiques**
1592 S. Broadway
303/777-7761

**Gateway Antiques & Art**
357 Broadway
303/744-8479

**Antique Center on Broadway**
1235 S. Broadway
303/744-1857

**Talisman Antiques**
1248 S. Broadway
303/777-8959

**Antiques by Corky**
1449 S. Broadway
303/777-8908

**Warner's Antiques**
1401 S. Broadway
303/722-9173

**Uniquittes**
1415 S. Broadway
303/777-6318

**Calamity Jane Antiques**
1445 S. Broadway
303/778-7104

**Cravings/Upland Interiors**
1460 S. Broadway
303/777-1728

**Antique Exchange Co-op**
1500 S. Broadway
303/777-7871

**Antiques of Denver**
1534 S. Broadway
303/733-9008

**Sleepers Antiques**
1564 S. Broadway
303/733-8017

**Packrat Antiques**
1594 S. Broadway
303/778-1211

**Times Shared**
1160 E. Colfax Ave.
303/863-0569

**Decorables & Antiques Best**
5940 E. Colfax Ave.
303/399-8643

**Country Club Antiques**
408 Downing St.
303/733-1915

**Artifact Room**
2318 S. Colorado
303/757-2797

**Buckboard**
3265 S. Wadsworth Blvd.
303/986-0221

**Wayside Antiques**
3795 S. Knox Ct.
303/783-3645

**Borgman's Antiques & Things**
1700 E. 6th Ave.
303/399-4588

**Mountain Man Antiques**
3977 Tennyson St.
303/458-8447

**Country Line Antiques**
1067 S. Gaylord St.
303/733-1143

**Victoriana Antique Jewelry**
1512 Larimer St. #39R
303/573-5049

**Red's Antique Galleries**
5797 E. Evans Ave.
303/753-9187

**Sandpiper Antiques**
1524 S. Broadway
303/777-4384

**Shepton's Antiques**
389 S. Broadway
303/777-5115

**American Vogue Vintage Clothing**
10 S. Broadway
303/733-4140

**Antique Brokers**
1388 S. Broadway
303/722-3090

**Collector's Choice Antiques**
2920 E. Colfax Ave.
303/320-8451

**Reckollections Indoor**
5736 E. Colfax Ave.
303/329-8848

**Treasured Scarab**
25 E. Dakota Ave.
303/777-6884

**East West Designs**
600 Ogden St.
303/861-4741

**Antique Zoo**
1395 S. Acoma St.
303/778-9191

**Hampden Street Antiques**
8964 E. Hampden Ave.
303/721-7992

**Collectible Chair Co.**
2817 E. 3rd Ave.
303/320-6585

**Starr Antiques**
2940 E. 6th Ave.
303/399-4537

**Feathered Nest**
935 E. Cedar Ave.
303/744-6881

**Railroad Memories**
1903 S. Niagara St.
303/759-1290

**APIRY**
585 Milwaukee St.
303/399-6017

**Denver Doll Emporium**
1570 S. Pearl St.
303/733-6339

**Queen City Architectural**
4750 Brighton Blvd.
303/296-0925

**Sixth Avenue Antiques**
2900 E. 6th Ave.
303/322-5773

**And Etcetera Antiques**
1065 S. Gaylord St.
303/744-0745

**Broadway Antiques & Auction**
511 Broadway
303/825-7533

**Collectors Corner**
10615 Melody Dr.
303/450-2875

**Belleli Antiques & Fine Arts**
210 Clayton St.
303/355-2422

**Finders Keepers Antiques**
1451 S. Broadway
303/777-4521

**Frontier Gallery**
1500 S. Broadway
303/733-4200

**La Cache**
400 Downing St.
303/871-9605

**Eron Johnson Antiques Ltd.**
451 Broadway
303/777-8700

**French Country Antiques Ltd.**
2906 E. 6th Ave.
303/321-1977

**Metropolitan Antique Gallery**
1147 Broadway
303/623-3333

**Mer-Sadies Antiques**
1345 S. Broadway
303/765-5440

## *Great Places To Stay*

### Capitol Hill Mansion
1207 Pennsylvania St.
1-800-839-9329

The Capitol Hill Mansion is located in the most architecturally outstanding area of the City, surrounded by historic houses of pioneers, governors, financiers, mining magnates and other families of wealth and power. Built in 1891, it is one of the last splendid homes erected before the Great Silver Crash. The elegant exterior of ruby sandstone is expressed in a Richardsonian Romanesque style: high turrets, balconies, soaring chimneys and a grand curved porch. The entry interior of meticulously-crafted patterned plaster and golden oak paneling opens to a dramatic sweeping staircase, punctuated by an exquisite stained and beveled glass window. Inviting public parlors in rich green tones and exceptional guest rooms, each individually decorated, complete the appointments to this truly grand mansion.

## *Interesting Side Trips*

### Byers-Evans House
Corner of 13th Ave. & Bannock St.
303/620-4933

The Byers-Evans House was built in 1883 by Rocky Mountain News publisher, William Byers. It was sold in 1889 to the family of William Gray Evans, an officer of the Denver Tramway Company. Guided tours take visitors through this elegant residence, richly filled with original family furnishings.

## 12 DURANGO

**Southwest Book Trader**
175 E. 5th St.
970/247-8479

**Time Traveler**
131 E. 8th St.
970/259-3130

**Wildflowers Antiques**
742 Main Ave.
970/247-4249

**Comstock Mercantile**
638 Main Ave.
970/259-5069

**Treasures by Therese**
111 E. 30th St.
970/259-5034

**Appaloosa Trading Co.**
501 Main Ave.
970-259-1994

### *Great Places To Stay*

**Blue Lake Ranch**
16000 Hwy. 140
(Hesperus)
970/385-4537
Email: bluelake@frontier.net
Web site: www.frontier/nbluelake
Rates: $65-245
Reservations taken Mon.-Sun. 8 a.m.-8 p.m.
*Directions: Blue Lake Ranch is 15 minutes west of Durango. To protect the guests' privacy, there is no highway signage for Blue Lake Ranch. Use your odometer to find the gravel driveway. From the north, east or west: Take Hwy. 140 south at Hesperus. Go 6 1/2 miles to find the driveway to the right. From the south: Take Hwy. 170 in New Mexico north, which turns into Colorado Hwy. 140 at the state line. Continue north and note the junction of Hwy. 141 and Hwy. 140. Blue Lake Ranch is 1 3/10 miles north of this junction on the left.*

Blue Lake Ranch has evolved from a simple 1910 homestead into a luxurious European-style Country Estate. From the elegantly appointed Main Inn to the secluded garden cottages, there are unsurpassed views of Blue Lake, and the gardens of the 13,000-foot La Plata Mountains. A year-round destination acclaimed for its spring and summer gardens, the ranch offers spectacular fall color and becomes a winter wonderland with the first snowfall. There is absolute privacy and quiet without another house in sight. Guests enjoy fishing for trophy trout in the lake, strolling in the gardens, where over 10,000 iris bloom annually, and exploring the ranch's private wildlife preserve.

The Main Inn is the original restored homestead house and serves as Ranch headquarters. In the summer a European-style breakfast buffet is served in the dining room and on the garden patios. The buffet offers a delicious selection of cheeses, meats, cereals, fruits, seasonal berries, pastries, juices, Southwestern dishes and fresh roasted coffee or tea. Afternoon tea is served at 5 p.m. on the garden patios.

The four guest rooms in the Inn are all comfortably separated from one another. The Garden Room entered through the library hall has a window seat, fireplace and private deck in a garden overlooking the lake. The Oriental-style bath has a shower room with a deep-soaking tub. Situated at the top of a circular staircase, The Rose Room provides 360-degree views of the lake, gardens and mountains through dormer windows, has a queen bed and sitting area. The Victorian Room is furnished with an 1850s handcarved four poster canopied double bed and has a Dutch door to the garden. The private unattached bath has a six-foot-long claw footed tub.

In addition to the four rooms in the Inn, Blue Lake Ranch has a 3 bedroom, 3 bath log cabin on the lake, a cottage in the woods, two suites in a renovated barn and a turn of the century homestead house on the banks of the La Plata River.

**Note: Dr. Shirley Isgar, Innkeeper at Blue Lake Ranch, delights in recounting this amusing tale. At the Country Inn, an elusive trout lured a first-time fisherman physician in waders a bit too far out into the lake. While concentrating on landing an incredible rainbow trout, he didn't realize he had sunken into the soft mud up to his thighs. Meanwhile, a guest (a malpractice lawyer) was watching from the cabin directly on the lake. Finally the physician, not being able to move, cried for help and the lawyer pulled him into shore...minus his boots. Who gets the bill?*

**The Historic Strater Hotel**
699 Main Ave.
1-800-247-4431 or 970/247-4431
Open year round

Built in 1887 and furnished throughout with authentic Victorian antiques, the Strater Hotel has been catering to travelers for 108 years. Selected by *Diversion Magazine* as " Colorado's finest Victorian Hotel," the Strater offers 93 beautiful guest rooms, a restaurant, and a saloon all set in the melodramatic aura of the 1800s gold rush days.

### *Interesting Side Trips*

**Durango & Silverton Narrow Gauge Railroad**
479 Main Ave./Durango & Silverton Train Depot
970/247-2733
Call for schedule & tickets

When you ride the DURANGO & SILVERTON NARROW GAUGE RAILROAD, you'll experience a legacy of mountain railroading history that has remained virtually unchanged for over a century.

This historic steam-powered train once carried food, provisions and silver. Today the Silverton takes visitors on a spectacular scenic trip through the San Juan Mountains. Witness relics of the 1800s that line the railroad's tracks, or even catch a glimpse of bears, elk, bald eagles, and many other species of Rocky Mountain wildlife. It's one train ride you won't soon forget.

**Animas Museum**
31st St & West 2nd Ave.
970/259-2402
Mon.-Sat. 10-6 May through Oct.

Located in the residential neighborhood in the old Animas City section of town, Durango's only history museum is somewhat out of the public eye. But what surprises are in store for those who venture off the beaten path of north Main to visit the museum! Cloistered within the sandstone walls of the 90-year-old museum building are untold treasures of the San Juan Basin's rich and colorful heritage. Does an 1880s hand-crafted saddle made in Animas City intrigue you? Perhaps a porcelain Victorian doll, a D&RG railroad lantern, a pair of Buckskin Charlie's beaded moccasins or a Zuni polychrome olla is more to your liking. These objects and many more can be seen in the museum's exhibits.

## 13 ENGLEWOOD

**Van Dyke's Antiques**
3663 S. Broadway
303/789-3743
Mon.-Sat. 10-5, Sun. 1-4
303/973-0110 for after hour appointments
*Directions: Denver Metro Area — Take I-25 to Hwy. 285 (Hampdon Ave) west to Broadway, exit south on Broadway, 1 1/2 blocks on west side of street.*

For specific information see review at the beginning of this section.

**QMyan's Popourri Antiques**
3665 S. Broadway
303/781-7724

**Rocky Mountain Clocks & Repair**
2739 S. Broadway
303/789-1573

## 14 ESTES PARK

**Bountiful**
125 Moraine Ave. #B
970/586-9332

**Cottage & Gardens**
7461 County Road 43
970/586-0580

**Little Victorian Attic**
157 W. Elkhorn Ave.
970/586-8964

## 15 FORT COLLINS

**Nostalgia Antiques**
2216 Northridge Ct.
970/221-5139

**Bell Tower Antiques**
2520 N. Shields St.
970/482-2510

**Happenstance**
136 W. Mountain Ave.
970/493-1668

**Collins Antique Mart**
6124 S. College Ave.
970/226-3305

**Front Range Antique Mall**
6108 S. College Ave.
970/282-1808

**Yesterday's Treasures**
272 N. College Ave.
970/493-9211

**Windswept Farm**
5537 N. County Road 9
970/484-1124

**Foothills Indoor Flea Market**
6300 S. College Ave.
970/223-9069

**Bennett Antiques & Accessories**
1220 S. College
970/482-3645

**Nesch Brass & Antiques**
201 N. Link Lane
970/221-0787

**Never Open Antiques**
1746 E. Mulberry St.
970/495-0401

## 16 GEORGETOWN

**Antique Emporium**
501 Rose St.
303/569-2727

**Cobweb Shoppe of Georgetown**
512 6th St.
303/569-3112

**Nora Blooms's Antiques**
614 6th St. #B
303/569-0210

**Powder Cache Antiques**
612 6th St.
303/569-2848

**Stuff & Such**
601 14th St.
303/569-2507

## 17 GLENWOOD SPRINGS

**Anita's Antiques & Elegant**
1030 Grand Ave.
970/928-9622

**Forever Elegant**
815 Grand Ave.
970-928-0510

**Glenwood Books & Collectibles**
720 Grand Ave.
970-928-8825

**Antiques Etc.**
212 6th St.
970/945-6129

**Strange Imports**
291 County Road 119
970/945-1484

**First Class Trash**
3330 S. Glen Ave.
970/945-0533

## 18 GRAND JUNCTION

**Guy Kelly Washburn Antiques**
600 White Ave.
970/241-6880

**Antique Emporium**
140 W. Main St.
970/242-1563

**American Heritage Antiques**
117 N. 6th St.
970/245-8046

**Great American Antqs. Store**
439 Main St.
970/242-2443

**Finders Trove**
558 Main St.
970/245-0109

## 19 GREELEY

**Antiques at Lincoln Park**
822 8th St.
970/351-6222

**Blossom Tyme Gifts & Antiques**
1201 11th Ave.
970/352-4379

**Create Antiques**
2200 Reservoir Rd.
970/353-1712

**Foster's Antiques & Clock Shop**
1329 9th Ave.
970/352-9204

## 20 GUNNISON

**Chars**
119 S. Main St.
970/641-2494

### *Great Places To Stay*

**Eagle's Nest Bed and Breakfast**
206 N. Colorado
970/641-4457
Open every day
*Directions: Take Hwy. 50 to the Holiday Inn in Gunnison. Located directly behind the Holiday Inn on the corner of Colorado and Virginia.*

Hugh and Jane McGee are retired school teachers from a northern Chicago suburb. They now enjoy their new vocation as proprietors of the Eagles Nest B&B in Gunnison.

The upstairs of the McGee home has a large suite, private bath and breakfast nook or reading room for relaxing. The front porch beautifully displays Hugh's own works of art—stained glass. Hugh's superb culinary masterpieces - Western Eggs Benidict, Vegetable Omelets and French Toast "keeps folks raving!" Jane also finds time to be a Mary Kay cosmetics consultant. It is advisable to call well ahead for reservations.

## 21 HOTCHKISS

**Beulah B's**
1091 A Hwy. #133
970/872-3051

**Cowboy Collectibles**
448 Bridge St.
970/872-3025

**The Ark II**
101 W. Bridge St.
970/872-2226

**Country Home Store**
264 W. Bridge St.
970/872-4647

**Olde Town Hall Antiques**
503 N. 2nd St.
970/872-3500

## 22 LITTLETON

**Colorado Antique Gallery**
5501 S. Broadway
303/794-8100
Mon.-Sat. 10-6, Thurs. 10-8, Sun. 12-6

For more specific information see review at the beginning of this section.

**Creamery**
2675 W. Alamo Ave.
303/730-2747

**Olde Littleton Antique Co-op**
2681 W. Alamo Ave.
303/795-9965

**Olde Towne Antiques & Vintage**
2500 W. Main St.
303/347-9258

**Remember When Antiques**
2569 W. Main St.
303/798-2989

**Colorado Antique Gallery**
5501 S. Broadway
303/794-8100

## 23 LOVELAND

**Lynn Allee Down Antiques**
1220 Langston Lane
970/667-9889

**Bonser Antique Mall**
315 E. 4th St.
970/669-8005

**Canyon Collectibles**
5641 W. U.S. Hwy. 34
970/593-9227

**Country Shed Antiques**
136 E. 4th St.
970/667-9448

**Country Wishes & Wants**
120 E. 4th St.
970/635-9132

**Diamonds & Toads**
137 E. 4th St.
970/667-9414

**Grandma's Attic**
214 E. 4th St.
970/667-1807

**Kottage**
333 Cleveland Ave.
970/667-1110

**Nostalgia Corner**
140 E. 4th St.
970/663-5591

**Rocky Mt. Antiques Inc.**
3816 W. Eisenhower Blvd.
970/663-7551

**Bill's Antiques & Flea Market**
339 E. 4th St.
970/663-4355

**Ed's Antique Furniture Sales**
1400 Falls Court
970/669-3545

**North Fork Antique Flea Market**
3121 W. Eisenhower Blvd.
970/203-1522

## 24 LYONS

**Left-Hand's Antique & Western**
228 E. Main
303/823-5738

**Ralston Brothers Antiques**
426 High St.
303/823-6982

**Left-Hand Trading Co.**
401, 405 & 228 Main
303/823-6311

## 25 MANITOU SPRINGS

**Nothing New**
116 Canon Ave.
719/685-9353

### *Interesting Side Trips*

**Miramont Castle**
Capitol Hill Ave. off Ruxton Ave.
719/685-1011

Are you fascinated by old buildings? Do you love history? Are you interested in the unusual? If so, tour Miramont Castle! The world-famous "castle" was constructed in 1895, and currently hosts more than 42,000 visitors annually. The four-story structure has 46 rooms (28 of them open to the public), two-foot-thick stone walls, and incorporates nine distinctly different styles of architecture over 14,000 square feet of floor space!

Miramont Castle has played an important role in the history of Manitou Springs. Originally built by a wealthy French priest, over the years the castle has been both a sanitarium and an apartment house.

Today you can tour the historic Miramont Castle and marvel at the Drawing Room with its gold ceiling and 200-ton Peachblow sandstone fireplace. You can enjoy a quiet moment in the eight-sided Montcalm Chapel, visit the new miniature museum, or take in the grandeur of the 400-square-foot Marie Francolon bedroom. Relax in the Queen's Parlor enclosed tearoom, which offers tasty menu items and striking views of the surrounding mountains.

## 26 MONTROSE

**Black Bear Antiques**
62281 Hwy. 90
970/249-5738

**C & D Antiques**
1360 Townsend Ave.
970/249-6155

## 27 MORRISON

**El Mercado**
120 Bear Creek Ave.
303/697-8361

**Little Bits of Yesterday**
309 Bear Creek Ave.
303/697-8661

**Morrison Antiques**
307 Bear Creek Ave.
303/697-9545

**Western Trail Antiques & Gifts**
205 Bear Creek Ave.
303/697-9238

## 28 NEDERLAND

**Off Her Rocker Antiques**
4 East First St.
303/258-7976

## 29 NIWOT

**Lockwood House Antiques**
198 2nd Ave.
303/652-2963

**Niwot Antique Emporium**
136 2nd Ave.
303/652-2587

**Wise Buys Antiques**
190 2nd Ave.
303/652-2888

**Niwot Trading Post**
149 2nd Ave.
303/443-0184

## 30 PUEBLO

**Silver Lining Antiques**
27050 U.S. Highway 50 E.
719/545-3575

**Blazing Saddle Antiques**
118 S. Union Ave.
719/544-5520

**Mid 30s Glass Shop**
225 S. Union Ave.
719/544-1031

**Cardinelli's Antiques**
525 N. Santa Fe Ave.
719/544-9016

**Oldies But Goodies Antq. Shop**
113 W. 4th St.
719/545-4661

**Victorianna's**
213 S. Union Ave.
719/583-8009

**A Touch of the Past**
3369 S. Interstate 25
719/564-1840

**Lane's House of Glass Inc.**
111 Colorado Ave.
719/542-2210

**Quilt Shop Antiques**
111 E. Abriendo Ave.
719/544-4906

**Trail Antiques**
28018 E. U.S. Hwy. 50
719/948-2001

**Silver Lining Antiques**
27050 U.S. Hwy. 50 E.
719/545-3575

**Why Not Antiques**
1240 Berkley Ave.
719/544-4104

**Abriendo Antiques**
130 W. Abriendo Ave
719/543-3036

**Because You Love Antiques**
118 W. 3rd St.
719/544-5567

**Highlander Antiques**
330 S. Union Ave.
719/544-6040

**Trolley Stop Antiques**
818 W. 4th St.
719/543-1261

## 31 SALIDA

**Carriage House Antiques**
148 N. F St.
719/539-4001

**Jacobson's Antiques**
7535 W. U.S. Hwy. 50
719/539-2093

**Old Log Cabin Antiques**
225 E. Rainbow Blvd.
719/539-2803

**Hartman's Furn. & Antqiues**
11384 W. U.S. Highway 50
719/539-4083

## 32 SILVERTON

Silverton, Colorado, and its surrounding countryside are a playground where the scenery uplifts the spirit and sends energy levels climbing. The town is a National Historic Landmark, representing the Victorian era.

Having never suffered the catastrophic fires that most old mining towns have endured, Silverton is one of the best preserved, with most of its original homes and businesses still standing. Among the original buildings to explore is the San Juan County Historical Society Museum, a 1902 structure that once housed the county jail. The museum provides an excellent introduction to the town and its history.

On the "wilder" side of town is Blair Street, infamous for once offering Silverton and its visitors 40 saloons and brothels. These businesses appeared in abundance in mining and railroad towns at the turn of the century. Now serving as a location for many western movie shots, the street has earned an additional reputation since the heyday of its original activities.

Tantalized by the history and the longing for gold that the town and its premises encourage, you should be well prepped for the Old Hundred Gold Mine Tour. Local miners have established this one-hour train ride tour into an authentic gold mine deep within a mountain. Experienced miners guide the tours.

For the adventurous, a trip can be planned aboard a coal-fired, steam-operated train of the Durango & Silverton Narrow Gauge Railroad, which has served Silverton since 1882. Part of the year a railroad-operated bus shuttles passengers from Silverton to Durango for return the same day by rail, allowing a new perspective of the fabulous views offered by the surrounding landscape. Another option is to make the complete Durango-Silverton-Durango loop, stopping over for one or more nights in Silverton.

### *Great Places To Stay*

**Alma House**
220 East 10th Street
970/387-5336
Open year round

European style.

### *Favorite Places To Eat*

**The French Bakery**
1250 Greene Street
970/387-5423
*Directions: From Denver, take I-70 west to Exit 37 (before Grand Junction), CO 141 south to U.S. 50 South to U.S. 550 (at Montrose), U.S. 550 South to Silverton. Located on the first floor of Teller House Hotel.*

The French Bakery is located on Greene Street, which just happens to be the main fairway through the tiny town of Silverton. Along this street, attractive Victorian period buildings and homes patiently pass the years.

The building housing the bakery is also home to the Teller House Hotel, which is on the second floor of the two-story brick building. Built by Silverton Brewery owner, Charles Fischer, the upstairs has been a hotel since its construction in 1896. It is listed as a National Historic Landmark and retains its original woodwork, high ceilings and many of its original Victorian furnishings.

The French Bakery, on the first floor below, serves a hearty southwestern breakfast, soup, deli sandwich or gourmet pizza for lunch. The bakery has long been hailed as a favorite dining spot by hotel guests and drop-ins.

## 33 VAIL

**Englishman Fine Art & Antiques**
143 E. Meadow Dr. #205
970/476-3570

**Finishing Touch of Vail Inc.**
122 E. Meadow Dr.
970/476-1656

**Lodge & Cabin Dry Goods Co.**
100 E. Meadow Dr.
970/476-1475

## 34 VICTOR

**Assay Office Antiques**
113 South Third
719/689-2712
Open 7 days a week end of May to September 15, 11-5; open by appointment in the winter
*Directions: Take Hwy. 67 to Victor. At the corner of Victor Ave. and 3rd St., turn right. The shop is situated in the middle of the block on the west side.*

Assay Office Antiques gets its name from the building's younger days as an assayer's office. For those of you who haven't a clue what an assayer is, here's an explanation. Back in the gold rush days, Victor was the largest gold mining district in the United States. The miners, speculators, the hopeful and the lucky, would bring their samples to the local assayer's office where it was tested for its true gold content.

Today within the walls of this turn-of-the-century building, trades of the past can still be found (and offered for sale). The shop carries a nice selection of gold mining gear, such as picks, pans, weights and measuring devices. Apart from the relics related to the history of the town, you can turn up old railroad items, some nice primitives, old toys, glassware and other interesting collectibles.

## 35 WINDSOR

**Memory Lane Antiques**
426 Main St.
970/686-7913

## 36 YUMA

**The Farmstead**
46999 County Rd. E.
970/848-2643

**Albany Street Antique & Gift**
203 S. Albany St.
970/848-5214

**Kaliko Kreations**
419 S. Houston
970/848-0807

# Connecticut

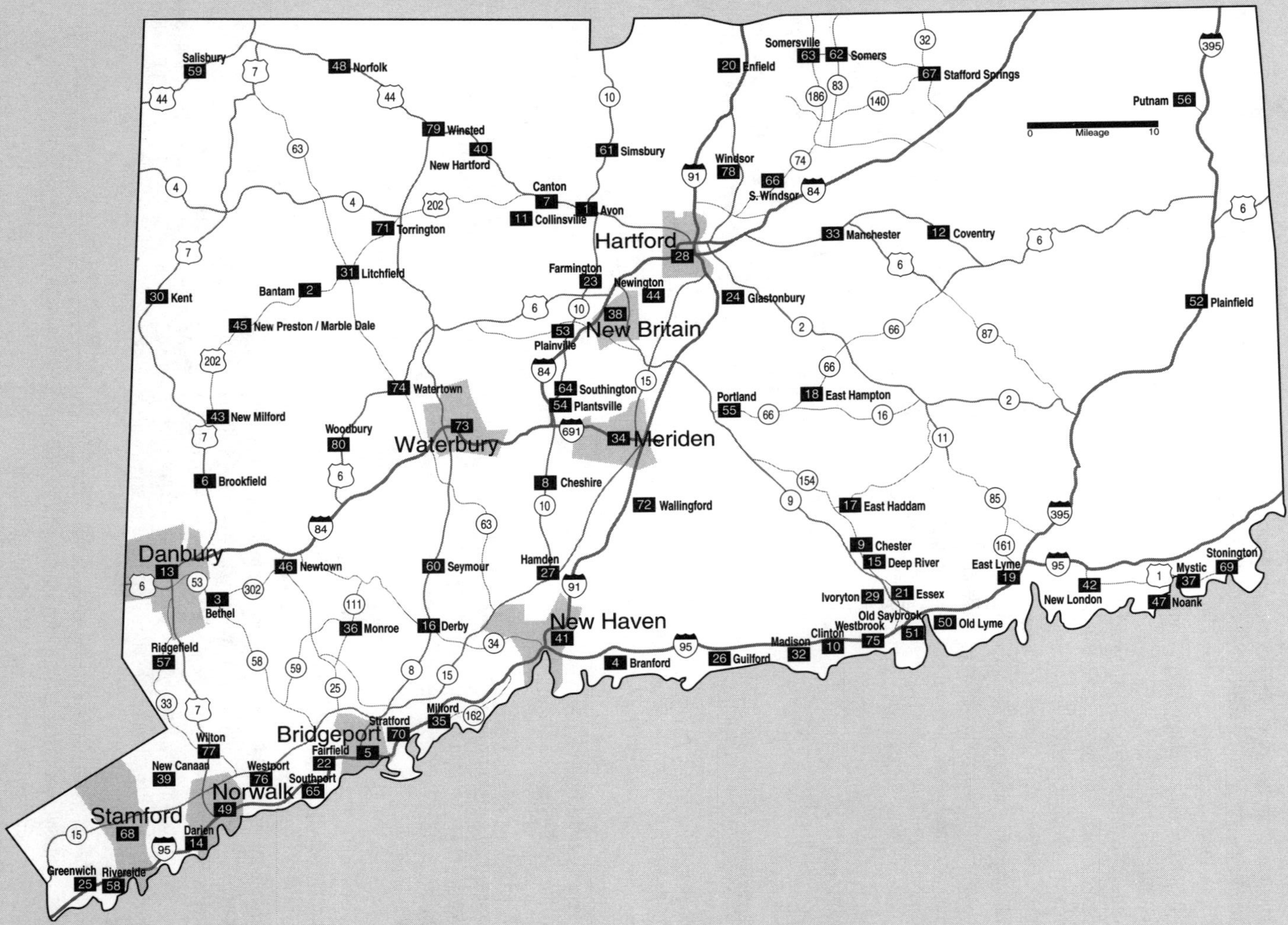

# Interest compounds daily for collectors at Old Bank Antiques

Old Bank Antiques is just as its name implies, an old bank. I have always been fascinated with buildings such as these, mostly because they hold something I would like to have — *a lot of money*.

Years ago if you had walked into this "Old Bank." the vaults would have been shut and tightly locked, protecting the loot from bank robbing bandits who often rode into town unexpectedly. Today, the doors are opened wide, welcoming all to view a different kind of bounty. Displayed within are small antique pieces such as flow blue, limoges, lamps, sterling, china, music boxes, toys, firearms and art.

Throughout this three-story building, thirty antique dealers offer a distinguished collection of 18th-20th century furnishings and smalls, with over 300 pieces of furniture ready to go in oak, mahogany, pine and wicker. The shop is also one of the few places that always has big tables and *sets* of chairs.

*Old Bank Antiques is located at 66 Main St. in East Hampton. For additional information see listing #18 (East Hampton).*

*A converted bank building serves to protect a different sort of loot, heirloom antiques and furniture.*

*In an atmosphere of old money, a collection of 18th-20th century furniture is featured, with over 300 pieces ready to go. Oak, mahogany, pine and wicker selections are available at Old Bank Antiques.*

*The Old Mill Inn is cozily nestled in the Connecticut countryside. The area is loaded with bucolic charm and natural beauty, an ideal escape from the world.*

# The Old Mill Inn is the charm of Connecticut

This warm and inviting private home was originally built in the mid-1800s. It was enlarged and renovated 100 years later by an owner of the Mill, who raised a family of seven in its gracious rooms. The second-floor guest wing has five bedrooms complete with down comforters, full-size robes and bath sheets, fresh fruit and purified drinking water. There is a quiet, comfortable reading room, a large sun deck which is perfect for soaking up rays or stargazing by telescope at night. Downstairs is another guest room, a parlor with fireplace, and a dining room with handpainted walls of flowering shrubs and trees, which merge with a similar vista through the window wall that overlooks a deep expanse of lawn bordered by flowering shrubs and trees. The entire property is surrounded by giant maple trees that open onto the green, and guests can wander down the path through the woods to the private beach on the Scantic River. There, they'll find hammocks, swings, canoes, picnic tables, fishing and bicycles, and a spa for evening soaking of any sore muscles from the day's activities.

*Your hosts are Stephanie and Jim.*

Nearby attractions are only minutes away and include antique shops, restaurants, numerous museums and historic homes. In the immediate area are two golf courses, an equestrian center and a motor speedway.

** Note: David and I stayed with Stephanie and Jim during our antiquing tour to Brimfield, Massachusetts. These guys are so much fun and made our stay something special to remember. We definitely recommend The Old Mill Inn.*

*The Old Mill Inn Bed & Breakfast is located at 63 Maple St. in Somersville. For additional information see listing #63 (Somersville).*

*Although enlarged and renovated by owners of the mill years ago, The Old Mill Inn Bed and Breakfast originally dates from the mid-1800s.*

*Amenities abound for guests who enjoy the great outdoors. Paths through the woods lead to a beach with boating, fishing , picnicking, bicycling equipment and areas for just plain old relaxing.*

# Connecticut

## 1 AVON

**D & W Collectibles**
13 E. Main St.
860/676-2180

**Moosavi Persian Rugs**
45 E. Main St.
860/676-0082

## 2 BANTAM

**Bradford House Antiques**
895 Bantam Road
860/567-0951

**TNT Antiques & Collectibles**
898 Bantam Road
860/567-8823

**Old Carriage Shop Antique Center**
920 Bantam Road
860/567-3234

**Weston Thorn**
940 Bantam Road
860/567-4661

## 3 BETHEL

**Saltbox Antiques**
123 Greenwood Ave.
203/744-6097

## 4 BRANFORD

**Yesterday's Threads Vintage**
206 Meadow St.
203/481-6452

**Oldies But Goodies**
781 E. Main St.
203/488-7230

**Taken For Granite Antiques**
409 Leetes Island Road
203/488-0557

**C & R Antiques**
62 Knollwood Dr.
203/488-9860

**Clock Tower Antiques**
824 E. Main St.
203/488-1919

## 5 BRIDGEPORT

**Sweet Memories**
2714 Fairfield Ave.
203/330-0558

**Tinker's Treasures**
2980 Fairfield Ave.
203/579-4243

**Olivia's Attic**
3004 Fairfield Ave.
203/332-0253

**All That Glitters**
3000 Fairfield Ave.
203/333-5836

## 6 BROOKFIELD

**Sugar Hollow Antiques**
797 Federal Road
203/775-5111

**Antiques International**
934 Federal Road
203/740-2336

**Old Favorites Antiques**
9 Arrowhead Road
203/775-3744

## 7 CANTON

**Balcony Antiques**
81 Albany Turnpike
860/693-6440

**On The Road Bookshop**
163 Albany Turnpike
860/693-6029

**Canton Green Antique Store**
181 Albany Turnpike
860/693-0008

**Antiques at Canton Village**
Canton Village Rte. 44
860/693-2715

**Lila Sklar Antiques**
Canton Vlge-Rte. 44
860/651-9111

**Griffin Brothers & Co.**
10 Front
860/693-9007

**Cob-Web Shop**
20 Dyer Cemetery Road
860/693-2658

**Canton Barn Antiques-Auctions**
75 Old Canton Rd. (Off Route 44)
860/693-0601

### *Great Places To Stay*

**Special Joys**
41 N. River Road
1-800-750-3979

Discover the ambiance of the old and the new at this Victorian 3 Diamond AAA rated B&B that also houses an antique doll and toy shop and museum where treasures of the past blend charmingly with the attractive, sophisticated decor of a small country inn. Modern amenities, flower gardens, a solarium lit dining area, full breakfast and a relaxed atmosphere add to the comfort of your stay.

## 8 CHESHIRE

**Cartophilians**
430 Highland Ave.
203/272-1143

**Chez Angele**
150 Main St.
203/271-9883

**Granny's Attic**
192 S. Main St.
203/272-8262

**Magnolia Shoppe**
908 S. Meriden Road
203/272-3303

## 9 CHESTER

**Spiritus Mundi Antiques**
122 Middlesex Ave. (Rt. 154)
860/526-3406

**One of a Kind Antiques**
21 Main St.
860/526-9736

**Nilsson Spring St. Studio &Gallery**
3 Spring St.
860/526-2077

**William L. Schaeffer/Photographs**
41 Main St.
860/526-3870

### *Favorite Places To Eat*

**Restaurant Du Village**
59 Main St.
860/526-5301

Country French cuisine prepared by Chef/Owners Michael & Cynthia Keller, served in an intimate setting. "Best restaurant in Ct.," ZAGAT survey and "Best French in State,", CONNECTICUT Magazine. Dinner only. Reservations recommended.

**Mad Hatter Bakery & Cafe**
23 Main St.
860/526-2156

Bakery specializing in hearth-baked sourdough breads and old-fashioned pastries. Cafe serves up an eclectic, mostly Mediterranean menu for breakfast, lunch and weekend dinners. Closed Tuesday.

**Inn At Chester**
318 W. Main St. (Route 148)
860/526-9541

The Inn at Chester boasts two restaurants: The Post and Beam features fine dining, serving New American cuisine in casual elegance. Dunk's Landing is a comfortable tavern serving lighter fare. Open 7 days including Sunday brunch.

## 10 CLINTON

**Clinton Antique Center**
78 E. Main St.
860/669-3839

**Antiques on Main Street**
104 E. Main St.
860/664-9163

**Waterside Antiques & Gifts**
109 E. Main St.
860/669-0809

**Square-Riggers Antique Center**
350 E. Main St.
860/664-9001

**John Street Antiques**
23 W. Main St. #A
860/669-2439

**Loft**
59 W. Main St.
860/669-4583

**Hey-Day Antiques**
9 Rocky Ledge Dr.
860/669-8800

**Van Carter Hale Fine Art**
36 W. Main St.
860/669-4313

**Barker & Chambers Antiques On Main**
100 E. Main St. (Rt. 1)
860/664-9163

**Miller's Antiques**
327 E. Main St. (Rt. 1)
860/669-3533

**Wooden Wheelbarrow**
327 E. Main St. (Rt. 1)
860/669-3533

### *Great Places To Stay*

**Captain Dibbell House**
21 Commerce St.
860/669-1646
Web site: clintonct.com/dibbell

The Captain Dibble House Bed & Breakfast offers guests the opportunity to experience the warmth and hospitality of a lovingly preserved 1866 Victorian. The house is situated on a historic residential street in a small seacost town just two blocks from the harbor. Crossing the wisteria covered footbridge leading to the front porch sets the mood. Guests can relax in the spacious parlor in front of the fireplace or on the gazebo after strolling through the gardens or gazing into the water garden. Four comfortable guest rooms are uniquely decorated ranging from the Victorian Captain's Room with its formal furnishings to the casual Garden Room with its painted and stenciled walls, original wood floor and wicker furniture. All are furnished with a mixture of antiques and family heirlooms and have ceiling fans (air conditioners in the summer), private baths and fresh flowers from the gardens. There's a refrigerator stocked with complimentary beverages, afternoon or evening home baked snacks and hot beverages. Freshly baked savories will tempt you at breakfast and then its off for a day of exploring quaint towns, antiquing, or enjoying the beach.

## 11 COLLINSVILLE

**The Collinsville Antiques Co.**
Historical Collins Axe Factory
P.O. Box 473
860/693-1011

## 12 COVENTRY

**CCS Antiques & Gifts**
2799 Boston Turnpike
860/742-6099

**Memory Lanes Countryside**
2224 Boston Turnpike, Rt. 44
860/742-0346

## 13 DANBURY

**Red White & Blue Antiques**
49 South St.
203/778-5085

**Antiques & Collectibles**
49 South St.
203/791-1275

**Antique Palace Emporium Inc.**
7 Backus Ave.
203/798-8569

**Antiquity**
66 Sugar Hollow Rd.
203/748-6244

## 14 DARIEN

**Knock on Wood**
355 Post Road
203/655-9031

**Antiques of Darien**
1101 Boston Post Road
203/655-5133

**Emy Jane Jones Antiques**
770 Post Road
203/655-7576

**Sebastian Gallery**
833 Post Road
203/656-3093

**Windsor Antiques Ltd.**
1064 Post Road
203/655-2330

**H. P. McLane Antiques**
110 Post Road #R
203/655-2280

**Catherine Reiss**
1072 Post Road
203/655-8070

**Fred Heintz Antiques**
1101 Post Road
203/656-4393

## 15 DEEP RIVER

**Detour**
Old Piano Factory
860/526-9797

**Irish Country Pine**
246 S. Main
860/526-9757

**James E Elliott Antiques**
453 Winthrop Road
860/526-9455

**Riverwind Antique Shop**
68 Main St.
860/526-3047

**Way We Wore**
116 Main St.
860/526-2944

**Deep River Design**
381 Main St. (Rt. 154)
860/526-9270

**Slater & Sons Irish Country Antiques**
Corner of Main & Union Streets
860/525-9757

## 16 DERBY

### The Derby Antique Center, Inc.
181 Main Street
203/734-7614
Tues.-Thurs. 10-2, Fri.-Sat. 10-5, closed Sun.-Mon.
*Directions: The Derby Antique Center is located on Connecticut Route 34N., 500 feet from Exit #15 north or Route 8 south. Route 8 runs north and south through Connecticut. The shop is on the right side traveling north on Main St. in Derby, which is also Connecticut Route 34 north and south.*

There's lots of expertise in antiques here at The Derby for shoppers to draw on as they browse through this large store. Although owner Peter Petrino has had the store only four years himself, he grew up working with the past owner and learned the business inside-out before taking the reins. The former owner also comes back from Florida in the summers to work in the store and greet old, familiar faces. The Derby handles "everything," as Peter says, but seems to get in a lot of musical instruments, besides the furniture, china, collectibles, jewelry, etc.

## 17 EAST HADDAM

**Howard & Dickinson Antiques**
48 Main St.
860/873-9990

**Iron Horse Antiques & Nostalgia**
64 Main St.
860/267-7623

## 18 EAST HAMPTON

Nestled in the south central hills of Connecticut lies the quaint, historic town of East Hampton. Formerly known as Chatham, the area was originally famous for its ship-making and bell industries. Today, the old town center has developed into a cluster of antique shops and eateries making for a pleasant afternoon of antique shopping.

### Old Bank Antiques
66 Main St.
860/295-9416
Wed.-Sun. 10-5, Fri. until 8 p.m., or by appointment
*Directions: Route 91 exit 25 N.; connects with Route 2 East, Exit 13, right onto Route 66, left at 3rd light.*

For specific information see review at the beginning of this section.

**Antiques at Seventy Main St.**
70 Main St.
860/267-9501

**Past & Present Antiques**
81 Main St.
860/267-0495

## 19 EAST LYME

**Judy's Unfound Treasures**
180 Boston Post Road #A
860/739-7440

**Country Life Antiques**
55 W. Main
860/739-8969

**Book Barn**
41 W. Main
860/739-5715

**G-Tiques Antiques**
179 Boston Post Road
860/739-1946

## 20 ENFIELD

**Hazard Antique Center**
287 Hazard Ave.
860/763-0811

## 21 ESSEX

**Arne E Ahlberg Antiques**
145 Westbrook Road
860/767-2799

**American Heritage Antiques**
251 Westbrook Road
860/767-8162

**Francis Bealey American Arts**
3 S. Main St.
860/767-0220

**Hastings House**
4 N. Main St.
860/767-8217

**Phoenix Antiques**
10 Main St.
860/767-5082

**Valley Farm Antiques**
134 Saybrook Road
860/767-8555

***Favorite Places To Eat***

### Griswold Inn
36 Main St.
860/767-1776

Famous for meat pies, homemade sausage, fresh seafood and prime rib. World famous marine art collection. Twenty-seven guest rooms.

## 22 FAIRFIELD

**Reminisce With Kathy**
238 Post Road
203/254-0300

**James Bok Antiques**
1954 Post Road
203/255-6500

**Winsor Antiques**
43 Ruance St.
203/255-0056

**Our Place Antiques**
111 Post Road
203/254-3408

## 23 FARMINGTON

**Farmington Lodge Antiques**
185 Main St.
860/674-1035

**Samovar Antiques**
780 Farmington Ave. #F
860/677-8772

**Antiq's**
1839 New Britain Ave.
860-676-2670

### *Great Places To Stay*

**Farmington Inn**
827 Farmington Ave.
860/677-2821

The 'quintessential' Farmington Inn is a lovely two-story inn of seventy-two rooms including plush suites, an inviting cozy fireplaced lobby decorated in antiques and original paintings. Guests are treated to Victoria's Cafe, the private breakfast room, where a sumptuous daily continental breakfast is served complimentary with an overnight stay.

## 24 GLASTONBURY

**Always Buying Antiques**
By Appointment Only
860/646-6808

**Tobacco Shed Antiques**
119 Griswold St.
860/657-2885

**Black Pearl Antiques**
2217 Main St.
860/659-3601

**Perfect Finish**
27 Commerce St. #C
860/657-2295

## 25 GREENWICH

**Elaine Dillof Antiques**
71 Church St.
203/629-2294

**Church Street Antiques**
77 Church St.
203/661-6309

**Greenwich Ave. Antiques**
369 Greenwich Ave.
203/622-8361

**Henri-Burton French Antqs**
382 Greenwich Ave.
203/661-8529

**Guild Antiques**
384 Greenwich Ave.
203/869-0828

**Michael Kessler Antiques**
40 E. Putnam Ave.
203/629-1555

**Manderley Antiques**
134 E. Putnam Ave.
203/861-1900

**Provinces De France**
22 W. Putnam Ave.
203/629-9798

**Rue Fauborg**
44 W. Putnam Ave.
203/869-7139

**Hallowell & Co.**
340 W. Putnam Ave.
203/869-2190

**Eggplant & Johnson Inc.**
58 William St. #A
203/532-0409

**Consign It Inc.**
115 Mason St.
203/869-9836

**Maison La Belle**
15 E. Elm St.
203/622-0301

**Classic Antique Consignment**
173 Hamilton Ave.
203/869-0916

**Antan Antiques**
E. Putnam Ave.
203/661-4769

**Surrey Collectibles**
563 Steamboat Road
203/869-4193

**Fieldstone Antiques**
260 Mill St.
203/531-0011

**French Country Living**
34 E. Putnam Ave.
203/869-9559

**Greenwich Antiques-Consignment**
249 Railroad Ave.
203/629-1500

**Tudor House Antiques**
30 E. Putnam Ave.
203/661-7010

### *Great Places To Stay*

**Stanton House Inn**
76 Maple Ave.
203/869-2110

Built in 1840, The Stanton House Inn is a converted mansion that is now a bed and breakfast inn, located in the prestigious village of Greenwich, Connecticut. The Inn offers elegant surroundings and a satisfying continental breakfast. The twenty-four guest rooms are bright and cheery, decorated primarily with Laura Ashley-style waverly fabrics with period antiques and reproductions.

## 26 GUILFORD

**Arne E Ahlberg Antiques**
1090 Boston Post Road
203/453-9022

**Guilford Antique Center**
1120 Boston Post Road
203/458-7077

**Gustave D Balacos**
2614 Boston Post Road
203/488-0762

## 27 HAMDEN

**Donald Barese Fine Art**
47 Wakefield St.
203/281-7438

**T Melillo Antiques**
2373 Whitney Ave.
203/281-3787

**Gallery 4**
2985 Whitney Ave.
203/281-6043

**Mill River Antiques**
3551 Whitney Ave.
203/407-1800

**Nancy Stiner Antiques**
1715 Whitney Ave.
203/248-7682

**Sleeping Giant Antiques**
3551 Whitney Ave.
203/288-4464

**Timeless Furniture II**
1656 Whitney Ave.
203/287-1904

**Unbroken Circle Antiques**
2964 Dixwell Ave.
203/248-3788

## 28 HARTFORD

### The Unique Antique

Hartford Civic Center
860/522-9094
Mon.-Sat. 10-7:30, Sun. by chance
*Directions: Located right in the center of Hartford, the Hartford Civic Center adjoins the Sheraton Hotel. Exit I-91 at the downtown exit. The high-rise Sheraton is visible from either I-84 or I-91.*

This is the place to stop if you are in the market for very high-end antique and estate jewelry. The Unique Antique is an antique shop in a mall and carries one of the largest selections of antique/estate jewelry in the East. Owner Joanne Douglas brings a lifetime of experience in this field to her shop and customers. She has been in the business for 20 years, but her grandmother was an antique jewelry dealer, and Joanne grew up with an antique store in the house. She gets her stock from sources in New England, mainly through dealers and individuals who bring pieces in to her. If you want anything from "diamonds down to costume," The Unique Antique is a "must."

**Carol's Antiques & Collectibles**
453 Washington St.
860/524-9113

**Bacon Antiques**
95 Maple Ave.
860/524-0040

#### *Interesting Side Trips*

### The Mark Twain House

351 Farmington Ave.
860/493-6411
Open year round with peak season and off-season hours.

From sun-dappled days of playing on the Mississippi River at Hannibal, Missouri, to the winter wonderland of Hartford, Connecticut, is a long way, but American author and humorist Mark Twain (Samuel Langhorne Clemens), built a Victorian mansion in Hartford for his family, where they all lived from 1874 to 1891. Now a National Register Historic Landmark (since 1963), the Mark Twain House is a showplace, a museum, a piece of American history and a very rare piece of American decorative art.

Twain wrote seven major works (including *Tom Sawyer, Adventures of Huckleberry Finn, The Prince and the Pauper, Life on the Mississippi*, and *A Connecticut Yankee in King Arthur's Court*) while living in this remarkable High Victorian building. Designed by Edward Tuckerman Potter, the 19-room mansion features an important collection of fine and decorative arts, and the only remaining domestic interiors by Louis Comfort Tiffany and his design firm, Associated Artists. Now restored to its 19th century glory, the house is a museum and research center with a collection of some 10,000 objects, and offers a full program of literary, musical, family oriented, scholarly, and educational programs.

Mark Twain's Carriage House, also designed by Potter, was home to the Clemenses' coachman and his family, along with horses, carriages and a sleigh. For a time, Twain did his writing in a makeshift study in the Carriage House. The buildings share a lawn with the home of 19th century author Harriet Beecher Stowe, who was Clemens' neighbor.

## 29 IVORYTON

#### *Great Places To Stay*

### Copper Beech Inn

46 Main St.
860/767-0330
Open year round, except first week of January
Rates: $105-175
Web site: www.copperbeechinn.com

The Copper Beech Inn takes its name from the magnificent copper beech tree that fronts the property, one of the oldest and largest of its kind in Connecticut. The 1880s home was built as an elegant Victorian country cottage, complete with carriage barn, root cellar, and terraced landscaping. Surrounded by turn-of-the-century gardens and native woodlands, the house was rescued from disrepair and vacancy in the 1970s, and restored and opened as the Copper Beech Inn.

The Inn has thirteen guest rooms, all with telephones and air conditioning. Four rooms are in the Main House. Those have been lovingly restored and decorated with country and antique furnishings. They have old fashioned baths, kept intact, to lend a note of nostalgia.

There are nine charming, traditional guest rooms in the renovated Carriage House. Several have four-poster or canopy beds. Some of the rooms have soaring cathedral ceilings, in which the original supporting beams have been left exposed. All Carriage House rooms have television, whirlpool baths and doors leading out onto decks.

An enticing complimentary buffet breakfast - including fresh fruit, home-made pastries, breads, cereal, juice, coffee and tea - is set for all house guests. A plant filled, Victorian-style conservatory offers a delightful spot for an aperitif before dinner, or for quiet moments anytime. Dinner at The Copper Beech Inn is in the hearty, French country style. Fresh flowers, sparkling silver and soft candlelight create an atmosphere of romance and warm elegance. The restaurant has been recognized with the 1998 AAA Four Diamond Award.

The Lower Connecticut River Valley is a wonderful place to explore quiet New England countryside, small museums and antique shops. The Inn itself has a small gallery offering fine antique oriental porcelain. The quaint nearby villages of Essex, Old Lyme and Chester are among the most charming in Connecticut. In spring and summer, the area abounds with water associated activities; there are fine beaches within a 20 minute drive from the Inn. The area also enjoys superb theatre, including the Ivoryton Playhouse, Goodspeed Opera House and Goodspeed-at-Chester.

## 30 KENT

**Company Store Antiques**
30 Kent Cornwall Road
860/927-3430

**R.T.Facts Garden & Architectural**
22 S. Main St.
860/927-5315

**Foreign Cargo & American Antiques**
Main St.
860/927-3900

**Golden Thistle**
Main St.
860/927-3790

**Harry Homes Antique**
3 Carter Road
860/927-3420

**Kent Antiques Center**
Kent Station Square
860/927-3313

**Main Street Antiques**
8 N. Main St.
860/927-4916

### *Great Places To Stay*

**Chaucer House**
88 N. Main St. 7
860/927-4858

Both of the innkeepers at this beautiful Colonial style inn are from the same small village in Kent, England. How ironic that they found themselves in Kent, Connecticut. The Inn offers three guest accommodations and is within walking distance to antique shops and restaurants.

**Mavis' Bed and Breakfast**
230 Kent Cornwall Road
860/927-4334

Mavis' B&B is a stunning 1860s Greek Revival home with five bedrooms, two of which have fireplaces. The family room has 30x31 ft. beamed ceilings, the dining room overlooks the terrace and rose gardens. There is also a cottage available with dining and kitchen area. Mavis' sits on two acres of property with a fine stream, barn and many plants.

## 31 LITCHFIELD

**Linsley Antiques**
499 Bantam Road
860/567-4245

**Barry Strom Antiques**
595 Bantam Road
860/567-9767

**Thomas M McBride Antiques**
62 West St.
860/567-5476

**Jeffrey Tillou Antiques**
33 West St.
860/567-9693

**Barry Strom Antiques**
503 Bantam Road
860/567-2747

**Roberta's Antiques**
469 Bantam Road
860/567-4041

## 32 MADISON

**Crescent Antiques**
60 Boston Post Road
203/245-9145

**Mildred Ross**
294 Boston Post Road
203/245-7122

**Kirtland H. Crump Clockmaker**
387 Boston Post Road
203/245-7573

**Madison Trust Antique**
891 Boston Post Road
203/245-3976

**Fence Creek Antiques**
916 Boston Post Road
203/245-0151

**Nosey Goose**
33 Wall St.
203/245-3132

## 33 MANCHESTER

**Yesterday's Treasures**
845 Main St.
860/646-8855

**Lest We Forget Antiques**
503 E. Middle Turnpike
860/649-8187

**Vintage & Jewels & Collectibles**
190 Middle Turnpike W.
860/645-1525

## 34 MERIDEN

**Dee's Antiques**
600 W. Main St.
203/235-8431

**Fair Weather Antiques**
763 Hanover Road
203/237-4636

## 35 MILFORD

**The Stock Transfer**
554 Boston Post Road
203/874-1333
Tues.-Sat. 10-4
*Directions: From I-95 North: Take Exit 37 (High St.) and turn right to Route 1. Turn left and go 1/2 block. The shop is on the right. From I-95 South: Take Exit #36 (Plains Road) to Route 1. Turn left and go 1/2 mile. The shop is on the right. From Merritt Parkway: Take Exit 54 to the first Milford Exit and go to Route 1. Turn right and go 1/2 block. The shop is on the right in "The Courtyard."*

Nanci has been in business for 17 years at The Stock Transfer. With 2400 square feet of space, it is the largest shop of its kind in the area, and, says Nanci, they carry "everything." Shoppers can find furniture, crystal, china, jewelry, oriental rugs, paintings and lots more.

**Ray's Antiques**
16 Daniel St.
203/876-7720

**New Beginnings**
107 River St.
203/876-8332

**Antiques of Tomorrow**
93 Gulf St.
203/878-4561

**Something of Bev's**
400 Bost Post Road-Colony Center
203/874-4686

**Geoffrey Flett Antiques**
1027 Bridgeport Ave.
203/874-1698

**Milford Green Antiques Gallery**
22 Broad St.
203/874-4303

**Retro-Active**
30 Broad St.
203/877-6050

**Treasures & Trifles**
580 Naugatuck Ave.
203/878-7045

## 36 MONROE

**Addie's Cottage**
144 Main St.
203/261-2689

**Barbara's Barn**
418 Main St.
203/268-9805

**Strawberry Patch Antiques**
418 Main St.
203/268-1227

**Anna's Antiques & Consignment**
266 Main St. #A
203/452-1866

**Yesteryears Antiques**
650 Main St.
203/459-9458

## 37 MYSTIC

**Briar Rose Antiques**
27 Broadway Ave.
860/536-4135

**Tradewinds Gallery**
20 W. Main St.
860/536-0119

**Sonny's Toys & Collectibles**
6 Hendel Dr.
860/536-0646

### *Great Places To Stay*

**Pequot Hotel Bed & Breakfast**
Burnett's Corner
711 Cow Hill Road
860/572-0390
Open year round
Rates $95-130

It just doesn't seem like stagecoaches ever ran anywhere but the old West-certainly not through New England-but the Pequot Hotel Bed & Breakfast is an authentically restored 1840 stagecoach stop. This stately Greek Revival landmark, located in the center of the Burnett's Corners historic district, still has its original hardware, moldings and fireplaces. Two of the three guest rooms, all with private baths, have 12-foot-high coved ceilings and Rumford fireplaces. There is a rare book collection in the library, wicker furniture on the screened porch, and two parlors for guests' use. More than 20 acres of trails and woods, open fields, ponds, spacious lawns, and gardens surround the hotel.

**Six Broadway Inn**
6 Broadway
860/536-6010
Web site: www.visitmystic.com/sixbroadway

Six Broadway Inn is the only bed and breakfast in the heart of Historic Downtown Mystic. The innkeepers, Jerry and Joan, restored the 1854 homestead to classic Victorian splendor. Guests are invited to enjoy the tranquility of the parlor, the gazebo, and the 1/2 acre grounds, or to stroll only blocks away to the Mystic Seaport Museum or by the Mystic River. The Inn graciously offers sophisticated accommodations with a superb location in a village reminiscent of an era gone by.

**Steamboat Inn**
73 Steamboat Wharf
860/536-8300
Web site: www.localnews.com/buspages/steamboa/

Steamboat Inn is Mystic's only waterfront inn. Elegant and intimate accommodations with fireplace, whirlpool baths and continental breakfast. Rooms are directly on the Mystic River in Historic Downtown Mystic only steps from numerous fine shops and restaurants.

### *Interesting Side Trips*

**Mystic Seaport**
75 Greenmanville Ave.
860/572-5331
Web site: www.mystic.org
Open daily year round except Christmas Day
*Directions: Mystic Seaport is located midway between New York and Boston in Mystic, Connecticut. Take I-95 to Exit 90. Proceed one mile south on Route 27.*

This place is absolutely fascinating! You don't even have to like sailing to be amazed by all the glimpses into our country's history that are preserved here at this private museum. In 1929 three residents of Mystic - Dr. Charles K. Stillman, Edward E. Bradley and Carl D. Cutler - formed the Marine Historical Association, Inc., in order to establish a museum and preserve the rapidly disappearing remnants of America's maritime past. The museum's name was changed in 1978 to Mystic Seaport. So, Mystic Seaport is an indoor/outdoor museum which includes historic ships, boats, buildings and exhibit galleries relating to American maritime history. The exhibit area is located on 17 acres along the Mystic River. Primary emphasis is on the maritime commerce of the Atlantic coast during the 19th century. The village area architecture, gardens, and demonstrations depict life in a maritime community from 1850 to 1921. Located on an estuary three miles from the open sea, the Museum is divided into three main areas: Preservation Shipyard, where museum staff maintain the Museum's unique historic ships and small boats, while preserving the traditional skills of wooden shipbuilding; the outdoor Village Exhibits, representing elements of life and work in 19th century New England seaport communities, and aboard the ships that sailed from them; and the Gallery exhibits, presenting fabulous collections of maritime art and artifacts, and special changing exhibitions on important aspects of America's relationship with the sea.

## 38 NEW BRITAIN

**Vintage Shop**
61 Arch St.
860/224-8567

**Universal Stamp & Coin**
304 Broad St.
860/827-9439

## 39 NEW CANAAN

**Evans-Leonard Antiques**
114 Main St.
203/966-5657

**Silk Purse**
118 Main St.
203/972-0898

**Main St. Cellar Antiques**
120 Main St.
203/966-8348

**New Canaan Antiques**
120 Main St.
203/972-1938

**Sallea Antiques**
66 Elm St.
203/972-1050

**Courtyard Antiques**
150 Elm St.
203/966-2949

**English Heritage Antiques, Inc.**
13 South Ave.
203/966-2979

**Elisabeth De Bussy Inc.**
By Appointment Only
203/966-5947

**Manor Antiques**
110 Main St.
203/966-2658

**Severed Ties, Inc.**
111 Cherry St.
203/972-0788

## 40 NEW HARTFORD

**Rose Marie**
202 Main St.
860/693-3979

**New Hartford Junction**
510 Main St.
860/738-0689

## 41 NEW HAVEN

**Edwin C Ahlberg Antiques**
441 Middletown Ave.
203/624-9076

**W Chorney Antiques**
827 Whalley Ave.
203/387-9707

**Antiques Market**
881 Whalley Ave.
203/389-5440

**Antique Corner**
859 Whalley Ave.
203/387-7200

**Second Time Around**
970 State St.
203/624-6343

**Patti's Antiques**
920 State St.
203/865-8496

**Village Francais**
555 Long Wharf Dr.
203/562-4883

**Harold's Antiques, Inc.**
873 Whalley Ave.
203/389-2988

**Sally Goodman, Ltd.**
902 Whalley Ave.
203/387-5072

## 42 NEW LONDON

**Captains Treasures**
253 Captains Walk
860/442-2944

## 43 NEW MILFORD

**Chamberlain's Antiques**
469 Danbury Road
860/355-3488

**Retro**
267 Kent Road
860/355-1975

**Accent Antiques**
Church St.
860/355-7707

**This N That Shop**
27 Old State Road
860/350-4001

**Ida's Antiques**
329 Danbury Road
860/354-4388

## 44 NEWINGTON

**Connecticut Antique Wicker**
1052 Main Rear
860/666-3729

**Doll Factory Vintage Clothing**
2551 Berlin Turnpike
860/666-6162

**Trellis Antiques & Gifts**
39 Market Square
860/665-9100

## 45 NEW PRESTON/MARBLE DALE

**Earl Slack Antiques**
Wheaton Road (Marble Dale)
860/868-7092

**Grampa Snazzy's Log Cabin**
270 Litchfield Turnpike (New Preston)
860/868-7153

**Martell & Suffin Antiques**
1 Main St. #A (New Preston)
860/868-1339

**Reece Antiques**
15 E. Shore Road (New Preston)
860/868-9966

**Room With A View**
13 E Shore Road (New Preston)
860/868-1717

**Recherche Studio**
166 New Milford Turnpike
860/868-0281

## 46 NEWTOWN

**McGeorgi's Antiques**
129 S. Main
203/270-9101

**Poverty Hollow Antiques**
78 Poverty Hollow Road
203/426-2388

## 47 NOANK

**The Antiquary**
215 Park
860/928-4873

### *Great Places To Stay*

**Palmer Inn**
25 Church St.
860/572-9000
Open year round
Rates $125-185

On a prime piece of real estate just off Long Island Sound is a soaring, magnificent home that reveals the extravagance and superb craftsmanship of turn-of-the-century architecture. Two miles from Mystic Seaport, shipyard craftsmen built a grand seaside mansion for shipbuilder Robert Palmer in 1906. The house, described by the architects as a "Classic Colonial Suburban Villa," features a hip roof with dormers, a balustrade, dentil cornices, pilasters, Palladian windows, and a huge portico with two-story Ionic columns. These architectural details remain intact on the outside, while inside guests enjoy and marvel at 13-foot ceilings, a mahogany staircase and beams, brass fixtures, intricate woodwork, stained-glass windows, and original wall coverings, all of which have been restored. The six guest rooms with private baths are filled with family heirlooms and antiques, as well as modern luxuries. Balconies offer views of Long Island Sound, while fireplaces warm the chilly Connecticut winter evenings.

## 48 NORFOLK

### *Great Places To Stay*

**Greenwoods Gate**
105 Greenwoods Road E.
860/542-5439
Web site: www.bbhost.com/greenwoodsgate

The Federal era architecture of Greenwoods Gate sets the tone for relaxation, warmth and romance. Greenwoods Gate is conveniently located in the picture perfect village of Norfolk, CT, one half mile east of the Village Green. The home has a charming character all its own, having been carefully and lovingly furnished throughout with an eclectic blend of fine antiques, period pieces and collections, all combined to provide guests with a wondrous country experience.

**Manor House**
69 Maple Ave.
860/542-5690

Treat yourself to an elegant retreat at the Manor House, an 1898 Victorian Tudor estate. Designated Connecticut's most romantic hideaway and included in *10 Best B and Bs* in the country, this historic mansion is described by *Gourmet* as "quite grand with its Tiffany windows". The antique decorated guestrooms are furnished with four poster, brass, sleigh, spindle or lace canopy beds, covered with luxurious down comforters. Several rooms have fireplaces, private balconies, a jacuzzi or a deluxe soaking tub. The hearty breakfast includes honey harvested from their own hives, pure local maple syrup and homemade bread. During the day, there is so much to see and do - music festivals, summer theater, antique and craft shops, vineyards, museums, gardens, hiking, biking, water sports, tennis, riding stables, carriage and sleigh rides, alpine and cross country skiing. They can even arrange an appointment with a massage therapist.

**Mountain View Inn**
67 Litchfield Road
Route 272
860/542-6991

Nestled high in the Berkshire Hills of Northwest Connecticut, Norfolk with its village green, bell towers and postcard landscapes, reflects New England's spirit at its best. Golf, tennis, fishing, hiking, cross country and downhill skiing are available nearby. Mountain View Inn, located 1/4 mile south of the Village Green, is a historic Victorian style, full service country inn. Individually appointed guestrooms offer spacious, comfortable accommodations filled with period antiques.

## 49 NORWALK

**Pak Trade**
14 Wall St.
203/857-4165

**Eagle's Lair Antiques**
565 Westport Ave.
203/846-1159

**Old Well Antiques**
135 Washington St.
203/838-1842

**Koppel's Antique Warehouse**
24 1st St.
203/866-3473

## 50 OLD LYME

**Antique Association-Old Lyme**
11 Halls Road
860/434-5828

**Elephant Trunk**
11 Halls Road
860/434-9630

**Treasures**
95 Halls Road
860/434-9338

**The Cooley Gallery**
25 Lyme St.
860/434-8807

**Morelock Antiques**
At the Village Shops on Lyme St.
860/434-6333

**Antiques on Lyme**
At the Village Shops on Lyme St.
860/434-3901

**Antiques Associates**
11 Halls Road
860/434-5828

**Treasures, Consignments**
Halls Road
860/434-9338

### *Great Places To Stay*

**Old Lyme Inn**
85 Lyme St.
1-800-434-5352
Open year round except for first two weeks of January
Rates: $86-158
*Directions: Going south on I-95, take Exit 70 and turn right off of the ramp. Going north on I-95, turn left off of the ramp, right at the second light. Follow this road (Rte. 1) to the second light and the inn is on the left.*

Situated on the main street in Old Lyme's historic district, Old Lyme Inn represents the classic traditions of excellence in dining and lodging that is the very heart of a small Connecticut town. The original building, constructed around 1850 by the Champlain family, was a 300-acre working farm until the Connecticut Turnpike cut through Old Lyme in the early 1950s. Some guests still remember when the place housed a riding academy in the 1920s, where it is reputed that Jacqueline Bouvier Kennedy Onassis took lessons. Prior to that, around the turn of the century, many of Old Lyme's famous impressionist artists hauled their painting wagons into the beautiful fields and Connecticut woodlands behind the inn. Townspeople also remember lively square dancing in the old barn that burned (only the foundation remains) about 300 yards behind the still remaining 1850s yellow barn.

When the turnpike arrived, the Champlain family home was sold and became the Barbizon Oaks, named after the Barbizon School for painters that Old Lyme emulated, and the 300-year-old oak tree that still stands on a hill behind the inn. It became a boarding establishment, and survived a major fire that was the beginning of a spiral into disrepair. Its staircase and interior walls disappeared, and it became an Italian restaurant of questionable reputation. When Diana Field Atwood bought it in 1976, the second floor was still charred and the building was ready for demolition. The kitchen, then in the basement, was a hazard to its occupants - including the dead rat found in one of the ovens. The only access to the second floor was up a rickety fire escape supported by a metal milk crate and pulled down with one hand!

But when Diana bought it, she restored the inn to its current beauty. Walls and staircases were rebuilt, marble fireplaces were found and everything was redone from the basement to the attic. Now it offers not only fine dining, but 13 guest rooms with private baths and Empire and Victorian antiques. The inn's facilities include four separate dining rooms and a cocktail lounge, with seating from 2 to 70. In combination with the guest rooms, the inn handles conferences, wedding parties, rehearsal dinners and other special events.

Guests can spend time in the Victorian Bar that came out of one of Pittsburgh's oldest taverns. It has never been refinished, retaining its original beveled glass mirrors and scores of dart holes from many games in the past. The mirror over the bar's fireplace was purchased at an auction for $5 - no one else wanted it! The marble mantles in the bar and parlor came from a lady in Wetherfield who had saved them when her family's home was being razed.

Many of the paintings in the inn represent the Old Lyme School of artists who resided up the street at Florence Griswold's home (now the Lyme Historical Society) at the turn of the century. There are also paintings purchased from current artists at Lyme Art Association shows, and some lovely watercolors in the Champlain rooms, from unknown artists of Old Lyme, found at tag sales.

The Empire Room (the main dining room) was an addition to the original building, added around the time of the Barbizon Oak period. The large pier mirror was found in an old Norwich mansion undergoing the wrecker's ball. Curly maple balustrades from an old Pennsylvania home march up the front staircase. Nineteenth century chestnut paneling covers the walls in the private dining room. In the front hall, the original paintings and stenciling were done by Gigi Horr-Liverant. This type of wall painting was done quite often during the mid-1800s by itinerant artists; they usually painted local scenes, so the inn's wall murals represent several of the old buildings on Lyme St., and going up the stairs - Hamburg Cove in Lyme and Tiffany's Farm, the only working dairy farm owned by one of Connecticut's former legislators.

Over the years the inn has been awarded multiple prestigious awards and tributes: three star reviews by the *New York Times* on three separate visits; three stars from *Connecticut Magazine;* five stars from the *Norwich Bulletin;* wonderful stories in *Signature, Travel & Leisure, Redbook, Town & Country,* and many more; feature billing in *Bon Appetite* and on a separate cover of the same magazine; feature stories in *Connoisseur, Food & Wine,* and *NewYork Magazine*. And for three years in a row, the inn's pastry chef won the "Ultimate Chocolate Dessert" contest in Hartford.

**Bee and Thistle Inn**
100 Lyme St.
860/434-1667 or 1-800-622-4946
Rates: $75-210
*Directions: By Amtrak from Boston or New York: Train stops at Old Saybrook Station. By car from Boston or Providence: Take I-95 south to Exit 70, turn right off the ramp. The inn is the third house on the left. From New York City: Take the New England Thruway (I-95 North) to Exit 70. At the bottom of the ramp turn left. Take the first right onto Halls Road (Route 1 North). to the "T" in the road and turn left. The inn is the third house on the left. From Hartford: Take I-91 south to Route 9 South to I-95 North. Take Exit 70 and turn left off of the ramp. Take the first right onto Halls Road (Route 1 North). Go to the "T" in the road and turn left. The inn is the third house on the left.*

The Bee and Thistle is somewhat more formal than many bed and breakfasts, but the effort is worth it. With landscaped and natural areas along the Lieutenant River in the historic district of Old Lyme, the inn states that it is "a return to early American gracious living." The house was built in 1756 for Judge Noyes, very close to the Post Road. Around the turn of the century the Hodgson family moved it back from the road to its present location. They added the lovely sunken garden, the porches and the kitchen area. It remained a private home until the late 1930s, when Henrietta Greenleaf Lindsay found herself a widow with a large house to support. Her friend, Elsie Ferguson, an actress at the Goodspeed Opera House, suggested Henrietta take in boarders. Because it was Elsie's idea, Henrietta named her boarding house the Bee and Thistle after the Ferguson clan emblem in Scotland. The logo is still used today.

Dining is a highlight and specialty of the house, with appropriate evening dinner attire required and jackets required on Saturdays. But for that little extra effort, guests will enjoy four star creative American cuisine that has been voted the "Best Restaurant" and "Most Romantic Place" to dine in Connecticut by *Connecticut Magazine* Readers' Choice Poll. Candlelit dining areas showcase the food; wine comes from a large selection; desserts are award-winning; it is an experience many visitors enjoy simply as an evening out. Breakfast is served either on the porches or in the privacy of individual rooms. Luncheon is the chance for the chefs to use their imaginations.

To work off the excesses of the dining room, a walk down Lyme St. leads to historic homes, museums, galleries, fine antique shops, and beautiful private homes. A short drive away are numerous attractions and sites.

## 51 OLD SAYBROOK

**Antiques at Madison**
869 Middlesex Turnpike
860/388-3626

**Antiques Depot**
455 Boston Post Road
860/395-0595

**Corner Cupboard Antiques**
853 Middlesex Turnpike
860/388-0796

**Essex-Saybrook Antiques Village**
345 Middlesex Turnpike
860/388-0689

**Joseph Goclowski Antiques**
223 Hidden Cove Road
860/399-5070

**Old Saybrook Antiques Cntr**
756 Middlesex Turnpike
860/388-1600

**Presence of the Past**
488 Main St.
860/388-9021

**Sweet Pea Estate Jewelry**
851 Middlesex Turnpike
860/388-0289

**Van's Elegant Antiques**
998 Middlesex Turnpike
860/388-1934

**Essex Town Line Antiques Village**
985 Middlesex Turnpike
860/388-5000

**Little House of Glass**
1560 Boston Post Road. (Rt. 1)
860/399-5127

**James Demorest Oriental Rugs**
5 Great Hammock Road
860/388-9547

**Weatherbee Hill Antiques**
1340 Boston Post Road (Rt.1)
860/388-0442

***Favorite Places To Eat***

**Cuckoo's Nest**
1712 Boston Post Road (Route 1)
860/399-9060

Authentic Mexican & Cajun cuisine, served in an antique-filled barn. Voted Connecticut's Best Mexican Restaurant five years in a row. Outside patio. Open 7 days, lunch and dinner.

## 52 PLAINFIELD

**Plainfield Trading Post**
260 Norwich Road
860/564-4115

## 53 PLAINVILLE

**Winter Associates**
21 Cooke St.
860/793-0288

**March Hare Antiques**
188 W. Main St.
860/747-2526

**Fireglow Antiques**
12 W. Main St.
860/793-1600

## 54 PLANTSVILLE

**Village Antique Shop**
61 Main St.
860/628-2498

**West Main Antiques**
9 W. Main St.
860/620-1124

**Nothing New**
69 W. Main St.
860/276-0143

**Plantsville General Store**
780 S. Main St.
860/621-5225

**Al Judd & Associates**
40 W. Main St.
860/628-5828

**G. W. G. Antiques**
758 Main St.
860/620-0244

## 55 PORTLAND

**Robert T Baranowsky Antiques.**
66 Marlborough
860/342-2425

**Tall Tale Antiques**
Portland Colbalt Road
860/342-2444

**Taverin Antiques**
1118 Portland Cobalt Road
860/342-3779

## 56 PUTNAM

**Riverside Antiques**
58 Pomfret St., Bldg. 2A, Suite 101
860/928-6020
Regular hours Wed.-Sun. 10-5
Apr. 1-Aug.30, Wed.-Sun. 10-5, except Sat. 11-5

Nov. 1-Dec. 23, daily 10-5
*Directions: From Interstate 395 take exit 95. Go right onto Kennedy Dr. At the first traffic light, left onto Pomfret St., 200 yards on the left directly across from WINY Radio Studio.*

Located on the western edge of the extensive Putnam Antiques District, Riverside Antiques is housed in the Wilkinson Mill (Hale Mfg. Co.) ca. 1830, a stone and brick structure formerly used for the manufacture of woolen goods. Riverside Antiques is a co-op featuring 20+ dealers selling a full range of quality antiques and collectibles, complimented by an on-site Clock Repair Shop.

Riverside Antiques has long been recognized for reasonable prices, product variety, dealer following and handicapped accessibility.

**Grams & Pennyweights**
626 School St. Rt.44
860/928-6624

**Grandpa's Attic**
10 Pomfret St.
860/928-5970

**Antiques Marketplace**
109 Main St.
860/928-0442

**Brighton Antiques**
91 Main St.
860/928-1419

**J B Antiques**
37 Front St.
860/928-1906

**Antique Corner**
112 Main St.
860/963-2445

**Jeremiah's Antique Shoppes**
26 Front St.
860/963-8989

**Remember When**
80 Main St.
860/963-0422

**Mission Oak Shop**
109 Main St.
860/928-6662

## 57 RIDGEFIELD

### The Red Petticoat Antiques

113 West Lane, Route 35
203/431-9451
Tues.-Sat. 10-5:30, Sun. 12-5:30, closed Mon.

In April, 1777, a young girl saved her home (which is now The Red Petticoat Antiques) on West Lane, Ridgefield from being burned and plundered, and protected a wounded Patriot from being captured by British soldiers, by waving her red petticoat from the window in pretended sympathy with the Tories. The wounded Patriot had an important message to deliver to General George Washington, but was too weak to travel, so the girl sewed the message into the red petticoat and delivered it to Dobb's Ferry. Soon after, Washington expressed his gratitude by sending her some lovely red silk for a new petticoat, hoping it would replace the one she had sacrificed so bravely for her country...or so the story is told.

Continuity and tradition are important parts of the fabric of the Northeast, and The Red Petticoat antique store is built on American history and its own tradition, making it a perfect setting in which to sell historical objects. To begin with, the building itself is a home that was built in 1740, in one of the most beautiful settings in New England. For another, antiques have been sold at the sign of The Red Petticoat for as long as most people can remember. One of the oldest owners and sellers was Florene Maine, who knew and taught people about some of the finest English furniture ever made. After her death, the house remained an antique shop and the present owners, Ralph and Gloria Pershino, bought it. Now the antique selection is much more eclectic, with seven rooms of 18th and 19th century antique furnishings, folk art, iron and wicker, ephemera, oriental rugs, lamps, and fine furniture reproductions by Douglas Dimes.

A specialty of the house is advertising ephemera, which draws a great number of the shop's customers. Many people come to The Red Petticoat just for this. They have customers who are either employed by companies or whose families have started major companies, and the Perschinos call them when particular advertisements come in, usually items from the late 1800s to the early 1900s. A major part of the Perschinos' business is repeat customers, who particularly like to shop at the store for accessories and gifts. They cater to a varied clientele, who either shop by phone, or who come into the store and browse through the room settings. There is a beautiful sunroom filled with antique wicker, a huge fireplace where the old kitchen once was, decked out with tools and iron from the past. There is a staircase leading to a cozy room upstairs, with the entire stairway furnished with Wallace Nutting vintage pictures - seven rooms of 18th and 19th century antique furnishings and much more, all in a beautiful country setting in this historical antique house.

**Hunter's Consignments**
426 Main St.
203/438-9065

**Horologists of London Clocks**
450 Main St.
203/438-4332

**Consignments by Vivian**
458 Main St
203/438-5567

**Silk Purse**
470 Main St.
203/431-0132

**Attic Treasures Ltd.**
58 Ethan Allen Hwy.
203/544-8159

**Country Gallery Antiques**
346 Ethan Allen Hwy.
203/438-2535

**Route 7 Antiques**
659 Danbury Road
203/438-6671

**Ridgefield Antiques Center**
109 Danbury Road
203/438-2777

**Branchville Antiques & Collectibles**
32 Ethan Allen Hwy.
203/544-9940

**Cromlix Antiques & Consign.**
454 Main St.
203/431-7726

**Village Emporium**
384 Main St.
203/438-8767

## 58 RIVERSIDE

**Classiques Antiques & Consignment**
1147 E. Putnam
203/637-8227

**Estate Treasures of Greenwich**
1162 E. Putnam
203/637-4200

**Maury Rose Antiques**
1147 E. Putnam Ave.
203/698-2898

## 59 SALISBURY

**Buckley & Buckley**
84 Main St.
860/435-9919

**Salisbury Antiques Center**
46 Library St.
860/435-0424

## 60 SEYMOUR

**Seymour Antique Co.**
26 Bank St.
203/881-2526

**Chrisandra's**
249 West St.
203/888-7223

## 61 SIMSBURY

**Simsbury Antiques**
744 Hopmeadow St.
860/651-4474

**Back Fence Collector**
1614 Hopmeadow St.
860/651-4846

**William III Antiques**
21 Wolcott Road
860/658-1121

## 62 SOMERS

**Antiques & Folk Art Shoppe**
62 South Road - Route 83
860/749-6197

**Somer House Designs & Antiques**
62 South Road - Route 83
860/763-4458

**Genora's Furn & Antiques**
Maple St.
860/749-3650

## 63 SOMERSVILLE

### *Great Places To Stay*

**The Old Mill Inn Bed & Breakfast**
63 Maple St.
860/763-1473
Open daily
Rates: $85-95
*Directions: From the north or south: Take I-91 to Exit 47E, then proceed east on Route 190 five miles to the Somersville traffic signal. Turn right on Maple St., past the old mill (red brick buildings with a waterfall on the left), to the second house on the left, #63 Maple St. From the west: Take Route 190 east under I-91, then follow the above directions. From the east: Take Route 190 west through Somers, then go 2 miles to the traffic signal at Somersville, then south to #63 Maple St.*

For specific information see review at the beginning of this section.

## 64 SOUTHINGTON

**Albert Judd & Associates Antiques**
40 W. Main St.
860/628-5828

## 65 SOUTHPORT

**Chelsea Antiques**
293 Pequot Ave.
203/255-8935

**Ten Eyck-Emerich**
342 Pequot Ave.
203/259-2559

**Pat Guthman Anqitues**
281 Pequot Ave.
203/259-5743

## 66 SOUTH WINDSOR

**Treasure Trunk Antiques**
1212 Sullivan Ave.
860/644-1074

**Country Barn Collectibles**
1135 Sullivan Ave.
860/644-2826

**Horace Porter Antique Shop**
728 Deming St.
860/644-0071

**Time Past**
673 Main St.
860/289-2119

## 67 STAFFORD SPRINGS

**Mallard's Nest**
17 Crystal Lake Road
860/684-3837

**Smith's Collectibles**
107 W. Stafford Road
860/684-5844

## 68 STAMFORD

**Antique & Artisan Center**
69 Jefferson St.
203/327-6022
Mon.-Sat., 10:30-5:30; Sun. 12-5
*Directions: Traveling North on I-95 take Exit 8, turn right at second light on Canal St. Take first left onto Jefferson St. Antique & Artisan Center is located in second building on the right.*

Antique & Artisan Center is housed in a converted historic ice house. Catering to the discriminating shopper, the market is considered to be one of New England's finest. Within 22,000 square feet, over 100 dealers display their wares in spacious room settings. Period and decorative furnishings, exquisite porcelains, glass, silver, art and bronzes are just a sampling of the fine quality pieces you will find here.

**Stamford Antiques Center**
735 Canal St.
1-888-329-3546
Mon.-Sat. 10:30-5:30, Sun. 12-5
*Directions: I-95 South; Exit 7, left onto Canal St. I-95 North; Exit 8, 2 blocks right onto Canal St.*

Owner Debbie Schwartz said her career in the antiques business started in the carriage. "I'm a third-generation antiques dealer. My grandparents sold Tiffany lamps, my parents were called 'second-generation antiques.' " Her mother, Jeri Schwartz, has written a book on antiques, is a columnist for *Country Living* magazine and is a licensed appraiser.

The building, a one-time factory turned antique shop, is an architectural beauty with its pillars and sawtoothed roof featuring hundreds of skylights. The painted honey-colored concrete floors complement the wares of interior designer Gordon McCunis and his associate, Jay, who have taken a booth to display paintings, pillows, fabrics and furnishings.

Outer aisles are filled with chandeliers suspended from the ceiling stretching the length of one aisle into infinity. The center aisle displays showcases of museum-quality antiques such as orientalia, silver, porcelain and collectibles. "We have high end up to Tiffany lamps and then linen for $10," Debbie said. "We display blue and white porcelain, samplers, every single century furniture you can imagine. You name it, we have it. Antiquers can spend the day. This is antique heaven."

**Finders Keepers**
22 Belltown Road
203/357-1180

**Good Riddance Girls**
44 Four Brooks Road
203/329-0009

## 69 STONINGTON

**Water St. Antiques**
114 Water St.
860/535-1124

**Collections**
119 Water St.
860/535-9063

**Grand & Water Antiques**
135 Water St.
860/535-2624

**Mary Mahler Antiques**
144 Water St.
860/535-2741

**Peaceable Kingdom Antiques**
145 Water St.
860/535-3434

**Orkney & Yost Antiques**
148 Water St.
860/535-4402

**Neil Bruce Eustace**
156 Water St.
860/535-2249

**Pendergast N Jones**
158 Water St.
860/535-1995

**Quester Maritime Gallery**
77 Main St.
860/535-3860

**Marguerite Riordan**
8 Pearl St.
860/535-2511

**Findings-A Collection by Patrick Gallagher**
68 Water St.
860/535-1330

**Church St. Antiques**
5 Church St.
860/572-0457

**Antiques Limited**
530 Stonington Road (Route 1)
860/535-1017

## 70 STRATFORD

**4 Seasons Antiques**
427 Honeyspot Road
203/380-2450

**Main St. Antiques**
2399 Main St.
203/377-5086

**Natalie's Antiques & Collectibles**
2403 Main St.
203/377-1483

**Stratford Antique Center**
400 Honeyspot Road
203/378-7754

## 71 TORRINGTON

**Remember When**
66 Main St.
860/489-1566

**Americana Mart**
692 S. Main St.
860/489-5368

**Northwood Antiques**
47 Main St.
860/489-4544

**Wheatfield Antiques**
83 Main St.
860/482-3383

## 72 WALLINGFORD

**Wallingford General Antiques**
202 Center St.
203/265-5567

**Curiosity Shop**
216 Center St.
203/294-1975

**Wallingford Center St. Antiques**
171 Center St.
203/265-4201

**Connecticut Coin Gallery**
428 N. Colony St.
203/269-9888

**Images-Heirloom Linen**
32 N. Colony St.
203/265-7065

**Hunt's Courtyart Antiques**
38 N. Main St.
203/294-1733

**Antique Center of Wallingford**
28 S. Orchard St.
203/269-7130

**Rick's Antiques**
428 N. Colony St.
203/269-9888

## 73 WATERBURY

**Brass City Antiques**
2152 E. Main St.
203/753-1975

**Mattatucks Antiques**
156-158 Meriden Road
203/754-2707

**Century Antiques**
1015 W. Main St.
203/573-8092

## 74 WATERTOWN

**Treasures & Trash**
755 Thomaston Road
860/274-2945

**Corner Curio**
413 Main St.
860/945-9611

**Fannie Rose Vintage Clothing**
737 Main St.
860/274-0317

## 75 WESTBROOK

**Westbrook Antiques**
1119 Boston Post Road
860/399-9892

**Shops at Tidewater Creek**
433 Boston Post Road
860/399-8399

**Trolley Square Antiques**
1921 Boston Post Road
860/399-9249

**The Source**
374 Essex Road (Route 153)
860/399-6308

## 76 WESTPORT

### George Subkoff
260 Post Road E.
203/227-3515

Ultra-quality upscale is about the only way to describe one of the most famous dealers in Manhattan and in Connecticut collecting circles. George Subkoff's showroom is on Post Road in Westport, just past Main St. and the central downtown area, across from a picture postcard New England church. His antiques are not for the faint of heart nor light of wallet. Most are of Continental provenance, with a few early American pieces.

George has been in the business for 35 years, a third-generation antique dealer. He specializes in, as he puts it, "quality, quality, quality" - mostly furniture of the 17th through the mid-19th centuries. A world renowned dealer who sells to very well known decorators, George is an avid collector of trompe l'oeil. He often buys privately at auctions and has multiple sources who offer him the select pieces they receive. You never know what you're going to find in his showroom as you browse through the two floors of paintings, lighting fixtures, etc. As George is fond of saying, "Every day is an adventure," whether buying, selling, or hunting.

**Jordan Delhaise Gallery**
238 Post Road E.
203/454-1830

**Todburn**
243 Post Road W.
203/226-3859

**Family Album**
283 Post Road E.
203/227-4888

**Glen Leroux Collections**
68 Church Lane
203/227-8030

**Riverside Antiques Center**
265 Riverside Ave.
203/454-3532

**Bungalow**
4 Sconset Square
203/227-4406

**Leslie Allen A Home**
3 Kings Hwy. N.
203/454-4155

**Aladdin Of Westport**
9 Post Road W.
203/222-8770

**Audrey Morgan Interiors**
19 Post Road W.
203/227-1344

**Leonce Consignment & Antiques**
1435 Post Road E.
203/254-8448

**Prince of Wales, Inc.**
1032 Post Road E.
203/454-2335

***Great Places To Stay***

### The Inn at National Hall
Two Post Road W.
203/221-1351 or 1-800-NAT-HALL
Web site: www.integra.fr/relaischateaux/nationalhall
Rates: $195-475, including breakfast

Neither its sensible name nor its formidable red-brick exterior prepares guests for the delightful mix of whimsy, privacy, history, elegance and luxury that is found in this magnificent 15-bedroom bed & breakfast, first-class restaurant, boardroom/conference room and residents' drawing room. The Italianate structure was built in 1873 by Horace Staples, chairman of the First National Bank of Westport, founder of Staples High School and owner/operator of a lumber and hardware business with offices at National Hall, and a fleet of commercial sailing vessels. The Saugatuck River was an active waterway in those days and this sailing fleet was berthed alongside National Hall. The building originally housed the First National Bank on the first floor, the local newspaper on the second floor, and the town's meeting hall on the third floor - hence its unofficial name, National Hall.

In 1884 the third floor public space was converted into classrooms for a short while until Staples High School was completed. The third floor, with its panoramic views of the Saugatuck River, served as the town's location for graduations, dances, theatrical productions, as well as public meetings. At the turn of the century, the space was even large enough for basketball games and other athletic events. National Hall remained the focal point of Westport's business district and social scene until the 1920s. In 1926 the hall was sold for $25,000 (the National Bank had moved by then) and by 1929 the Connecticut State Police maintained offices in the building, sharing it with many of the first tenants. In 1946 the building was renovated and reopened as the Fairfield Furniture Store on all three floors. This business remained for 34 years, closing its doors in 1980.

In 1987 Arthur Tauck, president of Westport-based Tauck Tours, purchased the 120-year-old structure and began its meticulous, five-year, $15 million renovation. Local artists were recruited to do the elaborate stenciling and hand-painted decor throughout the structure. After taking a masterclass from the renowned English artist Lyn Le Grice, the local artists were assigned individual rooms and areas to work on. San Francisco-based artists John Wullbrandt and Jeff Patch, with Joszi Meskan Associates, supervised the local artists and are personally responsible for the hand-painted decor in several of the rooms, as well as the mural and interior artwork in the restaurant. One of the most notable features - and everybody's favorite - is the tiny elevator decorated with a *trompe l'oeil* library!

### *Favorite Places To Eat*

**Coffee An'**
343 N. Main St.
203/227-3808

This is the end of the line for donut nuts! Go between 7 and 9 a.m., mingle with the crowds, and watch the regulars at the twin counters on either side of the store and at the seats along the front window. They've got their dunking-sipping-reading-the-paper-routine down to a science - you'd never guess there were so many ways to dunk and eat donuts! And take your appetite - there's no way you can eat just one!

The genius responsible for this morning ritual is Derek Coutouras, who starts cooking in the back room every morning at 4 a.m., working at the fry kettles, hanging freshly cooked donuts on dowels to cool, drizzling on the glaze and sprinkling sugar. Up front, Mrs. Coutouras and a team of speed-demon waitresses man the counters and cash register. They can barely keep up with the demand for chocolate, glazed, plain, jelly-filled and powdered sugar donuts, but the real *piece de resistance* is the cinnamon buns - about six inches wide and three inches high, veined with lodes of dark, sweetened cinnamon, with a faintly brittle glaze of sugar - billowing, yeasty spiral too big for dunking or even picking up whole. It takes half an hour just to work your way through it, washed down with three or four cups of good coffee. To die for!

## 77 WILTON

**Wilton Antiques Shows**
Managed by Marilyn Gould
MCG Antiques Promotions, Inc.
10 Chicken St.
203/762-3525

The most exciting antiques venue in the east...where more fine dealers show more notable antiques covering a broader spectrum of the market and at a range of prices than can be found anywhere. These outstanding shows offer the opportunity for significant buying; making a trip to Wilton always worthwhile. For a complete listing of show dates and locations call for brochure.

**Connecticut Trading Co.**
Old Ridgefield Road
203/834-5008

**Old & New Collectibles**
146 Danbury Road
302/762-8359

**Wayside Exchange Antiques**
300 Danbury Road
203/762-3183

**Simply Country**
392 Danbury Road
203/762-5275

**Vallin Galleries**
516 Danbury Road
203/762-7441

**Frances Hills Antiques**
1083 Ridgefield Road
203/762-3081

**Greenwillow Antiques**
26 Cannon Road
203/762-0244

**Emerald Forrest**
951 Danbury Road
203/544-9441

**Escape Design**
436 Danbury Road
203/834-9774

## 78 WINDSOR

**Nadeau's Auction Gallery**
184 Windsor Ave.
860/246-2444

**Olde Windsor Antique Gallery**
184 Windsor Ave.
860/249-4300

**Patti's Treasures & Antiques**
73 Poquonock
860/687-1682

**Great Eastern Antiques Gallery**
184 Windsor Ave.
860/724-0115

### *Great Places To Stay*

**Charles R. Hart House**
1046 Windsor Ave.
860/688-5555
Rates $65 and up
Web site: www.ntplx.net/~harthous
*Directions: Take I-91 north or south to Exit 36. Proceed east on Route 178 to Route 159 (7/10 mile). Turn right on Route 159 south, proceed 1/5 mile to Country Lane on the left, enter the first driveway on the left.*

Tucked away in Connecticut's oldest town, the Charles R. Hart House was first constructed as a simple farmhouse. It was later added to and embellished with Queen Anne fixtures and appointments. In 1896 Charles R. Hart, a well-known Hartford merchant, carefully restored the house in the colonial revival style by adding luxurious Lincrustra wall coverings, ceramic tiled fireplaces and an elegant Palladian window. The Hart family maintained ownership until the 1940s, when it became the homestead for a pheasant farm! Today it has been fully restored and furnished with period antiques, including an extensive collection of clocks.

## 79 WINSTED

**Laurel City Coins & Antiques**
462 Main St.
860/379-0325

**Verde Antiques & Books**
64 Main St.
860/379-3135

## 80 WOODBURY

**Wayne Pratt, Inc.**
346 Main St. S.
203/263-5676
Open daily 10-5, Sun. 12-5

Wayne Pratt, owner of Wayne Pratt Antiques, has long been recognized as one of the most prestigious antique dealers in America and abroad. On occasion, you may find Wayne exhibiting his wonderful "finds" at upscale antique shows across the country. On any other day, you can visit his showroom where you are assured of finding authentic and distinctive pieces of furniture, silver, rugs, art, porcelains, decorative lamps and other antique accessories.

**Art & Peggy Pappas Antiques**
113 Main St. S.
203/266-0374

**Gothic Victorian Antiques**
137 Main St. S.
203/263-0398

**Tucker Frey Antiques**
451 Main St. S.
203/263-5404

**Frank Jensen Antiques**
142 Middle Road Turnpike
203/263-0908

**Country Bazaar**
451 Main St. S.
203/263-2228

**Country Loft**
557 Main St. S.
203/266-4500

**Jean Reeve Antiques**
813 Main St. S.
203/263-5028

**Grass Roots Antiques**
12 Main St. N.
203/263-3983

**British Country Antiques**
50 Main St. N.
203/263-5100

**Woodbury Antiques**
745 Main St. N.
203/263-5611

**Mill House Antiques**
1068 Main St. N.
203/263-3446

**Monique Shay Antiques**
920 Main St. S.
203/263-3186

**Antiques on the Green**
6 Green Circle
203/263-3045

**Joel Einhorn**
819 Main St. N.
203/266-9090

**Eagle Antiques**
615 Main St. N.
203/266-4162

**Madeline West Antiques**
373 Main St. S.
203/263-4604

**Carriage House**
403 Main St. S.
203/266-4021

**G. Sergeant Antiques**
88 Main St. N.
203/266-4177

**Daria of Woodbury**
82 Main St. N.
203/263-2431

**Taylor Manning Antiques**
107 Main St. N.
203/263-3330

**West Country Antique**
334 Washington Road
203/263-5741

**Rosebush Farm Antiques**
267 Good Hill Road
203/266-9114

**Harold E. Cole Antiques**
Middle Quarter Road
203/263-4909

**Jenny Lynn Shop**
113 Main St. S.
203/263-0284

**Nancy Fierberg Antiques**
289 Main St. S.
203/263-4957

**Rosebush Farm Antiques**
267 Good Hill Road
203/266-9114

**Rosebush Farm Antiques**
289 Main St. S.
203/266-9115

### *Visiting Historic Lighthouses of Connecticut*

Living in a lighthouse ranks right up there with running away to join the circus. Although automation has replaced the jobs of lighthouse keepers, many lighthouses of all shapes and sizes can still be found in Connecticut.

Old Lighthouse Museum, Stonington. A photographic journey to other lighthouses is among the exhibits in the Stonington light station on the east side of the harbor. The stone tower and the keeper's house attached to it were built in 1840.

Sheffield Island Lighthouse, South Norwalk. The slate-roofed granite lighthouse, on a 53-acre island bird sanctuary, has ten rooms on four levels that you can explore. A picnic area outside and regular ferry service to the island make the adventure even more fun.

Several boat operators, such as Captain John's of Waterford/Old Saybrook, provide harbor tours and visits to lighthouses.

The New London Ledge Light, a mile offshore at the entrance to New London's harbor, is among other lighthouses that can be reached by boat. Its beacon and eerie foghorns are automated now, but local legend says that the ghost of an old lighthouse keeper still keeps watch there.

The New London Light, at the entrance to the harbor, is the fifth-oldest in the country, dating from 1760. The original building was replaced by the present structure, an 80-foot octagonal tower, in 1801. Its Fresnel lens, now automated, has flashed its warning signals since before the Civil War.

Other lighthouses a short boat ride away from New London are at Great Captain Island, off Greenwich; Penfield Reef, off Fairfield; Stratford Shoal, off Stratford; Southwest Ledge, off New Haven, and Morgan Point, off Noank.

Avery Point Light, on the Groton campus of the University of Connecticut, was built in 1941 and was never lit. It services the Coast Guard today as a research and development center, finding ways to make every lighthouse do its job better.

*For additional information, call 1-800-CT-BOUND, 1-800-282-6863.*

# Delaware

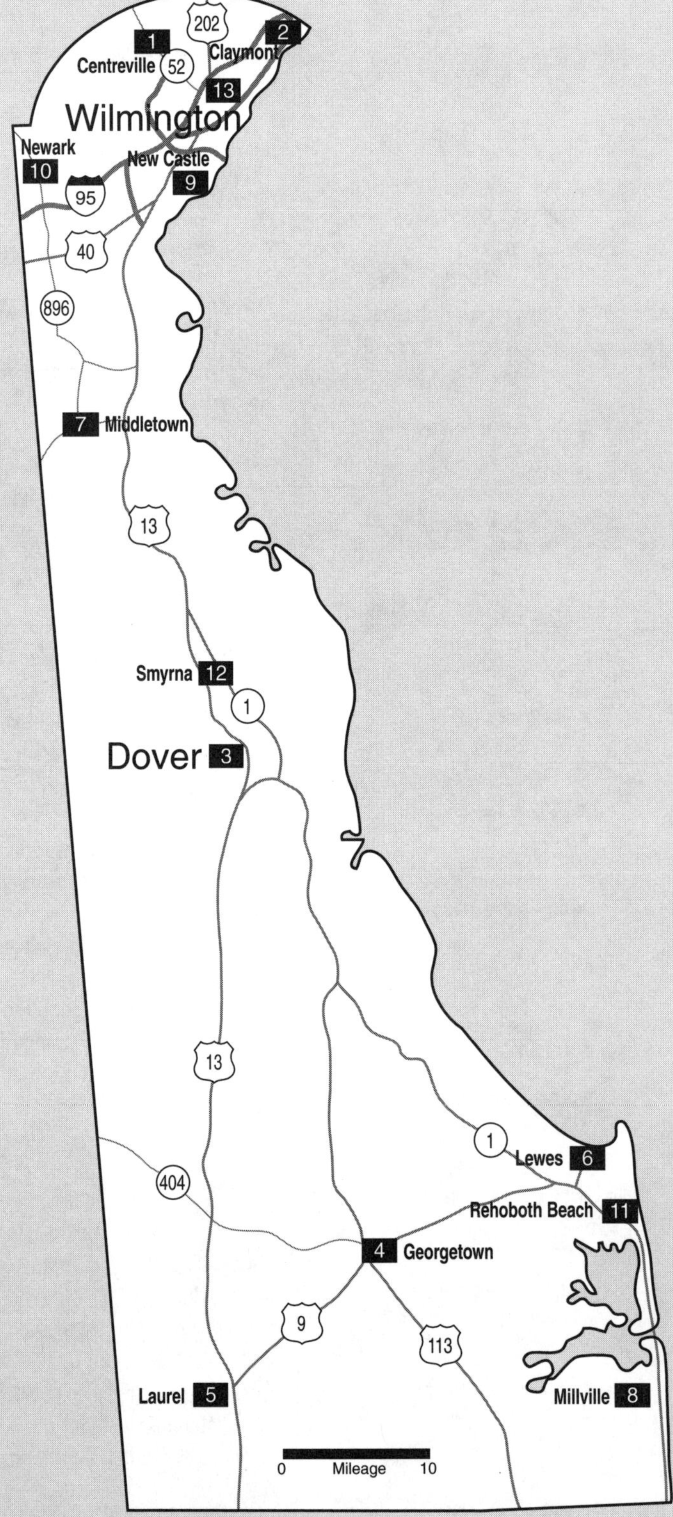

1
202
2
Centreville
52
Claymont
13
Wilmington
Newark
New Castle
10
9
95
40
896
7 Middletown
13
Smyrna 12
1
Dover 3
13
1
Lewes 6
404
Rehoboth Beach 11
4 Georgetown
9
113
Laurel 5
Millville 8
0 Mileage 10

*Darley Manor Inn's front parlor provides a serene and graceful atmosphere. Once the home of famous illustrator Felix Darley, suites are named for authors.*

# Historic Darley Manor Inn:

## Classic authors and artists are the inspiration for elegantly appointed suites

Darley Manor Inn located at 3701 Philadelphia Pike in Wilmington, Delaware was once the home of America's most famous illustrator, Felix Darley. This 1790's Historic Register home features six suites decorated in Classic Colonial antiques and reproductions. The North-South Writers Suite features Civil War period antiques and collectibles, including the porch rail from the Confederate White House in Richmond, Virginia. Additional suites are the Dickens or Cooper Room, overlooking the gardens and lawn; the Darley Suite, named for the famous illustrator; the Irving Suite, located on the third floor and overlooking the backyard; and the Wren's Suite, the most private and largest of all the suites provides a cozy fireplace and separate sitting room.

Situated in the beautiful wine country of Delaware, nearby Interstates 495, 95 and Route 2020 give quick and easy access to Winterthur, Longwood Gardens, Brandywine Art Museum, Historic Philadelphia, good restaurants and great antique shopping.

*Rates begin at $79 per night and vary with the season. For additional information on Darley Manor Inn visit their web site at www.dca.net/darley/ or call the innkeepers at 1-800-824-4703.*

*Darley Manor Inn is on the National Register for historic homes, minutes away from many local attractions.*

## 1 CENTREVILLE

**Twice Nice Antiques**
5714 Kennett Pike, Route 52
302/656-8881

**Barbara's Antiques & Books**
5900 Kennett Pike, Route 52
302/655-3055

## 2 CLAYMONT

**AAA Claymont Antiques**
2811 Philadelphia Pike
302/798-1771

**Lamb's Loft**
16 Commonwealth Ave.
302/792-9620

## 3 DOVER

**Ancestors Inc.**
1025 S. Dupont Hwy.
302/736-3000

**Delaware Made**
214 S. State St.
302/736-1419

**Dover Antique Mart**
4621 N. Dupont Hwy.
302/734-7844

**Then Again**
28 W. Loockerman St.
302/734-1844

**Paul's Antique Furniture**
4304 N. Dupont Hwy.
302/734-2280

**Antiques Art & Collectibles**
329 W. Loockerman St.
302/736-0739

**Kilvington Antiques**
103 S. Bradford St.
302/734-9124

**Harmics Antique Gallery**
5409 N. Dupont Hwy.
302/736-1174

**Robert's Antique Lamps**
2035 S. Dupont Hwy.
302/697-3414

**Flamm Antiques**
1958 Mitten St.
302/734-5623

## 4 GEORGETOWN

**Bailey's Bargains**
Route 113
302/856-2345

**Brick Barn Antiques**
Route 9
302/684-4442

**Candlelight Antiques**
406 N. Dupont Hwy.
302/856-7880

**Collector's Corner**
101 E. Market St.
302/856-7006

**Gas Station**
546 N. Dupont Hwy.
302/855-1127

**Georgetown Antiques Market**
105 E. Market St.
302/856-7118

**Passwaters Antiques**
6 Primrose Lane
302/856-6667

**Generations Antiques**
Route 9
302/856-6750

## 5 LAUREL

Front Street is Laurel's oldest street, following an old Indian trail along Broad Creek. The town was plotted in 1802 after the sale of the Indian reservation that had occupied much of the land. The town was named for the abundance of laurel growing in nearby woods. Today it is the site of a rapidly expanding flea market—the largest in Delaware—that complements the traditional farmers' markets and auctions of the region. Laurel is the site of an annual Watermelon Festival.

**O'Neal's Antiques**
Route 13 & 466
302/875-3391

**Delmar Antiques**
Route 13
302/875-2200

**Golden Door**
214 E. Market St.
302/875-5084

**Bargain Carnival**
310 N. Central Ave.
302/875-1662

## 6 LEWES

Settled by the Dutch in 1631, Lewes (pronounced "Lewis") is Delaware's oldest settlement and is located on the Delaware Bay rather than on the Atlantic Ocean. Known for its fishing marinas, Lewes is also the southern terminal of the Cape May-Lewes Ferry that crosses the mouth of the Bay between Delaware and New Jersey. Lewes is the site of an enclave of historic buildings and homes, many carefully restored. (see Lewes Historical Complex below)

**Heritage Antique Mall**
130 Hwy. One, S. Bound Lane
302/645-2309

**Classic Country Antiques**
Route 9
302/684-3285

**Antique Corner Downtown**
142 C Second St.
302/645-7233

**Auntie M's Emporium**
116 W. 3rd St.
302/644-1804

**Auntie M's Emporium**
203 B Second St.
302/644-2242

**Art & Antiques**
130 Hwy. One, Booth #8
302/645-2309

**Old & Gnu Antiques**
1503 Hwy. One N.
302/645-8080

**Swan's Nest**
107 Kings Hwy.
302/845-8403

**G. C. Vernon Fine Art**
1566 Hwy. One N.
302/645-7905

**Jewells Antique & Jewelry**
118 2nd St.
302/645-1828

**Lewes Mercantile Antique Gallery**
109 2nd St.
302/64-7900

### *Interesting Side Trips*

### Lewes Historical District

**Burton-Ingram House**
Oldest section built c. 1789. Furnished with Chippendale and Empire antiques.

**Blacksmith Shop**
An old frame building, now an extension to the gift shop.

**Doctor's Office**
Greek Revival structure showing a turn-of-the-century doctor's office.

### Early Plank House

Early Swedish-style construction, furnished as a settler's cabin. May be the oldest surviving building in the area.

### Ellegood House

Serves as a gift shop.

### Hiram Burton House

Ca. 1780 and furnished with items from the collection of John Farrace.

### Rabbit's Ferry House

An early 18th-century Sussex County farmhouse.

### Thompson Country Store

Built around 1800 in Thompsonville, DE. Operated continuously by the Thompson family from 1888 to 1962. Moved to Lewes, repaired and reopened in 1963.

The entrance fee for the Lewes Historical Complex also includes the Lightship Overfalls Museum. A sea-going lightship, like the one that was anchored on the Overfalls Shoal, this lightship used to be the Boston Light. It was given to Lewes in the 1960s. Located on the canal in Lewes by the U.S. Lifesaving Station.

Walking tours of the historic area begin at the Thompson Store, Shipcarpenter St. and W. Third St. Reservations required for groups. Open mid-June until Labor Day, Tuesday-Saturday. For information call the Lewes Historical Society, 302/645-7670.

## 7 MIDDLETOWN

**Butler & Cook Antiques**
13 E. Main St.
302/378-7022

**G. W. Thomas Antiques**
2496 N. Dupont Pkwy.
302/378-2414

**Daniel Bennett Shutt Inc.**
123 W. Main St.
302/378-0890

**Mac Donough Antique Center**
2501 N. Dupont Pkwy.
302/378-0485

## 8 MILLVILLE

**Hudson's General Store**
Route 26 & Road 348
302/539-8709

## 9 NEW CASTLE

New Castle, on the Delaware River just south of Wilmington, is an undiscovered jewel of the Eastern Seaboard. Cobblestone streets date from the Colonial era, as do the proud homes that line them. "A Day in Old New Castle" is held annually in May, and there are also Christmas time candlelight tours.

New Castle was founded by the Dutch on their way up the Delaware River. It was later conquered by the Swedes and then by the British. In 1682, it was the first landing site in North America of William Penn.

**Opera House Antiques**
308 Delaware St.
302/326-1211

**Yesterday's Rose**
204 Delaware St.
302/322-3001

**Lynch Antiques/Caroline's Ginger Jar**
1 E. Second St.
302/328-5576

**Cobblestones**
406 Delaware St.
302/322-5088

**Raven's Nest**
204 Delaware St.
302/325-2510

***Great Places To Stay***

### William Penn Guest House

206 Delaware St.
302/328-7736

Named in honor of Pennsylvania's Quaker founder, William Penn, this guest house was built in the same year of Penn's arrival to New Castle in 1682. In fact, Penn himself once stayed at the home as an overnight guest. Constructed of brick, this three-story building has been restored to its original architectural features, including wide-planked floors. Three guest rooms are available overlooking the green in the center of town. Revolutionary War sites, walking tours, shopping and dining are within walking distance.

### Armitage Inn

2 The Strand
302/328-6618

The Armitage Inn sets on the bank of the Delaware River only a few feet from the spot where William Penn first stepped into the new world. Built in 1732, the inn includes the main house, a wing, and a garden cottage. It is believed that the inn began life as a one-room dwelling built during the 1600s. The room was incorporated into its expansion in 1732. Within this room is an original brick walk-in cooking fireplace. Guest rooms are historically decorated and furnished with period antiques. Guests are welcome to enjoy the common areas including the parlor, library, screened porch and garden.

## 10 NEWARK

**Chapel Street Antiques**
197 Chapel St.
302/366-0700

**Classic Crafter**
5 Polly Drummond Shopping Center
302/369-1160

**Main Street Antiques**
280 E. Main St.
302/733-7677

## 11 REHOBOTH BEACH

**Affordable Antiques**
4300 Hwy. One
302/227-5803

**Antiques Village Mall**
221 Hwy. One
302/644-0842

**Garage Sale Antiques**
1416 Hwy. One
302/645-1205

**Stuart Kingston Inc.**
502 N. Boardwalk
302/227-2524

***Great Places To Stay***

**Chesapeake Landing Bed and Breakfast**
101 Chesapeake St.
302/227-2973

Nestled in a forest of pine and bamboo on the shore of Lake Comegy is Chesapeake Landing. This romantic and secluded setting feels like a mountain retreat or a tropical hideaway, it is only steps from the Atlantic Ocean. A sparkling pool, gourmet breakfast, comfy fire, and poolside den contribute to a very special getaway. Sunset refreshments, lakeside dock, and a lifetime of collecting, all add to a wonderful experience any time of the year. Four guest accommodations with private baths. $150-225

**Lighthouse Inn**
20 Delaware Inn
302/226-0407

The Lighthouse Inn is located in the heart of Rehoboth Beach. This wonderful old house was built around the turn of the century and its location is ideal for those who enjoy leaving their car parked and touring the town. The Lighthouse Inn is one-half block from the beach and just blocks from all the fine restaurants and bars. A fabulous breakfast awaits you...the smell of freshly-brewed coffee leads you to a supreme continental cuisine served on the enclosed porch. Sunday brings a special treat with a hot breakfast consisting of eggs or waffles with topping, Vermont maple syrup, sausage or ham, assorted pastries, bagels, English muffins, cereal, yogurt, fresh fruit and more! The main house has six newly decorated rooms named for cities famous for lighthouses. The inn has a sitting room with fireplace, TV/VCR and a small library of movies. You can relax with your friends at days end on the enclosed porch or by the fireplace.

## 12 SMYRNA

Smyrna began about 1700 as an English Quaker settlement called Duck Creek Village, one mile north of the current town. The Smyrna Landing wharfs were centers of commerce in the 1800s. Many examples of Federal and Victorian architecture can be found in the town. Smyrna is eight miles west of the Delaware Bay and Bombay Hook Wildlife Refuge.

**A Bit of The Past**
3511 S. Dupont Blvd.
302/653-9963

**Attic Treasures**
2119 S. Dupont Blvd.
302/653-6566

**Eileen Gant Antiques**
5527 Dupont Pkwy.
302/653-8996

**Smyrna Antiques Mart**
3114 S. Dupont Blvd.
302/659-0373

**Tin Sedan**
12 N. Main St.
302/653-3535

**C & J Antiques**
Route 13
302/653-4903

**What Nott Shop**
5786 Dupont Hwy.
302/653-3855

## 13 WILMINGTON

**Sheepish Grin, Inc.**
Nancy and Bill Settel
Open by appointment
302/995-2614
Fax: 302/995-2899

I first met Bill and Nancy at the Heart of Country Show in Nashville, Tennessee. For those of you who read about Sheepish Grin in last years edition, I had mistakenly called Nancy's husband by the wrong name-"George"-instead of Bill. I wanted to set the record straight before the rumors started flying-Nancy was at that time and still is married to Bill. There has been no divorce and re-marriage in the family, although Nancy jokingly says that George could be the name of her husband in her next life and that I'm just ahead of my time. None-the-less, for now it's BILL. And BILL and NANCY are a great team.

They specialize in early painted country furniture and accessories such as old tins, iron, pantry boxes, rag dolls and primitive angels. They also are the manufacturers of the original Colonial Grunge Nubbie Candles (18th-century-looking candles). These candles are fabulous decorator items, and the Settels sell them wholesale to shops all over the world and to folks like me - I have 3 of each scent. (I still think Bill looks like "a George").

**"sweet potato cabin"**
antiques and mighty fine folk art
Shop: 302/995-2614
Home: 302/995-1808
Open by appointment
*Directions: One block off I-95.*

Nancy and Bill Settel, owners of the Sheepish Grin, have just opened one of the best shops, or should I say "warehouses," for early country furnishings in the U.S. and quiet possibly the world! Okay, so I'm getting a little carried away with that one, but their "stuff" is so wonderful! Sugar buckets, blanket chests, baskets, cupboards, cabinets and much, much more - most in original paint. An absolute must stop-but don't forget to call first.

**Golden Eagle**
1905 N. Market St.
302/651-3480

**Next To New Shop**
2009 Market St.
302/658-0020

**Brandywine Antiques**
2601 Pin Oak Dr.
302/475-8398

**Wright's Antiques**
802 W. Newport Pike
302/994-3002

**Merrill's Antiques**
100 Northern Ave.
302/994-1765

**Twice Nice Antiques**
5714 Kennett Pike
302/656-8881

**Brandywine Trading Co.**
804 Brandywine Blvd.
302/761-9175

**Impulse Antiques**
216 Main St. (Stanton)
302/994-7737

**Bellefonte Shoppe**
901 Brandywine Blvd.
302/764-0637

**Willow Tree**
1605 E. Newport Pike
302/998-9004

**Brandywine Treasure Shop**
1913 N. Market St.
302/656-4464

**Holly Oak Corner Store**
1600 Philadelphia Pike
302/798-0255

**Country Corner**
641 W. Newport Pike
302/998-2304

**Doyle Antiques**
601 S. Maryland Ave.
302/994-1424

**Resettlers Inc.**
5801 Kennett Pike
302/658-9097

**Barbara's Antiques & Books**
5900 Kennett Pike
302/655-3055

**Browse & Buy**
1704 Philadelphia Pike
302/798-5866

**Jackson-Mitchell Inc.**
5718 Kennett Pike
302/656-0110

**Brandywine Resale Shop**
900 Brandywine Blvd.
302/764-4544

**La Femme Mystique Boutique**
Trolley Square Shopping Center
302/651-9331

## *Great Places To Stay*

**Darley Manor Inn**
3701 Philadelphia Pike
(Claymont Community)
302/792-2127, 1-800-824-4703
Web site: www.dca.net/darley/

For specific information see review at the beginning of this section.

## *Interesting Side Trips*

**Winterthur**
Museum Garden Library
1-800-448-3883

Henry Francis du Pont's world-renowned collection of decorative arts made or used in America from 1640-1860, are showcased in two buildings on the property. The Galleries at Winterthur offer an introductory exhibition, Perspectives on the Decorative Arts in Early America. The Period Rooms offer visitors guided tours of rooms decorated as they might have been in days gone by. Spread over almost 1,000 acres, the Garden features native and exotic plants, ponds, woods and meadowland. Year-round programming includes the annual Point-to-Point races in May and the Yuletide tour. Reservations required for some tours. Located on DE 52, six miles northwest of Wilmington.

**Hagley Museum**
302/658-2400

Features the original du Pont mills, estate and gardens on 230 acres along the Brandywine River. Daily demonstrations and exhibits depict American life at home and at work in the 19th century. First du Pont family home, French garden, antique automobiles, first Dupont Company office and working machine shop highlight the visit. Three miles northwest of Wilmington via DE Routes 52 and 141.

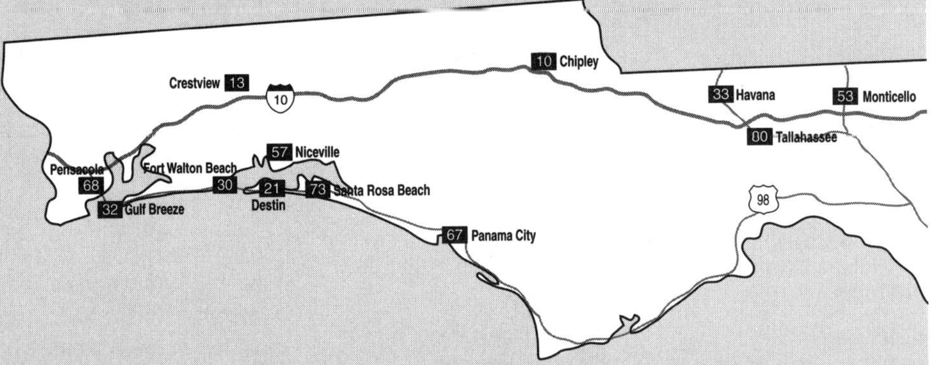
Crestview 13
10
10 Chipley
33 Havana
53 Monticello
80 Tallahassee
57 Niceville
Pensacola
68
Fort Walton Beach
30
21
Destin
73 Santa Rosa Beach
32 Gulf Breeze
98
67 Panama City

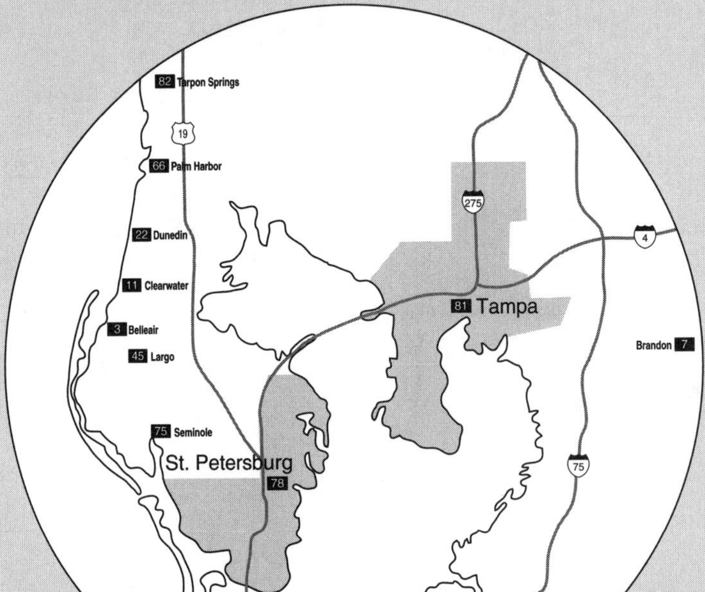
82 Tarpon Springs
19
66 Palm Harbor
22 Dunedin
11 Clearwater
3 Belleair
45 Largo
75 Seminole
St. Petersburg
78
275
81 Tampa
4
Brandon 7
75
275

# Florida

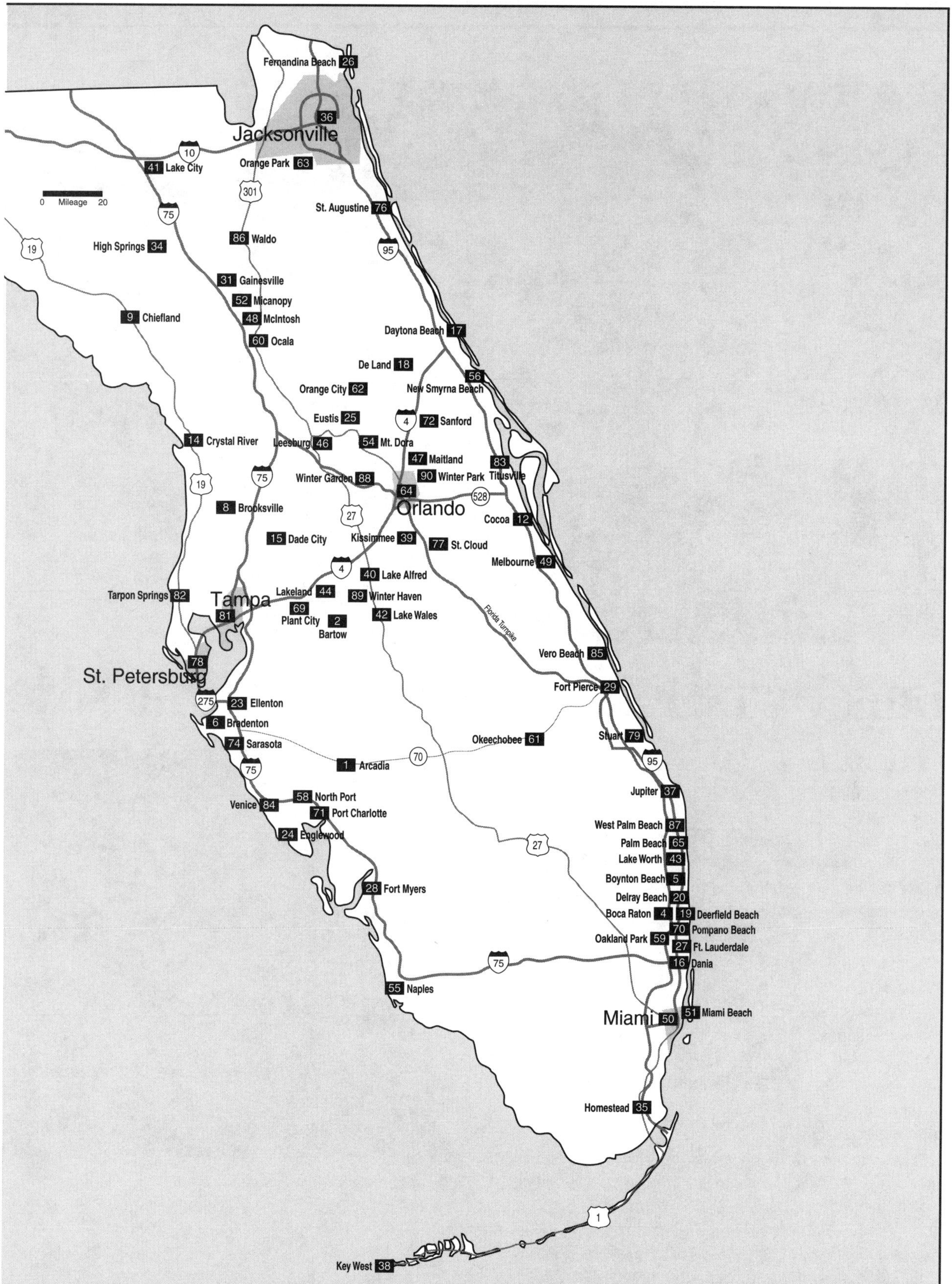
Fernandina Beach 26
36
Jacksonville
10
41 Lake City
Orange Park 63
0 Mileage 20
301
75
St. Augustine 76
86 Waldo
19
High Springs 34
95
31 Gainesville
52 Micanopy
9 Chiefland
48 McIntosh
60 Ocala
Daytona Beach 17
De Land 18
56
Orange City 62
New Smyrna Beach
4
72 Sanford
Eustis 25
14 Crystal River
Leesburg 46
54 Mt. Dora
47 Maitland
83
90 Winter Park
Titusville
19
75
Winter Garden 88
64
528
Orlando
8 Brooksville
27
Cocoa 12
15 Dade City
Kissimmee 39
77 St. Cloud
Melbourne 49
4
40 Lake Alfred
Tarpon Springs 82
Tampa
Lakeland 44
89 Winter Haven
69
81
Plant City
2
Bartow
42 Lake Wales
Florida Turnpike
Vero Beach 85
78
St. Petersburg
Fort Pierce 29
275
23 Ellenton
6 Bradenton
Okeechobee 61
Stuart 79
74 Sarasota
1 Arcadia
70
95
75
Jupiter 37
58 North Port
Venice 84
71 Port Charlotte
West Palm Beach 87
24 Englewood
27
Palm Beach 65
Lake Worth 43
Boynton Beach 5
28 Fort Myers
Delray Beach 20
Boca Raton 4
19 Deerfield Beach
70 Pompano Beach
Oakland Park 59
27 Ft. Lauderdale
75
16 Dania
55 Naples
Miami 50
51 Miami Beach
Homestead 35
1
Key West 38

*Butterpat's tasteful china and pottery selections are temptingly arranged.*

# Butterpat's: Extraordinarily flavorful style

A beautiful display of antiques and fine collections awaits those who visit Butterpat's Antiques. The warmth and charm of the shop is created from the gathering of all the wonderful collections assembled by the owners. Not your ordinary array of antiques and collectibles, Butterpat's specializes in the rare and exquisite. Among the selections you'll find Majolica, mercury glass, English lusters, Coors, "Rosebud" pottery, McCoy, Quimper, papier mache, unusual wooden boxes, and my favorite: architectural details and garden ornaments.

*Majolica lovers will rejoice at the intriguing selection of pieces.*

*Row upon row of antique treasures are displayed for your browsing pleasure.*

*Butterpat's is located at 2439 Edgewater Dr. in Orlando. For additional information please call 407/423-7971.*

*Key West at its best: Blue Parrot Inn is your charming centrally-located base for excursions into the heart of Key West where beaches, shops and galleries beckon. The Blue Parrot pool is kept to the soothing temperature of bathwater, no matter what the season.*

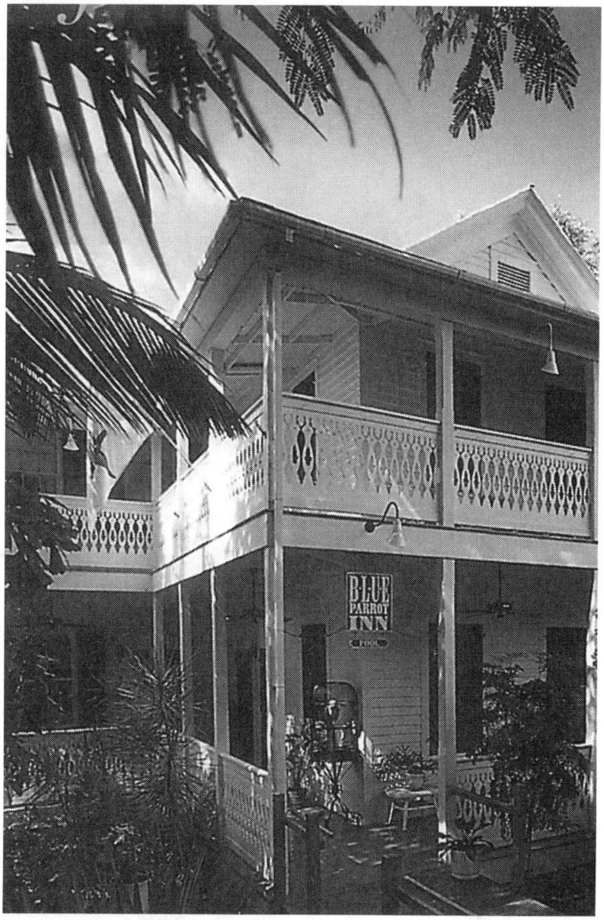


*Palms gently brush the rooftops of the sweeping verandas.*

# The Blue Parrot offers a little bit of paradise for lazy days, crazy nights on the town, and a world of wonderful memories

*Guests can share a little sailor talk with Blue Parrot himself.*

Key West and the Florida Keys are the only car-accessible islands of the Caribbean and the 3-hour drive from Miami is absolutely amazing: the Gulf on one side of the road and the ocean on the other. It is also the perfect setting for the Blue Parrot Inn which has been located in the heart of "Historic Downtown" Key West since 1884.

The inn is a relaxed, friendly home reflecting classic Bahamian charm with an overlay of Victorian gingerbread. Sweeping verandas provide outside access to the rooms. It is located just off U.S. Hwy. 1 (Truman Ave.), and only two blocks from the famous Duval St. beaches, restaurants, shops and galleries.

Morning comes with its own clean, tropical sweetness as you awaken to the sounds of Mozart, heliconia and softly whooshing palm fronds. Freshly-brewed coffee and home-baked muffins are served by the pool. Evenings offer fond memories of paintbox sunsets and walks down Old Town lanes and historic alleys under the spell of a tropical moon. And after everything, the quiet comfort of the Blue Parrot Inn where sweet dreams are only a prelude to an even sweeter tomorrow.

*The Blue Parrot Inn is located at 916 Elizabeth St. in Key West. For additional information see listing #38 (Key West) or call the innkeepers at 1-800-231-BIRD for specific rates.*

*The owner of the Historic Chipley Antique Mall chose to restore the facade to match a 1907 photograph of the former mercantile business.*

# Historic finds: Chipley Antique Mall

Historic Chipley was settled in the 1880s as a railroad town and was named for Colonel Chipley who built the railroad across the panhandle of Florida. The center of town is known as the Historic District boasting vintage store fronts and meticulously restored buildings dating back to the 1800's.

This beautifully resurrected area is home to Historic Chipley Antique Mall. The mall is located in what once was the town mercantile store. The owners have restored the front of the building to resemble its appearance in a 1907 photograph. Within this 10,000 square foot mall over 50 dealers display an array of antiques and collectibles including depression glass, pottery, flow blue and other fine porcelains as well as quality furnishings from several styles and eras.

The mall promotes special events throughout the year such as dealer day sales. This has become a very popular occasion among the many customers who frequent the mall. It's that one special day when the customer can deal one-on-one with the booth operator. Guest speakers often frequent the mall and Harry Rinker, distinguished author and lecturer has been among the celebrity guests. Don't be surprised when you drop in to find the staff decked out in vintage attire.

*Hobby horses, basketry, wicker furniture and antiques galore fill the Historic Chipley Antique mall.*

*Historic Chipley Antique Mall is located at 1368 N. Railroad Ave. just 2 miles north of I-10 at Exit 18. One block west of Hwy. 77 and ten blocks west of Hwy. 231, a major north-south route from the midwest. The mall is open seven days a week, Mon.-Sat., 9 to 5, and Sun. 11-5. For additional information the mall phone number is 850/638-2535. Web site: www.antiqnet.com/chipley*

Florida

*Palm breezes fan the porches of the Addison House, situated in the historic district of Fernandina Beach, Amelia Island.*

# Sea, sun and sweet dreams at the Addison House

The Addison House located in the historic district of Fernandina Beach on beautiful Amelia Island is a stunning circa 1876 home. The guest rooms feature private porches, and whirlpool tubs. Each afternoon beverages and home-made goodies are offered on the veranda overlooking the courtyard. The island offers the perfect getaway and the innkeepers, the Gibson family, are dedicated to providing a special place to stay. Special arrangements can be made for romantic desserts, picnic lunches, anniversary or honeymoon packages.

*The Addison House is located at 614 Ash St. in Fernandina Beach. This 1876 home offers thirteen guest rooms. Rates begin at $115. For additional information on the Addison House please call the innkeepers at 1-800-942-1604 or visit their web site at www.addisonhousebb.com.*

*Romantic, airy, light-filled rooms furnished gracefully create an environment that welcomes the traveler and promises a very special stay. Private porches are an added feature of each room. Whirlpool tubs provide another comfort to the road weary.*

# Florida

## 1 ARCADIA

**Townsend Antiques**
5 E. Oak St.
941/494-2137

**Maddy's Antiques**
101 W. Oak St.
941/494-2500

**Glacier Melt—Antiques & Unusuals**
114 West Oak St.
941/993-4489

**Hidden Treasures**
33 W. Magnolia Hwy. 70
941/491-0060

**The Crested Duck**
121 W. Oak St.
941/491-8600

**The Collectors Addict**
109 West Oak St.
941/993-2228

**Arcadia Tea Room**
117 W. Oak St.
941/494-2424

**Hitching Post Antiques**
24 W. Oak St.
941/993-9963

**Orange Blssm & Picket Fence Antqs.**
15 S. Polk Ave.
941/491-0008

**Old Opera House Mus. Antq. Mall**
106 West Oak St.
941/494-7010

**Forgotten Things**
132 West Oak St.
941/491-0053

**Mary's Attic**
12 W. Oak St.
941/993-2533

**My Friend & Me**
305 W. Oak St.
941/993-4438

**Three Amish Shoppe & More**
12 N. Desoto Ave.
941/993-4151

## 2 BARTOW

**Dolene's Downtown**
290 E. Main St.
941/534-3311

**Philip's Antiques**
330 E. Main St.
941/533-2365

**Bartow Antiques**
280 S. Wilson Ave.
941/534-1094

**Apple Blossom**
318 E. Main St.
941/534-1717

**Yates Antiques**
875 E. Main St.
941/533-7635

## 3 BELLEAIR

**Belleair Bluffs Antiques**
428 Indian Rocks Road N.
813/586-1488

**Collum Antiques**
580 Indian Rocks Road N.
813/581-6585

**Royal Crown Antiques Etc.**
562 Indian Rocks Road N.
813/584-6525

**Encore Events**
562 E. Indian Rocks Road N.
813/585-7242

**Treasures & Dolls**
518 Indian Rocks Road N.
813/584-7277

**Posh Pineapple Antiques**
560 Indian Rocks Road N.
813/586-3006

**Merndale Antiques**
562D Indian Rocks Road N.
813/581-1100

**Lejan's Antqs. @ Remember When**
570 Indian Rocks Road N.
813/586-7515

**Neil's Furniture/Antique Shop**
568 Indian Rocks Road N.
813/586-3232

**Jean's Locker Collectibles**
596 Indian Rocks Road N., #17A
813/585-8460

**Back Door Antiques**
596 Indian Rocks Road N.
813/581-2780

**Victoria's Parlour**
596 Indian Rocks Road N.
813/581-0519

**Music Box**
784 Indian Rocks Road N.
813/581-1359

**Provence Art & Antiques**
2620 Jewell Road
813/581-5754

**Antiques & Specialities**
566 Indian Rocks Road N.
813/584-4370

**Elaine's Antiques**
596 Indian Rocks Road N.
813/584-6143

**Antiques & Design**
560 Indian Rocks Road N.
813/584-8843

**Belleair Coins**
730 Indian Rocks Road N.
813/581-6827

**Jewel Antiques Mall**
2601 Jewel Road
813/585-5568

## 4 BOCA RATON

**Village Rose**
7044 Beracasa Way
561/750-7070

**Art Nouveau Antiques**
6000 A Glades Road #168
561/347-2885

**C-Trois & Co**
2831 N. Federal Hwy.
561/347-1169

**Maybe Shop Antiques**
221 E. Palmetto Park Road
561/392-5680

**Country Pine**
161 N.W. 11th St.
561/368-8470

**Country Tyme Antiques**
672 Glades Road
561/391-7749

**Find A Deal Antiques Gallery**
2621 N. Federal Hwy.
561/362-9022

**Unusual Usuals**
2831 N. Federal Hwy.
561/367-6083

**Luigi's Objects D'Art Gallery**
6018 S.W. 18th St., Suite C9
561/394-4968

## 5 BOYNTON BEACH

**A & B Antiques & Collectibles**
2951 S.W. 14th Place
561/731-2213

**Mrs. Hilda's Antique Shop**
524 E. Ocean Ave.
561/735-0333

**Red Tag Furnishings**
531 Ocean Ave.
No Phone Listed

**Consignment Shoppe**
411 E. Boynton Beach Blvd.
561/736-8767

**Pat's Accents**
528 E. Ocean Ave.
561/374-9040

**Treasures & Antiques**
640 E. Ocean Ave.
561/364-1272

## 6 BRADENTON

**Leach-Wells Galleries Antiques**
316 12th St. W.
941/747-5453

**Dotty's Depot**
1421 12th Ave. W.
941/749-1421

**Antiques on the Avenue**
2931 Manatee Ave. W.
941/749-1360

**George M. Hicks Antiques**
5206 Manatee Ave. W.
941/749-1866

## 7 BRANDON

**Nostalgia Station Antiques**
514 Limona Road
813/681-5473

**Victoria's Attic Antiques**
714 W. Lumsden Road
813/685-6782

**Somewhere In Time**
720 W. Lumsden Road
813/684-0588

**Remember When Antiques**
408 N. Parsons Ave.
813/654-8323

**About Antiques**
728 W. Lumsden Road
813/684-2665

**Sweet Memories Antiques**
608 N. Parsons Ave.
813/685-3728

**Cottage Corner Antiques**
616 N. Parsons Ave.
813/654-2193

**American Country Antiques**
745 Sandy Creek Dr.
813/681-9592

## 8 BROOKSVILLE

Brooksville, originally known as Melendez and then Benton, is a wonderful city of hills, ranging in elevation from 175 to 274 feet. Coupled with its condensed area (2.77 square miles) and its long history of successful planters, growers, and cattlemen, Brooksville is more a reflection of "the Old South" than other West Coast towns. Its Southern background is reflected in its name, honoring South Carolina Congressman Preston Brooks who is best noted for hitting abolitionist Senator Charles Sumner on the head with his cane.

**Barnette's Antique Mall**
2 N. Broad St.
352/544-0910

**Antiques at the Corner**
10431 Broad St.
352/796-7518

**Hillhouse Antiques**
406 E. Liberty St.
352/796-8489

**Cabin Creek Antiques**
770 E. Jefferson St.
352/799-8770

**Red Rooster Antiques & Collectibles**
838 E. Jefferson St.
352/799-4636

**Old World Antiques**
31 S. Main St.
352/796-2729

### *Great Places To Stay*

**Verona House**
201 South Main St.
1-800-355-6717
Web site: www.bbhost.com/veronabb

Verona House is a 1925 Sears and Roebuck catalog house in the historic downtown area of Brooksville. With picturesque tree lined streets and rolling hills, Brooksville, unlike most of Florida, has many hills and canopied streets with large oak trees. A small southern town of 7500 people and "a quiet getaway from the fast pace of City life", your hosts Bob & Jan Boyd will extend southern hospitality and share with you the historical background of their town. There are four guests rooms decorated in cherished pieces, a fireplace and hot spa. Each morning enjoy Jan's fresh baked casserole and muffin or bread, accompanied with fruit and juice. Canoeing, horseback riding, golf, tennis, antique stores, coffee house and Roger's Christmas House are nearby. Special weekends are scheduled around local antique, craft and entertainment festivals.

### *Interesting Side Trips*

At Liberty and Saxon Avenue is the famous Roger's Christmas House, 103 Saxon Avenue. Mary Roger's Christmas gift shop has grown into an amazing complex of houses filled with decorations, displays, and attractions.

## 9 CHIEFLAND

**Kip's Trading Post**
914 N. Young Blvd. (U.S. 19)
352/493-1083

**Elaine's Treasure House**
1708 N. Young Blvd.
352/493-1306

## 10 CHIPLEY

**Historic Chipley Antique Mall**
1368 N. Railroad Ave.
850/638-2535

For specific information see review at the beginning of this section.

## 11 CLEARWATER

**Able Antiques**
1686 Clearwater Largo Road
813/581-5583

**Banyan Tree's Trunk**
1775 Clearwater Largo Road
813/587-0799

**Pack Rat Corner**
617 Cleveland
813/443-2721

**Singletree Antiques**
1411 Cleveland
813/447-1445

**Iron Gate Antiques**
703 Court St.
813/443-4730

**Savoy Antiques**
924 N. McMullen Booth Road
813/726-1111

**Antique Pine Imports**
13585 49th St. N.
813/572-0956

## 12 COCOA

**Country Life**
313 Brevard Ave.
407/639-3794

**Forget-Me-Not**
404 Brevard Ave., #A
407/632-4700

**Antiques & Old Lace Mall**
1803 N. Cocoa Blvd.
407/631-5787

**Gould's Old Time General Store**
307 Delannoy Ave.
407/632-2481

**Past Gas Co.**
308 Willard St.
407/636-0449

## 13 CRESTVIEW

**Yesteryear's Attic**
1407 Ferdon Blvd. S.
850/682-9296

**Pappy T's**
388 Main St. N.
904/689-2323

## 14 CRYSTAL RIVER

**Heritage Antiques Mall**
103 N.W. U.S. Hwy. 19
352/563-5597

**Trader Jack's Antiques**
706 S.E. U.S. Hwy. 19
352/795-5225

**Crystal River Antiques**
756 N.E. U.S. Hwy. 19
352/563-1121

**Cobblestone Alley Antiques**
657 Citrus Ave.
352/795-0060

## 15 DADE CITY

**Ivy Cottage**
14110 7th St.
352/523-0019

**Remember When Antique Mall**
14129 7th St.
352/521-6211

**Church Street Antiques**
14117 8th St.
352/523-2422

**Corner Emporium**
14136 8th St.
352/567-1990

**Sugarcreek Antiques**
37846 Meridian Ave.
352/567-7712

## 16 DANIA

**Mark First Antique Guns**
1 N. Federal Hwy.
954/925-0856

**Antique Center of Dania Inc.**
3 N. Federal Hwy.
954/922-5467

**Antique Jewels by Paula**
3 N. Federal Hwy.
954/926-1060

**E & F Antiques & Collectibles**
3 N. Federal Hwy.
954/929-3119

**Gallery Picture Frames, Inc.**
3 N. Federal Hwy.
954/920-2086

**Goldie Kossow Antiques, Inc.**
3 N. Federal Hwy.
954/921-5569

**Linda's Antique Collectibles**
3 N. Federal Hwy.
954/920-2030

**Madeleine France's Past Pleasures**
3 N. Federal Hwy.
954/921-0022

**Michael T. Pye**
3 N. Federal Hwy.
954/922-5467

**Murray's Antiques**
3 N. Federal Hwy.
954/921-0470

**Crown Antiques**
10 N. Federal Hwy., #A
954/923-4764

**Lorraine's Collectibles**
13 N. Federal Hwy.
954/920-2484

**Memorable Moments Antiques**
15 N. Federal Hwy.
954/929-7922

**Rose Antiques**
17 N. Federal Hwy.
954/921-0474

**Cameo Antiques**
18 N. Federal Hwy.
954/929-0101

**Athena Gallery**
19 S. Federal Hwy.
954/921-7697

**Collectomania**
19 N. Federal Hwy.
954/926-7999

**Daddy's Antiques & Collectibles**
19 N. Federal Hwy.
954/920-4001

**Dania Antique & Jewelry Arcade**
19 N. Federal Hwy.
954/925-9400

**Doe's Treasures**
19 N. Federal Hwy.
954/923-3081

**Glass Antique Or Not**
19 N. Federal Hwy.
954/925-7667

**Jackie's Fine Things**
19 N. Federal Hwy.
954/456-5655

**Antique Tony's & Furniture**
24 N. Federal Hwy.
954/920-4095

**Dania Antique Emporium**
25 N. Federal Hwy.
954/927-1040

**Tamara's Treasures**
25 N. Federal Hwy.
954/927-1040

**Pyewackett's Antiques**
26 N. Federal Hwy.
954/926-7975

**The Garden Path**
27A N. Federal Hwy.
954/929-7766

**Attic Treasures**
32 N. Federal Hwy.
954/920-0280

**Aries Antiques**
47 N. Federal Hwy.
954/923-2239

**Audrey Arovas Antiques**
47 N. Federal Hwy.
954/920-0706

**Grand Central Station**
47 N. Federal Hwy.
954/925-8181

**Memory Lane**
52 N. Federal Hwy.
954/922-0616

**Davidson Antiques**
53 N. Federal Hwy.
954/923-8383

**Beaudet Antiques**
56 N. Federal Hwy.
954/922-5040

**Royal Red Antiques**
56 N. Federal Hwy.
954/925-6111

**English Accent Antiques**
57 N. Federal Hwy.
954/923-8383

**Allison Jaffee Antiques**
60 N. Federal Hwy.
954/923-3939

**Antique Fancies**
60 N. Federal Hwy.
954/929-4473

**Antique Galleries Mall**
60 N. Federal Hwy.
954/920-2801

**Celia & Louis Kleinman Antiques**
60 N. Federal Hwy.
954/920-2801

**Iris Fields of Dania**
60 N. Federal Hwy.
954/926-5658

**Scintillations Antiques Ltd.**
67 N. Federal Hwy.
954/921-8325

**Gordon's of London**
71 N. Federal Hwy.
954/927-0210

**Ambiance Antiques & Design**
19 N. Federal Hwy., Booth #7
954/925-9400

**A to Z Antiques**
11 N. Federal Hwy.
954/927-2707

**Barbra's Place, Inc.**
249 S. Federal Hwy.
954/927-8083

**Dick's Toys & Collectibles**
3 N. Federal Hwy.
954/922-5467

**Gary Slade**
47 N. Federal Hwy.
954/925-8181

**J. J. Haag, Ltd.**
3 N. Federal Hwy.
954/922-5467

**Murray's Antiques**
3 N. Federal Hwy.
954/921-0470

**Anzardo's Fine Arts & Antiques**
14 N.W. 1st Ave.
954/922-6140

**F & N Antiques**
63 N. Federal Hwy.
954/923-3910

**Wilburn's Inc**
68 N. Federal Hwy.
954/922-3188

**Hattie's Antiques & Collectibles**
3 N. Federal Hwy.
954/929-4290

**Antiquety Farms Antiques**
6 N.W. 1st Ave.
954/925-0402

**Aunty Q's, Inc.**
27 N. Federal Hwy.
954/925-3446

**Connie's Place**
3 N. Federal Hwy.
954/922-5467

**Friendly Shoppers**
3 N. Federal Hwy.
954/922-5467

**House of Hirsch Antiques**
75 N. Federal Hwy.
954/925-0818

**Maurizio's Antiques**
8 N. Federal Hwy.
954/929-9954

**Talya's Antiques**
3 N. Federal Hwy.
954/923-6512

## 17 DAYTONA BEACH

**Arlequin Antiques**
122 S. Beach St.
904/252-5498

**Bagwell's Flowers & Antiques**
909 S. Ridgewood Ave.
904/257-4423

**Browse About Shop**
6296 S. Ridgewood Ave.
904/322-6900

**House of Gamble Antique Mall**
1102 State Ave.
904/258-2889

**Kay's Antiques**
522 Seabreeze Blvd.
904/252-1656

**AAAB As Antiques**
114 S. Beach St.
904/252-1040

**Bagwell's Flowers & Antiques**
312 S. Peninsula Dr.
904/252-7687

**Daytona Flea & Antique Market**
1425 Tomoka Farms Road
904/252-1999

**Jerry's Antiques**
1311 Center Ave.
904/252-8952

**Lets Talk Antiques**
140 N. Beach St.
904/258-5225

**Maxwell Galleries**
228 Carswell Ave.
904/238-0076

**Olde Loved Things**
900 Ridgewood Ave.
904/252-7960

**My Nanna's Antiques**
2008 Schultz Ave.
904/239-5992

**Silver Coast**
222 E. Intl. Speedway Blvd.
904/252-5775

### *Great Places To Stay*

**Live Oak Inn**
444 S. Beach St.
1-800-831-1871

Live Oak Inn stands where Mathias Day founded Daytona. Two carefully restored houses-both listed on the national register of historic places (1871-1881) are among Florida's top ten historic inns, and are the cornerstone of Daytona's historic district. Each of Live Oak Inn's twelve rooms celebrates one of the people or events which helped shape Florida's history. All rooms have private bathrooms, king or queen size beds, and either Jacuzzi or Victorian soaking tubs with showers.

## 18 DE LAND

**Cratina's Frameshop & Antiques**
108 S. Woodland Blvd.
904/736-8392

**Rivertown Antique Mall**
114 S. Woodland Blvd.
904/738-5111

**Sylva's Antiques**
428 S. Woodland Blvd.
904/734-4821

**Estate Furniture**
114 N. Woodland Blvd.
904/740-1104

**Outhouse Antiques**
1765 N. Woodland Blvd.
904/736-1575

**Muse Book Shop**
112 S. Woodland Blvd.
904/734-0278

**De Land Antq. Mall/Temple of Time**
142 S. Woodland Blvd.
904/740-1188

**Angevine & Son**
2999 S. Woodland Blvd.
904/734-6347

**Our Hearts In The Country**
136 N. Woodland Blvd.
904/736-4528

**Florida Victorian Archt.**
112 W. Georgia Ave.
904/734-9300

## 19 DEERFIELD BEACH

**A Moment In Time Antiques & Collectibles**
3575 West Hillsboro Blvd.
954/427-7223
Tues.-Sat. 10:30-5:30
*Directions: From I-95 go to Hillsboro Blvd., then head west to Powerline Road in the Shoppes of Deer Creek.*

Shellee grew up in the art business. Her dad was a 3rd generation art dealer, so it was only natural that she follow in his footsteps. In her shop, the art is carefully blended with a selection of other wonderful things.

Her exquisite taste and flair for decorating are evident throughout this beautifully arranged store. In settings reminiscent of Country Living magazine, you'll find country, early American and painted furniture accented with pottery, copper pots, old tools, washboards and other old iron and rustic pieces. If you're not into country, there are plenty more offerings of Limoges, Royal Doulton, vintage jewelry and such.

**Absolutely Fabulous**
337 S.E. 15th Terrace
954/725-0620

**Antiques Unusual**
100 S. Federal Hwy.
954/421-8920

**Cove Cottage Antiques Inc.**
1645 S.E. 3rd St.
954/429-0408

**Joyce M Dudley Antiques**
839 S.E. 9th St.
954/428-8500

**Hillsboro Antique Mall & Tea Room**
1025 E. Hillsboro Blvd.
954/571-9988

## 20 DELRAY BEACH

**Martha T Bartoo**
430 E. Atlantic Ave.
561/279-0399

**Estate Galleries**
1201 N. Federal Hwy.
561/276-0029

**Antique Buying Center**
1201 N. Federal Hwy.
561/379-7360

**Second Chance Emporium**
2101 N. Federal Hwy.
561/276-6380

**Finders Keepers Antiques**
88 S.E. 4th Ave.
561/272-7160

**Antiques Plus**
130 N. Federal Hwy.
No Phone Listed

## 21 DESTIN

**Smith's Antique Mall**
12500 Emerald Coast Pkwy.
904/654-1484

**Clements Antiques of Fla.**
9501 U.S. Hwy. 98 W.
904/837-1473

**Antiques on the Harbor**
202 Hwy. 98 E. (Near the Harborwalk)
904/837-6463

## 22 DUNEDIN

**P Kay's Downtown**
359 Scotland St.
813/734-1731

**The Highlands**
362 Scotland St.
813/547-1637

**Cindy Lou's**
330 Main St.
813/736-3393

**Vyctoria's**
365 Main St.
813/736-0778

## 23 ELLENTON

### Old Feed Store Antique Mall
4407 Hwy. 301
941/729-1379
Mon.-Sat. 10-5 (closed Sun.)
*Directions: Traveling I-75, take exit 43. Go west 9/10 mile on Hwy 310. Turn left on 45th Avenue.*

You'll never guess where this shop got its name. Okay, so I gave you a hint. Somewhere in the early to mid 1920s, the Old Feed Store Antique Mall was just as its name implies, the old feed store in Ellenton. Today, you'll find no evidence of grains, seeds or beans. What you will find are 65 dealers displaying a wide selection of oak, mahogany and walnut furnishings, exquisite glass and crystal items, jewelry, mirrors, china and much more.

(The Gamble Plantation, a historic mansion and grounds is located approximately 200 yards from the mall.)

## 24 ENGLEWOOD

**Rujean's Collectibles Past & Present**
Corner Route 41 & Biscane Dr.
941/426-5418

**Linda's Charming Choices**
145 W. Dearborn St.
941/474-1230

**The Paisley Pelican Artisan & Antique Mall**
447-449 W. Dearborn St.
941/473-2055

**Coins, Jewelry & Antiques**
140 N. Indiana Ave. (S.R. 776)
941/475-4740

**"A Bull in a China Shop"**
395 W. Dearborn St.
941/474-5004

## 25 EUSTIS

**Cowboys**
120 N. Bay St.
352/589-1449

**Merry's Silver Vault**
32 S. Eustis St.
352/589-4321

**Old South Antique Mall**
320 S. Grove St.
352/357-5200

**Palm Village Shoppes**
100 E. Magnolia Ave.
352/589-7256

**Ye Olde Kracker House**
517 E. Orange Ave.
352/357-3291

## 26 FERNANDINA BEACH

One of America's few remaining unspoiled island paradises, Amelia Island is the southernmost of the chain of Atlantic coast barrier islands that stretch from North Carolina to Florida. Its rich history, thirteen miles of uncrowded beaches, lush, natural setting, moss-covered oaks, unparalleled golf, boating, and fishing, stunning sunrises and sunsets, and friendly "locals" make it more than just a place for antiquing.

Birthplace of the modern shrimping industry, Fernandina Beach, located near the north end of the island, hosts its annual "Isle of Eight Flags Shrimp Festival" the first weekend of each May. The event attracts hundreds of artists, artisans, and craftsmen from across the country ... and more than 150,000 visitors ... each year.

**Yesterday's Child**
14 N. 4th St.
904/277-0061

**Fleur De Lis**
14 S. 2nd St.
904/261-1150

**Eight Flags Antique Warehouse**
21 N. 2nd St.
904/277-7006

**Country Store Antiques**
219 S. 8th St.
904/261-2633

**Plantation Shop**
4828 First Coast Hwy.
904/261-2030

**Amelia Island Antique Mart**
1105 S. 8th St.
904/277-3815

### *Great Places To Stay*

**Addison House**
614 Ash St.
1-800-943-1604

For specific information see review at the beginning of this section.

**Bailey House**
28 S. 7th St.
904/261-5390

Built in 1895 in historic Fernandina Beach on Amelia Island, the Bailey House, a Queen Anne Victorian home is listed on the National Register of Historic Places. The wrap-around porch, turrets, widows walk, stained glass, heart pine floors, grand staircase, and six fireplaces, all contribute to the charm. All five bedrooms, entrance hall, parlor and the dining room are decorated with authentic period furnishings.

### *Favorite Places To Eat*

**1878 Steak House**
"Authentic 19th Century Atmosphere"
12 N. 2nd St.
904/261-4049

**Beech Street Grill**
"A Jacksonville Magazine Top 25 Selection"
801 Beech St.
904/277-3662

**Brett's Waterway Cafe**
"A Tradition in the Making"
1 South Front St. - at the foot of Centre St.
904/261-2660

**The Cafe**
"At the Ritz-Carlton"
4750 Amelia Island Pkwy.
904/277-1100

**Captain Van's Seafood**
"Fresh Cooked Seafood"
1214 Beech St.
904/261-5581

**The Crab Trap**
"Serving Fernandina Beach Over 15 Years"
31 N. 2nd St.
904/261-4749

**DJ's Seafood Restaurant**
"Dining Inside & Out"
3199 S. Fletcher Ave.
904/261-5711

**Down Under Restaurant**
"Fernandina's freshest seafood with a spectacular view of the Intracoastal"
A1A at the Intracoastal Waterway - Under the Bridge
904/261-1001

**The Florida House Inn**
"Serving the Florida Traveler Since 1857"
22 S. 3rd St.
904/261-3300

**The Golden Grouper Cafe**
"Fresh Seafood - Grilled, Broiled, Baked & Fried"
5 S. 2nd St.
904/261-0013

**The Grill at the Ritz Carlton**
"Florida's only AAA Five Diamond Restaurant"
4750 Amelia Island Pkwy.
904/277-1100

**Horizon's Continental Cuisine**
"Continental Cuisine - Casual Elegance"
803 Ash St.
904/321-2430

**Island Bar-B-Q**
"Lewis Williams' Original"
2045 S. Fletcher Ave.
904/277-3894

**Kabuki Japanese Steakhouse & Sushi Bar**
"Where the show is good...and the food is great!"
18 N. 2nd St.
904/277-8782

**The Marina Restaurant**
"A 10-Time News-Leader 'Best of the Best' Selection"
18 N. 2nd St.
904/261-9976

**Pompeo's**
"Italian Continental Cuisine and Seafood Restaurant"
302 Centre St.
904/261-7490

**Shakespeare's Kitchen**
"A Coffee House"
316 Centre St. (Upstairs)
904/277-2005

**Slider's Oceanfront Restaurant & Lounge**
"The Seaside Inn"
1998 S. Fletcher Ave.
904/261-0954

**The Southern Tip**
"A Jacksonville Magazine Top 25 Selection"
A1A at Palmetto Walk Shopping Village
904/261-6184

## 27 FORT LAUDERDALE

**Carl Stoffer's Antiques**
3699 N. Dixie Hwy.
954/564-9077

**Gemini Antiques**
4117 N. Dixie Hwy.
954/563-9767

**Jims Antiques Ltd.**
1201 N. Federal Hwy.
954/565-6556

**June Sharp Antiques**
3000 N. Federal Hwy.
954/565-8165

**Lilywhites Antiques & Interior**
3020 N. Federal Hwy.
954/537-9295

**Down East Antiques**
3020 N. Federal Hwy.
954/566-5023

**Malouf Tower Antiques**
2114 S. Federal Hwy.
954/523-5511

**Teddy Bear Antiques**
4136 S.W. 64th Ave.
954/583-7577

**Antiques Limited**
2125 S. Federal Hwy.
954/525-3729

**Glausiers Antiques**
2130 S. Federal Hwy.
954/524-3524

**Las Olas Arts & Antiques**
611 E. Las Olas Blvd.
954/527-2742

**Coo-Coo's Nest**
1511 E. Las Olas Blvd.
954/524-2009

**Lomar Collectibles**
3291 W. Sunrise Blvd.
954/581-1004

**Victorian Reflections Inc.**
1348 Weston Road
954/389-4498

**Perry & Perry**
3313 N.E. 33rd St.
954/561-7707

**Nostalgia Mall**
2097 Wilton Dr.
888/394-7233

### *Great Places To Stay*

**Caribbean Quarters**
3012 Granada St.
954/523-3226

Nestled just a few yards from the heart of Fort Lauderdale's famous promenade and beach, this exquisite setting offers a very high degree of comfort and service that would enchant the most discerning of travelers. The interior setting boasts 16-inch pillow top mattresses with spaciously ventilated rooms, decorated in light shades of pastels and Caribbean colors, comfortable wicker and rattan furnishings. Built in 1939 and totally renovated in 1998, this superior, luxury bed and breakfast captures the romantic charm of a by-gone era. A small intimate three-story property embraces all the Southern Florida and Caribbean architectural qualities for which Southern Florida was famous for in the late thirties and early forties. All units are non-smoking, fully air-conditioned and have private bathrooms, direct dial phones with dual jacks for computers or fax machines, remote controlled color TV with VCR, guest movie library, coffee maker and daily maid service. Some units offer private balcony, living room and full kitchen facilities. The tropical courtyard features a hot tub/Jacuzzi, sun deck, patio, barbecue grills, shuffleboard, ping pong table, darts and numerous other games. An extended continental breakfast is so extensive that a menu is required.

## 28 FORT MYERS

**Old Times Antiques**
1815 Fowler St.
941/334-7200

**Yesterday & Today**
1609 Hendry St.
941/334-6572

**Flowers To Fifties**
2229 Main St.
941/334-2443

**Margie's Antique Market Place**
2216 Martin Luther King Blvd.
941/332-3321

**Heartland Antiques**
12680 McGregor Blvd.
941/482-3979

**Valerie Sanders Antiques**
12680 McGregor Blvd.
941/433-3229

**Blough's Antiques**
12680 McGregor Blvd., #3
941/482-6300

**Era Antiques**
12691 McGregor Blvd.
941/481-8154

**Bayview Collectibles & Antiques**
12695 McGregor Blvd.
941/432-0988

**Absolutely The Best Antique Empor.**
12695 McGregor Blvd., #1
941/489-2040

**Judy's Antiques**
12710 McGregor Blvd.
941/481-9600

**George Brown Antiques**
12710 McGregor Blvd.
941/482-5101

**Tit For Tat This & That**
12717-2 McGregor Blvd.
941/489-3255

**Laura's Aura**
2218 1st St.
941/334-6633

**Pappy Antique N' Good Junque**
1079 N. Tamiami Trail
941/995-0004

**Bea's Antique Shop**
1535 N. Tamiami Trail
941/995-0130

## 29 FORT PIERCE

**Fredericks Antiques**
2872 N. U.S. Hwy 1
561/464-0048

**Red Rooster Attic**
3128 N. U.S. Hwy 1
561/466-8344

**Treasure Coast Antique Mall**
4343 N. U.S. Hwy 1
561/468-2006

**Red Barn Antiques Mall**
4809 N. U.S. Hwy 1
561/468-1901

**Antiques Etcetera**
211 Orange Ave.
561/464-7300

**Olde Town Antique Mall**
116 N. 2nd St.
561/468-9700

## 30 FORT WALTON BEACH

**King Arthur Classic's**
30 Eglin Pkwy. S.E.
904/243-9197

**Rose Harbor Interiors**
85A Eglin Pkwy. N.E.
904/664-0345

**Garden Gate Antique Mall**
85B Eglin Pkwy. N.E.
904/664-0164

**Fran's Treasure Trove**
167 A&B Eglin Pkwy. N.E.
904/243-2227

**Willow Tree**
169B Elgin Pkwy. N.E.
904/243-4991

**Abrams Antiques**
86 N Eglin Pkwy.
904/664-0770

**Bailey's Antiques**
136 Miracle Strip Pkwy.
904/244-2424

**Darby Mitchell Antiques**
158 Miracle Strip Pkwy.
904/244-4069

**White Sands Antiques**
161 Miracle Strip Pkwy.
904/243-6398

**Country Junkshun**
1303 Beverly St.
904/864-4735

**Abrams Antique Cottage**
147 Hollywood Blvd. N.E.
904/664-0011

**Rose Garden Antiques**
151 A Elgin Pkwy.
904/243-2268

**Fort Walton Beach Antique Mall**
167 Miracle Strip Pkwy. S.E.
904/243-6255

**Magnolia Tree**
151 Eglin Pkwy. S.E.
904/244-2727

**Village Emporium**
149 Hollywood Blvd. N.E.
904/302-0111

**Li'l Darlings By JW**
100 Beal Parkway S.W.
904/244-2551

## 31 GAINESVILLE

**Browse Shop**
433 S. Main St.
352/378-5121

**Reruns**
807 W. University Ave.
352/336-0063

**My Mother's Place**
2441 N.W. 43rd St., #24A
352/376-4580

## 32 GULF BREEZE

**Annais Antique Mall**
4531 Gulf Breeze Pkwy.
904/916-1122

## 33 HAVANA

**Antique Center**
104 N. Main St.
850/539-0529

**Berry Patch**
117 6th Ave.
850/539-6988

**H & H Antiques**
302 N. Main St.
850/539-6886

**Antiques & Accents**
213 N.W. 1st St.
850/539-0073

**My Secret Garden**
127 E. 7th Ave.
850-539-8729

**McLauchlin House**
201 W. 7th Ave.
850/539-0901

**Hallway Annex**
110 E. 7th Ave.
850/539-8822

**Sticks 'N Stitches**
108 E. 7th Ave.
850/539-8070

**Kudzu Plantation**
102 E. 7th Ave.
850/539-0877

**Havana's Cannery**
115 E. 8th Ave.
850/539-3800

**Antique Center**
104 N. Main St.
850/539-0529

## 34 HIGH SPRINGS

In 1883 the Savannah, Fla., and Western Railroad was extended from Live Oak to Gainesville and a post office and railroad station were established under the name of Santaffey, which was the common spelling of the nearby Sante Fe River. In 1888 the name was changed to High Springs and in the next few years the town prospered as a result of phosphate mining in the area. In 1893 the town was incorporated and the railroad completed its connection to Tampa. The community of High Springs was built and prospered because of honest hard work of men and women who toiled on the railroad, in the mines, and in the fields.

In cooperation with the University of Florida, High Springs is now involved in the restoration of her downtown area. The two adjacent buildings which now house The Great Outdoors Trading Company and Cafe were restored in 1986. Built circa 1895, the trading company building was generally known as the Old Opera House. The bottom floor housed many different mercantile firms over the years and the top floor where the stage performances, silent movies, and dances were held. The cafe building was originally built as a barber shop circa 1915. *(see the Great Outdoors Trading Company and Cafe listed under Great Places To Eat.)*

**Bus Stop Antiques**
205 N.W. Santa Fe Blvd.
904/454-2478

**Burch Antiques Too**
60 N. Main St.
904/454-1500

**High Springs Antiques Cntr**
145 N. Main St.
904/454-4770

**Sophie's Antiques & Gifts**
215 N. Main St.
904/454-2022

**Wisteria Corner Antique Mall**
225 N. Main St.
904/454-3555

**Main St. Antique Mall**
10 S. Main St.
904/454-2700

**Palm Springs Antiques**
220 S Main St.
904/454-5389

**Platz Antiques & Collectibles**
625 S. Main St.
904/454-4193

**Victorian Village**
1700 U.S. 441 S.
904/454-1835
*Numerous shops all located within a Victorian Village*

**The Painted Lady Antiques, Treasures & Coffee House**
30 N.E. 1st Ave.
904/454-5511

**Wendy's Treasure Chest**
280 N.E. 1st Ave.
904/454-0408

**Aristocratic Attic**
5 N.W. 1st Ave.
904/454-1496

**Apple Creek Mercantile**
55 N.W. 1st Ave.
904/454-2178

**Heartstrings**
65 N.W. 1st Ave.
904/454-4081

**A Step In The Past**
75 N.W. 1st Ave.
904/454-5389

### *Great Places To Stay*

**Grady House**
420 N.W. 1st Ave.
904/454-2206

Built in 1917 the Grady House served as lodging for railroad workers at a time when the railroad was a major industry in High Springs. The name, derived from a long-standing High Springs family, was also home to many young married couples in the High Spring area. Today, this historic home is owned by innkeepers Ed and Diane Shupe. Ed's primary interest is art. He is especially proud of the Honeymoon Suite, which houses his collection of classic nudes. Diane enjoys cooking. The breakfast menu includes homemade scones, banana bread, herbed eggs and cheese grits. Fresh fruit is always included. She is also a CPA, so she tells the guests that she is the "bean-counter" and Ed is the artist. She loves to read and dabbles in writing. She hopes to write a novel someday.

**The Rustic Inn**
3105 S. Main St.
904/454-1223

Indulge yourself in solitude at The Rustic Inn nestled on a ten-acre ranch style setting. Enjoy a stroll along the nature trails, take a dip in the pool, play cards, games, or just curl up and read a book from the library. Enjoy magnificent sunsets from the comfort of a rocking chair on the front porch. The Rustic Inn offers six rooms, each of which carries out a chosen endangered species theme.

### *Favorite Places To Eat*

**Great Outdoors Trading Company & Cafe**
65 N. Main St.
904/454-2900

Try the Oatmeal Pancakes for breakfast, or maybe French Toast with real Maple Syrup—just two of the many special treats offered here. For lunch choose from the extensive menu and daily Chef's Specials. The Cafe offers a range of salads and vegetarian dishes for non-meat eating friends. For dinner the atmosphere is casual, comfortable, and candlelit. Evening specials include dishes such as Tofu Bombay, Mediterranean Chicken or Steak cooked the Chef's very special way. At the end of a fabulous meal try a sinful homemade dessert with gourmet coffees or teas.

Once a week a musician plays for dinner and on weekends live music is heard in the "Old Opera House" upstairs. Before you leave be sure to visit The Great Outdoors Trading Company Store where you'll find maps and guides, rock candy, chocolate, British candy, jams and jellies...even a kayak!

## 35 HOMESTEAD

**Bayleaf Peddler**
813 N. Homestead Blvd.
305/247-9200

**Renaissance Interiors**
69 N.W. 4th St.
305/247-5283

**Albury Road Antiques**
115 N. Krome Ave.
305/242-1366

**Book Nest**
115 N. Krome Ave.
305/242-1366

**Forever Antiques**
115 N. Krome Ave.
305/248-0588

**Sian San Antiques & Collectibles**
115 N. Krome Ave.
305/246-8010

**Yesterday's Memories**
115 N. Krome Ave.
305/247-0191

**Time Line Vintage Clothing**
115 N. Krome Ave.
305/248-6511

**Jo Crafton Antiques**
123 N. Krome Ave.
305/245-1700

**Crouse's Homestead Antiques**
137 N. Krome Ave.
305/247-5555

**Cam's Antiques**
140 N. Krome Ave.
305/245-3320

**Autumn Leaf Cottage**
229 N. Krome Ave.
305/246-3513

**Cobblestone Antiques**
501 N. Krome Ave.
305/245-8831

**Ages Ago**
102 S. Krome Ave.
305/245-7655

**Jacobsen's Antiques & Collectibles**
144 N. Krome Ave.
305/247-4745

**Roby's Antiques & Collectibles**
229 N. Krome Ave.
305/246-3513

**Antique Clocks & Gifts**
1316 N. Krome Ave.
305/247-9555

## 36 JACKSONVILLE

### Carriage House Antique Mall
8955 Beach Blvd.
904/641-5500
Mon.-Sat. 10-6, Sun. 12-6
*Directions: Located on Beach Blvd. at Southside Blvd.*

Carriage House Antique Mall offers visitors that "Jack-of-all-trades" atmosphere with its spectrum of items and services. Once inside the mall, you can roam through aisles of glassware including decanters, goblets, china, crystal, and depression pieces. A wide selection of collectibles and gifts are also housed within the mall.

**Tappin Book Mine**
705 Atlantic Blvd.
904/246-1388

**Antique House**
1841 Dean Road
904/721-0886

**Somewhere In Time Antiques**
1341 University Blvd. N.
904/743-7022

**Springfield Antiques**
1755 N. Pearl St.
904/355-2897

**Little Shop of Antiques**
2010 Forbes St.
904/389-9900

**Ina's Antiques**
3572 Saint Johns Ave.
904/387-1379

**Frontier**
5161 Beach Blvd.
904/398-6055

**Uncle Davey's Americana**
6140 St. Augustine Road
904/730-8932

**Gallery of Antiques**
7952 Normandy Blvd., #1
904/783-6787

**Audrey's Attic At Five Points**
1036 Park St.
904/355-8642

**Olde Gallery**
3921 Hendricks Ave.
904/396-2581

**Canterbury House Antiques**
1776 Canterbury St.
904/387-1776

**Antiques Are Forever**
2 Independent Dr.
904/358-8800

**Judy Judy Judy**
1633 San Marco Blvd.
904/396-1537

**Grandma's Things**
5814 St. Augustine Road
904/739-2075

**Olde Albert's**
5818 St. Augustine Road
904/731-3947

**White House Antiques**
214 4th Ave. S.
904/247-3388

**China Cat Antiques**
226 4th Ave. S.
904/241-0344

**Orange Tree Antiques**
4209 St. John Ave.
904/387-4822

**Interiors Market**
5133 San Jose Blvd.
904/733-2223

**Avonlea Antiques**
11000 Beach Blvd.
904/645-0806

**Don's Antiques**
5121 San Jose Blvd.
904/739-9829

**Shop of M. Miller**
1036 Park St.
904/384-3724

**Bayard Country Store**
12525 Phillips Hwy.
904/262-2548

**Antique Wooden Horse**
6323 Phillips Hwy.
904/739-1008

**Annie's Antiques**
9822 Beach Blvd.
904/641-3446

**Lovejoy's Antique Mall**
5107 San Jose Blvd.
904/730-8083

#### *Great Places To Stay*

### Cleary-Dickert House
1804 Copeland St.
903/387-4003
Web site: members.aol.com/idjo/index.htm

Upon arrival at this stately mansion, you will be greeted by owners, Joseph Cleary, who prides himself in being a true Englishman and, his wife, the ebullient Southern lady, Betty Dickert. Join them in getting acquainted in the warm, flower-decked porch overlooking the St. John River. Each suite, (one award-winning), consists of a separate sitting room, private bedroom and bath. Relax, have some tea, enjoy the warm and inviting atmosphere and smell the fresh cut flowers. In keeping with English tradition, each suite has facilities for a late night beverage. Join Betty and Joe in the formal dining room each morning for a delicious breakfast. The food varies from Southern to English gourmet recipes, complete with an assortment of breads and jams. If privacy is desired, breakfast may be served in your suite, upon request. An authentic English tea is brewed and served in the afternoon. Wine and cheese is also served.

### House on Cherry Street
1844 Cherry St.
904/384-1999

The House on Cherry Street is a beautiful Colonial home situated on the St. John's River. Decorated with period antiques, oriental rugs, tall case clocks, a large decoy collection, baskets, pewter and numerous other unique collectibles. The home is a true "antiquers" dream get-a-way. Bedrooms have sitting areas, woven coverlets and canopied beds, four rooms; one twin room with private bath and three queen rooms with private baths, each with sitting room area.

## 37 JUPITER

**Axe Antiques**
275 AH A 1A (SR811)
561/743-7888

**Patricia Ann Reed Fine Antiques**
126 Center St., Suite B-7
561/744-0373

## 38 KEY WEST

**Wanted Store**
1219 Duval St.
305/293-9810

**Sam's Treasure Chest**
518 Fleming St.
305/296-5907

**Joseph's Antiques**
616 Greene St.
305/294-9916

**China Clipper**
333 Simonton St.
305/294-2136

**Commodore Antiques**
500 Simonton St.
305/296-3973

**Just Good Stuff**
1100 White St.
305/293-8599

### *Great Places To Stay*

**Blue Parrot Inn**
916 Elizabeth Inn
1-800-231-BIRD
Web site: blueparrottinn.com

For specific information see review at the beginning of this section.

**Heron House**
512 Simonton Street
1-800-294-1644
Web site: www.heronhouse.com

Heron House is a bit of a half-breed - it possesses all of the charm of a Key West guesthouse, while at the same time, it is operated with all the professionalism of a small luxury hotel. It consists of four historical buildings with twenty-three rooms total. One of the oldest homes was built in 1856 representing one of the few remaining examples of "Conch Architecture" in Key West, and is in fact, the oldest house on Simonton St. The Innkeepers Fred Geibelt and Robert Framarin have gone out of their way to bypass the ordinary at this fabulous Key West get-a-way.

Stained glass transoms above beautiful French doors invite you into your accommodations, where cool tile floors, granite baths and custom "signature wall" in teak, oak or cedar await. Private decks and balconies merge with private gardens to allow interior and exterior spaces to blend. Multi-level decks provide areas to sun, to lounge, or just enjoy the beauty of your surroundings.

You should not miss a stroll through the tropical gardens and take in the beauty of the hand grown, rare orchids set amidst the trees.

**William Anthony House**
P. O. Box 107
1-800-613-2276
Web site: www.WmAnthonyHse.com

This beautifully renovated historic inn is the winner of two awards for preservation and new construction. Four luxury suites, one with separate bedroom, and two guest rooms are available. Suites have sitting and dining areas. A spa, lovely gardens and pond, porches and decks offer the opportunity to relax and appreciate the warm Florida weather.

## 39 KISSIMMEE

**Euro Classics**
3645 Old Dixie Hwy.
407/846-2122

## 40 LAKE ALFRED

**Biggar Antiques**
140 W. Haines Blvd.
941/956-4853

**Potpourri Antiques**
144 W. Haines Blvd.
941/956-5535

**Picket Fence**
135 E. Pierce St.
941/956-3471

**Barn Antiques**
State Road 557
941/956-1362

## 41 LAKE CITY

**Webb's Antique Mall**
I-75 @ Exit 80
904/758-9280

Florida's largest antiques mall.

**Britannia Antiques**
Hwy. 90
904/755-0120

**Nancy's Antiques**
412 N. Marion St.
904/752-0272

**Remember When**
420 N. Marion St.
904/755-6007

**The Pink Magnolia**
202 Duval St.
904/752-4336

**Antiques Antiques**
4447 U.S. Hwy. 90, Suite 1
904/758-4744

## 42 LAKE WALES

**Inglenook Antiques & Collectibles**
3607 Alt. 27 N.
941/678-1641

**Bittersweet Memories**
113 E. Park Ave.
941/676-4778

**Liberty Antiques**
130 E. Park Ave.
941/678-0730

**Once Upon A Tyme Antiques**
201 N. Scenic Hwy.
941/676-0910

**Bruce's Antiques**
201 N. Scenic Hwy.
941/676-4845

**Wisteria Cottage**
229 E. Stuart, Suite 11
941/676-6730

## 43 LAKE WORTH

**Mickey's Antiques**
12 S. J St.
561/582-7667

**Ada's Olde Towne Antique Mall**
25 S. J St.
561/547-1700

**P & G Antiques**
702 Lake Ave.
561/547-6326

**Lake Avenue Antiques**
704 Lake Ave.
561/586-1131

**Tuesday Gallery**
705 Lake Ave.
561/586-1180

**Hawkins Antiques & Art**
712 Lake Ave.
561/582-4215

**Yesterday's Antique Mall**
716 Lake Ave.
561/547-3816

**Roussos & Sons Antiques**
801 Lake Ave.
561/585-2100

**Antique Palace**
808 Lake Ave.
561/582-8803

**Carousel Antiques Center**
813 Lake Ave.
561/533-0678

**Heritage Antiques**
621 Lake Ave.
561/588-4755

## 44 LAKELAND

**Agape Antique Center**
243 N. Florida Ave.
941/686-6882

**Silver Cloud Shop**
701 N. Florida Ave.
941/687-4696

**Celebration Gallery**
1037 S. Florida, #106
941-686-9999

**Somewhere In Time-Nonstalgia**
1715 S. Florida Ave.
941/688-9472

**Peacock Antiques**
234 N. Kentucky Ave.
941/686-7947

**A Keslinger Antiques Complex**
244 N. Kentucky Ave.
941/683-4444

**Sissy's Gallery**
314 N. Kentucky Ave.
941/687-6045

**My Cottage Garden**
327 N. Kentucky Ave.
941/688-9686

**Bubba's Country Store**
3720 County Line Road
941/647-5461

**Frog Pond**
3403 Providence Road
941/858-1979

**Roger A Cheek Gallery**
218 E. Pine St.
941/686-5495

**Casey Lynn Antiques**
214 Traders Alley
941/682-2857

**Reflections Of The Past**
215 Traders Alley
941/682-0349

## 45 LARGO

**Nearly New Shop**
623 W. Bay Dr.
813/586-2196

**Time & Again**
814 W. Bay Dr.
813/586-3665

**Details**
1260 W. Bay Dr.
813/585-6960

**Brenda's Styling**
39 Clearwater Largo Road
813/582-9839

**Country Village**
11896 Walsingham Road
813/397-2942

**T & T Antiques**
12790 66th St. N.
813/531-8072

## 46 LEESBURG

**Leesburg Antique Mall**
403 W. Main St.
352/323-3396

**Victorian Rose**
415 W. Main St.
352/728-8388

**Smith's Antiques & Collectable**
717 W. Main St.
352/787-1102

**Ruth's Antiques**
1223 W. Main St.
352/787-7064

**Mary's Treasure Chest**
2300 W. Main St.
352/326-3181

**Curiosity Shop**
1310 N. Shore Dr.
352/787-6870

**Morning Glori Antique Mall**
1111 S. 14th St. (Hwy. 27)
352/365-9977

## 47 MAITLAND

**Cranberry Corners**
203 E. Horatio Ave.
407/644-0363

**Pence & Pound House**
630 S. Maitland Ave.
407/628-4911

**Bestenwurst Antiques**
145 S. Orlando Ave.
407/647-0533

**Halley's Antiques Mall**
473 S. Orlando Ave.
407/539-1066

## 48 MCINTOSH

**Creekside Antiques/Collectibles**
Hwy. 441 & Ave. E
352/591-4444

**Book Barn/O. Brisky's**
Hwy. 441 & Ave. F
352/591-2177

**Fort McIntosh Armory**
Hwy. 441 & Ave. G
352/591-2378

**Harvest Village**
22050 N. U.S. Hwy 441
352/591-1053

## 49 MELBOURNE

**Hometown Expressions**
712 E. New Haven Ave.
407/676-0692

**Born Again**
724 E. New Haven Ave.
407/768-8442

**Melbourne Antique Mall**
806 E. New Haven Ave.
407/951-0151

**Finders Keepers**
809 E. New Haven Ave.
407/676-5697

**Antiques Anonymous**
811 E. New Haven Ave.
407/724-5666

**Red Lion Antiques**
821 E. New Haven Ave.
407/726-8777

**Just For You**
829 E. New Haven Ave.
407/768-2636

**Age of Elegance**
932 E. New Haven Ave.
407/728-8870

**Antique Connection**
568 W. Eau Gallie Blvd.
407/255-1333

**Effie's Antiques & Collectibles**
819 E. New Haven Ave.
407/728-7345

**Eclectibles Unlimited**
825 E. New Haven Ave.
407/768-9795

**Helen's Antique & Modern**
847 E. New Haven Ave.
407/723-8830

**Antique Mall & Collectibles**
3830 W. New Haven Ave.
407/727-1761

**Betty's Antiques**
2001 Melbourne Court
407/951-2258

## 50 MIAMI/NORTH MIAMI

**Aunt Hattie's Attic**
10828 N.E. 6th Ave.
305/751-3738

**Len's 7th Ave. Antiques**
4950 N.W. 7th Ave.
305/754-5601

**J R Antiques**
5987 S.W. 8th St.
305/264-6614

**Gloria's Place**
2231 S.W. 22nd St.
305/285-2411

**Escala Antiques & Gifts**
2385 S.W. 22nd St.
305/857-9955

**Hidden Place**
1092 S.W. 27th Ave.
305/644-0469

**Antique Center**
2644 S.W. 28th Lane
305/858-6166

**ITO**
2685 S.W. 28th Lane
305/856-1361

**Antiques & Gifts by Roses**
6350 S.W. 40th St.
305/667-8703

**Well Design**
6550 S.W. 40th St.
305/661-1386

**Robin's Nest Antiques**
6703 S.W. 40th St.
305/666-7668

**Echoes of the Past Antiques**
12325 N.E. 6th Ave.
305/895-8462

**Manetta's Antiques**
5531 S.W. 8th St.
305/261-8603

**Harris Antique Shop**
8747 N.W. 22nd Ave.
305/693-0110

**Antiques Paradise**
2371 S.W. 22nd St.
305/285-7885

**Ralph's Antiques**
3660 S.W. 22nd St.
305/441-1193

**Arenas Antiques**
1131 S.W. 27th Ave.
305/541-0900

**Charlotte's International**
2650 S.W. 28th Lane
305/858-9326

**Twery's Inc**
160 N.E. 40th St.
305/576-0564

**Nostalgiaville**
6374 S.W. 40th St.
305/669-1608

**Beall's Antiques & Collectibles**
6554 S.W. 40th St.
305/663-2103

**Old Paris**
7125 S.W. 47th St.
305/666-7008

**Antiques & Tribal**
7165 S.W. 47th St., #B319
305/661-1094

**Suarez Graciela**
7209-7217 S.W. 48th St.
305/667-3431

**Pine Mine**
7262 S.W. 48th St.
305/663-4432

**Dietel's Antiques**
2124 S.W. 67th Ave.
305/266-8981

**1800's Antiques & Accessories**
4666 S.W. 72nd Ave.
305/668-9777

**Drummond of Perth Antiques**
4691 S.W. 72nd Ave.
305/665-3345

**Antiques & Country Pine**
4711 S.W. 72nd Ave.
305/665-7463

**Malina's Victorian Country**
4836 S.W. 72nd Ave.
305/663-0929

**Ideas & More Inc.**
4467 S.W. 75th Ave.
305/265-8538

**Joylot Antiques**
921 N.E. 79th St.
305/754-9136

**Golden Era Antiques**
1640 N.E. 123rd St.
305/891-1006

**Dietel's Antiques**
6572 Bird Road
305/666-0724

**Spencer Art Gallerie**
4441 Collins Ave.
305/532-7577

**Alhambra Antiques Center**
3640 Coral Way
305/446-1688

**Oldies But Goodies**
17842 S. Dixie Hwy.
305/232-5441

**B & H Antiques**
12777 W. Dixie Hwy.
305/899-0921

**Gloria Allison Antiques**
7207 S.W. 48th St.
305/666-3900

**Antiquario Fine Furniture**
7219 S.W. 48th St.
305/663-8151

**Gilbert's Antiques Inc.**
7265 S.W. 48th St.
305/665-2006

**Ceramic by Design**
4664 S.W. 72nd Ave.
305/663-5558

**British Connection Antiques**
4669 S.W. 72nd Ave.
305/662-9212

**Bonnin Ashley Antiques, Inc.**
4707 S.W. 72nd Ave.
305/667-0969

**General Consignment**
4762 S.W. 72nd Ave.
305/669-0800

**General Consignment**
4215 S.W. 75th Ave.
305/261-3200

**Eclectique**
6344 Bird Road
305/666-7073

**F. & D. Lopez-Del Rincon Art**
803 82nd St.
305/861-5997

**Tania Sante's Classic**
6556 Bird Road
305/662-4975

**A & J Unique Antiques**
2000 Biscayne Blvd.
305/576-5170

**Midori Gallery Antique**
3170 Commodore Plaza
305/443-3399

**Alba Antiques**
3656 Coral Way
305/443-5288

**Ye Olde Cupboard**
17844 S. Dixie Hwy.
305/251-7028

**Washington Square Antiques**
19090 W. Dixie Hwy.
305/937-0409

**Victoria's Armoire Country**
4077 Ponce De Leon Blvd.
305/445-3848

**Stone Age Antiques**
3236 N.W. South River Dr.
305/633-5114

**Olde Tyme Shoppe**
1549 1/2 Sunset Dr.
305/662-1842

**Antiques & Art**
10143 S.W. 79th Court
305/663-3224

**Valerio Antiques**
2901 Florida/Coconut Grove
305/448-6779

## 51 MIAMI BEACH

**Collectors Art Gallery**
730 Lincoln Road
305/531-4900

**Circle Art & Antiques**
1014 Lincoln Road
305/531-1859

**Bolero**
1688 Meridian Ave.
305/534-3759

**Senzatempo**
815 Washington Ave.
305/534-8882

## 52 MICANOPY

**The Shop**
Cholokka Blvd.
352-466-4031

**Chateau Des Antiques**
Cholokka Blvd.
352/466-4505

**Among The Ivy**
Cholokka Blvd.
352/466-8000

**Delectable Collectibles**
Cholokka Blvd.
352/466-3327

**Smiley's Antique Mall**
I-75 @Exit 73, CR 234
352/466-0707

**Baytree Antiques Inc.**
Cholokka Blvd.
352/466-3946

**Sun Glo Farm Antiques**
16319 S.E. County Road 234
352/466-3037

**Micanopy Country Store**
108 Cholokka Blvd.
352/466-0510

**Antique Alley**
110 Cholokka Blvd.
352/466-0300

**Savino's Antiques**
203 Cholokka Blvd.
352/466-3663

**Elena's Antiques**
206 E. Cholokka Blvd.
252/466-4260

**Roberts Antiques**
208 Cholokka Blvd.
352/466-3605

**House Of Hirsch Too Antiques**
209 E. Cholokka Blvd.
352/466-3774

## 53 MONTICELLO

### Southern Friends Antique Mall

I-10, exit 33 (U.S. Hwy. 19)
904/997-2559
Mon.-Sat. 10-6, Sun. 1-6
*Directions: From I-10, take exit 33 (U.S. Hwy. 19). The store has no street number.*

The name suggests true Southern hospitality. Southern Friends Antique Mall opened its doors in March of 1997 and has done a wonderful job of filling this 7,500-square-foot store with quality antiques. No reproductions or crafts are accepted by the 50 dealers who work to create an authentic representation of glassware, pottery, porcelain, quilts, linens, books, clocks and more. For you Civil War buffs, Southern Friends has a nice offering of Civil War memorabilia as well.

**Bush Baby**
280n N. Cherry St.
904/997-6108

**Rosewood Flowers & Antiques**
Hwy. 19
904/997-6779

**Mister Ed's**
Hwy. 27
904/997-5880

**Court House Antiques**
205 E. Washington St.
904/997-8008

## 54 MOUNT DORA

Mount Dora is described as a bustling village in the rolling hills of Central Florida overlooking lovely Lake Dora. Known for the Historic Lakeside Inn, it's filled with nineteen antique stores, twenty-two specialty gift shops and stylish boutiques. You can enjoy a sandwich at a sidewalk deli, fajitas in a parrot-filled cafe, high tea in an English garden or gourmet meals in several fine restaurants.

Tour the town on a trolley or buggy ride, cruise the Dora Canal, walk Palm Island, swing at Gilbert Park, play tennis, shuffleboard or just enjoy a park bench.

Listed by Money Magazine as one of the three best places in the United States to retire, Mount Dora is less than an hour from Walt Disney World, Sea World and Universal Studios. Located on Hwy. 441 just thirty minutes northwest of Orlando or thirty minutes west of Sanford on Hwy. 46.

**Mt. Dora Antique Mall**
315 N. Donnelly St.
352/383-0018

**Baker Street Gallery**
110 E. 5th Ave.
352/383-4199

**Caroline's Antiques**
331 N. Donnelly St.
352/735-4003

**Oliver Twist Antique Furniture**
404 N. Donnelly St.
352/735-3337

**Corner Nook Antiques**
426 N. Donnelly
352/383-9555

**Verandah Antique Galleries**
427 N. Donnelly
352/735-0330

**Old Village Antiques**
439B N. Donnelly
352/383-1820

**Olde Bostonian Antiques & Gift**
442 N. Donnelly
352/383-3434

**My Secret Garden**
404B N. Donnelly St.
352/735-0995

**Wild Rose Antique Mini Mall**
140 E. 4th Ave.
352/383-6664

**Southern Exotic Antiques**
116 W. 5th Ave.
352/735-2500

**Renninger's Antique Center**
20651 U.S. Hwy. 441
352/383-8393

**Cottage Artwork & Antiques**
605 N. Donnelly Ave.
352/735-2700

**Rosecreek Antiques & Gifts**
418 N. Donnelly St.
352/735-0086

**Stairway to the Stars**
411 Donnelly St.
352/383-9770

**Purple Pineapple**
317 N. Donnelly St.
352/735-2189

**Courtyard Antiques**
142 E. 4th Ave.
352/735-1915

**Di Antiques**
122 E. 4th St.
352/735-1333

**Old Town Bookshop**
127 W. 5th Ave.
352/383-0878

### *Great Places To Stay*

**Christopher's Inn**
539 Liberty Ave.
352/383-2244

**Darst Victorian Manor**
485 Old Hwy. 441
352/383-4050

**Farnsworth House**
1029 E. Fifth Ave.
352/735-1894

Built in 1886, the Farnsworth House is only ten blocks away from on the of the best antiquing areas in Florida. Three suites are available in the main house and two theme efficiencies are located in the carriage house. After a full day of antiquing and exploring the quaint historic town of Mt. Dora, guests can relax on the screened porch over-looking a beautifully landscaped yard.

**Lakeside Inn**
3rd & Alexander
352/383-4101

**Magnolia Inn**
347 E. Third Ave.
1-800-776-2112
Web site: magnolia.cde.com

Magnolia Inn features true southern hospitality and charm at its finest. Relaxation and romance are found at this inn where guests can escape the hectic life outside this one acre estate in downtown Mt. Dora. Lounge in a hammock by the garden wall, swing under the majestic magnolia, unwind in the gazebo spa, or curl up with a good book in the chaise lounge. Park at the inn and walk to many antique shops, boutiques, bookstores, tearooms, and exceptional restaurants found along flower-box lined streets. Perhaps you would like a romantic evening carriage ride, a historic trolley tour, hot air balloon ride, or boat ride. Fishing, water sports, tennis, golf, and nature trails are all available nearby. Guestrooms are beautifully decorated and each has its own private bath. Breakfast is included and varies daily. Eggs Benedict, gourmet blueberry french toast, and citrus pancakes are some of the favorites. Only thirty minutes from many Orlando areas, but the uniqueness of Mt. Dora and the pampering you receive at Magnolia Inn might keep you from the big-city activities!

**Mount Dora Historic Inn**
221 E. 4th Ave.
1-800-927-6344
Web site: www.lcia.com/clients/inn/

Re-live the elegance of the past at the lovely Mount Dora Historic Inn. Nestled in a secluded setting in romantic downtown Mount Dora, the inn is only 25 minutes from Orlando. Enjoy the gracious hospitality, authentic period antiques, and relaxed atmosphere of this charming bed and breakfast. Originally built in the late 1800s as a downtown merchant's home, the inn has been lovingly restored to it's original beauty, by the proprietors, Lindsay and Nancy Richards. The efforts of their labor of love have resulted in a memorable ambiance of warmth and embraceable character. The Mount Dora Historic Inn features fine, beautifully appointed rooms with private baths, each decorated with individuality, and an emphasis on complete guest comfort and tranquillity. From the hearty breakfast to the nightly turndown service, you will be welcomed to the return of a bygone era.

**Seabrook B&B**
644 N. Donnelly St.
352/383-4800

**Simpson's B&B**
441 N. Donnelly St.
352/383-2087

**Upper Room**
3rd & Donnelly Streets
352/735-5203

### *Favorite Places To Eat*

**A Taste of Home**
411 N. Donnelly St.
352/735-1717
Sandwiches, Soups & More

**Gable's Restaurant & Lounge**
322 N. Alexander St.
352/383-8993
Fine Dining

**Goblin Market**
321B N. Donnelly St. (in alley)
352/735-0059
Casual Dining

**La Cremerie**
425 N. Donnelly St.
352/735-4663
Ice Cream, Coffee, Cappuccino

**Park Bench Restaurant**
116 E. 5th Ave.
352/383-7004
Gourmet, Featuring Seafood

**Sinfully Sweet**
633 N. Baker St.
352/735-1926
Chocolate, Ice Cream, Yogurt

**Windsor Rose English Tea Room**
144 W. 4th Ave.
352/735-2551

### *Interesting Side Trips*

**Antique Extravaganza**
Renninger's Twin Markets
352/383-8393
January 15-17

**Antique Extravanganza**
Renninger's Twin Markets
352/383-8393
February 19-21

**Annual Mount Dora Antiques Show And Sale**
Downtown Mount Dora
March
Contact Clay Oliver at 352/735-3337 for exact dates.

**Antique Fair**
Renninger's Twin Markets
April, May, June, July, August, September, October
Call 352/383-8393 for exact dates.

**Antique Extravaganza**
Renninger's Twin Markets
November
Call 352/383-8393 for exact dates.

## 55 NAPLES

**Lovejoy Antiques**
960 2nd Ave. N.
941/649-7447

**Rocking Horse Antiques**
950 3rd Ave. N.
941/263-6997

**Antiques-Glenna Moore**
465 5th Ave. S.
941/263-4121

**Gabriel's South**
555 5th Ave. S.
941/643-0433

**Baldwins at Fifth**
604 5th Ave. S.
941/263-2234

**Thompson-Strong Antiques**
605 5th Ave. S.
941/434-6434

**Naples Trading Co.**
810 6th Ave. S.
941/262-0376

**Yahl Street Antique Mall**
5430 Yahl St.
941/591-8182

**Ivy House Antiques**
639 8th St. S.
941/434-9555

**Bailey's Antiques & Country**
606 9th St. N.
941/643-1953

**Margie's Antiques**
153 10th St. S.
941/262-3151

**Antique Guild**
183 10th St. S.
941/649-0323

**Catherine's Collectibles Inc.**
255 13th Ave. S.
941/262-4800

**Recollections New & Old**
639 8th St. S.
941/649-1954

**Barney's Island Antiques**
348 Capri Blvd.
941/394-2848

**Lovejoy Antiques**
950 Central Ave.
941/649-7447

**Granny's Attic**
1971 County Road 951
941/353-0800

**Wizard of Odds II**
4584 Mercantile Ave.
941/261-4459

**Debbie's Monkey Business**
2033 Pine Ridge Road, #3
941/594-8686

**Black Bear Cove Inc.**
1661 Trade Center Way
941/598-1933

## 56 NEW SMYRNA BEACH

**Victoria Station**
402 Canal St.
904/426-8881

**New Smyrna Antiques**
419 Canal St.
904/426-7828

**Coronado Antiques**
512 Canal St.
904/428-3331

**Kellys Country Store**
569 Canal St.
904/428-2291

**Jeff's Antiques**
507 S. Dixie Freeway
904/423-2554

**Lion D'or Antiques**
511 N. Orange St.
904/428-1752

## 57 NICEVILLE

**Steven's Yesterday's Furnishings**
98 Nathey @ Hwy. 85 N.
904/678-6775

**Gee Gee's Antiques**
1209 N. Partin Hwy. 285
904/678-2689

**Little Ole Lady Trading Post**
314 Bayshore Dr.
904/678-7424

**The Early Attic**
119 Jones Ave.
904/678-9089

## 58 NORTH PORT

**Rujan's Antiques & Collectibles**
13640 Tamiami Trail
941/426-5418

## 59 OAKLAND PARK

**C Strange Antiques**
3277 N. Dixie Hwy.
954/565-6964

**Yesteryears Today**
3689 N. Dixie Hwy.
954/568-0362

**Affordable Treasures**
1051 N.E. 45th St.
954/938-4567

**Antique Exchange**
3493 N. Dixie Hwy.
954/564-3504

**Vintage Fabrics & Etc**
3500 C N.E. 11th Ave.
954/564-4392

## 60 OCALA

**Stuf N Such**
1310 Hwy. 484
352/245-7744

**Ocala Antique Mall**
3700 S. Pine Ave.
352/622-4468

**Antique Attic**
507 S.E. Fort King St.
352/732-8880

**A Corner of Yesterday**
521 S.E. Fort King St.
352/622-1927

**ABS Antiques Co.**
4185 W. Hwy. 40
352/351-1009

**Camellia House Antiques**
1317 S.E. Fort King St.
352/629-8085

**Antique Emporium Inc.**
6500 S. Pine Ave.
352/351-1003

## 61 OKEECHOBEE

**Peddlers Cove**
216 S.W. 4th St.
941/467-1939

**Fort Drum Antique Mall**
30950 Hwy. 441 N.
941/763-6289

**Silver Spoon**
401 S.W. Park St.
941/763-0609

**My Other House**
10017 N. Hwy. 441
941/357-3447

**Curiosity Shop**
118 S.E. Park St.
941/467-6411

## 62 ORANGE CITY

**Curiosity Corner Furniture & Antiques**
746 N. Volusia Ave.
904/775-3122

**Antiques & Things**
1427 S. Volusia Ave.
904/775-4900

**Orange City Mighty Mall**
747 N. Volusia Ave.
904/775-1666

## 63 ORANGE PARK

**Victoria's Timely Treasures**
835 Park Ave.
904/269-0907

**Old Towne Antiques**
2020 Carnes St.
904/269-2318

## 64 ORLANDO

**Butterpat's**
2439 Edgewater Dr.
407/423-7971

For specific information see review at the beginning of this section.

**Swanson's Antiques**
1217 N. Orange Ave.
407/898-6050

**William Moseley Gallery**
1221 N. Orange Ave.
407/228-6648

**Designer House, Inc.**
1249 N. Orange Ave.
407/895-9060

**Antique Exchange**
1616 N. Orange Ave.
407/896-3793

**A & T Antiques**
1620 N. Orange Ave.
407/896-9831

**Allison's Antiques**
1804 N. Orange Ave.
407/897-6672

**Jack Lampman Antiques**
1810 N. Orange Ave.
407/897-1144

**Rock & Roll Heaven**
1814 N. Orange Ave.
407/896-1952

**1817 Antiques**
1817 N. Orange Ave.
407/894-6519

**Penny Edwards Antiques**
1616A N. Orange Ave.
407/896-2499

**Troy's Treasures**
1612A N. Orange Ave.
407/228-6648

**Fee Fi Fauk**
1425 N. Orange Ave.
407/895-9060

**Marge Leeper Collection**
1618 N. Orange Ave.
407/894-2165

**Flo's Attic**
1800 N. Orange Ave.
407/895-1800

**Antiques Arcade**
1806 N. Orange Ave.
407/898-2994

**Two Timer**
1815 N. Orange Ave.
407/894-4342

**Floraland**
1808 N. Orange Ave.
407/898-2301

**D L Times Two Antiques**
1827 N. Orange Ave.
407/894-6519

**DeJavu Vintage Clothing**
1825 N. Orange Ave.
407/898-3609

**Golden Phoenix**
1826 N. Orange Ave.
407/895-6006

**A. J. Lillun Antiques**
1913 N. Orange Ave.
407/895-6111

**Red's Antiques & Collectibles**
1827 N. Orange Ave.
407/894-6519

**Victorian Gallery**
1907 N. Orange Ave.
407/896-9346

**Pieces of Eight Antique Emporium**
2021 N. Orange Ave.
407/896-8700

**Corner Cupboard**
4797 S. Orange Ave.
407/857-1322

**B'S Antiques**
1214 N. Mills Ave.
407/894-6264

**Millie's Glass & China Shop**
5512 Edgewater Dr.
407/298-3355

**Backstreet Bodega**
817 Virginia Dr.
407/895-9444

**Apple Core Antiques & Gifts**
3327 Curry Ford Road
407/894-2774

**A Antique Shop By Flo's Attic**
310 E. New Hampshire St.
407/894-0607

**Orlando Antique Exchange**
420 W. 27th St.
407/839-0991

**Backstreet Bodega**
1909 N. Orange Ave.
407/895-9444

**Oriental Unlimited & Antiques**
2020 N. Orange Ave.
407/894-2067

**Back Street**
2310 N. Orange Ave.
407/895-1993

**White Wolfe Cafe & Antiques**
1829 N. Orange Ave.
407/895-9911

**Annie's Antique Alley**
2010 N. Orange Ave.
407/896-0433

**Bangarang**
2309 N. Orange Ave.
407/898-2300

**And So On**
1807 N. Orange Ave.
407/898-3485

**College Park Antique Mall**
1317 Edgewater Dr.
407/839-1869

**Virginia Rose**
542 Virginia Dr.
407/898-0552

**Laughing Gargoyle Antiques**
322 W. Colonial Dr.
407/843-8070

**Antique Mall**
361 E. Michigan St.
407/849-9719

**Em's Attic**
1530 S. Primrose Dr.
407/896-0097

**Myrtee B's Antiques**
321 Ivanhoe Blvd. N.
407/895-0717

## 65 PALM BEACH

**Deco Folies**
210 Brazilian Ave.
561/822-8960

**Art & Antiques**
117 N. County Road
561/833-1654

**Kofski Antiques**
315 S. County Road
561/655-6557

**Island Trading Co.**
105 N. County Road
561/833-0555

**Rose Pennm, Inc.**
301 S. County Road
561/835-9702

**F. S. Henemader Antiques**
316 S. County Road
561/835-9237

**R.J. King & Co.**
6 Via Parigi
561/659-9029

**Bellon Antiques**
309 Peruvian Ave.
561/659-1844

**Christian Du Pont Antiques Inc.**
353 Peruvian Ave.
561/655-7794

**Spencer Gallerie**
240 Worth Ave.
561/833-9893

**L'Antiquaire**
329 Worth Ave.
561/655-5774

**Brighton Pavillon**
340 Worth Ave.
561/835-4777

**Barzina**
66 Via Mizner
561/833-5834

**Letitia Lundeen Antiques**
5 Via Parigi
561/833-1087

**Lars Bolander Ltd.**
375 S. County Road
561/832-2121

**Fleur-De-Lis Antiques**
326 Peruvian Ave.
561/655-2295

**Vilda B. De Porro**
211 Worth Ave.
561/655-3147

**Meissen Shop**
329 Worth Ave.
561/832-2504

**Yetta Olkes Antiques**
332 S. County Road
561/655-2800

**Devonshire**
340 Worth Ave.
561/833-0796

**Galerie Haga Antiques**
2 Via Parigi
561/833-2051

## 66 PALM HARBOR

**Generations Antiques**
1682 Alt. 19 N.
813/787-0067

**Cierra-Jordan Antique & Gift**
1026 Florida Ave., Suite C
813/781-0305

**Miss B'S Antiques & Collectibles**
1710 Alt. 19 N.
813/787-0388

**The Gift Connection**
1001 Omaha Circle
813/781-0103

## 67 PANAMA CITY

**Antique Cottage**
903 Harrison Ave.
850/769-9503

**The Eclectic Emporium**
2113 E. 3rd. St.
850/914-9114

**Sentimental Treasurers of the Past**
18400 Panama City Beach Pkwy.
850/233-1224

**J & M Doll Castle & Collectibles**
1700 Bayview Ave.
850/872-0092

**Shady Oaks Antiques**
3706 W. Hwy. 98
850/785-3308

**Elegant Endeavors**
2609 E. Business 98
850/769-1707

**Antique Mall**
Hwy. 77
850/271-9810

## 68 PENSACOLA

**American Antique Mall**
2019 N. T St.
904/432-7659

**Turn of the Century Antiques**
2401 N. T St.
904/434-1820

**Heirlooms**
2706 N. T St.
904/438-2279

**Burch Antiques**
3160 N. T St.
904/433-5153

**Burch Antiques**
2410 N. T St.
904/433-5153

**This Ole House**
712 S. Palafax St.
904/432-2577

**Hamilton House Antiques**
4117 Barrancas Ave.
904/456-2762

**Warehouse Antiques**
60 S. Alcaniz St.
904/432-0318

**Ragtime Antiques**
3113 Mobile Blvd.
904/438-1232

**Dusty Attic**
1113 N. 9th Ave.
904/434-5568

**Baily Attic**
9204 N. Davis Hwy.
904/478-3144

**9th Ave. Antiques Mall**
380 N. 9th Ave.
904/438-3961

**East Hill Antique Village**
805 E. Gadsden St.
904/435-7325

**Cleland Antiques-Seville Square**
412 E. Zarragossa St.
904/432-9933

**L L Sloan Antiques**
115 S. Florida Blanca St.
904/434-5050

**Status Symbol**
698 Hindberg, Suite 106
904/432-6614

**Lind House Estate Jewelers**
217 S. Alcaniz St.
904/435-3213

## 69 PLANT CITY

### Bay Antiques & Clock Repair

109 East Reynolds St.
813/759-6638
Tues.-Sat. 10-5
*Directions: Traveling I-4 between Tampa and Lakeland, exit at #13. Go south on Hwy 39. Turn left on Reynolds Street (U.S. 92 East). Pass through 2 traffic lights. The shop is the second on the right.*

If old clocks are your forte then stop for a visit at Bay Antiques & Clock Repair. Tom Smiley, known as the resident clock "Doc", can answer all your questions (or at least try to) and even repair your old clock if needed. If you're in the market to purchase an old timepiece the shop has a nice selection to choose from.

Glyn (Tom's better half) is the antique addict. She brings to the shop not only some very nice antique pieces from which to choose, but a wealth of knowledge. She can answer most any question you may have about your selection of glassware, jewelry, furniture or linens. With a large library of reference books as her guide, Glyn will share plenty of information with you.

If you're an animal lover, be sure to say hello to "Sweet," the dedicated and lovable dachshund who greets customers at the door (unless he happens to be taking a nap).

### The Olde Village Shoppes Mini Mall and Le Bistro Cafe

108 S. Collins St.
813/752-3222
Tues.-Sat. 10-5:30, closed Sun. & Mon.

It takes a person of great vision to take an old, dilapidated building and turn it into a thing of beauty. That is just what Victoria Hawthorne has accomplished. She saw beyond the crumbling bricks, broken windows and littered interior. Hawthorne envisioned an enclosed European Style Shopping Village. She and her husband purchased the historic building in 1996 and began the work to fulfill her dream. The results are spectacular.

The quaint shops are connected by a red brick walkway with overhead ceilings of sky blue and big puffy clouds. All the shops have European facades or are a part of a beautiful English garden with a bubbling fountain. The 56 shops are filled with such eclectic treasures as stained glass pieces, antique Victorian lamps, Gone With The Wind memorabilia, paintings, fine antique furnishings, glassware, vintage jewelry, imported tiles from around the world and porcelain dolls, just to name a few.

Le Bistro Cafe gives shoppers a respite from the day's hectic pace. Chef Christopher, trained at the American Culinary Art Institute, prepares fresh soups, sandwiches, salads and seafood. Catering is available as well as High Tea, by reservation.

Vickie Hawthorne's dream to promote the revival of downtown Plant City is off to a remarkable start. Take some time to discover for yourself The Olde Village Shoppes and enjoy the beautiful surroundings of historic Plant City.

*Dale Gardner contributed to this story.*

## 70 POMPANO BEACH

**Heritage Clock Shop**
713 E. Atlantic Blvd.
954/946-4871

**Antique Market Place**
721 E. Atlantic Blvd.
954/943-6221

**Emporium Antiques**
1642 E. Atlantic Blvd.
954/946-0120

**Memories**
2692 E. Atlantic Blvd.
954/785-1776

**Purnie's Antiques**
25 N. Ocean Blvd.
954/941-6154

## 71 PORT CHARLOTTE

**Port Charlotte Gold & Silver**
2221D Tamiami Trail
941/629-3745

**Westchester Gold Fabricators**
3361A Tamiami Trail
941/625-0666

**Visions Unlimited**
3750A Tamiami Trail
941/625-6418

## 72 SANFORD

**Arts & Ends**
116 E. 1st St.
407/330-4994

**Granny Squares**
118 E. 1st St.
407/323-3919

**Granny's on Magnolia**
201 E. 1st St.
407/322-7544

**Junk Exchange**
118 Palmetto Ave.
407/330-7748

**Two Doves & A Hound Antiques**
205 E. 1st St.
407/321-3690

**Antiques Etc.**
205 E. 1st St., Suite C
407/330-1641

**Yester Years**
205 E. 1st St. #A
407/323-3457

**Bennington & Bradbury Antiques**
210 E. 1st St.
407/328-5057

**Somewhere In Time**
222 E. 1st St.
407/323-7311

**Delilah's**
301 E. 1st St.
407/330-2272

**Sanford House Inc.**
616 W. 1st St.
407/330-0608

**Sanford Antiques**
700 W. 1st St.
407/321-2035

**Helen's Den**
205 N. Palmetto Ave.
407/324-3726

**Park Avenue Antique Mall**
1301 S. Park Ave.
407/321-4356

## 73 SANTA ROSA BEACH\GRAYTON BEACH\SEASIDE\SEAGROVE BEACH

**Bayou Arts & Antiques**
105 Hogtown Bayou Lane
904/267-1404

**Martha's Plantation Shop**
1727 S. County Hwy. 393
904/267-2944

**Gunby's**
4415 Scenic Rt. 30-A E.
904/231-5958

**Grandma's Stuff**
35 Musset Bayou Road
904/267-1999

**Ole Outpost**
687 S. Church St.
904/267-2551

**Tidewater Antiques**
Emerald Coast Plaza, Suite 33
904/267-9599

**Hogtown Landing**
Hwy. 393 N. & Cessna Park
904/267-1271

**Tea Tyme Antiques**
Hwy. C-30A & Tanglewood Dr.
904/267-3827

**"S" House Antiques**
3866 W. Hwy. C-30A & Satinwood
904/267-2231

**Fernleigh, Ltd.**
Hwy. C-30A (Seaside Town Center)
904/231-5536

## 74 SARASOTA

### Mark of Time
24 S. Lemon Ave.
1-800-277-5275
Mon.-Thurs. 10:30-5:30, Fri. 11-4, Sat. 10-2
*Directions: Traveling on I-75, take exit 39 onto Fruitville Road (SR 780), going west for 5 miles into downtown. Turn left onto Lemon Ave., and proceed through two STOP signs and a traffic light. The shop is on the right.*

Located in the heart of Sarasota's antique district, Mark of Time specializes in rare antique clocks. The shop recently acquired a Ferdinand Lapp Centennial Clock, circa 1876. This one-of-a-kind clock and cabinet was created by Ferdinand Lapp especially for the Centennial International Exhibit in Philadelphia. Mark of Time also offers expert clock and watch repair. Antique furnishings and accessories are available along with the many fine selections of clocks.

**Bargain Box Consignment Shoppe**
4406 Bee Ridge Road
941/371-1976

**Daddy Franks**
907 Cattleman Road
941/378-1308

**Miller's Antiques**
970 Cattleman Road
941/377-2979

**Talk of the Town**
4123 Clark Road
941/925-3948

**Alley Cat Antiques**
1542 4th St.
941/366-6887

**Treasures & More**
1466 Fruitville Road
941/366-7704

**Shadow Box**
1520 Fruitville Road
941/957-3896

**Li Lou**
1522 Fruitville Road
941/362-0311

**Sarasota Antiques & Upholstery**
1542 Fruitville Road
941/366-9484

**Dotty's Accents & Antiques**
1555 Fruitville Road
941/954-8057

**Queen Anne's Lace Antiques**
2246 Gulf Gate Dr.
941/927-0448

**Sanders Antiques**
22 N. Lemon Ave.
941/366-0400

**Design Shop**
34 S. Lemon Ave.
941/365-2434

**A. Parker's Books**
1488 Main St.
941/366-2898

**A World Coin & Jewelry Exch.**
1564 Main St.
941/365-5415

**Rosie Ogrady's Antqs. & Fine Gifts**
32 S. Palm Ave.
1-800-793-4193

**Hartman, William**
48 S. Palm Ave.
941/955-4785

**Apple & Carptr. Gllry. Fine Art**
64 S. Palm Ave.
941/951-2314

**Kevin L. Perry, Inc.**
127 S. Pineapple Ave.
941/366-8483

**NEW England Antiques**
500 S. Pineapple Ave.
941/955-7577

**Beverly's Antiques & Collectibles**
510 S. Pineapple Ave.
941/953-6887

**Creative Collections**
527 S. Pineapple Ave.
941/951-0477

**Jack Vinale's Antiques**
539 S. Pineapple Ave.
941/957-0002

**Yesterday's Browse Box**
2864 Ringling Blvd.
941/957-1422

**Bacon & Wing**
1433 State St.
941/371-2687

**Remember Gallery**
1239 S. Tamiami Trail
941/955-2625

**British Pine Emporium**
4801 S. Tamiami Trail
941/923-7347

**Antiques And Country Pine**
5201 S. Tamiami Trail
941/921-5616

**Franklin Antiques & Collectibles**
3512 N. Lockwood Ridge Road
941/359-8842

**Crissy Galleries**
640 S. Washington Blvd. Ste. 150
941/957-1110

**Yellow Bird of St. Armands, Inc.**
640 S. Washington Blvd., Suite 230
941/388-1823

**Steven Postan's Antiques**
2305 Whitfield Park Dr.
941/755-6063

**Cherubs Of Gold**
2245 Ringling Blvd.
941/366-0596

**Sarasota Trading Co.**
522 S. Pineapple Ave.
941/953-7776

**Orange Pineapple**
533 S. Pineapple Ave.
941/954-0533

**Avenue Antiques**
606 S. Pineapple Ave.
941/362-8866

**Antiques & Collectibles Vault**
1501 2nd St.
941/954-4233

**Raymond's Second Hand World, Inc.**
5624 Swift Road
941/925-7253

**Caroline's Used Furn. & Antiques**
4511 S. Tamiami Trail
941/924-7066

**Shah Abba's Fine Oriental Rugs**
4801 S. Tamiami Trail
941/366-6511

**Coral Cove Antique Gallery**
7272 S. Tamiami Trail
941/927-2205

**Methuselah's Antiques**
322 S. Washington Blvd.
941/366-2218

**Robert A. Blekicki Antiques**
640 S. Washington Blvd.
941/365-4990

**Century Antiques**
3626 Webber St.
941/921-0056

**Coco Palm Glty. Art & Antiques**
1255 N. Palm Ave.
941/955-1122

**Franklin Antiques & Collectibles**
3512 N. Lockwood Ridge Road
941/359-8842

## 75 SEMINOLE

### Cobweb Antiques
7976 Seminole Blvd.
813/399-2929
Mon.-Sat. 10-5, closed Mondays May through September
*Directions: Traveling I-275, take exit 15; go west on Gandy Blvd. (Becomes Park Blvd.) to Seminole Blvd. (Alt. 19). Turn right onto Seminole Blvd. Drive two blocks north. Make a left into Temple Terrace. Located on the northwest corner of Seminole Blvd. and Temple Terrace.*

Cobweb Antiques is one of those "have all," "do all," "be all" kind of shops. They carry antique furniture, pottery, jewelry, watches, clocks, china, silver, books, postcards, prints, paintings, mirrors, lamps, linens, vintage clothing, antique firearms and related items. And if that weren't enough, they do estate liquidations, appraise firearms, real estate and antique automobiles. I wonder if these guys ever take a vacation.

**The Fox Den**
6020 Seminole Blvd.
813/398-4605

**Cobwebs Antiques**
7976 Seminole Blvd.
813/399-2929

**Evon's Antiques**
7480 90th St.
813/391-3586

**Vintage Antiques**
6920 Seminole Blvd.
813/399-9691

**Adams Emporium**
8780 Seminole Blvd.
813/397-7938

**The Hen Nest**
5485 113th St. N.
813/398-1470

## 76 ST. AUGUSTINE

St. Augustine, America's Oldest City, is a time capsule capturing nearly 500 years of fascinating history. Located on the uppermost Atlantic Coast of Florida, the city exudes a playful charm with a refreshing mixture of antiquated romance, youthful vibrance and Southern sweetness. St. Augustine was founded in 1565 and is the oldest continuously occupied European settlement in the continental United States. Evidence of the magic and mystery spanning five centuries in St. Augustine is revealed in more than sixty historic sites, including massive forts, missions and living history museums. Just minutes from historic downtown lie the Beaches of Anastasia Island, which stretch along twenty-four miles of sun-swept shores. There you will find the waves sprinkled with water enthusiast sailing, surfboarding and windsurfing. Incredibly fresh seafood and global delicacies are served in more than one hundred fifty eateries in St. Augustine. Options range from waterfront restaurants and shrimp shacks to gourmet bistros and turn-of-the-century Victorian mansions. The strong Minorcan heritage makes spicy tastes such as pilau and datil pepper sauce savory specialities. The nation's oldest city is truly a place where history comes alive.

**Centuries Past**
9C King St.
904/824-9588

**Bettye's Baubles & Books**
60 Cuna St.
904/823-9363

**Antique Warehouse**
6370 U.S. Hwy. 1 N.
904/826-1524

**Carriage House Antiques**
5A Sanchez Ave.
904/829-8505

**Riverside Antiques**
58 Charlotte St.
904/824-5424

**Barclay-Scott Antiques**
4 Rohde Ave.
904/824-7044

**Conch House Antiques**
600 Anastasia Blvd.
904/825-1255

**Second Hand Rose**
13 Anastasia Blvd.
904/824-7800

**Joy's Antiques**
72 San Marco Ave.
904/823-0706

**Down Memory Lane**
56 San Marco Ave.
904/823-1228

**San Marco Antique Mall**
63 San Marco Ave.
904/824-9156

**Ravenswood Antiques**
81 San Marco Ave.
904/824-1740

**Debra Williams**
Lightner Mall-Back of Lightner Museum
904/824-1552

**North Country Antiques**
Lightner Antique Mall
904/829-2129

**All Precious & Pleasant Riches**
203 S Ponce De Leon Blvd.
904/824-3156

**Anastasia Antique Center**
201 Anastasia Blvd.
904/824-7126

**Lovejoy's Antique Mall**
1302 N. Ponce De Leon Blvd.
904/826-0200

**Wolf's Head Books**
48 San Marco Ave.
904/824-9357

**Grandma's Attic**
60 San Marco Ave.
904/829-9871

**Country Store Antiques**
67 San Marco Ave.
904/824-7978

**First Encounter Antiques**
216 San Marco Ave.
904/823-8855

**Blue Max Antique Shop**
Lightner Mall
904/826-0963

**Second Time Around Antiques**
Lightner Antique Mall
904/825-4982

### *Great Places To Stay*

**Carriage Way Bed & Breakfast**
70 Cuna St.
1-800-908-9832
Web site: www.carriageway.com

Carriage Way is a beautifully restored 1883 Victorian home in the heart of the St. Augustine historic district. It is within walking distance of the waterfront, shops, restaurants and historic sites. The rooms are decorated with antiques and reproductions. Private baths have showers or antique claw foot tubs. The atmosphere is leisurely and casual. Complimentary beverages, newspaper, cookies, and a full gourmet breakfast is offered. Roses, fruit and cheese tray, gourmet picnic lunch, carriage rides and sweetheart packages can be arranged especially for you.

**Casa De La Paz Bayfront Bed & Breakfast**
22 Avenida Menendez
1-800-929-2915
Web site: www.oldcity.com/delapaz

In keeping with the Flagler Era, Casa de la Paz graces St. Augustine's bayfront and historic district with its' elegant Mediterranean architecture. (Centrally located to all sites, fine restaurants, shopping and miles of ocean beach.) Each guest room is distinctive in style and furnishings reminiscent of the early 1900s. All have a queen or king bed, cable TV, phone and private bath. From your room or veranda you will enjoy views of passing boats on Matanzas Bay or the beautifully walled Spanish garden courtyard. Awake to the fragrant aromas of a freshly baked breakfast and specially blended coffee. A delicious full breakfast typically includes a savory quiche, muffins or cakes, fresh fruit and homemade applebutter.

**Casa De Solana**
21 Aviles St.
904/824-3555

A lovingly renovated colonial home in the heart of St. Augustine's historical area, within walking distance of restaurants, museum and quaint shops. There are four antique-filled guest accommodations. All are suites, some with fireplaces, others with balconies that overlook the beautiful garden, and others have a breathtaking view of the Matanzas Bay. (All have private baths)

**Casa de Suenos B&B**
20 Cordova St.
1-800-824-0804

Casa de Suenos Bed and Breakfast, the "House of Dreams." is a beautiful turn-of-the-century Mediterranean home built during Florida's Golden Age. It is located on the romantic Carriage Route, still traveled today by horse-drawn carriages. You'll be just steps from charming shops, fine restaurants and fascinating landmarks. Six lovely rooms, include two suites (each with a private bath), and special touches such as terry robes, decanters of sherry and fresh flowers. Several rooms have relaxing whirlpool baths. Casa de Suenos exquisite rooms and suites are decorated with quality antiques and objets d'art. There is a gorgeous Honeymoon/ Anniversary Suite and a "Dream Suite." Enjoy sumptuous, full breakfasts in the lovely, bay-windowed dining room. During weekends and holidays you'll be serenaded by a guitarist.

**Old Mansion Inn**
14 Joyner St.
904/824-1975

This historic mansion home is on the National Register of Historic Sites. Constructed in 1872, it is the oldest and most architecturally significant structure in the area. Conveniently located opposite the Visitors Center and within walking distance of all historic sites, attractions and fine restaurants. An English Style breakfast is served in the formal dining room of the mansion.

**St. Francis Inn**
279 St. George St.
1-800-824-6062
Web site: www.stfrancisinn.com

Located in St. Augustine's restored historic district, the inn is rich in Old World charm and modern comforts. Built in 1791, it is constructed of coquina limestone which is made up of broken shells and coral. The entrance faces a courtyard containing lush banana trees, bougainvillea, jasmine and other exotic flora. Two courtyards, several balconies, porches and patios are perfect places for guests to read, write or paint. Each accommodation in this Spanish Colonial home is unique; all have private baths, antiques or quality reproductions, several have fireplaces, two person whirlpool tubs and kitchenettes. A two bedroom, two bath cottage (formerly the slave quarters and later the cookhouse for the main building) is ideal for a family or couples. Inn guests enjoy a hearty, complimentary breakfast, private parking, complimentary admission to the Nation's Oldest House, use of Inn bikes and swimming pool.

**The Cedar House Inn**
79 Cedar St.
1-800-233-2746
Open year round. Reservations taken from 10-8:30 daily
*Directions: Northern: From I-95 S, take SR 16 (exit 95) east to U.S. 1 (Ponce de Leon Blvd.). Turn right and go to the third traffic light. Turn left on King Street and go through two traffic lights. Turn right on next street (Granada Street) and go one block to Cedar Street. Turn right. The inn is the second house on the left. Southern: From I-95 N, take SR 207 (exit 94) east to U.S. (Ponce de Leon Blvd.). Turn left and go to the second traffic light. Turn left on King Street and go through two traffic lights. Turn right on the next street (Granada Street) and go one block to Cedar Street. Turn right. The Inn is the second house on the left.*

The Cedar House Inn is located in St. Augustine, the oldest town in the United States. Built in 1893, this Victorian inn has been characterized by family lore and love. As a remembrance to Russ and Nina Thomas' grandparents, each of the six guest rooms are named in their honor. Additionally, the rooms are decorated with family heirlooms and memorabilia from the particular grandparent's life. Tess' Room, often called the "angel room" by guests, was named for Russ' maternal grandmother. During the 1920s, she was an actress on early radio, the co-founder of the first Girl Scout troop in Paterson, N.J., and known to many as an "angel." "Tess's room reflects her life and love of people," explains Russ. It is often requested by new brides and grooms.

On one such occasion, a honeymoon couple booked the suite for a one night's stay between their wedding reception and their departure for the Bahamas the next day. They arrived late at night and departed early, apparently never needing to use the key nor ever having glanced at the key's name tag. Departing in a rush, they forgot to turn in the key. For the next week, Russ and Nina joked about how Tess' key was on a honeymoon.

Meanwhile, on the islands, the honeymooners were in quite a dismay. It seems upon checking into their hotel the groom had slipped the room key into his pocket. When they reached the room, try as he might, the key he took out of his pocket wouldn't open the door. He and his bride promptly marched down to the hotel lobby, confronted the desk clerk and displayed the offending key. One glance, and the clerk explained that this was not his hotel's key and asked who is "Tess" anyway. Which is exactly what the bride wanted to know "...and who is Tess??!!" Fortunately, after a few embarrassing moments, the groom fished into his other pocket, found the real hotel key, unraveled the mystery, and saved his new marriage.

## 77 ST. CLOUD

**A & D Antiques & Collectibles**
1032 New York Ave.
407/891-0331

**Troy's Treasures**
1037 New York Ave.
407/957-0588

**Caesar's Treasure Chest**
1116 New York Ave.
407/892-8330

**Forget Me Not Antiques**
1122 10th St.
407/892-7701

## 78 ST. PETERSBURG

**Nana's Other Place**
260 1st Ave. N.
813/827-0813

**Nana's Place**
428 4th St. N.
813/823-4015

**Rosemary's Antiques**
770 4th Ave. N.
813/822-1221

**B & G Antiques**
1018 4th St. N.
813/823-2452

**4th Street Antique Arcade Inc.**
1535 4th St. N.
813/823-5700

**Sunken Gardens Antique Gallery**
1825 4th St. N.
813/822-5117

**Dessa Antiques**
2004 4th St. N.
813/823-5006

**More Friends Antiques**
1219 9th St. N.
813/896-5425

**Patty & Friends Antiques**
1225 9th St. N.
813/821-2106

**Person's Antiques Too**
1250 9th St. N.
813/895-1250

**Memory Lane**
2392 9th St. N.
813/896-1913

**Suzette's Antiques**
3313 W. Maritana Dr.
813/360-2309

**Main House Antique Center**
4980 38th Ave. N.
813/522-2492

**Carrousel Antiques**
7033 46th Ave. N.
813/544-5039

**Bennie's Barn**
3700 58th Ave. N.
813/526-4992

**Ma's Glass Barn**
5822 60th Ave. N.
813/546-2459

**Tudor Antiques**
601 Central Ave.
813/821-4438

**Elephant Trunk**
627 Central Ave.
813/823-2394

**Stuart Galleries**
647 Central Ave., #1
813/894-2933

**David Ord Antiques & Fine Art**
649 Central Ave.
813/823-8084

**Jackie's Place**
657 Central Ave.
813/544-1844

**Urbana**
665 Central Ave.
813/824-5669

**Hauser Antiques**
7204 Central Ave.
813/343-5511

**Burr Antiques**
7214 Central Ave.
813/345-5727

**Blue Bear Antiques**
7214 Central Ave.
813/345-8851

**Cappy's Corner Antiques**
7215 Central Ave.
813/345-4330

**Antique Shoppe**
7223 Central Ave.
813/341-1199

**Harpies' Bazaar**
7240 Central Ave.
813/343-0409

**Antique Depot**
2835 22nd Ave. N.
813/327-0794

**Park Street Antique Center**
9401 Bay Pines Blvd.
813/392-2198

**Beach Drive Antiques**
134 Beach Dr. N.E.
813/822-3773

**Abbey Road Antiques**
1581 Canterbury Road N.
813/345-6852

**Karen's Place**
9999 Gandy Blvd. N.
813/576-0764

**Pink House of Collectibles**
1515 4th St. N.
813/894-2746

**Gas Plant Antique Arcade**
1246 Central Ave.
813/895-0368

**Echo Antiques**
1209 Central Ave.
813/898-3246

**Antique Exchange**
2535 Central Ave.
813/321-6621

### *Great Places To Stay*

**Bay Shore Manor Bed & Breakfast**
635 12th Ave. N.E.
813/822-3438
Email: baymanor@aol.com

The Bay Shore Manor is one of the oldest buildings in the Old Northeast Neighborhood located across from Northshore Park and the beach. The Bay Shore Manor opened for business in 1928 and is now hosted by the German Gross family. Each suite is nicely furnished and has its own bath. On hot summer days you'll love to sit outside and look to the Bay. Guests are served a delicious German style breakfast that consists of: coffee, tea, milk, orange juice, homemade bread and rolls, butter, cold cuts, cheese, honey, marmalade, eggs and cereal.

## 79 STUART

**Pastimes Furniture**
2380 N.W. Bay Colony Dr.
561/335-0590

**Custom Woods**
650 N.W. Buck Henry Way
561/692-0702

**A Certain Ambiance**
522 Colorado Ave.
561/221-0388

**Beckoning Antiques**
614 Colorado Ave.
561/288-5044

**Partners Antique Mall**
6124 S.E. Federal Hwy.
561/286-6688

**Time Will Tell**
3 S.W. Flagler Ave.
561/283-6337

**Collections**
53 S.W. Flagler Ave.
561/288-6232

**Bon Bon Antiques**
2681 S.E. Ocean Blvd.
561/288-0866

**Partners Mall**
6124 S. East Federal Hwy.
561-286-6688

## 80 TALLAHASSEE

**Grant's Collectibles**
2887 W. Tharpe St., #C
904/575-2212

**Early American Antiques**
2736 Pecan Road
904/385-2981

**Killearn Antiques**
1415 Timberland Road
904/893-0510

**Old World Antiques**
929 N. Monroe St.
904/681-6986

**Country Collection**
1500 Apalachee Pkwy.
904/877-0390

## 81 TAMPA

**Paris Flea**
3115 W. Bay to Bay Blvd.
813/837-6556

**Hunter's Find Antiques**
3224 W. Bay to Bay Blvd.
813/251-6444

**L'Exquisite Antiques**
3413 W. Bay to Bay Blvd.
813/837-8655

**Your Treasures**
3413 W. Bay to Bay Blvd.
813/837-8655

**Cox/Feivelson**
3413 W. Bay to Bay Blvd.
813/837-8655

**Neta Winders**
3901 W. Bay to Bay Blvd.
813/839-0151

**A Silver Chest**
203 S. Dale Mabry Blvd.
813/228-0038

**Antique Mall of Palma Ceia**
3300 S. Dale Mabry Blvd.
813/835-6255

**Flo's Antiques**
4301 W. El Prado Blvd.
813/837-5871

**Larry R. Engle Antiques**
4303 W. El Prado Blvd.
813/839-0611

**Tureville Antiques**
4303 W. El Prado Blvd., #A
813/831-0555

**Grandma's Place**
4305 W. El Prado Blvd.
813/839-7098

**Antique & Art By Patty**
4305 W. El Prado Blvd., #A
813/832-6129

**Frantiques**
1109 1/2 W. Waters Ave.
813/935-3638

**The Antique Room**
4119 S. Macdill Ave.
813/835-8613

**Decades Ago-go**
1514 E. 7th Ave.
813/248-2849

**Grandma's Attic**
1901 N. 13th St.
813/247-6878

**Antique Mall of Tampa**
1102 E. Busch Blvd.
813/933-5829

**Floriland Antique Center**
9309 N. Florida Ave.
813/935-9257

**Smith's Trading Post**
1781 W. Hillsborough Ave.
813/876-2292

**Timeless Treasures**
2305 W. Linebaugh Ave.
813/935-8860

**Brushwood**
3006 W. Swann Ave.
813/873-8022

**Ceia Palma Porcelain & Art**
1802 S. Macdill Ave.
813/254-7149

**South Mac Dill Antique Mall**
4004 S. Macdill Ave.
813/832-3766

**Cracker House**
4121 S. Macdill Ave.
813/837-2841

**Uptown Threads**
1520 E. 8th Ave.
813/248-5470

**Lorene's Antiques & Collectibles**
9840 Angus Dr.
813/249-0901

**Red Rooster Antiques**
6420 N. Central Ave.
813/238-2615

**Greg's Unique Antiques**
708 E. Grove Ave.
813/977-1990

**Boyd Clocks**
937 S. Howard Ave.
813/254-7862

**Huckleberry's Cottage Antiques**
3808 W. Neptune St.
813/258-0707

**Gaslight Antiques**
3616 Henderson Blvd.
813/870-0934

## 82 TARPON SPRINGS

Turn-of-the-century street lights, brick streets and sidewalks, towering oaks, the beautiful Anclote River, historic bayous, recreational parks, and beaches on the Gulf of Mexico are just a few of the many sights that greet you when you enter Tarpon Springs by vehicle or boat. Located in the center of town is the Tarpon Springs Downtown Historic District, listed on the National Register of Historic Places. This seven-block area features buildings from the late 1800s that house shops, art galleries, restaurants, and music venues that proudly welcome visitors from all over the world.

**Angelic Antiquities & Accents**
104 E. Tarpon Ave.
813/942-8799

**Carter's Antique Asylum**
106 E. Tarpon Ave.
813/942-2799

**Through The Looking Glass Antiques**
132 E. Tarpon Ave.
813/942-2851

**Beehive**
104 E. Tarpon Ave.
813/942-8840

**Antiques On The Main Inc.**
124 E. Tarpon Ave.
813/937-9497

**Menzer's Antiques**
134 E. Tarpon Ave.
813/938-3156

**Antiques Forever**
143 E. Tarpon Ave.
813/938-0078

**Court of Two Sisters**
153 E. Tarpon Ave.
813/934-9255

**Vintage Department Store**
167 E. Tarpon Ave.
813/942-4675

**Victorian Ivy**
151 E. Tarpon Ave.
813/942-6080

**Tarpon Avenue Antiques**
161 E. Tarpon Ave.
813/938-0053

### *Great Places To Stay*

**Bed and Breakfast on the Bayou**
976 Bayshore Dr.
813/942-4468

You'll love your stay at this beautiful contemporary home situated on a quiet bayou. Fish for a big old red or watch the blue herons and pelicans nesting in a bird sanctuary behind the B&B. Go for a swim in your hosts solar-heated pool or soak your cares away in a whirlpool spa. Then take a stroll through the famous Sponged Docks or do some antiquing in town. The inn is located just minutes from a white sandy beach with breathtaking sunsets.

**Fiorito's East Lake Bed & Breakfast**
421 Old East Lake Road
813/937-5487

Just off a quiet road that runs along Lake Tarpon's horse country, this meticulously maintained home on two and a half acres offers respite for the visitor. The guest room and bath are decorated in tones of blue, enhanced with beautiful accessories. Fresh fruit, cheese omelet, homemade bread and jam, and a choice of beverage is served on the tree-shaded, screened terrace. The hosts will be happy to direct you to the Greek Sponge Docks in Tarpon Springs for deep-sea fishing, golf courses, beaches and great restaurants which abound in the area.

**Heartsease**
272 Old East Lake Road
813/934-0994

You'll find plenty of "heartsease", meaning peace of mind and tranquility at this beautiful guest suite. Wicker and pine furniture and a green and rose color scheme create a light and airy feeling. Amenities include a private entrance, mini kitchen with a microwave, stocked with breakfast goodies, a color TV and private bath. The suite overlooks the pool and tennis courts. Pluck an orange or grapefruit from a tree and then settle in the gazebo, an ideal place to relax. Only twenty miles from Busch Gardens and five miles from the beach.

## 83 TITUSVILLE

**C C's Antique Mall**
4547 S. Hopkins Ave.
407/383-2204

**Crows Nest**
4521 S. Hopkins Ave.
407/383-1007

**Banana Alley-1913 Shop**
106 Main St.
407/268-4282

**Dusty Rose Antique Mall**
1101 S. Washington Ave.
407/269-5526

**Linger Awhile Antiques & Gifts**
326 S. Washington Ave.
407/268-4680

**River Road Mercantile**
342 S. Washington Ave.
407/264-2064

## 84 VENICE

**Buttercup Cottage**
227 Miami Ave. W.
941/484-2222

**Albee Antiques**
602 E. Venice Ave.
941/485-0404

**Treasures In Time**
101 W. Venice Ave.
941/486-1700

## 85 VERO BEACH

**Red Barn Antiques**
5135 N. U.S. Hwy 1
561/778-9860

**Gaslight Collectibles**
6235 U.S. Hwy 1
561/569-0033

**Company Store & Antique Mall**
6605 N. U.S. Hwy 1
561/569-9884

**Antique Alley**
1171 Commerce Ave.
561/569-5068

**Olde Towne Antiques**
1708 Old Dixie Hwy.
561/778-5120

**Antique Time**
3600 69th St.
561/567-0900

## 86 WALDO

**Waldo Antique Village**
17805 N.E. U.S. Hwy. 301
352/468-3111

**Red Barn of Waldo**
455 S.W. 3rd Way
352/468-2880

**Casa Las Brujas Antiques**
State Road 24
352/468-2709

**Laura's Antiques & Collectibles**
State Hwy. 24
352/468-2016

**Past Reflections**
250 N. Main St.
352/468-2528

## 87 WEST PALM BEACH

### Boomerang Modern
3301 S. Dixie Hwy.
561/835-1865
Tues.-Sat. 11-5 and by appointment
*Directions; On I-95, take exit 50 (Southern Blvd.). Go east 1 mile to South Dixie Hwy. Then go north 1/2 mile to Boomerang Modern located on the left.*

Boomerang Modern offers mid-20th style and design within the largest collection of blonde, streamline Heywood Wakefield furniture in the Southeast. Early and rare pieces designed by Gilbert Rhode, Leo Jiranek and renowned streamline automotive designer, Count Alexis de Sakhnoffsky, are featured.

Also offered are decorative objects and accessories by leading artisans and designers of the mid-twentieth century, along with funky, 50s lamps, ceramics and glass.

**Tinson Antique Galleries & Appraisers**
718 S. Dixie Hwy.
561/833-0700

**Argosy**
1913 S. Dixie Hwy.
561/832-5753

**Cassidy's Antiques**
3621 S. Dixie Hwy.
561/655-2313832-8017

**Antique Row's Little House**
3627 S. Dixie Hwy.
561/833-1552

**Bittersweet of Palm Beach, Inc.**
3630 S. Dixie Hwy.
561/655-2313

**Land's End Antiques**
3634 S. Dixie Hwy.
561/833-1751

**James & Jeffrey Antiques**
3703 a S. Dixie Hwy.
561/832-1760

**Cashmere Buffalo**
3709 S. Dixie Hwy.
561/659-5441

**E. Nelson Antiques**
3715 S. Dixie Hwy.
561/659-4726

**Old-Timers Antique Mall**
3717 B Dixie Hwy.
561/832-5141

**Lu Lu's Stuff**
3719 S. Dixie Hwy.
561/655-1529

**Dennis Joel Fine Arts**
3720 S. Dixie Hwy.
561/835-1991

**Brass Scale**
3721 S. Dixie Hwy.
561/832-8410

**ART Lane's Time And Again**
3725 S. Dixie Hwy.
561/655-5171

**Time And Again**
3725 S. Dixie Hwy.
561/655-5171

**Elephant's Foot**
3800 S. Dixie Hwy.
561/832-0170

**Michael Maclean Antiques & Est.**
3803 S. Dixie Hwy.
561/659-0971

**Greta S. Decorative Antiques**
3803-1/2 S. Dixie Hwy.
561/655-1533

**Floral Emporium**
3900 S. Dixie Hwy.
561/659-9888

**Time Worn Treasures**
4211 S. Dixie Hwy.
561/582-8064

**Real Life Antiques**
5105 S. Dixie Hwy.
561/582-8064

**R. B. Antiques**
5109 S. Dixie Hwy.
561/533-5555

**Deco Don's**
5107 S. Dixie Hwy.
561/588-2552

**John Cantrell & Margaret**
7729 S. Dixie Hwy.
561/588-8001

## 88 WINTER GARDEN

**Shirley's Antiques**
12900 W. Colonial Dr.
407/656-6406

**Trailside Antiques**
12 W. Plant St.
407/656-6508

**Antiques**
1075 S. Vineland Ave.
407/656-5166

**Winter Garden Country Store**
403 S. Dillard St.
407/656-0023

**Page's Pastiques Inc**
741 Tildenville School Road
407/877-3845

## 89 WINTER HAVEN

**Classic Collectibles & Antiques**
279 W. Central Ave.
941/294-6866 or 1-800-287-6866

**Antique Mall Village**
3170 U.S. Hwy. 17 N.
941/293-5618

**Joan Alach Antiques**
326 W. Central Ave.
941/293-8510

**Robert Holley Antiques & Gifts**
318 W. Central Ave.
941/299-3131

**Mimi's Bargain Corner**
3240 Dundee Road
941/324-5275

## 90 WINTER PARK

**Per Se Antiques & Collectibles**
116 E. Park Ave.
407/628-5231

**Antique Buff**
334 Park Ave. N.
407/628-2111

**Mimi's Antiques**
535 Park Ave. N.
407/645-3499

**Carols Antiques & Collectibles**
171 E. Morse Blvd.
407/645-2345

**Our Antiques Market**
5453 Lake Howell Road
407/657-2100

**Orange Tree Antiques Mall**
853 S. Orlando Ave.
407/644-4547

**American Antiques**
1500 Formosa Ave.
407/647-2260

**Chintz & Co.**
515 Park Ave. N.
407/740-7224

**Ferris-Reeves Galleries**
140 E. Morse Blvd.
407/647-0273

**Ginger's Antiques**
2695 W. Fairbanks Ave.
407/740-8775

**Winter Park Antique Mall**
2335 Temple Trail
407/628-5384

# Georgia

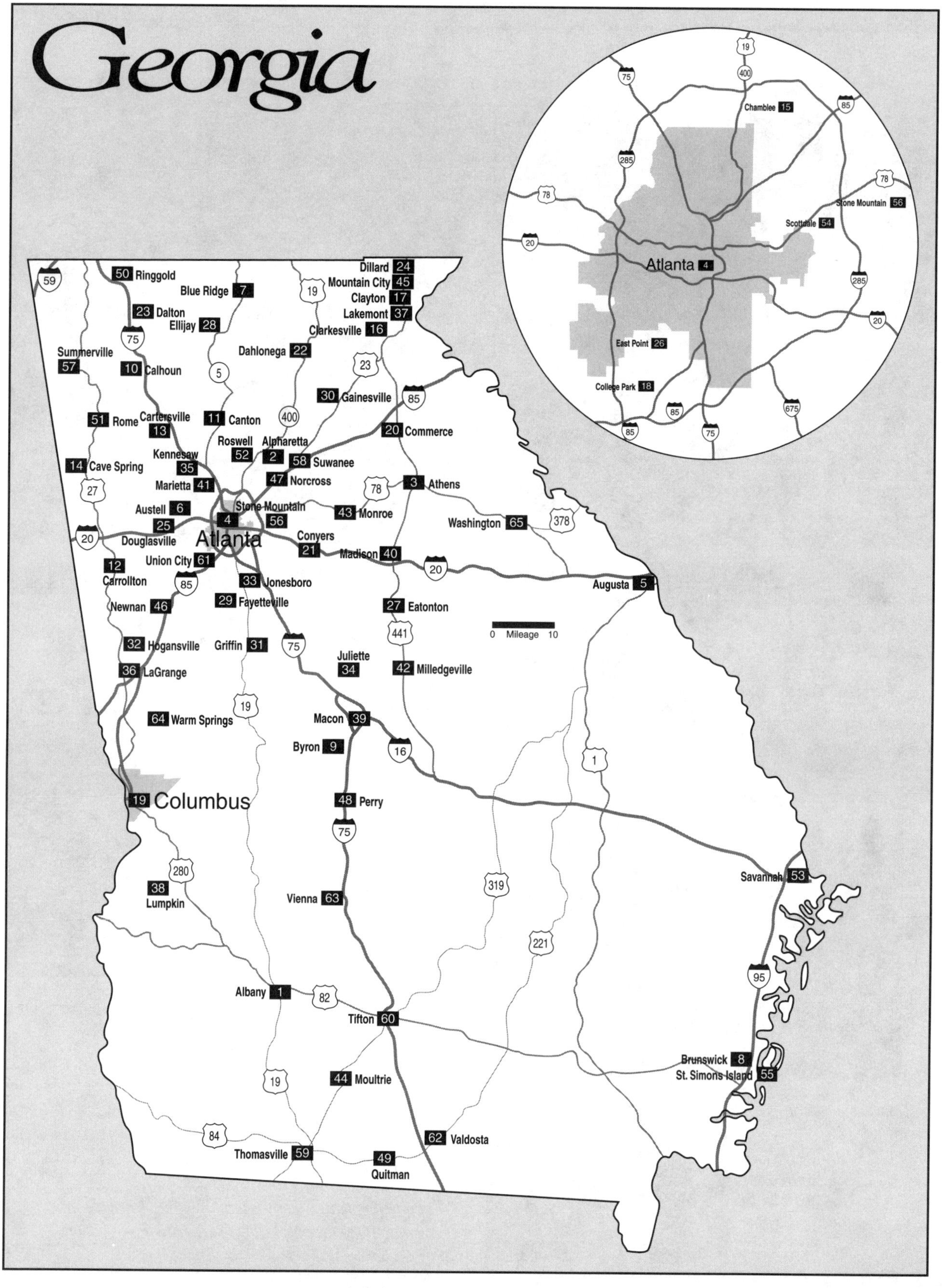

Chamblee 15
Stone Mountain 56
Scottdale 54
Atlanta 4
East Point 26
College Park 18
19
400
75
85
285
78
20
675
50 Ringgold
Blue Ridge 7
Dillard 24
Mountain City 45
Clayton 17
Lakemont 37
Clarkesville 16
23 Dalton
Ellijay 28
Dahlonega 22
Summerville
57
10 Calhoun
30 Gainesville
51 Rome
Cartersville
13
11 Canton
20 Commerce
Roswell
52
Alpharetta
2
58 Suwanee
Kennesaw
35
14 Cave Spring
47 Norcross
Marietta 41
3 Athens
Austell 6
Stone Mountain
56
43 Monroe
25
Douglasville
Atlanta
Conyers
21
Washington 65
Madison 40
Union City 61
12
Carrollton
33 Jonesboro
Augusta 5
29 Fayetteville
Newnan 46
27 Eatonton
0 Mileage 10
32 Hogansville
Griffin 31
Juliette
34
42 Milledgeville
36 LaGrange
64 Warm Springs
Macon 39
Byron 9
19 Columbus
48 Perry
38
Lumpkin
Vienna 63
Savannah 53
Albany 1
Tifton 60
Brunswick 8
St. Simons Island 55
44 Moultrie
62 Valdosta
Thomasville 59
49
Quitman
59
5
27
378
441
16
1
280
319
221
95
82
84

A variety of garden accents are offered in addition to the fine antiques and furnishings at Roswell Antique Gallery.

Snacks, TV and comfy chairs make up the husband recovery area.

# Something for everyone at the accommodating Roswell Antique Gallery

Are you looking for something a little different in the way of an antiquing experience? Roswell Antique Gallery will be worth your stop. The gallery has 30,000 square feet, 240 quality dealer spaces, and plenty of room outside to accommodate even the most lavish traveler's bus-sized recreational vehicle. What makes the gallery unique is the focus on quality and the assurance that the merchandise is period antique, no reproductions are allowed. If questionable, a product's authenticity is judged by three impartial experts before being added to the inventory, giving the customer a quality selection dating prior to the 1950s.

*Jack Nix (right) and his son Bill are the knowledgeable owners.*

Boasting "something for everyone" would be appropriate for the Roswell Antique Gallery. They offer a concession area, a Kid's Korner with a television, and a "husband recovery area" for wives who cannot bear to leave before visiting every square foot the gallery has to offer.

*The Roswell Antique Gallery is located in the Crabapple Shopping Center at 10930 Crabapple Road in Roswell. For additional information see listing #52 (Roswell).*

# Historic Savannah glows with old world charm, captivates with graceful Southern manners

*Built in 1878, Magnolia Place is one of the fabulous homes, now a grand inn, located in the Historic District of Old Savannah.*

Savannah, the city of warmth and grace, recently gained notoriety for the book *Midnight in the Garden of Good and Evil* by author John Berendt. But, the city, founded in 1733 by the Englishman James Edward Oglethorpe, has been welcoming visitors for more than 250 years. Savannah lends a charm and spirit unparalleled among the world's tourist destinations. *Conde Nast Traveler* has named Savannah one of the top ten cities to visit in the United States. Paris newspaper *Le Monde* called Savannah one of the most beautiful cities in North America.

Home to one of the nation's largest urban National Historic Landmark Districts, Savannah is located deep in the Sun Belt, where spring flows in around February and is followed shortly thereafter by an explosion of color as azaleas bloom in abundance by mid-March.

A true old world city, Savannah retains Oglethorpe's original design of 24 squares (22 survive) representing the crowning jewels of Savannah's 2.2 square mile historic district. Oglethorpe's city plan, where each square was an area of fortification as well as a place for public gathering, has been heralded as a masterpiece of urban design. Beautiful homes surround these lovely squares, replete with gardens and courtyards. Ancient moss-draped oaks line the picturesque boulevards forming an emerald canopy over the historic district.

Integral to Savannah are its historic inns. They represent the core of the historic district and offer a glimpse of life in old Savannah. From colonial English architecture to Italianate, each is unique while retaining the elegance of this historic city.

*Director Clint Eastwood poses with the owners of the Clay Café while filming "Midnight."*

Just as memorable as the city itself, is the graciousness of the people who live there. Every day is a party in Savannah. When the sun goes down the city comes alive with music, great food and laughter. A perfect ending to a perfect day of exploring and antiquing in Old Savannah.

*For a listing of antique shops and bed and breakfasts in Historic Savannah see listing #53 (Savannah).*

# Georgia

## 1 ALBANY

**Treasure House Antiques**
800 N. Slappey Blvd.
912/436-9874

**Bennett's Home Place**
910 N. Slappey Blvd.
912/436-0040

**Cottage Antiques**
526 Pine Ave.
912/435-7333

## 2 ALPHARETTA

**Old Milton Antique Mall**
27 S. Main St.
770/752-0777

**Main St. Antiques**
53 S. Main St.
770/663-1355

**A Flea Antique**
222 S. Main St.
770/442-8991

**Murf's Applecart Market**
735 Mayfield Road
770/740-0308

**Crabapple House Antiques**
765 Mid Broadwell Road
770/343-9454

**Crabapple Home Place Antiques**
12680 Crabapple Road
770/475-2799

**Crabapple Corners**
790 Mayfield Road
770/475-4545

**Laura Ramsey Antiques**
220 S. Main St.
770/475-2085

**Sweetapple Antiques Crabapple**
780 Mayfield Road
770/663-6555

**Shops of the Gin**
780 Mayfield Road
770/475-3647

## 3 ATHENS

One of Athens' most cherished landmarks is a unique failure. The double-barreled cannon was cast at the Athens Foundry in 1862 to the specifications of John Gilleland, a local house-builder.

Each barrel was to be loaded with a cannonball connected to the other by an eight-foot chain. When fired, the balls were supposed to separate, pull the chain taut and sweep across the field, mowing down Yankees.

A contemporary reported that when test-fired, the projectile "had a kind of circular motion, plowed up an acre of ground, tore up a cornfield, mowed down saplings, then the chain broke sending the two balls in opposite directions. One of the balls killed a cow in a distant field, while the other knocked down a chimney on a log cabin." The observers "scattered as though the entire Yankee army had been turned loose in that vicinity," end of quote.

Athens displays its unusual weapon in a special park on the City Hall lawn, with the cannon pointing north, "just in case."

Another beloved landmark is a "Tree that Owns Itself," perched atop a hill approached by a cobblestone street.

**Antiques Etc.**
10 Huntington Road, #3B
706/354-7863

**Archipelago Antiques**
1676 S. Lumpkin St.
706/354-4297

**Young's Antiques**
1379 Prince Ave.
706/353-6997

**Jingles**
1737 S. Lumpkin St., #B
706/549-6843

**Swap Shop**
1739 Lexington Road
706/613-6037

**Sam's Antiques**
1957 W. Broad St.
706/548-3764

**Stolls Studio**
135 Towns Grocery Road
706/549-4263

## 4 ATLANTA

**Cheshire Antiques**
1859 Cheshire Bridge Road
404/733-5599
Open daily 11-7, closed Christmas & Thanksgiving
*Directions: Located 1 mile from I-85. Take Monroe Dr. or Lenox Road exit, go 2 blocks north from Piedmont Road. Located in the Shopping Center.*

Within 7,000 sq. ft. of space, 35 dealers offer exceptional sought-after items such as Hull, Fostoria, Fiesta, Roseville, McCoy and fine porcelains and glassware. In addition, the shop has dealers who specialize in toys, sterling and exquisite glassware.

**Turnage Place Antiques**
3097 Piedmont Road
404/239-0378

**Buckhead Antiques**
3207 Early St.
404/814-1025

**Irish Country Pine Ltd.**
511 E Paces Ferry Road
404/261-7924

**Jeff Littrell Antiques & Interiors**
178 Peachtree Hills Ave.
404/231-8662

**Now & Again**
56 E. Andrews Dr.
404/262-1468

**Plantation Shop**
96 E. Andrews Dr.
404/841-0065

**Reed Savage Antiques**
110 E. Andrews Dr.
404/262-3439

**Regals Antiques**
351 Peachtree Hills Ave.
404/237-4899

**Toby House**
517 E. Paces Ferry Road
404/233-2161

**Antiques Etc.**
1044 N. Highland Ave.
404/874-7042

**Providence**
1409 N. Highland Ave.
404/872-7551

**Boomerang**
1145 Euclid Ave.
404/577-8158

**Allan Arthur Oriental Rugs**
25 Bennett St.
404/350-9560

**Beaman Antiques**
25 Bennett St.
404/352-9388

**Bittersweet Antiques**
45 Bennet St.
404/351-6594

**H Moog Antq Porcelains**
2300 Peachtree Road, Suite B 105
404/351-2200

**Interiors Market**
55 Bennett St.
404/352-0055

**John Eric Riis Designs Ltd.**
875 Piedmont Ave. N.E.
404/881-9847

**Peurifoy Antiques**
2300 Peachtree Road, Suite C103
404/355-3319

**Shelton Antiques**
2267 Peachtree Road N.E.
404/351-5503

**J Michael Stanley**
2265 Peachtree Road N.E.
404/351-1863

**Woodward & Warwick**
45 Bennett St.
404/355-6607

**Anne Flaire Antiques**
900 Huff Road N.W.
404/352-1960

**Bull & Bear Antiques**
1189 Howell Mill Road N.W.
404/355-6697

**Howell Mill Antiques**
1189 Howell Mill Road N.W.
404/351-0309

**O'Callaghan Antiques**
1157 Foster St. N.W.
404/352-2631

**Robert Mixon Antiques**
1183 Howell Mill Road N.W.
404/352-2925

**Acquistions**
631 Miami Circle N.E.
404/261-2478

**Antique Paintings**
631 Miami Circle N.E.
404/264-0349

**Bobby Dodd Antiques**
695 Miami Circle N.E.
404/231-0580

**Granny Taught Us How**
1921 Peachtree Road
404/351-2942

**Milou's Market**
1927 Cheshire Bridge Road N.E.
404/892-8296

**Jacqueline Adams Antiques**
2300 Peachtree Road, Suite B-110
404/355-8123

**Nottingham Antiques**
45 Bennett St.
404/352-1890

**Robuck & Co Antiques**
65 Bennett St.
404/351-7173

**Stalls at Bennett Street**
116 Bennett St.
404/352-4430

**Walker McIntyre Antiques**
2300 Peachtree Road, Suite B101
404/352-3722

**House Of Treasures**
1771 Centra Villa Dr. S.W.
404/752-7221

**Atlanta Antiques Exchange**
1185 Howell Mill Road N.W.
404/351-0727

**Garwood House Ltd.**
1510 Ellsworth Industrial Blvd. N.W.
404/892-7103

**Pine Cottage**
1189 Howell Mill Road N.W.
404/351-7463

**Provenance**
1155 Foster St. N.W.
404/351-1217

**Another Time-Antiques**
1382 Dresden Dr. N.E.
404/233-2500

**Antique Collections**
1586 Piedmont Road N.E.
404/875-0075

**Freeman Galleries & Graham Antqs.**
631 Miami Circle N.E. #15
404/237-0599

**Canterbury Antiques Ltd.**
660 Miami Circle N.E.
404/231-4048

**Dearing Antiques**
709 Miami Cr. N.E.
404/233-6333

**Out of the Attic Antiques**
1830 Cheshire Bridge Road N.E.
404/876-0207

**Pine & Design Imports**
721 Miami Circle N.E.
404/266-3741

**Thames Valley Antiques**
631 Miami Circle N.E.
404/262-1541

**Williams Antiques**
699 Miami Circle N.E.
404/231-9818

**Sandy Springs Galleries**
233 Hilderbrand Dr. N.E.
404/252-3244

**The Levison & Cullen Gallery**
2300 Peachtree Road, Suite C101
404/351-3435

**Designer Antiques Ltd.**
25 Bennett St.
404/352-0254

**A Cherubs Attic**
2179 Cheshire Bridge Road N.E.
404/634-9577

**Act 2**
3070 Cambellton Road S.W.
404/629-9966

**Architectural Accents**
2711 Piedmont Road N.E.
404/266-8700

**Back To Square One**
1054 N. Highland Ave. N.E.
404/815-9970

**Consignment Shop**
1185 Howell Mill Road N.W.
404/351-6025

**Century Antique Rugs**
727 Miami Circle N.E.
404/816-2412

**Gables Antiques**
711 Miami Circle N.E.
404/231-0734

**English Accent Antiques**
22 Bennett St. N.W.
404/351-9433

**Joseph Konrad Antiques**
693 Miami Circle N.E.
404/261-3224

**Red Barons Antiques**
6450 Roswell Road N.E.
404/252-3770

**Red Baron's Private Reserve**
631 Miami Circle N.E.
404/841-1011

**Twickenham Gallery, Inc..**
631 Miami Circle, Suites 24 & 26
404/261-0951

**Antiquities Historical Gallery**
3500 Peachtree Road N.E.
404/233-5019

**Antiques of Vinings**
4200 Paces Ferry Road N.W., #230
770/434-1228

**20th Century Antiques**
1044 N. Highland Ave.
404/892-2065

**Gallery Momoyama**
2273 Peachtree Road
404/351-0583

**A Flea Antique II**
1853 Cheshire Bridge Road N.E.
404/872-4342

**Antiquish Things**
3734 Roswell Road N.E.
404/261-0911

**Atlanta Camera Exchange**
2793A Clairmont Road N.E. #203
404/325-9367

**Big Chandelier**
484 14th St. N.W.
404/872-3332

**Cache Antiques**
1845 Cheshire Bridge Road N.E.
404/815-0880

**Davis & Fille Ltd. Antiques**
1151 Foster St. S.W.
404/352-5210

**Designer Antiques Ltd.**
25 Bennett St. N.W.
404/352-0254

**Jane Marsden Antiques**
2300 Peachtree Road N.W., #A102
404/355-1288

**Mayfair Antiques**
631 Miami Circle N.E.
404/816-4532

**Tara Antiques**
2325 Cheshire Bridge Road N.E.
404/325-4600

### *Great Places To Stay*

**Gaslight Inn**
1001 St. Charles Ave. N.E.
404/875-1001
Web site: www.gaslightinn.com

This extravagantly decorated B&B inn has been featured in *Better Homes & Gardens* magazine and on CNN's Travel Guide Show. *Frommer's Official Guide to Atlanta* lists the inn among the "Best Bets" and says "the most exquisite interior is found at the Gaslight Inn". Located in Atlanta's Virginia-Highland neighborhood and within walking distance of numerous restaurants, antique shops, galleries, and theaters, this inn is an oasis with a spectacular southern-styled walled garden. Other amenities include antique glass light fixtures, six working fireplaces and detached carriage house rooms.

**The Woodruff B&B Inn**
223 Ponce De Leon Ave.
1-800-473-9449
Email: RSVP@mindspring.com

Atlanta's Woodruff Bed and Breakfast Inn is centrally located in Midtown adjacent to many fine restaurants, cultural activities, and convention centers. This 1900s house abounds with original antiques, hardwood floors and stained glass windows. The Woodruff's history may make you smile or make you blush. Bessie Woodruff along with a staff of fine young ladies once operated a licensed massage parlor rumored to have catered to some of Atlanta's finest politicians.

**Ansley Inn**
253 15th St.
1-800-446-5416

Built in 1907 as the home of famous Atlanta clothier George Muse, the Ansely Inn is a landmark in Ansley Park. It is within walking distance of the Atlanta Botanical Garden, Symphony Hall and the High Museum of Art. While close to midtown Atlanta office buildings, the inn is situated among other stately homes on a quiet tree-lined residential street. The inn offers the amenities normally found in much larger properties with the personal attention found only in the very best.

### *Favorite Places To Eat*

**Mary Mac's Tea Room**
224 Ponce de Leon Ave. N.E.
404/876-1800

There seems to be something inversely proportional in the more of a lack of sophistication and elegance, to the more enjoyable and tasty cooking of food. Such is the case at Mary Mac's in Atlanta. It's a lunchroom with no frills and low prices where you write your own order for the waitress to pick up. But it is one of the tops in regional cuisine in the South. They even have a dessert called Carter Custard, made with peanuts and named after a well-known Georgia resident!

Mary Mac's is most noted for its fast service, fried chicken, and vegetables. Once you are seated at one of the plain laminated tables, you check the day's menu (printed on pastel paper), then write your order on a tiny pad. The waitress flies by, grabs the order, and is instantly back with the food! Do order the fried chicken, and eat as many different vegetables as you can get down. It is a breathtaking, belt-tightening experience.

## 5 AUGUSTA

**Antique World Mall**
1124 Broad St.
706/722-4188

**Broad Street Antique Mall**
1224 Broad St.
706/722-4333

**Attic Antiques**
2301 Peach Orchard Road
706/793-1839

**Antiques & Furnishings**
1421 Monte Sano Ave.
706/738-4400

**Riverwalk Antique Depot**
505 Reynolds St.
706/724-5648

**Antique Market**
3179 Washington Road
706/860-7909

**Antiques & Stuff Inc.**
4471 Columbia Road, #4
706/863-7195

**Charleston Street Antiques**
1423 Monte Sano Ave.
706/738-6298

**Merry's Trash & Treasures**
1236 Broad St.
706/722-3244

**Marketplace Antiques**
1208 Broad St.
706/724-6066

**Downtown Antique Mall**
1243 Broad St.
706/722-3571

**Quaint Shop**
1918 Central Ave.
706/738-7193

**Aunt Sissy's Antiques**
421 Crawford Ave.
706/736-0754

**Ann Spivey Antiques**
2611 Central Ave.
706/733-5889

**Antique Gallery of Augusta**
2055 Walton Way
706/667-8866

**Consignment Shop**
1421 Monte Sano Ave.
706/738-1340

**Days Gone By**
1401 Monte Sano Ave.
506/667-8579

*Great Places To Stay*

**Azalea Inn**
312-316 Greene St.
706/724-3454
Web site: www.theazaleainn.com

Discover the Azalea Inn and enjoy turn of the century charm in this restored Victorian bed and breakfast. The inn provides upscale Victorian accommodations and elegance, presented with a personal touch. King and queen guest suites feature fireplaces, private baths with large Jacuzzi tubs, and 11-foot ceilings. The elegant decor includes antiques and period style furnishings.

**The Partridge Inn**
2110 Walton Way
1-800-476-6888

The Partridge Inn is Old South indeed, offering charming white wicker, potted palms, and sunny porticoes for pure lyric. The Veranda Bar & Grill sings its own praise to the inn's glorious past, offering a quarter mile of covered verandas for comfortable, unique dining. Wall-to-wall sepia and black and white photographs, comfortable rattan, and overstuffed couches provide an atmosphere of relaxation and the comforts of home.

**Perrin Guest House Inn**
208 Lafayette Dr.
1-800-668-8930

The Perrin Place is an old cotton plantation home established in 1863. The plantation's original tract has long since become the Augusta National, home of The Masters, while the three acres of the home place remain a little spot of magnolia heaven. For guest, Perrin offers ten beautifully appointed bedrooms featuring fireplaces, Jacuzzi, period antiques and gracious surroundings. Treat yourself to the pleasure of a front porch rocker, and the comfort of a cozy parlor.

## 6 AUSTELL

**Grapevine**
2787 Bankhead Hwy.
770/944-8058

**Ramona's Antiques & Things**
2805 Bankhead Hwy.
770/941-2993

**Whistle Stop Antiques**
2809 Bankhead Hwy.
770/739-8366

**Wishful Thinking**
5850 Bankhead Hwy.
770/745-1194

**Antiques & More**
4434 Powder Springs Road, #B
770/439-6605

**Busters Antiques**
6289 Bankhead Hwy.
770/944-7844

## 7 BLUE RIDGE

**Sammy's Antiques**
662 E. Main St.
706/632-3991

**Blue Ridge Antique Mall**
285 Depot St.
706/632-5549

**Blue Ridge Antiques**
631 E. Main St.
706/632-7871

**Main Street Antiques**
631 E. Main St.
706/632-7788

## 8 BRUNSWICK

**Miss Milley's Antiques/Tea Room**
1709 Reynolds
912/265-5300

**Hildergard's Antique Collectibles**
1515 Newcastle St.
912/265-8378

**Loves Antiques**
1508 Bay St.
912/265-9221

**Piddlers**
1505 Martin Luther King Blvd.
912/265-0890

**Victorian Place**
1412 Gloucester St.
912/265-3175

**Carriage Trade**
1529 Newcastle St.
912/261-0507

**Wisteria Lane**
211 Gloucester St.
912/261-2210

**Brown's Antiques**
1527 Norwich St.
912/265-6099

## 9 BYRON

**Lord Byron Antiques & Collectibles**
100 W. Heritage Blvd.
912/956-2789

**BIG Peach Antq. & Collectibles Mall**
Hwy. 49
912/956-6256

**Little Peach Antiques & Gifts**
Highway 49
912/956-4222

## 10 CALHOUN

**Ridley's Antiques**
209 S. Wall St.
706/629-8684

**Sam's Antiques & Auction Barn**
3051 U.S. 41 Hwy. S.W.
706/629-6856

**Calhoun Antique Mall**
1503 Red Bud Road N.E.
706/625-2767

**Showcase Antiques**
1017 Hwy. 53 East S.E.
706/602-1233

**Magnolia House**
309 Belwood
706/625-2942

**Wall Street Trading**
117 S. Wall St.
706/625-0011

## 11 CANTON

**Beaver's Antiques**
370 E. Marietta St.
770/720-2927

**Cherokee Antiques**
210 Lakeside Dr.
770/345-2989

**Chamberhouse**
145 W. Main St.
770/479-2463

## 12 CARROLLTON

**Antiques & Stuff**
4552 Carrollton Villa Rica Hwy.
770/832-1855

**Linda's Antiques**
269 Cross Plains Hulett Road
770/836-8051

**Antique Mall**
106 Adamson Square
770/832-2992

**Cotton Gin Antiques**
4640 E. Hwy. 166
770/834-3196

**Carrollton Antique Mall**
109 City Hall Ave.
770/832-0507

**Oak Mountain Mall**
2093 S. Hwy. 16
770/838-0037

**Ben's Antiques & Collectibles**
4098 N. Hwy. 27
770/832-8050

## 13 CARTERSVILLE

**Antiques Downtown**
9 E. Main St.
770/382-1744

**Cartersville Antique Mall**
1277 Joe Frank Harris Pkwy. S.E.
770/606-0035

**Ruff's Antiques**
525 Hwy. 61 S.E.
770/387-0084

**Spring Place antiques**
1329 Joe Frank Harris Pkwy. S.E.
770/387-1345

## 14 CAVE SPRING

**County Roads Antique Mall**
19 Rome Road
706/777-8397

**Appletree Antiques**
24 Broad St.
706/777-8060

**411 Antiques & Uniques**
22 Alabama St.
706/777-0411

## 15 CHAMBLEE

### Eugenia's Authentic Antique Hardware

5370 Peachtree Road
770/458-1677 or 1-800-337-1677
Fax: 770/458-5966
Mon.-Sat. 10-6

This is a store that should be invaluable to anyone who buys antiques. Eugenia's specializes in one-of-a-kind, hard-to-find hardware items. But what sets them apart is that all their hardware is authentic—no new pieces or reproductions. Owners Eugenia and Lance Dobson search out every piece, clean and polish everything they buy for the store. They carry an extensive line of authentic antique door hardware, both interior and exterior, dating back to the 19th century, primarily 1840-1960. Here is just a short list of some of the items Eugenia's carries:

* bath and powder room accessories: soap, cup and toothbrush holders, towel bars, faucets, cast iron claw feet, wire soap baskets, cabinet latches and hinges

* furniture hardware: handles, pulls and knobs in Hepplewhite, Queen Anne, arts and crafts, Art Deco, Victorian, colonial, Eastlake, Art Nouveau, Chippendale

* door hardware, both interior and exterior: thumb latch entry sets, glass rosette sets, Victorian cast iron dead bolts, mortise locks, rim locks, elbow locks, door plates

* other accessories: sconces, door knockers, mechanical door bells, curtain/drapery tie-backs, hooks, letter slots, finials, switch/receptacle plates, pocket door hardware, brass bed finial balls, trunk/chest hardware, casters, decorative wrought iron pieces, old keys, door stops

* fireside shop: andirons, firesets, fire fenders, firescreens, cast iron grates

**A Little Bit Country Antiques**
5496 Peachtree Road
770/452-1726

**Happy Happy Shoppe**
5498 Peachtree Road
770/458-8700

**Pennsylvania John's**
5459 B Peachtree Road
770/451-8774

**Way We Were Antiques**
5493 Peachtree Road
770/451-3372

**24 Carat Antiques**
5360 Peachtree Industrial Blvd.
770/451-2224

**Antique City**
5180 Peachtree Industrial Blvd.
770/458-7131

**Blue Max Antiques**
5180 Peachtree Industrial Blvd.
770/455-3553

**Atlanta Antq. Center & Flea Markets**
5360 Peachtree Industrial Blvd.
770/458-0456

**Cannon Mall Antiques**
3509 Broad St.
770/458-1662

**Antique Haus**
3510 Broad St.
770/455-7570

**Blanton House Antiques**
5449 Peachtree Road
770/458-1453

**Broad Street Antique Mall**
3550 Broad St.
770/458-6316

**Rust & Dust Co.**
5486-92 Peachtree Road
770/458-1614

**Helen's Antiques & Collectibles**
5494 Peachtree Road
770/454-9397

**Moose Breath Trading Co.**
5461 Peachtree Road
770/458-7210

**Biggar Antiques**
5576 Peachtree Road
770/451-2541

**End of the Row Antiques**
5485 Peachtree Road
770/458-3162

**Liza's Cafe**
2201 American Industrial Blvd.
770/452-7001

**The Cameo Estate Jewelry**
3535 Broad St.
770/457-9925

**Baby Jane's**
5350 Peachtree Road
770/457-4999

**Antique Asylum**
5356 Peachtree Road
770/936-0510

**Atlanta Vintage Books**
3660 Clairmont Road N.E.
770/457-2919

**Chamblee Antique Row**
3519 Broad St.
770/455-4751

**Great Gatsbys**
5070 Peachtree Industrial Blvd.
770/457-1905

**Murphys Antiques**
5180 Peachtree Industrial Blvd.
770/451-6143

**Townsend Fine Antique Clocks**
3524 Broad St.
770/986-8981

**Metropolitan Artifacts**
4783 Peachtree Road
770/986-0007

**24 Carat Antiques**
5180 Peachtree Industrial Blvd.
770/451-2224

## 16 CLARKESVILLE

**Barbara's Antiques**
Hwy. 197
706/947-1362

**Dixie Galleries Antiques**
1404 Washington Square
706/754-7044

**Wonders' Antiques**
On The Square - Washington St.
706/754-6883

**Parker Place Antiques & Gifts**
On The Square - Washington St.
706/754-5057

**Once Upon A Time Co.**
On The Square - 1440 N. Washington
706/754-5789

**Nostalgia Antiques & Collectibles**
On The Square - 1417 Washington St.
706/754-3469

**Mustang Village Antiques**
6357 State Hwy. 17
706/754-3179

## 17 CLAYTON

**Berry Patch Antiques**
Hwy. 441 N.
706/782-7216

**Heritage Antiques**
Hwy. 441 S.
706/782-6548

**Second Hand Rose Antiques**
Charlie Mountain Road
706/782-1350

**Mountain Peddlers**
E. Savannah St.
706/782-4633

**Rhonnettes**
W. Savannah St.
706/782-6963

**Shiloh Post Cards**
Main St.
706/782-4100

**Timpson Creek Millworks**
Hwy. 76 W.
706/782-5164

### *Favorite Places To Eat*

### Green Shutters Tea Room
Old Hwy. 441 (south of Clayton)
706/782-3342

If you've never experienced the utter delight and pure pleasure of eating great food in the absolute "quiet" of the real, undisturbed country, then take a break and eat at the Green Shutters Tea Room. Hidden in the mountains of north Georgia, this little jewel has been serving three meals a day for the past forty or so years. Get there early and enjoy breakfast on the back porch overlooking a meadow with a split-rail fence, and watch the sunrise slowly paint the dewy grass with tiny jewels of light while the rooster crows. Eat crisp-crust biscuits slathered in homemade jelly and honey fresh from the hive; crispy pan-fried country ham; grits swimming in butter, eggs any way you like and steaming hot coffee.

Stop for lunch or dinner in the indoor dining room, and sink into crunchy fried chicken, country ham, biscuits, and all the southern-style vegetables you can imagine. Everything is served country/family style, in bowls that are passed whenever needed. Green Shutters is open from the day school closes until the day school starts, or until it gets too cold, so call first to see if they're cooking.

## 18 COLLEGE PARK

**Mu Mac Antiques**
3383 Main St.
404/768-6121

**Royal Touch Antiques**
3395 Main St.
404/669-9525

**Sarah's Antiques**
2815 Roosevelt Hwy.
404/761-2881

**Gallen's Antiques**
1682 Virginia Ave.
404/761-5166

**Good & Plenty Antiques**
3827 Main St.
404/762-5798

## 19 COLUMBUS

**Beavers Antiques**
1409 Warm Spring Road
706/327-2123

**Farmhouse Furniture**
3808 River Road
706/323-4325

**Grannys Thrift Shop**
308 10th St.
706/324-3378

**Scavengers**
1147 Brown Ave.
706/324-3539

**English Patina**
1120 10th Ave.
706/576-4300

**That Added Touch of Columbus**
1103 13th St.
706/327-2330

**The Tea Caddy**
1231 Stark Ave.
706/327-3010

**Glass Porch Antiques**
3852 Gentian Blvd.
706/569-7777

**Keeping Room**
4518 Reese Road
706/563-2504

**Charles & Di Antiques**
7870 Veterans Pkwy.
706/324-3314

**Peaches & Cream**
1443 17th St.
706/327-7485

## 20 COMMERCE

### *Great Places To Stay*

### The Pittman House
81 Homer Road
706/335-3823

Built by rural mail carrier T. C. Pittman in 1890, this stunning home is located in Northeast Georgia about one hour from anything important in the Northeast Georgia Mountains. You can visit college campuses, attend major sporting events, fish to your hearts content, golf on championship golf courses (3 or 4 in immediate area), and antique at many shops in the area. There are many discount shops in the shopping malls five minutes away.

## 21 CONYERS

**Collectors Choice**
908 Commercial St. N.E.
770/388-9434

**Conyers Antique Junction**
939 Railroad St. N.W.
770/922-5445

**Horse Crazy**
936 Center St. N.E.
770/860-1966

## 22 DAHLONEGA

**Do-Drop-In Antiques**
87 N. Chestatee St.
706/867-6082

**Golden Memories Antiques**
8 Public Square
706/864-7222

**Rockhouse Market Place**
Hwy. 52 E. & Rockhouse Road
706/864-0305

**Quigley's Antiques & Rare Books**
103 N. Chestatee St. N.W.
706/864-0161

### *Great Places To Stay*

**Stanton Storehouse**
78 Meaders St. N.
706/864-6114

Situated two blocks from the historic courthouse and Public Square, the inn is a short stroll to all the downtown attractions and restaurants. The inn's three suites are situated on the second floor of this Folk Victorian Storehouse built in 1884. A full gourmet breakfast is served each morning and afternoon tea may be enjoyed in the Rose and Herb Garden. Clawfoot and whirlpool tubs, fireplace, English & American antique furnishings, original hand-finished heart of pine floors complete the decor.

### *Favorite Places To Eat*

**The Smith House**
84 S. Chestatee
706/864-3566

The Smith House is a first-come, first-served, no holds barred kind of place; no reservations are accepted, and on weekends the place is packed. It's an elbow-to-elbow kind of atmosphere, with communal tables, shared by whomever is fortunate enough to get a seat! Pay one price and eat all you want. There is no menu, no choices. Everything that the kitchen has prepared that day is brought to the tables in large serving dishes, and it's a constant passing game. You can always count on fried chicken, bolstered either by Brunswick stew or catfish and hushpuppies, plenty of southern-style vegetables and warm breads.

The history of The Smith House began before the Civil War, during Georgia's gold rush—yes, I mean Georgia! This southern love affair with the golden stuff attracted prospectors from all over America, one of whom was wealthy Vermonter Captain Frank Hall. Hall staked a claim just east of Dahlonega's public square, and struck a fashionably rich lode. Dahlonega authorities, so the legend goes, would not allow their town's heart to be stripped open, so the stubborn Yankee decided if he couldn't have the wealth, nobody could. He promptly built an ostentatious mansion, complete with carriage house and servants' quarters, right on top of the vein! In 1922, long after Captain Hill's feud with Dahlonega had ended, Henry and Bessie Smith bought the house to operate it as an inn. For $1.50 travelers got a room and three meals! Mrs. Smith was a sensational cook, and praise for her culinary creations soon spread far and wide, especially about her fried chicken, country ham and fresh vegetables. When Fred and Thelma Welch took over ownership in 1946, The Smith House became known for its family-style offerings. Today, although the rooms have been spruced up a little, the food has not changed. It's still old-fashioned north Georgia cooking. As of yet, nobody has tried to dig up Captain Hall's gold.

## 23 DALTON

**Jot M Down Store**
311 N. Glenwood Ave.
706/226-2872

**Simply Outrageous**
114 W. Cuyler St.
706/272-4744

## 24 DILLARD

**Appalachian Trader**
Hwy. 441
706/746-5194

**Olde Feed Store Mall**
1093 Franklin St.
706/746-6525

**Black Rock Antiques**
Hwy. 441
706/746-2470

**Yesterday's Treasures**
6 Depot St.
706/746-3363

**Pine Cone Antiques of Dillard**
Hwy. 441
706/746-2450

**Stikeleathers**
Hwy. 441
706/746-6525

**Treasures Old & New Antiques**
Hwy. 441
706/746-6566

**Village Peddler**
Hwy. 441
706/746-5156

## 25 DOUGLASVILLE

**Antiques Plus**
6554 Church St.
770/489-1669

**Homespun & Sweet Antiques**
6118 Fairburn Road
770/949-1020

**Your Cup Of Tea**
5848 Bankhead Hwy.
770/489-7908

## 26 EAST POINT

**Dragon's Lair**
1605 White Way
404/762-7020

**Amazing Grace Elephant Co.**
1613 White Way
404/767-2423

**Sara Goen's Antiques**
1603 White Way
404/762-1234

## 27 EATONTON

Welcome to Eatonton and Putnam County, home of Brer Rabbit and the Uncle Remus Tales. As you drive through the tree-lined streets, you will witness some of the most unique styles of Antebellum architecture in the South, or you might even catch a glimpse of Sylvia, the ghost that occupies Panola Hall, the former home of Dr. Benjamin Hunt. Eatonton is proud of the many people it has produced. Two of the most famous are Joel Chandler Harris, creator of the Uncle Remus Tales; and Alice Walker, author and Pulitzer Prize winner for her book, *The Color Purple.*

**Fox Hunt Antiques**
109 N. Jefferson Ave.
706/485-6402

**Crystal Palace Flea Market**
1242 Madison Road
706/485-9010

## 28 ELLIJAY

**East Towne Antiques**
715 River St.
706/636-1931

**Victorian Attic**
40 N. Main St.
706/636-3700

**Cartecay Trading Post**
Big Creek Road
706/635-7009

**Old Hotel Antique Mall**
11 North Ave.
706/276-2467

**Antiques & More**
6 River St.
706/635-7738

**Ole Harpers Store**
3 miles out 52 W.
706/276-7234

**Coosawattee Mini Mall**
215 S. Main St.
706/636-4004

## 29 FAYETTEVILLE

**Brannon Antiques**
165 W. Lanier Ave.
770/461-9160

**Attic Treasures Antiques**
235 S. Glynn St.
770/460-8114

**Fayette Collectibles**
105 E. Stonewall Ave.
770/460-6979

## 30 GAINESVILLE

**Antiquities In Time**
330 Bradford St. N.
770/534-3689

**Fourth Colony Antique Shop**
5170 Browns Bridge Road
770/536-6423

**Antiques & Uniques**
2145 Cleveland Road
770/536-1651

**Antique Nook**
1740 Cleveland Road
770/536-0646

**Brickstore Antiques**
1744 Cleveland Road
770/532-8033

**Curiosity Shop**
2714 Old Cornelia Hwy.
770/536-7088

**Queen City Antiques**
112 Bradford St. N.E.
770/535-8884

**Stuff Antiques**
4760 Dawsonville Hwy.
770/889-8183

**Gainesville Antique Gallery**
131 Bradford St.
770/532-4950

## 31 GRIFFIN

**Dovedown Antique Mall**
315 W. Solomon St.
770/412-6121

**Complements**
522 W. Solomon St.
770/229-2561

**J Newton Bell Jr Antiques Inc.**
417 S. 6th St.
770/227-2516

**Solomon House Antiques**
103 N. 13th St.
770/229-5390

**Nearly New Store**
1003 W. Taylor St.
770/229-8397

**Country Cottage**
1975 Atlanta Road
770/227-0476

**Treasures Antiques & Furniture**
233 N. Hill St.
770/228-0053

## 32 HOGANSVILLE

**Ray Cheatham's Enterprises**
304 E. Main
706/637-6227

**Liberty Hill Antiques**
301 S. Hwy. 29
706/637-5522

## 33 JONESBORO

**Jonesboro Antique Shoppe**
203 N. Main St.
770/478-4021

## 34 JULIETTE

In Juliette the primary color is green, as in *Fried Green Tomatoes*. They are now served hot at the Whistle Stop Café, the actual film location of the movie. Other notable stops in this area include the Piedmont Wildlife Refuge, Lake Juliette and the 1847 Jarrell Plantation Historic Site.

**Garments Praise & Antiques**
McCrackin Road
912/994-0011

**Southern Grace**
420 McCrackin St.
912/994-0057

## 35 KENNESAW

**By-Gone Treasures**
2839 S. Main St.
770/428-2262

**Garner's Antiques**
2950 Moon Station Road
770/428-6481

**Kennesaw Mountain Military**
1810 Old Hwy. 41
770/424-5225

**Big Shanty Antique Mall**
1720 N. Roberts Road
770/795-1704

## 36 LAGRANGE

**B J's Quiet Country Barn**
29 Old Hutchinson Mill Road
706/845-7838

**Lemon Tree Shoppes**
204 Morgan St.
706/882-5382

**B. A. Evans Home House**
2106 Hamilton Road
706/882-1184

**Main Street Antique Mall**
130 Main St.
706/884-1972

## 37 LAKEMONT

### THE LAKEHOUSE on Lake Rabun
Lake Rabun Road
706/782-1350
404/351-5859
Fri., Sat., and Sun. 11-6 May 1-Oct. 30. Closed Winter months
*Directions: From Clayton, GA. go south on Hwy. 441 approximately 4 miles to Wiley Junction. Turn sharp right and go 50 yards to old Hwy. 441. Turn left and go approximately 1 mile to Alleys Store in Lakemont. Continue approximately 1/4 mile to a fork in the road. Take the right fork (Lake Rabun Road) and go approximately 2 miles to THE LAKEHOUSE antique shop. (On the left across from the historic Rabun Hotel.)*

THE LAKEHOUSE antique shop on beautiful Lake Rabun in the northeast Georgia mountains is a multi-dealer shop with two floors of antiques and mountain (rustic) furniture. The shop specializes in Adirondack furnishings for the mountain cabin and lake home. They also carry a line of mountain twig furnishings by Buz Stone. Bamboo fly rods, outboard motors, old camp paddles, blankets, birchbark items along with local folk ark and paintings complete the inventory at this unique mountain shop.

## 38 LUMPKIN

### Nana's Nook
South Side of Court House Square
912/838-4131
Tues.-Sat. 11-5, Sunday by chance and closed Mon.
*Directions: Nana's Nook is located on the south side of the Court House Square, Lumpkin, Georgia. Lumpkin is 35 miles south of Columbus, Georgia on U.S. 27.*

Nana's Nook, owned and operated by Dolores Harris and Gina Mathis, a mother and daughter team, has no consignors or dealers. It was a life-long dream of Dolores (Nana) to own an antique shop when she retired after having taught 30 years of elementary school music. Daughter Gina, talked her into opening the shop. Their goal is to have affordable antiques and collectibles for everyone's taste and budget. The two have "decorated" the shop as you would your own home and have been complimented numerous times by customers on its "at home" feel and "no dust" atmosphere. While visiting Lumpkin, be sure to enjoy the other shops and tourist sights such as Westville Historic Village and Providence Canyon State Park. The town of Lumpkin offers two great places to eat, Dr. Hatchett's Drugstore Museum and Michele's Country Cooking Buffet.

**Browse-A-Bout**
Broad St.
912/838-6793

**Town Square Antiques**
104 Broad St.
912/838-0400

### *Interesting Side Trips*

### The Village of Westville
Intersection of U.S. 27 and GA. 27
912/838-6310
Tues.-Sat. 10-5, Sun. 1-5

Westville is a functioning living history village of relocated, authentically restored, original buildings and landscape. The Village of Westville realistically depicts Georgia's pre-industrial life and culture of 1850 for your educational benefit.

Stroll down the streets and watch craftsmen at work producing items for their neighbors in the Village. Hear the "clang" of the blacksmith's hammer and anvil, and smell the gingerbread and biscuits cooking on the stove and fireplace. Try your hand at making seasonal crafts, such as candles, syrup, and soap. Here, you family will "glimpse the forgotten dreams" of 150 years past.

## 39 MACON

Welcome to America's Dreamtown, historic Macon, your southernmost stop on Georgia's Antebellum Trail. Founded in 1823 on the banks of the Ocmulgee River, Macon is a dreamtown for those looking for a wealth of antebellum treasures. Wide avenues, created by Macon's original town planners, lead you through what has been called "a city in a park." In fact, Macon was designed to resemble the ancient gardens of Babylon, providing large parks and garden squares. Today, some 200,000 Yoshino cherry trees throughout the city make Macon the Cherry Blossom Capital of the World!

**Village Antique Mall**
2390 Ingleside Ave.
912/755-0075
Email: vam2@mindspring.com
7 days a week until 6. Extended hours at Christmas. Accepts all major credit cards.
*Directions: Located only three minutes from I-75 in the heart of Georgia. Northbound, take Exit 52, cross 41 South, turn left onto 41 North, turn right at the 5th traffic light (Rogers Ave.) come to the next traffic light and turn left onto Ingleside Ave. You will find Village Antique Mall at the end of the block on the left. From exit 54 southbound, go to second traffic light and turn right onto Ingleside Ave. They will be on the left after the first traffic light at the end of the block.*

Specializing in pieces rarely found in the area, Village Antique Mall offers the discriminating shopper items from the arts and crafts era, such as Stickley, Limbert, Van Briggle and Niloak. Twenty-five expert antique dealers specialize in fine china, oil paintings, 30s & 40s mahogany furnishings as well as period pieces offered by Sherwood Antiques. Considered by its customers to be one of the finest antique malls in the middle Georgia area, this shop prides itself as offering only the finest in true antiques and collectibles.

**Dealer of quality care products for your antiques: Howards Products, Kramers Antiques Improver, Bri-Wax and more.*

**Eclectic Era Antique Place**
1345 Hardeman Ave.
912/746-1922

**Catherine Callaway Antiques**
3164 Vineville Ave.
912/755-9553

**Yellow House Antiques**
2176 Ingleside Ave.
912/742-2777

**Kennington's Antiques**
5296 Riverside Dr.
912/477-1422

**Antiques & Nostalgia**
612 Poplar St.
912/746-8668

**Colonial Collection**
1346 Hardeman Ave.
912/746-1922

**Kathryn's Fine Furniture**
623 Cherry St.
912/755-8700

**Purple Door**
6394 Zebulon Dr.
912/477-7170

**Exmoor Antiques**
2370 Ingleside Ave.
912/746-7480

**McLean Antiques**
2291 Ingleside Ave.
912/745-2784

**Mallard Nest Antiques**
5860 Bankston Lake Road
912/788-8606

**Amal's Antiques**
3108 Vineville Ave.
912/746-1878

**Attic Treasures**
2989 Columbus Road
912/742-6072

**Edwards House**
2376 Ingleside Ave.
912/741-9825

**Payne Mill Village Antiques**
342 Rose Ave.
912/741-3821

**Steve Popper Gift & Antique**
1066 Magnolia Dr.
912/743-2234

**Old Mill Antique Mall**
155 Coliseum Dr.
912/743-1948

## 40 MADISON

**Old Madison Antiques**
184 S. Main St.
706/342-3839

**Attic Treasures Antiques**
121 S. Main St.
706/342-7197

## 41 MARIETTA

**Railway Antiques & Design Center**
472 N. Sessions St. N.W.
770/427-8505

**Antique Accents**
67 Church St.
770/426-7373

**Keeping Room**
77 Church St.
770/499-9577

**Hill House Antiques**
85 Church St.
770/425-6169

**Southern Traditions Antiques**
93 Church St.
770/428-6005

**Heather's Neste**
95 Church St.
770/919-8636

**Willow Antiques**
105 Church St.
770/426-7274

**Mountain Mercantile**
107 Church St.
770/429-1663

**Mountain Mercantile**
115 Church St.
770/429-1889

**Antique Store of Marietta**
113 Church St.
770/428-3376

**Trading Memories**
686 Roswell Road
770/421-9724

**Back Home Antiques**
1450 Roswell Road
770/971-5342

**A Classy Flea**
1355 Roswell Road
770/579-2555

**Marietta Antiques Exchange**
1505 Roswell Road
770/565-7460

**Abe's Antiques**
1951 Canton Road
770/424-0587

**Water Spaniel Collectibles**
7 Whitlock Ave.
770/427-0277

**Du Pre's Antique Mkt**
17 Whitelock Ave. N.W.
770/428-2667

**Lamps of Yesteryear, Inc.**
5 Powder Springs St.
770/424-6015

**Ari's I Antiques**
19 Powder Springs St.
770/425-0811

**Juniper Tree Collectibles & Antqs.**
15 West Park Square
770/427-3148

**Antiques & Interiors**
685 Johnson Ferry Road
770/565-7903

**Victoria's Garden**
21 West Park Square
770/419-0984

**Antique Corner**
110 S. Park Square
770/428-4294

**Antiques on the Square**
146 S Park Square
770/429-0434

**Antiquity Mall**
815 Pine Manor
770/428-8238

**Elizabeth Cottage**
825 Church Street Extd. N.W.
770/424-6818

**My Favorite Things**
1355 Roswell Road, #200
770/992-7589

**Papa's Antiques**
721 Roswell St. N.E.
770/590-0109

## 42 MILLEDGEVILLE

**J & K Fleas Antiques**
2937 N. Columbia St.
912/454-3006

**Jeans Antique Shop**
2205 Irwinton Road
912/452-1550

**Sugartree**
1045 N. Jefferson St. N.E.
912/452-7914

**Browsing Barn**
169 Sparta Hwy. N.E.
912/452-7740

**Carolyn's Antiques**
1415 Vinson Hwy. S.E.
912/453-9676

### *Great Places To Stay*

**Maras Tara**
330 W. Greene St.
912/453-2732

Straight from the pages of *Gone With The Wind*, this beautiful 171 year old home boasts massive columns surrounding three sides of the home. With over 5,000 square feet of finished space, the Maras Tara has two parlors, a library and is filled with pre-Civil War antiques. Conveniently located in the center of the historic district.

## 43 MONROE

**Primitive Touch**
136 N. Broad St.
770/267-9799

**Road Side Bargain Shop**
2183 Hwy. 78 N.W.
770/267-6227

**Picket Fence**
120 N. Broad St.
770/267-3350

**Green Leaf Consignment, Flea Mkt.**
530 S. Madison Ave.
770/267-0952

**Marvin's Antiques**
104 Walker St.
770/267-2271

**Walton County Flea Market**
216 Davis St.
770/267-9927

## 44 MOULTRIE

**Olde Harmony Antiques**
15 2nd Ave. S.E.
912/985-5679

**R & R Antiques**
4246 Tallokas Road
912/985-3595

**Southland Country Antiques**
123 1st St. S.E.
912/985-7212

**Southland Antiques & Gifts**
120 1st St. S.E.
912/890-2092

**Sid's**
112-114 1st St. N.E.
912/985-8300

## 45 MOUNTAIN CITY

**Lana's Country Store**
Hwy. 441 - Depot St.
Seasonal Shop

**Rocking Horse Antiques**
Hwy. 441 - Depot St.
706/746-6979

**Blue Antler**
Hwy. 441 - Depot St.
706/746-7381

## 46 NEWNAN

**Homespun Heart**
50 Farmer St.
770/253-0480

**R J's Antiques & Collectibles**
17 Augusta Dr.
770/251-0999

**Green Door**
53 Southerland Dr.
770/251-9993

**Three Crowns Antiques Ltd.**
733 E. Hwy. 34
770/253-4815

**Amelia's Collectibles**
182 Jefferson St.
770/251-6467

**Jefferson House Antiques & Gifts**
51 Jefferson St.
770/253-6171

### *Great Places To Stay*

**The Old Garden Inn**
51 Temple Ave.
706/304-0594

The Old Garden Inn is a neo-classic Greek Revival mansion located in one of five historic districts of Newnan. While housed in a wonderful old home, the innkeepers focus is always the relaxation and comfort of each guest. The atmosphere is casual while the surroundings are serene and elegant. The cozy guestrooms offer bubbles, lotions, and romantic candles.

## 47 NORCROSS

**Georgia Antique Center & Market**
6624 Dawson Blvd.
770/446-9292

**Pride of Dixie Antique Market**
1700 Jeurgens Court
770/279-9853

**Antiques Market**
6 Jones St.
770/840-8365

## 48 PERRY

**Antiques From The Shed**
1139 Macon Road
912/987-2469

**Perry Antique Mall**
351 Gen. C. Hodges Blvd.
912/987-4001

**Rainbows End**
1126 Macon Road
912/987-0994

## 49 QUITMAN

**Backward Glance**
111 E. Screven St.
912/263-4430

**Bank of Antiques**
108 S. Lee St.
912/263-5537

**Blairs Flowers & Gifts**
110 W. Screven St.
912/263-8902

**Bargain Place**
401 E. Screven St.
912/263-4120

**Coin Quest**
113 E. Screven St.
912/263-8083

**Keeping Room Antiques**
313 E. Screven St.
912/263-4411

**Quitman Antique Mall**
101 E. Screven St.
912/263-4808

**McCord's Antiques**
311 E. Screven St.
912/263-9004

### *Great Places To Stay*

**Malloy Manor Bed & Breakfast**
401 W. Screven St.
912/263-5704 or 1-800-239-5704
Rates: $55-85
*Directions: Go west on U.S. Hwy. 84 off I-75 at the Quitman, Georgia Exit, about halfway between Atlanta and Orlando.*

Malloy Manor is the place to go to experience a unique blend of Victorian elegance and Old South southern hospitality! At this three-story, 1905 Victorian home listed on the National Register of Historic Places, you can literally stop and smell the roses, or any other flowers for that matter, because this city is situated in the middle of a "fragrance zone." Quitman is Georgia's camellia city; Valdosta, Georgia's azalea city, and Thomasville, Georgia's rose city.

You can imagine yourself in pre-Civil War times enjoying the balmy days on the large wrap-around porch outfitted with rockers and a swing, or gliding gracefully across the entrance that features leaded glass in sidelights and transom, with more leaded glass sidelights in the upper sitting room. All the staircases, wainscoting and moldings are original, and each room holds not only antiques and lace curtains, but a working fireplace! The parlor features a windup Victrola, and the music room houses an old upright piano. Three suites are available, each with sitting room and private bath. Also there is a pair of rooms that share a sitting room and bath. Gourmet lunches and dinners are served next door at The Booth House restaurant, in a restored Victorian home.

Antiquers can explore all of Quitman—the entire town is on the National Historic Register!—and there are multiple antique shops and fascinating old homes. The Brooks County Cultural Arts Museum, open every afternoon, features local artistry and Civil War and local artifacts.

## 50 RINGGOLD

**Gateway Antiques Center**
4103 Cloud Springs Road
706/858-9685
Open 7 days a week 9-8
*Directions: Last exit in Georgia or first exit south of Chattanooga, I-75 exit 142 - 200 yards on right.*

Gateway Antiques Center, appropriately named for its location in Georgia, is a whopping 40,000 sq. ft. wonderland of antiques and collectibles. Considered by some to be the South's largest antique mall (I certainly won't argue that), the store has 300 dealers, 400 showcases and a true sampling of every antique imaginable. The mall specializes in offering a large variety of smalls for the traveler.

**Autumn Oak Antique Mall**
383 Bandy Lane
706/965-7222

**Barn Gallery Antiques**
Alabama Road
706/935-9044

**Joel's Antiques**
4192 Bandy Road
706/965-2097

**My Favorite Things**
7839 Nashville St.
706/965-8050

**Huskey's Antiques**
3218 Boynton Dr.
706/937-4881

**Golden Oak Gallery**
5546 Boynton Dr.
706/86602526

## 51 ROME

**Apple Cart Antiques**
1572 Burnett Ferry Road
706/235-7356

**Antique Musique**
2358 Old Kingston Hwy.
706/291-9230

**Heritage Antique Mall**
174 Chatillon Road
706/291-4589

**Masters Antiques**
241 Broad St.
706/232-8316

**Northside Antiques**
1203 Calhoun Ave.
706/232-6161

**Smart Shop**
1943 N. Broad St.
706/234-5667

**Three Rivers Antq. Shop**
109 Broad St.
706/290-9361

**Grandpa's Attic**
516 Shorter Ave.
706/235-8328

**Chisholm & Thomason Ltd.**
14 E. 3rd Ave.
706/234-0533

**West Rome Trading Post**
1104 Shorter Ave.
706/232-3525

**Skelton's Red Barn Antiques**
10 Burton Road
706/295-2713

## 52 ROSWELL

**Roswell Antique Gallery**
10930 Crabapple Road (Crabapple Square Shopping Center)
770/594-8484 or 1-888-JACK NIX
Fax: 770/594-1511
Open daily, Mon.-Sat. 10-6, Sun. 1-6, closed Thanksgiving Day and Christmas Day
*Directions: Located 2.8 miles west of Hwy. 400 at the intersection of Crabapple Road and Crossville Road (next to Van Gogh's Restaurant).*

For specific information see review at the beginning of this section.

**Arts & Antiques**
938 Canton St.
770/552-1899

**Roswell Clock & Antique Co.**
955 Canton St.
770/992-5232

**Moss Blacksmith Shop**
1075 Canton St.
770/993-2398

**Elizabeth's House**
1072 Alpharetta St.
770/993-7300

**Shops of Distinction**
11235 Alpharetta Hwy.
770/475-3111

**Smith's Antiques & Consignments**
1154 Alpharetta St.
770/518-9689

**European Antiques**
938 Canton St.
770/552-1899

**Victorian Dreams**
944 Canton St.
770/998-9041

**Mulberry House Antiques**
1028 Canton St.
770/998-6851

**Corner Collections**
1132 Canton St.
770/641-9422

**Historic Roswell Antique Market**
1207 Alpharetta St., #C
770/587-5259

**Irish Antique Shop**
679 Atlanta St.
770/998-3499

**Cotton Blossom**
944 Canton St.
770/642-2055

## 53 SAVANNAH

For specific information on historic Savannah, see review at the beginning of this section.

**Alex Raskin Antiques**
441 Bull St.
912/232-8205

**A Second Chance**
3326 Skidaway Road
912/236-4576

**Arthur Smith Antiques**
1W. Jones St.
912/236-9701

**Alexandra's Antique Gallery**
320 W. Broughton St.
912/233-3999

**Antique Alley**
121 E. Gwinnett St.
912/236-6281

**Blatner's Antiques**
347 Abercorn St.
912/234-1210

**Bozena's European Antiques**
230 W. St. Julien St., #A
912/234-0086

**Contents**
205 W. River St.
912/234-7493

**Jere's Antiques**
9 N. Jefferson St.
912/236-2815

**Kenneth Worthy Antiques Inc.**
319 Abercorn St.
912/236-7963

**Historic Savannah Antique Market**
220 W. Bay St.
912/238-3366

**Memory Lane Antiques & Mall**
230 W. Bay St.
912/232-0975

**Old Arch Antiques & Collectibles**
235 W. Boundary St.
912/232-2922

**Pinch of the Past**
109 W. Broughton St.
912/232-5563

**V & J Duncan Antique Maps**
12 E. Taylor St.
912/232-0338

**D & B Collection**
408 Bull St.
912/238-0087

**Treasure Trove**
3301 Waters Ave.
912/353-9697

**Fiesta & More**
224 W. Bay St.
912/238-1060

**Peddler Jim's Antiques**
39 Montgomery St.
912/233-6642

**Attic Antiques**
224 W. Bay St.
912/236-4879

**Southern Antiques & Interiors**
28 Abercorn St.
912/236-5080

**Carriage House Antiques**
135 Bull St.
912/233-5405

**Japonica**
13 W. Charlton St.
912/236-1613

**Jimmie's Attic Antiques**
14 C Bishop Court
912/236-9325

**Carson Davis Ltd.**
7 W. Charlton St.
912/236-2500

**Melonie's**
202 E. Bay St.
912/231-1878

**Mulberry Tree**
17 W. Charlton St.
912/236-4656

**Once Possessed Antiques**
130 E. Bay St.
912/232-5531

**Scrooge & Marley Antiques**
230 Bull St.
912/236-9099

**Willows**
101 W. Broughton St.
912/233-0780

**Seventh Heaven Antique Mall**
3104 Skidaway Road
912/355-0835

**Olde Savannah Estates**
3405 Waters Ave.
912/351-9313

**17 South Antiques**
4401 Ogeechee Road
912/236-6333

**Junk House Antiques**
5950 Ogeechee Road
912/927-2354

**Cobb's Galleries**
417 Whitaker St.
912/234-1582

**Yesterday Today & Tomorrow**
1 W. Victory Dr.
912/232-3472

### *Great Places To Stay*

**Ballastone Inn and Townhouse**
14 E. Oglethorpe Ave.
1-800-822-4553

This antebellum mansion, circa 1838, has twenty-four guest rooms/suites with private baths (some have whirlpools) and is furnished with period antiques. Continental breakfast-plus served in room, bar or courtyard. Four blocks from Savannah River Front. Recommended by *NY Times, Brides, Glamour, Gourmet and Conde Nast Traveler.*

**Eliza Thompson House**
5 W. Jones St.
1-800-348-9378

Located on Jones St., the most beautiful street in Savannah according to *Southern Living Magazine*, this lovely Federal style inn has twenty-three large guest rooms beautifully restored with antiques, heart of pine floors, fireplaces and one of the most stunning courtyards in the city. An extended continental breakfast and wine and cheese reception is offered in the late afternoon, plus dessert and coffee in the late evening.

**Foley House Inn**
14 W. Hull St.
1-800-647-3708

Located on Chippewa Square, where Forrest Gump was filmed, this inn has nineteen spacious rooms, beautifully appointed with period furniture, fireplaces, color TV, some rooms have oversized whirlpool baths. Continental breakfast served in your room, courtyard or in the stunning lounge. Nearby golf and tennis can be arranged.

**The Forsyth Park Inn**
102 W. Hall St.
912/233-6800

This Queen Anne Victorian mansion, circa 1893, has a wide verandah overlooking a beautiful historic park. The inn focuses on lovely architectural details such as antique marble, fireplaces, carved oak floors and a grand staircase.

**The Gastonian**
220 E. Gaston St.
1-800-322-6603

This 1868 Historic inn is furnished with English antiques, operating fireplaces and in-room Jacuzzi baths with showers. Fruit and wine is served upon arrival; nightly turndown with cordials and sweets. Full, hot sit-down breakfast; sundeck with hot tub.

**The Grande Toots Inn**
212 W. Hall St. at Tattnall
1-800-835-6831

One of Savannah's newest Victorian inns, located two blocks from beautiful Forsythe Park. This charming 1890s mansion is well located for guests exploring Historic Savannah. It has been lovingly restored and is elegantly furnished to offer luxurious lodging. Breakfast each morning; tea and cordials in the afternoon. Private garden and verandas.

**Hamilton-Turner Inn**
330 Abercorn St.
1-888-448-8849
Email: homemaid@worldnet.att.net

One of the finest examples of Second French Empire styles of architecture in the United States, this inn has fourteen luxurious bedrooms and suites furnished with Empire, Eastlake and Renaissance Revival period antiques. Several have working fireplaces and balconies overlooking Lafayette Square in the heart of the Historic District. A full southern breakfast and afternoon tea await guests.

**Jesse Mount House**
209 West Jones St.
912/236-1774

Built in 1854, this beautiful Georgian townhouse is decorated with antiques and artwork from around the world. The Jesse Mount House offers modern comforts with historic charm.

**Kehoe House**
12 Habersham St.
1-800-820-1020

A magnificent Victorian mansion located in the heart of the Historic District. Restored to its full turn-of-the-century perfection as a European-style inn, this combination of luxurious guestrooms and gracious public spaces offers a unique experience in timeless elegance and personalized service.

**Lion's Head Inn**
120 E. Gaston St.
1-800-355-LION

A stately 19th-Century home in quiet neighborhood within walking distance to all attractions and amenities. Each guest room is exquisitely appointed with four-poster beds, private baths, fireplaces, TVs, and telephones. Enjoy a deluxe Continental breakfast, turndown service and wine and cheese reception.

### Park Avenue Manor
107-109 W. Park Ave.
912/233-0352

Park Avenue Manor is a restored 1879 Victorian bed & breakfast graced with charm and beauty that beacons the professional and reserved traveler. This pristine inn is furnished with antiques, period prints, porcelains, and has the ambiance of true southern living. The inn, adjacent to Forsyth Park, is ideally located to shopping, dining and the business district.

## 54 SCOTTDALE

**Old Mill Antiques**
3240 E. Ponce De Leon Ave.
404/292-0223

**Yesterday's Antiques**
3252 E. Ponce De Leon Ave.
404/292-3555

**Grandma's Treasures**
3256 E. Ponce De Leon Ave.
404/292-6735

## 55 ST. SIMONS ISLAND

**Low Country Walk**
1627 Frederica Road
912/638-1216

**Antiques & Interiors Inc.**
1806 Frederica Road
912/638-9951

**Shaland Hill Gallery**
3600 Frederica Road
912/638-0370

**J. Atticus**
3600 Frederica Road
912/634-0606

**D'Amico's**
208 Redfern Village
912/638-2785

**Frederica Antiques**
10 Sylvan Dr.
912/638-7284

**Sainte Simone's**
536 Ocean Blvd.
912/634-0550

**Island Annex**
545 Ocean Blvd.
912/638-4304

**One Of A Kind**
320 Mallory St.
912/638-0348

**Village Mews**
504 Beachview Dr.
912/634-1235

**Mimi's Antiques & Gifts**
3600 Frederica Road
912/638-5366

**Olde World Antiques**
3600 Frederica Road, #14
912/634-6009

**Peppercorn Collection**
276 Redfern Villiage
912/638-3131

## 56 STONE MOUNTAIN

**Country Manor Antiques**
937 Main St.
770/498-0628

**C M Becker Ltd. Antiques**
1100 2nd St.
770/879-7978

**Paul Baron's Antiques**
931 Main St.
770/469-8476

**Remember When Collectibles**
6570 Memorial Dr.
770/879-7878

**Stone Mountain Relics Inc.**
968 Main St.
770/469-1425

## 57 SUMMERVILLE

Soon after retiring as a Baptist preacher in 1965, the Reverend Howard Finster received instructions from the Lord to convert the swampland surrounding his lawnmower and bicycle repair shop in Summerville into "Paradise Garden." Working with cast-off materials, Finster created sculpture illustrating Scriptural messages, sidewalks embedded with glass and tools, edifices composed of bicycle parts and bottles, and a "Wedding Cake" chapel. He also began to paint in response to God's instructions. His distinctive sermon art combines visual imagery with texts from the Bible and other sources.

Now one of America's most popular self-taught artists, Finster's works came to the world's attention through exhibitions, as well as a 1980 *Life* magazine article that included his work.

The National Endowment for the Arts recognized Finster's work with a 1982 visual Artist Fellowship in Sculpture, which he used to enhance his "Paradise Garden." Since then, the Garden has become a popular site for art lovers, tourists and advocates of self-taught artists. In October 1994, Finster made several major pieces from the Garden available to the High Museum of Art in Atlanta to ensure their long-term preservation.

### Cherokee Antique Market
132 S. Commerce St.
706/857-6788
Mon.-Sat. 10-5, Sun. 1:30-5
*Directions: From the north: 40 miles south of Chattanooga, Tennessee on U.S. Hwy. 27. Exit I-75 at Ringgold (exit 140). Go south on Georgia 151 to U.S. 27. From the south: 25 miles north of Rome, Ga., on U.S. Hwy. 27. Exit I-75 at Adairsville (exit 128). Follow Georgia 140 west to U.S. 27, then north to Summerville. The store is located at the junction of U.S. Hwy. 27 and Georgia Hwy. 48 in Summerville.*

In the heart of Confederate territory, Cherokee Antique Market deals in rare Civil War documents and antiques, as well as flow blue, majolica, and other fine porcelains. A nice selection of fine furniture, primitives, linens, books and collectibles are also available at the 6400 square foot store featuring sixteen dealers.

**TLC Antiques**
5 N. Commerce St.
706/857-6723

## 58 SUWANEE

**Early Attic Antiques**
4072 Suwanee Dam Road
770/945-3094

**Pierces Corner Antiques**
597 Main St.
770/945-0111

## 59 THOMASVILLE

**Thomasville Antique Mall**
132 S. Broad St.
912/225-9231

**Firefly Antiques**
125 S. Broad St.
912/226-6363

**Antique Parlor**
1835 Smith Ave.
912/228-7432

**Collectors Corner**
326 S. Broad St.
912/228-9887

**James S. Mason Antiques**
309 W. Remington Ave.
912/226-4454

**Town & Country Antiques**
119 S. Madison St.
912/226-5863

**Times Remembered**
209 Remington Ave.
912/228-0760

**Brass Ring**
124 S. Stevens St.
912/226-0029

**Ross' Woodshop**
Hwy. 319 S.
912/226-8786

**Southern Traditions**
302 Gordon St.
912/227-0908

**Kelly's Flea Market**
210 W. Jackson St.
912/225-9054

### *Great Places to Stay*

**Serendipity Cottage**
339 E. Jefferson St.
1-800-383-7377
Web site: www.bbhost.com/serendipity

Step back to a slower, gentler time when Victorian ladies and gentlemen enjoyed evenings on welcoming porches with white wicker furniture and large potted ferns. This 4600 square foot home, located in a quiet, convenient, residential area, offers the best of both worlds-a combination of days past and present (all updated comforts).

## 60 TIFTON

**Judy's Antiques & Collectibles**
332 S. Main St.
912/387-8591

**Carey Antiques & Furniture**
506 S. Main St.
912/386-8914

**Things**
511 S. Main St.
912/382-7726

**Sue's Antique Mall**
I-75 @ Exit 23
912/388-1856

## 61 UNION CITY

**Robinson's Antiques**
6425 Roosevelt Hwy.
770/964-6245

## 62 VALDOSTA

**Joli Antiques**
1006 Slater St.
912/244-0514

**Martha's Antiques**
1915 Baytree Place
912/241-8627

**Odds & Ends Antique**
1919 Baytree Place
912/244-6042

**Landmark**
1110 N. Patterson St.
912/247-2534

**Worth Keeping Antiques**
1809 Remonton
912/241-7633

## 63 VIENNA

**Exit 36 Antique Mall**
1410 E. Union St.
912/268-1442

**Joel's Antiques & Collectibles**
215 N. 6th St.
912/268-2919

**Olde Shoppe Upstairs**
108 A Union St.
912/268-9725

**Vienna Antiques**
101 N. 7th St.
912/268-2851

## 64 WARM SPRINGS

"It was the best holiday I ever had..."—Franklin D. Roosevelt, commenting upon returning from Warm Springs, Georgia in March 1937. President Franklin D. Roosevelt made Warm Springs world-famous when he became a regular visitor and built his only home, The Little White House, there. He was often seen riding around Meriwether County in his little blue roadster. Even before Roosevelt's day, visitors came seeking the warm mineral springs which were believed to have curative powers.

**Antiques & Crafts Unlimited Mall**
Santa Fe Art Gallery
Alternate 27
706/655-2468

Located two miles north of Warm Springs, Georgia on U.S. Hwy. 27 Alternate, Antiques & Crafts Unlimited Mall is open year long for your shopping pleasure. There are 114 shops, including the Santa Fe Art Gallery. Antiques & Crafts Unlimited Mall is open daily from 9:00 to 7:00 April through October and 9:00 to 6:00 November through March. Antiques & Crafts Unlimited Mall is closed on Christmas Day. You will find a wide variety of antiques & collectibles including quality furniture, depression glass, elegant glass, collectibles of all kinds, plus a few quality crafts.

The Sante Fe Art Gallery is located inside of Antiques & Crafts Unlimited Mall. You will be able to view and purchase art by regional artist Arthur Riggs. His work is very unique and much sought after. Don't miss this Art Gallery when you are in the area. Also you will find art by Roberta Geter in the Santa Fe Art Gallery. Roberta is a young budding artist, who is proving to be very talented.

You will also find art located elsewhere in the building by Roberta Jacks of Monroe, Louisiana. Roberta has a unique style of her own. You must see her art to really appreciate it.

Visit them on the World Wide Web at: http://www.users.dircon.co.uk/~andyc/ANTIQUES

**Llewellyn's**
5634 Spring St.
706/655-2022

**Veranda**
10 Broad St.
706/655-2646

## 65 WASHINGTON

**Colonial Antiques**
721 E. Robert Toombs Ave.
706/678-2635

**Carl's Antiques & Collectibles**
722 E. Robert Toombs Ave.
706/678-2225

**Heard House Gallery**
32 E. Robert Toombs Ave.
706/678-3604

**Sunny Daze Antique & Gift Shop**
4151 Lexington Road
706/274-3286

**Ye Olde Lamplighter**
222 E. Robert Toombs Ave.
706/678-2043

# Idaho

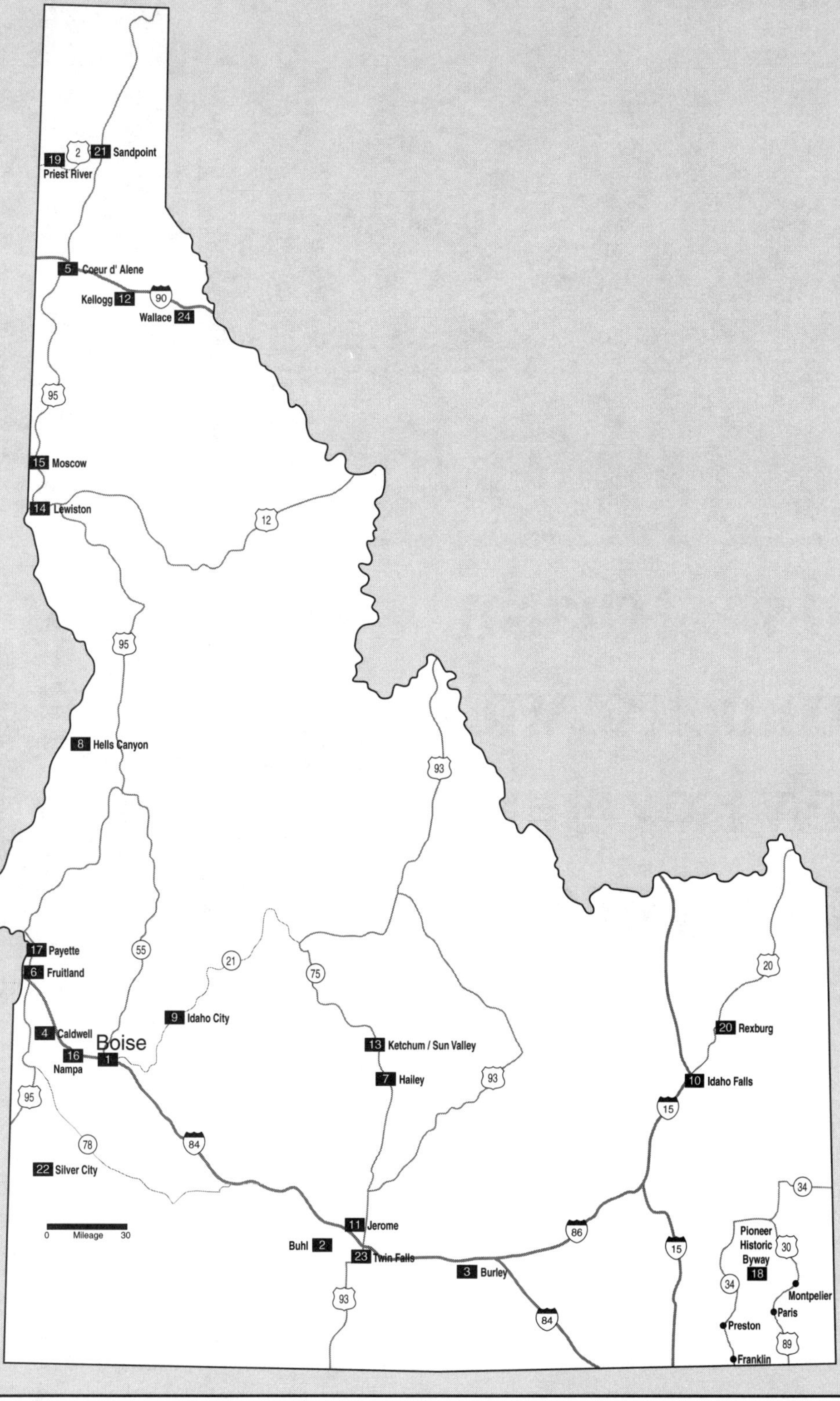

2
21 Sandpoint
19
Priest River
5 Coeur d' Alene
Kellogg 12
90
Wallace 24
95
15 Moscow
14 Lewiston
12
95
8 Hells Canyon
93
17 Payette
6 Fruitland
55
21
75
20
9 Idaho City
4 Caldwell
Boise
16
1
Nampa
13 Ketchum / Sun Valley
7 Hailey
93
20 Rexburg
10 Idaho Falls
95
15
78
84
22 Silver City
34
0 Mileage 30
11 Jerome
Buhl 2
23 Twin Falls
86
15
Pioneer Historic Byway 18
30
3 Burley
34
93
Montpelier
Paris
84
Preston
89
Franklin

*The Jameson has banquet facilities available to serve up to 80 guests, cozy Victorian guest rooms, and an old-fashioned saloon with mirrored back-bar.*

# Old west charm, complete with lovely lady ghost, at the Jameson

The historic Jameson Restaurant and Saloon opened its doors in 1900 as a small-town hotel and traditional saloon. It is now restored to its former elegance, offering guests the charm of the Victorian era. The bedrooms are on the third floor, and are very Victorian in appearance with heavy wooden furniture, chunky hand-carved wooden headboards and carpets in Victorian patterns. It is in room three that Maggie, who once stayed at the hotel as a long-term guest in the early part of the century, often returns for a visit. The hotel staff knew very little about Maggie except that she often received letters from New York and London. The letters arrived frequently for years until one day, early in the 1930s, Maggie checked out of the hotel headed for the East Coast. A few weeks later, word was received that she had either been murdered in a train robbery or died violently in an accident.

Several months later the staff noticed room fans and lights were turned off by an invisible hand. Hot showers turned cold and guests found themselves locked in their rooms with the key on the outside! Strangest of all, someone was using the sheets and towels in room three, despite the fact that it was locked and empty.

The puzzled owners decided to consult a psychic who agreed there was a spirit at the hotel: a woman who had died violently and who, because she had no home of her own, had "checked back in." To this day, Maggie makes her presence known. She still steals keys, turns off the water and joins guests for social gatherings. She is always friendly and welcomed by the current owners and their guests.

*The Jameson is located at 304 6th Street in Wallace. For additional information please call the innkeepers at 208-556-1554.*

*The Beale House Bed and Breakfast was originally occupied from 1904 until 1926 by the family of mining attorney Charles W. Beale. Jim and Linda See began restoring the home in 1987.*

# The Beale House majestically welcomes guests

## Historic home in a town filled with houses on the Historic Register

The Beale House, a prominent turn-of-the-century dwelling, has many unique features and impressive architectural details. This stately 1904 Colonial Revival home is listed on the National Register of Historic Places, as is the entire town of Wallace. Original parquet floors, antique furnishings, and memorabilia contribute to an atmosphere of comfortable elegance reminiscent of bygone days. A massive Palladium window in the library area provides a scenic view of the grounds and mountains. Each of the five second-floor guest rooms has its own distinctive charm — one with a fireplace, another with a balcony, still another with two full walls of windows. Guests are invited to peruse the collection of historic photographs aquired from prior owners, as well as from the renowned Barnard-Stockbridge Photographic Collection housed at the University of Idaho.

*Inspired use of elegant furnishings in this beautifully-restored home provide a gracious style of hospitality.*

*Breakfast is served in the serenity of the dining room, where the clock on the wall ticks at the slower pace than the outside world.*

*The Beale House Bed & Breakfast is located at 107 Cedar St. in Wallace. For additional information please call the innkeepers at 1-888-752-5151. Rates begin at $75.*

# Idaho

## 1 BOISE

**Acquired Again**
1306 Alturas St.
208/338-5929

**Forget Me Not Antiques**
1603 N. 13th St.
208/344-0678

**Perkins & Perkins Antiques**
1516 Vista Ave.
208/344-6153

**Collection Connection**
1612 N. 13th St.
208/343-6221

**American Nostalgia Antiques**
1517 N. 13th St.
208/345-8027

**Antique Village**
944 Vista Ave.
208/342-1910

**Early Attic**
2002 Vista Ave.
208/336-7451

**Hobby Horse Antiques**
231 Warm Springs Ave.
208/343-6005

**Antiques Hub**
2244 Warm Springs Ave.
208/336-4748

**Carol's Antiques & Collectibles**
10670 Overland Road
208/322-5059

**Collector's Choice**
5150 Franklin Road
208/336-2489

**Collector's Choice Too**
5284 Franklin Road
208/336-3170

**Elliott's Great Stuff**
1006 Main St.
208/344-9775

**Nifty 90's Antique Shop**
2422 Main St.
208/344-3931

**Boise Antique & Unique**
350 N. Milwaukee St.
208/377-3921

**5th Street Antiques**
225 N. 5th St.
208/344-7278

**Victoria's Antiques**
9230 Ustick Road
208/376-8016

**Wild Hare Bookshop**
3397 N. Cole Road
208/377-5070

**Memory Lane Antiques**
5829 Franklin Road
208/384-0074

### *Great Places To Stay*

### Idaho Heritage Inn
109 West Idaho
208/342-8066
Open year round. Reservations requested.
*Directions: Exit I-84 at Broadway in Boise; then follow north to Idaho St.*

The Idaho Heritage Inn was built in 1904 for one of Boise's early merchants, Henry Falk. It remained in the Falk family until it was purchased in 1943 by then governor Chase A. Clark. Lovingly restored by its present owners, the inn is now listed on the National Register of Historic Places.

All rooms at the inn have been comfortably and charmingly provided with private baths, period furniture and crisp linens. The spacious main floor common rooms include a formal dining room, living room and sun room, featuring diamond-paned French doors, oak flooring and Oriental carpets.

Guests of the inn enjoy a complimentary breakfast of fresh-squeezed juice, choice of beverage, fresh fruit in season, and a delectable entree which may include baked German pancakes, apricot cream cheese stuffed French toast, or apple skillet cake.

Surrounded by other distinguished turn-of-the-century homes, the inn is conveniently located within walking distance of downtown, 8th Street Marketplace and Old Boise (a historic shopping district).

### J J Shaw House Bed & Breakfast Inn
1411 W. Franklin St.
208/344-8899

This beautiful three story brick and sandstone residence is accented with original leaded glass and interesting bay windows. Architectural details reminiscent of the 1900s include columns, decorative moldings and French doors. A variety of living areas are available to guests. Gourmet breakfasts are served in the dining room or sun porch. J J Shaws is within walking distance to fine restaurants, Hyde Park and Idaho's State Capitol. The Boise River offers unlimited outdoor activities and snow skiing just sixteen miles away.

## 2 BUHL

**Claudia's Country Cabin**
3917 N. 1500 E.
208/543-5315

**Granny's Drawers**
219 Broadway Ave. N.
208/543-6736

## 3 BURLEY

South of Burley is an eerie and dreamlike landscape where people have been doing a double-take for centuries. It's called City of Rocks and it's now a national reserve.

There's little warning of what is to come as you drive the gravel road over rolling hills of desert sage. Suddenly, huge granite columns loom up 60 stories high!

The area has a poignant history that can still be glimpsed. Here is where would-be Californians parted from the Oregon Trail and headed southwest over desert plains and high mountain passes. The impressive spires became a memo board of hope, fear and determination; many of the inscriptions written in axle grease can still be read.

Rumor has it that there's gold among the mammoth rocks. On his deathbed, a stagecoach robber confessed to burying his treasure at the City of Rocks. It has never been found.

The City of Rocks is a bit out of the way, but well worth the effort. Oakley, a village en route, is listed on the National Register of Historic Places because of its many intricate stone and wood structures built before the turn of the century. No other town in Idaho has such a concentration of old buildings.

A good starting point is the Oakley Co-op Building on the corner of Main and Center Streets. Near the city park is a jail cell that once held the noted outlaw, "Diamondfield" Jack Davis.

**Golden Goose**
1229 Overland Ave.
208/678-9122

## 4 CALDWELL

**Alan Vulk Auction Service**
523 Main St.
208/454-2910

**Caldwell Auction**
4920 Cleveland Blvd.
208/454-1532

## 5 COEUR D ALENE

**Coeur D'Alene Antique Mall**
3650 N. Government Way
208/667-0246

**Coeur D'Alene Antique Mall**
408 W. Haycraft Ave., #11
208/664-0579

**Good Things**
204 N. 3rd St.
208/667-6958

**Crow's Nest Antiques**
416 E. Sherman Ave.
208/667-1679

**Lake City Antique Mall**
401 N. 2nd St.
208/664-6883

**Sherman Antiques & Collectibles**
415 E. Sherman Ave.
208/666-1809

**Worthington's Fine Antiques**
210 Sherman Ave., #103
208/765-7753

**Timeless Treasures Antiques**
823 N. 4th St.
208/765-0699

**Wiggett Marketplace**
119 N. 4th St.
208/664-1524

**Ciscos-Hunters of the Past**
212 N. 4th St.
208-769-7575

**Dicker-N-Swap Secondhand**
810 N. 4th St.
208/666-9042

**One of a Kind**
413 Sherman Ave.
208/664-5145

**Cisco's - II**
317 Sherman
208/765-7997

### *Great Places To Stay*

**Amors Highwood House**
1206 Highwood Lane
1-888-625-3470
Web site: www.amors.com

Highwood House is nestled in towering Ponderosa Pines, half a mile from Coeur d'Alene National Forest and five minutes from Lake Coeur d'Alene and Fernan Lake. The home features a newly decorated master suite with king size bed with a down comforter and private bathroom. For your enjoyment the inn offers mountain bikes or table tennis, then relax in the Gazebo covered spa. Awaken to the aroma of fresh brewed coffee and look forward to a hearty full breakfast in the dining room or the adjoining deck.

**Baragar House Bed and Breakfast**
316 Military Dr.
1-800-615-8422
Web site: www.baragarhouse.com

This charming Craftsman-style bungalow in historic Fort Sherman was built by a limber baron. The spacious common area, comfortably furnished, has an antique parlor furnace, a victrola, and a lovely piano. The beautiful neighborhood viewed through the exquisite antique beveled, leaded, windows shows the lovely, mature trees native to this area. The rooms are decorated in themes: the "Country Cabin" is delightful with its decor of mountain stream and cloud murals. The "Garden Room" is floral, with a canopied window seat and unique antique vanity. The "Honeymoon Suite" in Victorian decor is especially appealing with its over-sized bathroom offering a claw-foot tub under a bay window and curved glass shower. All rooms have private use of indoor spa/sauna, and "sleep under the stars" of a professionally applied solar system. Wonderful "wreck your diet" breakfasts.

**Berry Patch Inn**
1150 N. Four Winds Road
208/765-4994
Web site: www.bbhost.com/berrypatchinn

The Berry Patch Inn offers a restorative atmosphere for the guest that needs "to get-away-from-it-all", whether for an evening or an extended stay. Your hostess, Ann Caggiano, a world traveled proprietress, offers her beautiful mountain top chalet home, nestled in a forest of tall pines, for that perfect diversion to everyday life. Only three miles from the center of the town, the Berry Patch has private road access and is very serene and quiet, ideal for a fabulous honeymoon escape. Guests are invited to take a walk on the two acres, and stop by the seasonal fruit orchard, berry patches and green gardens to take in the sounds of nature and munch on the sun-warmed berries. For those who enjoy the more quiet wonders of nature, this mountain is a bird watcher's paradise, and occasionally you will hear the call of the wild. An authentic Sioux Tepee on the property offers a place for quiet contemplation and communication with nature. Nordstrom's store (Spokane) praised this bed and breakfast in their "Rediscover the Northwest" 1993 promotion, while *Country Magazine* gave national acclaim in "Perfect Place to Stay while Touring America's Countryside" (1994) and just recently it was hailed as one of the top 20 Inns of the Rockies by *National Geographic Traveler* (March 1997).

**Gregory's McFarland House Bed and Breakfast**
601 E. Foster Ave.
208/667-1232
Web site: www.bbhost.com/mcfarlandhouse

In 1989, McFarland House won a Special Heritage Preservation Award presented by the Cranbrook Archives, Museum and Landmark Foundation for the preservation and restoration of this circa 1905 home. It was also the featured bed and breakfast in the August 6, 1989 travel section of the *Los Angeles Times*, in which Jerry Hulse, Travel Editor, wrote, "Entering Gregory's McFarland House is like stepping back 100 years to an unhurried time when four posters were in fashion and lace curtains fluttered at the windows and the notes of a vintage piano echoed through the house." A perfect romantic and peaceful get-a-way.

**The Roosevelt Inn**
105 Wallace Ave.
208/765-5200
Open year round
*Directions: Call ahead.*

The Roosevelt Inn, named after the 26th president, Theodore Roosevelt, was built in 1906. Included in the National Register of Historic Places, this beautiful red brick building with its steeple shaded by maple trees, offers traditional elegance and Hungarian hospitality.

Two charmingly furnished parlors and dining area featuring lovely leaded glass windows and a hand-painted mural welcome you on the main floor. Each of the cozy guests rooms are decorated with antiques and provide views of the lake.

The Roosevelt Inn is located within a short walking distance to area restaurants, shops and boutiques. The nature trails of beautiful Tubbs Hill are also within easy access.

## 6 FRUITLAND

**Now & Then**
7190 Elmore Road
208/452-5500

**Riverview Antiques & Collectibles**
1125 N.W. 16th St.
208/452-4365

**Suzy's Nu-2-U**
200 S.W. 3rd
208/452-5878

***Great Places To Stay***

**Elm Hollow Bed & Breakfast**
4900 Hwy. 95
208/452-6491
Open year round
*Directions: Traveling I-84, take Exit 3. Drive toward Parma. Elm Hollow is at the bottom of the dip between Glenway and Fairview. Make a left onto the driveway, just before milepost 58. Only two and one half miles south of I-84; makes for a convenient stop-over for travelers.*

Nestled against a hillside overlooking fertile Idaho farms and orchards, Elm Hollow Bed & Breakfast gives the weary traveler a true taste of home. Guests to this country retreat experience the relaxing atmosphere of old-fashioned hospitality and good Dutch cooking.

The Guest Room offers spacious comfort with queen size beds and loveseat, and a full bookcase provide the touches of home for a cozy evening.

For a romantic getaway, the Barn (a renovated section of the old dairy barn) offers privacy and a great view of the countryside.

Mornings at Elm Hollow start with a choice of Continental breakfast with home-baked breads and sweet rolls, or a full and hearty country meal, served family style in the dining room.

## 7 HAILEY

**Hailey's Antique Market**
P.O. Box 1955
208/788-9292
Locations: Inside—Hailey Armory;
Outside—Roberta McKercher Park

1999 Show Dates
July 2, 3 & 4
September 3, 4 & 5

**Lone Star Designs**
109 S. Main St.
208/788-9158

## 8 HELLS CANYON

**Seven Devils and A Hell of A Canyon**

Over one mile deep, Hells Canyon is North Americas deepest river gorge, deeper even than the Grand Canyon. Walls of black, crumbling basalt thrust straight up, forcing boaters and fishermen on the Snake River to crane their necks for blue sky. Looking down upon the canyon are the mighty Seven Devils, an awe-inspiring mountain range that crests over

1 ½ miles above the river.

## 9 IDAHO CITY

Idaho City was, at one time, the largest city in the Northwest-a rough and tumble, rip-roaring mining town that epitomized the "boom or bust" lifestyle of gold rushers. Gold often took precedence over human life. It's said that of the 200 men and women buried in picturesque Boot Hill, only 28 died of natural causes.

### A One Step Away Bed and Breakfast and Antique Shop
112 Cottonwood St.
208/392-4938

Nestled on a quiet little street on the south side of town, "One Step Away" is a quaint bed and breakfast with an exquisite antique shop adjoining it. Rooms are tastefully furnished in 1800s elegance and named after early settlers of Idaho City. The Jenny Lind Chamber is dedicated to the famous lady of the Nightingale Theater; the Miner's Room is named in honor of all the men who left their native homes in search of fortunes and were the first to settle in the area, and the Beth Parkinson Suite serves as a tribute to the previous owner of the house.

A gourmet breakfast is served on antique china and silver pieces of the era. The antique-filled dining room is available for meals, or room service is provided if you prefer.

### Idaho City Hotel
Corner of Montgomery and Walulla
208/392-4290

In 1929, the Idaho City Hotel was a boarding house run by Mrs. Mary Smith. Since that time it has been completely renovated to retain its quaint charm and rustic flavor. Five guest rooms are available. The hotel has a wonderful wraparound porch and a tin roof.

## 10 IDAHO FALLS

A spectacular waterfall provides the scenic centerpiece for Idaho Falls, a growing city surrounded by gold and green croplands and rustic barns.

This community of 50,000 people is further blessed by 39 parks ranging from small corner parks, where business people stop to chat and eat lunch, to large parks such as Tautphaus Park which houses a nationally renowned zoo.

The Rotary International Peach Park located along the greenbelt features granite lanterns, gifts to the city from its sister city in Japan.

**Cross Country Store**
4035 Yellowstone Hwy.
208/529-0766

**Antique Gallery**
341 W. Broadway St.
208/523-3906

**Scavenger Shop**
202 1st St.
208/523-7862

**A Street Village**
548 Shoup Ave.
208/528-0300

**Country Store Boutique**
4523 E. Rire Hwy.
208/522-8450

## 11 JEROME

**Frontier Antiques**
149 W. Main St.
208/324-1127

**Antiques & Things**
137 E. Main St.
208/324-8549

**Vintage Vantities**
921 S. First St.
208/324-3067

**Rose Antique Mall**
130 E. Main St.
208/324-2918

## 12 KELLOGG

Driving east on I-90 from Coeur d'Alene, you'll find yourself in the Silver Valley, the largest silver producing area in the world and a bonanza for history buffs.

Silver Valley has been transformed not once but twice, first by the ambition and sacrifice of intrepid miners. Today, Kellogg offers different treasures—a Bavarian-theme village, murals, statues, a mining museum, and unique events.

**Willow's Antiques**
119 McKinley Ave.
208/556-1022

## 13 KETCHUM-SUN VALLEY

### Antique Peddlers' Fairs
Location: Warm Spring Resort
208/344-6133
*Directions: At the base of Bald Mountain*
Call for specific dates

**Antiques Etc.**
431 Walnut Ave. N.
208/726-5332

**Legacy Antiques & Imports**
491 10th St.
208/726-1655

**Polly Noe Antiques**
471 Leadville Ave. N.
208/726-3663

**Angel Wings**
320 Leadville Ave. N.
208/726-8708

**Charles Stuhlberg Gallery**
511 East Ave. N.
208/726-4568

## 14 LEWISTON

**Bargain Hunter Mall**
1209 Main St.
208/746-6808

**Somewhere in Time**
628 Main St.
208/746-7160

**Marsh's**
1105 36th St. N.
208/743-5778

**Yesturdays Antiques & Florist**
925 Preston Ave.
208/743-0345

## 15 MOSCOW

**Second Hand/First Hand**
107 S. Main St.
208/882-5642

**Bill's Antiques**
5010 Harden Road
208/882-4812

**Now & Then**
321 E. Palouse River Dr.
208/882-7886

## 16 NAMPA

### Old Towne Antique Mall-Coffee House
1212 1st St. S.
208/463-4555
Mon.-Sat., 10-6; Sun. 10-3 (seasonal)
Coffee House: Mon.-Fri. 8-6; Sat. 10-6; Sun. 10-3 (seasonal)
*Directions: Traveling I-84 Exit 36. Travel south on Franklin Blvd. to stop sign. Turn right on 11th Ave. Drive approximately 1 ½ miles, then under railroad overpass. Immediately turn left on 1st St. south at light. Located 1 and ½ blocks on left (Historic Downtown). We are 25 miles east of Boise, Idaho.*

Located in historic downtown Nampa, Old Towne Antique Mall is more than just an antique shop. It has a coffee shop inside serving delicious espresso. The dealers who display their wares are usually on hand to answer any questions you may have.

A wide variety of merchandise is available such as nostalgic paper goods, vintage clothing, china, pottery, along with a complete line of furnishings from early country to Victorian to depression.

**Yesteryear Shoppe**
1211 1st St. S.
208/467-3581

**Victorian Shoppe**
911 12th Ave. S.
208/465-7565

**Village Square Antiques**
1309 2nd St. S.
208/467-2842

## 17 PAYETTE

**Lambsville Collectibles**
101 S. 16th St., Hwy. 95
208/642-1727

**Yesterdays Cupboard**
220 N. Main St.
208/642-3711

## 18 PIONEER HISTORIC BYWAY

Southeast Idaho's Pioneer Historic Byway gives motorists a nostalgic glimpse, through rustic ranches and roadside communities, of a West long past. The route begins in Franklin, Idaho's oldest white settlement, and retraces the steps of Idaho's earliest pioneers. Franklin's center is now designated by the state as a historic district, and two buildings are on the National Historic Register—the Franklin Co-op Building built in the 1860s, and the Hatch home, a classic of pioneer architecture.

Nearby are the remnants of Idaho's first flour mill and one of the oldest homes in the state, a two-story edifice built almost entirely of rock.

After passing through the rustic town of Preston, you'll come to the Bear River Massacre Site, now a national landmark. More Indians were killed here in one battle than in any other in the United States.

The byway continues on to Montpelier, home of the fascinating Rails and Trails Historical Museum. Just south of Montpelier is the small town of Paris. The Romanesque Mormon Tabernacle, complete with intricate wood ceilings and stone carvings, was built in 1889 of red sandstone snow-sledded to Paris from a quarry 18 miles away.

Between Montpelier and the Utah border, Butch Cassidy made a quick but impressive visit by robbing the local bank.

Another astounding drive is the Bear Lake-Caribou Scenic Byway running through Paris. It begins on Highway 89 at the Utah state border and passes mammoth Bear Lake.

The Scenic Byway continues at Montpelier on Highway 30 and at Soda Springs on Highway 34. The drive, in its entirety from the Utah border to the Wyoming border, is 111 miles or 2 ½ hours. Along the way are numerous attractions—Bear Lake State Park, the Paris Museum, the Cache National Forest, the Caribou Forest, the carbonated waters and spouting geysers of Soda Springs and the Blackfoot Reservoir.

## 19 PRIEST RIVER

**Mercer's Memories**
221 Main St.
208/448-1781

**Joodle Bug's**
120 Wisconsin
208/448-2442

## 20 REXBURG

North of Idaho Falls on Highway 20 is the historic and charming town of Rexburg, home to several diverse and noteworthy attractions.

Just a block off Main St. you'll find a gray stone Tabernacle now listed on the National Register of Historic Places. At Porter Park is the only restored authentic wooden carousel in Idaho.

But Rexburg is probably best known for a nearby, unusual tourist site: a dam which collapsed in June 1976, dumping eight billion gallons of roaring flood water into the unsuspecting valley below. A visit to the dam site on the Teton River will give you an idea of the power that was unleashed. An understanding of the flood's effect on local people, and their ability to rebuild their fertile valley, can be gained at a unique museum outside Rexburg.

Rexburg is also home to the Idaho International Folk Dance Festival. The week-long event features dance groups from around the world. Dancers and musicians gather here from Europe, Asia, South America and the south Pacific to share the vibrant and expressive spirit of their homelands. Perhaps no other event in Idaho boasts such international flavor. The dancing begins July 26th and concludes August 3rd each year.

**Country Keepsakes**
12 E. Main St.
208/359-1234

**Mainstreet Antiques Mall**
52 E. Main St.
208/356-5002

## 21 SANDPOINT

**Antique Arcade**
119 N. 1st Ave.
208/265-5421

**Antique Collective**
504 W. Oak St.
208/263-6499

### *Great Places To Stay*

**Angel of the Lake Bed & Breakfast**
410 Railroad Ave.
1-800-872-0816

A century ago Sandpoint's first mayor built a beautiful home on the shores of Lake Pend Oreille in North Idaho. Today this very special place is a step back in time as you feel the romance of another era. Take a short scenic walk to the many shops and restaurants in downtown Sandpoint or a leisurely stroll along the lake. In winter, world class Schweitzer Mountain, rated 7th in North America, is a 20 minute drive away.

**Schweitzer Mountain Bed and Breakfast**
110 Crystal Court
1-888-550-8080

Even if you're not a skier, there's something very cool about staying at a mountain resort. The first thing you notice about the new bed and breakfast at Schweitzer - the only on-mountain bed and breakfast - is the silence. At night, it's interrupted only by the sound of the wind or the occasional rumbling of a snowplow. With the lack of noise, getting a good night's sleep is a cinch. It also makes it easy to concentrate on a good book, if you opt not to battle the elements on the ski hill. The Schweitzer Mountain Bed and Breakfast sits high on the mountain, at the end of a road that at certain times of the year is accessible only by four-wheel drive. Or, it might be reached by a determined driver of a front-wheel drive. The feeling of being up where the birds fly only increases after you climb the stairs to the guest quarters on the third and fourth floor of the 5,000 sq. ft. gorgeously decorated home. There are five rooms, all with private baths, all named for the area's ski runs. A "must" stay over on your antique trail.

## 22 SILVER CITY

Silver City, high in the Owyhee Mountains, is an evocative ghost town chock-full of historic buildings and atmosphere. This "Queen of Idaho Ghost Towns" appears just as she was during her boom times with over 70 rustic buildings remaining intact.

## 23 TWIN FALLS

The Oregon Trail pioneers, who trudged through South Central Idaho on their way to Oregon, would be astounded at the sight of present day Twin Falls. Poised near the edge of spectacular Snake River Canyon, the city is the commercial center of scenic Magic Valley, one of America's most productive agricultural areas.

Driving down inside the canyon is an experience, a world apart from the terrain high above. The Perrine Bridge spanning the canyon is 1,500 feet long and 486 breathtaking feet above the river. This is the location of Evil Knievel's attempted jump across the canyon in a rocket cycle.

In town are two museums of note. The Herrett Museum on the College of Southern Idaho campus has in its collection over 3,000 North and Central Native American artifacts, ranging from 12,000-year-old relics to contemporary Hopi Kachina Dolls.

**Anne Tiques Etc.**
325 Main Ave. E.
208/736-0140

**Second Time Around**
689 Washington St. N.
208/734-6008

**Snow's Antiques & Sleigh Works**
136 Main Ave. N.
208/736-7292

**Treasures from the Past**
227 Main Ave. E.
208/733-2976

**Back Door Antiques**
195 Washington St. N.
208/733-7639

**Every Blooming Thing**
266 Blue Lakes Blvd.
208/733-8322

**Dudley Studio**
1062 Blue Lakes Blvd.
208/733-7110

## 24 WALLACE

**The Wallace Corner**
525 Cedar St.
208/753-6141

**Wallace Antiques**
506 Bank St.
208/752-2011

### *Great Places To Stay*

**Beale House Bed and Breakfast**
107 Cedar St.
1-888-752-7151

For specific information see review at the beginning of this section.

**The Jameson**
304 6th St.
208/556-1554

For specific information see review at the beginning of this section.

# Illinois

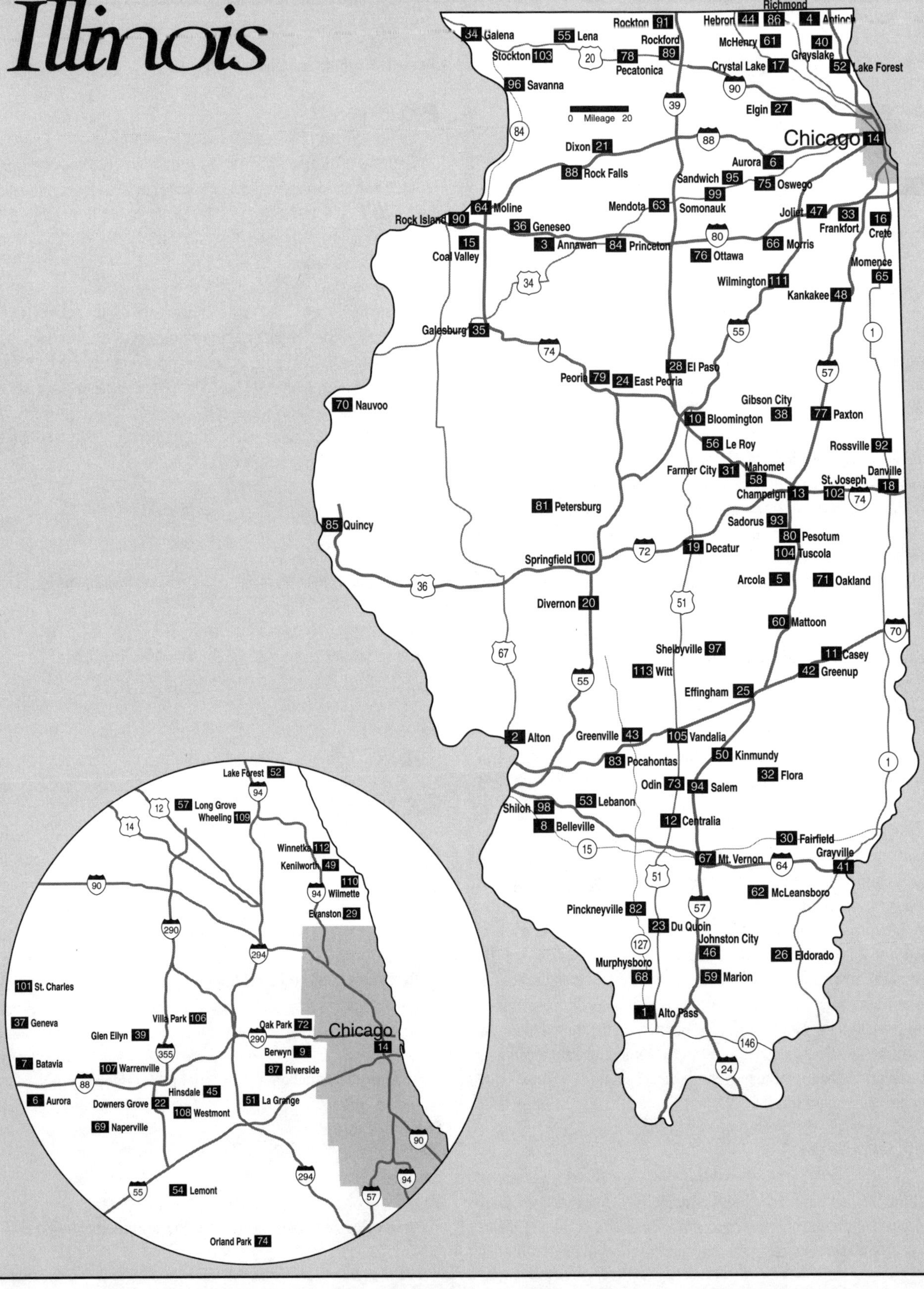

34 Galena
55 Lena
Rockton 91
Rockford 89
Hebron 44
86
Richmond
4 Antioch
McHenry 61
40 Grayslake
Stockton 103
78 Pecatonica
Crystal Lake 17
52 Lake Forest
96 Savanna
Elgin 27
0 Mileage 20
Chicago 14
Dixon 21
Aurora 6
88 Rock Falls
Sandwich 95
75 Oswego
99 Somonauk
Mendota 63
64 Moline
Rock Island 90
36 Geneseo
Joliet 47
33 Frankfort
16 Crete
15 Coal Valley
3 Annawan
84 Princeton
76 Ottawa
66 Morris
Momence 65
Wilmington 111
Kankakee 48
Galesburg 35
28 El Paso
Peoria 79
24 East Peoria
70 Nauvoo
Gibson City 38
10 Bloomington
77 Paxton
56 Le Roy
Rossville 92
Farmer City 31
Mahomet 58
Danville 18
Champaign 13
St. Joseph 102
81 Petersburg
85 Quincy
Sadorus 93
80 Pesotum
Springfield 100
19 Decatur
104 Tuscola
Arcola 5
71 Oakland
Divernon 20
60 Mattoon
Shelbyville 97
11 Casey
42 Greenup
113 Witt
Effingham 25
2 Alton
Greenville 43
105 Vandalia
83 Pocahontas
50 Kinmundy
32 Flora
Odin 73
94 Salem
Shiloh 98
53 Lebanon
8 Belleville
12 Centralia
30 Fairfield
67 Mt. Vernon
Grayville 41
62 McLeansboro
Pinckneyville 82
23 Du Quoin
Johnston City 46
26 Eldorado
Murphysboro 68
59 Marion
1 Alto Pass
Lake Forest 52
57 Long Grove
Wheeling 109
Winnetka 112
Kenilworth 49
110 Wilmette
Evanston 29
101 St. Charles
37 Geneva
Villa Park 106
Glen Ellyn 39
Oak Park 72
Chicago 14
Berwyn 9
7 Batavia
107 Warrenville
87 Riverside
Hinsdale 45
6 Aurora
Downers Grove 22
51 La Grange
108 Westmont
69 Naperville
54 Lemont
Orland Park 74

# Findings of Geneva:

## In the midst of a beautiful downtown, you'll discover rare and precious books, china, fancy table and bed linens, collectable art, toys and more

"Findings" has been open approximately 2 years at the busy intersection of Route 38 (State St.) and Third St., in Geneva's beautiful downtown shopping district. It is owned by Marv and Jan Barishman, who operate it on a daily basis; from 10:30 to 6 p.m. Tuesday through Saturday, 12 to 5 p.m. on Sunday, and closed on Mondays.

> "The customer is always dealing with the owners in this shop, and has an opportunity to source information, as well as friendly discussion surrounding the items displayed here."

The shop has become well known for its finer and unusual older books, covering a wide range of collectable topics. Sharing the spotlight is collectable glass, pottery, sterling and finer linens. It is not unusual to find prints hanging on the walls done by collected artists; as well as a wide selection of older postcards, world's fair items, paper collectibles, magazines, pocket knives, and toys.

The customer is always dealing with the owners in this shop, and has an opportunity to source information, as well as friendly discussion surrounding the items displayed here. Buying and selling items is a daily occurence in this old-fashioned environment, and one can hear a pleasant interchange of price negotiating during many of the purchase and sale transactions. The store is actively buying many items regularly. The most sought-after items are pre-1900 leather bound and "marbelized" books, fancy cutwork tablecloths, whitework bed linens, table scarves and damask napkins. Active buying is always taking place in Franciscan Pottery's "Desert Rose," "Ivy" and "Apple" dinnerware; Hall China's "Crocus" pattern, and McCoy Pottery, Fostoria, Heisey, and Cambridge glass; and illustrated children's books like "Little Black Sambo" and those illustrated by N.C. Wyeth or Jessie Wilcox Smith.

*Findings of Geneva is located at 307 W. State St. (Rte. 38) in Geneva. For additional information see listing #37 (Geneva).*

## 1 ALTO PASS

### Austin's of Alto Pass
Route 127 and Alton Pass Road
618/893-2206
Sat., 10-5; Sun., 1-5; other times, call for appointment.
*Directions: Alto Pass, Ill., is located on Illinois Hwy. 127. Travel 16 miles south from Murphysboro, Ill., or 8 miles north from Jonesboro, Ill., on Hwy. 127. To reach Alto Pass from Carbondale, Ill., take Route 51 south to Makanda Road; turn right; then make a quick left onto Old Hwy. 51 South. Travel approximately 5 miles to Alto Pass Road and turn right to stop sign at Skyline Dr. Turn right onto Skyline and follow through town to old grade school building on the left.*

This one-owner shop is located in a beautifully restored brick grade school built in 1927. A large selection of hand- picked, restored furniture and lots of unusual old wares are available to the discriminating shopper.

## 2 ALTON

**Gabriel's Old Post Office Mall**
300 Alby St.
618/462-8204

**Dormann's Gifts & Interiors**
330 Alby St.
618/462-2654

**Alton Landing Framery**
100 Alton St.
618/465-1996

**Alton Landing Antiques**
110 Alton St.
618/462-0443

**1900's Antiques Co.**
7 E. Broadway
618/465-2711

**Prairie Peddler**
200 State St.
618/465-6114

**Carol's Corner/Frank's Steins**
16 E. Broadway
618/465-2606

**Cane Bottom My Just Desserts**
31 E. Broadway
618/462-5881

**Cracker Factory Mini Mall**
203 E. Broadway (2nd Floor)
618/466-9008

**Thames on Broadway**
205 E. Broadway (Lower Floor)
618/462-1337

**Country Meadows**
207 E. Broadway
618/465-1965

**Antiques & Collectibles**
301 E. Broadway
618/462-3656

**Simple Treasures**
301 E. Broadway
618/462-3003

**Jim's Attic**
301 E. Broadway
618/463-7699

**River Bend Replicas**
301 E. Broadway
618/462-8206

**The Second Reading**
301 E. Broadway
618/462-2361

**Unusual Place**
301 E. Broadway Ave.
618/474-2128

**Wildwood**
301 E. Broadway
618/465-4012

**Mississippi Mud Pottery**
310 E. Broadway
618/462-7573

**Granny's Time**
319 Broadway
618/462-5440

**Jack's Cllbls./Jeanne's Jewels**
319 Broadway
618/463-0451

**Heartland Antiques**
321 E. Broadway
618/465-6363

**Jan's Antiques**
323 E. Broadway
618/465-2250

**Steve's Antiques**
323 E. Broadway
618/465-7407

**Sloan's Antiques**
401 E. Broadway
618/463-0808

**Alton Antique Center**
401 E. Broadway (Lower)
618/463-0888

**Old Bridge Antique Mall**
435 E. Broadway
618/463-9907

**Rubenstein's Antiques**
724-26 E. Broadway
618/465-1306

**Debbie's Decorative Antiques**
108 George & Broadway
618/465-6018

**River Winds**
117 Market St.
618/465-8981

## 3 ANNAWAN

### Annawan Antique Alley
309 North Canal St.
309/935-6220
(Jan.-March; Mon.-Sat. 10-5, Sun. 12-4) (April-Dec.; Mon.-Sat. 9-5:30, Sun.s 12-4)
*Directions: From Interstate 80, take Exit 33. Go south on Illinois 78. The first left driveway (about 1 block from Exit 33).*

Tucked away in the quiet, small town of Annawan, Ill., the Annawan Antique Alley adopted its name from its former life as a bowling alley. Located just one block from I-80 the "alley" is a convenient "antique stop." This multi-dealer antique mall offers furnishings, quilts, Tiffany and Tiffany-style lamps, statuary, and a lot more of the items you would expect to find in a quality antique mall.

## 4 ANTIOCH

**Green Bench Antiques**
924 Main St.
847/838-2643

**Collection Connection**
400 Lake St.
847/395-8800

**Antioch Antique Mall**
42189 N. Lake Ave.
847/395-0000

**Williams Brothers Emporium**
910 Main St.
847/838-2767

**Park Avenue Antique Mall**
345 Park Ave.
847-838-1624

## 5 ARCOLA

**Green Barn Antiques**
111 N. Locust St.
217/268-4754

**Emporium Antiques**
201 E. Main St.
217/268-4523

## 6 AURORA

**Treasures Old & New**
355 E. End Trail
630/896-0161

**Peddler Showcase**
566 Parker Ave.
630/851-4200

## 7 BATAVIA

**Yesterdays**
115 S. Batavia Ave.
630/406-0524

**Savery Antiques**
14 N. Washington
630/879-6825

**Just Good Olde Stuff Inc.**
8 E. Wilson St.
630/879-2815

**Kenyon & Co.**
215 E. Wilson St.
630/406-0665

**Village Antiques**
416 E. Wilson St.
630/406-0905

## 8 BELLEVILLE

**Antiques & Things**
704 N. Douglas Ave.
618/236-1104

**Traditional Manor**
1101 N. Illinois St.
618/235-4683

**Eagle Collectibles Inc.**
22 E. Main St.
618/257-1283

**Belleville Antique Mall**
208 E. Main St.
618/234-6255

**Ben's Antique Mall**
225 E. Main St.
618/234-0904

## 9 BERWYN

**BBMM Antiques**
6710 Cermak Road
708/749-1465

**Silver Swan Antiques**
6738 16th St.
708/484-7177

**Antique Treasure Chest**
6746 16th St.
708/749-1910

**Past Time Antiques**
7100 16th St.
708/788-4804

**Josie's Antiques & Collectibles**
2135 Wisconsin Ave.
708/788-3820

## 10 BLOOMINGTON

**Bloomington Antique Mall**
102 N. Center St.
309/828-1211

**Antique Mart/Joce Williams Inc.**
907 S. Eldorado Road
309/662-4213

**A Gridley Antiques**
217 E. Front St.
309/829-9615

### *Great Places To Stay*

**The Burr House**
210 E. Chestnut St.
1-800-449-4182

A Civil War Era brick home constructed in 1864, situated near downtown Bloomington in central Illinois, the Burr House B&B is located in the city's Historic District across from Franklin Park. Six rooms are available, including one suite with a private bath and sitting room, three rooms with private bath and two with a shared bath. The home has three marble fireplaces, ornate plaster ceilings, inlaid wood floors and a formal dining room where breakfast is served. A variety of stately trees and an outdoor private terrace is all surrounded by a wrought iron fence. Attractions within walking distance include antique shops, fine dining, retail shops and the communities museum and historic sites.

## 11 CASEY

**Perisho's Antiques**
104 E. Colorado Ave.
217/932-4493

## 12 CENTRALIA

**Kim Logan**
1829 Gragg St.
618/532-8495

**Lofty Affair**
Walnut Hill Road
618/532-0186

**Cedar House Antiques & Collectibles**
I-57 & Hwy. 161 (Exit 109)
618-533-0399

**J & M Resales**
1180 Medlin Road
618/532-6031

## 13 CHAMPAIGN

**First St. Antiques**
206 S. 1st St.
217/359-3079

**Good Time Antiques**
1519 N. Highland Ave.
217/359-6234

**Carrie's**
204 N. Neil St.
217/352-3231

**Partners In Time Antiques**
311 S. Neil St.
217/352-2016

**Capricorn Antiques**
720 S. Neil St.
217/351-6914

**Gray's Antiques & Collectibles**
723 S. Neil St.
217/351-9079

**Vintage Antiques**
117 N. Walnut St.
217/359-8747

## 14 CHICAGO

### Salvage One Architectural Artifacts

1524 South Sangamon St.
312/733-0098
Tues.-Sat. 10-5, Sun. 11-4
*Directions: From O'Hare Airport, downtown Chicago, north and west Suburbs, take Dan Ryan Expressway, 90/94 east; exit 18th St. Exit and turn right (west); right (north) on Halsted; left (west) on 16th St.; go three blocks and right (north) on Sangamon St. From Midway, Indiana, Michigan, and South Chicago, take Dan Ryan Expressway 90/94 West; exit Canalport/Cermak Road Exit; proceed north on access road (Ruble St.); left (west) on 16th St., go five blocks and right (north) on Sangamon St.*

Salvage One was founded in 1980 and purchased in 1986 by Leslie Hindman Auctioneers, the Midwest's leading auction house. It has since grown to be the largest architectural salvage company in the country. "Today the popularity of using salvaged architectural materials is not limited to people restoring vintage homes or even choosing to construct a historically accurate design. The vast majority of people buying architectural elements are adding them to enhance their homes or surroundings," says Anne McGahan, of Salvage One.

The staff at Salvage One travels the continent in search of the finest architectural treasures available. At the time of this printing the group had purchased a stunning collection of 13, 14th-century Italian pink marble columns and capitals, a late 17th-century Chinese pottery water carrier, an early French pine butcher's table, a pair of cast iron garden urns with elaborate rococo designs and a Chinese teakwood lantern with hand-painted glass panels.

Salvage One offers over 6,000 interior and exterior doors, an enormous selection of vintage hardware, stained, leaded and beveled glass windows and doors, garden ornaments, fabricated furniture, bathroom fixtures, lighting, and one of the nation's largest inventories of period American and Continental fireplace mantels and accessories, acquired from across the U.S., England, and France.

Brochures, photographs, condition reports and worldwide shipping are available for Salvage One customers.

**Turtle Creek Antiques**
850 W. Armitage Ave.
773/327-2630

**Daniels Antiques**
3711 N. Ashland Ave.
773/868-9355

**Ray's Antiques**
1821 W. Belmont Ave.
773/348-5150

**Armitage Antique Gallery**
1529 W. Armitage Ave.
773/227-7727

**Lincoln Antique Mall**
3141 N. Lincoln Ave.
773/244-1440

**Antique House**
1832 W. Belmont Ave.
773-327-0707

**S & F Johnson Antiques**
1901 W. Belmont Ave.
773/477-9243

**Kristina Maria Antiques**
1919 W. Belmont Ave.
773/472-2445

**Phil's Antique Mall**
2040 W. Belmont Ave.
773/528-8549

**Father Time Antiques**
2108 W. Belmont Ave.
773/880-5599

**Good Old Days**
2138 W. Belmont Ave.
773/472-8837

**Belmont Antique Mall West**
2229 W. Belmont Ave.
773/871-3915

**Quality Antiques & Gifts**
6401 N. Caldwell Ave.
312/631-1134

**Wrigleyville Antique Mall**
3336 N. Clark St.
773/868-0285

**Camden Passage Antiques Mkt**
5309 N. Clark St.
773/989-0111

**Michael Fleming Antiques**
5221 N. Damen Ave.
773/561-8696

**Wallner's Antiques**
1229 W. Diversey Pkwy.
773/248-6061

**Stanley Antiques**
3489 N. Elston Ave.
773/588-4269

**Aged Experience Antiques**
2034 N. Halsted St.
773/975-9790

**Hyde-N-Seek Antiques**
5211 S. Harper Ave., #D
773/684-8380

**Portals Limited**
230 W. Huron St.
312/642-1066

**Tompkins & Robandt**
220 W. Kinzie St., 4th Floor
312/645-9995

**Nineteen Thirteen**
1913 W. Belmont Ave.
773/404-9522

**Belmont Antique Mall**
2039 W. Belmont Ave.
773/549-9270

**House of Nostalgia**
2047 W. Belmont Ave.
773/244-6460

**Danger City**
2129 W. Belmont Ave.
773/871-1420

**Kaye's Antiques**
2147 W. Belmont Ave.
773/929-8187

**Olde Chicago Antiques**
2336 W. Belmont Ave.
773/935-1200

**Stanley Galleries Antiques**
2118 N. Clark St.
773/281-1614

**Acorn Antiques & Uniques Ltd.**
5241 N. Clark St.
773/506-9100

**Collectables On Clybourn**
2503 N. Clybourn
773/871-1154

**Shop Front Antiques**
5223 N. Damen Ave.
773/271-5130

**International Antiques**
2300 W. Diversey Ave.
773/227-2400

**Pilsen Gallery Arch**
540 W. 18th St.
312/829-2827

**Silver Moon**
3337 N. Halsted St.
773/883-0222

**Sandwich Antiques Market**
1510 N. Hoyne Ave.
773/227-4464

**Antiques Centre at Kinzie Square**
220 W. Kinzie St.
312/464-1946

**Griffins & Gargoyles Ltd.**
2140 W. Lawrence Ave.
773/769-1255

**Haily's Antiques & Collectibles**
5508 W. Lawrence Ave.
773/202-0555

**Steve Starr Studios**
2779 N. Lincoln Ave.
773/525-6530

**Urban Artifacts**
2928 N. Lincoln Ave.
773/404-1008

**Red Eye**
3050 N. Lincoln Ave.
773/975-2020

**Gene Douglas Antiques**
3419 N. Lincoln Ave.
773/561-4414

**Lake View Antiques**
3422 N. Lincoln Ave.
773/935-6443

**Benkendorf Antique Clocks**
900 N. Michigan Ave.
312/951-1903

**U.S. #1 Antique**
1509 N. Milwaukee Ave.
773/489-9428

**Crossings Antiques Mall**
1805 W. 95th St.
773/881-3140

**Malcolm Franklin Inc.**
34 E. Oak St.
312/337-0202

**David McClain Antiques**
2716 W. 111th St.
773/239-4683

**Decoro**
224 E. Ontario St.
312/943-4847

**Architectural Artifacts Inc.**
4325 N. Ravenswood Ave.
773/348-0622

**Garrett Galleries**
1155 N. State St.
312/944-6325

**Sara Breiel Designs**
449 N. Wells St.
312/923-9223

**Pimlico Antiques Ltd.**
500 N. Wells St.
312/245-9199

**Gibell's & Bits**
5512 W. Lawrence Ave.
773/283-4065

**Time Well**
2780 N. Lincoln Ave.
773/549-2113

**Chicago Antique Center**
3045 N. Lincoln Ave.
773/929-0200

**Harlon's Antiques**
3058 N. Lincoln Ave.
773/327-3407

**Zigzag**
3419 N. Lincoln Ave.
773/525-1060

**Lincoln Ave. Antique Co-op**
3851 N. Lincoln Ave.
773/935-6600

**Antiques on the Ave.**
104 S. Michigan Ave., 2nd Floor
312/357-2800

**Modern Times**
1538 N. Milwaukee Ave.
773/772-8871

**Little Ladies**
6217 N. Northwest Hwy.
773/631-3602

**Russell's Antiques**
2404 W. 111 St.
773/233-3205

**Therese Chez Antiques**
3120 W. 111th St.
773/881-0824

**Time Square Ltd.**
6352 S. Pulaski Road
773/581-8216

**Gallery 1945**
300 N. State
312/573-1945

**First Arts & Antiques**
7220 W. Touhy Ave.
312/774-5080

**Rita-Bucheit Ltd.**
449 N. Wells St.
312/527-4080

**O'Hara's Gallery**
707 N. Wells St.
312/751-1286

**Chicago Riverfront Antique Market**
2929 N. Western Ave.
773/252-2500

**Penn Dutchman Antiques**
4912 N. Western Ave.
773/271-2208

**Memories & More**
10143 S. Western Ave.
773/238-5645

**Grich Antiques**
10857 S. Western Ave.
773/233-8734

**An Antique Store**
1450 W. Webster Ave.
773/935-6060

**Rich Oldies & Goodies**
4642 N. Western Ave.
773/334-7033

**A & R**
8024 S. Western Ave.
773/434-9157

**Cluttered Cupboard**
10332 S. Western Ave.
773/881-8803

**R J Collectibles**
11400 S. Western Ave.
773/779-8828

**Jazz'e Junque**
3831 N. Lincoln Ave.
773/472-1500

## 15 COAL VALLEY

### Country Fair Mall
504 W. 1st Ave. (Hwy. 6)
309/799-3670
Mon. & Thurs. 10-6; Tues., Fri., & Sat. 10-5; Sun. 12-5 (Closed Wed.)
*Directions: Traveling I-280 west to Exit 5B (Moline Airport) to Hwy. 6 east. Mall is 1 3/4 mile on the north side of the highway.*

No one goes away empty handed at Country Fair Mall. Kent Farley, the owner, has created a two-star attraction for antiquers. For the discriminating shopper, one location provides upscale antiques; no reproductions, no sifting through the ordinary. The second location houses 150 to 170 booths of a "Shopper's Haven." Treasure hunters should be prepared to dig!

## 16 CRETE

**Third Generation Antiques**
831 W. Exchange
708/672-3369

**Season's**
1362 Main St.
708/672-0170

**Gatherings**
1375 Main St.
708/672-9880

**Village Antiques and Lamp Shop**
595 Exchange
708/672-8980

**Woodstill's Antiques**
610 Gould St. (Beecher)
708/946-3161

**Farmer's Daughter**
1262 Lincoln St.
708/672-4588

**Indian Wheel Co.**
1366 Main St.
708/672-9612

**The Marketplace**
550 Exchange
708/672-5556

**The Finishing Touch**
563 Exchange
708/672-9520

## 17 CRYSTAL LAKE

**Way Back When Antiques**
4112 Country Club Road
815/459-1360

**Penny Lane Antiques**
6114 Lou St.
815/459-8828

**Railroad St. Market**
8316 Railroad St.
815/459-4220

**Aurora's Antiques**
8404 Railroad St.
815/455-0710

**Carriage Antiques & Collectibles**
8412 Railroad St.
815/455-0710

**Country Church Antiques**
8509 Ridgefield Road
815/477-4601

**Carriage's Antiques**
5111 E. Terra Cotta Ave.
815/356-9808

## 18 DANVILLE

**Queen Ann's Cottage**
407 Ann St.
217/443-5958

**Treasures Unique**
1327 Main St.
217/443-4280

**Bob's Antiques**
53 N Vermilion St.
217/431-3704

**Two's Company**
109 N. Vermilion St.
217/446-7553

## 19 DECATUR

**China House Antiques**
801 W. Eldorado St.
217/428-7212

**Collector's Shop**
2345 S. Mount Zion Road
217/864-3000

**Nellie's Attic Antique Mall**
3030 S. Mount Zion Road
217/864-3363

**Calliope House**
560 W. North St.
217/425-1944

### *Great Places To Stay*

**Younker House Bed and Breakfast**
500 W. Main St.
217/429-9718

The Younker House is a beautiful Victorian brick home located in the historic district of downtown Decatur. The home was once the residence of Dr. Williams Barnes, who was well known for housing the largest butterfly collection in North America. The home has won several awards for historical preservation and is on the historic register.

## 20 DIVERNON

**Lisa's I & II Antique Malls**
I-55 and Route 104
217/628-1111; 217/628-3333
Daily 10 -6, closed Thanksgiving and Christmas.

*Directions: Both Lisa's I & II Antique Malls are located on Interstate 55 at Route 104 (Exit 82), 10 miles south of Springfield, Ill.*

Promising 40,000 square feet of rambling room, these two malls exhibit a full array of antiques and collectibles. No crafts are to be found among the quality selection of antiques which includes: furniture (oak, cherry, walnut, pine, mahogany), early American, glassware, old toys, jewelry and much, much more.

If you are looking for something "large" to take home, the old Stagecoach is for you. It's quite a showpiece and it's FOR SALE! Delivery is available at Lisa's I & II (I wonder if that means the Stagecoach, too?).

**Country Place Antiques**
RR1 Frontage Road
217/628-3699

## 21 DIXON

**Brinton Ave. Antique Mall**
725 N. Brinton Ave.
815/284-4643

**Dixon Antique Station**
1220 S. Galena Ave.
815/284-8890

**E & M Antique Mall**
1602 S. Galena Ave.
815/288-1900

## 22 DOWNERS GROVE

**Mr. Chips Crystal Repair**
743 Ogden Ave.
630/964-4070

**Asbury's**
1626 Ogden Ave.
630/769-9191

**Country Cellar**
2101 Ogden Ave.
630/968-0413

## 23 DUQUOIN

**Main St. Antiques Mall**
211 E. Main
618/542-5043

**Mulberry Tree Antqs., Cllbls. & Gifts**
24 S. Mulberry St.
618/542-6621

## 24 EAST PEORIA

**Charley's**
1815 Meadows Ave.
309/694-7698

**Pleasant Hill Antique Mall**
315 S. Pleasant Hill Road
309/694-4040

**Southern Knights**
125 E. Washington St.
309/694-4581

**Cowboy Antiques**
1107 E. Washington St.
309/699-3929

**Antiques Inclusive**
2469 E. Washington St.
309/699-0624

## 25 EFFINGHAM

**Antik Haus**
915 N. Henrietta St.
217/342-4237

**Red Coach Antiques**
608 W. Fayette Ave.
217/342-6280

## 26 ELDORADO

**Eldorado Antique Mall**
935 4th St.
618/273-5586

**Little Egypt Antiques**
1212 State St.
618/273-9084

## 27 ELGIN

**Antique Corner**
475 Walnut Ave.
847/931-0310

**State St. Market**
701 N. State St.
847/695-3066

**The Antique Emporium @ The Milk Pail**
Rt. 25 ( 1/2 Mi. North of I-90–Dundee)
847/468-9667

## 28 EL PASO

**Century House Antiques**
11 & 2nd St./ I-39 Exit 14
309/527-3705

**El Paso Antique Mall**
I-39 & Rt. 24
309/527-3705

## 29 EVANSTON

**Eureka!**
705 W. Washington
847/869-9090
Tues.-Sat. 11-5
*Directions: From Chicago, take any main artery north to Evanston. Evanston is the first suburb north of Chicago along the lake. When going north or south along the Tri-State (Route 294) or on the Edens Expressway (Route 94), exit at Dempster (east). Go east 15-20 minutes to Ridge Ave. in Evanston (stoplight). Turn right (south); go 1 street past Main St. Turn left onto Washington, and go 3 blocks to 705. Located 1 block south of Main, 1 block west of Chicago Ave., 3 blocks east of Ridge.*

Now, this shop could quite possibly be a first - "No Repro's" in the way of collectibles. The owner claims "this is the best nostalgia shop in Chicagoland! Early advertising, paper ephemera, world's fair collectibles, black memorabilia, and oddball items can all be found throughout this fun shop. Men will love it!

**Harvey Antiques**
1231 Chicago Ave.
847/866-6766

**Another Time Another Place**
1243 Chicago Ave.
847/866-7170

**Pursuit of Happiness**
1524 Chicago Ave.
847/869-2040

**Sarah Bustle Antiques**
821 Dempster St.
847/869-7290

**Village Bazaar**
503 Main St.
847/866-9444

**Edward Joseph Antiques**
520 Main St.
847/332-1855

**Rusty Nail**
912 1/2 Sherman Ave.
847/491-0360

## 30 FAIRFIELD

**Riverside Antiques**
Hwy. 15 E.
618/842-3570

**Robinson's Antiques**
Route 15
618/842-3626

**Dickey's Antiques**
Hwy. 15 E., Rt. 5
618/842-2820

**La Jean's Country Antiques**
U.S. 45 S.
618/847-4525

## 31 FARMER CITY

**Main St. Antiques**
115 S. Main St.
309/928-9208

**Margaret's Attic to Basement**
117 S. Main St.
309/928-3023

**Salt Creek Emporium**
120 Main St.
309/928-2844

**Farmer City Antiques Center**
201 S. Main St.
309/928-9210

**Renaissance Art Studio**
211 S. Main St.
309/928-2213

**The Junction**
E. Rt 150 & 54
309/928-3116

## 32 FLORA

**Eileen's Antiques**
526 E. Fourth St.
618/662-6171

**Wallace Antiques**
504 E. North Ave.
618/662-8252

## 33 FRANKFORT

**Antiques Unique**
100 Kansas St.
815/469-2741

**The Trolley Barn**
11 S. White St.
815/464-1120

## 34 GALENA

*Directions: From Chicago, travel I-90 (Northwest Tollway) to U.S. 20 at Rockford. Follow U.S. 20 west to Galena: also from Chicago, take I-88 to I-39. Travel I-39 north to U.S. 20 at Rockford. Go U.S. 20 west to Galena.*

Once mired in decay and forgotten river routes, Galena, Illinois, has been revived. Some of America's most enticing countryside surrounds this small town of historic manor houses, handsome brick mercantile and business buildings, and churches accented with the craft and love shown in hand-carved altars and pulpits. The enchanting qualities of Galena are echoed in the fact that many leading Chicago CEOs have chosen to retire to this spot.

Galena and Jo Daviess County swell with more than 50 antique shops (making this the main Midwestern antiquing center), 50 bed and breakfasts, 12 galleries, 25 private studios, along with 150 specialty shops. Billed and living up to fame, Galena is one of the most popular destinations in the Midwest. Weekends find bed and breakfasts booked, so travelers should make reservations early. November and March are the only reliably slow months during the year.

**Glick Antiques**
112 N. Main St.
815/777-0781

**Reds Antiques & Collectibles**
11658 W. Red Gates Road
815/777-9675

**Hawk Hollow**
103 S Main St.
815/777-3616

**Galena Shoppe**
109 Main St.
815/777-3611

**My Favorite Things**
116 S. Main St.
815/777-3340

**Touch-Banowetz Antiques**
117 S. Main St.
815/777-3370

**Karen's**
209 S. Main St.
815/777-0911

**Cedar Chest**
213 S. Main St.
815/777-9235

**Sparrow**
220 S. Main St.
815/777-3060

**J G Accent Unlimited**
221 S. Main St.
815/777-9550

**Village Merchantile**
225 S. Main St.
815/777-0065

**Beneath The Dust**
302 S. Main St.
815/777-3202

**Tin-Pan Alley**
302 S. Main St.
815/777-2020

**EGK Collectibles**
305 S. Main St.
815/777-0180

**Belle Epoque**
306 S. Main St.
815/777-2367

**Crickets**
404 S. Main St.
815/777-6176

**A Peace of the Past**
408 S. Main St.
815/777-2737

**Galena Antique Mall**
8201 State Route 20 W.
815/777-3440

***Great Places To Stay***

### Avery Guest House Bed & Breakfast
606 S. Prospect St.
815/777-3883

This 1848 Pre Civil War home is beautifully decorated in period decor. It was once owned by Major George Avery who served with General Grant during the Civil War. Located just two and one half blocks from Galena's Historic Main St.

### Bielenda's Mars Ave. Guest Home
515 Mars Ave.
815/777-2808

The Bielenda's Mar Ave. Guest House was built in 1855 in the Federal style by J. C. Packard, owner of the town's dry good store. During 1930 the home served as Maybelle's Tea Room (first tea room in town). The three guest rooms are large with queen sized beds and private baths. Relax on the porch in a swing and enjoy the scenery.

### Brierwreath Manor Bed & Breakfast
216 N. Bench St.
815/777-0608

The elegant Brierwreath Manor Bed & Breakfast is listed on the National Historic Register. The home was built in 1884 and has antique furnishings to reflect that era. The Mayor's Room, named for former mayor Frank Einsweiler, who once owned the home, is a rose colored two room suite with gas log fireplace. The Heirloom Suite is a Victorian splendor featuring two beds and a claw-foot tub.

### Craig Cottage
505 Dewey Ave.
815/777-1461

'Craig Cottage', named after Captain Nathan Boone Craig (who married Daniel Boone's granddaughter) built this brick and limestone house in 1827. It has since been restored and featured in *Country Living* magazine, Hallmark Christmas cards and tour of homes for Galena. The house is very quaint, private, peaceful and well equipped. It overlooks a wooded valley and is within walking distance of Historic Galena.

### Park Ave. Guest House
208 Park Ave.
1-800-359-0743

This Queen Ann Victorian "Painted Lady" features original ornate woodwork, pocket doors, transoms, 12 foot ceilings, and an open staircase. Three guest rooms feature private baths, queen-sized beds, fireplaces, and antique decor. During the summer, enjoy the extensive perennial gardens alongside a unique gazebo, or sip a cool drink on the screened wrap-around porch. Experience an old fashioned opulent Christmas - you'll find a miniature Dickens Village with over seventy houses, twelve full sized trees, and yards of beautiful garlands with while lights glowing softly. Take a short stroll to Grant Park or across the footbridge to Main St. where you'll find plenty of shopping and fine restaurants.

**Victorian Mansion**
301 S. High St.
1-888-815-6768

Higher Ground Victorian Mansion is an elegant Italianate Victorian home set amidst an acre of trees and gardens. Accommodations include eight bedrooms with beautiful ornate Victorian beds and marble topped dressers. All bedrooms have a private bath and two have marble fireplaces. Relaxing comes easily in two large parlors and library with a fireplace. The music parlor has a turn-of-the century Victrola and an antique pump organ. Old time movies are availabe in the TV/movie parlor. A full breakfast is served in a lovely dining room that seats fourteen people around four tables. The Mansion is located on a hilltop which provides a commanding view of the countryside from the second floor porch. Downtown Historic Galena is two blocks away accessed by a flight of stairs known as the school house stairs.

### *Favorite Places To Eat*

**American Old-Fashioned Ice Cream Parlor**
102 N. Main St.
815/777-3121

An 1846 soda fountain with 50 flavors of ice cream and yogurt, sherbet, shakes, floats, sodas, sandwiches, snacks. Coke memorabilia. Trolley tickets. '50s music.

**Backstreet Steak & Chophouse**
216 S. Commerce
815/777-4800

Dinner nightly: fine steaks, pork and lamb chops, veal and seafood. BBQ ribs a speciality.

**Boone's Place**
305 S. Main
815/777-4488

Lunch and dinner daily, breakfast on weekends, in an 1846 historic building with antique decor. Full expresso bar. Specializing in "made from scratch" gourmet sandwiches, stuffed potatoes, soups, salads, homemade deep dish pie, ice cream and cheesecakes.

**Grant's Place**
515 S. Main St.
815/777-3331

Civil War theme restaurant on second floor over winery. Lunch and dinner daily. Gourmet sandwiches, seafood and steaks.

**Fried GreenTomatoes**
1031 Irish Hollow Road
815/777-3938

Upscale country Italian dining in an historic brick farmstead two miles southeast of Galena just off Blackjack Road. Black Angus steaks, chops, fresh seafood. Full bar, detailed wine list.

**Jakels' Backerei Cafe & Break Shop**
200 S. Main St.
815/777-0400

European bakery. Breakfast and lunch daily. Hearth-baked breads, Danish, tortes.

## 35 GALESBURG

**East Main Antiques**
125 E. Main St.
309/342-4424

**Hwy. Antique Shop**
224 E. Main St.
309/343-1931

**Antique Corporation**
674 E. Main St.
309/342-9448

**Attic Antique Shop**
169 E. Water St.
309/342-7956

**Galesburg Antique Mall**
349 E. Main St.
309/343-9800

**Rug Beater Antiques**
137 E. Main St.
309/343-2001

**Rail City Antiques**
665 E. Main St.
309/343-2614

**General Store Antiques**
940 E. North St.
309/342-2926

**Ziggy's Antiques**
674 E. Main St.
309/342-9448

## 36 GENESEO

**Geneseo Antique Mall**
117 E. Exchange
309/944-3777

**Heartland Antique Mall**
4169 S. Oakwood Ave.
309/944-3373

## 37 GENEVA

**Findings of Geneva Antiques**
307 W. State St. (Route 38)
630/262-0959
Email: findings g@aol.com

For specific information see review at the beginning of this section.

**A Step in the Past**
122 Hamilton St.
630/232-1611

**Geneva Antiques Ltd.**
220 S. 3rd St.
630/208-7952

**Geneva Antique Market**
227 S. 3rd St.
630/208-1150

**Fourth St. Galleries**
327 Franklin
630/208-4610

## 38 GIBSON CITY

**Wil E Makit Antiques**
305 E. 1st
217/784-4598

**Red Barn Antiques**
620 E. 11th St. (Rt. 54 & 11th)
217/784-8752

**The Silver Lion**
107 N. Sangamon
217/784-8220

## 39 GLEN ELLYN

**Patricia Lacock Antiques**
526 Crescent Blvd.
630/858-2323

**Stagecoach Antiques**
526 Crescent Blvd.
630/469-0490

**Finders Keepers**
558 Crescent Blvd.
630/469-5320

**Marcia Crosby Antiques**
477 Forest Ave.
630/858-5665

**Royal Vale View Antiques**
388 Pennsylvania Ave.
630/790-3135

**Pennsylvania Place**
535 Pennsylvania Ave.
630/858-1515

## 40 GRAYSLAKE

**Grayslake Trading Post**
116 Barron Blvd.
847/223-2166

**Yesterday Once More**
299 W. Belvidere Road
847/223-4944

**Duffy's Attic**
22 Center St.
847/223-7454

**Antique Warehouse**
2 S. Lake St.
847/223-9554

## 41 GRAYVILLE

**Antiques & More**
1 Mile N. of I-64
618/375-4331

**Prairie Town Antiques**
101 N. Main
618/375-7306

## 42 GREENUP

**Cumberland Road Collectibles**
100 W. Cumberland
217/923-5260

**Western Style Town Antique Mall**
113 E. Kentucky St.
217/923-3514

## 43 GREENVILLE

**County Seat Mall Inc.**
105 N. Third St.
618/664-8955

## 44 HEBRON

**Prairie Ave. Antiques**
9936 Main St.
815/648-4507

**Hebron Antique Gallery**
10002 Main St.
815/648-4080

**Grampy's Antique Store**
10003 Main St.
815/648-2244

**Lloyd's Antiques & Restorations**
10103 Main St.
815/648-2202

**Nancy Powers Antiques**
12017 Maple Ave. (Rt. 173)
815/648-4804

**Scarlet House**
9911 Main St.
815/648-4112

**Back In Time Antiques**
10004 Main St.
815/648-2132

**Watertower Antiques**
9937 Main St.
815/648-2287

## 45 HINSDALE

**Yankee Peddler**
6 E. Hinsdale Ave.
630/325-0085

**Aloha's Antique Jewelry**
6 W. Hinsdale Ave.
630/325-3733

**Griffin's in the Village**
16 E. 1st St.
630/323-4545

**Fleming & Simpson Antiques**
53 S. Washington St.
630/654-1890

## 46 JOHNSON CITY

**"Little Shop in the Woods"**
Corinth Road
618/982-2805

**Seagle's Creative Collectibles**
Liberty School Road
618/983-8130

**Shamrock Antiques**
306 W. Broadway
618/983-6661

**Some Things Special Antiques**
1805 Benton Ave.
618/983-8166

## 47 JOLIET

Joliet is home to four Riverboat Casinos, the historic Rialto Theatre and is situated on the Heritage Corridor of the I&M Canal that runs from Chicago to La Salle-Peru, Illinois. There are numerous restaurants in the area that run the gamut from fast food to fine dining. There are a large number of motels at the Houbolt Road and Larkin Ave. exits off of I-80 and at the Rt. 30 Exit off of I-55.

The largest and best antique show in the Midwest is the Sandwich Antiques Market, about 30 miles from Joliet. There is one show a month from May to October; you can call the Chicago office for the 1998 show dates (773/227-4464) or contact them on the internet at this address: www.antiquemarkets.com

**Uniques Antiques, Ltd.**
1006 W. Jefferson St.
815/741-2466

*Directions: Uniques Antiques, Ltd. at 1006 W. Jefferson St. in Joliet, Illinois is conveniently located near two interstates. You can reach it from I-55 at the Rt. 52 east exit 253 and go straight east for 4.8 miles; Rt. 52 is W. Jefferson St. as it goes through Joliet. You can also reach it from I-80 at the Larking Ave. N. exit 130B. Take Larkin Ave. N., turn right (east) at the 3rd stoplight and go 1.5 miles to Uniques.*

Uniques Antiques, Ltd. is a single-owner shop that has 3,000 sq. ft. of a wide variety of clean, quality, and well-displayed antiques and collectibles. Everything is guaranteed to be what it is represented as; 99% of the merchandise is 30 years old or older. The owner, Ron Steinquist, stands behind the authenticity of his merchandise. You will find everything from smalls to furniture: advertising items and signs, china, clocks, cameras, crocks, dolls, glassware, jugs, lamps, mirrors, military items, milk bottles, phonographs, pocket watches, pottery, prints, political pins, radios, sheet music, toys, telephones, vases, wristwatches from the 40s, World's Fair items, and much more. In addition there is one room of "Boys Toys" that specializes in auto-related items, hunting, fishing, etc. You can almost smell the testosterone in this room!

Special services that are available at Uniques Antiques, Ltd. are: clock and watch repair, chair caning, radio repair, and stain removal from porcelain and pottery. China repair will be available in the near future.

## 48 KANKAKEE

**Kankakee Antique Mall**
145 S. Schuyler Ave.
815/937-4957

**Bellflower Antique Shop**
397 S. Wall St.
815/935-8242

**Blue Dog Antique**
440 N. 5th Ave.
815/936-1701

**Indian Oaks Antique Mall**
N. Rt. 50 & Larry Power Road
(Bourbonnais)
815/933-9998

## 49 KENILWORTH

**Smith & Ciffon**
626 Green Bay Road
847/853-0234

**Kenilworth Antique Center**
640 Green Bay Road
847/251-8003

**Federalist Antiques**
515 Park Dr.
847/256-1791

**Indian Oaks Antique Mall**
N. Rt. 50 & L. Power Road (Bourbonnais)
815/933-9998

## 50 KINMUNDY

**Buckboard Antiques**
253 S. Madison
618/547-3731

**Lil's Antiques**
301 E. Third St.
618/547-3604

## 51 LA GRANGE

**Corner Shop**
27 Calendar Court
708/579-2425

**Patterns of the Past**
15 W. Harris Ave.
708/579-5299

**Victorian Vanities**
19 W. Harris Ave.
708/354-1865

**Rosebud Antiques**
729 W. Hillgrove Ave.
708/352-7673

**Antiques & More**
2 S. Stone Ave.
708/352-2214

**Another Time Around**
10 S. Stone Ave.
708/352-0400

## 52 LAKE FOREST

**Country House**
179 E. Deerpath Road
847/234-0244

**Lake Forest Antiquarians**
747 E. Deerpath Road
847/234-1990

**Samlesburg Hall Ltd. Antiques**
730 Forest Ave.
847/295-6070

**Spruce Antiques**
740 N. Western Ave.
847/234-1244

**Lake Forest Antique Inc.**
950 N. Western Ave.
847/234-0442

**Anna's Mostly Mahogany**
950 N. Western Ave.
847/295-9151

**On Consignment Ltd. Antiques**
207 E. Westminster Road
847/295-6070

**Snow-Gate Antiques Inc.**
234 E. Wisconsin Ave.
847/234-3450

## 53 LEBANON

**General Store Antique Mall**
112 E. St. Louis St.
618/537-8494

**The Shops at 111**
111 W. St. Louis St.
618/537-4162

**Grandma's Attic**
119 W. St. Louis St.
618/537-6730

**Mom & Me**
200 W. St. Louis St.
618/537-8343

**The Cross Eyed Elephant**
201 W. St. Louis St.
618/537-4491

**Town & Country**
205 W. St. Louis St.
618/537-6726

**Peddler Books**
209 W. St. Louis St.
618/537-4026

**And Thistle Dew**
210 W. St. Louis St.
618/537-4443

**Heritage Antiques**
218 W. St. Louis St.
618/537-2667

**Owings Antiques**
326 W. St. Louis St.
618/537-6672

## 54 LEMONT

Thirty minute southwest of Chicago, Lemont has over 40 dealers in 8 antique stops. Specialty stores display the works of local craftsmen and artisans. A cookie jar museum and historical museum are located nearby.

### ANTIQUES ON STEPHEN STREET

**Carroll & Heffron Antiques & Collectibles**
206 Stephen St.
630/257-0510
Mon.-Sat., Sun. 12-4

Proud to be a part of the little international village of Lemont, the store has an always-changing inventory of almost everything: furniture, toys, glassware, books, artwork, and more.

**Myles Antiques**
119 Stephen St.
630/243-1415
Daily 10-4

Affordable elegance with a fine selection of European and American furniture, quality home decorating accessories, and Fenton art glass. Discover treasures from the past or that special something for that special someone.

**Bittersweet Antiques & Country Accents**
111 Stephen St.
603/243-1633
Daily 10-4

Located in an 1885 Limestone building filled with country primitives, painted furniture, decoys, fishing lures and woodenware. In addition they offer antique country decorator items, candles, lamps, wreaths, silks, etc. Sourcing available to find your special "wants."

**Pacific Tall Ships**
106 Stephen St.
1-800-690-6601

Unique maritime gallery specializing in handcrafted museum quality sailing ships of the world. Included with the ships are your choice of several different custom-built cases to enhance the decor of your home or office.

**ANTIQUES ON MAIN STREET**

**Greta's Garrett**
408 Main
603/257-0021
Tues.-Sat. 11-4

Antiques, collectibles, art pottery, fine glass, jewelry, Lenox china, linens, jewelry, old books, etc. Specializing in appraisal service and estate sales. We buy. Free Estimates.

**Lemont Antiques**
228 Main St.
630/257-1318
Daily 10-5 or by appointment

Set in the restored 1862 Gerharz Funeral Store. Restoration and referral service, clock repair, antiques & collectibles, furniture, china, glass, clocks, dolls, jewelry, salt and pepper shakers, linens, lamps, cookie jars, collector plates, Russian curios and primitives.

**Main St. Antique Emporium**
220 Main St.
630/257-3456
Mon.-Fri., 11-8; Sat. 10-5; Sun. 11-5

Two stores in one, filled with antiques, collectibles, stamps, postcards, lamps, toy trains, and unique things. We also refurbish lamps. Multi-dealer shop.

**ANTIQUES ON CANAL STREET**

**Antique Parlour**
316-318 Canal St.
630/257-0033
Tues.-Sun. 11-5

Set in the 2400-square-foot 1928 Dodge Car Showroom. Engraved with the "Bicentennial Mural" wall. Victorian & Country fine furniture and homethings, 1840s to 1940s, antique guide books, plate holders, Victorian paper goods, silk lampshades.

***Favorite Places to Eat***

**Lemont's Famous Christmas Inn**
107 Stephen St.
630/257-2548
Tues.-Sat. starting at 11 a.m., Sun. 9 a.m.-2 p.m.

Lunch and dinner in a Christmas atmosphere. Featured in "Best Decorations in Chicagoland." Sunday's breakfast buffet is a great way to start your antiquing day in Lemont.

**Old Town Restaurant**
113 Stephen St.
630/257-7570
Tues.-Sun, 11-8, Closed Monday

Lunch, dinner, family-style European cuisine, including Polish, Lithuanian, Hungarian, German. Carry-outs. Homemade bakery the specialty. Sunday brunch.

**The Strand Cafe & Ice Cream Parlor**
103 Stephen St.
630/257-2112
Weekdays 11-10, weekends 8-10

Fantastic food, breakfast, lunch or dinner! Serving the best Cajun food outside New Orleans. Best ice cream parlor in the U.S.A. and the best chocolate soda in the world. Bob Gerges plays the concert piano, honky tonk piano and accordion Fri.-Sun., 6 p.m. to closing. Tony Price plays the concert piano and sings every day for lunch.

**Nick's Tavern**
221 Main St.
630/257-6564
Mon.-Sat. 11-10:30

An antique in its own right, Nick's Tavern has been serving Lemont for more than 50 years. Home of "The Best Biggest Cheeseburger" in the state.

### *Interesting Side Trip*

**The Cookie Jar Museum**
111 Stephen St.
708/257-2101

In 1975, Lucille Bromberek successfully completed a treatment program for alcoholism. Although she had no idea what to do with her life now that she'd recovered, she bolted up in bed one night "because a little voice inside my head told me to start collecting cookie jars." Four years later, she opened the only known cookie jar museum in the civilized world.

"I traveled throughout the country and found them at garage sales, antique shows, and flea markets," she remembers. As her reputation grew, people began sending her C-jars, as she fondly calls them, from all over the United States and abroad. Soon her home was overflowing, not unlike one of her overfilled collectibles.

Today the museum is in an office building and boasts a Wedgewood jar that's over a century old; rare Belleek china shamrock-and-pineapple containers from Ireland; a Crown Milano jar worth $3000 and petite, hand decorated biscuit jars, some of which have gold filigree, and others of which are made of exquisite cranberry glass.

"Most C-jars cost from $1 to $2,000, although prices have risen dramatically since I started. Jars I paid $5 for are now worth at least $125." For instance, those made from Depression glass, which was cheap in the thirties, can now fetch up to $8,000. "a few go for as high as $23,000, such as the McCoy 'Aunt Jemima' that belonged to Andy Warhol." That's a lot of dough for something that holds empty calories. Most in the two-thousand-plus collection are from twenty to fifty years old.

But the real fun of the museum is the perusal of Bromberek's piquant groupings. In the Pig Sty, Miss Piggy shares shelf space with peers dressed in black tie, chef's togs, and a nurse's uniform. There's even a jar depicting a farmer giving slop to the porkers.

Other cookie jar menagerie members include dogs, owls, turkeys, bears, camels, cows, fish, and a whale. "The lambs and the lions and the cats and mice are shelved together and get along beautifully." One of Bromberek's favorites is the "Peek-a-Boo" jar, a ceramic rabbit in pajamas. "They made only a thousand."

The museum has cookie jar trolleys, ships, trains, cars, airplanes, and even a gypsy wagon and a spaceship to help visitors along on their journeys. And, of course, there are the usual seasonal themes: a jack-o'-lantern, a Santa Claus, and a jar commemorating the annual downfall of many a dedicated dieter, Girl Scout cookies.

Nursery rhyme characters range from the old woman who lived in the shoe to the cow who jumped over the moon, and visitors will find Dennis the Menace, Howdy Doody, and W.C. Fields as well. Bromberek has devoted three shelves to a Dutch colony and its population. Some of her arrangements tell a story, such as the one in which Cinderella is followed by a castle and then a pumpkin coach. "Turnabouts," with different faces on each side, include Mickey/Minnie Mouse, Papa/Mama Bear, and Pluto/Dumbo.

No cookie jar museum would be complete without homage paid to the treats they hold. a giant Oreo and a Tollhouse cookie, bags depicting Pepperidge Farm and Famous Amos munchies, and the Keebler elf are all represented here. Other enterprising containers include the Quaker Oats box, a Marshall Field's Frango Mint bag, the real-estate logo for Century 21, and an Avon lady calling on a Victorian-style house. For the health conscious, there are strawberry and green-pepper-shaped jars (at least the container's nonfattening). And you can really get caught with your hand in cookie jars that play music when opened.

Although Bromberek collects cookie cutters, cookie cook books, cookie plates, and measuring spoons that work for other comestibles besides cookies, the jars remain her true passion. "If they could talk, the stories they'd tell!" she half-jokes. "They come alive when I'm not there. The chefs and grannies stir up their favorite recipes for a grand gala affair. They come out of their little house C-jars, go to the barn, turn on the radio C-jar and dance up a storm." She claims she sometimes finds them in different spots in the morning. Well, okay. Leave the appetite at home, however. "There's not a cookie on the premises."



## 55 LENA

**St. Andrew's Antiques**
12075 W. Oak St.
815/369-5207

**Cubbies Bull Pen**
211 N. Schuyler St.
815/369-2161

**Rebecca's Parlor Antiques**
208 S. Schuyler St.
815/369-4196

**Raccoon Hollow Antiques**
7114 U.S. Route 20 W.
815/233-5110

## 56 LE ROY

**On The Park Antiques Mall**
104 E. Center St.
309/962-2618

**Party Line Antiques**
301 W. Oak
309/962-8269

## 57 LONG GROVE

**Mrs. B & Me**
132 N. Old McHenry Road
847/634-7352

**Curiosity Shop**
350 N. Old McHenry Road
847-821-9918

**Emporium of Long Grove**
227 Robt Parker Coffin
847/634-0188

**Especially Maine Antiques**
231 Robt Parker Coffin
847/634/3512

**Carriage Trade**
427 Robt Parker Coffin
847/634-3160

## 58 MAHOMET

**Country Crossroads**
103 S. Lincoln St.
217/586-5363

**Olde Town Gallery**
401 E. Main
217/586-3211

**Victorian House**
408 E. Main St.
217/586-4834

**Tin Rabbit**
415 E. Main St.
217/586-4178

**Willow Tree Antiques**
421 E. Main St.
217/586-3333

## 59 MARION

**Collector's Choice**
500 S. Court St.
618/997-4883

**Old Homeplace**
112 E. Deyoung St.
618/997-2454

**Treasure Trove**
1616 Emory Lane
618/993-2213

**Kerr's Antiques**
213 N. Hamlet St.
618/993-6389

**Spotlight Antiques**
1301 Interprise Way
618/993-0830

**Oldies But Goodies**
503 N. Madison St.
618/993-0020

**Guesswhat & Co.**
103 N. Market St.
618/997-4832

**Jenny Lee Antiques**
314 Red Row
618/993-5054

**B & a Collections & Antique Clock Repair**
1420 Julianne Dr.
618/997-2047

## 60 MATTOON

**Country Charm Antiques**
816 Charleston Ave.
217/235-0777

**Mattoon Antique Mart**
908 Charleston Ave.
217/234-9707

**Patti Re's Artistic Creations**
Rt. 4 Box 11A
217/235-4857

**Maple Tree Corner Antiques**
1316 Lafayette Ave.
217/235-4245

## 61 McHENRY

**The Crossroad Merchant**
1328 N. Riverside Dr.
815/344-2610

## 62 McLEANSBORO

**Melba's Antiques**
601 S. Washington St.
618/643-3355

**Southfork Antique Mall**
105 E. Broadway
618/643-4458

## 63 MENDOTA

**Prairie Trails Antique Mall**
704 Illinois Ave.
815/539-5547

**Apple Tree Junction**
701 Illinois Ave.
815/539-5116

**Heartland Treasures**
714 Illinois Ave.
815/538-4402

**Little Shop on the Prairie**
702 Illinois Ave.
815/538-4408

## 64 MOLINE

**Mostly Old Stuff**
1509 15th St.
309/797-3580

**Victorian House Antiques**
1925 6th Ave.
309/797-9755

**Mississippi Manor Antique Mall**
2406 6th Ave.
309/764-0033

## 65 MOMENCE

**Cal-Jean Shop**
127 E. Washington
815/472-2667

**Days of Yesteryear**
Hwy. I-17
815/472-4725

## 66 MORRIS

**Judith Ann's**
117 W. Jackson St.
815/941-2717

**Morris Antique Emporium**
112 W. Washington St.
815/941-0200

## 67 MT. VERNON

**Darnell's Antiques**
Route 148
618/242-6504

**Flota's Antiques**
901 S. 10th St.
618/244-4877

**Olde World Antiques**
2515 Broadway
618/242-7799

**Variety House Antiques**
410-412 S. 18th St.
618/242-4344

## 68 MURPHYSBORO

**Virginia's Antiques**
1204 Chestnut St.
618/687-1212

**Old & in the Way**
1318 Walnut St.
618/634-3686

**Phoebe Jane's Antiques**
1330 Walnut St.
618/684-5546

## 69 NAPERVILLE

**Nana's Cottage**
122 S. Webster
1-800-690-2770

## 70 NAUVOO

**Country Cottage Antiques**
1695 Knight St.
217/453-6478

**Old Nauvoo Antique Mall**
1265 Mulholland St.
217/453-6769

**Rita's Romantiques**
2592 N. Sycamore Haven Dr.
217/453-6480

### *Great Places To Stay*

**The Ancient Pines**
2015 Parley St.
217/453-2767

Surrounded by orchards, a winery, herb gardens, perennials, and old roses, this stunning home has ornate brick details, stained glass windows, pressed metal ceilings, and carved woodwork. The rooms are furnished with antiques. Within walking distance of antique shops.

## 71 OAKLAND

**Outback Antique Store**
2 E. Main
217/3462584

## 72 OAK PARK

**Treasures N Trinkets**
600 Harrison St.
708/848-9142

**Antiques Etc. Mall**
125 N. Marion
708/386-9194

## 73 ODIN

**Lincoln Trail Antiques**
U.S. Hwy. 50
618/775-8255

**Vernon's Antiques**
Box 57, Rt. 50
618/775-8360

## 74 ORLAND PARK

**Beacon Hill Antique Shop**
14314 Beacon Ave.
708/460-8433

**Old Bank Antique Shop**
14316 Beacon Ave.
708/460-7979

**Emporium Antique Shop**
14320 Beacon Ave.
708/460-5814

**Favorite Things**
14329 Beacon Ave.
708/403-1908

**Olde Homestead Ltd.**
14330 Beacon Ave.
708/460-9096

**Cracker Barrell Antiques**
9925 W. 143rd Place
708/403-2221

**General Store**
14314 S. Union Ave.
708/349-9802

**Station House Antique Mall**
12305 W. 159th St. (Lockport)
708/301-9400

## 75 OSWEGO

**Bob's Antique Toys**
23 W. Jefferson St.
630/554-3234

**Oswego Antiques Market**
72 S. Main St.
630/554-9779

**Oswego Antiques Market II**
78 S. Main St.
630/554-9779

**Old Oak Creek Shoppes**
4025 U.S. Hwy. 34, #B
630/554-3218

## 76 OTTAWA

**Gramma's Attic Antique Mall**
219 W. Main St.
815/434-7332
Mon.-Sat. 9:30-5
*Directions: From Interstate 80, take the Ottawa Exit south on Hwy. 23 to Main St. Located south of Downtown courthouse, go right (west) 1/2 block, south side of the street.*

From the name given to this establishment, one might come to the conclusion that it is a cozy little place filled with great "old things." But you can't judge a book by its title! This building swells to four floors and is a restored 150-year-old former hotel. That would date its existence back to 1847, when Illinois was the pioneer west in still young America. It was a time when gunbelts were slung over bedposts, "ladies of the night" were escorted upstairs, whiskey flowed and bar-room brawls extended out into the streets. Today, thanks to the restoration efforts of Woody Jewett, Gramma's Attic, one of Ottawa's newest antique malls is a "gem" of a place to shop. Thirty-four dealers present a large selection of antique glassware, furniture, quilts, dolls, jewelry, collectibles, books and more.

## 77 PAXTON

**Cheesecloth & Buttermilk**
124 S. Market St.
217/379-3675

**Antique Mall & Tea Room**
931 S. Railroad Ave.
217/379-4748

## 78 PECATONICA

**Antiques at Hillwood Farms**
498 N. Sarwell Bridge Road
815/239-2421

## 79 PEORIA

**Mia's Antiques & Uniques**
1507 E. Gardner Lane (Heights)
309/685-1912

**U Name It**
3205 W. Harmon Hwy.
309/677-6710

**Whaley's Clock Shop**
218 W. McClure Ave.
309/682-8429

**Abe's Antiques**
2001 N. Wisconsin Ave.
309/682-8181

**Backdoor Antiques & Collectibles**
725 S.W. Washington
309/637-3446

**The Illinois Antique Center**
308 S.W. Commercial St.
309/673-3354

## 80 PESOTUM

### Wildflower Antique Mall
511 S. Chestnut
217/867-2704
Mon.-Sat. 9-6, Sun. 10-5
*Directions: Exit 220 - I-57 & Rt. 45*

Stepping into Wildflower Antique Mall gives you a feeling of nostalgia. This true "sense for the past" is created by 55 dedicated and experienced dealers whose quality merchandise is displayed throughout this 5300 square foot mall. Selections are nicely diverse and neatly arranged; showcased in such a way as to provide you with unique decorating ideas. A convenient stop for travelers, the mall is located just off I-57, Exit 220 in Pesotum.

## 81 PETERSBURG

**Salem Country Store**
Route 97 S.
217/632-3060

**Petersburg Peddlers**
113 S. 7th St.
217/632-2628

**Fezziwig's**
110 E. Sheridan St.
217/632-3369

**Estep & Associates**
320 N. 6th St.
217/632-4154

**Stanis Sayre Antique Store**
511 S. 6th St.
217/632-7016

## 82 PINCKNEYVILLE

***Great Places To Stay***

### Oxbow Bed & Breakfast
Route 1, Box 47
618/357-9839
Year round 7-11
*Directions: Oxbow is located on Hwys. 13/127, 1 3/4 miles south of Perry County Courthouse. If traveling I-64, take Exit 50 (Hwy. 127), and drive approximately 23 miles south. If driving I-57, take Exit 77 (Hwy. 154), then go 28 miles east.*

A true vision of craftsmanship, Oxbow Bed & Breakfast was created by taking old barns and silos and turning them into perfect retreats for anyone in search of the more relaxed life. The barns were moved from various sites throughout the area to the present property, then painstakingly reconstructed and restored.

An older barn (settled behind the main house) is a retreat for honeymooners or others wanting to escape the crowds. During the summer months, take a dip in the swimming pool creatively constructed from old silo staves.

## 83 POCAHONTAS

**Annabelle's Antiques Academy**
Academy & National
618/669-2088

**T G Antiques Mall**
IH 70 & Hwy. 40
618/669-2969

**Wagon Wheel Antiques**
202 National St.
618/669-2918

**Village Square Antiques**
202 State St.
618/669-2825

## 84 PRINCETON

**Midtown Antique Mall**
I-80 Exit 56
815/872-3435

**Sherwood Antique Mall**
1661 N. Main St.
815/872-2580

## 85 QUINCY

**Broadway Antique Mall**
1857 Broadway
217/222-8617

**Pawnee**
501 Hampshire St.
217/222-8090

**R & W Antiques**
117 N. 4th St.
217/222-6143

**June's Antiques**
121 N. 4th St.
217/223-9265

**Old Town Antiques**
2000 Jersey St.
217/223-2963

**Brocks Antiques**
516 Main St.
217/224-7414

**Yester Year Antique Mall**
615 Maine St.
217/224-1871

**Carriage House Antiques**
805 Spring St.
217/228-2303

**Vintage Home Furniture**
208 S. 10th
217/224-5166

## 86 RICHMOND

**A Little Bit Antiques**
5603 Broadway
815/678-4218

**Happy House Antiques**
5604 Broadway
815/678-4076

**Once Upon a Time**
5608 W. Broadway
815/678-6533

**Old Bank Antiques**
5611 Broadway
815/678-4839

**Hiram's Uptown Antiques**
5613 Broadway
815/678-4166

**a Step Above**
5626 Broadway
815/678-6906

**Cat's Stuff**
5627 Broadway
815/678-7807

**Serendipity Shop**
9818 Main St.
815/678-4141

**Antiques On Broadway**
10309 N. Main St.
815/678-7951

**Emporium-1905**
10310 N. Main St.
815/678-4414

**Marilyn's Touch**
10315 N. Main St.
815/678-7031

**Ed's Antiques**
10321 N. Main St.
815/678-2911

## 87 RIVERSIDE

**Riverside Antique Market**
30 East Ave.
708/447-4425

**J P Antiques**
36 East Ave.
708/442-6363

**Arcade Antiques & Jewelers**
25 Forest Ave.
708/442-8110

**Arcade Antiques & Furniture**
7 Longcommon Road
708/442-8999

## 88 ROCK FALLS

**Rock River Antique Center**
2105 E. Rt. 30
815/625-2556

## 89 ROCKFORD

**Homestead Antiques**
3712 N. Central Ave.
815/962-7498

**Peddler's Attic**
2609 Charles St.
815/962-8842

**Houtkamp Art Glass Studio**
120 N. Main St.
815/964-3785

**Krenek's Clock Haven**
2314 N. Main St.
815/965-4661

**Eagle's Nest Antiques**
7080 Old River Road
815/633-8410

**Forgotten Treasures**
4610 E. State St.
815/229-0005

**East State St. Antique Mall #2**
5301 E. State St.
815/226-1566

**East State St. Antique Mall**
5411 E. State St.
815/229-4004

## 90 ROCK ISLAND

**Rock Island Antique Mart**
1608 2nd Ave.
309/793-6278

**Old Hat Antiques**
1706 3rd Ave.
309/794-9089

**Iron Horse Antiques & Gifts**
533 30th St.
309/793-4500

**Jackson's Antiques**
1310 30th St.
309/793-1413

### *Great Places To Stay*

**The Potter House**
1906 7th Ave.
1-800-747-0339

Stay in either the main house or the adjacent cottage at this turn-of-the-century home listed on the National Register of Historic Places. Look for the old-fashion details, from brass doorknobs to embossed leather wallcovering and stained and leaded glass windows. Even the bathrooms are distinctive. One has its original nickel plated hardware. You'll notice other historic homes in the area which you can tour on foot, by carriage or by trolley.

**The Victorian Inn**
702 20th St.
1-800-728-7068

Nestled in the Heart of Old Rock Island on nearly an acre of wooded gardens is the gracious Victorian Inn Bed and Breakfast.The Broadway Historical Area begins at the Victorian Inn where old fashioned trolly and walking tours crisscross the neighborhood. The inn built in 1876 offers five guestrooms with private baths.

## 91 ROCKTON

**Big D's Antiques**
110 N. Blackhawk Road
815/624-6300

**Nichols Antiques**
212 W. Main St.
815/624-4137

## 92 ROSSVILLE

**Fife & Drum**
15 E. Attica St.
217/748-4119

**Scarce Glass**
101 S. Chicago St.
217/748-6352

**Hall Closet**
103 S. Chicago St.
217/748-6766

**Heritage House**
104 S. Chicago St.
217/748-6681

**Market Place**
106 S. Chicago St.
217/748-6066

**Smith's Antiques & Collectibles**
107 S. Chicago St.
217/748-6728

**Freeman's Folly**
110 S. Chicago St.
217/748-6720

## 93 SADORUS

**Antique & Curiosity Shop**
101 S. Vine St.
217/598-2200

**This 'N'That Shop**
119 E. Market St.
217/598-2462

## 94 SALEM

**Freeman Creek Antiques**
3242 Hotze Road
618/548-6677

**Little Lulu's**
216 E. Main St.
618/548-0219

## 95 SANDWICH

**Sandwich Antique Market**
2300 E. Rt. 34 – Village East Plaza
815/786-6122

**Quackers Country Accents**
127 S. Main St.
815/786-6429

**Sandwich Antiques Mall**
108 N Main St.
815/786-7000

## 96 SAVANNA

### Pulford Opera House Antiques Mall/J.T. Bradley's
324 Main St.
815/273-2661
Mon.-Thurs., 10:30-5:30; Fri.-Sat., 10:30-8: Sun., 11-6
Memorial Day through Labor Day: Mon.-Sat., 9:30-8; Sun., 11-6
*Directions: Hwy. 84, "Great River Road," is a major highway running north/south along the Mississippi River. (Savanna is mid-distance between the Quad cities and Dubuque, Iowa.) Route 84 is called Main St. in downtown Savanna. The mall is located on Main St..*

The Pulford Opera House Antique Mall was built at the turn of the century and is the largest antique mall in northwestern Illinois. In 1905, the Opera House was the site of the murder of a local attorney, followed by the suicide of the Opera House owner, Botworth Pulford, a week later. Some folks attribute the occasional strange noises and occurrences throughout the house to their "ghosts." Apart from the spiritual visitors that frequent the Pulford Opera House are thousands of antique enthusiasts who flock to this 27,000-square-foot establishment, noted for its quality antiques. Located four doors south is J. T. Bradley's, the mall's companion store. This restored 1880s eatery offers soups, sandwiches, a salad bar, pastries and many entrees along with 30 more booths of antiques. a total of 120 dealers from Illinois, Iowa and Wisconsin provide the fine antiques displayed for purchase throughout both locations.

## 97 SHELBYVILLE

**Hidden Antiques. at the Hub**
111 E. Main St.
217/774-2900

**Pat's Antiques**
133 E. Main St.
217/774-4485

**Wooden Nickel Antiques**
140 E. Main St.
217/774-3735

**Auntie Darling's Daydreams**
225 N. Morgan St.
217/774-5510

**Jake's Antiques**
W. Route 16
217/774-4223

**Kinfolk**
RR 1
217/774-2557

**Jakes Warehouse**
1501 W. South 8th St.
217/774-4201

## 98 SHILOH

### Mueller's Antiques & Collectibles
522 N. Main St.
618/632-4166
Thurs.-Sun., 1-5
*Directions: Traveling Interstate 64, exit at #19 B (S.R. 158). Go north to traffic lights (Old S.R. 50). Turn left, and go approximately 1/4 mile to Shiloh Road (Main St.). Turn left going 1/4 mile to shop on the left.*

Some of us collect antique glassware, linens, primitives, etc. but the owners at Mueller's Antiques collects buildings. Not necessarily buildings of a historic nature, but buildings full of history. On the main street of town in Shiloh, Ill., you'll find six farm buildings filled to the rafters with antiques. Everything imaginable can be found in here, so bring a big truck and a hefty wallet - you won't go away empty handed.

## 99 SOMONAUK

### House of 7 Fables
300 E. Dale St.
815/498-2289
Daily 10-5, but call ahead to avoid disappointment.
*Directions: Somonauk is on U.S. Route 34 (Ogden Ave.) which runs parallel to and between Interstates 80 and 88, approximately 22 miles east of Interstate 39. The shop is at the corner of North Sagamore and Dale Streets, 1/2 block north of Route 34. The shop is a red house with white trim, white letters "ANTIQUES."*

House of Seven Fables is, itself one of those treasures that collectors love to find. The half dozen or more buildings that make up the shop are all painted brick red with white trim and are rescued antiques themselves.

Owner Merwin Shaw got hooked on antiques back in the 1930s, when he "dusted, polished and steel-wooled antiques for a lady here in

Somonauk." as he tells it.

Not only is the store, with all its items for sale, crammed to the rafters with finds in just about every category, but the repair areas - yes, repair areas - are just as interesting, because much of the repair work done here is a lost or dying art. There are hobby horse and toy restoration workshops, a wicker repair workshop, and an antique picture framing area. The shop handles vintage lighting, but they also do restoration and wiring of old pieces.

Inside one of the buildings, stuffed among the Windsors and firkins stacked in front of a window area, are several moonshine jugs, and green glass sits on the window ledge. Another window holds pink and red glass, with rockers, tables and baskets in front.

Antique chandeliers and bird cages hang from the ceiling in another corner over a hodgepodge of furniture covered with paintings and potted plants. Another corner, with shelves and cabinets running floor to ceiling, holds hundreds of vintage tins: coffee, tea, milk, liquor, all shapes, sizes, colors, configurations. Another wall is more elegant in tone, with framed pictures of all kinds hung in an orderly arrangement over a few choice pieces of furniture. Then there are the showcases - antiques themselves - filled with colored pressed glass cruets, rose bowls, toothpick holders, butter molds, complete sets of dishes, and perfume bottles, all arranged by color. It's a visual feast!

Bigger pieces of early American furniture that shoppers will find include Colonial pine cupboards, Shaker rockers, and hutch-top dry sinks decorated with accessories like salt glaze pottery, apothecary items and Norwegian tins.

There's usually something for everyone, and more importantly, there is a place to bring your treasures when they need tender loving care.

## 100 SPRINGFIELD

**Old Georgian Antique Mall**
830 S. Grand Ave. E.
217/753-8110

**Antiques Antiques**
2851 Green Valley Road
217/546-1052

**AAron's Attic Antiques**
1525 W. Jefferson St.
217/546-6300

**Renaissance Shop**
2402 W. Jefferson St.
217/787-8125

**Silent Woman Antique Shop**
2765 W. Jefferson St.
217/787-3253

**Eastnor Gallery of Antiques**
700 E. Miller St.
217/523-0998

**House of Antiques**
412 E. Monroe St.
217/544-9677

**Antiques Unique**
617 E. Monroe St.
217/522-0772

**Springfield Antique Mall**
3031 Reilly Dr.
217/522-3031

**Barrel Antique Mall**
5850 S. 6th St.
217/585-1438

**Ruby Sled-Antiques & Art**
1142 S. Spring St.
217/523-3391

**Pastime Antiques**
6279 N. Walnut St.
217/487-7200

**Murray's Oxbow Antiques**
2509 S. Whittier Ave.
217/528-8220

## 101 ST. CHARLES

**Riverside Antiques**
410 S. 1st St.
630/377-7730

**Consign-Tiques**
214 W. Main St.
630/584-7535

**Brown Beaver Antiques**
219 W. Main St.
630/443-9430

**Antique Market III**
413 W. Main St.
630/377-5599

**Studio Posh**
17 N. 2nd Ave.
630/443-0227

**Market**
12 N. 3rd St.
630/584-3899

**Memory Merchant Antiques**
15 S. 3rd St.
630/513-0340

**Antique Market I**
11 N. Third St.
630/377-1868

**Antique Market II**
303 W. Main (Rt. 64)
630/377-5798

## 102 ST. JOSEPH

**Peach's Antiques**
228 E. Lincoln
217/469-8836

**Pine Acres Trees & Herbs**
E. of Sidney on 2300 E.
217/688-2207

**The Village Shoppe**
228 E. Lincoln
217/469-8836

## 103 STOCKTON

**Grandpa & Grandma Antiques**
118 W. Front Ave.
815/947-2411

**Cornerstone Creations**
101 N. Main St.
815/947-2358

**Tredegar Antique Market**
208 E. North Ave.
815/947-2360

**Glick's Antiques**
3602 E. Woodbine St.
815/858-2305

## 104 TUSCOLA

**Wood Tin & Lace**
604 S. Main St
217/253-3666

**Prairie Sisters Antique Mall**
102 W. Sale St.
217/253-5211

**Prairie Church Antique Mall**
568 36th E.
217/253-3960

## 105 VANDALIA

**Back When Antiques**
118 N. Elm
No Number Listed

**Cuppy's Antique Mall**
& Old Fashioned Soda Fountain
618/283-0080

**Treasure Cove Antique Mall**
302 W. Gallatin
618/283-8704

**Wehrle's Antiques**
Rt. 51
618/283-4147

## 106 VILLA PARK

**Astorville Antiques**
51 S. Villa Ave.
630/279-5311

**Memories from the Attic**
119 S. Villa Ave.
630/941-1517

## 107 WARRENVILLE

### Lil' Red Schoolhouse Antiques and Collectibles
3 S. 463 Batavia Road
630/393-1040
Mon.-Sat. 10-5, Sun. 11-5
*Directions: From Chicago, take 290 (Eisenhower Expressway) west to I-88. Continue on I-88; exit at Winfield Road. Travel north to second stoplight (Amoco and Mobile stations); turn left, go 2 blocks to STOP sign. Turn right, 4th building on the right (opposite the fire station).Coming on Route 59, turn east on Butterfield Road, to Batavia Road. Turn right (south) to shop on left hand side.*

Settled among a grove of wonderful trees which give way to a lawn tumbling down to the Du Page River, sets the Lil' Red Schoolhouse. It was built in 1836 when teachers were required to be single ladies. There are ten rooms and two porches which make up the schoolhouse's construction. The desk, the chalkboard, the pencils and the rulers have all been replaced with quality antiques and collectibles. You'll find tables, chairs (many dating to the early 1900s and beyond), lamps, glassware, early tools and a hodgepodge of other wonderful things.

The Lil' Red Schoolhouse schedules outdoor sales and special events during each season (dealers take note).

### Route 59 Antique Mall
3 S. 450 Route 59
630/393-0100
Mon.-Sat. 10-6, Sun. 11-4:30
*Directions: 1 mile north of I-88, Just south of Butterfield Road, 1 mile from Cracker Barrel.*

Route 59 Antique Mall is the premier mall in Chicago's western suburbs. Featuring the wares of over sixty quality dealers, you will enjoy browsing through an excellent selection of furniture, home accents, primitives, glassware, architectural items, art deco, 50s items, and much more. In their two years of existence the owners are frequently complimented for the ever-changing variety of items and pleasant shopping atmosphere. Stop and see why Route 59 Antique Mall is a favorite spot for local antiquers and treasure hunters just passing through.

## 108 WESTMONT

**Tony's Collectibles**
141 S. Cass Ave.
630/515-8510

**Elite Repeat**
123 E. Ogden Ave.
630/960-0540

**Old Plank Road Antiques**
233 W. Ogden Ave.
630/971-0500

**Zeke's Antiques & Leo's Lamps**
135 W. Quincy St.
630/969-3852

## 109 WHEELING

**Kerry's Clock Shop**
971 N. Milwaukee Ave.
847/520-0335

**Lundgren's**
971 N. Milwaukee Ave.
847/541-2299

**The Crystal Magnolia**
971 N. Milwaukee Ave.
847/537-4750

**Shirley's Dollhouse**
971 N. Milwaukee Ave.
847/537-1632

**My Favorite Place**
971 N. Milwaukee Ave.
847/808-1324

**O'Kelly's Antiques**
971 N. Milwaukee Ave.
847/537-1656

**County Faire Antiques**
971 N. Milwaukee Ave.
847/537-9987

**Antiques of Northbrook**
971 N. Milwaukee Ave.
847/215-4994

**Coach House Antiques**
971 N. Milwaukee Ave.
847/808-1324

**Antiques Center of Illinois**
1920 S. Wolf Road
847/215-9418

## 110 WILMETTE

**Shorebirds**
415 1/2 4th St.
847/853-1460

**Buggy Wheel**
1143 Greenleaf Ave.
847/251-2100

**Collected Works**
1405 Lake Ave.
847/251-6897

**Raven & Dove Antique Gallery**
1409 Lake Ave.
847/251-9550

**Heritage Trail Mall**
410 Ridge Road
847/256-6208

**Josie's**
545 Ridge Road.
847/256-7646

## 111 WILMINGTON

### Wilmington Antique Dealers Association

Wilmington offers days of treasure hunting in the century old buildings of N. Water St. There are 3 multi-level antique malls and 9 additional antique shops featuring over 100 dealers with a wide variety of antiques and collectibles. These shops along with a diner and "The best burgers in Will County" at RTM's, specialty shops with bakery, coffee, teas and ice cream make N. Water St. an enjoyable and rewarding adventure.

Snuggled within 20 minutes of three major interstate routes on the Kankakee River, Wilmington is easily accessible. From I-80 take the I-55 exit south to sixth 238, then left on Strip Mine Road. to Rte. 53, left again to second light then left on Water St. From I-57 take the Peotone/ Wilmington exit 327 to Route 53 then left to second light, and left on Water St.

**Mill Race Emporium**
110 N. Water St.
Multi-level, multi-dealer
Antiques and collectibles
815/476-7660

**Water St. Mall**
119-121 N. Water St.
Multi-level, multi-dealer
Full line-Fenton-Heisey-
carnival-pottery-toys-
Discover-Visa-Mastercard
815/476-5900

**Abacus Antiques**
113-115 N. Water St.
Art Deco-50s items-
furniture-more
815/476-5727

**The Opera House Antiques**
203 N. Water St.
Antiques-Collectibles
Primitives
Discover-Visa-Mastercard
815/476-0872

**R. J.'s Relics**
116-118-120 N. Water St.
Multi-level, multi-dealer
space and showcase rental.
Knives-Military-Books-
Sports cards-Jewelry-
Vintage clothing-Furniture
and much more
Discover-Visa-Mastercard
815/476-6273

**Paraphernalia Antiques**
112-114-124 N. Water St.
Jewelry-Irish Pine-
European Imports
815/476-9841

**Stuff-N-Such**
Antiques-collectibles-
crafts
815/476-0411

**O'Koniewski's Treasures**
General Line-anything
unusual and interesting
815/476-1039

## 112 WINNETKA

**Jack Monckton Gallery**
1050 Gage St.
847-446-1106

**Arts 220**
895 1/2 Green Bay Road
847/501-3084

**Antique Heaven**
982 Green Bay Road
847/446-0343

**Pied a Terre**
554 Lincoln Ave.
847/441-5161

**Robertson-Jones Antiques**
569 Lincoln Ave.
847/446-0603

**Country Shop**
710 Oak St.
847/441-8690

**West End Antiques**
619 Green Bay Road
847-256-2291

**Knightsbridge Antiques**
909 Green Bay Road
847/441-5105

**M Stefanich Antiques Ltd.**
549 Lincoln Ave.
847/446-4955

**Heather Higgins Antiques**
567 Lincoln Ave., #A
847/446-3455

**Stuart Antiques**
571 Lincoln Ave.
847/501-4454

## 113 WITT

**Hole in the Wall**
3 E. Broadway
217/594-7132

**Mystique Antiques**
510 N. Main St.
217/594-2802

**Country Store Antiques**
411 E. Ford St.
217/594-7275

# Indiana

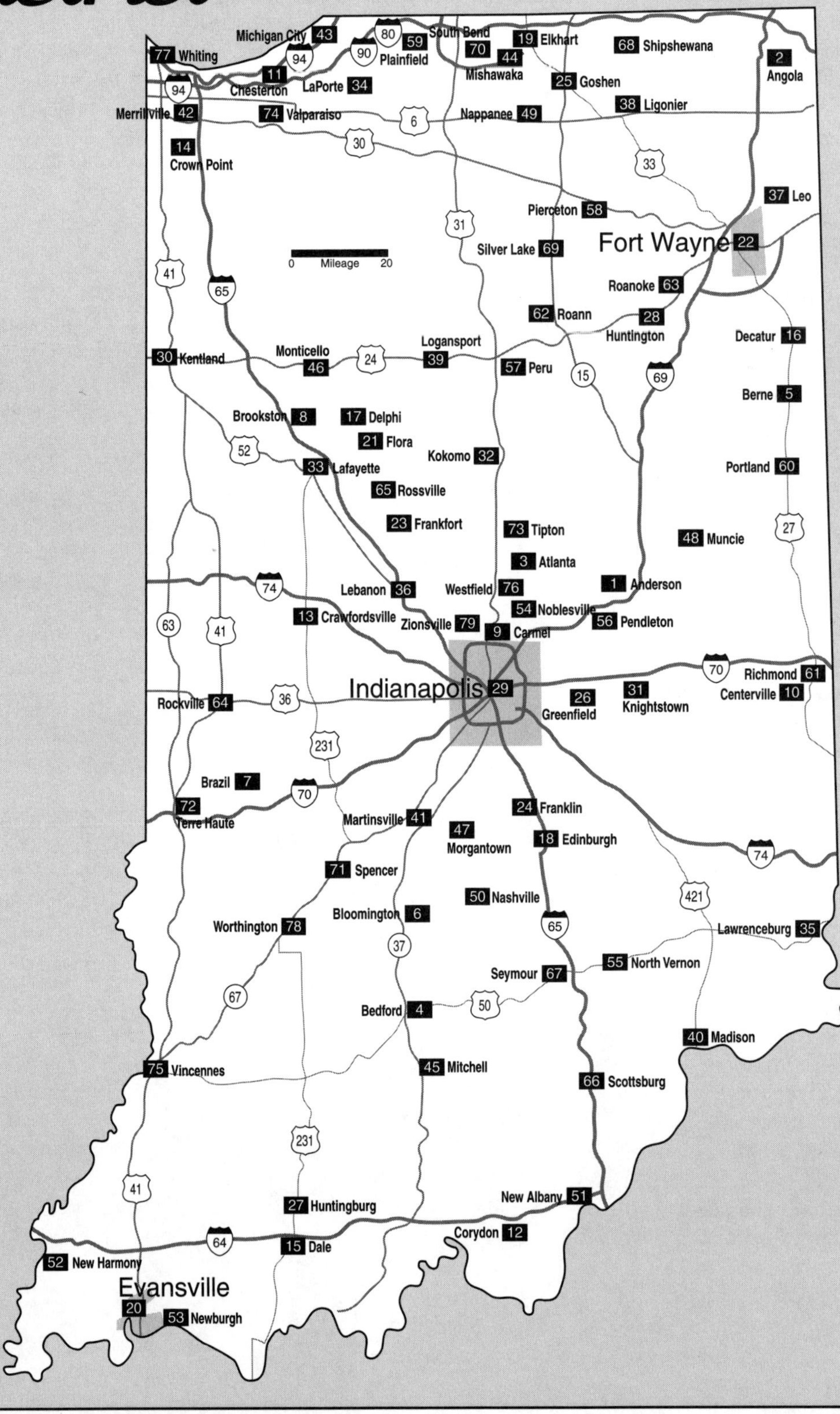
77 Whiting
Michigan City 43
80
94
90
59 Plainfield
South Bend
70
44
Mishawaka
19 Elkhart
68 Shipshewana
2 Angola
11 Chesterton
LaPorte 34
25 Goshen
38 Ligonier
Merrillville 42
74 Valparaiso
6
Nappanee 49
30
14 Crown Point
33
37 Leo
Pierceton 58
31
Silver Lake 69
Fort Wayne 22
0 Mileage 20
41
65
Roanoke 63
62 Roann
28 Huntington
Decatur 16
30 Kentland
Monticello 46
24
Logansport 39
57 Peru
15
69
Berne 5
Brookston 8
17 Delphi
21 Flora
52
Kokomo 32
33 Lafayette
Portland 60
65 Rossville
23 Frankfort
73 Tipton
48 Muncie
27
3 Atlanta
74
Lebanon 36
Westfield 76
1 Anderson
54 Noblesville
13 Crawfordsville
Zionsville 79
56 Pendleton
63
9 Carmel
Indianapolis 29
70
Richmond 61
Centerville 10
Rockville 64
36
26 Greenfield
31 Knightstown
231
Brazil 7
72 Terre Haute
Martinsville 41
24 Franklin
47 Morgantown
18 Edinburgh
71 Spencer
50 Nashville
421
Worthington 78
Bloomington 6
65
Lawrenceburg 35
37
Seymour 67
55 North Vernon
67
Bedford 4
50
40 Madison
75 Vincennes
45 Mitchell
66 Scottsburg
New Albany 51
27 Huntingburg
64
15 Dale
Corydon 12
52 New Harmony
Evansville
20
53 Newburgh

From the American flag on the front porch of The Allison House, to the quaint shops — Nashville is a gem of an Indiana town.

# The Allison House is work of art in artist colony town

In the early 1990s, the rolling hills and spectacular fall colors of this time-forsaken area brought many artists from far and wide to be inspired by its beauty. Turning the country village of Nashville into an artist colony, T.C. Steele and other award winning impressionist artists dubbed the "Hoosier Group" were among the first to discover this artists haven.

Nashville is still known as the home of artists. In galleries and shops you will find everything from fine paintings and pottery to weavings, stained glass, and charming country crafts. But don't stop there — this town has nearly 350 quaint shops selling not only art, but antiques, fine clothing and great souvenirs. A buggy or trolley ride can get you around the town to complete your shopping. Hearty country food has made Nashville famous. You can enjoy such wonderful treats as fried biscuits and apple butter. In 1868, Frank Taggart built the dry goods store which is now Nashville's oldest commercial building, housing Hobnob Corner at 17 W. Main St., a restaurant featuring fresh, hearty homemade fare. Enjoy a collection of Hohenberger photos in an old-time drugstore setting boasting a swatch of wallpaper from the 1890s.

In a town full of history, The Allison House (built in 1883) stands as a fine example of this charming scenic area. An American flag floats from its staff from the porch of the inn, pots of geraniums sit on wicker tables and firewood is stacked beside the door. "Neighborliness is contagious," says innkeeper Tammy Galm as she serves breakfast on a deck screened by pole beans. The Galms figured rightly that inn lovers would appreciate this small-town setting. After they purchased the house in 1985, they completely gutted and rebuilt the building, more than doubling its original size. There are five guest rooms newly remodeled and individually decorated with an emphasis on comfort and charm.

A full breakfast is served each morning. Fortified with calories, shoppers can work them off in search of antiques, a cornhusk doll or perhaps a ceramic pig with a red bandana.

*The Allison House is located at 90 S. Jefferson St. in Nashville. For additional information, call the innkeepers at 812-988-0814.*

Indiana

# Antiquers: Discover a very special part of Indiana

Delphi, Indiana is the center of a circle that encompasses several cities, each filled with unique shops. On leaving Delphi in any direction within a twenty-mile radius, the antiquer will encounter at least 20 locations at which to shop. The cities within the circle have organized a co-op to promote themselves, a membership that is ever-growing, but includes shops within or between the cities of Flora, Brookston, Rossville, Monticello and Delphi.

Each city within the co-op recognizes the others' ability to draw a crowd. Monticello is home of the famous Indiana Beach; Brookston has an annual popcorn and apple festival; Rossville has a summer's-end festival with roads closed and street vendors in operation. Flora has an annual pork producer cook-off, with an old car "cruise in," oldies music, and a lot of activity. The area also has the Wabash and Erie Canal digs every summer. Visit the area. You'll be a satisfied antiquer!

## *A quick reference guide to antiquing in the Delphi area*

### FLORA, BROOKSTONE, ROSSVILLE

**John's Toys & Antiques**
4160 N. County Road O.E.V.
Frankfort • 765/659-9017, 659-3519

**Wertz Antiques**
IN 18 W. of IN 75
Flora • 291/967-3056

**Bill's Clockworks**
8 W. Columbia
Flora • 219/967-4709, 888/742-5625
Web site: www.qlink.com/clockworks

**Rolling Wheels**
Antiques and Collectibles
8136 West St. Rd. 26 or 4 miles west of Rossville
765/379-2649

**Back Through Time Antiques Mall**
9 W. Main St. (at flasher)
Rossville • 765/379-3299

**Pappy's Rossville Antique Mall**
54 E. Main St.
Rossville • 765/379-9000

### MONTICELLO

**Beth's Antiques**
12355 N. Upper Shore Dr.
219/583-3002
Web site: www.monti.net

**Uptowne Antiques Mall**
134 S. Main St.
219/583-5359

**Blossom Station**
101 W. Broadway
219/583-5359

**Main Street Antiques Mall**
127 N. Main St.
219/583-2998

**Turquoise 'N' Treasures**
400 W. Fisher
219/583-8413

**Creative Clutter**
Antiques, Furniture, Gifts
2702 W. Shafer Dr.
219/583-336

**Inntwinned Inn Time**
U.S. 421 S.
Upper level Sportsman Inn
219/583-5133

### DELPHI

**J & B Furniture Store**
113 S. Washington St.
765/564-9204

**Delphi Antique Mall**
117 Washington St.
765/564-3990

**Lil' Bit of Country**
125 S. Washington St.
765/564-6241

**Teddy's Emporium**
115 E. Main St.
756/564-3742

**Town Square Mall**
110 W. Main St.
756/564-6937

**Times Past Antiques and Art**
124 S. Main St.
765/564-6317

**Crouch's Victorian Antiques**
404 E. Main St.
765/564-4195

**Linda's Treasure Trove**
**Ruby's Cottage Antiques**
1816 N. Wells
765/564-3649

## 1 ANDERSON

**Jerry's Junkatique**
509 E. 8th St.
765/649-4321

**Harold's Hideaway**
2023 Lindberg Road
765/642-7880

**Anderson Antique Mall**
1407 Main St.
765/622-9517

**Abby's**
1231 Meridian St.
765/642-8016

**Antiques by Helen Marie**
909 Raible Ave.
765/642-0889

***Great Places To Stay***

### Plum Retreat
926 Historic W. Eighth St.
765/649-7586

Innkeepers John and Marilyn Bertacchi have a philosophy, "Come to the Plum Retreat as strangers, leave as friends." "We love sharing this beautiful home and enjoy telling about its history and the life of the previous owners," says John and Marilyn. "But more than that, we enjoy people and chatting with them about their lives and pampering our guests to make their stay as pleasant as possible."

The architectural style is Victorian, circa 1892. This peaceful get-a-way is decorated in wonderful antiques and has three guest rooms available.

## 2 ANGOLA

**Angola Mini Mall**
109 W. Gale St.
219/665-7394

**Olde Towne Mall**
101 W. Maumee St.
219/665-9920

**Then & Now Mini Mall**
200 W. Maumee St.
219/665-6650

**Angola Antique Depot**
208 W. Maumee St.
219/665-2026

**Angola Antique Depot**
611 W. Maumee St.
219/665-2026

## 3 ATLANTA

### The Wooden Indian Antiques
115 W. Main St.
765/292-2722
Summer (April-December. Sat.-Wed. 11-5), Winter (January-March , Fri.-Sun. 12-5), other times by chance or appointment
*Directions: Located in downtown Atlanta next to the railroad tracks. Atlanta is 5 miles south of Tipton on State Route 19 and 12 miles north of Noblesville on State Route 19. U.S. 31 is 5 miles west of Atlanta. The road to Atlanta from U.S. 31 (approximately 296th St.) is 20 miles north of I-465 (on north edge of Indianapolis) and 20 miles south of Kokomo.*

As you might have surmised, The Wooden Indian Antiques shop specializes in wood. They stock from 800 to 1,000 pressed back chairs and although they are not always in pristine condition, choices are limitless. There is something for everyone; including the do-it-yourselfer. They also do chair caning, a diminishing art.

The next time someone asks, "It that chair taken," you can tell them, "yes but there are many, many more where that one came from at The Wooden Indian Antiques."

## 4 BEDFORD

### Brown Hen Antique & Craft Mall
Route 11, Box 646
812/279-9172
Mon., Thurs., Sat. 10-5, Fri. 10-6, Sun. 12-5.
*Directions: Located three miles south of 16th St. in Bedford on Hwy. 37/50 just south of Hickory Hill Restaurant & Dalton's RVs.*

Brown Hen Antiques & Craft Mall definitely has something to cackle about. The "old" Brown Hen Mall was leveled by a tornado in 1991; however, hanging over the check-out counter was a large painting of a brown hen. An inspection of damage found the shop completely gone, but the brown hen survived with only minor damage. Today, this "brown hen" has a place of honor in the new Brown Hen shop, which offers an eclectic array of antiques and collectibles.

**Zollman's Finery**
917 15th St.
812/275-2216

## 5 BERNE

**Berne Antique Mall**
105 W. Water St.
219/589-8050

**Karen's Treasures**
444 E. Main St.
219/589-2002

**Pandora's Box**
Stone City Mall F-6
812/275-6534

## 6 BLOOMINGTON

**The Garret**
403 W. Kirkwood Ave.
812/339-4175
Mon.-Wed., Fri. & Sat. 9-6, Thurs., Sun. By appointment or chance
*Directions: Highways 37, 45, 48 and 446 all go into Bloomington. Go to the Court House Square in downtown. One street south is Kirkwood (also called 5th Street). The Garret is 2 blocks west on the corner of Kirkwood and Madison.*

The Garretts have been in the antiquing business nearly forty years and, according to them, their shop is "simply the largest, oldest, and most diversified shop in the area." The three floors of this unique shop, house not only a world of wonderful antiques, but a rock and mineral shop as well. The specialties of The Garret are lighting and furniture.

**Cowboys & Indians**
110 E. Kirkwood Ave.
812/323-1013

**Grant St.**
213 S. Rogers St.
812/333-6076

**Odds & Olds**
2524 S. Rogers St.
812/333-3022

**Bloomington Antique Mall**
311 W. 7th St.
812/332-2290

**Elegant Options Antique Gallery**
403 N. Walnut St.
812/332-5662

**Different Drummer**
2964 E. 2nd St.
812/337-1776

### *Great Places To Stay*

**Quilt Haven**
711 Dittemore Road
812/876-5802

This quaint New England saltbox home is nestled in some of Indiana's finest woodlands but less than fifteen minutes from downtown Bloomington.

Fall asleep to a cricket's lullaby, and awaken to the trill of a titmouse or a glimpse of a pileated woodpecker making his round. The three antique filled guest rooms are beautifully decorated and each displays a collection of the innkeepers hand-sewn quilts. A full gourmet breakfast is served each morning.

## 7 BRAZIL

**Brazil Antique Mall**
105 E. National Ave.
812/448-3275

**Crestline Antiques**
531 E. National Ave.
812/448-8061

**Stuff N Things Antiques**
U.S. Hwy. 40 E.
812/448-3861

**His & Hers**
RR 12
812/448-3153

## 8 BROOKSTON

There is a great antique shop located in Brookston as well as others in the immediate area. See review at the beginning of this section for a complete listing.

## 9 CARMEL

**Matty's Antiques**
210 W. Main St.
317/575-6327

**Heritage of Carmel**
250 W. Main St.
317/844-0579

**Acorn Farm Country Store**
15466 Oak Road
317/846-6257

**Antique Emporium**
1055 S. Range Line Road
317/844-8351

## 10 CENTERVILLE

**Tom's Antique Center**
117 E. Main St.
765/855-3296

**Now & Then Antiques**
139 E. Main St.
765/855-2806

**Wheeler's Antiques**
107 W. Main St.
765/855-3400

**Webb's Antique Mall**
200 Union St.
765/855-2489

## 11 CHESTERTON

**Antiques 101**
101 Broadway
219/929-1434

**Kathy's Antique Shop**
530 Indian Boundary Road
219/926-1400

**Yesterday's Treasures Antique Mall**
700 Broadway
219/926-2268

**Russ & Barb's Antiques**
222 W. Lincoln Ave.
219/926-4937

**Emma's Antiques & Gifts**
428 S. Calumet Road
219/929-4427

### *Great Places To Stay*

**Gray Goose Inn**
350 Indian Boundary Road
219/926-5781

The Gray Goose Inn sits on 100 wooded acres overlooking a private lake. The decor is Williamsburg with a mixture of antiques, fine reproductions, tapestries and fine prints. Guest rooms are tastefully decorated from Shaker, 18th century English, French Country to English Victorian. A gourmet breakfast is served in the dining room overlooking the lake where guests can enjoy the wildlife such as Canadian geese and ducks. Walking trails ring the lake for nature lovers.

## 12 CORYDON

**Griffin Bldg. Antique Mall**
113 E. Beaver St.
812/738-3302

**John's Try'Al**
110 N. Elm St.
812/738-1924

**Red Barn Antique Mall**
215 Hwy. 62 W.
812/738-2276

### *Great Places To Stay*

**Kinter House Inn**
101 S. Capitol Ave.
812/738-2020
Fax: 812/738-7430
Open year round

All the elements which made Kinter House Inn the finest hotel in Corydon are still preserved today. The current owners have restored this three-story brick Italianate to its 1873 grandeur.

## 13 CRAWFORDSVILLE

**Cat's Meow**
4030 State Road 32 E.
765/362-0053

**Fireside Antique Mall**
4035 State Road 32 E.
765/362-8711

**Cabbages & Kings**
124 S. Washington St.
765/362-2577

## 14 CROWN POINT

**Gard Gallery Antiques**
700 N. Sherman St.
219/663-0547

**Dan's Antiques**
8703 E. 109th Ave.
219/663-4571

**Antique Shoppe**
Old Courthouse Shops
219/663-1031

**Antique Mall of Crown Point**
103 W. Joliet St.
219/662-1219

## 15 DALE

**Lincoln Heritage Antiques**
Hwy. 231
812/937-4840

## 16 DECATUR

**Family Tree Antiques**
618 Adams St.
219/728-2880

**Memories Past Antique Mall**
111 E. Jefferson St.
219/728-2643

**Red Duck Antiques**
132 N. 2nd St.
219/728-2224

**Town House Antiques**
222 N. 2nd St.
219/724-2920

**Yvonne Marie's Antique Mall**
152 S. 2nd St.
219/724-2001

## 17 DELPHI

There are eight antique shops located in Delphi as well as others in the immediate area. See review at the beginning of this section for complete listing.

## 18 EDINBURGH

**Edinburgh Antiques, Crafts & Collectibles**
101 W. Main Cross
812/526-0054

**Pac Rats**
109 W. Main Cross
812/526-8891

**Back In Time Antiques**
126 E. Main Cross
812/526-5409

## 19 ELKHART

**Caverns of Elkhart**
111 Prairie Court
219/293-1484

**Elkhart Antique Mall**
51772 State Road 19
219/262-8763

## 20 EVANSVILLE

**Different Things**
2107 W. Franklin St.
812/423-3890

**A King's Antique Shoppe**
504 N. Garvin St.
812/422-5865

**Em Siler Antiques**
513 N. Green River Road
812/476-2656

**Daylight Country Store**
12600 N. Green River Road
812/867-6932

**Lori's Antiques**
12747 N. Green River Road
812/867-7414

**Pack Rat**
305 N. Main St.
812/423-7526

**American & European Antiques**
402 N. Main St.
812/421-1720

**Walkway Mall**
518 Main St.
812/421-9727

**1001 Antiques**
711 N. Main St.
812/422-0291

**Rick Tremont Antiques**
608 S.E. 2nd St.
812/426-9099

**Bill's Antiques**
601 E. Virginia St.
812/422-0810

**Paxson's Antiques**
1355 Washington Ave.
812/476-6790

**Franklin Street Antique Mall**
2123 W. Franklin St.
812/428-0988

**Inside Out**
12747 N. Green River Road
812/867-7414

**Puckett's Treasures & Collectibles**
Washington Square Mall
812/473-2988

**The Tuesday Shop**
7521 Old State Road
812/867-6332

**Whispering Hills Antiques**
10600 Hwy. 65
812/963-6236

***Great Places To Stay***

**River's Inn Bed and Breakfast**
414 S.E. Riverside Dr.
812/428-7777 or 1-800-797-7990
Fax: 812/421-2902
Open year round

Built in 1866 and furnished throughout with fine antiques and collectibles this three-story Italianate home overlooks the Ohio River. Third floor rooms have balconies from which you can view the river or the beautiful gardens below. Johnny Walker potato pie is often served at breakfast.

## 21 FLORA

There are two antique shops located in Flora as well as others in the immediate area. See review at the beginning of this section for a complete listing.

**Bill's Clockworks**
Repair and sales of antique clocks
8 W. Columbia St. (Hwy. 18)
219/967-4709
1-888-742-5625
Web site: www.qklink.com/clockworks
Mon.-Fri. 9-6, Sat. 9-5
*Directions: From Chicago: (I-65 S) Take Exit 188 (SR 18 Brookston/Fowler). Turn east through Brookston and Delphi. Approximately 26 miles, at second four-way flasher on right in center of Flora.*
*From Indianapolis west side (I-70) or points south (I-65N) north on I-165 to Exit 72 (SR 26 Lafayette/Rossville) Turn right (east) through Rossville to SR 75 (approximately 17 miles), turn left (north) 8 miles to Flora & SR 18. Turn right then just before next flasher in center of town.*
*From Indianapolis/N.E. side, or from points East (I-70 and I-74). Take I-465 around N.E. side of city to Exit 27 (U.S. 421 N. Frankfort/Zionsville). Turn north on U.S. 421 approximately 48 miles to SR 18, turn left (west) on SR 18 to Flora, 7 miles (U.S. 421 turns into SR 29 at SR 28, continue north on SR 29). To left of 4-way in town.*
*From Ft. Wayne/Michigan/Northern Ohio: Take I-69 S. to Exit 64 (SR 18 Marion) Go west on SR 18 approximately 55 miles.*

Owner Bill Stoddard has had a lifelong interest in clocks. When he was a small boy, his grandfather, who had a small clock collection, showed Bill how to wind and regulate clocks. At the age of eight he acquired his first timepiece and so began his love for collecting. Bill and his mother, while cleaning out an attic, discovered a broken Waterbury octagon lever wall clock, ca. 1880. Several years later, he saved up money mowing lawns and had the clock repaired.

Throughout his teen years, Bill's love for collecting clocks grew. In April, 1991 Bill opened his own clock shop in his home in Indianapolis. By 1995 Bill had moved to Flora where he opened shop in the former Rainbow Cafe. He enjoys repairing many different types of clocks, particularly early American weight driven clocks. Bill says he enjoys his work because he gets to repair each clock, treating it as if it were his own, enjoying it while it's in the shop, then seeing the smile on the customers face when their time-piece is clean, shiny and repaired. And the best part — he gets paid for doing something he truly loves.

## 22 FORT WAYNE

**Betty's Antiques**
1421 Broadway
219/424-0504

**Old Clock Shop & Antiques**
3331 Butler Court
219/483-2061

**Karen's Antique Mall**
1510 Fairfield Ave.
219/422-4030

**Candlelight Antiques**
3205 Broadway
219/456-3150

**Wagenhaus Furniture Gallery**
3920 N. Clinton St.
219/484-9420

**Nature's Corner Antique Mall**
2305 Spy Run Ave.
219/493-5236

## 23 FRANKFORT

There is a great antique shop located in Frankfort as well as others in the immediate area. See review at the beginning of this section for a complete listing.

## 24 FRANKLIN

**Jeri's Antiques**
56 E. Jefferson St., #C
317/738-3848

**Peddler's II**
90 W. Jefferson St.
317/736-6299

**Countryside Antiques**
4251 N. State Road 135
317/422-9206

**Lighthouse Antique Mall**
62 W. Jefferson St.
317/738-3344

**Town Square Antiques**
104 W. Jefferson St.
317/736-9633

## 25 GOSHEN

### Carriage Barn Antiques
1100 Chicago Ave.
219/533-6353
Mon.-Fri. 9:30-5, Sat. 9:30-4
*Directions: From 80/90 Indiana Toll Road, Exit 101 at Bristol. Turn south on State Road 15 to Goshen. Go right (west) on U.S. 33 to K.F.C. (Indiana Ave.). Turn right and continue for 2 1/2 blocks to the old Bag Factory. Park behind the log house. Look for arched entry into brick building.*

Looking for a piece of furniture like Grandma used to own? Unless Grandma is 125-225 years old, you're not likely to find it here in the Carriage Barn. Their circa 1780-1890 furniture is displayed in room settings with appropriate accessories and quilts.

Fine replica tin, copper, and brass lighting accentuate these fine old furnishings. If you are a true antique enthusiast, you can't help but feel a pang for the past as you browse through this truly unique antique haven.

**Goshen Antique Mall**
107 S. Main St.
219/534-6141

***Great Places To Stay***

### Front Porch Inn
320 S. Fifth St.
219/533-4258

This 1800s Italianate Victorian home is located in Goshen's historic district near downtown shopping, churches and government offices. If your interest is bicycling you will enjoy the location on the city's Greenway which winds its way through the town from Goshen College to many parks, along the Mill Race, and downtown. Guest rooms are spacious and newly decorated. Located in Amish country, a short drive from Shipshewana, Middlebury and Nappanee.

### Indian Creek Bed & Breakfast
20300 CR 18
219/875-6606

This new Victorian style home is filled with family antiques and collectibles and has been lovingly decorated throughout. The guest rooms, named after the innkeeper's grandchildren, have either queen or full size beds, private baths and each is uniquely different. Indian Creek is within driving distance of the beach and Shipshewana Flea Market.

## 26 GREENFIELD

**Carriage House Antiques**
210 Center St.
317/462-3253

**Red Ribbon Antiques**
101 W. Main St.
317/462-5211

**Bob's Antiques**
113 W. Main St.
317/462-8749

**Sugar Creek Antique Mall**
2244 W. U.S. Hwy. 40
317/467-4938

**Reflections of Time**
14 W. Main St.
317/462-3878

**J W Riley's Emporium**
107 W. Main St.
317/462-5268

**The Red Rooster**
1001 W. Main St.
317/462-0655

## 27 HUNTINGBURG

### Mulberry Tree Antiques and Collectibles
4625 S. State Route 162
812/482-1822
Wed.-Sun. 10-5, Mon.-Tues. by appointment
*Directions: Traveling I-64, take Exit 63 north approximately 7 miles. The Mulberry Tree is centrally located in the county, 1/2 mile north of State Highways 162 and 64, 5 miles north of Ferdinand, 5 miles south of Jasper, or 5 miles east of Huntingburg.*

This shop's "claim to fame" is their quality antiques and excellent dealers. Mulberry Tree is owner-operated and friendly, providing two good reasons to stop in for a visit!

**Parker House Antiques**
307 E. 4th St.
812/683-5352

**Goodthings**
517 E. 4th St.
812/683-4815

**Country Corner**
3rd & Geiger St.
812/683-4849

**Locker Antiques**
314 E. 4th St.
812/683-4149

**Enchantingly Yours**
330 E. 4th St.
812/683-5437

**Judy Ann's Antiques**
S.E. Corner 4th & Main
812/683-4993

**B-K Antiques**
507 E. 4th St.
812/683-2534

**Antique Boutique**
3582 S. 75 W.
812/683-2850

**Green Tree Antiques**
312 E. 4th St.
812/683-4448

**Yesterdays Antiques & Collectibles**
320 E. 4th St.
812/683-4422

**Gene's Antiques**
330 4th St.
812/683-4199

**Lamb's 'n Ivy**
421 E. 4th St.
812/683-5533

## 28 HUNTINGTON

**S & B Antiques & Collectibles**
434 N. Jefferson St.
219/356-1302

## 29 INDIANAPOLIS

### Colonial Antiques
5000 W. 96th St.
317/873-2727
Fri.-Sat. 10-5; other days by appointment
*Directions: Take I-465 north to Michigan Road (Exit 421). Exit north and go 1 block to 96th Street. Colonial Antiques is 1 mile west on the right.*

Once, not long ago, architectural treasures were destroyed, fallen prey to the wrecking ball in order to build society's latest needs—a new high rise, a service station, a grocery store, or even a cement parking lot. Today these treasures have been sought after and salvaged by decorators, builders and collectors. Colonial Antiques specializes in these unique, mostly one-of-a-kind finds including lighting, mantels, hardware and more.

**Bluemingdeals Antiques & Jazzy Junk**
4601 N. College Ave.
317/924-4765

**Neat Antiques & More**
4907 N. College Ave.
317/921-1916

**Barn Village Antiques**
5209 N. College Ave.
317/283-5011

**D T Hollings Antiques Inc.**
1760 E. 86th St.
317/574-1777

**North Indy Antique Mall**
7226 E. 87th St., #E
317/578-2671

**Hope's Shop**
116 E. 49th St.
317/283-3004

**Abe's Attic Treasures**
1431 S. Meridian St.
317/636-4105

**Red Barn Galleries**
325 E. 106th St.
317/846-8928

**Antique Centre**
3422 N. Shadeland Ave.
317/545-3879

**Margie's Menagerie**
4905 N. College Ave.
317/931-1400

**Recollections Antiques**
5202 N. College Ave.
317/283-3800

**A Rare Find Gallery**
4040 E. 82nd St., #10C
317/842-5828

**Finds Antiques**
1764 E. 86th St.
317/571-1950

**Sayger Antiques**
711 E. 54th St.
317/251-1936

**Trash to Treasures**
5505 N. Keystone Ave.
317/253-2235

**Midland Arts & Antiques**
907 E. Michigan St.
317/267-9005

**Blue Sun Gallery**
922 E. Westfield Blvd.
317/255-8441

**Antiques N More**
3440 N. Shadeland Ave.
317/542-8526

**Antique Mall**
3444 N. Shadeland Ave.
317/542-7283

**Nostalgia**
7501 Somerset Bay, #B
317/926-0097

**Indianapolis D/Town Antiques**
1044 Virginia Ave.
317/635-5336

**Fountain Square Antique Mall**
1056 Virginia Ave.
317/636-1056

**Manor House Antique Mall**
5454 U.S. 31 S.
317/782-1358

**Quality Antiques**
1105 Shelby St.
317/686-6018

**Southport Antique Mall Inc.**
2028 E. Southport Road
317/786-8246

**Mobile Merchant**
1052 Virginia Ave.
317/264-9968

**D & D Antique Mall**
6971 W. Washington St.
317/486-9760

#### *Great Places To Stay*

### Tranquil Cherub
2164 N. Capitol Ave.
317/923-9036

This 95-year-old Greek Revival home has four guests rooms each with private bath and unique charm. Guests often wander through the antique filled rooms, enjoy the 1914 player piano or relax with a good book in the upstairs sitting room. Breakfast is served in the beautiful dining room near the fire. Weather permitting you may eat on the outside deck overlooking the garden and Koi ponds.

## 30 KENTLAND

**Pastyme Peddlers**
210 & 213 N. 3rd St.
219/474-9306

**Dad's Trash & Treasures**
506 E. Seymour St.
219/474-3231

## 31 KNIGHTSTOWN

**Knightstown Antique Mall**
136 W. Carey St.
765/345-5665

**Lindon's Antique Mall**
32 E. Main St.
765/345-2545

**The Glass Cupboard**
115 E. Main St.
765/345-7572

**Michael Bonne Coppersmith Shop**
103 E. Main St.
765/345-7831, 765/345-5521

**Hats Off**
102 E. Main St.
765/345-7788

**Nostalgia Nook**
6 E. Main St.
765/345-7937

**J. W. Riley's Emporium**
121 E. Main St.
765/345-7480

### *Great Places To Stay*

**Main Street Victorian**
130 W. Main St.
765/345-2299

This stunning Victorian cottage offers a unique decor with a romantic ambiance. Lace, stained glass windows and soft light complete the three guest rooms, each decorated in beautiful colors and antique furnishings. The cottage is located within "Antique Alley" making it a perfect place to rest after a full day of antiquing.

**Old Hoosier House**
7601 S. Greensboro Pike
1-800-775-5315

Central Indiana's first and favorite country bed and breakfast, the Old Hoosier House is ideally suited for sightseeing and shopping Indiana's "Antique Alley." The architectural style is Victorian, circa 1836, and is furnished in antique decor throughout. Four guest rooms are available; breakfast is included as well as afternoon tea.

## 32 KOKOMO

**White Bungaloo Antique Mall**
906 S. Main St.
765/459-0789

**C & L Antiques**
841 S. Main St.
765/452-2290

**Ol' Hickory & Lace Antiques.**
913 S. Main St.
765/452-6026

**Wild Ostrich Antiques**
929 S. Main St.
765/452-3990

**Roninger's Then & Now Store**
4410 S. 00 EW
765/453-0521

**Cricket Box**
907 S. Main St.
765/459-8790

**Treasure Mart Mall**
3780 S. Reed Road
765/455-9855

## 33 LAFAYETTE

**Buck's Collectibles & Antiques**
310 S. 16th St.
765/742-2192
Mon.-Sat. 10-5
*Directions: Enter Layfayette either on Interstate 65 or State Road 52. If entering on Interstate 65, exit on State Road 26 west. Travel west on State Road 26 which is South St. after crossing State Road 52. Travel South St. until the 5-points intersection before South St. heads downtown. At the 5-points intersection turn left onto 16th St. and the antique mall will be on the right side of the corner of 16th St. and Center St.*

Buck's Collectibles & Antiques is filled to the brim with primitives, Coca Cola, antique dolls, collector dolls, antique furniture, pottery, Occupied Japan, monon and nickel plate railroad, advertising, Keen Kutter tools, antique tools, and case knives all supplied by a mix of 45 dealers from around the Greater Lafayette area. This antique mall is definitely a must stop if you are interested in browsing or purchasing the unique and unusual.

**Leonard's Antiques & Books**
1324 N. 14th St.
765/742-8668

**Alley Gifts & Collectibles**
638 Main St.
765/429-5758

**Lee-Weises Antiques**
1724 N. 9th St.
765/423-2754

**Koehler Bros. General Store**
3431 State Road 26 E.
765/447-2155

**Pack Rat Antiques**
424 Main St.
765/742-7490

**Antique Mall of Lafayette**
800 Main St.
765/742-2469

**Chesterfield Antiques & Collectibles**
210 N. 6th St.
765/742-2956

**Lamb & Heart Americana**
3433 State Road 26 E.
765/447-1863

## 34 LaPORTE

The city of LaPorte is brimming with a rich historical heritage. Start here for the antique tour of LaPorte County; follow the tour with a visit to the LaPorte County Historical Society Museum. Housed in the LaPorte County Courthouse, the museum displays everything from a 1,000 piece antique firearms collection to old musical instruments to re-created shops and offices. Don't leave town until you've followed LaPorte's Stroll Along the Avenues walking tour of historic homes and elegant architecture. The Door Prairie Museum, south of LaPorte, displays a distinguished collection of automobiles spanning 100 years.

**Corner Cupboard**
108 Lincolnway
219/326-9882

**It's A Wonderful Life**
708 Lincolnway
219/326-7432

**Walnut Hill Antiques**
613 Michigan Ave.
219/326-1099

**Coachman Antique Mall**
500 Lincolnway
219/326-5933

**Antique Junction Mall**
711 Lincolnway
219/324-0363

## 35 LAWRENCEBURG

**Shumways Olde Mill Antique**
232 W. High St.
812/537-1709

**Livery Stable Antique Mall**
318 Walnut St.
812/537-4364

## 36 LEBANON

**Cedars of Lebanon Antiques**
126 W. Washington St.
765/482-7809

## 37 LEO

**Leo Antique Exchange**
11119 Grabill Road
219/627-2242

**Cellar Antique Mall**
15004 A State Road 1
219/627-6565

**Shades of Country**
51004 State Road 1
219/627-2189

## 38 LIGONIER

**Creative Visions**
115 S. Cavin St.
219/894-3449

**Mad Hatter Antiques**
254 W. U.S. Hwy. 6
219/894-4995

## 39 LOGANSPORT

**A-1 Preowned Items**
112 Burlington Ave.
219/739-2121

**Market Street Antiques**
222 E. Market St.
219/735-0131

**Yesteryear Antiques & Collectibles**
525 E. Market St.
219/753-7371

**Homewood Antiques**
1075 N. State Road 25
219/722-2398

## 40 MADISON

**Broadway Antique Mall**
701 Broadway St.
812/265-6606

**Lumber Mill Antique Mall**
721 W. 1st St.
812/273-3040

**Wallace's Antiques**
125 E. Main St.
812/265-2473

**Antiques on Main**
129 E. Main St.
812/265-2240

**Best Friends**
133 E. Main St.
812/265-5548

**Main St Antique Mall**
210 E. Main St.
812/273-5286

**Antiques Etc.**
224 E. Main St.
812/273-6768

**Old Town Emporium**
113 E. 2nd St.
812/273-4394

**Madison Antique Mall**
401 E. 2nd St.
812/265-6399

### *Great Places To Stay*

**Main Street B&B**
739 W. Main St.
1-800-362-6246

Main Street Bed and Breakfast is a graceful, Classic-Revival home built circa 1843 located in Madison's historic district. This charming accommodation has three tastefully decorated, spacious guest rooms, all with private baths. While there is an atmosphere of elegance in the home and its furnishings, the mood is relaxed and friendly. A delicious full breakfast awaits guests in the morning. Restaurants, shops, historic homes, and the Ohio River are all within walking distance.

**Schussler House Bed and Breakfast**
514 Jefferson St.
812/273-2068 or 1-800-392-1931
Open year round
Rates $75-120

The Schussler House was built in 1849 for Charles Schussler a local physician who used the residence for his office and home.

Today, this Federal and Greek Revival home is an elegant bed and breakfast featuring antique and reproduction furniture throughout the three guest rooms and common areas. A gourmet breakfast is served in the dining room

## 41 MARTINSVILLE

**Emporium**
110 N. Main St.
765/349-9060

**Morgan County Auction & Flea Mkt.**
128 N. Main St.
765/342-8098

**Gateway Collectibles**
96 E. Morgan St.
765/342-8983

**Creative Accents, Inc.**
166 E. Morgan St.
765/342-0213

## 42 MERRILLVILLE

**Carriage House**
420 W. 73rd Ave.
219/769-2169

## 43 MICHIGAN CITY

### The Antique Market
3707 N. Frontage Road
219/879-4084
Mon.-Sat. 10-5, Sun. 12-5, closed major holidays
*Directions: Take I-94 to Exit 34B and U.S. Hwy. 421 north. Go 1 block to stoplight and turn right, then take another quick right onto Frontage Road (access road to The Antique Market).*

Easily accessible from I-94 and Hwy. 142, The Antique Market with its more than 85 dealers is one of the few remaining markets or malls that has not conformed by adding crafts and reproductions to its line of antiques and collectibles. If you are a true antique enthusiast, you will enjoy shopping among the fine old treasures.

**Road House Antiques**
3900 W. Dunes Hwy.
219/878-1866

**Mona's Treasure Chest**
4496 Wozniak Road
219/874-6475

**E T World Antiques**
7326 Johnson Road
219/872-9002

**Days Gone By Antiques**
10673 W. 300 N.
219/879-7496

**Stocking Bale Antiques Mall**
227 W. 7th St.
219/873-9270

## 44 MISHAWAKA

**Antiques Etc.**
110 Lincoln Way E.
219/258-5722

**Interiors Etc.**
301 Lincoln Way E.
219/259-7717

**Pack Rat Pats**
3005 Lincoln Way E.
219/259-5609

**Ed's Collectables**
126 N. Main St.
219/255-5041

## 45 MITCHELL

**Ma Nancy's Antiques**
609 W. Main St.
812/849-2203

**Checkerberry**
615 W. Main St.
812/849-3784

**Persimmon Tree Antiques**
619 W. Main St.
812/849-5300

**Mitchell Antique Mall**
706 W. Main St.
812/849-4497

## 46 MONTICELLO

There are seven antique shops located in Monticello as well as others in the immediate area. See review at the beginning of this section for a complete listing.

## 47 MORGANTOWN

**Morgantown Antiques**
49 E. Washington St.
812/597-0412

**Miller's Antiques**
Route 1 Box 5A
812/597-6024

**Yesterday's Antique & Auction Service**
149 W. Washington St.
812/597-5525

## 48 MUNCIE

**Off-Broadway Antique Mall**
2404 N. Broadway Ave.
765/747-5000

**Walker Antiques**
4801 E. Memorial Dr.
765/282-0399

## 49 NAPPANEE

Imagine yourself leisurely driving over scenic country backroads and broad flat prairie lands, past picturesque farms, stopping for handmade quilts and crafts. All this and more quietly awaits you in Northern Indiana Amish Country. Take the Heritage Trail, a 90-mile loop through the heart of mid-America, which is even easier to enjoy with a self-guided tour complete with map, guidebook and audio cassette tape with directions. Between the towns of Middlebury, Shipshewana, and Nappanee you'll sense the influence of one of the largest Amish settlements in the United States. To receive a full listing of accommodations and attractions along the Trail or make lodging reservations, call Northern Indiana Amish Country at 1-800-860-5957.

### Borkholder Dutch Village
71945 C. R. 101
219/773-2828, Fax 219/773-4828
Mon.-Sat. 10-5 winter, 9-5 summer
*Directions: Located 1/4 mile north of U.S. 6, 1 1/2 miles west of State Road. 19; or 13 miles east of U.S. 31, then 1/4 mile north off U.S. 6.*

In 1987, Freeman Borkholder, owner of Borkholder American Vintage Furniture, decided to purchase a facility to showcase the local crafts and antiques for which Nappanee is well known. He bought, believe it or not, high rise chicken houses, completely renovated them, and created Borkholder Dutch Village. It is an authentic country-style marketplace, complete with a flea market, an arts and crafts mall, a restaurant, antique mall, events center and village shops.

The Dutch Village is open six days a week (see hours above) and a huge antique auction is held every Tuesday at 8 a.m. At the auction and throughout the antique mall, you can find quality furniture, including bedroom and dining room suites, dry sinks, roll-top desks, iceboxes, hall trees, buffets and more. And you can add a taste of the past to your life with antique dinnerware, jewelry, dolls and vintage clothes.

Stroll through the arts and crafts mall, where you'll find quilts, wood carvings, shelving, dolls, framed artwork, knitted and crocheted items, new and used household goods, floral arrangements and many other hand-crafted items.

For lunch, visit the Dutch Kitchen, where you can indulge in a soda fountain treat, like a Green River or a Phosphate, enjoy a homemade lunch and top it off with Amish Apple Dumplings or another scrumptious dessert.

**AAA Antique Shop**
Hwy. 6 W.
219/773-4912

**Main Street Antiques Mall**
160 N. Main St.
219/773-5158

**Antiques on the Square**
106 S. Main St.
219/773-5770

**Nappanee Antique Mall**
156 S. Main St.
219/773-3278

**Amishland Antique Mall**
106 W. Market St.
219/773-4795

## 50 NASHVILLE

**Lee's Antiques**
S. Jefferson, #45 A
812/988-1448

**Brown County Antique Mall II**
3288 E. State Road 46
812/988-1025

**Grandma Had One Antique Center**
216 S. Van Buren St.
812/988-1039

### *Great Places To Stay*

**Allison House Inn**
90 S. Jefferson
812/988-0814

For specific information see review at the beginning of this section.

## 51 NEW ALBANY

**Old New Albany Antique Mall**
225 State St.
812/948-1890

## 52 NEW HARMONY

**New Harmony Antique Mall**
500 Church St.
812/682-3948

**Donna Smith's Heirlooms, Etc.**
527 Church St.
812/682-5027

**Antiques Showrooms In The Mews**
531 Church St.
812/682-3490

**Treasure Trove**
514 S. Main St.
812/682-4112

### *Great Places To Stay*

**Raintree Inn Bed and Breakfast**
503 West St.
1-888-656-0123
Web site: www.raintree-inn.com

In New Harmony, one of Indiana's most unique and historic communities, a late Victorian Mansion has been reborn as a premier bed and breakfast establishment dedicated to providing quality service and excellent accommodations. Raintree Inn's magnificent interiors and furnishings are just part of its appeal. Whether your interests are in history, shopping, art, theatre, relaxation or a romantic getaway, innkeepers Scott and Nancy McDonald will help you get the most out of your New Harmony experience. Tastefully furnished guestrooms each with large comfortable beds and private baths combined with a sumptuous full breakfast to insure that your visit to New Harmony is both pleasant and memorable.

## 53 NEWBURGH

**Rivertown Antiques**
1 W. Jennings St.
812/853-2562

**Generations**
218 W. Jennings St.
812/853-7270

**Little Red Barn Antiques**
10044 W. State Route 662
812/853-8096

**Country Gentleman Antiques**
103 State St.
812/858-9544

## 54 NOBLESVILLE

**Durwyn Smedley Antiques**
853 Conner St.
317/776-0161

**Olde House Antiques**
293 S. 8th St.
317/773-6951

**Lazy Acres Antiques**
77 Metsker Lane
317/773-7387

**Noblesville Antique Mall**
20 N. 9th St.
317/773-5095

**Bound To Be Found Antiques**
74 N. 9th St.
317/776-1993

## 55 NORTH VERNON

**Country Corner Market**
4250 N. State Hwy. 7
812/346-1095

**Olde Store Antiques**
162 E. Walnut St.
812/346-1925

**Cornett's**
246 E. Walnut St.
812/346-8995

**North Vernon Antique Mall**
247 E. Walnut St.
812/346-8604

## 56 PENDLETON

**Bob Post Antiques**
104 W. State St.
765/778-7778

**Pendleton Antique Mall**
123 W. State St.
765/778-2303

**Grandma's Treasures**
128 W. State St.
765/778-8211

## 57 PERU

**Annie's Attic**
57 N. Broadway
765/473-4400

**Peru Antique Mall**
21 E. Main St.
765/473-8179

## 58 PIERCETON

**Beebe's Antique Shop**
Downtown Pierceton
219/594-2244

**Old Theater Antique Mall**
103 N. 1st St.
219/594-2533

**Antiques at the Sign of the Gas Light**
130 N. 1st St.
219/594-2457

**Curiosity Shop**
112 S. 1st St.
219/594-2785

**Gregory's Antiques**
State Road 13
219/594-5718

## 59 PLAINFIELD

**Gilley's Antique Mall**
5789 E. U.S. Hwy. 40
317/839-8779

**Avon Antiques**
7673 E. U.S. Hwy 36
317/272-4842

**Little Dave's Everything Store**
10107 W. Washington
317/839-6040

**Haunted Bridge Antique. Mall**
184 N. State Road 267
317/272-6956

## 60 PORTLAND

**Farmstead Antiques**
Hwy. 275
219/726-4930

**Carlson's Antiques**
212 N. Meridian St.
219/726-7919

## 61 RICHMOND

**Scott Lure Co. & Trading Post**
1449 E. Chester Road
765/935-5091

**Foster's E Street Gallery**
825 N. E St.
765/935-9055

**Ft. Wayne Furniture Store**
193 Fort Wayne Ave.
765/966-9372

**The Silhouette Shop**
126 S. 4th St.
765/935-7887

**Top Drawer Antique Mall**
801 Promenade
765/939-0349

**John's**
823-825 Promenade
765/962-0214

**Kate's Furniture**
131 Richmond Ave.
765/966-5246

**At The Garden Gate**
111 S. 3rd
765/939-0777

## 62 ROANN

**Covered Bridge Merc. Co.**
165 N. Chippewa Road
765-833-7473

**Mom & Pop's Jazzy Junk**
175 N. Chippewa Road
765/833-2233

**Royal Attic Design**
180 N. Chippewa St.
765/833-5333

**Roann Antique Mall**
200 N. Chippewa St.
765/833-6242

## 63 ROANOKE

### Antiques from BC At Lonsdale
10979 N. Roanake Road
219/672-9744
Open daily 10-5, by chance and any time by appointment
*Directions: Just 7 miles south of I-69, take Exit 102 to Hwy. 24 South until you reach 1100 North, then turn right and go to the next corner. The shop is located in the front of the school building on the southeast corner.*

Located in a 1915 school building, this shop specializes in quality country and formal furniture dating from the 18th-20th century. Additionally, they offer decorative paintings and accessories to enhance your home.

## 64 ROCKVILLE

**Covered Bridge Mall**
115 S. Jefferson St.
765/569-3145

**Rockville Antique Mall**
411 E. Ohio St.
765/569-6873

**Aunt Patty's Antiques**
U.S. Route 36
765/569-2605

**Bart's Corner**
Walker Ramp Road
765/344-6112

## 65 ROSSVILLE

There are three antique shops located in Rossville as well as others in the immediate area. See review at the beginning of this section for a complete listing.

## 66 SCOTTSBURG

**Country Cousins Antiques**
Hwy. 31 S.
812/752-6353

**Scottsburg Antique Mall**
4 N. Main St.
812/752-4645

## 67 SEYMOUR

**Broadway Antiques**
219 N. Broadway St.
812/522-9538

**Remember When Antiques**
317 N. Broadway St.
812/522-5099

**Lucille's House of Antiques**
603 S. Chestnut St.
812/522-5541

**Crossroads Antique Mall**
311 Holiday Square
812/522-5675

## 68 SHIPSHEWANA

**Log House Country Store**
255 Depot
219/768-4652

**Berry's Hitching Post**
250 E. Middlebury
219/768-7862

**Fisher's Antiques**
155 Morton
219/768-4213

**Haarer's Antiques**
165 Morton
219/768-4787

## 69 SILVER LAKE

**Attic Antiques**
107 N. Jefferson
219/352-2744

**D & J Antiques**
102 S. Jefferson
219/352-2400

**Twin Lakes Antiques**
7208 W. State Road 114
219/982-2939

## 70 SOUTH BEND

**Thieves Market Mall**
Crossroad Shopping Center
219/273-1352

**Anthony's Antiques**
1606 W. Ewing Ave.
219/287-8180

**A-Antiques Ltd.**
1009 N. Frances St.
219/232-1134

**Antiques & Things**
2210 Huron St.
219/282-2550

**Light Owl Antiques**
529 Lincoln Way W.
219/287-1184

**Victorian Galleries**
2011 Miami St.
219/233-3633

**AAA Quality Antiques**
1763 Prairie Ave.
219/232-1099

**Unique Antique Mall**
50981 U.S. Hwy. 33
219/271-1799

**Antique Avenue Mall**
52345 U.S. Route 31 N.
219/272-2558

### *Great Places To Stay*

**The Book Inn**
508 W. Washington
219/288-1990
Fax 219/234-2338
Web site: members.aol.com/bookinn
*Directions: Exit #77 off the I-80/90 Toll Road.*

Built by Martha and Albert Cushing in 1872, this home was one of the earliest residences in the historic district of South Bend. Cushing was a local businessman with interests in several enterprises, including a drug and bookstore at 101 North Michigan Street. The house is listed as an outstanding example of Second Empire architecture by the Indiana Historic Site Preservation Committee. Sometimes called French Victorian, the mansard roof with ornamental arched dormer windows creates an impression of massive elegance. The entry doors with double leaf wood and applied decoration reportedly won first place for design at the 1893 Columbian Exposition in Chicago.

Inside you will find twelve foot ceilings and handhewn, irreplaceable butternut woodwork that welcome you into this elegant mansion. The Book Inn has been a designer showcase and every room offers comfortable bed and breakfast accommodations. The five sleeping rooms all have private bathrooms.

The Book Inn is located in the historic West Washington District of downtown South Bend, Indiana. The original owners, the Cushings, must have watched in wonder when Clement Studebaker built his home, Tippecanoe Place, "right next door" in 1888. Studebaker's forty-room 'feudal castle' is now an elegant restaurant where you can explore the mansion and enjoy a wonderful meal.

"High ceilings, large comfortable beds with beautiful linens, lovely antique furnishings, picture books, novels, cozy reading chairs, fresh flowers, lush terry robes, private bath - everything I could possibly want. The entire house, from the well-stocked library and kitchen to the dining room set with crystal, linen, great coffee, and tasty breakfast fare, is a weary traveler's dream. Peggy and John made be feel welcome, relaxed and pampered."

*(Guest) Suzanne Peck*
*America's Favorite Inns, B&Bs & Small Hotels*

## 71 SPENCER

**River Valley Sales**
27 E. Franklin St.
812/829-4948

**Hillside Cottage and Antiques**
870 W. Hillside Ave.
812/829-4488

**Maxine's**
56 E. Jefferson
812/829-6369

**Spencer Antique Mall, Inc.**
165 S. Main St.
812/829-0785

**Robinson House Galleries**
3 N. Montgomery St.
812/829-9558

## 72 TERRE HAUTE

There's something for everyone in Terre Haute! Enjoy a walking tour through the lovely Farrington Grove Historical District, near downtown Terre Haute, where over 800 homes offer visitors a wealth of historic architectural detail and colorful histories.

Take a step back even further in time at the new Native American Museum located on the east side of Terre Haute in Dobbs Park. This museum lets you explore Native American cultures through exhibits, programs, and a Native American heirloom garden.

**Hoosier Antiques & Clocks**
1630 S. 3rd St.
812/238-0562
Mon.-Sat. 10-5, Sun. by chance or appointment
*Directions: Traveling I-70 exit at U.S. 41 (Exit 7) and proceed 1.2 miles north on 3rd St. Turn right at either Hulman St. or Osborne St. Parking is at the rear off the alley. Traveling U.S. 40 drive 1.2 miles south of the Court house at Wabash Ave. and 3rd St. In Terre Haute, 3rd St. is U.S. 41 and Wabash Ave. is U.S. 40.*

Hoosier Antiques & Clocks is located in a charming, shingled cottage built in the early 1900s. The shop carries a general line of antiques and collectibles and specializes in antique clocks. All clocks are in running condition.

**Swank Antiques**
1126 N. 8th St.
812/235-7734

**Antiques Crafts & Things**
137 W. Honey Creek Pkwy.
812/232-8959

**E Bleemel Flour & Feed**
904 Poplar St.
812/232-2466

**Lowry's Antiques**
1132 Poplar St.
812/234-1717

**Ancient Tymes Antiques Mall**
1600 S. 3rd St.
812/238-2178

**Antiques Inc.**
2000 S. 3rd St.
812/235-4829

**Gatherings**
1429 S. 25th St.
812/234-8322

**Shady Lane Antique Mall**
9247 S. U.S. Hwy. 41
812/299-1625

**Granny's Daughter**
11746 S. U.S. Hwy. 41
812/299-8277

**Nancy's Downtown Mall**
600 Wabash Ave.
812/238-1129

**North Side Collectables**
2323 Lafayette Ave.
812/466-9091

**Colonial Antiques**
Farmersburg, So. on U.S. 41
812/696-2600

**Anderson Antiques**
1612 S. 3rd St. (U.S. 41)
812/232-2991

**Antiques, Tim Weir**
1641 S. 25th St.
812/234-6515

**Kasameyer Antiques & Collectibles**
5149 So. U.S. 41 (7th & 41)
812/299-1672

## 73 TIPTON

**Dezerland**
114-116 S. Main
765/675-8999

**Foster's Last Stand**
122 N. Main St.
765/675-3391

## 74 VALPARAISO

**Sydow Antiques**
153 W. Lincolnway
219/465-1777

**Accents Etc.**
202 E. Lincolnway
219/464-3739

**Valparaiso Antique Mall Inc.**
212 E. Lincolnway
219/465-1869

## 75 VINCENNES

**Yesteryear**
305 Main St.
812/882-2459

**Hitching Post**
1717 Washington Ave.
812/882-9372

**Old Town Attic Antiques**
1804 Washington Ave.
812/882-0903

## 76 WESTFIELD

**Antiques Galore & More**
110 E. Main St.
317/867-1228

**Welcome House Antiques Etc**
202 E. Main St.
317/867-0077

**Jonathan Westfield Co.**
120 N. Union St.
317/896-3566

**R Beauchamp Antiques**
16405 Westfield Blvd.
317/897-3717

**Westfield Antique Mall**
800 E. Main, Hwy. 232
317/867-3327

## 77 WHITING

**Granny's General Store**
1309 Community Court
219/659-7538

**Blue Ribbon Antiques**
1858 Indianapolis Blvd.
219/659-4502

**Just Little Things**
1600 119th St.
219/659-3438

## 78 WORTHINGTON

**Carriage House Antiques**
318 S. Jefferson St.
812/875-3219

## 79 ZIONSVILLE

**Brown's Antique Shop**
315 N. 5th St.
317/873-2284

**Sow's Ear**
76 S. Main St.
317/873-2785

**Captain Logan**
150 S. Main St.
317/873-9999

**Zionsville Antiques**
75 N. Main St.
317/873-1761

**Indiana Folkart & Antiques**
120 S. Main St.
317/873-4424

**Helen Kogan Antiques & Lghting**
195 S. Main St.
317/873-4208

### *Great Places To Stay*

**Brick Street Inn**
175 S. Main St.
317/873-9177
Email: www.Brickstinn@aol.com

Capture the essence of Midwestern hospitality and country living at Brick Street Inn, a historic 5-room circa 1865 home. The style is relaxed, which means all the comforts with a casual attitude. The attention to detail is not just how it looks, but how if feels...cozy, romantic, friendly, the inn is a secret that unfolds. Rooms feature down comforters, fluffy robes and an eclectic mix of new and old furnishings. Your hosts provide fresh flowers, mouth watering goodies and a gourmet breakfast. Set in historic Zionsville which quietly borders metropolitan Indianapolis, the inn is privy to some of the best shopping and dining in Central Indiana.

# Iowa

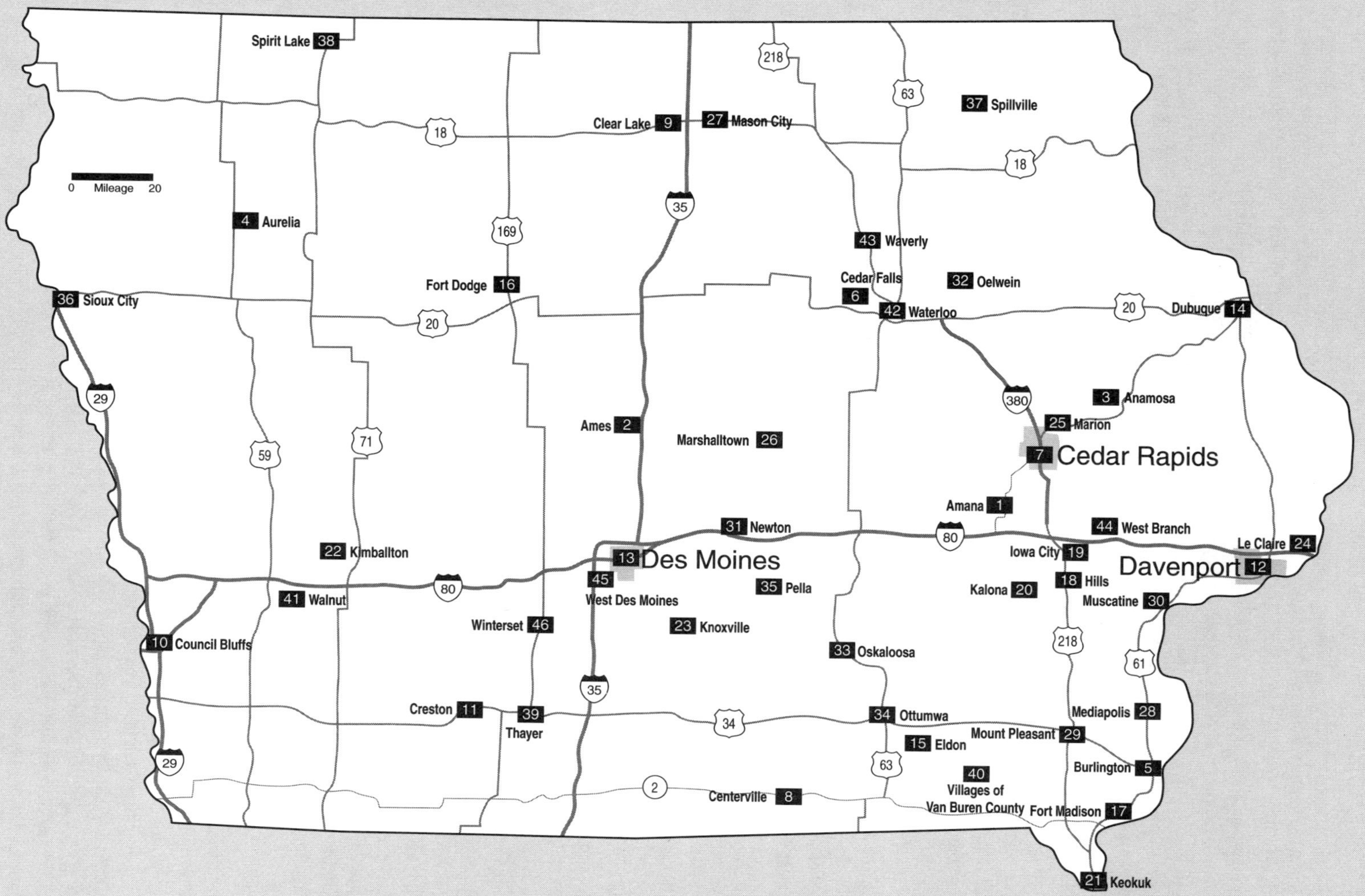

Spirit Lake 38
37 Spillville
Clear Lake 9
27 Mason City
0 Mileage 20
4 Aurelia
43 Waverly
Cedar Falls
6
32 Oelwein
Fort Dodge 16
36 Sioux City
42 Waterloo
Dubuque 14
3 Anamosa
Ames 2
Marshalltown 26
25 Marion
7 Cedar Rapids
Amana 1
31 Newton
44 West Branch
Le Claire 24
22 Kimballton
13 Des Moines
Iowa City 19
Davenport 12
45
West Des Moines
35 Pella
18 Hills
Kalona 20
41 Walnut
Muscatine 30
Winterset 46
23 Knoxville
10 Council Bluffs
33 Oskaloosa
Creston 11
39
Thayer
34 Ottumwa
Mediapolis 28
Mount Pleasant 29
15 Eldon
Burlington 5
40
Villages of
Van Buren County
Centerville 8
Fort Madison 17
21 Keokuk

# Iowa

Let's take a trip through history and celebrate the 10th anniversary of "Main Street" Iowa. Over the past decade, the preservation-based downtown revitalization program of the National Trust for Historic Preservation has helped Iowa not only to preserve, but celebrate and share its heritage and culture through the "Main Street" program. All across the state each year, "Main Street" towns keep their pasts alive. Annual heritage festivals help Iowans and visitors appreciate the lifestyles of our ancestors with food, costumes, events and music of times past. Visiting these "Main Street" communities is like an annual vacation in a time machine! You'll see unique shops intermingled with historic buildings...festivals, food and fun from America's Heartland...pride, personality and friendliness of hearty, happy people. Consider this your special invitation to stop by, stay a while and catch the spirit on "Main Streets" all across Iowa.

## 1 AMANA

Iowa's Amana Colonies are seven closely situated villages that comprise a unique settlement running along the Iowa River valley, through lush farming country. Amana's early settlers left Germany in 1842 seeking religious freedom. They settled near Buffalo, N. Y., but in 1855 they moved to Iowa and established seven villages known as the Amana Colonies on 26,000 acres of wooded hills. There they lived under a religious communal system, sharing work, meals, worldly goods and religious services. In 1932 the villagers voted to end the communal way, and they created the Amana Church Society to direct their faith, which is now known as the Community of True Inspiration. They created the Amana Society to operate the 26,000 acres of land and businesses that were formerly held by the commune. All the villagers became stockholders in the Society, bought their own homes, and some founded their own businesses.

The first village to be settled was named "Amana," from the Song of Solomon (4:8), which means "to remain true." There were seven villages in the original Colonies; today there are a total of nine. Visitors may recognize the name Amana from an appliance they may own. Amana Refrigeration was founded by Amana people and is located in the village of Middle Amana! Just 93 miles east of Des Moines, the other villages are West Amana, East Amana, South Amana, High Amana, and Homestead. There is also a section of South Amana called Upper South, and another village called Little Amana, that were not part of the original colony.

Colony villagers have all remained true to a simpler way of life that still revolves around old-world craftsmanship and handcrafted furniture, clock-making, black smithing, world-famous cooking, and locally manufactured goods. These items are sold in numerous stores and shops, including the many quality antique shops that are an added attraction of the Colonies. For the past 150 years, Amana residents have quarried their own sandstone, made their own bricks, and cut their own timber for more than 400 buildings that cover the villages. They farmed, built woolen and calico mills for clothing and fabric, established cabinet shops to build furniture, and craft shops to supply daily necessities. Today they still produce products at the furniture factories, the woolen mill, and in most of the craft shops, where artisans make baskets, brooms, candles, ironwork, pottery and more.

Community life called for community kitchens, and the Amana Colonies have become well-known for superb food, wines and beer. In the tradition of communal kitchens, food is served family style. German specialties include Wienerschnitzel and Sauerbraten, as well as traditional Midwestern food. The bakeries are known for breads and pastries, the many wineries for their fruit wines, and the brewery for award-winning "German style" beer.

The Colonies remain Iowa's leading visitor attraction because of their heritage and hospitality. People come from around the world to see the historic villages and to buy their products, to tour the museums and to enjoy a piece of Germany in the American colonies.

### *Great Places To Shop*
### *(Antiques in the Amana Colonies)*

### *Main Amana*

**Antiques and Things**
F St. (next to Colony Cone)
319/622-6461
Open daily 9-5

Antiques, collectibles, doll house and crafts

**Carole's**
4521 220th Trail (Main St.)
319/622-3570
Open daily Summer 9-6, winter 10-5

Upstairs: old-new-used-abused

**Erenberger Antiques**
4514 F St.
319/622-3230
Mon.-Sat. 11-5, Sun. 12-5

Primitives and pine furniture are the main items featured in this original Amana home built in 1856. Early pine and painted furniture are displayed, along with small primitive antique accessories including greenware, pottery, tin, copper, pewter, stickware, baskets, decoys, quilts and more.

**Renate's Antique Gallery**
4516 F St.
319/622-3859
Mon.-Sat. 10-5, Sun. 12-5

Eight rooms of exploring fun are in this original, two-story Amana home built in 1870. Each room displays something different. In the entry room Renate has her loom where she makes rag rugs (some days visitors can watch). There's china and glass in the dining room, bowls in the kitchen, furniture in the bedroom and primitives in the family room. Renate's specializes in pottery and antiques from the Amana Colonies.

**Smokehouse Square Antiques**
4503 F St.
319/622-3539
Mon.-Sat. 10-5, Sun. 11-5, Summer 9:30-5:30, Sun. 11-5

Smokehouse Square Antiques has added a new dimension to antiquing in the Colonies. The mall is home to more than 29 of eastern Iowa's finest antique dealers. The inventory is constantly changing, but you will always find furniture, glassware, china, pottery, stoneware, graniteware, silver, jewelry, quilts and linens, books and paper, pictures and mirrors, and many advertising items, plus toys and children's collectibles, primitives, folk art, tools, decoys, fishing collectibles, 1950s memorabilia and railroad items.

**Tick Tock Antiques**
220th Trail (across from Amana General Store)
319/622-3730

Collectibles, glassware, primitives

### *West Amana*

**Cricket on the Hearth Antiques**
404 6th Ave. W.
319/622-3088
Wed.-Sun. 10-5 May-Oct.

Unique country gifts, collectibles and antiques

**West Amana General Store**
511 F St.
Located on top of the hill
319/622-3945
Open daily 10-5, Summer 9-5

Antiques, furniture and a nice line of gifts

### *South Amana*

**Fern Hill Gifts and Quilts**
103 220th Trail
Located at the corner of Hwy. 6 and 220
319/622-3627
Mon.-Sat. 9:30-5, Sun. 12-4

Antiques, quilts, supplies, dolls, bears and everlastings

**Granary Emporium**
1063 4th Ave.
319/622-3195
Open daily 10-5

Antiques, glassware, furniture, primitives

### *High Amana*

**High Amana Store**
1308 G St.
Located on Hwy. 220 (Amana Colonies Trail, 4 miles west of Main Amana)
319/622-3797
Open daily

Built in 1857 of sandstone quarried at the edge of high Amana, the high Amana Store was the original "one stop" shopping center of its time for local residents and area farmers. Over the years it has sold everything from fabric and notions to bicycles and appliances to kerosene, and even served as the local post office. In a setting of original pressed tin ceilings, glass display showcases and comb-painted drawer fronts, the store today offers traditional Amana Colonies arts and crafts, quilts, products of Iowa, glassware, unique toys and books, cards, gourmet food products, herbs, spices and more.

### *Great Places To Stay In The Amana Area*

**Babi's B & B**
2788 Hwy.
South Amana
319/662-4381

**Corner House B & B**
404 F St.
West Amana
319/622-6390 or 1-800-996-6964

**Dusk To Dawn B & B**
2616 K St. Box 124
Middle Amana
319/622-3029

**Baeckerei B & B**
6 Trail, Box 127
South Amana
319/622-3597 or 1-800-391-8650

**Die Heimat Country Inn**
Box 160, 4430 V St.
Homestead
319/622-3937

**Rawson's B & B**
Box 118
Homestead
319/622-6035 or 1-800-637-6035

### *Interesting Side Trips*

**Herbert Hoover Presidential Library and Birthplace**
Located in West Branch just 30 miles east of Amana Colonies just off of I-80
Open daily
319/643-5301

Kalona: Amish and Mennonite community that offers an opportunity to see the differences between the Amanas (not Amish) and Kalona, which is "Amish-land."
Located about 30 miles south and east of the Amana Colonies
319/656-2519

## 2 AMES

**Memories On Main Antique Mall & Old-Fashioned Ice Cream Parlor**
203 Main St.
515/233-2519
Open daily, Memorial Day-Labor Day 10-8;
Labor Day-Memorial Day 10-6, Mon. until 8, special Christmas hours
*Directions: Located 3 miles from I-35. From Exit 111 B: Take Hwy. 30 west, Duff Ave. north, then left on Main St. From Exit 113: Take 13th St. west, Duff Ave. south, right on Main St.*

Great ice cream, great antiques and collectibles, an unbeatable combination! You get both at M.O.M.'s, as it's known in Ames. The 1940s soda fountain serves great ice cream treats made the old-fashioned way, while Fancy That Lamp Shop features fine fabric and glass shades suitable for antique and vintage lamps. The mall itself offers a constantly changing array of items, from fine furniture to fun collectibles like lamps, glass, china, dinnerware, linens, pottery, figurines, decorative accessories, kitchen collectibles, primitives, crocks, cast iron, dolls, children's items, vintage clothing, records, books, sheet music and more!

**Pak-Rat**
110 S. Hyland Ave.
515/296-0230

**Coin Castle II, Inc.**
236 Main St.
515/232-7527

**Victorian Showcase Mall**
26772 241st St.
515/232-4818

## 3 ANAMOSA

**This Old Farm Antiques**
110 S. Elm St.
319/462-2856

**Country Creek Cove**
110 E. Main St.
319/462-3788

**Antiques of Anamosa**
122 E. Main St.
319/462-4195

**Memory Shoppe**
203 E. Main St.
319/462-6085

## 4 AURELIA

**C & M Antiques**
Highway 7 W.
712/434-2217

**Brown's Antiques**
116 Main St.
712/434-2337

**Forgotten Favorites**
128 Main St.
712/434-2069

**Vogt's Antiques & Toys**
141 Main St.
712/434-5380

**Cedars Antiques**
2235 W. 9th St.
712/434-2244

## 5 BURLINGTON

**A-1 Antiques & Uniques**
1234 Agency St.
319/752-5901

**Privy Antiques**
2500 Division St.
319/752-8320

**Call & Haul Antiques**
401 N. Front St.
319/754-6389

**Antique Mall**
800 Jefferson St.
319/753-6955

**Antiques & Things**
806 Jefferson St.
319/753-5096

**Casey's World Antiques**
6212 Summer St.
319/752-3265

**5th St. Antique Mall & Collectibles**
211 N. 5th St.
319/752-0498

## 6 CEDAR FALLS

**Jackson's**
2229 Lincoln St.
319/277-2256

**Gilgen's Consignment Furniture**
115 W. 16th St.
319/266-5152

**Cellar Antiques**
4912 University Ave.
319/266-5091

## 7 CEDAR RAPIDS

**Antique Wicker & Collectibles**
1038 3rd Ave. S.E.
319/362-4868

**Wellington Square Antique Mall**
1200 2nd Ave. S.E.
319/368-6640

**Gingerbread**
92 16th Ave. S.W.
319/366-8841

**Cellar Door-Stable on Alley**
2900 1st Ave. N.E.
319/366-1638

## 8 CENTERVILLE

**Summer Antiques**
1099 N. 18th St.
515/856-2680

**Taste of Country**
300 W. State St.
515/856-5705

# Iowa

## 9 CLEAR LAKE

**Yesteryear House of Antiques**
112 N. 8th St.
515/357-4352

**Whispering Oaks Antiques**
2510 S. 8th St.
515/357-5094

**Good Olde Days**
809 5th Pl. N.
515/357-6575

**Keepsake Antiques**
308 Main Ave.
515/357-7553

**Antiques on Main**
309 Main Ave.
515/357-3077

**Jada Consignment Shop**
309 Main Ave., #B
515/357-2555

**Jo's Antiques**
311 Main Ave.
515/357-8120

**Legacy Antiques**
315 Main Ave.
515/357-4000

**Antique Alley**
19 S. 3rd St.
515/357-7733

**Cornerstone Antiques**
22 S. 3rd St.
515/357-3899

## 10 COUNCIL BLUFFS

**Collins Antiques**
607 S. Main St.
712/328-2598

**Jantiques**
729 S. Main St.
712/323-6624

## 11 CRESTON

**Jessie's Antique Gems**
1481 130th St.
515/782-5366

**Two Bricks Shy Antiques**
Hwy. 34 E.
515/782-2725

**Timeless Treasures Antiques**
1313 U.S. Hwy. 34
515/782-6517

## 12 DAVENPORT

**Trash Can Annie Antiques**
421 Brady St.
319/322-5893

**Riverbend Antiques**
425 Brady St.
319/323-8622

**Raphael's Emporium**
628 N. Harrison St.
319/322-5053

**Upper Level Antiques**
321 E. 2nd St.
319/324-2133

**Lampsmith Antique**
5102 W. Locust St.
319/391-8552

**Bird In Hand**
1121 Mound St.
319/322-1082

**Antiques By Judy**
401 E. 2nd St.
319/323-5437

**Antique America**
702 W. 76th St.
319/386-3430

## 13 DES MOINES

**Brass Armadillo, Inc.**
701 N.E. 50th Ave.
515/282-0082

**R & S Enterprises**
1601 E. Grand Ave.
515/262-9384

**Soda City Collectables**
1244 2nd Ave.
515/282-0345

**Bartlett's Antiques**
820 35th St.
515/255-1362

**Christine's**
309 E. 5th St.
515/243-3500

**Corner Collectors**
1903 46th St.
515/274-4106

**Emily's Attic/Emily's Closet**
4800 Maple Dr.
515/262-3933

**Madaline's Gifts & Antiques**
3000 E. 9th St.
515/266-0204

**Majestic Lion Antique Center**
5048 N.W. 2nd St.
515/282-5466

**Murray's Antiques**
1805 Army Post Road
515/285-8840

**Time Passages Ltd.**
980 73rd St.
515/223-5104

## 14 DUBUQUE

**Bob's Antiques**
3271 Central Ave.
319/583-6061

**Collector's Corner**
340 W. 5th St.
319/588-0886

**Harbor Place Antiques**
98 E. 4th St.
319/582-6224

**Antiques at the Schoen's**
144 Locust St.
319/556-7547

**Old Towne Shoppe**
163 Main St.
319/583-1962

**Antiques on White**
902 White St.
319/557-2141

## 15 ELDON

**American Gothic Antiques & Tearoom**
408 Elm St.
515/652-3338

For a nostalgic antiquing experience American Gothic Antiques & Tearoom offers antiques in the front 1500 square feet of the store, and a restaurant and ice cream shop in the back. Homemade pies are the house specialty. Everything is housed in an historic old hardware store that is over 100 years old - a true antique itself!

## 16 FORT DODGE

**Antique Emporium**
Crossroads Mall
515/955-4151

**Old Harvester Gifts & Antiques**
1915 1st Ave. N.
515/955-6260

**Downtown Antiques Mall**
102 S. 14th St.
515/573-3401

**Michehl's Memory Furniture**
1731 Paragon Ave.
515/576-0148

**Pine Cupboard**
25 S. 12th St.
515/576-7463

**Young's Antiques & Collectibles**
814 1st Ave. S.
515/576-4733

## 17 FORT MADISON

For an old army post, Fort Madison is a swinging, adventurous place even today! It was the site of the first outpost west of the Mississippi River, when flintlock rifles and cannons were the main armaments. Today visitors can take the narrated Olde Towne Express and buy antiques galore in the Downtown Riverfront district. You can watch—and maybe walk—the world's longest double-deck swingspan bridge in action, or take your chances on firmer ground at the Catfish Bend Casino.

**Sixth & G Antique Mall**
602 Ave. G
319/372-6218

**Memory Lane Antique Mall**
820 Ave. G
319/372-4485

**Wishing Well Antiques**
3510 Ave. L
319/372-5237

**Devil's Creek Antiques**
2495 Hwy. 61
319/372-7101

### *Great Places To Stay*

**Mississippi Rose & Thistle Inn**
532 Ave. F
319/372-7044
Open daily 8-10
Rates: $70-90
*Directions: Fort Madison is easily reached by U.S. 61, a major connection to I-80 and I-70. The inn is located between Burlington, Iowa (18 miles north) and Keokuk, Iowa (20 miles south). Both are reached by U.S. 61, and the inn is located 2 blocks north of the highway. Turn on 5th St., go 2 blocks, turn left on Avenue F (a one-way street). Go 1 block and the inn is on the left side at the corner of Avenue F and 6th St.*

This lovely, historic brick Italianate mansion was built in 1881 by Dennis A. Morrison, a partner in Morrison Plow Works. The Morrison family owned the first automobile in Fort Madison, a 1902 Stanley Steamer. Today, the inn has been carefully restored to its past splendor, extravagance and elegance. Guests can gaze upon ornate woodwork and marble fireplaces, walk on Oriental carpets, and enjoy period antiques. After a day exploring, riverboat gambling, antiquing, golfing, and picnicking, guests can return to the inn for afternoon wine and hors d'oeuvres in the parlor or on the wraparound porch, then choose a book from the library and retire with a glass of sherry from your own private stock! Candlelight dinners and gourmet picnic baskets are available with advance notice.

Each bedroom has its own distinctive charm and decor. The Lillian Austin Room is furnished with an old-fashioned brass bed, antique oak dresser and clawfoot tub. The Celsiana Room holds an old-fashioned white and brass bed, antique walnut dresser and clawfoot tub. The Mary Rose Room offers a clawfoot tub, white and brass bed and antique Eastlake dresser. And the Tara Allison Room charms guests with a white and brass bed, sitting alcove, balcony and whirlpool.

## 18 HILLS

**Antiques In The Old White Church**
120 Oak St.
319/679-2337

## 19 IOWA CITY

**Granny's Antique Mall**
315 E. 1st St.
319/351-6328

**Antique Mall of Iowa City**
507 S. Gilbert St.
319/354-1822

**Watt's Antiques & Collectibles**
1603 Muscatine
319/337-4357

**Ackerman's Newton Road Antiques**
814 Newton Rd.
319/338-8449

**Antique Christmas Shop**
1600 Sycamore St.
319/679-2337

**European Vintage Lace Shop**
5011 Lower West Branch Road S.E.
319/351-2801

**Sweet Livin'**
224 S. Linn St.
319/337-5015

**Avenue B Antiques**
511 B Ave.
319/656-2500

## 20 KALONA

**Kalona Antique Co. Plus**
**Antique Furniture Warehouse**
Corner of 4th & C
211 4th St.
319/656-4489 Days
319/656-5157 Evenings
Mon.-Sat. 9am-5pm, Closed Sun. & Major Holidays
*Directions: Located just 18 miles south of Iowa City, Iowa on Hwy. 1, or 9 miles west of Hwy. 218 (The Avenue of the Saints) on Hwy. 22.*

The Kalona Antique Company is housed in an old 1890s Baptist Church in downtown Kalona, Iowa, the home of the largest Amish settlement west of the Mississippi River. The Kalona Antique Co. showcases the wares of 19 dealers on 2 floors offering a quality selection of antiques, quilts and collectibles. Ken and Brenda Herington own and operate the Kalona Antique Co. and Furniture Warehouse. They specialize in oak, pine and walnut furniture. The Furniture Warehouse, just one block south of the Kalona Antique Co. features original finish furniture. The shop offers wholesale prices to dealers and will open after hours for dealers traveling through the area.

**Main Street Antiques**
413 B Ave.
319/656-4550

**Courtyard Square**
417 B Ave.
319/656-2488

**Woodin Wheel Antiques & Gifts**
515 B Ave.
319/656-2240

**Fifth Street Antiques**
303 5th St.
319/656-2080

**Heart of the Country Antiques**
203 5th St
319/656-3591

**Weathervane**
411 5th St.
319/656-3958

**Yoder's Antiques**
435 B Ave.
319/656-3880

**Avenue B Antiques**
511 B Ave.
319/656-2500

## 21 KEOKUK

**Showcase Antique Mall**
800 Main St.
319/524-1696

**Treasures & Trash**
1803 S. 7th St.
319/524-1112

## 22 KIMBALLTON

**Attic Antiques**
114 N. Main St.
712/773-3255

**Mama Bear**
117 N. Main St.
712/773-2430

**Mercantile**
122 N. Main St.
712/773-3777

**Country Corner**
200 N. Main St.
712/773-2300

**D Johnson Antiques**
209 N. Main St.
712/773-3939

## 23 KNOXVILLE

**Antiques Or Others**
1253 Hwy. 14
515/842-4644

## 24 LE CLAIRE

**Riverview Antiques**
510 Cody Road
319/289-4265

**Rare Find Antiques**
114 N. Cody Road
319/289-5207

**Memory Lane**
110 S. Cody Road
319/289-3366

## 25 MARION

**Country Corner Antiques**
786 8th Ave.
319/377-1437

**Remember When Antiques**
847 8th Ave.
319/373-3039

**Antiques of Marion**
1325 8th Ave.
319/377-7997

**Scott's Antiques Furniture**
1060 7th Ave.
319/377-6411

**Park Place Hotel Antiques**
1104 7th Ave.
319/377-2724

**Marion Center Antique Mall**
1150 7th Ave.
319/377-9345

**Eckhart's Antique Furniture**
560 10th St.
319/377-1202

**Sanctuary Antique Center**
801 10th St.
319/377-7753

**Harmening Haus**
915 10th St.
800/644-3874

**Cooper's Antiques**
997 10th St.
319/377-3995

## 26 MARSHALLTOWN

**Charley's Antiques**
3002 S. Center St.
515/753-3916

**Marshall Relics**
14 E. Main St.
516/752-7060

**Main Street Antique Mall**
105 W. Main St.
515/752-3077

**Granny's Country Mall**
3201 Village Circle
515/752-6966

## 27 MASON CITY

**Olde Central Antique Mall**
317 S. Delaware Ave.
515/423-7315

**Wilson Antiques**
317 S. Delaware Ave.
515/423-5811

**Cobweb Corners Antiques**
715 N. Federal Ave.
515/423-2160

**North Federal Antique**
1104 N. Federal Ave.
513/423-0841

## 28 MEDIAPOLIS

**Patriot Antiques**
Hwy. 61
319/394-9137

**Heirloom Antiques**
Hwy. 61 S.
319/394-3444

**Lamp Post Antiques**
318 Wapello St. N.
319/394-3961

## 29 MOUNT PLEASANT

**Iris City Antique Mall**
Hwy. 34 W.
319/385-7515

**Old & New Things Plus**
110 S. Main St.
319/385-7311

**Lori's Loft**
2001 E. Washington St.
319/986-9980

## 30 MUSCATINE

**River Bend Cove**
418 Grandview Ave.
319/263-9929

**Market Place**
1919 Grandview Ave.
319/263-8355

**Melon City Antique Mart**
200 E. 2nd St.
319/264-3470

**River's Edge Antiques**
331 E. 2nd St.
319/264-2351

**Manley's Antiques**
417 E. 2nd St.
319/264-1475

**Lost Treasures**
419 E. 2nd St.
319/262-8658

**Old Blue Bldg. Antiques**
821 Park Ave.
319/263-5430

**Koosli Antiques**
208 E. 2nd St.
319/264-8625

## 31 NEWTON

**Pappy's Antique Mall**
103 1st Ave. W.
515/792-7774

**Tripp Thru The Past**
3928 N. 4th Ave. E.
515/792-5514

**Skunk Valley Antique Mall**
7717 Hwy. F 48 W.
515/792-2361

## 32 OELWEIN

### Amish Settlement
Rural Buchanan County
319/283-1105
Mon.-Sat. 8-5 year round, closed New Year's, Epiphany, Good Friday, Ascension Day, Thanksgiving Day and Christmas Day

Visitors to the Amish Settlement are given a glimpse of the life that fascinates most Americans. The Amish teach separation from the world, which includes living without modern conveniences, something most Americans find unbelievable. The Amish till the soil with horse-drawn equipment, and their doctrine forbids the use of electricity and telephones. They make most everything they need on a daily basis, and they sell baked goods, quilts, and handmade furniture at their farm homes in the Settlement.

**West Charles Antiques**
17 W. Charles St.
319/283-3591

## 33 OSKALOOSA

**Rock & Shell Shop**
117 A Ave. W.
515/673-3816

**Tyme & Again**
113 High Ave. E.
515/673-5857

**Antique Shop**
117 High Ave. E.
515/673-0895

**Old Friends Antiques**
123 N. Market
515/673-0428

## 34 OTTUMWA

**Phil Taylor Antiques**
224 Fox Sauk Road
515/682-7492

**Nancy's Unique Antiques**
510 E. Main St.
515/682-8661

## 35 PELLA

When you drive into Pella, Iowa, you'll probably double check the map, because you'll feel like a giant wind has blown you across the ocean to Holland! It looks and sounds like Holland, with windmills and wooden shoes, Dutch pastries and Klokkenspel, courtyards and sunken gardens, and acres and acres of tulips! In Pella the Old and New worlds combine completely every May and December at the Tulip Time Festival and Sinterklass (Santa Claus) Day. And the recently renovated and reopened Pella Opera House, built in 1900, provides year-round musical and theatrical performances by nationally known performers.

**Beekhuizen Antiques**
913 W. 8th St.
515/628-4712

**Country Lane Antqs. & Collectibles**
752 190th Ave.
515/628-2912

**Red Ribbon Antique Mall**
812 Washington St.
515/628-2181

## 36 SIOUX CITY

**Red Wheel Furniture & Antiques**
By Appointment Only
712/276-3645

**Old Town Antiques & Collectibles**
1024 4th Hwy.
712/258-3119

**Heritage House Antiques**
3900 4th Ave.
712/276-3366

**Gas Light Antiques**
1310 Jennings Hwy.
712/252-2166

**Collectors Cupboard**
500 S. Lewis Blvd.
712/258-0087

**Shirley's Stuff & Antiques**
1420 Villa Ave.
712/252-1565

**Antiques Sioux City Inc.**
1014 4th St.
712/252-1248

**Dealin Antiques & Collectibles**
509 8th St.
712/252-1060

## 37 SPILLVILLE

***Great Places To Stay***

### Taylor-Made Bed & Breakfast
330 Main St.
319/562-3958

Built in 1890, this Victorian home featuring four antique filled guest rooms is located across the street from the world-reknown Bily Clock Museum.

## 38 SPIRIT LAKE

**Spirit Lake Antique Mall**
2015 18th St.
712/336-2029

**Heritage Square Antiques**
1703 Hill Ave.
712/336-3455

**Rubarb Antiques**
2009 Hill Ave.
712/336-2154

**Ardie's Attic**
1612 Ithaca Ave.
712/336-4233

## 39 THAYER

### L & H Antique Mall

301 S. 3rd Ave. (mailing address)
Hwy. 34 (shop location)
515/338-2223, 1-888-338-7178
Tues.-Sat. 10-5, Sun., 12-5, closed Mon., holidays and the week between Christmas and New Year's.
*Directions: Located on Hwy. 34, 14 miles west of Osceola and 17 miles east of Creston.*

Lee and Helen Spurgeon, the owners of L & H Antique Mall, celebrate their sixth anniversary in their shop this year. They started out with 3200 square feet and 20 dealers. Last year they added 1100 square feet and eight more dealers. Who knows how high they'll go? And if you look closely in the shop, among the depression glass, Hull pottery, furniture, tools, black memorabilia, Fox and Parrish prints and country crafts, you'll see an engraved walnut plaque congratulating Helen on her selection to the National Directory of Who's Who in Executive and Professionals. Congratulations to the Spurgeons!

## 40 VAN BUREN COUNTY

### The Villages of Van Buren County

1-800-868-7822
Email: Villages@netins.net
Web site: www.netins.net/showcase/villages

These former riverboat ports, located along the Des Moines River in the southeast corner of Iowa just north of the Missouri border, are quaint, quiet villages that still maintain the atmosphere and relaxed lifestyle of the past century. Populated today with resident artists and craftspeople, antiques sellers and history buffs, these villages offer visitors relaxation and renewal in a setting that preserves and illuminates our history.

The villages in Van Buren Country include Selma, Birmingham, Stockport, Douds, Leando, Kilbourn, Lebanon, Pittsburg, Milton, Cantril, Keosauqua, Bentonport, Vernon, Mount Sterling, Bonaparte and Farmington, plus several lakes and state parks.

### Bentonport National Historic District

Scenic Byway J-40 in Van Buren County
319/592-3579
Tues.-Sun. 10-5, April-October. Some businesses open daily or for longer season

This 1840s river town, with its 100-year-old bridge and walkway, was already thriving when Iowa became a state. Mormon craftsmen, on their western trek to Utah, helped construct some of its buildings; the ruins of old mills along the Des Moines River are evident even today. Visitors can stroll through shops in historic buildings that feature antiques, locally made handcrafted items from working artisans, and American Indian artifacts. Then they can camp at riverside parks and campgrounds or stay at the historic bed and breakfast, eat at the cafe, view the rose garden, or launch into the river at the boat ramp and dock that are available.

***Great Places to Shop, Eat and Stay in Bentonport***

### Greef General Store

Downtown Bentonport
319/592-3579

Antique mall features quality furniture, primitives, etc., plus art and a collection of Indian artifacts.

### Country Peddlers

Downtown Bentonport
319/592-3564

Specializes in originally designed folk art.

### The Hot Pot Cafe

Downtown Bentonport
319/592-3579

Sandwich shop serves soup and sandwiches, drinks, homemade goodies, ice cream and Dutch treats.

### Mason House Inn and Antique Shop of Bentonsport

Route 2, Box 237
1-800-592-3133
Rates: $54-74

The Mason House Inn was built by Mormon craftsmen on their way to Utah in 1846, the year Iowa became a state. It remains the oldest steamboat river inn in the Midwest still serving overnight guests, quite a record when you consider that it has been in continual service to travelers for 150 years! With the state's only fold-down copper bathtub (that really raises questions, doesn't it!), it has, according to local legend, hosted such notables as John C. Fremont, Abraham Lincoln and Mark Twain. The Inn offers nine guest rooms, five with private bath.

Outback Antiques is also located on the premises.

***Bonaparte National Historic Riverfront District***

The history of Iowa's riverboat era is predominant in Bonaparte. The historic buildings in its downtown district have been carefully preserved and restored in a renaissance of cultural revival. Two of the 1800s mills are still in existence. The old flour and grist mill of 1878 is now the location of one of southeast Iowa's finest restaurants, The Bonaparte Retreat. Bonaparte Mill Antiques is next door in the former Meek's Woolen Mill, and other historic buildings in the district house a variety of businesses. The Aunty Green Museum is just down the street, where visitors can see a collection of historic memorabilia.

### *Great Places to Shop and Eat in Bonaparte*

**Bonaparte Mill Antiques**
319/592-3274
Tues.-Sun. 11-7

Antiques and collectibles

**Bonaparte Retreat Restaurant**
319/592-3339
Lunch served 11-1 every day except holidays; dinner served at 5 every day except holidays and Sundays.

Located in a restored grist mill.

**Milton, Cantril, Lebanon Triangle**
Van Buren County

Another opportunity for people to see firsthand the simple but beautifully crafted life of the Amish and Mennonites is available in the villages of Milton, Cantril and Lebanon, a triangular area in the western end of Van Buren County. Mennonites have settled in the Cantril community, offering several businesses that are open to visitors, including a general store that features bulk groceries and yard goods. In the Milton and Lebanon areas, visitors can watch the Amish practice the trades of horseshoeing, blacksmithing, buggy and harness making, furniture making, sawmill work, and other old world crafts that are a daily part of the Amish lifestyle. Candy and dry goods stores are open to visitors in the Milton area.

**Daughtery's Coffee Shop**
Cantril
319/397-2100
Mon.-Fri. 7-5

Antiques, lunch, coffee and donuts

### *Great Places to Shop and Eat in Farmington*

**Borderline Antiques**
103 Elm
319/878-3714
Thurs.-Sat. 10-4:30

**Bridge Cafe and Supper Club**
319/878-3315
Mon. & Tues. 6-4, Wed.-Sat. 6-9, Sun. 7-2

"Traditional Iowa fare since 1932"

### *Great Places to Shop, Eat and Stay in Keosauqua*

**Hotel Manning**
100 Van Buren St.
319/293-3232 or 1-800-728-2718
Open year round
Rates $35-65

Hotel Manning, named for a founder of Keosauqua, was built in 1839 to house a bank and general store. The second and third stories were added in the 1890s and the entire edifice took on a style known as "steamboat gothic," with verandas spanning the width of the first two floors. The grand hotel opened on April 27, 1899 and has been in continuous use as a hotel since then! Guests and visitors can marvel at the lobby's ceilings, original pine woodwork and antique fixtures. The lobby also holds a rare Vose rosewood grand piano, a specially commissioned grandfather clock, and outstanding examples of early pine and oak furniture. The 18 guest rooms, 10 with private bath, are filled with handsome antiques.

**Top of the Hill Antiques**
319/293-3022

Their antiques can also be found at the Greef Store in Bentonsport.

**The Village Creamery**
319/293-3815
Summer: 11-10 daily, winter 11-5 daily

Soft ice cream products, sandwiches, etc.

## 41 WALNUT

**Farm Fresh Antiques**
200 Antique City Dr.
712/784-2275

**Country Treasure's Mall**
202 Antique City Dr.
712/784-3090

**Heart of Country**
207 Antique City Dr.
712/784-3825

**Everybody's Attic Antiques**
210 Antique City Dr.
712/784-3030

**Corn Country Antiques**
212 Antique City Dr.
712/784-3992

**Victorian Rose Antiques**
216 Antique City Dr.
712/784-3900

**Antique Furniture Emporium**
226 Antique City Dr.
712/784-3839

**Walnut Mercantile Co.**
230 Antique City Dr.
712/784-2225

**Simple Pleasures-Antiques**
309 Antique City Dr.
712/784-3999

**Don's Antiques**
310 Antique City Dr.
712/784-2277

**Bear Trap Antiques**
608 Highland St.
712/784-3779

**Barn Mall**
615 Highland St.
712/784-3814

**Walnut Antique Mall**
514 Pearl St.
712/784-3322

**Granary Mall**
603 Pearl St.
712/784-3331

**Village Blacksmith**
610 Pearl St.
712/784-3332

**Forget-Me-Nots**
209 Antique City Dr.
712/784-3040

## 42 WATERLOO

**Calico Hen's House**
1022 Alabar Ave.
319/234-1266

**Tovar's Hidden Treasures**
1642 Burton Ave.
319/232-0769

**Grandpa Harry's**
620 Commercial St.
319/232-5900

**Toad's Treasures**
622 Commercial St.
319/233-6506

**Pilot House Antiques**
1621 Falls Ave.
319/232-5414

**Pink Pig (Washburn)**
7114 Laporte Road
319/296-3000

**Black's Antiques**
501 Sycamore St.
319/235-1241

**Antique Galleries**
618 Sycamore St.
319/235-9945

**Buehner's Antiques**
627 Sycamore St.
319/232-5710

**Gathering**
1910 Forest Ave.
310/236-3352

## 43 WAVERLY

**Apple Cottage Gifts & Antiques**
103 Bremer Ave.
319/352-0153

**Round Barn Antiques**
R.R. 2
319/352-3694

## 44 WEST BRANCH

**Memories Restored**
111 E. Main St.
319/643-7330

**Main Street Antiques & Art**
110 W. Main St.
319/643-2065

## 45 WEST DES MOINES

### Antique Jamboree
Location: Valley Junction, 5th Street area
Call for dates.

For more than eighteen years, important antique dealers from across the Midwest have presented their wares at the West Des Moines Antique Jamboree. The show promoters insist upon exceptional antiques; no reproductions or crafts. Therefore, the discriminating shopper will be delighted to find nice porcelains, art glass, period to formal furnishings and more.

### Valley Junction
*Directions: Take I-235 to the 63rd Street exit. Go south and follow the Valley Junction signs.*

In 1893 Valley Junction bustled with horse-drawn traffic, a trolley line, eight-foot wooden sidewalks, and dirt streets lined with three banks, three drug stores and several "boarding houses" of questionable character! By 1900 the Chicago, Rock Island and Pacific Railroad made Valley Junction a popular stop, with 26 passenger trains arriving and departing daily. Today visitors can enjoy more than 120 specialty stores, art galleries, antique shops and restaurants, each with a unique historic character.

One of the places in Valley Junction that is an absolute "must see" for anybody, any age, is the Valley Junction Train Station and Toy Train Museum. Centerpiece of the museum is the colossal 1,000 square foot toy train layout, designed by renowned Broadway set designer Clarke Dunham, and built in New York by Dunham Studios. Eleven Lionel trains, powered by state-of-the-art electronics, run on four different elevations where viewers of all sizes can watch and discover minute details at every eye level. There's the candy factory with its arteries of pipes, valves, tanks and Life Saver watertower. There are animated figures working and playing in a four-season wonderland, concrete arch viaducts, tunnels through spectacular mountains, towns and villages where tiny figures recreate daily life and fun all across America. Over 2,000 feet of track, connected by bridges and viaducts, loop through a scale-model of America's rural and urban landscapes. You'll see freight trains hauling grain and delivering goods to industrial areas; passenger trains carrying workers and tourists to the layout's metropolitan cities. Surrounding the central layout are dozens of custom-built oak and glass showcases where museum owner Doug DuBay displays his personal, extensive collection of antique trains, tiny houses and railroad memorabilia.

From there visit the Valley Junction Toy Train Station—a collector and hobbyist shopping paradise! Shelf after shelf of Lionel equipment and layout accessories are there for viewing, dreaming and buying. After seeing the museum and its fantastic possibilities, it's no wonder that most visitors don't leave the Toy Train Station empty-handed! The museum and Toy Train Station are open Mon.-Sat. 10-5 and Sun. 12-5. The address is 401 Railroad Place, 515/274-4424.

### Fifth Street Mall
115 5th St.
515/279-3716

Fifth Street Mall presents quality antiques and collectibles with showcases full of great merchandise. They also have a 1940s original soda fountain.

**Elinor's Wood 'N' Wares**
102 5th St.
515/274-1234

**"Prezzies"**
513 Elm St.
515/255-1915

**Station**
104 5th St.
515/255-6331

**Joy's Treasures**
108 5th St.
515/279-5975

**Antique Mall**
110 5th St.
515/255-3185

**Diane's Antiques**
110 5th St.
515/255-3185

**Cherry Stone**
111 5th St.
515/255-6414

**Country Caboose Antiques**
113 5th St.
515/277-1555

**David Meshek Antique Lighting**
115 5th St.
515/277-9009

**Time Passages Ltd.**
980 73rd St.
515/223-5104

**Especially Lace**
202 5th St.
515/277-8778

**Alverdas Antiques**
211 5th St.
515/255-0931

**Pegasus Gallery**
218 5th St.
515/277-3245

**Valley Junction Mall**
333 5th St.
515/274-1419

**Lanny's**
404 5th St.
515/255-0700

**Antique Collectors Mall**
1980 Grand Ave.
515/224-6494

**A Okay Antiques**
124 5th St.
515/255-2525

**Century Shop**
333 5th St.
515/255-9449

## 46 WINTERSET

**Madison County Mercantile**
58 W. Court Ave.
515/462-4535

**East Coast Connection**
116 S. 1st Ave.
515/462-1346

# Kansas

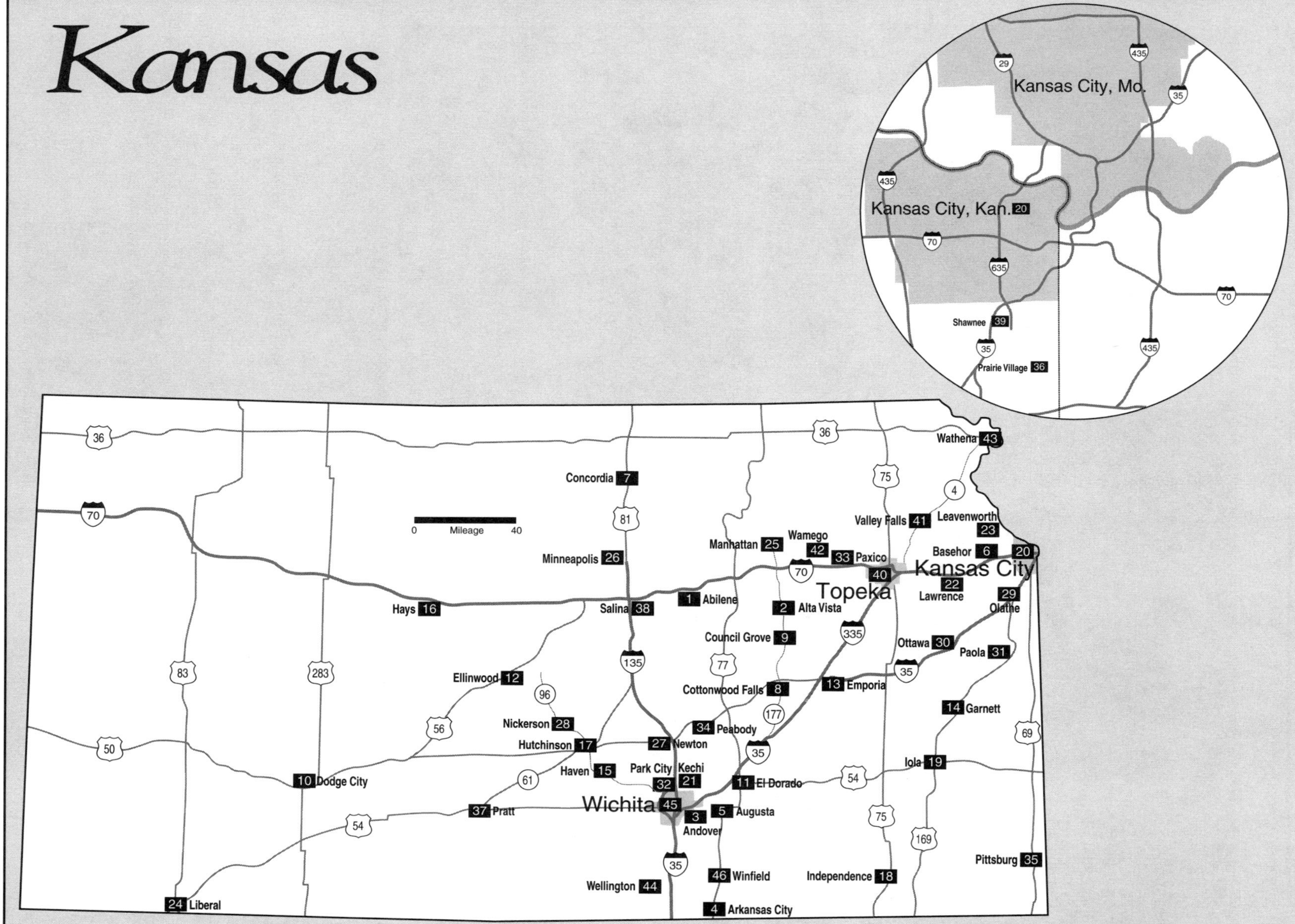

Kansas City, Mo.
Kansas City, Kan. 20
Shawnee 39
Prairie Village 36
Wathena 43
Concordia 7
Valley Falls 41
Leavenworth 23
Manhattan 25
Wamego 42
33 Paxico
Basehor 6
20
Kansas City
Minneapolis 26
40
Topeka
22 Lawrence
29 Olathe
Hays 16
Salina 38
1 Abilene
2 Alta Vista
Council Grove 9
Ottawa 30
Paola 31
Ellinwood 12
Cottonwood Falls 8
13 Emporia
14 Garnett
Nickerson 28
34 Peabody
Hutchinson 17
27 Newton
Haven 15
Park City 32
Kechi 21
11 El Dorado
Iola 19
10 Dodge City
37 Pratt
Wichita 45
3 Andover
5 Augusta
46 Winfield
Independence 18
Pittsburg 35
Wellington 44
24 Liberal
4 Arkansas City
0 Mileage 40

*A wide selection of furniture awaits you at the Wooden Heart, along with architectural accents.*

# Wooden Heart Antiques is the heartbeat of Wichita

*The Wooden Heart occupies two floors of a warehouse in Wichita.*

Wooden Heart Antiques & Refinishing occupies a large two-story warehouse in Wichita. The two floors of antique oak, walnut and mahogany furniture as well as a large selection of wonderful old architectural items invites visitors to a wonderland of history. Items range from very rough to fully restored. Special services include furniture stripping, repairing and refinishing. For more information you can visit Wooden Heart's web site at: www.feist.com/~woodenheart.

*Charming antique coffee mill*

*Wooden Heart Antiques is located at 141 S. Rock Island St. in Wichita. For additional information, see listing #45 (Wichita).*

*This ornately carved oak beauty features elaborately carved griffins. The mythical half lion, half eagle, supports the glass-doored cabinets on top.*

# Wichita castle has European touch

*Salve:*

This Latin message greets all guests to the Castle Inn Riverside. Carved in stone over the drive, it is one of the many details that will speak to you during your stay. Built in 1888 by Burton Harvey Campbell, this architectural masterpiece was fashioned after a castle located in the foothills of Scotland. It is more than mortar and limestone, it is the result of one man's dream and several architects' expertise.

The stonework is known as "rough rock face," a style that presents the roughest natural surface of the gray limestone, which came from the Butler Country quarry. Materials also came from farther away. The original floors were created in Chicago by Behl and Company; the hardware was ordered directly from the factory in New York, and the stairwell, fireplaces, lamps and fixtures were imported from Europe.

For 20 years, the mansion remained the property of Campbell. In 1910 Walter Morris purchased the estate for less than a third of what it cost to build.

Fifty years later it became the property of Maye Crumm, who began calling it Crumm Castle. For a time it housed the Belle Carter High School, an institution begun and operated by Crumm.

In April 1973, the castle was entered on the National Register of Historic Places as "a building of architectural significance."

*The 28-room castle was built from 1886-88 for a cost of $90,000 by Colonel Burton Harvey Campbell. At the time, Campbell was one of Wichita's wealthiest residents, and he spared no expense in building the castle.*

*The high ceilings, the spaciousness of the grand foyer, and the 250-year-old staircase (imported from London) all combine with the 650-year-old Grecian fireplace to add history and hospitality.*

In the '70s, the upkeep of the castle became a constant struggle. To raise funds for its survival, the 19-room mansion was opened to the public for tours of all but the rooms occupied by the Crumm family.

In 1994, the castle, a historic and beloved member of the Wichita community was existing on borrowed time. It was then that Terry and Paula Lowry purchased the property. Out of respect for Campbell and his vision, they returned his name to the castle.

They invested all their time, energy and resources into restoring this majestic structure to its original beauty. Damaged stones were painstakingly taken apart and replaced with pieces created by expert masons. The woodwork and floors have been brought back to their original luster. The roof has been reslated with tiles from Vermont. The plumbing was replaced with safer materials and the upstairs ballroom has been converted to luxurious suites.

Like many before them, the Lowrys had a dream of making the castle their home, but their dream is much larger. They want to share its beauty with the rest of the world.

This luxury inn features 14 uniquely appointed guest rooms, each a distinctive theme based on the heritage of the castle. Amenities include Jacuzzi tubs for two (six rooms), complimentary wine and hors d'oeuvres, and an assortment of homemade desserts and gourmet coffees served each evening. *Salve* ... the castle bids you welcome!

*The Castle Inn Riverside is located less than five minutes from downtown Wichita and approximately 15 minutes from Mid-Continent Airport. For your meeting needs, the castle offers a carefully-designed conference in the original castle cellar.For additional information, call the innkeepers at 316/263-9300.*

# Caffee's tempts shoppers with antiques, then treats them in The Tea Room

*Spacious and artful display areas often feature collectibles which rest appropriately on antique furniture.*

Caffee's Antique Mall occupies 7900 square feet in the old JC Penney building at 505 Delaware St. in downtown Historic Leavenworth. Renovation began Jan. 1, 1998 to add 900 square feet to the first level. A total of ten new booths, three new shelf units, a larger showcase area, and a combination consignment/dance floor area were created. A total of 60 vendors rent space on three levels at Caffee's Antique Mall, therefore, new antiques and collectibles arrive daily. The first floor is home to The Tea Room, where lunch is served Monday through Saturday, and the site of many special parties and functions. Caffee's Antique Mall and The Tea Room host meetings and other functions in a separate meeting area.

Within walking distance of Caffee's Antique Mall there are four other quality antique shops, a new flea market, and an "everything" shop. Just two blocks to the east, visitors will find the historic Leavenworth Landing shopping area and the new Riverside Park.

*Caffee's Antique Mall is located at 505 Delaware St. in Leavenworth. For additional information on Caffee's Antique Mall see listing #23 (Leavenworth).*

*Right: If The Tea Room menu isn't enough to tempt passersby, an elegant tray displays sinful dessert selections.*

*Far right: A couple enjoys the friendly service and ambience of The Tea Room.*

## 1 ABILENE

If you "like Ike," you're in the right place. After he returned from World War II, General Dwight D. Eisenhower told a hometown crowd "the proudest thing I can claim is that I am from Abilene." At the Eisenhower Center in Abilene, visit the home, library and final resting place of the former president and five-star general.

And don't miss Kirby House, a fully restored 1855 gingerbread mansion that is now a wonderful family restaurant, and the Seelye Mansion, a twenty-five room Georgian mansion built in 1905.

**Downtown Antique Mall**
313 N. Buckeye Ave.
913/263-2782

**Chisholm Trail Antiques**
1020 S. Buckeye Ave.
913/263-2061

**Liddle Shoppe**
306 N. Cedar St.
913/263-0077

**Abilene Antique Plaza**
418 NW 2nd St.
913/263-4200

**Family Antiques**
1449 2700th Ave.
913/598-2356

**Buckeye Antique Mall**
310 N. Buckeye
913/263-7696

**Chicken Crossing Antiques**
1975 Hawk Road
913/263-3517

**5th & Cedar Antiques Etc.**
421 N. Cedar
913/263-3919

**Prairie Antiques**
301 N. Cedar
785/263-1119

**Splinters & Rags**
612 S. Buckeye
913/263-4615

## 2 ALTA VISTA

### Alta Vista Antiques
902 N. Main St.
785-499-5375
Thurs., Fri., Sat., 10-5, Sun. 1-5
*Directions: Sixteen miles south from I-70*

Located in a little Victorian house decorated in room settings.

## 3 ANDOVER

**Andover Antique Mall**
656 N. Andover Road
6 Mi. E. of Wite
316/733-8999

## 4 ARKANSAS CITY

**Antiques Plus Mall**
120 N. Summit St.
316/442-5777

**Summit Antique Mall**
208 S. Summit St.
316/442-1115

**Mylissas Garden Antiques**
309 S. Summit St.
316/442-6433

## 5 AUGUSTA

### White Eagle Antique Mall
10187 S.W. U.S. Hwy. 54
316/775-2812
Mon.-Sat. 10-9, Sun. 12-7
*Directions: Located 2.5 miles west of Augusta on the south side of U.S. Hwy. 54. Travelers on U.S. Hwy. 77 take U.S. Hwy. 54 west at Walnut St. stoplight in Augusta.*

White Eagle Antique Mall, billed as "A Collector's Dream Come True," is no disappointment. The mall features that hard-to-find, early petroleum and gas station memorabilia. With over 100 dealers, this place is attractively filled to the brim with high quality glassware, primitives, vintage clothing, old books, jewelry, lamps, old toys, pottery, tools, large and small furniture and other exceptional antiques.

**Like A Rose**
343 Main St.
316/775-5860

**Circa 1890**
10257 S.W. River Valley Road
316/775-3272

**Two Fools Antiques**
429 State St.
316/775-2588

**Pigeons Roost Mall**
601 State St.
316/775-2279

**Serendipity**
529 State St.
316/775-6117

## 6 BASEHOR

***Great Places To Stay***

### Bedknobs & Biscuits
15202 Parallel
913/724-1540
Rates: $50-70

A little bit of country close to Bonner Springs and Kansas City. A warm, inviting beamed gathering room; featuring walls covered in hand-painted vines. Stenciling throughout the house, lovely quilts, lace curtains and colorful stained glass is yours to enjoy. Complimentary cookies in the evening and a huge country breakfast is served in the morning.

## 7 CONCORDIA

**General Store Antiques**
317 W. 5th St.
913/243-7280

**Dans Antiques**
101 E. 6th St.
913/243-3820

**Chapter I Books**
120 E. 6th St.
913/243-1423

**Antique Mall**
128 E. 6th St.
913/243-2313

## 8 COTTONWOOD FALLS

### *Great Places To Stay*

**Grand Central Hotel**
215 Broadway
316/273-6763 or 1-800-951-6763

Most of us rarely think of hills in connection with Kansas, but hidden among the state's Flint Hills is an elegant hotel that is a luxurious surprise when you stumble across it. The Grand Central Hotel bills itself as "very exclusive, very distinctive, very, very special." Located one block west of National Scenic Byway 177 in historic Cottonwood Falls, the hotel was built in 1884 and has been fully restored to its original grandeur. It offers ten suites, each beautifully appointed and oversized, and decorated with a western flair. In fact, each suite is "branded" with historic brands of the area's local ranchers! It offers full dining and complete catering services, and is often the suite of choice for weddings, receptions, small board and business conferences, corporate outings, and, of course, private accommodations. It caters to the business trade with concierge and room service, plus V.I.P. robes and a business center; but the hotel also offers hunting trips, bicycle tours, horseback riding, and tours of the surrounding Flint Hills.

**1874 Stonehouse Bed & Breakfast on Mulberry Hill**
Rural Route 1, Box 67A
316/273-8481
Rates $75

If you've ever wondered about the landscape that nurtured Dorothy and Toto, here's your chance to spend some time at one possibly. The 1874 Stonehouse on Mulberry Hill offers three lovely rooms with private baths on the second floor, with two common rooms and a stone fireplace. But that's not nearly all. On its 120 acres guests can spend all day, or several days, exploring old stone fences, a river valley that crosses the property, acres of woods (more than 10 acres), a pond, the ruins of an old stone barn and corral, an abandoned railway right-of-way, and a decrepit "hired hands place." The inn and its grounds are a magnet for fishermen and hunters, equestrians and naturalists, antiquers and photographers, cyclists and hikers, bird watchers and historians, and maybe even a little girl in pigtails and her funny little dog.

## 9 COUNCIL GROVE

Council Grove was the last outfitting post between the Missouri River and Santa Fe on the Santa Fe Trail. In 1825, the U.S. Government negotiated with the Osage Indians for a passage across their lands. The stump of Council Oak still stands where the treaty was signed. At the Last Chance Store, you can still visit the last supply stop on the Santa Fe Trail. And if you're hungry, try some tasty family recipes at the Hays House Restaurant, the oldest continuously operated restaurant west of the Mississippi.

**Prairie Pieces**
217 W. Main St.
316/767-6628

**Faded Roses**
307 E. Main St.
316/767-5217

### *Great Places To Stay*

**The Cottage House Hotel**
25 N. Neosho St.
1-800-727-7903

**Flint Hills B&B**
613 W. Main St.
316/767-6655

Flint Hills Bed and Breakfast is located on the Santa Fe Trail in Historic Council Grove. The house is an American Four Square built in 1913 by the Jacob Rhodes family. It still has its original yellow pine and oak woodwork and hardwood floors. Each room is antique filled and has a personality of its own. Get acquainted with other guests in the sitting room furnished with TV, coffee pot, and refrigerator, or relax outside on the porch swing. In the morning you will join other guests in the main dining room where you will be served a full country breakfast. Afterwards you may want to tour one of Council Grove's eighteen registered historic sites or enjoy one of the two beautiful lakes.

### *Favorite Places To Eat*

**Hays House 1857 Restaurant**
112 W. Main St.
316/767-5911
Summer 7-9, winter 7-8

Oldest restaurant west of the Mississippi; National Register Historic Landmark; nationally acclaimed restaurant featured in many magazines and newspapers; outstanding steaks, breads and dessert made from scratch daily.

## 10 DODGE CITY

**Ole Jem's**
212 S. 2nd Ave.
316/227-6162

**Collectors Cottage**
106 E. Wyatt Earp Blvd.
316/225-7448

**Curiosity Shoppe**
1102 W. Wyatt Earp Blvd.
316/227-3340

### *Interesting Side Trips*

Relive the 1870s heyday of the rip-snortin', gun-slingin' Wild West at Dodge City's Boot Hill Museum and Front Street complex. More than five million Texas longhorn cattle were driven to the "Cowboy Capital." Miss

Kitty still runs the Longbranch Saloon, gunslingers have "high noon" shootouts and an authentic stagecoach still boards passengers for a ride along Front Street.

## 11 EL DORADO

**North Ward Junction Antiques**
518 North Star
316/321-0145
1-800-286-0146
Mon.-Sat. 10-5:30, Sun. 1-4
Accepts all major credit cards - offers dealer discounts.
*Directions: From I-35 Exit 71 (east); turn left on Central Ave., go 2 1/2 miles into El Dorado. Turn left at the courthouse onto Star. Go five blocks north.*
*From Hwy. 54 east of El Dorado, come into town on Central Ave. heading west, turn right at the courthouse; go five blocks north.*

This shop began life in 1884 as the North Ward School. No longer catering to the educational concerns of fidgety boys and girls, this 4,000-square-foot shop provides fifteen quality antique dealers the opportunity to display their wares in decorated room-like settings. A large selection of furniture is available along with accent pieces of porcelain, china, glassware, elegant table settings, linens, prints and much, much more.

**Cinnamon Tree**
1417 W. Central Ave.
316/321-0930

**Leather Works**
1630 W. Central Ave.
316/321-7644

**Blast From The Past**
527 N. Washington St.
316/321-3434

**Haverhill Antiques**
811 S. Haverhill Rd.
316/321-3199

**Silver Bell Antiques**
204 W. Carr
316/321-3913

## 12 ELLINWOOD

**James J. Elliott Antiques**
1 N. Main
316/564-2400

**Our Mother's Treasures**
14 N. Main
316/564-2218

**Starr Antiques**
104 E. Santa Fe
316/564-2400

## 13 EMPORIA

Emporia is a city with over 130 years of history as an agricultural and railroad community. It still maintains its small town Middle American charm, exemplified by brick streets, tree-lined avenues and many beautiful old Victorian homes.

Emporia was also the home of two-time Pulitzer Prize winner, William Allen White, owner of *The Emporia Gazette*. White became famous overnight for his opposing editorial reviews against the Populist Party.

**Wild Rose Antique Mall**
1505 East Road 175
316/343-8862
Tues.-Sat. 11-5, Sun. 1-5, closed Mon.
*Directions: 3 miles east of Emporia on I-35 at exit #135 (Thorndale exit)*

Terry McCracken, owner and shopkeeper at the Wild Rose Antique Mall, has collected antiques since her childhood. Up until seven years ago, she had never sold a one of them. When she decided to retire as a real estate broker (she added that she's not that old); she opened a booth at a mall in Topeka. Her success prompted her to open her own shop in Emporia where she presented high-end antique glassware, quilts, jewelry, china, pottery, linens, primitives and furnishings. Today, thanks to all the folks who enjoyed shopping at Wild Rose, Terry has expanded. Her new shop allows space for more dealers with a broader selection of antiques. Three dealers specialize in items from the Victorian era. Congratulations, Terry!

### *Great Places To Stay*

**Plumb House Bed and Breakfast**
628 Exchange St.
316/342-6881
Rates $35-75
*Directions: Call from your location.*

Built in 1910 and once the home of George and Ellen Plumb, this bed and breakfast offers classic Victorian charm. Its original beveled glass windows and pocket doors are still intact, and the home is furnished throughout with Victorian era antiques.

Guests may choose from the Horseless Carriage with large windows overlooking a garden; the Garden Suite offering views from a balcony; the Rosalie Room, the Loft, or Grannie's Attic filled with over 250 dresses, hats, gloves, shoes, and jewelry. Everything you need for dress-up tea parties.

## 14 GARNETT

**Country Peddler**
146 E. 5th Ave.
913/448-3018

**Corner Stone Antiques**
146 E. 5th Ave.
913/448-3737

**Goodies Antiques**
121 E. 4th Ave.
913/448-6712

**Emporium on the Square**
415 S. Oak St.
913/448-6459

# Kansas

## 15 HAVEN

### The Home Place Antiques
7619 S. Yoder Road
316/662-1579
Tues.-Sat.; 10-5
*Directions: 4 1/2 miles south of Hwy. 50; 1 1/2 miles north of Hwy. 96.*

The Home Place Antiques is located in a barn built in 1909 and sits on a fourth-generation farm, thus creating the perfect atmosphere for selling antiques. The "old barn" is full of antiques, from furniture (lots of it) to dishes, to pottery, to a little of everything.

## 16 HAYS

**Antique Mall**
201 W. 41st St.
913/625-6055

**Littles Antiques**
717 Vine St.
913/628-3393

### *Interesting Side Trips*

Old Fort Hays was built to protect military roads, guard the mails and defend construction gangs on the Union Pacific Railroad. See the original blockhouse, guardhouse and officers' quarters. "Buffalo Bill" Cody supplied the fort with buffalo meat, and General Custer's ill-fated 7th cavalry was stationed here.

## 17 HUTCHINSON

**Antique Memories**
25 E. 1st St.
316/665-0610

**Unique Antiques**
1831 E. 4th Ave.
316/669-8678

**Yesterdays Treasures**
436 Hendricks St.
316/662-0895

**Cow Creek Antiques**
127 S. Main St.
316/663-1976

**Nu-Tu U**
201 S. Main St.
316/662-4357

**Book Collector**
404 N. Main St.
316-665-5057

**Finders Keepers II**
412 N. Main St.
316/663-5457

**Brokers Antiques**
820 S. Main St.
316/665-7040

**GAI Marche Ltd.**
2528 N. Main St.
316/662-6323

**Armstrong's Antiques**
121 S. Main St.
316/664-5811

**Bluebird Antiques**
112 S. Main St.
316/663-1519

**Old Tyme Things**
129 S. Main St.
316/665-6024

**Jim's Antique Bottles**
1310 13th Terrace
316/662-7784

**The Antique Connection**
419 N. Poplar
No Phone Listed

**The Shoppe**
1000 S. Main St.
316/663-7789

**Wild Horse Primitives & Antiques**
123 S. Main St.
316/662-6773

**Wood N Horse**
15 E. 1st St.
1-800-293-6607

## 18 INDEPENDENCE

If you're a fan of "Little House on the Prairie," visit a replica of the house where Laura Ingalls Wilder lived and found inspiration for her books. The cabin was rebuilt where it originally stood near Independence.

**Attic Treasures**
211 E. Main St.
316/331-6401

**Southwest Wood Shop**
1813 W. Main St.
316/331-1400

**Susie's Vintage Villa**
2919 W. Main (Hwy. 160)
316/331-6811

### *Great Places To Stay*

### The Rosewood Bed and Breakfast
417 W. Myrtle St.
316/331-2221
Rates: $50-60
*Directions: Located 1 block north of Hwy. 75/169 at 11th St. and Myrtle St.*

This stately home was built in 1915 for William Gates, general manager of Prairie Oil and Gas. Leaded glass windows and wrap-around porches still embrace the home. Decorated throughout in period antiques, the Victorian Rose room creates a picture of a romantic time gone by. A white iron bed piled high with pure white and soft pink dressings is the focus of the room, with a large bay window providing the morning sun. The Royal Orchid, preferred by honeymooners, has a black canopy bed. The Desert Blossom is the whimsical room, decorated in a Southwestern flair.

Breakfast is served in the dining room near the bay windows and fireplace.

## 19 IOLA

### *Great Places To Stay*

**Northrup House Bed & Breakfast**
318 East St.
316/365-8025
Rates: $60-70

The Northrup House, a Queen Anne Victorian, was built in 1895 by Lewis Northrup, a prominent Iola businessman and community leader. The interior features stained glass windows, beautiful oak woodwork, crystal chandeliers and pocket doors. The house is furnished with elegant antiques. The guests are welcome to use the parlors, dining room and porches.

## 20 KANSAS CITY

**Palmers Antique**
761 Central Ave.
913/342-8299

**Glenn Books**
1710 Central Ave.
913/321-3040

**Happy House Antiques**
1712 Central Ave.
913/321-8909

**Treasures From Grannys Attic**
6000 Leavenworth Road
913/334-0824

**Antique & Craft City Mall**
1270 Merriam Lane
913/677-0752

**Adventure Antiques**
1306 Merriam Lane
913/831-6005

**Andersons General Store**
1713 Minnesota Ave.
913/321-3165

**Old World Antiques**
4436 State Line Road
913/677-4744

**Show Me Antiques**
4500 State Line Road
913/236-8444

**State Line Antique Mall**
4510 State Line Road
913/362-2002

**Collectors Emporium**
3412 Strong Ave.
913/384-1875

**Past Renewed**
4356 Victory Dr.
913/287-2817

## 21 KECHI

**Country Antiques Kechi**
201 E. Kechi Road
316/744-0932

**Anderson Antiques**
309 E. Kechi Road
316/744-8482

**Cherishables**
311 E. Kechi Road
316/744-9952

**Primitives Plus**
127 Foreman
316/744-1836

**Jo's Antiques**
210 E. Kechi Road
316/744-1581

**Aunt B's**
130 E. Kechi Road
316/744-3505

**Daisy Patch Antiques**
134 E. Kechi Road
316/744-1144

**Rememberings**
132 E. Kechi Road
316/744-3400

**The Five Little Ladies**
128C E. Kechi Road
316/744-8874

## 22 LAWRENCE

**Quantrill's Antique Mall & Flea Market**
811 New Hampshire St.
913/842-6616
Daily 10-5:30
*Directions: Located 3 miles south of the I-70 East Kansas Turnpike Exit. One block east of Massachusetts St. Two blocks from Riverfront Outlet Mall.*

Quantrill's is the oldest antique mall in the state of Kansas. This massive 3-story natural limestone structure dates back to 1863. With 150 dealers covering 20,000 square feet, their inventory list is just as impressive. You'll find furniture, toys, jewelry, glassware, pottery, books, lunch boxes, dolls, advertising memorabilia, buttons, crocks and Fiesta. From their list of the unusual, they offer retro '60s and '70s items, tobacco, military and '50s dinettes and other nostalgic items.

**Topiary Tree Inc.**
15 E. 8th St.
913/842-1181

**Antique Mall**
830 Massachusetts St.
913/842-1328

**B & S Antiques**
1017 Massachusetts St.
913/843-9491

**Strong's Antiques**
1025 Massachusetts St.
913/843-5173

## 23 LEAVENWORTH

**Caffee's Leavenworth Antique Mall**
505 Delaware St.
913/758-0193
Mon.-Sat. 10-6
*Directions: Located in Historic Downtown Leavenworth.*

For specific informative see review at the beginning of this section.

**Bob's Antiques**
511 Delaware St.
913/680-0101

**Ginny's Antiques**
206 S. 5th St.
913/651-8426

**Carol's Cupboard**
207 S. 5th St.
913/651-0400

**Weakleys Antique Furniture**
1433 Kingman St.
913/682-5816

**River Front Antique Shop**
401 S. 2nd St.
913/682-3201

**Trumpet Vine**
1700 2nd Ave.
913/651-8230

**June's Antiques**
612 Cherokee
913/651-5270

## 24 LIBERAL

**Randy's Antiques**
1 S. Kansas Ave.
316/624-0641

**Yesterdays Treasure**
406 E. Pancake Blvd.
316/624-1683

### *Interesting Side Trips*

Take a stroll along Dorothy's Yellow Brick Road in Liberal. See the original miniature farmhouse used in the 1939 classic film "The Wizard of Oz," or go through a full-sized replica of Dorothy's house. Liberal also is the home of Kansas' largest aviation museum, the Mid-America Air Museum. There are more than 80 vintage aircraft on display. And the world-famous International Pancake Race is held in Liberal each Shrove Tuesday.

## 25 MANHATTAN

**Pop's Collectables**
315 S. 4th St.
785/776-1433

**Gumbo Hill Antique Shop**
6590 Gumbo Hill Road
785/539-5778

**On The Avenue**
405 Poyntz Ave.
785/539-9116

**Antique Emporium of Manhattan**
411 Poyntz Ave.
785/537-1921

**Under The Avenue Antique Mall**
413 Poyntz Ave.
785/537-1921

**Zeandale Store**
R.R. 3
785/537-3631

**Tuttle's Antique Market**
2010 Tuttle Creek Blvd.
785/537-4884

**Time Machine Antique Mall**
4910 Skyway Dr.
785/539-4684

## 26 MINNEAPOLIS

**Griffin's Antiques & Collectibles**
703 E. 10th
913/392-2821

**Blue Store Emporium**
307 W. Second St.
913/392-3491

## 27 NEWTON

**Wharf Road**
413 N. Main St.
316-283-3579

**Stuart's Antique Gallery**
709 N. Main St.
316/284-0824

**The Curiosity Shop**
106 W. Broadway
316/283-5555

## 28 NICKERSON

**Johnson's Antique Warehouse**
#2 Nickerson St.
316/442-3225

### *Great Places To Stay*

**Hedrick Exotic Animal Farm/Bed and Breakfast**
7910 N. Roy L. Smith Road
316/422-3245
1-800-618-9577
Daily 8-10
*Directions: 50 miles northwest of Wichita on Hwy. 96; 8 miles west of Hutchinson on Hwy. 96. From I-70, go south on 135 at Salina to McPherson. Take Hwy. 61 to Hutchinson, Take Hwy. 96 west 8 miles. Located on the north side of Hwy. 96.*

Looking for a little bit out of the ordinary place to stay? Then book your reservations here. Hedrick's Bed and Breakfast offers a relaxing, country atmosphere in a picturesque Old West town front nestled in the midst of a farm. But cows and horses aren't the only animals you'll find here. It wouldn't be out of the ordinary to find camels, zebras, llamas, kangaroos, and ostriches. And Jeffrey, the tallest animal found on the farm, will practically kiss you for an apple slice. In case you haven't guessed, Jeffrey's a giraffe.

You can arrange for the staff to take you on a guided tour where you can actually touch and feed the animals. Camel rides, pony rides, hayrack rides and campfire wiener roasts can also be arranged.

The decor of each guest room depicts an animal on the farm, with personal touches such as zebra sheets, rugs from Peru and much more. True to the western heritage of Kansas, the inn reflects the image of Main Street in the Old West, complete with swinging "bar" doors. An outside balcony which completely surrounds the inn is accessible from each room. A great place to bring the kids.

## 29 OLATHE

**Rosebriar Limited**
11695 S. Black Bob Road
913/829-3636

**Heirloom Antiques**
2135 N.E. 151 St.
913/780-3478

**Aggies Attic Antiques**
301 1/2 W. Park St.
913/768-0058

**Flutterby**
1313 E. Santa Fe St.
913/780-1644

## 30 OTTAWA

**Over The Hill Collectibles**
120 S. Main St.
785/242-8016

**Down Home Antiques**
202 S. Main St.
785/242-0774

**Gables Antiques**
503 N. Main St.
785/242-7144

**Outback Antiques**
534 N. Main St.
785/242-1178

**Silver Arrow Trading Post**
1630 S. Main St.
785/242-0019

**Ottawa Antique Mall & Restaurant**
202 S. Walnut St.
785/242-1078

## 31 PAOLA

**Park Square Emporium**
18 S. Silver St.
913/294-9004

**Magdelenas Antiques & Collectibles**
8 S. Silver St.
913/294-5048

**Special Occasions**
23 W. Wea St.
913/294-8595

## 32 PARK CITY

**Recollections**
1530 S. 61st St.
316/744-8333

**Poor House Antiques**
1542 N. 61st St.
316/744-9935

**Teddys Antiques & Collectibles**
1550 E. 61st St.
316/685-0435

**Annie Antiques & Collectibles**
1600 S. 61st St.
316/744-1999

**Howe's Homestead**
8416 N. Broadway
316/755-0371

**Park City Antique Mall**
6227 N. Broadway
316/744-2025

## 33 PAXICO

**Paxico Variety Shop**
203 Main St.
913/636-5292

**Main Street Antiques**
204 Main St.
913/636-5200

**Time Warp Antiques**
207 Main St.
913/636-5553

**Mill Creek Antiques**
109 Newbury Ave.
913/636-5520

**Paxico Antiques**
111 Newbury Ave.
913/636-5426

## 34 PEABODY

This little town of 1,400 probably has preserved its architectural heritage better than any other community in the state. Gutted by two fires in its first 14 years of existence, Peabody was rebuilt in 1885 with limestone fire walls between the buildings.

"That's what saved our town," said the town historian, Koni Jones. "You can see that the buildings are still the way they were in the 1880s. One of our slogans is 'It really is a step back in time.' "

The town was named for a railroad executive who donated a library to the fledgling community in 1874. It was the first free library in Kansas, and today the original building is the Peabody Historical Museum.

Visitors downtown can also browse an antique store, try a Phosphate at a 1920s soda fountain, enjoy flavored coffees and teas at the Jackrabbit Hollow Bookstore, or dine in restaurants that once were a bank in 1887 and a chicken hatchery in 1885.

**Tumbleweed Antiques**
101 N. Walnut St.
316/983-2200

**Sharon's Korner Kitchen**
(1887 old bank)
128 N. Walnut St.
316/983-2307

**Turkey Red Restaurant**
(an old chicken hatchery)
101 S. Walnut St.
316/983-2883

**Jack Rabbit Hollow Books**
113 N. Walnut St.
316/983-2600

## 35 PITTSBURG

**Marilyns Ceramics Crafts**
710 W. Atkinson Road
316/231-4131

**Georges Antiques**
210 S. Broadway St.
316/232-6340

**Treasure Village Antiques**
212 S. Broadway St.
316/231-4888

**Browsery-Collector Antiques**
216 S. Broadway St.
316/232-1250

**Friday's Child**
615 N. Broadway St.
316/235-0403

**Antique Shop**
2305 N. Broadway St.
316/231-4090

## 36 PRAIRIE VILLAGE

**Mission Road Antique Mall**
4101 W. 83rd St.
913/341-7577

## 37 PRATT

**Peggys Antiques**
208 S. Main St.
316/672-5648

**Brick Street Antique Mall**
212 S. Main St.
316/672-6770

**Mom's Attic**
607 S. Main St.
316/672-7656

**Higgin's Antiques**
617 Champa
316/672-6655

## 38 SALINA

**Auld Lang Syne &**
**Auld Lang Syne, too**
1-101 N. Santa Fe
too-110 N. Santa Fe
913/825-0020
913/827-4222
Mon.-Sat. 10-5, Sun. 1-5
*Directions: Corner of Santa Fe and Iron*

Two shops to double your antiquing pleasure. Auld Lang Syne is located in the former First National Bank Building complete with a center courtyard for relaxing. Auld Lang Syne, too is across the street. Both shops display the wares of ninety dealers offering a selection of antiques and collectibles of various styles and periods

**Treasure Chest of Salina**
N. Broadway
913/827-9371

**Furniture Clinic**
405 S. Clark St.
913/827-5115

**Stan & June's Heirlooms**
201A S. 5th St.
913/823-6627

**Fourth Street Mini Mall**
127 S. 4th St.
913/825-4948

**Forever & Ever Antiques & Collectibles**
108 N. Santa Fe Ave.
913/827-4222

**Daddy & Me**
116 S. Santa Fe Ave.
913/452-9976

## 39 SHAWNEE

**O'Neills Classics - Antiques & Uniques**
11200 Johnson Dr.
913/268-9008
Tues.-Fri. 10-5:30, Sat. 10-4:30, closed Sun. & Mon.
*Directions: One mile from I-35, on the north side of Johnson Dr., just a block west of its intersection with Nieman Road.*

Located in the historic town of Shawnee, O'Neill's carries a general line of antiques and collectibles. Antique chairs, tables, dressers, pictures, elegant glassware and the such are just a few of the items one may find in this quaint 1400 sq. ft. store. The oldest piece in the store dates to around 1830 with collectibles up through 1960s.

Local residents frequent the store often, but the owners, Mike & Cyndee Bohaty, love meeting new antique friends who stop in while traveling. Cyndee grew up around antiques and was once a member of Questers, a national association of people interested in antiquing. When Cyndee and Mike were married they loved going to auctions - Cyndee jokingly laughs that they couldn't afford anything else. Today, they still love auctions as evidenced by the wonderful pieces available in their store.

**Gene Switzer Antiques**
6711 Antioch Road
913/432-3982

**Armoires & More**
12922 W. 87th St.
913/438-3868

**Memory Lane Antiques**
5401 Johnson Dr.
913/677-4300

**Past & Present Antiques**
5727 Johnson Dr.
913/362-6995

**Petersons Antiques**
7829 Marty St.
913/341-5065

**J & M Collectables**
7819 W. 151st St.
913/897-0584

**June's Antiques**
612 Cherokee
913/651-5270

**Consignment Shop**
4740 Rainbow Shop
913/384-2424

**Mission Road Antique Mall**
4101 W. 83rd St.
913/341-7577

**Lincoln Antiques**
5636 Johnson Dr.
913/384-6811

**Drake's Military Antiques**
8929 Johnson Dr.
913/722-1943

**Antiques & Oak**
10464 Metcalf Ave.
913/381-8280

**Zohners Antiques**
10200 Pflumm Road
913/894-5036

### *Interesting Side Trips*

### Old Shawnee Town

As visitors pass through the gates into Old Shawnee Town, they are enveloped by the 1880s atmosphere of the town. From the blacksmith's shop to the sod house, the setting makes visitors become a part of life on the Kansas frontier.

Furniture, tools and household items are just a few of the goods to see on the walk through town. The original Shawnee jail - the first in Johnson County - stands in Old Shawnee Town for people of all ages to explore.

For those who decide to make it a day at the site, the central grassy area serves as an ideal spot for picnics and group gatherings.

### Johnson County Historical Museum

From pioneer trail utensils to the coming of the television, the Johnson County Historical Museum brings the area's history to life.

The experiences of prairie pioneers come alive at the Hands-on History display in the museum. After donning the traditional attire of calico dresses or overalls, kids can try their hand at mixing pretend biscuits or discovering how to harness an oxen team.

## 40 TOPEKA

**Shade Tree Antiques**
1300 S.W. Boswell Ave.
913/232-5645

**B & J Antique Mall**
1949 S.W. Gage Blvd.
913/273-3409

**Cobweb**
2508 S.W. 15th St.
913/357-7498

**Antiques Unique**
1222 S.W. 6th Ave.
913/232-1007

**Packrat Antiques**
3310 S.W. 6th Ave.
913/232-6560

**Reflections Antiques**
2213 S.W. 10th Ave.
913/232-4619

**Antique Plaza Of Topeka**
2935 S.W. Topeka Blvd.
913/267-7411

**Darlas World Antiques & Collectibles**
3688 S.W. Topeka Blvd.
913/266-4242

**Topeka Antique Mall**
5247 S.W. 28th Court
913/273-2969

**Dickerson Antiques**
5331 S.W. 22nd Place
913/273-1845

**Antique Elegance**
2900 S.W. Oakley Ave.
913/273-0909

**Pastense**
3307 S.W. 6th Ave.
913/233-7107

**Kansan Relics & Old Books**
3308 S.W. 6th Ave.
913/233-8232

**History House**
215 S.W. Topeka Blvd.
913/235-1885

**Rose Buffalo Antiques & Cllbls.**
3600 S.W. Topeka Blvd.
913/267-7478

**Wheatland Antique Mall**
2121 S.W. 37th St.
913/266-3266

**Washburn View Antique Mall**
1507 S.W. 21st St.
913/234-0949

**Saltbox**
507 S.W. Washburn Ave.
913/233-6264

## 41 VALLEY FALLS

### Valley Falls Antiques

423 Broadway
913/945-3666
Tues.-Sat. 10-5, Sun. 12-5, closed Mon.
*Directions: Located halfway between Topeka and Atchison, Kan., 30 miles either direction, via Hwy. 4. In Valley Falls, go downtown. The store is easily found at the corner of Walnut St. and Broadway.*

Halfway between Topeka and Atchison, Kansas, sits Valley Falls, "Antique Capital of Jefferson County." Among the three established shops and the one opening this year, Valley Falls Antiques presents its shoppers the expected assortment of goods, in addition to some not-so-usual items.

The shop is housed in a historic bank building built in 1872, and within its walls you can shop for antique furniture, primitives, glassware and collectibles. Delores Werder, owner and shopkeeper, admits that original artwork is a passion for her. She prefers to purchase pieces with some unusual quality. Among her display of art, you will find prints, paintings and block prints.

## 42 WAMEGO

**Carriage House Antiques & Collectibles**
210 Lincoln St.
913/456-7021

**Wagon Wheel Antiques**
409 Lincoln St.
913/456-8480

**Antique Emporium of Wamego**
511 Lincoln St.
913/456-7111

**Fulkerson's Antiques**
206 Maple St.
913/456-9175

## 43 WATHENA

### *Great Places To Stay*

### Carousel Bed & Breakfast

Route 1
913/989-3537
Daily 7-10 p.m.
*Directions: Approximately 15 miles west of I-29 and Hwy. 36 interchange. The B&B driveway comes off of Hwy. 36 three miles west of Wathena and 4 miles east of Troy, Kan. (60 miles north of Kansas City and 9 miles west of St. Joseph, Mo.)*

Located on a country hillside with a gorgeous panoramic view of the glacial hills, the Carousel Bed and Breakfast has been beautifully restored to its 1917 splendor by innkeeper Betty Price, her husband, and her sister, Ginnie. The trio was the restoration crew responsible for the Victorian elegance evident throughout the home. Ginnie was the painter, Betty hung all the wallpaper while Mr. Price ran all the errands. If you look closely at the stairway spindles, you might observe a rather heavy coating of paint on them. It seems that Ginnie, in her efforts to perform the perfect task, got carried away and painted them five times! That night she dreamed that the stairway reached all the way to heaven and that she was painting every one of them.

This labor of love is especially evident in the Victorian parlor where personal touches have created a soothing environment for guests to relax. Victorian furnishings are placed throughout the home, further enhancing its aura.

Breakfast is served beginning at 7 a.m. for early birds who are eager to venture out into the beautiful surroundings that embrace The Carousel.

## 44 WELLINGTON

**Antiques Plus Mall**
1112 E. Hwy. 160
316/326-5700

**Dianne Wagoner's Antqs. & Cllbls.**
Hwy. 81, 1 Mi. N. of Wellington
316/326-2665

**Pastime Treasures Antique Mall**
221 N. Washington
316/326-3440

## 45 WICHITA

In 1865, Jesse Chisholm and James Mead established Wichita near a village of grass lodges built by the Wichita Indians. The settlement around their trading post soon attracted passing drovers along the Chisholm Trail, and Wichita boomed into a wide-open cowtown. Today you'll find remnants of Western history almost everywhere you look. Step back to the early years of the booming cattle town at Old Cowtown Museum. The

44 restored buildings and authentic characters will give you a true sense of Wichita in the 1870s. Visitors can see Wichita's first jail, a fully stocked general store, a one-room school, a saloon, a railroad depot, and also watch a blacksmith demonstrate his craft.

Across town is the historic Old Town District. It's one part of town you won't want to miss. This newly renovated warehouse district is packed full of antique shops, a variety of delightful restaurants, galleries and great night spots. And from May through October enjoy the Wichita Farm and Art Market, an open-air market of fresh produce, arts, and crafts.

**Wooden Heart Antiques**
141 S. Rock Island St.
316/267-1475
Mon.-Sat 10-5, Sun. 12-5
*Directions: I-135 to U.S. Hwy. 54 W. Exit off U.S. Hwy. 54 on Washington St. North on Washington St. to Waterman St. Left (west) on Waterman St. across RR tracks to Rock Island St. Right (north) on Rock Island St. to 141 S. Rock Island St.*

For specific information see review at the beginning of this section.

**White Eagle Antique Mall**
10187 S.W. U.S. Hwy. 54
316/775-2812
Mon.-Sat. 10-9, Sun. 12-7
*Directions: Travelers through Wichita on I-135 should take the East 54 (Kellogg) exit. Go east on U.S. Hwy. 54 (Kellogg) 16 miles. The mall is located on the south side of U.S. Hwy. 54.*
*Travelers on I-35 (Kansas Turnpike) use Exit 50 and go east on U.S. Hwy. 54 (Kellogg) 11 miles. The mall is located on the south side of U.S. Hwy. 54.*

White Eagle Antique Mall billed as "A Collector's Dream Come True," is no disappointment. The mall features that hard-to-find, early petroleum and gas station memorabilia. With over 100 dealers, this place is attractively filled to the brim with high quality glassware, primitives, vintage clothing, old books, jewelry, lamps, old toys, pottery, tools, large and small furniture and other exceptional antiques.

**Green Dragons Books**
2730 Boulevard Plaza
316/681-0746

**Park City Antique Mall**
6227 N. Broadway St.
316/744-2025

**River City Basket Co.**
509 E. Douglas Ave.
316/265-1068

**Santa Fe House & Old Town Gallery**
630 E. Douglas Ave.
316/265-4736

**Gay 90s Antique Shop**
1303 N. Broadway St.
316/263-7421

**M Ballard & Co.**
920 Buffum St.
316/267-7831

**Douglas Avenue Antiques**
517 E. Douglas Ave.
316/263-6454

**S A Phillip Company**
1109 E. Douglas Ave.
316/267-5730

**Legacy Antiques**
105 S. Emporia St.
316-267-2730

**Paradise Antique Mall**
430 E. Harry St.
316/269-4441

**A & A Antique Mall**
2419 Maple St.
316/945-4250

**A Little Everything Antqs**
2301 S. Meridian Ave.
316/945-3150

**Ice House Antiques**
136 S. Oliver Road (Kechi)
316/744-2331

**Dorothys Antiques & Collectibles**
1515 E. Pawnee St.
316/265-6035

**Vanderkellen Galleries**
701 E. 2nd St. N.
316/264-0338

**Hephner Antiques**
737 S. Washington St., #3
316/264-3284

**Variety Plus & Mills Stream**
110 W. Harry St.
316-262-4299

**KIS Antiques**
724 N. Main St.
316/267-1357

**Hewitts Antiques**
228 N. Market St.
316/264-2450

**Reflections**
550 N. Rock Road
316/267-7477

**Somewhere In Time**
30 N.W. Pkwy.
316/681-1007

**Yesterdays**
535 N. Woodlawn St.
316/684-1900

**Country Sentiments**
200 S. 61st St.
316/744-9403

**Grannys Shanty**
405 N. West St.
316/942-6222

### *Great Places To Stay*

**The Castle Inn Riverside**
1155 N. River Blvd.
316/263-9300
1-800-580-1131

For specific information see review at the beginning of this section.

## 46 WINFIELD

**B & B Antiques**
1102 E. 5th
316/221-0457

**Antique Mall of Winfield**
1400 Main St.
316/221-1065

**Jenny's Treasures**
919 Manning St.
316/221-9199

**Virginia Jarvis Antiques**
701 Main St.
316/221-1732

**Antiques Plus Mall**
1820 Main St.
316/221-6699

# Kentucky

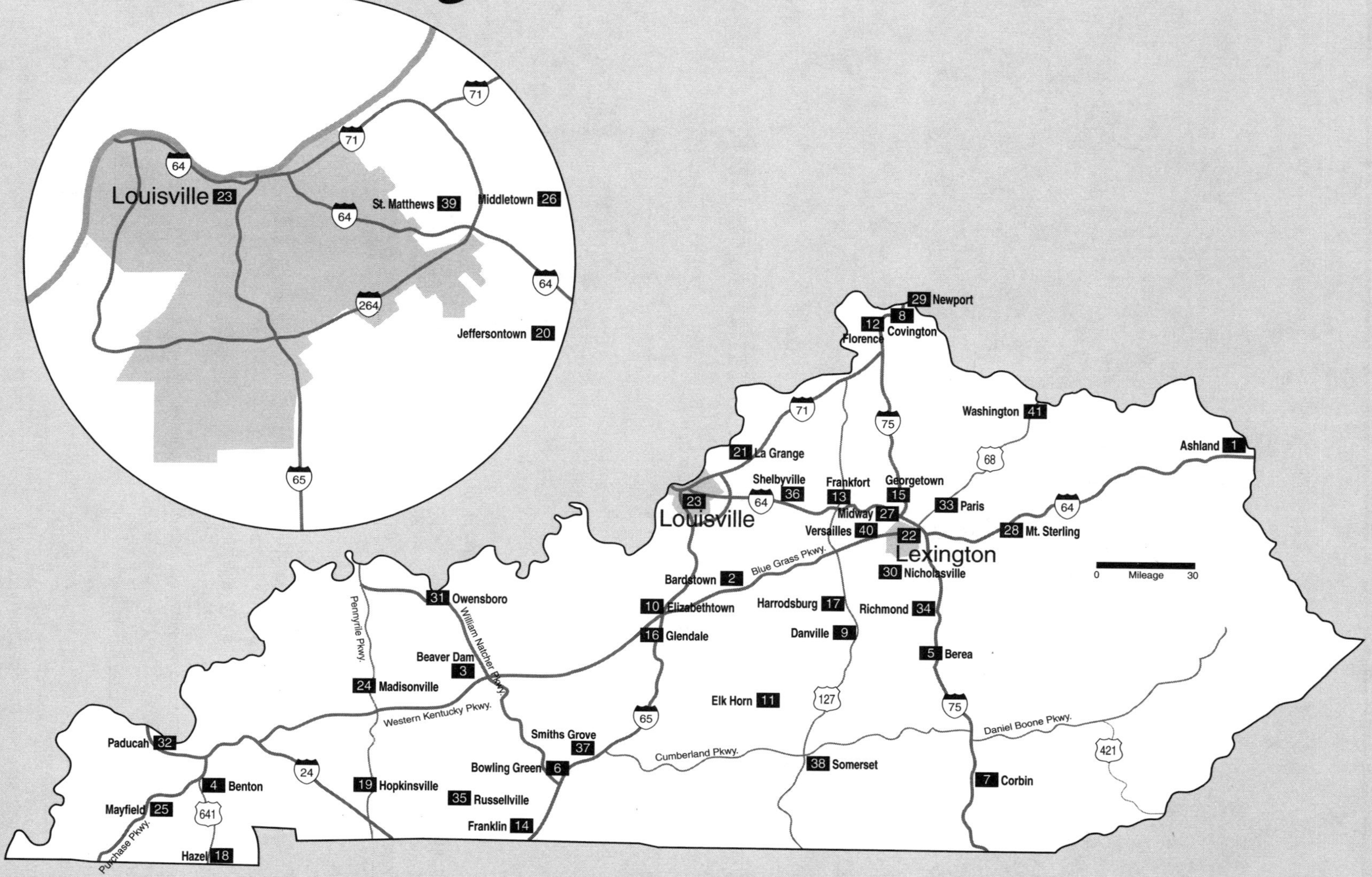
Louisville 23
St. Matthews 39
Middletown 26
Jeffersontown 20
64
71
264
65
29 Newport
12
8
Covington
Florence
Washington 41
Ashland 1
21 La Grange
Shelbyville
36
Frankfort
13
Georgetown
15
33 Paris
Midway 27
Versailles 40
22
Lexington
28 Mt. Sterling
30 Nicholasville
Louisville
23
Bardstown 2
Blue Grass Pkwy.
0 Mileage 30
31 Owensboro
10 Elizabethtown
16 Glendale
Harrodsburg 17
Richmond 34
Danville 9
5 Berea
Beaver Dam
3
24 Madisonville
Elk Horn 11
William Natcher Pkwy.
Western Kentucky Pkwy.
Pennyrile Pkwy.
Paducah 32
Smiths Grove
37
Bowling Green 6
Cumberland Pkwy.
38 Somerset
Daniel Boone Pkwy.
7 Corbin
4 Benton
19 Hopkinsville
35 Russellville
Mayfield 25
Franklin 14
Hazel 18
Purchase Pkwy.
75
68
127
421
24
641

# The sun shines bright on Kentucky's Blackridge Hall

This Southern Georgian style mansion situated on five acres in the heart of horse country exemplifies the high style and elegant living of a true Kentucky horse farm. Blackridge Hall's grand entry looks out upon the rolling bluegrass landscape. It is surrounded by horse farms and is just an eight-minute drive from the Kentucky Horse Park and twenty minutes from Keeneland, Lexington and Rupp Arena. For the antique shopper, there's Midway, a community known for its antique shops, as well as numerous quaint antique shops in Georgetown. Nearby is the Factory Stores of America Outlet Mall, and the Toyota Motor Co., which offers tours of its plant.

Blackridge Hall, built on a ridge which has a view of the Lexington lights at night, was completed in 1991 and features 10,000 square feet of living space.

Five guest suites/rooms are available and all have names which indicate their decor. The Colonial Williamsburg master suite is a large, plush suite with Jacuzzi, fireplace, living room and sitting area. The Fox and Hound and Thoroughbred guest rooms both have private baths.

Guests will love the tiled sunroom and the elegant formal dining room, where proprietor Jim D. Black serves breakfast on fine china, with sterling flatware and crystal stemware. The furnishings throughout the house are 18th century and 19th century antiques and reproductions and include rice-carved queen-size beds.

*Blackridge Hall Bed & Breakfast is located at 4055 Paris Pike in Georgetown. For additional information please call the innkeepers at 800-768-9308. Rates begin at $119.*

*Relax in the Great Room by listening to quiet music, curling up with a good book in front of the fireplace, or meeting with other guests and sharing experiences.*

*Off the double curved staircase in the Grand Marble Entry Hall, you will discover the Colonial Williamsburg master suite with its custom fireplace, mahogany rice carved four poster bed, Jacuzzi and a private sitting room.*

Kentucky

# Georgetown and Scott County: The Antique Capital of Kentucky

## Over 100,000 square feet of antique malls and shops

Located just north of the crossroads of I-75 and I-64. Georgetown was founded in 1790 by the Baptist minister Elijah Craig, The Reverend Craig is perhaps best known for his world-famous invention, bourbon whiskey.

Today, Georgetown is a blend of old and new. Noted for its profusion of historic houses and perhaps the finest antique shopping in the state, it is also one of Kentucky's fastest growing communities and the American home of Toyota's Camry, Avalon and Sienna production facility. Mid-July to mid-August, Georgetown is also host to the Cinncinnati Bengals training camp.

Georgetown offers beautiful horse farms, Irish fieldstone fences, the meandering Elkhorn and Eagle creeks and rolling fields of tobacco and cattle. You'll find small quaint communities like Stamping Ground and Sadieville. Elkhorn Creek, the inspiration for Walt Whitman's "Leaves of Grass," offers both canoeists and fishermen a rewarding and relaxing experience.

Georgetown and Scott County offer a complete range of overnight accomodations (more than 800 rooms) from clean and affordable motels to unique bed and breakfasts. All of this, plus you are just five minutes from the world famous Kentucky Horse Park.

Georgetown and Scott County is host to numerous craft shows and other events which include:

Double Stink Hog Farm Pumpkinfest
Fister's By-Water Farm Autumnfest
Festival of the Horse (with arts and crafts)
Cinncinnati Bengals Training Camp
Morgan's Raid Civil War Reenactment
Under the Trees Antique Show
Bluegrass Cycling Club's Horsey Hundred
Kentucky Gala Driving Event

*For additional information, contact Georgetown/Scott County Tourism Commission, 401 Outlet Center Dr., Ste. 240, Georgetown, KY 40324. Call the commission at 888/863-8600, 502/863-2561(fax) and e-mail: gtown@mis.net or www.georgetownky.com.*

***Antique Malls and Shops***

Central KY Antique Mall • 114 E. Main St.• 502/863-4018
Bee's Den of Antiquity • 100 E. Main St. • 502/863-7536
Georgetown Antique Mall (3 buildings) • 124 W. Main St. • 502/863-9033
Gretchen's Antiques • 119 S. Broadway • 502/863-2538
Pooh's Place • 122 E. Main St. • 502/867-3930
Kollector's Corner • 1365 Lexington Road • 502/863-5829
Cox's Collectibles • Hwy. 62 • Oxford • 502/863-1407
Olde Barn Antiques • 222 N. Broadway • 502/863-2013
Oxford Antiques • 5 miles east of Georgetown • Hwy. 62 • 502/863-3965
The Vault Antiques • 201 E. Main St. • 502/863-2728
The Wee Shop • 3830 Cynthia Road • 502/863-0841
Trojan Antiques • 130 N. Broadway • 502/867-1823
Wyatt's Antique Center • 149 E. Main St. • 502/863-0331

*Visit this unique antique-filled area of Kentucky and find part of America's heritage to take home with you.*

## 1 ASHLAND

**Tunnel Hill Antique Shoppe**
1827 6th St.
606/324-6880

**Miners Coins & Antiques**
830 29th St.
606/325-9425

**Vintage Hall**
By Appointment Only
606/329-1173

**Treasured Possessions/Antq. Mall**
1430 Winchester Ave.
606/324-4798

## 2 BARDSTOWN

**Town and Country Antiques**
118 N. 3rd St.
502/348-3967

**Scarlett's Fever**
Appointment Only
502/349-9211

### *Great Places To Stay*

**Arbor Rose Bed & Breakfast**
209 E. Stephen Foster Ave.
1-888-828-3330

The Arbor Rose is a late Victorian style home thoroughly renovated in 1993. The original structure was built in 1820 and contains five fireplaces, some of which were designed by Alexander Moore, master craftsman of My Old Kentucky Home. Five guest suites all have private baths. Homemade cookies and beverages are available at all times in the common area, as well as TV, phone, fax and a computer hook-up. Located in Historical Bardstown, the Arbor Rose provides easy accessibility to shopping and all the local attractions. Each room comes with a full "Country Gourmet" breakfast and weather permitting it is served on the garden terrace by a pond stocked with Japanese Koi and a garden complete with Hummingbirds.

**Jailer's Inn**
111 W. Stephen Foster Ave.
502/348-5551 or 1-800-948-5551
Open February through December, closed January

Ever wondered what it would be like to spend a night or two in jail? Well you can—sort of—if you stay at the Jailer's Inn in Bardstown! This 1819 building (listed on the National Register) was originally built as a jail, with prisoners housed and the jailer living below. In 1874 prisoners were moved to a new jail built right behind this old one, and the old building became the jailer's official permanent residence. Believe it or not, both buildings were used for the original purposes until 1987! The complex was then declared the oldest operating jail in the state of Kentucky! Now the 1819 building has been completely renovated into six individually decorated guest rooms filled with antiques, original rugs and heirlooms. Guest quarters range from the Victorian Room and the Garden Room to the former women's cell, which is decorated in prison black and white and features two of the original bunk beds plus a more modern waterbed. One room even has a Jacuzzi. Guests are treated to a filling continental-plus breakfast and refreshments.

**Kenmore Farms**
1050 Bloomfield Road
1-800-831-6159

Kenmore Farms was established in the 1860s as the Victorian residence of a prominent Kentucky horse farm. This stately home features antiques throughout, oriental rugs, and gleaming wood, from the poplar floors to the cherry stairway. The decor and Southern hospitality creates a relaxing and enjoyable atmosphere. Within driving distance of Derby Museum and Churchill Downs, Keeneland Racetract, Kentucky Horse Park and the Shaker Village at Pleasant Hill.

**The Mansion Bed & Breakfast**
1003 N. Third
502/348-2586

The home was placed on the National Register of Historic Places in 1979, described in the nomination as a 'truly dignified, aristocratic and striking example of Greek Revival architecture.' Overnight guests at The Mansion are treated to a deluxe continental breakfast served in the dining room on china, silver and crystal. The Mansion also boasts a rich history. The home is on the site where the first Confederate flag, the 'Stars and Bars', was raised in Kentucky.

## 3 BEAVER DAM

Ohio County is older than the Commonwealth of Kentucky and was named for the Ohio River, which was originally its northern boundary. It is the fifth-largest county in Kentucky—located 23 miles south of Owensboro, 40 miles north of Bowling Green, 100 miles southwest of Louisville, and 90 miles north of Nashville, Tennessee.

**Downtown Antique Mall**
103 N. Main St.
502/274-4774

**Casey's Antiques & Collectibles**
116 N. Main St.
No Phone Listed

**Past & Presents Antiques**
930 N. Main St.
502/274-3360 or 502/274-7124

**Tomorrow's Treasures Doll Shop**
108 N. Main St.
502/274-7946

**Knob Hill Antiques**
282 Knob Hill Road
502/274-3065

**Pat's Antiques & Collectibles**
Hwy. 269 off Hwy. 231
502/274-3076

**Flower Land Antiques**
1202 N. Main St.
502/274-4488

**Reflections**
340 S. Main St.
502/274-7980

**Beaver Dam Auction**
200 E. 3rd St.
502/274-3349

**Papa's Playhouse**
724 Buttermilk Lane
502/274-7558

**Lee's**
116 Main
502/274-3108

**Capp's Mini Mall**
110 W. 3rd
502/274-7367

**Central Park Antiques**
Jefferson St. (McHenry)
502/274-7200

## 4 BENTON

**Answer**
321 Main St.
502/527-1078

**The Antique Mall**
600 Main St.
502/527-2085

**Antiques Et Cetera**
1026 Main St.
502/527-7922

**Treasured Memories**
1207 Main St.
502/527-0039

**Benton Antiques & Collectibles**
103 W. 13th St.
502/527-5424

**Twin Lakes Antique Mall**
6953 U.S. Hwy. 641 N.
502/362-2218

**The Strawberry Patch**
2391 U.S. Hwy. 68 W.
502/527-8186

## 5 BEREA

**McCray's Antiques**
408 Chestnut St.
606/986-2520

**Chestnut St Antique Mall Inc.**
420 Chestnut St.
606/986-2883

**Bay Window Antiques**
436 Chestnut St.
606/986-2345

**Something Olde**
437 Chestnut St.
606/986-6057

**Bratchers Antiques & Lamp Repair**
438 Chestnut St.
606/986-7325

**Place In Time**
440 Chestnut St.
606/986-7301

**Todds Antique Mall**
7435 Hwy. 21 E.
606/986-9087

**Impressions of Berea**
116 McKinney Dr.
606/986-8177

**Howards Antique Mall**
573 Mount Vernon Road
606/986-9551

**Teresa's Antiques & Art Gallery**
702 Prospect St.
606/986-9147

## 6 BOWLING GREEN

**River Bend Antique Mall**
315 Beech Bend Road
502/781-5773

**Daniel's Wicker**
2125 Bill Dedmon Road
502/842-6926

**Werner-Lowe Ltd**
1232 U.S. 31 W. Bypass
502/796-2683

**Timeless Treasures**
5521 Russellville Road
502/781-3698

**Greenwood Mall**
Scottsville Road
502/781-9655

### *Great Places To Stay*

**Bowling Green B&B**
3313 Savannah Dr.
502/781-3861

This lovely brick two-story home, furnished with antiques, sits next to a woods and is a comfortable walk to a charming duck pond. Relax by the fireside in winter in the comfortable den with books, TV, video or organ. In summer enjoy the covered patio or walk the pleasant, safe streets. Western Kentucky University, restaurants, shopping and entertainment are all nearby. Hosts are a chemistry professor and retired nurse and teacher who enjoy people, travel and photography.

## 7 CORBIN

**Past Times Antique Mall, Inc.**
135 W. Cumberland Gap Pkwy.
606/528-8818
Daily 9-6 Mon.-Sat., 11-6 Sun.
*Directions: From I-75: take Exit 29 east. At the first traffic light make a right turn. Past Times is located behind Burger King and Super 8 Motel.*

Past Times houses some interesting things in its 14,000 square feet of space. Its 95 booths hold the general consignment of furniture, primitives, collectibles, etc., with a great deal of glassware, railroad and mining memorabilia, plus a very active trade in antique knives, period safety razors, etc.

**Meadow Land Antiques & Collectibles**
3475 Cumberland Falls Hwy.
606/523-2803

## 8 COVINGTON

**The World's Largest Outdoor Sale**
August 14-17

Covington is the northern starting point...and the roadside bargains extend south to Alabama! Pack a lunch and hop in the car for this 450-mile shopping adventure. 513/357-MAIN.

**Sentimento Antiques & Collectibles**
525 Main St.
606/291-9705

**Philadelphia Street Antiques**
526 Philadelphia St.
606/431-6866

## 9 DANVILLE

History abounds in the picturesque community of Danville, 35 miles southwest of Lexington. The Rhodes House (305 North Third, where Raintree County was filmed in 1956) is just one of the 50 sites on the city's walking tour. The visitor center is in the beautiful Greek Revival McClure-Barbee House (304 S. Fourth, Monday through Friday, 9 a.m. to 4 p.m., 1-800-755-0076). Danville's internationally recognized Great American Brass Band Festival is in mid-June.

Ten constitutional conventions took place at Constitution Square State Historic Site (134 South Second) between 1784 and 1792. The park includes the original pre-1792 post office (the first west of the Alleghenies!), Governor's Circle, and replica meetinghouse, courthouse and jail. You'll also see the 1817 Fisher's Row houses, now an art gallery; the historical society museum in the Watts-Bell House featuring a great collection of vintage clothing.

**Leigh & Company Estate Liquidators**
128 & 130 S. 4th St.
606/236-2137

**Antique Mall of Historic Danville**
158 N. 3rd St.
606/236-3026

**Annie's Loft**
By Appointment Only
606/236-6735

## 10 ELIZABETHTOWN

Elizabethtown, 35 miles south of Louisville, has a wealth of American history including ties to Abraham Lincoln's family. The walking tour on Thursdays (free, June through September, 7 p.m.) has costumed characters from the town's past such as Carrie Nation, General George Custer and Sarah Bush Lincoln.

Around the corner is the 1825 Brown-Pusey House, the town's first haven for travelers. This stately Georgian colonial building housed General Custer and his wife in the 1870s.

**Back Home**
251 W. Dixie Ave.
502/769-2800

**Irene's Antiques**
407 E. Dixie Ave.
502/737-2552

**Addington Antiques**
711 W. Park Road
502/769-6456

**Buckboard Antiques**
125 Hillsdale Dr.
502/737-0589

**Heartland Antique Mall**
1006 N. Mulberry
502/737-8566

**Touch of the Past Antiques**
9 Houchens Plaza
502/765-2579

**Goldnamers**
210 N. Main St.
502/766-1994

**Elizabethtown Antique Mall**
516 N. Main St.
502/769-3959

## 11 ELKHORN

**Piece of the Past**
466 Elkhorn
502/465-3171

## 12 FLORENCE

**Heirloom Antique Gallery**
6614 Dixie Hwy.
606/371-5566

**Kelly's Antiques**
7610 U.S. 25
606/371-0303

## 13 FRANKFORT

Frankfort, chosen the state capital in 1792, is nestled among the rolling hills of the Bluegrass in a beautiful Kentucky River valley. Much of Kentucky's history has been written here—old frontiersman Simon Kenton pleaded relief from taxes, Henry Clay practiced his oratory, former Vice President Aaron Burr was charged with treason—the stories go on and on.

**Button Box**
123 Brighton Park Blvd.
502/695-7108

**Ron-Jo's Antiques & Collectibles**
227 Broadway St.
502/223-5466

**Poor Richard's Books**
233 W. Broadway St.
502/223-8018

**Old Capitol Antiques**
239 W. Broadway St.
502/223-3879

**Treadle Works**
333 W. Broadway St.
502/223-2571

**Rail Fence Antiques**
415 W. Broadway St.
502/875-5040

**Gift Box**
1500 Louisville Road
502/223-2784

## 14 FRANKLIN

A surveyor's mistake created the Kentucky-Tennessee "Triangular Jag," a small piece of land that forms Simpson County's southern border. The muddy waters of legal ownership made the area a safe place for duelists to avoid the law. The Sanford Duncan Inn, six miles south of Franklin, was a popular overnight stop for guests such as General Sam Houston, before meeting at nearby Linkumpinch to settle their "gentlemanly disputes."

Franklin's downtown historic district includes the Simpson County Archives & Museum in the old jailer's residence, with wall drawings left by Civil War soldiers held prisoner here (free, Monday-Friday, 206 North College, 502/586-4228).

**Strickly Country Antique Mall**
5945 Bowling Green Road
502/586-3978

**Main St. Antiques & Collectibles**
207 N. Main St.
502/586-6104

**Two Sisters Antiques**
Wal-Mart Shopping Center
502/586-0099

**Heritage Antique Mall**
111 W. Washington St.
502/586-3880

**P J's General Store**
205 W. Cedar st.
502/586-8340

**Classic Image**
101 W. Cedar St.
502/586-8886

**Country Cottage**
1037 N. Main St.
502/586-6742

## 15 GEORGETOWN

Georgetown was founded in 1790 by the Baptist minister Elijah Craig. He is best known for his world famous invention, "bourbon" whiskey. You'll see where he drew water when you visit Royal Spring Park (Water and West Main). Also see the mini-local history museum in an authentic 1874 log cabin built by former slave Milton Leach. Don't miss great antique shopping downtown in one of the most picturesque Victorian areas in the state.

**Den of Antiquity**
100 W. Main St.
502/863-7536

**Central Kentucky Antique Mall**
114 E. Main St.
502/863-4018

**Pooh's Place**
122 E. Main St.
502/867-3930

**Georgetown Antique Mall**
124 W. Main St.
502/863-9033

**Trojan Antiques Gallery**
130 N. Broadway St.
502/867-1823

**Wyatts Antique Center**
149 E. Main St.
502/863-0331

**The Vault Antique & Collectibles Mall**
201 E. Main St.
502/863-2728

### *Great Places To Stay*

**Blackridge Hall**
4055 Paris Pike
502/863-2069 or 1-800-768-9308
Rates: $119-179

For specific information see review at the beginning of this section.

## 16 GLENDALE

Don't miss the charming Historic Register community of Glendale, 7 miles south of Elizabethtown off I-65, Exit 86. Antique malls, shops and a country store line the street bisected by the L & N railroad crossing. Enjoy great food at The Whistle Stop, 502/369-8586, or The Depot, 502/369-6000. Most shops are open Tuesday through Saturday 11:00 a.m.-6:00 p.m. The annual Glendale Crossing Festival is in October.

**Log Cabin Antique Shop**
101 Jaggers Road
502/369-6001

**Ivy Gate**
1 block off Main St.
502/369-6343

**Crow's Nest**
138 Main St.
502/369-6060

**Side Track Shops**
212 E. Main St.
502/369-8766

**Sisters**
1 Block off Main St.
502/369-8604

**A Step Back Antiques**
College St.
502/369-6122

**Through The Grapevine**
1 Block off Main St.
502/369-7925

**Bennies Barn**
434 E. Main St.
502/369-9677

**Glendale Antique Mall**
103 W. Railroad Ave.
502/369-7279

**Ramona's Antiques**
122 E. Railroad Ave.
502/369-9652

## 17 HARRODSBURG

Once a frontier territory, Harrodsburg was founded in 1774 as the first permanent English settlement west of the Allegheny Mountains. On the walking and driving tours, spanning more than 200 years of history, you'll pass by stately pre-Civil War homes, churches and businesses representing various architectural styles. Morgan Row, 220-232 S. Chiles, is the oldest rowhouse standing in Kentucky. While on Main, don't miss a stroll through Olde Towne Park featuring a cascading fountain.

A highlight of the historic community is Beaumont Inn, built on the site of the Greenville Springs Spa. It was constructed in 1845 as one of the South's most prestigious girls schools. Since 1919, it has operated as a country inn under four generations of the same family (638 Beaumont Inn Dr., 606/734-3381).

**North Main Center Antique Mall**
520 N. Main St.
606/734-2200
Mon.-Sat. 10-5, Sun. 1-5, closed Wed.

Owner Nena Inden has loved antiques since she was a teenager, so what better business to get into than owning an antique store? She has over 22,000 square feet filled with Victorian pieces, primitives, china, glassware, '50s collectibles, jewelry, silver, old prints, frames, and children's toys.

But the real treat would be to see Nena and husband Christian's home, fabulous Ashfeld Manor. This 1891 stone mansion, complete with a four-story tower, is about 8,000 square feet of breathtaking old-world craftsmanship and opulence. Every room is made of a different wood, with hand-carved fireplaces, French chandeliers, and original wainscotting.

**Old Kentucky Restorations**
122 W. Lexington St.
606/734-6237

**Granny's Antique Mall**
1286 Louisville Road
606/734-2327

**Main Street Antiques**
225 S. Main St.
606/734-2023

**Tomorrows Another Day**
117 Poplar St.
606/734-9197

**J Sampson Antiques. & Books**
107 S. Main St.
606/734-7829

**The Antique Mall of Harrodsburg**
540 N. College St. (Hwy. 127)
606/734-5191

### *Great Places To Stay*

**Canaan Land Farm Bed and Breakfast**
4355 Lexington Road
1-800-450-7307

Located off Highway 68, near Shakertown, Canaan Land Farm B&B is a working sheep farm where guests can enjoy a variety of barnyard animals. Canaan Land, circa 1795, is on the National Register of Historic Places and is also designated a Kentucky Historic Farm. In 1995, a historic log house was restored on the property, giving the B&B six rooms with private baths, and three working fireplaces. Amenities: antiques, featherbeds, large pool, hot tub, and hammocks in the shade. Peaceful, secluded and romantic.

## 18 HAZEL

Easily reached by antique hounds in four states (Tennessee, Kentucky, Arkansas and the Missouri Bootheel), Hazel is western Kentucky's oldest and largest antique shopping district. Located on U.S. Highway 641 at the Kentucky/Tennessee state line just east of the fabulous Land Between The Lakes, this tiny turn-of-the-century community has been transformed into an antique shopper's heaven. Almost all the storefronts are now antique shops or malls, offering a smorgasbord of antiques and collectibles.

There are several annual festivals and open houses in Hazel targeted for antique lovers.

* Freedom Fest-July 4, 1999, with decorations, fireworks, and special deals on antiques throughout town.

* Hazel's Celebration-Oct. 4, an old-time country street festival. Hazel's population is 500; this festival draws 8,000! There's food, entertainment, art, cloggers, even the winning lottery ticket is drawn here!

* Christmas Open house (sponsored by the Antique Dealers Association)-Saturday after Thanksgiving, all the shops in town have refreshments, decorations and carolers.

**Miss Bradie's Antiques and Christmas**
304 Dees St. (Dees and Main)
502/492-8796
Daily except Thanksgiving Day and Christmas Day, Mon.-Sat. 10-5, Sun. 12:30-5

Here's a good stop for early Christmas shoppers. Miss Bradie's specializes in antiques and decorative accessories and also features a year-round Christmas room. Owner Jo McKinley is an authorized dealer for Christopher Radko glass ornaments, Old World Christmas, Annalee Dolls and Boyds Bears. Indulge your shopping habit and get those pesky Christmas shopping chores out of the way at the same, enjoyable time!

**Ginger's Antiques and Refinishing**
310 Main St., P.O. Box 37
502/492-8138
Daily Mon.-Sat. 10-4:30, Sun. 1-4:30

Among the many antique shops in Hazel is Ginger's. They offer not only the wares of 12 dealers, but folks can visit Ginger's 3rd Floor Candy Store. The candy store is like an old-fashioned general store, with big glass jars full of Mrs. Burton's Gourmet candy, lots of jams and jellies, different kinds of honey, and all the luscious things that used to fascinate kids in an old-fashioned candy store! They also have a soda fountain in the candy store, so shoppers can quench their thirst after all that buying!

**Miss Martha's Antiques**
302 Main St.
502/492-8145
Daily 10-4:30

Bill Price has been offering a general variety of antiques, including primitives, kitchen collectibles and furniture, to the public for 14 years. During these years, he has had the opportunity to see and hear lots of funny stories from his customers and shoppers. Here's one of the stories he has to tell:

Two ladies came into my shop several years ago late on a Saturday afternoon. They had spent the day at the Heart of Country Show in Nashville and had decided to come to Hazel on their way home. They had obviously had a good time and had probably stopped somewhere for a lunch that had included a couple of Bloody Marys. One of the ladies immediately began picking up items and talking about how much cheaper things were here than at the show (naturally!). She began making a pile of things on my check-out counter. She would put something on the counter then go back for more. Each time she put something in her pile, her friend would say, "Oh, Roger's gonna kill you!" The first lady would find something else she wanted and her friend would say, "Oh, Roger's gonna kill you!" This went on for a while, and after about three or four of these comments, the happy shopper stopped and looked at her friend. "Listen," she said, "When I first started going out on these shopping trips, Roger used to worry about how much money I had with me or whether or not I had the checkbook with me. Later, he'd be nervous if I went out and took the credit card with me. Now when I get home, the only thing Roger asks is, "Is anybody shipping anything?"

**Country Collectibles**
Main St., P.O. Box 258
502/492-8121
Tues.-Sat. 10-4:30, Sun. 1-4:30, closed Mon.

This collection cache offers the shopping public Victorian furnishings, primitives and glassware.

**Hazel Antique Mall & Flea Market**
Route 2, Box 169AAA
502/492-6168
Mon.-Sat. 8-5

An all-purpose, well-rounded antique shop and flea market, the mall is located approximately 2 miles north of Hazel's antique district on U.S. Highway 641.

**Horse's Mouth Antiques**
308 Main St., Box 207
502/492-8128
Daily 10-4:30

The name of the shop makes you grin, but if you're into crystal, silver, china, old kerosene lamps and Aladdin lamps, you won't want to miss this stop!

**Decades Ago Antique Mall**
317 Main St.
502/492-8140
Open year round Mon.-Sat. 10-4:30, Sun. 1-4:30

Decades Ago—it sounds like the beginning of a bedtime story, doesn't it? It is a multi-dealer mall with more than 90 exhibitors plus showcases filled with wonderful antiques and collectibles.

**Memory Lane Antiques**
P.O. Box 155
502/492-8646
Open daily 10-4:30 Mon.-Sat., 1-4:30 Sun.

For the past two years Larry Elkins' mall has offered 25 booths that carry a variety of furniture, glass, collectibles, primitives and other items, catering to both the individual shoppers and to dealers.

**Tooters Antique Mall**
209 3rd St.
502/492-6111
Mon.-Sat. 10-4:30, Sun 1-4:30 (winter) and
Mon.-Sat. 10-5:30, Sun. 1-4:30 (summer)

Snacks and drinks are available when you take a break from strolling through this 8,000 square foot, multi-dealer mall with showcases and more than 40 booths.

**Retro-Wares**
306 Main St., P.O. Box 251
502/492-8164
Mon.-Sat. 10:30-4:30, Sun. 1-4:30

Situated in the heart of Hazel's antique district, this is the place to find those neat chrome and vinyl retro things. The shop specializes in mid-century furnishings and art deco, with a large collection of costume jewelry, limited edition Barbies, and fashion flashbacks.

**Idle Hour Antiques**
Main St., P.O. Box 42
502/492-8180
By appointment or by chance

Idle Hour Antiques is another Hazel Shop that specializes in Victorian furnishings and collectibles.

**Charlie's Antique Mall & Soda Fountain**
303 Main St.
502/492-8175
Daily 10-4:30 Mon.-Fri., 10:30-5 Sat., 1-4:30 Sun.

This 60-dealer mall offers not only an appealing variety of antiques, but an assortment of fountain treats as an added dividend. They serve ice cream, sodas, shakes, and malts at the old-fashioned soda fountain, so you can rest and revive between browsing and buying!

## 19 HOPKINSVILLE

**Hopkinsville Antique Mall**
1010 S. Main St.
502/887-9363

**Country Boy Stores**
Newstead Road
502/885-5914

**Aunt Mary's Antiques**
2180 Madisonville Road. (Hwy. 41)
502/885-9623

**The Snoop Shop**
Main St.
502/889-0360

**Quidas Antiques**
1301 E. 9th St.
502/886-6141

**Forget-Me-Nots Antiques**
110 E. 6th St.
502/885-5556

**Butler's Antiques**
601 E. 17th St.
502/889-9603

## 20 JEFFERSONTOWN

**Madge's Antiques**
3515 Chenowith Run Road
502/266-5622

## 21 LA GRANGE

**Heirlooms**
110 E. Main St.
502/222-4149

**Iron Horse Antiques**
119 E. Main St.
502/222-0382

**Primrose Antiques**
123 E. Main St.
502/222-8918

**Three Peas In Pod**
125 E. Main St.
502/222-2139

## 22 LEXINGTON

### Boone's Antiques of Kentucky, Inc.
4996 Old Versailles Road
606/254-5335
Mon.-Sat. 8:30-5:30
*Directions: From Highway 75: Follow all the signs to the airport, then pass the entrance on Man-of-War. Stay on Highway 60 west. Boone's is located on Highway 60 west, 1 1/2 miles from the airport, 3/4 miles from Keeland Race Track. From Highway 64: Take Highway 60 east when approaching Castle. Go to the top of the hill to the caution light, then right on Old Versailles Road.*

Boone's offers 27,000 square feet of English, French and American Antiques. They carry everything from furniture and rugs to porcelains and unusual accent pieces.

**Pless Antiques**
247 N. Broadway St.
606/252-4842

**Blue Grass Antique Market**
760 Winchester Road
606/258-2105

**Country Antique Mall**
1455 Leestown Road
606/233-0075

**Gift Box**
171 N. Lowry Lane
606/278-2399

**Heritage Antiques**
380 E. Main St.
606/253-1035

**Lexington Antique Gallery**
637 E. Main St.
606/231-8197

**Clock Shop**
154 W. Short St.
606/255-6936

**Antique Mall at Todds Square**
535 W. Short St.
606/252-0296

**Mike Maloney Antiques**
303 Southland Dr.
606-275-1934

**O'Loves Collectible Antiques**
410 W. Vine St., #149
606/253-0611

**Cowgirl Attic**
220 Walton Ave.
606/225-3876

**Blue Grass Bazaar**
246 Walton Ave.
606/259-0303

## 23 LOUISVILLE

Some people call it "Louaval," others say "Louieville," but regardless of how you pronounce it, you'll find plenty of things to see and do in Kentucky's largest city. Louisville is a blend of restored historic sites and sparkling new structures, fine arts and architecture, horses and sports, and more park acreage than any other city in the country.

The excitement in Louisville comes to a fevered pitch each year during the Kentucky Derby Festival, one of the country's largest civic celebrations, beginning with the "Thunder Over Louisville" fireworks extravaganza and ending with the "Run for the Roses," the one and only Kentucky Derby (April 19 through May 5, 502/584-6383).

Louisville is a treat for antique shopping. The largest malls are Den of Steven, Joe Ley Antiques, and Louisville Antique Mall.

### St. James Court Art Show
October 3-5
For more information call: 502/635-1842

Historic Old Louisville marks the spot for this treasure hunting adventure also known as one of the largest outdoor art shows in the nation! Explore tree-lined streets of this grand 'ole Victorian neighborhood to unearth a king's ransom of trinkets and treasures. This one is more than a must-see, it's a must-BE!

**Tin Horse Antiques**
1040 Bardstown Road
502/584-1925

**Archibald Geneva Galleries**
1044 Bardstown Road
502/587-1728

**Alines Antiques**
1130 Bardstown Road
502/473-0525

**As Time Goes By**
1310 Bardstown Road
502/458-5774

**Steve Tipton**
1327 Bardstown Road
502/451-0115

**Discoveries**
1315 Bardstown Road
502/451-5034

**David R Friedlander Antiques**
1341 Bardstown Road
502/458-7586

**Charmar Galleries**
2005 Frankfort Ave.
502/897-5565

**All Booked Up**
1555 Bardstown Road
502/459-6348

**Another Antique Shop**
1565 Bardstown Road
502/451-5876

**Century Shop**
1703 Bardstown Road
502/451-7692

**Steve White Gallery**
945 Baxter
502/458-8282

**Swan Street Antique Mall**
947 E. Breckinridge St.
502/584-6255

**Architectural Salvage**
618 E. Broadway
502/589-0670

**Antiques On Broadway**
821 Broadway
502/584-4248

**Louisville Antique Mall**
900 Goss Ave.
502/635-2852

**Red Geranium Shop**
1938 Harvard Dr.
502/454-5777

**Jan's Antique Shop**
704 Lyndon Lane
502/426-0828

**Antique Galleries**
8601 W. Manslick Road
502/363-3326

**Joe Ley Antiques Inc.**
615 E. Market St.
502/583-4014

**Annie's & Mine**
12123 Old Shelbyville Road
502/254-9366

**Red Barn Mall**
12125 Old Shelbyville Road
502/245-8330

**Holland House**
129 D Saint Matthews Ave.
502/895-2707

**2023 Antiques**
2023 Frankfort Ave.
502/899-9872

**Henderson Antiques**
2044 Frankfort Ave.
502/895-6605

**John Henry Sterry Antiques**
2144 Frankfort Ave.
502/897-1928

**Bittners**
731 E. Main St.
502/584-6349

**Highland Antiques**
940 Baxter Ave.
502/583-0938

**Zigafoos..Antiques & Beyond**
1287 Bardstown Road
502/458-2340

**Forevermore**
1734 Bonnycastle Ave.
502/473-0021

**Isaacs & Isaacs**
3937 Chenoweth Square
502/894-8333

**Kathryn's**
1008 Goss Ave.
502/637-7479

**Candyjack's Antique Store**
703 Lyndon Lane
502/429-6420

**Madalyn's Antiques**
8026 New La Grange
502/425-9700

**Towne House Antiques**
612 E. Market St.
502/585-4456

**Middletown Antiques**
11509 Old Shelbyville Road
502/244-1780

**Pieces of Olde Antiques**
11405 Old Shelbyville Road
502/244-3522

**Schumann Antiques**
4545 Taylorsville Road
502/491-0134

**Annie's Attic**
3812 Frankfort Ave.
502/897-1999

**Scott F. Nussbaum Antiques**
2023 Frankfort Ave.
502/894-9292

**Elizabeth's Timeless Attire**
2050 Frankfort Ave.
502/895-5911

**Nanny Goat Strut Antiques**
638 E. Market St.
502/584-4417

**Baxter Ave. Antique Mall**
623-625 Baxter Ave.
502/568-1582

**Hanna's Place Antiques**
1126 Bardstown Road
502/589-3750

**Antiques at the Loop**
1940 Harvard Dr.
502/584-4248

**J.C. & Co. Dreamlight**
1004 Barret Ave.
502/456-4106

**Frances Lee Jasper Rugs**
1330 Bardstown Road
502/459-1044

**Children's Planet**
1349 Bardstown Road
502/458-7018

**The Weekend Antiques**
2910 Frankfort Ave.
502/897-1213

**Attic Treasures**
600 Baxter Ave.
502/587-9543

**The Eclectic Jones**
1570 Bardstown Road
502/473-0396

**Annie's Attic**
12410 Shelbyville Road
502/244-0303

**Mary Lou Duke**
2916 Frankfort Ave.
502/893-6577

**Louisville Visual Art Assoc.**
3005 River Road
502/896-2146

## *Great Places To Stay*

### Inn at the Park Bed and Breakfast
1332 S. 4th St.
1-800-700-7275
Web site: www.bbonline.wom/ky/innatpark

You will find this 7,400 square foot restored Victorian mansion nestled in among other equally beautiful homes in the Historic Preservation District of Old Louisville. Inn At The Park boasts a grand, sweeping staircase, twelve and a half foot ceilings, crown moldings, fireplaces and private stone balconies. Relax in an atmosphere of a bygone era and enjoy mouth-watering breakfasts, leisurely walks in Central Park, adjacent to the inn, and romantic, fireside evenings.

### Rocking Horse Manor Bed and Breakfast
1022 S. 3rd St.
1-888-HOR-SEBB
Web site: www.bbonline.com/ky/rockinghorse

Built in 1888, the Rocking Horse Manor B&B is one of the finest Victorian mansions in "Old Louisville". It has all the elegance of a bygone era plus all the modern conveniences for today's traveler. Take a step back in time with a visit to the parlor or library, or if you choose, use the third floor sitting area equipped with a mini-office for those that can't leave work behind. If a romantic getaway is your plan, choose the room with a cast wrap queen size bed and whirlpool for two. Awaken each morning to a wonderful full gourmet breakfast offering homemade breads, quiches, fresh fruits and muffins.

**Aleksander House Bed & Breakfast**
1213 S. First St.
502/637-4985

Aleksander House is a gracious in-town Victorian Italianate home built in 1882. It is centrally located in historical "Old Louisville" near shops, restaurants, museums and many attractions. The three-story brick building is completely restored and is listed on the National Registry of Historical Landmarks. Inside are fourteen foot ceilings, original hardwood floors, light fixtures, stained glass and fireplaces. The walls of the spacious dining room are lined with French Toile paper and prints of 19th century French impressionists. Sumptuous breakfasts are served along with specially blended coffees, an assortment of fine teas, homemade granolas, muffins and jams. Two sweeping staircases lead to the second and third floor guest rooms each uniquely decorated in eclectic or period furnishings with fine linen and comforters.

## 24 MADISONVILLE

**Ole House Antique Mall**
343 E. Center St.
502/821-4020

**Kesterson's Antiques**
502 Hall St.
502/821-7311

**Country Store Antiques & Crafts**
455 S. Madison Ave.
502/825-1556

## 25 MAYFIELD

**Mayberry Antique Mall**
114 W. Broadway St.
502/247-1979

**Country Corner**
Hwy. 97/Sedalia Road
502/247-9361

**Remember When Antiques**
200 S. 6th St.
502/247-7228

**Collectors Shop**
104 W. South St.
502/247-1706

**Sarah's Grapevine**
112 W. Broadway St.
502/247-9034

## 26 MIDDLETOWN

**Annie's Attic**
12410 Shelbyville Road
502/244-0303

## 27 MIDWAY

**Gordon H. Greek Antiques**
204 N. Gratz St.
606/846-4336

**Midway Antiques Gallery**
138 E. Main St.
606/846-5669

**D Lehman & Sons**
100 Winter St. N.
606/846-4513

## 28 MT. STERLING

**Monarch Mill Antiques**
101 S. Maysville St.
606/498-3744

**Smokehouse Antiques**
310 E. Main St.
606/498-7585

**Mt. Sterling Antique Mall**
16 E. Main St.
606/498-5868

## 29 NEWPORT

**R & L Collectibles & Etc.**
602 Monmouth St.
606/431-2230

**471 Antique Mall**
901 E. 6th St.
606/431-4753

**Peluso Antique Shop**
649 York St.
606/291-2870

## 30 NICHOLASVILLE

**Antiques on Main**
221 N. Main St.
606/887-2767

**Coach Light Antique Mall**
213 N. Main St.
606/887-4223

## 31 OWENSBORO

**Spend A Buck Galleries**
210 Allen St.
502/685-5025

**Second Avenue Antiques**
109 E. 2nd St.
502/683-0308

**Peachtree Galleries Antiques**
104 W. 2nd St.
502/683-6937

**Peachtree Galleries**
105 W. 2nd St.
502/926-1081

**Plantation Antiques**
113 E. 2nd St.
502/683-3314

**Owensboro Antique Mall**
500 W. 3rd St.
502/684-3003

**Downstairs Attic Country Store**
2753 Veach Road
502/684-1819

**Antiques & Collectibles**
724 W. 2nd St.
No Phone

## 32 PADUCAH

**Michael Stewart Antiques**
136 Lone Oak Road
502/441-7222
Open by chance or appointment
*Directions: From I-24 take Exit 7. Travel east on Lone Oak Road 1 1/2 miles. The shop is located on the right side of the street, a 1/2 block before Broadway.*

Michael Stewart specializes in 18th and 19th century furniture, paintings, books, maps and accessories. The shop handles primarily English and American furniture, and occasionally French. Civil War and 19th century maps, 19th century American and European paintings, and leather-bound 19th century books, either in complete sets or single volumes, are found here.

**American Harvest Antiques**
632 N. 6th St.
502/442-4852
Wed. 10-5, Sat. 10-4 or anytime by appointment
*Directions: Traveling I-24: Take Exit 4. Travel east approximately 5 miles toward historic downtown Paducah. Turn left on North 6th St. American Harvest is located at the end of the block on the corner of North 6th and Park Ave.*

This interesting arrangement was originally a four-dealer group that has now, unfortunately, had to become three because of one member's health. The four women who started the shop have all been dealers and friends for many years, traveling and buying together all over the region. They decided to open the shop together because their tastes and ideas are similar and because, as one said, "We just love it!"

Lisha Holt, Sharon Clymer and Brenda Jones, along with retired member/dealer Wilma Becker, opened American Harvest antiques in historic downtown Paducah in an old grocery building. They also have the historic shotgun house next door filled with antiques. These ladies specialize in early American country furniture and accessories-from large pieces on down-with original paint or surface.

**Farmer's Daughter Antiques**
6330 Cairo Road
502/444-7619 or 502/443-5450
Wed.-Sat. 10-5, Sun. 1-5, closed Mon.-Tues.
*Directions: From I-24 take Exit 3 onto Hwy. 305 south. The shop is just 1 1/2 miles from I-24 on Cairo Road.*

This cutely-named shop holds 2,400 square feet of browsing pleasure for all who stop to look around. Noted for its wide variety of quality antiques such as oak and country furniture, kitchen wares, tools, old toys, fishing collectibles, decoys, quilts, linens, advertising memorabilia and more. Jane's love for "old things" is evident in her creative design of display throughout the store. This is a "must stop" for the decorator who loves country furnishings and accessories at a reasonable price.

**American Quilter's Society National Show and Contest**
Held in April each year.
For more information call: 502/898-7903

More than $80,000 in prizes draws the best quilters and their heirlooms to this national competition. Exhibits and workshops complete this quilt-crazy festival in Paducah, home of the museum of American Quilter's Society.

**Antiques Cards & Collectibles, Inc.**
203 Broadway St.
502/443-9797

**Broadway House Antiques**
229 Broadway St.
502/575-9025

**Market Antiques & Collectibles Shop**
401 Jefferson St.
502/443-6480

**Sherry & Friends Antique Mall**
208 Kentucky Ave.
502/442-4103

**Shirley's Antiques**
217 Kentucky Ave.
502/444-7599

**Anthony Barnes Antiques**
111 Market House Square
502/442-1891

**Wood Whittlers**
201 Ohio
502/443-7408

**Things Unique & Antique**
133 S. 3rd St.
502/575-4905

**Vick's Attic**
133 S. 3rd St.
502/575-4905

**Giller Antiques**
405 Jefferson
502/444-6786

**Fleur de lis Antiques**
219 Kent Ave.
502/443-6103

**The Rose Antiques**
215 Broadway St.
502/443-2483

**Cynthia's Playhouse & Antiques**
218 Broadway St.
502/442-5770

**Grandma & Grandpas Treasures**
200 Kentucky Ave.
502/443-6505

**Once Upon A Time Antiques**
212 Kentucky Ave.
502/443-1062

**D. Beverly Johnson**
2201 Kentucky Ave.
502/443-1034

**Market Square Antiques**
113 Market House Square
502/444-9253

**Affordable Antiques, Inc. II**
933 S. 3rd St.
502/442-1225

**Chief Paduke Antiques Mall**
300 S. 3rd St.
502/442-6799

**Marshall's Antiques**
113 N. Second
502/442-2052

**Lamon's Antiques**
1616 S. Sixth St.
502/443-7225

***Great Places To Stay***

**The 1857's Bed and Breakfast**
127 Market House Square
502/444-3960 or 1-800-264-5607
Rates: $65-85

This three-story, friendly-featured brick Victorian home offers everything needed for a complete and secluded weekend getaway. Listed on the National Register of Historic Places, the first floor holds Cynthia's Ristorante. Two guest rooms and a bath are on the second floor, and the third floor holds a family room and game room with hot tub and billiards table. All this is located in the Downtown Historic District, with antique stores, carriage rides, a quilt museum, lots of restaurants, and the Market House Cultural Center within walking distance. Guests may choose to book the entire second floor with private bath, if they want true privacy.

## 33 PARIS

**Loch Lea Antiques**
410 Main St.
606/987-7070

**Green Apple Gift Shop**
600 Main St.
606/987-7512

**Antiques Arts & Collectibles**
627 Main St.
606/987-0877

**Fairbanks Antiques**
Main St.
606/987-0877

## 34 RICHMOND

Historic Richmond, off I-75 south of Lexington, has a variety of attractions to enjoy. This was Daniel Boone's site for his wilderness outpost, the birthplace of Kit Carson, and home of the fiery abolitionist Cassius Marcellus Clay. Civil War buffs will want to take the Battle of Richmond driving tour (1-800-866-3705). And, along the way, stop at the 1780 Valley View Ferry on Kentucky 169.

**Lena's Antiques**
2047 Berea Road-U.S. Hwy. 25
606/623-4325

**Waterstreet Mall**
129 S. 1st St.
606/625-1524

**Gift Box**
139 N. Keeneland Dr.
606/624-0025

**Olde Tyme Toys**
209 W. Main St.
606/623-8832

**Memories Antiques**
401 North St.
606/625-0909

**Country Porch Antiques**
2529 Doylesville Road (Union City)
606/625-0851

**Old Country Store**
Ashland Ave.
606/625-1275

## 35 RUSSELLVILLE

For a community of its size, Russellville boasts the largest historic district in Kentucky. The Southern Bank of Kentucky at Sixth and Main was the site of the first documented bank robbery by Jesse James, with a re-enactment each October during the Logan County Tobacco Festival.

The Bibb House Museum, a circa 1822 Georgian mansion, was built by Major Richard Bibb, an early abolitionist and Revolutionary War officer. The collection of antebellum antiques includes Belter and Duncan Phyfe originals (183 West 8th, 502/726-2508).

Check out Libby's Family Entertainment, eight miles west on U.S. 68. Friday night is the Country Jamboree, while Saturday nights' "Live at Libby's" show is syndicated to more than 65 radio stations in the United States and Canada.

**Diamond D Auction**
208 N. Bethel St.
502/726-7892
Call for auction dates

David and I first heard about the Diamond D Auction from Leon Tyewater (a great auctioneer with a wife who can really cook). We were stuck in Nashville, Tennessee, for a few days so we decided to check out this little country auction which was only an hour's drive away. It's one of those "sleeper" auctions. You know the kind—when you walk in and at the first glance you see nothing—then about 30 minutes into the sale something pops up that you can't live without! I'm sitting there minding my own business when out of the blue the most wonderful cupboard crosses the auction block. An authentic Tennessee piece from Piney Flats with its original dark oak finish, yellow paint inside, complete with perfect rat holes, and old glass doors— a true "virgin." Of course I bought it! For $550 wouldn't you?

**Russellville Antique Mall**
141 E. 5th St.
502/726-6900

**Russellville Flower Shop**
104 S. Franklin St.
502/726-7608

**Betty's Antiques**
103 Bethel Shopping Center
502/725-8222

### *Interesting Side Trip*

**Shaker Museum**
S. Union (U.S. 68)
502/453-4167
March-December 15: Mon.-Sat. 9-5, Sun. 1-5

Shaker Museum at South Union, 15 miles east of Russellville on U.S. 68, is the site of the last Western Shaker community (1807-1922). The 1824 Centre House showcases the fine craftsmanship of this inventive communal group with hundreds of original artifacts. Have lunch at Shaker Tavern, 502/542-6801, Tuesday through Saturday from 11:30 a.m. to 2 p.m.; Sunday and dinner by reservation; also a bed and breakfast. Events include the Shaker Festival in late June.

## 36 SHELBYVILLE

You'll find a charming area of antique and specialty shops amid the late-Victorian, National Register Downtown District at I-64, Exit 35 between Louisville and Frankfort. Shelbyville is home to world-renowned Wakefield-Scearce Galleries, located within the historic Science Hill buildings, with an outstanding inventory of English and European antiques (Washington St., 502/633-4382).

The area is also known for wonderful regional restaurants. There's Science Hill Inn, 502/633-2825; the Claudia Sanders Dinner House, originally operated by the Colonel, at 3202 Shelbyville Road/U.S. 60 West, 502/633-5600; and the Old Stone Inn in Simpsonville, once a stagecoach inn, on U.S. 60 East, 502/722-8882.

**Country Cottage Collectibles**
137 Frankfort Road
502/633-5341

**Main St. Antique Mall**
514 Main St.
502/633-0721

**Antiques For You Mall**
528 Main St.
502/633-7506

**Tam Antiques**
610 Main St.
502/633-3106

**Old Mill Shop Antiques**
117 7th St.
502/633-2733

**Shelbyville Antique Mall**
524 Main St.
502/633-0720

**Corner Collectibles & Antiques**
629 Washington St.
502/633-4838

**Something Unique**
By Appointment Only
502/633-3621

## 37 SMITHS GROVE

**Smiths Grove Antique Mall**
604 S. Main St.
502/563-4921

**The Corner Cupboard**
133 S. Main St.
502/563-6221

**Pony Express**
105 S. Main St.
502/563-5130

**Ye Olde Bank Antiques**
108 E. First St.
502/563-9313

**Wright House Antiques Etc.**
124 First St.
502/563-9430

**Wanda's Antiques & Collectibles**
131 N. Main St.
502/563-6444

**Anytime Antiques**
133 N. Main St.
502/563-9111

**Village Grove Antiques**
135 N. Main St.
502/563-9100

**Martin's Antiques**
Hwy. 68-80
502/563-2575

**Cotton Corner**
Main St.
502/563-4607

## 38 SOMERSET

**North 27 Antique Mall**
3000 N. Hwy. 27
606-679-1923

**Cumberland Antique Mall**
6494 S. Hwy. 27
606/561-8622

**Pitman Creek Antique Mall**
6940 S. Hwy. 27
606/561-5178

**Gift Box Uniques Inc.**
207 E. Market St.
606/679-8041

**Somerset Antique Mall**
209 E. Market St.
606/679-4307

## 39 ST. MATTHEWS

**Elaine Claire**
211 Clover Lane
502/895-0843

**Sarah Few McNeal Co.**
2866 Frankfort Ave.
502/895-2752

## 40 VERSAILLES

**Irish Acres**
4205 Fords Mill Road
606/873-6956

**Mason Antiques**
408 Lexington Road
606/873-4792

**Olde Towne Antique Mall**
161 N. Main St.
606/873-6326

**Farm House Antiques & Gifts**
175 N. Main St.
606/873-0800

### *Great Places To Stay*

**Rose Hill Inn**
233 Rose Hill
1-800-307-0460

Rose Hill Inn is a two story Kentucky Gothic mansion on three acres within walking distance of downtown Versailles. The home was built about 1820 and it is rumored that both Confederate and Union troops used the manor during the Civil War. The first floor has fourteen-foot ceilings and original woodwork. Fireplaces warm the atmosphere and coffee, tea and treats are always available. All bedrooms are invitingly furnished and have private baths. One has a Jacuzzi tub/shower, one a claw-foot tub and the cottage (original summer kitchen) has been updated to include two full size beds, kitchen and bath. Smells from the morning's breakfast call you to the dining room for a delicious meal, either at a table for two or conversing with other guests at the larger dining table. Afterwards, some time on the front porch is always a favorite.

## 41 WASHINGTON

**House of Three Gables**
2027 Old Main St.
No Phone #

**Alice's Antiques & Jewels**
2028 Old Main St.
606/564-4877

**Peiis**
2029 Old Main St.
606/759-5533

**Iron Gate**
2103 Old Main St.
606/759-7074

**Strawberry Patch Antiques & Gifts**
2109 Old Main St.
606/759-7001

**Washington Hall Antiquities**
2111 Old Main St.
606-759-7409

**Phyllis Antique Lamp & Dollhouse**
2112 Old Main St.
606/759-7423

**1790 Row House Mall**
2117 Old Main St.
606-759-7025

# Louisiana

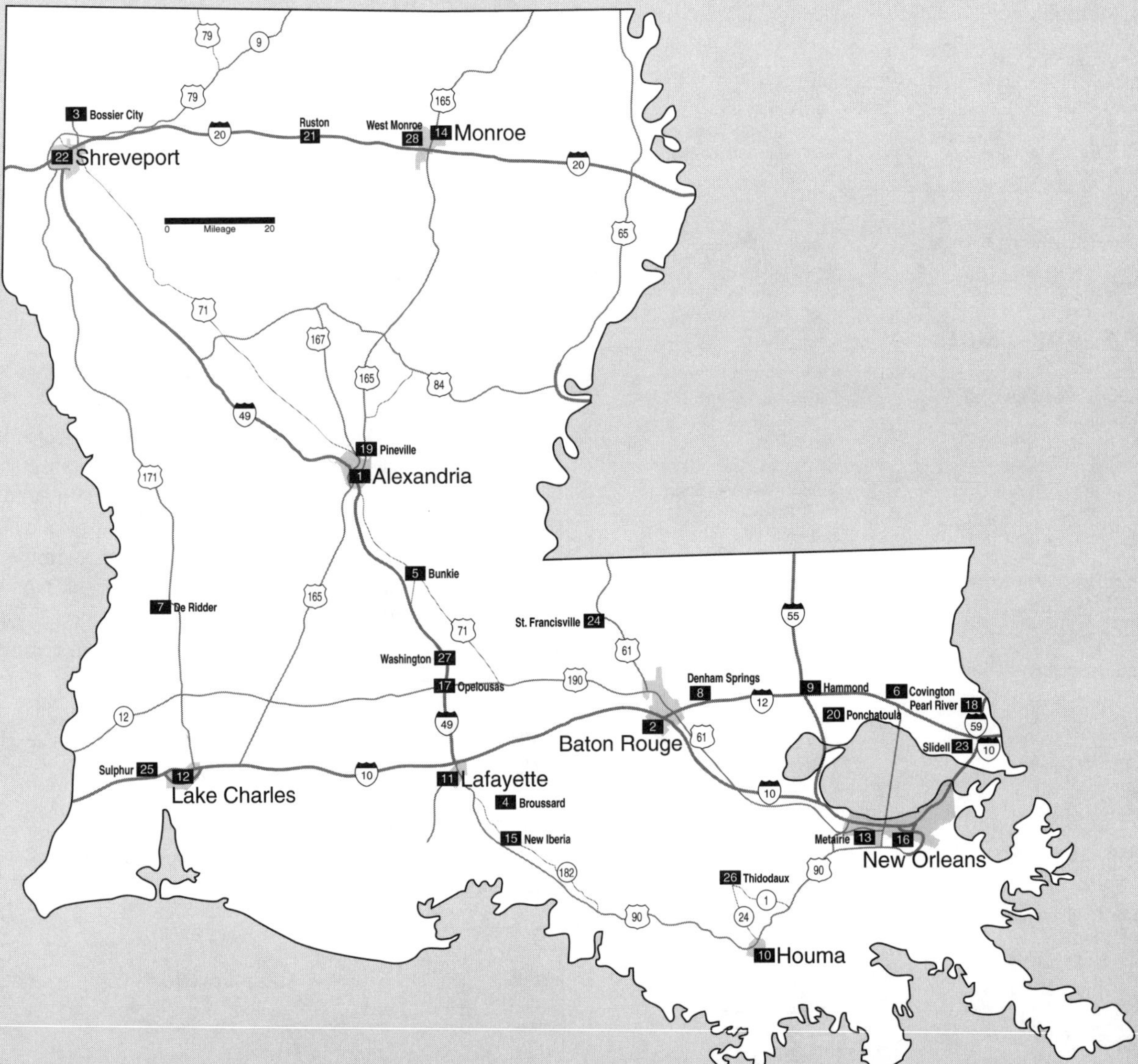

3 Bossier City
22 Shreveport
Ruston 21
West Monroe 28
14 Monroe
0 Mileage 20
19 Pineville
1 Alexandria
5 Bunkie
7 De Ridder
St. Francisville 24
Washington 27
17 Opelousas
Denham Springs 8
9 Hammond
6 Covington
Pearl River 18
20 Ponchatoula
2 Baton Rouge
Slidell 23
Sulphur 25
12 Lake Charles
11 Lafayette
4 Broussard
15 New Iberia
Metairie 13
16 New Orleans
26 Thidodaux
10 Houma

## 1 ALEXANDRIA

**Ancient Slots**
3609 N. Bolton Ave.
318/473-2184

**Eclectic**
5528 Jackson St. Ext.
318/487-1728

**Eclectic II**
5416 Masonic Dr.
318/487-1728

**B & N Collectibles Antiques**
2000 Rapides Ave.
318/487-8910

**Hirsch House Antiques**
1216 Jackson St.
318/442-7764

**Dantzlers Flea Market**
5416 Masonic Dr.
318/443-1589

**Miss Lily's**
1900 Rapides Ave.
318/448-0186

**Sally Foster Designs**
1307 Windsor Place
318/445-5480

## 2 BATON ROUGE

### Louisiana Purchases Auction Company
637 St. Ferdinand St.
504/346-1803

The company specializes in on-site estate auctions and tag sales. Clients should call for the next auction date because, as owner Wayne Welch says, "We never know when it will be!" He never knows what customers will do, either, as this story he tells proves:

"I once had a lady wanting to buy a piece of stained glass. At the time I had over 180 pieces. She arrived around 10 a.m. and by 2 p.m. she finally decided on one. She really wanted this piece, knowing full well it would not fit. But she bought it anyway. About 20 minutes later she came back, crying like a baby. 'It just won't fit,' she sobbed. As everyone knows, all sales are final, but this lady had already bought more glass from me than she had windows, so I asked her if she had brought the piece back. She said "no" because of our policy. I then asked if she would be home after I closed the shop that day. After work I went over to her house and looked at the space she wanted to use the newly purchased piece of glass in. I told her to come by the store the next afternoon and I took the piece back and cut it down to fit. She came that afternoon, got it, took it home, and it fit perfectly. She is now my greatest advertisement!"

**Cavalier House**
8655 Bluebonnet Blvd.
504/767-9007

**Jean Petit Antiques**
3280 Drusilla Lane
504/924-3801

**Kornmeyer Furniture Co. Inc.**
7643 Florida Blvd.
504/926-0137

**Merchant's Landing**
9800 Florida Blvd.
504/925-1664

**Lagniappe Antiques**
2175 Dallas Dr.
504/927-0531

**Great Heritage Antiques**
5905 Florida Blvd.
504/923-1861

**AAA Antiques**
9800 Florida Blvd.
504/925-1664

**Country Time Clocks & Gifts**
11242 Florida Blvd.
504/272-4663

**Guillot's Furniture Repair**
1906 N. Foster Dr.
504/357-6033

**Aladdins Lamp Resale Shop**
2714 Government St.
504/338-1933

**The Antique Group**
2963 Government St.
504/387-5543

**Estate Auction Gallery**
3374 Government St.
504/383-7706

**Shades of the Past Antiques**
3374 Government St.
504/383-6911

**The Decorator's Gallery**
3378 Government St.
504/383-7708

**Blue Pearl Antiques**
3875 Government St.
504/346-8508

**Atkinson Antiques**
8868 Greenwell Springs Road
504/924-1941

**Potluck Antiques**
10044 Hooper Road
504/262-8311

**Best Kept Secrets**
5425 Highland Road
504/763-9066

**Farm and Village**
6636 Florida Blvd., Suite 10
504/924-7555

**Absolutely Genius**
7317 Jefferson Hwy.
504/929-9862

**Keepsake Antiques & Collectibles**
10912 Joor Road
504/261-3540

**Wayside House Antiques Inc.**
1706 May St.
504/344-2633

**Goudeau Antiques**
1284 Perkins Road
504/383-7307

**Stewart's Inessa Antiques**
8630 Perkins Road
504/769-9363

**I M Causey and Co. Inc.**
501 Government St.
504/343-3421

**Confederate States Military Antqs.**
2905 Government St.
504/387-5044

**Audubon Station & Co.**
3153 Government St.
504/383-3599

**River City Books**
3374 Government St.
504/383-1003

**Westmoreland Antique Gallery**
3374 Government St.
504/383-7777

**Lynns Antiques & Collectibles Inc.**
3582 Government St.
504/334-9048

**Designers Custom Lamps**
4375 Government St.
504/344-4674

**Hearth & Home Antqs. & Cllbls.**
10136 Greenwell Springs Road
504/272-7544

**Collectors Choice**
13612 Hooper Road
504/261-1835

**Highland Road Antiques**
16257 Highland Road
504/752-8446

**Fetzers Interiors & Fine Antiques**
711 Jefferson Hwy.
504/927-7420

**Barkers Antique Jewelry**
7565 Jefferson Hwy.
504/927-4406

**Dixon Smith Interiors**
1655 Lobdell Ave.
504/927-4261

**Classic Jewelers Inc**
7610 Old Hammond Hwy.
504/927-6299

**Antique Emporium**
4347 Perkins Road
504/344-5856

**Sylvia's**
12648 Perkins Road
504/769-7143

**Country Bumpkin Antiques**
13166 Perkins Road
504/769-5138

**Fireside Antiques**
14007 Perkins Road
504/752-9565

**Eagles Nest Antiques**
15127 Perkins Road
504/753-4748

**Plank Road Antiques**
11728 Plank Road
504/778-0280

**Grandpa's Cellar**
832 St. Phillip St.
504/344-7030

**Landmark Antq. Plaza Inc.**
832 St. Phillip St.
504/383-4867

**Country Emporium**
10349 Sullivan Road
504/261-6959

**Lums Place**
7607 Tom Dr.
504/923-0745

## 3 BOSSIER CITY

**Cajun Crafters Junction**
1882 Airline Dr.
318/747-6555

## 4 BROUSSARD

### *Great Places To Stay*

**La Grande Maison**
302 E. Main St.
318/837-4428
Open year round
*Directions: 10 miles south of I-10 or 5 miles south of the airport, exit at Broussard, turn left at light. It is the large Victorian building on the right.*

Built in 1911, the La Grande Maison was once the residence of the Paul and Lawrence Billeaud family. This Victorian style home features several lovely porches and is situated on a beautifully landscaped lot with large oak trees.

The home was purchased in 1994 by Norman and Brenda Fakier. It has been completely restored to its current grand style and is listed on the National Historic Register.

The bed and breakfast offers several lovely rooms, all with private bath. A full breakfast is included.

## 5 BUNKIE

**By-Gone Days Antiques**
105 W. Magnolia St.
318/346-4940

**Griffins Antiques**
228 S.W. Main St.
318/346-2806

## 6 COVINGTON

**French House Antiques**
735 E. Boston at Lee Lane
504/893-4566

**Antiques on Consignment**
315 N. Columbia St.
504/898-0955

**Antique Obsession**
421 N. Columbia St.
504/898-3667

**Merlyn Fine Antiques**
609 E. Gibson
504/892-6099

**Country Corner Shop**
205 Lee Lane
504/892-7995

**Walker House Ltd.**
221 Lee Lane
504/893-4235

**A Few of My Favorite Things**
316 Lee Lane
504/867-9363

**Lee Lane Antique Mall**
326 Lee Lane
504/893-4453

**Claiborne Hill Antiques**
72022 Live Oak St.
504/892-5657

**Chocolate Tulips**
714 E. Rutland St.
504/893-5506

**Countryside**
828 E. Rutland
504/893-7622

**Chimes Antiques**
125 N. Theard St.
504/8892-8836

**Homespun Antiques**
204 W. 21st Ave.
504/892-3828

**Past Restored**
2380 W. 21st Ave.
504/892-7475

## 7 DE RIDDER

**Secret Attic**
109 S. Washington St.
318/463-4649

**Uptown Deridder**
113 N. Washington St.
318/463-7200

## 8 DENHAM SPRINGS

**Louisiana Purchases Antique Mall**
239 N. Range Ave.
504/665-2803
Mon.-Sat. 10-5, Sun. 12-5
(after hours appointments available by calling 504/346-1803)
*Directions: Located off of I-12 in Denham Springs. Take I-12 to Exit #10 and go north about 2 miles. When you cross a railroad track, you will be in "Antique Village." The mall is the last shop on the left at the traffic light.*

Louisiana Purchases is one of two malls and a restaurant located under one roof, and shoppers can walk through each shop to get to the other one. In all there are 27 dealers, with several specializing in different items such as antique copper, primitives and antique stained glass. The other mall is La Maison Antique Mall, and the Brass Lantern Restaurant serves the biggest burger in town.

**Romantique**
104 N. Range Ave.
504/667-2283

**Live Oak Antiques**
111 N. Range Ave.
504/665-0488

**Benton Brothers Antique Mall**
115 N. Range Ave.
504/665-5146

**Enchanted Attic**
123 N. Range Ave.
504/664-3655

**Diamond Mine**
201 N. Range Ave.
504/664-6463

**Way Back When Antiques**
208 N. Range Ave.
504/667-4169

**Painted Lady Antiques**
215 N. Range Ave.
504/667-1710

**Hart To Heart Antiques**
219 N. Range Ave.
504/667-4018

**La Maison Antiques**
235 N. Range Ave.
504/664-4001

**Backwards Glance**
222 N. Range Ave.
504/667-9779

**Antiques Plus**
226 N. Range Ave.
504/664-3643

**Theater Antiques**
228 N .Range Ave.
504/665-4666

## 9 HAMMOND

**Dec's Antiques**
100 E. Thomas St.
504/345-1960

## 10 HOUMA

**Heritage House**
1714 Barrow St.
504/872-3017

**Bayou Antiques**
2011 Bayou Blue Road
504/873-7500

**Country Antiques**
2036 Coteau Road
504/868-4646

**Antq Gallery of Houma Inc.**
3382 Little Bayou Black
504/857-8237

## 11 LAFAYETTE

### Gateway Antiques, Inc.
200 Northgate Dr.
318/235-4989
Mon.-Sat. 10-5, closed Sun.
*Directions: Traveling I-10: Take Exit #103A to the first traffic light (East Willow). Take a left at the East Willow light and make another left behind Montgomery Ward in the Northgate Mall. This is Northgate Dr. and the shop is in back of the Montgomery Ward parking lot. It can be seen at the East Willow light if you look to your left.*

Gateway Antiques concentrates mostly on smalls and glassware, pottery, toys, perfume bottles, jewelry, jars and boxes, pieces of Roseville, Hull and Fiestaware, with some tools added for good measure.

**Accent Studios Inc.**
805 W. University Ave.
318/233-0186

**Coin & Treasure Co.**
2474 W. Congress St.
318/237-2646

**Stewart's**
1000 Coolidge Blvd.
318/232-2957

**Bouligny Interiors Inc.**
331 Doucet Road
318/984-2030

**Clock House**
326 Duhon Road
318/984-1779

**Fazy's**
1416 Eraste Landry Road
318/269-5800

**Ole Fashion Things**
402 S.W. Evangeline Thruway
318/234-4800

**Ruins and Relics**
900 Evangeline Dr.
318/233-9163

**Antiques & Interiors Inc.**
616 General Mouton Ave.
318/234-4776

**Kings Rowe Antiques**
326 Heymann Blvd.
318/261-5934

**Auntie Em's**
410 Jefferson St.
318/233-9362

**Gerts Antiques Etc.**
1306 Jefferson St.
318/261-2311

**Lafayette Antique Market**
2015 Johnston St.
318/269-9430

**Antiques Et Cie**
3601 Johnston St.
318/981-9847

**Julia Martha Antiques Et Cie**
3601 Johnston St.
318/981-9847

**Artisans of Louisiana**
3603 Johnston St.
318/988-4280

**Gala's Unique Antiques & Gifts**
922 Kaliste Saloom Road
318/235-7816

**Treasures**
924 Kaliste Saloom Road
318/234-9978

**Granny's Attic**
410 Mudd Ave.
318/237-6418

**Gateway Antiques Inc.**
200 Northgate Dr.
318/235-4989

**Renaissance Market**
321 Oil Center Dr.
318/234-1116

**La Jolie**
1326 W. Pinhook Road
318/233-5319

**Graham's Antiques & Accents**
1891 W Pinhook Road
318/234-5045

**Crowded Attic**
512 N. University Ave.
318/237-5559

**Hallmark Interiors & Antiques**
412 Travis St.
318/234-5997

**Crowded Attic**
512 N. University Ave.
318/233-0012

**Accent Studios Inc**
805 W. University Ave.
318/233-0186

***Great Places To Stay***

### Alida's, A Bed and Breakfast
2631 S.E. Evangeline Thruway
1-800-922-5867

Alida's, A Bed & Breakfast, can best be described as a haven for the weary traveler to relax, unwind and enjoy the gracious, warm and constant attention lavished on its guests by the hosts, Tanya and Douglas Greenwald. From the deep, deep clawfoot tubs, designed for soaking, to the lively conversation during the evening social hour, to the sumptuous breakfast fit for a king, the highlight of your journey will be your stay at this lovely home. The local area features world famous Cajun restaurants.

# Louisiana

## 12 LAKE CHARLES

**Harry's Hodge Podge**
701 14th St.
318/436-6219

**Chapman Antiques & Collectibles**
748 Bank St.
318/436-2726

**Curiosity Antique Mall**
831 Kirkman St.
318/491-1170

**Lacey Jade & Co.**
3612 Kirkman St.
318/478-4304

**Kelly's Flea Market**
332 N. Martin Luther King Hwy.
318/439-0382

**Reflections**
608 A E Prien Lake Road
318/479-1974

**Nantiques**
2508 Ryan St.
318/439-0366

**Bayou Furniture Inc.**
1104 Alamo St.
318/477-6456

**Somewhere In Time**
2802 Hodges St.
318-494-0176

**Antics & Attics**
1908 Kirkman St.
318/436-5265

**My Sister's Closet**
3735 Kirkman St.
318/474-4733

**Yesterday Today & Tomorrow**
138 W. Prien Lake Road
318/478-1010

**My Favorite Things**
216 S. Ryan St.
318/439-1900

## 13 METAIRIE

**Sisters Antiques**
114 Codifer Blvd.
504/828-6701

**Olde Metairie Antq. Mall**
1537 Metairie Road
504/831-4514

**Unique Galleries & Auction**
4040 Veterans Memorial Blvd.
504/885-9000

**Rare Bits**
800 Metairie Road
504/837-6771

**Steve M Burgamy**
2011 Metairie Road
504/831-9265

## 14 MONROE

**B & W Antiques**
407 Desiard St.
318/387-9025

**Collectiques**
815 Desiard St.
318/387-5974

**R J Wills Antique Shop**
1907 S. Grand St.
318/323-6150

**Clarence's Old Stuff**
424 Desiard St.
318/323-1306

**Cottonland Crafters Mall**
1119 Forsythe Ave.
318/323-2325

**Camille Wood Antiques**
217 Hudson Lane
318-323-8979

## 15 NEW IBERIA

**Jaja's Just Things**
609 Charles St.
318/367-2141

**Rose Antique Ville**
2007 Freyou Road
318/367-3000

**Magnolia Antiques**
203 E. Main St.
318/365-5285

**Janie's Vintage Jewelry**
105 E. Saint Peter St.
318/365-8323

**Lantiques**
311 W. Saint Peter St.
318/364-8517

**Bo's Attic Antiques**
231 Pollard Ave.
318/364-1093

**Kimberly Interiors Inc.**
105 E. Saint Peter St.
318/365-8323

## 16 NEW ORLEANS

### Didier, Inc.
3439 Magazine St.
504/899-7749

This exclusive shop on Magazine Street specializes in period American furniture (1800-1840) and the accompanying decorative arts. Primarily the furniture is from Boston, Philadelphia, New York City and Baltimore. Everything is housed in an 1850s period home, completely restored to that era. The shop has clients who have been with them since 1970. Their decorative arts consist of period prints, paintings, glass and porcelain - absolutely no reproductions.

**Bienville Antique Shoppe**
4600 Bienville St.
504/488-2428

**Cass-Garr Company**
237 Chartres St.
504/522-8298

**Button Shoppe**
328 Chartres St.
504/523-6557

**Lucullus**
610 Chartres St.
504/528-9620

**Animal Art Antiques**
617 Chartres St.
504/529-4407

**O'Suzanna's**
1231 Decatur St.
504/581-5006

**Legarage Antiques & Clothing**
1234 Decatur St.
504/522-6639

**Framboyan**
624 Dumaine St.
504/558-9241

**Antiques by Ruppert**
1018 Harmony St.
504/895-6394

**Whisnant Galleries**
222 Chartres St.
504/524-9766

**Blackamoor Antiques Inc.**
324 Chartres St.
504/523-7786

**Ray J Piehet Gallery-Antiques**
608 Chartres St.
504/525-2806

**Molieres Antique Shop**
612 Chartres St.
504/525-9479

**Adrian's Antiques**
618 Conti St.
504/525-4615

**Collectible Antiques**
1232 Decatur St.
504-566-0399

**Tomato Warehouse**
1237 Decatur St.
504/524-2529

**Ruebarb Gallery**
1101 First at Magazine St.
504/523-4301

**Kohlmaier & Kohlmaier**
1018 Harmony St.
504/895-6394

**Ole Hickory Antique Clock Repair**
216 Hickory Ave.
504/737-2937

**Stan Levy Imports Inc.**
1028 Louisiana Ave.
504/899-6384

**Java Nola**
1313 Magazine St.
504/558-0369

**Shop of Two Sisters**
1800 Magazine St.
504/586-8325

**Aaron's Antique Mall**
2014 Magazine St.
504/523-0630

**Audubon Antiques**
2025 Magazine St.
504/581-5704

**Dodge-Fjeld Antiques**
2033 Magazine St.
504/581-6930

**Jim Smiley Vintage Clothing**
2001 Magazine St.
504/528-9449

**Mr. Anthony's Town & Country Antiques**
2049 Magazine St.
504/451-7314

**Renaissance Shop**
2104 Magazine St.
504/525-8568

**Shades of Light**
2108 Magazine St.
504/524-6500

**Eclectique Antiques**
2112 Magazine St.
504/525-4668

**Belle Mina Antique**
2127 Magazine St.
504/523-3222

**Bernard Regenbogen Furniture Store**
2208 Magazine St.
504/522-6351

**Christopher's Discoveries**
2842 Magazine St.
504/899-6226

**Susan Taylor Interiors**
3005 Magazine St.
504/891-0123

**Antiques Etc.**
8400 Jefferson Hwy.
504/737-3503

**Charbonnet & Charbonnet Antiques**
2929 Magazine St.
504/891-9948

**Lee Ali Interiors Unlimited**
1800 Magazine St.
504/586-8325

**Antebellum Antiques**
2011 Magazine St.
504/558-0208

**Hands**
2023 Magazine St.
504/522-2590

**Antiques Magazine**
2028 Magazine St.
504/522-2043

**Miss Edna's Antiques**
2035 Magazine St.
504/524-1897

**Attic Treasures**
2039 Magazine St.
504/588-1717

**Bep's Antiques**
2051 Magazine St.
504/525-7726

**Mona Mia's**
2105 Magazine St.
504/525-8686

**Bush Antiques**
2109 Magazine St.
504/581-3518

**Antique Vault**
2123 Magazine St.
504/523-8888

**Magazine Antique Mall**
2205 Magazine St.
504/524-0100

**Dombourian Oriental Rugs Inc.**
2841 Magazine St.
504/891-6601

**Antiques & Things**
2855 Magazine St.
504/897-9466

**Magazine Arcade Antiques**
3017 Magazine St.
504/895-5451

**As You Like It Silver Shop**
3029 Magazine St.
504/897-6915

**The Private Connection**
3927 Magazine St.
504/593-9526

**Grand Antiques**
3125 Magazine St.
504/897-3179

**Empire Antiques**
3420 Magazine St.
504/897-0252

**Blackamoor Antiques Inc.**
3433 Magazine St.
504/897-2711

**Custom Linens**
3638 Magazine St.
504/899-0604

**Brass Image**
3801 Magazine St.
504/897-1861

**Wirthmore Antiques**
3900 Magazine St.
504/899-3811

**Jean Bragg Antiques**
3901 Magazine St.
504/895-7375

**Aux Belles Choses**
3912 Magazine St.
504/891-1009

**C Susman-Estate Jewelry**
3933 Magazine St.
504/897-9144

**Judy, A Gallery**
3941 Magazine St.
504/891-7018

**Country at Heart**
3952 Magazine St.
504/891-5412

**Dellwen Antiques**
3954-56 Magazine St.
504/897-3617

**Davis Gallery**
3964 Magazine St.
504/897-0780

**Gizmo's**
4118-4122 Magazine St.
504/897-6868

**Shaker Shop**
3029 Magazine St.
504/895-8646

**Finders Keepers**
3118 Magazine St.
504/895-2702

**Esfahani Oriental Rugs**
3218 Magazine St.
504/895-5550

**French Collectibles**
3424 Magazine St.
504/897-9020

**Didier Inc.**
3439 Magazine St.
504/899-7749

**K & K Design Studios**
3646 Magazine St.
504/897-2290

**Uptowner Antiques**
3828 Magazine St.
504/891-7700

**Collector Antiques**
3901 Magazine St.
504/895-7375

**Orient Expressed Imports Inc.**
3905 Magazine St.
504/899-3060

**Mimano**
3917 Magazine St.
504/895-9436

**Anne Pratt**
3937 Magazine St.
504/891-6532

**Jacqueline Vance**
3944 Magazine St.
504/891-3304

**The Sitting Duck Gallery**
3953 Magazine St.
504/899-2007

**Mac Maison Ltd.**
3963 Magazine St.
504/891-2863

**Neal Auction Co.**
4038 Magazine St.
504/899-5329

**Emil Moore & Co. LLC**
4119 Magazine St.
504/891-1198

**Talebloo Oriental Rugs**
4130 Magazine St.
504/899-8114

**Sigi Russell Antiques**
4304 Magazine St.
504/891-5390

**Custom Woodwork & Antiques**
4507 Magazine St.
504/891-1664

**Carol Robinson Gallery**
4537 Magazine St.
504/899-6130

**Jon Antiques**
4605 Magazine St.
504/899-4482

**19th Century Antiques**
4838 Magazine St.
504/891-4845

**Wirthmore Antiques**
5723 Magazine St.
504/897-9727

**Enoch's Framing & Gallery**
6063 Magazine St.
504/899-6686

**Apropos**
3806 Magazine St.
504/899-3500

**Au Vieux Paris Antiques**
7219 Perrier St.
504/866-6677

**Diane Genre Oriental Art & Antiques**
233 Royal St.
504/525-7270

**Dixon & Dixon**
237 Royal St.
504/524-0282

**Royal Antiques Ltd.**
309 Royal St.
504/524-7033

**Jack Sutton Antiques**
315 Royal St.
504/522-0555

**Keil's Antiques**
325 Royal St.
504/522-4552

**J Herman Son Galleries**
333 Royal St.
504/525-6326

**Berta's and Mina's Antiquities**
4138 Magazine St.
504/895-6201

**Top Drawer Auction & Appraisals**
4310 Magazine St.
504/832-9080

**Fraza Framing & Art Gallery**
4532 Magazine St.
504/899-7002

**Modell's Rostor & Polsg Inc.**
4600 Magazine St.
504/895-5267

**Melange Sterling**
5421 Magazine St.
504/899-4796

**Pettie Pence Antique**
4904 Magazine St.
504/891-3353

**The Tulip Tree**
5831 Magazine St.
504/895-3748

**Le Wicker Gazebo**
3715 Magazine St.
504/899-1355

**Driscoll Antiques & Restorations**
8118 Oak St.
504/866-7795

**French Antique Shop Inc.**
225 Royal St.
504/524-9861

**Brass Monkey**
235 Royal St.
504/561-0688

**Rothschild's**
241 Royal St.
504/523-5816

**Robinson's Antiques**
313 Royal St.
504/523-6683

**Rothschild's**
321 Royal St.
504/523-2281

**Royal Co.**
325 Royal St.
504/522-4552

**Waldhorn - Adler**
343 Royal St.
504/581-6379

**Manheim Galleries**
409 Royal St.
504/568-1901

**Cynthia Sutton**
429 Royal St.
504/523-3377

**Gerald D Katz Antiques**
505 Royal St.
504/524-5050

**Royal Art Gallery Ltd.**
537 Royal St.
504/524-6070

**M. S. Rau Inc.**
630 Royal St.
504/523-5660

**Regency House Antiques**
841 Royal St.
504/524-7507

**Barakat**
934 Royal St.
504/593-9944

**W M Antiques**
1029 Royal St.
504/524-1253

**Riccas Architectural Sales**
511 N Solomon St.
504/488-5524

**Harper's Antiques**
610 Toulouse St.
504/592-1996

**Moss Antiques**
411 Royal St.
504/522-3981

**Jack Sutton Co. Inc.**
501 Royal St.
504/581-3666

**Le Petit Soldier Shop**
528 Royal St.
504/523-7741

**Harris Antiques Ltd.**
623 Royal St.
504/523-1605

**L.M.S. Fine Arts & Antiques**
729 Royal St.
504/529-3774

**Patout Antiques**
922 Royal St.
504/522-0582

**Sigles Antiques & Metalcrafts**
935 Royal St.
504/522-7647

**Centuries Old Maps & Prints**
517 Saint Louis St.
504/568-9491

**Nina Sloss Antiques & Interiors**
1001 State St.
504/895-8088

**The Westgate**
5219 Magazine St.
504/899-3077

### *Great Places To Stay*

**Bywater Guest House**
908 Poland Ave.
504/949-6381
1-888-615-7498
Email: bywatergh@aol.com
Web site: members.aol.com/bywatergh
*Directions: A relaxed, comfortable atmosphere in an 1872 Eastlake Victorian home located in the Bywater National Historic District, 1 mile from the French Quarter.*

Located on the site of the Audey Plantation, later known as the Faubourg Washington, Bywater Guest House is located one and one-half miles down river from the French Quarter. The house was built in 1872, in the Victorian style by Michael Darby, an American engineer. The main building construction shows styles influenced by Charles Eastlake. The site also holds the original kitchen, or cookhouse, which by law had to be a separate structure, and one of the first three car garages in the City of New Orleans. The house is furnished in antique and reproduction appointments and original artwork.

The Innkeepers at Bywater Guest House take pride in providing a relaxed, comfortable environment for their guests. Amenities for the three guest rooms include; comfortable queen size beds with feather mattresses and down duvets, writing tables and Queen Anne style chairs. The full breakfast includes a hot entree, fresh fruit and juice, coffee, tea and breads.

**Dusty Mansion**
2231 General Pershing St.
504/895-4576
Open year round
Rates $50-75

Just six blocks from the St. Charles Ave. streetcar, Dusty Mansion is ideally located for weekend exploration and enjoyment of New Orleans. This is a homey, casual inn on a quiet residential street just on the edge of the Garden District in the historic Bouligny Plantation District. It's a turn-of-the-century, two-story frame house with wide front porch and porch swing, original hardwood floors and cypress woodwork and doors. The four guest rooms (two with private bath) have romantic ceiling fans and are filled with antiques and reproduction pieces. The four beds are queen-sized and are either brass, canopied, sleigh or white enameled iron. A continental-plus breakfast is served in the dining room, and afterwards you can explore, relax and catch some rays on the sundeck, read or nap on the shaded patio, play pool or table tennis, and later, ease into the hot tub secluded in the gazebo.

## 17 OPELOUSAS

**Doucet's Acadiana Antiques**
1665 N. Main St.
318/942-3425
Mon.-Fri. 9:30-5, Sat.9-3:30, closed Sun.-Mon.
*Directions: From I-49 take the Opelousas exit and follow the signs to Hwy. 182 N. (Main is also known as Hwy. 182 N.). The shop is located across from Soileau's Dinner Club.*

Doucet's is a well-heeled shop that has been providing superior pieces since 1928. They handle only fine 18th and 19th century antiques, paintings and collectibles from France and England. This is truly a shop to visit if you are looking for high end French or English period pieces.

**Opelousas Antique Mall**
353 E. Landry St.
318/942-5620

## 18 PEARL RIVER

**Anns Place Antiques**
39613 Pecan Dr.
504/641-2754

## 19 PINEVILLE

**Peck's Antiques**
706 Pearce Road
318/640-0006

**Jessie's Antique Barn**
5632 Hwy. 28 E.
318/473-8347

**Beaten Path Antiques**
6892 Hwy. 28 E.
318/445-9425

**Handmaiden & Friends**
318 Maryhill Road
318-640-3727

**Peck's Antiques**
706 Pearce Road
318/640-0006

## 20 PONCHATOULA

**Remember When Antiques**
223 W. Pine St.
504/386-6159
Wed.-Sun. 10-5

This large and spacious mall carries everything from Victorian to primitives, but concentrates primarily on furnishings and glassware accessories.

**Ponchatoula Antiques**
400 W. Pine St.
504/386-7809
Wed.-Sun. 10-5

This mall carries antiques, but their main focus is on fountains and statuary! They handle new fountains (not antique ones) and statuary in a variety of themes, and have at least 200 fountains on display at all times. The statuary is the free-standing yard and garden variety. If you're looking to add a touch of the exotic or a touch of luxury to your yard and garden, look here first.

**Alford's General Store**
114 E. Pine St.
504/386-0111

**Layrisson Walker Ltd.**
123 E. Pine St.
504/386-8759

**Yesteryear Antiques**
165 E. Pine St.
504/386-2741

**Ellen's Antiques & Collectibles**
179 E. Pine St.
504/386-3564

**Country Market**
10 W. Pine St.
504/386-9580

**Needful Things**
101 W. Pine St.
504/386-2918

**Memory Lane**
105 W. Pine St.
504/386-2812

**Country Carosel Antiques**
120 W. Pine St.
504/386-2271

**Oldies and Goodies**
138 W. Pine St.
504/386-0150

**Red Baron Antiques Inc.**
139 W. Pine St.
504/386-8792

# Louisiana

**Wholesale Antiques**
152 W. Pine St.
504/386-8086

**Courtyard Antiques**
155 W. Pine St.
504\386-9569

**Ma Meres**
165 W. Pine St.
504/386-0940

**Roussel's Specialty Shop**
177 W. Pine St.
504/386-9097

**Remember When**
223 W. Pine St.
504/386-6159

**Ponchatoula Antiques Inc**
400 W. Pine St.
504/386-7809

**C J's Antiques & Collectibles**
160 S.E. Railroad Ave.
504/386-0026

**Roussel's Annex**
138 N. 6th St.
504/386-9096

## 21 RUSTON

**Deep South Antiques**
Hwy. 167 N.
318/255-5278

**Michael's Furniture Mart**
305 W. Mississippi Ave.
318/251-9409

**Railroad Depot**
101 E. Railroad Ave.
318/255-3103

**Acorn Creek Antiques**
1323 S. Service Road W.
318/255-1831

**Times Past Antiques**
103 N. Trenton St.
318/254-8279

**Park Ave Antique Mall**
108 N. Vienna St.
318/255-4866

**Pot Luck**
202 N. Vienna St.
318/254-1331

## 22 SHREVEPORT

**Hudson House Antiques**
3118 Gilbert
318/865-2151

**Bullock's**
1723 Highland Ave.
318/226-9168

**Heirloom Antiques**
3004 Highland Ave.
318/226-0146

**Caloways Antiques & Bygones**
811 Jefferson Place
318/221-5493

**Hudson House Antiques**
109 Kings Hwy.
318/868-9579

**D&B Russell-Books**
129 Kings Hwy.
318/865-5198

**Kings Ransom**
133 Kings Hwy.
318/865-4811

**Enchanted Gardens**
2429 Line Ave.
318/227-1213

**Katie-Beths Antiques**
3316 Line Ave.
318/868-5246

**Arrangement**
3322 Line Ave.
318/868-6812

**Hinton Gallery**
3324 Line Ave.
318/868-0018

**Jack Farmer Antiques**
6018 Line Ave.
318/869-3297

**Then & Now**
6030 Line Ave.
318/865-6340

**Corrente Oriental Antiques**
6401 Line Ave.
318/868-3833

**Golden Pineapple**
6104 Line Ave., #5
318/868-3691

**London Gallery-Antiques**
6401 Line Ave.
318/868-3691

**Pilgrim's Progress**
6535 Line Ave.
318-868-3383

**Red Caboose Antiques**
855 Pierremont Road
318/865-5376

**Estate Sale Consignment**
2847 Summer Grove
318/687-7525

**Lost & Found Antiques**
2847 Summer Grove
318/687-1896

**Gozas Gallery Inc.**
5741 Youree Dr.
318/868-3429

**Antique Mall**
546 Olive St.
318/425-8786

**Nigel's Heirloom Antique Gallery**
421 Texas St.
318/226-0146

## 23 SLIDELL

**Recollections**
2265 Carey St.
504/641-9410

**Barbara's Victorian Closet**
124 Erlanger St.
504/641-6316

**Magnolia House Antiques**
228 Erlanger St.
504/641-3776

**Bon MeNage Gallery**
1922 1st St.
504/646-0488

**La Jolie Maison**
1944 1st St.
504/649-7055

**Wishing Well**
1952 1st St.
504/646-0801

**Vintage Antiques & Collectibles**
1958 1st St.
504/649-5968

**First Street Antiques**
1960 1st St.
504/643-6727

**Little Green House Antiques**
1732 Front St.
504/643-5176

**Slidell Trading Post**
40137 Hwy. 190 E.
504/643-1606

**Slidell Antq Market**
806 Cousin St.
504/649-0579

**Victorian Tea Room**
228 Carey St.
504/643-7881

**Something Old/Something New**
1929 2nd St.
504/649-8088

**Parc Antique Mall**
2019 2nd St.
504/649-0410

**The Antique Store**
1944 1st St.
504/649-7055

**Horaist "A Design Experience"**
1654 Front St.
504/643-3030

## 24 ST. FRANCISVILLE

**C & D Collectible Now & Then**
217 Ferdinand St.
504/635-3606

**Honeysuckles**
11739 Ferdinand St.
504/635-3367

**Something Special**
11911 Ferdinand St.
504/635-9804

**Pretty Things Antiques**
11917 Ferdinand St.
504/635-0308

*Great Places To Stay*

**Barrow House**
524 Royal St.
504/635-4791

This beautiful, picturesque building is sitting right in the middle of the historic district of St. Francisville, a wonderful location for exploration. The two-story section was built in 1809 in the salt-box style, while the one-story wing and Greek Revival facade were added in 1855. The inn offers guests one suite and four double rooms, three of them with private baths. Antiques from the 1860s fill every nook and cranny of the historic building and guests are served wonderful dinners in the formal dining room.

## 25 SULPHUR

**Miss Peggy's Antiques & Collectibles**
208 S. Huntington St.
318/527-5027

**Costwold**
2223 Maplewood Dr.
381/625-3367

**Sherry's Antique & Gift Shop**
210 W. Napoleon St.
318/528-3346

**Finders Keepers**
414 E. Napoleon St.
318/527-7070

## 26 THIBODAUX

**Dodge City Mall**
1213 Canal Blvd.
504/447-4411

**Erwin's Antique Bank**
413 W. 4th St.
504/446-5827

**Sweet Memories**
602 Green St.
504/446-1140

**Andree's Antiques**
416 Jackson St.
504/447-5889

**Angela's Antiques**
517 Jackson St.
504/446-3641

**Terry's Antiques**
5504 W. Main St.
504/449-1600

**Lafourche Antiques and Co.**
424 Saint Mary St.
504/449-1635

**Bryson's Angels**
511 St. Phillip
504/447-1800

**Mainstreet**
606 W. 3rd St.
504/449-1001

**Debbie's Antiques**
705 W. Third
504/633-5680

## 27 WASHINGTON

**O'Connors Antiques School Mall**
210 S. Church St.
318/826-3580

**Cajun Antiques**
400 S. Main St.
318/826-3710

## 28 WEST MONROE

**Anderson Collection**
204 Trenton St.
318/388-0366

**Cotton's Collectables**
255 Trenton St.
318/322-6479

**River Run Antiques**
303 Trenton St.
318/324-0517

**Sanderson's Antiques**
310 Trenton St.
318/325-0089

**Martha's Unfinished Furniture**
311 Trenton St.
318/323-1454

**Trenton Street Images**
312 Trenton St.
318/322-2691

**O'Kelley's Antiques**
313 Trenton St.
318/329-9409

**Potpourri de Marie Tante**
314 Trenton St.
318/325-0103

**Imperial Galleries Antiques & Fine Arts**
317 Trenton St.
318/361-9458

**Chandler's Antiques**
318 Trenton St.
318/322-3925

**Virginia's Antiques**
320 Trenton St.
318/324-9885

**Old Trenton Country Store**
323 Trenton St.
318/323-7152

**Sawyer's Antiques**
4352 Whites Ferry Road
318/397-1292

**The Side Track**
101 Trenton St.
318/323-9501

**Trenton Street Antique Mall**
215 Trenton St.
318/325-9294

**Marie's Antiques & Glass**
224 Trenton St.
318/388-0908

**Memory Lane Antiques**
301 Trenton St.
381/323-3188

**Sanderson's Antique Mall**
308 & 310 Trenton St.
318/325-0089

**Trenton Street Gallery**
319 Trenton St.
318/329-9200

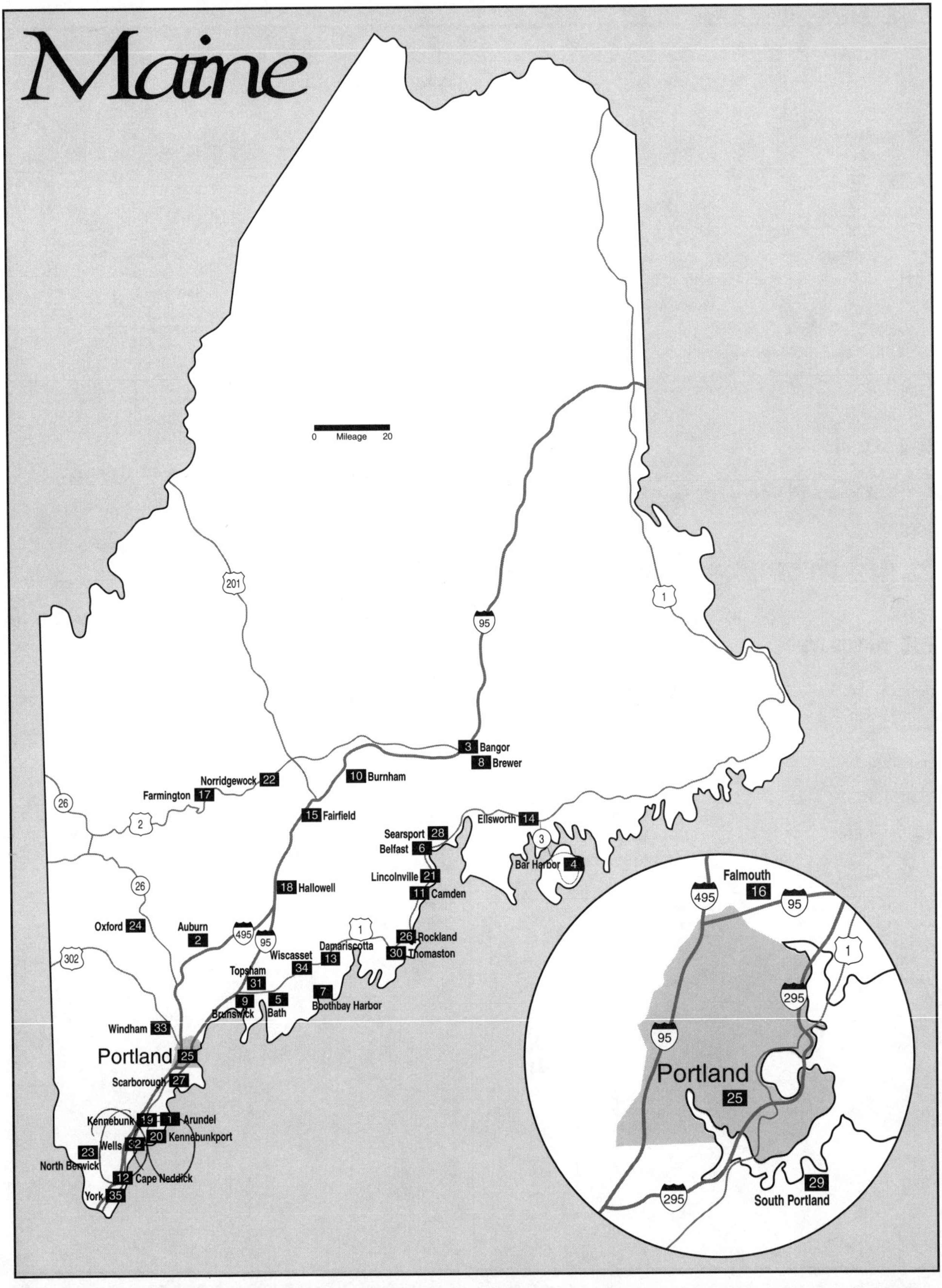

Maine
0 Mileage 20
201
1
95
3 Bangor
8 Brewer
Norridgewock 22
10 Burnham
Farmington 17
26
2
15 Fairfield
Searsport 28
Ellsworth 14
Belfast 6
3
Bar Harbor 4
Lincolnville 21
11 Camden
18 Hallowell
26
Oxford 24
Auburn 2
495
95
1
26 Rockland
30 Thomaston
Damariscotta 13
302
Wiscasset 34
Topsham 31
7 Boothbay Harbor
9 Brunswick
5 Bath
Windham 33
Portland 25
Scarborough 27
Kennebunk 19
1 Arundel
20 Kennebunkport
Wells 32
23 North Berwick
12 Cape Neddick
York 35
Falmouth 16
495
95
1
295
95
Portland 25
295
29 South Portland

# The Galen C. Moses House in Bath is a stylish Victorian B&B on the National Register of Historic Homes

The historic town of Bath offers both remarkable antique shopping and an incredible bed & breakfast. In 1994 former antique dealers James Haught and Larry Kieft moved from the antique business (except who really ever gets "out" of antiques!) into the bed and breakfast field - and they did it with a bang! They purchased the 1874 Galen C. Moses house and immediately made it the talk of the town.

*Stained glass detail in the stairwell.*

The house was designed by Francis Fassett for Galen C. Moses (1835-1915) and redesigned in 1901 by John Calvin Stevens, one of Fassett's apprentices. The vernacular Italianate has an interior that is both Victorian and Colonial Revival. There are so many original, unique touches and finishes that I can't begin to list them all, but I will give you just a taste of what's in store when you visit: stained glass windows, elaborately carved mantels, window seats, arched windows, claw-foot tubs, and on the third floor, a full movie theater (vintage 1930s) complete with a projection booth and sixteen tiered seats facing a makeshift stage. During World War II, officers from the Brunswich Navel Air Station were invited to view movies (some of them supposedly "blue") as part of the local effort to build morale.

The three guest rooms, all with private baths, are upstairs (second floor) and continue the uniqueness of the house. The Victorian Room has bay windows and a white marble fireplace. The Moses Room holds an antique wash stand and the original plaster frieze on all four walls. The Vintage Room as been furnished with oak and walnut pieces of the period which compliment the 1874 built-in washstand. And if all this doesn't overdose you on antiques, there are eight antique shops within blocks of the house, plus six antique shows per year in Bath.

Wait.There's more! Besides the rooms filled with antiques and the elegant gardens, the house contains a number of spirits, other than the sherry served at 5 p.m.! The ghosts are friendly and seem to make their presence felt on a regular basis. A full breakfast is served each morning, and the fare depends entirely on the cook's mood. Juice, coffee and muffins are always available for early risers or late sleepers, but the full meal can range from fresh fruit and blueberry pancakes to mushroom quiche or sour cream and chive omelets. It's an adventure all the way at the Moses House in Bath!

*For additional information on the Galen C. Moses House see listing #5 (Bath) or visit their web site:http://www.galenmoses.com*

*Throughout the history of the Galen C. Moses House, entertaining guests has been an important function of the owners.*

# Maine

## 1 ARUNDEL

**Arundel Antiques**
1713 Portland Road
207/985-7965

**Bacons**
1740 Portland Road
207/985-1401

**Nothing New Antiques**
2796 Portland Road (Route 1)
207/286-1789

## 2 AUBURN

### Orphan Annie's Antiques
96 Court St.
207/782-0638
Mon.-Sat. 10-5; Sun. 12-5
*Directions: Take Exit 12 off the Maine Turnpike. Go left after the exit three miles into town. At the third stoplight, turn right onto Court St. The shop is down four blocks on the right, across from the county courthouse.*

For lovers of art glass, this is a shop you don't want to miss! Owner Dan Poulin has been in the antique business for 20 years, the last ten dealing primarily in art glass. This shop is full of such jewels as Tiffany, Stuben, Quezal, Imperial and numerous other styles in American glass; French glass pieces by Galle, Daum Nancy, D'Argental, Loetz and Czech glass. He specializes in art glass from the 1890s to the 1930s, getting most of the glass from private sources and some at auction.

The shop also offers over 100 pieces of Roseville, vintage clothing, along with a three-story warehouse filled to the brim with antique furnishings.

**Rower J. Morin & Son Inc.**
195 Turner St.
207/782-7511

## 3 BANGOR

**Alcott Antiques**
30 Central St.
207/942-7706

**Maritime International**
89 Central St.
207/941-8372

**Maritime International**
89 Central St.
207/941-8372

**Ireland's Antiques**
650 Main St.
207/945-5902

**Dave's Furniture Co.**
100 Center St.
207/942-5291

## 4 BAR HARBOR

**Bar Harbor Antiques**
128 Cottage St.
207/288-3120

**Olde Stuffe & Things**
7 Everard Court
207/288-2203

**Shaw Antiques**
3 Cromwell Harbor Road
207/288-0114

**Super's Junkin Co.**
Town Hill Route 102
207/288-5740

***Great Places To Stay***

### Bar Harbor Inn
Newport Dr.
1-800-248-3351

Built as a private club in 1887, the Bar Harbor Inn was designed by Boston architect William Ralph Emerson. The inn rests on an estate style, seven-acre property, in the center of the historic village of Bar Harbor. The main inn is tastefully decorated in the traditional inn style with many rooms featuring views of Frenchman's Bay. The Oceanfront Lodge has 64 deluxe rooms with oversized beds and private balconies directly overlooking the ocean.

### Black Friar Inn
10 Summer St.
207/288-5091

The Black Friar Inn is a uniquely restored Victorian home surrounded by a perennial flower garden. Mantels, bookcases, windows and finely crafted woodwork from turn-of-the-century 'cottages' on Mount Desert Island shape every part of the inn. Seven romantic guest rooms are tastefully furnished with period antiques. Fine linens dress the beds and each room has a private bath. During the months of May, June and September the innkeepers offer professional guided trips on some of the most beautiful trout and salmon waters in the state of Maine.

### Breakwater 1904
45 Hancock St.
1-800-238-6309

In 1904, John Innes Kane, the great grandson of John Jacob Astor, built a magnificent 'summer cottage' and named it 'Breakwater'. Located on over four acres of lush lawns, beautiful gardens, and natural woods, this ocean front English Tudor estate was completely renovated and restored to its original grandeur in 1991, and placed on the National Historic Register March 26, 1992. The inn features six guest chambers, eleven working fireplaces and nine spacious common areas.

### The Canterbury Cottage
12 Roberts Ave.
207/288-2112
Web site: www.acadia.net/canterbury

A small bed and breakfast with comfortable, tastefully decorated rooms on a quiet side street within easy walking distance to in-town and harbor activities. Owners share a lifetime of island knowledge with guests while breakfast is served in the dining room.

**Castlemaine Inn**
39 Holland Ave.
1-800-338-4563

Castlemaine Inn is nestled on a quiet side street in the village of Bar Harbor, only minutes from the magnificent Acadia National Park and within easy reach of galleries, shops and restaurants. The inn has twelve charming rooms and four comfortable suites. Some rooms have queen canopy beds, queen four poster beds and king size beds. Many rooms have fireplaces and private balconies. All rooms have private baths.

**Cleftstone Manor**
92 Eden St.
1-888-288-4951
Web site: www.acadia.net/cleftstone

The Cleftstone Manor is an 1884 Victorian mansion featuring sixteen guestrooms, each with a private bath. The inn is furnished with Victorian antiques and period pieces, creating an atmosphere reminiscent of turn-of-the-century.

**Hatfield Bed & Breakfast**
20 Roberts Ave.
207/288-9655

Hatfield Bed & Breakfast is located on a quiet side street in Bar Harbor, two blocks from the center of town and two and one half blocks from the waterfront. The inn is only minutes from beautiful Acadia National Park and the Ferry Terminal Nova Scotia. Hatfield's eclectic mix of antique and country decor and the unpretentious, down home hospitality of Innkeepers Jeff and Sandy Miller bring true meaning to the term 'relaxed atmosphere'. Jeff and Sandy serve up a full, hearty breakfast.

**The Holland Inn**
35 Holland Ave.
207/288-4804
Web site: www.downeast.net/com/holland

The 1895 Holland House is the only in-town traditional Maine farmhouse B&B. Offering five recently restored rooms with private baths, each one illuminates the gracious simplicity and comfort of a county farm. The generous yards and gardens surrounding the inn fill each window with light and a fresh summer breeze. Relax on the sun porch or under the shaded Maples in the backyard. Stroll to the town pier or your favorite restaurant. Your hosts Evin and Tom will treat you with friendly down-east hospitality and endless activities to fill your days. Cottages also available.

**Inn At Canoe Point**
Route 3, Eden St.
207/288-9511
Web site: www.innatcanoepoint.com

This secluded waterside inn is situated among the pines on two acres tucked into a quiet cove. Located only moments away from lively Bar Harbor and next door to the unspoiled natural attractions of Acadia National Park. Situated directly on Frenchman's Bay you can walk among the trees, sit on the rocks and watch the boats sail by, or relax in front of the granite fireplace and enjoy the views of the sea and mountains. From the surrounding deck you can look out over the ocean and listen to the roaring surf.

**Stratford House Inn**
45 Mount Desert St.
207/288-5189

The Stratford House Inn is one of the few remaining summer 'cottages' that amplify the grand and elegant life of Bar Harbor at the turn of the century. Built in 1900 by the noted Boston book publisher Lewis A. Roberts, The Stratford House Inn is styled with the romantic charm of an English Tudor Manor. The inn boasts ten beautifully decorated bedrooms, each with its own individual charm and style. In the mornings, guests are treated to a continental breakfast in the elegant dining room.

**The Maples Inn**
16 Roberts Ave.
207/288-3443
Web site: www.acadia.net/maples

Enjoy classic tranquility in this 1903 Victorian inn, located on a quiet tree-lined street near downtown Bar Harbor. Stroll to the water's edge, just two blocks away. All five guest rooms and two room suites with a fireplace, have down comforters and all rooms are designed in a traditional decor. Some of the inn's breakfast entrees have been featured in *Gourmet* and *Bon Appetit* magazines and have recently been published in the inn's own cookbook called *Cats Can't Cook*, written by Bailey the Wonder Dog.

**Twin Gables Inn**
P. O. Box 282
207/288-3064

At Twin Gables Inn, you can experience all the natural delights of Acadia National Park while enjoying the country comfort and charm of a completely restored 100 year old inn. Each of the six cheerful guest rooms provides a private bath and some have beautiful mountain and ocean views. Share good conversation with other guests during the 'forget about lunch' breakfast from a menu that includes the house specialty...raspberry pancakes.

## 5 BATH

East of Brunswick along Coastal Route One is the shipbuilding city of Bath. Here is the site of Bath Iron Works, which produces many vessels for the United States Navy and the Merchant Marine. It is an impressive sight to see such massive ships under construction. Spectators can get a bird's eye view from the Route One Carlton Bridge, which spans the mighty Kennebec River. Bath is the business hub for many nearby resort areas along the Kennebec. Its downtown business district features wonderful brick sidewalks and street lamps reminiscent of the nineteenth century, while old sea captains' and shipbuilders' homes line the avenues. Visitors will also find a waterfront public park and several specialty and antique shops.

Between 1862 and 1902, Bath was the nation's fifth largest seaport, and nearly half of the United States' wooden sailing vessels were built here. During that era, more than 200 private shipbuilding firms flourished along a four-mile stretch of waterfront, producing large numbers of vessels. Exhibits describing the Maine shipbuilding traditions are displayed at the Maine Maritime Museum on the banks of the Kennebec in Bath. The Museum is a must for travelers interested in our nautical heritage.

**Brick Store Antiques**
143 Front St.
207/443-2790

**Countryside Antiques & Books**
170 Front St.
207/442-0772

**Cobblestone & Co.**
176 Front St.
207/443-4064

**Pollyanna's Antiques**
182 Front St.
207/443-4909

**Front Street Antiques**
190 Front St.
207/443-8098

**Atlantic Coast Antiques**
Sanford Road
207/443-9185

**Timeless Treasures Antiques**
104 Front St.
207/442-0377

**Trifles Antiques**
42 High St.
207/443-5856

***Great Places To Stay***

**The Galen C. Moses House**
1009 Washington St.
207/442-8771, 888/442-8771
Web site: www.galenmoses.com
Email: galenmoses@clinic.net.
Open year round
Rates $65-95
*Directions: Take the Maine Turnpike (I-95) to Exit 6A (I-295). After Portland, I-295 rejoins I-95. Continue to Exit 22 (Route 1, Brunswick and Bath). Entering Bath, stay right for the last exit before the Bridge (marked "Historic Bath") and proceed to Washington St. Turn left and drive 6 blocks to 1009 Washington St., which is on the right.*

For specific information see review at the beginning of this section.

## 6 BELFAST

Once a prosperous shipbuilding center, Belfast exhibits more than its share of exquisite Federal and early Victorian sea-merchants' mansions, many of them now operated as gracious inns and bed and breakfasts. White clapboard, aged brick, gingerbread trim, large lawns and enormous overarching oaks, elms and maples give the town a stately air. The charm is complimented by the "all-of-a-piece" flow of late 19th century brick shop fronts down Main Street to the bay and the attractive and neatly maintained Waterfront Heritage Park.

**Anna's Antiques**
Route 1
207/338-2219

**Landmark Architectural Antiques**
108 Main St.
207/338-9901

**Hall Hardware Co.**
Searsport Ave., U.S. Route 1
207/338-1170

**Apex Antiques**
208 High St.
207/338-1194

## 7 BOOTHBAY HARBOR

**Bay Street Studio East Side**
2 Bay St.
207/633-3186

**Palabra Shops**
85 Commercial St.
207/633-4225

**Marine Antiques**
43 Townsend Ave.
207/633-0862

**Opera House Village Antiques**
Townsend Ave.
207/633-6855

### *Great Places To Stay*

**Anchor Watch**
3 Eames Road
207/633-7565
Web site: www.maineguide.com/boothbay/anchorwatch

Lighthouse beacons, lobster boats, rock shores and fir trees of many islands provide the view this inn is famous for. Bedrooms are set among lots of fir, maple and oak trees making the rooms sunny in winter, and cool in summer with lots of leaf color in fall. Boating, hiking on Monhegan Island and other land preserves and shopping are popular activities; and of course, restaurants feature excellent food prepared by many award-winning chefs. Lobsters are abundant and can be consumed picnic style while watching the boats bring in their catch or in a fancy restaurant with Newburg sauce. Rooms at the Anchor Watch are comfortable and cheerful, and decorated with quilts and stenciling. The kitchen and social rooms have pine floors, pleasing blue and white colors, a cozy fireplace and lots of windows facing the water. The side lawn slopes to the water and the pier provides sunbathing, fishing or even swimming. Breakfast is an enjoyable experience as you join others from around the world, or take a tray to the deck or your room. The delicious full breakfast includes lots of fresh fruit, granola, hot egg casserole and muffins or breads. Coffee lasts as long as the guests linger over fascinating conversations. Within an hours drive are white sandy beaches, the famous L. L. Bean and shopping malls of Freeport, Pemaquid Point Lighthouse and Museum, Owl's Head Light, Maine Maritime Museum, and the Farnsworth Art Gallery.

**Five Gables Inn**
Murray Hill Road
1-800-451-5048
Web site: www.maineguide.com/boothbay/5gables

Taking its name from the prominent windowed gables along its front, the Five Gables Inn sits on a sloping lawn overlooking Linekin Bay and East Boothbay, a quiet shipbuilding village. Once a twenty-two room, three bath hotel, the stately structure underwent a tasteful remodeling that reduced the rooms to sixteen, all with private baths. Five have working fireplaces. Furnishings are traditional with uncluttered country details. A gourmet buffet breakfast is prepared by the owner/chef.

**Harbour Towne Inn on the Waterfront**
71 Townsend Ave.
1-800-722-4240
Web site: www.acadia.net/harbourtowneinn

Harbour Towne Inn, the finest B&B on the waterfront, combines the convenience of village lodging coupled with the charm of a country inn. The inn is a handsomely refurbished Victorian townhouse with spectacular penthouse lodging available. Deluxe Continental breakfast is served.

**Jonathan's Bed and Breakfast**
15 Eastern Ave.
207/633-3588

Jonathan's is situated on the edge of a lovely woods, a short walk to the harbor, abounding in shops, boating, fishing and restaurants. After a hearty breakfast of fresh fruit, homemade muffins and special entree, the hosts will help guests plan a day of sightseeing throughout the beautiful coastal region. Return late afternoon to cool harbor breezes on the deck, sherry or lemonade, or, in wintertime, hot tea and a roaring fire in the parlor.

## 8 BREWER

**Center Mall**
39 Center St.
207/989-9842

**Paul Noddin Antiques**
171 Wilson St.
207/989-6449

## 9 BRUNSWICK

**Robbins Antique & Art Gallery**
343 Bath Road
207/729-3473

**Dionne's Antique Shop**
92 Merrymeeting Road
207/725-4263

**Days Antiques**
153 Park Row
207/725-6959

**Antiques at 184 Pleasant**
184 Pleasant St.
207/729-8343

**Waterfront Flea Market**
14 Main St.
207/729-0378

### *Great Places To Stay*

**Bethel Point Bed & Breakfast**
Bethel Point Road 2387
207/725-1115

Peaceful oceanside comfort in a 150 year old house furnished with antiques. Perfect view of islands and ocean birds while you watch seals at play and lobster boats at work. Opportunity for ocean swimming and shoreline walks to explore and find treasures from the sea. Easy drive to area's specialties such as Bowdoin College, Popham Beach, L. L. Bean and local restaurants featuring seafood delicacies.

## 10 BURNHAM

**Houston-Brooks Auctioneers**
Horseback Road
207/948-2214 or 1-800-254-2214
Fax: 207/948-5925
*Directions: Off of I-95, take Exit #37 and take a right off the ramp. Follow the road 1 1/2 miles to Clinton Village. Take a right on Route 100 and follow for 7 miles to Burnham. Take a right at the store (signs are posted) and go 3 2/10 miles to the four corners. Take a right (signs are posted here, too) and the auction hall is the next place on the left.*

Among the best-known auction houses in New England, Houston-Brooks is a family business that has been auctioning antiques for 27 years. Auctioneer and co-owner Pamela Brooks is one of the few practicing women auctioneers in the state. She's been at it 20 years herself; learning the art from working with her dad, who started the company. The auctions pull lots of customers from all over the region, especially from New England, upstate New York and Canada. Auctions are held every Sunday, and they offer a wide range of antique furniture, glass, collectibles, art and other items. According to Pam, they always have odd pieces come through. She says that the worst part of holding a weekly auction is that it's like running a never-ending race; you sell everything on Sunday and then wonder if you're going to have anything come in for the next week!

## 11 CAMDEN

Slightly larger than Kennebunkport - Camden's population is right at 4,000 - Camden is one of those rare places that is so stereotypical picturesque that it really looks "postcard perfect." Harbors, sailboats, softly mellowed houses, tree-lined streets and roads with dappled sunlight, breathtaking views around each bend in the road - this is Camden.

This is also sailboat country, and to really get a feel for the area, every visitor must spend at least a couple of hours out on Penobscot Bay. There are a variety of cruise options on both schooners and motor vessels, with trips running from just an hour too all day. If you are staying more than a little while, overnight, three-day and six-day cruises of the Maine coast are available on classic windjammers. You can also take weekend and week-long courses in sailing and earn a certificate that says "Learned to Sail in Maine."

When you shop, you'll find many more hand-loomed sweaters and handcrafted jewelry than you will tee shirts. And the food is not to be missed - all of the famous Maine fare, from lobsters, scallops and mussels to clams, haddock, salmon and swordfish. Here's a most interesting and refreshing end note: Camden has no fast-food franchises! So it really is "postcard perfect!"

**Downshire House Clocks**
49 Bayview St.
207/236-9016

**Hard Alee**
51 Bayview St.
207/236-3373

**Star Bird**
17 Main St.
207/236-8292

**Schueler Antiques**
10 High St.
207/236-2770

### *Great Places To Stay*

**A Little Dream**
66 High St.
207/236-8742
Web site: www.obs-us.com/obs/english/books/chesler/ne/05/bnb/meb122.htm

Sweet dreams and little luxuries abound in this lovely white Victorian with wicker and flower filled wrap-around porch. Set on two acres of rolling lawns and lovely perennial gardens, it overlooks two small castles with distant views of Penobscot Bay. Noted for it's lovely breakfast, beautiful rooms, and charming atmosphere, A Little Dream's English-Country-Victorian decor has been featured in *Country Inns* magazine, and in *Glamour's* "40 Best Getaways Across the Country." Located in the historic district, just a few minutes from shops and harbor, it is listed on the National Register of Historic Places. All rooms have special touches such as imported soaps and chocolates.

**Castleview by the Sea B&B**
59 High St.
1-800-272-8439

Located on the waterside of the oceanview section of Camden's historic district, this gorgeous inn offers spectacular glass walled views of Camdens only two castles and the sea, right from your bed! Count the stars across the bay and wake up to bold Maine Coast views. Bright and airy charm of classic 1856 cape architecture, wide pine floors, beams, clawfoot tubs, skylights, ceiling fans and stained glass. Private balconies.

**Edgecombe-Coles House**
64 High St.
1-800-528-2336

Edgecombe-Coles house is a classic example of a nineteenth century summer home. Situated on a quiet hillside overlooking Penobscot Bay, it offers an escape from summer's traffic. A lovely private place, Edgecombe-Coles House is a short walk from Camden's picturesque harbor with its fine restaurants, shops and recreational facilities. Visitors can view the ocean from the front porch or drive less than a mile to Camden Hills State Park where there are miles of uncrowded hiking trails.

## Swan House

49 Mountain St.
1-800-207-8275
Web site: www.swanhouse.com

Swan House is a small, intimate inn nestled at the foot of scenic Mt. Battie. This 1870 Victorian offers a private haven in a lovely, quiet setting. It's location in the residential village, away from the busy, nonstop Route 1 traffic, Swan House could be considered one of Camden's best kept secrets. A short walk down the hill leads to the picturesque harbor, unique and interesting shops and excellent restaurants. Swan House offers six guest rooms all with private baths and tastefully decorated. A delicious breakfast is served on the glass enclosed front porch. Relax and unwind in one of the parlors or discover the shaded gazebo - a perfect place to catch up on a favorite book. For the outdoor enthusiast, hike the many trails of Camden Hills State Park, one of which starts directly behind the inn and leads to Mt. Battie's summit.

## The Victorian by the Sea

P.O. Box 1385
1-800-382-9817

By the Sea, by the sea, by the beautiful sea is a century old Queen Anne Victorian restored to its original charm with spacious rooms, queen size beds, private baths, waterviews, and fireplaces. Decorated in period decor the inn provides a quiet atmosphere in a unique country setting. Relax on the beautiful porch and enjoy spectacular views of the gardens, the ocean, and the islands off the coast. Wake up to a full country breakfast to start off your day. Off Route 1 and 300 feet from the shore.

## Windward House Bed & Breakfast

6 High St.
207/236-9656

Windward House is located on Historic High Street in the picturesque sea coast village of Camden, the 'Jewel of the Maine Coast' where the mountains meet the sea. This beautifully restored 1854 Greek Revival home has eight tastefully decorated guest rooms, all with queen beds and private baths. Located within one block of harbor, village, shops and restaurants.

## 12 CAPE NEDDICK

**Columbary Antiques**
RR 1
207/363-5496

**Cranberry Hill Antiques**
RR 1
207/363-5178

**Gold Bug**
Route 1 & Clarke Road
207/351-2707

## 13 DAMARISCOTTA

Damariscotta is a classic Maine coastal village nestled along the eastern side of the Damariscotta River.

Oyster shell heaps, some reaching 30 feet in height, attest to this area being a centuries-old sanctuary for native American people. During the mid-1800s, Damariscotta was home to Metcalf and Norris, pioneer clipper ship builders. From their yards came the Flying Scud, famous for her 76-day passage to Melbourne.

**1839 House**
370 Bristol Road
207/563-2375

**Patricia Anne Reed Fine Antiques**
148 Bristol Road
207/563-5633

**Loons Landing Antiques**
Courtyard Shops
207/563-8931

**Arsenic & Old Lace**
Main St.
207/563-1414

**Cooper's Red Barn**
Waldoboro Road
207/563-3714

## 14 ELLSWORTH

**Mill Mall Treasures**
Bangor Road, Route 1A
207/667-8055

**His & Hers Antiques**
Bucksport Road
207/667-2115

**Eastern Antiques**
52 Dean St.
207/667-4033

**Sandy's Antiques**
111 Oak St.
207/667-5078

**Big Chicken Barn Books & Antiques**
RR 3
207/667-7308

## 15 FAIRFIELD

**Trading Post**
194 Main St.
207/453-2526

**Julia-Poulin Antiques**
199 Route 201
207/453-2114

## 16 FALMOUTH

**Scottish Terrier Antiques**
89 Hillside Ave.
207/797-4223

**Port 'N' Starboard Gallery**
53 Falmouth Road
207/781-4214

**Gerald Bell Antiques**
124 Gray Road
207/797-9386

## 17 FARMINGTON

### The Old Barn Annex Antiques
30 Middle St., #3
207/778-6908

Always presenting outstanding quality and exceptional antiques. If you can't visit them in Maine, be sure to watch for The Old Barn Annex Antiques on exhibit at finer antique shows.

## 18 HALLOWELL

**Dealer's Choice Antique Mall**
108 Water St.
207/622-5527

**Brass & Friends Antiques**
154 Water St.
207/626-3287

**James H Lefurgy Antiques & Books**
168 Water St.
207/623-1771

**Josiah Smith Antiques**
181 Water St.
207/622-4188

**Manny's Antiques**
202 Water St.
207/622-9747

**Berdam & Newsom Antiques**
151 Water St.
207/622-0151

**Acme Antiques**
165 Water St.
207/622-2322

**Johnson-Marsano Antiques**
172 Water St.
207/623-6263

**James J. LeFurgy Antiques**
168 Water St.
207/623-1771

## 19 KENNEBUNK

**Heritage House Antiques**
10 Christensen Lane
207/967-5952

**Antiques on Nine**
75 Western Ave., Route 9
207/967-0626

**Paper Collectibles**
58 Portland Road
207/985-0987

**Rivergate Antique Mall**
RR 1
207/985-6280

**Victorian Lighting**
29 York St.
207/985-6868

***Great Places To Stay***

### Arundel Meadows Inn
P.O. Box 1129
207/985-3770
Web site: www.biddeford.com/arundel-meadows-inn/

This old farmhouse located two miles north on Route 1 from the center of Kennebunk, combines the charm of antiques and art with the comfort of seven individually decorated bedrooms with sitting areas—two are suites, three have fireplaces, some have cable television, and all have private bathrooms. Full homemade breakfasts and afternoon teas are prepared by co-owner Mark Bachelder, a professionally trained chef.

## 20 KENNEBUNKPORT

Kennebunkport, with its little population of just 1,100, offers something for just about everyone, but especially for those who love the sea and a little seclusion. Scattered among its beaches, harbors, boat yards, rocky coasts, manicured streets, quaint shops and historic churches are the magnificent homes of 18th and 19th century sea captains, shipbuilders and wealthy summer residents. Many of these homes are now bed and breakfasts; indeed, few towns can match Kennebunkport for number, variety, and quality of its inns and the experience of the town's innkeepers. There are also several restored seaside hotels from another era that dot the scenic landscape of the town.

If you want a good introduction to the history of the Kennebunks (the name of the townsfolk), visit the Brick Store Museum. The museum shop features quality reproductions and books on local history and crafts. Another way to visit the area's past is to tour White Columns, a gracious Greek Revival mansion (1851-1853) with original furnishings that is maintained by the Kennebunkport Historical Society.

There's all sorts of things to do and see around Kennebunkport. Many of the historic buildings on Dock Square and elsewhere now house galleries and artists' studios, as well as many interesting little shops. The Seashore Trolley Museum has a collection of over 225 trolleys from around the world, and offers a three-mile ride on an antique electric trolley. And all visitors should take at least one offshore excursion and indulge in whale-watching, sightseeing and cruising. There's also canoeing, golfing, cross-country skiing, hiking or biking.

**Old Fort Inn**
8 Old Fort Ave.
207/967-5353

**Times Past & Past Times**
11 Pier Road
207/967-0266

**Antiques Workshop**
64 North St.
207/967-5266

**Antiques USA**
RR 1
207/985-7766

**Arundel Antiques**
1713 Portland Road
207/985-7965

**Anna Benjamin Antiques**
Old Limerick Road
207/985-2312

### *Great Places To Stay*

**1802 House B&B Inn**
15 Locke St.
1-800-932-5632
Web site: www.bbhost.com/1802inn

This nineteenth century inn is situated along the fifteenth fairway of the Cape Arundel Golf Club. Like so many New England homes, the inn has been added to over the years. The second story was added just after the turn of the nineteenth century. The structure was converted into an inn in 1977 and since that time, the original barn was converted to a gourmet kitchen and guest dining room. The six guest rooms are located in the original part of the house, each configured and decorated differently, each offering a fireplace or a double whirlpool tub, and some rooms offer both. The luxurious three room suite provides the ultimate in comfort and privacy.

**Captain Lord Mansion**
P.O. Box 800
207/967-3141
Web site: www.captainlord.com

The Captain Lord Mansion was built during the War of 1812 as an elegant private residence and is situated at the head of a sloping green overlooking the Kennebunk River. Large guest rooms, luxurious appointments, oversize antique four poster beds and gas fireplaces create a true haven for romantic and celebratory escapes. A three-course breakfast is served "family style" giving lots of opportunity to share with fellow travelers. Awarded both AAA 4 Diamonds & Mobil 4 Stars. Many "quiet season" events and activities. Walk to shops, galleries and restaurants. River view rooms.

**Inn At Harbor Head**
41 Pier Road
207/967-5564

The nostalgia of a bygone era lingers in this picturesque fishing village. Your artist/innkeeper has beautifully decorated the rambling shingled inn with various sculptures, marine paintings, oriental carpets, antique furniture and handpainted murals on guestroom walls. Beautifully appointed beds are king or queen. The library is perfect for reading or watching ocean and harbor activities, while a stroll past the gardens will take you to the water's edge.

**Maine Stay Inn & Cottages**
34 Main St.
1-800-950-2117
Web site: www.mainstayinn.com

Maine Stay is a beautiful 1860 Victorian inn with Italianate hiproof, accentuated by a Queen Anne period flying staircase, wrap-around porch, bay windows, and masterful architectural detail. The Maine Stay offers a variety of accommodations, suites in the main house, to delightful one-bedroom cottages, some with fireplace and separate kitchens. Cottage guests may have a breakfast basket delivered to their door. The living room is a comfortable place to sit and meet fellow travelers.

**The Captain Jefferds Inn**
5 Pearl St.
1-800-839-6844
Web site: www.captainjefferdsinn.com

Hospitality abounds in this gracious 1804 Federal style mansion. Originally built by Daniel Walker, the property was given as a wedding present to his daughter Mary, and her husband, Captain William Jefferds, in 1805. Each of the sixteen guest rooms are named, designed and decorated in the spirit of the Bartholomew's favorite places. The Italian suite has a king size verdi-gris iron bed, fireplace and indoor water garden. Other rooms in the inn include the Charleston, the Chatham, the Adare and the Monicello. Six have fireplaces, all have private baths and are furnished with antiques and period reproductions. Each morning a full, gourmet breakfast is served by candlelight in front of a warm fire or, in the summer months, on the sunny terrace overlooking the gardens. Located in Kennebunkport's magnificent historic district, within easy walking distance to many fine shops, restaurants and galleries.

**The Waldo Emerson Inn**
207/985-4250
Web site: www.bbhost.com/waldoemersoninn

This interesting inn has had several famous owners. The original Dutch grambrel was constructed by Waldo Emerson in 1753 and is the oldest remaining house in Kennebunk. Waldo, great-uncle of Ralph Waldo Emerson, the poet/essayist, made a tidy profit building clipper ships on the river behind the house. It was inherited, through marriage, by Theodore Lyman, who made a fortune building ships on the site and added the enormous addition in 1784 as a wedding gift for his second wife. Theodore sold the home in 1804, to build the now-famous Lyman Estate and Greenhouses in Waltham, Massachusetts. The house was purchased by John Bourne, father of fifteen children, one of whom was George Washington Bourne, the builder of the famous "Wedding Cake House" next door. The inn is a wonderful recollection of the past. You enter directly into the 245-year-old keeping room, with its hand-hewn oak timbers hung with dried flowers, pewter, and copper. During your stay, please stop by Mainely Quilts, innkeeper Maggie Carver's shop in the carriage house. You will likely find her working on her latest creation. Her heirloom quality quilts and wall hangings, often taking hundred of hours to create, grace homes all over the world.

## 21 LINCOLNVILLE

**Blue Dolphin Antiques**
164 Atlantic Hwy.
207/338-3860

**Deer Meadows**
RR 1
207/236-8020

**Painted Lady**
RR 1
207/789-5201

**Andrews & Andrews**
71 Cross St.
207/338-1386

## 22 NORRIDGEWOCK

**Black Hill Antiques & Collectibles**
Main St.
207/634-5151

**Victoria Shoppe Antique Mall**
Main St.
207/634-3130

## 23 NORTH BERWICK

### Brick House Antiques
Corner Route 9 & Main St.
207/676-2885
Open every day

Located seven miles from Wells and Ogunquit, Brick House Antiques is literally a treasure trove of hand picked antiques. Reverse painted lamps, Bohemian glass, Art Nouveau, fine porcelain, quality furniture, steins and objects of art are some of the examples that may be found in one of Maine's finest antique shops.

## 24 OXFORD

**Kall Us Antiques**
Route 26
207/743-9788

**Meetinghouse Antiques**
Route 26
207/539-8480

**Undercover Antique Mall**
Route 26
207/539-4149

### *Great Places To Stay*

### The Inn at Little Creek
Route 121
207/539-4046 or 1-888-539-4046
Open year round
Rates $35-75
*Directions: Take the Maine Turnpike to Exit 11 (Gray) to Route 26 N. Travel Route 26 north approximately 30 minutes to Oxford. Take Route 121 south. The inn is located on Route 121 S., 1 1/4 miles off of Route 26 in the village of Oxford.*

This bed & breakfast truly stands out from all the others. It was started only two years ago by Ken Ward and Diane Lecuyer, and already has return guests from around the world. What sets it apart is that it is furnished in a Native American/Southwestern flavor, complete to the serving of buffalo meat and Native American teas for breakfast. And all this is tucked away in the southwestern end of Maine!

Running a B&B has been a dream of Ken's since he was 18 years old. When he and Diane decided to open the inn, they spent a year traveling around the country, visiting B&Bs, to see just what was available. They knew they wanted something totally different so, since Diane is part Native American, they decided to include her heritage as the main focus of their inn. Although Diane is associated with the Iroquois Nation of the Northeast, they used the Southwestern feel because most non-Native Americans only know that side of the culture. The inn is furnished in the soft, muted pastel palette of the Southwest that is familiar to most people (as opposed to the harsher, more vivid palette that is also part of the Southwestern culture). But they have not focused on any specific tribes, using instead artifacts and accessories from all over North America. In this way, they use their B&B to help educate people about Native Americans in general. They are not yet selling Native American artifacts and antiques, but may in the future.

As to where one obtains buffalo meat in Maine? Well, surprise, there are two buffalo ranches in the state, one of which is conveniently near the inn and operated by a friend of Ken and Diane's. Diane is the cook and prepares all the buffalo meat dishes. The Native American teas are brought in from the Dakotas and served to the inn's guests for breakfast.

Although The Inn at Little Creek is new on the B&B scene, it has already established a following and is certainly a welcome addition and change of pace. So visit Ken and Diane and soak up a little culture and history while you relax in the "wilds" of Maine.

## 25 PORTLAND

**Shipwreck & Cargo Co.**
207 Commercial St.
207/775-3057

**Seavey's**
249 Congress St.
207/773-1908

**Anna's Used Furniture & Collectibles**
612 Congress St.
207/775-7223

**Antiques at Zinnias**
662 Congress St.
207/780-6622

**Venture Antiques**
101 Exchange St.
207/773-6064

**F. O. Bailey Co. Inc.**
141 Middle St.
207/774-1479

**West Port Antiques**
8 Milk St.
207/774-6747

**Geraldine Wolf Antique Jewelry**
26 Milk St.
207/774-8994

**Magpie's**
610 Congress St.
207/828-4560

**Nelson Rarities, Inc.**
1 City Center, #8
207/775-3150

**O'Brien Antiques**
38 High St.
207/774-0931

**Tucker's Furniture & Antiques**
255 Congress St.
207/761-0719

**Andrew Nelson & Co.**
1 City Center, #8
207/775-1135

### *Great Places To Stay*

**Inn at St. John**
939 Congress St.
1-800-636-9127

The Inn at St. John is a most unique 100 year old inn noted for its European charm and quiet gentility, centrally located in Portland, just a short walk to the Old Port Waterfront and Art District. Built in 1897, the inn offers tastefully decorated rooms with traditional and antique furnishings.

## 26 ROCKLAND

**Katrin Phocas Ltd. Antiques**
19 Main St.
207/236-8654

**Hall Antiques**
432 Main St.
207/594-5031

**Mainly Paper**
474 Main St.
207/596-0077

**Early Times Antique Center**
Route 90 in Rockport
207/236-3001

**Antique Treasures**
Midway on Route 90
207/596-7650

**Jordan's Antiques**
187 Pleasant St.
207/594-5529

## 27 SCARBOROUGH

**Centervale Farm Antiques**
200 U.S. Route One at Oak Hill
207/883-3443 or 1-800-896-3443
Open year round, 10-5 (Nov.-June closed Mondays)
*Directions: Maine Turnpike, Exit 6, then take Route 1 north 6 miles south of Portland via 295.*

Delight in this New England barn filled with country antiques, furniture, paintings, rugs, lamps plus all sorts of accessories. An ell connected to the barn extends the wonderful selection to include porcelain, glassware, silver, toys up to and beyond "you-name-it."

**A Scarborough Fair Antiques**
264 U.S. Route 1
207/883-5999

**Top Knotch**
14 Willowdale Road
207/883-5303

**Cliff's Antique Market**
RR 1
207/883-5671

## 28 SEARSPORT

**Pumpkin Patch Antiques**
15 W. Main St./Route 1
207/548-6047

**Red Kettle Antiques**
RR 1
207/548-2978

**Searsport Antique Mall**
RR 1
207/548-2640

### *Great Places To Stay*

**Brass Lantern Inn**
81 W. Main St.
1-800-691-0150

Sunlight pours through the windows of this beautiful Sea Captain's home nestled at the edge of the woods on a rise overlooking Penobscot Bay. The inn is furnished with a combination of antiques, reproductions and contemporary furniture. Ornate woodwork, marble fireplaces and tin ceilings enhance the inn's ambiance. Guests awake to the smell of freshly ground coffee and homemade bread or muffins. A full gourmet breakfast is served in the formal dining room. Blueberry pancakes and maple syrup are one of the favorites.

**Old Glory Inn**
Route 1 (89 W. Main St.)
207/548-6232

Old Glory Inn, a Colonial sea captain's home was built prior to 1830 on land acquired by the Gilmore family in 1784. Constructed of brick and set on two acres, the inn is a fine example of New England architecture. The 'Captain's Suite' plus two additional guestrooms, each with a private bath, allow you to enjoy the beach. Breakfast is included and served in the keeping room. Country antiques and artist made Santas are available in the shop on the premises.

### Watchtide "B&B by the Sea"

190 W. Main St.
1-800-698-6575
Web site: www.agate.net/~watchtyd/watchtide.html

This circa 1795 Early-American New England Cape home is situated on three and a half ocean side acres with a magnificent seascape of Penobscot Bay. Once owned by General Henry Knox, this home has hosted many Presidential wives and was often frequented by Eleanor Roosevelt. A fan which belonged to Mary Todd Lincoln is one, of many, of the collections of this estate. Angels to Antiques gift shoppe is located in the adjacent barn with guest discounts.

## 29 SOUTH PORTLAND

**Mulberry Cottage**
45 Western Ave.
207/775-5011

**G L Smith Antiques Art Collectibles**
378 Cottage Road
207/799-5253

**Brass House Antiques**
580 Main St.
207/773-7662

## 30 THOMASTON

Located on the St. George River is Thomaston, once an important port and home to many prominent sea captains. Beautiful homes still exist to mark the rich heritage of the town. General Henry Knox, chief-of-staff and Secretary of War for President George Washington, once resided in Thomaston. Today a replica of his mansion, Montpelier, offers visitors a chance to see the home as it was in the days when it housed the General's family.

### David C. Morey American Antiques

103 Main St.
207/354-6033 or 207/372-6660
Wed., Fri. & Sat., 10-5 or by appointment anytime

Honoring the American craftsmen, David C. Morey Antiques presents 18th century American country furnishings and accessories in this 2,000 square foot shop.

**Wee Barn Antiques**
4 1/2 Georges St.
207/354-6163

**Ross Levett Antiques**
111 Main St.
207/354-6227

**Anchor Farm Antiques**
184 Main St.
207/354-8859

**The Rose Cottage**
187 Main St.
207/354-6250

## 31 TOPSHAM

**Red Schoolhouse Antiques**
8 Middlesex Road
207/729-4541

**Affordable Antiques**
49 Topsham Fair Mall, #21
207/729-7913

**Lisbon Road Antiques**
1089 Lewiston Road
207/353-4094

## 32 WELLS

### Reed's Antiques & Collectibles

U.S. Route 1
207/646-8010, 1-800-891-2017
Daily 10-5
*Directions: Exit 2, ME Turnpike, Left on Route 1*

In two short years Reed's has become known as the number one multi-dealer shop in Maine for quality antiques and collectibles. Open year round, seven days a week, this customer-friendly store has merchandise ranging from Meissen to Mickey Mouse, Sevres to Star Wars, Neo-lithic artifacts to Nouveau art. Whether you are shopping for a personal treasure, a choice resale item or a special gift, you're sure to find it at Reed's. Come join the thousands of other satisfied customers from all over the world who have made Reed's their must stop shop. When a Maine native says "This is the best shop in New England" they must be doing it right!

### MacDougall-Gionet Antiques & Associates

U.S. Route One; 2104 Post Road
207/646-3531
Daily 9-5, closed Mon.

Known as New England's most exciting period antiques center, MacDougall-Gionet's sixty quality dealers pack the barn full of names such as Hepplewhite, Chippendale and Sheraton. Here you will find items such as camphorwood chests, tavern tables, Pennsylvania dower chest in original salmon and smoked paint, an original mustard and stenciled dressing table, a turquoise inlaid secretary desk and the list goes on. Stop in and see for yourself the marvelous inventory of fine antiques.

**Farm**
294 Mildram Road
207/985-2656

**R Jorgensen Antiques**
502 Post Road, Route #1
207/646-9444

**Bomar Hall Antiques & Collectibles**
1622 Post Road
207/646-4116

**Art Smith Antiques**
1755 Post Road
207/646-6996

**Peggy Carboni Antiques**
1755 Post Road
207/646-4551

**Smith-Zukas**
1755 Post Road
207/646-6996

**Wells Antique Mart**
RR 1
207/646-8153

**Country Mouse D & A**
2077 Sanford Road
207/646-7334

**Wells Union Antique. Center**
1755 Post Road
207/646-6996

**R. Sherwood Antiques**
1755 Post Road
207/646-2445

**Eastmoor Antiques**
1823 Post Road
207/646-2663

## 33 WINDHAM

**Barn**
71 Route 115
207/892-9776

**Smokey's Den Antiques**
133 Roosevelt Trail
207/892-6775

## 34 WISCASSET

Wiscasset is an inspiring community for artists and writers, as well as shoppers and sightseers. Located on the west bank of the Sheepscot River at the western edge of Lincoln County, the town's attractions include two decaying four-masted schooners which were beached along the banks of the Sheepscot in 1932. Luther Little and Hester, as they are called, were built during World War I and saw active service during the 1920s as cargo vessels.

Other points of interest in this charming town are the distinguished and stately mansions which used to belong to sea captains and shipping merchants. Several of these are open to the public during the summer months. Scenic boat rides and train trips leave from the waterfront area to provide unique views of coastal wildlife and marvelous views.

### Parkers of Wiscasset Antiques

Coastal Route One
207/882-5520
North and South Buildings open April-December
Seven days a week 9-5; after Columbus day, 10-4

A dream come true; two buildings filled to overflowing with anything you might desire in the antique line. At Parkers of Wiscasset Antiques, you will find folk art, toys, early pottery, Quimper, country and primitives, furniture, quilts and rugs, paintings, Indian jewelry as well as the unusual; Irish lace baby bonnet, 18th century iron toaster, early brass trivet and human hair art in a frame are just a few of the recent offerings. If you're looking for the ordinary as well as the unique, we recommend you visit Parkers of Wiscasset Antiques.

**Marston House American Antiques**
Main St.
207/882-6010

**Patricia Stauble**
Main St.
207/882-6341

**Two at Wiscasset**
Main St.
207/882-5286

**Nonesuch House Antiques.**
1 Middle St.
207/882-6768

**Maine Antiques**
RR 1
207/882-7347

**Maine Trading Post**
RR 1
207/882-7400

**Wiscasset Bay Gallery**
Water St.
207/882-7682

## 35 YORK

### York Antiques Gallery

Route 1
207/363-5002
Daily 10-5 year round
*Directions: Easy access from I-95, just 9/10 of a mile north from the Yorks, Ogunquit Exit (last exit before toll).*

Intrigue and artistry are the hallmarks of the collection found at York Antique Gallery. Showcased in this multiple dealer shop are 18th and 19th century country and formal furniture in addition to accessories. Shoppers will also discover a surprising assortment of other goods including textiles, paintings/prints, nautical items, decoys/hunting, advertising, folk art, Indian, military/fire, as well as out of print reference books.

### Marie Plummer & John Philbrick

44 Chases Pond Road
207/363-2515

Offerings of exceptional quality and a unique display of early antiques, makes this shop grandly unique. Just a sampling of the superior items available are: c. 1780 New England pine pipe box, an 18th century Westwald jug, and an 18th century New England maple rope bed.

**Barn at Cape Neddick Antiques**
RR 1
207/363-7315

**Bell Farm Antiques**
RR 1
207/363-8181

**Maritime Antiques**
935 U.S. Route 1
207/363-4247

**Olde Stuff Shop**
RR 1
207/363-4517

**York Village Crafts Antiques & Gifts**
211 York St.
207/363-4830

# Maryland/D.C.

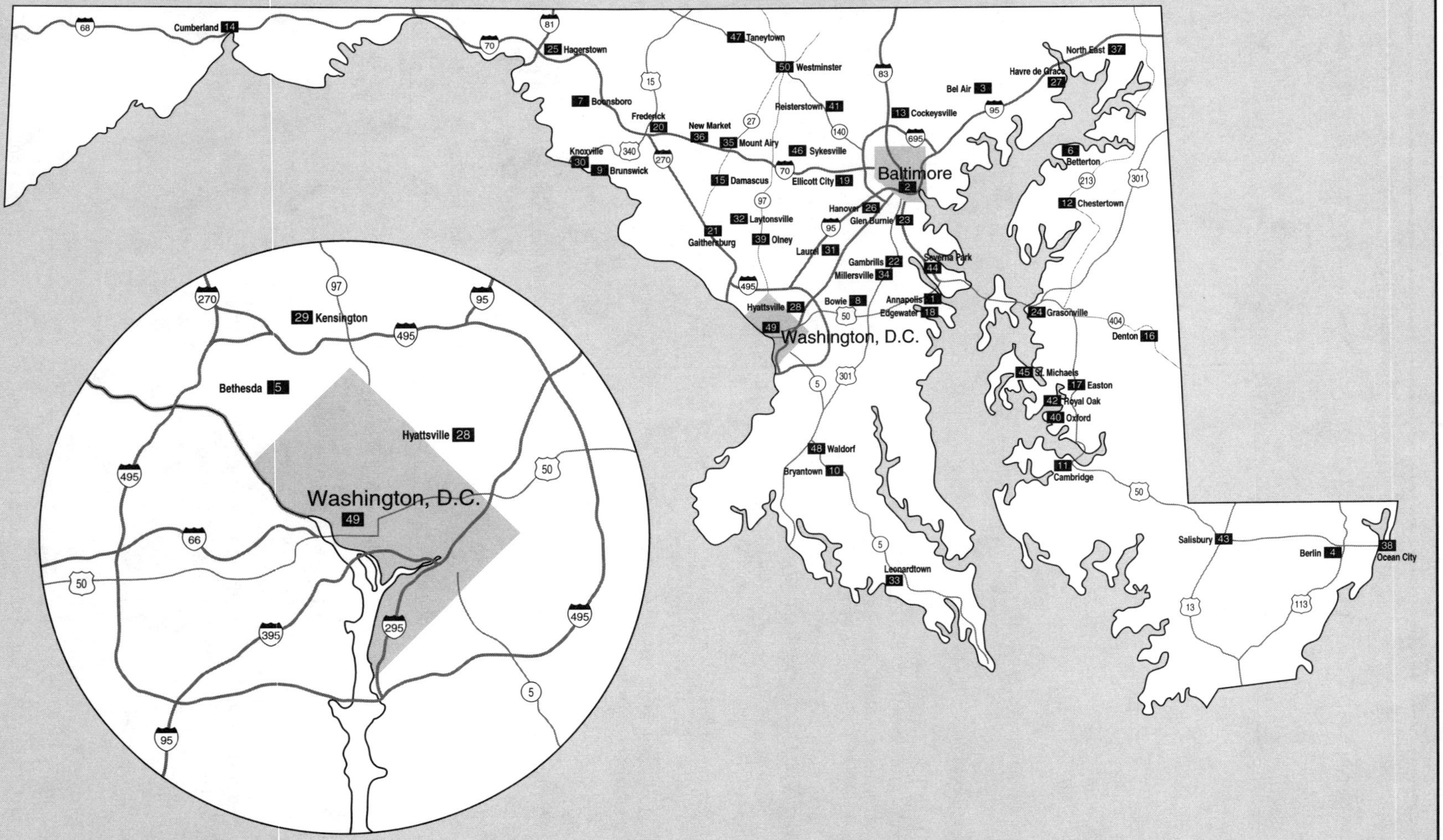
Cumberland 14
25 Hagerstown
47 Taneytown
50 Westminster
7 Boonsboro
Frederick 20
New Market 36
35 Mount Airy
Reisterstown 41
46 Sykesville
13 Cockeysville
Bel Air 3
Havre de Grace 27
North East 37
6 Betterton
12 Chestertown
Knoxville 30
9 Brunswick
15 Damascus
Ellicott City 19
Baltimore 2
32 Laytonsville
39 Olney
21 Gaithersburg
Hanover 26
Glen Burnie 23
Laurel 31
Gambrills 22
Millersville 34
Severna Park 44
Annapolis 1
Edgewater 18
Bowie 8
Hyattsville 28
49 Washington, D.C.
24 Grasonville
Denton 16
45 St. Michaels
17 Easton
42 Royal Oak
40 Oxford
11 Cambridge
48 Waldorf
Bryantown 10
Leonardtown 33
Salisbury 43
Berlin 4
38 Ocean City
29 Kensington
Bethesda 5
Hyattsville 28
Washington, D.C. 49

# Making a Difference

## Timothy Albrecht
## Grapevine of Bethesda

Timothy Albrecht has always had a personal interest in antiques and tableware. He can remember collecting at the age of 10. Tim applied for a position at the Grapevine at the age of 16 and was turned down. Today, he owns the store now known as the Grapevine of Bethesda.

The Grapevine of Bethesda consigns and sells antiques, Persian rugs, and oil paintings. The store specializes in French and Continental furniture pieces as well as tableware. Most merchandise at the Grapevine of Bethesda is dated between 1850 and 1920. You can find anything from place plates to finger bowls at the Grapevine. You can find most place settings of 12 and the shop carries English and Continental porcelain. Beautiful oil paintings can also be bought or consigned here. Many of these paintings can be researched for history or has a auction trail.

The Grapevine has been in existence for fifty years. Past owners had impeccable qualities of honesty and fairness which traits are carried on today. First owned by Linda Gore, a very distant relative of Al Gore, the shop was located on Brookville Road and then moved to Bethesda. Ms. Gore owned the business for 23 years before selling to the second owner, Mrs. Grant. Timothy Albrecht is the third owner and has operated this highly reputable business for three years.

This unique shop is located on the corner of Wilson Road and Old Georgetown Road in the heart of Bethesda. There is a store front window with an entrance at each street side. Cafe Bethesda, a French cooking school, is located next door (and is known as one of the best 50 restaurants in Washington, D.C.)

Most of The Grapevine's clientele are individuals interest in fine art or spend a lot of time entertaining. Diplomats, high society, and world travelers often shop at this reputable antique store. Many of The Grapevine's clientele bring pieces for consignment due to liquidation or the accumulation of fine pieces acquired from a heritage.

The Grapevine of Bethesda is a member of ADAM, Maryland Antique Association, an affiliate of Maryland Retail Association. Benefits of membership with the association, says Mr. Albrecht, are the "opportunities to share notes with other antique dealers and members, and the advantage of buying pieces among themselves."

Approximately every two months, the Grapevine of Bethesda hosts a workshop called "The Art of Entertaining." Clients are invited to listen to knowledgeable speakers talk on subjects such as Russian porcelain, English porcelain or style and tableware.

Mr. Albrecht's future goal for his antique business is to fine tune his collection and services; learn more about his fine collectibles; and to continue to look for quality merchandise and fine pieces that his clientele are searching for. His long term goal is to become a professional appraiser. He is currently attending appraisal school.

*Antiquers will find a dizzying array of seemingly limitless choices of fine antiques and furnishings at the Grapevine of Bethesda.*

When asked what he enjoys most about his business, Mr. Albrecht says "the interesting people . . most of whom are mature, well traveled individuals who often have tales to tell of their travels and the pieces they bring in for consignment." Mr. Albrecht says "Washington is a wonderful city, offering a large variety of collectibles and antiques."

Timothy Albrecht loves history and is a collector himself. His interest and love for collecting is reflective in the fine quality pieces his store offers. The Grapevine of Bethesda's hours of operation are Tuesday through Saturday, 10 a.m.-5 p.m.

*The Grapevine of Bethesda is located at 7806 Old Georgetown Road, Bethesda, MD 20814; for additional information call the shopkeeper at 301/654-8690.*

## 1 ANNAPOLIS

Founded in 1649, Annapolis is often referred to as a "museum without walls," for the number of historic homes and buildings that have been restored and are open to the public. The city has served as Maryland's State Capitol since 1694, and was the nation's capital from November 1783 to August 1784.

**AA West Annapolis Antiques**
14 Annapolis St.
410/268-8762

**Country Finds**
103 Annapolis St.
410/267-9366

**Clockmaker Shop**
1935 Generals Hwy.
410/266-0770

**Baldwin & Claude Antiques**
47 Maryland Ave.
410/268-1665

**Sixth Street Studio**
422 6th St.
410/267-8233

**Third Millennium Designs**
57 Maryland Ave.
410/267-6428

**Walnut Leaf Antiques**
62 Maryland Ave.
410/263-4885

**Maryland Ave. Antiques**
82 Maryland Ave.
410/268-5158

**DHS Designs Inc.**
86 Maryland Ave.
410/280-3466

**Annapolis Antique Gallery**
2009 West St.
410/266-0635

**Ron Snyder Antiques**
2011 West St.
410/266-5452

### *Great Places To Stay*

**The Gatehouse Bed & Breakfast**
249 Hanover St.
410/280-0024

Overlooking the U.S. Naval Academy in Annapolis, the Gatehouse Bed & Breakfast is a towering, three story Georgian home, offering elegant accommodations. The Gatehouse provides five luxuriously appointed guest rooms: four with queen sized beds and private baths, and one with double bed and shared bath. Fresh flowers, bath amenities, and down-soft robes are provided in each room. Full breakfast is served daily.

**Jonas Green House B&B**
124 Charles St.
410/263-5892
Web site: www.bbhost.com/ighouse

This charming old home, dating from the 1690s and early 1700s, is one of Annapolis' two oldest residences. It was the home of Jonas Green and his wife, Anne Catherine Greene. Jonas was a colonial printer and patriot, from 1738 until his death in 1775. The home has been continuously occupied by their family ever since. The current owners are Jonas' five great-grandsons. Much of the original house fabric survives. It still maintains its original floor, fireplace surrounds, and old cooking fireplace.

## 2 BALTIMORE

A 14-block area in Eastern Baltimore, fronting on the Patapsco River with the deepest harbor in the area, this active post is one of the original communities that joined "Baltimore Town" to become the city of Baltimore. The first settlers came in 1724, and the grid plan was laid out by Edward Fell in 1761. Many of the cobblestone streets retain their English-inspired names, including Thames And Shakespeare. Fells Point's famed shipyards produced the renowned Baltimore clippers used as privateers, along with frigates and sloops used by the Continental Navy. The Broadway Market, along with scores of charming antiques shops and restaurants, still welcomes visitors from foreign lands—as well as locals intent on shopping or dining.

**Antique Amusements**
**A-1 Jukebox & Nostalgia Co.**
208 S. Pulaski St.
Phone & Fax 410/945-8900
Toll-Free Order Line 1-888-694-9464
Web site: members.aol.com/jukeboxusa/
Mon. - Fri. 10 -5 and some Sat. Closed on Sun. From 5:30 p.m.-8:30 p.m. Mon.-Fri., they offer customers in home service and installation for the items they sell.
*Directions: Located one mile west of Oriole Park at Camden Yards in West Baltimore. From Oriole Park take Lombard St., (it's one way west), 1 mile to Pulaski St. and turn left 1 1/2 blocks, on the right side. From I-95 northbound or southbound take Exit #50 north to Wilkens Ave. and turn right. At the 5th traffic light turn left onto S. Pulaski St. 2 blocks north on the left side.*

Antique Amusements A-1 Jukebox & Nostalgia Company has been in business for eighteen years selling and servicing jukeboxes. If you have a jukebox to sell they also buy jukeboxes. They will even rent a jukebox to you for your next party or company event. Their jukebox inventory consists of New Compact Disc Wurlitzer jukeboxes and Original Seeburg jukeboxes from the '50s, '60s, and '70s. It's important to know that more 45 R.P.M. records, (the 7 inch singles with the big hole), are currently being made now than at any time in the past and that's because so many folks are purchasing new Wurlitzer and original jukeboxes for their homes and businesses. Their $4.95 "Singles" Record Catalog lists ten thousand 45 R.P.M. records, and on any given order they can supply at least an 80% fill. They carry many replacement parts for Wurlitzer and Seeburg jukeboxes and all of the repair and parts manuals including schematics for: Rock-Ola; Rowe/Ami; Seeburg; and Wurlitzer jukeboxes. They also carry a complete line of classic style diner booths, chairs, stools, and tables. Some of the most unique items include: Edison Cylinder Machines from the turn of the last century, (they actually reproduce sound by playing a wax cylinder); reproduction barber poles which light-up and have a rotating pole, (made of glass and metal just like the originals); reproduction metal signs, (very limited production), mostly soft drink signs, some with thermometers; and a line of stained glass hanging light fixtures, (top quality). Antiques Amusements A-1 Jukebox & Nostalgia Company currently occupies 5,000 sq. ft. of space in a five story brick building known as the Cambridge Building. They are planning to move the entire business operation to Howard County, Maryland during 1998.

If you would like to see color pictures of their unique and beautiful items, please visit their Web Site at: http://members.aol.com/jukeboxusa/. The Web Site has taken the place of the old catalog, which they no longer use. Domestic and World Wide Shipping is available. Visa, Mastercard, and Personal Checks in U.S. Dollars are accepted.

**The Karmic Connection**
508 W. Broadway
410/558-0428

**Along The Way, Ltd.**
1719 Aliceanna St.
410/276-4461

**Saratoga Trunk**
1740 Aliceanna St.
410/327-6635

**Portebello Square Inc.**
28 Allegheny Ave.
410/821-1163

**Memory Lane Antiques**
607 S. Broadway
410/276-0865

**Oh! Susanna**
620 S. Broadway
410/327-1408

**A Squirrel's Nest**
313 Eastern Blvd.
410/391-3664

**Modest Rupert's Attic**
919 S Charles St.
410/727-4505

**Olde Touch**
2103 N. Charles St.
410/783-1493

**Thompson's Antiques**
430 Eastern Blvd. (Essex)
410/686-3107

**Reginald Fitzgerald Antiques**
1704 Eastern Blvd.
410/534-2942

**Constance**
1709 Aliceanna St.
410/563-6031

**Auntie Qs**
1721 Aliceanna St.
410/276-7660

**Velveteen Rabbit**
20 Allegheny Ave.
410/583-1685

**Collectors Item**
4903 Belair Road
410/483-2020

**Off Broadway Antiques**
614 S. Broadway
410/732-6522

**Hattie's Antiques & Collectibles**
726 S. Broadway
410/276-1316

**Craig Flinner Gallery**
505 N. Charles St.
410/727-1863

**Silver Mine**
1023 N. Charles St.
410/752-4141

**Sabina & Daughter**
1637 Eastern Ave.
410/276-6366

**Ramm Antiques & Collectibles**
811 Eastern Blvd.
410/687-5284

**John's Art & Antiques**
1733 Eastern Blvd.
410/675-4339

**Sunporch Antiques**
6072 Falls Road
410/377-2904

**American Pie**
1704 Fleet St.
410/276-0062

**Davids-Gans Co., Inc.**
910 W. 36th St.
410/467-8159

**R & H Antiques**
1720 Fleet St.
410/522-1621

**Antique Man**
1731 Fleet St.
410/732-0932

**Angela R. Thrasher Antiques**
833 N. Howard St.
410/523-0550

**Three Rag Picker Collection**
5722 Harford Road
410/254-0033

**DJ's Antiques & Collectibles**
7914 Harford Road
410/665-4344

**Hamilton House Antiques**
865 N. Howard St.
410/462-5218

**Cross Keys Antiques**
801 N. Howard St.
410/728-0101

**Dubeys Art & Antiques**
807 N. Howard St.
410/383-2881

**Fisher Interiors P G**
817 N. Howard St.
410/669-9292

**Heritage Antiques**
829 N. Howard St.
410/728-7033

**E A Mack Antiques. Inc.**
839 N. Howard St.
410/728-1333

**Wintzer Galleries**
853 N. Howard St.
410/462-3313

**Sindler Fine Arts & Antiques**
809 Howard St.
410/728-3377

**Antique Toy & Train World**
3626 Falls Road
410/889-0040

**J & M Antiques**
1706 Fleet St.
410/732-2919

**The Bowery of Antiques**
1709 Fleet St.
410/732-2778

**Mystery Loves Company**
1730 Fleet St.
410/276-6708

**In The Groove Antiques**
1734 Fleet St.
410/675-7174

**Old Treasure Chest**
3409 Greenmount Ave.
410/889-0540

**Valley Gun**
7719 Harford Road
410/668-2171

**Dusty Attic**
9411 Harford Road
410/668-2343

**Gaines McHale Antiques**
836 Leandenhall St.
410/625-1900

**Antiques at 805**
805 N. Howard St.
410/728-8419

**Antique Treasury**
809 N. Howard St.
410/728-6363

**Thaynes Antiques**
823 N. Howard St.
410/728-7109

**Imperial Half Bushel**
831 N. Howard St.
410/462-1192

**Amos Judd & Son Inc.**
841-843 N. Howard St.
410/462-2000

**Drusilla's Books**
859 Howard St.
410/225-0277

**Yakov's Antiques**
861 N. Howard St.
410/728-4517

**Connoisseurs Connection**
869 N. Howard St.
410/383-2624

**L A Herstein & Co.**
877 N. Howard St.
410/728-3856

**Antique Warehouse at 1300**
1300 Jackson St.
410/659-0663

**Collectiques**
1806 Maryland Ave.
410/539-3474

**French Accents**
3600 Roland Ave.
410/467-8957

**A & M Antique & Modern Jewelry**
708 N. Rolling Road
410/788-7000

**Heirloom Jewels**
5100 Falls Road, # 14
410/323-0100

**Antique Exchange Inc.**
318 Wyndhurst Ave.
410/532-7000

**Consignment Galleries Inc.**
6711 York Road
410/377-3067

**Keepers Antiques**
222 W. Read St.
410/783-0330

**Christie's Fine Art**
100 W. Road, #310
410/832-7555

**Early Attic Furniture**
415 E. 32nd St.
410/889-0122

**Harris Auction Galleries Inc.**
875 N. Howard St.
410/728-7040

**Regency Antiques**
893 N. Howard St.
410/225-3455

**Antique Furniture Co.**
3524 Keswick Road
410/366-2421

**Nostalgia Too**
7302 N. Point Road
410/477-8440

**Turnover Shop Inc.**
3547 Chestnut Ave.
410/366-2988

**Grrreat Bears**
1643 Thames
410/276-4429

**Mel's Antiques**
712 S. Wolfe St.
410/675-7229

**Alex Cooper Oriental Rugs**
908 York Road
410/828-4838

**Michaels Rug Gallery**
415 E. 33rd St.
410/366-1515

**Another Period in Time**
1708 Fleet St.
410/675-4776

**Cuomo's Antiques & Interiors**
871 N. Howard St.
410/383-9195

**Mt. Vernon Antique Flea Market**
226 W. Monument St.
410/523-6493

**Shirley Balser 16-20th Century Paintings, Prints & Books**
By Appointment Only
410/484-0880

### *Great Places To Stay*

**Gramercy Mansion Bed & Breakfast**
1400 Greenspring Valley Road
1-800-553-3404
Web site: www.angelfire.com/md/gramercy/

Gramercy, a majestic Tudor style mansion and estate, situated on 45 acres in Maryland's Greenspring Valley, provides an Olympic size pool, tennis court, extensive woodland trails, Honeybrook Stream, a working organic farm, and classic flower gardens. In addition to five spacious public rooms with fireplace, the mansion offers antiques, oriental carpets, artwork, high ceilings, a stunning grand staircase, chandeliers and a serene outdoor terrace. Railroad magnate, Alexander Cassatt, brother of Impressionist painter Mary Cassatt, presented this historic house as a wedding present to his daughter. Later occupants included the Brewster family, descendants of Benjamin Franklin, and the Koinonia Foundation, a predecessor of the Peace Corps. The Carriage House and Gramercy Mansion are also available for weddings, meetings, seminars and parties.

**Betsy's Bed & Breakfast**
1428 Park Ave.
410/383-1274

An elegant home in the architecturally significant downtown neighborhood of Bolton Hill, this four story 'petite estate' overlooks a quiet tree-lined street with a brass rail and white marble steps. Inside you will marvel at the high ceilings with medallions, carved marble mantels, a center staircase that rises to a skylight. Throughout the house, the expansive walls are hung with handsome brass rubbings, family heirloom quilts and coverlets.

## 3 BEL AIR

**Country Schoolhouse Antiques**
1805 E. Churchville Road
410/836-9225

**Antiques Bazaar**
117 N. Main St.
410/836-7872

**Oak Spring Antiques**
1321 Prospect Mill Road
410/879-0942

**Back Door Antiques**
106 N. Main St.
410/836-8608

**Bel Air Antiques Etc.**
122 N. Main St.
410/838-3515

## 4 BERLIN

**Something Different**
2 S. Main St.
410/641-1152

**Sassafrass Station**
111 N. Main St.
410/641-0979

**Findings**
104 Pitts St.
410/641-2666

**Brass Box**
27 N. Main St.
410/641-1858

**Stuarts Antiques**
5 Pitts St.
410/641-0435

## 5 BETHESDA

### Grapevine of Bethesda
7806 Old Georgetown Road
301/654-8690
Tues.-Sat., 10-5
*Directions: Located in downtown Bethesda at the intersection of Old Georgetown Road/Wilson Lane, Arlington and St. Elmo. Store has Georgetown Road entrance and Wilson Lane parking.*

For specific information see review at the beginning of this section.

**Cordell Collection Furniture**
4922 Cordell Ave.
301/907-3324

## 6 BETTERTON

***Great Places To Stay***

### Lantern Inn
115 Ericsson Ave.
410/348-5809
Open year round
*Directions: Off of Maryland 213 between Chestertown and Galena. Turn north on Still Pond Road (Maryland 292) to Betterton's Beach. Left 2 blocks to inn.*

The inn was constructed in 1904 and is located in a small Victorian resort town. Thirteen guest rooms reflect the heyday of Betterton when excursion boats brought vacationers from Baltimore and Philadelphia. A large front porch offers relaxation in the beautiful surroundings. The inn is conveniently located near Dixon's Furniture Auction and many fine antique shops.

## 7 BOONSBORO

**Fitz Place**
7 N. Main St.
301/432-2919

**Antique Partners**
23 S. Main St.
301/432-2518

**Auction Square Antiques & Collectibles**
7700 Old National Pike
301/416-2490

## 8 BOWIE

**Bets Antiques & Uniques**
8519 Chestnut Ave.
301/464-1122

**Fabian House**
8519 Chestnut Ave.
301/464-6777

**House of Hegedus**
8521 Chestnut Ave.
301/262-4131

**Welcome House**
8604 Chestnut Ave.
301/262-9844

**Keller's Antiques**
8606 Chestnut Ave.
301/805-9593

**Olde Friends & Memories**
13006 9th St.
301/464-2890

**Treasure House Antiques**
13010 9th St.
301/262-2878

## 9 BRUNSWICK

**Antiques N Ole Stuff**
2 E. Potomac
301/834-6795

**Jimmy Jakes Antique Center**
24 W. Potomac St.
301/8334-6814

## 10 BRYANTOWN

***Great Places To Stay***

### Shady Oaks of Serenity Bed and Breakfast
7490 Serenity Dr.
1-800-597-0924, 301/932-8864
Open year round
*Directions: For specific directions to Shady Oaks of Serenity, please call the Innkeeper who will provide specific directions from your location.*

Shady Oaks of Serenity is a Georgia Colonial Victorian situated on three acres and surrounded by trees. This secluded home is off the beaten path, yet within a 45 minute drive of the nation's capitol and Annapolis, Md., home of the U.S. Navel Academy. Just down the road is the Amish country with antiques and unique shops, several historic churches, the renowned Dr. Mudd Home and Gilbert Run Park, a favorite county stop. Also, this retreat may be of interest to small groups of 25 or less for meetings.

Decorated with various themes, each room has a private bath and king size bed for a peaceful night's rest. Visitors are welcome to gather in the family room, the front porch or enjoy an evening on the deck. Kathy and Gene cordially invite you to be a guest in their home and visit their historic county. The morning brings fresh coffee, homemade muffins or breads and a variety of fresh fruit.

## 11 CAMBRIDGE

Established in 1684 as a port on the Choptank River, Cambridge has a rich history as a ship building center, mill town, Civil War "underground railroad" stop, and internationally known packing and canning center. The historic district reflects the commercial and economic history of the town, with fascinating 18th and 19th century Georgian and Federal buildings clustered in the 100 and 200 blocks of High Street. Large mansion houses are located on Mill, Oakley and Locust Streets (many in the Queen Anne and Colonial Revival styles), while rhythmic rows of modest gable-front homes dating from the turn of the century are found along Vue de L'eau, West End, Willis and Choptank Streets. Skipjacks and other sailing vessels are often seen on scenic Cambridge Creek.

**Heirloom Antique Gallery**
419 Academy St.
410/228-8445

**Packing House Antique Mall**
411 Dorchester Ave.
410/221-8544

**Bay Country Antique Co-op**
415 Dorchester Ave.
410/228-3112

**Jones Antiques**
518 High St.
410/228-1752

**A J's Antiques Mall**
2923 Ocean Gateway
410/221-1505

**Artwells Mall**
509 Race St.
410/228-0997

**Another Man's Treasure**
114 Belvedere Ave.
410/228-4525

## 12 CHESTERTOWN

The county seat of Kent County was created in 1706 and designated as one of Maryland's official ports in 1707. This river town had grown elegant, prosperous and daring by the 1770s. Residents angry over the Boston Port Act staged their own tea party—in broad daylight—against the British brigantine Geddes in 1774. This daring event is re-enacted each June as the Chestertown Tea Party. Chestertown is a wonderful place to explore on foot, and visitors may stroll past Federal town houses, Georgian mansions, a stone house supposedly constructed from a ship's ballast and many fine antiques and specialty shops. Chestertown is also home to Washington College, which was chartered in 1782 and named after George Washington with his expressed consent.

**Crosspatch**
107 S. Cross St.
410/778-3253

**Red Shutters**
337 High St.
410/778-6434

**Seed House Gallery**
860 High St.
410/778-2080

**Childrens Exchange**
306 Park Row
410/778-1467

**Chestertown Antique & Furn. Ctr.**
6612 Churchill Road (Route 213)
410/778-5777

### *Great Places To Stay*

### Brampton
25227 Chestertown Road
410/778-1860
Email: brampton@friend.ly.net

The Brampton Bed & Breakfast is one of the finest inns on Maryland's Eastern Shore. Built in 1860 as a plantation house, Brampton still retains nearly all of its original details. The thirty-five acres of grounds that surround Brampton with century old trees and boxwood plantings provide a quiet, pastoral setting for a peaceful escape. The historic bed & breakfast inn is tucked between the Chester Ricer and The Chesapeake Bay, just one mile south of historic Chestertown. You can pass the time antiquing, shopping, bird watching, crabbing, hunting, fishing and horseback riding, or just relax on one of the front porch swings. All rooms are spacious and well appointed with beautiful period furnishings.

### Inn At Mitchell House
8796 Maryland Pkwy.
410/778-6500

Nestled on ten rolling acres, surrounded by woods and overlooking 'Stoneybrook Pond', this historic manor house, built in 1743, greets you with warmth and affords a touch of tranquility. The five bedroom inn with parlors and numerous fireplaces provides a casual and friendly atmosphere. Depending upon the season, you may be awakened in the morning by birdsong or migrating geese. At sunset, sighting white-tailed deer, red fox, or a glimpse of a soaring eagle add to the scene.

### Lauretum Inn
954 High St.
1-800-742-3236

Lauretum Inn sits atop a tree graced knoll on six acres in Chestertown. A long winding lane invites you to the inn and reveals a stunning example of nineteenth century Queen Anne Victorian architecture. The original owner, U.S. Senator George Vickers (1801-1879), lovingly built this gracious country manor and called it 'Lauretum Place.' Lauretum features a delightful screened-in porch, charming rooms, fireplaces, and the pleasant company of other guests.

## 13 COCKEYSVILLE

**Cuomo's Interiors & Antiques**
10759 York Road
410/628-0422

**Abundant Treasures Gallery**
10818 York Road
410/666-9797

**Pack Rat**
10834 York Road
410/683-4812

**Hunt Valley Antiques**
10844 York Road
410/628-6869

**Bentley's Antiques Show Mart**
10854 York Road
410/667-9184

**Alley Shoppes**
10856 York Road
410/683-0421

**Decorative Touch**
11008 York Road
410/527-1075

**Corner Cottage Antiques**
11010 York Road
410/527-9535

**Kendall's Antique Shop**
3417 Sweet Air Road
410/667-9235

## 14 CUMBERLAND

**Historic Cumberland Antique Mall**
55 Baltimore St.
301/777-2979

**Yesteryear**
62 Baltimore St.
301/722-7531

**Ye Olde Shoppe**
315 Virginia Ave.
301/724-3537

**Auntie's Antiques & Collectibles**
328 Virginia Ave.
301/724-3729

**Goodwood Old & Antique Furniture**
329 Virginia Ave.
301/777-0422

**Queen City Collectibles**
28 N. Centre St.
301/724-7392

## 15 DAMASCUS

**Appleby's Antiques**
24219 Ridge Road
301/253-6980

**Flo's Antiques**
28314 Kemptown Road
301/253-3752

**Bea's Antiques**
24140 Ridge Road
301/253-6030

## 16 DENTON

**Attic Antiques & Collectibles Mall**
24241 Shore Hwy.
410/479-1889

**Denton Antique Mall**
24690 Meeting House Road
410/479-2200

## 17 EASTON

**Windsor Gallery**
21 Goldsborough St.
410/820-5246

**Wye River Antiques**
23 N. Harrison St.
410/822-3449

**Camelot Antiques Ltd.**
7871 Ocean Gateway (Route 50)
410/820-4396

**Sullivan's Antique Warehouse**
28272 Saint Michaels Road
410/822-4723

**Delmarva Jewelers**
210 Marlboro Ave.
410/822-5398

**Foxwell's Antiques & Collectibles**
7793 Ocean Gateway (Route 50)
410/820-9705

**Stock Exch. Antique & Consignment Mall**
8370 Ocean Gateway (Route 50)
410/820-0014

**American Pennyroyal**
5 N. Harrison St.
410/822-5030

**Chesapeake Antique Center-The Gallery**
29 S. Harrison St.
410/822-5000

**Easton Maritime Antiques**
27 S. Harrison St.
410/763-8853

**Picket Fence Antiques**
218 N. Washington St.
410/822-3010

**Kathe & Company**
20 S. Harrison St.
410/820-9153

**Lanham Merida Antiques & Interiors**
218 N. Washington St.
410/763-8500

**Antique Center of Easton**
Ocean Gateway (Route 50)
410/820-5209

**Oxford Antiques & Art Gallery**
21-A N. Harrison St.
410/820-0587

**Tabot Antiques**
218 N. Washington St.
410/476-5247

**Tharpe House Antiques and Decor. Arts**
30 S. Washington St.
410/820-7525

**The Flo-Mir**
23 E. Dover St.
410/822-2857

**Wings Antiques**
7 N. Harrison St.
410/822-2334

### *Great Places To Stay*

**Ashby 1663**
27448 Ashby Dr.
410/822-4235

Situated on an eastern shore peninsula, Ashby 1663 defines tranquility. The 23 acre waterfront estate features crape myrtle, magnolia, oak and tulip trees. Guest are greeted by sounds of nature including bobwhites, mocking birds and waterfowl. Each of the guest rooms include a private bath and may feature a fireplace, whirlpool tub or deck. A full breakfast, evening cocktails and use of the lighted tennis court, heated pool, exercise room, canoe and paddle boat are complimentary.

**Gross' Coate Plantation 1658**
11300 Gross Coate Road
1-800-580-0802

Built in 1760 by William Tilghman, Gross' Coate is a unique part of American history. A fine example of Georgian architecture it is extremely romantic, comfortable, and extraordinarily beautiful. The historic mansion and its dependencies, framed by emerald lawns and immense trees, beckon guests to 18th century plantation life at its finest. The plantation is located along the scenic banks of the Wye River as it converges with Gross' Creek and Lloyd Creek.

## 18 EDGEWATER

**Rafters Antique Mini-Mall**
1185 Mayo Road
410/798-1204

**Londontown Antiques**
1205 Mayo Road
410/698-6192

## 19 ELLICOTT CITY

Unique and well-preserved, this 19th-century mill town on the Patapsco River has sloping streets and sturdy granite buildings reminiscent of English industrial towns. Ellicott City was a summer destination for Baltimore residents and notable visitors who came by train, including Robert E. Lee and H. L. Mencken. Antiques shops, specialty boutiques and restaurants are abundant in this small town.

**American Military Antiques**
8398 Court Ave.
410/465-6827

**Antique Depot**
3720 Maryland Ave.
410/750-2674

**Halls Antiques & Collectibles**
8026 Main St.
410/418-9444

**A Caplans Antiques**
8125 Main St.
410/750-7678

**Cottage Antiques**
8181 Main St.
410/465-1412

**Catonsville Village Antiques**
787 Oella Ave.
410/461-1535

**Rebel Trading Post**
3744 Old Columbia Pike
410/465-9595

**Shops at Ellicott Mills**
8307 Main St.
410/461-8700

**Maxine's Antiques & Collectibles**
8116 Main St.
410/461-5910

**Ellicott's Country Store**
8180 Main St.
410/465-4482

**Historic Framing & Collectibles**
8344 Main St.
410/465-0549

**Oella Flea Market**
787 Oella Ave.
410/461-1535

**Wagon Wheel Antique Shop**
8061 Tiber Aly
410/465-7910

## 20 FREDERICK

Antiques hunters and history lovers will find much to enjoy in Frederick. The city had a role in the Revolutionary War, War of 1812 and Civil War. Much of the historic district includes business and residences in and around the original 1745 city grid, with Market St. the north-south axis and Patrick St. the east-west axis. A wealth of commercial, residential, public and religious structures in the architectural styles spanning two centuries contribute to this historic and culturally significant city.

### Off The Deep End

712 East St.
301/698-9006
Mon.-Sat., 10-7; Sun., 10-6
*Directions: *From Washington, D.C.: From I-270 to Maryland Route 15 N., take 7th St. (east) Exit. Proceed to Stop sign at East St. Take a left onto East St. for 1/2 block. The shop is located on the right.*
**From Baltimore: I-70 W. To Route 15 N. Then proceed as above.*
**From Pennsylvania: Maryland Route 15 S. to 7th St. (east) Exit. Then proceed as above.*

With over 3,000 square feet of space, a wide array of antique furniture and accessories are on display. Antique toys, collectibles, vintage clothing, plus intriguing '50s memorabilia and "bizarre" items form a part of this massive collection. You will also want to browse through the over 14,000 old and used books in stock.

**Warehouse Antiques**
47 E. All Saints St.
301/663-4778

**Brass & Copper Shop**
13 S. Carroll St.
301/663-4240

**Cannon Hill Place**
111 S. Carroll St.
301/695-9304

**Gaslight Antiques**
118 E. Church St.
301/663-3717

**Collage Antiques**
7 N. Court St.
301/694-0513

**Eastside Antiques**
221 East St.
301/663-8995

**Antique Galleries**
3 E. Patrick St.
301/631-0922

**J & T Antiques**
29 E. Patrick St.
301/698-1380

**Family S Choice Side Antiques**
Route 15 & Biggs Ford Road
301/898-5547

**Old Glory Antique Market Place**
5862 Urbana Pike
301/662-9173

**Antique Station**
194 Thomas Johnson Dr.
301/695-0888

**Catoctin Inn & Antiques**
3619 Buckeystown Pike
301/831-8102

**The Consignment Warehouse**
35 S. Carroll St.
301/695-9674

**Carroll St. Mercantile**
124 Carroll St.
301/620/4323

**Homeward Bound**
313 E. Church St.
301/631-9094

**Antique Imports**
125 East St.
301/662-6200

**Emporium at Creekside Antiques**
112 E. Patrick St.
301/662-7099

**Carroll Creek Antiques Etc.**
14 E. Patrick St.
301/663-8574

**Craftworks Antiques**
55 E. Patrick St.
301/662-3111

**Flea Factory**
Route 15 & Biggs Ford Road
301/898-5052

**Frederick's Best**
307 E. 2nd St.
301/698-1791

#### *Great Places To Stay*

### The Turning Point Inn

3406 Urbana Pike
301/874-2421 or 301/831-8232
Rates: $75 weekdays, $85 weekends
Open year round

Shaded by four acres of trees and gardens, this exquisite antique-filled bed and breakfast country inn offers a delightful spot for a getaway or special occasion. With five spacious bedrooms having private baths, guests find additional comfort in the large living and dining room. A basket of fruit greets each guest, as well as the full country breakfast. Tuesday-Friday, lunch and dinner is served.

## 21 GAITHERSBURG

**Emporium of Olde Towne**
223 E. Diamond Ave.
301/926-9148

**Old Town Antiques**
223 E. Diamond Ave.
301/926-9490

**Becraft Antiques**
405 S. Frederick Ave.
301/926-3000

**Yesteryear Antique Farms Inc.**
7420 Hawkins Creamery Road
301/948-3979

**Peking Arts Inc.**
7410 Lindbergh Dr.
301/258-8117

**Days of Olde Antiques**
710 State Route 3 Northbound
410/987-0397

**Julia's Room**
9001 A Warfield Road
301/869-1410

**Gate House Antiques**
21125 Woodfield Road
301/869-4480

**Gaitherburg Antiques**
5 N. Summit Ave.
301/670-5870

**Griffith House Antiques**
21415 Laytonsville Road
301/926-4155

## 22 GAMBRILLS

**Holly Hill Antiques**
382 Gambrills Road
410/923-1207

**Days of Olde Antiques**
710 Maryland Route 3 N.
410/987-0397

## 23 GLEN BURNIE

**Rosies Past & Present**
7440 Balt Annapolis Blvd.
410/760-5821

**Curiosity Unlimited Inc**
7450 Balt Annapolis Blvd.
410/768-8697

**Neatest Little Shop**
7462 Balt Annapolis Blvd.
410/760-3610

**Fourth Crane Antiques**
310 Crain Hwy. S.
410/760-9803

## 24 GRASONVILLE

**Going Home Unq Gft Antiques**
3017 Kent Narrow Way S.
410/827-8556

**Dutch Barn Antiques**
3712 Main St.
410/827-8656

**Enchanted Lilly**
4601 Main St.
410/827-5935

**Eastern Bay Trading Co.**
4917 Main St.
410/827-9286

## 25 HAGERSTOWN

**Halfway Antiques & Collectibles**
11000 Bower Ave.
301/582-4971

**Beaver Creek Antique Market**
40 East Ave.
301/739-8075

**Ravenswood Antique Center**
216 W. Franklin St.
301/739-0145

**Country Village of Beaver Creek**
20136 National Pike
301/790-0006

**Antique Crossroads**
20150 National Pike
301/739-0858

**Country Lanes**
326 Summit Ave.
301/790-1045

### *Great Places To Stay*

**Beaver Creek House**
20432 Beaver Creek Road
301/797-4764

Comfort, relaxation, and hospitality await you at this turn-of-the-century country Victorian home, located in the historic area of Beaver Creek, Maryland. Choose from five guest rooms, and enjoy a country breakfast served on the spacious wrap-around screen porch or in the elegantly appointed dining room. Stroll through the country garden, or linger by the fish pond and gaze at the mountain. Nearby are the National Historic parks of Antietam and Harper's Ferry.

**Lewrene Farm Bed & Breakfast**
9738 Downsville Pike
301/582-1735

This authentic 125-acre farm offers lodging in a charming turn-of-the-century farmhouse. The grounds provide a woods to stroll through, a gazebo to relax in, and a platform swing. Local attractions include Antietam Battlefield, Harper's Ferry, Fort Frederick, and the Appalachian Trail. In the winter, skiing is available at the nearby Whitetail Resort.

**Sundays Bed & Breakfast**
39 Broadway
1-800-221-4828
Web site: www.sundaysbnb.com

This elegant 1890 Queen Anne Victorian home is situated in the historic north end of Hagerstown. Relax in any of the many public rooms and porches or explore the many historic attractions, antique shops, golf courses, museums, shopping outlets, and ski areas that are nearby. You'll experience special hospitality and many personal touches at Sundays. A full breakfast, afternoon teas and desserts, evening refreshments, fruit baskets, fresh flowers, special toiletries, and late night cordial and chocolate are just some of the offerings at Sundays.

**Wingrove Manor Inn**
635 Oak Hill Ave.
301/797-7769
Web site: www.interaccess.com/wingrovemanor/index.html

The Wingrove Manor is a beautifully restored bed and breakfast minutes from the Antietam Battlefield, Whitetail Ski Resort, and championship golf courses. Relax in wicker rockers stretched across a large southern porch surrounded by twenty three white columns, ceramic tiled floors, and beauty that is breathtaking. Inside, you will enjoy marble fireplaces, winding staircase, oriental rugs, crystal chandeliers, and white towering columns all reflecting the home's lineage.

## 26 HANOVER

**AAA Antiques Mall, Inc.**
Maryland's Largest
2659 Annapolis Road
Routes 295 & 175 (Between Severn & Jessup)
410/551-4101

Be prepared to spend the day at Maryland's largest antiques mall offering over 58,000 square feet of quality, affordable antiques and collectibles.

You will find plenty of fine furniture from all periods as well as glassware from the brilliant, depression and elegant periods. The mall also offers a fine selection of art glass and pottery. If you are in the market for military, movie, black memorabilia or any number of yesterday's treasures, this is the place to be.

Located only minutes from Baltimore and Washington, AAA Antiques Mall, Inc. offers plenty of free parking and welcomes bus tours. Wheelchair accessible-wheelchair on premises. If you need more information or require overnight accommodations, please feel free to call the mall at 410/551-4101.

## 27 HAVRE DE GRACE

**Eclections**
101 N. Washington St.
410/939-4917

**Franklin St. Antiques & Gifts**
464 Franklin St.
410/939-4220

**Investment Antiques & Collectibles**
123 Market St.
410/939-1312

**Splendor In Brass**
123 Market St.
410/939-1312

**Streets Uniques**
2132 Pulaski Hwy.
410/273-6778

**Bank of Memories**
319 Saint John St.
410/939-4343

**Wonder Back Antiques**
331 N. Union Ave.
410/939-6511

**Golden Vein**
408 N. Union Ave.
410/939-9595

**Washington St. Books & Antiques**
131 N. Washington St.
410/939-6215

### *Great Places To Stay*

**Currier House Bed & Breakfast**
800 S. Market St.
1-800-827-2889
Web site: www.currier-bb.com

Currier House is located in the heart of Havre De Grace's historic residential district and overlooks the juncture of the Chesapeake Bay and the Susquehanna River. The original portion of the house that now forms the dining room and an upstairs bedroom and bath, dates from the 1790s. The house was first occupied by the Currier's in 1861. Over the years, the house was enlarged and modernized. Its decor now reflects Havre De Grace's late historical period when the town was a regional recreational center that attracted waterfowl hunters and horsemen who wagered at the local track.

## 28 HYATTSVILLE

**Annas Antiques & Bits & Pieces**
5312 Baltimore Ave.
301/864-5953

**Ellingtons**
1401 University Blvd. E.
301/445-1879

**Maryland Precious Metals**
By Appointment Only
301/779-3696

## 29 KENSINGTON

**Barrington Antique**
10419 Fawcett St.
301/949-1994

**Phyllis Van Auken Antiques Inc.**
10425 Fawcett St.
301/933-3772

**Jantiques**
10429 Fawcett St.
301/942-0936

**James of Kensington**
3706 Howard Ave.
301/933-8843

**Kensington Station Antiques**
3730 Howard Ave.
301/946-0222

**Nancy T.**
3730 Howard Ave.
301/942-8446

**Pen Haven**
3730 Howard Ave.
301/929-0955

**Villa Accents**
3730 Howard Ave.
301/942-7944

**ABS Consignment & Collectibles**
3734 Howard Ave.
301/946-9646

**Oriental Antiques by Susan Akins**
3740 Howard Ave.
301/946-4609

**Sally Shaffer Interiors**
3742 Howard Ave.
301/933-3740

**Jill Americana & Co.**
3744 Howard Ave.
301/946-7464

**Pritchard's**
3748 Howard Ave.
301/942-1661

**Antique Market II**
3750 Howard Ave.
301/933-4618

**Dianes Antiques**
3758 Howard Ave.
301/946-4242

**Mariea's Place**
3758 Howard Ave.
301/949-2378

**Antique Scientific Instruments**
3760 Howard Ave.
301/942-0636

**Kensington Antique Market Center**
3760 Howard Ave.
301/942-4440

**Antiques And Uniques**
3762 Howard Ave.
301/942-3324

**Antique Market**
3762 Howard Ave.
301/949-2318

**Paul Feng Antiques**
3786 Howard Ave.
301/942-0137

**European Antiques**
4080A Howard Ave.
301/530-4407

**Ambiance Galleries Ltd.**
4115 Howard Ave.
301/656-1512

**Sparrows**
4115 Howard Ave.
301/530-0175

**Paris-Kensington**
4119 Howard Ave.
301/897-4963

**Onslow Square Antiques**
4125-4131 Howard Ave.
301/530-9393

**Gonzales Antiques**
4130 Howard Ave.
301/564-5940

**Great British Pine Mine**
4144 Howard Ave.
301/493-2565

**Lighting by Estate Gallery Antiques**
4217 Howard Ave.
301/493-4013

**Chelsea & Co.**
4218 Howard Ave.
301/897-8886

**Furniture Mill Inc.**
4233 Howard Ave.
301/530-1383

**Victoria Antiques**
4265 Howard Ave.
301/530-4460

**Time Frames**
10408 Montgomery Ave.
301/929-8419

**For Cats Sake Inc.**
10513 Metropolitan Ave.
301/933-5489

**All Books Considered**
10408 Montgomery Ave.
301/589-2575

**International Parade**
10414 Montgomery Ave.
301/933-1770

**Lionel Buy, Sell, Repair**
3610 University Blvd. W.
301/949-5656

**Potomac Trade Post & Antique Guns**
3610 University Blvd. W.
301/949-5656

## 30 KNOXVILLE

**Schoolhouse Antiques**
847 Jefferson Pike
301/620-7470

**Garrett's Mill Antiques**
1331 Weverton Road
301/834-8581

## 31 LAUREL

**Antique Center**
8685 Cherry Lane
301/725-9174

**Dark Horse Antiques Mall**
8687 Cherry Lane
301/953-1815

**Antique Alley**
99 Main St.
301/490-6500

**David's Antiques & Gifts**
353 Main St.
301/776-5636

**Main Street Corner Shoppe Inc.**
401 Main St.
301/725-3099

**Geary's Antiques**
508 Main St.
301/725-7733

**L & L Antiques & Gifts**
512 Main St.
301/725-7539

**Antique Market**
9770 Washington Blvd. N.
301/953-2674

## 32 LAYTONSVILLE

**Griffith House Antiques**
21415 Laytonsville Road
301/926-4155

**Ludingtons Antiques**
21520 Laytonsville Road
301/330-4340

**Red Barn Antique Shops**
6860 Olney Laytonsville Road
301/926-3053

## 33 LEONARDTOWN

**Maryland Antiques Center**
593 Jefferson St.
301/475-1960

**Antiques on the Square**
337 N. Washington St.
301/475-5826

## 34 MILLERSVILLE

**Arundel Way Antiques**
1004 Cecil Ave.
410/923-2977

**Red Barn Antiques**
241 Najoles Road
410/987-2267

## 35 MOUNT AIRY

**Trading Post Antiques**
13318 Glissans Mill Road
301/829-0561

**Country House**
309 N. Main St.
301/829-2528

## 36 NEW MARKET

Located on the old National Pike, New Market's Main Street was an important stop for 19th-century travelers headed west and for cattle drivers going to the eastern markets. Though the town was laid out in 1788 and patrolled by Confederate forces during the Civil War, it has survived the years well enough to be a largely intact rural town with many early buildings restored for combined use as antiques shops and homes. Unique buildings include the Prosser House, Ramsburg House and Fehr-Schriss House.

**Comus Antiques**
#1 N. Federal St.
301/831-6464

**Before Our Time**
1 W. Main St.
301/831-9203

**Fleshman's Antiques**
2 W. Main St.
410/775-0153

**John Due Antiques**
13 W. Main St.
301/831-9412

**Jo's Antiques**
21 W. Main St.
301/831-3875

**Shaws of New Market**
22 W. Main St.
301/831-6010

**Victorian Jewelry**
33 Main St.
301/865-3083

**C W Wood Books**
42 W. Main St.
301/865-5734

**Main St. Antiques**
47 W. Main St.
301/865-3710

**Tomorrow's Antiques**
50 W. Main St.
301/831-3590

**Browsery Antiques**
55 W. Main St.
301/831-9644

**Thomas Antiques**
60 W. Main St.
301/831-6622

**Antiques Folly**
105 W. Main St.
301/607-6513

**R P Brady Antiques**
3 E. Main St.
301/865-3666

**Smith's Tavern Antiques**
Main & Fifth St.
301/865-3597

**Mimi's Antiques**
3 Strawberry Alley
301/865-1644

**Arlenes Antiques**
41 W. Main St.
301/865-5554

**Glen Moore & Violet**
45 W. Main St.
301/865-3710

**1812 House**
48 W. Main St.
301/865-3040

**Mr. Bob's**
52 W. Main St.
301/831-6712

**Iron Bell**
59 W. Main St.
301/831-9589

**Village Tea Room & Antique Shop**
81 W. Main St.
301/865-3450

**Finch's Antiques**
122 W. Main St.
301/685-3926

**Thirsty Knight Antiques**
9 E. Main St.
301/831-9889

**Rossig's Frame Shop**
1 N. Strawberry Alley
301/865-3319

**Grange Hall Antiques**
1 8th Alley
301/865-5651

***Great Places To Stay***

**National Pike Inn**
9 W. Main St.
301/865-5055
Open year round

Located on Main Street amidst antique shops, this 1796-1804 Federal style inn offers five guest rooms decorated with individual themes. The large Federal Sitting Room surrounds guests in comfort. For a private outdoor retreat, step into the enclosed courtyard. The Colonial dining room is the location for the hearty morning breakfast. Create a memory in New Market.

## 37 NORTH EAST

**JB's Collectibles**
32 S. Main St.
410/287-0400

***Great Places To Stay***

**The Mill House**
102 Mill Lane
410/287-3532
Open year round

A tidal creek authenticates the early 1700 Mill House, which is filled with antique furnishings. Guests can take strolls through the spacious lawn, or settle back before the crackling fire in the parlor. Also, antique shops and restaurants are within an easy walk.

## 38 OCEAN CITY

**Bookshelf Etc.**
8006 Coastal Hwy.
410/524-2949

**GG's Antiques**
9 Somerset St.
410/289-2345

**Edgemoor Antiques**
10009 Silver Point Lane
410/213-2900

**Brass Cannon**
204 S. Saint Louis Ave.
410/289-3440

***Great Places To Stay***

**Inn on the Ocean**
10th St. and the Ocean
1001 Atlantic Ave.
1-888-226-6223

Inn on the Ocean is a perfect blend of elegance, hospitality and quiet graciousness. All rooms are magnificently decorated for luxury and comfort. From the wrap-around oceanfront verandah you can watch the waves and world go by. In winter, a fireplace welcomes you in the living room. Expanded continental breakfast, afternoon refreshments, bicycles, beach equipment and health club facilities are complimentary.

## 39 OLNEY

**Briars Antiques**
4121 Briars Road
301/774-3596

**Hyatt House Antiques**
16644 Georgia Ave.
301/774-1932

**Liz Vilas Antiques**
16650 Georgia Ave.
301/924-0354

**Barry Rogers**
16650 Georgia Ave.
301/570-0779

**Olney Antique Village**
16650 Georgia Ave.
301/570-9370

**Jimmy's Village Barn**
16650 Georgia Ave.
301/570-6489

**Nicco's Antiques**
16650 Georgia Ave.
301/924-3745

## 40 OXFORD

**Americana Antiques**
111 S. Morris St.
410/226-5677

**Anchorage House Antiques**
Oxford Road
410/822-8978

**Donald D. Donahue Sr.**
111 S. Morris St.
410/226-5779

**Oxford Salvage Co.**
301 Tilghman St.
410/226-5971

**Vintage Shop**
202 S. Morris St.
410/226-5712

## 41 REISTERSTOWN

**Curiosity Shoppes**
17 Hanover Road
410/833-3434

**Now N Then**
208 Main St.
410/833-3665

**New England Carriage House**
218 Main St.
410/833-4019

**Derby Antiques**
222 Main St.
410/526-6678

**Relics of Olde**
222 Main St.
410/833-3667

**Things You Love Antiques**
234 Main St.
410/833-5019

**Margie's Antiques & Dolls**
237 Main St.
410/526-5656

**Tina's Antiques & Jewelry**
237 Main St.
410/833-9337

## 42 ROYAL OAK

**Bellevue Store**
5592 Poplar Lane
410/745-5282

**Oak Creek Sales**
25939 Royal Oak
410/745-3193

## 43 SALISBURY

**Henrietta's Attic**
205 Maryland Ave.
410/546-3700

**Springhill Antiques**
2704 Merritt Mill Road
410/546-0675

**Peddlers Three**
Old Quantico Road
410/749-1141

**Holly Ridge Antiques**
1411 S. Salisbury Blvd.
410/742-4392

## 44 SEVERNA PARK

**Antiques in the Park**
540 Balto Anap Blvd.
410/544-2762

**Taylor Antiques**
557 Balton Anap Blvd.
410/647-1701

**Memory Post Antique Boutique**
Riggs Ave.
410/315-9610

**Anatiues Market Place**
4 Riggs Ave.
410/544-9644

**Adair & Halligan**
5 Riggs Ave.
410/647-0103

## 45 ST. MICHAELS

St. Michaels began in 1778 as a planned development backed by a Liverpool merchant firm, and was small but firmly established by the end of the Revolutionary War. Surrounded by tributaries of the Chesapeake Bay, St. Michaels is a delightful waterfront town and easy to explore on foot. Historic buildings span a period of two centuries, with many Federal period houses built in the early 19th century, including the Cannonball House, the Old Inn and the Kemp House. Many restaurants, specialty shops, bed and breakfasts, and inns welcome visitors to the town. The harbor has been developed into a marina, but commercial watermen also use it, as they have for generations.

**Freedom House Antiques**
121 A S. Fremont St.
410/745-6140

**Hodgepodge**
308 S. Talbot St.
410/745-3062

**Nina Lanham Ayres Antiques**
401 S. Talbot St.
410/745-5231

**Sentimental Journey Antiques**
402 Talbot St.
410/745-9556

**Pennywhistle Antiques**
408 S. Talbot St.
410/745-9771

**Saltbox Antiques**
310 S. Talbot St.
410/745-3569

### *Great Places To Stay*

**Wades Point Inn on the Bay**
Wades Point Road
1-888-923-3466
Web site: www.wadespoint.com

This country bed and breakfast inn overlooking Chesapeake Bay, is ideal for those seeking country serenity and the splendor of the bay. All rooms enjoy a waterview. The inn's 120 acres of fields and woodland, a dock for fishing and crabbing, and the ever changing view of boats, birds and water lapping the shoreline, provide a peaceful setting for relaxation and recreation. Interesting shops and fine dining, the famed Chesapeake Bay Maritime Museum and other attractions are nearby.

## 46 SYKESVILLE

**Alexandra's Attic**
7542 Main St.
410/549-3095

**All Through The House**
7540 Main St.
410/795-6577

**Village Antique Shoppe**
7543 Main St.
410/795-0556

**My Bear-IED Treasures**
7543 Main St.
410/795-0556

**TLC Creations**
7615 Main St.
410/549-1425

**Yesterday Once More**
6251 Sykesville Road
410/549-0212

**Clocks & Collectibles**
7311 Springfield Ave.
410/549-1147

## 47 TANEYTOWN

**Margaret J Maas**
202 E. Baltimore St.
410/756-2480

## 48 WALDORF

**Country Connection**
2784 Old Washington Road
301/843-1553

**Heritage Designs**
3131 Old Washington Road
301/932-7379

**Madatics Attic**
3141 Old Washington Road
301/645-6076

## 49 WASHINGTON D.C.

### Amaryllis Vintage Company, Inc.
4922 Wisconsin Ave.
202/244-2211
Daily 11-7.
*Directions: Traveling I-495 take Exit #33. Travel south on Connecticut Ave. to Fessenden St. (approximately 3 1/2 miles). Turn right on Fessenden. Go to Wisconsin Ave.; turn left on Wisconsin, the shop is 1/2 block on the right.*

With pieces from the 1840s to 1940s, this shop carries furniture and accessories. The most popular furnishing styles include Empire, Mission and Art Deco. Mirrors, lamps, rugs, paintings and jewelry add to the selection. Bridal Registry, gift certificates, and local delivery are available. A 90-day-same-as-cash credit line can be established for qualified applicants.

### Dunnan's, Inc.
3209 O St., N.W.
202/965-1614
Daily 11-4
*Directions: Located in Historic Georgetown off Wisconsin Ave.*

With hundreds of antique items and accessories, this Historic Georgetown shop offers a wide selection and variety. Furniture, lamps, memorabilia, advertising, in addition to jewelry, collectibles and art, make up the eclectic array of wares. Inventory varies as a result of frequent deliveries.

**Antiques-On The Hill**
701 N. Carolina Ave. S.E.
202/543-1819

**Tiny Jewel Box**
1147 Connecticut Ave. N.W.
202/393-2747

**Antiques Anonymous**
2627 Connecticut Ave. N.W.
202/332-5555

**Mom & Pop Antiques**
3534 Georgia Ave. N.W.
202/722-0719

**Logan's Antiques**
3118 Mount Pleasant St. N.W.
202/483-2428

**Justine Mehlman Antiques**
2824 Pennsylvania Ave. N.W.
202/337-0613

**Proud American (Georgetown)**
1529 Wisconsin Ave. N.W.
202/625-1776

**Rooms with a View**
1661 Wisconsin Ave. N.
202/625-0610

**VIP Antiques**
1665 Wisconsin Ave. N.W.
202/965-0700

**Consignment Galleries**
3226 Wisconsin Ave. N.W.
202/364-8995

**Chevy Chase Antique Center**
5215 Wisconsin Ave. N.W.
202/364-4600

**Ruff & Ready Furnishings**
1908 14th St. N.W.
202/667-7833

**Retrospective Inc.**
2324 18th St. N.W.
202/483-8112

**Cherishables**
1608 20th St. N.W.
202/785-4087

**Old Print Gallery Inc.**
1220 31st St. N.W.
202/965-1818

**Adam A Weschler & Son**
909 E St. N.W.
202/628-1281

**Janis Aldrige Inc.**
2900 M St. N.W.
202/338-7710

**Cherub Antiques Gallery**
2918 M St. N.W.
202/337-2224

**Mission Possible**
5516 Connecticut Ave. N.W.
202/363-6897

**Dalton Brody Ltd.**
3412 Idaho Ave. N.W.
202/244-7197

**Two Lions Antiques**
621 Pennyslvania Ave. S.E.
202/546-5466

**Rooms & Gardens**
3677 Upton St. N.W.
202/362-3777

**Julie Walters Antiques**
1657 Wisconsin Ave. N.W.
202/625-6727

**Blair House Antiques**
1663 Wisconsin Ave. N.W.
202/338-5349

**China Gallery & Gifts**
2200 Wisconsin Ave. N.W.
202/342-1899

**Amaryllis Vintage Co Inc.**
4922 Wisconsin Ave. N.W.
202/244-2211

**Antiques & Gifts Boutique**
5300 Wisconsin Ave. N.W.
202/237-2060

**Brass Knob**
2311 18th St. N.W.
202/332-3370

**Uniform**
2407 18th St. N.W.
202/483-4577

**Adams Davidson Galleries Inc.**
By Appointment Only
202/965-3800

**Wash. Dolls House & Toy Museum**
5236 44th St. N.W.
202/363-6400

**Antique Textile Resource**
1730 K St. N.W., Suite 317
202/293-1731

**Frank Milwee**
2912 M St. N.W.
202/333-4811

**Michael Getts Antiques**
2918 M St. N.W. (Georgetown)
202/338-3811

**Susquehanna Antiques Co. Inc.**
3216 O St. N.W.
202/333-1511

**Second Store Books & Antiques**
2000 P St. N.W.
202/659-8884

**Kelsey's Kupboard**
3003 P St. N.W.
202/298-8237

**Affrica**
2010 R St. N.W.
202/745-7272

### *Great Places To Stay*

**Morris-Clark Inn**
1015 L St. N.W.
202/898-1200
Rates $115-185
Year-round accommodations

Built in 1864 and the only area inn listed independently in the National Register of Historic Places, it originally stood as two detached Victorian mansions. One presents an ornate Chippendale porch topped by a mansard roof, 1980s restoration united the structures creating an elegant small hotel. Original interior includes 12-foot-high mahogany-framed mirrors and elaborately carved marble fireplaces. All rooms offer Victorian, neoclassical, or country decor. *Gourmet* has featured the inn's well-respected restaurant.

**Adams Inn**
1744 Lanier Place, N.W.
202/745-3600
Year-round accommodations

This three-story townhouse built in 1908 nestles among antique shops in the surrounding blocks. Guest rooms have individual and distinctive home-style furnishings and accessories. Public rooms include breakfast room, parlor, television lounge. A seat amid the flowers of the garden patio, or taking in the view from the front porch, enhance each stay. Refreshments are complimentary.

### *Interesting Side Trips*

**Washington Dolls' House & Toy Museum**
5236 44th St. N.W.
202/244-0024
Tues.,-Sat., 10-5; Sun., 12-5
*Directions: One block west of Wisconsin Ave. between Jenifer St.and Harrison St.*

The Washington Dolls' House and Toy Museum began as a private collection belonging to doll house historian, Flora Gill Jacobs. Her extensive antique collection of doll houses, toys and games were researched and dated; all are representative of either the architecture, decorative arts, or social history of the time of their creation.

## 50 WESTMINSTER

**Seven East Main St.**
7 E. Main St.
410/840-9123

**Locust Wines & Antiques**
10 E. Main St.
410/876-8680

**White's Bicycles**
10 W. Main St.
410/848-3440

**Ain't That A Frame**
31 W. Main St.
410/876-3096

**Westminster Antique Mall**
433 Hahn Road
410/857-4044

# Massachusetts

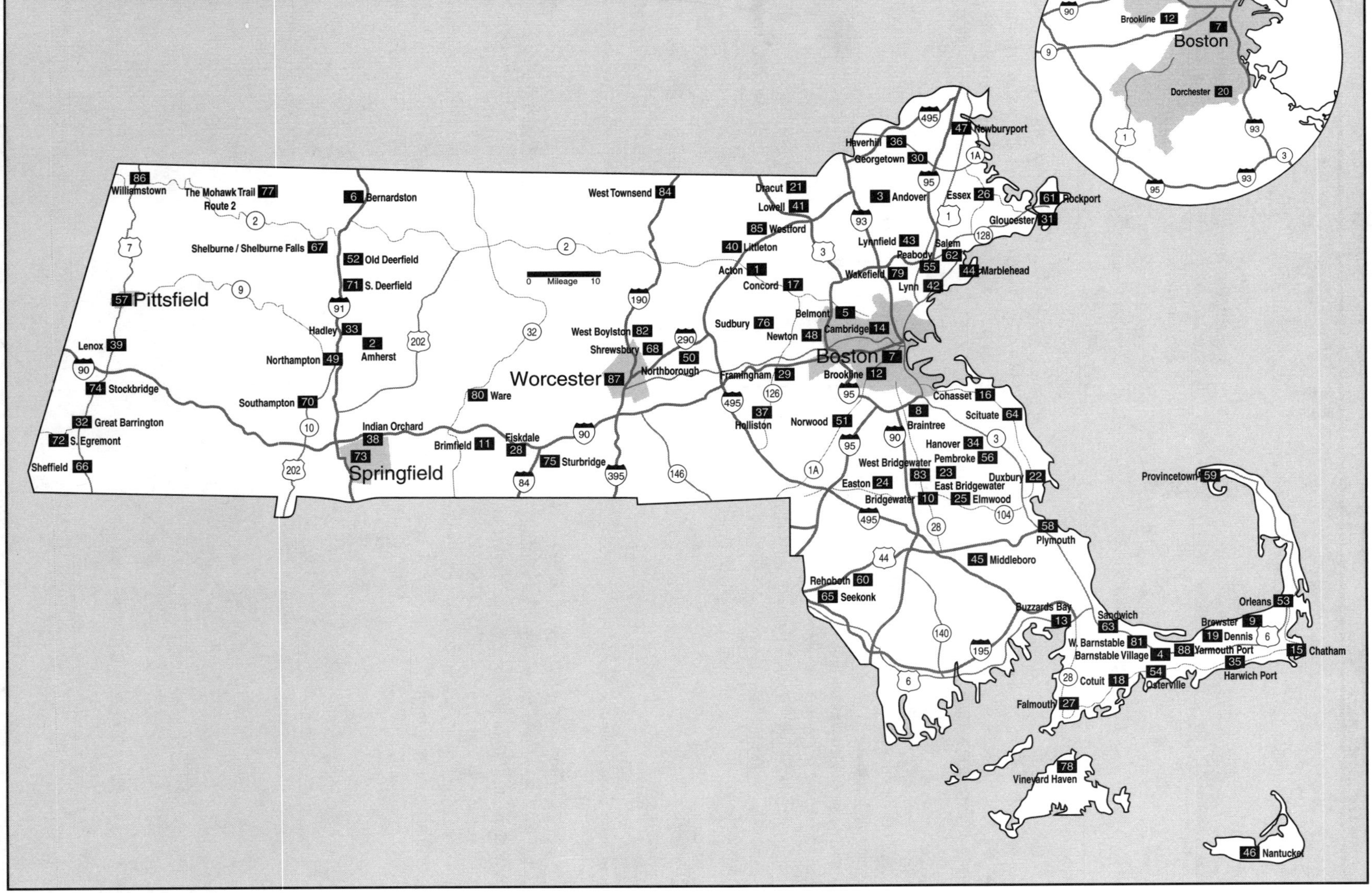

3¼" Kewpie doll with fly on her toe sits beside a tiny 2¾" high Doodles pup.

Left: 10½" Limoges cache pot from the famous factory in France.

Cast iron fisherman doorstop next to a Hubley cast iron cornucopias motif doorstop.

# Showcase Antique Center: Where history comes alive

Linking history and the future through modern technology, Showcase Antique Center offers not only the physical, visual delight of strolling through selections of 180 showcase dealers, but modern conveniences of worldwide shipping, 24-hour fax, answering machine, Email, website cyber store on the Internet and merchandise listings faxed back 24-hours a day.

Located at the entrance to Old Sturbridge Village, the selections feature art glass, sterling, jewelry, paintings, toys, primitives, advertising, art, pottery, Royal Bayreuth, tools, china, Shaker, medical, Indian, furniture and much, much more. Some of the items most recently found at Showcase Antique Center were a Dedham pottery crab plate, Vienna bronze hunter on horseback with dogs, milk glass phrenological of George Washington in cast iron frame with a milk glass inkwell, Bavarian clothes cabinet with original floral design, pictorial Navajo mat made by Lorretta Chee, "Salisbury Cathedral" oil on canvas and a sterling kettle on a stand signed Alexander Clark Co., London.

*Showcase Antique Center is located along Route 20, at the entrance to Old Sturbridge Village. For additional information see listing #75 (Sturbridge).*

*French brass go-to-bed is adorned with four stones.*

*Period match safe advertises Wrigley's gum.*

*Composition Santa was made in Germany.*

*Stunning blond furnishings with sleek lines complement the collectibles in this display at Main Street Antique Center. Over 126 dealers from eight states display their wares here.*

# Full line of antiques and friendly shopkeepers at Main Street Antique Center on Cape Cod

Main Street Antique Center is located in the heart of Dennisport Village on historic old Cape Cod. The perfect setting for selling antiques, Richard or Vince (the shopkeepers) are always on hand to help with any questions you might have regarding their full line of antiques and collectibles.

*A country hen cookie jar nests on an antique table, surrounded by a colorful quilt and collectibles.*

In the beginning, Main Street Antiques was a moderate size shop of 50 dealers, mostly exhibiting in cases. In 1997 the shop moved next door to a larger building increasing to 126 dealers from eight states. Americana to interesting smalls can be found in the spacious new area. All merchandise is beautifully presented, focusing on quality and diversity. Conveniently located along Route 28, the shop is easy to get to from Route 6 and Route 134. Additional antique shops are located nearby.

*To reach this truly unique shop on the Cape take Route 6 to Exit 9 (Route 134), proceed south on Route 134 and go 2 miles to Route 28. Turn left on Route 28, go 1.3 miles. For additional information call the shop at 508-760-5700 and see listing #19 (Dennis/Dennisport) for more shop listings.*

*Artful presentation delights the senses at the Main Street Antique Mall, where you're likely to find anything from a major furniture piece to irresistable smalls.*

# Massachusetts

## 1 ACTON

**Seagull Antiques**
481 Great Road
978/263-8260

**Encores Antiques**
174 Great Road
978/263-1515

## 2 AMHERST

### Black Walnut Inn
1184 N. Pleasant St.
413/549-5649
Fax: 413/549-5149
Open year round 7-8
Rates: $95-125
*Directions: Traveling north on I-91: Take Exit 19 (marked Amherst) onto Route 9 E. Go 4.6 miles and turn left (Staples will be on your right) onto Route 116 N. Go 3 miles to the first traffic light and turn right onto Route 63 (Meadow St.). The next light is North Pleasant St. and Black Walnut Inn is the brick house on the right. Traveling south on I-91: Take Exit 24, turn right onto Route 5; continue for 1 mile. Turn left on Route 116 S. for 6 miles. Turn left at the first Amherst light onto Route 63 (Meadow St.). The next light is North Pleasant St. and Black Walnut Inn is on the right.*

The Black Walnut Inn, a stately 1821 Federal style brick house shaded by tall black walnut trees, stands on the corner of North Pleasant and Meadow Streets in Amherst, just a few minutes from the campuses of Amherst College and the University of Massachusetts. Although the double doors, crowned with a large fan window, give the house an imposing facade, inside you'll find coziness and comfort. Each guest room is furnished with a mix of antiques and period-piece reproductions, all distinctive in size, furnishings, and history. Touches like the turn-of-the-century mulberry color chosen for the Mulberry Room, cherry Windsor-style and sleigh beds, antique dressing tables, a spinning wheel, a cast iron canopy bed, original wood wainscotting, exposed post and beam and fine wood floors all add rich, historical detail to an already historic house. A full breakfast, including homemade muffins and jams and fresh squeezed orange juice is genially served by hosts, Edd and Marie Twohig, who also offer guests tea, coffee and goodies from 2-8 p.m. on request. The barn that goes with the Black Walnut Inn is the last one in western Massachusetts of the scientific agricultural design.

**Kay Baker's Antiques**
233 N. Pleasant St.
413/549-4433

**Main St. Antiques & Books**
321 Main St.
413/256-0900

**Grist Mill Antiques**
Route 116 S. Amherst
413/253-5296

**Amherst Glass & Antiques**
754 Main St.
413/253-9574

**Amherst Antiques Center**
308 College St.
413/253-1995

## 3 ANDOVER

**Andover Antiques Inc**
89 N. Main St.
978/475-4242

**Rose Cottage Antiques**
68 Park St.
978/475-6214

**Necessities**
185 N. Main St.
978/475-7992

**Bider's Antiques**
6 Park St.
978/475-8336

**Limoges Antiques**
20 Post Office Ave.
978/470-8773

**Collen's**
68 Park St.
978/474-8983

**New England Gallery, Inc.**
350 N. Main St.
508/475-2116

## 4 BARNSTABLE VILLAGE

### Beech Wood
### A Romantic Victorian Inn
2839 Main St., Route 6A
1-800-609-6618, 508/362-6618
Email: bwdinn@virtualcapecod.com
Web site: www.virtualcapcod.com/market/beechwood/
*Directions: For specific directions to Beech Wood please call the innkeepers who will be happy to provide specific directions from your location.*

Sometimes you dream about getting away from it all—whiling away a summer afternoon with a glass of lemonade out on the porch, or relaxing in front of the fireplace with a mug of hot chocolate. Beech Wood is the place where these fantasies become reality.

A tall hedge shields the gabled-roofed Victorian from Main St., making it a peaceful respite. Two sprawling beech trees embrace the grounds, and a wide porch wraps around three sides of the house; a perfect spot for lounging, or even making friends with the resident golden retrievers, Hobbes and Star.

Innkeepers Debbie and Ken Taugot have made sure that the inn is as comfortable as it is pretty. The seven guest rooms are each strikingly different, from the elegant Rose Room with its canopy bed and fireplace, to the airy Lilac Room with its clawfoot bathtub, to the cozy third-floor Garrent Room with its brass bed.

If you want to find out a bit more about the Cape Cod area on your visit, head down to the inn's parlor, where you will find ample guides to local restaurants, information on sightseeing, and able advice from Debbie and Ken.

There's plenty to do in Barnstable, but the highlight is really antiquing. There are dozens of shops, craft stores, and the like, just a stone's throw away from Beech Wood.

If you'd rather stay put, play croquet or badminton on Beech Wood's broad lawn, or treat yourself to a few quiet moments on the porch swing. But before you decide, don't forget about breakfast. Each morning, guests are served a bountiful breakfast in the dining room. Start with muffins or breads, followed by fresh fruit, and a hearty entree. It is here that guests gather for spirited conversation, to plan their days, or just slowly ease into the morning. And midday brings a respite of afternoon tea, with beverages and treats the civilized way. Beech Wood will feel like your home away from home.

**Esprit Decor**
3941 Main St. (Route 6A)
508/362-2480

**Harden Studios**
3264 Main St. (Route 6A)
508/362-7771

**Salt & Chestnut**
651 Main St. (Route 6A)
503/362-6085

**Village Antiques**
3267 Main St. (Route 66)
508/362-6633

## 5 BELMONT

**Fancy That**
4 Trapelo Road
617/489-3497

**Cross & Griffin**
468 Trapelo Road
617/484-2837

**Antiques by Olde Mystic**
367 Trapelo Road
617/489-4147

**In Place**
3 Bartlett Ave.
617/489-4161

**Belmont Antique Exchange**
243 Belmont St., #A
617/484-9839

**As Time Goes By**
97 Trapelo Road
617/489-3212

**Consignment, Etc.**
352 Trapelo Road
617/489-4077

## 6 BERNARDSTON

**Carriage Barn Antiques**
Route 5, 727 Brattleboro Road
413/648-9406

## 7 BOSTON

**Devonia Antiques**
43 Charles St.
617/523-8313

**George Gravert Antique**
122 Charles St.
617/227-1593

**Bradstreet's Antiquarins**
51 Charles St.
617/723-3660

**Regency Antiques**
70 Charles St.
617/742-3111

**Eugene Galleries**
76 Charles St.
617/227-3062

**Antiques at 80 Charles**
80 Charles St.
617/742-8006

**Elegant Findings Antiques**
89 Charles St.
617/973-4844

**Upstairs Downstairs Antiques**
93 Charles St.
617/367-1950

**Towne & Country Home**
99B Charles St.
617/742-9120

**Antiques at 99 Charles**
99A Charles St.
617/367-8088

**Boston Antique Co-op I**
119 Charles St.
617/227-9810

**Boston Antique Co-op II**
119 Charles St.
617/227-9811

**Marika's Antique Shop**
130 Charles St.
617/523-4520

**Danish Country**
138 Charles St.
617/227-1804

**Stephen Score**
73 Chestnut St.
617/227-9192

**Charles River St. Antiques**
45 River St.
617/367-3244

**Buddenbrooks Fine & Rare Books**
31 Newbury St.
617/536-4433

**Small Pleasures**
142 Newbury St.
617/267-7371

**Marcoz Antiques**
177 Newbury St.
617/262-0780

**Nostalgia Factory**
51 N. Margin St.
617/236-8754

**Autrefois Antiques**
125 Newbury St.
617/424-8823

**Gallagher-Christopher Antiques**
84 Chestnut St.
617/523-1992

**Newbury St. Jewelry & Antiques**
255 Newbury St.
617/236-0038

**Brookline Village Antiques**
1 Design Center Place, Suite 325
617/734-6071

**Akin Lighting Company**
28 Charles St.
617/523-1331

**Streamline Antiques**
1162 Washington St.
617/298-3326

**Commonwealth Antiques**
121 Charles St.
617/720-1605

**Alberts-Langdon Inc.**
126 Charles St.
617/523-5954

**Antiques on Tremont**
550 Tremont St.
617/451-3329

**Camden Co.**
211 Berkeley St.
617/421-9899

**Cameron Adams Antiques**
37 River St.
617/725-1833

**Comeno's Fine Arts**
9 Newbury St., #2
671/262-9365

**Cove Hollow Antiques**
138 St. James Ave.
617/266-7850

**David L. O'Neal Antiquarian**
234 Clarendon St.
617/266-5790

**Howard Chadwick**
40 River St.
617/227-9261

**Hyacinth's**
91 Charles St.
617/367-0917

**India Antiques & Musical Instruments**
279 Newbury St.
617/266-6539

**Jerry Freeman Ltd.**
211 Berkleley St.
617/236-4945

**JMW Gallery**
144 Lincoln St.
617/338-9097

**Lannan Ship Model Gallery**
540 Atlantic Ave.
617/451-2650

**Machine-Age Corp.**
354 Congress St.
617/482-0048

**Newbury Galleries**
18 Arlington St.
617/437-0822

**Polly Latham Antiques**
96 Charles St.
617/723-7009

**S. W. Alan Antiques**
131 Charles St.
617/720-7808

**Shreve Crump & Low Co.**
330 Boylston St.
617/267-9100

**Twentieth Century Ltd.**
73 Charles St.
617/742-1031

### *Favorite Places To Eat*

**No Name Restaurant**
15½ Fish Pier
617/338-7539

It's places like No Name Restaurant that you look for in every city you visit. Because you know that not only will you have a delightful dining experience, but the trip and the atmosphere alone will create memories that bear retelling over and over. No Name is the name. There is no sign outside; none is needed. It started years ago as a luncheonette with a counter and a few tables, strictly for wharf workers. But word got around about its inexpensive, simple, fresh seafood, and No Name expanded. There is still a dingy luncheonette counter for single diners, but most tourists are seated in the new, paneled dining room with nautical decor and harbor view. Tables are crowded and communal. Customers yell out their orders, and waiters yell back and practically toss food from the kitchen. Start with the fish chowder—nothing but fish! Main course choices are scrod, sole, bluefish, scallops, clams or salmon. Side orders are homemade tartar sauce and fresh-cut slaw with a light, milky dressing. For dessert there's strawberry-rhubarb or blueberry pie, plain or a la mode. Very straightforward, very New England!

## 8 BRAINTREE

**Second Thoughts Antiques**
871 Washington St.
781/849-6750

**Out of the Wood**
230 Quincy Ave.
781/356-5030

**Antiques & Things**
826 Washington St.
781/843-4196

## 9 BREWSTER

**William Baxter Antiques**
3439 Main St.
508/896-3998

**Pflock's Antiques**
598 Main St.
508/896-3457

**Monomoy Antiques**
3425 Route 6A
508/896-6570

**Heirloom Antiques**
2660 Main St.
508/896-2080

**Mark Lawrence**
1050 Main St.
508/896-8381

**Kings Way Books & Antiques**
774 Main St.(Route 6A)
508/896-3639

**Gaskill Antiques**
134 Main St.
508/385-6663

**Eve's Place**
564 Main St.
508/896-4914

**Breton House Antiques**
1222 Stoney Brook Road
508/896-3974

**Barbara Grant Antiques & Books**
1793 Main St.
508/896-7198

**Donald B Howes Antiques**
1424 Main St.
508/896-3502

**Kingsland Manor Antiques**
440 Main St.
508/385-9741

**Homestead Antiques**
2257 Main St. (Route 6A)
508/896-2917

**Huckleberry's Antiques**
2271 Main St. (Route 6A)
508/896-2670

**Pink Cadillac Antiques**
3140 Main St. (Route 6A)
508/896-4651

**Punkhorn Bookshop**
672 Main St. (Route 6A)
508/896-2114

**Shirley Smith & Friends**
2926 Main St. (Route 6A)
508/896-4632

## 10 BRIDGEWATER

**Antiques Etc.**
1278 Bedford St.
508/697-3005

**Central Market**
27 Central Square
508/697-2121

**Fond Memories**
34 Central Square
508/697-5622

**Hidden Treasures**
50 Central Square
508/697-2828

**Harvest Hill Antiques**
450 Plymouth St.
508/697-7160

**Old Dutch Cottage**
1 Broad St.
508/697-1586

**Pandora's Box**
10 Broad St.
508/697-8185

**Hatfield House Antiques**
136 Birch St.
508/697-5869

## 11 BRIMFIELD

**Brimfield Antiques & Collectibles Show**
The Granddaddy of Them All!
May, July, September
Call 413/245-9329 for dates

The Brimfield "Strip" is a quarter of a mile long - and what a quarter of "land" it is! All adjacent to one another are 23 major fields offering both antique and collectible buyers the opportunity to select millions of items from any style and period. It's the one single place on earth where you can find both the familiar and unfamiliar in gizmos and gadgets, furniture, folk art, pottery, war memorabilia, garden decor, graniteware, books, toys, scores of glassware and other stuff! This monumental phenomenon started as a small show of about 60 to 75 dealers in 1959.

# Massachusetts

Within a few short years it had grown to become the largest antique and collectible show in the world. And it certainly is not uncommon to find folks from around the world at Brimfield. Antiquers from countries such as Germany, England, Australia, and Canada (just to name a few) are seen throughout the week examining and purchasing the wonderful wares.

If you are a serious antiquer who loves the thrill of the hunt - you must make plans to attend the Brimfield Shows.

Submitted by Bob Brown, author of Brimfield: The Collector's Paradise

**Sturbridge Road Antiques**
109 Sturbridge Road
413/245-6649

## 12 BROOKLINE

**Turnip & Brig's**
313 Washington St.
617/232-9693

**Erinn's Antiques**
185 Corey Road
617/734-4522

**Autrefois Antiques**
130 Harvard St.
617/566-0113

**Antique Company**
311 Washington St.
617/738-9476

**Cypress Trading Post**
146 Cypress St.
617/566-5412

**Gurari Antique Prints**
91 Marion St.
617/864-0404

**Vintage Jewelry, Gifts, Antiques**
1382 Beacon St., #B
617/739-3265

**Lost Engine Antiques**
14 Allston
617/254-4678

**Antiquers III**
171 Harvard St., #A
617/738-5555

**A Room with a Vieux Antiques**
200 Washington St.
617/277-2700

**Appleton Antique Lighting**
195 Harvard St.
617/566-5322

**Dreaming of Vieux**
214 Washington St.
617/277-6200

**Towne Antiques**
256 Washington St.
617/731-3326

## 13 BUZZARDS BAY

**Heirlooms Etc.**
95A Main St.
508/759-1455

**Grey Goose**
95C Main St.
508/759-3055

**Brier Rose Antiques**
95B Main St.
508/759-5588

**Almost Antiques**
89 Main St.
508/759-2111

**Marketplace**
61 Main St.
508/759-2114

## 14 CAMBRIDGE

**European Country Antiques**
146 Huron Ave.
617/876-7485

**Easy Chairs**
375 Huron Ave.
617/491-2131

**James & Devon Booksellers**
12 Arrow St.
617/868-0752

**Cambridge Antique Market**
201 Monsignor O'Brien Hwy.
617/868-9655

**Harvard Antiques**
1654 Massachusetts Ave.
617/354-5544

**City Lights Antique Lighting**
2226 Massachusetts Ave.
617/547-1490

**Antiques on Cambridge Street**
1076 Cambridge St.
617/234-0001

**Hurst Gallery**
53 Mount Auburn St.
617/491-6888

**Penny Scale Antiques**
1353 Cambridge St.
617/576-6558

**Sadye & Co.**
182 Massachusetts Ave.
617/547-4424

**Offshore Trading Co.**
1695 Massachusetts Ave.
617/491-8439

**All & Everything**
2269 Massachusetts Ave.
617/354-8641

**Consignment Galleries**
2040 Massachusetts Ave.
617/354-4408

**Justin Tyme**
91 River St.
617/491-1088

## 15 CHATHAM

**Spyglass**
618 Main St.
508/945-9686

**Agnes of Cape Cod**
Balfour Lane 17C
508/945-4099

**Aquitain Antiques**
35 Cross St.
508/945-9746

**Archer Antiques**
595 Main St.
508/945-7500

**Bayberry Antiques**
300 Orleans Road (Route 28)
508/945-9060

**House on the Hill Antiques**
17 Seaview St. (at Main St.)
508/945-2290

**Amazing Lace**
726 Main St.
508/945-4023

**Carol's Antiques & Collectibles**
1278 Main St.
508/945-1705

**Rose Cottage Antiques**
1281 Main St.
508/945-3114

**Bob's Antiques**
1589 Main St.
508/945-4606

**Chatham Antiques**
1409 Main St. (Route 28)
508/945-1660

**1736 House Antiques**
1731 Main St. (Route 28)
508/945-5690

## 16 COHASSET

**3 A Antiques Center**
130 Cushing Hwy.
781/383-9411

**Reflections**
808 Jerusaleum Road
781/383-6465

**Green Gage Plum**
819 Cushing Hwy.
781/383-1778

**Victoria's by the Sea**
87 Elm St.
781/383-2087

**Lilac House Antiques**
26 South Main
781/383-2598

**Cohasset Antiques**
Route 3A
781/383-6605

**Carousel Antiques**
93 Ripley Road
781/383-9654

**Country House Antiques**
818 Cushing Hwy. (Route 3A)
781/383-1832

## 17 CONCORD

**Upstairs Antiques**
23 Walden St.
978/371-9095

**Ford Crawford Antiques**
1/2 Main St.
978/369-8870

**North Bridge Antiques**
45 Walden St.
978/371-1442

**Concord Antiques**
32 Main St. D/Stairs
978/369-8218

**Soft Antiques**
1/2 Main St.
978/369-8870

## 18 COTUIT

**Acorn Acres Antiques**
4339 Route 28
508/428-3787

**Sow's Ear Antique Co.**
4698 Route 28 & 130
508/428-4931

**Remember When**
4015 Route 28 Falmouth Road
508/428-5650

**Cotuit Antiques**
4404 Route 28 Falmouth Road
508/420-1234

**Antiques of Tomorrow**
45 Main St.
508/428-6262

**1849 House**
809 Main St.
508/428-2258

**Isaiah Thomas Boosk & Prints**
4632 Route 28
508/428-2752

**Paper Junction**
215 Main St.
508/428-8061

## 19 DENNIS/DENNISPORT

**Main Street Antique Center**
691 Route 28 (Dennisport)
508/760-5700

For specific information see review at the beginning of this section.

**Red Lion Antiques**
601 Main St.
508/385-4783

**Village Peddler Antiques**
601 Main St.
508/385-7300

**Antiques 608**
608 Main St.
508/385-2755

**Antiques Center of Cape Cod**
243 Main St.
508/385-6400

**Johanna**
606 Main St.
508/385-7675

**Old Town Antiques**
593 Main St.
508/385-5202

**Audrey's Antiques**
766 Main St.(Route 6A)
508/385-4996

**Dovetail Antiques**
543 Main St.(Route 6A)
508-385-2478

**Gloria Swanson Antiques**
632 B Main St.
508/385-4166

**Antiques Ctr Warehouse**
243 Main St. (Route 6A)
508/385-5133

**Second Hand Rose**
668 Main St. (Dennisport)
508/394-6620

**Side Door**
103 Main St. (Dennisport)
508/394-7715

**Lilac Hedge Antiques & Home Furniture**
620 Main St. (Route 6A)
508/385-0800

**The Cape Cod Galleries**
632 Main St. (Route 6A)
508/385-5436

**Leslie Curtis Antiques & Design**
838 Main St. (Route 6A)
508/385-2931

**Southside Antique Center**
691-A Route 28
508/394-8601

**East Dennis Antiques**
1514 Main St. (Route 6A)
508/385-7651

**Webfoot Farm Antiques**
1475 Main St. (Route 6A)
508/385-2334

**Recollections**
623 Main St. (Route 6A)
508/385-7504

## 20 DORCHESTER

**Avenue Antiques**
863 Dorchester Ave.
617/265-7100

**Darkhorse Antiques**
2297 Dorchester Ave.
617/298-1031

**Time Traders Antiques**
857 Dorchester Ave.
617/288-9000

**Streamline Antiques**
1162 Washington St.
617/298-3326

## 21 DRACUT

**James McKenna Antique Clocks**
16 Hovey St.
978/937-8283

## 22 DUXBURY

**Gordon & Genevieve Deming Antiques**
125 Wadsworth Road
781/934-5259

**Wickham Books**
285 Saint George St.
781/934-6955

**Folk Art Antiques**
447 Washington St.
781/934-7132

**Simon Hill Antiques**
453 Washington St.
781/934-2228

**Duxbury Antiques**
285 St. George St.
781/934-2127

## 23 EAST BRIDGEWATER

**Elmwood Antiques & Country Store**
734 Bedford St.
(Intersection of Routes 106 and 18)
508/378-2063
Tues.-Sat. 11-5, Sun. 12-5
*Directions: Travel I-95 to Route 24 S. Take Exit 16, Route 106 east to Route 18. Elmwood Antiques is on the corner of Routes 106 and 18.*

A 10-dealer group shop, Elmwood Antiques & Country Store offers mail order service from the U.S. to Europe. They carry a variety of items, including advertising, furniture, glass, china, Royal Doulton, Disney collectibles, toys, trains, dog collectibles, Coca-Cola memorabilia, military items and prints. While visiting, be sure to see their 132-year-old working post office.

**Attic Treasures**
582 West St.
508/378-7510

**Red house Antiques**
355 Bedford St.
No phone # available

**Hartman House Antiques**
334 Bedford St.
508/378-7388

**Antiques at Forge Pond**
35 N. Bedford St.
508/378-3057

**Victorian Gardens & Books**
76 N. Bedford St.
No phone # available

**Ye Olde Tyme Shoppe**
280 N. Bedford St.
508/378-3222

## 24 EASTON

**Barbara Bailey Antiques**
143 Washington St.
508/238-9770

**Orchid Antiques**
593 Turnpike St.
508/238-6146

## 25 ELMWOOD

**Mrs. Swifts & Moore**
741 Bedford St.
508/378-9383

## 26 ESSEX

Essex is a mecca for antiques hunters. But be warned: You'll find it impossible to resist the enticing aroma of fried clams that pervades the main street. Local restaurants pay homage to the tasty bivalve, which was first cooked here.

**White Elephant's Shop**
32 Main St.
978/768-6901

**Chebacco Antiques**
38 Main St.
978/768-7371

**Main Street Antiques**
44 Main St.
978/768-7039

**APH Waller & Sons**
140 Main St.
978/768-6269

**Ro-Dan Antiques**
67 Main St.
978/768-3322

**Annex Antiques**
69 Main St.
978/768-7704

**Emmons & Martin Antiques**
2 Martin St.
978/768-3292

**Howard's Flying Dragon Antiques**
136 Main St.
978/768-7282

**Westerhoff Antiques**
144 Main St.
978/768-3830

**Neligan & Neligan**
144 Main St.
978/768-3910

**North Hill Antiques**
155 Main St.
978/768-7365

**Ellen Neily Antiques**
157 Main St.
978/768-6436

**L A Landry Antiques**
164 Main St.
978/768-6233

**Susan Stella Antiques**
166 Main St.
978-768-6617

**Antiques & Elderly Things**
199 Western Ave.
978/768-6328

**Essex Antiques & Interiors**
235 John Wise Ave.
978/768-7358

**Friendship Antiques**
John Wise Ave.
978/768-7334

**J. E. Rider Antiques**
164 Main St.
978/768-7441

**Joshua's Corner Antiques**
2 Southern Ave.
978/768-7716

**South Essex Antiques**
166 Eastern Ave.
978/768-6373

## 27 FALMOUTH

### Hewins House Bed & Breakfast

20 Hewins St., Village Green
508/457-4363 or 1-800-555-4366
Best time to call is 9-7 daily
Open year round
*Directions: Take Route 28 south to Falmouth. Route 28 veers to the left at "Queens Byway" and becomes Main St. Falmouth. Make the left at "Queens Byway". (There is a pillar with a "Keep Right" sign in the middle of the road.) The next right is Hewins St., and Hewins House is right on the corner of Route 28 and Hewins.*

Built around 1820 by John Jenkins, a wealthy merchant and sea captain, Hewins House today remains much as it was in the 19th century. The Federal era building, home of some of Falmouth's most prominent families, features wide pine floors, the original staircase, and a black and white floor cloth in the foyer that was made by current owner, Mrs. Albert Price, who also planned the formal gardens and restored a side porch to provide access to the garden area. Within easy walking distance are downtown shopping, restaurants, antique stores, tourist attractions, and a free shuttle that goes to the ferry docks that service Martha's Vineyard.

**The Village Barn**
606 Route 28A
508/540-3215

**Enseki Antiques**
73 Palmer Ave.
508/548-7744

**Chrisales Country Home**
550 W. Falmouth Hwy.
508/540-5884

**Antiques in West Falmouth**
634 Route 28A
508/540-2540

**Antiquarium**
204 Palmer Ave.
508/548-1755

**Beach Rose**
35 N. Main St.
508/548-1012

**Aurora Borealis Antiques**
104 Palmer Ave.
508/540-3385

## 28 FISKDALE

**Commonwealth Cottage**
*See Sturbridge #70*

**Faxon's Antique Shows**
60 Mount Dan Road
508/347-3929

## 29 FRAMINGHAM

**Framingham Centre Antiques**
931 Worcester Road (Route 9)
508/620-6252

**Wex Rex Collectibles**
Tropical Isle Plaza (Route 9 E.)
508/620-6181

## 30 GEORGETOWN

**A F Scala Antiques**
28 W. Main St.
978/352-8614

**Sedler's Antique Village**
51 W. Main St.
978/352-8282

**Elmwood Antiques**
22 E. Main St.
978/352-9782

**Puddle Duck**
10 E. Main St.
978/352-4655

## 31 GLOUCESTER

**Tally's Trading Post**
108 Eastern Ave.
978/283-8662

**Beauport Antiques**
43 Main St.
978/281-4460

**Jer-Rho Antiques**
352 Main St.
978/283-5066

**Main St. Art & Antiques**
124 Main St.
978/281-1531

**Salt Island Antiques**
269 Main St.
978/283-2820

## 32 GREAT BARRINGTON

### The Coffman's Country Antiques Market
Jennifer House Commons
Stockbridge Road, Route 7
413/528-9282
Daily 10-5
*Directions: Located in the southwestern "Berkshires," Coffman's is located on Route 7 between Great Barrington and Stockbridge.*

A feast for serious, upscale antique lovers, Coffman's Country Antiques Market hosts over 100 quality antique dealers in room settings on three floors. Known for its distinctive, authentic American country antiques, Coffman's handles only merchandise produced before 1949 and only the upper end.

**Elise Abrams Antiques**
11 Stockbridge Road
413/528-3201

**Bygone Days**
969 Main St.
413/528-1870

**Snyder's Store**
945 Main St.
413/528-1441

**Reuss Antiques Gallery**
420 Stockbridge Road (Route 7)
413/528-8484

**Memories**
306 Main St.
413/528-6380

**Red Horse Antiques**
117 State Road
413/528-2637

**Emporium Antique Center**
319 Main St.
413/528-1660

**Carriage House**
389 Stockbridge Road
413/528-6045

**Le Perigord**
964 S. Main St. (Route 7)
413/528-6777

**Paul & Susan Kleinwald Inc.**
578 S. Main St. (Route 7)
413/528-4252

**Donald McGrory Oriental Rugs**
24 Railroad St.
413/528-9594

**Mullin-Jones Antiquities**
525 S. Main St. (Route 7)
413/528-4871

**The Kahn's Antique & Estate Jewelry**
38 Railroad St.
413/528-9550

**The Country Dining Room Antiques**
178 Main St. (Route 7)
413/528-5050

**Corashire Antiques**
Route 7 & 23 @ Belcher Square
413/528-0014

**Reeves Antiques**
420 Stockbridge Road
413/528-5877

## 33 HADLEY

**Hadley Antique Center**
Route 9
413/586-4093

**North Hadley Antiques**
Route 47 - 399 River Dr.
413/549-8776

## 34 HANOVER

**La Petite Curiosity Antiques**
195 Washington St.
978/829-9599

**Lloyd Antiques**
140 Broadway
978/826-9232

## 35 HARWICH/HARWICHPORT

**Mews Antiques at Harwichport**
517 Main St.
508/432-6397

**Diamond Antiques & Fine Art**
103 Main St. (Route 28) W. Harwich
508/432-0634

**A London Bridge Antiques**
9 Pleasant Lake Ave. (Route 124)
508/432-6142

**Old Cape Antiques**
1006 Main St. (Route 28) S. Harwich
508/432-8885

**Barn at Windsong**
243 Bank St.
508/432-8281

**Syd's A & J**
338 Bank St. (Harwich)
508/432-3007

**Harwich Antique Center**
10 Route 28
508/432-4220

## 36 HAVERHILL

**Graham & Sons Antiques**
420 Water St.
978/374-8031

**Antique World**
108 Washington St.
978/372-3919

**Tom's Place**
4 Auburn St.
978/373-3820

**Parker's Antiques**
110 River St.
978/373-2332

**Elmwood Antiques**
229 Kenoza Ave.
978/374-7778

**Paul Martin Antiques**
266 River St.
978/521-0909

## 37 HOLLISTON

**Yankee Picker**
86 Church Rear
508/429-9825

**Wilder Shop**
400 Washington St.
508/429-4836

**Antiques Plus**
755 Washington St.
508/429-9186

**Holliston Antiques**
798 Washington St.
508/429-0428

## 38 INDIAN ORCHARD

**Cat's Paw Antiques**
45 Parker St.
413/543-5254

**Oldies from the Estate**
10 Parker St.
413/543-6065

**Tri-Town Antiques**
524 Main St.
413/543-5020

**Sherman Alden Antiques**
520 Main St.
413/543-1820

**Cabotville Collectors**
8 1/2 Parker St.
413/543-6095

## 39 LENOX

**Charles L Flint Antiques**
56 Housatonic St.
413/637-1634

**Past & Future**
38 Church St.
413/637-2225

**Stone's Throw Antiques**
51 Church St.
413/637-2733

### *Great Places To Stay*

**Seven Hills Country Inn**
40 Plunkett St.
413/637-0060 or 1-800-869-6518
Open daily
*Directions: Take Exit 2 off I-90 (Massachusetts Turnpike) and follow Route 20 west for approximately 3 miles. You will see a blue sign on the right that says "Seven Hills." That sign will be pointing to the left, which is Plunkett St. Seven Hills Inn is 1 mile down Plunkett St. on the left.*

Not just a fair-weather haven, Seven Hills Inn works year round to customize just about anything for vacations, banquets, weddings, business retreats and conferences. Furnished with care-worn antiques, and boasting hand-carved fireplaces, leaded glass windows and high ceilings, nothing has changed since the inn was originally built and known as Shipton Court, one of the original Berkshire cottages. The inn is comprised of 15 manor house and 37 terrace house guestrooms, including 3 handicapped accessible ones, on 27 acres in the heart of the Berkshires. There's also a 60-foot swimming pool and two hard-surface tennis courts. Ideally situated to take advantage of the Bershires' seasonal and cultural activities and scenery, Seven Hills Inn is surrounded with such offerings as fall foliage festivals, cider pressings, hayrides, downhill and cross-country skiing, historic homesites and museums. Tanglewood, Jacobs Pillow Dance Theatre, and, next door is the Edith Wharton estate, home of Shakespeare and Company.

## 40 LITTLETON

**Van Wyck's Antiques**
325 Great Road
978/952-2878

**Upton House Antiques**
275 King St.
978/486-3367

**Sunflower Antiques**
537 King St.
978/486-0606

**Littleton Antiques**
476 King St.
978/952-0001

**Hamlet Antiques**
161 Great Road
978/952-2445

**Flowers & Spice & Everything**
2 Mannion Pl.
978/486-3687

**Blue Cape Antiques**
620 Great Road
978/486-4709

**Frederic Gallery**
510 King St.
978/486-9183

## 41 LOWELL

**Whitney House Antiques**
913 Pawtucket St.
978/458-0044

**Hank Garrity Antiques**
331 Broadway St.
978/453-6497

**Vintage Co.**
17 Shattuck St.
978/453-9096

## 42 LYNN

**Diamond District Antiques**
9 Broad St.
781/586-8788

### *Great Places To Stay*

**Diamond District Breakfast Inn**
142 Ocean St.
781/599-4470 or 1-800-666-3076
Fax: 781/599-2200
*Directions: Located about 8 1/2 miles north of Boston and Logan International Airport, near the intersection of Routes 1A and 129.*

Just 300 feet off of a 3.5 mile stretch of beach, the Diamond District Breakfast Inn offers guest rooms with private baths, ocean swimming, walking and biking paths, and business services. Recently listed on the National Register as a Historic District, the inn is a 1911 Georgian style mansion with 17 rooms, sitting on one half acre in Boston's North Shore, also known as Lynn's "Diamond District." Once the private estate of P. J. Harney, a Lynn shoe manufacturer, the original house plans and specifications remain with the house, as do some original fixtures. Features include a three-story staircase, established gardens, hardwood floors, antiques and Oriental rugs, an 1895 rosewood Knabe concert grand piano, and a custom-made Chippendale dining room table and chairs.

## 43 LYNNFIELD

**B & D Antiques & Collectibles**
451 Broadway
781/598-4653

## 44 MARBLEHEAD

### Wicker Unlimited

108 Washington St.
781/631-9728
Mon.-Sat. 10-5, Sun. 12-6
*Directions: Take Route 128 north from Massachusetts Turnpike (I-95) about 20 miles to Route 114 E. (Exit 25 A Marblehead). Go east on 114 through Salem into Marblehead (Route 114 E. becomes Pleasant St.). Follow Pleasant St. all the way to end "T" intersection. Turn left on Washington St. and look to your right. The store can be seen in old town. From 128 to Marblehead is 6 miles.*

Marla Segal bought her first piece of wicker at the ripe old age of 15. The purchase of that single wicker rocker inspired her to the point of hopeless infatuation. After serving several years as an apprentice at a Boston firm, where she learned to repair wicker, Marla decided to open up her own shop. She quickly earned the reputation as an honest and knowledgeable dealer. Today, she supplies both veteran and new collectors with wicker she acquires from all parts of the country. "I try to match the lifestyle of the person to the right piece of wicker," she explains.

However, Marla's interests are unlimited, so a full array of American antiques and collectibles is also found in Wicker Unlimited. Quilts, Fiesta, Roseville, Limoges, linens, rugs, and even garden tools are just a small sampling of what might be available. Country pine, mahogany, oak or walnut—it's always a surprise to see what has been discovered in some of the great, old New England estates that surround the area.

**Calico**
92 Washington St.
781/631-3607

**Old Town Antique Co-op**
108 Washington St.
781/631-9728

**Heeltapper Antiques**
134 Washington St.
781/631-7722

**Marblehead Antiques**
118 Pleasant St.
781/631-9791

**Honest Ladies-Good Buy**
120 Pleasant St.
781-631-7555

**Antiquewear-Buttons**
82 Front St.
781/639-0070

**Evie's Corner**
96 Washington St.
781/639-0007

**Sack's Antiques**
38 State St.
781/631-0770

## 45 MIDDLEBORO

**Sam's Antique Centre**
51 Centre St.
508/947-9550

**Middleboro Antiques Co.**
11 N. Main St.
508/947-1844

**Christina's Antiques**
19 S. Main St.
508/947-5220

**Milady's Mercantile**
21 S. Main St.
508/946-2121

**Barewood**
282 W. Grove St.
508/947-4482

## 46 NANTUCKET

### Nantucket Island

Step off the ferry or the plane and you're in another world. Thirty miles off Cape Cod, this crescent-shaped island retains a quiet charm found in past days when whaling ships made the island haven their home. You'll find lots to explore on foot or on bicycle: unspoiled beaches and the solitary lighthouses, peaceful byways and lanes, historic mansions, and open-air farmers' stands.

Nantucket Town abounds with elegant restaurants and antiques, craft and specialty stores. Sea captains' houses line the cobblestone streets. The Whaling Museum, a former spermaceti factory, now overflows with artifacts and memorabilia from the island's once-thriving industry. Whale-watching trips, deep-sea fishing charters, and numerous excursion boats leave from Straight Wharf.

The island's magic continues year round. In late April, the Daffodil Festival features millions of yellow flowers planted by islanders as a celebration of spring.

### Wayne Pratt, Inc.

28 Main St.
508/228-8788
(Seasonal)

Offering the discriminating shopper the opportunity to purchase antiques of exceptional quality and design. When traveling in Connecticut, be sure to visit their 3,000 sq. ft. showroom located in Woodbury.

**Weeds**
14 Centre St.
508/228-5200

**Celtic Pine**
118 Orange St.
508/228-6866

**Nantucket House Antiques**
1 S. Beach St.
508/228-4604

**Jewelers Gallery of Nantucket**
21 Center St.
508/228-0229

**Frank Sylvia Jr Antiques**
0 Washington St.
508/228-2926

**Sylvia**
6 Rays Court
508/228-0960

**Antiques Depot**
14 Easy St.
508/228-1287

**Modern Arts**
67 Old South Road
508/228-2358

**Forager House Collection**
20 Center St.
508/228-5977

**Gallery at 4 India**
4 India St.
508/228-8509

**Manor House Antiques**
31 Center St.
508/228-4335

**Letitia Lundeen Antique**
34 Center St.
508/228-8566

**Nantucket Country**
38 Center St.
508/228-8868

**Nina Hellman**
48 Center St.
508/228-4677

**Val Maitino Antiques**
31 N. Liberty St.
508/228-2747

**Tonkin of Nantucket Antiques**
33 Main St.
508/228-9697

### *Favorite Places To Eat*

**Atlantic Cafe**
15 S. Water St.
508/228-0570

Atlantic Cafe is one of those kinds of eating places where anybody can go at any time and feel comfortable, because it really doesn't matter how you look. They have a huge menu of all-American food, and eventually everyone you know will come in. You can bring the kids, the in-laws, the weekend guests, all in shorts, or grunge clothes, or whatever—it doesn't matter!

**Jared Coffee House**
29 Broad St.
508/228-2400

Jared Coffee House is a legend and a landmark in Nantucket—one of those "see and be seen" places. The formal dining room serves breakfast and dinner (steaks, fish, stuffed shrimp and desserts). An informal pub serves lunch and dinner (fish and chips, tuna, burgers, etc.). A must-do tourist destination.

## 47 NEWBURYPORT

**Newburyport Estate Jewelers**
7 State St.
978/462-6242

**Olde Port Book Shop**
18 State St.
978/462-0100

**Flukes & Finds & Friends**
37 State St.
978/463-6968

**Lady Di's Antiques**
21 Water St.
978/462-5858

**Sam's Treasured Memories**
39 Water St.
978/462-0024

**Annex**
49 Water St., #R
978/462-8212

**Seacoast Antiques**
115 Merrimac St.
978/463-3106

**Shandell Antiques**
12 Federal St.
978/463-0681

**Pleasant Village Antiques**
40 Pleasant St.
978/463-8605

## 48 NEWTON

**Marcia & Bea**
1 Lincoln St.
617/332-2408

**Sonia Paine Antiques Gallery**
373 Boylston St.
617/566-9669

**Give & Take Consignments**
799 Washington St.
617/964-4454

**Dining Room Showcase**
833 Washington St.
617/527-8368

**Antique Gallery-Eugene O'Neill**
381 Elliot St.
617/965-5965

**Antique Nook**
381 Elliot St.
617/969-1060

**Antique Treasures**
381 Elliot St.
617/965-8141

**Belle Maison**
51 Langley Road
617/964-6455

**Consignment Galleries**
1276 Washington St.
617/965-6131

**Eric's Antiques**
381 Elliot St.
617/332-3744

**Madeleine C. Scanlon Antiques**
381 Elliot St.
617/964-8853

**Marcy's Antiques Ltd.**
381 Elliot St.
617/244-3237

**Ruth Feldman Antiques**
381 Elliot St.
617/527-7121

**Shirley Van Antiques**
381 Elliot St.
617/969-1846

**Steve's Antique Shop**
381 Elliot St.
617/969-2403

**Tactile**
381 Elliot St.
617/527-4938

**Touch of Glass**
381 Elliot St.
617/527-4865

**Acorn Antiques**
289 Elliot St.
617/527-8511

## 49 NORTHAMPTON

**Antiques Corner**
5 Market St.
413/584-8939

**Antique Center of Northampton**
9 1/2 Market St.
413/584-3600

**American Decorative Arts**
3 Olive St.
413/584-6804

**Up In The Attic**
11 Market St.
413/587-3055

**C. J. Sprong & Co.**
300 Pleasant St.
413/584-7440

**Family Jewels**
56 Green St.
413/584-0613

**Collector**
11 Bridge St.
413/584-6734

## 50 NORTHBOROUGH

**Tins & Things**
28 Main St.
508/393-4647

**Elegant Junk**
94 Main St.
508/393-8736

**Bell Tower Antiques**
56 W. Main St.
508/393-5477

**Cyrus Gale Antiques**
20 Main St.
508/393-7300

## 51 NORWOOD

**Norwood Antiques & Restorations**
483 Washington St.
781/769-9198

**Wise Owl**
637 Washington St.
781/769-5255

**Brenda's Antiques**
644 Washington St.
781/762-3227

**Applegate Antiques**
721 Washington St.
781/769-8892

**Norwood Trading Post**
1182 Washington St.
781/762-2186

## 52 OLD DEERFIELD

In "Historic Deerfield, an Introduction," the author produces a setting of long ago:

"Deerfield is a beautiful ghost, haunted by the drama and violence of its early history as well as by more recent spirits who have witnessed the joys and sorrows of life in a small New England town over 300 years ago. Unlike other ghosts, Deerfield is no disembodied spirit eluding our sight and grasp. The town retains material evidence of Native American habitations from several millennia, the 17th century English town plan of compact village and broad meadows, 18th and 19th century houses filled with the relics of hearth and home that reveal to us so many intimate details of life in early New England. Twenty-four of the houses along The Street in Deerfield were here when revolution broke out against England in 1775. Another twenty-three buildings had been erected before 1850. Their contents date from the time of Deerfield's first English settlement in 1669 to the flourishing of the Arts and Crafts movement in the early 20th century."

In 1952 Mr. and Mrs. Henry N. Flynt, wanting to assure the future of the village of Deerfield, incorporated Historic Deerfield, Inc. (then known as the Heritage Foundation) to preserve Deerfield, open its old houses to visitors, and use the buildings and their collections to foster education in and understanding of the American past.

When the Flynts founded Historic Deerfield in 1952, they had four houses open to the public in which they attempted to offer visitors a view of life in Deerfield in the colonial and early national periods. Although they had acquired a few choice antiques for display in these buildings, most of their furnishings were country pieces. In the 1950s their collection grew under the influence of antiques dealers, museum curators, and fellow collectors. They turned increasingly to high style furniture and began to form special collections of early American silver, English ceramics and Chinese export porcelain, and textiles, needlework, and costume. By the end of the decade the Flynts and Historic Deerfield had become widely recognized for the national importance of these collections. They are displayed in sympathetic settings in six historic buildings along The Street.

Today, Historic Deerfield offers workshops, lecture series, antiques forums, summer archaeological excavations and educational programs for students and visitors of all ages.

Daily guided museum tours and walking tours through the village highlight Deerfield and America's history for tourist and travelers from all over the world.

Among the accommodations for dining and lodging is the 1884 Deerfield Inn. The inn has 23 guest rooms, three dining rooms, a coffee shop and full-service bar. There are facilities on the premises for weddings, private parties and small business meetings. The inn is open throughout the year, 413/774-5587.

All in all, there is plenty to see. Thirteen museum houses dating from circa 1720 to 1850 display more than 20,000 objects made or used in America from 1600 to 1900. Highlights of the collections include American furniture with special emphasis on the Connecticut River Valley; English and Chinese ceramics; American and English silver; and American and English textiles.

For further information, call 413/774-5581

Contributed by Southern Antiques Magazine, May 1995

**5 & 10 Antique Gallery**
Routes 5 & 10 (Old Deerfield)
413/773-3620
Web site: antiques510.com
Daily 10-5, Jan.-May, Closed Wed.
*Directions: Exit 26 off I-91, 2A E., right at Dunkin' Donuts, right at first light, 1 1/4 mile on Routes 5 & 10. Exit 24 off I-91, 7 miles north on Routes 5 & 10, 1 mile north of Historic Deerfield, Mass.*

The 5 & 10 Antique Gallery is a bit of history within itself. The shop has provided quality antiques for the past 20 years. Featuring two levels of 18th, 19th and early 20th century furnishings, fine porcelain, china, glassware, silver, linens, primitives, toys, dolls, books, antique reference books, Sotherby catalogues, tools, kitchen ware, and showcases of smalls and collectibles all within the beautiful setting of Old Deerfield.

**Lighthouse Antiques**
Routes 5 & 10
No Phone Listed

## 53 ORLEANS, EAST ORLEANS, SOUTH ORLEANS

**Lilli's Antique Emporium**
Route 6 A
508/255-8300

**Continuum**
7 Route 28
508/255-8513

**Antique Center of Orleans**
34 Main St.
508/2240-5551

**Pleasant Bay Antiques, Inc.**
540 Chatham Road (Route 28)
508/255-0930

**Countryside Antiques**
6 Lewis Road
508/240-0525

**East Orleans Antiques**
204 Main St.
508/255-2592

**The Clock Shop at Pleasant Bay**
403 S. Orleans Road
508/240-0175

## 54 OSTERVILLE

**A Stanley Wheelock Antiques**
870 Main St.
508/420-3170

**Farmhouse**
1340 Main St.
508/420-2400

**Hollyhocks**
891 Main St.
508/420-0484

## 55 PEABODY

**Chuck Watts Antiques**
18 Main St.
978/532-7400

## 56 PEMBROKE

**Magic Garden Antiques**
74 Congress
781/826-7930

**North River Antiques Center**
236 Water St.
781/826-3736

**Endless Antiques**
95 Church St.
781/826-7177

**Good Riddance Antiques**
95 Church St.
781/826-8955

**Red Lion Antiques**
95 Church St.
781/829-8782

## 57 PITTSFIELD

**Greystone Gardens**
436 North St.
413/442-9291

**Potala**
148 North St.
413/443-5568

**Memory Lane Antiques**
446 Tyler St.
413/499-2718

**Fontaine Auction Gallery**
1485 W. Housatonic St.
413/448-8922

**Craftsman Auctions**
1485 W. Housatonic St.
413/448-8922

### *Interesting Side Trips*

**Hancock Shaker Village**
413/443-0188 or 1-800-817-1137
*Directions: Hancock Shaker Village is located in western Massachusetts in the heart of the Berkshires. It is at the junction of Routes 20 and 41 west of Pittsfield. Convenient to the Massachusetts Turnpike, Taconic State Parkway and New York Thruway, it is a one-hour drive from Albany and a three-hour drive from New York or Boston. The Village is located near Tanglewood, the Norman Rockwell Museum, Clark Art Institute and many other major cultural attractions.*

Shakers' "City of Peace," beckons you to discover the way of life of America's most successful communitarian society. Now a living history museum, the village was an active Shaker community from 1790 to 1960.

Members held all property in common and practiced celibacy, equality and separation of the sexes, and pacificism as they sought to create "heaven on earth". Putting their "hands to work and hearts to God", the Shakers created a society based in spirituality but rich in practicality and ingenuity. Discover their unique approach to life and the remarkable fruits of their labors at Hancock Shaker Village.

Explore the extraordinary 1826 Round Stone Barn, the remarkable 1830 communal Brick Dwelling, and eighteen other restored buildings which span three centuries. From the early water-powered laundry and machine shop to the heated 1916 automobile garage, you will marvel at Shaker design, workmanship, inventiveness and efficiency. Envision the Shakers worshiping in ecstatic dance and song in the sparse simplicity of the 1793 Meetinghouse. Learn about 20th-century Shaker life amidst the worldly decor and comforts of the Trustees' Office and Store.

Appreciate Shaker industriousness as you watch artisans and farmers at work. Chat with gardeners as they harvest herbs, vegetables, and seeds in the heirloom gardens.

Try a spinning wheel, loom, or quill pen in the Discovery Room. Enjoy a candlelight dinner in the quiet of the matches, sheep shearing and harvest activities. Explore Shaker archaeological sites. Savor the order and tranquility of the "City of Peace".

## 58 PLYMOUTH

**Dillon & Co. English Country**
12 North St.
508/747-2242

**Chiltonville Antiques**
40 State Road
508/746-2164

**North Plymouth Antiques**
398 Court St.
508/830-0127

**Plymouth Antiques Trading Co.**
8 Court St.
508/746-3450

**Antique House**
184 Water St.
508/747-1207

**Village Braider**
48 Sandwich St.
508/746-9625

**Thyme Collections Center**
15 Main St.
508/746-6970

### *Interesting Side Trips*

**Plimoth Plantation**
Plimoth Plantation Hwy.
Accessible via Route 3
508/746-1622

It's places like Plimoth Plantation and other living history museums that let us know just how remarkable our ancestors really were. Plimoth Plantation offers a chance to see Plymouth as it was when America's most famous immigrants, the Pilgrims, first colonized the New World. It also gives an in-depth look into the lives of the Wampanoag Indians, on whose land the Pilgrims settled. Key parts of the museum are the 1627 Pilgrim Village, where people represent actual Pilgrims in everyday life and settings, like house building, food preparation and gardening; the Carriage House Crafts Center, where you can watch period goods being reproduced using materials and tools like those of the 17th century; Hobbamock's Wampanoag Indian Homesite, where Native Americans describe the effects of the colonists' arrival on their own ancestors and how the events continue to affect their people today. Some of the staff are in native attire, and the area itself is a re-creation of one family's homesite. Don't forget to check out the Mayflower II, a reproduction of the ship that brought the Pilgrims to Plymouth, located on the waterfront adjacent to Plymouth Rock.

## 59 PROVINCETOWN

**Provincetown Antique Market**
131 Commercial St.
508/487-1115

**West End Antiques**
146 Commercial St.
508/487-6723

**Scott Dinsmore Antiques**
179 Commercial St.
508/487-2236

**Clifford-William Antiques**
225 Commercial St.
508/487-4174

**Small Pleasures**
359 Commercial St.
508/487-3712

**Remembrances of Things Past**
376 Commercial St.
508/487-9443

**Alan's Attic**
194 Commercial St.
508/487-4234

**194 Memory Lane**
194 Commercial St.
508/487-4234

**Emporium Antiques**
220 Commercial St.
508/487-1948

**Julie Heller Gallery**
2 Gosnold St.
508/487-2169

**Sagamore Antiques**
Corner Route 6A & Westdale Park
508/888-5186

## 60 REHOBOTH

**Madeline's Antiques**
164 Winthrop St.
508/252-3965

**Mendes Antiques**
Route 44 - 52 Blanding Road
508/336-7381

**Sleepy Hollow Antiques**
309 Winthrop St.
508/252-3483

**Wooden Keyhole**
582 Winthrop St.
508/336-7475

## 61 ROCKPORT

**Hanna Wingate of Rockport**
11 Main St.
978/546-1008

**Woodbine Collection**
35 Main St.
978/546-9324

**Rockport Trading Co.**
67 Broadway
978/546-8066

**Rockport Quilt Shoppe**
2 Ocean Ave.
978/546-1001

**Ye Olde Lantern Antiques**
28 Railroad Ave.
978/546-6757

## 62 SALEM

**Filigree & Fancy Antiques**
4 Wharf St.
978/745-9222

**Burke Antiques**
11 Central
978/744-2242

**Asia House**
18 Washington Square
978/745-8257

**AAA Olde Naumkeag Antiques**
1 Hawthorne Blvd.
978/745-9280

**Pickering Wharf Antiques**
71-73 Wharf St.
978/740-6734

**Union Street Antiques**
1 E. India Square Mall
978/745-4258

**Salem Antiques**
266 Canal St.
978/744-7229

## 63 SANDWICH

**Sandwich Antique Center**
131 Route 6A
508/833-8580

**Paul Madden Antiques**
16 Jarves St.
508/888-6434

**May Pope Lane**
161 Old Kings Hwy.
508/888-1230

**H Richard Strand Antiques**
2 Grove St./Town Hall Square
508/888-3230

**Brown Jug**
155 Main St.
508/833-1088

**Coco Plum Garden Antique**
18 Liberty St.
508/1-888-9001

# Massachusetts

**Nodding Violet**
25 Jarves
508/888-7756

**Ezra Weston**
433 St. 6A, E. Sandwich
508/833-2228

**Horsefeathers Antiques**
454 Route 6A, E. Sandwich
508/888-5298

**Keepers of the Past**
198 Old King's Hwy.
508/888-8278

**Old Time Shop**
379 Route 6A (E. Sandwich)
508/888-2368

**Shawme Pond Antiques**
13 Water St. (Route 130)
508/888-2603

## 64 SCITUATE

**Quarter Deck**
206 Front St.
781/545-4303

**Greenhouse Antiques**
182 First Parish Road
781/545-1964

**Echo Lake Antiques**
165 Front St.
781/545-7100

**Gatherings**
131 Front St.
781/545-7664

**Quarter Deck**
51 Cole Pkwy.
781/544-3301

**Bird In Hand Antiques**
157 Front St.
781/545-1728

**Needful Things Antiques**
161 Front St.
781/544-0299

## 65 SEEKONK

**Antiques at Hearthstone House**
15 Fall River Ave. (Route 114A)
508/336-6273

**Vinny's Antiques Center**
380 Fall River Ave.
508/336-0800

**Consignment Barn**
394 Fall River Ave.
508/336-3228

**Ruth Falkinburg Doll Shop**
208 Taunton Ave.
508/336-6929

**Lost Treasures Antiques**
1460 Fall River Ave.
508/336-9294

**County Squire Antiques**
1732 Fall River Ave.
508/336-8442

**Grist Mill Country Store**
879 Arcade Ave.
508/336-8232

**Amanda Lynn's Antiques**
640 Fall River Ave.
508/336-5205

**Bittersweet Memories**
642 Fall River Ave.
508/336-9300

**John George Antiques**
370 Tauton Ave.
508/336-6057

**Leonard's Antiques & Reproductions**
600 Tauton Ave.
508/336-8585

## 66 SHEFFIELD

**David M. Weiss**
Main St. (Route 7)
413/229-2716

**Darr Antiques & Interiors**
28 S. Main (Route 7)
413/229-7773

**Corner House Antiques**
Main St. (Route 7)
413/229-6627

**1750 House Antiques**
S. Main (Route 7)
413/229-6635

**Frederick Hatfield Antiques**
99 S. Main (Route 7)
413/229-7986

**Anthony's Antiques**
102 Main St. Rear (Route 7)
413/229-8208

**Saturday Sweets**
755A N. Main (Route 7)
413/229-0026

**Centuryhurst Berkshire Antiques**
Main St. (Route 7)
413/229-3277

**Cupboards & Roses**
Main St. (Route 7)
413/229-3070

**Ole T J's Antique Barn**
Main St. (Route 7)
413/229-8382

**Kuttner Antiques**
Main St. (Route 7)
413/229-2955

**Berkshire Gilder's Antiques**
15 Main St. (Route 7)
413/229-0113

**Jenny Hall Antiques**
Route 7
413/229-0277

**Dovetail Antiques**
Route 7
413/229-2628

**Classic Images Art & Antiques**
527 Sheffield Plain
413/229-0033

**Le Trianon**
1854 N. Main St.(Route 7)
413/528-0775

**North Main Street Antique**
655 Route 7
413/229-9029

**May's Everything Shop**
655 Route 7
413/229-2037

## 67 SHELBURNE/SHELBURNE FALLS

**Shea Antiques**
69 Bridge St.
413/625-8353

**Strawberry Field**
1204 Mohawk Trail
413/625-2039

**Rainville Trading Post**
251 Main St.
413/625-6536

**Orchard Hill Antiques**
108 Colrain Road
413/625-2433

**Yankee Pastime Antiques**
Route 112 N. Colrain Road
413/625-2730

**Amstein's Antiques**
46 Crittendon Hill Road
413/625-8237

**Charlemont House Gallery**
6 State St.
413/625-2800

**Blacksmith Shoppe**
44 State St.
413/625-6291

**Merry Lion**
6 State St.
413/625-2800

**Shelburne Country Shop**
Mohawk Trail
413/625-2041

## 68 SHREWSBURY

**The Antique Center of Shrewsbury**
510 Boston Turnpike Road (Route 9)
508/845-9600

## 69 SOMERVILLE

**Londontowne Galleries**
380 Somerville Ave.
617/625-2045

**Karma Antiques**
248 Beacon St.
617/864-5875

**Warped Collectibles**
236 Elm St.
617/666-3129

## 70 SOUTHAMPTON

### Southampton Antiques
172 College Hwy. (Route 10)
413/527-1022 Fax: 413/527-6056
Sat. 10-5. Appointments welcome, closed August

Meg and Bruce Cummings offer the largest selection of authentic antique American oak and Victorian furniture in New England — no reproductions, no imports and authenticity guaranteed. They have three large barns with five floors of merchandise for customers to browse through, sigh over, touch, examine and take home.

Instead of having a store catalog, they offer customers a custom-made video for $25, designed to meet particular specifications and needs. Each video is individually made and includes price quotes, style description, condition, approximate age and dimensions.

"We focus on high style American Victorian walnut, rosewood, mahogany, and turn-of-the-century oak," say the Cummings. "Furniture found in our barns is in three categories: 'as found' original varnish, superb original finish and refinished. We are very proud of our refinished product and feel that our refinishing process has reached a quality second to none."

Among the pieces regularly offered by the Cummings are curio cabinets, hall trees, desks, wicker, swivel chairs, bedroom suites, lockside chests, conference tables, clocks, bookcases, lamps, side-by-sides, library tables, beds, roll-top desks, Victorian sofas, marble-top furniture, sets of chairs, and square and round dining tables. Their specialties include Victorian Renaissance Revival, turn-of-the-century oak and Victorian Rococo.

## 71 SOUTH DEERFIELD

**Yesterdays Antique Center**
Routes 5 & 10
413/665-7226

**Antiques at Deerfield**
Routes 5 & 10
No Phone Listed

**House of the Ferret**
Routes 5 & 10
413/665-0038

**Antiques by Sandra Pavoni**
Routes 5 & 10
413/665-0511

## 72 SOUTH EGREMONT

**Red Barn Antiques**
72 Main St.
413/528-3230

**Howard's Antiques**
Hillsdale Road (Route 23)
413/528-1232

**Bruce & Sue Gventer: "Books"**
By Appointment
413/528-2327

**Geffner/Schatzky Antiques**
Route 23
413/528-0057

**The Splendid Peasant Ltd.**
Route 23 at Sheffield Road
413/528-5755

## 73 SPRINGFIELD

**Fancy That**
699 Sumner Ave.
413/739-5118

**Lady In Red Antiques**
712 Sumner Ave.
413/734-6100

**A-1 Antique Store**
752 Summer Ave.
413/732-6855

**Tri-Towne Collectibles**
524 Main St.
413/543-5020

**Prestige Antiques**
435 White St.
413/739-2190

**Cat's Paw Antiques**
45 Parker St.
413/543-5254

**Antiques on Boland Way**
1500 Main St.
413/746-4643

**Susan T's Antiques**
705 Sumner Ave.
413/827-8910

**Patti's Antiques & Treasures**
532 Main St.
413/543-8484

## 74 STOCKBRIDGE

**Greystone Gardens**
The Mews
413/298-0113

**John R. Sanderson Rare Books**
8 W. Main
413/298-5322

***Great Places To Stay***

### Inn at Stockbridge
P.O. Box 618, Route 7 N.
413/298-3337
Daily 8-9
Rates:$75-225
*Directions: On Route 7, 1 1/2 miles north of Stockbridge Center. Off the Massachusetts Turnpike, take Exit 2, Route 102 West to Route 7 North. Travel Route 7 North for 1 1/4 miles.*

Graciously operated by Alice and Len Schiller, the Inn at Stockbridge offers eight guest rooms with private baths, including two suites. Settled on 12 secluded acres, the Colonial Revival style home, complete with Georgian detailing and classical columns, has remained structurally unchanged since its construction in 1906 as a vacation home for a Boston attorney. Each morning a full breakfast is served on a grand mahogany table set with china, silver, crystal, linen and lighted candles. Often after a refreshing dip in the pool, guests are treated to afternoon wine and cheese, and can spend a quiet evening browsing the inn's extensive library.

### *Interesting Side Trips*

**Charles H. Baldwin & Sons**
1 Center St.
West Stockbridge
413/232-7785
Tues.-Sat. 9-5, occasionally open Sun.

As a counterpoint to overindulged chocoholics, West Stockbridge offers a vanilla lover's nirvana. In the tiny storefront of Charles H. Baldwin & Sons, vanilla connoisseurs can see vanilla being made according to the methods used by the Baldwin family since 1888. The shop itself dates back to the late 1700s; the oak barrels in which the extract is aged, over 100 years. The whole place smells like, well, vanilla. Shoppers can watch family members draw the spice from the casks into gallon jugs, then use the vintage, soldered-steel measuring cup with a spring-operated siphon to pour the fragrant brandy-colored liquid into tiny bottles, which are capped and labeled by hand. In the rear of the store is the "laboratory," where more family members blend almond, anise, peppermint and lemon extracts or their special vanilla sugar. Purchases are rung up on a 19th century cash register, and money is kept in a 100-year-old safe that opens with an antique brass key. A true piece of "living history."

## 75 STURBRIDGE

**Showcase Antique Center, Inc.**
Route 20
At The Entrance To Old Sturbridge Village
508/347-7190 Fax: 508/347-5420
Merchandise listings faxed back 24 hrs.: 508/347-2400
Web site: www.showcaseantiques.com
Email: showcase@hey.net
Mon., Wed.-Sat. 10-5, Sun. 12-5, closed Tue.
Extended hours during Brimfield Antique Shows
*Directions: Located on Route 20 in Sturbridge, just one mile west from Exit 9 off I-90 (Massachusetts Turnpike) and from Exit 3B off I-84.*

For specific information see review at the beginning of this section.

**Fairground Antique Center**
362 Main St.
508/347-3926

**Antique Center of Sturbridge**
426 Main St.
508/347-5150

**Sturbridge Antique Shops**
200 Charlton Road
508/347-2744

**This & That**
446 Main St.
508/347-5183

**Airport Antiques**
22 New Boston Road
508/347-3304

### *Great Places To Stay*

**The Wildwood Inn Bed & Breakfast**
121 Church St.
413/967-7798 or 1-800-860-8098
Open daily
Rates: $50-80

The Wildwood Inn Bed & Breakfast is located very near Sturbridge. For specific information see Ware #80.

**Commonwealth Cottage**
11 Summit Ave.
508/347-7708
Mon.-Sun. All year
Rates: $85-145
*Directions: From Massachusetts Turnpike (I-90): Take Exit 9 to Route 20 W. towards Brimfield. After passing the intersection of Route 148 on the right, take the next left onto Commonwealth Ave. At the "Heritage Green" sign, veer left and you'll see Commonwealth Cottage straight ahead. From I-84 E.,: Take Exit 3 B, (Route 20 W./Palmer). Follow Route 20 west and proceed as before. From Brimfield: Follow Route 20 east into Sturbridge. Make a right onto Commonwealth Ave., then proceed as above. (Be careful—Commonwealth Ave. appears quickly. Just after the sign for 630 Main St. in front of the gray building of shops on the left, and a yellow clapboard house on the right.)*

Sitting on a knoll surrounded by 200-year-old maple trees, almost in the heart of Sturbridge's attractions, is the charming Queen Anne Victorian home known as Commonwealth Cottage. Lovingly run by Wiebke and Bob Gilbert, the Commonwealh is comfortably furnished with period pieces and family hand-me-downs. A variety of guest rooms is available, most with queen-sized beds and private bath. Each room has its own personality, like the M&M Room, named after both Wiebke and Bob's grandmothers and furnished with many of their cherished belongings. Or Uncle Sam's baroque-themed room, and Mr. Bigelow's Room, named after Bob's dad and filled with lots of greens, wicker and an actual picket fence for the queen headboard. In addition to a sumptuous breakfast, complete with the house's own jams and jellies, guests are treated to afternoon tea.

### Interesting Side Trips

**Old Sturbridge Village**
Route 20 W.
508/347-3362
Website: www.osv.org
*Directions: Route 20, Sturbridge, Mass., Exit 2 off I-84. (After 7 p.m. use Exit 3 B), Exit 9 off the Massachusetts Pike.*

Old Sturbridge Village is another amazing piece of living history. It is an extraordinary outdoor museum that brings to life a working community of the 1830s, down to the smallest details. The largest history museum in the northeast, Old Sturbridge is a re-created community on over 200 acres, with more than 40 restored structures, carefully relocated from as far away as Maine. The museum concept was conceived by a member of the Wells family in 1936 as the families of Albert B. And Joe Cheney Wells tried to decide what to do with both men's extensive collections of furniture, tools, utensils, paperweights, glassware, and 19th century clocks. After several major interruptions, including a hurricane and World War I, the museum opened to the public in 1946. In the ensuing 50 years the museum has grown and developed, been redefined and researched. Each exhibit and program is meticulously grounded in historical research, which provides a clearer understanding of the region's past.

By exploring the museum, visitors can experience daily life in an early 19th century country village in New England — from the rustic farmhouse kitchen to the elegant parlor in the finest house on the village common, from the blacksmith shop to a rural printing office and bookstore, examining along the way home furnishings and decorative arts, costume and dress, food and cooking utensils, and implements and devices of all sorts. By choosing to recreate the life and times of the 1830s, the museum founders have chosen a transitional era in New England when life was changing from an agrarian society to an industrial one, when water and steam power was replacing man and animal power, when exploration was increasing through better mass transportation, and the Northeast was moving into the industrial age. The exhibits show these changes in New England: farming with its seasonal tasks and customs; women's lives and their households; mill neighborhoods with their sawmills and gristmills; artisans and rural industry; the center village, more attuned to changes emanating from the cities; community events; and the story of Old Sturbridge Village itself, which celebrated its 50th anniversary in 1996 and is a major force in the field of historic preservation and restoration.

### 76 SUDBURY

**Flashback Furnishings**
88 Boston Post Road
978/443-7709

**Pairs of Chairs, Etc.**
345 Boston Post Road
978/443-3363

**Sudbury Art & Antiques**
730 Boston Post Road
978/443-0994

**Smith & Jones Inc.**
12 Clark Lane
978/443-5517

### 77 THE MOHAWK TRAIL

For an antidote to the hectic pace of modern life, travel the back roads of the northwest corner of Massachusetts, where you'll find charming villages, swimming holes, and covered bridges. The Mohawk Trail, now Route 2, began as a Native American trail, was widened by the early settlers, then was developed as America's first scenic automobile route. The trail is most spectacular in autumn, when the trees turn to brilliant crimsons, oranges and yellows.

A fragrant stop is Shelburne Falls, where the Bridge of Flowers, an old trolley bridge, is planted with masses of blossoms.

### 78 VINEYARD HAVEN/MARTHA'S VINEYARD

Once you've experienced the Vineyard's charm, you'll find it hard to leave. New England's largest island has soft sandy beaches, pine forests, rolling hills and moors, and a number of delightful towns.

Oak Bluffs is famous for its Methodist campground with brightly painted Victorian gingerbread cottages, built in the mid-1800s as a religious retreat. The town also features the Flying Horses, the oldest working carousel in America. Vineyard Haven is a picturesque turn-of-the-century community and a year-round ferry port. Edgartown, once a prosperous whaling port, is now a yachting center filled with stately mariners' homes. The town's Old Whaling Church is a performing arts center. All three towns have bistros, boutiques, and galleries.

Head "up island" and you'll discover the classic New England town of West Tisbury and the rolling hills of Chilmark. At the outermost point of the island are the dramatic color-streaked clay cliffs of Gay Head National Monument.

**C. W. Morgan Maine Antiques**
Beach Road
508/693-3622

**Bramhall & Dunn**
19 Main St.
508/693-6437

**Chartreuse**
State Road
508/696-0500

**Pyewacket's Flea Circus**
63 Beach Road
508/696-7766

**Early Spring Farm Antiques**
93 Lagoon Pond Road
508/693-9141

**All Things Oriental**
Beach Road
508/693-8375

**Summer Old Summer New**
76 Main St.
508/693-8333

More shopping in Martha's Vineyard Oak Bluffs

**Now & Then Shop**
176 Circuit Ave.
508/696-8604

**Pik-Nik Antiques at Four Gables Inn**
New York Ave.
508/696-8384

**Federal House Antiques**
469 New York Ave.
508/693-8602

**Tuckernuck Antiques**
101 Tuckernuck Ave.
508/696-6392

More shopping in Martha's Vineyard West Tisbury

**Hull Antiques**
Edgartown Road
508/693-5713

**M. M. Stone**
527 State Road
508/693-0396

**Forget-Me-Not Antiques**
State Road
508/693-1788

**The Granary Gallery**
The Red Barn Emporium
508/693-0455

More shopping in Martha's Vinyard Menemsha

**Over South**
Basin Road
508/645-3348

More shopping in Martha's Vinyard Edgartown

**Vintage Jewelry**
Main St.
508/627-4509

**Arbor Antiques**
222 Upper Main St.
508/627-8137

**Past & Presents**
37 Main St.
508/627-3992

**Past & Presents**
12 N. Water St.
508/627-6686

### *Favorite Places To Eat*

**The Black Dog Tavern**
Beach St., Vineyard Haven Harbor
508/693-9223

**The Black Dog Bakery**
Water Street, Vineyard Haven Harbor
508/693-4786

Home of the Black Dog T-shirt, The Black Dog Bakery offers "only the best" breads, pies, cookies and more, while The Black Dog Tavern offers an eclectic menu of fresh seafood, pasta salads, and American ethnic thrown in.

## 79 WAKEFIELD

**Iron Horse Antique Gallery**
951 Main St.
781/224-1188

**Back Track Antiques**
239 North Ave.
781/246-4550

## 80 WARE

**The Wildwood Inn Bed & Breakfast**
121 Church St.
413/967-7798 or 1-800-860-8098
Open daily
Rates: $50-80
*Directions: From Massachusetts Turnpike (I-90): Take Exit 8. Turn left off the exit ramp onto Route 32 N. Follow Route 32 N. for 8 miles to Junction Route 32 N. and Route 9 E. (A movie theater is in front of you.) Take a right onto Routes 32 N. and 9 E. At the second light, take a left onto Church St. (If you reach the fire station, you missed the left turn!) Wildwood Inn is on the right, 3/4 mile up Church St., across from the Highland St. sign.*

Midway between Boston and the Berkshires, near the southern gateway to New England, the town of Ware is located right on Highways 9 and 32, two of the beautiful foliage routes of New England, and just a short ride from Exit 8 of the Massachusetts Turnpike.

Waiting to greet you in Ware is a homey, 1880 Victorian inn furnished with American primitive antiques, handmade heirloom quilts, and early cradles. Located on a maple tree-canopied street lined with stately Victorian homes, Wildwood Inn offers a wrap-around porch for lazing away the afternoon, or two landscaped acres for strolling. You can even wander the adjacent 100-acre park, or canoe, bike or ski nearby. The Brimfield Antique Market is a 20-minute drive on "no traffic" back roads. It's also an easy drive to the Five College area, Old Sturbridge or Deerfield, Yankee Candle Complex, the Basketball Hall of Fame, or beautiful Quabbin wilderness. Seven of the nine guest rooms have private baths, and there is a two-bedroom suite with bath and parlor.

## 81 WEST BARNSTABLE

**Bird Cage Inc.**
1064 Main St.
508/362-5559

**Maps of Antiquity**
1022 Route 6A
508/362-7169

**Salt & Chestnut**
651 Route 6A
508/362-6085

## 82 WEST BOYLSTON

**Robert & Co. Antiques**
271 W. Boylston St.
508/835-6550

**West Boylston Antiques**
277 W. Boylston St.
508/835-8853

**Wexford House Gifts**
9 Crescent St.
508/835-6677

**Yankee Heritage Antiques**
44 Sterling St. (Junction 12 & 110)
508-835-2010

**Obadiah Pine Antiques**
160 W. Boylston St.
508/835-3806

## 83 WEST BRIDGEWATER

**Upstairs Downstairs Antiques**
118 S. Main St.
508/586-2880

**One Horse Shay Antiques**
194 S. Main St.
508/587-8185

**America's Attic**
221 W. Center St.
508/584-5281

**Cherry Lane Antiques**
26 W. Center St.
508/559-0359

**West Bridgewater Antiques**
220 S. Main St.
508/580-5533

**Armen Amerigion Antiques**
223 W. Center St.
508/580-1464

**Carriage House Antiques**
102 W. Center St.
508/584-3008

**West Bridgewater Antiques**
165 W. Center St.
508/584-9111

## 84 WEST TOWNSEND

**Delaney Bros. Clocks**
435 Main St.
978/597-8340

**Hobart Village Antique Mall**
445 Main St.
978/597-0332

**Antq. Associates @ West Townsend**
473 Main St.
978/597-8084

## 85 WESTFORD

**Antiques**
301 Littleton Road
978/392-9944

**Westford Valley Antiques**
434 Littleton Road
978/486-4023

**Wolf's Den Antiques**
139 Concord Road RM. 225
978/692-3911

## 86 WILLIAMSTOWN

**Saddleback Antiques**
Route 7 S.
413/458-5852

**Village Flowers Country Store**
Route 43, 112 Water St.
413/458-9696

**The Library Antiques**
70 Spring St.
413/458-3436

**Greenbrier**
Route 7
413/458-2248

**The Amber Fox**
622A Main St. (Route 2)
413/458-8519

**Collectors Warehouse**
105 North St.
413/458-9686

## 87 WORCESTER

**Ragtime Ann-tiques**
70 James St.
508/752-6638

**Collector's Corner**
1 Greenwood
508/754-2062

**Pastiche**
113 Highland St.
508/756-1229

**A & A Antiques**
276 Plantation St.
508/752-6567

**Encore Consignment Shop**
417 Park Ave.
508/757-8887

## 88 YARMOUTH PORT

**Design Works**
159 Main St.
508/362-9698

**Ryan Cooper Maritime Antiques**
161 Main St.
508/362-0190

**Minden Lane Antiques**
175 Main St.
508/362-0220

**Constance Goff Antiques**
161 Main St.
508/362-9540

**Stephen H. Garner Antiques**
169 Main St. (Route 6A)
508/362-8424

**Nickerson's Antiques**
162 Main St.
508/362-6426

**King's Row Antiques**
175 Main St.
508/362-3573

**Lookout Farm Antiques**
175 Main St.
508/362-0292

**Crooks Jaw Inn**
186 Main St.
508/362-6111

# Michigan

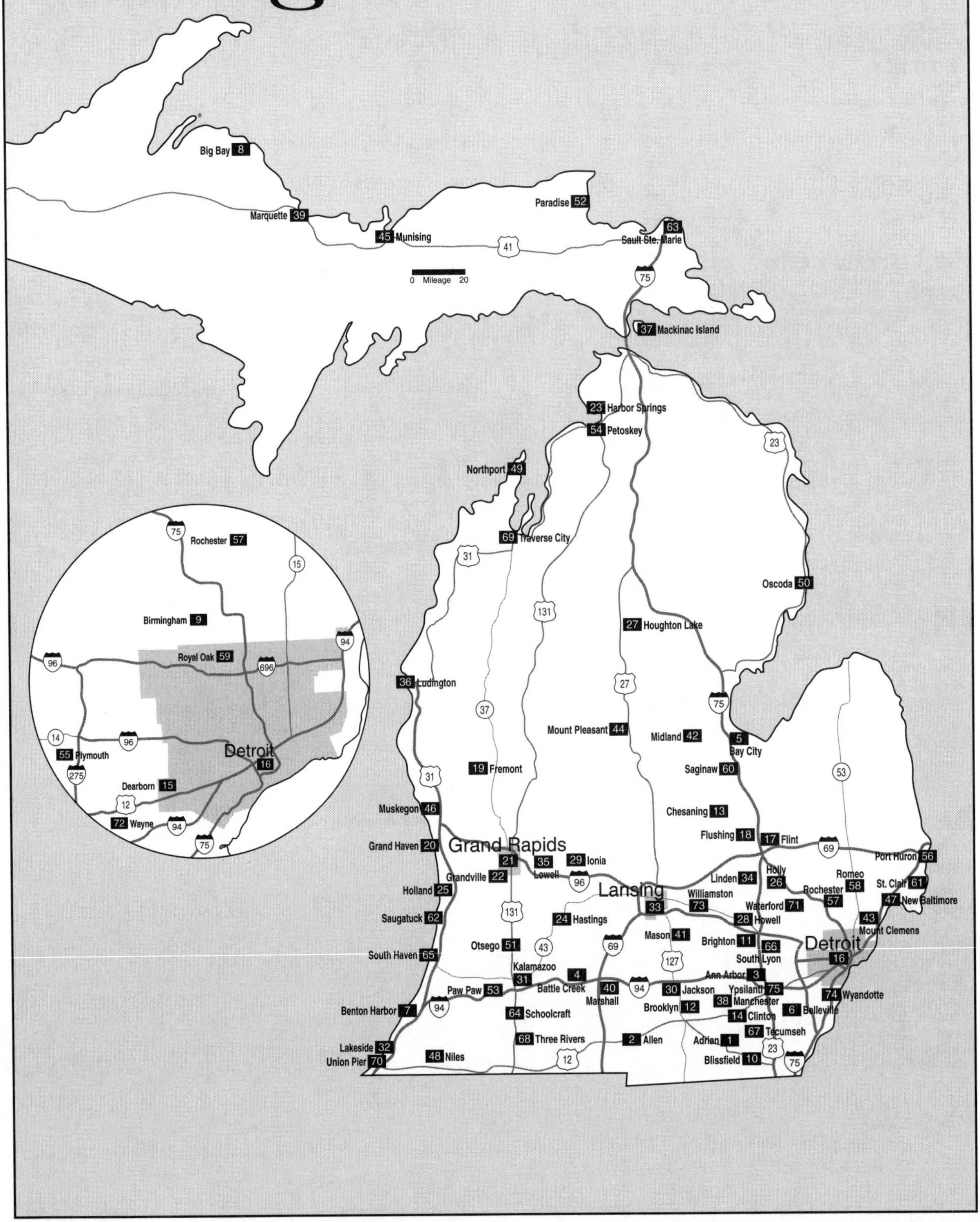

Big Bay 8
Marquette 39
45 Munising
Paradise 52
63
Sault Ste. Marie
41
0 Mileage 20
75
37 Mackinac Island
23 Harbor Springs
54 Petoskey
23
Northport 49
69 Traverse City
31
Oscoda 50
131
27 Houghton Lake
36 Ludington
27
37
75
Mount Pleasant 44
Midland 42
5
Bay City
19 Fremont
Saginaw 60
31
53
Muskegon 46
Chesaning 13
Flushing 18
17 Flint
69
Grand Haven 20
Grand Rapids
21
35
29 Ionia
Lowell
96
Port Huron 56
Grandville 22
Holly 26
Romeo
Holland 25
Lansing
Linden 34
Rochester 58
St. Clair 61
33
Williamston
73
Waterford 71
Rochester 57
47 New Baltimore
Saugatuck 62
131
24 Hastings
28 Howell
43
Mount Clemens
Mason 41
Brighton 11
66
South Lyon
Detroit
16
Otsego 51
43
69
127
South Haven 65
Kalamazoo
31
4
Battle Creek
40
Marshall
94
30 Jackson
Ann Arbor 3
Ypsilanti 75
Paw Paw 53
38 Manchester
74 Wyandotte
Benton Harbor 7
94
64 Schoolcraft
Brooklyn 12
6 Belleville
14 Clinton
67 Tecumseh
Lakeside 32
68 Three Rivers
2 Allen
Adrian 1
Union Pier 70
48 Niles
12
23
Blissfield 10
75
75
Rochester 57
15
Birmingham 9
94
96
Royal Oak 59
696
14
96
Detroit
55 Plymouth
16
275
Dearborn 15
12
72 Wayne
94
75

# A memorable trip to the past begins beneath the beams of Walt's Barn

There's nothing romantic about livestock or farm implements, but the barns that house them—faded red or weathered gray—are another story.

Whether it's simply their sturdy architecture or nostalgia for a simpler country lifestyle, it seems that barns have been adapted very successfully as antiques shops.

From a distance, Walt's Barn in Traverse City appears as quaint and untouched as when it was first built on Nelson Road in 1910. Primitives lie scattered across the yard and, in summer, among the flowers. The barn itself leans a bit, the windows are crooked, the road line seems to wander.

This unique shop is owned and operated by Walt and Susan Feiger. Susan, with the help of her mother, Marian Trager, first opened the barn to sell off family antiques and clear it of "junk," which the Feigers inherited when they bought the building stuffed to the rafters.

Even after the success of the initial sale, she had to be convinced by family members that she'd found her calling. But by 1967 she was in business for the summer trade, and before long, her shop gained the enviable reputation as "the barn with everything."

Walt's Barn has three floors crammed top to bottom. When you visit, give yourself plenty of time. You'll want to browse leisurely through the building and the fine antiques it holds.

A huge cabinet holds an assortment of butter pats, Limoges and early pressed glass. Another is filled with flow blue, orientalia and a touch of stick sponge. Even jewelry—everything from Victorian to George Jensen and Taxco—has a place in the barn.

Walt Feiger, a license plate collector who joined the business when he retired, is known across the country for his gas station memorabilia, slot machines and advertising signs. He does 30 percent of his business through interstate sales.

Although the barn and its inventory are absolutely vintage, the Feigers are state-of-the-art antiques dealers. Susan does appraisals using a mini-cassette and the couple finds their computer invaluable as a research and advertising tool, especially when used with a digital camera that allows them to send photos of a gas pump or globe to a prospective customer anywhere around the world.

*By Marilyn Flaherty*
*Marilyn Flaherty is an area antiques dealer and appraiser.*

*Walt Feiger, a license plate collector who joined the business when he retired, is known across the country for his gas station memorabilia.*

*Walt's Antiques is located on M-37 (Old Mission Peninsula) 8 miles north of Traverse City, Michigan. Turn west 1/4 mile on Nelson Road to 2513. The shop is open Mon.-Sat. 10-5:30, Sun. 12-5:30. The phone number is 616-223-4123 or 616-223-7386.*

# Michigan

## 1 ADRIAN

**Birdsall Depot Antiques**
4106 N. Adrian Hwy.
517/265-7107

**Marshs Antique Mall**
136 S. Winter St.
517/263-8826

## 2 ALLEN

**Michiana Antiques**
100 W. Chicago Road
517/869-2132

**Hand & Heart Antiques**
109 W. Chicago Road
517/869-2553

**Sandy's Simple Pleasures**
109 W. Chicago Road
517/869-2875

**Allen Old Township Hall Shops**
114 W. Chicago Road
517/869-2575

**Andy's Antiques**
118 W. Chicago Road
517/869-2182

**Peddlar's Alley**
164 W. Chicago Road
517/869-2280

**Olde Chicago Pike Antiques Mall**
211 W. Chicago Road
517/869-2719

**A Horse of Course**
108 Prentiss
517/869-2527

**Greentop Country Antique Mall**
8651 W. Chicago Road
517/869-2100

**Allen Antique Mall**
9011 W. Chicago Road
517/869-2788

**Capital Antiques**
U.S. Hwy. 12
517/869-2055

## 3 ANN ARBOR

### Ann Arbor Antiques Market

Margaret Brusher, Promoter
5055 Ann Arbor Saline Road
313/662-9453

Thirty years ago, Margaret Brusher was a pioneer in the antique market, holding her first show at the local Ann Arbor Farmer's Market with 68 dealers participating. Nowadays, the monthly market draws over 350 dealers and a national (sometimes international) clientele.

So why has Ann Arbor stood the test of time? First is the Brusher's market tough standards of authenticity, with every item guaranteed. Second, the market has shown a tendency to change as the antiques market in general changes. Where once, booth after booth was filled with country furniture and related accessories, desirous at the time, today's Ann Arbor represents variety and quality, irrespective of style or period to reflect the diversity of the customer. (For show dates, call the number listed above).

**Rage of the Age**
314 S. Ashley St.
313/662-0777

**Treasure Mart**
529 Detroit St.
313/662-1363

**Past Presence Antiques**
303 S. Division St.
313/663-2352

**Antiques Market Place**
210 S. 1st St.
313/913-8890

**Antelope Antiques & Coins**
206 S. 4th Ave.
313/663-2828

**Graces Select Antiques**
122 S. Main St.
313/668-0747

**Arcadian Too Antiques & Collectibles**
322 S. Main St.
313/994-8856

**Maple Ridge Antiques**
490 S. Maple Road
313/213-1577

**Antique Mall of Ann Arbor**
2739 Plymouth Road
313/663-8200

**Kaleidoscope Books & Collectibles**
217 S. State St.
313/995-9887

**Lotus Gallery**
1570 Covington Dr.
313/665-6322

**Dixboro General Store**
5206 Plymoth Road
1-800-DIXBORO

### *Great Places To Stay*

### Woods Inn

2887 Newport Road
313/665-8394
Rates: $50-60

Here's a place to relax in the Michigan woods. The Woods Inn is an 1859, two-story wood and stone Early American home with four spacious guest rooms, plus an ample kitchen, dining room, parlor and large screened porch filled with wicker furniture. There are three acres of pine and hardwoods for guests' strolling pleasure, complete with sprawling gardens, a barn, and one of the few remaining smokehouses in Michigan. The inn is filled with Early American pieces and period collections of ironstone, colored art glass, and Staffordshire figurines.

## 4 BATTLE CREEK

**Old Beckley School Antiques**
3019 B Dr. N.
616/979-1842

## 5 BAY CITY

**Mid Michigan Retail Sales**
614 Garfield Ave.
517/893-6537

**Everybody's Attic**
606 E. Midland St.
517/893-9702

**Owl Antiques**
703 E. Midland St.
517/892-1105

**Hen In the Holly**
110 3rd St.
517/895-7215

**Little House**
924 N. Water St.
517/893-6771

**Bay City Antiques Center**
1010 N. Water St.
517-893-1116

**Downtown Antiques Market**
1020 N. Water St.
517/893-0251

## 6 BELLEVILLE

**Antiques on Main**
430 Main St.
313/699-8285

## 7 BENTON HARBOR

**Good Old Times Antiques**
3076 E. Napier Ave.
616/925-8422

**Antique Exchange**
4823 Territorial Road
616/944-1987

## 8 BIG BAY

### *Great Places To Stay*

### Big Bay Point Lighthouse Bed & Breakfast
3 Lighthouse Road
906/345-9957

Lighthouses have this mysterious pull and fascination for just about everybody, so imagine the thrill of staying in a lighthouse that's a bed & breakfast! In 1986, the two-story brick building and its adjoining 60-foot high square light tower at Big Bay Point were adapted to a bed and breakfast. It is now an 18-room inn with seven guest rooms (five with private bath) and a common living room with a fireplace, a dining room, a library, and a sauna in the tower. Not only do guests get great accommodations and a really nice place to poke around, but they can also go up in the tower and see the original 1500-pound Third Oder Fresnel Lens-the second largest ever used on the Great Lakes.

## 9 BIRMINGHAM

**Watch Hill Antiques**
330 E. Maple Road
248/644-7445

**Cece's**
335 E. Maple Road
248/647-1069

**Lesprit**
336 E. Maple Road
248/646-8822

**Patrick Vargo Antiquarian**
250 Martin St.
248/647-0135

**Chase Antiques**
251 E. Merrill St.
248/433-1810

**Cowboy Trader**
251 E. Merrill St.
248/647-8833

**Leonard Berry Antiques**
251 E. Merrill St.
248/646-1996

**O'Susannah**
570 N. Woodward Ave.
248/642-4250

**Merwins Antiques Gallery**
588 N. Woodward Ave.
248/258-3211

**Chelsea Antiques Ltd.**
700 N. Woodward Ave.
248/644-8090

**Troy Corners Antiques**
251 E. Merrill St.
248/594-8330

**Classic Country Antiques**
2277 Cole St.
248/258-5140

**La Belle Provence**
185 W. Maple Road
248-540-3876

**Madelines Antique Shop**
790 N. Woodward Ave.
248/644-2493

**Hagopian World of Rugs**
850 S. Woodward Ave.
248/646-1850

## 10 BLISSFIELD

**Blissfield Antiques Mall**
103 W. Adrian St.
517/486-2236

**J & B Antiques Mall**
109 W. Adrain St.
517/486-3544

**Triple Bridge Antiques**
321 W. Adrian St.
517/486-3777

**Memories on Lane St.**
104 S. Lane
517/486-2327

**Greens Gallery Of Antiques**
115 S. Lane
517/486-3080

**Estes Antiques Mall**
116 S. Lane
517/486-4616

## 11 BRIGHTON

**Nostalgia Days Gone By Antiques**
116 W. Main St.
810/229-4710

**Mill Pond Antique Galleries**
217 W. Main St.
810/229-8686

**Entre Nous Antiques**
323 W. Main St.
810/229-8720

**Hidden Treasures**
7925 Winans Lake Road
810/231-7777

## 12 BROOKLYN

**Pine Tree Centre Antique Mall**
129 N. Main St.
517/592-3808

**Memory Lane Antique Shop**
12939 S. M-50
517/592-4218

**Muggsies Antiques**
13982 U.S. Hwy. 12
517/592-2659

## 13 CHESANING

### Fancy That Antiques & Uniques
324 W. Broad St.
517/845-7775 or 1-800-752-0532
Fax: 517/845-4190
April-December 10-6 Mon.-Sat., 12-5 Sun., January-March weekends 11-5 Sat., 12-5 Sun.; or by appointment
*Directions: From I-75/U.S. 23, the shop is located north of Flint, Michigan. Use Exit 131, which is M-57. Head west 18 miles on M-57. Located 2 miles east of M-52 on M-57, and 21 miles east of U.S. 27. 30 miles from Flint and Saginaw and 40 miles from Lansing.*

Nothing but true antiques are allowed in the multi-level Fancy That Antiques & Uniques. No reproductions will be found among the crystal, china, silver, toys or two large cases of jewelry. You can also browse through art glass that includes Tiffany, French Cameo, Moser, Lotton and Loetz; cut glass and perfume bottles; American art pottery like Roseville and Rookwood; country primitives, quilts, linens, European porcelains and Nippon. An interesting and unique service that this shop offers is atomizer repairs-those squeezy bulbs on the ends of perfume bottles that squirt out the good-smelling stuff! The shop also offers estate sales and appraisal services.

## 14 CLINTON

**First Class Antique Mall**
112 E. Michigan Ave.
517/456-6410

**Turn of the Century Light Co.**
116 W. Michigan Ave.
517/456-6019

**Wooden Box**
141 W. Michigan Ave.
517/456-7556

**Oak City Antiques**
1101 W. U.S. Hwy. 12
517/456-4444

## 15 DEARBORN

**A & D Antiques & Oriental Rugs**
13333 Michigan Ave.
313/581-6183

**Retro Image Co.**
14246 Michigan Ave.
313/582-3074

**Village Antiques**
22091 Michigan Ave.
313/563-1230

**Michelangelo Woodwkg. & Furn.**
1660 N. Telegraph Road
313/277-7500

## 16 DETROIT

**Grand River Sales**
4837 Grand River Ave.
313/361-3400

**New World Antique Gallery**
12101 Grand River Ave.
313/834-7008

**Marketplace Gallery**
2047 Gratiot Ave.
313/567-8250

**Dumouchelle Art Galleries Co.**
409 E. Jefferson Ave.
313/963-6255

**Relics**
10027 Joseph Campau St.
313/874-0500

**Antique & Resale Shop**
4811 Livernois Ave.
313/898-1830

**Park Antiques**
16235 Mack Ave.
313/884-7652

**In-Between**
16237 Mack Ave.
313/886-1741

**Another Time Antiques**
16239 Mack Ave.
313/886-0830

**Xavier's**
2546 Michigan Ave.
313/964-1222

**Michigan Ave. Antiques**
7105 Michigan Ave.
313/554-1012

**Mike's Antiques**
11109 Morang Dr.
313/881-9500

**Mingles**
17330 E. Warren Ave.
313/343-2828

**Detroit Antique Mall**
828 W. Fisher Freeway
313/963-5252

## 17 FLINT

**Sue's Antiques**
G3106 N. Center Road
810/736-0800

**Reminisce Antique Gallery**
3124 S. Dort Hwy.
810/744-1090

**Westwood Antiques & Gifts**
4123 W. Coldwater Road
810/785-1300

## 18 FLUSHING

**Trudy's Antiques**
113 N. McKinley Road
810/659-9801

**Antq. Center R & J Needful Things**
G6398 W. Pierson Road
810/659-2663

## 19 FREMONT

**Brass Bell Antique Mall**
48 W. Main St.
616/924-1255

**Rolling Ladder Antique Mall**
10 W. Main St.
616/924-0420

## 20 GRAND HAVEN

### Carriage House Antiques
122 Franklin Ave.
616/844-0580
Tues.-Sat. 11-5, Sun. 1-5, closed Mon., closed January & February
*Directions: From U.S. Hwy. 31 - travel west on Franklin Ave. in downtown Grand Haven. Parking and entrance in rear.*

This quaint shop is located in a restored 1892 carriage house. The owners have been in the antiques business for 20 years so experience is a plus for shopping here. Specializing in true antiques from the 1830s to the 1930s, this two-story, 2,000 square feet shop offers quilts, linens, estate jewelry, glassware and a large selection of Victorian and country furnishings.

**Whims and Wishes**
216 Washington Ave.
616/842-9533

**West Michigan Antique Mall**
13279 168th Ave.
616/842-0370

## 21 GRAND RAPIDS

**Antiques by the Bridge**
445 Bridge St. N.W.
616/451-3430

**Bygones**
910 Cherry S.E.
616/336-8447

**Heartwood**
956 Cherry St. S.E.
616/454-1478

**Classic Woods Refinishing**
966 Cherry St. S.E.
616/458-3700

**Turn of the Century Antiques**
7337 S. Division Ave.
616/455-2060

**Scavengers Hunt**
210 E. Fulton St.
616/454-1033

**Nobody's Sweetheart Vintage**
953 E. Fulton St.
616/454-1673

**Marlene's Antiques & Collectibles**
1054 W. Fulton St.
616/235-1336

**Perception**
7 Ionia Ave. S.W.
616/451-2393

**Mary's Used Furnishings**
732 Leonard St. N.W.
616/774-8792

**Ms. Doll's Gifts & Collectibles**
150 Madison Ave. S.E.
616/336-8677

**Home Sweet Home**
2712 Kraft S.E.
616/949-7788

**Cherry Hill Antique Emporium**
634 Wealthy St. S.E.
616/454-9521

**Plaza Antique Mall**
1410 28th St.
616/243-2465

**Scavenger Hunt Too**
2 Jefferson Ave. S.E.
616/454-9955

**Brooknelle Antiques**
4600 Knapp St. N.E.
616/363-3687

**Marlene's Antiques & Collectibles**
1054 W. Fulton St.
616/235-1336

**Village Antiques & Lighting**
1334 Burton St. S.W.
616/452-6975

## 22 GRANDVILLE

**Sherrie's Antiques**
3948 20th St. S.W.
616/249-8066

## 23 HARBOR SPRINGS

**TLC Summer Place Antiques**
811 S. Lake Shore Dr.
616/526-7191

**Huzza**
136 E. Main St.
616/526-2128

**Joe De Vie**
154 E. Main St.
616/526-7700

**Lesprit**
195 W. Main St.
616/526-9888

**Pooter Olooms Antiques**
339 State St.
616/526-6101

**Elliott & Elliott**
292 E. 3rd St.
616/526-2040

## 24 HASTINGS

**Carlton Center Antique Market**
2305 E. Carlton Center Road
616/948-9618

**Davals Used Furn & Antiques**
2020 Gun Lake Road
616/948-2463

**Hastings Antique Mall**
142 E. State St.
616/948-9644

## 25 HOLLAND

**Dutch Colonial Inn**
560 Central Ave.
616/396-3664

**Antiques & Etc.**
383 Central Ave.
616/396-4045

**Nob-Hill Antique Mall**
A1261 Graafschap Road
616/392-1424

**Possessions Gifts & Antiques**
287 Howard Ave.
616/395-8207

**Twig's**
184 S. River Ave.
616/392-2775

**Stonegate Antiques & Gifts**
1504 S. Shore Drive
616/335-3646

**Tulip City Antique Mall**
3500 U.S. Hwy. 31
616/786-4424

**Brick House Antiques**
112 Waukazoo Drive
616/399-9690

### *Great Places To Stay*

### Dutch Colonial Inn Bed and Breakfast

560 Central Ave.
616/396-3664
Open year round
*Directions:From Chicago: Take I-196 north to Exit 44. Follow Business 196 to U.S. 31 (Muskegon). From U.S. 31, veer left on Central Ave. (1st stoplight). The inn is 1¼ miles on the right. From Detroit: Take I-94 to U.S. 131 north, turn onto M 89 towards Allegan. Continue on M 89 to M 40. M 40 becomes State St. in Holland. Continue north on State St. until 23rd St. Turn left from 23rd St. to Central Ave. From Grand Rapids: Take I-196 to exit 52. Follow 16th St. west turning left onto Central Ave.*

What was once a wedding gift in 1928 is today a bed and breakfast inn offering Dutch hospitality. The decor is eclectic from Victorian Country to 1930s Chic. The inn offers five guest suites (one a cozy hideaway), whirlpool tubs for two, a common area with fireplace and an open porch for relaxing.

## 26 HOLLY

**Arcade Antiques**
108 Battle Aly
810/634-8800

**Balcony Row**
216 S. Broad St.
810/634-1400

**Holly Crossing Antiques**
219 S. Broad St.
810/634-3333

**Water Tower Antiques Mall**
310 S. Broad St.
810/634-3500

**Home Sweet Home**
101 S. Saginaw St.
810/634-3925

**Holly Antiques on Main**
118 S. Saginaw St.
810/634-7696

## 27 HOUGHTON

**Macvicar Antiques**
9103 W. Houghton Lake Dr.
517/422-5466

**Antique Mall**
418 Shelden Ave.
906/487-9483

## 28 HOWELL

**Adams Antique Mall**
203 E. Grand River Ave.
517/546-5360

**Egnash Antiques & Auctions**
202 S. Michigan Ave.
517/546-2005

**Lake Chemung Oldies**
5255 W. Ri Circle
517/546-8875

**Victorian Gardens**
128 E. Sibley St.
517/546-6749

## 29 IONIA

### Grand River Antiques

7050 S. State Road
616/527-8880
Daily 10-5
*Directions: When traveling I-96, exit 3 M-66. Drive 1/4 mile north on M-66 to the light. Grand River Antiques is across from The Corner Landing Restaurant.*

Any day of the week antique hounds can visit the 20-plus dealers at Grand River Antiques. Housed in an old fresh fruit market, everything offered is authentic; no reproductions are allowed. There is a large collection of furniture, country primitives, vintage clothing, glassware and advertising collectibles. Art Perkins, who owns Grand River antiques, along with wife Marcia, restores old trunks.

**Ionia Antique Mall**
415 W. Main St.
616/527-6720

**Fire Barn Antiques**
219 W. Washington St.
616/527-2240

**Checkerboard Antiques**
524 W. Lincoln Ave.
616/527-1785

## 30 JACKSON

**Jackson Antique Mall**
201 N. Jackson St.
517-784-3333

**Gumper Antiques**
3801 Stonewall Road
517-789-7982

**Stevens Antiques & Flea Market**
5166 Page Ave.
517/764-1194

## 31 KALAMAZOO

### Kalamazoo Antiques Market

130 N. Edwards
616/226-9788
Mon.-Sat. 11-6, Sun. 1-5
*Directions: From U.S. 131, take Exit #36 or #38 east to downtown. From I-94, take Exit # 78 north to downtown. Once in downtown, take Michigan Ave. to Edwards (behind Wendy's).*

In the early 1890s the Kalamazoo Antique Mall was a carriage maker's shop. Today it holds the wares of 32 dealers who offer a broad selection of high quality antiques from Victorian to early country along with a great array of collectibles.

This is a "must stop" since the market is located next to an architectural salvage, two garden shops, near two antique shops and three microbreweries and only one block from the famous Kalamazoo Downtown Mall. Stay at the Radisson Hotel and rest up for two or three days of shopping.

**J Ps Coins Collectibles & Antiques**
420 S. Burdick St.
616/383-2200

**Alamo Depot Crafts**
6187 W. D Ave.
616/373-3886

**Emporium**
313 E. Kalamazoo
616/381-0998

**Souk Sampler**
4614 W. Main St.
616/342-9124

**Wild Goose Chase**
4644 W. Main St.
616/343-5933

**Crosstown Collectibles**
7616 E. Michigan Ave.
616/385-1825

**Red Wagon Antiques**
5348 N. Riverview Dr.
616/382-5461

**Warehouse Distributors**
6471 Stadium Dr.
616/372-1175

**Aldon Antiques**
608 Summer St.
616/388-5375

**Aaron & Assoc.**
824 S. Westnedge Ave.
616/342-8834

**Attic Trash & Treasures**
1301 S. Westnedge Ave.
616/344-2189

**Heritage Architectural Salvage**
150 N. Edwards St.
616/385-1004

## 32 LAKESIDE

**Lakeside Antiques**
14876 Red Arrow Hwy.
616/469-7717

**Rabbit Run Antiques & Interiors**
15460 Red Arrow Hwy.
616/469-0468

## 33 LANSING

**Antique Connection**
5411 S. Cedar St.
517/882-8700

**Tom's Furniture & Antiques**
319 E. Grand River Ave.
517/485-8335

**Classic Arms Company**
1600 Lake Lansing Road
517/484-6112

**Pennyless In Paradise**
1918 E. Michigan Ave.
517/372-4526

**Slightly Tarnished-Used Goods**
2006 E. Michigan Ave.
517/485-3599

**Triola's**
1114 E. Mt. Hope Road
517/484-5414

**Unique Furniture Store**
1814 S. Washington Ave.
517/485-8404

**Mid Michigan Mega Mall**
15487 U.S. Hwy. 27
517/487-3275

**Airport Antqiues**
5124 N. Grand River Ave.
517/886-9795

## 34 LINDEN

**Thimbleberry Antiques**
100 W. Broad
810/735-7324

**Linden Emporium**
115 N.E. Bron Ave.
810/735-7987

**Tangled Vine**
131 N.E. Bron Ave.
810/735-4611

## 35 LOWELL

**Cranberry Urn Antique Shop**
208 E. Main St.
616/897-9890

**Flat River Antique Mall**
210 W. Main St.
616/897-4172

**Main Street Antiques**
221 W. Main St.
616/897-5521

### *Great Places To Stay*

**McGee Homestead Bed & Breakfast**
2534 Alden Nash N.E.
616/897-8142
Daily 24 hrs. Mar. 1-Dec. 31
Rates: $38-58
*Directions: Take Exit 52 off I-96 north. Go 7 miles through Lowell to Bailey Dr. turn left. At Alden Nash, turn right for 2 miles to McGee Homestead.*

This 1880s brick farmhouse (just like Grandma's) is set on five acres and surrounded by orchards. There is a big ol' barn filled with petting animals, making it a great place to stay if you have children.

The guest area of the bed and breakfast has its own entrance, sitting room with fireplace, parlor and small kitchen. Four spacious guest rooms are individually decorated with antiques and all have private baths. A big country breakfast with eggs fresh from the McGee Farm is served each morning.

There is a golf course next door, the largest antique mall in Michigan five miles away and it's only 18 miles to Grand Rapids.

## 36 LUDINGTON

**Coles Antiques Villa**
322 West Ludington Ave.
616/845-7414
(March-April & Nov.-Dec.) Fri.-Sat. 10-5, Sun. 1-5
(May-Aug.) Mon.-Sat. 10-6, Sun. 12-5
*Directions: Going north on U.S. 31: From McKegon, exit for Old U.S. 31, turn left on Old U.S. 31 (Pere Marquette Road), follow to the intersection of U.S. 10. Turn left (west), head toward Lake Michigan. Go straight through downtown Ludington (3 stop lights 1 block apart). Cole's Antiques Villa is 2 blocks ahead on the right, just before House of Flavors Restaurant. Coming south on U.S. 31: from Traverse City, go west on U.S. 10 at Scottsville junction. Coming from the east: Take U.S. 10 straight west to downtown Ludington and follow the previous direction.*

This group of dealers offers a great selection of furniture, glassware, china, pottery, quilts, linens, paper products, jewelry, fishing and military memorabilia, advertising collectibles, country decoratives, tools and kitchenware. They also hold two antiques shows and sales each year: one on the third weekend in October at the West Shore Community College, and another the first weekend in February at Lands Inn.

**Antique Store**
127 S. James St.
616/845-5888

**Sunset Bay Antiques**
404 S. James St.
616/843-1559

**Country Charm Gifts & Antiques**
119 W. Ludington Ave.
616/843-4722

**Sandpiper Emporium**
809 W. Ludington Ave.
616/843-3008

**Christa's Antiques & Collectibles**
1002 S. Madison St.
616/845-0075

**Washington Antiques**
102 2nd St.
616/843-8030

## 37 MACKINAC ISLAND

### *Great Places To Stay*

**Haan's 1830 Inn**
Huron St.
906/847-6244
Rates: $80-120
Open mid-May to mid-November
(Winter address: 3418 Oakwood Ave., 708/526-2662)

According to a survey conducted under the National Historic Preservation Act of 1966, Haan's 1830 Inn is the oldest example of Greek Revival architecture in the Northwest Territory. It is the oldest building used as an inn in the state of Michigan. Each of the seven guestrooms (five with private bath) is furnished with antiques from the mid-19th century and artifacts from the island's fur-trading period. The inn has been featured in numerous publications, including the *Chicago Tribune* and *Innsider*. It is located only a short distance from Mackinac Island's downtown area, old Fort Mackinac, and the ferry docks.

## 38 MANCHESTER

**Manchester Antique Mall**
116 W. Main Blvd.
313/428-9357

**Eighteenth Century Shoppe**
122 W. Main Blvd.
313/428-7759

**Raisin Valley Antiques**
201 E. Main St.
313/428-7766

## 39 MARQUETTE

**Collector Lower Harbor Antiques**
214 S. Front St.
906/228-4134

**Summer Cottage**
810 N. 3rd St.
906/226-2795

**Antique Village**
2296 U.S. Hwy. 41 S.
906/249-3040

**Fagans**
333 W. Washington St.
906/228-4311

## 40 MARSHALL

**Marshall House Center**
100 Exchange St.
616/781-7841

**McKee Monument & Mercantile**
200 Exchange St.
616/781-8921

**J H Cronin Antique Center**
101 W. Michigan Ave.
616/789-0077

**Hildor House Antiques**
105 W. Michigan Ave.
616/789-0009

**Keystone Antiques**
110 E. Michigan Ave.
616/789-1355

**Smithfield Banques**
117 E. Michigan Ave.
616/781-6969

**Little Toy Drum Antiques**
135 W. Michigan Ave.
616/781-9644

**J & J Antiques**
206 W. Michigan Ave.
616/781-5581

**Pineapple Lane Antiques**
209 W. Michigan Ave.
616/789-1445

**Heirlooms Unlimited**
211 W. Michigan Ave.
616/781-1234

**Finders Keepers Antiques**
858 E. Michigan Ave.
616/789-1611

**Cornwells Turkeyville USA**
15½ Mile Road
616/781-4293

**Olde Homestead Antique Mall**
15445 N. Dr. N.
616/781-8119

## 41 MASON

**Art & Shirley's Antiques**
1825 S. Aurelius Road
517/628-2065

**Old Mill Antiques Mall**
207 Mason
517/767-1270

**Carriage Stop**
208 Mason
517/676-1530

**Front Porch**
208 Mason
517/676-6388

**Mason Antiques Market**
208 Mason
517-676-9753

## 42 MIDLAND

### Michigan Antique Festival
2156 Rudy Court
517/687-9001

Antique show and sale, collectible market, memorabilia, oddities and Folk Art, 1000 outside and inside vendors - May, July and September. Call for exact dates.

**Big Jim's Antiques**
4816 Bay City Road
517/496-0734

**Linda's Cobble Shop**
2900 Isabella St.
517-832-9788

**Dad's Antiques**
3004 S. Poseyville Road
517/835-7483

**Corner Cupboard**
2108 E. Wheeler St.
517/835-6691

## 43 MOUNT CLEMENS

**Estate Antiques**
1142 Southbound Gratiot Ave.
810/468-9888

## 44 MOUNT PLEASANT

**Riverside Antiques**
993 S. Mission St.
517/773-3946

**Mount Pleasant Antique Center**
1718 S. Mission St.
517/772-2672

## 45 MUNISING

**Bay House**
111 Elm Ave.
906/387-4253

**Old North Light Antiques**
M 28 E.
906/387-2109

## 46 MUSKEGON

### Downtown Muskegon Antique Mall
1321 Division, Suite 10
616/728-0305
Mon.-Sat. 11-6, Sun. 1-6
*Directions: Exit U.S. 31, west on Laketon, one block west of Henry St. turn right on Division. Located at the corner of Division and Western, across the street from Muskegon Lake.*

Downtown Muskegon Antique Mall is now bigger and better! Their new location in the old Shaw Walker Industrial Building offers 12,000 sq. ft. with 40 dealers displaying a general line of antiques and collectibles. Quality "pickings" arrive daily as excited dealers fill their booths to the brim with treasures for your selecting!

**Old Grange Mall**
2783 E. Apple Ave.
616/773-5683

**Country Peddler**
2542 W. Bard Road
616/766-2147

**Home Town Treasures**
3117 Heights Ravenna Road
616/777-1805

**Memory Lane Antique Mall**
2073 Holton Road
616/744-8510

**Kensington Antiques**
2122 Lake Ave.
616/744-6682

**Mandy's Antiques**
1950 E. Laketon Ave.
616/777-1428

**Airport Antique Mall**
4206 Grand Haven Road
616/798-3318

## 47 NEW BALTIMORE

**Charlottes Web Antiques**
36760 Green St.
810/725-7752

**Heritage Square Antique Mall**
36821 Green St.
810/725-2453

**Days Gone By**
50979 Washington St.
810/725-0749

**Washington Street Station**
51059 Washington St.
810/716-8810

## 48 NILES

**Michiana Antique Mall**
2423 S. 11th St.
616/684-7001

**Antiques and More**
2429 S. 11th St.
616/683-4222

**Bookouts Furniture**
2439 S. 11th St.
616/683-2960

**Niles Antique Mall**
220 Front St.
616/683-6652

**Yankee Heirlooms**
211 N. 2nd St.
616/684-0462

**Four Flags Antique & Craft Mall**
218 N. 2nd St.
616/683-6681

**River City Antique Mall**
109 N. 3rd St.
616/684-0840

**Old Time Outfitters, Ltd.**
16 S. 12th St.
616/683-3569

## 49 NORTHPORT

**Grandma's Trunk**
102 N. Mill St.
616/386-5351

**Heathman Antiques & Finery**
210 Mill St.
616/386-7006

**5th St. Antiques**
211 N. Mill St.
616/386-5421

**Back Roads Antiques & Collectibles**
116 S. Nagonaba Ave.
616/386-7011

**Bird N Hand**
123 Nagonaba
616/386-7104

**Cobweb Treasures Antiques**
393 S. West
616/386-5532

## 50 OSCODA

**McNamara Antique Mall**
2083 N. U.S. Hwy. 23
517/739-5435

**Ryland Company**
2091 N. U.S. Hwy. 23
517/739-0810

**Antique Mall**
4239 N. U.S. Hwy. 23
517/739-4000

**Wooden Nickel Antiques**
110 E. Park Ave.
517/739-7490

## 51 OTSEGO

**Otsego Antique Mall**
114 W. Allegan St.
616/694-6440

**Harry J's**
123 W. Allegan St.
616/694-4318

**Heritage Antique Mall**
621 Lincoln Road
616/694-4226

**Mercantile**
504 Lincoln Road
616/692-3630

## 52 PARADISE

### *Interesting Side Trip*

### Village of Sheldrake, near Paradise

*Directions: Go west on Route 28 through Hiawatha National Forest, turn north on Route 123. Or take the scenic route along the shore of Lake Superior. From Paradise, Sheldrake can be reached by taking the Whitefish Point Road north.*

Although Sheldrake is on the Michigan Historic Register, the village is no longer on the map. It's on Whitefish Bay, four miles north of Paradise, which is 60 miles north and west of Sault Sainte Marie, the largest town on Michigan's Upper Peninsula. Sheldrake is an old logging village that once had about 1,500 people and about 150 buildings. Now only about a dozen buildings are still standing, and they are owned by Brent Biehl, an entrepreneur from Detroit who moved his family to Sheldrake in the 1960s and who has developed a small manufacturing plant for wood products that employs a dozen people. Biehl, his wife, and their six now-grown children have been, for the most part, the only year-round residents of the village, although they have renovated some of the wooden houses and do summer rentals.

Actually, that statement should be qualified: the Biehl family is the only live, year-round family in the village. Everybody else is a ghost! And there seem to be lots of them, mostly former residents. There's the old sea captain who stands on the dock, wearing a cap and cape smoking a pipe. There's the retired city engineer from Detroit who sits in a chair on the front porch of his old house and who turns on the lights in the house in the winter when nobody's home. There's the dark, bearded logger who used to walk through the older parts of one house and sit on the couch so people renting the house could see him. The ghost often opened and closed doors and walked around, but never did anything else.

The Biehls themselves have seen so many ghosts over the past 30 years that they have become rather blase about the whole situation. Figures appear and disappear regularly, voices are heard, pictures fall off walls, bathroom faucets turn on for no visible reason, smells of food cooking waft through the houses, "just the garden variety poltergeist things," says Biehl.

## 53 PAW PAW

**Paw Paw Antique Gallery**
404 E. Michigan Ave.
616/657-5378

## 54 PETOSKEY

**Jedediahs Antiques & Collectibles**
422 E. Mitchell St.
616/347-1919

**Joie De Vie**
1901 M 119
616/347-1400

**Joseph's World Art & Antiques**
2680 U.S. 31 S.
616/347-0121

**Longton Hall Antiques**
410 Rose St.
616/347-9672

### *Great Places To Stay*

**Stafford's Perry Hotel**
Gaslight District, Bay at Lewis
616/347-4000 or 1-800-456-1917
*Directions: From Detroit or the Upper Peninsula: Take I-75 to the Indian River exit, then take M 68 west to U.S. 31 and turn south. From Chicago: Follow I-94 to I-96 and then pick up U.S. 131 at Grand Rapids. U.S. 131 ends at Petoskey's northwest side.*

The Perry Hotel opened in 1899 to the rave reviews of the thousands of summertime visitors who flocked to northern Michigan for its clean air, water and relaxing atmosphere. The Perry was built next to the downtown train depot, and many Perry guests spent the afternoons on the large front porch greeting friends and relatives as they arrived at the station. The hotel is now filled with antiques and reproductions that reflect the grandeur of the Edwardian era. Just out the back door is the Gaslight District, which has all manner of art studios, antique galleries and shops, or, for the more athletic, just 20 minutes away is world-class skiing, golf, boating, cross-country trails and beaches.

**Stafford's Bay View Inn**
2011 Woodland Ave.
616/347-2771 or 1-800-258-1886
Fax: 616/347-3413
Web site: stafford@freeway.net or innbook.com/staffbay.html

Just a mile north of Petoskey, and owned and operated by the same Stafford family as the Perry Hotel in downtown Petoskey, is the Bay View Inn. Built in 1886, it is one of only three locations in the nation where guests can participate in a Chatauqua: a summertime educational program that includes lectures, concerts, plays, musicals, various spiritual speakers and Sunday church services. Encased in a sprawling, elegant, airy building, all 31 guest rooms have been decorated with Victorian antiques, wallpapers, quilts and modern amenities such as whirlpool tubs, fireplaces and private balconies overlooking the bayside gardens. The entire inn is filled with antiques, and with the staff dressed in period costumes, it's like walking back in time.

## 55 PLYMOUTH

**Uptown Antiques**
120 E. Liberty St.
313/459-0311

**Upstairs Downstairs Antiques**
149 W. Liberty St.
313/459-6450

**In My Attic**
157 W. Liberty St.
313/455-8970

**Plymouth Antiques Mall**
198 W. Liberty St.
313/455-5595

**Memory Lane Antiques**
336 S. Main St.
313/451-1873

**Robin's Nest Antique Mall**
640 Starkweather St.
313/459-7733

## 56 PORT HURON

**Antique Collectors Corner**
1603 Griswold St.
810/982-2780

**Citadel Antique Gallery**
609 Huron Ave.
810/987-7737

**Yesterdays Treasures**
4490 Lapeer Road
810/982-2100

**Wooden Spool**
2513 10th Ave.
810/982-3390

## 57 ROCHESTER

**Antiques By Pamela**
319 S. Main St.
248/652-0866

**Watch Hill Antiques**
329 S. Main St.
248/650-5463

**Tally Ho!**
404 S. Main St.
248/652-6860

**Chapman House**
311 Walnut Blvd.
248/651-2157

## 58 ROMEO

**Village Barn**
186 S. Main St.
810/752-5489

**Town Hall Antiques**
205 N. Main St.
810/752-5422

**Romeo Antique Mall**
218 N. Main St.
810/752-6440

**Remember When Antiques**
143 W. Saint Clair St.
810/752-5499

## 59 ROYAL OAK

**Royal Oak Auction House & Gallery**
600 E. 11 Mile Road
248/398-0646

**Antique Connection**
710 E. 11 Mile Road
248/542-5042

**Lovejoys Antiques**
720 E. 11 Mile Road
248/545-9060

**The White Elephant Antique Shop**
724 W. 11 Mile Road
248/543-5140

**Royal Antiques**
1106 E. 11 Mile Road
248/548-5230

**Decades**
110 W. 4th St.
248/546-9289

**Trumbull's Antique Emporium**
112 E. 4th St.
248/584-0006

**Dandelion Shop Antiques**
114 W. 4th St.
248/547-6288

**Red Ribbon Antiques**
418 E. 4th St.
248/541-8117

**Delgiudice Fine Arts & Antiques**
515 S. Lafayette Ave.
248/399-2608

**Antiques & Fine Jewelry by Helen**
107 S. Main St.
248/546-9467

**Antiques on Main**
115 S. Main St.
248/545-4663

**Pinks-N-Lace**
1000 N. Main St.
248/543-3598

**Heritage Co. II Archl Artifacts**
116 E. 7th St.
248/549-8342

**Troy Street Antiques**
309 S. Troy St.
248/543-0272

**Yellow House Antiques**
125 N. Washington Ave.
248/541-2866

**North Washington Antiques**
433 N. Washington Ave.
248/398-8006

**Vertu**
511 S. Washington Ave.
248/545-6050

**Antiques & Rare Old Prints**
516 S. Washington Ave.
248/548-5588

## 60 SAGINAW

**Salt Marsh**
220 N. Center Road
517/793-4861

**Adomaitis Antiques**
412 Court St.
517/790-7469

**Antique Market Place**
418 Court St.
517/799-4110

**Dee Jays Antiques**
418 Court St.
517/799-4110

**Little House**
418 Court St.
517/792-9622

**Ron's Antiques**
12025 Gratiot Road
517/642-8479

**Antique Warehouse , Inc.**
1910 N. Michigan Ave.
517/755-4343

## 61 SAINT CLAIR SHORES

**Adam's English Antiques**
19717 9th Mile
810/777-1652

**Jennifer's Trunk**
201 N. Riverside Ave.
810/329-2032

**Rivertown Antiques**
201 N. Riverside Ave.
810/329-1020

**John Moffett Antiques**
1102 S. 7th St.
810/329-3300

**Antique Inn**
302 Thornapple St.
810/329-5833

## 62 SAUGATUCK

**Country Store Antiques**
120 Butler
616/857-8601

**Taft Antiques**
240 Butler
616/857-2808

**Centennial Antiques**
3427 Holland St.
616/857-2743

**Handled With Care**
403 Lake
616/857-4688

**Fannies Antique Market**
3604 64th St.
616/857-2698

**Handled With Care-Everlasting**
3483 Washington Road
616/857-3044

## 63 SAULT STE MARIE

**Lagalerie Antiques**
1420 Ashmun
906/635-1044

## 64 SCHOOLCRAFT

**Fox Antiques Co.**
113 N. Grand St.
616/679-4018

**Ron's Grand St. Antiques & More**
205 N. Grand St.
616/679-4774

**Schoolcraft Antique Mall**
209 N. Grand St.
616/679-5282

**Norma's Antiques & Collectibles**
231 S. Grand St.
616/679-4030

**Prairie Home Antiques**
413 N. Grand St.
616/679-2062

## 65 SOUTH HAVEN

**Sunset Junque Antiques**
856 Blue Star Memorial Hwy.
616/637-5777

**Black River Antiques & Gifts**
516 Phoenix St.
616/637-8042

**Anchor Antiques Ltd.**
517 Phoenix St.
616/637-1500

**Antiques & Accents**
209 Center St.
616/639-1960

## 66 SOUTH LYON

**South Lyon Corner Store**
101 S. Lafayette St.
248/437-0205

**Pegasus Antiques & Collectibles**
105 N. Lafayette St.
248/437-0320

**Cabbage Rose**
317 N. Lafayette St.
248/486-0930

## 67 TECUMSEH

**Tecumseh Antique Mall**
112 E. Chicago Blvd.
517/423-6441

**Harold Robert Antiques**
154 E. Chicago Blvd.
517/423-6094

**Tecumseh Antique Mall II**
1111 W. Chicago Blvd.
517/423-6082

**Hitching Post Antiques Mall**
1322 E. Monroe Road
517/423-8277

**L & M Antique Mall**
7811 E. Monroe Road
517/423-7346

## 68 THREE RIVERS

**Antoinette's Gft Baskets & Antiques**
51 N. Main St.
616/273-3333

**Old Town Antique & Craft Hall**
60 N. Main St.
616/273-2596

**Links To The Past**
52631 N. U.S. Hwy. 131
616/279-7310

## 69 TRAVERSE CITY

**Devonshire Antiques**
5085 Barney Road
616/947-1063

**Antique Emporium**
565 W. Blue Star Dr.
616/943-3658

**Fascinations**
140 E. Front St.
616/922-0051

**Painted Door Gallery**
154 E. Front St.
616/929-4988

**Antique Company**
4386 U.S. Hwy. 31 N.
616/938-3000

**Custer Antiques**
826 W. Front St.
616/929-9201

**Wilson's Antiques**
123 S. Union St.
616/946-4177

**Chums Corner Antique Mall**
4200 U.S. Hwy. 31 S.
616/943-4200

## 70 UNION PIER

### Antique Mall & Village, Inc.
9300 Union Pier Road
616/469-2555
Daily 10-6
*Directions: From Indiana and Illinois: Take I-94 to Union Pier Road, Exit 6, then west (turn right) onto Union Pier Road. The Antique Mall & Village is 500 feet from Exit 6 on the left, just past St. Julian Winery. From northern Michigan: Take I-94 to Union Pier Exit 6, then turn left onto Union Pier Road. Antique Mall & Village is 100 feet from exit 6, immediately turn left.*

At the Antique Mall & Village, dealers from four states bring together some of the finest Victorian, primitives and collectibles for your shopping pleasure. The Mall is the first installment of a complete Village close to Lake Michigan in the heart of Harbor County. It is the area's largest, offering 15,000 square feet of quality antiques. They have patio dining when you need to replenish your energy for more shopping, offering sandwiches and salads.

**Plum Tree**
16337 Red Arrow Hwy.
616/469-5980

**Frog Forest Findings**
16100 York Road
616/469-7050

## 71 WATERFORD

**Great Midwestern Antique Emporium**
5233 Dixie Hwy.
248/623-7460

**Shoppe of Antiquity**
7766 Highland Road #M59
248/666-2333

## 72 WAYNE

**Heritage Colonial**
32224 Michigan Ave.
313/722-2332

**J Wofford Co.**
32536 Michigan Ave.
313/721-1939

**Blue Willow Antiques**
34840 Michigan Ave.
313/729-4910

**Sanders Antiques**
35118 Michigan Ave.
313/721-3029

## 73 WILLIAMSTON

**Main Street Shoppe Antiques**
108 W. Grand River Ave.
517/655-4005

**Jolly Coachman**
115 W. Grand River Ave.
517/655-6064

**Old Plank Road Antiques**
126 W. Grand River Ave.
517/655-4273

**Corner Cottage Antiques**
120 High St.
517/655-3257

**Putnam Street Antiques**
122 S. Putnam St.
517/655-4521

**Canterbury Antiques**
150 S. Putnam St.
517/655-6518

**Antiques Market of Williamston**
2991 Williamston Road
517/655-1350

**Grand River Merchants**
2991 N. Williamston Road
517/655-1350

## 74 WYANDOTTE

**J & J Antiques**
1836 Biddle St.
313/283-6019

**Yesterday's Treasures**
258 Elm St.
313/283-5232

**Tony's Junk Shop**
1325 Fort St.
313/283-2160

**Thomas Antiques**
93 Oak St.
313/283-1880

**Lovejoy Antiques**
95 Oak St.
313/282-3072

**Etcetera Antiques**
99 Oak St.
313/282-3072

**Old Gray House Antiques**
303 Oak St.
313/285-2555

## 75 YPSILANTI

**Remington Walker Design Associates**
19 E. Cross St.
313/485-2164

**Jim MacDonald Antiques**
29 E. Cross St.
313/481-0555

**Renewed Interest Antiques**
33 E. Cross St.
313/482-4525

**Thomas L. Schmidt Antiques**
7099 McKean Road
313/485-8606

**Materials Unlimited**
2 W. Michigan Ave.
313/483-6980

**Schmidts Antiques**
5138 W. Michigan Ave.
313/434-2660

**Griffin's Collectibles**
629 Lynne Ave.
313/482-0507

# Minnesota

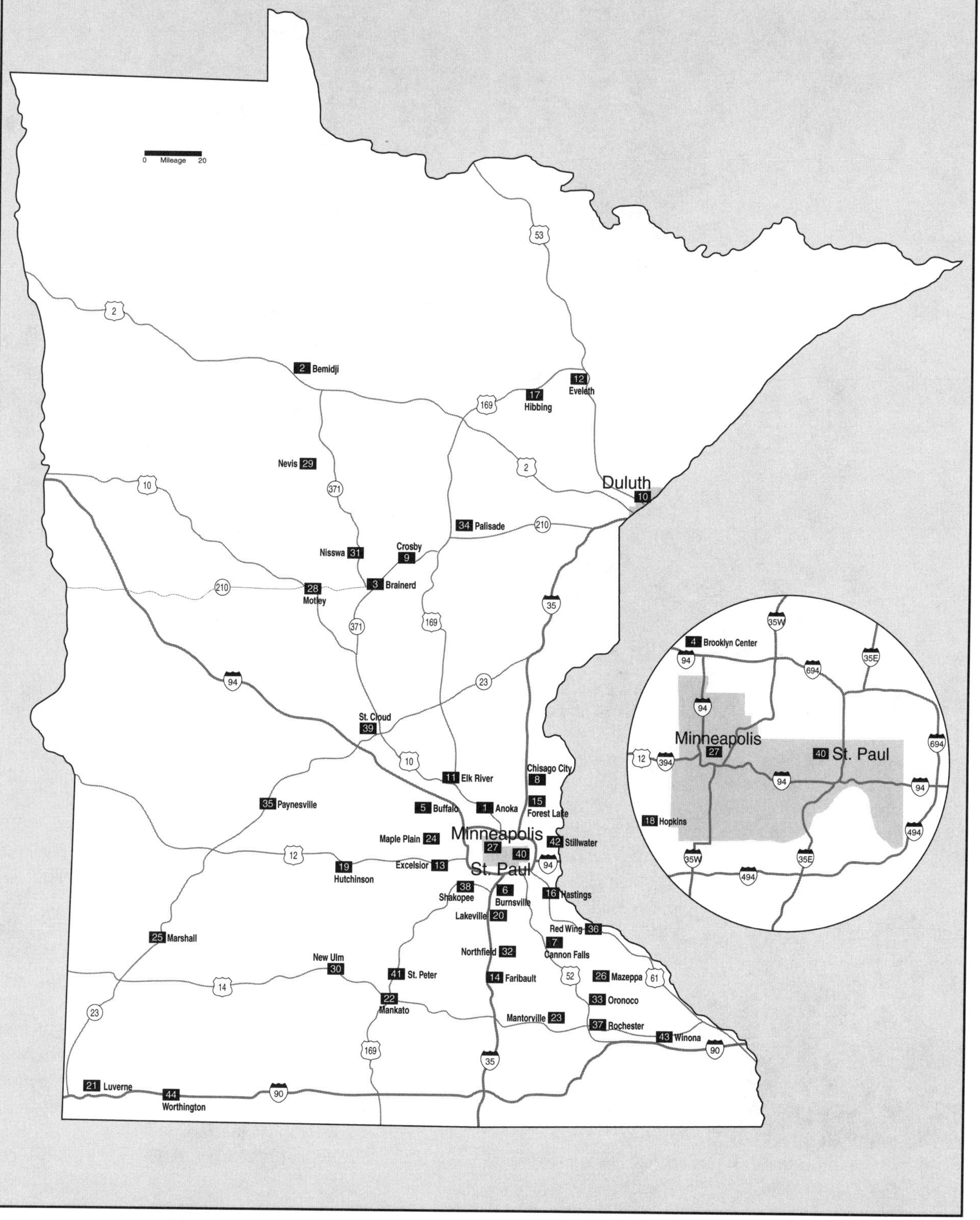

0 Mileage 20
53
2
2 Bemidji
12 Eveleth
169
17 Hibbing
2
Duluth
10
Nevis 29
10
371
34 Palisade
210
Crosby
9
Nisswa 31
3 Brainerd
210
28
Motley
35
371
169
94
23
St. Cloud
39
10
11 Elk River
Chisago City
8
35 Paynesville
5 Buffalo
1 Anoka
15
Forest Lake
Maple Plain 24
Minneapolis
27
42 Stillwater
40
12
19
Hutchinson
Excelsior 13
St. Paul
94
38
Shakopee
6
Burnsville
16 Hastings
Lakeville 20
Red Wing 36
25 Marshall
7
Cannon Falls
Northfield 32
New Ulm
30
14
41 St. Peter
14 Faribault
52
26 Mazeppa
61
22
Mankato
33 Oronoco
23
Mantorville 23
37 Rochester
43 Winona
90
169
35
21 Luverne
44
Worthington
90
4 Brooklyn Center
35W
94
694
35E
94
Minneapolis
27
40 St. Paul
12
394
694
94
94
18 Hopkins
494
35W
35E
494

*This famous house belongs to American Gothic Antiques owner Jane Eiklenberg. The house appears in the background of the painting "American Gothic."*

# American Gothic Antiques shares story and exquisite antique selections with antiquers

This 45-plus dealer shop located in a lovely old building on Stillwater's main street was named from Grant Wood's famous 1930s painting entitled "American Gothic."

*Grant Wood's famous painting is the inspiration for the shop's name.*

What's so unusual is the story behind the naming of this shop. The house in the painting's background belonged to Janie (Johnston) Eiklenborg's (the shop owner) great-grandmother. Janie says her great granny sat on the porch and actually watched as Mr. Wood doodled and sketched the details for this famous painting. The house located in Eldon, Iowa, is still owned by the family, and Janie's sister Mari Beth lives there today. "It's been a fun story to share with customers," says Janie, "and we're so proud to have been a part of it."

Oh, my goodness, I got so carried away with this story that I almost forgot to tell you about the shop. Inside American Gothic Antiques, dealers display exquisite selections of Victorian and oak furnishings, country furniture and accessories, as well as a choice group of primitive items. On a smaller scale, there are generous offerings of vintage clothing and jewelry, glassware and other collectibles. "Thanks for sharing your story with us, Janie."

*American Gothic Antiques is located at 236 S. Main St. in Stillwater. For additional information see listing #42 (Stillwater).*

## 1 ANOKA

**Round Barn**
3331 Bunker Lake Blvd. N.W.
612/427-5321

**Antiques on Main**
212 E. Main St.
612/323-3990

**Amore Antiques**
2008 2nd Ave.
612/576-1871

**Yours Mine & Ours Antiques**
2014 2nd Ave.
612/422-4959

**Cats Den of Antiques**
2010 2nd Ave.
612-323-3613

## 2 BEMIDJI

**Bargain Junction**
3220 Adams N.W./Hwy. 2 W.
218/751-5036

**Back N Time Antiques**
1105 15th St. N.W.
218/759-0206

**Louise's Antiques**
RR 8 #597
218/751-3577

**Brier Patch Antiques**
RR 3 #546
218/751-8832

**Anntiques**
301 3rd St. N.W.
218/751-2144

**Oelrichs Antique Shop**
1114 America Ave. N.W.
218/751-5126

## 3 BRAINERD

**Karen's Antiques & Things**
Downtown
218/825-7355

**Hyland Antiques**
1466 Hwy. 371 N.
218/828-8838

**Antiques On Laurel**
711 Laurel
218/828-1584

**Bargains on 7th**
211 S. 7th St.
218/829-8822

**Antiques & Accents-Brainerd**
214 S. 7th St.
218/828-0724

## 4 BROOKLYN CENTER

### *Great Places To Stay*

### Inn on the Farm
6150 Summit Dr. N.
1-800-428-8382

The Inn on the Farm at Earle Brown Heritage Center offers a bed and breakfast experience you'll never forget. Housed in a cluster of historic farm buildings the inn is located on the grounds of a beautifully restored Victorian gentleman's country estate, just 10 minutes from the heart of downtown Minneapolis. You may choose from eleven exquisitely furnished and beautifully decorated bedrooms, each with private whirlpool bath.

## 5 BUFFALO

**Behind The Picket Fence**
30 Central Ave.
612/682-9490

**Division Street Antiques**
7 Division St.
612/682-6453

**Vintage Mall**
8 E Division St.
612/682-0600

**Buffalo Bay Antiques**
11 E. Division St.
612/682-1825

**Buffalo Nickel Antique Mall**
Hwy. 55
612/682-4735

**Waldon Woods Antiques**
2612 State Hwy. 55 S.E.
612/682-5667

**Annie's Attic**
1205 State Hwy. 25 N.
612/682-2818

## 6 BURNSVILLE

### Robinson Cruise O Antiques
1509 W. 152nd St.
612/435-7327
Available all hours and all days, call ahead
*Directions: From Minneapolis, go south on Hwy. 35 W. to Burnsville, to County Road 42 W. From County Road 42 W., go until exit onto County Road 5. Turn west on 152nd St.*

In Juanita Robinson's backyard in Burnsville, Minnesota, you will find a dry-docked 35-foot cruiser which has become Robinson Cruise O Antiques.

According to Mrs. Robinson, the boat was built in the late thirties by Mr. Olson, a steel worker by trade. It weighs between 12 and 18 tons and is all steel except the after cabin, which was a later addition. It was designed as a paddle wheeler, but with one critical problem: it would not back up! So the boat was hauled to the backyard until Mr. Olson's death.

In the '50s it was sold to Mr. Batcher who modified it, removed the paddle wheel, and built an after cabin. Proving to be too much to handle, the old boat was sold to the Robinsons who used it for weekend recreation.

After 15 years of use the Robinson Cruise O was dry-docked in the Robinson's 2-acre backyard. Time and disuse took their toll until Mrs. Robinson restored the old boat and converted it into an antique shop.

Primitives form a large part of her inventory, but she also displays dolls, hurricane lamps, dish and kitchen goods, as well as brass, stained glass and buttons. This old boat may not be seaworthy any more, but the old Robinson Cruise O is certainly worth seeing.

**Hagen's Furniture & Antiques**
2041 W. Burnsville Pkwy.
612/894-5500

**Touch of Countree**
14150 Nicollet Ave.
612/435-3688

## 7 CANNON FALLS

**Schaffer's Antiques Downtown**
Downtown
507/263-5200

**Country Side Antique Mall**
Old Hwy. #525
507/263-0352

**Fourth Street Antiques**
106 4th St.
507/263-7249

## 8 CHISAGO CITY

**Chisago Antique Co-op**
10635 Railroad Ave.
612/257-8325

**Glyer Block Antiques**
10675 Railroad Ave.
612/257-3043

**Kichi-Saga Antiques & Art**
10645 Railroad Ave.
612/257-8273

## 9 CROSBY

**Linda's Collectibles**
10 W. Main St.
218/546-8233

**Den of Antiquity**
108 W. Main St.
218/546-5385

**Alice's Antiques**
22 First St. N.W.
218/546-6685

**Crosby Collectible Co-op**
Main St.
218/546-5385

**Hallett Antique Emporium**
28 W. Main St.
218/546-5444

**C & H Odds & Ends**
425 Mesaba
218/546-5899

**Iron Hills Antiques & Gun**
128 W. Main St.
218/546-6783

## 10 DULUTH

**Brass Bed Antiques**
329 Canal Park Dr.
218/722-1347

**Sunset Antiques**
2705 E. 5th St.
218/724-8215

**Antiques on Superior St.**
11 W. Superior St.
218/722-7962

**Antique Collectible Emporium**
314 E. Superior St.
218/722-1275

**Old Town Antiques & Books**
102 E. Superior St.
218/722-5426

**Antique Centre-Duluth**
335 Canal Park Dr.
218/726-1994

**Greysolon Arms**
1920 Greysolon Rd.
218/724-8387

**Neil Shakespeare Antiques**
38 E. Superior St.
218/723-8100

**Canal Park General Store**
10 Sutphin St.
218/722-7223

**Woodland Antiques**
1535 Woodland Ave.
218/728-1996

## 11 ELK RIVER

**Art Barn**
20700 Hwy. 169
612/441-7959

**Antique Clock Doctor**
7808 N.E. River Road
612/441-3456

**Antiques Downtown**
309 Jackson Ave.
612/441-1818

**Historical Fragments**
7808 N.E. River Road
612/441-5889

## 12 EVELETH

**Wildrose Antiques & Collectibles**
616 Grant Ave.
218/744-3053

**Garden Cottage**
7687 Wilson Road
218/744-4803

## 13 EXCELSIOR

**Antiquity Rose & Dining Room**
429 2nd St.
612/474-2661

**Excelsior Coin & Collectibles**
449 2nd St.
612/474-4789

**Collectors Choice**
227 Water St.
612/474-6117

**Country Look-In Antiques**
240 Water St.
612/474-0050

**John Ferm Coins**
449 2nd St.
612/474-9223

**Mary Oneal & Co.**
221 Water St.
612/470-0205

**Leipold's Gifts & Antiques**
239 Water St.
612/474-5880

## 14 FARIBAULT

**Curiosity Shop Antiques**
3052 Cedar Lake Blvd.
507/334-5959

**Dimestore Antique Mall**
310 Central Ave. N.
507/332-8699

**Collectors Antique Gallery**
409 Central Ave. N.
507/332-7967

**Country Antiques**
212 Central Ave. N.
507/332-2331

**Keepers Antique Shop**
403 Central Ave. N.
507/334-7673

**Stoeckels Antique Clocks & Dolls**
615 3rd St. N.W.
507/334-7772

## 15 FOREST LAKE

**Now Showing Antiques & Collectibles**
119 Lake St. N.E.
612/464-2286

**Signs of the Past**
4864 210th St. N.
612/786-4201

**Muriel & Friends Antiques**
1031 Lake St. S.E.
612/464-1954

**Gold-Dusters**
143 Lake St. N.E.
612/464-4442

## 16 HASTINGS

**Carroll's Antiques**
107 2nd St. E.
612/437-1912

**Cherished Treasures**
116 2nd St. E.
612/480-8881

**Madeline's**
205 2nd St E
612/480-8129

**Olde Main St. Antiques**
216 2nd St. E.
612/438-9265

**Hastings Antique Market**
375 33rd St. W.
612/437-7412

**Village General Antiques**
14570 240th St. E.
612/437-8150

### *Great Places To Stay*

**Hearthwood Bed & Breakfast**
17650 200th St. E.
612/437-1133

Tucked into the bluffs of the Mississippi River Valley between the historic cities of Hastings and Red Wing, this six bedroom home blends a quaint timber facade with Cape Cod architectural influences. A rural setting of oak, paper birch, and other upland plants nestle the visitor into a sense of one with nature. Come and walk the two nature trails on this estate. One is for the adventurous while the other is for a casual romantic stroll.

## 17 HIBBING

**Northland Antiques & Collectibles**
11192 Hwy. 37
218/263-4427

**Ct Antiques**
Hwy. 37
218/262-1891

**Antique Treasure Trove**
3798 S. Pintar Road
218/263-7246

**Anties Attic Antiques**
1621 13th Ave. E.
218/262-3159

## 18 HOPKINS

**K & C Trains**
1409 Cambridge St.
612/935-5007

**Blake Antiques**
1115 Excelsior Ave. E.
612/930-0477

**Mary Francis**
901 Main St.
612/930-3283

**Hopkins Antique Mall**
1008 Main St.
612/931-9748

## 19 HUTCHINSON

**Schaffers Antiques**
16457 Hwy. 7
320/587-4321

**Main Street Antiques**
122 Main St. N.
320/587-6305

**Barb's Country Collectibles & Antiques**
12634 Ulm Ave.
320/587-9144

## 20 LAKEVILLE

**Hot Sam's Antiques & Furniture**
22820 Pillsbury Ave.
612/469-5922

**Nampara Farm Antiques**
10196 234th St. E.
612/985-5665

## 21 LUVERNE

**Duane's Glassware & Antiques**
Brown Church/Estey and Main St.
507/283-2586

**Hillside Antiques**
County Road 4-RR 3, Box 22B
507/283-2985

**Larry's Furniture Refinishing**
RR 1 Box 84
507/283-2275

## 22 MANKATO

**Arts & Antiques Emporium**
1575 Mankato Place
507/387-6199

**Northwind Antiques**
110 E. Washington St.
507/388-9166

**Antique Mart**
529 S. Front St.
507/345-3393

**Earthly Remains**
731 S. Front St.
507/388-5063

**Save Mor Antiques & Jewelry**
816 N. 2nd St.
507/345-5508

## 23 MANTORVILLE

This quaint little town in the picturesque valley of the middle fork of the Zumbro River, with its wealth of architectural heritage, Mantorville, Minn., was named to the National Register of Historic Places in 1975. A visit here opens the door to many historical pursuits.

This tiny town is probably most famous for one of its limestone buildings constructed in 1854, the Hubbell House Hotel. In its early days, the hotel was a 16x24-foot-long structure and was the only building in town having a double roof, thereby allowing room in the chamber for guests.

In 1856, the present three-story structure was built, and it immediately became an important stopping place along the trail from Mississippi to St. Peter. Senator Alexander Ramsey, General Ulysses S. Grant, Dwight D. Eisenhower, American journalist Horace Greeley, Roy Rogers and Mickey Mantle were but a few of the many guests who took relaxation in the pleasant facilities provided at the Hubbell House.

In 1946, Paul Pappas purchased the old hotel and opened its doors as a first-class restaurant. Although times have changed, early American hospitality is still available at the Hubbell House. Excellent food and outstanding service are still provided for the many visitors who happen upon this wonderful little town called Mantorville.

**Grand Old Mansion Bed & Breakfast**
No address listed
507/635-3231

**Carl's Cut Crystal**
5th St.
507/635-5690

**Pfeifer's Eden Bed & Breakfast**
RR 1 (7 miles from Mantorville)
507/527-2021

**The Chocolate Shoppe**
5th St.
507/635-5814

**Memorabilia Antiques**
5th St.
507/635-5419

## 24 MAPLE PLAIN

### Country School House Shops
5300 U.S. Hwy. 12
612/479-6353
Daily 10-6
*Directions: Located 25 miles west of Minneapolis. Go west from Minneapolis on Interstate 394 (U.S. Hwy. 12) to Maple Plain.*

Plan to spend some time here because there is just so much to see. Set in an old 3-story schoolhouse are 100 dealers who have something for every shopper.

If collectibles and memorabilia are your forte, you'll find them here: toys, dolls, games, coins, glassware, china, books—you name it.

There are also antique household furnishings, rugs, clocks, and lamps, the latter of which can be repaired by their staff.

The Coffee Cabin Cafe located in the shop offers lunch, dessert, and gourmet coffee when you feel your energy flagging.

**Gingerbread House of Antiques**
1542 Baker Park Road
612/479-1562

**Steeple Antique Mall**
5310 Main St.
612/479-4375

## 25 MARSHALL

**Bev's Antiques**
107 5th St.
507/537-1933

**General Store**
349 Main St. W.
507/537-0408

**Orphanage Antiques Strawberry**
351 Main St. W.
507/532-3998

## 26 MAZEPPA

### Bed and Browse and Robby's Antiques
1st St.
507/843-4317
Year round; call for reservation information.
*Directions: From Minneapolis, head south on Minnesota Hwy. 52 until south of Zumbrota, Minn., then east on Country Road 60 to Mazeppa. Turn north on 1st St. to third block.*

The Robinsons of Burnsville, Minn., lived a busy life as foster care givers and were anxious to find a retreat from the visits of social workers, personal care attendants, and all of the comings and goings associated with such charitable works. They finally found asylum in an old building on a street corner in quaint Mazeppa, Minnesota.

Juanita Robinson recalls, "For 6 years of summer weekends, Luke, our adopted son, played while I hammered and sawed and painted...." It is a two-story building, the first floor of which is now Robby's Antiques. The second floor is now the "getaway."

The building, which is on the National Historic Register, has a brick front with stone walls on the interior, and has been an overnight haven for treasure hunters and weary travelers for the past three years. Guests bring their own food, or eat in nearby cafes.

There are some intriguing curiosities upstairs at the Bed and Browse, including a 100-year-old duck boat that has been converted to a display cabinet; an old English zinc bathtub that is now used for reading or napping, and the "in-house outhouse" door made of stained glass (backed by wood to insure privacy).

Downstairs at Robby's Antiques you'll find more treasures, such as stained glass, buttons and collectibles galore. Bed and Browse is also a convenient stopover for antiquing adventures in nearby Red Wing, Wabasha, Oronoco, Lake City and Rochester.

## 27 MINNEAPOLIS

**Great Northern Antiques & Vintage**
5159 Bloomington Ave. S.
612/721-8731

**J & H Used Furniture & Antiques**
2421 W. Broadway Ave.
612/588-3049

**Ross Frame Shop**
4555 Bryant Ave. S.
612/823-1421

**Euro Pine Imports**
4416 Excelsior Blvd.
612/929-2927

**Hollywood North**
4510 Excelsior Blvd.
612/925-8695

**Park Avenue Antiques**
3004 W. 50th St.
612/925-5850

**Complements**
3020 W. 50th St.
612/922-1702

**Loft Antiques**
3022 W. 5th St.
612/922-4200

**Cupboard Collectables**
3840 W. 50th St.
612/929-9244

**Illyricun Antiques**
430 1st Ave. N.
612/338-3345

**Tiques & Treasures Antiques**
117 4th St. N.
612/359-0915

**Wooden Horse**
3302 W. 44th St.
612/925-1148

**Durr Ltd.**
4386 France Ave. S.
612/925-9146

**A Anderson**
3808 Grand Ave. S.
612/824-1111

**Plaza Antiques**
1758 Hennepin Ave.
612/377-7331

**Finishing Touches Antiques**
2520 Hennepin Ave.
612/377-8033

**H & B Gallery**
2729 Hennepin Ave.
612/874-6436

**J Oliver Antiques**
2730 Hennepin Ave.
612/872-8952

**Cobblestone Antiques Inc.**
2801 Hennepin Ave.
612/823-7373

**Shades on Lake**
921 W. Lake St.
612/822-6427

**Antiques Minnesota Inc.**
1516 E. Lake St.
612/722-6000

**Muzzleloaders Etcetra Inc.**
9901 Lyndale Ave. S.
612/884-1161

**Spiderweb Antiques**
6525 Penn Ave. S.
612/798-1862

**Indigo**
530 N. 3rd St.
612/333-2151

**American Classics Antiques**
4944 Xerxes Ave. S.
612/926-2509

**Getchell's Antiques**
5012 Xerxes Ave. S.
612/922-6222

**Antiques at Anthonies**
801 E. 78th St.
612/854-4855

**Annabelle's Gifts & Antiques**
2907 Pentagon Dr.
612/788-3700

**C. W. Smith Antiques**
4424 Excelsior Blvd.
612/922-8542

**Hazen's Used & Rare Records**
3318 E. Lake St.
612/721-3854

**Past Present Future**
336 E. Franklin Ave.
612/870-0702

**Tom's Antiques**
3801 Chicago Ave.
612/823-6076

**Waldon Woods Antiques**
213 Washington Ave. N.
612/338-2545

**Battlefield Military Antiques**
3915 Hwy. 7
612/920-3820

**Len's Antiques**
1108 E. Lake St.
612/721-7211

**Theatre Antiques**
2934 Lyndale Ave. S.
612/822-4884

**Sherry's Old Stuff Antiques**
9139 Old Cedar Ave. S.
612/854-5086

**Antiques Riverwalk**
210 3rd Ave. N.
612/339-9352

**Architectural Antiques Inc.**
801 Washington Ave. N.
612/332-8344

**Park Ave. Antiques**
4944 Xerxes Ave. S.
612/922-0887

**American Island**
3505 W. 44th St.
612/925-9006

**Arteffects**
13 5th St. N.E.
612/627-9107

**Antique Clock Shop**
1516 E. Lake St.
612/722-9590

**East Lake Antiques & Collectibles**
1410 E. Lake St.
612/721-6589

**Minneapolis Uptown Antiques**
2512 Hennepin Ave.
612/374-4666

**Sherry's Old Stuff Antiques**
9139 Cedar Ave. S.
612/854-5086

**Uptown Antique & General Store**
2833 Hennepin Ave.
612/879-0019

## 28 MOTLEY

**Wilson House Antiques**
Box 315
218/352-6629

**Pat's Place**
Box 173
218/352-6410

**Olde Tyme Trading Post**
681 Hwy. 10 S.
218/352-6273

## 29 NEVIS

**Danny's Arcade Ice Cream & Antiques**
115 Main St.
218/652-3919

## 30 NEW ULM

New Ulm was established in 1848 by German settlers, and ties to the old country still run deep. Downtown shops sell delicious fudge and traditional German crafts. In the town square is a 45-foot glockenspiel, one of a few free-standing carillon clocks in the world. Outside of town is Harkin Store, an authentic restoration stocked with the goods, sights and smells of an 1870s general store.

**Antiques Plus**
117 N. Broadway St.
507/359-1090

**Antique House**
327 N. Broadway St.
507/354-2450

**Cherry Lane Antiques**
1440 Cherry St.
507/354-4870

**Heritage Antiques**
16 N. Minnesota St.
507/359-5150

**Neidecker Antiques**
1020 N. State St.
507/354-6459

## 31 NISSWA

**International Country Antiques**
Nisswa Square
218/963-0311

## 32 NORTHFIELD

Drive the Outlaw Trail Tour into Northfield, the escape route of notorious bank robbers Frank and Jesse James, who tried to rob Northfield bank but were foiled by alert townsfolk. The restored bank, one of many buildings in the Historic Downtown District, is now a museum.

**Old Stuff Gallery**
200 Division St.
507/645-7821

**Terrell's Antiques**
200 Division St.
507/645-5878

**Three Acres Antiques**
302 Division St.
507/645-4997

**Cherubs Cove Inc.**
307 Division St.
507/645-9680

**Remember When Antiques**
418 Division St.
507/645-6419

**Seven Gables Books & Antiques**
313 Washington St.
507/645-8572

## 33 ORONOCO

The tiny town of Oronoco (population 700) is famous for the large antique show and flea market which comes to town every third week-end in August. Thirteen hundred dealers from the U.S. and Canada display their wares amongst a crowd of 30 to 40,000 prospective buyers.

**Antiques Oronoco**
Hwy. 52
507/367-2220

Gordon and Yvonne Cariveau are professionals when it comes to antiques. Of course, it helps to have been in the business for the past twenty years.

Eight years ago, the Cariveau's built a large shop, about 4,000 square feet of showroom space, plus a restoration area. Last year a 1,500 square foot wholesale outlet was added.

Antiques are displayed in department store style settings; according to colors, catagories, etc. The inventory is pre-1950s, specializing in early 1900s.

**Berg's Antique Store**
50/420 Minnesota Ave. S.
507/367-4413 or 507/367-4588
Open flexible days/hours. Call for appointment. (When possible, main buildings 9-5, Tue.-Sat.)
*Directions: Traveling on State Hwy. 52 (6 miles North of Rochester). Exit onto Minnesota Ave. S. (Main St.). Berg's is located next to the bridge in the largest (brick) building in town.*

Berg's is an original in more ways than one. With the same owner and location since 1963, it specializes in original finishes and rough oak and pine pieces. "Nothing has been redone," boasts owner Mary Lou Berg.

These original finished pieces are exceptional, highly sought after, and hard to find—except here. You'll also find thousands of "smalls" to suit your fancy. What you won't find here are crafts, gifts, or reproductions.

Because the shop is so specialized, the hours vary, and Mary Lou recommends that you call ahead for an appointment. If you feel impulsive enough to just drop by, your best chances are between 9 and 5 Tuesday through Saturday.

**Greta's Country Antiques**
1005 1st St. S.E.
507/367-2315

**Antiques Oronoco**
Hwy. 52
507/367-2220

**Cathis Country Store & Antiques**
230 S. Minnesota Ave.
507/367-4931

## 34 PALISADE

**Old River Road Antiques**
Route 2, Box 190
218/845-2770
Open by chance or appointment—open most days during the summer, and open most weekends during the spring and fall.
*Directions: 4 miles north of the Hwy. 169 and Hwy. 210 junction toward Grand Rapids, Minnesota. 12 miles north of Aiken, Minnesota, on Hwy. 169.*

Both this smaller version and the original barn built in 1913 are constructed of the salvaged wood from the old steamboat, Irene, which once traveled along the Mississippi River. It seems fitting that since its reconstruction in 1983, it has sat on the spot where the river road was once located.

The heritage of Old River Road Antiques provides an interesting introduction to the shop which carries many newly restored furnishings. Mr. Hlidek (the "h" is silent) restores the antique furniture, and the shop is a showcase for his work.

Other interesting items listed among what Ms. Hlidek terms her "fun junk" are Wade porcelain animals from England and her extensive button collection.

## 35 PAYNESVILLE

**Koronis Antiques**
26753 N. Hwy. 55
320/243-4268

**Country Porch Antiques**
399th St.-Hwy. 55
310/243-4027

**Antique Cellar**
104 Washburne Ave.
320/243-7605

**Paynesville Antique Mall**
104 Washburne Ave.
320/243-7000

**Jeanne's Antiques & Collectibles**
109 Washburne Ave.
320/243-7381

## 36 RED WING

In Red Wing shop for antiques, the latest fashions and more in the Pottery District, where Red Wing stoneware was once made. On a self-guided walking tour, see the restored T.B. Sheldon Auditorium Theatre, a historic hotel and Goodhue County Historical Museum. More sights are visible from the river by excursion boat or from the Red Wing Shoe Company Observation Deck.

**Mona Lisa Antiques & Gardens**
1228 W. Main St.
612/388-4027

**Memories**
2000 W. Main St.
612/388-6446

**Old Main Street Antiques**
2000 W. Main St.
612/388-1371

**Dorothy's Antiques**
1604 Old W. Main St.
612/388-7024

**Ice House Antiques**
1811 Old W. Main St.
612/388-8939

**Al's Antique Mall**
1314 Old W. Main St.
612/388-0572

**TEA House Antiques**
927 W. 3rd St.
612/388-3669

**Hiawatha Valley Ranch**
29665 Hwy. 61 Blvd.
612/388-4033

### *Great Places To Stay*

### Pratt-Taber Inn
706 W. Fourth St.
612/388-5945

As an elegant reminder of its heritage, the Pratt-Taber Inn serves its guests a taste of Victorian style. Built in 1876, the interior is of fine woods like butternut and walnut. Particular attention was paid to rich details during construction, including the woodwork throughout and the trim on the wonderful porch, which is so representative of the style. Three fireplaces in the parlors are also expressive of such elegance. The richness continues in the inn's furnishings. The six bedrooms boast Renaissance Revival and Victorian style antiques.

Enjoy a gourmet breakfast before taking a walk to nearby downtown Red Wing, or to the banks of the Mississippi River. If you prefer, you can tour the area aboard an old San Francisco cable car that has been mounted to a truck chassis. If your timing is right, you can watch as eagles migrate through the area. An estimated 4,000 were sighted last year.

## 37 ROCHESTER

**Old Stonehouse Antiques**
1901 Bamber Valley Road S.W.
507/282-8497

**Sentimental Journeys Unlimited**
110 W. Center St.
507/281-6616

**Timeless Treasures**
7 1st Ave. S.W.
507/288-3398

**Mayowood Galleries**
Kahler Hotel/ 2nd Ave S.W.
507/288-2695

**Collins Antique Feed & Seed Center**
411 2nd Ave. N.W.
507/289-4844

**Just A Little Something**
305 6th St. S.W.
507/288-7172

**Old Rooster Antique Mall**
106 N. Broadway
507/287-6228

**Peterson's Antiques & Stripping**
111 11th Ave. N.E.
507/282-9100

**Iridescent House**
227 1st Ave. S.W.
507/288-0320

**Mayowood Galleries**
3705 Mayowood Road S.W.
507/288-6791

**Blondell Antiques**
1408 2nd St. S.W.
507/282-1872

**Antique Mall on Third**
18 3rd St. S.W.
507/287-0684

**John Kruesels General Merchandise**
22 3rd St. S.W.
507/289-8049

**Broadway Antiques**
324 S. Broadway
507/288-5678

## 38 SHAKOPEE

### Lady Di Antiques
126 S. Holmes St.
612/445-1238
Daily 10-5

Downtown Shakopee, Minnesota, offers the discriminating shopper a superb selection at Lady Di Antiques. Owner Diane Sullivan, well known in Minnesota for her expertise in promoting high-end antique shows, has consolidated her sense of style and taste into this versatile shop.

Merchandise runs the gamut from vintage clothing to dolls and toys, to distinctive furnishings and decorative accessories.

**Something Olde**
120 Holmes St.
612/445-3791

### *Interesting Side Trips*

### Historic Murphy's Village
2187 East Hwy. 101
612/445-6900
*Directions: On the banks of the Minnesota River, one mile east of Shakopee on Minnesota Hwy. 101 – 30 minutes from the Minneapolis/St. Paul International Airport and 23 minutes from the Mall of America.*

In a quiet village nestled along the shores of the scenic Minnesota River, pioneers long ago learned to thrive in a sometimes hostile, sometimes hospitable new world. As they carved a life for themselves in the wilderness, the stories of their determination and dignity, and their spirit and ingenuity filled this new land.

Today, more than 100 years later, the spirit of that time lives on. Historic Murphy's Village is a unique living history museum that preserves and interprets 19th century life in the Minnesota River Valley. Dedicated to the lives of children and adults, both past and present, Historic Murphy's Village is not only a land that remembers time, but a land where history comes alive with each new day.

The idyllic wooded setting that stretches along one and a half miles of scenic river valley brings alive the charm and challenges of life in the 19th century. Families, history buffs and adventurers of all ages can step into this historic village, which features the rich diversity of early American life.

Each homestead, among the 40 different buildings at Murphy's, represents the coming together of the many groups that settled in the Minnesota River Valley between 1840 and 1890—Czech, Danish, English,

French, German, Irish, Norwegian, Polish and Scandinavian. In addition, Murphy's Historic Village includes 16 Native American mounds that are estimated to be more than 2000 years old.

Visitors can stroll on their own or ride on horse-drawn trolleys. Their journey will cover the very early days of the fur trade era when people traveled by footpath and canoes, to the bustling village complete with its shops, homes, church, town hall and railroad depot. Throughout the village, costumed interpreters are prepared to spin a tale, demonstrate their craft and explain the daily life of the men, women and children who settled in the valley more than a century ago. Day-to-day activities such as cooking, weaving, spinning and woodworking take place in their homes and on their farmsteads. Visitors will hear how villagers lived and learned together during that rugged pioneer era.

Music and entertainment also often fill the daily Village routine. Musicians and crafts people are a common sight, while folks gather at the blacksmith shop or general store for a chat with tour guides and costumed interpreters.

## 39 SAINT CLOUD

**Kays Antiques**
713 Germain
320/255-1220

**Paper Collector Art Gallery**
26 7th Ave. N.
320/251-2171

**Depot Antique Mall**
8318 State Hwy. 23 & I-94
320/253-6573

### *Great Places To Stay*

### Edelbrock House
216 N. 14th Ave.
320/259-0071

Located in Saint Cloud just south of the famous Minnesota lakes and forests, the Edelbrock House offers guests the opportunity to step back in time to an 1880 yellow brick Victorian farmhouse brimming with antiques, collectibles and country decor. Excellent home cooking and personal pampering will make you fall in love with Edelbrock House.

## 40 SAINT PAUL

**Victoria Grande Gardens**
818 Grand Ave.
612/228-0228

**Cottage Interiors**
1129 Grand Ave.
612/224-2933

**Anything & Everything Inc.**
1208 Grand Ave.
612/222-7770

**Oxford Antiques**
58 Hamline Ave. S.
612/699-1066

**Antiques White Bear Inc.**
4903 Long Ave.
612/426-3834

**Wicker Shop**
2190 Marshall Ave.
612/647-1598

**Danny's Antiques**
1076 Maryland Ave. E.
612/776-6287

**Granny Smiths Antiques & Crafts**
7600 147th St. W.
612/891-1686

**Antique Mart**
941 Payne Ave.
612/771-0860

**Antique Lane on Payne**
946 Payne Ave.
612/771-6544

**Golden Lion Antiques**
983 Payne Ave.
612/778-1977

**Emporium Antiques**
1037 Payne Ave.
612/778-1919

**Grand Old House**
517 Selby Ave.
612/221-9191

**Oldies But Goodies**
1814 Selby Ave.
612/641-1728

**Able Antiques**
226 7th St. W.
612/227-2469

**Wescotts Station Antiques**
226 7th St. W.
612/227-2469

**Alladdin's Antique Alley**
239 7th St. W.
612/290-2981

**John's Antiques**
261 7th St. W.
612/222-6131

**Ann & Larry's Antiques**
2572 7th Ave. E.
612/773-7994

**Nakashian-Oneil Inc.**
23 6th St. W.
612/224-5465

**Taylor & Rose**
251 Snelling Ave. S.
612/699-5724

**French Antiques**
174 W. 7th St.
612/293-0388

**Antiques Minnesota Midway**
1197 University Ave. W.
612/646-0037

**Recollections**
4754 Washington Square
612/426-8811

**Robert J. Riesbery**
343 Salem Church Road
Sunfish Lake
612/457-1772

**J & E Antiques**
1000 Arcade St.
612/771-9654

## 41 SAINT PETER

**Collective Memories**
216 S. Minnesota Ave.
507/931-6445

**Tate Antiques**
817 N. Minnesota Ave.
507/931-5678

## 42 STILLWATER

### American Gothic Antiques
236 S. Main St.
612/439-7709
Mon.-Thurs. 10-5, Fri. & Sat. 10-8, Sun. 11-5
*Directions: On Interstate 94, 10 miles east of St. Paul, exit onto Hwy. 95 North at the Wisconsin border. Travel 8 miles north along the St. Croix River to Stillwater, Minnesota.*

For specific information see review at the beginning of this section.

**DeAnna Zink's Antiques**
9344 60th St. N.
612/770-1987
Thurs.-Sat. 12-6, other days and hours by chance or appointment. Monday is "dealer day" from approximately 9-6 (discounts on everything).
*Directions: Drive Interstate 694 to Hwy. 36 E. Take Hwy. 36 E. 1 1/4 miles to Demontreville Trail. Get off to the left (north). Get on service road (60th St.), and continue east 1/2 mile to the big gray farmhouse on the hill. (From Stillwater: Take Hwy. 36 W. to Keats; veer onto 60th St.; continue west for 1/2 mile.)*

Once inside this 1870s farmhouse, you'll be delighted to find, not only what DeAnna refers to as a "general" line of antique furniture and accessories, but a choice selection of fine glassware, prints, and porcelains. Moreover, the display of Victorian and primitive pieces, which are DeAnna's specialty, are not to be missed.

Treat yourself to coffee and munchies while roaming the aisles of this charming shop.

**One of a Kind**
102 Main St. N.
612/430-0009

**Gabrielle**
114 N. Main St.
612/439-5930

**Main Street Antiques Stillwater**
118 Main St. N.
612/430-3110

**Country Charm Antiques**
124 Main St. S.
612/439-8202

**River City Antiques & Collectibles**
124 Main St. S.
612/439-3889

**Past and Present Antiques**
208 Main St. S.
612/439-6198

**Stillwater Antiques**
101 S. Main St.
612/439-6281

**St. Croix Antiquarian Books**
232 S. Main St.
612/430-0732

**Mulberry Point Antiques**
270 Main St. N.
612/430-3630

**Antique Radio Company**
301 Main St. S.
612/432-3919

**Midtown Antique Mall**
301 Main St. S.
612/430-0808

**More Antiques**
312 Main St. N.
612/439-1110

**Architectural Antiques Inc.**
316 Main St. N.
612/439-2133

**Mill Antiques**
410 Main St. N.
612/430-1816

**Rivertown Antiques**
501 Main St. N.
612/439-8188

**Battle Hollow Antiques**
6148 Osgood Ave.
612/439-3414

## 43 WINONA

**Markham's Antiques**
1459 W. 5th St.
507/454-3190

**A-Z Chair Caning**
160 Main St.
507/454-0366

**R D Cone Antiques Mall**
66 E. 2nd St.
507/453-0445

**Traveling Treasures**
1161 Sugar Loaf Road
507/452-5440

**Country Comfort Antiques**
79 W. 3rd St.
507/452-7044

**Haviland Matching Service**
467 E. 5th St.
507/454-3283

## 44 WORTHINGTON

**Hodgepodge Lodge**
214 8th St.
507/376-4542

**LBJ Antiques**
760 W. Shore Dr.
507/376-5004

**Margaret's Specialty Antiques**
802 3rd Ave.
507/372-2239

**Martin's Antiques**
259 Kragness Ave.
507/372-5678

**Remember When**
1321 Milton Ave.
507/376-3548

# Mississippi

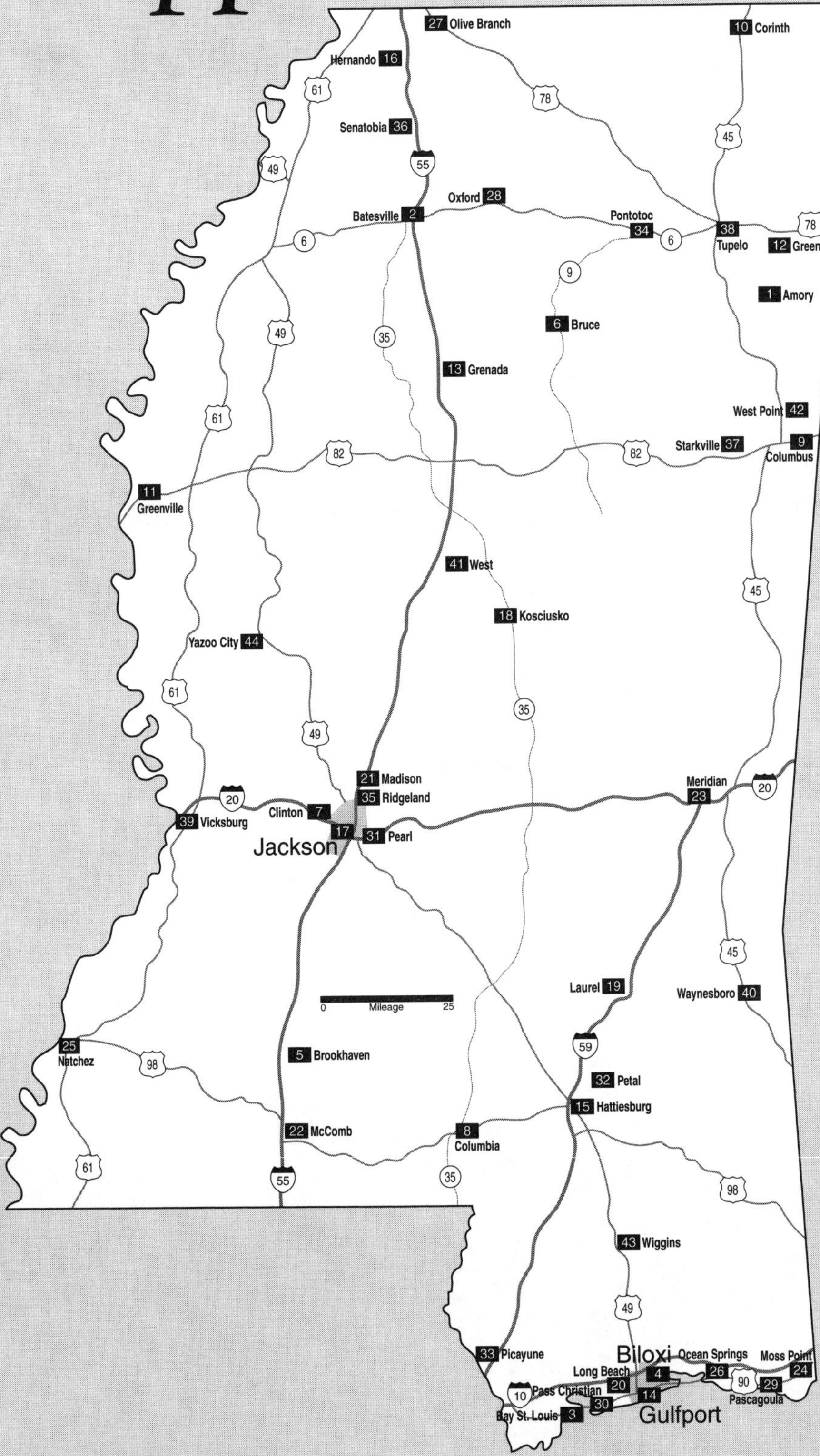

*Spend some time relaxing on the splendid 64-foot porch of the Red Creek Inn — admire the handsome magnolias which cradle the space, enjoy the fragrant breeze, and soak up the atmosphere of Southern hospitality.*

# Long Beach: A great 'home port' between New Orleans & Mobile

Red Creek Inn Vineyard & Racing Stable is a circa 1899 "raised French cottage" centrally located for antiquing in Biloxi and Ocean Springs to the east, and Pass Christian and Bay St. Louis to the west. Located on 11½ acres of fragrant magnolias and ancient live oaks, you'll love swinging on Red Creek's 64 foot front porch, before hitting the nearby beaches, casinos, or historical sites...just minutes away!

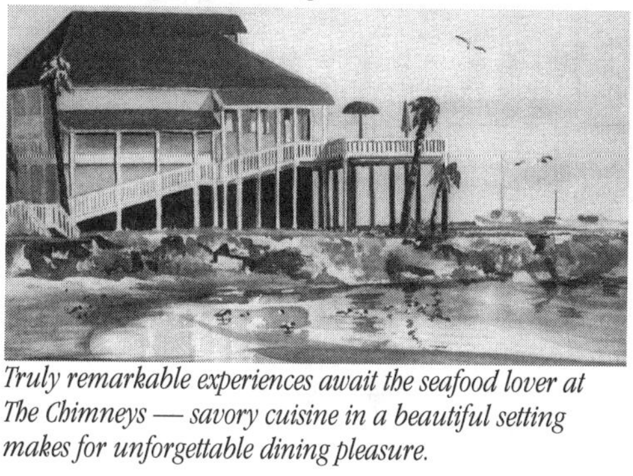

*Truly remarkable experiences await the seafood lover at The Chimneys — savory cuisine in a beautiful setting makes for unforgettable dining pleasure.*

Breakfasts at Red Creek are memorable. But, for superb local seafood, The Chimneys can't be beat. With a splendid view of the Long Beach small craft harbor, this local landmark also features a quaint bar and a 20' x 50' deck. For casual elegant ambience, deep in the "Old South" tradition, The Chimneys gets our vote.

*For additional information on Red Creek Inn, call 1-800-729-9670 or 228/452-3080 and for information on The Chimneys,*

*You'll enjoy a generous breakfast at The Red Creek Inn Vineyard & Racing Stable. The dining room features tasteful decor and a relaxed elegance that is the hallmark of a graceful lifestyle.*

*Visitors are keenly aware of the Southern heritage that is preserved for future generations to appreciate at Linden.*

# Find majestic tranquility at Linden in Natchez

Rising gracefully from the top of a gentle slope and set behind mossy oaks, this stunning mansion is the epitome of dignity, comfort, and hospitality. Linden is a Federal plantation home and has one of the finest collections of Federal furniture in the South. The home's front doorway was copied for "Tara" in Gone With the Wind.

Mrs. Jane Gustine Conner purchased the estate in 1849 and her descendants have lived in the home ever since. Today it is owned by Mrs. Jeanette Feltus, and her children are the sixth generation of the Conner family to reside there.

Linden's stately dining room...a magnificent cypress punkah, painted white, hangs over the Hepplewhite banquet table, set with many pieces of family coin silver and heirloom china. On the walls are three Havell editions of John James Audubon's bird prints. Each of the seven bedrooms is furnished with antiques and canopied beds. All bedrooms have private baths and are central heated and air-conditioned. Most of the bedrooms open onto the galleries where old-fashioned rocking chairs welcome its guests to relax.

Linden has been home to many outstanding Mississippi statesmen such as: Thomas B. Reed, first U. S. Senator from the then new state of Mississippi; Mrs. Margaret Conner Martin, wife of General W. T. Martin of Confederate fame; Michael Conner, Governor of Mississippi, and Mrs. Percy Quinn, wife of Senator Percy Quinn.

Articles featuring this historic mansion have appeared in: *Southern Living, Colonial Homes, Reader's Digest, Ghosts of the South*, and *Modern Maturity* to mention a few.

*Linden is located at 1 Linden Place in Natchez, Mississippi.*
*Call 1-800-2-LINDEN, 601/445-5472 or fax 601/442-7548 for reservations or additional information.*

# Service and flair are specialties at Interior Spaces

Located in the metropolitan area of Jackson, Miss., Interior Spaces is an upscale antique market dealing with English, French, and American antiques. Beautifully displayed rooms entice the eye with assorted home accessories, original art, prints, mirrors, rugs, architectural elements and lamps. A wide price range makes this a "must see" stop for the discriminating buyer.

*Beautiful displays entice the shopper.*

The staff includes several interior decorators, ready to assist you at your request. To complete your decorating needs, Interior Spaces offers an "in home" decorating service for a nominal fee.

*Open Monday through Saturday, 10-5:30, Interior Spaces is located at 1220 E. Northside Dr., Suite 120 in Jackson, Miss. For additional information see listing #17 (Jackson).*

*Sought-after American, French and English antiques are presented in a range of prices that merits the attention of the serious antique shopper. You'll find just the right accent in an outstanding selection of accessories for the home.*

# Mississippi

## 1 AMORY

**The Park Antiques**
109A S. Main St.
601/257-2299

**Jerry's Antiques & Collectibles**
300 N. Main St.
601/256-8790

**Amory Mini-Mall**
105 N. Main St.
601/256-8003

## 2 BATESVILLE

**Collector Antiques & Things**
111 Public Square
601/563-1916

## 3 BAY SAINT LOUIS

**Beach Antique Mall**
108 S. Beach Blvd.
601/467-7955

**Paper Moon**
220 Main St.
601/467-8318

**Lighthouse Antiques**
131 Main St.
601/467-1455

**Charters Antiques**
125 Main St.
601/467-4665

**Cummings Antiques**
131 Main St.
601/467-1648

**Bay Shoppe Gallery, Inc.**
136 Main St.
601/466-2651

**Evergreen Antiques**
201 Main St.
601/467-9924

**M. Schon Antiques**
110 S. 2nd St.
601/467-9890

## 4 BILOXI

**Beauvoir Antique Mall & Flea**
190 Beuvoir Road
601/388-5506

**Memories Annex**
918 A St.
601/374-6708

**Nixon Antique Gallery Ltd.**
993 Howard Ave.
601/435-4336

**Tu J's Treasures Ltd.**
819 Jackson St.
601/435-5374

**Russenes**
128 Porter Ave.
601/432-0903

**Spanish Trail Books**
781 Vieux Marche Mall
601/435-1144

### *Great Places To Stay*

**The Father Ryan House Bed and Breakfast**
1196 Beach Blvd.
601/435-1189 or 1-800-295-1189

Circa 1841. National Register. One-time home and study of Father A. J. Ryan, poet laureate of the Confederacy. Private balconies overlooking white sand beaches and the Gulf. Nine rooms on 3 floors. Private bath. Period antiques. Pool and courtyard. Southern breakfast.

## 5 BROOKHAVEN

**Brookwood Gifts & Antiques**
706 Hwy. 51 N.
601/833-3481

**This N That**
1383A Union St. Ext. N.E.
601/835-1512

## 6 BRUCE

**Collins Antiques**
S. Tyson Road
601/983-7194

## 7 CLINTON

**Trash and Treasures**
590 Springridge Road
601/924-3224

**Brick Street Antiques**
312 N. Jefferson St.
601/924-5251

**Pette's Place**
300 Monroe
601/924-2147

**Cindy's**
406 Monroe
601/924-7078

## 8 COLUMBIA

**Neat Stuff**
919 High School Ave.
601/736-5061

**The Tiger Lily**
Main St.
601/731-2511

## 9 COLUMBUS

**Vintage Vignettes & Framery**
413 Main St.
601/327-5655

**Riverhill Antiques**
122 3rd St. S.
601/329-2669

**Love-Lincoln Carriage House**
714 3rd Ave.
601/328-5413

### *Great Places To Stay*

**Amzi Love Bed and Breakfast Inn**
305 Seventh St. S.
601/328-5413

Circa 1848. National Register. Italian-style villa in Historic district. Romantic English garden. Five bedrooms with baths. Home is steeped in history and features original furnishings and old scrapbooks. Southern breakfast.

### Liberty Hall
Armstrong Road
601/328-4110

Circa 1832. National Register. Nineteenth century portraits are displayed, along with such interesting documents as the old planter's diary that recounts the trials of running a 6,000-acre plantation. Picnic lunches, dinner with advance reservations, hiking and fishing.

## 10 CORINTH

**Junkers Parlor Antiques**
2003 Hwy. 72 E.
601/287-5112

**Hammond House Antiques**
1004 Fillmore St.
601/286-6786

### *Great Places To Stay*

### The General's Quarters
924 Fillmore St.
601/286-3325

Circa 1872. Victorian home located in the Historic district of old Civil War town. Suite contains 140-year-old canopy bed. Lounge on second floor, veranda, parlor and beautiful garden. Furnished with period antiques. Evening snack. Southern breakfast.

### Madison Inn
822 Main St.
601/287-7157

Turn-of-the-century house in downtown residential area. Four suites, with sitting room and private bath. Beautiful courtyard, aquarium, in-ground pool. Continental breakfast.

### Robbins Nest Bed and Breakfast
1523 Shiloh Road
601/286-3109

Circa 1869. Southern Colonial-style home surrounded by oak, dogwood and azaleas. Situated on two acres. Three guest rooms with antiques and private baths. Generous breakfast served on the back porch where guests may relax in antique wicker furniture.

## 11 GREENVILLE

**Dust & Rust**
603 Hwy. 82 E.
601/332-4708

**Lina's Interiors**
525 S. Main St.
601/332-7226

**Wilsons Junk Tique & Woodwork**
Hwy. 82 E.
601/335-7525

**Town & Country Antique Barn**
Hwy. 82 E.
601/335-2436

## 12 GREENWOOD

**Russells Antique Jewelry**
229 Carollton Ave.
601/453-4017

**Warehouse Antiques**
229 Carollton Ave.
601/453-0785

**Olde World Antiques**
301 W. Market St.
601/455-9678

**Patsy's Hodge Podge**
511 Lamar St.
601/455-4927

**Heritage House Antiques**
311 E. Market St.
601/455-4800

**Finchers, Inc.**
512 W. Park Ave.
601/453-6246

**Antique Wholesalers**
527 W. Park Ave.
601/455-4401

**Corner Collection**
412 Walthall St.
601/453-8387

## 13 GRENADA

**Maw & Paws Antiques**
1079 Hebron Church Road
601/226-3672

**Donna's Antiques & Gifts**
N. Main St.
601/226-2595

## 14 GULFPORT

**Ronnie G's Antq. & Furniture Restorations**
240 Courthouse Road
601/896-7391

**Artiques**
1130 Cowan Road
601/897-2273

**Old Things**
15415 Landon Road
601/832-6945

**Dear Hearts**
10425 Old High #49
601/832-6017

**Back In Time Antique Mall**
205 Pass Road
601/868-8246

**Handsboro Trading Post**
504 E. Pass Road
601/896-6787

**Ward Antique Brass**
711 E. Pass Road
601/896-5436

**Right Stuff Antiques**
1750 E. Pass Road
601/896-8127

**Antique House**
1864 E. Pass Road
601/896-3435

**Alstons Antiques & Gifts**
2208 25th Ave.
601/868-3985

**Circa 1909 Antiques**
2170 E. Pass Road
601/897-7744

## 15 HATTIESBURG

**Early Settler Antiques & Collectibles**
5330 Hwy. 42
601/582-8212

**Old High School Antiques**
846 N. Main St.
601/544-6644

**Calico Mall**
309 E. Pine St.
601/582-4351

**The Antique Mall**
2103 W. Pine St.
601/268-2511

**Tin Top Antiques**
1005 Bouie St.
601/584-7018

**Riverwalk Marketplace**
5619 Hwy. 42
601/545-7001

### *Great Places To Stay*

**Tally House**
402 Rebecca Ave.
601/582-3467

Circa 1907. National Register. Tally House has welcomed five Mississippi governors as overnight guests. The 13,000-square-foot home has an intriguing collection of antiques, cozy animals and birds to enjoy.

## 16 HERNANDO

**Buddy's Antiques**
151 Commerce
601/429-5338

**Harper's Antiques**
2610 Hwy. 51 S.
601/429-9387

### *Great Places To Stay*

**Shadow Hill**
2310 Elm St.
601/449-0800

Originally opened as a tea room in 1923, this quiet country retreat is located on six acres and features large rooms, antiques, fireplaces and a wide front porch overlooking a deep, shaded lane.

## 17 JACKSON

**Interior Spaces**
Maywood Mart
1220 E. Northside Dr., Suite 120
601/981-9820
Mon.-Sat. 10-5:30
*Directions: Traveling I-55, Exit 100. If traveling north on I-55: Take Exit 100. Go through the first stop light on Frontage Road. Located on the right in Maywood Shopping Center. If traveling south on I-55: Take Exit 100. Go to the first stop light. Turn left on Northside Dr. Then turn left on Frontage Road. Located on the right in Maywood Shopping Center.*

For specific information see review at the beginning of this section.

**Oriental Shoppe**
110 Highland Village (I-55 N.)
601/362-4646

**Jo's Antiques**
680 Commerce St.
601/352-3644

**Primos Annelle & Associates**
4500 Highland Village (I-55 N.)
601/362-6154

**Ax Antiques & Trading Post**
3953 Hwy. 80 E. (Pearl)
601/939-5887

**Antique Mall of Richland**
731 Hwy. 49 S.
601/936-9007

**Kuntry Junkshun**
1135 Raymond Road
601/373-6503

**St. Martin's Gallery**
2817 Old Canton Road
601/362-1977

**Caldwell Antiques**
1048 Old Brandon Road
601/939-4781

**Jim Westerfield Antiques**
4429 Old Canton Road
601/362-7508

**Bobbie King Dressing Up**
667 Duling Ave.
601/362-9803

**Stately Home Antiques**
737 N. State St.
601/355-1158

**C W Fewel & Co.**
840 N. State St.
601/355-5375

**Elephants Ear**
3110 Old Canton Road
601/982-5140

**High Street Collection**
1217 Vine St.
601/354-5222

**Interiors Market**
659 Duling Ave.
601/981-6020

**The Antique Market**
3009 N. State St.
601/982-5456

**Oliver Antiques**
730 Lakeland Dr.
601/981-2564

### *Great Places To Stay*

**The Fairview Inn**
734 Fairview St.
601/948-3429, 1-888-948-1908
Rates $100-150, $15 each additional person
*Directions: I-55 exit #98A on Woodrow Wilson; left, first traffic light at North State; left, one block past second traffic light at Fairview St. Inn is first property on left.*

The Fairview Inn is Southern hospitality at its best. Constructed in 1908, at the turn of the century, Fairview is one of Jackson's landmark mansions and one of the few architecturally designed houses of that period remaining in the city. It was built for Cyrus C. Warren, vice president of the Warren-Goodwin Lumber Company, and was designed by the Chicago architectural firm of Spencer and Powers. Robert Closson Spencer was a prominent member of the Prairie School and a close associate of Frank Lloyd Wright. Walter Burley Griffin was his star employee.

Both the main house, whose front entrance facing Fairview Street is supported by modified Corinthian columns, and the carriage house facing Oakwood Street, are Colonial Revival, a style associated with the formality and elegance of Southern tradition. The classical detail and ordered proportions of the Palladian influence on Georgian architecture are also apparent in Fairview, and have caused it to be compared with Mount Vernon, although there are significant differences between the two structures. In recognition of its architectural character, Fairview was placed on the National Register of Historic Places in 1979.

The property was purchased in 1913 by Felix Gunter, president of the Jackson Board of Trade (forerunner of the Jackson Chamber of Commerce), and then by W. E. Guild, treasurer of the Finkbine Lumber Company, in 1921. In 1930, Fairview was purchased by D. C. Simmons, and has been a Simmons family home ever since. D. C. Simmons, associated for many years with Deposit Guaranty Bank and Trust Company and the Mississippi Baptist Hospital's Board of Trustees, lived in the house until his death in 1964, and his widow, Annie Belle Ferguson Simmons, continued to live in the house until her death in 1972. Their son, William J. Simmons purchased the property from his parents' estate in 1972. He and his wife, Carol, are the present owners and residents.

The inn's eight guest rooms and suites are all elegantly decorated with antiques and reproductions, fine linens, and collectibles. Amenities include private baths, phones, data ports, voice mail, TV and VCR, sitting rooms, toiletries, and air conditioning. Some rooms have in-room Jacuzzis.

Each gourmet meal at The Fairview Inn is meticulously prepared by Chef Todd McClellan, a graduate of the Johnson & Wales University. Fresh flowers, live music, and a five-course, five star meal can make your evening one to remember.

The inn is a AAA Four Diamond Award winning bed and breakfast and was recently chosen as one of four "dream vacations" by *Travel & Leisure*. For a look inside Fairview Inn, visit them on the internet at: www.fairviewinn.com

## 18 KOSCIUSKO

**Antiques & Interiors Mall**
301 W. Jefferson St.
601/289-3600

**Peeler House Antiques**
117 W. Jefferson St.
601/289-5165

### *Great Places To Stay*

**Redbud Inn**
121 N. Wells St.
601/289-5086 or 1-800-379-5086

Circa 1884. National Register. Queen Anne-style Victorian two-story, listed on Best Places to Stay in the South and top ten bed and breakfast inns in Mississippi. Furnished in period antiques. Antique shop. Tea Room. Near downtown Historic Square. Southern breakfast.

## 19 LAUREL

**Southern Collections Mall**
317 Central Ave.
601/426-2322

**Antiques Mart**
427 Oak St.
601/425-0009

### *Great Places To Stay*

**The Mourning Dove Bed and Breakfast**
556 N. Sixth Ave.
601/425-2561 or 1-800-863-3683

Circa 1907. National Register. Classic four-square one block from the Lauren Rogers Museum of Art and located in the Historic District. Features two private cottages.

## 20 LONG BEACH

**Red Creek Inn Vinyard & Racing Stable**
7416 Red Creek Road
228/452-3080 or 1-800-729-9670

For specific information see review at the beginning of this section.

**Oak Leaf Shoppe**
410 Jeff Davis Ave.
228/868-9433

**Doll Hospital**
110 E. 5th St.
228/863-1024

## 21 MADISON

**Talk of the Town**
120 Depot Dr.
601/856-3087

**Uptown Antiques Etc.**
111 Depot Dr.
601/853-9153

**Inside Story**
2081 Main St.
601/856-3229

**Madison Antiques Market**
100 Post Oak St.
601/856-8036

## 22 McCOMB

**Traditions-Art & Antiques**
125 S. Broadway St.
601/249-3038

**A J Sales**
205 E. Georgia Ave.
601/684-8249

**J & E Antiques**
127 S. Magnolia St.
601/249-3309

**Whistle Stop Antiques**
228 N. Railroad Blvd.
601/249-3990

**Bell Remnants, Inc.**
232 N. Railroad Blvd.
601/684-0529

**Finders Limited**
239 Louisiana Ave.
601/684-5062

## 23 MERIDIAN

**Lincoln Ltd. Bed and Breakfast**
601/482-5483 or 1-800-633-6477

Convenient to downtown Meridian. Home is filled with the host's collection of family heirlooms. Features a pre-Civil War mahogany-canopied bed, as well as a sun porch and patio.

**A & I Place**
2223 Front St.
601/483-9281

**Booker's Antiques**
Hwy. 19 S.
601/644-3272

**Cabin Antiques**
8343 Russell Topton Road
601/679-7922

**Z's Antiques**
1607 24th Ave.
601/482-0676

**Old South Antique Mall**
100 N. Frontage Road
601/483-1737

**Wayside Shop**
5523 Poplar Springs Dr.
601/485-2205

**House Of Antiques & Collectibles**
1725 17th Ave.
601/485-5462

**Century House Antiques**
2101 24th Ave.
601/482-5504

## 24 MOSS POINT

**Fishers Antiques**
5136 Elder St.
601/475-5731

**Pass-Point Antiques**
3806 Main St.
601/475-7863

## 25 NATCHEZ

**Antique Lantern**
145 Homochitto St.
601/445-9955

**As You Like It Silver Shop**
410 N. Commerce St.
601/442-0933

**H Hal Garner Antiques**
610 Franklin St.
601/445-8416

**Simonton Antiques**
631 Franklin St.
601/442-5217

**Antique Mall**
700 Franklin St.
601/442-0130

**Natchez Antiques & Collectibles**
701 Franklin St.
601/442-9555

**Lower Lodge Antiques**
712 Franklin St.
601/442-2617

**Rendezvous Antiques & Gifts**
401 Main St.
601/442-9988

**Natchez Gun Shop**
533 S. Canal St.
601/442-7627

**Country Bumpkin**
502 Franklin St.
601/442-5908

**Antiquarian**
624 Franklin St.
601/445-0388

**Mrs. Holder's Antiques**
636 Franklin St.
601/442-0675

**Sharp Designs & Works of Art**
703 Franklin St.
601/442-5224

**Pippens Limited Antiques**
708 Franklin St.
601/442-0962

**Antiques-Washington Villae**
824 Hwy. 61 N.
601/442-8021

**Tass House Antiques**
111 N. Pearl St.
601/446-9917

### *Great Places To Stay*

**Linden Bed and Breakfast**
1 Linden Place
601/445-5472 or 1-800-1-LINDEN

For specific information see review at the beginning of this section.

**Mark Twain Guest House**
25 Silver St.
601/446-8023

Circa 1830. National Register. Three rooms, two rooms overlooking the Mississippi River and one with balcony and fireplace. Large shared bathroom. Entertainment downstairs in saloon on weekends. Near casino and restaurants.

## 26 OCEAN SPRINGS

**Temptations**
1508 Government St.
601/875-7896

**Artifacts European Antiques**
1202 Government St.
601/872-4545

**Lumbee Antiques**
6510 Washington Ave.
601/872-2881

**Old Biloxey Antiques**
6011 Washington Ave.
601/872-7110

**Clocksmith**
12401 Hanover Dr.
601/875-6613

**B.J. & Friends**
3100 Bienville Blvd.
601/872-0509

**Magnolia Antiques**
1013 Government St.
601/875-4404

### *Great Places To Stay*

**Oak Shade Bed and Breakfast**
1017 La Fontaine
601/875-1050

Spacious and completely private retreat situated amidst the quiet charm of old Ocean Springs. The room has a private entrance and a private bath. Library. Southern breakfast.

**Who's Inn**
623 Washington Ave.
601/875-3251

Gallery rooms are furnished with art and sculpture by Southern artists. Handicapped accessible. Located in the center of downtown Historic District. Stocked refrigerator in each room, private baths, three blocks from beach, bikes available. Continental breakfast.

### The Wilson House Inn
6312 Allen Road
601/875-6933 or 1-800-872-6933

Circa 1923. Six guest rooms with private baths, white pine floors, fireplaces, 10-inch-wide wraparound porch, brick patio. One king bed, two queen beds, two full beds and one room with two twin beds. Southern breakfast.

## 27 OLIVE BRANCH

**Old Towne Antiques & Gifts**
9117 Pigeon Roost Road
601/893-2323

**Olive Branch Bazaar**
9119 Pigeon Roost Road
601/895-9496

**Memes Attic**
9121 Pigeon Roost Road
601/895-8616

## 28 OXFORD

Directions: From I-55 South toward Jackson, Miss., exit onto Hwy. 6 West. At South Lamar, you have reached downtown Oxford's antique district.

### Bea's Antiques
1315 N. Lamar Blvd.
601/234-9405
Mon.-Sat. 9-5

Antiques, used furniture, quilts, glassware, mirrors, pictures, lamps and much more. Bea's buys estates.

### The Bird In the Bush/The Oxford Collection
1415 University Ave. E.
601/234-5784
Mon.-Sat. 9-5:30

A multi-dealer mall featuring affordable antiques and collectibles, nostalgic accessories, a variety of reproduction antiques, linens, quilts, and more.

### Creme de la Creme
319 N. Lamar Blvd.
601/234-1463
Mon.-Sat. 10-5:30

A unique collection of shops featuring American, English, and French antiques and collectibles, distinguished home accessories, original art, children's furniture and gifts and a design and sew shop.

### Inside Oxford
1220 Jefferson Ave.
601/234-1444
Mon.-Fri. 9-5:30, Sat. 10-5:30

French, English and American furniture both in the main showroom and in the warehouse. Oriental rugs, lamps, framed art, oil paintings and mirrors, chandeliers, accessories and gifts.

### Material Culture, Inc.
405 S. Lamar Blvd.
601/234-7055
Tues.-Sat. 10-5, Mondays by appointment

Featuring all things Southern, plus early to mid-nineteenth century American furniture and decorative arts, antique Persian carpets, folk art, fine crafts, vintage linens, handcrafted jewelry, antique architectural elements and materials, quilts and silver.

**Tommy's Antiques & Imports**
Hwy. 6 E.
601/234-4669

**Ruffled Feathers**
Hwy. 6 W.
601/236-1537

**Old House Juntiques**
Hwy. 30
601/236-7116

**Weather Vane**
137 Courthouse Square
601/236-1120

**Willaims on the Square**
116 Courthouse Square
601/236-3041

## *Great Places To Stay*

### Barksdale-Isom House
1003 Jefferson Ave.
601/236-5600 or 1-800-236-5696

Circa 1838. National Register. Constructed entirely of native timber cut from the grounds and handworked by Indian and slave labor. Classic example of planter-style architecture.

### Puddin Place
1008 University Ave.
601/234-1250

Circa 1892. Beautifully restored. Suite accommodations with private bath, fireplaces, antiques, collectibles and historic mementos. Short walk to historic town square, Ole Miss campus and Rowan Oak. Southern breakfast.

### The Oliver-Britt House
512 Van Buren Ave.
601/234-8043

Circa 1905. Greek Revival. Five second-floor bedrooms, all with private baths and antiques. Breakfast at Smitty's, an Oxford tradition, on weekdays. Southern breakfast.

## 29 PASCAGOULA

**Samuels Antiques**
824 Denny Ave.
601/762-8593

**Bernard Clark's White House Antqs.**
2128 Ingalls Ave.
601/762-3511

**Wixon & Co. Jewelers**
1803 Jackson Ave.
601/762-7777

**J & B Antiques**
3803 Willow St.
601/769-0542

## 30 PASS CHRISTIAN

### The Blue Rose Restaurant and Antiques
120 W. Scenic Dr.
601/452-7004

The Blue Rose Restaurant and Antiques in Pass Christian sits majestically on Scenic Drive across from the Pass Christian Yacht Harbor.

The house, built in 1848, was originally a one-and-a-half story frame, five-bay coastal cottage with a gallery with square columns wrapped around three full sides of the house, and consoles carrying overhanging cornices over each bay. It has distinctive pilastered dormers and numerous rear ells attaching the former outbuildings and enclosing gallery.

Mr. Fitzpatrick, who built the home, was a merchant marine. He and his wife had four children, three girls and one boy. Their daughter, Nettie, was a nun and Kitty was the postmaster in the city of Pass Christian. Hugh was the supervisor for Beat 3 for many years and Lettie is believed to be a "ghost" at The Blue Rose. Lettie was mentally retarded and rarely allowed on the first floor of the house. It was rumored that at night, when everyone was asleep, Lettie would roam around the first floor with her terrier puppy. She died at the age of 11 or 12, of yellow fever. None of the other children had offspring and the house eventually went to a niece.

During World War II the house was converted into apartments and later sold to a man from Louisiana. The Blue Rose is now owned by Philip LaGrange, who is the fourth owner of the house in its history.

The house is listed on the National Register of Historic Places. The National Trust of Historic Preservation has described it as "the most significant antebellum home on the western portion of Pass Christian's beach front."

The broad front porch is now glassed in with breath taking views of the harbor and Gulf Coast waters. Interior areas are graced by stained glass, intricate woodwork, and high ceilings. The antique store, featuring fine antiques, estate silver and collectibles, is on the eastern portion of the house. The restaurant, featuring the finest cuisine on the Gulf Coast, is on the western portion of the house.

**Wicker N Wood**
254 E. Beach – Hwy. 90
601/452-4083

**Old Community Antique Mall**
301 E. 2nd St.
601/452-3102

**Blue Rose Antiques**
120 W. Scenic Dr.
601/452-7004

#### *Great Places To Stay*

### Inn at the Pass
125 E. Scenic Dr.
601/452-0333 or 1-800-217-2588

Circa 1879. National Register. On the beach of the Mississippi Gulf Coast. Victorian antiques, fireplaces, kitchenette, golf packages, restaurants and shops within walking distance. Original art in all rooms.

## 31 PEARL

**McClain's Antiques**
3834 York Road
601/679-5076

**Memory Lane Antique Mall**
413 N. Bierdeman Road
601/932-1946

## 32 PETAL

**Ruthie's Attic**
101 Pine St.
601/583-0429

## 33 PICAYUNE

**Pirates Plunder**
127 W. Canal St.
601/798-0885

**Pineros Antiques**
210 W. Canal St.
601/798-9615

**Edwards Antiques & Gallery**
335 W. Canal St.
601/798-3376

**Abundant Treasures**
111 N. Main St.
601/799-5871

**Just Stuff**
300 W. Canal St.
601/749-0461

**Nicholson Antique Trading Post**
73 Emmett Meitzler Road
601/798-7844

## 34 PONTOTOC

**Mason Jar Antique Mall**
34 Liberty
601/489-7420

**Court Square Antique Mall**
42 Liberty
601/488-8844

## 35 RIDGELAND

### Antique Mall of the South
367 Hwy. 51
601/853-4000
Mon.-Sat. 10-6, Sun. Noon-6
*Directions: Located one mile north of I-55/County Road intersection (I-55 Exit 103). One mile north of Jackson, Miss.*

This 14,000-square-foot antique mall is known to have the "finest quality antiques in the South." The inventory here will impress even the choosiest antique collector.

There is a distinct selection of furniture, including Early American, Country, Empire, Victorian, as well as "lots of oak." For collectors of fine glassware, they offer Fenton, flow blue, depression glass, and the finest cut glass pieces around. Hummel collectors will be delighted to find a selection of their favorite figurines available here. The locomotive hobbyist searching for that new locomotive to add to his collection just may find it here among the dandy selections of trains and accessories.

For an outstanding representation of quality antiques and collectibles, a "must stop" on your antiquing trail is the 50-dealer Antique Mall of the South.

**Village Antiques**
554 Hwy. 51, Suite D
601/856-6021

**Copper Kettle**
637A Hwy. 51
601/856-7042

## 36 SENATOBIA

**Dot Mitchell Antiques**
123 Lively St.
601/562-4392

**Home Sweet Home**
220 W. Main St.
601/562-0027

***Great Places To Stay***

### Spahn House
401 College St.
601/562-9853

Circa 1904. This gracious 15-room Southern mansion, situated on a picture-perfect shady street, is beautifully restored. Four guest rooms, jacuzzi baths, common areas. Honeymoon package. Lunch or dinner. Southern breakfast.

## 37 STARKVILLE

**Back Roads Antiques**
Old Crawford Road
601/323-4763

**Ginis Attic Antiques**
1221 Old Hwy. 82 E.
601/323-8790

**Watsons Village Antiques**
1237 Old High, #82E
601/323-5526

**Tin Top Antiques**
891 Old West Point Road
601/323-2032

***Great Places To Stay***

### The Caragen House
1108 Hwy. 82 W.
601/323-0340

Circa 1890. Steamboat Gothic design, the only one of its kind in Mississippi. Located inside the city limits on 22 acres. Five bedrooms with private baths, king beds, and refreshment center.

## 38 TUPELO

**Red Door Antique Mall & Collectibles**
1001 Coley Road
601/840-6777

**Cottage Book Shop**
214 N. Madison
601/844-1553

**Main Attraction**
214 W. Main St.
601/842-9617

**Nostalgia Alley**
214 W. Main St.
601/842-2757

**Chesterfield's**
624 W. Main St.
601/841-9171

**George Watson Antiques**
628 W. Main St.
601/841-9411

**Murphey Antiques Ltd.**
1120 W. Main St.
601/844-3245

**My Granny's Attic**
Appointment Only
601/844-4614

**Pam Antiques & Lamp Shop**
2229 W. Main St.
601/844-3050

**Skyline Antiques**
Old 78 E.
601/680-4559

**Rain Station Antiques**
202 S. Park St.
601/840-2030

**Peppertown Antiques**
Hwy. 78
601/862-9892

**The Treasure Chest**
4097 W. Main St.
601/840-2015

**Silver Web Antiques**
810 Harrison, #3
601/842-4022

***Great Places To Stay***

### The Mockingbird Inn
305 N. Gloster
601/841-0286

Seven guest rooms represent the decor from different corners of the world. Private bath and queen-size beds. Common rooms. Evening soft drinks, coffee, tea, bottled water and juices are complimentary. Southern breakfast.

## 39 VICKSBURG

### Yesterday's Treasures Antique Mall
1400 Washington St.
601/638-6213
Mon.-Sat. 10-5, closed Sun.

A multi-dealer mall in historic Downtown Vicksburg, offering furniture, glassware, Civil War relics, old books, pottery, quilts and linens, toys, collectibles, and much more!

**Old Feldhome Antiques**
2108 Cherry St.
601/636-0773

**River City Antiques**
1609 Levee St.
601/638-4758

**Washington St. Antique Mall**
1305 Washington St.
601/636-3700

**Yesterdays Treasures Antique Mall**
1400 Washington St.
601/638-6213

***Great Places To Stay***

### Balfour House
1002 Crawford St.
601/638-7113
Open year round

"Beneath the flickering glow of candlelight, elegant ladies and dashing Confederate officers danced one cold December evening in 1862, until a courier rushed in to announce that Union gunboats had been sighted on the Mississippi River. The officers bade their ladies a hasty good-bye and left to prepare for the defense of the city." (An eventful night at Balfour House)

Each December, Balfour House is host to a gala evening of music and festive re-enactment of the last grand ball before the siege of Vicksburg. Among Balfour House's other year-round accomplishments is its distinction as a National Register property and designated Mississippi landmark. Additionally, it is considered one of the finest Greek Revival structures in the state according to the Mississippi Department of Archives and History. This bed and breakfast establishment was certainly abuzz with activity during the siege of Vicksburg. In fact, and obviously so once you see, Balfour House became business headquarters for the Union Army after the fall of the city.

The 1982 restoration of the house complied obediently to the Secretary of the Interior's Standards for Rehabilitation, and in this obedience, the house's walls surrendered a cannonball and other Civil War artifacts. The three-story elliptical staircase and patterned hardwood floors were also restored in 1982. The work on these projects was honored with the 1984 Award of Merit from the state historical society.

With such a notable history, Balfour House would be a star stop for any Civil War, architectural or antique lover's tour of Vicksburg. Even so, the bed and breakfast offers delights matching the history of the home. The bedrooms are authentically decorated, and upon stepping out of your guest room each morning, you are invited to partake of a full Southern-style breakfast which is always generous and hearty. During the day, you might enjoy following the guided tour of the home, which will enlighten you on all of its history and beauty.

### Annabelle Bed and Breakfast
501 Speed St.
601/638-2000 or 1-800-791-2000

Circa 1868. Located in Vicksburg's Historic Garden District, this stately Victorian-Italianate residence is elegantly furnished with period antiques and rare family heirlooms. Private full baths. Southern breakfast.

### The Corners
601 Klein St.
601/636-7421 or 1-800-444-7421

Circa 1872. National Register. Original parterre gardens, a 70-foot gallery across the front with a view of the Mississippi River, double parlor, formal dining room and library. Five rooms with fireplaces and eight rooms with whirlpool tubs, private bath. Southern breakfast.

### Cedar Grove Mansion Inn
2200 Oak St.
601/636-1000 or 1-800-862-1300

Circa 1840. National Register. Greek Revival mansion overlooking the Mississippi River. Gardens, fountains and gazebos. Original antiques. Four-Diamond AAA Rating. Gourmet candlelight dining and piano bar.

### Duff Green Mansion
1114 First East St.
601/636-6968 or 1-800-992-0037

Circa 1856. National Register. Used as a hospital for Confederate soldiers. Furnished with period antiques and reproductions. Honeymoon and anniversary package. Southern breakfast.

### Floweree
2309 Pearl St.
601/638-2704

Circa 1870. National register. Fine example of Italianate architecture. Listed on Historic American Building Survey. Southern breakfast.

### The Stained Glass Manor
2430 Drummond St.
601/638-8893 or 1-800-771-8893

Circa 1906. National Register. "The Stained Glass Manor" of Spanish design features 32 stained glass windows, fine oak paneling and spectacular staircase. The interior glows from the light through the delicate panes of rose, salmon, rust, gold, blue and green.

## 40 WAYNESBORO

**Four Generations**
124 Mississippi Dr.
601/735-5721

**Old French House**
515 Mississippi Dr.
601/735-0353

## 41 WEST

***Great Places To Stay***

### The Alexander House
11 Green St.
1-800-350-8034
Open year round
*Directions: From I-55, take Exit 164, between Jackson, Miss., and Memphis, Tenn. Go 3 miles off the interstate. Located on the second paved road to the right after leaving the interstate exchange.*

An incident from the rooms of The Alexander House as recounted by Ruth Ray and Woody Dinstel.

**The Blinking Cat**

"Guests at The Alexander House often ask to photograph our rather elegant rooms and some of the more valuable or interesting antiques. We say, 'Be our guests.' One morning a guest was going through the rooms with a camcorder. She was in Miss Anne's room when she became excited and called everyone to her. She had a garbage can with an embossed cat as decoration in her viewfinder, and she cried out, 'The cat blinked at me.' We all gathered, but no one saw any blinking, no matter how hard we stared. A week or so later, this lady called from her home in Alabama to say when they showed the film on their television, the cat definitely blinked. Her husband even processed one frame that definitely showed the eyes closed! There is no streak of light across the frame. Needless to say, we have obtained a copy of the video, to show doubters the proof of the blinking cat."

Tucked lovingly into the heart of Mississippi is the town of West, which ironically is located east of Interstate 55. Among that town's historic buildings is The Alexander House. The unique events occurring in Miss Anne's room regarding "The Blinking Cat" are enough to entice the curious to spend a night or two peeping around corners to see embossed cats wink. Nevertheless, the opulent atmosphere and furnishings of this bed and breakfast allure anyone with a taste to be pampered and surrounded by the uncommon and exquisite. That pampered feeling certainly comes from being luxuriously housed within the historic district of West. The Alexander House was constructed as early as 1880. In 1994, the owners, Ruth Ray and Woody Dinstel, opened the restored home in its period grandeur. As a guest, you will be treated to a complimentary, Southern-style (hearty portions) breakfast in the authentically furnished, two-story home.

Gourmet lunches and dinners are available by reservation.

## 42 WEST POINT

**Aunt Teek's**
743 E. Brame Ave.
601/494-2980

**Treasure Nook**
111 Commerce St.
601/494-1103

**Antique Mall**
415 Hwy. 45 N.
601/494-0098

**Once Upon A Time Antiques**
910 Hwy. 45 Alt St.
601/494-7811

**Antiques on the Main**
123 E. Main St.
601/494-2010

**Wisteria**
411 E. Main St.
601/494-4205

## 43 WIGGINS

**Serendipity Shop**
203 E. Pine Ave.
601/928-5020

## 44 YAZOO CITY

**Main Street Antiques**
211 N. Main St.
601/746-9307

**Chesire Cat**
305 S. Main St.
601/746-8401

# Missouri

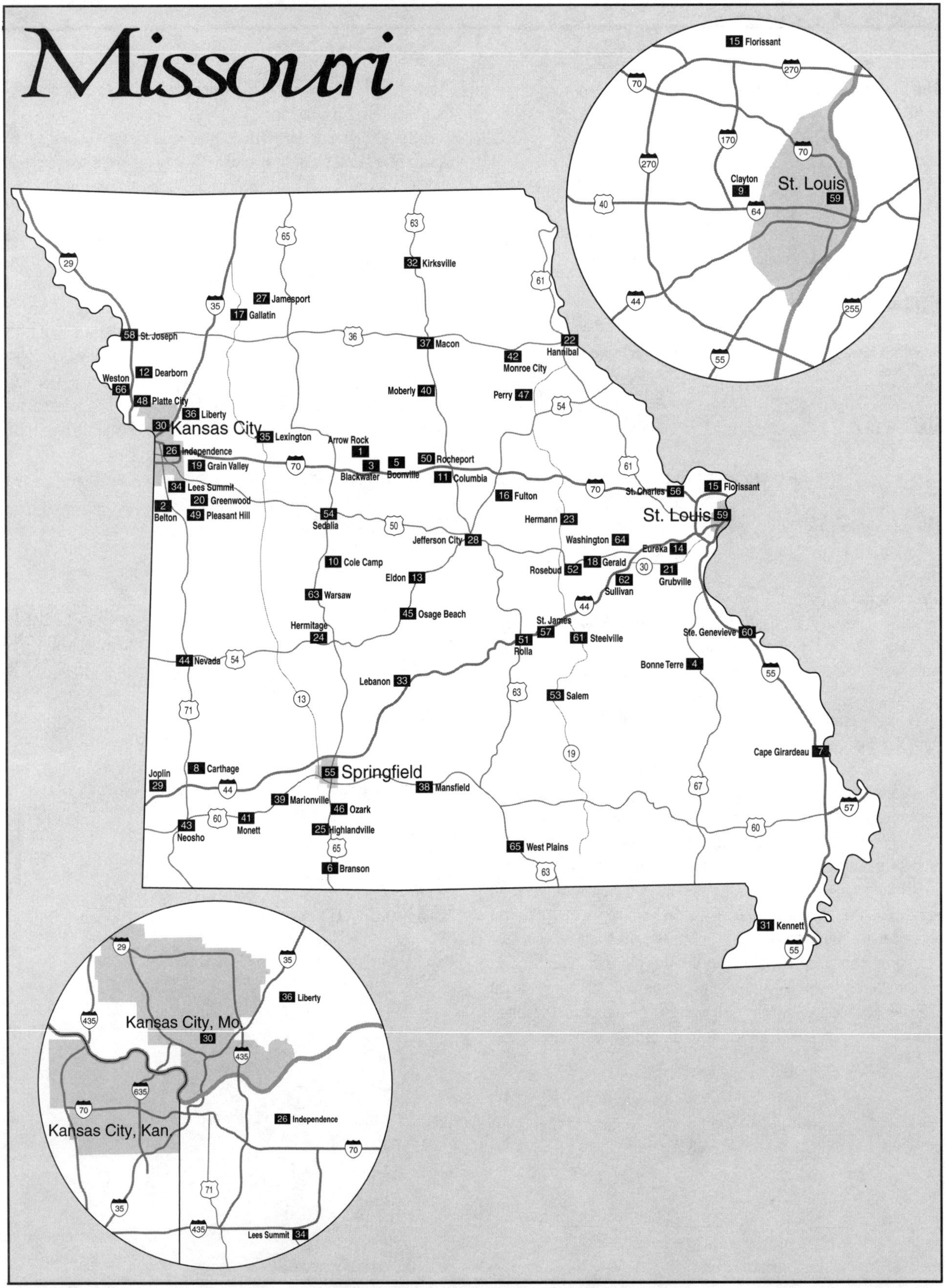
15 Florissant
270
70
170
270
Clayton
9
St. Louis
59
40
64
44
255
55
63
65
32 Kirksville
29
61
35
27 Jamesport
17 Gallatin
58 St. Joseph
36
37 Macon
22 Hannibal
42 Monroe City
12 Dearborn
Weston
66
Moberly 40
Perry 47
48 Platte City
36 Liberty
54
30 Kansas City
35 Lexington
Arrow Rock
1
26 Independence
19 Grain Valley
70
3 Blackwater
5 Boonville
50 Rocheport
11 Columbia
61
34 Lees Summit
20 Greenwood
2 Belton
49 Pleasant Hill
16 Fulton
St. Charles 56
15 Florissant
54 Sedalia
50
Hermann 23
St. Louis 59
Jefferson City 28
Washington 64
10 Cole Camp
Eureka 14
18 Gerald
Rosebud 52
30
21 Grubville
Eldon 13
62 Sullivan
63 Warsaw
44
45 Osage Beach
Hermitage 24
St. James 57
51 Rolla
61 Steelville
Ste. Genevieve 60
44 Nevada
54
Bonne Terre 4
Lebanon 33
71
13
63
53 Salem
19
Cape Girardeau 7
8 Carthage
Joplin 29
55 Springfield
44
38 Mansfield
67
39 Marionville
46 Ozark
57
60
43 Neosho
41 Monett
25 Highlandville
65
60
65 West Plains
6 Branson
63
31 Kennett
55
29
35
36 Liberty
435
Kansas City, Mo.
30
435
635
70
Kansas City, Kan.
26 Independence
70
71
35
435
Lees Summit 34

*Judging by the inviting decor, you'd never guess that the Woodstock Inn was once a turn-of-the-century factory.*

# A warm Woodstock welcome

## Relaxing inn serves as home base while visiting Independence

Formerly a turn-of-the-century doll and quilt factory, the Woodstock Inn B&B is situated in the famous historical district of Independence. There are 11 guest rooms, each with a distinct personality and private bath. Guests start the morning off with the house specialty—gourmet Belgian waffles—or another special breakfast entree. Then it's off to visit the Truman Home, the Truman Library and Museum, the National Frontier Trails Center, the Old Stone Church, the RLDS Temple and Auditorium, Jackson Square, and all the rest.

But when you get ready for dinner, please ask innkeepers Todd and Patricia Justice for suggestions, or you might make the same mistake that some guests did in a story the Justices' tell: "There's a very nice-looking building right up the street from our B&B. It looks like a very large house, with nice landscaping and green awnings over the windows. The sign by the door says 'Speaks.' Early one evening a pair of hungry and weary guests walked in our door wanting to check in. After the whole check-in process, the first words out of their mouths were, 'Where can we get something to eat? We are starving!' We suggested a few places just a couple of miles away, but the lady said right away, 'Oh, but what about that really nice restaurant on the left, right up the street?' We looked at each other, then looked at the couple and said, 'We really don't think you want to eat there!' She then asked, 'Why? It looks really nice! Have you heard anything bad about the food?' Todd said, 'It's a nice looking place but...it's a funeral home!' Needless to say our guests didn't eat dinner, or any other meal, there!"

*Woodstock Inn Bed & Breakfast is located at 1212 W. Lexington St. in Independence, Missouri. Call the innkeepers at 816/833-2233 for reservations or additional information.*

*Start the day with the Woodstock Inn's specialty of the house, gourmet Belgian waffles.*

*Innkeepers Todd & Patricia delight in greeting guests.*

*What's your pleasure? You're sure to find what you're looking for here at the Ozark Antique Mall and Collectibles. Over 17,000 square feet of merchandise competes for your attention — from furniture to Fiestaware.*

# Ozark Antique Mall and Collectibles filled with unique treasures

## Be prepared to come early and spend plenty of time browsing for that special item

Over 100 dealers have their wares displayed throughout the 17,000 square feet of Ozark Antiques. There is an endless variety of merchandise to choose from, with a very helpful staff happy to aid shoppers as they pore through large collections of primitives, pottery, furniture and thousands of pieces of depression glass. Other specialty lines include military items, fishing gear, gas pumps, Coca Cola memorabilia, toys, advertising, architectural salvage items, ball cards, Aladdin lamps, cookie jars, Ertl, radios, trains, tins, Fiesta ware, marbles, knives and dolls.

*Ozark Antique Mall and Collectibles is located at 200 S. 20th St. in Ozark, Missouri. For additional information and directions to the shop see listing #46 (Ozark).*

*Wonderful items can be found in abundance at the Ozark Antique Mall and Collectibles. A case of antique shirt collars rests atop a display of advertising memorabilia. Washboards, Mickey Mouse figures, dolls, knives, tin signs and kerosene lamps vie for your attention.*

## 1 ARROW ROCK

The year was 1804. Lewis and Clark were in the midst of their legendary explorations of the U.S. when they noted the bluff and the nearby salt licks in their journals and maps. Native Americans had for centuries gathered the flint from the bluff for arrowheads, hence the name Arrow Rock. After Lewis and Clark, westbound explorers and traders stopped at Arrow Rock Spring in 1829, some of them settled and founded the town. Today, Arrow Rock is basically untouched by time. The 70 people who currently live in the town are steeped in its history and in the recreation and preservation of its past.

Visitors to Arrow Rock can tour a restored 1834 tavern, a gunsmith's shop and home, the old print shop, frontier artist George Caleb Bingham's home, a museum dedicated to medical doctor John Sappington, who was a pioneer in the treatment of malaria, and more. Then you can experience live entertainment at Arrow Rock's award-winning Lyceum Theatre. Once a church, the theater is now a beautiful 420-seat complex where professional actors from around the country stage Broadway-caliber shows each summer. Also, visit shops filled with antiques, specialty gifts, and old-time crafts. Eat to your heart's content-everything from simple country fare to gourmet delights. Stay at a gracious bed and breakfast, or camp outdoors overlooking the Missouri River Valley.

### *Great Places To Shop*

**Arrow Rock Antiques**
Located on Main St.
816/837-3333

18th and 19th century formal and high country furniture and accessories.

**McAdams' Ltd.**
816/837-3259
Apr.-Dec., Wed.-Sun., 10-5. or by appointment

Once the bank building in a bustling stop on the Sante Fe Trail, this historic building now holds a unique blend of European and American antiques with a distinctive line of new merchandise. Antique, estate and traditional new jewelry have been a McAdams' specialty for 20 years.

**Pin Oak Antiques**
301 Main St., on the Boardwalk
816/837-3244
Wed.-Sun. or by appointment

A full line of antique country furniture and accessories at reasonable prices. Two floors of antiques, including a basement "rough room."

**The Village Peddler Antiques**
One-half mile north of Arrow Rock on Hwy. 41
816/837-3392
Wed.-Sun. 10-5 or by appointment

A general line of furniture and smalls.

### *Favorite Places To Eat*

**Arrow Rock Emporium**
Located on the Boardwalk
816/837-3364

A tea room atmosphere featuring home-cooked sandwich platters, flavored coffee, and delicious ice cream specialties.

**Grandma D's Cafe**
One block south of Main St.
816/837-3335

Enjoy dining surrounded by antiques and unique gifts. Sandwiches, salads, homemade soups, pies, and sweet breads.

**The Old Arrow Rock Tavern**
Located on Main St. one block from the Lyceum Theatre

Built in 1834, The Old Tavern continues to serve the public as it did in the glory days of the Sante Fe Trail. One of the oldest restaurants west of the Mississippi, the Old Tavern fare includes catfish, country ham, and fried chicken, with an ample selection in wine, beer and spirits. Reservations requested.

**The Old Schoolhouse Cafe**
Located in the Old Schoolhouse
816/837-3331

Enjoy homemade breakfast and lunch specialties located at the westside basement entrance in The Old Schoolhouse.

**The Evergreen Restaurant**
Located one block north of Main St. on Hwy. 41
816/837-3251

Enjoy gracious dining with a European touch in a restored 1840s home.

## 2 BELTON

**Dusty Attic Antiques & Collectibles**
319 Main St.
816/331-3505

**1802**
320 Main St.
816/322-7107

**Jaudon Antique Mall**
20406 S. State Road, #D
816/322-4001

## 3 BLACKWATER

### Rose Hill
21495 Hwy. 41
816/846-3031
Wed.-Sat., 10-5; Sun.-Tues., by chance or appointment
*Directions: From I-70 west, Exit #89. Travel 6 miles north through Blackwater on Route "K" to Hwy. 41, then go 1/2 mile north on Hwy. 41 to Rose Hill. From I-70 east, exit #98. Travel 7 miles north on Hwy. 41 toward Arrow Rock. Rose Hill is 1/2 mile on the right after you pass Route "K."*

Visitors to Rose Hill get a special treat, so take your cameras. The shop of Rose Hill is located behind the Kusgen's home and is set up inside in fashion groupings, by rooms. They have bedrooms decorated with beds, wardrobes, chests and accessories; a living room with antique furniture and accessories; and a kitchen with a working model woodburning stove (not for sale). Kitchen items include old utensils, depression glass, and stoneware bowls.

The special treat is growing on the property at Rose Hill. Its Missouri's largest known sugar maple tree, recognized by the Missouri Dept. Of Conservation. The tree has a circumference of 13 feet 8 inches, soars 62 feet tall, and spreads out 88 feet. The Missouri Forestry Department estimates the tree to be 150 years old. A film about the tree has been televised in Missouri by PBS and a plaque was presented to the Kusgens by the Missouri Department of Conservation, attesting to the claim of the state's largest sugar maple tree.

## 4 BONNE TERRE

**Bonne Terre Antiques**
1467 State Hwy. 47
573/358-2235

***Great Places To Stay***

### Victorian Veranda
207 E. School St.
573/358-1134 or 1-800-343-1134
Daily 8-10:30 except Dec. 24-25
Rates $55-85
*Directions: From St. Louis: Take I-55 south to U.S. 67. Turn south on U.S. 67 to Bonne Terre Exit. Turn right on Hwy. 47, then left on Allen Street in Bonne Terre. Turn right on Main St., then take an immediate left on East School St. to the inn. Only 45 miles from south St. Louis.*

Just one of the unique and historic buildings and homes in Bonne Terre, Victorian Veranda is a large old home with a big wraparound porch and four guest rooms decorated in Victorian and country decor, all with private baths. Victoria's Room has six large windows and Victorian accessories, and a Jacuzzi for two. The Victorian Boot and Lace Room holds a wrought iron queen bed and is filled with Victorian high top boots and Battenburg lace. The Drake Room is furnished in the Mallard duck theme, all greens and burgundies, with a claw-foot tub for playing with your own rubber duckie; The Countryside Room is bursting with Americana and country charm, complete with Charles Wysocki prints and country pine queen bed.

## 5 BOONVILLE

**Itchy's Stop & Scratch Flea Market**
1406 W. Ashley Road
816/882-6822

**Key to your Heart Antiques**
1420 W. Ashley Road
816/882-8821

**Hi-Way 5 Antique Mall**
1428 W. Ashley Road
816/882-3341

**Reichel and Co.**
1436 W. Ashley Road
816/882-3533

**Reichel Antique & Auction Corner**
1440 W. Ashley Road
816/882-5292

**McMillan Ltd. Antiques**
417 E. Spring St.
816/882-6337

## 6 BRANSON

**Finders Keepers Flea Market**
204 N. Commercial St.
417/334-3248

**Apple Tree Mall**
Hwy. 76
417/335-2133

**Somewhere In Time**
Hwy. 76
417/335-2212

**Mothers & Mine Antiques**
Mutton Hollow
417/334-2588

**Apple Pie Ltd.**
3612 Shepherd Hill Expressway
417/335-4236

**Twin Pines Antiques**
1120 W. State Hwy. 76
417/334-5830

**Antique City**
Hwy. 76 W.
417/338-2673

## 7 CAPE GIRARDEAU

**Campster School Antiques**
3298 Bloomfield Road
573/339-1002

**Another Time Another Place**
715 Broadway St.
573/335-0046

**Ohaira**
1001 Independence St.
573/334-8020

**Witness Designs**
31 N. Main St.
573/334-0333

**Antique Furn & Crafts Mall**
18 N. Sprigg St.
573/339-0840

**Peddlers Corner**
111 N. Sprigg St.
573/334-1213

**Heartland Antique Emporium**
701 William St.
573/334-0102

**Hansen's Collectibles**
709 William St.
573/334-4410

**A Antique Center Mall**
2127 William St.
573/339-5788

**Smother's Antiques**
467 Oakshire Dr.
573/243-1498

## 8 CARTHAGE

**Goad Unique Antique Mall**
111 E. 3rd St.
417/358-1201

**Accent Angels & Antiques**
342 Grant St.
417/359-5300

**Jerdon Ltd.**
311 S. Main St.
417/358-3343

**Carthage Rt. 66 Antique Mall**
1221 Oak St.
417/359-7240

**Oldies & Oddities Mall**
331 S. Main St.
417/358-1752

**Spring River Antiques**
222 Grant St.
417/358-4407

## 9 CLAYTON

Listed as a part of St. Louis.

## 10 COLE CAMP

### Stone Soup Antiques & Uniques
111 S. Maple St.
816/668-3624
Fax: 816/668-4458
Mon.-Sat., 10-5; Sun. 12-5
*Directions: U.S. 65 20 miles south of Sedalia, east Hwy. 52, 1/2 block south of 4-way stop.*

Here's a shop that takes its name - Stone Soup - from an old children's story. They offer an eclectic collection of antiques, collectibles, glassware (including depression glass, china and figurines), and country crafts in a "unique" 1906 lumber barn, complete with loft, that began its life as an old mercantile building. They also have a nice selection of furniture, including a bed that belonged to Walt Disney's parents!

**Tara Storm**
Maple St.
No Phone

**Antiques & Stuff**
Hwy. 52
816/668-4720

## 11 COLUMBIA

### Columbia Emporium
810 E. Broadway
573/443-5288
Fax: 573/449-6782
Thurs.-Sat. and Mon. 11-5:30, Tues.-Wed. 11-4, closed Sun.
*Directions: Travel west on I-70 (between St. Louis and Kansas City) to Columbia. Exit 126 south on Providence to Broadway. Turn left on Broadway. Columbia Emporium is located in downtown Columbia between 8th and 9th Streets. The shop is a lower level-one. Look for the black and gold sign.*

This upscale emporium offers shoppers a large showroom of art, antiques and jewelry; specializing in large "ornate" 100-year-old furniture, and antique and estate jewelry.

**Mary Watson Antiques & Interiors**
923 E. Broadway Ave.
573/449-8676

**Grandma's Treasures**
2000 Business Loop
573/499-0883

**Midway Antique Mall**
I-70 & Hwy. 40 Exit 121
573/445-6717

**Gates Antiques**
11105 Mexico Gravel Road
573/474-4067

**Museumscopes Antiques**
2507 Old #63 S.
573/449-8523

**Ice Chalet Antique Mall**
3411 Old #63 S.
573/442-6893

**McAdams Ltd.**
32 S. Providence Road
573/442-3151

**Itchys Stop & Scratch**
1907 N. Providence Road
573/443-8275

**Friends Together Antiques**
4038 E. Broadway
573/442-6759

## 12 DEARBORN

**Lickskillet Antique Mall & Shops**
214 Main St.
816/992-8776

**Moore Antiques**
108 W. 3rd
816/992-3788

**Yesterday's Memories**
110, 112, 114 W. 3rd
816/992-8941

**Outpost Trading Co.**
201 W. 3rd
816/992-3402

## 13 ELDON

**Red's Antique Mall**
Hwy. 52 & Bus. 54 S.
573/392-3866

**Past & Present**
106 S. Maple St.
573/392-2256

## 14 EUREKA

**Remember When Antiques**
126 S. Central Ave.
314/938-3724

**Oldys & Goodys Antique Mall**
127 S. Central Ave.
314/938-5717

**Firehouse Gallery & Shops**
131 S. Central Ave.
314/938-3303

**Olde Thyme Shoppe**
224 N. Central Ave.
314/938-3818

**Ice House Antiques**
19 Dreyer
314/938-6355

**Eureka Antique Mall**
107 E. 5th St.
314/938-5600

**Great Midwest Antique Mall**
100 Hilltop Village Center Dr.
314/938-6760

**Accent on Antiques**
120 S. Virginia Ave.
314/938-3200

**Owl's Nest Antiques**
128 S. Virginia Ave.
314/938-5030

**Gingerbread House**
138 S. Virginia Ave.
314/938-5414

**Aunt Sadie's Antique Mall**
515 N. Virginia Ave.
314/938-9212

**Wallach House Antiques**
510 West Ave.
314/938-6633

**Cherokee Chief Trading Post**
529 N. Virginia Ave.
314/772-4433

## 15 FLORISSANT

### Gittemeier House Antiques
1067 Dunn Road
314/830-1133
Daily Mon.-Sat. 10-4, Sun. 12-4
*Directions: From Hwy. 270, take Exit 27(New Florissant Road). Gittemeier House is located on the service road (1067 Dunn Road) behind the Shell Station.*

It's always fun to visit an antique shop that is as old, or older, than the merchandise inside! Gittemeier House is a seven room, two-story 1860 Federal style house where the focus inside is on Victorian furniture - lots of impressive, towering wardrobes, marble topped pieces, glassware, all sorts of things from that elegant, extravagant age of Victoria!

**Age of Reflection**
306 Rue St. Francis
314/972-1700

**Junkle John's Antiques**
525 Rue St. Francis
314/830-0095

**The Sisters Three**
525 Rue St. Francis
314/837-4748

**Village of the Blue Rose**
519 Rue St. Francis
No Phone

**Florissant Treasure House**
126 Rue St. Francis
No Phone

**Victorian Country Antiques**
1067 Dunn Road
314/921-4606

## 16 FULTON

**Cornerstone Antique Mall**
537 Court St.
573/642-6700

**Country Clipper Antiques**
1225 S. Hwy. 54
573/642-0393

**Kings Row Antiques**
Jct. Route F & Hwy. 54
573/642-5335

**Willing House Antiques**
211 Jefferson St.
573/642-7525

**Lutz & Doters**
505 Nichols St.
573/642-9350

## 17 GALLATIN

**Towne Square Antiques**
120 W. Grant St.
816/663-2555

**Goat Mountain Antiques**
Hwy. 6
816/663-2731

## 18 GERALD

***Great Places To Stay***

### The Bluebird Bed & Breakfast
For more specific information see listing under Rosebud #52

### River House Bed & Breakfast
For more specific information see listing under Rosebud #52

## 19 GRAIN VALLEY

**Sambos Antiques**
504 S. Main St.
816/224-4981

**Primitives Plus**
508A Main St.
816/224-3622

**Main Street Mall Antiques**
518 S. Main St.
816/224-6400

**The Collector's Corner**
513 Main St.
816/443-2228

## 20 GREENWOOD

**Gate House Antiques & Tea Room**
302 Allendale Lake Road
816/537-7313

**Country Heritage Antiques**
16005 S. Allendale Lake Road
816/537-7822

**Greenwood Antiques & Country Tea Room**
5th & Main on 150 Hwy.
816/537-7172

**Traditions**
5th & Main on 150 Hwy.
816/537-5011

**Little Blue Antiques**
409 W. Main St.
816/537-8688

**Greenwillow Farm Antiques**
15202 S. Smart Road
816/537-6527

## 21 GRUBVILLE

### Grubville Guitars
314/274-4738
Fax: 314/285-9833
By appointment only
*Directions: Located 35 minutes southwest of St. Louis off Hwy. 30 on State Road Y between Highways 270 & 44.*

A truly interesting shop on your antiquing trek, Grubville Guitars owned by Glenn Meyers, sells and restores used and vintage acoustic and electric guitars, basses, mandolins, banjos, violins and tube type amplifiers.

A musician for most of his life, Glenn thoroughly enjoys his work and has been interested in vintage instruments for 30 years. Most of his business is by word of mouth and his list of clients extends not only from the U.S. but from around the world.

Under Glenn's watchful eye the restoration and repair work is completed by two local guitar builders whose experience allows them to do any work necessary.

Being curious of this unusual fascination of Glenn's, I asked him what he considered to be a vintage instrument. He explains, "Vintage means certain instruments from the 1960s back to the 1700s. For instance, I recently worked on a style 1-42 Martin guitar that was made in 1898. A beautiful instrument with small body, ivory bridge, ivory tuners, Brazilian rosewood - back and sides - and abalone inlayed around the select spruce top. Martin began building guitars in the early 1800s and to this day builds some of the best instruments available." Glenn also noted that there is a difference in sound between the new and old instruments. "It has to do with the construction techniques used by the best makers, he says. Some of the woods available thirty years ago, are no longer available or are in short supply, such as Brazilian rosewood which is now banned as an import into the United States." Although Glenn prefers the sound of the old instruments, he says there are modern builders today who are reproducing the vintage sound and taking the art to a new level of excellence.

Sounds like Glenn really knows his business. Now we all know who to call the next time we pick up that old mandolin at an auction. You know the one you loved but passed up because it needed repairs.

## 22 HANNIBAL

Hannibal, Missouri, is synonymous with famous author and humorist Mark Twain. Twain's boyhood home, Hannibal, is the setting for the adventures of Tom Sawyer and Huck Finn. Near the riverfront is Twain's childhood home, restored to its exact mid-1800s appearance. The adjacent museum holds manuscripts and memorabilia, including one of his famous white suits. Nearby is the New Mark Twain Museum, featuring original Norman Rockwell paintings. Close by are Judge Clemens' law office, Becky Thatcher's house, and diorama and wax museums depicting Twain's famous characters.

Hannibal is full of interesting shops, and city tours take visitors into two impressive river mansions. The best way to see the sights is by river boat cruise or open-air tram, horse-drawn wagon or trolley. South of town, the Mark Twain Outdoor Theatre recreates some of his best-known works. Visitors can also explore the underground cave named for Twain, or visit the 18,600 acre Mark Twain Lake and the surrounding state park, where Twain's birthplace- - a two-room cabin- -is preserved.

**Mrs. Clemens Antique Mall**
305 N. Main St.
573/221-6427
Daily Spring-Fall 9-5/Winter 9:30-4:30
*Directions: Enter Hannibal on Route 79, 61, or 36. Mrs. Clemens Antique Mall is located 3 miles from I-72 in the Historic District, 1/2 block from the Mark Twain Home and Museum.*

Mrs. Clemens Antique Mall has over 40 dealers displaying a large selection of dolls, advertising items, pottery, cut and pressed glass, period furniture and an electric train booth of 1950s and prior trains and accessories. Mrs. Clemens is also a franchised dealer of Anheuser-Busch collectibles and a member of the Anheuser Busch Collectors Club. When you need to take a break, you have at your fingertips an ice cream parlor and snack bar in the mall, with an old back board and marble top counters. Eight flavors of premium, hand-dipped ice cream, sodas and snacks are served at old ice cream tables with matching chairs.

**Mark Twain Antiques**
312 N. Main St.
573/221-2568

**American Antique Mall**
119 S. Main St.
573/221-3395

**Market Street Mall**
1408 Market St.
573-221-3008

**Smith's Treasure Chest LLC**
315 S. 3rd St.
573/248-2955

**Cruikshank House Antiques**
1001 Hill St.
573/248-0243

**Swag-Man Antiques**
211 Center St.
573/221-2393

## 23 HERMANN

Hermann is a piece of the Old World in the middle of Missouri. The Germans who founded Hermann wanted a town that was "German in every particular." They carefully chose a site that reminded them of their beloved Rhine Valley and set about creating a city where German culture could flourish in the new world. Their vision was a grand one. Tucked away in the Ozark foothills, Hermann offers world-famous festivals, four thriving wineries, two historic districts, wonderful antique shops and delicious cuisine, served with a generous helping of Old World hospitality.

### *Great Places To Shop*

**Ace of Spades**
112 E. First St.
573/486-3060

Garden art and handmade copper jewelry.

**Antiques Unlimited**
117 E. 2nd St.
573/486-2148

Large selection of refinished antique furniture, primitives and collectibles.

**Burger Haus**
Hwy. 19 and 13th Terrace
573/486-2828
Daily

Furniture reproductions. Also handcrafted and painted items by local woodworker and artist, Os and Va.

**Deutsche Schule Arts & Crafts**
German School Building
573/486-3313
Daily 10-5

Handmade crafts with 150 artisans from the area. Specializing in quilts. Many other items, including pottery.

**Die Hermann Werks**
214 E. 1st St.
573/486-2601
Mon.-Sat., 9-5, Sun. 11-4

Specializing in European giftware and Christmas ornaments.

**J.H.P. Quilts and Antiques**
101 Schiller St.
573-486-3069
Mon.-Sat. 10-4; Sun. 12-4

Specializing in country furniture, primitives, antique quilts, stoneware and accessories.

**Jaeger Primitive Arms**
415 E. 1st St.
573/486-2394
Mon.-Sat. 9:30-5:30; Sun. 11:30-5

Specializing in black powder guns.

**Jewel Shop (Das Edelstein Geshaft)**
230 E. 1st St.
573-486-2955
Tues.-Sat. 9-5

Fine jewelry.

**Pottery Shop**
108 Schiller St.
573/486-3552/3558

Handmade porcelain and stoneware by local potter. Special orders accepted for dinnerware, tiles, and mugs.

**Rag Rug Factory**
113 E. 5th St.
573/486-3735
Daily or by chance/appointment

Rag rugs and other handwoven items.

**Sweet Stuff & Shepardson's Antiques**
210 Schiller St.
573/486-3903
Thurs.-Mon.

An eclectic blend of gourmet foods and coffees, antiques.

**White House Hotel Museum & Antiques**
232 Wharf St.
573/486-3200 or 573/486-3493
By chance or appointment

Antique collectibles, dolls.

**Wilding's Antiques and Museums**
523 W. 9th St.
573/486-5544

Country antiques. Museum houses permanent collection of Clem Wilding's wood carvings.

**Wissmath Baskets**
Rt. 1, Box 74
573/486-2090

Mail order or call for information. Specializing in handwoven baskets, deer antler baskets and 1-inch miniature baskets.

**Wohlt House**
415 E. First St.
573/486-2394
Mon.-Sat., 10-5

Antiques, locally handmade crafts, dried and fresh flower arrangements and wreaths.

***Great Places To Stay***

**Drei Madel Haus**
108 Shiller St.
573/486-3552 or 573/486-3558

1840's brick house in old town

**Edelweiss B & B**
800 18th St.
573/486-3184

Unique house with fabulous view.

**Gatzmeyer Guest House**
222 E. Second St.
573/486-2635 or 573/252-4380

Circa 1880s in Historic District

**German Haus B & B**
113 N. Market
573/486-2222

Circa 1840s.

**Hermann Hill Vineyard & Inn**
711 Wein St.
573/486-4455

Spectacular views and private balconies.

**John Bohlken Inn**
201 Schiller St.
573/486-3903

American country decor, homemade German pastries for breakfast.

**Kolbe Guest House**
214 Wharf St.
573/486-3453 or 573/486-2955

Circa 1850 with river view.

**Market Street B & B**
210 Market St.
573/486-5597

Turn of the century Victorian home.

**Mary Elizabeth House**
226 W. 6th St.
573/486-3281

1890s Victorian House

**Meyer's Fourth Street B & B**
128 E. Fourth St.
573/486-2917

Circa 1840s. Centrally located.

**Mumbrauer Gasthaus**
223 W. Second St.
573/486-5246

Circa 1885 in the heart of the Historic District.

**Patty Kerr B & B**
109 E. Third St.
573/486-2510

Circa 1840. Light breakfast. Outdoor tub.

**Pelze Nichol Haus (Santa Haus)**
Hwy. 100, 1.3 miles east of Missouri River bridge
573/486-3886

Primitive Christmas decor in 1851 Federalist brick home.

**Reiff House B & B**
306 Market St.
573/486-2994 or 1-800-482-2994

Circa 1871 in Historic District.

**Schau-ins-Land**
573/486-3425

Stone home that was once an 1889 winery.

**White House Hotel B & B**
232 Wharf St.
573/486-3200 or 573/486-3493

1868 historic hotel next to Missouri River with antique shop and ice cream parlor on premises.

***Favorite Places To Eat***

**Buckler's Deli & Pizza**
100 Schiller St.
573/486-1140 or 573/486-3514

See how the Bucklers turned an old bank into a unique deli.

**Downtown Deli and Custard Shop**
316 E. 1st St.
573/486-5002
Daily until 10 p.m.

Featuring salads, sandwiches served on fresh baked breads and homemade pies. Hand-dipped and soft-serve ice cream.

**Vintage 1847 Restaurant**
**Stone Hill Winery**
573/486-3479
Daily, lunch from 11 a.m.; dinner from 5 p.m.

Recommended by many food critics as one of America's finest restaurants. Casual dining in the original carriage house of the winery.

## 24 HERMITAGE

**H. Bryan Western Collectables**
Located at the corner of Spring St. and Hwy. 54
1-800-954-9911
Fax: 417/725-1572
Open daily 9-6
*Directions: Hermitage is in southwest Missouri, and H. Bryan Western Collectables is on Hwy. 54 at the corner of Spring St.*

"Real men shop at H. Bryan's Western Collectables," could be the motto at this Midwestern exchange. This home/shop combo was originally established during the 1940s as a watch repair/jewelry store. The present owners spent much of their formative years visiting the shop and learning the trade. It became a full-time profession when they purchased the business in 1995. Through the years, the shop has broadened its specialties to include the buying, selling and trading of vintage watches, collectible cigar lighters, Zippos, as well as antique and new knives for the collector or investor.

## 25 HIGHLANDVILLE

**Tuxedo Cat Antique Mall**
8180 Hwy. 160 S.
417/443-5000

## 26 INDEPENDENCE

**Country Meadows Antique Mall**
4621 Shrank Dr.
816/373-0410
Mon.-Sat. 9-9, Sun. 9-6
*Directions: From points north of K.C. Airport: south on I-435 to I-70 E. to Lee's Summit Road. Exit south on Lee's Summit Road to 40 Hwy. & east to Country Meadows Mall (3 blocks east of Lee's Summit Road on 40 Hwy.). From points south of Grandview: Take 71 N. to I-470 (this becomes 291 N.). Exit at 40 Hwy. W. Country Meadows is approximately 1 mile west of 291 on 40 Hwy. From points West, by way of I-70: Take Lee's Summit Road Exit S to 40 Hwy E. Country Meadows is east 3 blocks on 40 Hwy.*

Country Meadows Antique Mall offers a stunning array of antiques and collectibles. This two-story mall is brimming with diverse treasures from the past and present. Antiques from over 400 dealers fill hundreds of booths and showcases at Country Meadows, where 40,000 square feet full of history will keep you shopping for hours. Stop in and enjoy lunch in the Tea Room, which is open daily. Convenient location, ample parking and friendly, knowledgeable staff will add to your shopping pleasure.

**Shermans Odds & Endtiques**
109 W. Lexington Ave.
816/461-6336

**Liberty House Antiques**
111 N. Main St.
816/254-4494

**Black Flag Antiques Inc.**
118 S. Main St.
816/833-1134

**Keeping Room**
213 N. Main St.
816/833-1693

**Classic Treasures**
108 W. Maple Ave.
816/254-5050

**Sermon-Aderson Inc.**
210 W. Maple Ave.
816/252-9193

**Sermon-Aderson Inc.**
10815 E. Winner Road
816/252-9192

**Adventure Antiques**
11432 E. Truman Road
816/833-0303

***Great Places To Stay***

**Woodstock Inn Bed & Breakfast**
1212 W. Lexington Ave.
816/833-2233
Year round
Rates $54-99
*Directions: From points north or the K.C. Airport: Take I-435 east (to St. Louis) to the 23rd St. Exit. Go left 2 1/2 miles to Crysler. Be in*

*the left turn lane and go left 6 blocks. Crylser becomes Lexington and the Woodstock Inn is on the left at the end of the 6 blocks. From points west by way of I-70: Follow I-70 east through Kansas City to the I-435 North exit. Follow I-435 N. to the first exit (23rd Street exit). Make a right turn and follow 23rd St. 2 miles to Crysler St. After Crysler turns into Lexington, you will see a large auditorium on the right. The inn is on the left. From Branson, Springfield and points southeast: Follow U.S. 30 N. to I-70. Turn west on I-70 and follow it to Exit 12 or Noland Road. Turn right on Noland Road and follow it to 23rd St. (about 1.6 miles). Turn left on 23rd St. and go to Crysler St. (the first stop light). Turn right on Crysler. After about 7 blocks Crysler will turn into Lexington. After that, you will see a large auditorium on the right. The inn is on the left.*

For specific information see review at the beginning of this section.

## 27 JAMESPORT

The Amish first came to the Jamesport area in 1953 making it the largest Amish community in Missouri. The town is home to numerous antique and crafts shops, including Amish stores that specialize in commodities particular to Amish needs. Other town attractions include the Harris Family Log Cabin, located in the city park. The cabin was built in 1836 by Jesse and Polly Harris, one of the first white couples to settle in the area. Great-grandsons Ray and Herb Harris, both in the their 70s now, reconstructed the cabin at its present site.

### *Great Places to Shop*

**Antiques Americana**
One block north of 4-way stop next to library
660/684-5500 or 660/359-2408

Early American house contains antiques, collectibles, crafts, furniture, vintage clothing, primitives and gift items.

**Balcony House Antiques**
East of 4-way stop
660/684-6725
Mon.-Sat. year round, Sun. Apr. 1-Dec. 31.

Features a full line of quality antiques and collectibles: glassware, furniture, Indian artifacts, quilts, etc. In stock there are over 500 titles of reference books (with price guides) on antiques and collectibles.

**The Barn Antiques & Crafts**
660/684-6711

Large selection of antiques, collectibles, porcelain dolls, willow furniture, quilts, baskets, Christmas shop.

**Broadway Pavilion Mall**
South of 4-way stop
660/684-6655

Antiques, collectibles, furniture, glassware, pottery, jewelry, large selection of old books.

**Carlyles & Pastime Antiques**
East of 4-way stop
660/684-6222

Distinguished gifts, collectible items, antique furniture, home decorating ideas.

**Colonial Rug and Broom Shoppe**
2 1/2 blocks west of 4-way stop
1-800-647-5586
Mon.-Sun. 8-6

See hand-woven rugs and brooms made daily. Purchase them already made or have them created to your own needs.

**The Country Station**
1 block east of 4-way stop
660/684-6454
Mon.-Sat. 10-4

Country furniture, needlework, dolls, doilies, antiques, collectibles and lots more.

**Country Treasures**
660/684-6338
Mon.-Wed. and Fri.-Sat., 10-4; closed Thurs. and Sun.

Baskets, old spools, Amish pictures, doilies, potpourris, candles, shelves, Amish made furniture, many items one of a kind.

**Downtown Oak & Spice**
660/684-6526
Mon.-Sat. 9-5

Woodcrafts, teas and spices, oak furniture, hand-dipped ice cream, baskets, Moser glass.

**Ellis Antiques**
Located at 4-way stop
660/684-6319
Year round Mon.-Sat., 8-5: Sun. 1-4

Country furniture and accessories, glass, china, jewelry, etc.

**Granny's Playhouse Antique Mall**
East of 4-way stop
660/684-6599 or 660/359-3021

A unique selection of Jewel Tea, collectible jewelry, porcelain dolls, quilts, wall hangings, chimes, all in 33 booths.

**Iris Collectibles**
Five blocks west of 4-way stop at corner of South and Elm
660/684-6626

Glassware, pottery, jewelry, and miscellaneous.

**Katie Belle's**
Two blocks west of 4-way stop

Antiques, collectibles, furniture and country gift items.

**Koehn's Country Naturals**
855 Hwy. F
660/684-6830

"The Herb Lovers Nook"

**Leona's Amish Country Shop**
660/684-6628
7 days, 9-whenever

Dinner bells, Amish dolls and quilts, antiques and collectibles.

**Marigolds**
3 blocks west of downtown (The Orange House)
660/684-6122

Retail and wholesale. A house full of primitive country. Birdhouses, benches, mirrors, and lots of folk art.

**The Olde Homestead**
Two doors south of Post Office
660/684-6870

Rustic, primitive, western folk art.

**Pastime Antiques I & II**
660/684-6222

Antique furniture, finished and unfinished. Custom birdhouses, old fashion candies.

**Rolling Hills Store**
Hwy. 190
4 1/2 miles south of Jamesport

Local made Amish furniture.

**Ropp's Country Variety**
1 1/4 miles south of Jamesport

Amish shop.

**Sherwood Quilts and Crafts**
3 miles east on F and one mile south on U

Large selection of handmade quilts, rugs, and baskets. Amish shop.

**This-N-That**
S. Broadway
1 block north of 4-way stop
660/684-6594
Mon.-Sat. 9-5

Antique furniture, glassware, jewelry and collectibles.

**Warren House Antiques**
East of 4-way stop
660/684-6266
Daily 10-5

Antique Mall, 27 booths, antiques and collectibles - dishes, furniture, tools, primitives and more.

***Great Places To Stay***

**Country Colonial Bed & Breakfast**
660/684-6711 or 1-800-579-9248

Originally built in the 1800s, this house has been restored to an era past with a veranda and three bedrooms, each with a private bath. Since the bed & breakfast is centrally located near the shops, you can spend your day shopping, and at night, relax by playing parlor games, reading one of the 500 antique books in the library, or playing the baby grand piano. In the morning awake to a full country breakfast.

**Marigolds Inn**
Located 3 blocks west of downtown next to Marigold's Shoppe
660/684-6122

Opening Spring of 1997. Twelve rooms, each individually decorated in folk art themes.

**Nancy's Guest Cottage Bed and Breakfast**
660/684-6156

The cottage is filled with antique memories of yesteryear. Family style country breakfast is included. Located 2 blocks east of the 4-way stop, 2 blocks north on 190 and 2 blocks east.

**Oak Tree Inn Bed & Breakfast**
4 miles on Hwy. F east of Jamesport
660/684-6250

Relax in an original 3-story Amish-built home set in a wondrous 20 acre grove of tall majestic oak trees.

***Favorite Places To Eat***

**Anna's Bake Shop**
Route 1, Box 34A, west end of town (Amish owned)
Mon.-Sat. 8-6, Closed Sun., closed from Christmas until Feb.

Fresh baked donuts, pies, breads, cinnamon and dinner rolls, cakes and much more.

**Black Crow Soda Fountain**
Corner of Main & Broadway
660/684-6789

An old fashion ice cream parlor. Soup and sandwiches along with their famous "Darla's BBQ beef brisket special".

**Country Bakery**
Located 1/2 mile south of Jamesport on Hwy. 190, Route 2, Box 177B
Closed Thurs. and Sun. (Amish owned)

Large selection of home-made baked goods.

**Gingerich Dutch Pantry and Bakery**
Located at 4-way stop
Mon.-Sat. 6-9
660/684-6212

(Mennonite owned) Specializing in Amish style meals, homemade pies and baked goods, made fresh daily. Tasty sandwiches to home cooked dinner specials.

## 28 JEFFERSON CITY

**Old Munichberg Antique Mall**
710 Jefferson St.
573/659-8494

**Twin Maples Collections**
1125 Jefferson St.
573/636-2567

**Bare Necessities Collectibles**
804 E. Hight St.
573-636-5509

**Missouri Boulevard Antique**
1415 Missouri Blvd.
573/636-5636

## 29 JOPLIN

**Southside Antique Mall**
2914 E. 32nd St.
417/623-1000

**Uniform Shoppe**
1052 S. Main St.
417/624-6650

**Connie's Antiques. & Collectibles.**
3421 N. Range Line Road
417/781-2602

**Country Heart Village**
4901 S. Range Line Road
417/781-2468

**Gingerbread House**
RR 7
417/623-6690

## 30 KANSAS CITY

**Bellas Hess Antique Mall**
715 Armour Road
816/474-4790

**Belle Chelsea Antiques**
4444 Bell St.
816/561-1056

**Estate Pine Gallery**
4448 Bell St.
816/931-6661

**Olde Theatre Archl. Salvage Co.**
2045 Broadway St.
816/283-3740

**Cummings Corner Antiques**
1703 W. 45th St.
816/753-5353

**River Market Antique Mall**
115 W. 5th St.
816/221-0220

**Molly & Otis O'Conner**
1707 W. 45th St.
816/561-6838

**Portobello Road & Camel Antiques**
1708 W. 45th St.
816/931-2280

**Lloyd's Antiques**
1711 W. 45th St.
816/931-7922

**Elizabeth Gibbs**
1714 W. 45th St.
816/561-7355

**Josephs Antiques**
1714 W. 45th St.
816/756-5553

**Parrin & Co.**
1717 W. 45th St.
816/753-7959

**Christopher Filley Antiques**
1721 W. 45th St.
816/561-1124

**Morning Glory Antiques**
1807 W. 45th St.
816/756-0117

**European Express**
1812 W. 45th St.
816/753-0443

**Andersons Antiques**
1813 W. 45th St.
816/531-1155

**Brown's Emporium**
1263 N. 47 St.
816/356-0040

**Mom's Ole Stuff**
10939 Hillcrest Road
816/765-6561

**J J McKee Antiquities**
222 W. 7th St.
816/361-8719

**Chabineaux's**
334 W. 75th St.
816/361-1300

**Waldo Galleria Antique Annex**
336 W. 75th St.
816/361-2396

**Old World Antiques Ltd.**
1715 Summit St.
816/472-0815

**Boomerang**
1415 W. 39th St.
816/531-6111

**Town Gallery**
3522 N.E. Vivion Road
816/454-3570

**Twentieth Century Consortium**
1004 Westport Road
816/931-0986

**Meirhoff's Antique Stained Glass**
210 Wyandotte St.
816/421-4912

**Sebree Galleries & Le Picnique**
301 E. 55th St.
816/333-3387

**5th Street Antique Mall**
302 W. 5th St.
816/472-9700

**Broyle's Antiques**
10605 Blue Ridge Blvd.
816/966-8888

**Crestwood Galleries Antiques**
301 E. 55th St.
816/333-3387

**General Store Antiques**
4200 Genessee St.
816/531-7888

**Red Room Antiques**
232 W. 75th St.
816/361-5933

**Jewelry Box Antiques**
2450 Grand Blvd.
816/472-1760

**Asiatica Ltd.**
4824 Rainbow Blvd.
816/831-0831

**Waldo Antiques & Imports**
226 W. 75th St.
816/333-8233

**Waldo Galleria**
334 W. 75th St.
816/361-2544

**Remember When Antiques**
349 N.W. 69 Hwy.
816/455-1815

**Poor Richard's Antiques Object**
401 E. 31st St.
816/531-4550

**Darlene's Antiques & Collectibles**
5502 Troost Ave.
816/361-9901

**Superlatives**
320 Ward Pkwy.
816/561-7610

**Smith & Burstert**
1612 Westport Road
816/531-4772

**River Market Antique Mall**
115 W. 5th St.
816/221-0220

**Antiquities & Oddities**
1732 Cherry St.
816/842-4606

**Brookside Antiques**
6219 Oak St.
816/444-4774

**Cheep Antiques**
500 W. 5th St.
816/471-0092

**Dottie Mae's**
7927 Wornall Road
816/361-1505

**M & B Antiques**
230 W. 7th St.
816/361-7300

## 31 KENNETT

### Bank of Antiques & Special Finds
201 First St.
573/888-4663
Mon.-Sat. 10-5, usually open til 8 on Thurs.
*Directions: 17 miles from I-55 (Hayti Exit) in downtown Kennett.*

Bank of Antiques & Special Finds, gets its name from its former life as a bank in downtown Kennett, MO. Built in 1916, this historical establishment houses a fine selection of glassware, dolls, furniture, jewelry, some collectibles, and more. Within the bookstore located in the shop, you can browse for new books and enjoy a delicious box lunch and a cup of gourmet coffee or hot tea. For those of you interested in "star" memorabilia, music artist Sheryl Crow donates her hand-me-downs to the shop. The proceeds of the clothing and shoe sale supports the local children's home.

**The Treasure Chest**
211 First St.
573/888-6772

## 32 KIRKSVILLE

**Poor Richard's Gifts & Collectibles**
713 S. Baltimore St.
816/627-4438

**Square Deal Antique Mall**
Hwy. 63 Route 2
816/665-1686

**Potpourri Antiques**
106 W. Harrison St.
816/665-8397

**Good Ole Days Antqs. & Collectibles**
1515 S. Baltimore St.
816/665-3540

**Wood Rail Antique Mall**
Hwy. 63 S.
816/665-1555

## 33 LEBANON

**Treasure Trove Antiques**
1231 W. Elm St.
417/532-6945

**Jefferson House Antiques**
364 N. Jefferson Ave.
417/532-6933

**Country Corner Antique. Mall**
585 N. Jefferson Ave.
417/588-1430

**Spring Holler Antiques**
15350 Glendale Road
417/532-9453

**Pleasant Memories Antique Mall**
25999 Hwy. 5
417/588-3411

**Jennissa Antiques & Gifts**
577 N. Jefferson Ave.
417/588-1029

**Griffith House Antiques**
115 E. Elm St.
417/532-8211

## 34 LEES SUMMIT

**American Heritage Antique Mall**
220 S.E. Douglas St.
816/524-8427

**Annie Sue's Antiques**
302 S.W. Main St.
816/246-8082

**Sandy's Mall**
101 S.W. Market St.
816/525-9844

**Exclusively Missouri Gifts & More**
200 S.W. Market St.
816/525-5747

## 35 LEXINGTON

**The Velvet Pumpkin**
827 Main St.
816/259-4545

**Victorian Peddler**
900 Main St.
816/259-4533

**Redgoose Antiques**
914 Main St.
816/259-2421

## 36 LIBERTY

**Liberty Square Antiques**
2 E. Franklin St.
816/781-7191

**Liberty Antique Mall**
Town Square-1 E Kansas
816/781-2796

**Kansas Street Antiques**
10 W. Kansas Ave.
816/781-1059

**Liberty Antique Mall**
1005 N. State Route 291
816/781-3190

**Anna Marie's Antiques Gft & Acces**
118 N. Water St.
816/792-8777

**Sandy's Antiques Ltd.**
131 S. Water St.
816/781-3100

**Antebellum Antiques**
7 N. Missouri St.
816-792-0779

## 37 MACON

**The Weathervane**
32429 Juniper Place
816/385-2941

**Ednamay's Antiques**
203 Jackson St.
816/385-3021

**Ugly Duckling Antiques**
1144 Jackson-Hwy. 63 N.
816/385-6183

**Colonel's Flea Market**
312 S. Missouri Hwy. 63
816/385-2497

**Carousel Antiques**
127 Vine St.
816/385-4284

**The Antique Parlor & Coffee Bar**
132 Vine St.
816/385-1168

## 38 MANSFIELD

Laura Ingalls Wilder, the greatly loved and internationally known authoress of the beloved "Little House" books, lived most of her life in Mansfield, Missouri. It is here at Rocky Ridge Farm that she wrote all nine of her famous books about her pioneer childhood and later life in Missouri. Her writing desk still stands in the home that Almanzo built for her. The home is on the National Register of Historic Places and is surrounded by apple, walnut and dogwood trees, many of which Laura planted.

Each year the residents of Mansfield relive the times of Laura Ingalls Wilder with their fall festival. There are costume and beard contests, a kiddie parade, a big parade, an arts and crafts fair, games for the children, surprises, entertainment from the bandstand, lots of good food, and gingerbread made from Laura's recipe. And of course, there are continuous tours all day through the Laura Ingalls Wilder Home and Museum. Call the Friendship House B&B for dates.

### *Great Places To Stay*

**Friendship House Bed & Breakfast and Antique Boutique**
210 W. Commercial
417/924-8511
Open year around
*Directions: For specific directions from your location, please call the Innkeepers.*

Friendship House is the charming rock home where Little House author Laura Ingalls Wilder celebrated birthdays and other special occasions with her close friend, Neta Seals.

Built in 1939, by Mr. and Mrs. Seals, the 16-room home was planned as a rooming house advertising "Modern Rooms." Lovingly preserved by its present owners, the tree-shrouded brownstone wears the soft patina of age and bespeaks the tranquility of days past.

Friendship House is ideally located, one half block from the Mansfield Town Square, and is a five minute drive from the Laura Ingalls Wilder Home and Museum.

Yours hosts, Sharon and Charlie Davis, offer visitors old-fashioned hospitality and comfortable ambience. Guests may relax with a refreshing iced drink on the charming sun porch or head straight for the swimming pool. Tall fences, stately trees, and a landscaped patio envelop this lush backyard hideaway in peace and privacy.

The living room, with its lace-covered windows and rich blend of antiques and period reproductions, is an inviting place of repose. Breakfast is served in the adjoining formal dining room, where Laura and Neta gathered with their husbands and friends to share meals and celebrations.

Upstairs, visitors are transported in time to the boarding house days of the 1930s. Cozy sleeping rooms open onto the airy central hall. Its restful decor and gleaming woodwork are a welcome change from the sterility of modern day motels. Each room is individually decorated and has its original porcelain sink. A full bath and water closet are shared by the guests.

## 39 MARIONVILLE

Beautiful Victorian homes and a rare, urban white squirrel population are the hallmarks of Marionville, Missouri. According to town legend, around 1854 a circus came to town and brought rare white squirrels with them (were they part of an act?). When the circus left, their squirrels didn't! Now there are thousands of them. They don't cross the highway; they don't run off to the woods - they like living right in the middle of town!

**Ole Mill Around**
Hwy. 60
417/463-7423

**Kountry Korner Antqs.s & Uniques**
Hwy. 60 & 265
417/463-2923

***Great Places To Stay***

### White Squirrel Hollow Bed & Breakfast

203 Mill St.
417/463-7626
24 hours a day, 7 days a week

Step back in time when you visit the White Squirrel Hollow Bed and Breakfast. It's a historical, romantic Victorian home built in 1896 by one of the Ozarks first famous families, and it's filled with original antique photos, prints and furnishings. It's also a theme B & B, so its 5,000 square feet are filled with six different atmospheres decorated in antique, purist decor. Guests can choose from the Victorian Honeymoon suite with a full lace canopy bed and private screened balcony; the Gold Coast Room reminiscent of the 1849 California Gold Rush days; the Elizabethan Room, fit for royalty with it's flocked wall paper, satin canopy-covered bed, mink spread and English antiques; Turkish Corners, with a tented canopy bed, fabulous view and exotic touches; the Wild, Wild West Room, with an atmosphere from the days of western adventure; and a cottage that offers a night on African safari. The main house also boasts inlaid hardwood floors, beaded woodwork, a spiral staircase and doorway spandrels that are all original and lavish. The large music room was once a conservatoire, but now houses an antique baby grand and a 600-piece antique book collection. And of course there are the rare white squirrels rambling all across the property for your pleasure!

## 40 MOBERLY

**Reed Street Antiques**
303 W. Reed St.
816/263-7878

**Jim' Country Barn Antiques**
RR 4
816/263-6714

**Moberly Plating & Antiques**
512 W. Rollins St.
816/263-5371

**Kierstle Haus Antiques**
Route 1 Box 56
816/263-7828

## 41 MONETT

### V. B. Hall Antiques

201 W. Main St.
417/235-1110
Daily Mon.-Sat. 9:30-5, Sun. 1-5

*Directions: From intersection of Highways 60 and 37 in Monett, turn north on 37, 2 blocks turn right, one block - you're there!*

The name V.B. Hall Antiques is very well known to the folks of Monett. Four generations of V. B.s have participated in the business community of this Missouri town, with V.B. Sr. even serving as town mayor for a term or two. The store, with 70 to 75 dealers in about 12,000 square feet of space, carries a large variety of items, from primitives to pottery, to glassware and a mixture of furnishings covering several periods and styles. The building itself is vintage 1947, beginning its life as a wholesale produce store.

**Banks Antiques**
103 N. Lincoln Ave.
417/235-6387

**Archer Antiques & Collectibles**
119 Commercial
417/235-3523

## 42 MONROE CITY

**Downtown Antique Mall**
208 S. Main St.
573/735-4522

**Downtown Antique Mall**
Business 36
573/735-3156

**Country Mini Mall**
Hwy. 24 & 36
573/735-4935

**Over The Hill Antique Mall**
101 S. Main St.
573/735-4966

## 43 NEOSHO

**Neosho Gllry & Flea Market**
900 N. College St.
417/451-4675

**Four Seasons**
322 S. Neosho Blvd.
417/451-3839

## 44 NEVADA

**Crossroads 71/54 Antique Mall**
1617 E. Ashland St.
417/667-7775

**Louise Fanning Antiques**
1231 E. Austin Blvd.
417/667-5903

## 45 OSAGE BEACH

**Osage Beach Flea Market**
Hwys. 42 & 54
573/348-5454

**Land Of Yesteryear**
Hwy. 54
573/348-3855

**Osage River Co. Store**
Hwy. 54
573/348-0819

**House of Stewart Antiques**
Hwy. 54
573/348-9248

## 46 OZARK

Most of the thousands of antiquers who come to Ozark, Missouri every summer are, as one antique shop owner puts it, "just coming in to browse, but some people are on a mission." Another says that Ozark is known as "the antique place to come," and that most of the visitors hit every store. There's plenty of stores to be found in Ozark, scattered throughout the city, but most are prominently collected at two sites: Missouri 14 and U.S.

65, and the Riverview Plaza locations on Missouri 14 northeast of the U.S. 65 intersections. Collectively all these stores contribute significantly to the city's tax revenues and tourism industry. Although the antique shops are not Ozark's only draw, they are important to the city's economy - so much so that the Ozark Chamber of Commerce promotes the shops on billboards and in tourist information mailings. Of course it doesn't hurt that Ozark is on the way to Branson, and picks up a great deal of traffic from that destination. From old dolls and battered school desks to yellowed newspaper front pages and expensive jewelry, any item you are looking for is likely to be somewhere among the booths of old stuff brought in from all over the country.

**Antique Emporium**
1702 W. Boat St.
Located at 65 & CC (behind Lambert's Cafe)
417/581-5555
Summer: Mon.-Sat. 9-9; Winter; Mon.-Thurs. and Sat. 9-6, Fri. 9-9, Sun. 9-5
*Directions: From I-44 exit 65 South. Antique Emporium is located approximately 9 miles south of I-44 on U.S. 65 on route to Branson, 9 miles south of Springfield.*

All antiques and no crafts are what you'll find among the 100 dealers in the 12,000-square-foot mall of Antique Emporium. They don't carry a lot of bigger furniture, mostly small period pieces, but shoppers will find a great deal of glass, primitives and collectibles, including Roseville, Fiesta, Candlewick, Fenton, Heisey, china, and ladies artifacts. In addition you'll find clocks, quilts, gas pumps, railroad items, advertising, antique hunting and fishing items and western collectibles.

**Ozark Antique Mall and Collectibles**
200 S. 20th St.
417/581-5233
Fax: 417/581-5233 (Call first to have us plug in fax)
Summer 9-6; Winter 9-5, daily
*Directions: At U.S. 65 and Hwy. 14 in Ozark, turn west and take the first left, which is 20th St. Look for Ozark Antique Mall on the right-hand side - it's the building with all the great old advertising signs and antiques out front in the southwest corner of Highways 65 and 14.*

For specific information see review at the beginning of this section.

**Finley River Heirlooms, Inc.**
105 N. 20th St.
417/581-3253

**Maine Streete Mall**
1994 Evangel St.
417/581-2575

**Pine Merchant Antiques**
140 N. 20th St.
417/581-7333

**Riverview Antique Center, Inc.**
909 W. Jackson
417/581-4426

**Scott's-Beckers' Hardware, Inc.**
1411 S. 3rd St.
417/581-6525; 1-800-991-0151

**Abbotsford Antiques**
200 S. 20th St.
417/581-8445

**Crossroads Antique Mall**
2004 Evangel St.
417/485-4941

**Norman's Antiques**
1781 W. Clay St.
417/581-7826

## 47 PERRY

**Huffman Trading Post**
Hwy. 19
573/565-3275

**Price Emporium**
113 W. Main St.
573/565-3159

**Packrats Unlimited**
124 E. Main St.
573/565-3594

**Country Store Antiques**
1007 E. Main St.
573/565-2822

**Lick Creek Antiques**
Main St.
573/565-3422

**Miss Daisy's Antique Shop**
Main St.
573/565-2737

**Elam Antique Shoppe**
110 S. Palmyra St.
573/565-2206

**Arlington Antiques**
Palmyra St.
573/565-2624

**Perry Main Street Antiques**
S. Palmyra St.
573/565-3246

## 48 PLATTE CITY

**I-29 Antique Mall**
Junction I-29 & H. H. Hwy.
816/858-2921
Daily 10-6

I-29 Antique Mall is located in historic Platte City, Missouri just 30 minutes north of downtown Kansas City on Interstate 29. The Platte City area features some of the best antique shopping in the Midwest, with three large malls offering a wide range of quality furniture, glassware, advertising items and much more. A favorite stop for dealers and collectors from across the country, I-29 Antique Mall is just 6 miles north of K.C. International Airport, with abundant food and lodging close by. Visit the Platte City area and see some of the best antiquing Missouri has to offer!

**W D Pickers Antique Mall**
Exit 20 I-29
816/858-3100

**Wellsbrooke Antiques**
500 Main St.
816/858-5306

## 49 PLEASANT HILL

**Cookie Jars & More**
113 S. 1st St.
816/987-5244

**First Street Antiques**
121 S. 1st St.
816/987-5432

**Sentimental Journey Antiques**
100 Wyoming St.
816/987-3661

**Downtown Antiques**
115 Wyoming St.
816/987-5505

## 50 ROCHEPORT

**Griffith's Antiques**
405 Clark
573/698-3503

**Richard Saunder's Antiques**
Columbia & 2nd St.
573/698-3765

**Missouri River Antiques & Books**
12851 W. High
573/698-2080

**Whitehorse Antiques**
12855 W. High
573/698-2088

**Farm Road Antiques**
370 N. Roby Farm Road
573/698-2206

**River City Antique Mall**
420 N. Roby Farm Road
573/698-2116

**Henderson's Antiques**
451 N. Roby Farm Road
573/698-4485

**Widow Lister Antiques**
405 2nd St.
573/698-2701

## 51 ROLLA

**Antique Corner**
606 Lanning Lane
573/368-5579

**Mary's Antiques**
13458 S. U.S. 63
573/364-5372

**Totem Pole Trading Post**
1413 Martin Spring Dr.
573/364-3519

**Hancock's Used Furniture**
102 S. Rucker Ave.
573/364-2665

## 52 ROSEBUD

### Apple Antiques
Hwy. 50
573/764-3148
Thurs.-Mon. 9:30-5, closed Tues.-Wed.

Owner Edna Weatherford handles glassware, furniture and collectibles in her store, and tells a very interesting story about the shop's name, Apple Antiques. "The name of my antique shop is very unique, indeed. The customers usually tend to believe 'Apple' is my last name. Actually, it has nothing to do with my name. The last year I taught school, my students made a project of naming my shop. They came up with 'Apple Antiques' - an apple for the teacher, find the apple of your eye, etc. The parts of the apple are all divisions within the shop: the seed - beginning of goodness; the core - innermost and loved; the fruit - no serpents allowed; the peel - delicious value inside; the stem - attached and treasured; and last but not least; the apple orchard - ripe with age.

"There are apples everywhere you look, even on a shoplifting sign, the last line of which says, 'But Eve paid dearly when she stole an apple!' The name 'Apple Antiques,' has proven to be very...fruitful!"

### Dinner Bell Antiques
Hwy. 50
573/764-3090
Mon.-Sat. 9:30-5, closed Sun.

Dinner Bell Antiques is nestled in a turn-of-the-century building full of antiques, collectibles, old tools, primitives, furniture, glassware and architectural antiques. According to owner Karen Jose, her store was the third building constructed in Rosebud when the railroad came through in 1900. In the past 96 years, the store has housed everything from shoe stores and farm implement stores to a drug store, a grocery, a barber shop, even the town post office.

### Quilts By Shirley
249 Hwy. 50 (located at Shirley's House of Beauty)
573/764-2422

Shirley Rice, owner of Quilts By Shirley, is a true artisan, one of a dwindling group of women who still quilt by hand. She began quilting as a little girl, taught by her mother, and they quilted together for years. Shirley didn't really begin quilting part-time until about thirteen years ago, when she lost one of her little girls and went back to quilting as a means of therapy. She is a full-time hairdresser, so she quilts nights, weekends—anytime she has a few spare moments.

Shirley makes all of the tops for her quilts, table runners, baby quilts, Christmas tree skirts and wall hangings herself, and she has a couple of ladies who help her with the actual quilting. She can make most tops in a day's time, she says, but the quilting may take as long as two or three months. Her personal favorite pattern is the Wedding Ring, but she makes them all: Lover's Knot, Lone Star, Dresden Plate, Log Cabin. If customers who come to her shop don't see exactly what they want, Shirley will custom make anything to the exact size and color.

Her husband has gotten into the quilting business with her by making a special quilting frame that is much easier to handle, set up, use and store than the traditional giant frame. Mr. Rice's frame is made from square metal tubing and the frame is 10 feet long but only three feet wide; its special feature is a rolling florescent light that rolls along the edge of the frame, providing shadow-free lighting along the entire frame.

***Great Places To Stay***

### The Wild Rose Bed & Breakfast
Route 1, off Idel Road
573/764-2849
Rates $55-65

The Wild Rose is a restored farmhouse filled with art and antiques, set on 25 beautifully landscaped acres just outside of Rosebud. The well-stocked lake is surrounded by pines and stately pin oaks, with trails winding through the woods and meadows. There are boats and fishing gear for the fishermen in the group (no license required), while anyone wanting to just unwind and commune with nature can sit by the peaceful Koi and goldfish pond near the house.

The library offers the beauty of stained glass windows, a fireplace and a collection of masks, with an additional fireplace in the cathedral-ceiling living room. Each bedroom has its own unique personality. The Victorian Rose is dominated by a high backed Victorian bed and rose-covered walls. The Rambling Rose combines wicker furniture and whimsical art work, dashed with tropical blues and pastels, plants and seashells. The English Rose has a wonderful 19th century English brass bed and antique camp table with two large wing chairs.

**The Bluebird Bed & Breakfast**
5734 Mill Rock Road
573/627-2515
Seven days a week

The Bluebird Bed & Breakfast offers a peaceful English Country setting for city-dwellers in need of a little R & R. Restful views, the chirping of birds, beautiful trees, flowering gardens and a well-stocked fishing pond provide the perfect escape.

There are four guest rooms, all comfortably appointed, each with its own unique theme. An old fashioned screened porch is ideal for bird watching, fish jumping, or simply cat-napping.

As is customary, continental and full breakfasts are served; gourmet dinners are available with 48 hours notice.

Only minutes from local flea markets, antique shops, caverns, and wine country, the Bluebird Bed & Breakfast can provide an effective reprise from an otherwise hectic world.

**River House Bed & Breakfast**
5339 Mill Rock Road
573/764-5262
Fax: 573/764-7262

This bed and breakfast is appropriately named for the Bourbeuse River that flows through the property, with the bedroom window and side deck overlooking the river. The cottage includes a kitchen, full bath, living and dining areas, and bathroom, all completely furnished in antiques, Americana and accessories. The old Franklin wood stove can even be used. A very private, self-contained cozy getaway. Breakfast is served upon request.

## 53 SALEM

**Bargain Barn**
506 E. Center St.
573/729-7354

**Antiques & Things**
806 E. Center St.
573/729-4062

**Gunny Sack**
300 E. 4th St.
573/729-8797

**Nina's Antique & Flea Market**
Hwy. 72 N.
573/729-2958

**Gateway Antiques**
900B S. Main St.
573/729-7766

**Fourth Street Mall**
215 E. 4th St.
573/729-8520

**Gateway Antiques**
402 W. 4th St.
573/729-5544

## 54 SEDALIA

**Country Village Mall**
4005 S. Limit Ave.
816/827-2877

**John's Used Furniture & Things**
4011 S. Limit Ave.
816/826-7801

**Millie's Pink Mall**
Hwy. 65-5915 Limit Ave.
816/826-5894

**Mapleleaf Antique Mall**
106 W. Main St.
816/826-8383

**Downtown Antiques**
516 S. Ohio Ave.
816/826-2266

**Sedalia Antique Shop**
804 W. 16th St.
816/826-1472

## 55 SPRINGFIELD

**Park Central Flea Market**
429 Boonville
417/831-7516
Daily Mon.-Sat. 10-5, Sun. 12-5
*Directions: Traveling I-44 from the west, turn east on Chestnut Expressway, or traveling I-44 from the east, turn south on Glenstone and west on Chestnut Expressway, or exit Hwy. 65, and turn west on Chestnut Expressway. Take Chestnut Expressway to Boonville and turn south to 429 Boonville.*

Having been in business for more than 20 years, Park Central Flea Market has lots of antiques and collectibles stashed in its two-story shop. They carry antique glassware, carnival glass, pottery, graniteware, pictures, primitives, toys and lamps.

**Aesthetic Concerns Ltd.**
326 N. Boonville Ave.
417/864-4177

**Country Corner Flea Market**
351 Boonville Ave.
417/862-1597

**Treasure Chest**
411 N. Boonville Ave.
417/863-1047

**Centerfield Sportscards**
427 Boonville Ave.
417/831-7675

**Downtown Furn Rest. & Collectibles**
419 Boonville Ave.
417/865-3230

**Fort No 5**
425 N. Boonville Ave., #5
417/865-9966

**By-Pass Antiques**
535 B N. W. Bypass
417/865-4992

**Bass Country Antique Mall**
1832 S. Campbell Ave.
417/869-8255

**Antique Warehouse & Mall**
2139 S. Campbell Ave.
417/886-9776

**Auction Barn**
1435 W. College St.
417/831-2734

**Another Man's Treasure**
1700 W. College St.
417/864-2811

**Nellie Dunn's Antiques**
211 E. Commercial St.
417/864-6822

**G & W Antiques & Collectibles**
400 W. Commercial St.
417/869-0061

**Century Galleries**
1355 E. Commercial St.
417/869-4137

**Antique Place**
1720A S. Glenstone Ave.
417/887-3800

**Cottage & Provence**
2744 S. Glenstone Ave.
417/887-1930

**Andrews Collectibles**
435 W. Kearney St.
417/831-3577

**Touche Designs Inc.**
2009 S. National Ave.
417/883-8633

**Furniture Stripping Ozarks Ltd.**
1263 E. Republic Road
417/883-8313

**Jerry's Antique Mall**
309 South Ave.
417/862-4723

**Knight's Stamps**
323 South Ave.
417/862-3018

**Sunshine Antiques**
1342 W. Sunshine St.
417/864-0069

**STD East Flea Market**
1820 E. Trafficway
417/831-6367

**Collections**
1112 E. Walnut St.
417/865-0552

**Great Discoveries**
416 W. Commerical St.
417/869-9101

**Mary II Antiques & Gifts**
3747 S. Cox Road
417/888-3099

**A Second Time Around Shoppe**
1736 N. Glenstone Ave.
417/831-1666

**STD East Flea Market**
651 S. Kansas
417/831-6331

**Coach House Antique Mall**
2051 E. Kearney St.
417/869-8008

**Apple Barrel Antiques**
2104 N. National Ave.
417/862-4635

**Viles Swap Shop**
3023 E. Republic St.
417/881-4042

**South Peer Antique Mall**
317 South Ave.
417/831-6558

**Springfield Antique Co.**
406 South Ave.
417/866-6995

**Anastasia & Co.**
1700 E. Sunshine St.
417/890-1714

**History Antiques**
1111 E. Walnut St.
417/864-8147

**Class Act Antiques**
224 E. Commercial St.
417/862-1370

## 56 ST. CHARLES

**Saint Charles Antique Mall**
1 Charlestowne Plaza
314/939-4178

**Fifth Street Antique Mall**
520 S. 5th St.
314/940-1862

**Royal Antiques**
101 N. Main St.
314/947-0537

**Aladdin's Lamp & Collectibles**
321 S. Main St.
314/946-8865

**Log House Antiques**
2431 W. Clay St.
314/724-1889

**Upstairs Mkt./Aimee B's Tea Room**
837 1st Capitol
314/949-9271

**Antiques & Oak**
319 N. Main St.
314/946-1898

**Hobbitts Hole Antiques**
323 N. Main St.
314/947-6227

**Kuhlmann's Antique Emporium**
324 N. Main St.
314/946-7333

**Mirabilia Gallery**
524 S. Main St.
314/947-9077

**Mamie Maples Emporium**
825 N. 2nd St.
314/947-0801

**Lauree's Vintage Jewelry**
827 N. 2nd St.
314/940-1711

**Charlestowne Antiques**
903 N. 2nd St.
314/946-7134

**Pioneer Antiques**
1410 N. 2nd St.
314/724-1539

**Rachel's Antiques**
1601 N. 2nd St.
314/925-1023

**Gina's at the Witt House**
426 S. Main St.
314/946-6106

**Memories of Yesteryear**
806 N. 2nd St.
314/724-2163

**French Connection Antiques**
826 N. 2nd St.
314/947-7044

**Bo's Primitive Peddler**
901 N. 2nd St.
314/724-9366

**Little Hills Antiques**
1125 N. 2nd St.
314/947-1770

**Wartimes Memorabilia**
1501 N. 2nd St.
314/949-9929

**McKinley Antique Mall**
1701 N. 2nd St.
314/946-8186

## 57 ST. JAMES

**Kracker Barrell Antiques**
108 N. Jefferson St.
573/265-3546

**Old Mill Store**
RR 2
573/699-4423

**Treasure Nook**
132 W. Washington St.
573/265-7416

**Forest City Popcorn Co.**
124 N. Jefferson St.
573/265-3383

**Heirlooms Past & Present**
107 W. Springfield St.
573/265-7938

## 58 ST. JOSEPH

No matter where you're bound, St. Joseph is the way to real adventure. Saddle up to glory at the Pony Express National Memorial, where "young, skinny, wiry fellows" like Buffalo Bill Cody and Johnny Fry started their 10-day relay dash to California with the mail. Follow the footsteps of 50,000 '49ers, who left here in the gold rush to "pick up a fortune." Walk in the front door of the house where Jesse James' infamous life came to an end and onto the recreated streets of ol' St. Jo at the Patee House Museum.

St. Jo isn't all rough and ready, though. Turn-of-the-century mansions are open for you to tour and even have high tea. Admire the works of the masters at the Albrecht-Kemper Museum of Art, and discover the secret gardens and stone bridges of the 26 miles of greenway linking the parks. Hunt through a nearly endless supply of beautiful antiques, and shop to your heart's content.

Located on the scenic river bluffs overlooking the Missouri River, born of the fur trade, nurtured by the "Westward Expansion," and brimming with a spirit of adventure, St. Joseph is a city you will never forget.

**Somersby Antiques**
501 N. Belt Hwy.
816/390-8864

**Creverling's**
1125 Charles St.
816/232-9298

**Horn's Antique Emporium**
502 Felix St.
816/364-3717

**Hatfield's Antique Mall**
2028 Frederick Ave.
816/233-9106

**Jerry's Antiques**
2512 Frederick Ave.
816/232-9881

**Coin-Jewelry-Antique Exchange**
3837 Frederick Ave.
816/232-8838

**Dakons Antiques**
1801 Garfield Ave.
816/233-2971

**Den of Antiquity**
1919 Holman St.
816/279-0942

**Penn Street Square**
1122 Penn St.
816/232-4626

**Corner Shoppe**
1503 Penn St.
816/232-0045

**Arnolds Antiques**
644 S. 6th St.
816/233-4416

**A & E Company**
1213 S. 22nd St.
816/279-6206

**Country House Antiques & Crafts**
1801 N. Woodbine Road
816/232-4455

## 59 ST. LOUIS

### Cherokee Antique Row

2014 Cherokee St.
314/664-7916 or 314/773-8810
Daily 11-4
*Directions: Take I-55 to Arsenal Street (near the Anheuser-Busch Brewery), turn south on Lemp, go 4 blocks and turn west on Cherokee Street.*

Here's your chance to shop from dawn till dusk in one spot! At Cherokee Antique Row you can visit 40 unique shops that sell many different varieties of items in a four-block area. Don't miss it!

**Dapple-Gray Antiques**
159 W. Argonne Dr.
314/965-0239

**Stock Exchange Consign. Shop**
2115 S. Big Bend Blvd.
314/645-3025

**Johns Furn. & Antiques**
7107 S. Broadway
314/351-6745

**Phillips Antiques**
8473 N. Broadway
314/867-0965

**White Swan Antiques**
7006 Bruno Ave.
314/781-7114

**English Garden Antiques**
1906 Cherokee St.
314/771-5121

**Looking Glass**
1915 Cherokee St.
314/773-1912

**Panorama Antiques & Collectibles**
1925 Cherokee St.
314/772-8007

**Neon Lady**
1926 Cherokee St.
314/771-7506

**Hammonds Books**
1939 Cherokee St.
314/776-4737

**Riverside Architectural Antiques**
1947 Cherokee St.
314/772-9177

**Lealee Antiques**
1950 Cherokee St.
314/772-9030

**Remember When Antiques**
1955 Cherokee St.
314/771-1711

**My Friends Closet**
2851 Cherokee St.
314/664-3993

**Hartmann's Treasures**
1960 Cherokee St.
314/773-5039

**Purple Cow**
2018 Cherokee St.
314/771-9400

**Henderson Co.**
2020 Cherokee St.
314/773-1021

**Haffner's Antiques**
2100 Cherokee St.
314/772-6371

**Odd Shop**
2101 Cherokee St.
314/773-8566

**Tfa-Things From The Attic**
2110 Cherokee St.
314/865-1552

**Glass Turtle**
2112 Cherokee St.
314/771-6779

**Southside Antiques**
2114 Cherokee St.
314/773-4242

**Nostalgia Shop**
2118 Cherokee St.
314/773-4907

**Homemaker Antiques**
2124 Cherokee St.
314/776-4267

**Victorian Village Antiques**
2125 Cherokee St.
314/773-8810

**Frank & Julia's**
2201 Cherokee St.
314/865-2995

**Antiques by Art of the Ages**
2205 Cherokee St.
314/776-0959

**Debbie Fellenz Antiques**
2224 Cherokee St.
314/776-8363

**Pennys Collectibles**
2307 Cherokee St.
314/771-2822

**Haffners Antiques**
2847 Cherokee St.
314/771-3173

**Claton Antiques**
6403 Clayton Road
314/725-9878

**Shaker Tree Antiques**
7713 Clayton Road
314/726-3233

**Legacy Antiques**
7715 Clayton Road (Clayton)
314/725-2209

**Regent Parade Consign Shop**
7721 Clayton Road (Clayton)
314/727-4959

**Finches Consign & Gifts**
7729 Clayton Road
314/725-2622

**Davis Place Antiques & Consign.**
7731 Clayton Road
314/727-9850

**M Js Consignment Shop**
7803 Clayton Road (Clayton)
314/863-8762

**Matti's Antiques**
7805 Clayton Road (Clayton)
314/721-5535

**Small World Antiques**
9752 Clayton Road
314/997-5854

**Jules L Pass Antiques Ltd.**
9916 Clayton Road
314/991-1522

**Antique & Art Appraisers of America**
9918 Clayton Road
314/993-4477

**Braun Antiques**
10315 Clayton Road
314/991-1798

**The Original Cast Lighting Inc.**
6120 Delmar Blvd.
314/863-1895

**Rothschild's Antiques**
398 N. Euclid Ave.
314/361-4870

**Kodner Gallery**
7501 Forsyth Blvd.
314/863-9366

**Books & Collectibles**
3196 S. Grand Blvd.
314/771-3196

**PSA Presentations**
131 W. Jefferson Ave.
314/822-8345

**Alamo Military Collectables**
716 Lemay Ferry Road
314/638-6505

**Ferrari's Consignment Shop**
7314 Manchester Road (Maplewood)
314/644-5755

**Post Card Shop**
12024 Manchester Road (Des Peres)
314/822-7174

**Brilliant Antiques**
8107 Maryland Ave. (Clayton)
314/725-2526

**Clark Graves Antiques**
132 N. Meramec Ave.
314/725-2695

**Tower Grove Antiques**
3308 Meramec St.
314/352-9020

**Sambeaus Ltd.**
4724 McPherson Ave.
314/361-4636

**West End Antiques Gallery**
4732 McPherson Ave.
314/361-1059

**West Monroe Antiques**
132 W. Monroe Ave.
314/821-2931

**Kodner Gallery**
9918 Clayton Road
314/993-4477

**Ziern Antiques**
10333 Clayton Road
314/993-0809

**Coyotes Paw Gallery**
6388 Delmar Blvd.
314/721-7576

**Fellenz Antiques**
439 N. Euclid Ave.
314/367-0214

**Switching Post**
7742 Forsyth Blvd.
314/725-7730

**J. Middleton Mid Century Modern**
3949 Gravois Ave.
314/773-8096

**Shackelford Antiques & More**
4519 S. Kingshighway Blvd.
314/832-6508

**A Country Place Antiques**
2930 Lemay Ferry Road
314/892-6677

**European Country Antiques Ltd.**
9621 Manchester Road
314/968-2550

**Four Seasons West Antiques**
4657 Maryland Plaza
314/361-2929

**Tin Roof Antiques**
2201 McCausland Ave.
314/647-1049

**This N That**
3305 Meramec St.
314/353-2365

**Alexander Furniture Co.**
3309 Meramec St.
314/481-2111

**Golden Harvest**
4732 McPherson Ave.
314/454-9330

**Martin's Galleries**
4736 McPherson Ave.
314/361-1202

**Pierce House Antiques**
139 W. Monroe Ave. (Kirkwood)
314/821-5140

**Designs In Gold**
11006 Olive Blvd.
314/567-3530

**Now And Then Antiques**
6344 S. Rosebury Ave.
314/721-3301

**Jack Parker Antiques**
4652 Shaw Ave.
314/773-3320

**St. Louis Architectural Art**
1600 S. 39th St.
314/773-2264

**South County Antique Mall**
13208 Tesson Ferry Road
314/842-5566

**Vinegar Hill Antique**
107 W. Pacific Ave.
314/962-0375

**Remember Me Vintage Clothing**
1021 Russell Blvd.
314/773-1930

**Tommy T's**
3010 Sutton Blvd.
314/645-7471

**Harley's Harps**
2271 Administration Dr.
314/567-1980 X206

**Warson Woods Antique Mall**
10091 Manchester Road
314/909-0123

## 60 ST. GENEVIEVE

**Mill Antique Mart**
301 N. Main St.
573/883-7333

**Sarah's Antiques**
124 Merchant St.
573/883-5890

**Kaegel's Country Collectibles**
252 Merchant St.
573/883-7996

**Collagé**
18 S. Third
573/883-9575

**Joyce & Choyse's Antiques & Collectibles**
58 S. 3rd St.
573/883-2358

**Dalton's Treasure Chest**
183 S. 3rd St.
573/883-9190

**Monias Unlimited**
316 Market St.
573/883-7874

**Mr. Frederic Ltd.**
195 Merchant St.
573/883-2717

**Zielinski's**
288 Merchant St.
573/883-7004

**Odile's Linen & Lace Etc.**
34 S. 3rd St.
573/883-2675

**The Summer Kitchen**
146 S. 3rd St.
573/883-3498

## 61 STEELVILLE

**Nancy's Antique Dolls-N-Stuff**
103 W. Main St.
573/775-3655

**Edie's Backwoods Antiques**
403 Main St.
573/775-2629

**Willies Moles**
105 E. Main St.
573/775-2722

**Down Memory Lane**
107 W. Main St.
573/775-3131

## 62 SULLIVAN

**Cntry Collectibles & Early Smithing**
5054 Hwy. K
573/468-8170

**White Lion Antiques**
5 Maple St.
573/468-2437

**Sullivan Showcase Antique Mall**
201 N. Service Road W.
573/468-3943

## 63 WARSAW

**This Old House Antiques & Crafts**
420 Commercial
816/438-3588

**Mule Barn**
Hwy. 7 & Truman Dam
816/438-3186

**Warsaw Antique Mall**
245 W. Main St.
816/438-9759

**Molly's Antiques**
616 W. Main St.
816/438-6911

**Swinging Bridge Antiques & Crafts**
Hwy. 7 & Main St.
816/438-7422

**Columns Antique Shop**
1129 N. Lay Ave.
816/438-6032

**Curiosity Shop**
406 W. Main St.
816/438-5034

**Lou's Quilts & Buckley's Antiques**
702 W. Main St.
816/438-7853

## 64 WASHINGTON

**Annie-Rose**
1110 Clock Tower Plaza
314/239-1970

**Feed Store Antique Mall**
101 E. Main St.
314/390-0115

**Attic Treasures**
100 W. Front St.
314/390-0200

**Waterworks Antiques**
1 Elbert Dr.
314/390-2344

**Tamm Haus Antiques**
5 W. 2nd St.
314/239-9699

## 65 WEST PLAINS

**Elledge House Antiques**
315 Broadway
417/256-2442

**Jefferson St. Flea Market**
310 Jefferson Ave.
417/256-4788

**Antique Corner**
313 Washington Ave.
417/256-2193

**Aid Downtown Antique Mall**
1 Court Square
417/256-6487

**Looking Back**
712 Porter Wagoner Blvd.
417/256-8586

## 66 WESTON

**J & L Antiques**
Hwy. 45 & P
816/386-2456

**J P's Antiques**
509 Main St.
816/386-2199

**Painted Lady Antiques**
540 Main St.
816/386-5580

**J P's Antiques**
424 Main St.
816/386-2894

**Tobacco Road**
400 Main St.
816/386-2121

**J P's Antiques**
523 Main St.
816/386-2828

**Tobacco Patch Country Store**
18260 State Route 45 N.
816/640-2627

# Montana

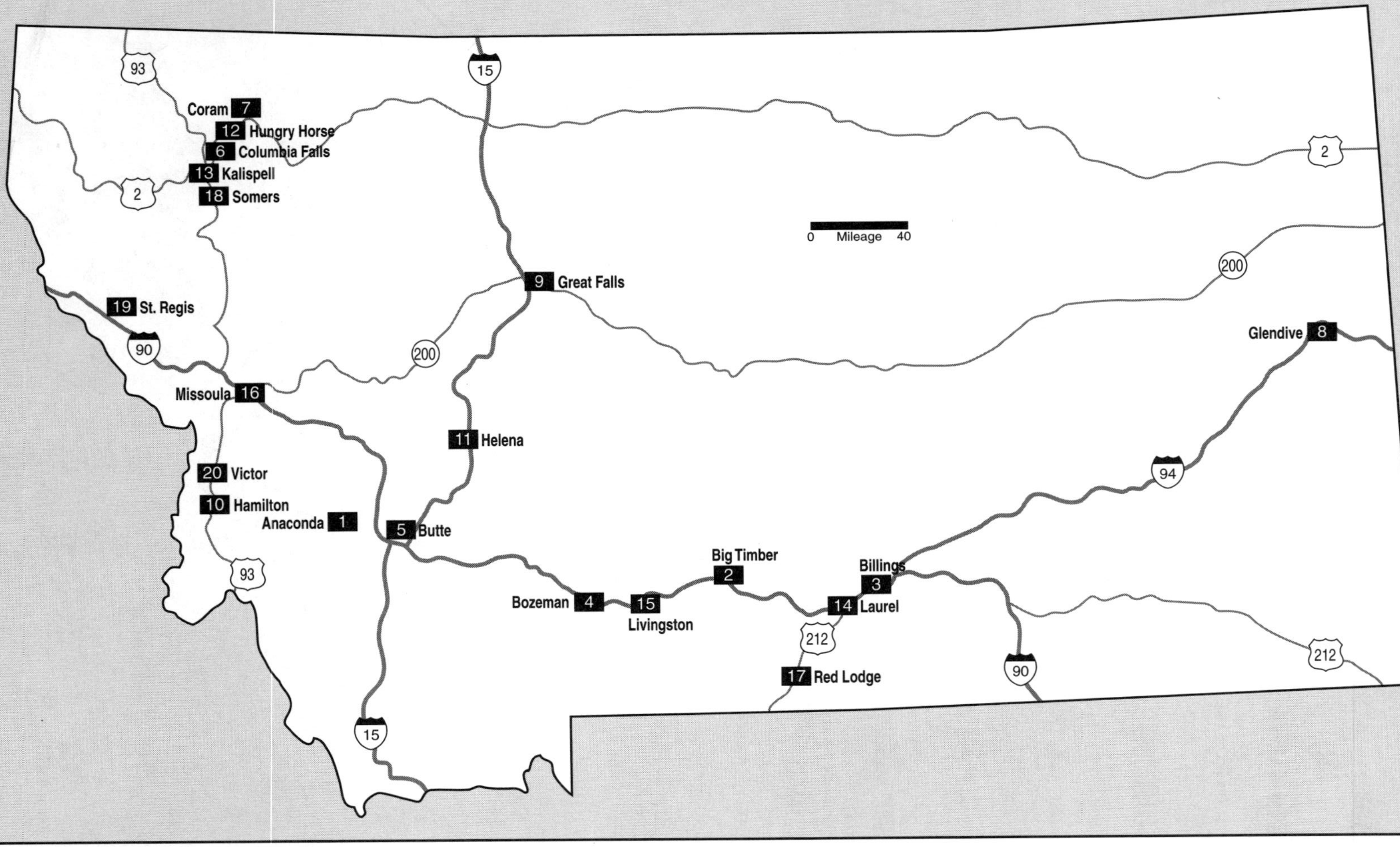
93
15
Coram 7
12 Hungry Horse
6 Columbia Falls
13 Kalispell
2
18 Somers
2
0 Mileage 40
9 Great Falls
200
19 St. Regis
90
200
Glendive 8
Missoula 16
11 Helena
20 Victor
94
10 Hamilton
Anaconda 1
5 Butte
Big Timber
2
Billings
3
93
Bozeman 4
15
Livingston
14 Laurel
212
212
17 Red Lodge
90
15

## 1 ANACONDA

Founded in 1883, this small town owes its existence to Marcus Daly and the Anaconda Copper Company. Smelting operations were suspended in 1980, but Anaconda has a firm grip on its role in Montana history. The town's landmark and a state park, "The Stack," stands 585 feet 1.5 inches tall. Visit the Copper Village Museum and Art Center for area history and a copper smelter display, and the Hearst Free Library, a classic 1889 period building donated to the city by George and Phoebe Hearst. Self-guided walking tour, brochure and bus tour of historic Anaconda begins at the Anaconda Visitor Center.

**Brewery Antiques**
125 W. Commercial St.
406/563-7926

**Park Street Antique Mall**
113 E. Park St.
406/563-3150

## 2 BIG TIMBER

Located at the foot of the Crazy Mountains, Big Timber offers a broad range of activities in a beautiful setting. Explore the Boulder Valley, fish blue-ribbon trout streams and stop by the Yellowstone River Trout Hatchery for an appreciation of cut-throat trout. Visit museums, galleries, antique shops and historic sites including Victorian Village, Montana Armory, Shiloh Rifle Manufacturing Co., Sweetgrass and Sage Gallery and the Crazy Mountain Museum.

**Crazy Mountain Art & Antiques**
14 Anderson
406/932-4797

## 3 BILLINGS

Montana's largest city, Billings is a regional business hub, as well as a cultural, medical, educational and entertainment center. Museums, art galleries, theaters and shopping are all part of the appeal of this vibrant city. Discover the elegantly restored, turn-of-the-century Moss Mansion providing a glimpse into the life of Preston B. Moss, one of Billings' most prominent early residents. Bordered on the north by distinctive rock formations known as rimrocks, Billings is a gateway to Little Bighorn Battlefield National Monument, Bighorn National Recreation Area, Yellowstone Park, the Yellowstone River and the Abrasroka-Beartooth Wilderness.

**Whispering Pines**
12 S. Broadway
406/446-1470

**Pickett Fence Antqs. & Collectibles**
645 Custer Ave.
406/254-1725

**Waterwheel Antiques**
2339 S. 56th Road
406/656-8350

**Magic City Floral**
1848 Grand Ave.
406/652-6960

**Antique Peddler**
1327 Main St.
406/256-7003

**Oxford Hotel Antiques**
2411 Montana Ave.
406/248-2094

**Billings Nursery**
2147 Poly Dr.
406/656-5501

**A-l Attic Dreams Antiques**
901 Terry Ave.
406/256-3051

**Yesteryears**
114-118 N. 29th St.
406/259-3314

**Rose Petal Antiques**
726 Grand Ave.
406/248-5801

**Buy the Book**
2040 Rosebud Dr., #5
406/652-1188

**Depot Antique Mall**
2223 Montana Ave.
406/245-5955

## 4 BOZEMAN

Visitors will find a small town atmosphere with big city amenities in Bozeman. This town, beautifully situated at the base of the Bridger Range, blends spectacular recreation with art galleries, museums, symphony, opera, history and many one-of-a-kind Western stores. Walk through the South Wilson Historic District, a residential area featuring houses that range from large mansions to small cottages. Visit the Gallatin Pioneer Museum for area history and artifacts.

**Country Mall Antiques**
8350 Huffine Lane
406/587-7688

**Davis Torres Furniture Collect**
14 W. Main St.
406/587-1587

**Cellar 105 Antiques & Gifts**
105 W. Main St.
406/587-3013

**The Antique Mall**
612 E. Main St.
406/587-5281

**Country Charm**
612 E. Main St.
406/587-5281

**Antiques Etc.**
25 N. Willson Ave.
406/587-9306

**The Attic**
212 S. Wallace
406/587-2747

**The Brass Monkey**
370 Lodgepole Lane
406/586-6855

**Sack's of Bozeman**
138 W. Mendenhall
406/587-7283

**Brass Monkey The Sandman**
370 Lodgepole Lane
406/586-6855

**Rocky Mountain Rug Gallery**
628 W. Main St.
406/585-7900

**Swenson's Furniture**
702 E. Main St.
406/587-8701

**Take 2**
7 S. Tracy Ave.
408/586-8324

**Old World Antiques**
1530 W. Main St.
406/582-1848

### *Great Places To Stay*

**Fox Hollow Bed & Breakfast**
545 Mary Road
406/582-8440 or 1-800-431-5010
Open year round

At Fox Hollow Bed & Breakfast, the wonder of Montana's big sky awaits. Sunsets are spectacular from the wraparound porch of this country-style home. Settle into an oversized guest room, each with a private bath. Soak in the hot tub while gazing into the cool starlit Montana night. Wake to the aroma of coffee brewing and a delicious gourmet breakfast.

**Torch and Toes Bed and Breakfast**
309 S. Third Ave.
406/586-7285 or 1-800-446-2138

This 1906 Colonial Revival home, found in the Bon Ton historic district, was built for Wilbur F. Williams, vice-president of the Bozeman Milling Company. Today, the Torch and Toes Bed and Breakfast retains its original high ceilings, oak wainscoting, and leaded-glass windows. Turn-of-the-century furnishings accentuate the house's original elements. Collections of gargoyles, mousetraps, and old postcards create a fanciful atmosphere. Each of four guest rooms (with private baths) presents an individual setting. During winter, a full breakfast is provided before the fireplace in the dining room. In summer, breakfast is served on the redwood deck.

## 5 BUTTE

Once known as "the richest hill on earth," Butte is steeped in mining history. Copper, gold, silver were all found here, and Butte became a melting pot of ethnic diversity as immigrants flocked to the mines for employment. The Anselmo Mine Yard in uptown Butte is the best surviving example of surface support facilities that once served the mines. Butte is the home of Montana Tech of the University of Montana, which grew out of Butte's mining heritage. Its Mineral Museum displays 1,500 specimens, including a 27.5 ounce gold nugget. Walking tour brochures of this historic city are available at the Butte Chamber of Commerce. This is also the place to catch a tour of Butte on a replica of an early-day streetcar, "Old No. 1." Three-story, 34-room Copper King Mansion, home of former copper king/politician William A. Clark, has been preserved as it was in the 1880s.

**Antiques on Broadway**
45 W. Broadway
406/782-3207

**Donut Seed Consignments**
120 N. Main St.
406/782-7123

**Rediscoveries Vintage Clothing**
55 W. Park St.
406/723-2176

**Rustic Montana Interiors**
27 W. Park St.
406/723-1500

**Debris Ltd.**
123 N. Main St.
406/782-9090

**D & G Antiques**
16 N. Montana St.
406/723-4552

**Someplace Else**
117 N. Main St.
406/782-2864

### *Great Places To Stay*

**The Scott Bed and Breakfast**
15 W. Copper
406/723-7030 or 1-800-844-2952

Built in 1897, this former boarding house for miners overlooking Butte's Historic Landmark District is today The Scott Bed and Breakfast. Extensively renovated, this historic setting offers the modern comforts of seven rooms, each with private baths. Explore nearby Copper King Mansion, as well as the World Museum of Mining.

## 6 COLUMBIA FALLS

A stop in this gateway city to Glacier National Park brings family fun and exploration. Enjoy championship golf in the summer; cross country skiing, ice skating and snowmobiling in the winter. The city also boasts a popular waterslide and whitewater rafting.

**Charmaine's Antiques & Collectibles**
35 5th St. W.
406/892-3121

**Pony Circus Antiques**
527 Nucleus Ave.
406/892-1965

### *Great Places To Stay*

**Bad Rock Country Bed & Breakfast**
480 Bad Rock Dr.
406/892-2829 or 1-800-422-3666

Bad Rock Country Bed & Breakfast is an elegant and charming home filled with Old West antiques, minutes from Glacier Park, on 30 acres in a gorgeous farming valley. Enjoy spectacular views of the 7200-foot-high Columbia Mountain, only 2 miles away. Experience the magic of quiet in the country and be pampered in the Bad Rock Bunny way. Soak in the secluded spa in a time reserved exclusively for you. Relax in one of the four new rooms made of hand-hewn square logs, with fireplaces and handmade lodgepole pine furniture, or settle into one of the four rooms in the home, all with private baths. Fantastic breakfasts are only one portion of the superb hospitality.

## 7 CORAM

### *Great Places To Stay*

**Heartwood**
400 Seville Lane
406/387-5541

The "Little Cabin" at Heartwood (a family homestead) is a cheerful, 1930s log cabin nestled among tall pines on 215 acres of secluded meadows and woodlands - completely surrounded by majestic mountains including views of the famous "Park Mountains" and located just seven miles from Glacier National Park. The "Little Cabin" is tastefully decorated with vintage furniture and accessories - yet remains very cozy and comfortable. The original (working) wood cookstove still occupies its place in the fully modern country kitchen. Accomodations include three bedrooms, living room, kitchen and large bathroom. Take advantage of nature trails, trout pond, nightly campfire, or just rest and relax.

## 8 GLENDIVE

**"Helen's Stuff"**
716 E. Bell St.
406/365-3405

**Tin Shed**
112½ Country Club Road
406/365-4553

**Alley Antiques**
616 N. Kendrick
406/365-3330

**Montana Antiques & Collectibles**
1111 W. Bell St.
406/365-4691

**Antiques & Such**
614 N. Meade
406/365-3018

## 9 GREAT FALLS

Great Falls is Montana's second-largest city, located on the Missouri River among the five falls that were both a magnificent spectacle and formidable barrier to early river travel. This area held significance for the Lewis and Clark Expedition. The explorers were forced to spend nearly a month portaging around the falls in June, 1805. Much of the Missouri River in this area remains as it was when Lewis and Clark first viewed it 190 years ago. The "Great Falls" of the Missouri is now the site of Ryan Dam, but may still be visited. Great Falls was also home of cowboy artist, Charlie Russell (1864-1926), whose original home and log studio are now part of the C. M. Russell Museum Complex. Soak up some local culture at the Montana Cowboys Bar and Museum or at Mehmke's Steam Engine Museum.

**Browsers Corner**
117 Central Ave.
406/727-5150

**G P Trading Company**
405 Central Ave.
406/727-0369

**The Bet Art & Antiques**
416 Central Ave.
406/453-1151

**Accents & Antiques**
1015 14th St. S.
406/727-6049

**Mary Beth Shop**
500 4th Ave. N.
406/452-4522

**Bill's Time Center**
827 9th St. S.
406/761-1074

**Bull Market Antq Mall**
202 2nd Ave. S.
406/771-1869

**Lucky Lee's**
8½ 7th St. S.
406/452-0358

**Now & Then Shop**
718 13th St. N.
406/452-0671

**Far Out Antiques**
301 24th St. N.W.
406/452-5211

**Janet's General Store**
115 Central Ave.
406/761-1655

**DeCoy Antiques**
500 5th Ave. S.
406/761-4684

## 10 HAMILTON

Located in the heart of the Bitterroot Valley, Hamilton is Montana's gateway to the Selway-Bitterroot Wilderness and a number of other recreational and historic attractions, including the Ravalli County Museum and Daly Mansion. Built in 1890 by Irish immigrant, Marcus Daly, one of Montana's colorful "copper kings," Daly Mansion with 42 rooms, 24 bedrooms, 15 baths and 5 Italian marble fireplaces, presides over 50 planted acres in Montana's scenic Bitterroot Valley.

**Clothes Tree**
301 Main St.
406/363-7003

**Hamtana**
Pennsylvania Ave.
406/363-2482

**Magpie Nest**
247 State St.
406/363-3167

**Howdy Antiques**
383 Owings Lane S.W.
406/363-2186

### *Great Places To Stay*

**Deer Crossing**
396 Hayes Creek Road
406/363-2232 or 1-800-763-2232

Relax on the deck with a steaming cup of coffee and watch the sun rise over the Sapphire Mountains at Deer Crossing, a bed and breakfast with Old West charm. Enjoy a luxury suite with double jacuzzi tub, one of the three gracious guest rooms or the bunk house. The hearty ranch breakfast features garden fresh vegetables. Nearby adventures include fly fishing, rafting, hiking, horseback riding, skiing and snowmobile riding.

## 11 HELENA

An 1864 gold strike touched off a boom era that transformed Helena into "Queen City of the Rockies" and Montana's capital city. Trace its history along Main Street, still known as Last Chance Gulch. View historic buildings and mansions dating back to the 1870s such as the Original Governor's Mansion built in 1888. This Victorian mansion was the official residence of nine governors between 1913 and 1959. Enjoy the Last Chance Tour Train, a one-hour narrated tour of historic downtown Helena.

**MT Antique Mall**
4528 U. S. Hwy. 12 W.
406/449-3334
Mon.-Sun. 10-5:30
*Directions: Located approximately 2 miles west of Helena on U. S. Hwy. 12 toward Missoula. From I-15, go through Helena following the signs for Hwy. 12 W. and Missoula.*

Listed on the National Register of Historic Places, Wassweiler Hotel and Bath House, built in 1883, is home to MT Antique Mall. Over 30 dealers display a wide selection of antiques and collectibles offering a variety of quality furniture, accessories, glassware, pottery, plus much more inside this former stopover for the cattle drovers, gold dust rovers, and "strike-it-rich" elite of Helena's boom days.

**Missouri River Chronicle Antiques**
1125 Helena Ave.
406/442-7887

**Days of Yore**
25 S. Last Chance Gulch St.
406/443-7947

**Quigleys Antiques**
5944 U.S. Hwy. 12 W.
406/449-8876

## 12 HUNGRY HORSE

**Grandpa's Attic**
8760 Hwy. 2 E.
406/387-4166

## 13 KALISPELL

Founded in 1891, Kalispell is now a bustling small city and home to much history, culture, commercial activity and outdoor recreation. The city's natural beauty and pleasant lifestyle draw a wide variety of residents and tourists. Get acquainted with the city on a walking tour of historic buildings and enjoy regional culture at the Hockaday Center for the Arts.

Wander through Conrad Mansion's Victorian elegance, built in 1895 as the home of C. E. Conrad, Montana pioneer, Missouri River trader, freighter and founder of the city of Kalispell.

**End of the Trail Trading Post**
1025 W. Center St.
406/756-3100

**Idaho St. Antiques**
110 E. Idaho St.
406/755-1324

**Kalispell Antiques Market**
48 Main St.
406/257-2800

**Arts & Antiques Mall**
40 2nd St. E.
406/755-1801

**Bazaar**
154 2nd Ave.
406/257-1878

**Antiques of Kalispell**
175 6th Ave.
406/257-4415

**Southside Consignments**
2699 U.S. Hwy. 93 S.
406/756-8526

**Glacier Antique Mall**
3195 U.S. Hwy. 93 N.
406/756-1690

**White Elephant**
3258 U.S. Hwy. 93 S.
406/756-7324

**Demersville Mercantile**
4010 U.S. Hwy. 93 S.
406/755-0917

**Stageline Antiques**
2510 Whitefish Stage Road
406/755-1044

**Mom's Place**
227 Main St.
406/257-4333

**Four Corners Country Collectibles**
105 Welf Lane
406/756-6541

**Somers Second Hand & Antiques**
210 Montana Hwy. 82
406/857-3234

### *Great Places To Stay*

**Creston Country Willows Bed & Breakfast**
70 Creston Road
406/755-7517 or 1-800-257-7517

Near Glacier Park, wonder at the majestic mountain views and quiet charm of Creston Country Willows' rural setting. This bed & breakfast provides four guest rooms with private baths. In addition, head for area recreations, such as golfing, fishing or hiking, after the complimentary full country breakfast.

**Stillwater Inn Bed & Breakfast**
206 4th Ave. E.
1-800-398-7024

Relax in the comfort of this lovely historic home built at the turn of the century. The Stillwater Inn offers four guest bedrooms, two with private bathrooms and two that share a bathroom. Start the day dining on the delicious gourmet breakfast. Within walking distance are antique shops, art galleries and the Charles Conrad Mansion.

## 14 LAUREL

Located at the junction of great rivers and highways, Laurel is a convenient stop for travelers. The Chief Joseph Statue and Canyon Creek Battlefield Marker in downtown Fireman's Park commemorate the 1877 battle between the Nez Perce Indians, led by Chief Joseph, and the U.S. Cavalry under the command of Col. Samuel Sturgis.

**Blue Bell Antiques**
210 E. Main St.
406/628-2002

**Huff Antiques**
405 Maple Ave.
406/628-4493

**Lind Antique Mall**
101 W. 1st St.
406/628-1337

## 15 LIVINGSTON

Downtown Livingston, a designated historic district on the National Register, encompasses 436 buildings, most within walking distance of one another. With the Yellowstone River flowing through town, Livingston is anglers' heaven, providing excellent floating and fishing access. Visit Park County Museum which is housed in a turn-of-the-century schoolhouse, featuring household displays, Indian artifacts, a stagecoach, sheep wagon and caboose. Located in a restored Northern Pacific Railroad station, Depot Center houses railroad and Western history exhibits and art shows.

**Save The Pieces**
119 W. Callender St.
406/222-8131

**Island Antiques**
1500 E. Park St.
406/222-8025

**Livingston Merctl & Trade Co**
W. Park St.
406/222-3334

**Doris Loomis Antiques**
E. River Road
406/222-0427

**Cowboy Connection**
108 N. 2nd St.
406/222-0272

**Authentic & Old Antiques**
5237 Hwy. 89 S., Suite 3
406/222-9571

**Grandma's Treasures**
211 S. Main St.
406/222-2177

**Jeannie's Alley Antiques**
118½ N. Yellowstone St.
406/222-1617

**Krohne Island Antiques**
1500 E. Park St.
406/222-8025

**Save the Pieces**
119 W. Callender St.
406/222-8131

**Vik's Antiques**
Off Hwy 89 S. at Merrill St.
406/222-0128

## 16 MISSOULA

Montana's cultural superstar and third largest city, Missoula presides over the north end of the Bitterroot Valley. Best known as the home of the University of Montana, Missoula is an eclectic mix of students, independent business people, professors, foresters, artists and writers. At the head of five scenic valleys and the junction of three great rivers, Missoula has no shortage of recreational opportunities. Missoula is home to the Montana Repertory theatre, Missoula's Children's Theatre, String Orchestra of the Rockies and Garden City Ballet. Take a Trolley Tour through the historic downtown/university area or a carousel ride at A Carousel for Missoula in Caras Park beside the Clark Fork River. Soak up some western Montana history at the Historical Museum at Fort Missoula. Wonder with admiration at St. Francis Xavier Church, built in 1889, the year Montana became a state, outstanding for its graceful steeple, paintings and stained glass.

**Ovilla**
115 W. Front St.
406/728-3527

**Jem Shoppe Jewelers**
105 S. Higgins Ave.
406/728-4077

**Birds Nest**
219 N. Higgins Ave.
406/721-1125

**Ma & Pa's Second Hand Store**
531 N. Higgins Ave.
406/728-0899

**Mr. Higgins Vintage Clothing**
612 S. Higgins Ave.
406/721-6446

**Herman's on Main Vintage Clothing**
137 E. Main St.
406/728-4408

**1776 Antiques**
214 E. Main St.
406/549-5092

**Montana Antique Mall**
331 Railroad St. W.
406/721-5366

**Mountain Mama's Antiques**
2002 S. Reserve St.
406/549-9281

**Horse Trader Antiques**
1920 S. Russell St.
406/549-6280

**Opportunity Resources Inc.**
2821 S. Russell St.
406/721-2930

**Montana Craft Connection**
1806 South Ave. W.
406/549-4486

**Magpie Antiques**
109 S. 3rd St. W.
406/543-4428

**Third Street Curiosity Shop**
2601 S. 3rd St. W.
406/542-0097

**Fran's Second Hand Store**
601 Woody St.
406/549-0440

## 17 RED LODGE

This historic mining town has roots that reach back to the European homes of its diverse founders. Situated at the base of the Beartooth Mountains, Red Lodge is one of Montana's premier ski destinations in winter; in summer, it draws hikers, anglers, campers, sightseers and Yellowstone Park visitors via the nearby Beartooth Highway. Enjoy native North American animals and the children's petting zoo at the Beartooth Nature Center. Take in the area's history at the Carbon County Museum, housed in the homestead cabin of John Garrison, subject of the movie Jeremiah Johnson. Explore buildings and houses on and off Main Street that were built between 1883 and 1910 during the coal mining boom. Remnants of the ethnic groups that settled Red Lodge are preserved in "Hibug" Town, Finn Town and Little Italy, whose ethnic traditions are celebrated every August during the 9-day Festival of Nations.

**Flower Shop**
20 N. Broadway Ave.
406/446-2330

**Mama Bear**
217 S. Broadway Ave.
406/446-2207

**Whispering Pines**
12 S. Broadway Ave.
406/446-1470

**Cabin**
105 S. Broadway Ave.
406/446-3386

**Montana Chinook**
6 S. Broadway Ave.
406/446-1810

## 18 SOMERS

**Laurie Levengood's Antiques**
4834 Hwy. 93 S.
406/857-3499

**Somers Second Hand & Antiques**
210 Montana Hwy., #82
406/857-3234

## 19 ST. REGIS

### Cold Creek Antiques
Cold Creek Road
406/649-2675

Discover a fine array of antique furniture, collectibles, glassware as well as a pleasing assortment of accessories and other items in Cold Creek Antiques, a cozy shop.

### The Place of Antiques
Downtown St. Regis
406/649-2397
Mon.-Sun 9-5
*Directions: From I-90, take Exit #33 into St. Regis.*

Featuring original finish and refinished antique oak furniture, The Place of Antiques prepares all of its refinished pieces. In addition to furniture, Red Wing items, depression glassware and advertising memorabilia enhance the shop's offerings brought together by over 70 dealers.

### Someplace In Time
Hwy. 135
406/649-2637

For a nostalgic stroll, Someplace In Time offers antique dolls, furnishings, in addition to many other delightful and attractive items.

## 20 VICTOR

Named for a Flathead Indian chief and nestled in the Bitterroot Valley, Victor offers endless recreational opportunities. Explore the Victor Heritage Museum, housed in the railroad depot.

**Antique Sellar**
275 Dinger Lane
406/642-3386

**Red Willow Dry Goods**
111 Main St.
406/642-3130

# Nebraska

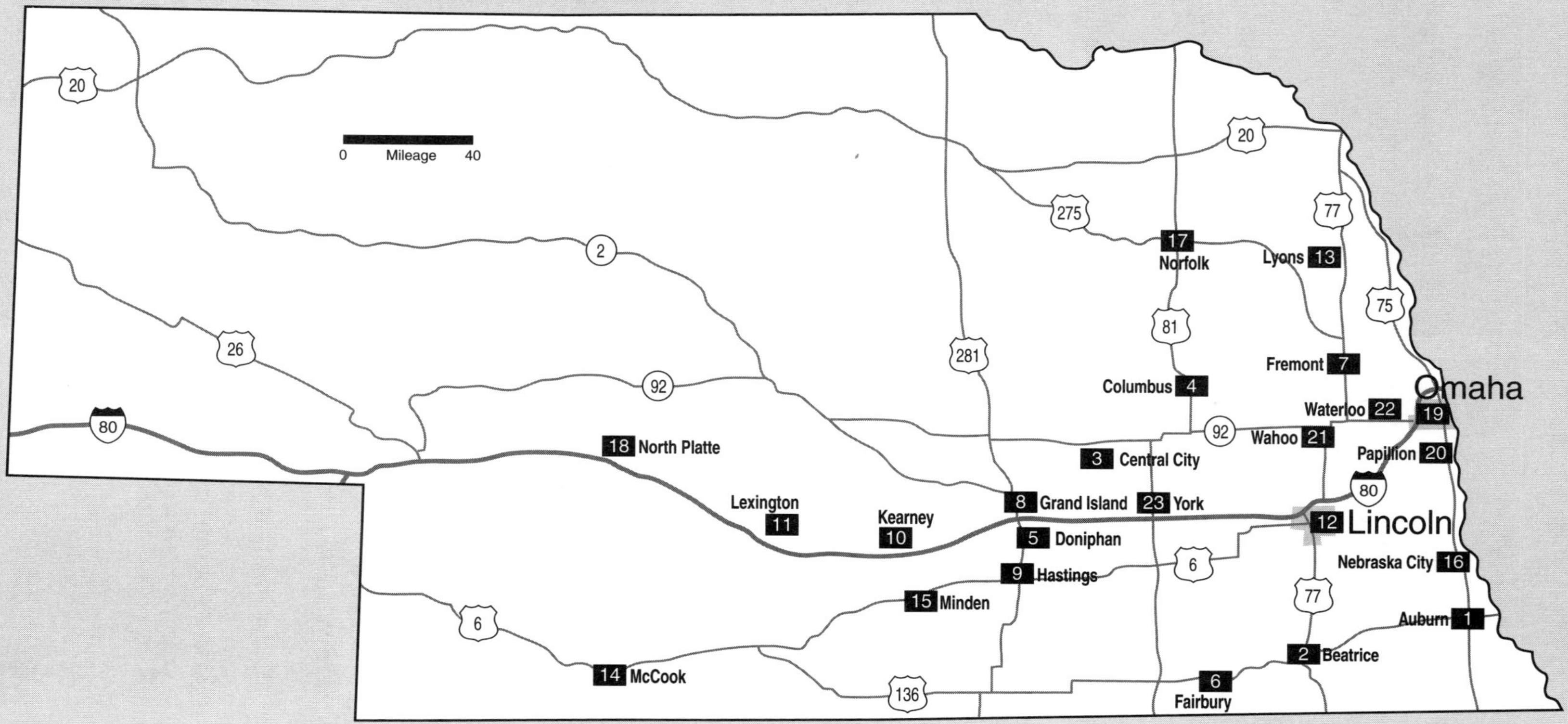

0 Mileage 40
20
275
17 Norfolk
77
13 Lyons
75
2
81
26
281
7 Fremont
4 Columbus
Omaha
92
22 Waterloo
19
80
92
21 Wahoo
18 North Platte
3 Central City
20 Papillion
80
8 Grand Island
23 York
11 Lexington
10 Kearney
12 Lincoln
5 Doniphan
6
9 Hastings
16 Nebraska City
77
15 Minden
1 Auburn
6
2 Beatrice
14 McCook
6 Fairbury
136

## 1 AUBURN

**Bobbi-Jon Antique Mall**
923 Central Ave.
402/274-5548

**Auburn Antique Center**
900 Central Ave.
402/274-3056

## 2 BEATRICE

**Bert's Bargains**
515 Ella St.
402/228-2670

**Riverside Antiques**
321 N. 9th St.
402/228-2673

**Third Street Antiques**
123 N. 3rd St.
402/228-2200

**Attic Treasures**
400 Court
402/228-2288

**Rowdy's Relics**
821 N. 11th St.
402/223-2807

## 3 CENTRAL CITY

**Hitching Post Antiques**
1607 16th St. (Hwy. 30)
308/946-2211

**Time and Again**
1401 15th St.
No Phone Listed

## 4 COLUMBUS

**Cottonwood Antique Mall**
2423 11th St.
402/564-1099

**Memory Lane Antiques**
1164 23rd Ave.
402/564-1870

## 5 DONIPHAN

**Robb Mercantile Company**
Main St.
402/845-2784

**Stars N' Stripes**
Main St.
402/845-6900

## 6 FAIRBURY

### Stagecoach Mall

510 E St.
402/729-4034
Mon.-Sat. 9-6, Sun. 12-5
*Directions: Stagecoach Mall is located 45 miles south of I-80 on Hwy. 15, at the intersection of Hwy. 136 and Hwy. 15.*

Located in historic downtown Fairbury, award-winning Stagecoach Mall offers antiques, collectibles, crafts, gifts and goodies! They've been featured in *Midwest Living Magazine* and the book *Day Trips in the Heartland: A Get-Away Guide to Unique Places and Fun in the Heartland*. Don't miss them!

**Linda's Attic**
522 D St.
402/729-5180

*Great Places To Stay*

### Personett House Bed and Breakfast Inn

615 6th St.
402/729-2902
Rates from $35

This bed and breakfast takes its name from Susie Personett, who ran a boarding house in the home from 1916 to 1941. During World War II the Jefferson County Chapter of the Red Cross acquired the house and used it for various war-related purposes, such as assembling clothing and first aid articles to be sent to England.

Offering guests seven lovely rooms with shared baths, the Personett House is just one block from downtown Fairbury.

## 7 FREMONT

Visit historic downtown Fremont, eastern Nebraska's Antique Capital! There are seven antique shops within walking distance. Fremont is home of the May Museum that has a general store, a historic school room, an 1860 settler's log cabin, and a 25-room mansion filled with antiques. Fremont also is the home station of the Fremont and Elkhorn Railway's Fevr Dinner Train (402/727-0615).

**John C. Antique Mall**
544 N. Main
402/727-7092

**C & E Antiques**
530 N. Main
402/721-2101

**Antique Alley**
105 E. 6th Street
402/727-9542

**Dime Store Days**
109 E. 6th St.
402/727-0580

**Memories Antiques**
225 E. 6th St.
402/753-0578

**Yankee Peddler West**
141 E. 6th St.
402/721-7800

**Hen House Gallery**
3305 N. Broad St.
402/721-5275

**Park Avenue Antiques**
515 Park Ave.
402/721-1157

## 8 GRAND ISLAND

### Great Exchange Flea Market

N.E. Corner of Hwy. 34 & S. Locust St.
308/381-4075
Mon.-Sat.10-5, Sun. 12-5
*Directions: Eastbound on I-80, Exit 312, go 4 1/2 miles north on Hwy. 281 to Hwy. 34, east 2 miles to S. Locust St. Westbound I-80, exit 318, go 4 miles north to Hwy 34, west 6 miles to Locust St.*

The Great Exchange Flea Market has over 12,000 sq. ft. of well lighted, clean floor area to browse. Certain areas are kept for specific themes, such as "The Paper Route" where you'll find new, used and collectible books, plus vintage magazines, newspapers, cookbooks, comics and tear sheets covering most of the paper collecting arena. A large area is set aside for furniture, mainly antique and collectible. A feature area of the market is Abby's Emporium which is the only craft area in the store. In this shop is a trip down memory lane including the tin roofs and picket fences. You'll find everything here from cabinets to doilies. Shelves and benches are loaded with treasures to decorate your home or put a smile on a friend's face.

Billed as the finest flea market in Nebraska, the Great Exchange Flea Market has 60 dealers offering everything from Hummels to handcuffs, depression glassware, pottery, primitives, toys, collectibles and more.

**Lana's Antique Mall**
112 W. 2nd St.
308/384-9876
Mon.-Sat. 10-5, Sun. 12-5
*Directions: From I-80, take Exit 281. Lana's is located 8 to 10 miles from I-80 on Highway 30 in Grand Island.*

Nine dealers fill this two-story mall that specializes in country and primitive furnishings and accessories. It's easy to see how a piece will look in your home, since the individual rooms are set up as actual furnished areas with items from the mall.

Point of Interest: People from all over the country come to Grand Island from March through the first week of April to watch the sandhill cranes on their migratory route.

**H & S Refinishing & Antiques**
327 N. Cleburn St.
308/381-8737

**Keith's Red Lamp Antiques & More**
108 W. 3rd St.
308/384-6199

**Clutter Bug Antiques**
219 W. 3rd St.
308/382-0369

**Chantilly Lace**
327 N. Cleburn St.
308/381-8737

**Prairie House**
2536 Diers Ave.
308/381-8838

**Time After Time**
324 W. 3rd St.
308/384-7009

**Heartland Antique Mall**
216 W. 3rd St.
308/384-6018

**Treasure Chest**
216 S. Wheeler
308/382-8817

**Fantasy Ceramics & Antiques**
106 W. 3rd St.
308/381-6454

**Country Trader**
505 N. Pine
308/384-8277

## 9 HASTINGS

**VIP Antiques**
1733 W. 2nd St.
402/463-5055
Fax: 402/463-3038
Mon.-Fri. 8-5, Sat. 12-4
*Directions: Traveling I-80, take Exit 312 to South Hwy. 281. Go 16 6/10 miles to 2nd and Burlington St. and turn right (west) on 2nd St. Go exactly 8/10 of a mile to the Total Convenience Store, which is on the left. Look up and you will see the VIP Antiques marquee. Turn left and go 1 short block and you are there.*

Vicki and Paul Bergman love to cater to antique dealers and collectors, and their 5,000 square foot warehouse is filled with a full line of antiques and other treasures especially suited for both groups. The selection is varied, the quality is excellent and the price is right! Sounds like my kind of shop.

**Antiques And**
706 W. 2nd St.
402/463-8010

**Berdina's Treasure Trove**
406 S. Maple
402/462-6596

**Centra-Whse. Antiques**
1733 W. 2nd St.
402/463-3455

**The Antic Shop**
3555 S. Baltimore
402/643-8002

**Country Market Antiques**
RR 1
402/462-6349

**Geranium Hill Antiques**
214 S. Burlington
402/463-4354

**Katie's Nearly Nu**
708 E. South St.
402/462-2000

### *Great Places To Stay*

**Grandma's Victorian Inn Bed & Breakfast**
1826 W. 3rd St.
402/462-2013
Rates from $60

An 1886 Victorian with a beautiful staircase and outstanding woodwork, Grandma's offers guests five rooms, each with private bath. The house is filled with antiques, with an accent on rocking chairs and queen-size beds in each guest room. Enjoy such simple, old-fashioned pleasures as sipping lemonade on the beautiful balcony, or relaxing on the front porch swings. Breakfast is served in the dining room, or, for an additional charge, can be served to you in bed!

## 10 KEARNEY

**Kaufmann's Antique & Collectible Emporium**
2200 Central Ave.
308/237-4972
Mon.-Sat. 10-5, Sun. 1-5
*Directions: Conveniently located off I-80. Go right 2 blocks from first stop light—over railroad overpass.*

Kaufmann's Antique & Collectible Emporium is Kearney's largest antique mall with over 65 dealers displaying fine glassware, furniture, vintage jewelry, dolls, early American pieces and much more. Plan to spend at least two to three hours to browse this 8,000 square foot former 20's variety store. One of our *favorite* antiquing spots.

**Great Plains Art & Antique**
131 S. Central Ave.
308/234-5250

**Antique Co-op**
229 Central Ave.
308/236-6990

**Dady's Antiques & Collectibles**
1809 Central Ave.
308/236-8319

## 11 LEXINGTON

**Kugler Antiques**
311 S. Washington St.
308/324-4267
Daily 10-6
*Directions: From I-80, take the Lexington exit, turn north and go 2 miles.*

Located in a town that claims the title of "Antique Center of Nebraska," Kugler Antiques is unique in its inventory of antique furniture, primitives, glassware, pottery, crocks, silver, coins and old guns. The shop prides itself on providing shoppers with authentic antiques and is well known for its unusual collections. One of the most interesting is a collection of old mannequins that might remind you of the old department store days, when window dressing was an art in itself.

**Bargain John's Antiques**
700 S. Washington St.
308/324-4576
Mon.-Sat. 8-7, Sun. 12-6
*Directions: Traveling I-80, take the Lexington exit to Hwy. 283. Follow Hwy. 283 into Lexington and turn left at the Pizza Hut off of Hwy. 283. The shop is located in the blue building.*

Bargain John's has been Nebraska's largest supplier of quality antique furnishings since 1968. They specialize in Victorian furniture from the 1840s to 1910. They also carry a small quantity of Mission oak pieces and a grand selection of Victorian art glass and cameo glass.

**Richardson Bargain Shed**
951 W. Walnut
308/324-4786

**Tinder Box**
909 N. Grant St.
308/324-3585

**Youngs Furniture & Auction**
1108 N. Adams St.
308/324-4594

**Leif's Antique Mall**
Van Buren St.
308/324-2242

**Memories Bed & Breakfast & Antqs.**
900 N. Washington St.
308/324-3290

**Memories Antique Shop**
900 N. Washington St.
308/324-3290

**Hofaker's Antiques**
Hwy. 283
308/324-4719

**Trinkets & Treasures**
E. Hwy. 30 & Jefferson St.
308/324-5344

## 12 LINCOLN

**Burlington Arcade**
210 N. 7th St.
402/476-6067
Mon.-Wed. and Sat. 10-6, Thurs.-Fri. 10-8, Sun. 1-5
*Directions: From I-80, take the 9th Street Exit to the historic Hay Market District, where Burlington Arcade is located.*

Voted "Lincoln's Best Antique Mall" in 1996, Burlington Arcade Antique Mall is housed in the old Taxi Cab Building in Lincoln's historic Hay Market District. The 30-plus dealers fill the 7,000-square-foot building with a mix of fine furniture, glassware, linen and jewelry. Great restaurants in the immediate area, combined with Burlington's treasures, make a day's outing a must for avid antiquers and history buffs.

**B B & R Antique Mall**
1709 O St.
402/474-7505
Mon.-Fri. 10-6, Sat. 10-5, Sun. 12-5
*Directions: From I-80, take the exit to 27th St. and travel south to O St. Turn right and the shop is located approximately 10 blocks down, near the intersection of O St. and 17th St. Parking is available behind the shop.*

This 42-dealer mall is celebrating its second anniversary this year. They have a large variety of antiques ranging from jewelry to furniture to collectibles from the 1930s to the 1960s—just a big mix of everything.

**Conner's Architectural Antiques**
701 P St.
402/435-3338
Mon.-Sat. 9:30-6, Sun. 1-5
*Directions: From I-80, take the 9th St. Exit. Conner's is located in the historic Hay Market District of Lincoln, across the street from the*

*old train depot.*

Housed in the old Beatrice Creamery building, Conner's Architectural Antiques offers 20,000 square feet of any and everything you'll need to decorate your home. You'll find lighting, stained glass windows, doors, fireplace mantles, old hardware, garden accents, fencing, wrought iron tables and much, much more.

Additionally, the shop offers a matching service with over 20,000 pieces of china and crystal patterns.

**Country Store**
2156 S. 7th St.
402/476-2254

**Indian Village Flea Market Emporium**
3235 S. 13th St.
402/423-5380

**Pack Rats A Cooperative**
1617 S. 17th St.
402/474-4043

**Continental Furniture Ltd.**
400 N. 48th St.
402/464-0434

**Scherer's Architectural Antiques**
6500 S. 56th St.
402/423-1582

**Bittersweet Antiques & Gifts**
2215 N. Cotner Blvd.
402/466-4966

**Second Wind**
1640 O St.
402/435-6072

**Q Street Mall**
1835 Q St.
402/435-3303

**Bailey Antiques Inc.**
710 B St.
402/476-8422

**Eastman's Antiques**
2236 Bradfield Dr.
402/475-6669

**Vel-Roy Antiques & Collectible**
648 N. 31st St.
402/477-7062

**Aardvark Antique Mall**
5800 Arbor Road
402/464-5100

**Antique Corner Cooperative**
1601 S. 17th St.
402/476-8050

**Coach House Antiques Inc.**
135 N. 26th St.
402/475-0429

**Applebee's Antiques**
3911 S. 48th St.
402/489-6326

**Gatherings Antiques& Gifts**
100 N. 8th (Haymarket)
402/476-1911

**Capitol Beach Antique Mall**
1000 W. O St.
402/474-1125

**Cornhusker Mall Antiques**
2120 Cornhusker Hwy.
402/438-5122

**13th Street Antiques**
915 S. 13th
402/477-3662

**Burnham House Antiques**
4600 J St.
402/489-1803

**Treasures & Tropics**
3845 S. 48th St.
402/486-3960

## 13 LYONS

**Kristi's Antiques, Inc.**
Hwy. 77
402/687-2339
Mon.-Sat. 10-5, by appointment for dealers

Dealers, take note! Kristi's caters to you, as well as to the general shopper. They specialize in wholesaling, with over 1,000 pieces of original finish oak and walnut furniture. They also handle quilts, graniteware, stoneware, country store items, and thousands of smalls.

## 14 McCOOK

**Kenny's Country Gifts & Antiques**
N. Hwy. 83
308/345-2817

**Huegels Hutch**
401 Norris Ave.
308/345-7564

**Accents Etc.**
307 Norris Ave.
308/345-7720

**The Glass House**
1503 W. Fifth St.
308/345-2547

## 15 MINDEN

Minden could be the ideal picture of sweet, romantic middle America: all old town square charm with antique stores and little businesses surrounded by Victorian mansions on manicured lawns, surrounded yet again by rolling, lush farmland.

It really is a cozy little Nebraska prairie town with an old and imposing courthouse complete with a big white dome! There are lots of prosperous businesses in the downtown district, including four antique shops.

Minden also has the Harold Warp Pioneer Village, one of the top museums of its kind in the country. This is an award-winning museum with 26 buildings holding 50,000 items that trace the development of everything from lighting and bathtubs to motorcycles and musical instruments from 1830 onwards. Among the buildings are seven historic structures, including an original livery stable complete with harness shop, and an authentic replica of a sod house. The museum also presents daily weaving, broom-making and other craft demonstrations.

**House of Antiques**
124 E. 5th St.
308/832-2200

**Vinegar Hill Antiques**
1161 25 Road
308/743-2445

## 16 NEBRASKA CITY

**Nebraska City Antique Mall**
800 Central Ave.
402/873-9805

**Carriage House**
512 Central Ave.
402/873-7410

**Peppercricket Farm Antiques**
Hwys. 2 and 75
402/873-7797

**Grandma Lu's**
117 S. 7th St.
402/873-5799

**Cindy's Dream Shop**
705 Central Ave.
402/873-5799

**The Antique Shop**
820 Central Ave.
402/873-3937

## 17 NORFOLK

### Norfolk Market Place
207 Norfolk Ave.
402/644-7824
Mon.-Sat. 10-5, closed Sun.
*Directions: Norfolk Market Place is located directly on Business Hwy. 275. Actually, Norfolk Ave. is Business 275!*

This is a year-round indoor flea market, so browsing doesn't have to wait for good weather! They specialize in antiques, collectibles, furniture, and (here's an unusual one!) old saddles, tack and buckles.

**Buck-A-Roo Antiques**
308 Northwestern Ave.
402/371-1240

**Antique Arcade**
Hwy. 81
402/379-0533

**Reals Clock Repair & Antiques**
127 Norfolk Ave.
402/371-4966

**Main Street Antiques**
715 Norfolk Ave.
402/371-6400

**Double (S) Antiques**
212 Northwestern Ave.
402/371-5404

## 18 NORTH PLATTE

### The Hayloft
2006 E. 4th St.
308/532-1300
Mon.-Fri. 10-5:30, Sat. 10-5, Sun. 1-5
*Directions: Traveling I-80, take Exit 177 or 179 to East 4th St.*

The Hayloft (sounds like a wonderful Nebraska name) offers a nice selection of antiques, collectibles, handcrafts, art and gift items.

**Antique Emporium**
2019 E. 4th St.
308/532-9003

**Dynamic Perfection**
120 Rodeo Road
308/532-7420

**Steele's Antique Depot**
620 N. Vine St.
308/532-8173

## 19 OMAHA

### Kirk Collection
1513 Military Ave.
1-800-398-2542 or 402/551-0386
Fax: 402/551-0971
Tues.-Sat. 10-5 and Mon. by appointment
*Directions: Take I-80 to I-480 North to 75 North to the Hamilton St. Exit. Go left on Hamilton 15 blocks to Military Ave. Take a right on Military Ave., and the shop is the second building on the right.*

The next time you're watching a movie like "Forrest Gump" or "Titantic," pay special attention, you may be looking at fabric purchased from The Kirk Collection.

The Kirk Collection started dealing in antique quilts and only moved into antique fabrics when owner Bill Kirk brought two trunkloads of fabric home from an auction and the Kirks had to find a market for it.

After a textile show in L.A., Bill visited the set of "Thirty-Something" where the designer bought $500 in fabric in under a minute and the Kirks realized costume designers us a lot of fabric. That led to a four-year relationship with "Quantum Leap," plus a lot work with "Homefront" and "Brooklyn Bridge" on television. Nancy Kirk jokes "we don't lose customers, they get canceled." Movie work followed with feature films including "Little Women," "Wyatt Earp," "Forrest Gump" and the new Tom Hanks film, "That Thing You Do" and "Titanic."

"When setting the time period for a film or TV show, directors know that men recognize the cars on the street, and women recognize the fabric in the costumes," says Nancy.

It took the National Quilting Association show in Lincoln to teach the Kirks that quilters also use a lot of fabric—but in little tiny pieces. They would come by the booth and ask for a quarter yard of fabric, and we would say "sorry, we don't cut fabric, because the costume designers wanted the longest lengths possible."

By the end of that three day show, we realized a quilter could spend $500 in nothing flat, but wanted it all in quarter yards. Needless to say, we cut fabric now. So much so, that the Kirks no longer do regular antique shows, but travel only for major quilt shows. They also send trunk shows of antique fabrics to quilt guilds and shops around the country. "That way the fabric can travel while we stay home." says Bill.

Now the majority of their business is done through their mail order catalog both nationally and internationally, and now on the World Wide Web at, at http://www.auntie.com/kirk, but customers can shop in their real live shop in Omaha.

**McMillan's Old Market Antiques**
509 S. 11th St.
402/342-8418

**Finders Keepers of Omaha**
423 S. 13th St.
402/346-1707

**A & A Antiques Co-Op Mall**
1244 S. 13th St.
402/346-2929

**Joe's 13th St. Co-op Antiques**
1414 S. 13th St.
402/344-3080

**Standing Bear Antiques**
1904 S. 13th St.
402/341-4240

**Cobweb Corners**
1941 S. 13th St.
402/334-2091

**Oberman's Furniture**
4832 S. 24th St.
402/731-8480

**Katelman Antiques**
39th & Farnam
402/551-4388

**Treasure Mart**
8316 Blondo St.
402/399-8874

**Omaha Auction Center**
7531 Dodge St.
402/397-9575

**Blue Ribbon Flea Market & Antique Mall**
6606 Grover St.
402/397-6811

**Honest John's Emporium**
1216 Howard St.
402/345-5078

**Ana's Attic**
4833 Leavenworth St.
402/556-7366

**Anderson O'Brien Gallery**
8724 Pacific St.
402/390-0717

**Meadowlark Antique Mall**
10700 Sapp Brothers Dr.
402/896-0800

**A to Z Antiques**
4224 Leavenworth St.
402/553-1860

**Bag Lady**
2630 N St.
402/738-8916

**Big Bear Refinishing & Antiques**
1524 Military Ave.
402/553-3011

**Life's Luxeries**
3127 N. 60th Street
402/554-0993

**Anchor Harbor Antiqs. & Cllbls.**
4815 S. 24th St.
402/731-0558

**A Bit of the Past**
6620 S. 36th St.
402/733-8832

**Cherishables**
1710 N. 120th St.
402/493-2948

**City Slicker Antiques & Such**
4973 Dodge St.
402/556-8271

**Franx Antiques & Art Inc.**
3141 Farnam St.
402/345-5266

**Antiques & Fine Art**
1215 Howard St.
402/341-9942

**Cosgrove Auction Furn. & Antqs.**
3805 Leavenworth St.
402/342-5254

**Antiques Plus**
6570 Maple St.
402/556-9986

**Brass Armadillo Antique Mall**
1066 Sapp Brothers Dr.
800/896-9140

**Vinton Street Antique Mall**
1806 Vinton St.
402/345-4499

**Antiques Thee Upstairs**
4832 S. 24th St.
402/731-8480

**Barb's Recollections**
2212 S. 13th St.
402/346-6111

**Candy's Finders Keepers**
423 S. 13th St.
402/346-1707

**Country Corner**
6621 Railroad Ave.
402/731-8707

**Morgan's Place Antiques**
2351 S. 27th Ave.
402/346-1688

**S W Antiques**
4339 S. 87th St.
402/593-0403

**Trader Todds**
1902 S. 13th St.
402/341-2475

**Collector's Paradise**
7006 Maple St.
402/571-0879

**Once Upon a Time**
5007 Underwood Ave.
402/553-8755

**Second Chance Antiques**
1125 Jackson St.
402/346-4930

## 20 PAPILLION

**Country at Heart**
114 N. Washington St.
402/339-5988

**Homestead Antiques**
122 N. Washington St.
402/339-1339

## 21 WAHOO

**Country Antiques**
526 N. Linden
402/443-3646

**Wahoo Mercantile**
1 Mi. N.E. of Wahoo on 92-77
402/443-4305

**Hart & Hand**
521 N. Broadway
402/443-3135

**Wahoo Bob's Antique Emporium**
7th & Linden
402/443-5084

**The Trading Post**
326 W. 11th
402/443-4474

## 22 WATERLOO

**Venice Antiques**
26250 W. Center Road
402/359-5782

**Black Horse Antiques**
301 3rd St.
402/779-2419

## 23 YORK

**I-80 & 81 Antique Mall**
2 Mi. N. Of I-80 on Hwy. 81
402/362-1975

# Nevada

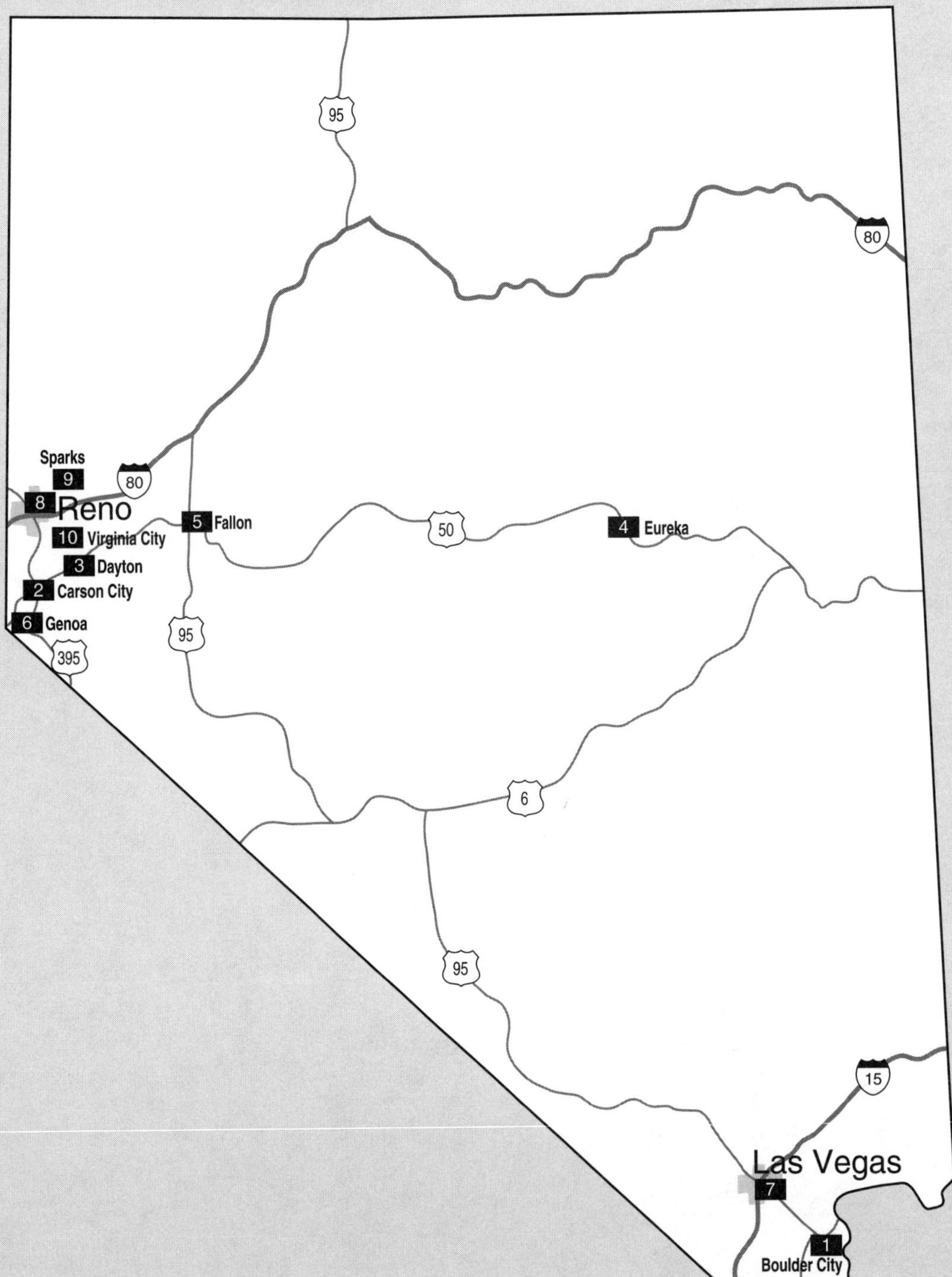

95
80
Sparks
9
8
Reno
80
5 Fallon
50
4 Eureka
10 Virginia City
3 Dayton
2 Carson City
6 Genoa
95
395
6
95
15
Las Vegas
7
1
Boulder City
95

## 1 BOULDER CITY

**Acks Attic**
530 Nevada Hwy.
702/293-4035

**Janean's Antiques**
538 Nevada Hwy.
702/293-5747

## 2 CARSON CITY

**Country Castle**
314 S. Carson St.
702/887-7447

**Bargain Barn**
2106 N. Carson St.
702/883-3124

**Gasoline Alley**
5853 S. Carson St.
702/883-1183

**Inglo Antiques & Collectibles**
224 S. Carson St.
702/885-0657

**Chapel Antiques**
112 N. Curry St.
702/885-8511

**Callis Corner**
202 N. Curry St.
702/885-9185

**Harrington's Hall Closet**
206 N. Curry St.
702/883-7707

**Frontier Antique Mall**
221 S. Curry St.
702/887-1466

**Art & Antiques**
201 W. King St.
702/882-4447

**Second Hand Rose**
5891 U.S. Hwy. 50 E.
702/883-6575

**Primrose Lane Antiques**
10112 U.S. Hwy. 50 E.
702/246-3372

### *Great Places To Stay*

### Deer Run Ranch Bed & Breakfast
5440 Eastlake Blvd.
Washoe Valley
702/882-3643
Rates: $80-95

#### An Excerpt From the Archives of Deer Run Ranch

"The original ranch, called the Quarter Circle J P, was purchased in 1937 by Emily and Jim Greil (Muffy's parents) for back taxes of $2,400. It and the "Goat Ranch" at the foot of Jumbo Grade two miles north of here were the only residences on the one-lane dirt road around this side of Washoe Lake. All the children in the valley went to the one-room schoolhouse in Franktown, directly across the lake, grades 1-8, one teacher.

Legend has it that the ranch springs, including our spring and pond, watered small truck gardens, the produce being carried by wagon up "Deadman's" (our main driveway) and Jumbo Grades to Virginia City during the height of the mining boom on the Comstock in the late 1800s.

Sometime after the end of World War I, prohibition became the law of the land, and the "Moonshiners" gravitated to isolated lands with plenty of water to set up their stills. The spring tunnels here on the ranch were used for that purpose, and at some point before the repeal of prohibition in 1933, government agents blew up the stills, destroying the tunnel at our spring. Excavations for our house unearthed pipes and other distillery relics, as well as some of the old shoring from the original spring."

*(Your hosts, David, an architect-builder, and Muffy Vhay, a professional artist-potter, are both longtime Nevada residents, and are knowledgeable about local lore and activities.)*

#### Deer Run Ranch As It Is Known Today

Step out of the urban life, and into the peace and tranquility of one of the most idyllic spots in Nevada. Deer Run Ranch Bed and Breakfast is the perfect hideaway for a private, secluded getaway any time of the year. Alfalfa fields surround the complex, which has spectacular views of Washoe Lake and the Sierra Nevada mountains to the west. Tall cottonwoods shade the pond deck, a favorite spot for watching the abundant wildlife that call Deer Run home.

The private guest wing has two comfortable guest rooms with queen beds and private baths, and guest sitting room with private entry. In these tranquil guest rooms you can sit on the window seats and look out at the Sierras: or you might want to sit by the cozy fireplace in the sitting room, which is decorated with Navajo rugs and paintings, and enjoy the extensive library collection.

A full ranch breakfast, served at the handmade table in the sitting room, might include house specialties like omelets Florentine or Provencal. Enjoy fresh-brewed coffee and imported teas, home-baked specialty breads and muffins. Breakfast is served on pottery plates made on the ranch in the studio.

## 3 DAYTON

**Wild Horse Trading Co.**
45 Main St.
702/246-7056

## 4 EUREKA

### *Interesting Side Trips*

Situated on the "Loneliest Road in America," Eureka is the best preserved town on Highway 50 through Nevada. A stroll down Main Street in Eureka will take you back 100 years ago when Eureka was a thriving mining camp. Visit the historic courthouse, the Eureka Opera House, and the Eureka Sentinel Newspaper Building (now a fine museum). Explore the side streets and discover dozens of historic buildings, each with its own fascinating story.

## 5 FALLON

**Fallon Antique Mall**
1951 W. Williams Ave.
702/423-6222

**Just Country Friends**
727 W. Williams Ave.
702/423-3315

## 6 GENOA

Did you know Genoa is the home of the famous "Genoa Candy Dance?"

The "Candy Dance" originated in 1919 as an effort to raise money to purchase street lights for the community of Genoa. Lillian Virgin Finnegan, native born Genoan, and daughter of Judge D. W. Virgin, suggested a dance with midnight supper at the Raycraft Hotel. As an added fundraiser, she encouraged the Genoa ladies to make a variety of candies to sell by the pound with samples passed around during the evening. The delicious candies proved to be the highlight of the evening and for the tiny town of Genoa, street lights became a reality.

The "Candy Dance" became an annual event, and each year the proceeds were used to keep Genoa's street lights burning. The dance and fair are held each year on the last full weekend in September.

Today, approximately 30,000 people attend this once-a- year, two day event when the Genoa candy makers and friends whip up approximately 3,000 lbs. of delicious candies such as nut fudge, plain fudge, turtles, almond roca, brittle, dipped chocolates, divinity and mints to name a few.

The "Genoa Candy Book," featuring prize winning candy recipes and a touch of Genoa's candy making history, is sold at the Candy Gazebo during the event.

**Antiques Plus**
2242 Main St.
702/782-4951

**Dake House Antique Emporium**
2242 Main St.
702/782-4951

***Great Places To Stay***

### Genoa House Inn

Jacks Valley Road
702/782-7075
Rates: $115-130

The Genoa House Inn is an authentic Victorian home on the National Register of Historic Places. Built in 1872 by A. C. Pratt, the town's first newspaper editor, the inn has a rich history of ownership.

The rooms here are distinct in their charm and individuality. One offers a private balcony, another a jacuzzi tub, yet another, a covered porch. All have private baths and are graced with period antiques and collectibles.

To add to the hospitality of the inn, innkeepers Linda and Bob Sanfilippo serve refreshments upon arrival. Early in the morning, coffee is delivered to your door, followed by a full breakfast served in the sunlit dining room; or if you prefer, in the privacy of your own room.

Genoa, the oldest settlement in Nevada, is nestled against the Sierra foothills with a panoramic view of Carson Valley. Activities such as soaring, ballooning, or cycling are always available. For those who prefer to keep their feet on the ground, there are casual walks in the old town, tours of the various Victorian homes and buildings, or visits to Nevada's oldest saloon. There are also attractions in nearby Lake Tahoe and Virginia City.

Capture the charm of a simpler time in the place where Nevada began, at the Genoa House Inn.

## 7 LAS VEGAS

### The Sampler Shoppes Antiques

6115 W. Tropicana
702/368-1170
Mon.-Sat., 10-6; Sun. 12-5
*Directions: Taking Exit #37 from I-15 for Tropicana, go west on Tropicana 2 1/2 miles to Jones Blvd. Located on the southwest corner.*

Just minutes from the Las Vegas "Strip" is the largest indoor antique mall in the state of Nevada. Occupying 40,000 square feet of floor space, this emporium displays a vast selection of quality furniture and antiques, books, toys, dolls, jewelry, and other collectibles.

With 200 dealers of distinction already represented, the mall is continuing to fill its available spaces, so there will be even more to delight the collector.

The "Pablo Picasso", located in the shoppes, serves coffee and light meals.

**Yesteryear Mart**
1626 E. Charleston Blvd.
702/384-6946

**Josette's**
1632 E. Charleston Blvd.
702/641-3892

**Fields of Dreams**
1647 E. Charleston Blvd.
702/385-2770

**Silver Horse Antiques**
1651 E. Charleston Blvd.
702/385-2700

**Corner House Antiques**
1655 E. Charleston Blvd.
702/387-0334

**Fancy That**
2032 1/2 E. Charleston Blvd.
702/382-5567

**Antonio Nicholas Antiques**
2016 E. Charleston Blvd.
702/385-7772

**Yanas Junk**
2018 E. Charleston Blvd.
702/388-0051

**Antiques By Sugarplums Etc.**
2022 E. Charleston Blvd.
702/385-6059

**Nicholson & Oszadlo**
2016 E. Charleston Blvd.
702/388-1202

**A Estate Antiques**
2026 E. Charleston Blvd., Suite A
702/388-4289

**Old Times Remembered**
2032 E. Charleston Blvd.
702/598-1983

**Judy's Antiques**
2040 E. Charleston Blvd.
702/386-9677

**Antiques by Sara**
3020 W. Charleston, Suite 4
702/877-4330

**Maudies Antique Cottage**
3310 E. Charleston Blvd.
702/457-4379

**Red Rooster Antique Mall**
1109 Western Blvd.
702/382-5253

**Ratliff's Antiques**
2532 E. Desert Inn Road
702/796-9686

**House of Antique Slots**
1236 Las Vegas Blvd. S.
702/382-1520

**Victorian Casino Antiques**
1421 S. Main St.
702/382-2466

**Romantic Notions**
6125 W. Tropicana Ave., Suite F
702/248-1957

**Valentinos Zootsuit Connection**
906 S. Sixth St., Suite B
702/383-9555

**Academy Fine Books**
2026 E. Charleston Blvd.
702/471-6500

**Antique Warehouse**
4175 Cameron St., #B1
702/251-3447

**B. Bailey & Co. Antiques**
1636 E. Charleston Blvd.
702/382-1993

**Buzz & Company**
2034 E. Charleston Blvd.
702/384-2034

**Sunshine Clocks Antiques**
1651 E. Charleston Blvd.
702/363-1312

**Vintage Antique Mall**
3379 Industrial Road
702/369-2323

**Antiquities International**
3500 Las Vegas Blvd. S.
702/792-2274

**Kathy's Antiques**
1115 Western Ave.
702/366-1664

**American Collectibles**
6125 W. Tropicana Ave., Suite F
702/248-1957

**VeNette's Table**
2040 E. Charleston Blvd.
702/386-9677

**Antique Plus**
6105 W. Tropicana Ave.
702/221-0903

**Antiques & Collectors Gallery**
6125 W. Tropicana Ave., #A
702/889-1444

**Bonnie's Antiques & Collectibles**
2030 E. Charleston Blvd.
702/385-3010

**Las Vegas Antique. Slot Machine**
4820 W. Montara Circle
702/456-8801

### *Favorite Places To Eat*

**Country Star American Music Grill**
On the Strip at Harmon between Tropicana and Flamingo
702/740-8400

Food and drink lovers will find a delightful choice of exciting new menues at the Country Star. This restaurant, backed by Vince Gill, Reba McIntire, and Wynonna, offers high-quality American cuisine at moderate prices and features country music memorabilia, a huge video wall, and CD "listening post" where guests can check out the latest country hits.

## 8 RENO

**Karen Hillary Antiques & Appraisals**
418 California Ave.
702/322-1800

**All R Yesterday**
125 Gentry Way
702/827-2355

**Antique Collective**
400 Mill St.
702/322-3989

**Antique Mall 1**
1215 S. Virginia St.
702/324-1003

**Reno Antiques**
677 S. Wells Ave.
702/322-5858

**Grant's Tomb**
721 Willow St.
702/322-6800

**Briar Patch Antiques**
634 W. 2nd St.
702/786-4483

**Antique Mall III**
1251 S. Virginia St.
702/324-4141

**Wells Avenue Antiques**
719 E. 2nd St.
702/324-0100

**Antique Marketplace**
1301 S. Virginia St.
702/348-6444

**Times Past Antiques**
855 S. Wells Ave.
702/329-0937

**Past & Present Antiques**
128 E. Sixth St.
702/329-4370

**Antique Mall II**
1313 S. Virginia St.
402/324-1980

## 9 SPARKS

**Victorian Square Antique Mall**
834 Victorian Ave.
702/331-2288

**Unique Antiques**
2160 Victorian Ave.
702/355-0133

**Heartfelt Handmade & Antiques**
1434 Victorian Ave.
702/356-8677

## 10 VIRGINIA CITY

**Comstock Antiques**
408 N. A St.
702/847-0626

**Peach House**
263 N. C St.
702/847-9084

**Lynch House Antiques**
Main St. (Gold Hill)
702/847-9484

### *Great Places To Stay*

**Gold Hill Hotel**
Hwy. 342
702/847-0111
Rates $35-135

Gracing the western countryside with quiet charm and elegance, Nevada's oldest hotel, Gold Hill Hotel, built in the late 1850s surrounds guests with period antiques. History and beauty combine in this setting where guests can relax in spacious rooms and soak in an antique claw foot tub. Some rooms have fireplaces—great for those chilly Nevada nights.

A wine list, with over 160 selections, complements the wonderful meals served at the Gold Hill Hotel.

# New Hampshire

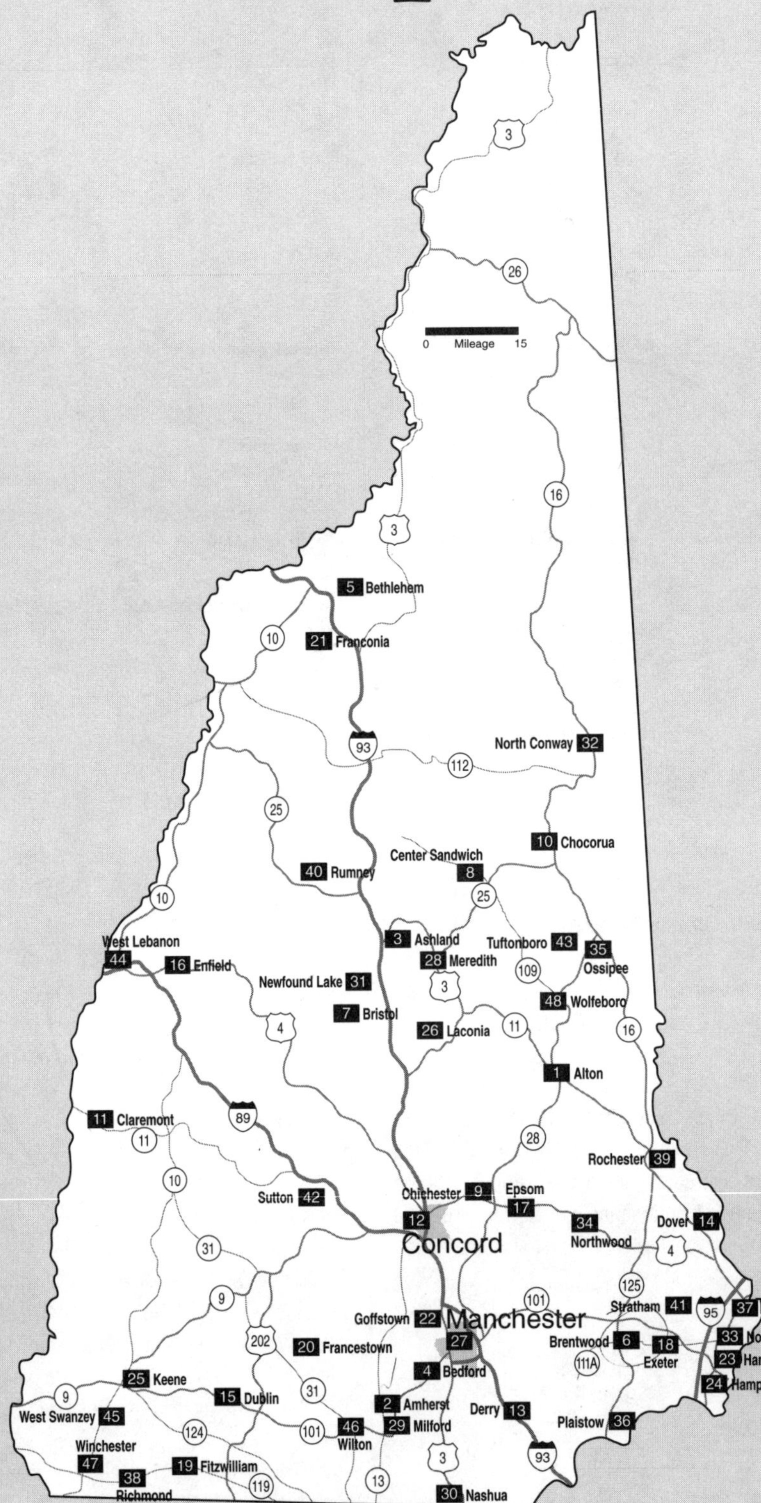

# New Hampshire

## 1 ALTON

**Cottontail Collectibles**
Main - Route 11
603/875-5456

**Homestead Place Antiques**
Jct. Routes 11 & 23
603/875-2556

## 2 AMHERST

**Needful Things**
112 State Route 101A
603/889-1232

**101 A Antique Center**
141 State Route 101
603/880-8422

**Antiques at Mayfair**
119 State Route 101A
603/595-7531

**Antiques at Mayfair**
121 State Route 101A
603/598-9250

**Iris Antiques**
141 State Route 101A
603/882-2665

**Mori Books**
141 State Route 101A
602/882-2665

**Consignment Gallery**
74 State Route 101A
603/673-4114

## 3 ASHLAND

**Antique House**
9 Highland
603/968-3357

## 4 BEDFORD

**Bell Hill Antiques**
Route 101
603/472-5580

## 5 BETHLEHEM

### Checkered Past Antiques

154 Guider Lane
603/444-6628
Open year round, Mon.-Sat., 10-5; Sun., 12-4; closed Wed. Nov.-June.
Email: kscope@ConnRiver.net
*Directions: Located at the junction of Route 302 and I-93 (Exit #40), Checkered Past is easily accessible. When exiting off I-93 or traveling Route 302 E., turn left at the Adair Country Inn sign and take Guilder Lane 4/10 of a mile to the end. When heading west on Route 302, immediately before the junction of I-93, turn right at the Adair Country Inn sign and follow Guilder Lane 4/10 of a mile to the end.*

In addition to Checkered Past's (what a great name!) ever-changing array of antiques, their heated 19th century barn holds hand-crafted, custom-made reproduction furniture.

**Curran's Antiques**
Main St.
603/869-2089

**Hundred Acre Wood**
Main St.
603/869-6427

**The Raven's Nest**
Main St.
603/869-2678

**3 of Cups**
Main St.
603/869-2606

### *Great Places To Stay*

### Wayside Inn

Route 302, P.O. Box 480
603/869-3364 or 1-800-448-9557
Daily 8-10; except Thanksgiving and Christmas
*Directions: Take Exit #40 off I-93. Go east on Route 302 for 6 3/10 miles. The inn is on the right side.*

Wayside Inn has a long and interesting history. It began in 1832, when the main building was built as a railroad boarding house for railroad workers (it sits across from the tracks). Around 1900 it became an inn for the general traveling public, and has remained open as such for nearly a century, making it the oldest continually operating inn in the area. The Victorian style building holds an extensive collection of antiques and quilts, and offers guests 28 rooms, all with private baths. There is an award-winning restaurant and lounge for guests' dining pleasure, and the restaurant gives diners a rare opportunity to enjoy Swiss specialties.

## 6 BRENTWOOD

### Crawley Falls Antiques

159 Crawley Falls Road
603/642-3417
*Directions: (From Massachusetts) Take I-495 N. to Exit #51B (Route 125). Follow Route 125 for approximately 16 miles. Look for the blinking light at the intersection of Routes 125 and 111A. Turn right at light, then make immediate left and go about 300 yards to shop parking lot. Shop is on the hill behind Lindy's Country Store. (From Route 101): Take Route 125 exit. south approximately 5 miles to Route 111A, left at blinking light.*

Visit this fabulous 18th Century homestead where the barn shop is filled with antique furniture and decorative accessories - primitive and vintage. The shop also features linens, china, artists' signed teddy bears (some made specially for the shop), sewing machines, trunks, ephemera and a wide selection of smalls. Displays not only show off the fine pieces in this shop, but are also artfully arranged to help you visualize ways to decorate your own home. Owner Donna Judah has created a warm and inviting atmosphere at Crawley Falls, complete with a children's area and sitting porch. No matter what your collecting interests, you surely will find something to take home with you at this wonderful shop.

## 7 BRISTOL

**Remember When**
Route 104 - 52 Summer St.
603/744-2191

**New Hampton Antiques Center**
Route 104
603/744-5652

## 8 CENTER SANDWICH

**New England Antiques & Collectibles Festival**
"A Show, Sale & Celebration of Old Time Living"
Sandwich Fairgrounds, Junctions 113 & 109
Call number below for dates.

New Hampshire's largest show, sale and celebration of old time living features over 200 exhibitors of antiques and collectibles. Emphasis is placed on family fun, live entertainment and nostalgia. Great buys can be found on garden decorations, architectural details, Fiesta ware, vintage toasters, radios, linens, tools, textiles, ephemera, robots, costume and bakelite jewelry, '50s kitsch, dolls, art pottery, series books and country furniture. Interactive demonstrations include hearthside cooking, bee keeping, blacksmithing, and soap making. Vintage car, truck and motorcycle show, sale and swap held simultaneously on 22-acre fairgrounds in a quaint New England village.

For more information call New England Antique Show Management, 603/539-1900.

## 9 CHICHESTER

**Austin's Antiques**
Route 4
603/798-3116

**Teachers' Antiques at Thunder Bridge**
11 Depot Road
603/798-4314

Two floors of painted country items, flow blue and Shaker smalls.

## 10 CHOCORUA

**Michael Dam Bookseller**
Route 16
603/323-8041

**Lucky Acres**
Route 16
603/323-8502

**Chocorua View Farm Antiques**
Route 16
603/323-8041

## 11 CLAREMONT

**La Deaus Annex**
38 Main St.
603/542-6352

**Farmor's Group Shoppes**
61 Main St.
603/542-2532

**Scottish Bear's Antiques Inc.**
54 Pleasant St.
603/543-1978

**Antique Center**
66 Pleasant St.
603/542-9331

## 12 CONCORD

**House & House Collectibles**
1 Eagle Square
603/225-0050

**Ol Speedway**
374 Loudon Road
603/226-0977

**Interior Additions**
38 N. Main St.
603/224-3414

**B & M Trading Post**
176 S. Main St.
603/753-6241

**Whispering Birches Antiques**
185 S. Main St.
603/753-8519

**Not Necessarily Antiques**
182 King St.
603/796-2240

## 13 DERRY

**Derry Exchange**
13½ Broadway
603/437-8771

**GRS Trading Post**
108 Chester Road
603/434-0220

**Antique & Used Furniture**
1 Pinkerton St.
603/437-4900

**Log Cabin**
182 Rockingham Road
603/434-7068

**Antique Store**
9 Grove St.
603/432-1070

## 14 DOVER

**Ubiquidous Antiques**
284 Central Ave.
603/749-9093

**Horse & Buggy Antiques**
34 Freshet Road
603/742-2989

**Timeless Appeal**
83 Washington St.
603/749-7044

## 15 DUBLIN

**Hedge House**
Main St. - Route 101
603/563-8833

**Peter Pap Oriental Rugs**
Route 101
603/563-8717

**Seaver & McLellan Antiques**
Route 101
603/563-7144

## 16 ENFIELD

### *Great Places To Stay*

**Mary Keane House**
Box 5, Lower Shaker Village
603/632-4241, 1-888-239-2153
Web site: mary.keene@valley.net
Open year round
*Directions: From I-89, take Exit #17. Bear right on Route 4 (east) for 1 1/2 miles. Turn right at the blinker light on Route 4A and go 3 miles. The Mary Keane House is on the left in the heart of Lower Shaker Village.*

Mary Keane House is a late Victorian style bed & breakfast located in the heart of historic Lower Shaker Village on the shore of Mascoma Lake. Expansive grounds, gardens, secluded beach and open and wooded hiking trails protected by 1200 acres of New Hampshire conservation district provide a peaceful and serene setting for a relaxing and stress-busting stay. Five spacious and light-filled one and two room suites (all with private baths) provide for your pleasure, antiques and comfort, elegance and whimsy. Watch the morning mist rise off the lake from your own balcony or enjoy the sunset from the glider swing on the west porch. The lakeside screened porch is the perfect spot to enjoy a summer afternoon conversation, book or nap while the living room with fireplace is the place to chase winter's chill. Full breakfast is served in the sunny dining room. They'll even pack you a picnic lunch for the antique trail or the hiking trail.

### *Interesting Side Trips*

**The Museum at Lower Shaker Village and Dana Robes' Workshop**
Route 4A
For Museum information call 603/632-4346
For Dana Robes' Wood Craftsmen information call 603/632-5385

Here in 1793 the Shakers established their Chosen Vale, a village of quietly majestic buildings, gardens and fields. Today, the Shaker heritage is preserved at the Museum at Lower Shaker Village and the Dana Robes Wood Craftsmen. Walking tours, exhibits, craft demonstrations, workshops, special programs and events, and extensive gardens bring new life to Shaker culture at the Museum. Reproduction Shaker furniture, and furniture inspired by Shaker design, is made by hand at Dana Robes' workshop.

## 17 EPSOM

**North Wind Antiques**
1782 Dover Road
603/880-0966

**Center Epson Antiques**
100 Dover Road
603/736-9972

**Epsom Trading Post**
Route #28
603/736-8843

## 18 EXETER

**Peter Sawyer Antiques**
17 Court St.
603/772-5279
Open by appt. or by chance, but most always open Mon.-Fri, 8-5

Offering appraisal and conservation services, Peter Sawyer Antiques specializes in important American clocks, particularly those of the New England area. They also offer a selection of fine 18th and 19th century New England furniture (emphasizing original state of preservation), American paintings, watercolors, drawing and folk art.

**Decor Antiques**
11 Jady Hill Circle
603/772-4538

**Scotch Thistle**
92 Portsmouth Ave.
603/778-2908

## 19 FITZWILLIAM

**Rainy Day Books**
Route 119
603/585-3448
Fax: 603/585-9108
Open early April-mid November, 11-5 Thurs.-Mon., and by appointment/chance, closed Tues.-Wed.

Antiquarian books showcased in an antique setting in the center of New Hampshire - it's a true antique lover's paradise! Rainy Day Books is a used and antiquarian bookstore housed in a 19th century barn and adjacent house in Fitzwilliam, the antique center of the southern Monadnock region. There are five other antiquarian book shops within half an hour's drive of Fitzwilliam. Rainy Day has a general stock of over 30,000 books, and a good selection of old prints and maps. In addition to the general stock, they also have sizable collections in the following special areas: amateur radio, American History/Civil War, audio engineering, children's, computer technology, cookbooks, fiber arts, outdoors, polar/mountaineering, radar and antenna engineering, radio and wireless, radio broadcasting, royalty, steam engines, surveying, town histories, and transportation. (Oh, and by the way, they have a great name.)

**Bloomin Antiques**
Route 12
603/585-6688

**Red Barn Antiques**
Old Richmond Road
603/585-3134

**Fitzwilliam Antiques**
Route 12
603/585-9092

## 20 FRANCESTOWN

**Mill Village Antiques**
195 New Boston Road
603/547-2050

**Stonewall Antiques**
532 New Boston Road
603/547-3485

## 21 FRANCONIA

**Colonial Cottage Antiques**
720 Blake Road
603/823-5614

### *Great Places To Stay*

**Blanche's Bed & Breakfast**
351 Easton Valley Road
603/823-7061
Open year round
Rates $40-85
*Directions: From I-93: Take Exit 38 to Route 116 south for 5 miles. From I-91: Take Exit 17 to Route 302 east. Go 7 miles to Route 112 east, then go 9 miles to Route 116 north, then approximately 6 more miles to Blanche's.*

Blanche's B&B gives guests a chance to relax in Victorian splendor while immersing themselves in an artistic atmosphere. Blanche's - named, by the way, for the family dog - is a restored 19th century Victorian farmhouse with views of the Kinsman Ridge. The artistic atmosphere is prevalent in the numerous decorative paintings scattered throughout the house, and an artist's working studio on the premises featuring hand painted canvas rugs. Steeped in the English B&B tradition, Blanche's offers antiques throughout, to compliment the cotton linens, down comforters, comfortable beds and great breakfast for the five guest rooms, one with private bath.

## 22 GOFFSTOWN

**Philip Davanza Clock Repair**
Addison Road
603/668-2256

**Griffin Watch & Antiques**
5 S Mast St.
603/497-2624

**Country Princess Antiques**
191 Mast St.
603/497-2909

**Goffstown Village Antiques**
9 N. Mast St.
603/497-5238

## 23 HAMPTON

**H G Webber**
495 Lafayette Road
603/926-3349

**Berg Antiques**
835 Lafayette Road
603/929-4911

**Northeast Auctions**
694 Lafayette Road
603/926-8222

## 24 HAMPTON FALLS

**Antiques New Hampshire**
Route 1, Lafayette Road
603/926-9603

**Antiques One**
Route 1, Lafayette Road
603/926-5332

**Barn Antiques at Hampton Falls**
Route 1, Lafayette Road
603/926-9003

**Antiques at Hampton Falls**
Route 1, Lafayette Road
603/926-1971

## 25 KEENE

**Fourteenth Division Antiques**
95 Main St.
603/352-5454

**Good Fortune**
114 Main St.
603/357-7500

**Colony Mill Marketplace**
222 West St.
603/357-1240

## 26 LACONIA

**Agora Collectibles**
373 Court St.
603/524-0129

**Almost All Antiques**
100 New Salem St.
603/527-0043

**LKS Regional Flea Mkt. & Antqs. Exchange**
38 Pearl St.
603/524-2441

**Barnless Bill Antiques**
30 Liscomb Circle
603/528-2443

**Glen & Ernie Antiques**
249 S. Main St.
603/524-2457

**Lake Village Antiques**
1073 Union Ave.
603/524-5591

## 27 MANCHESTER

**End of Trail Antiques**
420 Chestnut St.
603/669-1238

**Postcards from the Past**
571 Mast Road
603/668-5229

**Thistle Stop Antiques**
77 Pleasant St.
603/668-3678

**N H Bargain Mart**
334 Union St.
603/666-3644

**From Out of the Woods Furniture**
394 2nd St.
603/624-8668

## 28 MEREDITH

**Etcetra Shoppe**
Route 25
603/279-5062

**Alexandria's Lamp Shop**
62 Main St.
603/279-4234

**Burlwood Antique Center**
Route 3
603/279-6387

**Gordon's Antiques**
Route 3
603/279-5458

**Old Print Barn**
Winona Road
603/279-6479

## 29 MILFORD

**Elm Plaza Antique Center**
222 Elm St. (Route 101A)
603/672-7846

**Centurywood Antiques**
571 Elm St. (Route 101A)
603/672-2264

**New Hampshire Antique Co-op**
Elm St. (Route 101A)
603/673-8499

**Milford Antiques**
40 Nashua St. (Route 101A)
603/672-2311

**Golden Opportunities**
326 Nashua St. (Route 101A)
603/672-1223

**J C Devine Inc.**
20 South St.
603/673-4967

### *Great Places To Stay*

**Zahn's Alpine Guest House**
Route 13
603/673-2334
Fax: 603/673-8415
Located on Route 13 in Mont Vernon, New Hampshire on the Milford town line
Rates: Single $56, double $65 includes tax
Web site: www.intercondesign.com/zahns
*Directions: Zahn's Alpine Guest House is on a straight stretch of Route 13 with unimpeded visibility for almost a mile. On the left side (coming out of Milford, heading north) there is absolutely nothing at the roadside except the guest house's little cluster of signs (reflective at night), a lamp post (the only one), mail box, luminous green town line marker, and the mouth of the driveway. The building itself is obscured by trees, but there are five yard lanterns.*

Here's a twist that's a really nice change from the usual bed and breakfast. Bud and Anne Zahn have spent a lot of time in Austria, Bavaria and the South Tirol (northern Italy) over the past 30 years while importing antiques and leading bike/ski groups to Alpine Europe. Over the years they stayed primarily in small, out-of-the-way lodging places where the style of hospitality was quite different from anything stateside. They enjoyed this European experience so much that they decided to recreate such a place in the states - and so Zahn's Alpine Guest House was born.

They chose pine post and beams for the outer structure, which not only gave the house the heavy, timbered look of the old Alpine farmhouses, but lent itself perfectly to the deeply overhung roof (you don't have to close the windows when it rains), and the perimeter balcony. They shipped in a sea container full of antique farm furnishings, Alpine-authentic carpets, lampshades, wrought-iron lanterns and accessories. One of the highpoints that all guests comment on are the specially made mattresses and appropriate bedding that are exact replicas of the Alpine style. There are eight double rooms with private baths. One room has a conventional double bed. The others have European twin beds (three inches wider and six inches longer than usual). The top cover is an untucked, European style comforter inside a sheeting cover. When these beds are pushed together, the effect is that of an oversized double bed, and the space between the mattresses is minimal.

The Stube (evening and breakfast room) is, as in Europe, at the disposal of all the guests. Worth a visit just to examine something every American homeowner should consider is the Kachelofen - the hand-made-on-site, hand-decorated, two-ton tile oven. Almost all dwellings in Alpine Europe utilize these marvelous heaters which exploit masonry characteristics of "quick absorption, slow release of heat." The Zahns were fortunate to find a Bavarian Master Builder fairly nearby who could create one for the guest house.

Antiquers' constitute a strong portion of the clientele at Zahn's due to the literally hundreds of antique shops located within 15-20 minutes of the house.

## 30 NASHUA

**House of Joseph's Antiques & Collectibles**
523 Broad St.
603/882-4118
Tues.-Sun., 10-5
*Directions: From Route 3 N., take Exit #6 and bear left off the ramp onto Route 130 W. From Route 3 S., take Exit #6 and bear right off the ramp onto Route 130 W. Either way, go approximately 3 miles. The shop is a big red barn on the right.*

Housed in an actual, traditional red barn on Broad Street, this multi-dealer shop offers the discriminating antiquer an assortment of fine furniture, china, glass and collectibles. The shop has been in business for over 25 years, and holds a large selection of furniture and, among its many dealers, several who specialize in either oriental items, beer memorabilia, and glass pieces.

**L Morin Treasures**
191 W. Hollis St.
603/883-2809

**Past & Present**
202 Main St.
603/880-7991

**A A Antiques & Memorabilia**
214 Daniel Webster Hwy.
603/888-3222

**Gurette Cosve Antiques**
85 W. Pearls
603/880-0966

## 31 NEWFOUND LAKE

### *Great Places To Stay*

**The Inn On Newfound Lake and Pasquany Restaurant**
Route 3A
603/744-9111 or 1-800-745-7990 (reservations only)
Fax: 603/744-3894
Open daily 9-9
Rates $55-105
*Directions: Take I-93 N. (from Boston) to Exit #23. At the bottom of the ramp continue north on Route 104. At the small town of Bristol (approximately 6 miles) bear to the right (Route 3A). Continue on Route 3A approximately 6 miles, until you reach the inn, which is between the towns of Bristol and Plymouth.*

The Inn on Newfound Lake has been welcoming travelers since 1840. Formerly known as the Pasquaney Inn, it was the midway stop on the stage coach route from Boston to Montreal and now is the only remaining inn on the lake - at one time there were seven or eight. Located on seven and a half acres of lush New Hampshire countryside, the inn hugs the shore of Newfound Lake, the fourth largest lake in New Hampshire, and rated as one of the purest and cleanest bodies of fresh water in the world. As you can imagine, there is something to do outdoors in every season at the inn. Or if relaxation is what you're looking for, just kick back in one of the 31 extensively refurbished rooms. The main inn has 19 rooms, eleven with private baths and a common sitting room. Elmwood Cottage, which adjoins the main building by the veranda, contains 12 rooms, all with private baths and adjoining daybed rooms if needed. The cottage parlor has a full fireplace for added enjoyment. Besides the myriad outdoor activities and sports, indoor activities at the inn include shuffleboard, basketball, billiards, and table tennis, and a Jacuzzi and weight room.

When guests work up and appetite, they can go to the full-service Pasquaney Restaurant and tavern at the inn. The restaurant, complete with wood-burning stove, overlooks the lake for added atmosphere. Continental breakfast, lunch, dinner and Sunday brunch are available.

**The Cliff Lodge**
Route 3A
603/744-8660
*Directions: Take I-93 N. to Exit #23. At the bottom of the ramp take Route 104 N. When you reach the town of Bristol (approximately 6 miles), bear right on Route 3. Head north on Route 3 about 4 miles to the lodge.*

Here is a restaurant and cabins offering wonderful, casual country dining in a lodge perched on the side of a hill overlooking Newfound Lake. What better view could you ask for! It's a very romantic spot, and cabin rentals are available in the summer. A perfect weekend getaway, where you can enjoy the lake and surrounding countryside, eat great meals at your leisure, and never have to fight traffic!

## 32 NORTH CONWAY

**Sedler's Antiques**
30 Kearsarge
603/356-6008

**Antiques & Collectibles Barn**
Route 16
603/356-7118

**Aunt Aggie's Attic**
Route 16
603/356-0060

**Expressions by Robert N. Waldo**
Route 16
603/356-3611

**Richard M Plusch**
Route 16
603/356-3333

**John F Whitesides Antiques**
Route 16
603/356-3124

**North Conway Antiques & Collectibles**
3424 Main St.
603/356-6661

## 33 NORTH HAMPTON

**North Hampton Antique Center**
1 Lafayette Road
603/964-6615

**John Piperhousentz**
Sandy Point Road
603/778-1347

## 34 NORTHWOOD

**Parker-French Antique Center**
1st New Hampshire Turnpike
603/942-8852

**R S Butler's Trading Co.**
1st New Hampshire Turnpike
603/942-8210

**White House Antiques**
1st New Hampshire Turnpike
603/942-8994

**Willow Hollow Antiques**
1st New Hampshire Turnpike
603/942-5739

**Country Tavern Antiques**
Route 4
603/942-7630

**Coveway Corner Antiques**
Route 4
603/942-7500

**The Hay Loft Antique Center**
Route 4
603/942-5153

**Town Pump Antiques**
Route 4
603/942-5515

## 35 OSSIPEE

**Lakewood Station Antiques**
Route 16
603/539-7414

**Dow Corner Shop**
133 Mountain Road
603/539-4790

**Red Pine Antiques**
Route 16
603/539-6834

**Mountain Road Antiques**
Norman Drew Hwy.
603/539-7136

**The Stuff Shop**
25 Water Village Road
603/539-7715

**Treasure Hunt**
465 Route 16
603/539-7877

## 36 PLAISTOW

**Plaistow Commons Antiques**
166 Plaistow
603/382-3621

## 37 PORTSMOUTH

**Antiques Etc.**
85 Albany St.
603/436-1286

**Moose America Rustic Antiques**
75 Congress St.
603/431-4677

**Margaret Carter Scott Antiques**
175 Market St.
603/436-1781

**Silk Road Trading Company**
135 McDonough St.
603/433-1213

**Trunk Shop**
23 Ceres St.
603/431-4399

**Olde Port Traders**
275 Islington
603/436-2431

**Victory Antiques**
96 State St.
603/431-3046

## 38 RICHMOND

### The Yankee Smuggler Antiques

122 Fitzwilliam Road
603/239-4188
Fax: 603/239-4653
Open daily by chance or by appointment
*Directions: Located 1/2 mile east of Route 32 (Richmond Four Corners). From I-91: Take Exit 28 (Northfield) to Route 10 to Winchester. Take a right on Route 119 and go 6 miles to Richmond Four Corners (blinking light). Yankee Smuggler is the sixth house on the left.*

Ted and Carole Hayward are in their 40th year in the antique business and are still actively buying and selling quality country antiques, folk art and related accessories. Specializing in 18th and 19th century American country antiques with original painted surfaces, they carry large pieces of furniture like cupboards, tables, chest of drawers, desks, etc., as well as related accessories such as firkins, pantries, bowls, and picture frames, all in original paint - blue, red, green, mustard, and salmon, and grain, feather and sponge decorated. Visitors to The Yankee Smuggler can browse through two rooms in Ted and Carole's circa 1815 home, plus a large barn adjacent to the house. For the collector or dealer who wants something special they are open year round by chance or appointment, but they suggest visitors call ahead first - that way they can start a fresh pot of coffee!

## 39 ROCHESTER

**Elkins Trash & Treasures**
26 & 28 N. Main St.
603/332-1848

**Signal St. Antiques**
5 Signal St.
603/335-0810

**Four Corners Antiques**
204 Estes Road
603/332-1522

## 40 RUMNEY

**Courtyard Antiques**
Route 25
603/786-2306

**Willow Tree Antiques**
Route 25
603/786-2787

## 41 STRATHAM

### Compass Rose Antiques

17 Winnicut Road
603/778-0163
*Directions: Compass Rose is located 10 miles west of Portsmouth, just off Route 33.*

This charming shop carries a wide range of antiques with a focus on accessories. A few select furniture pieces are available, but what's lacking in furnishings is made up in the enormous offering of smalls. They carry exquisite lighting fixtures, glass, china, jewelry and much, much more. Antique weapons are also included among their inventory. Owners, Charles and Laurie Clark, have been in business for seventeen years, and the shop is actually located at their home. All of their items are "really" old (nothing modern) antiques from the 1800s.

Among the Clark's specialties are glass and china from the 1800s, "no depression or collectibles," says Laurie. Charles is the antique weapons expert and is a licensed gun dealer. Lighting fixtures, mainly whale oil lamps and lanterns, are also his forte.

**The Wingate Collection**
94 Portsmouth, Route 108
603/778-4849

## 42 SUTTON

**Sutton Mills Antiques**
90 Main St.
603/927-4557
Tues.-Sat. 10-6; Sun., 12-5; closed Mon.
*Directions: From I-89 North and South: Take Exit #10 and follow 114 S. for 4 miles. Turn right on Main St. and the store is 1/2 mile on the right.*

Sutton Mills is located in 1,900 square feet of an old, 19th century general store. This ten-dealer group features furniture, glass, old tools, estate and costume jewelry, coins and Americana.

## 43 TUFTONBORO

**Dow Corner Shop**
Route 171
603/539-4790

**Log Cabin Antiques**
Route 109A Ledge Hill Road
603/569-4249

## 44 WEST LEBANON

**Terry's Antiques**
Colonial Plaza-Airport Road
603/298-0556

**Colonial Antique Markets**
Route 12 A
603/298-7712

## 45 WEST SWANZEY

**Knotty Pine Antiques Market**
Route 10
603/352-5252

## 46 WILTON

**New England Antiques**
101 Intervale Road
603/654-5674

**Here Today**
71 Main St.
603/654-5295

**Noah's Ark**
Route 101
603/654-2595

## 47 WINCHESTER

**Latchkey Antiques**
4 Corners Plaza
603/239-6777

**Hearthside**
858 Keene Road
603/239-8697

## 48 WOLFEBORO

**The 44th Annual Wolfeboro Antiques Fair**
Brewster Academy, S. Main St.
Call number below for dates

Held for 44 continuous years, this show highlights 75 dealers in room settings and outdoors in a courtyard. Exhibitors offer high quality antiques ranging from estate jewelry, Oriental rugs, quilts, books and prints, to rustic, primitive and formal furniture, glass, paintings and silver. Located in Wolfeboro at Brewster Academy overlooking Lake Winnipesaukee & The Belknap Mountain Range. This picturesque community of New England white houses and country churches is also known as the "Oldest Summer Resort in America." This traditional antique fair and sale caters to tourists and summer residents alike.

For more information, call New England Antique Show Management, 603/539-1900.

**1810 House**
Route 28
603/569-8093

**Barbara's Corner Shop**
67 N. Main St.
603/569-3839

**Northline Antiques**
Northline Road
603/569-2476

# New Jersey

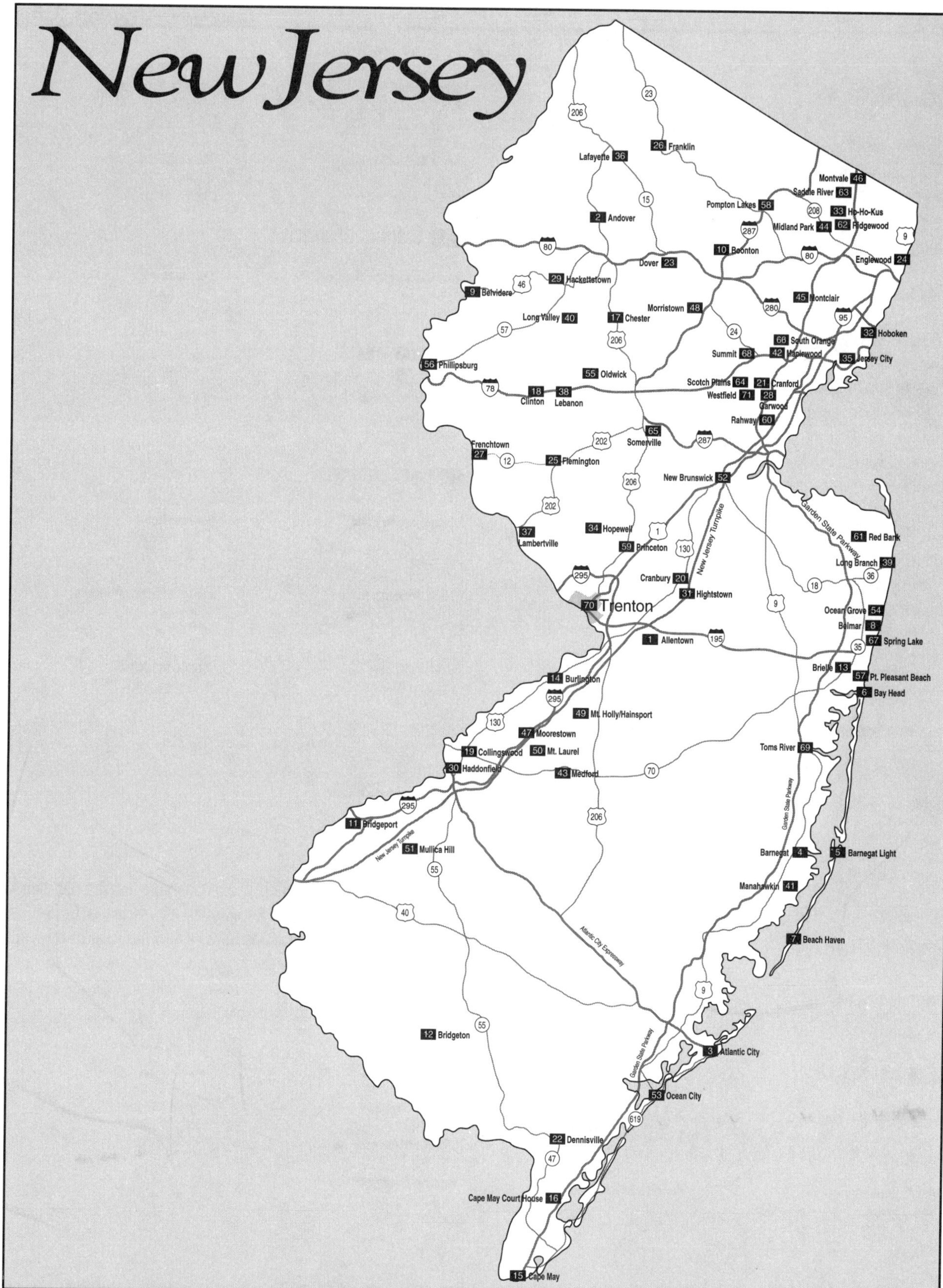

New Jersey
23
206
26 Franklin
Lafayette 36
15
Montvale 46
Saddle River 63
208
33 Ho-Ho-Kus
Pompton Lakes 58
2 Andover
287
Midland Park 44
62 Ridgewood
9
80
10 Boonton
80
Englewood 24
Dover 23
29 Hackettstown
46
9 Belvidere
45 Montclair
Morristown 48
280
95
Long Valley 40
17 Chester
57
24
32 Hoboken
66 South Orange
206
Summit 68
42 Maplewood
35 Jersey City
56 Phillipsburg
55 Oldwick
Scotch Plains 64
21 Cranford
78
18
38
Westfield 71
28
Clinton
Lebanon
Garwood
Rahway 60
65
287
Frenchtown
202
Somerville
27
12
25 Flemington
206
New Brunswick 52
Garden State Parkway
202
61 Red Bank
34 Hopewell
1
37
Lambertville
59 Princeton
130
New Jersey Turnpike
Long Branch 39
36
295
Cranbury 20
18
31 Hightstown
9
70 Trenton
Ocean Grove 54
Belmar 8
1 Allentown
195
67 Spring Lake
35
Brielle 13
14 Burlington
57 Pt. Pleasant Beach
6 Bay Head
295
49 Mt. Holly/Hainsport
130
47 Moorestown
Toms River 69
19 Collingswood
50 Mt. Laurel
30 Haddonfield
43 Medford
70
Garden State Parkway
295
11 Bridgeport
206
51 Mullica Hill
New Jersey Turnpike
Barnegat 4
5 Barnegat Light
55
Manahawkin 41
40
Atlantic City Expressway
7 Beach Haven
9
55
12 Bridgeton
3 Atlantic City
Garden State Parkway
53 Ocean City
619
22 Dennisville
47
Cape May Court House 16
15 Cape May

# New Jersey

## 1 ALLENTOWN

**Mill House Antiques**
38 S. Main St.
609/259-0659

**Brown Bear's Antiques**
35 S. Main St.
609/259-0177

**The Artful Deposit**
46 S. Main St.
609/259-3234

## 2 ANDOVER

### Great Andover Antique Company
124 Main St.
973/786-6384
Wed.-Sun. 10-5, closed Mon. & Tues.

Housed within a 2500-square-foot building constructed in 1868 and extending to two floors are the offerings of Great Andover Antiques Company. The shop specializes in 18th and 19th century furniture, American pottery, textiles, jewelry, lighting, Edison players, Victrolas, radios, Victorian furniture and complete bedroom sets. A large collection of stained glass is displayed in the 1,000 square foot former carriage house located on the property.

**3 Generations**
1 Gristmill Lane
201/786-7000

**Oriental Rugs & Antiques**
Hwy. 206
201/786-6004

**Scranberry Co-op**
Hwy. 206.
201/786-6414

**Red Parrot Antiques**
118 Route 206
201/786-5007

**Vintage Sam's**
124 Main St.
201/786-7955

**Andover Village Shop**
125 Main St.
201/786-6494

**Country and Stuff**
127 Main St.
201/786-7086

**Andover's Mixed Bag**
131 Main St.
201/786-7702

## 3 ATLANTIC CITY

**Princeton Antiques**
2917 Atlantic Ave.
609/344-1943

**Bayside Basin Antiques**
800 N. New Hampshire Ave.
609/347-7143

## 4 BARNEGAT

**Barnegat Antique Country**
684 E. Bay Ave.
609/698-8967

**Goldduster**
695 E. Bay Ave.
609/698-2520

**First National Antiques**
708 W. Bay Ave.
609/698-1413

**Federal House Antiques**
719 W. Bay Ave.
609/698-5490

**Lavender Hall**
289 S. Main St.
609/698-8126

**Babes in Barnegat**
349 S. Main St.
609/698-2223

**Forget Me Not Shoppe**
689 E. Bay Ave.
609/698-4336

**Blaze of Glory**
307 Main St. S.
609/597-8416

## 5 BARNEGAT LIGHT

**Americana by the Seashore**
604 Broadway
609/494-0656

**The Sampler**
708 Broadway
609/494-3493

## 6 BAY HEAD

**Fables of Bay Head**
410 Main Ave.
732/899-3633

## 7 BEACH HAVEN

**Somewhere in Time**
118 N. Bay Ave.
609/492-3034

**Summerhouse**
412 N. Bay Ave.
609/492-6420

**Courts Treasure Chest**
1500 Long Beach Blvd.
609/494-0910

**House of Seven Wonders**
7600 Long Beach Blvd.
609/494-9673

**Wizard of Odds**
7601 Long Beach Blvd.
609/494-9384

**Age of Antiquities**
8013 Long Beach Blvd.
609/494-0735

***Great Places To Stay***

### Amber Street Inn
118 Amber St.
609/492-1611

The inn built in 1885 as one of Beach Haven's original Victorian homes, was lovingly renovated and updated in 1991. Since then, the innkeepers, Joan and Michael Fitzsimmons have worked to establish the inn's reputation as a casually elegant, comfortable and romantic seashore retreat. The inn's six well appointed rooms, all with private baths, welcome guests with their individual charm and decor.

## 8 BELMAR

**Unique Designs**
809 Main St.
732/681-2060

**Aajeda Antiques**
1800 Main St.
732/681-2288

**Belmar Trading Post**
1735 State Route 71
732/681-3207

### *Great Places To Stay*

**The Inn at the Shore**
301 4th Ave.
732/681-3762

This stunning inn is located within sight of the Atlantic Ocean and Belmar's wide beautiful beaches and boardwalk, and steps away from serene Silver Lake, home to the first flock of swans bred in America. Only a short walk from the inn to fine restaurants, marina, river, lake, boardwalk and beaches.

## 9 BELVIDERE

**Painted Lady**
16 Greenwich St.
908/475-1985

**Uncommon Market**
228 Mansfield St.
908/475-1460

**H & H Liquidating Co.**
427 Mansfield St.
908/475-4333

**Major Hoops Emporium Antiques**
13 Market St.
908/475-5031

## 10 BOONTON

**Cupboard**
410 Main St.
973/402-0400

**Boonton Antiques**
521 Main St.
973/334-4416

**Claire Ann's Antiques**
815 Main St.
973/334-2421

**Fox Hill Exchange**
900 Main St.
973/263-2270

**Elizabeths Antiques Buying Center**
904 Main St.
973/263-9162

## 11 BRIDGEPORT

**Racoon Creek Antiques**
20 Main St., Box 132
609/467-3197
Thurs.-Sun. 12-5 or by appointment
*Directions: From the New Jersey Turnpike: Take Exit #1 and go 5 miles west on 322. Follow the signs to 20 Main St., Bridgeport. From I-95: Raccoon Creek Antiques is 30 minutes north of Wilmington, 30 minutes south of Philadelphia, and one mile from the base of Barry Bridge, which crosses the Delaware River on the "Jersey" side.*

If you are in the market for truly "old" antiques, Raccoon Creek is an absolute must on your trek. George Allen has 11 years of accumulation and selected buying savvy in the field of Americana, quilts, pottery and folk art. "I deal in items that are pre-1860s," says George. "All my stock is pre-industrial age, everything handmade— absolutely no reproductions of any kind." Examples of just some of his Americana include weather vanes, samplers and original painted furniture.

**Note: I've met up with George at several antique shows around the country. He's one of the nicest antique dealers in the business. At each of these shows, he always presents some very unusual pieces.*

## 12 BRIDGETON

**Kim Shell Gift Boutique**
404 Big Oak Road
609/451-4667

**Hudson House**
2012 Burlington Road
609/433-1414

**The Squirrel's Nest**
680 Shiloh Pike
609/455-6594

**Pony Point House/Candle Shop**
781 Shiloh Pike
609/451-6130

**Dutch Neck Village**
97 Trench Road
609/451-2188

## 13 BRIELLE

**Brielle Antique Center**
622A Green Ave.
732/528-8570

**Chappies Antiques**
406 Higgins Ave.
732/528-8989

**Relics**
604 Union Ave.
732/223-3452

## 14 BURLINGTON

**H. G. Sharkey & Company Antiques & Coffee House**
306 High St.
609/239-0200
Daily 8-8
*Directions: From I-295, Exit Burlington #54, go to High St. Located 1/2 block from the Delaware River.*

Housed in a historical building, specializing in antique jewelry and collectibles. A coffee house is also located on the premises.

**Antique Row**
307 High St.
609/387-3050

## 15 CAPE MAY

**Bridgetowne**
523 Broadway
609/884-8107

**Curious Collectibles**
719 Broadway
609/884-5557

**Promises Collectables**
301 N. Broadway
609/884-4411

**Bogwater Jim Antiques**
201 S. Broadway
609/884-5558

**Studio Victorian Antiques**
607 Jefferson
609/884-0444

**Cape Island Antiques**
609 Jefferson
609/884-6028

**Finishing Touches**
678 Washington
609/896-0661

**Antique Doorknob**
600 Park Blvd.
609/884-6282

**Rocking Horse Antique Center**
405 W. Perry St.
609/898-0737

**Hazard Sealander Antiques**
479 W. Perry St.
609/884-0040

**Millstone Antiques & Collectibles**
742 Seashore Road
609/884-5155

**Stephanie's Antiques**
318 Washington St.
609/884-0289

**Nostalgia Shop**
408 Washington St.
609/884-7071

**Midsummer Nights Dream**
668 Washington St.
609/884-1380

### *Great Places To Stay*

**Abigail Adams Bed & Breakfast**
12 Jackson St.
609/884-1371

Located just 100 feet from some of the widest beaches in Cape May, Abigail Adams's Bed and Breakfast by the sea, offers a breathtaking view of the ocean from many of the charmingly furnished guest rooms. Wake up to the sound of the waves and to the aroma of fresh coffee brewing in the country kitchen. Breakfast is substantial and served in the 1891 Victorian hand-stenciled dining room.

**Bedford Inn**
805 Stockton Ave.
609/884-4158
Web site: www.bbhost.com/bedfordinn

Just a half block to the beach and built in 1881 as a 'Mother-Daughter' twin home, the beautifully restored Bedford Inn offers a warm and peaceful getaway. Innkeepers Alan and Cindy Schmucker, have been welcoming guests to their home for more than 32 years. Enjoy the cozy fireplace in the Victorian parlor or laze away an hour or two on one of the old-fashioned verandahs. Each room and 'honeymoon' suite is furnished with authentic Victorian antiques and has a private bath.

**John Wesley Inn**
30 Guerney St.
609/884-1012
Open year round
*Directions: Go to the end of the Garden State Parkway in Cape May. Take Lafayette St. to the first traffic light (at Madison Ave.). Turn left and go two blocks to Columbia Ave. Take a right and continue down to Gurney St. (there is a monument in the center of the street) and turn left. The inn is the second building from the corner on the right.*

There is a real soap-opera story behind the recent history of the John Wesley Inn. Here it is in innkeeper Rita Tice's own words: "Once upon a time in 1983, we were all very happy with our three-apartment building in Cape May - "we" being my husband John, who loves to fish; my four teenagers, who loved the beach and making money with summer jobs, and myself, who also loved the beach and touring old Victorian homes. At least we were happy for a couple of years. But everything fell in—literally—in January 1985, when an active raw sewer main collapsed under the outhouse! Following a horrible two years of work, we opened as an inn. The building was actually lifted to add a perimeter foundation. Today, it is an award-winning grand Victorian, completely restored to its 1869 splendor."

Thoroughly recovered from a horrible experience, this grand old Victorian "lady" now offers visitors six guest rooms (four with private baths) and two apartments. The entire mansion is decorated in formal Victorian style, complete with white lace curtains and all American antiques. Guests can go from Victorian formality to barefoot freedom on the beach, which is a just one half block away, then come "home" and warm in front of the parlor fireplace, go to sleep in historical comfort, and wake up to an eye-opening continental breakfast and sea breezes. What a life!

**Mainstay Inn**
635 Columbia
609/884-8690
Web site: www.mainstayinn.com

'The jewel of them all has got to be the Mainstay,' according to *The Washington Post*. Built by a pair of wealthy gamblers in 1872, this elegant, exclusive clubhouse is now one of the premier bed and breakfast inns in the country. Guests enjoy 16 antique filled rooms and suites (some with fireplaces and whirlpool baths), three parlors, spacious gardens and rocker-filled verandahs. Breakfast and afternoon tea served daily.

## 16 CAPE MAY COURT HOUSE

**August Farmhouse**
1759 N. Route 9
609/465-5135

**Mallard Lake Antiques**
1781 N. Route 9
609/465-7189

**Quilted Gull**
1909 N. Route 9
609/624-1630

**Village Woodcrafter**
1843 N. Route 9
609/465-2197

## 17 CHESTER

**Chester Antique Center**
32 Grove St.
908/879-4331

**Beauty of Civilization Vintage Btq.**
30 Main St.
908/879-2044

**Delphinium's**
30 Main St.
908/879-8444

**Summerfields Antq. Furn. Warehouse**
44 Main St.
908/879-9020

**Pegasus Antiques**
98 Main St.
908/879-4792

**Marita Daniels Antiques**
127 Main St.
908/879-6488

**Black River Trading Co.**
15 Perry St.
908/879-6778

**Postage Stamp**
38 W. Main St.
908/879-4257

**Aunt Pittypat's Parlour**
57 E. Main St.
908/879-4253

**The Chester Carousel**
125 Main St.
980/879-7141

**Chester House**
294 E. Main St.
908/879-7856

**Spinning Wheel Antiques**
76 Main St.
908/879-6080

## 18 CLINTON

**Arts Resale**
Hwy. 31
908/735-4442

**Memories**
21 Main St.
908/730-9096

**Weathervane Antiques**
18 Main St.
908/730-0877

**Paddy-Wak Antiques**
19 Old High #22
908/735-9770

## 19 COLLINGSWOOD

**Ashwells Yesterdays Treasures**
738 Haddon Ave.
609/858-6659

**Collinswood Antiques**
812 Haddon Ave.
609/858-9700

**Unforgettables**
980 Haddon Ave.
609/858-4501

**Yesteryear Shop**
788 Haddon Ave.
609/854-1786

**Ellis Antiques**
817 Haddon Ave.
609/854-6346

## 20 CRANBURY

**Adams Brown Co.**
26 N. Main St.
609/655-8269

**Cranbury Collectibles**
60 N. Main St.
609/655-8568

**Cranbury Book Worm**
54 N. Main St.
609/655-1063

**David Wells Antiques**
60 N. Main St.
609/655-0085

## 21 CRANFORD

**Dovetails**
6 Eastman St.
908/709-1638

**Not Just Antiques**
218 South Ave. E.
908/276-3553

**Shirley Green's Antiques Ltd.**
8 Eastman St.
908/709-0066

**Nancy's Antiques**
7 Walnut Ave.
908/272-5056

**Cobweb Collectibles & Ephemera**
9 Walnut Ave.
908/272-5777

## 22 DENNISVILLE

### *Great Places To Stay*

### The Henry Ludlam Inn
1336 Route 47
609/861-5847
Open daily year round
*Directions: The inn is located on Route 47 in Dennisville. From Garden State Pkwy: Go south to the second Ocean City exit. Turn right onto Route 631 for about two miles. Turn left on Route 610 and follow the road to the end. Turn right on Route 47. The inn is about 1 1/2 miles on the right.*

This National Historic Registry entry claims more than 250 years of history! Two wings of the house were built at different times, between 1740 and 1804. This Federal-style house offers guests five rooms, all with private baths. It is filled with period antiques and the Federalist style in decor helps put guests into a historical frame of mind. The inn is located near many antique shops, museums, the Cape May Zoo and county historical sites.

## 23 DOVER

### Peddler's Shop
71 West Blackwell St.
973/361-0545
Fax: 973/366-4147
Wed. 2-7., Sat. 12-5, Sun. 9-5 or by appointment
*Directions: The Peddler's Shop is located between Hwy. 46 and Hwy. 10. Take Exit #35 off of I-80 and take Mt. Hope Ave. Cross Hwy. 46 and continue two blocks to Blackwell St. Turn right and the Peddler's Shop is approximately five blocks on the right.*

Since 1969 The Peddler's Shop has offered an unusual and rather distinctive array of items spread about its two floors of antiques. The shop is noted for its old lamps and lamp parts, furniture, glassware, dolls, trains, silver and books, and it has the largest watch fob collection in the east.

**At The Hop**
14 N. Morris St.
973/989-5225

**Sharp Shop**
34 W. Blackwell St.
973/366-2160

**The Iron Carriage Antique Center**
1 W. Blackwell St.
973/366-1440

**Corner Copia**
32 W. Blackwell St.
973/366-8999

# New Jersey

**Antiques Jungle**
12 W. Blackwell St.
973/537-0099

## 24 ENGLEWOOD

**Bizet Antiques & Unusual Finds**
6 S. Dean St.
201/568-5345

**Jewel Spiegel Galleries**
30 N. Dean St.
201/871-3577

**Chelsea Square Inc.**
10 Depot Square
201/568-5911

**Global Treasures**
120 Grand Ave.
201/569-5532

**Tony Art Gallery**
120 Grand Ave.
201/568-7271

**Portobello Road Antiques**
491 Grand Ave.
201/568-5559

**Antiques by Ophir Gallery**
12 E. Palisade Ave.
201/871-0424

**Crown House Antiques**
39 E. Palisade Ave.
201/894-8789

**Elvid Gallery**
41 E. Palisade Ave.
201/871-8747

**Royal Galleries Antiques**
66 E. Palisade Ave.
201/567-6354

**Rose Hill Auction Gallery**
35 S. Van Brunt St.
201/816-1940

## 25 FLEMINGTON

**Antiques Emporium**
32 Church St.
908/782-5077

**B & M Flemington Antiques**
24 Main St.
908/806-8841

**55 Main Antiques**
55 Main St.
908/788-2605

**Main St. Antique Center Inc.**
156 Main St.
908/788-8767

**International Show Case**
169 Main St.
908/782-6640

**Popkorn Antiques**
4 Mine St.
908/782-9631

**Furstover Antiques**
505 Stanton Station Rd.
908/782-3513

## 26 FRANKLIN

**The Munson Emporium**
33 Munsonhurst Road
973/827-0409

## 27 FRENCHTOWN

**Brooks Antiques**
24 Bridge St.
908/996-7161

**Jeanine-Louise Antiques**
8 Race St.
908/996-3520

**Frenchtown House of Antiques**
15 Race St.
908/996-2482

## 28 GARWOOD

**Classic Antiques**
225 North Ave.
908/233-7667

## 29 HACKETTSTOWN

**Family Attic Antiques Ltd.**
117 Main St.
908/852-1206

**Furnishings by Adam**
253 Main St.
908/852-4385

**Whispering Pines Antiques**
77 State Route 57
908/852-2587

**Main Street Bazaar**
128 Willow Grove St.
908/813-2966

## 30 HADDONFIELD

**General Store**
37 Ellis St.
609/428-3707

**Haddonfield Gallery**
1 Kings Court
609/429-7722

**Two in the Attic**
3 Kings Court
609/429-4035

**Adam's Antiques**
9 Kings Hwy. E.
609/770-1155

**Alice's Dolls**
9 Kings Hwy. E.
609/770-1155

**Haddonfield Antique Center**
9 Kings Hwy. E.
609/429-1929

**Owls Tale**
140 Kings Hwy. E.
609/795-8110

## 31 HIGHTSTOWN

**Olde Country Antiques**
346 Franklin St.
609/448-2670

**Empire Antiques**
278 Monmouth St.
609/585-1266

**Boat House Antiques**
161 E. Ward St.
609/448-2200

**Timekeeper**
York Road
609/448-0269

## 32 HOBOKEN

**Fat Cat Antiques**
57 Newark St.
201/222-5454

**Found in the Street**
86 Park Ave.
201/963-6494

**Sixth Street Antiques**
155 6th St.
201/656-5544

**Hoboken Antiques**
511 Washington St.
201/659-7329

**Erie Street Antiques**
533 Washington St.
201/656-3596

**House Wear Inc.**
628 Washington St.
201/659-6009

**Mission Postion**
1122 Washington St.
201/222-5001

**Little Cricket Antiques**
1200 Washington St.
201/222-6270

## 33 HO HO KUS

**Discovery Antiques**
618 N. Maple Ave.
201/444-9170

**Porreca & Chettle**
620 N. Maple Ave.
201/445-7883

**Camelot Home Furnishings**
9 N. Franklin Turnpike
201/444-5300

**Regal Antiques Ltd.**
181 S. Franklin Turnpike
201/447-5066

## 34 HOPEWELL

**H Clark Interiors**
31 W. Broad St.
609/466-0738

**Patsy's Antiques**
33 W. Broad St.
609/466-7720

**Ninotchka**
35 W. Broad St.
609/466-0556

**Antiques Etcetera**
47 W. Broad St.
609/466-0643

**Hopewell Antique Center**
Hamilton Ave.
609/466-2990

**Tomato Factory Antiques Center**
Hamilton Ave.
609/466-9860

**Your Aunt's Attic**
17 Seminary Ave.
609/466-0827

**Hopewell Antique Cottage**
8 Somerset St.
609/466-1810

## 35 JERSEY CITY

**Cliff's Clocks**
400 7th St.
201/798-7510

**L & L Antiques**
1170 Summit Ave.
201/656-6928

## 36 LAFAYETTE

**Mill Mercantile**
11 Meadows Road
973/579-1588

**Ivy Antiques**
Meadows Road
973/579-9602

**Silver Willow Inc.**
Meadows Road
973/383-5560

**Lafayette Mill Antique Center**
Route 15
973/383-6057

**Lamplighters of Lafayette**
156 State Route 15
973/383-5513

**Sweet Pea's**
12 Morris Farm Road
973/579-6338

## 37 LAMBERTVILLE

### Stoneman of the Delaware
Located inside Lambertville Antique Market
Route 29
609/397-0456
Wed.-Sun., 10-4
*Directions: Located 1 1/2 miles south of Lambertville on Route 29, River Road. Next to the Golden Nugget.*

Stoneman of the Delaware is located inside the Lambertville Antique Market. Specializing in Civil War, Revolutionary, Colonial, Victorian, Frontier through World War II and later; 1620-1960 historical collectibles, guns, parts, swords, bayonets, relics, coins, tokens, medals, arrowheads, marbles, old keys, jewelry, pottery, china, glassware and more. Don't Miss Museum Case #36.

Additionally, the market offers more than 100 showcases packed with all types of antiques and collectibles.

### Lambertville Antique and Auction Center
333 N. Main St.
609/397-9374
*Directions: From Philadelphia; Take I-95 N. into New Jersey. Exit at Route 29 North and follow 12 miles to Lambertville. Take a left at the light on Bridge St. Take the next right onto Main St. and follow one mile to 333 N. Main St. The building will be on the left.*

Year-round events including high-end arts and crafts, modern and general line auctions. Special events. Please call for information.

### Perrault-Rago Gallery
17 S. Main St.
609/397-1802
Tues.-Sun. 12-5 (usually), call to confirm
*Directions: From Philadelphia; Take I-95 N. into New Jersey. Exit at Route 29 N. and follow 12 miles to Lambertville. Take a left at the light on Bridge St. Take the next left onto S. Main St. and follow one block to 17 S. Main St. The building will be on the right.*

A memorable array of period furniture, decorative ceramics, metal, textiles and other accessories. Pottery, in particular, represents the finest "for sale" display in the country.

### David Rago Auctions, Inc.
333 N. Main St.
609/397-9374
Mon.-Fri. 9-5:30
*Directions: From Philadelphia; Take I-95 N. into New Jersey. Exit at Route 19 N. and follow 12 miles to Lambertville. Take a left at the light on Bridge St. Take the next right onto Main St. one mile. The building will be on the left.*

Specializing in 20th century Mission, Deco, and Postwar decorative arts and furnishings. Consignments wanted.

**Jim's Antiques Ltd.**
6 Bridge St.
609/397-7700

**Bridge St. Antiques**
15 Bridge St.
609/397-9890

**Karen & David Dutch's Antiques**
22 Bridge St.
609/397-2288

**Stefon's Antiques**
29 Bridge St.
609/397-8609

**Mill Crest Antiques**
72 Bridge St.
609/397-4700

**Fran Jay Antiques**
10 Church St.
609/397-1571

**Porkyard Antiques**
8 Coryell St.
609/397-2088

**Coryell St. Antiques**
51 Coryell St.
609/397-5700

**Lambertville's Center City Antiques**
11 Klines Court
609/397-9886

**Peter Wallace Ltd.**
5 Lambert Lane
609/397-4914

**Charles King Ltd.**
36 S Main St.
609/397-9733

**Golden Nugget Antique Flea Market**
State Hwy. #29
609/397-0811

**Prestige Antiques**
State Hwy. #29
609/397-2400

**JRJ Home**
7 N. Union St.
609/397-3800

**Yaroschuck Antiques**
10 N. Union St.
609/397-8886

**Artfull Eye**
12 N. Union St.
609/397-8115

**Lovrinic's Fine Period Antiques**
15 N. Union St.
609/397-8600

**Robin's Egg Gallery**
24 N. Union St.
609/397-9137

**The Second Floor**
29 N. Union St.
609/397-8618

**Miller-Topia Designers**
35 N. Union St.
609/397-9339

**Garden House Antiques**
39 N. Union St.
609/397-9797

**Kevin Sives Antiques**
43 N. Union St.
609/397-4212

**Meld**
53 N. Union St.
609/397-8487

**Olde English Pine**
202 N. Union St.
609/397-4978

**Best of France**
204 N. Union St.
609/397-9881

**Fox's Den**
7 N. Main St.
609/397-9881

### *Great Places To Stay*

**York Street House**
No. 42 York St.
609/397-3007
Web site: www.virtualcities.com
*Directions: Off I-95 exit 1 Route 29, Downtown Lambertville off Main St.*

This gracious 13-room Manor House situated on three quarters of an acre of land was built in 1909 by George Massey as a twenty-fifth wedding anniversary gift for his beloved wife. Massey was one of the early industrialists who settled his family in the historical river village of Lambertville just after the turn of the century. In 1911, the home was featured as *House and Garden* magazine's Home of the Year, with all the modern conveniences including a central vacuum that still stands in the cellar. In 1983, the home became a designer showcase.

Today the York Street House will comfort and surround you with its elegant and comfortable atmosphere. The heart of the inn features a winding three-story staircase leading to six gracious guestrooms, some with queen size canopy beds. From matching antique Waterford crystal sconces and chandelier in the sitting room, cut glass doorknobs on the second floor to the original tile and clawfoot master bath with its leaded stained glass window, the preservation of details will delight you at every turn.

A gourmet breakfast is served in the oak-trimmed dining room with its built in leaded glass china and large oak servers, looking out over the lawn and sitting porch. Feast your eyes on original art by Gilbert Bolitho, Jack B. Yeats, Rodriguez (Blue Dog), and Autorino.

The excitement starts two blocks away with antique shops, art galleries, bookstores and fine restaurants. Walk to New Hope, Pennsylvania with its artful atmosphere, theatre and gay clubs.

## 38 LEBANON

**Lebanon Antique Center**
U.S. Hwy. 22 E.
908/236-2851

## 39 LONG BRANCH

**Antiques & Accents**
55 Brighton Ave.
732/222-2274

**Hyspot Antiques & Collectibles**
61 Brighton Ave.
732/222-7880

**Take A Gander**
84 Brighton Ave.
732/229-7389

**Blue Cow Antiques**
194 Westwood Ave.
732/747-7738

## 40 LONG VALLEY

**German Valley Antiques**
6 E. Mill Road
980/876-9202

**Tavern Antiques**
5 Will Road
908/876-5854

## 41 MANAHAWKIN

**Manor House Shops**
160 N. Main St.
609/597-1122

**The Shoppes @ Rosewood**
182 N. Main St.
609/597-7331

**Cornucopia**
140 N. Main St.
609/978-0099

## 42 MAPLEWOOD

**Bee & Thistle Antiques**
89 Baker St.
973/763-3166

**Antiques by Greg Hawriluk**
48 Courter Ave.
973/378-9036

**Renaissance Consignment**
410 Ridgewood Road
973/761-7450

**Grey Swan**
411 Ridgewood Road
973/763-0660

## 43 MEDFORD

**Recollections**
6 N. Main St.
609/654-1515

**Spirit of 76**
49 N. Main St.
609/654-2850

**Regina's**
6 S. Main St.
609/654-2521

**Heather Furniture**
215 Medford Mount Holly
609/654-9506

**Toll House Antiques**
160 Old Marlton Pike
609/953-0005

**Yesterday & Today Shop**
668 Stokes Road
609/654-7786

## 44 MIDLAND PARK

**Brownstone Mill Antique Center**
11 Paterson Ave.
201/445-3074 or 201/612-9555
Wed.-Sat. 10:30-5, Tues. by appointment
*Directions: Take Route 4 West or Route 287 North to Route 208; exit Goffle Rd./Midland Park. Continue approximately 2 miles to the corner of Goffle Road/Paterson Ave.*

Features twenty unique shops under one roof.

**Tuc-D-Away Antiques**
229 Godwin Ave.
201/652-0730

**Time Will Tell**
644 Godwin Ave.
201/652-1025

**G F Warhol & Co.**
18 Goffle Road
201/612-1010

**Blue Barn**
60 Goffle Road
201/612-0227

## 45 MONTCLAIR

**Threadneedle Street**
195 Bellevue Ave.
973/783-1336

**Sablon Antiques**
411 Bloomfield Ave.
973/746-4397

**Americana Antiques**
411 Bloomfield Ave.
973/746-2605

**Past & Present Resale Shop**
416 Bloomfield Ave.
973/746-8871

**Gallery of Vintage**
504 Bloomfield Ave.
973/509-1201

**Ivory Bird Antiques**
555 Bloomfield Ave.
973/744-5225

**Antique Star**
627 Bloomfield Ave.
973/746-0070

**Buying Antiques**
629 Bloomfield Ave.
973/746-7331

**Milts Antiques**
662 Bloomfield Ave.
973/746-4445

**American Sampler Inc.**
26 Church St.
973/744-1474

**William Martin Antiques & Home**
41 Church St.
973/744-1149

**Garage Sale**
194 Claremont Ave.
973/783-0806

**Jackie's Antiques**
51 N. Fullerton Ave.
973/744-7972

**Earl Roberts Antiques & Interiors**
17 S. Fullerton Ave.
973/744-2232

**Noel's Place**
173 Glenridge Ave.
973/744-2156

**Station West Antiques**
225 Glenridge Ave.
973/744-9370

**Way We Were Antiques**
15 Midland Ave.
973/783-1111

## 46 MONTVALE

**Antique Mall**
30 Chestnut Ridge Road
201/391-3940

**Discovery Antiques**
30 Chestnut Ridge Road
201/391-9024

**Knox Gold Corp.**
30 Chestnut Ridge Road
201/930-0323

**Lost & Found Antiques Inc.**
30 Chestnut Ridge Road
201/391-0060

**Museum Shop**
30 Chestnut Ridge Road
201/573-8757

**Treasure Finders**
30 Chestnut Ridge Road
201/391-0006

## 47 MOORESTOWN

**Country Peddler Antiques**
111 Chester Ave.
609/235-0680

**George Wurtzel Antiques**
69 E. Main St.
609/234-9631

**Kingsway Antiques**
527 E. Main St.
609/234-7373

**Monique's Antiques**
400 Route 38 – Moorestown Mall
609/235-7407

**Her Own Place**
113 E. Main St.
609/234-2445

## 48 MORRISTOWN

**Associated Art**
31 Market St.
973/292-9203

**Morristown Antique Center**
45 Market St.
973/734-0900

**Marion Jaye Antiques**
990 Mount Kemble Ave.
973/425-0441

**Robert Fountain Inc.**
1107 Mount Kemble Ave.
973/425-8111

**Fearicks Antiques**
166 Ridgedale Ave.
973/984-3140

**Bayberry Antiques**
Route 202 (Harding Township)
973/425-0101

**Coletree Antiques & Interiors**
166 South St.
973/993-3011

## 49 MOUNT HOLLY/HAINSPORT

### Country Antique Center

1925 Route 38
609/261-1924
Email: ca1925@aol.com
Daily 10-5

*Directions: Traveling from I-295, take Exit #40 and travel east on Route 38 for 4.1 miles toward Mt. Holly. At the 8th light, take the jughandle to make a U-turn on Route 38. The shop's driveway is 50 feet from the U-turn on the westbound side of Route 38. Traveling the New Jersey Turnpike, take Exit #5/Mt. Holly. After the tolls, turn right onto Route 541 toward Mt. Holly. At the 4th light bear right onto the Route 541/Mt. Holly Bypass. Continue on the Bypass to the 3rd light (Route 38). Turn right onto Route 38 W. and go 3 lights. The shop's driveway is 50 feet from the 3rd light. Country Antique Center is just 30 miles from Philadelphia on Route 38.*

The Country Antique Center celebrated its 10th anniversary in March of this year. When the "co-op" first opened its doors on March 1, 1989, it offered the wares of 28 dealers. Now, with the connection of two separate buildings into one, they are represented by more than 100 dealers from Pennsylvania and New Jersey, offering only antiques and collectibles in 8,000 square feet of browsing room. The dealers specialize in primitives, jewelry, cut glass, Depression, Heisey and Clevenger glass; Roseville pottery, dolls, furniture, postcards and paper products.

**Carpet Baggers Doll Hospital**
Creek Road
609/234-5095

**Bills Bargains**
15 King St.
609-261-0096

**Center Stage Antiques**
41 King St.
609/261-0602

**Abode Antiques**
99 Washington St.
609/267-1717

**Ebenezer Antiques**
2245 Route 38 @ Creek Road
609/702-9447

**Fox Hill Antiques**
2123 Route 38
609/518-0200

**Rupp's Antiques**
2108 Route 38
609/267-4848

## 50 MOUNT LAUREL

**Collectors Express**
104 Berkshire Dr.
609/866-1693

**Creek Road Antique Centre Inc.**
123 Creek Road
609/778-8899

## 51 MULLICA HILL

The story of Mullica Hill began in the late 1600s, when English and Irish Quakers moved to the area and began establishing plantations. This Quaker community centered on the south bank of Raccoon Creek and was called Spicerville, in honor of Jacob Spicer, a prominent landowner. Originally only the north bank of the creek was known as Mullica Hill, and it was named after the town's pioneering Finnish settlers - Eric, John, Olag and William Mullica - who first purchased land here in 1704. Two of the homes the Mullica family built are still standing on North Main near the creek, nearly 300 years later!

Prior to the American Revolution, Mullica Hill was a coach town of little more than two scattered clusters of houses north and south of the creek, two taverns and a grist mill. Four of these structures still remain today. The town's first real period of growth began around 1780 and continued until the 1830s. Commercial development sprang up primarily in Spicerville (South Main) and four of the town's first churches were built here. Although a blacksmith shop, schoolhouse and one of the town's two taverns were on the north side, this neighborhood remained mostly agricultural. However, the entire village became known as Mullica Hill, probably because the hill itself was the most notable feature in the entire town. Many of the buildings from this era are still standing on Main Street today.

In the late 1800s a small mill district was established along the Raccoon Creek raceway. A woolen mill and an iron foundry operated here for several decades until fire and competition from larger industrial centers caused the area to decline drastically. Today only the 18th century gristmill remains - in a greatly altered state.

A second period of growth followed the Civil War and many noteworthy Victorian homes and public buildings were built throughout the entire village, including the town hall. Also, during this time Harrison Township established itself as one of the county's most productive agricultural areas. A railroad spur was built and very quickly the town became one of the nation's most active shipping points for agricultural commodities.

Throughout most of the 20th century Mullica Hill has served as the principal town and seat of government for Harrison Township, and its businesses catered to the needs of the surrounding farms. While agriculture today is still an important local industry, Mullica Hill's businesses are no longer so locally oriented. The town has emerged as a major antique and crafts center and is widely known for its nostalgic charm. Historic homes have been restored and the streets are now crowded with visitors from throughout the Eastern seaboard.

In 1991 the entire village of Mullica Hill was placed on the National Register of Historic Places and the New Jersey state Register of Historic Places. In 1992 Harrison Township established the village as a local historic district.

### The Warehouse

2 S. Main St.
609/478-4500
Wed.-Sun. 11-5

*Directions: From U.S. 95: Take Commodore Barry Bridge and 322 East to Mullica Hill. From the New Jersey Turnpike: Take Exit #2 then 322 East to Mullica Hill. From U.S. 295: Take Exit #11 then 322 East to Mullica Hill. The Warehouse is in the middle of town on Main St.*

This interesting, large, multi-dealer shop holds several divisions: an art gallery, jewelry store, candy store, furniture store, a large showcase shop, plus a cafe and tea room where you can recover when you realize that you've spent more than you should! And it's all packaged in a Civil War-era building.

**Raccoon's Tale**
6 High St.
609/478-4488

**Debra's Dolls**
20 N. Main St.
609/478-9778

**Elizabeth's of Mullica Hill**
32 N. Main St.
609/478-6510

**The Antique Center at Mullica Hill**
45 N. Main St.
609/478-4754

**Kings Row Antiques**
46 N. Main St.
609/478-4361

**The Queen's Inn Antiques**
48 N. Main St.
609/223-9433

**Murphy's Loft**
53 N. Main St.
609/478-4928

**Carriage House Antiques**
62 N. Main St.
609/478-4459

**The Country Christmas Shoppe**
86 N. Main St.
609/478-2250

**The Old Mill Antique Mall**
1 S. Main St.
609/478-9810

**The Front Porch**
21 S. Main St.
609/478-6556

**The Sign of Saint George**
30 S. Main St.
609/478-6101

**Dolls, Toys, and Free Museum**
34 S. Main St.
609/478-6137

**Wolf's Antiques**
36 S. Main St.
609/478-4992

**Deja Vu Antique & Gift Gallery**
38 S. Main St.
609/478-6351

**Antiquities at Mullica Hill**
43 S. Main St.
609/478-6773

**June Bug Antiques**
44 S. Main St.
609/478-2167

**Sugar & Spice Antiques**
45 S. Main St.
609/478-2622

**Clock Shop**
45 S. Main St. (Rear Shop)
609/478-6555

**Accesories**
46 S. Main St.
609/223-0100

**Lynne Antiques**
49 S. Main St.
609/223-9199

**Jane "D" Antiques**
50 S. Main St.
No Phone

**The Treasure Chest**
50 S. Main St.
609/468-4371

**Mullica Hill Art Glass**
53 S. Main St.
609/478-2552

## 52 NEW BRUNSWICK

**French Street Antiques**
108 French St.
732/545-9352

**Somewhere in Time**
115 French St.
732/247-3636

**Aaron Aardvark & Son**
119 French St.
732/246-1720

**Amber Lion Antiques**
365 George St.
732/214-9090

## 53 OCEAN CITY

**Joseph's Antiques**
908 Asbury Ave.
609/398-3855

**Curiosity Shoppe**
1119 Asbury Ave.
609/407-1251

**Sutton's Antiques**
1743 Asbury Ave.
609/399-0552

**Only Yesterday**
1108 Broadwalk
609/398-2869

**B's Fantasy**
11th St.
609/398-9302

## 54 OCEAN GROVE

### *Great Places To Stay*

### Cordova Hotel

26 Webb Ave.
732/774-3084 (in season); 212/751-9577 (winter)
Fax: 212/207-4720
Open May 15 through Sept. 30
*Directions: Take the Garden State Pkwy. to Exit #100 (from the south) or Exit #100B (from the north), then go 15 minutes on Route 33 E. to the end. Turn left for 100 feet then make an immediate right (Broadway) to the ocean. Turn left at the ocean and go to Webb. The inn is 1 1/2 blocks from the beach.*

This delightful century-old Victorian inn in historic Ocean Grove (National Register of Historical Places) has a friendly atmosphere with "Old World Charm." At the Cordova you feel like a member of an extended family as you chat with your hosts or other guests over breakfast. Quiet and family oriented, the Cordova was selected by *New Jersey Magazine* as "... one of the seven best places to stay on the Jersey Shore." Also featured in travel guide, *O'New Jersey* (1992). Full kitchen, living room, BBQ and picnic tables in a private garden are available for guests' use. Great for family gatherings!

Special weekday and 7-night rates, Saturday night wine and cheese parties, Murder Mystery Weekends, Comedy Night, Food Fests, annual Choir Festival (2000 voices), Tai Chi workshops, and work weekends (guests work/stay free) are especially popular. Call for details. The inn is near buses and trains.

# New Jersey

## 55 OLDWICK

**Magic Shop**
60 Main St.
908/439-2330

**Collections**
Route 523
908/439-3736

## 56 PHILLIPSBURG

**Gracys Manor**
1400 Belvidere Road
908/859-0928

**Harmony Barn**
2481 Belvidere Road
908/859-6159

**B & B Model A Ford Parts**
300 Firth St.
908/859-4856

**Lil's**
103 Foch Blvd.
908/454-3982

**Michael J Stasak Antiques**
376 River Road
908/454-6136

**Jensen Antiques**
State Hwy. #57
908/859-0240

## 57 POINT PLEASANT BEACH

**The Time Machine**
516 Arnold Ave.
732/295-9695

**Fond Memories Antiques**
625 Arnold Ave.
732/892-4149

**Wally's Follies Antiques**
626 Arnold Ave.
732/899-1840

**Classy Collectibles**
633 Arnold Ave.
732/714-0957

**Snow Goose**
641 Arnold Ave.
732/892-6929

**Clock Shop & Antiques**
726 Arnold Ave.
732/899-6200

**Feather Tree Antiques**
624 Bay Ave.
732/899-8891

**Company Store**
628 Bay Ave.
732/892-5353

**Antiques Etc.**
1225 Bay Ave.
732/295-9888

**Antique Emporium**
Bay Ave & Trenton
732/892-2222

**Ruddy Duck**
2034 Bridge Ave.
732/892-8893

**Shore Antique Center**
300 High #35
732/295-5771

**Bargain Outlet**
2104 Route 88
732/892-9007

**Willinger Enterprises Inc.**
626 Route 88
732/892-2217

## 58 POMPTON LAKES

**Charisma 7 Antiques**
212 Wanaque Ave.
973/839-7779

**P K's Treasures Ltd.**
229 Wanaque Ave.
973/835-5212

**Picker's Paradise**
269 Wanaque Ave.
973/616-9500

**Carrolls Antiques**
326 Wanaque Ave.
973/831-6186

**Sterling Antique Center**
222 Wanaque Dr.
973/616-8986

## 59 PRINCETON

**Gilded Lion**
4 Chambers St.
609/924-6350

**Girard Caron Interiors**
54 Constitution Hwy. W.
609/924-1007

**Eye For Art**
6 Spring St.
609/924-5277

**Tamara's Things**
4206 Quaker Bridge Road
609/452-1567

**Kingston Antiques**
4446 Route 27
609/924-0332

**East & West Chinese Antiques**
4451 Route 27
609/924-2743

## 60 RAHWAY

**Royal Treasures Antique Inc.**
69 E. Cherry St.
732/827-0409

**Tarnished Swan**
74 W. Cherry St.
732/499-7111

**Ken, Antiques**
1667 Irving St.
732/381-7306

## 61 RED BANK

**Copper Kettle Antiques**
15 Broad St.
732/741-8583

**Tower Hill Antiques & Design**
147 Broad St.
732/842-5551

**Tea & Vintage**
16 West St.
732/741-6676

**The Red Bank Antique Center**
195 W. Front St.
732/842-3393

**Antiques Associates**
205 W. Front St.
732/219-0377

**Gas Light Antiques**
212 W. Front St.
732/741-7323

**Monmouth Antiques Shoppes**
217 W. Front St.
732/842-7377

**Antique Gallery**
27 Monmouth St.
732/224-0033

**Two Broad Antiques**
160 Monmouth St.
732/224-0122

**Lone Arranger Outlet Store**
101 Shrewsbury Ave.
732/747-9238

**British Cottage Antiques**
126 Shrewsbury Ave.
732/530-0685

## 62 RIDGEWOOD

**Ridgewood Furniture Refinishing**
166 Chestnut St.
201/652-5566

**Irish Eyes Import**
1 Cottage Place
201/445-8585

**Marilyn of Monroe**
39 Godwin Ave.
201/447-3123

**Then and Now**
419 Goffle Road
201/670-7090

**Hahn's Antiques**
579 Goffle Road
201/251-9444

**Ivory Tower Inc.**
38 Oak St.
201/670-6191

## 63 SADDLE RIVER

**Carriage House Antiques**
7 Barnstable Court
201/327-2100

**Baldini Ricci Galleries Inc.**
24 Industrial Ave.
201/327-0890

**Richard Kyllo Antiques**
210 W. Saddle River Road
201/327-7343

## 64 SCOTCH PLAINS

**Antique Cottage**
1833 Front St.
908/322-2553

**Oakwood Furniture Co.**
1833 Front St.
908/322-3873

**Parse House Antiques**
1833 Front St.
908/322-9090

**Gallerie Ani' Tiques**
Stage House Village – Park & Front
908/322-4600

**Heritage Antiques Center**
364 Park Ave.
908/322-2311

**Seymour's Antiques & Collectibles**
1732 E. 2nd St.
908/322-1300

**Heinemeyers Collectibles & Antiques**
1380 Terrill Road
908/322-1788

## 65 SOMERVILLE

**Uptown Somerville Center**
Division St.
908/595-1294

**Somerville Center Antiques**
17 Division St.
908/526-3446

**Gallery**
30 Division St.
908/429-0370

**Incogneeto Neet-O-Rama**
19 W. Main St.
908/231-1887

**Country Seat Antiques**
41 W. Main St.
908/595-9556

## 66 SOUTH ORANGE

**Roberta Willner Antiques**
48 Crest Dr.
973/762-8844

**Aaltens Galleries Est. 1914**
461 Irvington Ave.
973/762-7200

**Carrie Topf Antiques**
50 W. South Orange Ave.
973/762-8773

## 67 SPRING LAKE

**Gallery III Antiques**
1720 State Hwy. #71
732/449-7560

**Spring Lake Antiques**
1201 3rd Ave.
732/449-3322

### *Great Places To Stay*

**Normandy Inn**
21 Tuttle Ave.
908/449-7172

The Normandy Inn was originally built as a summer home and rental property in 1888 by the Audenreid family of Philadelphia. This Italianate villa with Queen Anne modifications currently offers 17 guestrooms and 2 suites. Its present owners, Susan and Michael Ingino, have undertaken an extensive and authentic renovation of both the interior and the exterior of the house. Included in this renovation are colors used from the pallet of 'Century of Color' by Roger Moss.

**Victoria House**
214 Monmouth Ave.
1-888-249-6252
Web site: bbhost.com/victoriahouse

Victoria House is a Queen Anne style home built cc. 1882. The exterior has great vintage appeal with the original stained glass windows, Gothic shingles, gingerbread accents and perennial gardens. The guest parlor, filled with antiques of the Victorian era, invites you to explore the splendor of the past. Each of the nine beautifully appointed guestrooms portrays its own uniqueness with timeless antiques. Victoria House is just a short stroll to the lake, beach and village.

## 68 SUMMIT

**Plumquin Ltd.**
12 Beechwood Road
908/273-3425

**Summit Antiques Center Inc.**
511 Morris Ave.
908/273-9373

**The Second Hand**
519 Morris Ave.
908/273-6021

**Charming Home**
358 Springfield Ave.
908/598-1022

**Country House**
361 Springfield Ave.
908-277-3400

**Remmey's Consignment**
83 Summit Ave.
908/273-5055

**Antiques & Art by Conductor**
88 Summit Ave.
908/273-6893

## 69 TOMS RIVER

**Antique Outlet**
552 Lakehurst Road
732/286-7788

**Main St. Antique Center**
251 Main St.
732/349-5764

**Piggy Bank**
2018 Route 37 E.
732/506-6133

**Bulldog Glass Co.**
10 W. Gateway
732/349-2742

## 70 TRENTON

### Conti Antiques & Figurines

52 Route 33 (1 mile off I-295, Exit 64)
609/584-1080 or 609/586-4531
Mon.-Sat. usually 11-5; Sun. by appointment
*Directions: Located on State Hwy. 33 between Robbinsville (Route 130) and Trenton. Also, Exit 64 off I-295. Two miles from Trenton, 8 miles from Bordentown, 12 miles from Hightstown, 15 miles from Princeton. Call before coming!*

Richard Conti has been in business twenty two years, handling lots of smalls in his 1,400 square- foot shop. Most of his stock consists of furniture and figurines, which include Royal Doulton, Hummel, Boehm, Cybis, Ispanky, Precious Moments, Goebel and others. In addition to the shop and handling appraisals, Richard also holds auctions on an "as needed" basis.

**Greenwood Antiques**
1918 Greenwood Ave.
609/586-6887

**Armies of the Past Ltd.**
2038 Greenwood Ave.
609/890-0142

**Estate Galleries Ltd.**
1641 N. Olden Ave.
609/219-0300

**Canty Inc.**
1680 N. Olden Ave.
609/530-1832

**Antiques by Selmon**
10 Vetterlein Ave.
609/586-0777

## 71 WESTFIELD

**Betty Gallagher Antiques Inc.**
266 E. Broad St.
908/654-4222

**Westfield Antiques**
510 Central Ave.
908/232-3668

**Old Toy Shop**
759 Central Ave.
908/232-8388

**Linda Elmore Antiques**
395 Cumberland St.
908/233-5443

**Marylou's Memorabilia**
17 Elm St.
908/654-7277

**Back Room Antiques**
39 Elm St.
908/654-5777

**The Attic**
415 Westfield Ave.
908/233-1954

# New Mexico

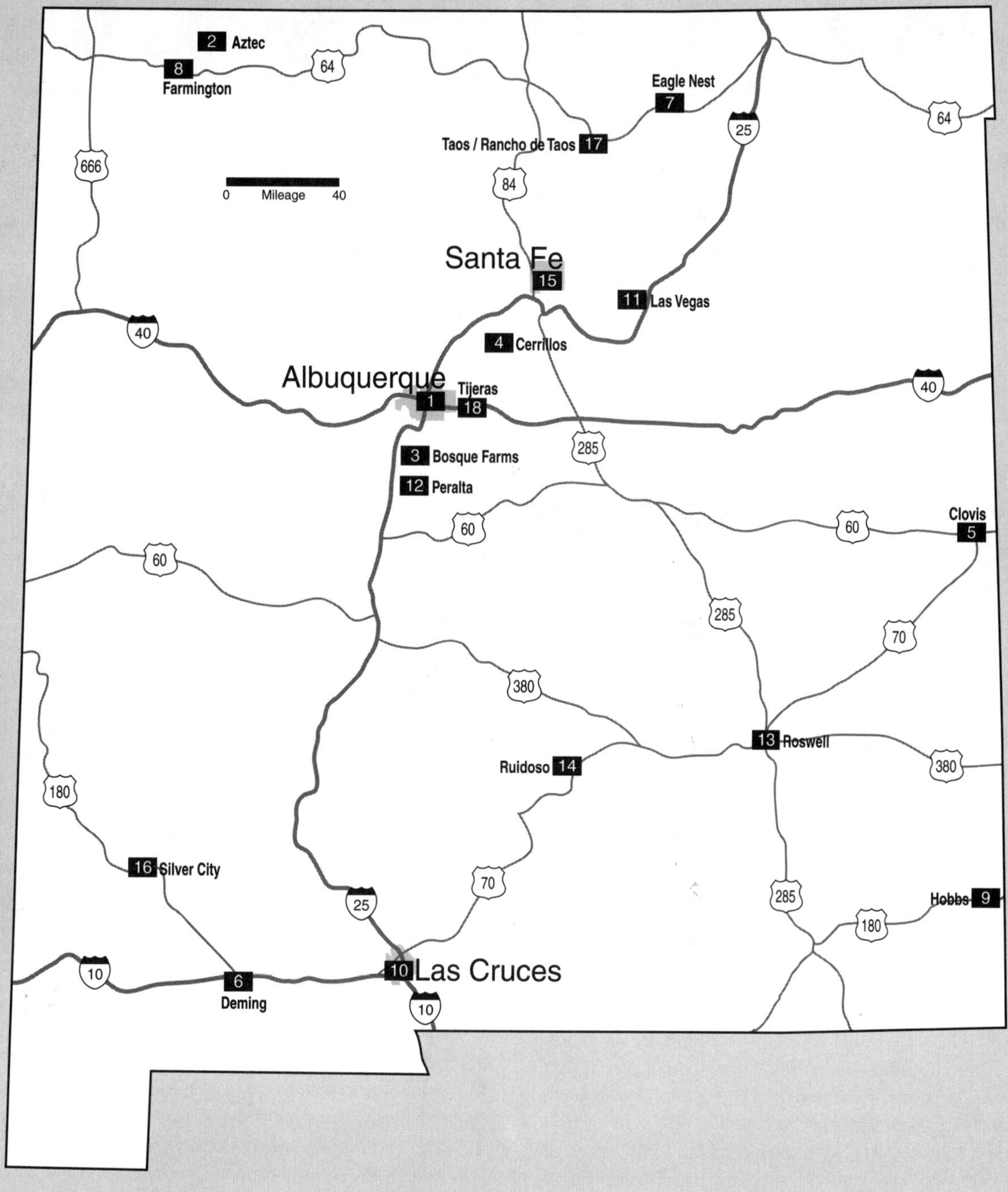

2 Aztec
8 Farmington
64
Eagle Nest
7
Taos / Rancho de Taos 17
25
666
0 Mileage 40
84
Santa Fe
15
11 Las Vegas
40
4 Cerrillos
Albuquerque
1
Tijeras
18
285
3 Bosque Farms
12 Peralta
60
Clovis
5
380
70
13 Roswell
Ruidoso 14
180
16 Silver City
Hobbs 9
10
6
Deming
10 Las Cruces

*Camp kitchen display includes vinyl-padded chairs and formica table, accompanied by an eggbeater, flour sifter and enamel-clad tin cookware.*

# In all New Mexico: Classic Century Square aims to be the biggest and the best

Classic Century Square is New Mexico's largest antiques and collectibles marketplace. With over 40,000 square feet of showroom space on three floors, one can only imagine the variety of treasures from which to choose. Filled to the rafters (literally), the mall has everything, music boxes, quilts and linens, glassware, pottery, advertising items, cast iron, framed prints and oils, war memorabilia, European dolls and Barbie dolls, fifties kitchen items, American Indian artifacts, furniture from every style and period, Star Wars collectibles and the list goes on and on.

An added draw to Classic Century Square has been the building's history and architectural features. Built in 1955 (art deco in design) the entire north side of the building is made of glass windows - shedding light on the spacious interior. In addition, the three story stairwell is a landmark in the Albuquerque area, as well as historical tidbits like the drums of sterile water stockpiled in the basement from the buildings days as a fallout shelter. A train museum located on the third floor is another popular attraction, especially for children.

Serious collectors often shop the market due to its outstanding inventory of "hot" collectibles. Decorators find it a good source for unique and interesting items not commonly found in other shops. Even set decorators for the movie industry, have found wonderful props at Classic Century Square. Marketing to the movie industry has generated interest and numerous inquiries over the years. One of their vendor's old trunks was purchased and tossed out of a window in a scene from *Billy the Kid*. With so much to look at, people can sometimes get overwhelmed, but the helpful and knowledgeable staff can quickly help folks find what they are looking for. "We stress service and pleasing the customer," says Bob Sloan. "There is something here for everyone. We know we are the biggest, but we also think we are the best."

*Jam-packed to the ceiling, this Century City Square case displays advertising memorabilia, lamps, scales, dolls, clocks, decorative ceramic ware and spoons.*

*Classic Century Square is located at 4616 Central Ave. S.E. in Albuquerque. See listing #1 for additional information.*

## 1 ALBUQUERQUE

### Classic Century Square
4616 Central Ave. S.E.
505/255-1850
Mon.-Sat. 10-6, Sun. 12-5; Closed Thanksgiving, Christmas and Easter
*Directions: West of San Mateo*

For specific information see review at the beginning of this section.

**Furniture on Consignment**
701 Candelaria Road N.E.
505/344-1275

**Antiques & Alike**
3904 Central Ave. S.E.
505/268-1882

**Cowboys & Indians Antiques**
4000 Central Ave. S.E.
505/255-4054

**Antiques on Central**
4009 Central Ave. N.E.
505/255-4800

**Ailene's & Donna's Antique Mall**
4710 Central Ave. S.E.
505/255-1850

**Anna's Grapevine Furniture**
5517 Central Ave. N.E.
505/268-3427

**Lawson's Antiques & Element Of Time**
2809 Chanate Ave. SW
505/877-0538

**Antique Manor**
1701 Eubank Blvd N.E.
505/299-0151

**Scottsdale Village Antiques**
3107 Eubank Blvd. N.E., Suite 7
505/271-1522

**Anglo American Antiques Ltd.**
2524 Vermont St. N.E.
505/298-7511

**Antiques Consortium**
7216 4th St. N.W.
505/897-7115

**Antiques & Treasures Inc.**
4803 Lomas Blvd. N.E.
505/268-6008

**Chatterelys Antiques & Natural Goods**
901 Rio Grande Blvd. N.W., D128
505/242-4430

**Old Oak Tree Antique Mall**
111 Cardenas Dr. N.E.
505/268-6965

**Dan's Place Antique Clocks**
3902 Central Ave. S.E.
505/268-1010

**Morningside Antiques**
4001 Central Ave. N.E.
505/268-0188

**Antique Specialty Mall**
4516 Central Ave. S.E.
505/268-8080

**Somewhere In Time**
5505 Central Ave. N.W.
505/836-8681

**Antique Connection**
12020 Central Ave. S.E.
505/296-2300

**Good Stuff The SW Antiques**
2108 Charlevoix N.W.
505/843-6416

**B's Antiques/Marie's Collectibles**
3107 Eubank Blvd. N.E., Suite 8
505/298-7205

**Consignment Interiors Etc.**
5850 Eubank Blvd. N.E.
505/293-0765

**Seddon's Rancho Chico Antiques**
6923 4th St. N.W.
505/344-5201

**Antique Co-op**
7601 4th St. N.W.
505/898-7354

**John Isaac Antiques Rio Grande**
2036 S. Plaza St. N.W.
505/842-6656

**Lawrence's**
4022 Rio Grande Blvd N.W., Suite D
505/344-5511

**Adobe Gallery**
413 Romero St. N.W.
505/243-8485

**Lindy's Ltd**
2035 12th St. N.W.
505/244-3320

**A Perfect Setting**
5901 Wyoming Blvd. N.E., Suite Y
505/821-7601

**Aah Such a Deal Antique Furniture**
7901 4th St. N.W.
505/898-1501

**Finders Keepers Antiques**
3902 Central Ave. S.E., #A
505/256-7684

**Granny's Attic**
4807 Lomas Blvd. N.E.
505/266-7607

**J & L Antiques & Gifts**
6305 Candelaria Road N.E.
505/884-2139

**Hanging Tree Gallery-Old Town**
416 Romero St. N.W.
505/842-1420

**Timeless Treasures**
2035 12th St. N.W.
505/891-8183

**White Dove Gallery**
2005 San Felipe Patio Market, #10
505/243-6901

**Eddie's Antique Shop**
119 Dartmouth Dr. S.E.
505/268-6153

**Gertrude Zachary's Antiques**
416 2nd St. S.W.
505/244-1320

**I-40 Antique Mall**
2035 12th St. N.W.
505/243-8011

**Route 66 Antique Connection**
12815 Central Ave. N.E.
505/296-2300

#### *Great Places To Stay*

### The Ranchette Bed and Breakfast
2329 Lakeview Road S.W.
505/877-5140 or 1-800-374-3230
Rates: $55-85
*Directions:Call ahead for specific directions from your locations.*

Just 15 minutes from historic old town Albuquerque, The Ranchette Bed and Breakfast seems a world away from the hustle and bustle of the city. With panoramic views of the Sandia and Manzano Mountains, the glorious Western sunsets, and the distant twinkle of the city lights, a sense of calm and beauty descends.

Whether you are lazing in the hot tub under the arbor, or riding the range on one of the majestic Arabian horses in residence, the atmosphere just naturally draws you in and calms you. If you like, you may bring and board your own horse. For those who prefer a more mechanical mode of transportation, walking and bicycle paths are adjacent to the property (bicycles are furnished by the Ranchette), but you'll have to bring your own Nikes!

Inside, all guest rooms are furnished with original art and antiques, writing desks, telephones, and terry robes. The living area offers a grand piano, a cozy fireplace and plenty of space to play games, plan the next day's activities, or just do nothing.

The food here is gourmet vegetarian fare, but if you have specific dietary needs, they'll be happy to accommodate you. They'll even provide picnic lunches or candlelight dinners upon request.

Whether you are on a family vacation or a romantic getaway, The

Ranchette Bed and Breakfast offers its own special brand of recreation and relaxation in a smoke-free and alcohol-free environment.

## 2 AZTEC

**Rocky Mountain Antiques**
107 S. Main St.
505/334-0004

**Downtown Antiques**
301 S. Main St.
505/334-5818

**Aztec Furniture Art & More**
201 E. Chaco
505/334-0033

## 3 BOSQUE FARMS

**Behind The Barn Antiques**
1435 Bosque Farms Blvd.
505/869-5212

## 4 CERRILLOS

### What-Not Shop Antiques
15 B First St.
505/471-2744
Daily 10-5

Situated on the Turquoise Trail and built in 1890 by Mr. Griffith, the shop offers Native American jewelry, rugs, pottery, jewelry, pocket watches and exquisite cut glass.

## 5 CLOVIS

### Marlene's Antiques & Gifts
1011 N. Norris St.
505/763-1396
Mon.-Fri. 9:30-5:30

Inside discover antique furniture, collectibles and a gift selection with limited edition collector items.

### Prairie Peddler Antiques
100 S. Main St.
505/763-7392
Mon.-Sat., 10-5

Housed in the 1931 former Raton Creamery, you'll find antique furniture, depression glass, primitives, Carnival, Roseville, elegant glassware, as well as cast iron pieces.

### Endless Trail
201 W. Grand Ave.
505/769-1839
Mon.-Fri., 10-5; Sat. 10-6

For the young-at-heart collector, check out the toys, Pez and magazines.

### Stitches of New Mexico—Antiques
927 N. Main St.
505/763-5018
Mon.-Fri., 10-5; Sat. 10-4

Inside Stitches of New Mexico, located in the Historic District of downtown, you'll find china, crystal, primitives, old books and records, RS Prussia, Carnival, cut glass, Depression glass, toys, linens, furniture, old pictures and wonderful tapestries.

**Furniture Corner**
123 W. Grand Ave.
505/762-1113

**Three Keys Antique Mall**
1709 Mabry Dr.
505/763-1740

## 6 DEMING

**Antique Bank of Deming**
122 E. Pine
505/544-4150

**Victorian Parlor**
105 S. Silver
505/546-2112

**Ox Yoke**
115 S. Silver
505/546-4077

**Historical Hotel Antiques**
124 S. Silver
505/544-7747

**Sanders Trading Post**
204 S. Gold
505/544-3482

## 7 EAGLE NEST

### Enchanted Circle Co., Antiques & Accommodations
124 E. Main St. (Hwy. 64)
505/377-3382
Daily 10-5 from May 15 to October 15. Call for winter hours.
*Directions: Traveling I-25 south from Raton, take Hwy. 64 W. through Cimarron to Eagle Nest.*

Located along The Enchanted Circle, a 100-mile scenic drive surrounding Wheeler Peak, Enchanted Circle offers antique shopping and overnight accommodations. Housed in the Main Street facility is the antique shop (the area's largest) specializing in china, silver, crystal, quilts, furniture and Southwestern artifacts. Apartments and suites on the second floor over the antique shop have antique furnishings and wood-burning stoves.

## 8 FARMINGTON

### Browsery
1605 E. 20th St.
505/325-4885
Mon.-Sat., 9:30-6

In business for 21 years, featuring furnishings such as antique wardrobes, chests, dressers, pianos and a full line of new Amish-made furniture.

**Antique Trove**
309 W. Main St.
505/324-0559

**Somewhere In Time**
115 W. Main St.
505/564-2711

**Dusty Attic**
111 W. Main St.
505/327-7696

**Sentimental Journey**
218 W. Main St.
505/326-6533

## 9 HOBBS

### Estelles Collectibles
3621 S. Eunice Hwy.
505/393-8633
Mon.-Sat., 9-5

This old house holds antique collectibles, furniture and primitives including irons, skillets, and churns.

### Antiques Unique
2420 N. Dal Paso St.
505/392-8527
Mon.-Fri., 8-5

An assortment of antiques including Depression glassware, pottery, primitives (such as irons, crocks, churns), crystal and some furniture will be found in this shop.

**Crafters Cottage & Antique Mall**
801 E. Bender Blvd.
505/397-4481

## 10 LAS CRUCES

**La Vieja**
2230 Avenida De Mesilla
505/526-7875

**Jones & Co. Jewelers**
1160 El Paseo St.
505/526-2809

**Main Street Antique Mall**
2301 S. Main St.
505/523-0047

**Things For Sale**
606 W. Picacho Ave.
505/526-7876

**S.O.B.'s Antiques**
928 W. Picacho Ave.
505/526-8624

**Coyote Traders**
1020 W. Picacho Ave.
505/523-1284

**Ross Bell Antiques**
1144 W. Picacho Ave.
505/523-2089

**High Class Junk Joint**
1150 W. Picacho Ave.
505/524-4314

## 11 LAS VEGAS

### Plaza Antiques
1805 On the Plaza
505/454-9447
Thurs.-Mon., 10-6; Sun. 12-4

Located on the historic Old Town Plaza, ten dealers display antique furniture, collectibles, primitives, glassware, pottery, vintage clothing and jewelry, western artifacts and much more.

**Virginia West-Antiques & More**
150 Bridge St.
505/454-8802

**Twentieth Century Store**
514 Douglas Ave.
505/425-3180

## 12 PERALTA

**Past & Present Treasures**
3617 Hwy. 47
505/869-4546

## 13 ROSWELL

### Monterey Antique Mall
1400 W. 2nd St.
505/623-3347
Daily 10-6

Ten-thousand square feet and thirteen dealers provide the gamut of antique items—jewelry, furniture, dolls, coins, plus much more.

**Byegones**
500 W. 2nd St.
505/622-1995

**Pedlar Way Upholstery & Antiques**
4506 W. 2nd St.
505/624-2521

## 14 RUIDOSO

### Camel House
714 Mechem Dr.
505/257-7479
Daily 9:30-5:30

Features Southwestern artifacts, antique beds, wagons, dressers, buffets, secretaries, pie and whiskey cabinets, tobacco cases, a wide selection of clocks, as well as bronzes. The shop offers Southwestern and Western artists including G. Harvey.

**House of Antiques**
2213 Sudderth Dr.
505/257-2839
Daily 10-5 except Tues. and Wed.

Victorian furniture, lamps, glassware and art glass are the specialties of this shop located in the walking tour section of midtown.

**Yesteryear Antiques**
122 N. Hwy. 7
505/378-4667

**Joyce's Junque**
650 Sudderth Dr.
505/257-7575

**Auntie Bo's**
2314 Sudderth Dr.
505/257-3683

## 15 SANTA FE

**Antique Warehouse**
530 S. Guadalupe
505/984-1159

**Scarlett's Antiques**
225 Canyon Road
505/983-7092

**Morning Star Gallery Ltd.**
513 Canyon Road
505/982-8187

**Kania-Ferrin Gallery**
662 Canyon Road
505/982-8767

**Architectural Antiques**
1117 Canyon Road
505/983-7607

**American Country Collection**
620 Cerrillos Road
505/984-0955

**Pegasus Antiques & Collectibles**
1372 Cerrillos Road
505/982-3333

**Doodlet's Shop**
120 Don Gaspar Ave.
505/983-3771

**Santa Kilim**
401 S. Guadalupe St.
505/986-0340

**Foreign Traders**
202 Galisteo St.
505/983-6441

**Foxglove Antiques**
260 Hyde Park Road
505/986-8285

**Pachamama**
223 Canyon Road
505/983-4020

**Casa Ana**
503 Canyon Road
505/989-1781

**Claiborne Gallery**
608 Canyon Road
505/982-8019

**Tiqua Gallery**
812 Canyon Road
505/984-8704

**The Bedroom**
304 Catron St.
505/984-0207

**La Puerta**
1302 Cerrillos Road
505/984-8164

**Stephen's A Consign Gallery**
2701 Cerrillos Road
505/471-0802

**Mary Corley Antiques**
215 N. Guadalupe St.
505/984-0863

**Rio Bravo**
411 S. Guadalupe St.
505/982-0230

**El Colectivo**
556 N. Guadalupe St.
505/820-7205

**In Home Furnishings**
132 E. Marcy St.
505/983-0808

**Peyton-Wright**
131 Nusbaum St.
505/989-9888

**Adams House**
211 Old Sante Fe Trail
505/982-5115

**James Reid Ltd.**
114 E. Palace Ave.
505/988-1147

**Susan Tarman Antiques & Fine Art**
923 Paseo De Peralta
505/983-2336

**El Paso Import Company**
418 Sandovol
505/982-5698

**Things Finer**
100 E. San Francisco St.
505/983-5552

**William R Talbot Fine Arts**
129 W. San Francisco St.
505/982-1559

**Canfield Gallery**
414 Canyon Road
505/988-4199

**Hampton Gallery**
236 Delgado
505/983-9635

**Henry C. Monahan**
526 Canyon Road
505/982-8750

**Reflection Gallery**
201 Canyon Road
505/995-9795

**Umbrello Showroom**
701 Canyon Road
550/984-8566

**Antiques on Grant**
126 Grant Ave.
505/995-9701

**American Country Collection**
620 Cerrillos Road
505/984-0955

**Arrowsmith's Relics of the Old West**
402 Old Santa Fe Trail
505/989-7663

**Wiseman & Gale & Duncan**
940 E. Palace Ave.
505/984-8544

**Hands of America**
401 E. Rodeo Road
505/983-5550

**Dewey Galleries Ltd.**
76 E. San Francisco St.
505/982-8632

**Vivian Wolfe Antiques**
112 W. San Francisco St.
505/982-7769

**Bizaare Bazaar Company**
137 W. Water St.
505/988-3999

**Economos Work of Art**
500 Canyon Road
505/982-6347

**Moondance Gallery**
707 Canyon Road
505/982-3421

**Ron Messick Fine Arts**
600 Canyon Road
505/983-9533

**Jane Smith**
550 Canyon Road
550/988-4775

**Nedra Matteucci Fenn Galleries**
1075 Paseo de Peralta
550/982-4631

### *Great Places To Stay*

**Guadalupe Inn**
604 Agua Fria St.
505/989-7422
Office hours: 8-9
Open year round
*Directions: From I-25, take St. Francis Dr. Exit and stay on St. Francis Dr. for 3.7 miles to Agua Fria Street. Turn right onto Agua Fria; proceed 3 blocks until the "604" sign then turn right.*

Pampered with family hospitality, enjoy a "truly Sante Fe" experience. Built on family property, the inn offers quiet, privacy and unique charm. Katchine, Hopi spirit dolls, enhance the local flavor of the decor. Fireplaces, patios and whirlpool tubs are available with some rooms. To the rear of the inn, a small garden makes a cozy nook for an outdoor breakfast.

**The Don Gaspar Compound**
623 Don Gaspar Ave.
505/986-8664
Open year round
Rates $85-220
*Directions: From east & south along I-25, take the Old Pecos Trail exit and go all of the way into town. Turn left on Paseo de Peralta, then left on Don Gaspar. The Compound is 1 1/2 blocks on the left. or from the north via 285, take St. Francis, turn left on Alameda and follow it to Don Gaspar. Turn right on Don Gaspar and go 4 1/2 blocks to the Compound.*

Built in 1912 in Santa Fe's Don Gaspar Historic District, the Compound is a classic example of Mission and Adobe architecture. Six private suites offer wood and gas-burning fireplaces (one is an adobe fireplace), saltillo and Mexican-tiled floors. Step into the secluded adobe-walled garden courtyard and relax to the trickle of the fountain while breathing in the scent of brilliant heirloom flowers.

## 16 SILVER CITY

**The Silver City Trading Co. Antique Mall**
205 W. Broadway
505/388-8989
Fax: 505/388-5263
Mon.-Sat., 10-6, Sun. 12-4
*Directions: From Lordsburg on I-10, take NM-90 north 42 miles. From Deming on I-10, take US-180 northwest 52 miles. From the north on I-25, you can take NM-152 south of Truth or Consequences, through Hillsboro, Kingston, and the Mimbres Mountains, joining US-180 eight miles east of Silver City (Inquire about road conditions in winter). The alternative is to take NM-26 from Hatch (the chile capital) to Deming and US-180. The antique mall is two blocks west of Hudson St. (NM-90) in Silver City's Historic District and near the campus of Western New Mexico University.*

The Silver City Trading Co. is housed in a 12,500 square foot building erected in 1897. The pressed tin ceilings testify to its longevity. Outstanding among the offerings of the 31 dealers are objects of art, utility and decoration associated with the Old West, as well as contemporary Native American craft production from both sides of the border. Other offerings include objects associated with mining, railroading, and ranching. Collectibles include coins, currency, dolls, toys, jewelry, vintage clothing, china, pottery, and glassware.

**Silver Creek Antiques**
614 N. Bullard St.
505/538-8705

## 17 TAOS/RANCHO DE TAOS

**Maison Faurie**
On The Plaza
505/758-8545

**Dwellings Revisited**
10 Bent St.
505/758-3377

**The Barn**
506 Kit Carson Road
505/758-7396

**Annabel's Strictly By Accident**
4153 State Road 68
505/751-7299

**P. Dunbar Antiques & Tribal Rugs**
222 Paseo Del Tueblo Norte
505/758-2511

**Horsefeathers, Etc.**
109 Kit Carson Road
505/758-7457

**Prints Old & Rare**
4155 State Road 68
505/751-4171

**Haciendo De San Francisco**
Saint Francis Plaza
505/758-0477

## 18 TIJERAS

**Another Place N Time**
Just South of I-40 on S S
505/281-1212

# New York

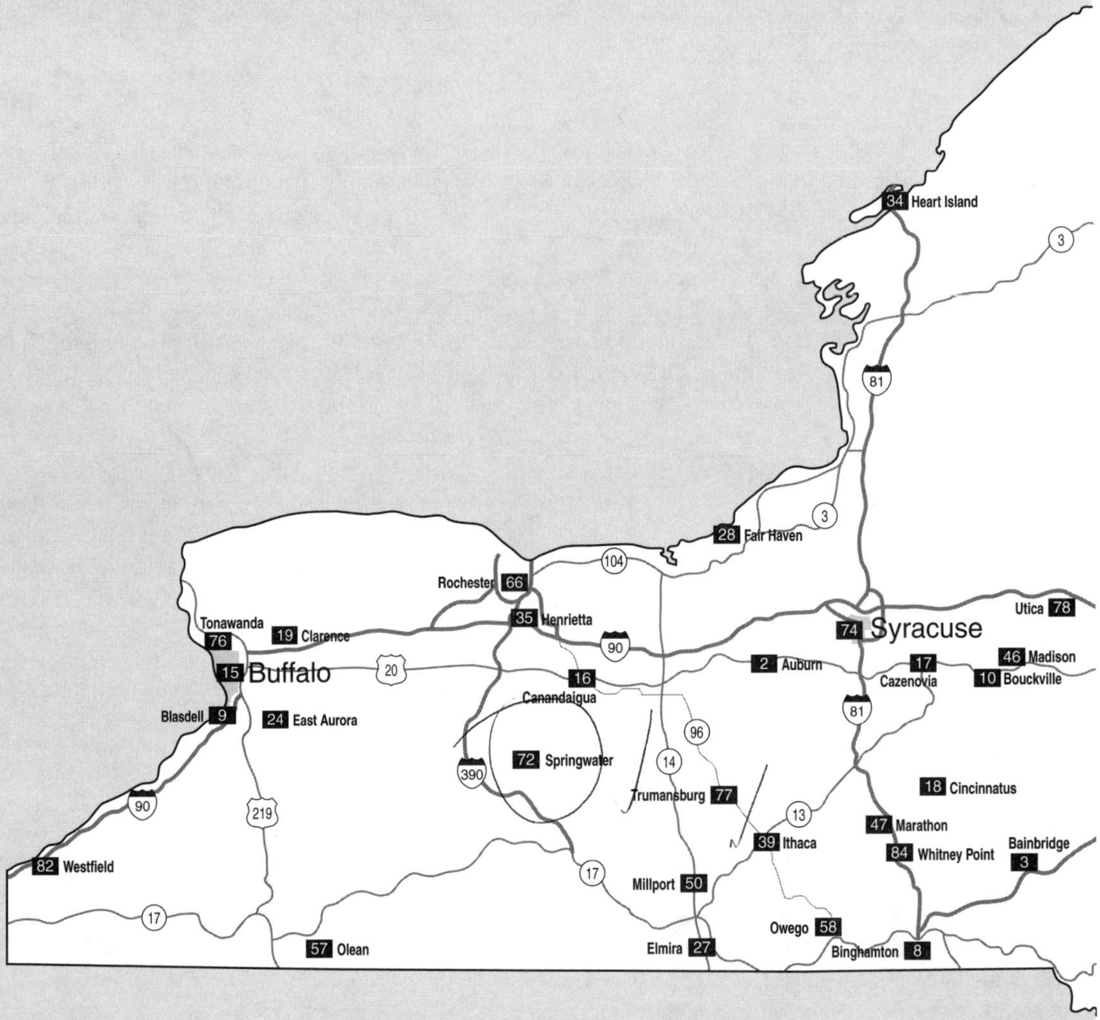
34 Heart Island
3
81
3
28 Fair Haven
104
Rochester 66
35 Henrietta
Utica 78
Tonawanda
76
19 Clarence
90
74 Syracuse
15 Buffalo
20
16
2 Auburn
17
46 Madison
Cazenovia
10 Bouckville
Canandaigua
81
Blasdell 9
24 East Aurora
96
72 Springwater
390
14
18 Cincinnatus
Trumansburg 77
90
219
13
47 Marathon
39 Ithaca
Bainbridge
84 Whitney Point
3
82 Westfield
17
Millport 50
17
Owego 58
57 Olean
Elmira 27
Binghamton 8

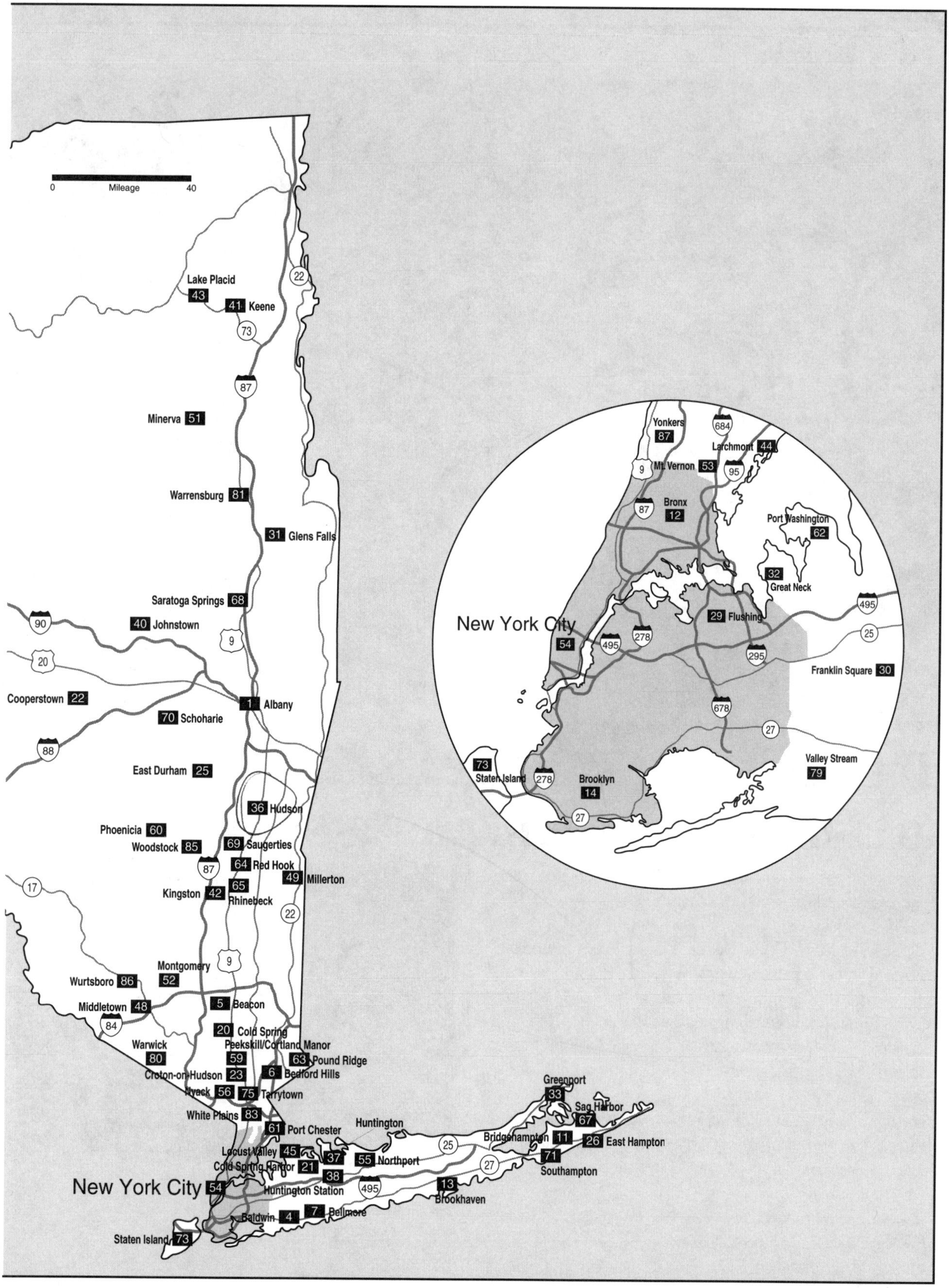
0 Mileage 40
Lake Placid 43
41 Keene
73
22
87
Minerva 51
Warrensburg 81
31 Glens Falls
Saratoga Springs 68
90
40 Johnstown
9
20
Cooperstown 22
1 Albany
70 Schoharie
88
East Durham 25
36 Hudson
Phoenicia 60
Woodstock 85
69 Saugerties
64 Red Hook
87
49 Millerton
17
Kingston 42
65 Rhinebeck
22
9
Montgomery 52
Wurtsboro 86
Middletown 48
84
5 Beacon
20 Cold Spring
Peekskill/Cortland Manor 59
Warwick 80
63 Pound Ridge
6 Bedford Hills
Croton-on-Hudson 23
Nyack 56
75 Tarrytown
White Plains 83
61 Port Chester
Huntington
Locust Valley 45
37
Cold Spring Harbor 21
55 Northport
38
Huntington Station
495
New York City 54
Baldwin 4
7 Bellmore
Staten Island 73
13 Brookhaven
25
27
Greenport 33
Sag Harbor 67
Bridgehampton 11
26 East Hampton
71 Southampton
Yonkers 87
684
Larchmont 44
9
Mt. Vernon 53
95
87
Bronx 12
Port Washington 62
32 Great Neck
495
New York City 54
29 Flushing
495
278
25
295
Franklin Square 30
678
27
73 Staten Island
278
Brooklyn 14
Valley Stream 79
27

*A full selection of vintage clothing is available in the shop, from the Victorian era to the 1970's you'll find garments to suit your fancy.*

# The Family Jewels Vintage Clothing Store caters to fashion designers, movie stars and you

Catering to men, women, and children, this store has been named "One of the best vintage stores in the United States" by *Vogue, In Style,* and *YM* magazines.

Filled with thousands of unique, one-of-a-kind antique wearables, the second floor shop embraces every area from the lacy Victorian to the bell-bottomed '70s. They carry a head-to-toe, inside-out selection from sexy lingerie to overcoats, even vintage fabrics and linens.

International design houses including Dolce and Gabbana, Georgio Armani, Ralph Lauren, and Adrienne Vittadini have shopped there looking for "inspiration" for their own designs.

Costume designers, wardrobe supervisors, and photographers have dressed the likes of Cindy Crawford, Uma Thurman, David Bowie, and Rosie O'Donnell from this smashing specialty store.

*Row upon row of vintage garments, from ladies' lacy unmentionables, ballgowns and hats to gentlemen's trousers and ties can be found here at The Family Jewels.*

*The Family Jewels Vintage Clothing Store is located at 832 Avenue of the Americas in New York City. See listing #54 (New York City) for additional information.*

## 1 ALBANY

**Vince Kendrick Jewelers**
475 Albany Shaker Road
518/438-6350

**Daybreak Antique Clothing**
22 Central Ave.
518/434-4312

**Zellers**
32 Central Ave.
518/463-8221

**Action Antiques & Used Furniture**
85 Central Ave.
518/463-0841

**S & S Antique & Used Furniture Co.**
85 Central Ave.
518/462-3952

**New Scotland Antiques**
240 Washington Ave.
518/463-1323

**Flamingo's 50s & 60s**
211 Lark St.
518/434-3829

**Pocket Change Antiques & Cllbls.**
4 Prospect Ave.
518/489-6413

**Yankee Peddler Thrift Shop**
265 Osborne Road
518/459-9353

## 2 AUBURN

**Ward's Antiques**
56 E. Gennesee St
315/252-7703

**Fingerlake's Antiques**
104 Grant Ave.
315/252-4934

**Roesch's Antiques & Collectibles**
7255 Grant Ave.
315/255-0760

**Auburn Trading Post**
24 McMaster St.
315/258-9492

**Auburn Antiques**
33 Walnut St.
315/252-9701

## 3 BAINBRIDGE

**Old Hickory Antique Center**
Route 7 at Gilford Road
607/967-4145

**Susquehanna Cafe & Antiques**
Route 7
607/967-4100

### *Great Places To Stay*

**Berry Hill Farms Bed and Breakfast**
242 Ward Loomis Road
607/967-8745 or 1-800-497-8745
Open all year
Gardens open from 8 a.m. to dusk
*Directions: From I-88, take Exit 8, Bainbridge. Go west on Route 206 for about 4 miles to West Bainbridge. Turn right on County Road 17 toward Oxford. Go 2.3 miles. Turn right on Ward-Loomis Road. Go 1/2 mile to the top of the hill.*

This secluded hilltop farm is surrounded by acres of woods and meadows. The 1820s farmhouse has been tastefully renovated, and is full of comfortable antiques. They have all the conveniences of home, and then some—flannel sheets, down comforters, extra pillows, fresh and dried flowers from the gardens and antiques everywhere.

The Berry Hill Farm gardens are already a local attraction. They are open to the public May to October. Combined with the spectacular view, you'll find them a "bit of heaven," "butterfly paradise," "food for the soul."

Guided tours are available to ensure you experience everything that Berry Hill has to offer. Altogether, there are hundreds of species of plants, so you will always find something in bloom, something to smell, and something to taste. Many of the flowers and plants are dried here on the farm to be used for herbal teas, cooking and for their dried flower business. Berry Hill Farms is conveniently located to many antique shops and auctions in the area.

## 4 BALDWIN

**Baldwin Antiques Centre**
906 Merrick Road
516/867-9842

**Arties Corner**
754 Sunrise Hwy.
516/867-4297

**Antique Quest**
87 Merrick Road
516/623-8351

## 5 BEACON

**Back in Time Antiques**
Located in Antiques and Uniques
346 Main St.
914/838-0623
914/737-8875

Back in Time Antiques features a nostalgic blend of antiques and collectibles, period furniture, unusual lamps, carnival and depression glass, books, Limoges, jewelry, marbles and much, much more.

The shop is located amongst 30 plus other antique, specialty and art shops on busy Main St.

**All That Jazz**
238 Main St.
914/838-0441

**Cold Spring Galleries Inc.**
324 Main St.
914/831-6800

**Dickinson's Antiques**
440 Main St.
914/838-1643

**East End Antiques**
444 Main St.
914/838-9030

**Early Everything**
470 Main St.
914/838-3014

**Beacon Hill Antiques**
474 Main St.
914/831-4577

**Tioronda Antiques**
15 Tioronda Ave.
914/831-3437

# New York

## 6 BEDFORD HILLS

**Raphael Gallery Paintings**
23 Depot Plaza
914/666-4780

**Bedford Salvage Co.**
2 Depot Plaza
914/666-4595

**Mark's Time**
132 Green Lane
914/242-0058

## 7 BELLMORE

**Antiques & Antiques**
111 Bedford Ave. N.
516/826-9839

**Austerns Antiques**
2970 Merrick Road
516/221-0098

**Ray's Antiques**
2962 Merrick Road
516/826-7129

## 8 BINGHAMTON

**Storekeeper**
95 Clinton St.
607/722-2431

**Clinton Mill Antique Center**
99 Clinton St.
607/773-2036

**Olde Breeze**
173 Clinton St.
607/724-2114

**Frog Alley**
300 Clinton St.
607/729-6133

**Interiors with Claudia**
310 Clinton St.
607/797-3200

**For Your Listening Pleasure**
368 Clinton St.
607/797-0066

**Mary Webster's Antique Frames**
12 Edwards
607/722-1483

**Buyers Unlimited**
140 Front St.
607/722-1725

**China Closet**
97 Clinton St.
607/724-3611

**Elysian Gems & Jewelry**
99 Clinton St.
607/724-0298

**Mad Hatter Antiques**
284 Clinton St.
607/729-6036

**Silver Fox Antiques**
304 Clinton St.
607/729-1342

**Rivers Twin Antiques**
352 Clinton St.
607/798-9395

**World Galleries**
591 Conklin Road
607/772-0900

**Antique Exchange**
22 Front St.
607/723-6921

**Bob Connelly & Sallie**
205 State St.
607/722-9593

## 9 BLASDELL

*Great Places To Stay*

**Morning Glory Bed & Breakfast**
45 Kent St.
716/824-8989

## 10 BOUCKVILLE

**Cobblestone Store**
Corner Route 20 & 46
315/893-7670

**By-Gones-Hinmans Motel**
Route 20
No Phone

**D & R Antiques**
Route 20
315/893-1801

**Gallery Co-Op**
Route 20
315/893-7752

**Jackie's Place**
Route 20
315/893-7457

**Stone Lodge Antiques**
Route 20
315/893-7270

**Bittersweet Bazaar**
Route 20
315/893-7229

**Bouckville Antique Corner**
Route 20
315/893-1828

**Depot Antiques**
Route 20
315/893-7676

**Elvira Stanton Antiques**
Route 20
315/893-7479

**Indian Opening Antique Center**
Route 20
315/893-7303

**Station House Antiques**
Route 20
315/893-7652

**Veranda Antiques & Art**
Route 20 & 12 B
315/893-7270

## 11 BRIDGEHAMPTON

**Beach Plum Antiques**
Main St.
516/537-7403

**Country Gear Ltd**
Main St.
516/537-1032

**John Salibello Antiques**
Montauk Hwy.
516/537-1484

**Legendary Collections**
Montauk Hwy.
516/537-2211

**English Country Antiques**
Snake Hollow Road
516/537-0606

**Inez G. MacWhinnie**
Main St.
516/537-7433

**House of Charm Antiques**
Montauk Hwy.
516/537-3335

**Kinnaman & Ramaekers**
2466 Montauk Hwy.
516/537-3838

**Urban Archeology**
Montauk Hwy.
516/537-0124

**Ruby Beets Antiques**
1703 Montauk Hwy.
516/537-2802

## 12 BRONX

**All Boro Estate Liquidators**
45 Bruckner Blvd.
718/402-8777

**Big Apple Antiques Inc.**
430 E. 188th St.
718/220-4018

**T & I Thrift World**
3980 White Plains Road
718/519-6724

**Larry's Antiques**
2419 Eastchester Road
718/779-2304

**F & J Furniture**
1007 Tiffany St.
718/378-2038

## 13 BROOKHAVEN

**Brook Store**
378 S. Country Road
516/286-8503

**Delancy St. East**
2527 Montauk Hwy.
516/286-2956

## 14 BROOKLYN

**Horseman Antiques Inc.**
351 Atlantic Ave.
718/596-1048

**In Days of Old Limited**
357 Atlantic Ave.
718/858-4233

**Atlantic Antique Center**
367 Atlantic Ave.
718/488-0149

**Circa Antiques Ltd.**
377 Atlantic Ave.
718/596-1866

**A Matter of Time**
380 Atlantic Ave.
718/624-7867

**Antiques and Collectibles Shop**
483 Atlantic Ave.
718/858-6903

**Easy Furniture Inc.**
871 Broadway
718/574-6400

**Aaa-Abbey Merchandising Co. Inc.**
618 Coney Island Ave.
718/253-8830

**Antiques Plus**
744 Coney Island Ave.
718/941-8805

**Smitty's New & Used Furniture**
744 Coney Island Ave.
718/854-3052

**Town & Country Antiques**
352 Atlantic Ave.
718/875-7253

**City Barn Antiques**
362 Atlantic Ave.
718/855-8566

**Time Trader**
368 Atlantic Ave.
718/852-3301

**Times & Moments**
378 Atlantic Ave.
718/625-3145

**Assaf Antiques**
383 Atlantic Ave.
718/237-2912

**Antiques by Ruth**
507 Atlantic Ave.
718/382-3269

**Broadway Top Class Furniture**
1275 Broadway
718/452-1100

**Scottie's Gallery**
624 Coney Island Ave.
718/851-8325

**Bernstein's**
744 Coney Island Ave.
718/342-3564

**Tyler Antiques**
744 Coney Island Ave.
718/331-1533

**All Boro Furniture**
779 Coney Island Ave.
718/272-0559

**Northeast Furniture & Antiques**
779 Coney Island Ave.
718/272-4133

**Finders Keepers Antiques & Tag**
784 Coney Island Ave.
718/941-4481

**Yava Furniture**
832 Coney Island Ave.
718/693-3322

**Roy Electric Antique Light Co.**
1054 Coney Island Ave.
718/434-7002

**Astor Antiques**
1067 Coney Island Ave.
718/434-9200

**Attic**
220 Court St.
718/643-9535

**New You Zd**
1211 Flatbush Ave.
718/856-4819

**Bibilo Furniture Store**
502 5th Ave.
718/832-6696

**Colonial Global Inc.**
6823 5th Ave.
718/748-4401

**Antiques & Decorations**
4319 14th Ave.
718/633-6393

**Park Hill Restoration**
375 Atlantic Ave.
718/624-0233

**Mel's Antique**
99 Smith St.
718/834-8700

**Grand Sterling Silver Co. Inc.**
4921 13th Ave.
718/854-0623

**Top Cash Antiques**
2065 E. 33rd St.
718/382-4418

**Frank Galdi Antiques**
247 Warren St.
718/875-9293

**C P Galleries**
779 Coney Island Ave.
718/462-3606

**Flatbush Galleries**
779 Coney Island Ave.
718/287-8353

**Sciarrino Antiques**
830 Coney Island Ave.
718/462-8134

**Once Upon A Time Antiques**
1053 Coney Island Ave.
718/859-6295

**Abbey Galleries**
1061 Coney Island Ave.
718/692-2421

**Charlotte's Nik Nak Nook Antiques**
1131 Coney Island Ave.
718/252-0088

**Action Furniture**
1171 Flatbush Ave.
718/284-2899

**People's Furniture**
1332 Flatbush Ave.
718/859-6850

**Juke Box Class & Vintage Slot**
6742 5th Ave.
718/833-8455

**Abboco**
8323 5th Ave.
718/238-6956

**South Portland Antiques**
753 Fulton
718/596-1556

**Gaslight Time Antiques**
5 Plaza St. W.
718/789-7185

**Ace New & Used Furniture**
575 Sutter Ave.
718/495-5711

**Discoveries**
8407 3rd Ave.
718/836-0583

**Dream Land Antiques**
619 Vanderbilt Ave.
718/230-9142

**Christmas Carol's**
492 Macon St.
718/919-9033

## 15 BUFFALO

**Bailey's Furniture**
3191 Bailey Ave.
716/835-6171

**Horsefeathers Architectural Antiques**
346 Connecticut St.
716/882-1581

**C Markarian & Sons Inc.**
3807 Delaware Ave.
716/873-8667

**Eaton Galleries**
115 Elmwood Ave.
716/882-7823

**Assets Antiques**
140 Elmwood Ave.
716/882-2415

**Source**
152 Elmwood Ave.
716/883-2858

**Lots of Stuff**
2703 Elmwood Ave.
716/874-1164

**American Militaria Collector**
2409 Harlem Road
716/891-5200

**Conley Interiors Inc.**
1425 Hertel Ave.
716/838-1000

**Coo Coo U**
1478 Hertel Ave.
716/837-3385

**A To Z Auction**
2150 William St.
716/896-3342

**Antiques Americana**
5600 Main St.
716/633-2570

**Erie West Antiques & Collectibles**
10 Michael Road
716/677-2119

**Antique Architectural Circus**
855 Niagra
716/885-5555

**Gallery of Treasures**
2180 Seneca St.
716/826-3907

**Scotty's Furniture**
3112 Bailey Ave.
716/835-6199

**Tres Beau Interiors**
489 Delaware Ave.
716/886-3514

**Lete Antiques-Carl Stone**
65 Elmwood Ave.
716/884-0211

**Taylor Gallery**
125 Elmwood Ave.
716/881-0120

**Jeffrey Thier Antiques**
152 Elmwood Ave.
716/883-2858

**MIX**
711 Elmwood Ave.
716/886-0141

**Dana E Tillou Gallery**
417 Franklin St.
716/854-5285

**Stock Exchange**
1421 Hertel Ave.
716/838-8294

**Just Browsin**
1439 Hertel Ave.
716/837-1840

**Melange Vintage Clothing**
1484 Hertel Ave.
716/838-9290

**Antique Architectural Circus**
86 Vermont St.
716/885-5555

**Jean's Creekview Antiques**
5629 Main St.
716/632-2711

**Attic Antiques & Collectibles**
550 Mineral Springs Road
716/822-0627

**Antique Jewelry Trojners**
296 Roycroft Blvd.
716/839-5453

### *Great Places To Stay*

**Beau Fleuve Bed & Breakfast Inn**
242 Linwood Ave.
1-800-278-0245

A grand, Stick-style Queen Anne Victorian in Buffalo's Linwood historic preservation district, the Beau Fleuve offers five tastefully-decorated guest rooms featuring antique and heirloom beds, down bedding, and decorator linens. A unique hand-crafted staircase and nine colorful stained glass windows reflect the Aesthetic Movement. Its signature motif, the sunflower, appears in the house in both wood carvings and art glass. The restored exterior is painted in authenic Aesthetic Movement colors. Continental or full breakfast by candlelight. House specialties include blueberry or raspberry pancakes, Belgian waffles, eggs benedict, french toast, or several varities of fritada.

## 16 CANANDAIGUA

**Richard Cuddeback**
22 Leeward Lane
716/394-4097

**Nostalgia Ltd.**
238 S. Main St.
716/396-9898

**Antiques Unlimited**
168 Niagara St.
716/394-7255

**Tall Pines Antiques**
3257 Route 5
716/394-7230

**Happy Clutter Antiques**
3735 State Route 5
716/394-4199

**Petticoat Junction Antiques**
103 Leicester St.
716/396-0691

**Kipling's Treasures**
116 S. Main St.
716/396-7270

**Harvest Mill**
40 Parrish St.
716/394-5907

**Antique Center-30 Dealers**
47 Saltonstall St.
716/394-2297

### *Great Places To Stay*

**Sutherland House Bed & Breakfast**
3179 State Route 21S
1-800-396-0375
Web site: www.sutherlandhouse.com

Sutherland House is an 1885 renovated Victorian centered on five private acres of quiet and solitude, surrounded by rolling farmland and mature trees. Don't forget to take a peek in the scrapbook that documents the transformation from haunted house to bed and breakfast.

## 17 CAZENOVIA

**Sallys Cellar**
58 Albany St.
315/655-3324

**Amanda Bury**
97 Albany St., Route 20
315/655-3326

**Old Everlasting Antiques**
1826 Ballina Road
315/655-3212

**Alexandra's Attic**
4010 Erieville Road
315/655-2146

**The Old Lamplighter Antiques**
3951 Number Nine Road
315/655-4991

**Web's Country House**
4031 Putnam Road
315/655-4177

## 18 CINCINNATUS

### *Great Places To Stay*

**Alice's Dowry B&B**
2789 Route 26
607/863-3934
Web site: www.bbonline.com/ny/alicesdowry/

This beautifully restored Italianate Victorian offers two guest rooms with antique decor. In season, the $1^1/_2$ acres provides the space to stroll and relax amongst the gardens or sit on the 'Painted Lady' Veranda in a wicker rocker. Full breakfasts, served on the sun porch at tables for two.

## 19 CLARENCE

**Christner's Antiques**
10715 Clarence Center Road
716/741-2826

**VI & Sis Antiques**
8970 Main St.
716/634-4488

**Antiques at the Barn**
9060 Main St.
716/632-6674

**Ruth's Antiques Inc.**
9060 Main St.
716/741-8001

**Uncle Sam's Antiques**
9060 Main St.
716/741-8838

**Charles M. Fisher**
10255 Main St.
716/759-6433

**Kelly Schultz Antiques & Oriental**
10225 Main St.
716/759-2260

**Up Your Attic Vintage Clothing**
10255 Main St.
716/759-2866

**Baumer Antiques**
10548 Main St.
716/759-6468

**Muleskinner Antiques**
10626 Main St.
716/759-2661

**Antique Emporium**
10225 Main St.
716/759-0718

**Clarence Hollow Antiques**
10863 Main St.
716/759-7878

**Antique Parlor**
10874 Main St.
716/759-2048

**Antique World & Market Place**
10995 Main St.
716/759-8483

**Clarence Antiques Co-op**
11079 Main St.
716/759-7080

**Kellys Antique Market**
11111 Main St.
716/759-7488

## 20 COLD SPRING

**Basso Brokerage Antiques**
12 Division St.
914/265-9650

**38 Main**
38 Main St.
914/265-3838

**As Time Goes By**
72 Main St.
914/265-7988

**Tin Man**
75 Main St.
914/265-2903

**Jacquie Antiques**
89 Main St.
914/265-7883

**Sarabeck Antiques**
91 Main St.
914/265-4414

**Once Upon a Time Antiques**
101 Main St.
914/265-4339

**Taca-Tiques**
109 Main St.
914/265-2655

**Others Oldies**
169 Main St.
914/265-2323

**Ground Zero Antiques Inc.**
290 Main St.
914/265-5275

**Dew Drop Inn Antique Center**
Route 9
914/265-4358

**Rick Lawler Antiques**
168 Route 9
914/265-2231

## 21 COLD SPRING HARBOR

**M. Nash & Company Inc.**
7 Main St.
516/692-7777

**Huntington Antique Cntr.**
129 Main St.
516/692-7777

**Candle Wycke Antiques Ltd.**
147 Main St.
516/692-3106

**Lyman Thorne Enterprises Ltd.**
169 Main St.
516/692-2834

**Arlene Coroaan Antiques**
7 Main St.
516/692-7777

## 22 COOPERSTOWN

The charming village of Cooperstown sits at the foot of Lake Otsego in the heart of the area made famous by author James Fenimore Cooper (1789-1851). The streets are lined with Victorian homes and storefronts decorated with hanging baskets and window boxes. The Fenimore House Museum includes the works of famed 19th and 20th century artists along with displays of Cooper memorabilia. Nearby, the Farmer's Museum, a living history center, recreates a 19th century village. This is the setting for one of the nation's premier sports shrines—the National Baseball Hall of Fame.

This red brick facility traces its beginnings back to a discovery in a dust-covered attic near Cooperstown. Here was found an undersized, misshapen, homemade ball stuffed with cloth, believed to be the baseball used by Abner Doubleday in the first game. The baseball was purchased by Cooperstown resident Stephen C. Clark, who conceived the idea of displaying it along with other baseball objects. The one-room exhibition attracted such public interest that plans for a national museum were drawn up, and the official National Baseball Hall of Fame was officially opened in 1939 to commemorate the game's 100th anniversary.

**Cooperstown Antique Center**
73 Chestnut St.
607/547-2435

General line of furniture and specializing in restored electrical lighting.

***Great Places To Stay***

**Brown-Williams House**
RR 1, Box 337
607/547-5569

Beautiful (c. 1825) Federal style inn, located 1½ miles from Cooperstown, offers guests charm and tranquility with the complete privacy of a 'true country gentleman's estate'. Immaculately kept, renovated by its owner to period Federal-Shaker style, the home offers a warm ambiance in this wood post and beam home. Its generous center hall, great room and dining rooms all have beautiful hand-painted wall furnishings and stenciling.

**Nineteen Church Street Bed & Breakfast**
19 Church St.
607/547-8384

This country home is located on a quiet street in the heart of Copperstown. Built circa 1829, the bed and breakfast features stenciled floors and Trompe L'oeuil paintings. The Baseball Hall of Fame back door is directly across the street. An easy walk to shopping and fishing, minutes by car or trolley to all Cooperstown attractions, including Fenimore House, Farmers' Museum, golf, Opera House, antiquing and horseback riding.

## 23 CROTON-ON-HUDSON

***Great Places To Stay***

**Alexander Hamilton House**
49 Van Wyck St.
914/271-6737
Fax: 914/271-3927
*Directions: From Route. 9, exit at Route. 129. Go east to light at Riverside Ave. Turn left onto Riverside for 1 block. Turn right on Grand St. Go 1 block. Turn left onto Hamilton which interesects Van Wyck right in front of #49. Go down the drive into the parking lot. Climb the porch steps and ring the bell.*

Westchester's first bed and breakfast, the Alexander Hamilton House, Circa 1889, is a stately Victorian home nestled on a cliff above the river, a short walk to the picturesque village of Croton-on-Hudson River Valley.

**Note: The Bridal Chamber at the Alexander Hamilton House was rated 4 Kisses in New York's Best Places to Kiss '92 & '94. Do you think five skylights, a king-sized bed, a Jacuzzi and a fireplace had anything to do with setting the mood?*

## 24 EAST AURORA

**Fire House Antiques**
82 Elm St.
716/655-1035

**Roycroft Campus Antiques**
37 S. Grove St.
716/655-1565

**Barn Shoppe**
368 Mills Road
716/652-1099

## 25 EAST DURHAM

***Great Places To Stay***

**Carriage House Bed & Breakfast**
Box 12A, Route 145
518/634-2284

This small, family owned and operated business, is located in the lower Catskill Mountains, with access to a host of nearby attractions, including five golf courses, a water park, horseback riding, mountain summer festivals, as well as Howes Caverns and Copperstown.

## 26 EAST HAMPTON

**Architrove, Inc.**
74 Montauk Hwy., #3
516/329-229
Fax: 516/309-1155
Daily 9-5, except Tues. & Wed. (Call for appointment on those days)
*Directions: Go 2 miles east of Wainslott on Route 27 (Montauk Hwy.) to the Red Horse Shopping Plaza.*

This tasteful, upscale establishment offers the discriminating buyer the best in antique lighting fixtures, chandeliers, and sconces.

**Christina Borg Inc.**
41 Main St.
516/324-6997

**Circle Antiques**
46 Main St.
516/324-0771

**Home James**
55 Main St.
516/324-2307

**Victory Gardens Ltd.**
63 Main St.
516/324-7800

**The Grand Alquistor**
110 N. Main St.
516/324-7272

**Antique Center of East Hampton**
251 Montauk Hwy.
516/324-9510

**Lars Bolander Antiques & Accessories**
5 Toilsome Lane
516/329-3400

**Pantigo House**
251 Pantigo Road
516/329-2831

**Country Green Antiques**
30 Race Lane
516/324-2756

**Maidstone Antiques**
512 Three Mile
516/329-7508

**Elaine's Room**
251 Partigo Road
516/324-4734

**Basil**
34 Park Place
516/324-4734

### *Great Places To Stay*

**East Hampton Point**
P. O. Box 847
516/324-9191

Whether you arrive on your own boat and anchor in the beautiful marina or stay the weekend in one of the exquisitely designed country cottages or come to dine at the fabulous new indoor-outdoor restaurant, you'll experience East Hampton at its most romantic. The spacious one-bedroom and two-bedroom cottages are each individually decorated in a charming country manner with a large living/dining room complete with modern kitchen.

## 27 ELMIRA

**AAAAAA Antiques By Proper**
33 Brookline Ave.
607/734-0153

**Maple Avenue Antiques**
352 Maple Ave.
607/734-0332

**Mark Twain Country Antiques**
400 Maple Ave.
607/734-0916

**A Touch of Country House Shops**
1019 Pennsylvania Ave.
607/737-6945

**Michael Watts Antiques**
558 Riverside Ave.
607/733-9126

**Sturdivant Gallery**
912 Southport St.
607/733-1903

## 28 FAIRHAVEN

### *Great Places To Stay*

**Black Creek Farm**
Mixer Road
315/947-5282
Fax: 315/947-5282
Hours: Bed and Breakfast open all year
Antique shop open weekends, 11-5, May 1-Sep. 15
*Directions: From New York State Route 104, turn north on Route 104 A. Go approximately 6 miles to Mixer Road, and turn left. The farm is 3/4 mile down Mixer Road. From Oswego, N.Y., go west on Route 104 to Route 104 A. Continue west through the village of Fair Haven to Mixer Road (about 2 miles). Turn right and go 3/4 mile to Black Creek Farm.*

This quiet, 20-acre farm is just 2 miles from Lake Ontario. Enjoy the tranquil surroundings of the fully restored 1888 Victorian farmhouse with four antique-filled, second floor rooms.Two of these rooms have private baths.

You may "help yourself to the big outdoors by strolling the lawns and gardens, playing croquet, or exploring the country lanes on a bicycle-built-for-two." You may, however, prefer to simply take a nap in the hammock under the weeping birch trees.

Now available is a new guest house built beside the two acre pond. Totally private and secluded, the guest house has everything you need for a romantic get-a-way.

The adjacent antique shop specializes in Victorian furniture, accessories, and collectibles. The owners refer to Black Creek Farm as "a 20-acre slice of serenity."

**Brown's Village Inn Bed and Breakfast and Antique Shop**
Stafford St.
315/947-5817
Tues.-Sun. 10-5,
*Directions: From Syracuse: Take Exit 34 A, Route 481 N. off the Thruway (Route 90). At Fulton, go west on Route 3 for about 14 miles to Route 104 A. Take a left and follow into Fair Haven. The in is on the 2nd street on the left after passing the State Park.*

Brown's Village Inn offers the perfect getaway near Fair Haven Beach. Fish the streams and lake for salmon, steel head or trout; enjoy boating, swimming and cross-country skiing in winter. The inn's four guest rooms and two full baths offer all the comforts of home but without the responsibilities. For more private accommodations, a guest cottage is available.

Relax on the deck, walk to nearby shops and restaurants, stroll under the shade trees or enjoy the flowers in the yard.

## 29 FLUSHING

**Auctions Room Ltd.**
11641 Queens Blvd.
718/263-2274

**Black Watch Rare Coins**
10412 Metropolitan Ave.
718/575-9779

**Comet Stamp & Coin Co., Inc.**
19207 Union Turnpike
718/479-0459

**OLD & New Shop Inc.**
7130 Myrtle Ave.
718/381-8814

**Raymond's Antiques**
8603 Northern Blvd.
718/335-0553

**Antique Shop**
15058 Northern Blvd.
718/886-8438

**Ezra's Antiques**
4101 162nd St.
718/353-2603

**MP Trading Co.**
4117 162nd St.
718/539-7019

**Feelings Antique Boutique**
4217 162nd St.
718/321-1939

**Queen's Collectibles**
4355 162nd St.
718/445-1316

**Peter Setzer Antiques**
4362 162nd St.
718/461-6999

**Rae's Antiques & Clocks**
4366 162nd St.
718/353-5577

**Antique Gallery**
3563 78th St.
718/478-1824

**Golden Oldies Ltd**
13229 33rd Ave.
718/445-4400

## 30 FRANKLIN SQUARE

### di Salvo Galleries Ltd.
1015 Hempstead Turnpike
516/326-1090
Tues.-Fri. 10-5, Sat. & Sun. 11-4
*Directions: From Long Island Expressway: Take Exit 34 (New York Park Road); go south approximately 3 to 4 miles. Make a right on Hempstead Turnpike. Proceed 1 1/2 blocks. di Salvo Galleries Ltd. is on the left.*

Di Salvo Galleries is the brainchild of two very successful individuals who pooled their individual talents, experience and their general love for fine antiques into a thriving showroom gallery that attracts the novice collector, to the most sophisticated individuals from the tri-state area.

One partner, Rosemarie DiSalvo was formerly a legal professional specializing in estate and trust administration. For more than 20 years, Rosemarie liquidated estates with values ranging from $500,000 to millions of dollars. Through the years, Rosemarie developed close associations with appraisers, major auction houses and antique dealers. These relationships have proved invaluable as resources in obtaining wonderful selections of furniture and decorative accessories that are fresh to the market.

Annemarie DiSalvo is a designer who was formerly employed for a well-known Manhattan interior design firm specializing in residential design. Her projects included penthouse apartments in New York City, large beach-front homes in the Hamptons and country estates in New Jersey and Connecticut. Annemarie's background and experience lends itself very well in assisting clients with design projects and helping them to make the right purchasing decisions.

Annemarie is a New York University graduate with a certificate (interior design) in fine arts and antique appraisal studies; her speciality is in antique rugs and antique furniture.

The di Salvo Gallery offers a wide variety of antique and vintage furniture, fine decorative accessories, art, porcelain, china, crystal, and antique and vintage linens. "Our inventory is selected based upon uniqueness and condition. Diversity is extremely important because our client's needs run the gamut of singles and newlyweds setting up their first home, to the baby boomers who are the biggest segment of our client base. These clients are voracious in purchasing the same furniture styles that their parents or grandparents owned," explains Annemarie. "Catering to the interior design community is our specialty, but we also welcome the general public."

**Estate Antiques**
967 Hempstead Turnpike
516-488-8100

## 31 GLENS FALLS

**Glenwood Manor Antiques Center**
Glenwood & Quaker Road
518/798-4747

## 32 GREAT NECK

**Charles Jewelers Inc.**
62 Allenwood Road
516/482-6688

**Barbara Hart Yesteryears**
4 Bond St.
516/466-8748

**Sabi Antiques**
112 Middle Neck Road
516/829-1330

## 33 GREENPORT

**Furniture Store**
214 Front St.
516/477-2980

**Friendly Spirits Antiques**
311 Front St.
516/477-8680

**Cracker Barrel Antiques**
74365 Main Road
516/477-0843

**Greenport Antique Center**
74365 Main Road
516/477-0843

**Primrose Lane**
74365 Main Road
516/477-8876

**Beall & Bell**
18 South St.
516/477-8239

## 34 HEART ISLAND

The legacy of Thousand Island's most tragic love affair can be found in Boldt Castle, a lavish, gilded-age mansion on Heart Island that dates back to the turn of the century. The castle motif is a monument to one man's love—hearts are carved in stone throughout the building and the island itself reshaped as a heart.

George Boldt, the owner of New York City's elegant Waldorf Astoria Hotel, decided to build a castle to symbolize his devotion to his young bride Louise.

As a poor boy in Germany, George Boldt had gazed longingly at castles along the banks of the Rhine, so he commissioned workers to build a similar structure. The 120-room castle took form as the workers ferried blocks of stone and marble and exotic woods onto the island. Towns along the shoreline buzzed with excitement.

But before it was complete, the young Mrs. Boldt died suddenly. The wealthy millionaire ordered all work to come to a halt and never returned to the island. The castle that was to have been a place of great joy fell into disrepair.

In 1977, the Thousand Islands Bridge Authority acquired the property, and gradually began a restoration process that continues to this day. From the outside, the castle is an impressive structure. From the inside, parts are yet unfinished, in a sad way evocative of the affair. Visitors can walk the island, admire the carved-stone cherubs, stroll down marble hallways, examine hand-crafted tile work and pause for a moment to consider lost dreams.

Today, Heart Island, near Alexandria Bay, is accessible by private craft and tour boats. For information call 315/482-9724.

## 35 HENRIETTA

**Wanderer's Antiques**
3204 E. Henrietta Road
716/334-0224

## 36 HUDSON

*Directions: Hudson is easily accessible from I-87 (15 minutes), I-90 (25 minutes), and the Taconic Pkwy.*
*Take a look inside some of Hudson's unique antique shops by visiting their Web Site at http://www.regionnet.com/colberk/hudsonantique.html*

With not a skyscraper or tall building in sight, Hudson is a conglomeration of architectural styles—Federal, Queen Anne, Greek Revival, Victorian and modern. It is a small city with a population of about 6,000 people. Within its downtown district over 40 antiques and collectibles shops are housed within the rich and diverse architecture of the river city. The city's grid design makes it readily accessible and its close proximity to New York draws the weekend shoppers and tourists to explore the many offerings of Hudson. Most can be found on Warren Street along with many restaurants, diners, coffee shops and the newly-renovated St. Charles Hotel.

**Americana Collectibles**
527 Warren St.
518/822-9026

**Antiques at 601**
601 Warren St.
518/822-0201

**Arenskjold Antiques Art**
537 Warren St.
518/828-2800

**The Armory Art & Antique Gallery**
State St. at N. 5th St.
518/822-1477

**Mark's Antiques**
612 Warren St.
518/766-3937

**David & Bonnie Montgomery**
526 Warren St.
518/822-0267

**Tom Noonan Antiques**
551 Warren St.
518/828-5779

**Northstar Antiques**
502 Warren St.
518/822-1563

**Atlantis Rising**
545 Warren St.
518/822-0438

**The British Accent**
537 Warren St.
518/828-2800

**The Carriage House**
454 Union St.
518/828-0365

**The Clock Man**
541 Warren St.
518/828-8995

**Days Gone By**
530 Warren St.
518/828-6109

**Doyle Antiques**
711 Warren St.
518/828-3929

**Ecclectables**
2 Park Place
518/822-1286

**Fern**
554 Warren St.
518/828-2886

**Foxfire, LTD.**
538 Warren St.
518/828-6281

**Judith Harris Antiques**
608 Warren St.
518/822-1371

**The Hudson Antiques Center**
536 Warren St.
518/828-9920

**Hudson Photographic Center**
611 Warren St.
518/828-2178

**Peter Jung Art & Antiques**
537 Warren St.
518/828-2698

**Kermani Oriental Rugs**
348½ Warren St.
518/828-4804

**Larry's Back Room Antiques**
612 Warren St.
518/477-2643

**Vincent R. Mulford**
711 Warren St.
518/828-5489

**Past Perfect**
4 Park Place
518/822-1083

**Pavillion Style Est. 1980**
521 Warren St.
518/828-4750

**Quartermoon**
528 Warren St.
518/828-0728

**Relics**
551 Warren St.
518/828-4247

**Riverhill**
610 Warren St.
518/828-2823

**Jeremiah Rusconi**
By Appointment Only
518/828-7531

**Savannah Antiques**
521 Warren St.
518/822-1343

**707 Antiques**
707 Warren St.
518/794-7883

**A. Slutter Antiques/20th Century**
556 Warren St.
518/822-0729

**Theron Ware**
548 Warren St.
518/828-9744

**Townhouse Antiques**
511 Warren St.
518/822-8500

**Uncle Sam Antiques**
535 Warren St.
518/828-2341

**Watnot Shop & Auction Service**
525 Warren St.
518/828-1081

**Benjamin Wilson Antiques**
513 Warren St.
518/822-0866

**K. West Antiques**
715 Warren St.
518/822-1960

## 37 HUNTINGTON

**Cracker Barrel Galleries Inc.**
17 Green St.
516/421-1400

**John Gennosa Antiques**
51 Green St.
516/271-0355

**Browsery Corner Shop**
449 E. Jericho Turnpike
516/351-9298

**Antique & Design Center**
830 W Jericho Turnpike
516/673-4079

**Nannyberry's Antiques**
32 Macarthur Ave.
516/421-5491

**Antiques and Jewels on Main**
293 Main St.
516/427-7674

**Ashbourne Antique Pine**
258 Main St.
516/547-5252

**Estate Jewels of Huntington**
331 New York Ave.
516/421-4774

## 38 HUNTINGTON STATION

**Browsery Antiques**
449 E. Jericho Turnpike Road.
516/351-8893

**Yankee Peddler Antqs. & Workshop**
1038 New York Ave.
516/271-5817

## 39 ITHACA

**Pastimes Antiques**
Dewitt
607/277-3457

**Asia House Gallery**
118 S. Meadow St.
607/272-8850

**City Lights Antiques Inc.**
1319 Mecklenburg Road
607/272-7010

**Bogie's Bargains**
608 W. Seneca St.
607/272-6016

**State Street Bargain House**
516 W. State St.
607/273-2303

**Celia Bowers Antiques**
1406 Trumansburg Road
607/273-1994

### *Great Places To Stay*

**Log Country Inn B&B of Ithaca**
P.O. Box 581
1-800-274-4771
Web site: www.logtv.com/inn

Escape to the rustic charm of a log house at the edge of 7,000 acres of State Forest. Awaken to the sound of birds and explore the peaceful surroundings. Easy access to hiking cross-country trails, Cornell, Ithaca College, Corning Glass Center, wineries, and antique shops. Check out their photo gallery at their web site. It is called: TODAY-AT LOG COUNTRY INN and is updated almost daily.

## 40 JOHNSTOWN

**Sir William Antiques**
Road Route 30A
518/762-4816

**Pillar**
222 N. Perry St.
518/762-4149

## 41 KEENE

### *Great Places To Stay*

**The Bark Eater Inn and Stable**
Alstead Hill Road
1-800-232-1607
Web site: www.tvenet.com//barkeater
Email: barkeater@tvenet.com
Open all the time
*Directions: From the south, take Exit 30 off I-87. Travel 17 miles west to Keene on Route 73. One mile west of Keene, heading toward Lake Placid, bear right onto Alstead Hill Road. The inn is ½ mile on the right. From the north, take Exit 34 off I-87. Proceed 25 miles south to Keene on Route 9 North. Turn right on Route 73, heading west. Bear right at the 1 mile point onto Alstead Hill Road.*

A gracious 150-year old farmhouse in the Adirondack Mountains is the setting for this unique cross country ski center and riding stable. Originally a stagecoach stopover, the rambling old inn with its 2 fireplaces, candlelight gourmet dinners, and graciously appointed accommodations offers a charming contrast to the vigorous outdoor activities that await you. Winter guests may choose cross-country or downhill skiing, bobsledding or ice climbing. If you're a beginner, Joe Pete Wilson (your host at Bark Eater) will assist you in your new adventure. You'll be in good hands, Joe Pete is a former Olympic and world competitor in nordic skiing, biathalon and bobsledding.

In summer, the inn is well known for its horseback riding program, which includes polo. Well trained horses, both English and western, are available for the rank beginner to the expert. Enthusiasts can ride for hours on miles of logging trails and back roads. For you "city slickers," riding lessons are available.

They also offer less demanding sports like shopping, dining and porch rocking (soon to be an Olympic sport!)

After a full day, you may choose one of eleven sleeping facilities, including one hand-hewn log cottage, deep in the woods.

By the way, "bark eaters" was a derisive term applied by the Mohawks to their northern neighbors, the Algonquins. Loosely translated it means, "they who eat trees."

## 42 KINGSTON

**Boulevard Attic**
400 Blvd.
914/339-6316

**Skillypot Antique Center**
41 Broadway
914/338-6779

**John Street Jewelers**
292 Fair St
914/338-4101

**Out Back Antiques**
72 Hurley Ave.
914/331-4481

**Catskill Mountain Antique Center**
Route 28
914/331-0880

**Lock Stock & Barrel**
Route 28
914/338-4397

**Stanz Used Items & Antiques**
743 Ulster Ave.
914/331-7579

**Wall Street Antiques**
333 Wall St.
914/338-3212

**Vin-Dick Antiques**
Route 209
914/338-7113

**Keystone Arts Antiques**
33 Broadway
914/331-6211

## 43 LAKE PLACID

### *Great Places To Stay*

**The Stagecoach Inn**
Old Military Road
518-523-9474

Serving Lake Placid visitors since 1833, the inn is the quintessence of the Adirondacks. Five birch-trimmed fireplaces, antiques and Indian art make up the decor.

## 44 LARCHMONT

**Dualities Galleries**
2056 Boston Post Road
914/834-2773

**Arti Antiques Inc.**
2070 Boston Post Road
914/833-1794

**Interior Shop**
2081 Boston Post Road
914/834-6110

**Briggs House Antiques**
2100 Boston Post Road
914/833-3087

**Post Road Gallery**
2128 Boston Post Road
914/834-7568

**Woolf's Den Antiques**
2130 Boston Post Road
914/834-0066

**Antiques Consign Collectibles**
2134 Boston Post Road
914/833-1829

**Thomas K Salese Antiques**
2368 Boston Post Road
914/834-0222

## 45 LOCUST VALLEY

**Finer Things**
24 Birch Hill Road
516/676-6979

**Treasured Times**
49 Birch Hill Road
516/759-2010

**Early & Co. Inc.**
53 Birch Hill Road
516/676-4800

**Oster Jensen Antiques Ltd.**
86 Birch Hill Road
516/676-5454

**Rena Fortgang Interior Design**
27 Forest Ave.
516/759-7826

**Country Cousin**
302 Forest Ave.
516/676-6767

## 46 MADISON

**Country Shop**
Route 20
315/893-7616

**Grasshopper Antiques**
Route 20
315/893-7664

**Madison Inn Antiques**
Route 20
315/893-7639

**Timothy's Treasures**
Route 20
315/893-7008

## 47 MARATHON

**Antiques & Accents**
73 Cortland St.
607/849-3703

**Riverbend Antique Center**
79 Cortland St.
607/849-6305

**Crosses Antique Center**
Route 11
607/849-6605

**Yesteryear Shoppe**
20 Main St.
607/849-6471

**Goldilocks**
36 Main St.
607/849-6144

## 48 MIDDLETOWN

**7-11 Antiques**
7 W. Main St.
914/344-4289

**Kaatskill Restoration & Antiques**
71 W. Main St.
914/343-6604

**Attic**
101 Monhagen Ave.
914/342-2252

## 49 MILLERTON

**Old Mill Of Irondale**
Route 22 NN
518/789-9433

**Country House Antiques & Interiors**
Main St.
518/789-3630

**Millerton Antique Center**
Main St.
518/789-6004

**Johnson & Johnson**
Route 22
518/789-3848

**Junk-Atique**
Route 22
518/789-4718

**Northeast Antiques**
Route 22
518/789-4014

## 50 MILLPORT

**Serendipity II**
3867 Route 14
607/739-9413
Mon.-Fri. 10-5, Sat.-Sun. 11-4
Open all year
*Directions: Approximately 5 miles from Exit 52 North off Route 17. Located at the north end of Pine Valley, between Watkins Glen and Route 17.*

Called "the little shop with the LARGE selection," this multi-dealer store offers a wide variety of glassware, especially depression and pressed glass. You'll also find an interesting assortment of furniture, lighting fixtures, books, and prints. They also offer a selection of sewing related items.

But, the most special service, and one for which they are well known, is their dedication to attention and care given to their customers.

**Millport Mercantile**
4268 S. Main St.
607/739-3180

## 51 MINERVA

**Mountain Niche Antiques**
Route 28 N.
518/251-2566

## 52 MONTGOMERY

**Clinton Shops**
84 Clinton St.
914/457-5392

**Montgomery Antique Mall**
40 Railroad Ave.
914/457-9339

**Marilyn Quigley-Lamplighter Antiques**
70 Union
914/457-5228

**Country Corner Antiques**
9 Bridge St.
914/457-5581

**Olde Towne Antique & Used Shop**
110 Clinton St.
914/457-1030

**Guns & Collectibles**
1092 Route 17 K
914/457-9062

**Antiques at Wards Bridge**
165 Wards St. Route (17 K)
914/457-9343

## 53 MOUNT VERNON

**Westchester Furniture Exchange**
78 W. 1st St.
914/668-0447

**Westchester Furniture & Antique Ctr.**
130 S. 4th Ave.
914/664-2727

**Classic Furniture & Antiques Inc.**
5 Gramatan Ave.
914/667-1651

**Veneque Collection**
115 S. 4th Ave.
914/667-5207

**Trend Antique & Genesis Books**
154 S. 4th Ave.
914/664-4478

**A Aadams Unlimited**
19-21 Mount Vernon Ave.
914/668-0374

## 54 NEW YORK CITY

**Hugo, Ltd.**
233 East 59th St.
212/750-6877
Fax: 212/750-7346
Hours: call for current schedule or appointment
*Directions: Located in the center of Manhattan, half a block from Bloomingdale's on 3rd Ave. and 59th St.*

Hugo Ltd. offers its patrons the nation's leading collection of documented and authenticated 19th century lighting and decorative arts.

With all offerings restored in-house to museum condition, this prestigious business prides itself on being a purveyor and consultant to the United States Senate and Treasury Department in Washington, D.C., as well as to the Metropolitan Museum of Art in New York City.

**Galleria Hugo**
304 E. 76th St.
212/288-8444
Fax: 212/570-9041
Hours: By appointment or chance, call ahead
Mon.-Fri., some Sat.
*Directions: Located in Manhattan's Upper East side, between 1st and 2nd Ave.*

This highly respected establishment, like its counterpart, Hugo Ltd., offers the nation's leading collection of 19th century documented and authenticated lighting. All in-house restoration is done using original finishes from that period-no plating or polishing.

Galleria Hugo is a supplier to major collections and museums.

**Cohen's Collectibles**
110 W. 25th St., Shop 305
Phone and fax: 212/675-5300
Web site: KingCohen@MSN.com
Daily 10-6
*Directions: Going north on 6th Ave., turn left onto 25th St. The building is a few hundred feet further, on the left.*

Located in the Chelsea Antique Building, Cohen's is the only open shop for "ephemera" in New York City.

The new and expanded shop buys and sells all types of airline and steamship nostalgia, sheet music, photographs, and autographs. For you photography buffs and postcard collectors, the shop offers over 4,000 photos and 5,000 postcards. This is also the place for Judaica and items pertaining to Black Heritage.

**The Family Jewels Vintage Clothing Store**
832 Ave. of the Americas
212/679-5023
Daily 11-7
*Directions: Located on the southeast corner of 29th St. and 6th Ave. (a.k.a. Avenue of the Americas).*

For specific information see review at the beginning of this section.

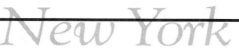

**Hege Steen Flowers**
360 Amsterdam Ave.
212/496-2575

**Portobello Antiques**
190 Ave. of Americas
212/925-4067

**Icon Jewelry and Antiques**
472 Ave. of Americas
212/647-0410

**Second Childhood**
283 Bleecker St.
212/989-6140

**Pierre Deux Antiques**
369 Bleecker St.
212/243-7740

**Clary & Co. Antiques Ltd.**
372 Bleecker St.
212/229-1773

**Kitschen**
380 Bleecker St.
212/727-0430

**Susan Parrish Antiques**
390 Bleecker St.
212/645-5020

**Avery Home Inc.**
2 Bond St.
212/614-1492

**IL Buco**
47 Bond St.
212/533-1932

**B M Arts Inc.**
367 W. Broadway
212/226-5808

**Antique Addiction**
436 W. Broadway
212/925-6342

**Antique Boutique**
712 Broadway
212/460-8830

**Agostino Antiques Ltd.**
808 Broadway
212/533-3355

**Jacobs Antiques**
810 Broadway
212/673-4254

**Abes Antiques Inc.**
815 Broadway
212/260-6424

**More & More Antiques**
378 Amsterdam Ave.
212/580-8404

**A K F Trading Ltd. Inc.**
472 Ave. of Americas
212/647-0410

**David J Air**
8 Beach St.
212/925-7867

**Niall Smith Antiques**
344 Bleecker St.
212/255-0660

**Distinctive Furnishings**
370 Bleecker St.
212/255-2476

**American Folkart Gallery**
374 Bleecker St.
212/366-6566

**Old Japan Inc.**
382 Bleecker St.
212/633-0922

**Treasures & Trifles**
409 Bleecker St.
212/243-2723

**Rhubarb Home**
26 Bond St.
212/533-1817

**What Comes Around Goes Around**
351 W. Broadway
212/343-9303

**Paracelso**
414 W. Broadway
212/966-4232

**Alice Underground Ltd.**
481 Broadway
212/431-9067

**William Roland Antiques**
808 Broadway Apt. 4J
212/260-2000

**Blatt Bowling & Billiard Corp.**
809 Broadway
212/674-8855

**Turbulence**
812 Broadway
212/598-9030

**Proctor Galleries**
824 Broadway
212/388-1539

**Howard Kaplan Antiques**
827 Broadway
212/674-1000

**Universe Antiques**
833 Broadway
212/260-9292

**David Seidenberg**
836 Broadway
212/260-2810

**Olden Camera & Lens Co. Inc.**
1265 Broadway
212/725-1234

**Penine Hart**
457 Broome St.
212/226-2761

**Gray Garden**
461 Broome St.
212/966-7116

**Henro Inc.**
525 Broome St.
212/343-0221

**Tibet West**
19 Christopher St.
212/255-3416

**Shady Acres Antiques**
Clark St. Road
315/252-3740

**Classic Antique Iron Beds**
518 Columbus Ave.
212/496-8980

**Welcome Home Antiques Ltd.**
562 Columbus Ave.
212/362-4293

**Historical Materialism**
125 Crosby St.
212/431-3424

**Bernard & S Dean Levy Inc.**
24 E. 84th St.
212/628-7088

**84th St Antiques Corp.**
235 E. 84th St.
212/650-1035

**Steve's Antiques**
206 W. 80th St.
212/721-2935

**Bijan Royal Inc.**
60 E. 11th St.
212/228-3757

**Philip Colleck of London Ltd.**
830 Broadway
212/505-2500

**Hyde Park Antiques Corp.**
836 Broadway
212/477-0033

**Cheap Jack's Vintage Clothing**
841 Broadway
212/995-0403

**Estelle Stranger**
2508 Broadway
212/749-0393

**Paterae Antiques & Decorations**
458 Broome St.
212/941-0880

**Sammy's**
484 Broome St.
212/343-2357

**Essex Gallery Ltd.**
104 Central Park S.
212/757-2500

**Christopher Street Flea Market**
122 Christopher St.
212/924-6118

**La Belle Epoque Vintage**
280 Columbus Ave.
212/362-1770

**Golden Treasury**
550 Columbus Ave.
212/787-1411

**Crosby Antiques Studio**
117 Crosby St.
212/941-6863

**A I D S Thrift Shop Inc.**
220 E. 81st St.
212/472-3573

**Better Times Antiques Inc.**
201 W. 84th St.
212/496-9001

**L J Wender Chinese Fine Art**
3 E. 80th St.
212/734-3460

**Alex's Now & Then Collectibles**
256 89th St.
212/831-4825

**James Hepner Antiques**
130 E. 82nd St.
212/737-4470

**David George Antiques**
165 E. 87th St.
212/860-3034

**Samuel Herrup Antiques**
12 E. 86th St.
212/737-9051

**Little Antique Shop**
44 E. 11th St.
212/673-5173

**William Albino Antiques**
55 E. 11th St.
212/677-8820

**Palace Galleries**
57 E. 11th St., 3rd Floor
212/228-8800

**Flores & Iva Antiques**
67 E. 11th St.
212/979-5461

**Maria Whitaker Ignez**
260 Elizabeth St.
212/941-6158

**Hebrew Religious Articles**
45 Essex St.
212/674-1770

**Columbus Circle Market**
58th & 8th
212/242-1217

**Charles G. Moore Americana Ltd.**
32 E. 57th St., 12th Floor
212/751-1900

**Megerian Rug Gallery**
262 5th Ave.
212/684-7847

**Sadigh Gallery & Ancient Art**
303 5th Ave.
212/725-7537

**Aaron Faber Gallery**
666 5th Ave.
212/586-8411

**Frederick P Victoria & Son Inc.**
154 E. 55th St.
212/755-2549

**James II Galleries Ltd.**
11 E. 57th St.
212/355-7040

**M D Flacks Ltd.**
38 E. 57th St.
212/838-4575

**Heritage East Inc.**
179 E. 87th St.
212/987-1901

**Once Upon A Time Antiques**
36 E. 11th St.
212/473-6424

**Big Apple Antiques Inc.**
52 E. 11th St.
212/260-5110

**Kings Antiques Corp.**
57 E. 11th St.
212/255-6455

**Retro-Modern Studio**
58 E. 11th St.
212/674-0530

**Metro Antiques**
80 E. 11th St.
212/673-3510

**Zane Moss Antiques**
10 E End Ave.
212/628-7130

**Tucker Robbins Warehouse**
366 W. 15th St.
212/366-4427

**Kermanshah Oriental Rugs**
57 5th Ave.
212/627-7077

**Alpine Designs Inc.**
230 5th Ave.
212/532-5067

**Chan's Antqs. & Furniture Co. Ltd.**
273 5th Ave.
212/686-8668

**Aaron's Antiques**
576 5th Ave.
1-800-447-5868

**Mercia Bross Gallery, Inc.**
160 E. 56th St. Gallery 8
212/355-4422

**Sheba Antiques Inc.**
233 E. 59th St.
212/421-4848

**Sheila Toma Gallery**
24 W. 57th St., Suite 803
212/757-1480

**Vojtech Blan Inc.**
41 E. 57th St., 6th Floor
212/249-4525

**Dalva Brothers Inc.**
44 E. 57th St.
212/758-2297

**Abraham Moheban & Son Antique**
139 E. 57th St.
212/758-3900

**Nesle Inc.**
151 E. 57th St.
212/755-0515

**Artifacts New York**
220 E. 57th St.
212/355-5575

**Iris Brown Antique Dolls Est. 1967**
253 E. 57th St.
212/593-2882

**Regal Collection**
5 W. 56th St.
212/582-7695

**I Freeman & Sons Inc.**
60 E. 56th St.
212/759-6900

**J M S & Eva Ltd.**
160 E 56th St., Gallery 8
212/593-1113

**Turner Antiques Ltd.**
160 E. 56th St. G#2
212/935-1099

**New Era Fine Arts & Antiques**
164 E. 56th St.
212/751-3473

**A Repeat Performance**
156 1st Ave.
212/529-0832

**R Anavian & Sons Gallery**
942 1st Ave.
212/879-1234

**Darrow's Fun Antiques**
1101 1st Ave.
212/838-0730

**Tamy's Antiques**
8 W. 47th St.
212/382-1112

**F Namdar Jewelry & Antique Co.**
10 W. 47th St.
212/921-7990

**Ira Moskovitz Estate & Antique Jewelry**
10 W. 47th St.
212/921-7759

**Alice Kwartler Antiques**
123 E. 57th St.
212/752-3590

**Golden Age Antique**
143 E. 57th St.
212/319-3336

**Krishna Gallery Asian Arts Inc.**
153 E. 57th St.
212/249-1677

**Lillian Nassau Ltd.**
220 E. 57th St.
212/759-6062

**Fil Caravans Inc.**
301 E 57th St
212/421-5972

**Ralph M Chait Galleries Inc.**
12 E. 56th St.
212/758-0937

**Antique Interiors by Nushin**
160 E. 56th St.
212/486-1673

**John Salibello Antiques**
160 E. 56th St.
212/580-9560

**Windsor Antique Inc.**
160 E. 56th St., G#67
212/319-1077

**Newel Art Galleries Inc.**
425 E. 53rd St.
212/758-1970

**Charles P Rogers Brass & Iron**
899 1st Ave.
212/935-6900

**Raphaelian Rug Co. Inc.**
1071 1st Ave.
212/759-5452

**N S Allan Ltd.**
Main Lobby at the Grand Hyatt
212/599-0620

**Expressions by Edith**
10 W. 47th St.
212/730-9584

**Galerie Spektrum**
10 W. 47th St.
212/840-1758

**Coin Dealer Inc.**
15 W. 47th St., Booth #12
212/768-7297

**Shans Premier Ancient Art**
31 W. 47th St., Suite 802
212/840-4805

**Antiques Corner Inc.**
608 5th Ave.
212/869-1411

**Anthony Frank Antiques**
124 E. 4th St.
212/477-1473

**Le Fanion**
299 W. 4th St.
212/463-8760

**Wyeth et Daphney**
151 Franklin St.
212/925-5278

**Stardust Antiques**
38 Gramercy Park N.
212/677-2590

**Boca Grande Furnishings**
66 Greene St.
212/334-6120

**Back Pages Antiques**
125 Greene St.
212/460-5998

**Bars & Backbars of N.Y.**
49 E. Houston St.
212/431-0600

**Cobweb**
116 W. Houston St.
212/505-1558

**Alphaville**
226 W. Houston St.
212/675-6850

**Jonathan Burden Inc.**
632 Hudson St.
212/620-3989

**Chameleon Antiques**
231 Lafayette St.
212/343-9197

**Second Hand Rose**
130 Duane St.
212/393-9002

**Lost City Arts**
275 Lafayette St.
212/941-8025

**Rooms & Gardens Inc.**
290 Lafayette St.
212/431-1297

**Euro Antiques & Gems**
36 W. 47th St.
212/997-5031

**Quilted Corner**
120 4th Ave.
212/505-6568

**Sundown & Antiques**
143 W. 4th St.
212/539-1958

**Urban Archeology Co.**
143 Franklin St.
212/431-6969

**Mobiller**
180 Franklin St.
212/334-6197

**Niall Smith Antiques**
96 Grand St.
212/941-7354

**Alice's Antiques**
72 Greene St.
212/874-3400

**Charterhouse Antiques**
115 Greenwich Ave.
212/243-4726

**B-4 It Was Cool Antiques**
89 E. Houston St.
212/219-0139

**American Antique Firearms**
205 W. Houston St.
212/206-1004

**Uplift Inc.**
506 Hudson St.
212/929-3632

**Kelter-Maice**
74 Jane St.
212/675-7380

**A & J 20th Century Designs**
255 Lafayette St.
212/226-6290

**B.Winsor Art, Antqs. & Gardn. Furn.**
272 Lafayette St.
212/274-0411

**Coming To America New York Inc.**
276 Lafayette St.
212/343-2968

**J. Marvec & Co.**
946 Madison Ave.
212/517-7665

**Old Print Shop Inc.**
150 Lexington Ave.
212/683-3950

**Maximilian's Grnd Pianos & Fine Art**
200 Lexington Ave., Main Floor
212/689-2177

**Antique Salon**
870 Lexington Ave.
212/472-0191

**S. Wyler Inc.**
941 Lexington Ave.
212/879-9848

**Deco Deluxe Inc.**
993 Lexington Ave.
212/472-7222

**La Cadet De Gascogne**
1015 Lexington Ave.
212/744-5925

**Malvina Solomon**
1021 Lexington Ave.
212/535-5200

**Mood Indigo**
181 Prince St.
212/254-1176

**J. Dixon Prentice Antiques**
1036 Lexington Ave.
212/249-0458

**Tout Le Monde**
1178 Lexington Ave.
212/439-8487

**F H Coin & Stamp Exchange**
1187 Lexington Ave.
1-888-FHCoins

**Lands Beyond Ltd.**
1218 Lexington Ave.
212/249-6275

**Jerry Livian Antique Rugs**
148 Madison Ave.
212/683-2666

**Bolour**
595 Madison Ave.
212/752-0222

**Ronin Gallery**
605 Madison Ave.
212/688-0188

**Macklowe Gallery**
667 Madison Ave.
212/644-6400

**Kim McGuire Antiques**
155 Lexington Ave.
212/686-0788

**The N Y Doll Hospital Inc**
787 Lexington Ave.
212/838-7527

**Lorraine Wohl Collection**
870 Lexington Ave.
212/472-0191

**Ellen Berenson Antiques**
988 Lexington Ave.
212/288-5302

**Nancy Brous Associates Ltd.**
1008 Lexington Ave.
212/772-7515

**Amy Perlin Antiques**
1020 Lexington Ave.
212/664-4923

**Bob Pryor Antiques**
1023 Lexington Ave.
212/861-1601

**Marckle Myers Ltd.**
1030 Lexington Ave.
212/288-3288

**Sylvia Pines Uniquities**
1102 Lexington Ave.
212/744-5141

**Garden Room**
1179 Lexington Ave.
212/879-1179

**Japan Gallery**
1210 Lexington Ave.
212/288-2241

**Las Venus**
163 Ludlow St.
212/982-0608

**Persian Shop Inc.**
534 Madison Ave.
212/355-4643

**Anita De Carlo Inc.**
605 Madison Ave.
212/288-4948

**F Gorevic & Sons Inc.**
635 Madison Ave., 2nd Floor
212/753-9319

**Lloyd Jensen Jewelers Ltd.**
716 Madison Ave.
212/980-3966

**Mayfair & Company**
741 Madison Ave.
212/737-4776

**Imperial Fine Oriental Arts**
790 Madison Ave.
212/717-5383

**Rosenblatt Minna Ltd.**
844 Madison Ave.
212/288-0250

**Devenish & Company Inc**
929-Madison Ave.
212/535-2888

**Stair & Company**
942 Madison Ave.
212/517-4400

**Florian Papp Inc.**
962 Madison Ave.
212/288-6770

**Koreana Art & Antiques Inc.**
963 Madison Ave.
212/249-0400

**Leigh Keno American Antiques**
980 Madison Ave.
212/734-2381

**Kenneth W Rendell Gallery**
989 Madison Ave.
212/717-1776

**Rafael Gallery**
1020 Madison Ave.
212/744-8666

**Burlington Antique Toys**
1082 Madison Ave.
212/861-9708

**Guild Antiques II**
1089 Madison Ave.
212/717-1810

**Eagles Antiques Inc**
1097 Madison Ave.
212/772-3266

**Betty Jane Bart Antiques**
1225 Madison Ave.
212/410-2702

**Wicker Garden Antique Store**
1318 Madison Ave.
212/410-7000

**Barry of Chelsea Antiques**
154 9th Ave.
212/242-2666

**America Hurrah Antiques**
766 Madison Ave.
212/535-1930

**Orientations Gallery**
802 Madison Ave.
212/772-7705

**Bardith Ltd.**
901 Madison Ave.
212/737-3775

**Alexander Gallery**
942 Madison Ave.
212/472-1636

**Antiquarium Fine Ancnt Arts**
948 Madison Ave.
212/734-9776

**Time Will Tell**
962 Madison Ave.
212/861-2663

**LEO Kaplan Ltd.**
967 Madison Ave.
212/249-6766

**Ursus Books Ltd.**
981 Madison Ave.
212/772-8787

**Edith Weber Antiques**
994 Madison Ave.
212/570-9668

**E Frankel Ltd**
1040 Madison Ave.
212/879-5733

**GEM Antiques**
1088 Madison Ave.
212/535-7399

**Guild Antiques II**
1095 Madison Ave.
212/472-0830

**Marco Polo Antiques**
1135 Madison Ave.
212/734-3775

**Carnegie Hill Antiques**
1309 Madison Ave., 2nd Floor
212/987-6819

**Frank Rogin Inc.**
21 Mercer St.
212/431-6545

**Something Else Antiques & Cllbls.**
182 9th Ave.
212/924-0006

**JAN Eleni Co.**
315 E. 9th St.
212/533-4396

**Atomic Passion**
430 E. 9th St.
212/533-0718

**Accents Unlimited**
65 W. 90th St.
212/799-7490

**John Rosselli International**
523 E. 73rd St.
212/722-2137

**Nelson & Nelson Antiques Inc.**
445 Park Ave.
212/980-5825

**James Robinson Inc.**
480 Park Ave.
212/752-6166

**Thomas**
41 Perry St.
212/675-7296

**Irreplaceable Artifacts**
14 2nd Ave.
212/473-3300

**Sapho Gallery Inc.**
1037 2nd Ave.
212/308-0880

**Alexanders Antiques**
1050 2nd Ave., Gallery 43, 44, 45 & 85
212/935-9386

**Paul Stamati Gallery**
1050 2nd Ave., Gallery #38
212/754-4533

**Federico Carrera Antiques**
1050 2nd Ave., Gallery 18
212/750-2870

**Hadassa Antiques Inc.**
1050 2nd Ave., Gallery 75
212/751-0009

**John Walker Antiques**
1050 2nd Ave.
212/832-9579

**Leah's Gallery Inc.**
1050 2nd Ave., #-42
212/838-5590

**Manhattan Art & Antiques Center**
1050 2nd Ave.
212/355-4400

**Archangel Antiques**
334 E. 9th St.
212/260-9313

**Upstairs Downtown Antiques**
12 W. 19th St.
212/989-8715

**Treasures & Gems**
250 E. 90th St.
212/410-7360

**Dixon Galleries Inc**
251 Park Ave. S.
212/475-6500

**Chinese Porcelain Co.**
475 Park Ave.
212/838-7744

**U S E D**
17 Perry St.
212/627-0730

**Rural Collections Inc.**
117 Perry St.
212/645-4488

**Love Saves The Day**
119 2nd Ave.
212/228-3802

**A A A Silver Buyer**
1050 2nd Ave.
212/755-6320

**A R Broomer Ltd.**
1050 2nd Ave., Gallery 81
212/421-9530

**Estate Silver Co. Ltd.**
1050 2nd Ave. Gallery 65
212/758-4858

**Flying Cranes Antiques**
1050 2nd Ave., Gallery 55 & 56
212/223-4600

**Hoffman-Giampetro Antiques**
1050 2nd Ave., Gallery 37
212/755-1120

**Kurt Gluckselig Antiques**
1050 2nd Ave., Gallery #90
212/758-1805

**LES Gallery Looms Inc.**
1050 2nd Ave., Gallery #59
212/752-0995

**Michaels Antiques & Jewelry**
1050 2nd Ave., Gallery #3
212/838-8780

**Natalie Bader**
1050 2nd Ave., Gallery 40 A
212/486-7673

**Rita Facks/Limited Additions Inc.**
1050 2nd Ave., G#94
212/421-8132

**J and P Timepieces Inc.**
1057 2nd Ave.
212/980-1099

**R & P Kassai**
1050 2nd Ave., Gallery #1
212/838-7010

**Sidney Bell Fine Arts**
1050 2nd Ave., G#16
212/486-0715

**Suchow & Siegel Antiques Ltd.**
1050 2nd Ave., Gallery #-81
212/888-3489

**Treasures & Pleasures**
1050 2nd Ave.
212/750-1929

**Robert Altman**
1148 2nd Ave.
212/832-3490

**Fairfield Antique Gallery**
1166 2nd Ave.
212/759-6519

**David Weinbaum**
1175 2nd Ave.
212/755-6540

**Oaksmiths & Jones**
1510 2nd Ave.
212/327-3462

**James Lowe Autographs Ltd.**
30 E. 60th St., Suite 304
212/759-0775

**Paris To Province**
207 E. 60th St.
212/750-0037

**GUY Regal Ltd**
210 E. 60th St.
212/888-2134

**David Duncan Antiques**
227 E. 60th St.
212/688-0666

**A Smith Antiques Ltd.**
235 E. 60th St.
212/888-6337

**Nelson & Nelson Antiques Inc.**
445 Park Ave.
212/980-5824

**Ostia Inc.**
1050 2nd Ave.
212/371-2424

**Rover & Lorber NYC, Inc.**
1050 2nd Ave., G#27
212/838-1302

**S Elghanayan Antiques**
1050 2nd Ave., Gallery #6
212/750-3344

**Tibor Strasser**
1050 2nd Ave., G#76
212/759-2513

**Time Gallery**
1050 2nd Ave., G#54
212/593-2323

**Unique Finds Inc**
1050 2nd Ave., G#36
212/751-1983

**A & R Asta Ltd.**
1152 2nd Ave.
212/750-3364

**Antique Accents**
1175 2nd Ave.
212/755-6540

**Elizabeth Street**
1190 2nd Ave.
212/644-6969

**Annex Antique Fair**
6th & 26th St.
212/243-5343

**Things Japanese**
127 E. 60th St
212/371-4661

**Objets Trouves Ltd.**
217 E. 60th St.
212/753-0221

**Victor's Antiques Ltd.**
223 E. 60th St.
212/752-4100

**Brahms-Netski Antique Passage**
234 E. 60th St.
212/755-8307

**James Grafstein Ltd.**
236 E. 60th St.
212/754-1290

**Luxor Gallery**
238 E. 60th St.
212/832-3633

**William Lipton Ltd.**
27 E. 61st St.
212/751-8131

**Dining Trade**
306 E. 61st St.
212/755-2304

**Town and Country Antiques**
306 E. 61st St.
212/752-1677

**Chrystian Aubusson**
315 E. 62nd St.
212/755-2432

**Objects Plus Inc.**
315 E. 62nd St., 3rd Floor
212/832-3386

**Paris Antiques**
315 E. 62nd St.
212/421-3340

**Emporium Antique Shop Ltd.**
20 W. 64th St.
212/724-9521

**Schlesch & Gaza**
158 E. 64th St.
212/838-3923

**Rita Ford Music Boxes Inc.**
19 E. 65th St.
212/535-6717

**Jean Hoffman Antiques**
207 E. 66th St.
212/535-6930

**Maya Schaper Cheese & Antiques**
106 W. 69th St.
212/873-2100

**Linda Morgan Inc.**
152 E. 70th St.
212/628-4330

**Salander Oreilly Galleries Inc.**
20 E. 79th St.
212/879-6606

**Godel & Co. Inc.**
39 A E. 72nd St.
212/288-7272

**Lantiquaire & Connoisseur Inc.**
36 E. 73rd St.
212/517-9176

**Ann-Morris Antiques**
239 E. 60th St.
212/755-3308

**Naga Antiques Ltd.**
145 E. 61st St.
212/593-2788

**Epel & Lacoze Antiques Inc.**
306 E. 61st St., 2nd Floor
212/355-0050

**Tender Buttons**
143 E. 62nd St.
212/758-7004

**Marvin Alexander Inc.**
315 E. 62nd St.
212/838-2320

**OLD Versailles Inc.**
315 E. 62nd St.
212/421-3663

**Wood & Hogan Inc.**
305 E. 63rd St., 5th Floor
212/355-1335

**Harvey & Co. Antiques**
250 E. 60th St.
212/888-7952

**French & Co. Inc.**
17 E. 65th St.
212/535-3330

**Bizarre Bazaar Antiques Ltd.**
130 1/4 E. 65th St.
212/517-2100

**Margot Johnson Inc.**
18 E. 68th St.
212/794-2225

**Victory Gardens Ltd.**
205 E. 68th St.
212/472-2472

**Leff Langham Art & Antiques**
19 E. 71st St.
212/288-4030

**George Glazer**
28 E. 72nd St.
212/535-5706

**Oriental Decorations**
253 E. 72nd St.
212/439-1573

**Hollis Taggart Galleries**
48 E. 73rd St.
212/628-4000

# New York

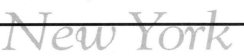

**Eric GUY Inc.**
503 E. 73rd St.
212/772-2326

**J Mavec & Co.**
946 Madison Ave.
212/517-7665

**Judith & James Milne Inc.**
506 E. 74th St.
212/472-0107

**Treillage Ltd.**
418 E. 75th St.
212/535-2288

**Peter Roberts Antiques Inc.**
134 Spring St.
212/226-4777

**Julian Antiques Restoration**
108 W. 25th St.
212/647-0305

**Design 18 Realty Inc.**
979 3rd Ave., 4th Floor
212/753-8666

**D & D Building / Palisander Ltd.**
979 3rd Ave., Suite 818
212/755-0120

**Evergreen Antiques Inc.**
1249 3rd Ave. (at 72nd)
212/744-5664

**Ghiordian Knot Ltd.**
1636 3rd Ave., Suite #-169
212/371-6390

**China Importing Co. Ltd.**
28 E. 10th St.
212/995-0800

**Reymer-Jourdan Antiques**
29 E. 10th St.
212/674-4470

**E 'Epoque**
30 E. 10th St.
212/353-0972

**Ritter-Antik Inc.**
35 E. 10th St.
212/673-2213

**Donzella 20th Century**
90 E. 10th St.
212/598-9675

**Regeneration Furniture Inc.**
223 E. 10th St.
212/614-9577

**Elliott Galleries**
155 E. 79th St.
212/861-2222

**Karen Warshaw Ltd.**
167 E. 74th St.
212/439-7870

**Woodard Greenstien**
506 E. 74th St.
212/794-9404

**H M Luther Inc.**
35 E. 76th St.
212/439-7919

**Classic Toys Inc.**
218 Sullivan St.
212/674-4434

**Ultimate European Rugs & Oriental**
969 3rd Ave.
212/759-6000

**Nicholas Antiques**
979 3rd Ave.
212/688-3312

**Place Des Artes Corp.**
979 3rd Ave.
212/750-8092

**Gordon Foster Antiques**
1322 3rd Ave.
212/744-4922

**Caldonia Antiques**
1685 3rd Ave.
212/534-3307

**The Tudor Rose Antiques**
28 E. 10th St.
212/677-5239

**Bernd H Goeckler Antiques Inc.**
30 E. 10th St.
212/777-8209

**Karl Kemp & Associates Ltd. Antqs.**
34 E. 10th St.
212/254-1877

**Martell Antiques**
53 E. 10th St.
212/777-4360

**Robert Gingold Antiques**
95 E. 10th St.
212/475-4008

**Cheapside Inc.**
280 E 10 th St
212/780-9626

**Renee Antiques Inc.**
8 E. 12th St.
212/929-6870

**Waves**
110 W. 25th St., 10th Floor
212/989-9284

**John Koch Antiques**
514 W. 24th St.
212/243-8625

**Tepper Galleries Inc.**
110 E. 25th St.
212/677-5300

**Cherubs Antiques & Collectibles**
110 W. 25th St., 11th Floor
212/627-7097

**John Gredler Antiques & House of Art**
110 W. 25th St., Room 702
212/337-3667

**Lubin Galleries Inc.**
110 W. 25th St.
212/924-3777

**Rocco, Vincent**
110 W. 25th St.
212/620-5652

**Vlasdimir's Antiques**
110 W. 25th St., Suite 207
212/337-3704

**Smith Gallery**
447 W. 24th St.
212/744-6171

**OLD Paper Archive**
122 W. 25th St.
212/645-3983

**LES Deux Inc.**
104 W. 27th St.
212/604-9743

**Sohell Oriental Rugs**
29 W. 30th St.
212/239-1069

**Kamall Oriental Rugs**
151 W. 30th St.
212/564-7000

**33rd Street Galleria**
100 W. 33rd St., 16th Floor
212/279-0462

**T & K French Antiques**
301 E. 38th St.
212/219-2472

**Kentshire Galleries Ltd.**
37 E. 12th St.
212/673-6644

**Dullsville Inc.**
143 E. 13th St.
212/505-2505

**Forty Fifty Sixty**
108 W. 25th St., 4th Floor
212/463-0980

**Chelsea Antiques Building**
110 W. 25th St.
212/929-0909

**Cohen's Collectibles & Ephemera**
110 W. 25th St., 3rd Floor
212/675-5300

**Le Chateau**
110 W. 25th St.
212/741-7570

**Shirley Mariaschin & Jerry Spiller**
110 W. 25th St.
212/989-3414

**This N That**
110 W. 25th St., Suite 613
212/255-0727

**Rene Kerne Antiques**
110 W. 25th St.
212/727-3455

**Garage Antique Show**
112 W. 25th St.
212/337-3704

**Lucille's Antique Emporium**
127 W. 26th St.
212/691-1041

**Metal Art Studio**
150 W. 28th St.
212/229-1130

**Ebison's Harounian Imports**
38 E. 30th St.
212/686-4262

**Joseph Solo Antiques**
1561 York Ave.
212/439-1555

**Pantry & Hearth**
121 E. 35th St.
212/889-0026

**Mary Efron Vintage**
68 Thompson St.
212/219-3099

**Lyme Regis Ltd.**
68 Thompson St.
212/334-2110

**Legacy**
109 Thompson St.
212/966-4827

**Deco Jewels Inc.**
131 Thompson St.
212/253-1222

**Ellen Lane Antiques Inc.**
150 Thompson St.
212/475-2988

**Stella Dallas**
218 Thompson St.
212/674-0447

**Zero To Sixties**
75 Thompson St.
212/925-0932

**LOU Ficherea & Ron Perkins**
50 University Plaza
212/533-1430

**Pall Mall Inc.**
99 University Plaza
212/677-5544

**World Collectible Center**
18 Versey St.
212/267-7100

**Fountain Pen Hospital**
10 Warren St.
212/964-0580

**Forty One**
41 Wooster St.
212/343-0935

**Interieurs**
114 Wooster St.
212/343-0800

**Sotheby's**
1334 York Ave.
212/606-7000

**Kendra Krienke**
By Appointment Only
212/580-6516

**Leo Design**
413 Bleecker St.
212/929-8466

**Arts & Antique Center**
160 E. 56th St., Gallery #7
212/229-0958

**Second Hand Rose**
130 Duane St.
212/393-9002

**Regeneration Furniture, Inc.**
38 Renwick St.
212/741-2102

**Garden Antiquary**
724 5th Ave., 3rd Floor
212/757-3008

**Antiques Corner**
608 5th Ave.
212/869-1411

**Roger Gross Ltd.**
225 E. 57th St.
212/759-2892

**Kendra Krienke Art**
230 Central Park W.
212/580-6516

**Primavera Gallery**
808 Madison Ave.
212/288-1569

**Everett Collection Inc.**
104 W. 27th St., 3rd. Floor
212/255-8610

### *Great Places To Stay*

**Incentra Village House**
32 Eighth Ave.
212/206-0007

Incentra Village House, built in 1841, occupies two red brick townhouses in New York's Greenwich Village Historic District. Offering an attractive alternative to Midtown's steel and glass, guests receive a warm welcome in the cozy double parlor which boasts two fireplaces, antique furniture, paintings, sculptures and a 1939 Steinway baby grand piano. To get to your room you'll wander down narrow corridors and up charming old stairways to one of twelve unique rooms. All studios and suites are pleasantly furnished and include a private bathroom, telephone, television and most include a working fireplace and kitchen or kitchenette. Each room is decorated according to cities that the founder lived in or to specific artwork or furniture in the room.

## 55 NORTHPORT

**Somewhere In Time Antiques**
162 Main St.
516/757-4148

**Wild Rose Antiques**
189 Main St.
516/261-0888

**TOP Notch Antiques**
76 Bayview Ave.
516/754-9396

**Country Shop**
171 Main St.
516/757-2362

**L E P Design & Consignment Shop**
160 Laurel Ave.
516/754-1831

**Scarlett's**
166 Main St.
516/754-0004

**Harbor Lights Antique Boutique**
110 Main St.
516/757-4572

**Antique Restoration by Julian**
108 W. 25th St., Suite #208
212/647-0305

## 56 NYACK

**Lisa's Antiques**
37 S. Broadway
914/358-7077
Fax: 914/358-1688
Tues.-Sun. 12-6
*Directions: From New York City and New Jersey, take Pallisades Pkwy. north to Exit 4 (9 West). Go north on 9 West about 6 miles to the yellow blinking light. Bear right and proceed to the south end of the Art, Craft, and Antiques area. From Upstate New York, take the NewYork Thruway South to Exit 11. Then go left on Route 59 (Main St.) to shopping area. From Westchester and Connecticut, cross the Tappan Zee Bridge to the first exit (10). Follow the sign for South Nyack to Clinton Ave. Go right 1 block to Broadway, then left to the shopping area.*

Part of the Hudson Valley Emporium Mall, this antique and collectibles shop specializes in oak furniture, glassware, old toys, and sterling silver. Other specialty items include postcards, metal lunch boxes, and a selection of African American prints.

**Ramapo Collectors**
4 N. Broadway
914/353-3019

**Elayne's Antiques & Collectibles**
6 S. Broadway
914/358-6465

**Gene Reed Gallery**
77 S. Broadway
914/358-3750

**Remembrances**
37 S. Broadway
914/358-7226

**Antiques & Country Pine**
41B N. Broadway
914/358-7740

**Towne Crier Antiques**
70 S. Broadway
914/358-5234

**Goldsmiths Treasure Mine**
79 S. Broadway
914/358-2204

**Acorn Antiques & Collectibles**
142 Main St.
914/353-5897

**Arlene Lederman Antiques**
142 Main St.
914/358-8616

**C D Antiques**
142 Main St.
914/358-1704

**Decorative Arts & Antiques Nyack**
142 Main St.
914/353-1644

**Hildegard's Antiques**
142 Main St.
914/353-2650

**J & J Antiques**
142 Main St.
914/353-3252

**Jeni Brandel's Antiques**
142 Main St.
914/353-3379

**Jo-Antiques**
142 Main St.
914/353-5154

**Kuku Antiques**
142 Main St.
914/353-1130

**Old Business Antiques**
142 Main St.
914/358-7008

**Room With A View**
142 Main St.
914/353-4072

**S & M Antiques**
142 Main St.
914/353-4774

**Vintage Gems & Antiques**
142 Main St.
914/353-2264

**Bruce Anderson Interior & Exterior**
145 Main St.
914/353-3992

**Gloria Paul Antiques**
152 Main St.
914/358-1859

**Allards**
167 Main St.
914/353-1884

**Levesque Antiques**
170-2 Main St.
914/353-4050

**ARK Shop**
190 Main St.
914/358-1039

**A Antique Center Upper Nyack**
366 Route 9 W.
914/358-3751

## 57 OLEAN

**E-Lites Antiques Inc.**
204 W. State St.
716/372-8661

**Olean Antique Center**
269 N. Union St.
716/372-8171

**Jerry's Antique Co-op**
1217 N. Union St.
716/373-3702

**Second Time Around**
126 Whitney Ave.
716/372-4308

## 58 OWEGO

**Hand of Man**
180 Front St.
607/687-2556

**Sally's Place**
196 Front St.
607/687-4111

**Cracker Barrel Antiques & Gift**
202 Front St.
607/687-0555

**Heritage Antiques**
36 John St.
607/687-3405

## 59 PEEKSKILL / CORTLAND MANOR

**Toddville Antique & Craft Center**
2201 Crompond Road
914/736-1117

**Rose Cottage**
44 N. Division St.
914/737-1845

**Garden Antiquary**
2551 Maple Ave.
914/737-6054

## 60 PHOENICIA

**Hernandez Edom Antiques**
Route 28
914/688-2124

**Phoenicia Antique Center**
Route 28
914/688-2095

**Bethkens Antiques**
Woodland Valley Road
914/688-5620

**Antique Store**
Route 28
914/688-5654

## 61 PORT CHESTER

**Simon-World Arts**
168 Irving Ave.
914/934-0113

**Greenberg's Antique Mall Port**
27 S. Main St.
914/937-4800

**Jacks Fabrics & Antiques**
33 S. Main St.
914/939-3308

**House of Weltz**
26 Poningo St.
914/939-6513

**Ninas Antiques Collectibles**
191 Westchester Ave.
914/939-6806

## 62 PORT WASHINGTON

### Port Antique Center
289 Main St.
516/767-3313
Tues.-Sat. 11-5, Sun. 12-5
*Directions: Long Island Expressway to Exit 36 N. Searingtown Road./Port Washington. Travel 4 miles north to Main St. Left onto Main St. and go about 1½ miles down the hill to shop on your right #289 Main St.. Travel time by car is 40 minutes from midtown Manhattan or 30 minutes by LIRR train.*

This charming quality multi-dealer shop is located in the heart of the Port Washington Antiques District. Located one block from Port Washington Harbor this shop offers a large selection of 19th and 20th century antiques and collectables.

Twenty four dealers in the shop carry a wide variety of quality antiques including art pottery such as Roseville, Weller, Rookwood, Fulper and McCoy in addition to a wide variety of china and porcelain with a special accent on Chintz and Majolica. If glass is your passion, Port Antique Center offers a beautiful array including depression and elegant glass as well as art glass such as Tiffany and Loetz.

The store abounds in both fine and costume jewelry offering a wide selection of antique watches as well as an extraordinary collection of colorful Bakelite jewelry. Come browse and enjoy collections of silver, kitchenware, toys, vintage clothing and memorabilia. If you happen to visit during the spring, summer or fall, the Harbor Association hosts an Antique Street Fair on the last Sunday of each month from April to October. Port Antique Center is surrounded by other antique shops and restaurants all within walking distance of each other and beautiful Port Washington harbor where you can stroll and relax in this beautiful bayside setting.

**Front Porch**
309 Main St.
516/944-6868

**Cat Lady Antiques**
164 Main St.
516/883-4334

**R E Steele Antiques**
165 Main St.
516/767-2283

**Nancy K. Banker Antiques**
279 Main St.
516/883-4184

**Pat Giles**
287 Main St.
516/883-1104

**Michael Mikiten**
287 Main St.
516/944-8767

**Red Door Antiques**
305 Main St.
516/883-5125

**Village Green**
306 Main St.
516/767-3698

**Baba Antiques & Collectibles**
292 Main St.
516/883-6274

## 63 POUND RIDGE

**Antiques & Tools Bus & Kitchen**
Scotts Corners
914/764-0015

**Peterson's Antiques Ltd.**
26 Westchester Ave.
914/764-5074

**Antiques & Interiors Inc.**
67 Westchester Ave.
914/764-4400

**Strap Hinge**
72 Westchester Ave.
914/764-1145

**Nancy Cody Antiques**
67 Westchester Ave.
914/764-4949

**Objects Trouvee Inc.**
69 Westchester Ave.
914/234-7600

## 64 RED HOOK

**Broadway Antiques & Collectibles**
30 N. Broadway
914/876-1444

**Cider Mill Antiques**
5 Cherry St.
914/758-2599

**Victorian Corner**
19 W. Market St.
914/758-1011

**Anntex Antiques Center**
23 E. Market St.
914/758-2843

**Rock City Relics Antique Center**
Route 199 & 308
914/758-8603

### *Great Places To Stay*

**The Grand Dutchess**
50 N. Broadway
914/758-5818

The Grand Dutchess is a Second-Empire Victorian mansion subtly updated to provide elegant and comfortable accommodations for the 20th Century traveler. An extensive collection of antique furniture and decoration provides the ambiance; firm queen-size beds provides the comfort; and a deliciously self-indulgent breakfast provides the sustenance.

**The Lombard's**
R.D. 3, Box 79
914/758-3805

Peter and Peggy Anne Lombard were professionals in the Broadway theater and as a consequence they have developed a theatrical clientele and theater is a favorite subject at the breakfast table. Guests browse the family photo gallery (which includes two former American presidents) and often end up prowling the in-house antique parlor or the 'primitive' room in the basement which boasts a huge original cooking hearth/fireplace. Barn and grounds are for exploring. Bikes are provided.

## 65 RHINEBECK

**Rhinebeck Antique Center**
7 W. Market St.
914/876-8168

**Hummingbird Jewelers**
20 W. Market St.
914/876-4585

**Gallery Shoppe**
9 Mill St.
914/876-2064

**Country Bazaar**
14 U.S. Hwy. 9 S.
914/876-4160

**Old Mill House Antiques**
144 U.S. Hwy. 9 N.
914/876-3636

## 66 ROCHESTER

**Treasure Hunters**
1434 Buffalo Road
716/235-5441

**Flower City Stamps and Coins**
1575 Dewey Ave.
716/647-9320

**Thomas R Paddock Oriental Rugs**
342 East Ave.
716/325-3110

**Upstate Gallery Antiques**
16 Gardiner Park Dr.
716/262-2089

**Antiques & Old Lace**
274 Goodman St. N.
716/461-1884

**Village Gate Square**
274 Goodman St. N.
716/442-9061

**Yankee Peddler Bookshop Vol II**
274 Goodman St. N.
716/271-5080

**Marilyn's Antiques**
500 Lyell Ave.
716/647-2480

**Worldwide Antiques & Imports**
631 Monroe Ave.
716/271-3217

**Aries Antiques**
739 Monroe Ave.
716/244-7912

**James Jewelry**
1315 E. Ridge Road
716/336-9960

**Jewelry & Coin Exchange**
2000 Ridge Road W.
716/227-6370

**Antique & Colledtibles Co-op Rochester**
151 Saint Paul St.
716/232-6440

**Warren Phillips Fine Art**
215 Tremont St.
716/235-4060

**Walt's Place**
1570 Dewey Ave.
716/254-1880

**Mission Oak Antiques**
378 Meigs St.
716/442-2480

**Eric Kase**
398 Westminster Road
716/461-4382

**Newell Distributors**
39 Branford Road
716/442-8810

**Michael Latragna**
1275 Clover St.
716/442-0725

**International Art Acquisitions Inc.**
3300 Monroe Ave.
716/264-1440

**Golden Oldies Antiques**
24 Bursen Court
716/266-2440

**Darcys Adventures In The Past**
149 Monroe Ave.
716/262-4776

**Carousel Antiques**
3409 Saint Paul Blvd.
716/266-3420

**Adventures In Past John**
149 Monroe Ave.
716/262-4776

**Jack Grecos Creekside Antiques**
1611 Scottsville Road
716/328-9150

**Household Sales by Mary Kay Roden**
20 Union Park
716/266-3524

**Chichelli Weiss Books & Antiques**
374 Meigs St.
716/271-3980

**Bettiques**
1697 Monroe Ave.
716/442-2995

## 67 SAG HARBOR

**Carriage House Antiques**
34 Main St.
516/725-8004

**Madison House Antiques & Artifacts**
43 Madison St.
516/725-7242

**Diana's Place**
Main St.
516/725-4669

**NED Parkhouse Antiques**
Main St.
516/725-9830

**Sage Street Antiques**
Sage St.
516/725-4036

**Carriage House Antiques**
34 Main St.
516/725-8004

## 68 SARATOGA SPRINGS

### Broadway Antiques Gallery
484 Broadway
518/581-8348
Daily 11-6 and extended summer hours.
*Directions: Take Route. 9 from either exit 13N or exit 15 to downtown. Broadway Antiques Gallery is 3 doors north of City Hall on the east side of Broadway in the center of downtown Historic Saratoga Springs.*

A cooperative effort of ten dealers brings you a wide variety of home furnishings and accessories. Over 3,000 square feet of antiques and unique gift items may be found in this shop.

**Ye Olde Wishin Shoppe**
353 Broadway
518/583-7782

**A Page In Time**
462 Broadway
518/584-4876

**Saratoga Antiques**
727 Route 29 E.
518/587-3153

**9 Caroline Antiques & Collectibles**
9 Caroline St.
518/583-9112

**Magnells Antiques**
53 Old Schuylerville Road
518/587-8888

**Regent St. Antique Center**
153 Regent St.
518/584-0107

**Saratoga Antiques**
727 Route 29 E.
518/587-3153

### *Great Places To Stay*

### Chestnut Tree Inn
9 Whitney Place
518/587-8681
Open April through November 1
*Directions: From I-87, take Exit 13 North. Take Route 9 North to the 5th traffic light (Lincoln Ave.) and turn right. Take the 1st left onto Whitney Place. The inn is the 2nd house on the left.*

Sample a more peaceful time in Saratoga's history at this fine traditional Victorian guest house. Situated conveniently near many of the city's attractions, the inn offers 10 rooms, most with private baths.

Continental breakfast is served each morning on the porch, and during July and August, guests may congregate there in the afternoons for wine, cheese, and crackers.

Sit and relax under what is reputed to be the last living chestnut tree in Saratoga.

## 69 SAUGERTIES

**Saugerties Antiques Center**
220 Main St.
914/246-8234

**Fancy Flea**
50 Market St.
914/246-9391

**Saugerties Antiques Gallery**
104 Partition St.
914/246-2323

**Acanthus**
112 Partition St.
914/247-0041

**Peacock Antiques**
2769 Route 32
914/246-7070

## 70 SCHOHARIE

**Cane Shoppe Antiques**
Barton Hill Road
518/295-8629

**Patent Country Shop & Antq. Emp.**
Route 145e East Cobleskill
518/296-8000

**Ginny's Hutch Antiques**
Route 30 Mdbg Schoh Road
518/295-7470

**Saltbox Antiques**
Stony Brook Road
518/295-7408

**Quest**
Vroman Road Route 30
518/295-8805

## 71 SOUTHAMPTON

**Southampton Antique Center**
640 N. High
516/283-1006

**Things I Love**
51 Jobs Lane
516/287-2756

**Elaines Antiques**
9 Main St.
516/287-3276

**Croft Antiques**
11 S. Main St.
516/283-6445

**Bob Petrillo's Brouserie**
30 Main St.
516/283-6560

**Old Town Crossing**
46 Main St.
516/283-7740

**Judi Boisson Antique American Quilts**
134 Mariners Dr.
516/283-5466

**Old Town Crossing Warehouse**
134 Mariners Dr.
516/287-4771

**Hampton Antiques**
116 N. Sea Road
516/283-3436

**John W Nilsson Inc.**
675 N. Sea Road
516/283-1434

### *Great Places To Stay*

### Caldwell's Carriage House
519 Hill St.
516/287-4720

Located in a historic shingled Colonial amid manicured lawns and lovely flower gardens, the Carriage House is one of the most unique accommodations in the Hamptons. Enter the suite through a private entrance leading to the sitting room with wide plank floors, window seat, and pull-out sofa. Full bath and efficiency kitchen on the ground level gives independence from the large bedroom above.

## 72 SPRINGWATER

### Canadice Farm Antiques
9034 Cratsley Hill Road
716/367-2771
Mon.-Fri. 10-5, Sat. & Sun. by chance or appointment
Easter through Thanksgiving
*Directions: From Route 390, exit at Avon/Lima. In Lima, turn right on 15 A through Hemlock, then left on Route 20 A. Go to County Road 37, then right and follow signs. From Rochester, go south on 65 (Clover St.). 65 becomes County road 37 at Routes 5 and 20 (West Bloomfield). Continue south to Route 20 A and follow signs. From Canandaigua, go west on 5 and 20 to West Bloomfield. Turn left and follow County Road 37 to 20 A in Honeoye.*

Along with a full line of antiques, this store offers an appraisal service, expertise in interior design as well as landscape design. They'll even help you design the wedding of your dreams. One stop shopping!

## 73 STATEN ISLAND

**Harborview Antiques**
1385 Bay St.
718/448-4649

**New Dorp Village Antiques**
517 & 519 Broadway
718/815-2526

**Faban General Mercandise & Antq. Store**
147 Canal
718/727-2917

**HEY Viv! Vintage Clothing**
125 Port Richmond Ave.
718/981-3575

**Rainbows End Gifts Antiques**
469 Port Richmond Ave.
718/273-3124

**Richmond Consignments**
1434 Richmond Road
718/980-4333

## 74 SYRACUSE

**Cerenas Antiques & Home Furniture**
2111 Brewerton Road
315/454-5543

**Antique Center of Syracuse**
1460 Burnet Ave.
315/476-8270

**Dacia of NY Vintage Furniture Shop**
2416 Court St.
315/455-2651

**Antique Underground**
247 W. Fayette St.
315/472-5510

**Lilac House**
1415 W. Genesee St.
315/471-3866

**Dewitt Antique Jwlry & Coin Co.**
4621 E. Genesee St.
315/445-1065

**Daltons Antiques**
1931 James St.
315/463-1568

**Antiques & Jewelry on Jefferson**
306 W. Jefferson St.
315/476-5926

**European Gallery & Frame Shop**
201 S. Main St.
315/458-6593

**Boom Babies Vintage Clothing**
489 Westcott St.
315/472-1949

**AAAA Antiques & Appraisals**
101 Wells Ave. E.
315/458-8193

**Ace Enterprise**
1200 Butternut St.
315/475-8006

**Colella Galleries**
123 E. Willow St.
315/474-6950

**Jerry Bonk Enterprises**
204 Rita Dr.
315/458-4649

**Karens Deco-Craft**
2101 Brewerton Road
315/455-2214

**Antique Exchange**
1600 Block N. Salina St.
315/471-1841

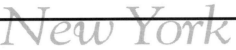

**Shades of Yesteryear Antiques**
658 N. Salina St.
315/423-9810

**Cash Corner**
1101 N. Salina St.
315/475-4045

### *Great Places To Stay*

**Giddings Garden Bed and Breakfast**
290 W. Seneca Turnpike
315/492-6389 or 1-800-377-3452
Always open
*Directions: From Route 81, north or south, take Exit 16 A (North 481 Dewitt). Stay on Route 481 to Exit 1 (Brighton Ave./Rockcut Road). Bare right onto Rockcut Road to the top of the hill. Turn left at the light onto Brighton. At the light, turn right onto East Seneca Turnpike for 1 miles. Bed and breakfast is on the right, at the corner of Milburn Drive.*

This elegantly restored Federal Tavern, circa 1810, offers such tasteful amenities as in-room fireplaces, private baths, and poster beds.

Outside, the lush gardens and lily ponds offer more opportunity for peaceful pleasure.

In the morning, guests may start the day with a full gourmet breakfast followed by relaxation or antique hunting. For those who choose the latter, a local map and listings are available.

## 75 TARRYTOWN

**Treasure Trove**
19 N. Broadway
914/366-4243

**Remember Me Antiques**
9 Main St.
914/631-4080

**Carol Master Antiques**
15 Main St.
914/332-8441

**North Castle Antiques**
28 Main St.
914/631-1112

**Spencer Marks**
Main St.
914/332-1142

**Michael Christopher's**
Main St.
914/366-4665

**Sam Said**
80 S. Broadway
914/631-3368

**Virginia's**
13 Main St.
No Phone

**Tarrytown Art & Antique Center**
19 Main St.
914/524-9626

**Traeger's Antiques**
35 Main St.
914/631-8694

**Hank's Alley**
15 N. Washington St.
914/524-9895

## 76 TONAWANDA

**Bronstein Antiques**
4049 Delaware Ave.
716/873-7000

## 77 TRUMANSBURG

**The Collection**
9-11 Main St.
607/387-6579 or 607/273-3480
Tues.-Sat. 11-5, Sun. 1-5, or by appointment
*Directions: The Collection is 10 miles north of Ithaca, N.Y., on Route 96 North, 15 miles south of New York's Thruway, Geneva Exit, Route 96 S.*

Featuring country Americana, 18th and 19th century country and formal furniture, primitives, quilts, folk art, early lighting, decorated stoneware and samplers. Insurance and estate appraisals.

**Ponzis Antiques**
9838 Congress St.
607/387-5248

### *Great Places To Stay*

**The Archway Bed and Breakfast**
7020 Searsburg Road
607/387-6175 or 1-800-387-6175
Open 7 days a week
*Directions: From New York State Route 96 in Trumansburg, go 1/2 mile south on 227 toward Watkins Glen. The bed and breakfast is on the corner of 227 and Searsburg.*

Owner Meredith Pollard relates that when they were formerly listed as simply "The Archway," they kept getting orders for cookies! They would reply, "We don't do cookies, but we make great muffins!"

This particular bed and breakfast borders a public golf course.

## 78 UTICA

**Antiques & Such**
210 Bleecker St.
315/724-0889

**Antique Clothing Company**
252 Genesee St.
315/724-3262

**Comeskey Stamp & Coin**
701 Noyes St.
315/724-9616

**Mister Jack's Antiques & Furniture**
250 Genesee St.
315/735-3815

**A A A Vintage Furnishings**
337 Genesee St.
315/738-1333

**A A Jewelry Buyers & Swap Shop**
400 South St.
315/724-3525

## 79 VALLEY STREAM

**Central Antiques**
233 N. Central Ave.
516/825-1043

**Shure Barnette Antiques Inc.**
904 Rockaway Ave.
516/825-9297

## 80 WARWICK

**Bearly Antiques**
18 Beverly Dr.
914/986-1996

**Antiques at the Clock Tower**
65 Main St.
914/986-5199

**Clock Tower Antique Center**
65 Main St.
914/986-5199

**Red Shutters**
34 Maple Ave.
914/986-5954

**1809 House**
210 Route 94 S.
914/986-1809

## 81 WARRENSBURG

### *Great Places To Stay*

### The Merrill Magee House
2 Hudson St.
518/623-2449

From the inviting wicker chairs on the porch to the candlelit dining rooms, the inn offers the romance of a visit to a Victorian country home. Antiques, lace and fine linens are found in each of the individually decorated rooms along with handmade quilts and working fireplaces. Enjoy an intimate dinner in the award winning dining room.

## 82 WESTFIELD

**Lakewood Antiques**
6940 Chestnut
716/326-6620

**Militello's Antiques**
31 Jefferson St.
716/326-2587

**The Leonards Antiques**
E. Main St.
716/326-2210

**Eley Place Antiques**
3 E. Main St.
716/326-2130

**Antique Marketplace**
25 E. Main St.
716/326-2861

**Saraf's Emporium**
58 E. Main St.
716/326-3590

**Priscilla B Nixon Antiques**
119 W. Main St.
716/326-3511

**Mollard Antiques**
120 E. Main St.
716/326-3521

**Candelight Lodge Antiques**
143 E. Main St.
716/326-2830

**Notaros Antiques**
161 W. Main St.
716/326-3348

**Landmark Acres-Antiques**
232 W. Main St.
716/326-4185

**Arundel Antiques**
9 Market St.
No Phone

**Dorothea Bertram**
53 S. Portage St.
716/326-2551

**J Miller Antiques**
81 S. Portage St.
716/326-6699

**Vilardo Antiques**
7303 Walker Road
716/326-2714

**Monroes Antiques & Collectibles**
69 E. Main St.
817326-3060

## 83 WHITE PLAINS

**Vintage By Stacey Lee**
305 Central Ave., Suite 4
914/328-0788

## 84 WHITNEY POINT

### Days Gone By
2659 Main St.
607/692-2713
Wed.-Mon.10-5, closed Tues.
*Directions: Traveling I-81 North: Take Exit 8. Travel south on Route 26 to Route 11, and take a left. Take a right at the red light onto Main St. Traveling I-81 S.: Take Exit 8 to Route 11 and turn left. Turn right at 2nd light onto Main St. The shop is in the old church between Aiello's and the Food King.*

Nancy Jackson, owner of Days Gone By, is a girl "after my own heart." Her antique shop is located in an old church. I've always wanted to own such a shop myself. The shop offers 20 quality dealers situated on three floors presenting everything from glassware to furniture, and primitives to collectibles. The staff is happy to assist you in finding something here or directing you to other local antique communities nearby.

## 85 WOODSTOCK

While Woodstock is famous for two rock concerts, one in 1969 and one in 1996, neither took place here. The first was held in Bethel, 50 miles southwest; the second in Saugerties, 10 miles northeast.

Yet Woodstock is a delightful artists' community, with galleries, antique shops and a selection of places to stop for lunch. Reminiscent of the sixties, long skirts, long hair and tie-dye tee shirts are ubiquitous. At the center of town, you might find a reader of tarot cards, with a line of people patiently waiting a turn.

## 86 WURTSBORO

**Wurtsboro Wholesale Antiques**
203 Sullivan St.
914/888-4411

## 87 YONKERS

**Ogrady, M**
356 Riverdale Ave.
914/964-8836

**Lynn's Used Furniture**
26 Warburton Ave.
914/966-7075

**Mitchel's Antiques**
800 Yonkers Ave.
914/423-2600

# North Carolina

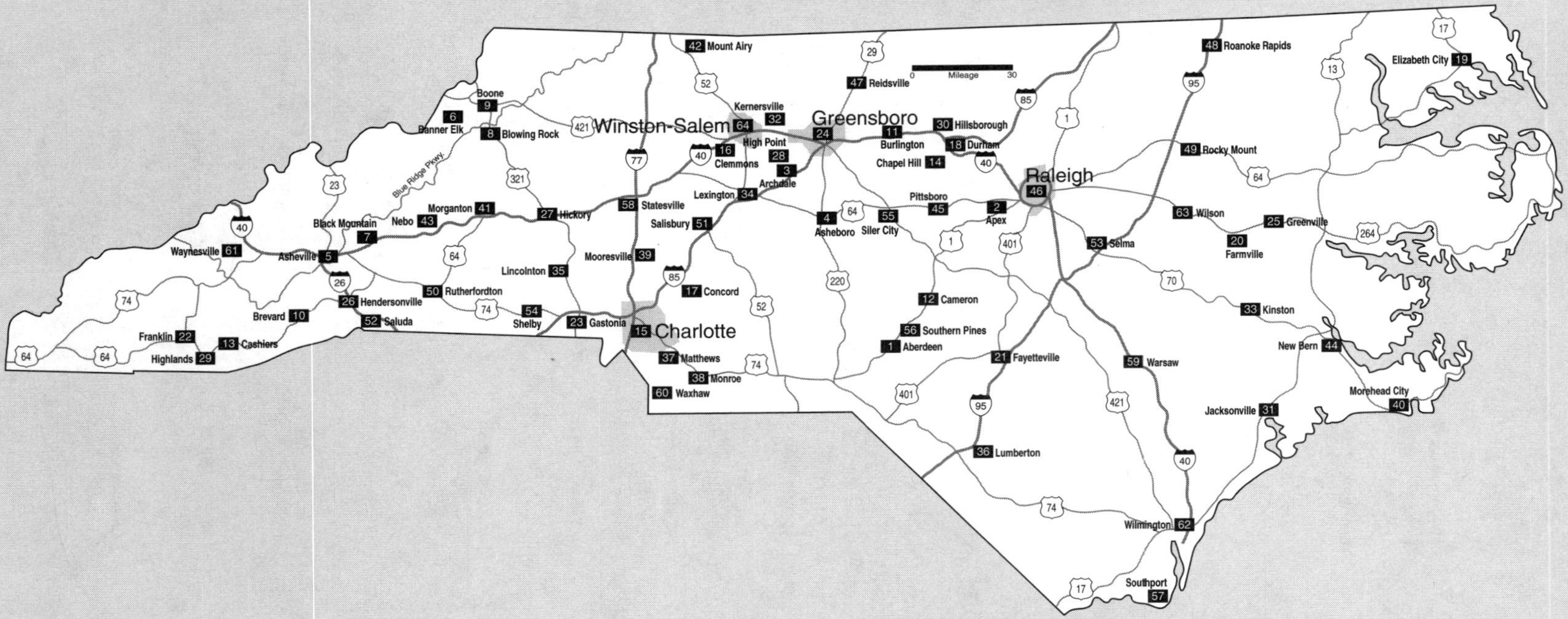

Oakwood Antiques Mall is known far and wide for having the largest selection of advertising memorabilia in the state of North Carolina.

The Lone Ranger rides again on this vintage advertising sign. No reproductions are allowed at the Oakwood Antiques Mall.

# Oakwood Antiques Mall is jam-packed with antiques collectibles and more

Inside the 10,000-square-feet of Oakwood Antiques Mall, more than 53 dealers have stuffed the aisles with a large variety of antiques and collectibles. No crafts or reproductions allowed. Marvel at the extensive collection of furniture, glass, toys, deco and '50s memorabilia. The shop is known to display the largest selection of antique advertising items in North Carolina.

*Oakwood Antiques Mall is located at 1526 Wake Forest Road in Raleigh, North Carolina. For additional information see listing #46 (Raleigh).*

*A rare National Cash register is one of the offerings from the more than 53 dealers of the antiques mall.*

*Looking as if she's right at home in the midst of the collectibles, an antique Dodge automobile makes her appearance at the Oakwood Antique Mall.*

# Merry Heart Cabin: A unique get-away vacation

One hour east of Asheville, nestled in the Blue Ridge mountains is a place called Merry Heart Cabin.

Overlooking a forest glen, this refurbished 110-year-old log cabin is yours exclusively. Merry Heart is the perfect spot for both couples and families, the best get-away-from-it-all spot in North Carolina.

Just 8 miles north of Interstate 40 and five minutes away from beautiful Lake James, Merry Heart provides everything necessary for a peaceful alternative to the "hurry up and relax" syndrome often experienced during a typical vacation.

Perfect for families desiring a quality-time environment or for couples seeking a romantic love nest, Merry Heart has it all. It is also a beautiful "safe haven" for individuals who desire a time out from life's busy pace.

*The Smarts raise a variety of animals on the farm, including smiling "Babydoll" sheep.*

Anything but a typical vacation cabin, Merry Heart recalls a simpler day in which a rich southern culture took its time to enjoy the fullness of life. It is a mood created when mankind and nature commune. Thus, Merry Heart Cabin-accented by its unique miniature animal farm including 24" sheep from England, 20" goats from Nigeria, 42" cattle from Ireland, 34" donkeys from Sardinia, and others, has become a renewal and resting spot for hundreds over the past four years.

Based upon the Bible scripture, "A merry heart doeth good like a medicine," the Smarts' hope to offer a dose of serenity to those who visit the cabin and farm.

Proprietors Leslie and Connie Smart state it simply, "Here at Merry Heart our desire is to offer an atmosphere of 'recreation', whether you choose to spend time at our miniature animal petting farm, horseback riding, rekindling your heart by the fire, soaking in your own private Jacuzzi or just enjoying the quiet intimacy of the quaint upstairs sleeping loft with beamed ceiling and spiral stairwell overlooking the living room with cozy fireplace."

Merry Heart is surrounded by such breathtaking scenery as was seen in the classic Michael Mann film "Last of the Mohicans" which was filmed just a five minute drive away from the cabin.

The cabin which is the centerpiece of Merry Heart was constructed in the late 1800s of hand-hewn logs and unites old time ambiance with the comfort of modern amenities such as air conditioning and gas heat.

From the rustic brick flooring to the high cedar-beamed ceiling, the cabin becomes a delightful home away from home.

Whether the guest have spent the day enjoying the nearby attractions or savoring a relaxing walk through the forest, a refreshing night awaits in the queen size bed in the unique sleeping loft or the two twin beds located on the lower level.

*Above: Guests find cozy comfort in the unique sleeping loft.*

*Left: Les and Connie Smart welcome you to Merry Heart Cabin.*

For the convenience of the guests, the cabin has a fully equipped kitchen with all staples, microwave, digital coffee maker, etc. All linens are provided as well.

Be sure to climb the knoll located at Merry Heart which provides a spectacular view over several ranges of the Appalachians, certain to enhance the peaceful mood created here. Oftentimes guests are treated to views of the gentle deer which come to feed in the glen during the early evening.

For those who enjoy the more rigorous activities, miles of exciting mountain biking and hiking trails are close by along "Old Highway 105" winding up to and overlooking the majestic Linville Wilderness Gorge area.

Hours of sightseeing are provided by such beautiful landmarks as Table Rock Mountain, Great Smokey Mountains National Park, Blue Ridge Parkway, Shortoff Mountain, Grandfather Mountain and Pisgah National Forest to name only a few.

Located about halfway between Statesville and Asheville, off I-40 and N.C. 126, Merry Heart Cabin is ideally situated to give access to Western North Carolina's attractions and yet far enough away to provide a relaxing retreat.

*For reservations, info, or a brochure call Les and Connie Smart, 1-888-736-0423 or visit their Web site at www.hci.net/~merryheart.*

## 1 ABERDEEN

**Cameron's Antique Station**
Hwy. 211 E. Ashley Heights
910/944-2022

**Cabbages & Kings**
111 W. Main St.
910/944-1110

**Honeycutt House**
204 E. Main St.
910/944-9236

**Town & Country Antique Mall**
1369 Sandhills Blvd. N.
910/944-3359

## 2 APEX

**Freewood Antiques**
541 New Hill Olive Chapel Road
919/362-6773

**That Unique & Wonderful Place**
104 N. Salem St.
919/387-9550

**Creative Expressions Gallery**
120 N. Salem St.
919/387-1952

**Olde Barn Antiques**
2708 Tingen Road
919/362-5266

## 3 ARCHDALE

### *Great Places To Stay*

**The Bouldin House Bed & Breakfast**
4332 Archdale Road
910/431-4909 or 1-800-739-1816
Fax: 910/431-4914
Rates: $85-95
*Directions: Take Exit 111 off Interstate 85. Turn north on Route 311 toward High Point. Turn left on Balfour Dr. Turn right on Archdale Road. The Boulding House is 2/10 mile on your left. Located four miles from downtown High Point, 20 minutes from Greensboro and 20 minutes from Winston-Salem.*

The Bouldin House offers guests a graceful version of country living on the lush, green acres of a former tobacco farm at the edge of North Carolina's bustling Piedmond Triad area. It took nearly two years to restore this fine country home to its original beauty. Today, that beauty resonates in the wainscottting of the hallways, in the finely crafted oak paneling of the dining room and in the decorative patterns and designs of the hardwood floors. Each bedroom features a fireplace, modern bath, king-size bed and large closets. The bedrooms also have personalities reflected in their names: "Warm Morning Room," "Doctor's Den," "Weekend Retreat," and "The Parlor."

The inn is only minutes from elegant restaurants, historic sites, abundant sports and entertainment events, and America's largest concentration of furniture showrooms.

## 4 ASHEBORO

**Nostalgia**
111 N. Church St.
336/625-0644

**Holly House Antiques & Collectibles**
207 E. Pritchard St.
336/625-4994

**Collectors Antique Mall**
211 Sunset Ave.
336/629-8105

**Andorra's Antiques Etc.**
305 Sunset Ave.
336/626-3699

**Weathervane**
239 White Oak St.
336/625-2404

**Cabin Creek Antiques**
3574 U.S. Hwy. 64 E.
336/626-0685

## 5 ASHEVILLE

**Fireside Antiques**
30 All Souls Crescent
704/274-5977
*Directions: Just one minute off I-40; take Exit 50B and the shop is located 1/4 mile on the left.*

Fireside Antiques is a direct importer of European antiques featuring four galleries of fine antiques, gifts and oriental porcelain. Specializing in English Georgian mahogany, English and Irish pine, Walnut and French furniture of the 17th, 18th, and 19th centuries, this is a must stop shop when traveling through Asheville.

**Pheasant on a Halfshell**
36 Battery Park Ave.
704/253-3577

**Lexington Park Antiques**
65 W. Walnut St.
704/253-3070

**King-Thomasson Antiques Inc.**
64 Biltmore Ave.
704/252-1565

**Village Antiques**
755 Biltmore Ave.
704/252-5090

**Chelsea's Gifts & Antiques**
6 Boston Way
704/274-4400

**Biltmore Antique Mall**
30 Bryson St.
704/255-0053

**Korth & Company**
30 Bryson St.
704/252-0906

**Pals**
24 N. Lexington Ave.
704/253-0440

**Catskill Antique Co.**
34 N. Lexington Ave.
704/252-2611

**Corner Cupboard Antique Mall**
49 N. Lexington Ave.
704/258-9815

**House of Alexander**
54 N. Lexington Ave.
704/251-0505

**Jim Knapp Antiques**
503 Haywood Road
704/258-0031

**Mac's Antiques**
602 Haywood Road
704/255-7809

**Interiors Marketplace**
2 Hendersonville Road
704/253-2300

**Old But Good**
2614 Hendersonville Road
704/687-3890

**Asheville Antiques Mall**
43 Rankin Ave.
704/253-3634

### *Great Places To Stay*

**Chestnut Street Inn**
176 E. Chestnut St.
1-800-894-2955

Chestnut Street Inn, located in the heart of the Liberty/Chester National Historic District, caters to those looking for an experience. The owner's love of people creates an inviting atmosphere to accompany the comfort and enchantment of the inn. Enjoy afternoon 'tea and crumpets', relax in the mountain breeze on one of the large porches, or take the five-minute walk to downtown Asheville for antiquing, sightseeing, or just selecting from several fine restaurants for dinner.

**The Inn on Montford**
296 Montford Ave.
1-800-254-9509
Web site: innonmontford.com

The Inn on Montford was designed by Richard Sharp Smith, supervising architect for Biltmore House. Today it is an elegant bed and breakfast furnished with English and American antiques dating from 1730 to 1910. Four exquisite rooms have private baths, queen size beds, fireplaces and telephones.

## 6 BANNER ELK

**Finders Keepers**
Green Mansions Village/Hwy. 105
704/963-7300

**Susanna's Antiques**
Hwy. 105
704/963-8685

**Marjon's Antiques**
10884 N. High, #1055
704/963-5305

**Elk River Trading Post**
Hwy. 194
704/898-9477

**Mill Pond Arts & Antiques**
920 Shawneehaw Ave.
704/898-5175

## 7 BLACK MOUNTAIN

**Aly Goodwin: The N. E. Horton Antique Quilt Collection**
100 Sutton Ave.
(Inside Black Mountain Antique Mall)
704/669-6218
Mon.-Sat. 10-5, Sun 1:30-5, year round
*Directions: Located off I-40, 15 minutes east of Asheville. Headed East on I-40, take Exit 64. Turn left to Black Mountain; at Sutton Ave. traffic light, turn left, immediately pull to right and park. Approximately one mile from interstate.*

Located in the Black Mountain Antique Mall, Aly Goodwin: The N. E. Horton Antique Quilt Collection specializes in antique quilts (c. 1780-1940) numbering over 300; as well as southern pottery and folk art, furniture, Victorian antique paintings, linens, books, tools and much more. The 7,000-square-foot Black Mountain Antique Mall is noted as being North Carolina's year-round antique show!

**Treasures & Trivia**
106 Broadway St.
704/669-5190

**L A Glenn Co Inc.**
109 Cherry St.
704/669-4886

**Hoard's Antiques**
121 Cherry St.
704/669-6494

**Cherry St. Antique Mall**
139 Cherry St.
704/669-7942

## 8 BLOWING ROCK

**Dreamfields of Blowing Rock**
Hwy. 105 Green Mt. Village
704/963-8333

**Blowing Rock Antique Center**
U.S. Hwy. 321 Bypass
704/295-4950

**Antique Rug Buyers of Florida**
999 N. Main St.
704/295-7750

**Hanna's Oriental Rugs & Gifts**
1123 Main St.
704/295-7073

**Family Heirlooms**
1125 Main St.
704/295-0090

**Village Antiques**
1127 Main St.
704/295-7874

**Old World Galleries**
1053 N. Main St.
704/295-7508

**Windwood Antiques**
1157 S. Main St.
704/295-9260

**Mystery Hill**
129 Mystery Hill Lane
704/264-2792

**Possum Hollow Antiques**
Opossum Hollow Road
704/295-3502

### *Great Places To Stay*

**Stone Pillar Bed & Breakfast**
144 Pine St.
P. O. Box 1881
704/295-4141
Web site: blowingrock.com/northcarolina
Daily 8-10
Rates $65-95
*Directions: From I-40, exit 123, to Hwy. 321 directly to Blowing Rock. At Sunset Dr. turn left into town. At Main St. tun right to Pine St. (second street on right); turn right on Pine. Inn is located at 144 Pine St.*

Nestled in the mountains of western North Carolina, just off the Blue Ridge Parkway, the town of Blowing Rock is home to Stone Pillar Bed & Breakfast. Located just 1/2 block from Main St., the Stone Pillar provides a relaxing home-like atmosphere in an historic 1920s house. Six guests rooms, each with private bath, offer a tasteful blend of heirlooms and antiques, accented by a few touches of modern.

# North Carolina

A full breakfast is created daily in the house kitchen and served family style to the Stone Pillar's guests. The living/dining area, with its working fireplace, offers an opportunity to meet fellow guest.

If you want an action-packed day of frantic activity such as hiking, skiing, sight-seeing, antiquing or prefer to just relax and enjoy the peace and quiet and fresh mountain air, the high country area is the ideal place to enjoy your perfect get away.

## 9 BOONE

**Antiques Unlimited Mall**
231 Boone Heights Dr.
704/265-3622

**Wilcox Emporium**
161 Howard St.
704/262-1221

**Boone Antique Mall**
631 W. King St.
704/262-0521

**Blowing Rock Antique Center**
877 W. King St.
704/264-5757

**Hidden Valley Antiques**
Hwy. 105 S.
704/963-5224

**Marines Interiors Inc.**
Hwy. 105 S.
704/963-4656

**Loafer's Glory**
U.S. Hwy. 321
704/265-3797

**Aunt Pymms Table Antiques**
U.S. Hwy. 421
704/262-1041

**Unique Interiors**
240 Shadowline Dr.
704/265-1422

## 10 BREVARD

**John Reynolds Antiques**
6 S. Broad St.
704/884-4987

**Open Door Antique Mall**
15 W. Main St.
704/883-4323

**Brevard Antique Mall**
57 E. Main St.
704/885-2744

**Carolina Connection Antiques**
5 W. Main St.
704/884-9786

**Whitewater Gardens**
259 Rosman Hwy.
704/884-2656

## 11 BURLINGTON

### Lionheart Antiques

120 E. Front St.
336/570-0830, 336/449-6595
Mon.-Wed. by chance or appointment, Thurs.-Sat. 10-5, Sun., 1-5
*Directions: Off I-40 and I-85, between Raleigh and Greensboro, North Carolina. Take Exit 145 to downtown Burlington. Turn right on Main St. and continue for 2 blocks. Turn right on Front St. Lionheart is on the left. Look for the lions.*

From its beginning at the turn of the century, the building housing Lionheart Antiques has been a showcase for fine furniture and decorative pieces for the home. Today, with the focus on antiques, the 5,000-square-foot showroom presents mahogany and glass cases displaying porcelain, crystal, boxes and scientific instruments. In the Garden and Architectural Room, a complete Columbia, S. C. post office serves as a backdrop for cast iron urns, fences, and gates from Europe. Many buying trips to Europe during the year keep the exciting and interesting pieces, from furniture to lamps and accessories, filling up the shop. Fair prices and a great variety is the reason shoppers return to Lionheart; or could it be because Boris, the Belgian Shepard greets them at the door?

**Eric Lane Antiques**
2602 Eric Lane
336/222-1496

**Robert Hodgin Antiques**
346 S. Worth St.
336/229-1865

**Antiques Art**
309 Trollinger St.
336/229-1331

**Burlwood Farm Antiques**
4758 Friendship Patterson Mill
336/226-5139

## 12 CAMERON

**Aunt Bertie's**
Hwy. 24-27
910/245-7059

**Crabtree Antiques**
Hwy. 24-27
910/245-3163

**Cranes Creek Antiques**
Hwy. 24-27
910/245-4476

**Ferguson House Antiques**
Hwy. 24-27
910/245-3055

**McKeithens Antiques**
Hwy. 24-27
910/245-4886

**McPherson's Antiques**
Hwy. 24-27
910/692-3449

**Old Greenwood Inn**
Hwy. 24-27
910/245-7431

## 13 CASHIERS

**Cobbies Interiors**
Route 64/Near Crossroads
704/743-2585

**Lyn K. Holloway Antiques**
Route 64 & 107
704/743-2524

**Trove Treasure**
Hwy. 64
704/743-9768

**Valley Gift Shop**
Hwy. 64 W.
704/743-2944

**Wormy Chestnut Antiques**
Hwy. 64
704/743-3014

**Rosemary's Antiques Etc.**
Hwy. 107
704/743-9808

**Cashiers East Antiques Mall**
Hwy. 107 S.
704/743-3580

**Not All Country Store**
Hwy. 107
704/743-3612

*Great Places To Stay*

**Millstone Inn**
Hwy. 64 W.
1-888-645-5786
Web site: www.millstoneinn.com

The Millstone Inn is situated on a cool, breezy 3,500 foot hilltop overlooking the Nantahalah Forest. The wood exterior, exposed beam ceilings, and stone fireplace in conjunction with the period and antique furnishings project a truly rustic elegance. The magnificent trees, waterfalls and wonderful views provide a casual and beautiful setting. There are many hiking trails, a trout pond, wild flowers and colorful birds to enjoy. A delicious full breakfast is served in the dining room overlooking Whiteside Mountain.

## 14 CHAPEL HILL

**Patterson's Mill Country Store**
5109 Farrington Road
919/493-8149

**Whitehall at the Villa Antique**
1213 E. Franklin St.
919/942-3179

**Countryside Antiques Inc**
9555 U.S. Hwy. 15-501 N.
919/968-8375

*Great Places To Stay*

**The Inn at Bingham School**
P.O. Box 267
919/563-5583

The inn is an award-winning restoration of a National Trust Property nestled among pecan trees and rolling farmland. Once a prestigious preparatory school for men, the inn is steeped in history. Offering a blend of old and new, you can select from five spacious guest rooms with modern private baths.

## 15 CHARLOTTE

**Blacklion Furniture, Gift & Design Showcases**
10605 Park Road
704/541-1148
*Directions: Conveniently located near Southpark and Carolina Place Malls off I-485 at Hwy. 51.*

Under one roof, in a convenient location, and in picturesque settings, Blacklion offers home decor from some of the most selective dealers in the Carolinas. A collection of distinctive show spaces feature: old world antiques, over 2,382 works of art, lawn and garden accents, lamps and rugs, as well as gifts and accessories. Twenty-three Interior Designers are available for expressing ideas, inspiration and practical solutions to your decorating needs.

**Antique Kingdom**
700 Central Ave.
704/377-5464

**The Galleria Gifts & Interiors**
1401 Central Ave.
704/372-1050

**Circa Interiors & Antiques**
2321 Crescent Ave.
704/332-1668

**English Room**
519 Fenton Place
704/377-3625

**Queen City Antqs., Collectibles & Jewelry**
3892 E. Independence Blvd.
704/531-6002

**Mary Frances Miller Antiques**
1437 E. Morehead St.
704/375-9240

**Karen's Beautiful Things**
8324 Pineville Matthews Road
704/542-1412

**Queen Charlotte Antiques Ltd.**
603 Providence Road
704/333-0472

**Gallery Designs Ltd.**
739 Providence Road
704/376-9163

**Antiques on Selwyn**
2909 Selwyn Ave.
704/342-2111

**Perry's at Southpark**
4400 Sharon Road
704/364-1391

**By-Gone Days Antiques Inc.**
3100 South Blvd.
704/527-8717

**Metrolina Expo**
7100 Statesville Road
704/596-4643

**Thompson Antique Co.**
7631 Wilkinson Blvd.
704/399-1405

**Clearing House Inc.**
701 Central Ave.
704/375-7708

**Crescent Collection Ltd.**
2318A Crescent Ave.
704/333-7922

**Tudor House Galleries Inc.**
1401 East Blvd.
704/377-4748

**Consignment Corner**
3852 E. Independence Blvd.
704/535-3840

**Treasure House**
5300 Monroe Road
704/532-1613

**Treasures Unlimited Inc.**
6401 Morrison Blvd.
704/366-7272

**Windwood Antiques**
421 Providence Road
704/372-4577

**Jenko's**
715 Providence Road
704/375-1779

**Colony Furn Shops Inc.**
811 Providence Road
704/333-8871

**Le-Dee-Das**
1942 E. 7th St.
704/372-9599

**Interiors Marketplace**
2000 South Blvd.
704/377-6226

**Chris' Collectibles**
7100 Statesville Road, B17
704/596-1592

**Dilworth Billiards**
300 E. Tremont Ave.
704/333-3021

*Great Places To Stay*

**The Elizabeth Bed & Breakfast**
2145 E. 5th St.
704/358-1368
Web site: www.bbhost.com/elizabethbnb

Built in 1923, this lavender painted 'lady' is in historic Charlotte's second-oldest neighborhood. European country-style rooms are beautifully appointed with antiques, ceiling fans, decorator linens and unique collections. Enjoy a delicious full breakfast, then relax in the garden courtyard or stroll beneath giant oak trees to convenient restaurants and shopping.

**The Homeplace Bed & Breakfast**
5901 Sardis Road
704/365-1936

Built in 1902, this completely restored home sits on 2 1/2 wooded acres. The Homeplace has 10-foot beaded ceilings, eight fireplaces, front and back stairways, all in original heart-of-pine woodwork. While touring the grounds you will see "The Barnplace", a 1930s log barn that was moved to the property in 1991. Two guest rooms with private bath and a suite are available.

## 16 CLEMMONS

*Great Places To Stay*

**Tanglewood Manor House Bed & Breakfast and Lodge**
P. O. Box 1040
336/778-6370

Circa 1859 home located within walking distance of the beach, river, rodeo, ruins and winery. On site activities include downhill skiing.

## 17 CONCORD

**Irbys Antiques**
244 McGill Ave. N.W.
704/788-1810

**Clock & Lamp Shoppe**
250 McGill Ave. N.W.
704/786-1929

**Memory Shoppe**
885 Old Charlotte Road
704/788-9443

**Antique Market of Concord**
14 Union St.
704/786-4296

**21 Union St-A Trading Co**
21 Union St.
704/782-1212

**Six O One Trading Post**
4018 U.S. Hwy. 601 S.
704/782-1212

**Dennis Carpenter Repro Ford**
4140 U.S. Hwy. 29 S.
704/786-8139

**Annies Cane Shop**
5680 U.S. Hwy. 601 S.
704/782-4937

## 18 DURHAM

**Chelsea Antiques**
2631 Durham Chapel Hill Blvd.
919/683-1865

**Antiques 1**
4422 Durham Chapel Hill Blvd.
919/493-7135

**Orig Illusions Antiques & Collectibles**
4422 Durham Chapel Hill Blvd.
919/493-4650

**Willow Park Lane**
4422 Durham Chapel Hill Blvd.
919/493-3923

**Attic Treasures**
2014 Granville Circle
919/403-8639

**Trash & Treasures**
2911 Guess Road
919/477-6716

**Antiques 1**
947 S. Miami Blvd.
919/596-1848

**James Kennedy Antiques Ltd.**
905 W. Main St.
919/682-1040

**White House Antiques**
3306 Old Chapel Hill Road
919/489-3016

**Twice Remembered**
4109 N. Roxboro Road
919/471-1148

**Sandpiper Antiques**
5218 Wake Forest Road
919/596-4949

**Finders Keepers**
2501 University Dr.
919/490-4441

**Maral Antiques & Interiors**
5102 Chapel Hill Road
919/493-7345

## 19 ELIZABETH CITY

**Pleasurehouse Antiques**
608 E. Colonial Ave.
919/338-6570

**Parker's Trading Post**
1051 U.S. Hwy. 17 S.
919/335-4896

**Pasquotank Antiques**
117 N. Water St.
919/331-2010

**Miller Antiques**
207 N. Water St.
919/335-1622

## 20 FARMVILLE

**The Hub Mall**
104 S. Main St.
919/753-8560
Mon.-Sat., 10-5:30
*Directions: Off I-95 on Hwy. 264 E. between Wilson, N.C., and Greenville, N.C.*

If you believe all rooms should be comfortable, timeless, unpretentious, as well as beautiful, then you will want to shop at The Hub. There you can furnish your home with antiques of enduring value. Since The Hub Mall is an alliance of dealers, you will be more likely to find the piece you are seeking. Each shopping trip becomes an aesthetic experience as you search for craftsmanship, artistry and one of a kind items in this large historically restored building in downtown Farmville.

**Rememberings**
119 S. Main St.
919/753-7333

**Jackie's Ole House**
RR 1
919/753-2631

## 21 FAYETTEVILLE

**Warpath Military Collectibles**
3805 Cumberland Road
910/425-7000

**Craft Market**
5012 Cumberland Road
910/424-0838

**Antique & Gift Center**
123 Hay St.
910/485-7602

**David R Walters Antique**
1110 Hay St.
910/483-5832

**Harris Auct. Gllry & Antique Mall**
2419 Hope Mills Road
910/424-0033

**Eastover Trading Co. Antique Mall**
Hwy. 301 N.
910/323-1121

**Country Junction**
Hwy. 87 S.
910/677-0017

**Antiques Unlimited of Eastover**
1128 Middle Road
910/323-5439

**Dimples & Sawdust Antique Dolls**
5409 Labrador
910/484-3655

**Tarbridge Military Collectibles**
5820 Ramsey St.
910/488-7207

**A A Antique Village**
5832 Ramsey St.
910/822-9822

**Unique Curtains & Antiques**
Stoney Point Road
910/424-1101

## 22 FRANKLIN

**Smoky Mt. Antique Mall**
4488 Georgia Road
704/524-5293

**R & S Furnshng. & Antique Mall**
354 E. Main St.
704/524-8188

**Friendly Village Antique Mall**
268 E. Palmer St.
704/524-8200

### *Great Places To Stay*

**Blaine House Bed & Breakfast and Cottage**
661 Harrison Ave.
704/349-4230

Blaine House, situated in the beautiful mountains of western North Carolina, reflects the serenity that is reminiscent of homes of yesteryear. A true bed and breakfast, this 1910 home has been restored to its original state revealing beautiful oak floors and beadboard ceilings and walls. Guest rooms are immaculate, well-appointed and throughtfully decorated with curios and relics to enhance their individual distinctiveness. Awake to the aroma of a Chef's choice breakfast that promises to be a truly memorable experience.

## 23 GASTONIA

**Past Time Antique Mall**
401 Cox Road
704/867-6535

**J & W Antiques**
181 W. Main Ave.
704/867-0097

**Willow Shoppe Ltd.**
1008 Union Road
704/866-9611

## 24 GREENSBORO

**Zenkes Inc.**
210 Blandwood Ave.
336/273-9335

**Caroline Faison Antiques**
18 Battleground Court
336/272-0261

**Carlson Antiques & Gifts**
507 N. Church St.
336/273-1626

**Elm Street Marketplace**
203 S. Elm St.
336/273-1767

**Antiques & Accessories on Elm**
323 S. Elm St.
336/273-6468

**Browsery Used Book Store**
506 S. Elm St.
336/370-4648

**Browsery Antiques**
516 S. Elm St.
336/274-3231

**Dramore Antiques**
526 S. Elm St.
336/275-7563

**Unexpected Antique Shop**
534 S. Elm St.
336/275-4938

**Rhynes Corner Cupboard**
603 S. Elm St.
336/378-1380

**Edlins Antiques**
604 S. Elm St.
336/274-2509

**Knight & Elliott**
909 N. Elm St.
336/370-4155

**E Freeman and Co.**
420 Eugene Court
336/275-8487

**Crumplers Antiques & Pottery**
442 N. Eugene St.
336/272-4383

**Saltbox Inc.**
2011 Golden Gate Dr.
336/273-8758

**Posh**
5804 High Point Road
336/294-1028

**Skinner & Company**
2908 Liberty Road
336/691-1219

**Spease House of Treasures**
350 McAdoo Ave.
336/275-2079

**Lavene Antiques**
4522 W. Market St.
336/854-8160

**Gallery Antiques**
801 Merritt Dr.
336/299-2426

**O'Henry Antiques**
3224 N. O'Henry Blvd.
336/375-0191

**Tyler-Smith Antiques**
501 Simpson St.
336/274-6498

**Cherrys Fine Guns**
3402 W. Wendover Ave., #A
336/854-4182

**House Dressing**
3608 W. Wendover Ave.
336/294-3900

**Byerlys Antiques Inc.**
4311 Wiley Davis Road
336/299-6510

# North Carolina

## 25 GREENVILLE

**Cable & Craft at Woodside**
Allen Road
919/756-9929

**Woodside Antiques**
Allen Road
919/756-9929

**Artisans Market**
2500 S. Charles St.
919/355-5536

**Tried & True Inc.**
924 Dickinson Ave.
919/752-2139

**Dapper Dans**
417 S. Evans St.
919/752-1750

**Red Oak Show & Sell**
264 W. Farmville Hwy.
919/756-1156

**Greenville Antique Mall**
E. N.C. Hwy. 33
919/752-8111

**Now & Then Designs**
801 Red Banks Road
919/756-8470

**Johnsen's Antiques & Lamp Shop**
315 E. 11th St.
919/758-4839

## 26 HENDERSONVILLE

**Old & New Shop**
3400 Asheville Hwy.
704/697-6160

**Richard D Hatch & Associates**
3700 Asheville Hwy.
704/696-3440

**Heritage Square Antiques**
Church & Barnwell
704/697-0313

**Antiques & Decorative Arts**
305 S. Church St.
704/697-6930

**Nancy Roth Antiques**
127 4th Ave. W.
704/697-7555

**Antiques Etc.**
147 4th Ave. W.
704/696-8255

**Scottie's Jewelry & Fine Art**
225 N. Main St.
704/692-1350

**Days Gone By Antiques**
303 N. Main St.
704/693-9056

**Calico Gallery of Crafts**
317 N. Main St.
704/697-2551

**Fourth & Main Antique Mall**
344 N. Main St.
704/698-0018

**Southern Comforts Antiques & Gifts**
628 Shawn Rachel Pkwy.
704/693-5310

**Wagon Wheel Antiques**
423 N. Main St.
704/692-0992

**Village Green Antique Mall**
424 N. Main St.
704/692-9057

**Mehri & Co. of New York**
501 N. Main St.
704/693-0887

**Honeysuckle Hollow**
512 N. Main St.
704/697-2197

**South Main Antiques**
119 S. Main St.
704/693-3212

**Hendersonville Antiques Mall**
670 Spartanberg Hwy.
704/692-5125

**JRD's Classics & Collectibles**
102 3rd Ave. E.
704/698-0075

### *Great Places To Stay*

**Melange Bed and Breakfast**
1230 5th Ave. W.
1-800-303-5253
Web site: www.circle.net/~melange

Melange is home to a blend of European and American cultures in a large New England colonial home from the 1920s. The house with its splendid gardens received its opulent French character in the early sixties when structural changes were made to the interior. Marble mantels and ornate mirrors from Paris, crystal chandeliers from Vienna, and hand painted porcelain accessories from Italy were imported. Fountains, Turkish tiles, a rose garden, colorful plants, enticing music, candles, old pictures, books and wonderful food underscore a cosmopolitan mindset. Four-color theme decorated rooms and a suite have private bath or Jacuzzi. Quiet and private. Paddleball court and fitness room. Less than 20 minutes walking to downtown Hendersonville and within thirty minutes drive to Biltmore Estate and Blue Ridge Parkway.

## 27 HICKORY

**Baker & Co. Antiques**
227 1st Ave. N.W.
704/324-2334

**Farm House Furnishings**
1432 1st Ave. S.W.
704/324-4595

**Collectors Cottage Antiques**
4164 Henry River Road
704/397-6386

**Norma's Antiques**
327 2nd Ave. N.W.
704/328-8660

**Southern Pride Antiques**
1949 Startown Road
704/322-6205

**Antiques and More**
1046 3rd Ave. N.W.
704/326-9030

**Hickory Antiques Mall**
348 U.S. Hwy. 70 S.
704/322-4004

**L & L Antiques**
4025 U.S. Hwy. 70 S.
704/328-9373

## 28 HIGH POINT

**Deep River Antiques**
2022 Eastchester Dr.
336/883-7005

**Wallace Antiques**
706 Greensboro Road
336/884-8044

**Antique & Vintage Furnishings**
652 N. Main St.
336/886-5126

**Kathryn's Collection**
781 N. Main St.
336/841-7474

**North Main Antiques & Collectibles**
1240 N. Main St.
336/882-2512

**Elisabeths Timeless Treasures**
1701 N. Main St.
336/887-3089

**Teague Pump Co. Inc.**
904 Old Thomasville Road
336/882-2916

**Randall Tysinger Antiques**
342 N. Wrenn St.
336/883-4477

## 29 HIGHLANDS

**A Country Home**
5162 Cashiers Road
704/526-9038

**Country Inn Antiques**
4th & Main/Highlands Inn
704/526-9380

**Home & Holiday**
4th St. on the Hill
704/526-2007

**Mirror Lake Antiques**
215 S. Fourth St.
704/526-2080

**C K Swann**
Hwy. 64 E.
704/526-2083

**Elephant's Foot Antiques**
Hwy. 64 & Foreman Road
704/526-5451

**Hanover House Antiques**
Hwy. 64 E.
704/526-4425

**Juliana's**
Main St.
704/526-4306

**I'm Precious Too!**
E. Main at Leonard
704/526-2754

**Stone Lantern**
309 Main St.
704/526-2769

**Royal Scot, Inc.**
318 Main St.
704/526-5917

**Scudders Galleries**
352 Main St.
704/526-4111

**Richard Guritz Antiques**
8 Mountain Brook Center
704/526-9680

**Fletcher & Lee Antiques**
10 Mountain Brook Center
704/526-5400

**Great Things**
Wright Square
704/526-3966

***Great Places To Stay***

### Colonial Pines Inn
541 Hickory St.
704/526-2060

Nestled on a secluded hillside just half a mile from Main Street, this gracious old home is surrounded by two acres of large rhododendron, hemlock, maple, and oak. Experience Highlands' clean, fresh air and enjoy lush views from wide porches. Sample berries from the garden, then visit the nature areas, ponds, fine boutiques and gourmet restaurants that are just a stroll away. Spacious suites and moderately priced rooms are filled with antique furnishings. A sumptuous breakfast is included and served in the dining room to the sounds of quiet classical, folk, or mountain tunes.

### Morning Star Inn
480 Flat Mountain Estates Road
704/526-1009

The Morning Star Inn is surrounded by waterfalls, gorgeous mountain scenery, trout-filled streams, and national forests. Prestigious golf courses and specialty and antique shops make this a couple's perfect getaway. The inn is on two private acres offering a gorgeous mountain view. Relax on the wicker-filled porch, enjoy wine and hors d'oeuvres in the large parlor with stone fireplace, and savor a gourmet breakfast in the sunroom.

## 30 HILLSBOROUGH

### Village Square Antiques & Auction
126 Antique St.
919/732-8799
Wed.-Sat. 11-5, Sun. 1-5
*Directions: Located I-85 Exit 164 & I-40 Exit 261 in the Daniel Boone Village.*

Located in the "Heart of North Carolina Antique Country" Village Square Antiques and Auctions is a jack-of-all-trades and master-of-ALL. The shop offers an outstanding selection of antiques such as depression glass, formal mahogany furniture, classic oak furniture, clocks, estate jewelry, carnival glass, lamps, chandeliers, old Fenton art glass, fine porcelain, Hawkes, Akro Agate children's dishes, sterling silver, cast iron and old tools, cut and elegant glass, oil paintings and prints, elegant mirrors, and this list could go on and on. All pieces are in the original finish or have been restored to its original beauty.

Village Square is both a retail and wholesale market, so dealers should definitely check this place out. L. B., the owner, has been known to give some deep discounts.

The shop also provides those "always needed" services of expert crystal repair, lamp repair and rewiring and chair caning. In addition, auctions are held periodically, but never on a set schedule.

Be sure to call ahead for auction dates.

**Court Square Shop**
108 S. Churton St.
919/732-4500

**Goldsmith & Precious Things**
116 Daniel Boone St.
919/732-6931

**Gatewood Antiques**
113 James Freeland Memorial Dr.
919/732-5081

**Hillsborough Antique Mall Inc.**
387 Ja-Max Dr.
919/732-8882

**Yesterday's Treasures**
361 Ja-Max Dr.
919/732-9199

**House of Treasures #2**
383 Ja-Max Dr.
919/732-0709

**Hillside Antiques & Collectibles**
392 Ja-Max Dr.
919/644-6074

**Depot Antiques & Collectibles**
409 Village St.
919/732-9796

**Butner Antique Barn**
111 Antique St.
919/732-4606

## 31 JACKSONVILLE

**B Js Antique Furniture**
333 Bell Fork Road
910/346-8693

**Jacksonville Antique Mall**
336 Henderson Dr.
910/938-8811

**Anchor Antiques & Lamp Shades**
117 S. Marine Blvd.
910/455-1900

**Basement**
237 S. Marine Blvd.
910/346-9833

## 32 KERNERSVILLE

**Collective Treasures**
4674 Kernersville Road
336/785-9886

**Curiosity Shoppe**
4710 Kernersville Road
336/785-4427

**Murphys Keepsake**
231 N. Main St.
336/993-4105

**Main Street Collectibles**
321 N. Main St.
336/996-6969

**Shouse Antiques**
419 S. Main St.
336/996-5108

## 33 KINSTON

**Just Stuff**
121 E. Gordon St.
919/523-1515

**Antique Market**
Hwy. 70 W. Bypass
919/527-8300

**Claydels Antiques**
1811 N. Queen St.
919/939-1710

## 34 LEXINGTON

**Candy Factory**
15 N. Main St.
336/249-6770

**Links Antique Shop**
2204 S. Main St.
336/249-9590

**Poor Boy Antiques**
1673 Old U.S. Hwy. 52
336/249-7226

**Harry's Antiques**
3185 N. U.S. Hwy. 6
336/249-1716

**B & D Antiques**
1506 Winston Road
336/249-0745

## 35 LINCOLNTON

**Antiques & Art**
231 E. Main St.
704/735-5224

**Antiques & Collectibles**
333 E. Main St.
704/732-0500

**Lincolnton Antique Mall**
2225 E. Main St.
704/732-3491

**Cynthia Rankin Antqs. & Interiors**
U.S. 321 Hwy. Bypass
704/735-4400

## 36 LUMBERTON

**Antiques Limited**
215 N. Elm St.
910/738-4607

**Lewis Durham Furniture**
307 W. 5th St
910/739-7327

**Bell's Antiques**
2201 W. 5th St.
910/671-0264

**Somewhere In Time Antiques**
4420 Kahn Dr.
910/671-8660

## 37 MATTHEWS

**Town & Country Antiques**
11328 E. Independence Blvd.
704/847-2680

**Antique Alley**
1325 Matthews Mint Hill Road
704/847-3003

**Matthews Antiques & Collectibles**
224 S. Trade St.
704/841-1400

## 38 MONROE

**Bloomin Furniture**
1401 N. Charlotte Ave.
704/289-4670

**Crow's Nest Consignment Mall**
5811 Hwy. 74
704/821-4848

**Mary's Country Furniture & Antiques**
2502 Old Charlotte Hwy.
704/289-2367

**Austins Collectibles**
4108 Old Camden Road
704/282-0144

## 39 MOORESVILLE

**Twice Treasured Antique Mall**
132 S. Main St.
704/664-6255

## 40 MOREHEAD CITY

**Seaport Antique Market**
509 Arendell St.
919/726-6606

**Cheeks Antiques**
727 Arendell St.
919/726-3247

**Coastal Treasures**
2210 Arendell St.
919/726-1570

**Ship & Shore Antiques**
4660 Arendell St.
919/726-0493

**Sea Pony**
411 Evans St.
919/726-6070

## 41 MORGANTON

**King's Depression**
1302 Bethel Road
704/437-7281

**Dale's Antiques**
Hwy. 18
704/437-4464

**Possibilities Antiques**
105 N. Sterling St.
704/433-0621

**Dogwood Antiques**
402 S. Sterling St.
704/438-4138

**Old Homestead Antiques**
2092 U.S. Hwy. 64
704/437-0863

**Southern Legacy**
106 W. Union St.
704/438-0808

## 42 MOUNT AIRY

Welcome to Mount Airy, also known as Mayberry, the birthplace of Andy Griffith. This small town was the model for the popular television series, "The Andy Griffith Show." While in the area you'll see such familiar sights as Pilot Mountain. In the downtown area, you can get a trim at Floyd's Barber Shop or go right next door for Andy's favorite porkchop sandwich at Snappy Lunch.

**Mayberry Junction Antiques**
1415 Fancy Gap Road
336/789-6743, 336/789-OPIE
Fri.-Sat. 10-5, Sun. 1-5, on Mon. (May thru October) 10-5
*Directions: From Interstate 77 take Exit 100 (Mount Airy). Go east on 89 for 7 miles. Go under bridge, right onto 52 North Bypass. On 52 N. go through two traffic lights. Take first left onto Fancy Gap Road. Look for Mayberry Junction billboard approximately 300 feet on the left.*

At Mayberry Junction you'll experience true small town hospitality. The coffee is always on the burner for you to enjoy as you're looking at anvils to washboards, or simply finding one of many hometown treasures.

## 43 NEBO

### *Great Places To Stay*

**Merry Heart Cabin**
1414 Merry Heart Lane
1-888-736-0423
Email: merryheart@hci.net
Web site: www.hci.net/~merryheart

For specific information see review at the beginning of this section.

## 44 NEW BERN

**Jane Sugg Antiques**
228 Middle St.
919/637-6985

**Tom's Coins & Antiques**
244 Middle St.
919/633-0615

**Middle Street Antique Market**
327 Middle St.
919/638-1685

**Elegant Days Antiques**
236 Middle St.
919/636-3689

**Cherishables**
712 Pollock St.
919/633-3118

**Will Gorges Antiques**
2100 Trent Blvd.
919/636-3039

**Seaport Antique Market**
504 Tryon Palace Dr.
919/637-5050

## 45 PITTSBORO

**Beggars & Choosers Antiques**
38 Hillsboro St.
919/542-5884

**52 Hillsboro St. Antiques**
52 Hillsboro St.
919/542-0789

**Edward's Antiques & Collectibles**
89 Hillsboro St.
919/542-5649

**Fields Antique Shoppe**
509 West St.
919/542-1126

## 46 RALEIGH

**Oakwood Antiques Mall**
1526 Wake Forest Road
919/834-5255
Tues.-Sat., 10-6; Sun. 1-5; closed Mon.
*Directions: From I-40 at Exit 299 (Hammond Road/Person St.) going toward downtown, go 3.7 miles to Texaco Canopy on the right side of the street. Oakwood is located in the strip with Texaco.*

For specific information see review at the beginning of this section.

**Leet Antiques, Ltd.**
709 Hillsborough St.
919/834-5255
Fax: 919/834-9066
Mon.-Fri. 10-6, Sat. 10-4
*Directions: Going towards Raleigh on I-40 (East), take the Wade Ave. Exit. Go down Wade Ave., take exit onto Glenwood Ave. (south). Go south on Glenwood Ave. to Hillsborough St., turn right onto Hillsborough St. (going west). Shop sits on south side of street between Boylan Ave. and Saint Mary's St.*

Leet Antiques, Ltd. is a direct importer of English and French Period antiques. Each item is hand-picked in Europe and no "container merchandise" is found in this exquisite shop. Instead, you will find majolica and Staffordshire, Oriental, crystal, colorful antique needlepoint rugs as well as a wide variety of gifts and accessories.

**City Antiques Market**
222 S. Blount St.
919/834-2489

**We've Lost Our Marbles Antiques**
406 Capital Blvd.
919/834-6950

**Gresham Lake Antique Mall**
6917 Capital Blvd.
919/878-9381

**Ordinary & Extraordinary**
115 W. Chatham – Ashworth Village
919/481-3955

**Carolina Antique Mall**
2050 Clark Ave.
919/833-8227

**Antiques Emporium**
2060 Clark Ave.
919-834-7250

**Acquisitions Ltd.**
2003 D Fairview Road
919/755-1110

**Antiques at Five Points**
2010 Fairview Road
919/834-4900

**Highsmith Antiques**
107 Glenwood Ave.
919/832-6275

**Aloma Crenshaw Antqs. & Interiors**
122 Glenwood Ave.
919/821-0705

**C & T Consignments**
122 Glenwood Ave.
919/828-2559

**Brideshead Antiques**
123 Glenwood Ave.
919/831-1926

**Ad Lib**
603 Glenwood Ave.
919/821-0031

**Carolyn Broughton Antiques**
3309 Garner Road
919/772-8555

**O C Cozart Ltd. Antiques**
318 S. Harrington St.
919/828-8014

**Shelton's Furniture Co.**
607 W. Morgan St.
919/833-5548

**Woody Biggs Antiques**
509 Dixie Trail
919/834-2287

**Elaine Miller Collections**
2102 Smallwood Dr.
919/834-0044

**Carolina Collectibles**
11717 Six Forks Road
919/848-3778

**Classic Antiques**
319 W. Davie St.
919/839-8333

**Gaston Street Antiques**
608 Gaston St.
919/821-5169

**Memory Layne Antiques Mall**
6013 Glenwood Ave.
919/881-2644

**Elisabeth's Space**
612 W. Johnson St.
919/821-2029

**Whitnee's Antiques**
1818 Oberlin Road
919-787-7202

**Woodleigh Place Interiors**
610 W. Peace St.
919/834-8324

**George R McNeill Antiques Inc.**
2102 Smallwood Dr.
919/833-1415

**Hillary's Interiors**
6301 Falls Road
919/878-6633

**Park Place Antiques at City Market**
135 E. Martin St.
919/821-5880

## 47 REIDSVILLE

**Uptown Antiques**
224 S.W. Market St.
336/349-4413

**Studebaker's of Rabbit Hill**
223 S. Scales St.
336/342-9400

**Auntie Q's Antique Mall**
211 S. Scales St.
336/349-5060

**Settle Street Station Antiques**
112 Settle St.
336/616-1133

## 48 ROANOKE RAPIDS

**Roanoke Valley Antiques**
Hwy. 158 W.
919/535-4242

**Odds & Ends**
1012 Roanoke Ave.
919/308-6960

**D & R Antiques**
518 Weldon Road
919/535-9172

**Past & Present Co.**
125 W. 9th St.
919/537-5843

**Curiosity Shop**
1346 Roanoke Ave.
919/535-1532

## 49 ROCKY MOUNT

**Carousel Antiques**
238 S.W. Main St.
919/442-5919

**Past 'N Present**
120 Tarboro St.
919/446-1272

**Godwin's**
1130 S. Wesleyan Blvd.
919/972-8972

## 50 RUTHERFORDTON

**William & Mary Antiques**
Hwy. 74 W.
704/287-4507

**Pastimes Antique Mall**
803 S. Main St.
704/287-9288

**Victorian Lace Antique Mall**
202 N. Main St.
704/287-2820

**Fiddlesticks Antique Mall**
1201 Hwy. 221 S.
704/286-0054

## 51 SALISBURY

**Eighteen Thirty-Nine Antiques**
218 W. Cemetary St.
704/633-1839

**Salisbury Emporium**
230 E. Kerr St.
704/642-0039

**Lillian's Library & Antiques**
3024 S. Main St.
704/636-4671

**Livery Stable**
210 E. Innes St.
704/636-2955

**Beggar's Bazaar**
102 S. Main St.
704/633-5315

## 52 SALUDA

**The Little Store**
Main St.
704/749-1258

**The Brass Latch**
23 Main St. – Nostalgia Courtyard
704/749-4200

**Ryan & Boyle Antiques**
Main St.
704/749-9790

**A Gardeners Cottage**
Main St. – Nostalgia Courtyard
704/749-4200

## 53 SELMA

**TWM's Antique Mall**
211 J.R. Road
919/965-6699
Mon.-Sat., 10-8; Sun., 10-6
*Directions: Exit 97 of I-95 (Selma). Located at the junction of I-95 and U.S. 70A just south of J. R. Outlet Stores.*

TWM's Antique Mall stocks a complete line of all types of antiques including furniture. Of additional interest, the mall also has a sterling silver tableware replacement service and also restores furniture.

## 54 SHELBY

**Kens Antiques**
1671 E. Marion St.
704/482-4062

**Bell's Antiques**
1502 New House Road
704/434-2254

**Antique Outlet**
6300 Polkville Road
704/482-8542

**Millie's Back Porch**
1201 S. Post Road
704/487-4842

## 55 SILER CITY

### *Great Places To Stay*

**Laurel Ridge Bed and Breakfast**
Route 1, Box 116
1-800-742-6049

A contemporary but rustic post and beam home located on twenty-six forested acres bordering the Rocky River. Centrally located in the heart of North Carolina, the Triad (furniture market), Research Triangle Park, North Carolina Zoo and Seagrove Pottery are within thirty minutes to one hour away. A professional chef with twenty-five years experience prepares the best breakfast in North Carolina using locally grown organic products.

## 56 SOUTHERN PINES

**Theater Antiques**
143 N.E. Broad St.
910/692-2482

**Gasoline Alley Antiques**
181 N.E. Broad St.
910/692-9147

**Thrifty Cobbler**
240 N.W. Broad St.
910/692-3250

**Down Memory Lane Collectibles**
795 S.W. Broad St.
910/693-1118

## 57 SOUTHPORT

**Curiosity Shop**
113 N. Howe St.
910/457-6118

**Waterfront Gifts & Antiques Ltd.**
117 S. Howe St.
910/457-6496

**Second Hand Rose**
702 N. Howe St.
910/457-9475

**Glass Menagerie Antiques**
1208 N. Howe St.
910/457-9188

**Antique Mall**
108 E. Moore St.
910/457-4982

**Northrop Antiques Mall**
111 E. Moore St.
910/457-9569

## 58 STATESVILLE

**Duck Creek Antiques & Collectibles**
2731 Amity Hill Road
704/873-3825

**Antique Mkt of Statesville**
114 N. Center St.
704/871-0056

**Westmoreland Antiques & Collectibles**
117 S. Center St.
704/871-1896

**Shiloh Antique Mini Mall**
Sharon School Road
704/872-2244

**Riverfront Antique Mall**
1441 Wilkesboro Road
704/873-9770

## 59 WARSAW

### *Great Places To Stay*

**The Squire's Vintage Inn**
748 N.C. Hwy. 24 & 50
910/296-1831
Weekend specials for two available
Call for Regular Rates
*Directions: Located just off I-40 on Hwy. 24.*

The Squire's Vintage Inn is located in the heart of Dublin County in a rural, intimate setting surrounded by nature. Beautiful gardens and lakes adorn the property while winding brick sidewalks and rustic paths, flanked by tall pines and towering oak trees, provide the perfect walk through nature.

Twenty four guests rooms are available at the inn with one king size Bridal Suite. A continental breakfast is served to all guest in their room or can be enjoyed in the sunken patio near the fountain shaded by pines.

The Peasant House, a two-bedroom, 1 ½ bath cottage with living room and kitchen, is also available by night, week or month. The country interior decor, brick patio, and fenced yard provide a setting for a pleasant and memorable stay.

(Also, see The Country Squire Restaurant below)

**The Country Squire Restaurant**
748 N.C. Hwy. 24 & 50
910/296-1727
Lunch: Mon.-Fri. 11:30-2, Sun. 12-2
Dinner: 5:30-until ?

The Country Squire Restaurant located next door to the Squire's Vintage Inn has been serving wonderful cuisine since 1961. Owner, Iris Lennon, has a unique way of making your dining experience a memorable one. Iris has her roots in Edinburgh, Scotland; however, she has lived many years along the coastline of Ayr where the beloved Scottish poet, Robert Burns was born. Endowed with the natural charm of her Scottish ancestry, she makes each guest feel special.

The spacious "Squire" (seating 456) creates the impression of outdoor living as decor changes with the season. The restaurant is divided into themed room settings such as the Jesters Court. In the medieval period, the court jester was summoned to entertain the manor lord and his guests around tables ladened with the best from the manor kitchens and cellars. The Jester's Court reflects this full tradition of warmth and conviviality through its rich exposed beams and traditional pine floors. The Mead Hall, a commodious room reflects the regions earliest English heritage with its brick floors, murals, tapestries, rough sawn paneling, and soft gas lighting.

Old cupboards, antiques, and fireplaces are strewn throughout the restaurant, creating a colonial dramatic setting. To every serving of food; romance, history, legend and atmosphere from all over the world has been blended. The Country Squire always welcomes guests with reflections of good taste.

## 60 WAXHAW

**Red Barn Gallery**
103 S. Church St.
704/843-1309

**The Junction**
100 E. South Main St.
704/843-3350

**Byrums Antiques**
101 Main St.
704/843-4702

**Waxhaw Antique Mart**
101 W. South Main St.
704/843-3075

**Ding-A Ling Antiques**
103 E. North Main St.
704/843-2181

**Farmhouse Antiques**
103 Main St.
704/843-5500

**The Rusty Hinge**
107 S. Main St.
704/843-4777

**Sherlock's**
108 E. South Main St.
704/843-3433

**Traders Path Antiques**
516 E. South Main St.
704/843-2497

**Victorian Lady**
8511 Prince Valiant Dr.
704/843-2917

## 61 WAYNESVILLE

**Magnolia Antique Mall**
322 Branner Ave.
704/456-5054

**Collector's Corner**
810 Delwood Ave.
704/452-2737

**Slow Lane Antiques**
71 N. Main St.
704/456-3682

**Antiques of Today & Tomorrow**
241 N. Main St.
704/456-8832

**Thad Woods Antiques Mall**
780 Waynesville Plaza
704/456-3298

## 62 WILMINGTON

**Floyds Used Furniture, Antqs. & Auction**
2230 Carolina Beach Road
910/763-8702

**Good Stuff**
5318 Carolina Beach Road
910/452-0091

**Michael Moore Antiques**
20 S. Front St.
910/763-0300

**Antiques of Old Wilmington**
25 S. Front St.
910/763-6011

**Golden Goose**
27 S. Front St.
910/341-7969

**About Time Antiques**
30 N. Front St.
910/762-9902

**Unique Americana**
127 N. Front St.
910/251-8859

**Betty B's Trash To Treasure**
143 N. Front St.
910/763-3703

**Virginia Jennewein**
143 N. Front St.
910/763-3703

**Antiquity Ltd. of Wilmington**
1305 N. Front St.
910/763-5800

**Antiques & Collectibles on Kerr**
830 S. Kerr Ave.
910/791-7917

**Cape Fear Antique Center**
1606 Market St.
910/763-1837

**Thieves Market**
6766 Market St.
910/392-9194

**Antiques & More**
6792 Market St.
910/392-3633

**Sentimental Journey Antiques**
6794 Market St.
910/790-5211

**Perry's Emporium**
3500 Oleander Dr.
910/392-6721

**Seven Seas Trading**
115 S. Water St.
910/762-3022

**McAllister & Solomon**
4402 Wrightsville Ave.
910/350-0189

### *Great Places To Stay*

**Rosehill Inn**
114 S. Third St.
1-800-815-0250
Web site: www.rosehill.com

Rosehill Inn offers travelers the warmth and security of returning home after a long day's journey. This beautiful house was built in 1848 by Henry Russel Savage, a prominent Wilmington businessman and banker. It was also the home of Henry Bacon, Jr., architect of the Lincoln Memorial in Washington, D.C. Rosehill Inn has been lovingly restored as an elegant, yet comfortable, bed and breakfast with an eclectic mix of antiques, fine linens, and beautiful gardens. Each of the large, luxurious guest rooms has been individually designed and decorated. The sparkling blue waters of the Atlantic Ocean, wide beaches, and world-class golf courses are within a twenty minute drive from the inn.

## 63 WILSON

**Fulford's Antique Warehouse**
320 Barnes St. S.
919/243-7727
Mon.-Fri. 8-5, Sat. 8-3
*Directions: Take I-95 at Hwy. 264 exit. Follow into Wilson. Continue to Lodge St. taking a left. The shop is then on the right at the corner of Lodge and Barnes St.*

Discover the treasures in the old Coca-Cola building now Fulford's Antique Warehouse. With 28 years of family experience, the Fulfords have stuffed 67,000-square-feet of their warehouse with an unimaginably enormous and varied collection of American, French, and English furniture, turn-of-the-century lighting, wrought iron furniture, tiger maple chests as well as a quaint selection of smalls. Across the street in the workshop, furniture repair and refinishing takes place.

**Fulford's Antiques**
2001 U.S. Hwy. 301 S.
919/243-5581
*Directions: I-95 to Hwy. 264 exit. Follow into Wilson, turn right on Forrest Hills Road at Golden Corral; continue to 301, turn left, next stop light on right.*

If you don't find what you're looking for at Fulford's Antique Warehouse, then at Fulford's Antiques (2nd location) you most assuredly will. Located in the old John Deere building, this shop offers an additional 7,000-square-feet for "plowing around."

**Albury Eagles Gallery Inc.**
104 Douglas St.
919/237-9299

**Bobby Langston Antiques**
2620 U.S. Hwy. 301 S.
919/237-8224

**Antique Barn & Hobby Shop**
2810 Forest Hills Road S.W.
919/237-6778

**Greater Wilson Antique Market**
4345 U.S. Hwy. 264
919/237-0402

**Jean's Olde Store & Antiques**
2007 U.S. Hwy. 301 S.
919/234-7998

**Marsha Stancil Antiques**
2020 U.S. Hwy. 301 S.W.
919/399-2093

**Boone's Antiques Inc.**
2014 U.S. Hwy. 301 S.W.
919/237-1508

**Boykin Antiques**
2013 Hwy. 301 S.
919/237-1700

***Great Places To Stay***

**Miss Betty's Bed and Breakfast Inn**
600 W. Nash St.
919/243-4447 or 1-800-258-2058

Wilson, "Antique Capital of North Carolina," is home to Miss Betty's Bed and Breakfast Inn which has been selected as one of the "Best Places to Stay in the South." Four exquisitely restored homes provide guests lodging amidst Victorian elegance in downtown's historic setting. Browse for antiques at Miss Betty's or any of the other numerous shops in the area. The tranquil atmosphere of Wilson in eastern North Carolina is ideal for enjoying golf, tennis, or swimming. Don't dare leave town without sampling the famous eastern Carolina barbecue.

## 64 WINSTON SALEM

**Pearl and Gearhart Antiques**
101 N. Broad St.
336/725-2102

**Brookstown Antiques**
1004 Brookstown Ave.
336/723-5956

**Brass Bed Antique Company**
451 W. End Blvd.
336/724-3461

**Karat Shop Inc.**
420 Jonestown Road
336/768-3336

**Timeless Treasures**
3510 S. Main St.
336/785-2273

**Country Road Antiques**
901 S. Marshall St.
336/659-7555

**Kim Taylor & Co.**
114 Oakwood Dr.
336/722-8503

**Village Green Antiques**
114A Reynolda Village
336/721-0860

**Winston-Salem Emporium**
217 W. 6th St.
336/722-7277

**D & B Antiques**
2840 Waughtown St.
336/788-4309

**Extraordinary Goods**
1000 Brookstown Ave.
336/773-1220

**Memoirs Ltd.**
1148 Burke St.
336/631-9595

**Snob Consignment Shop**
465 W. End Blvd.
336/724-2547

**Cross Keys Antiques**
468 Knollwood St.
336/760-3585

**Larry Laster Old & Rare Books**
2416 Maplewood Ave.
336/724-7544

**Marshall St. Antique Mall**
901 S. Marshall St.
336/724-9007

**Reynolda Antique Gallery**
114 Reynolda Village
336/748-0741

**Alice Cunningham Interiors**
3120 Robinhood Road
336/724-9667

**Oxford Antiques & Gifts**
129 S. Stratford Road
336/723-7080

# North Dakota

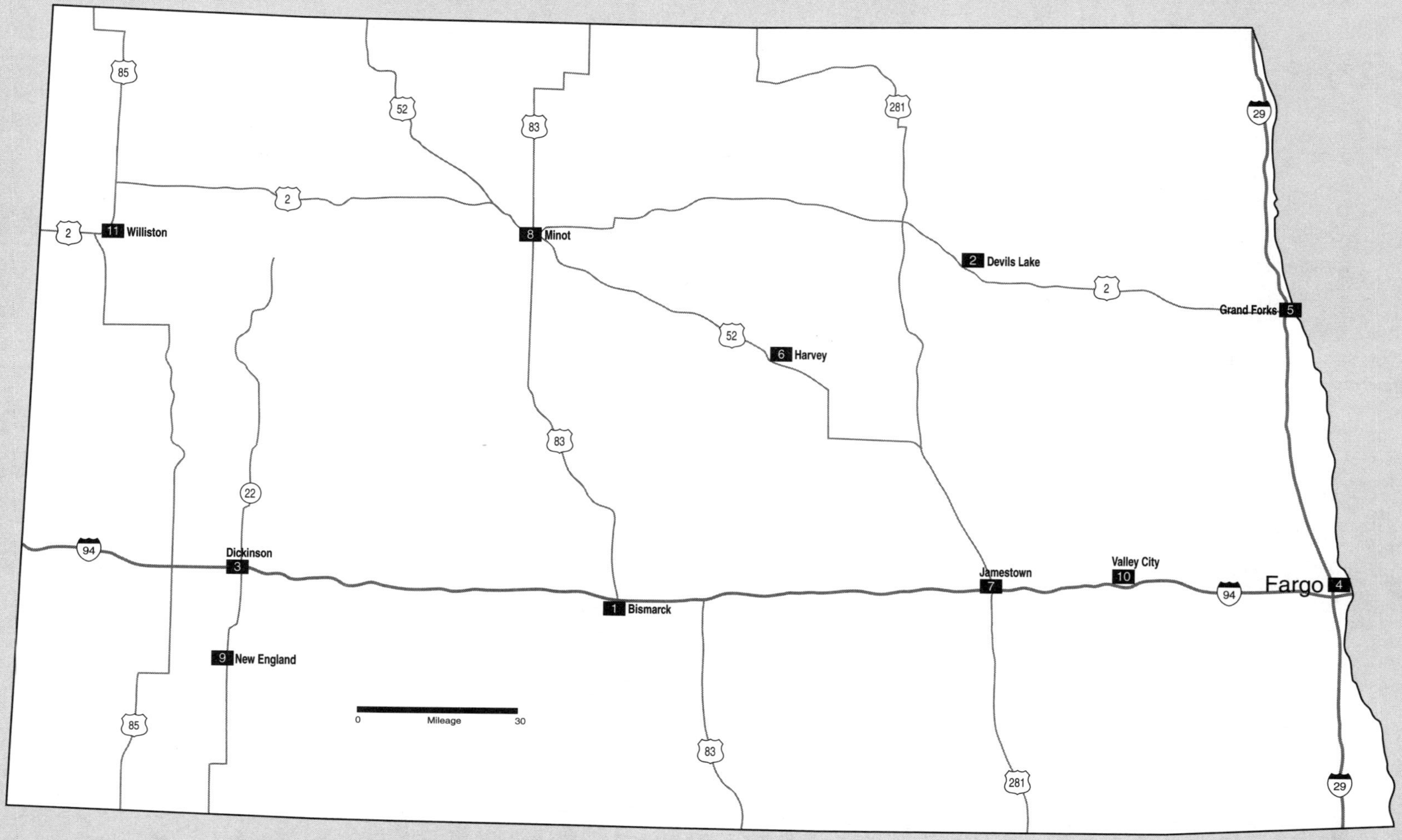

# North Dakota

## 1 BISMARCK

### Antique Interiors
200 W. Main Ave.
701/224-9551
Mon.-Sat. 10:30-5, Sun.1-4
*Directions: Downtown Bismarck*

Located in the Historic International Harvester Building, this shop specializes in interior design through the use of antiques. Fabrics to compliment any decor are also available.

### Wizard Of Odds 'N Ends
1523 E. Thayer Ave.
701/222-4175
Mon.-Sat. 10-5
*Directions: Find this shop near downtown Bismarck.*

"We're off to see the wizard, the wonderful Wizard of Odd 'N Ends." Located near downtown Bismarck, this shop offers such a stunning array of antiques and collectibles, you'll think you "really" are in the Emerald City.

### Antique and Coin Exchange
722 Kirkwood Mall
701/222-8859
Mon.-Fri. 10-9, Sat. 10-6, Sun. 12-6
*Directions: Exit I-94 at State St. Travel south on State St. It curves to Boulevard Ave. Go south on 7th Street to Kirkwood Mall. Shop is located in the mall.*

Specializing in "pack in your car" antiques. Large selection of smalls including dishes, coins, jewelry, etc.

**Antique Gallery**
1514 E. Thayer Ave.
701/223-8668

**Antique Mall**
200 W. Main Ave.
701/221-2594

**Country Home Sweet Home**
1144 Summit Blvd.
701/223-4897

**Downtown Furniture Co.**
117 N. 4th St.
701/255-6061

**Wood & Tiques**
1514 E. Thayer Ave.
701/255-4912

## 2 DEVILS LAKE

**Garden Gate**
410 4th St.
701/662-6388

**Antique Exchange**
By Appointment
701/662-8801

**Buds N Blossoms**
405 4th St.
701/662-8166

## 3 DICKINSON

**Carol's Antiques & Collectibles**
14 1st St. W.
701/225-4509

**Jackie's Antiques & Collectibles**
1331 Villard E.
701/227-1027

**Barry's 2nd H "Antiques"**
2221 Main St. S.
701/225-3701

**Collectors Corner**
14 1st St. W.
701/227-8411

## 4 FARGO

### Bonanzaville
W. Hwy. 10 (Main Ave.)
701/282-2822
Open 7 days a week June 1-Nov. 1; call for museum hours
*Directions: Tune into 530 AM radio for specific information.*

Relive the pioneer days in Bonanzaville. Antique cars, planes, farm machinery, school, church, stores, log and sod homes, dolls, Indian artifacts, museum and much, much more.

**Baker's Place Antiques**
114 Broadway
701/235-5334

**Grandpa's Antiques & Collectibles**
3041 Main Ave.
701/237-4569

**North Dakota Antiques Mall**
1024 2nd Ave. N.
701/237-4423

**Market Square Mall**
1450 25h St.
701/239-9814

**Lifetime Antique Furnishings**
18 8th St.
701/235-3144

**Fargo Antique Mall**
14 Roberts St.
701/235-1145

**Gramma's Antiques & Collectibles**
314 10th St. N.
701/239-4465

**A Place Called Traditions**
1201 S. University Dr.
701/280-1864

### Great Places To Stay

**La Maison des Papillons Bed and Breakfast**
423 8th St. S.
701/232-2041
Open year round
Rates $45-55
*Directions: From west on I-94: Take Exit 343 to Main Ave. (downtown), follow Main Ave. to 8th St. Take a right on 5th Ave. south. From north or south on I-29: Take Exit 65 to Main Ave.; once on Main Ave. follow previous instructions. From east on I-94: Take Exit 1 A (in Moorehead, Minnesota); follow 8th St. taking a right on 5th Ave. south.*

La Maison des Papillons Bed and Breakfast occupies a house built in 1899 on Historic 8th Street South of Fargo. If it could talk it would share many stories of the history of Fargo such as the fire that consumed most of downtown and raged only blocks away. When walking in the front door, visitors are struck with the warmth and friendliness of days gone by. The cozy grandeur of the ground floor and the intimate privacy of the second floor bedrooms give a restful welcome invitation to the weary of mind, body, and soul.

La Maison des Papillons has four guest rooms (three of which are ready for occupancy) on the second floor. Each room is named after a butterfly that is native to North Dakota. The Monarch is a double room with a half bath located on the north side of the house for lots of quiet. The Swallowtail is a double room with a beautiful stained glass window and bay window. The Fritillery is a single room overlooking the front yard and nearby park. All rooms share a large old fashioned bathroom occupied by a cast iron tub/shower with clawed feet.

## 5 GRAND FORKS

**Back Porch Antiques and Gifts**
205 DeMers Ave.
701/746-9369
Tues.-Sat. 10-6
*Directions: From I-29, take the DeMers Ave. exit (140). Go east on DeMers Ave. 3 1/2 miles. The shop is 1 block from Red River.*

The quaint name of the shop, Back Porch Antiques and Gifts, reveals a cozy, casual atmosphere. Potted red geraniums greet you at the door. Inside you will find a good representation of antique furniture, from headboards to foot stools; in oak, mahogany, walnut, cherry and other woods. Various periods and styles are included; such as Victorian, primitive and Art Deco. You will also discover antique linens, glassware, kitchen items, sewing implements and accessories. Fishing collectibles will catch the fancy of anglers. You can take home unusual gifts and decorative accessories as well.

**City Center Antique Mall**
16 City Center Mall
701/780-9076

**Sannes Antiques**
1020 Cottonwood Ave.
701/772-0541

**Victoria's Rose Antique Shop**
214 DeMers Ave.
701/772-3690

## 6 HARVEY

**Penny Pinchers**
604 Brewster St. E.
701/324-2551

## 7 JAMESTOWN

The city of Jamestown is known as the Buffalo City, thanks to its 60-ton giant, "The World's Largest Buffalo," a sculpture standing watch on a hill over I-94. Two dozen live buffalo roam the draws below this huge statue, and the National Buffalo Museum shares the high ground at the Frontier Village Complex.

Jamestown is the birthplace for some famous folk: torch singer Peggy Lee, Anne Carlsen, renowned for her work with the disabled, and the best-selling author of all time, writer Louis L'Amour.

**Treasure Chest**
213 1st Ave. S.
701/251-2891
Mon. 10-7, Tues.-Sat.10-5, or by appointment.
*Directions: Exit 2nd Jamestown exit off I-94. Travel north on 1st Ave. South.*

The name given to this antique shop could be considered synonymous with the name used by its former occupants in 1906, First Federal Savings "Bank". The Treasure Chest, as it is called today, holds a wealth of valuable antiques and collectibles, such as, Roseville, Rosemeade, Hull, Carnival, primitives and more.

**Antique Attic**
219 1st Ave. S.
701/252-6733
Mon.- Fri.12:30-5:30, Sat. 10-4
*Directions: Exit 2nd Jamestown exit off I-94. Travel north on 1st Ave. South*

There are 42 dealers offering, oak furniture, fine china, lamps, books & catalogs, fine glassware, dolls, linen & silver, as well as one of a kind items.

**On The Countryside**
Hwy. 281 S. & 25th St. S.W.
701/252-8941
Mon.-Fri. 10-9, Sat.10-6, Sun. 12-5.
*Directions: I-94 take 2nd exit, travel south to 25th St and. take a right.*

On The Country Side specializes in antique country furnishings, primarily cupboards. Other antique pieces along with decorative accessories are also available here. The Espresso Bar serves pastries soups, salads and ice cream.

**Wilma's Antiques**
221 7th St. N.E.
701/252-5145
Mon. 10-7, Tues.-Sat. 10-5 or by appointment
*Directions: Exit I-94 at Jamestown. Take Main to 7th N.E.*

Wilma's Antiques offers a large variety of antiques and collectibles specializing in everything old and wonderful.

**Antiques & Uniques**
Park Plaza Mall
Home Phone after 5 p.m.: 701/252-6682
(No phone in shop)

## 8 MINOT

**Home Sweet Home**
103 4th Ave. N.W.
701/852-5604
Mon.-Sat. 9:30-5, Sun. 12-4
*Directions: Situated near downtown Minot.*

Antiques in a historic setting. Home Sweet Home is located in an old house built in 1899. They offer "everything" (as the owner says) in the way of antiques and collectibles.

**Granny's Antiques & Gifts**
16 Main St. S.
701/852-3644
Mon.-Sat. 10-5:30
*Directions: Granny's is located in downtown Minot.*

Granny's Antiques offers furniture, glassware and collectibles along with a nice selection of Victorian items.

**Dakota Antiques**
8 4th St. N.E.
701/838-1150

**Downtown Mall**
108 Main St. S.
701/852-9084

**Minot Antiques**
1326 S. Broadway
701/852-6550

## 9 NEW ENGLAND

**Country Treasures**
Hwy. 22
701/579-4746
Hours: lives on premises and is open most of the time
*Directions: Located on Hwy. 22 on the east end of New England.*

This small, quaint shop specializes in quality smalls. Cookie jars, carnival, depression and pressed glass are represented here.

**Main Attractions**
709 Main St.
701/579-4419
Mon.-Sat. 10-4
*Directions: Exit from Hwy. 22 into New England. Located on Main St.*

At this shop, the "Main Attractions" are antique furniture, cookie jars, carnival glass and Dakota pottery.

## 10 VALLEY CITY

**E & S Antiques**
148 E. Main St.
701/845-0369
Mon.-Sat.9-5
*Directions: Located in downtown Valley City.*

Located in the old 1890s Opera House in downtown Valley City, this shop prides itself on offering exceptional antique furnishings and accessories.

**Unique Antiques**
164 E. Main St.
701/845-3549

**Kathleen's Kurio Kabinet**
114 3rd St.
701/845-3569

## 11 WILLISTON

**Collectors Corner**
109 Main St.
701/572-9313

**Larry Lynne Antiques**
715 3rd Ave. E.
701/572-3642

**Elizabeth's on Broadway**
12 E. Broadway
701/774-3835

# Ohio

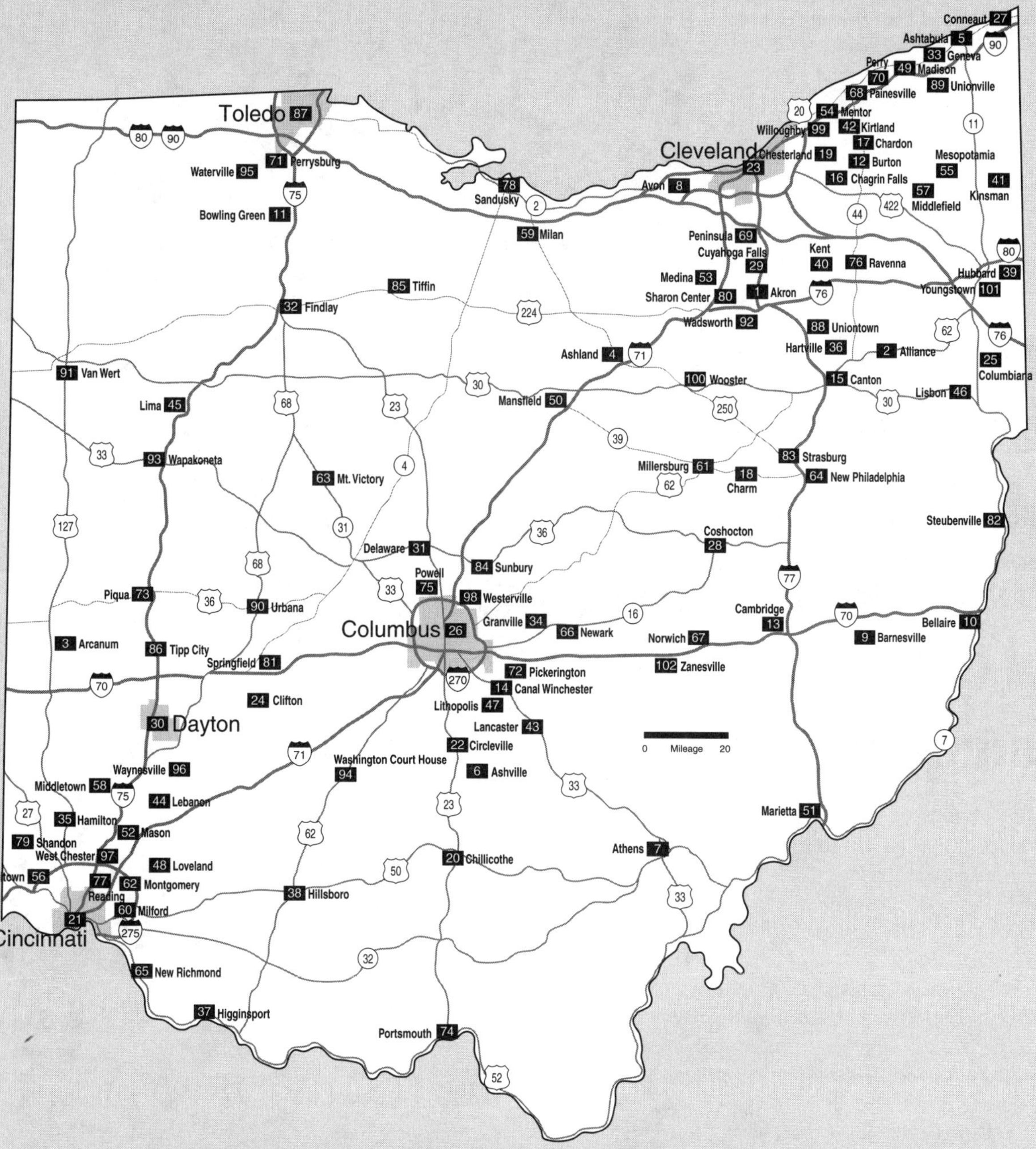

Toledo 87
80
90
71 Perrysburg
Waterville 95
75
Bowling Green 11
78
Sandusky
2
59 Milan
85 Tiffin
32 Findlay
224
91 Van Wert
Lima 45
68
23
30
Mansfield 50
33
93 Wapakoneta
63 Mt. Victory
4
31
127
Delaware 31
Powell
75
84 Sunbury
98 Westerville
68
33
Piqua 73
36
90 Urbana
Columbus 26
Granville 34
66 Newark
16
3 Arcanum
86 Tipp City
Springfield 81
70
270
72 Pickerington
14 Canal Winchester
Lithopolis 47
24 Clifton
30 Dayton
Lancaster 43
22 Circleville
71
Washington Court House
94
6 Ashville
Waynesville 96
Middletown 58
75
44 Lebanon
27
35 Hamilton
52 Mason
79 Shandon
West Chester 97
48 Loveland
Miamitown 56
77
62 Montgomery
Reading
21
60 Milford
275
Cincinnati
65 New Richmond
38 Hillsboro
62
23
33
20 Chillicothe
50
32
37 Higginsport
Portsmouth 74
52
Athens 7
33
Marietta 51
7
0 Mileage 20
Conneaut 27
Ashtabula 5
90
33 Geneva
Perry
70
49 Madison
68 Painesville
89 Unionville
20
54 Mentor
Willoughby 99
42 Kirtland
11
Cleveland
Chesterland 19
17 Chardon
23
12 Burton
Mesopotamia
55
16 Chagrin Falls
41
Avon 8
57
Kinsman
44
422
Middlefield
Peninsula 69
Cuyahoga Falls
29
Kent
40
76 Ravenna
80
Hubbard 39
Medina 53
Sharon Center 80
1 Akron
76
Youngstown 101
Wadsworth 92
88 Uniontown
62
76
Ashland 4
71
Hartville 36
2 Alliance
25
Columbiana
100 Wooster
15 Canton
Lisbon 46
30
250
39
83 Strasburg
Millersburg 61
18
Charm
64 New Philadelphia
62
36
Coshocton
28
Steubenville 82
77
Cambridge
13
70
Bellaire 10
Norwich 67
9 Barnesville
102 Zanesville

*The AAA I-70 Antique Mall in Springfield, Ohio features over 200 dealer booths and showcases in a state-of-the-art facility which has 30,000 square feet of fully air conditioned carpeted space to explore.*

# AAA I-70 Antique Mall is Disneyland of the antiques world

Located in the heartland of America, AAA I-70 Antique Mall in Springfield is truly one of "Ohio's Best." With two other antique malls within two miles of their front door, as well as the monthly Springfield Antique Show & Flea Market, the area is known as an "antique mecca" boasting more than 150,000 square feet of antiques and collectibles within three modern malls.

AAA I-70 Antique Mall is a 30,000 square foot (a monster of a place), 250 dealer mall with a vast assortment of antiques and collectibles displayed in a state-of-the-art, air conditioned single floor building. Beautiful locked showcases display many smalls such as R.S. Prussia, Flow Blue, Majolica, Weller, Roseville, toys, dolls and much more.

A real treasure hunt of yesteryear's history, AAA I-70 Antique Mall is one place where you can buy with confidence. The owners guarantee it to be what they say it is or your money back.

*AAA I-70 Antique Mall is located along State Route 41 in Springfield. For additional information see listing #81 (Springfield).*

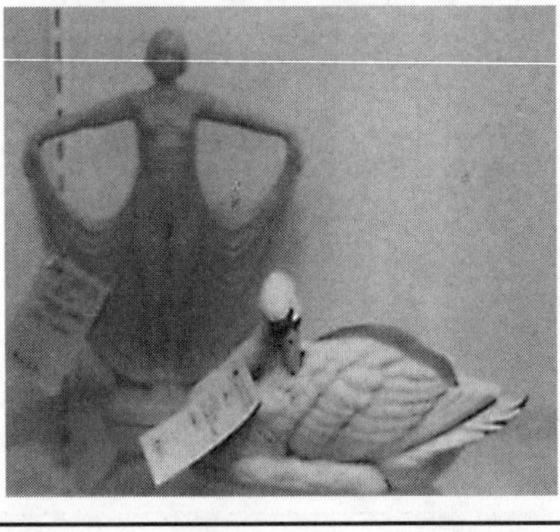

*The AAA I-70 Antique Mall's modern exterior (above) belies the time capsules within. Meticulously arranged displays include beautiful fine porcelain (left).*

*Aside from a comprehensive selection of furniture and decorative accessories, Hidden Treasures features a truly unique collection of icons and other religious items beautifully displayed.*

# Hidden Treasures discovered at historical home and barn in West Chester

Located in a large historical home and barn, surrounded by a beautifully landscaped garden, Hidden Treasures Antiques is stacked from floor to ceiling with a fine selection of furniture, artwork, and accessories.

*Magnificently carved oak sideboard, crowned with a lion's head holds a collection of silver trophies.*

This family owned business prides itself in offering personal service and commitment to its' customers as well as providing - you guessed it - "Hidden Treasures!"

*Hidden Treasures Antiques is located at 8825 Cincinnati-Dayton Road in West Chester. For additional information see listing #97 (West Chester).*

*Quaint country kitchen cabinet displays an old iron kettle, splatterware and bundt pans.*

# Plan a week-long antiquing vacation in Ohio's 'antique mecca': Ravenna

## Walking tour reveals quaint streets with discoveries such as quality antique shops, unique eateries and cozy bed and breakfasts

Ravenna, Ohio, is a town of antique shops, bed and breakfasts, and restaurants. Start on one end of Main Street and work your way, shop by shop, through town, occasionally taking a side street to reach a special place.

Begin at Copper Kettle Antiques. Spend some time admiring the tin ceilings and maple floors of this 1840 building. It still has its original central staircase, giving easy access to its 40 dealers in 6,000 square feet of space on two floors. You can browse through furniture, glassware, china, pottery, advertising memorabilia, Victrolas, primitives and tools, among other collectibles. Then wander next door to Hickory Way Antiques. They carry a wide variety of jewelry, furniture, paper items, glassware, leaded glass lamps, hand-painted lamp shades, Victorian lamps, primitives, and tools. Next is Farnsworth Antiques Associates, a 12-dealer mall featuring pottery, upscale furniture, lighting items, and a general mixture.

Fourth on your list should be Timeless Treasures. Owners Linda and Jeff Nicolaus specialize in glass and china, and walnut, cherry, and mahogany furniture from the mid-1800s through the 1940s, which is beautifully displayed in room settings making the shop one of the prettiest you've ever entered. Jeff designs and builds the mantels and shelves utilized in the shop and will take special requests to fill individual needs.

Next stop is Thyme Remembered. This unique shop blends a variety of old and new, country, primitives, and giftware in a quaint atmosphere.

By this time you will probably be ready for food, so you can start with Patricia's Family Tradition, just down the street on Main. They serve breakfast, lunch, dinner, sandwiches, and home-baked goods at reasonable prices. Or, you can hold on a little longer and make your way to Prospect Street and The Bello House Deli. They offer delicious soups, salads, and special sub sandwiches, served in an Italian Villa type setting. The atmosphere is friendly and the customers are treated like family.

A great way to work off that huge lunch is to head over to The Ohio Trader's Market & Antiques. Within 17,000 square feet, 40 dealers specialize in quality primitives, oak furniture, glassware, vintage clothing and furniture. The merchandise is neatly displayed in a friendly atmosphere of an old factory. People come not only to shop, but to admire the size of the building with gigantic windows.

The Upstairs Emporium, located on the second floor of The Ohio Trader's Mart, is a unique gift shop featuring one-of-a-kind decorator items from around the world beautifully displayed amidst silk flowers, concrete statuary, and fountains. The Emporium also features a year round Holiday Shoppe overflowing with Christmas items. Move on and shop for a while at The Added Touch, located within an old house whose rooms are filled with the house specialty—the unusual in china, glass, and furniture.

Your final stop for the day might be at the Rocking Horse Inn, where you can collapse for the night in comfort and homelike surroundings in one of its four guest rooms, complete with private baths. This bed and breakfast sits on land that was a part of the Western Reserve and the original platt of Ravenna. After buying the land in 1867, Rev. Edward Hubbell decided to build a grand home in the then-popular Stick style. Unfortunately, the construction got out of hand and was not completed until 1875 by Quincy Cook, who also built the mill on Main Street known today as Babcock Feed Mill, the oldest continuing operation in Ravenna. Following the death of Quincy's wife Charlotte in 1920, the house had several owners. The present owners, Jim and Carolyn Leffler, purchased the property in 1991 and opened it as the Rocking Horse Bed and Breakfast.

After a good nights sleep you're ready to spend the day at Ravenna's newest addition; AAA I-76 Antique Mall with more than 400 dealers within 50,000 square feet. You can fill the car (most likely a U-Haul) on this antiquing adventure!

# A Quick Reference to Shopping, Dining & Lodging in Ravenna

The Added Touch
315 N. Chestnut St.
330/297-0701

Copper Kettle Antiques
115 E. Main St.
330/296-8708

Farnsworth Antiques Associates
126 E. Main St.
330/296-8600
Mon.-Sat. 10-5, Sun. 12-5

Hickory Way Antiques
117 E. Main St.
330/296-5595
Daily 10-5

Timeless Treasures Antiques
129 E. Main St.
330/296-7800
Mon. & Wed.-Sat. 11-5
Sun. 12-5, Closed Tues.

Bello House Deli
684 S. Prospect St.
330/297-6415
Mon.-Fri. 11-2, Fri. & Sat. 5-8

Patricia's Family Tradition
250 W. Main St.
330/296-5201
Daily 6:30-4

Rocking Horse Inn
248 W. Riddle Ave.
330/297-5720

The Upstairs Emporium
645 S. Chestnut St.
330/296-7050
Wed.-Fri. 12-8, Tues., Sat., Sun. 9-5
Closed Mon.

Thyme Remembered
200 W. Main St.
330/296-0055

The Ohio Trader's Market & Antiques
645 S. Chestnut St.
330/296-7050
Tues.-Sun.

AAA I-76 Antique Mall
4284 Lynn Rd.
(Exit 38B Interstate 76)
1-888-476-8976

*The AAA I-76 Antique Mall in Ravenna, Ohio has it all. A fine selection of furniture, decorative home accessories such as picture frames, lamps, pottery and vessels of all sorts, cabinets, curios, chests and more.*

# Ohio's heritage found at Ravenna's newest antique mall

Arc-En-Ceil pottery, Cambridge glass, Cincinnati art pottery, Cowan pottery, Dagenhart glass, Erickson glass, Fenton art glass, Fostoria glass, Heisey glass, Hull pottery, Imperial glass, Lotus Ware, McCoy pottery, National cash registers, Nicodemus glass, Owens pottery, Peters & Reed pottery, Puriton pottery, Radford pottery, Rockwood pottery, Roseville pottery, Royal Copley, Shawnee pottery, Stanford pottery, Tiffin glass, Watt pottery, Weller pottery, Wheatley pottery, and Zanesville glass: what do all these items have in common? They were all made in Ohio and selections of these wonderful antiques and collectibles can be found at the newly opened AAA I-76 Antique Mall in Ravenna.

*Fine china fanciers will find it here.*

Ravenna has long been recognized as an "antique mecca." This town is chock full of antique shops, bed and breakfasts and wonderful restaurants. The addition of AAA I-76 with 50,000 square feet and 450 dealers will certainly lure travelers from nearby Interstate 76 to the charming town of Ravenna.

C. J. Hawley, owner of the new mall, is also an owner of the AAA I-70 Antique Mall in Springfield and says that this establishment will be similar in design to the Springfield mall. Hours of operation will be from 10 a.m. until 6 p.m. daily, according to Hawley, closing only three days of the year for Christmas, Thanksgiving and Easter.

*Get out the grocery list! The shelves are fully stocked with vintage tins, bottles and collectable comestibles at the AAA I-76 Antique Mall in Ravenna, Ohio.*

*For additional information including phone number and directions see listing #76 (Ravenna). The mall is located at 4284 Lynn Road.*

## 1 AKRON

Busy Akron gave the world Quaker Oats, Goodyear blimps, The All-American Soap Box Derby and, of course, rubber. Northeast Ohio's renowned "Rubber City" began as a nineteenth-century canal town. Within 100 years, it was a factory boom town. Dr. B. F. Goodrich's modest fire-hose plant had quietly launched Akron's rubber industry, but the burgeoning popularity of automobiles was assuring its prosperity.

**Annex Antiques & Cnsnmt Shop**
1262 S. Cleveland Massillon Road
330/666-5544

**Wizard of Odds II**
1265 S. Cleveland Massillon Road
330/666-1958

**Antiques Of Copley**
1463 S. Cleveland Massillon Road
330/666-8170

**Nanny's Antiques**
125 Ghent Road
330/865-1250

**Yellow Creek Barn**
794 Wye Road
330/666-8843

**Dreurey Lane Antiques**
7831 Main St.
330/882-6165

**Cuyahoga Valley Antiques**
929 N. Main St.
330/434-3333

**Coventry Antiques & Crafts**
3358 Manchester Road
330/644-7474

**Jerome's**
451 W. Market St.
330/535-5700

**West Hill Antiques**
461 W. Market St.
330/762-6633

**Courtyard Antiques**
467 W. Market St.
330/253-3336

**Fish Market Antique Center, Inc.**
474 W. Market St.
330/535-7799

**Stagecoach Antiques**
449 W. Market St.
330/762-5422

## 2 ALLIANCE

**Memory Lane Antiques**
20515 Alliance Sebring Road
330/823-8568

**Alliance Antiques**
319 E. Main St.
330/821-0606

**Attic Treasures Antiques & More**
248 E. Main St.
330/823-8920

**Towne Hall Antiques**
12347 Marlboro Ave. N.E.
330/935-0114

**Mack's Barn Antiques**
14665 Ravenna Ave N.E.
330/935-2746

**Bus Stop Antiques**
6727 Waterloo Road
330/947-2737

**Aunt Polly's Country Store**
1930 S. Freedom Ave.
330/821-9136

**New Baltimore Antique Center**
14725 Ravenna Ave. N.E.
330/935-3300

## 3 ARCANUM

**Smith's Antiques Store**
109 W. George St.
937/692-8540

**Stubblefield Antiques**
112 W. George St.
937/692-8882

**Staley's Antiques & Woodworking**
7 N. Sycamore St.
937/692-8050

## 4 ASHLAND

**The Gleaner**
1488 Ashland Cty. Road #995
419/281-2849

**Antiques on Main**
143 W. Main St.
419/289-8599

## 5 ASHTABULA

**C J's This N That**
4616 Main Ave.
440/992-9479

**Country Cottage**
3616 N. Ridge Road E.
440/992-9620

**Trash & Treasures Barn**
5020 N. Ridge Road W.
440/998-2946

**The Moses Antique Mall**
4135 State St.
440/992-5556

**The Way We Were**
1837 Walnut Blvd.
440/964-7576

## 6 ASHVILLE

**The Barn**
5201 S. Bloomfield Royalton
614/983-2238

**South Bloomfield Antique Mall**
5004 Walnut St. N.
614/983-4300

## 7 ATHENS

### Lamborn's Studio

19 W. State St.
614/593-6744; 1-800-224-5567
Mon.-Fri. 10:30-5:30, Sat. 10:30-5, Sun. 1-4
*Directions: Downtown Athens*

Located in a historically renovated building from the 1920s, Lamborn's offers fine antiques and collectibles scattered throughout the 5000-square-foot gallery that also features sculpture, prints, cards, stationery and local memorabilia.

Quality glassware, pottery and many fine old furniture pieces are available. Local artists exhibit hand painted furniture and tiles, as well as jewelry made from antique beads and glass. Photography buffs will enjoy the photography studio, which houses a private collection of old cameras. This very unique store is tucked away in the downtown area and is within walking distance of many shops and eateries.

### The Refurniture Pod
16416 U.S. Route 50 E.
614/592-1949
Hours vary, but appointments can be made by calling Lamborn's Studio at 614/593-6744.

Located just 6 miles from Athens, The Refurniture Pod is really an old barn built back in 1917. Inside, it's a furniture stripping and repair business—and a soon-to-be retail store specializing in furniture and collectibles.

As you might expect with this type of business, the hours of operation vary, but appointments may be made by calling Lamborn's Studio at the above number.

**Second Rose**
90 N. Court St.
614/592-4999

**Random House**
12 W. State St.
614/592-2464

**Canaanville Antiques**
16060 U.S. Hwy. 50
614/593-5105

## 8 AVON

**Country Heirs**
35800 Detroit Road
440/937-5544

**Country Side Antiques**
36290 Detroit Road
440/934-4228

**Jameson Homestead Antiques**
36675 Detroit Road
440/934-6977

**Woods & Goods**
36840 Detroit Road
440/934-6669

**Antique Gallery of Avon**
36923 Detroit Road
440/934-4797

**Sweet Caroline's**
37300 Detroit Road
440/934-4797

**Country Store**
2536 Stoney Ridge Road
440/934-6119

## 9 BARNESVILLE

### This Old House
118 N. Chestnut St.
740/425-4444
Mon.-Sat., 10-5, Sun., Noon-5
*Directions: Situated 6 miles south of I-70 at Exit 202, midway between Cambridge, Ohio, and Wheeling, W.V.*

This Old House, formerly known as the Smith House, was originally built in 1885 for Eli Moore, owner of the once-popular Moore's Opera House. A few years later, financial reverses forced him to sell to the Murphy family. The Murphy daughter married Carl Smith; thus the home became widely referred to as the Smith House.

This ten-room, Italianate-style brick home, listed on the National Register of Historic Places, features beautiful oak woodwork, fireplaces and ornate fretwood of the period. It provides the perfect setting for the presentation of fine antiques and gifts, such as pine furniture, lamps and shades, braided and woven rugs, Amish pictures and other wonderful decorative accessories.

**Antiques on the Main**
108 N. Chestnut St.
740/425-3406

**Barnesville Antique Mall**
202 N. Chestnut St.
740/425-2435

**East Main Flea Market**
511 E. Main St.
740/425-4310

## 10 BELLAIRE

**Collector's Corner**
3000 Belmont St.
740/676-8524

**Barn**
2095 Belmont St.
740/676-2613

## *Interesting Side Trips*

### Imperial Plaza
29th and Belmont St.
740/676-8300
Mon.-Sat., 9-5; Sun., 8-4
*Directions: Follow Ohio Route 7 south to 26th St. Exit. 3 miles from I-470, 4 miles from I-70.*

The Imperial Glass Factory was founded in 1901 with the goal of becoming the "most modern glass factory in America." The first glass was made for the mass market: jelly glasses with tin lids, pressed tumblers with horseshoe and star designs on the bottom, and assorted tableware.

The company later expanded and produced Nuart iridescent ware and imitation "Tiffany" style lampshades. Later, Nucut Crystal, handpressed reproductions of early English cut glass pieces, was made.

Hard times plagued the company during the Great Depression, but the Quaker Oats Company saved the company by ordering a premium piece which became the forerunner to the 'Cape Cod' pattern.

In 1937, the famous Candlewick pattern was introduced. Imperial Glass was chosen by the Metropolitan Museum of Art, the Smithsonian Institution and Old Sturbridge Village to produce authentic reproductions of famous glass items for sale to discriminating collectors.

Today, though Imperial is no longer producing glassware, it has a new lease on life through the efforts of Maroon Enterprises, Inc., the new owners. Businesses are invited to locate within the complex of Imperial Plaza. Below is a sampling of some of the shops you will find inside Imperial Plaza:

Heritage House: Handmade quilts, baskets, braided rugs, plus other samples of handicrafts people would consider themselves fortunate to own are found here. Often crafts people can be observed at work preparing the many items made on the premises.

Glass Museum: On display in this museum are many, many authentic early glass pieces from a great number of manufacturers. In the Ohio Valley, glass making thrived into the 1970s. Museum exhibits showcase local manufacturers and other famous makers.

Escott's Gallery: In addition to old and antique furniture, this gallery sells oil paintings, watercolors, sculptures in wood, bronze, terra cotta. Located in Escott's Gallery is Imperial Furniture Stripping/Refinishing. Repair services encompass resilvering mirrors, veneer, hand stripping and refinishing.

Flea Market: Each Sunday from 8:00 a.m. until 4:00 p.m. people flock to Imperial Plaza for the flea market. The selling area is a hefty 40,000 square feet. Many bargains and treasures lurk throughout the flea market.

## 11 BOWLING GREEN

**Millikin Antique Mall**
101 S. Main St.
419/354-6606

## 12 BURTON

**Gordon's Antiques**
Route 87 - On The Square
440/834-1426

**Spring Street Antiques**
13822 Spring St.
440/834-0155

## 13 CAMBRIDGE

**Judy's Antiques**
422 S. 9th St.
740/432-5855

**Tenth St. Antique Mall**
127 S. 10th St.
740/432-3364

**Guernsey Antique Mall**
623 Wheeling Ave.
740/432-2570

**Penny Court**
637 Wheeling Ave.
740/432-4369

**Country Bits & Pieces**
700 Wheeling Ave.
740/432-7241

## 14 CANAL WINCHESTER

### The Iron Nail Collectibles, Crafts & Herbs

47 W. Waterloo St.
614/837-6047
Mon.-Fri., 12-5:30; Sat., 11-5:30
*Directions: Located 10 minutes from downtown Columbus, Ohio, from I-70 east, take Route 33 east to Lancaster. Exit at Canal Winchester-Gender Road. Then take a left on Waterloo Road across from Winchester Shopping Mall. Another two miles to downtown Canal Winchester. The shop is one block west of High and Waterloo in a two-story brick house.*

This very diversified shop derives its name from owner, Peggy Eisnaugle, whose last name means "Iron Nail" in Dutch-German. The selection of antique headboards, mantelpieces, chests, chairs, and tables available here are sure to impress the discriminating antique shopper. The stock, however, is varied enough to meet the needs of those looking for more collectible items as well.

You'll find Raikes Bears and designer dolls by Virginia Turner. Interestingly, The Iron Nail also carries a line of fresh herbal products, edible and otherwise, many of which are from Peggy's own garden.

**Canal Country Coffee Mill**
154 N. High St.
614/837-4932

## 15 CANTON

**Somewhere In Time Antiques**
3823 Cleveland Ave. N.W.
330/493-0372

**Route 43 Antique Mall**
8340 Kent Ave N.E.
330/494-9268

**Oldies But Goodies**
101 Nassau St. W.
330/488-8008

**Treasure Trove Antiques**
4313 Tuscarawas St. W.
330/477-9099

**Andy's Antiques**
5064 Tuscarawas St. W.
330/477-3859

## 16 CHAGRIN FALLS

**Bell Corner Shop**
5197 Chillicothe Road
440/338-1101

**Chagrin Valley Antiques**
15605 Chillicothe Road
440/338-1800

**Market**
49 W. Orange St.
440/247-0733

**Chagrin Antiques Limited**
516 E. Washington St.
440/247-1080

**Martine's Antiques**
516 E. Washington St.
440/247-6421

**Hampton Antiques**
17578 Indian Hills Dr.
440/543-2530

**Erythea**
100 N. Main St.
440/247-1960

## 17 CHARDON

**Antiques on the Square**
101 Main St.
440/286-1912

**Steeplechase Antiques**
111 Main St.
440/286-7473

**Olden Dayes Shoppe**
129 Main St.
440/285-3307

**Elaine's Antqs. & Stained Glass**
11970 Ravenna
440/285-8041

**Bostwick Antiques**
310 South St.
440/285-4701

**Wedgwood Etc.**
By Appointment
440/285-5601

**Claridon Antiques**
13868 Mayfield Road
440/635-0359

## 18 CHARM

### *Great Places To Stay*

**Miller Haus Bed & Breakfast Inn**
P. O. Box 129
330/893-3602
Open year round
*Directions: From Berlin, take State Route 39 east 5 miles to County Road 114; turn right on County Road 114, then right onto County Road 135. Signs will direct. From Sugar Creek, take State Route 39 west 4 miles to County Road 114; turn left on County Road 114, then right onto County Road 135. Follow signs.*

The unhurried atmosphere of the Amish community is charmingly captured at Miller Haus Bed & Breakfast Inn. Situated on 23 acres, it is one of the highest points in Holmes County. Needless to say, the view is spectacular.

Darryl and Lee Ann Miller, with son Teddy, and Lee Ann's mother Ann, own and operate the inn. In fact Darryl, a mason/carpenter by trade, and his uncle built the Miller Haus.

Here, you'll find all the comforts of home, and more. Each of the nine guest rooms has its own unique personality, carefully selected antiques, and a private bath. The sitting/living/dining room area features a cathedral ceiling and a magnificent fireplace.

From the front porch you can watch Amish neighbors plow, plant and harvest crops, using horse drawn equipment.

The inn is ideally situated in the country, but close enough to drive to area Amish restaurants, cheese factories, quilt shops, antique stores and other area tourist attractions.

Isn't it appropriate that the Miller Haus, which is a culmination of a love story that brought together an "English" girl and an Amish boy, came to be located in a town called Charm?

## 19 CHESTERLAND

**The Second Time Around**
11579 Chillicothe Road, Route 306
440/729-6555

**Antiques Of Chester**
7976 Mayfield Road
440/729-3395

**Furniture & More**
12550 Chillicothe Road
440/729-0665

## 20 CHILLICOTHE

**Tygert House**
245 Arch St.
740/775-0222

**Country Peddler Store**
200 Burbridge Ave.
740/773-0658

**Antiques On Main Street**
145 E. Main St.
740/775-4802

**Cellar Room Antiques**
203 W. Water
740/775-9848

**American Heritage Antiques**
19 N. Paint St.
740/773-8811

## 21 CINCINNATI

**Drackett Designs & Antiques**
9441 Main St. (Montgomery)
513/791-3868
Tues.-Sat. 10-5 and by appointment
*Directions: Interstate 71 north of Cincinnati to Cross County Parkway Exit. After exiting, move to left lane and go north on Montgomery Road to Remmington Road. Turn right and they are on the corner of Remmington & Main. Parking lot behind house (also behind Montgomery Inn and across from Pomodori's Pizza).*

Located in an historic home built in 1846, Drackett Designs & Antiques specializes in 18th & 19th Century English antiques and accessories. The shop also offers interior design services.

**Every Now & Then Antiques**
430 W. Benson St.
513/821-1497

**Special Things Antique Mall**
5701 Cheviot Road
513/741-9127

**Primitive Kitchen**
9394 Butler Warren Lane Road
513/398-7139

**Country Manor**
7754 Camargo Road
513/271-3979

**Latin Quarter**
1408 Central Pkwy.
513/621-2300

**Wooden Nickel Antiques**
1410 Central Pkwy.
513/241-2985

**Briarpatch**
1006 Delta Ave.
513/321-0308

**Markarian Oriental Rugs Inc.**
3420 Edwards Road
513/321-5877

**Acanthus Antique & Decorative**
3446 Edwards Road
513/533-1662

**Boles Furniture**
1711 Elm St.
513/621-2275

**Phillip Bortz Jewelers**
34 E. 4th St.
513/621-4441

**Jamshid Antique Oriental Rugs**
151 W. 4th St.
513/241-4004

**Michael Lowe Gallery**
338 W. 4th St.
513/651-4445

**American Trading Co.**
3236 W. Galbraith Road
513/385-6556

**Peerson's Antiques**
4024 Hamilton Ave.
513/542-3849

**Mr. Furniture**
4044 Hamilton Ave.
513/541-1197

**Shadow Box Mini Mall**
3233 Harrison Ave.
513/662-4440

**Westwood Antiques & Fine Furn.**
3245 Harrison Ave.
513/481-8517

**Cheviot Trading Co.**
3621 Harrison Ave.
513/661-3633

**Covered Bridge Antique Mall**
7508 Hamilton Ave.
513/521-5739

**Bartoli Antiques**
7718 Hamilton Ave.
513/729-1073

**Treasures Inc.**
1971 Madison Road
513/871-8555

**English Traditions**
2041 Madison Road
513/321-4730

**Duck Creek Antique Mall**
3715 Madison Road
513/321-0900

**Drackett Design & Antiques**
9441 Main St.
513/791-3868

**Grosvenor Brant Antiques**
3407 Monteith Ave.
513/871-1333

**Regarding Books**
6095 Montgomery Road
513/531-4717

**Courtney's Corner**
7124 Montgomery Road
513/793-1177

**Aria's Oriental Rugs**
9689 Montgomery Road
513/745-9633

**Farr Furniture Co.**
8611 Reading Road
513/821-6535

**Glendale Antiques**
270 E. Sharon Road
513/772-0663

**Roth Furniture Co.**
1411 Vine St.
513/241-5491

**Byrd Braman**
338 Ludlow Ave.
513/872-0200

**Mount Healthy Antiques Gallery**
7512 Hamiton Ave.
513/931-1880

**Freeman Antiques**
7500 Hamilton Ave.
513/921-3222

**Teezer's Oldies & Oddities**
7513 Hamilton Ave.
513/729-1500

**Ferguson's Antique Mall**
3742 Kellogg Ave.
513/321-0919

**M J Nicholson Antiques**
2005 Madison Road
513/871-2466

**Federation**
2124 Madison Road
513/321-2671

**Greg's Antiques**
925 Main St.
513/241-5487

**Cannonball Express Antiques**
77175 Mile Road
513/231-2200

**Parlor Antiques by Benjamin**
6063 Montgomery Road
513/731-5550

**Architectural Art Glass Studio**
6099 Montgomery Road
513/731-7336

**Heriz Oriental Rugs**
9361 Montgomery Road
513/891-9777

**A B Closson Jr. Co.**
401 Race St.
513/762-5507

**Sales by Sylvia**
1217 Rulison Ave.
513/471-8180

**Springdale Coin & Antiques**
11500 Springfield Pike
513/772-2266

**Echos Past**
8376 Vine St.
513/821-9696

**Treadway Gallery Inc.**
2029 Madison Road
513/321-6742

## 22 CIRCLEVILLE

**The Country Wood Box**
7979 Bell Station Road
740/474-6617

**Brewer's Antique Mall**
105 W. Main St.
740/474-6257

**Gateway to Yesterday**
121 W. Main St.
740/474-4095

**Farm House Antiques**
29483 U.S. Route 23 S.
740/477-1092

**The Barn**
5201 S. Bloomfield Royalton
740/983-2238

**Peggy's Antiques**
109 E. Mound
740/474-4578

**Once Upon A Time Antiques**
130 W. Main St.
740/772-1164

**South Bloomfield Antique Mall**
U.S. Route 23
740/983-4300

## 23 CLEVELAND

**Ellen Stirn Galleries**
10405 Carnegie Ave.
216/231-6600

**Rastus Pl Black Memorabilia**
510 Euclid Ave.
216/687-8115

**Larchmere Antiques**
12204 Larchmere Blvd.
216/231-8181

**Princeton Antiques**
12628 Larchmere Blvd.
216/231-8855

**Loganberry Books**
12633 Larchmere Blvd.
216/795-9800

**Heide Rivshun Furniture**
12702 Larchmere Blvd.
216/231-1003

**Shaker Square Antiques Inc.**
12733 Larchmere Blvd.
216/231-8804

**Bingham & Vance Galleries**
12801 Larchmere Blvd.
216/721-1711

**Elegant Extras**
12900 Larchmere Blvd.
216/791-3017

**Studio Moderne**
13002 Larchmere Blvd.
216/721-2274

**Annie's**
10024 Lorain Ave.
216/961-3777

**Attenson's Coventry Antiques**
1771 Coventry Road
216/321-2515

**Gwynby Antiques.**
2482 Fairmount Blvd
216/229-2526

**Paulette's Antiques**
12204 Larchmere Blvd.
216/231-8181

**Dede Moore**
12633 Larchmere Blvd.
216/795-9802

**R & S Antiques**
1237 Larchmere Blvd.
216/795-0408

**Ashley's Antiques & Interiors**
12726 Larchmere Blvd.
216/299-1970

**Mark Goodman Antiques**
12736 Larchmere Blvd.
216/229-8919

**Bayswater Antiques**
12805 Larchmere Blvd.
216/231-5055

**Bischoff Galleries**
12910 Larchmere Blvd.
216/231-8313

**Blue Phoenix**
13017 Larchmere Blvd.
216/421-0234

**Metzger's-Ohio City**
3815 Lorain Ave.
216/631-5925

**Hommel's Furniture**
4617 Lorain Ave.
216/631-2797

**Century Antiques**
7410 Lorain Ave.
216/281-9145

**Artisan Antiques & Jewelry**
3095 Mayfield Road
216/371-8639

**Tudor House Antique Gallery**
5244 Mayfield Road
216/646-0120

**Ameriflag Antiques**
4240 Pearl Road
216/661-2608

**Ambrose Antiques**
1867 Prospect Ave. E.
216/771-4874

**Lee Fana Art Gallery**
845 S O M Cent
216/442-7955

**Yesterdays Treasures Antiques**
4829 Turney Road
216/441-1920

**Suite Lorain Antiques & Interiors**
7105 Lorain Ave.
216/281-1959

**Antique Emporium Eldon Ebel Prop.**
7805 Lorain Ave.
216/651-5480

**June Greenwald Antiques**
3098 Mayfield Road
216/932-5535

**American Antiques**
3107 Mayfield Road
216/932-6380

**Oriental Rug Warehouse**
4925 Pointe Pkwy.
216/464-2430

**Wolf's Gallery**
1239 W. 6th St.
216/575-9653

**South Hills Antique Gallery**
2010 W. Schaaf Road
216/351-8500

**Last Moving Picture Co.**
2044 Unclid Ave., Suite 410
216/781-1821

## 24 CLIFTON

**Webers Antiques Americana**
Route 343 & Clay
937/767-8581

**Clifton Antique Mall**
301 N. Main St.
937/767-2277

**Webers Antique Mall**
63 Clay
937/767-5060

## 25 COLUMBIANA

**Victorian Peacock**
139 N. Main St.
330/482-9139

**Philomeno's Antiques**
8 S. Main St.
330/482-0004

**Countryside Antiques**
16 S. Main St.
330/482-3259

**Vivian's Antiques & Collectibles**
24 S. Main St.
330/482-3144

**Glory Road Civil War Art**
103 S. Main St.
330/482-1812

**Historic Images Antiques**
8 S. Main St.
330/482-1171

**Stray Dog Antiques**
8 S. Main St.
330/482-1928

**Bunker Hill Antiques Etc.**
24 S. Main St.
330/482-9004

**Columbiana Antiques Gallery**
103 S. Main St.
330/482-2240

**Main Street Antiques**
13 E. Park Ave.
330/482-5202

## 26 COLUMBUS

### Yesteryear Antiques & Fine Art
268 South 4th St.
614/224-4232
Fax: 614/221-6610
*Directions: From I-70/71 traveling east, exit Fourth St., turn right 4 blocks, located at Main and Fourth St. Traveling west, exit Third and Fourth St., cross Third St., to Fourth St., turn left on Fourth St., four blocks down at Main and Fourth St. Fourth St. is one-way.*

Yesteryear Antiques & Fine Art is a variable treasure trove that will surely delight even the most particular shopper. Owners, John Blackburn and Gene Wagner, connoisseurs in their field, have assembled in the "full service store" a collection of merchandise that is uncompromising in quality, workmanship, and artistry.

They offer the customer superior selections of furniture and accessories from this century and the last; lighting fixtures, cut crystal, bronzes, pottery, and oil paintings are but a few of the many exceptional pieces presented here.

They also offer appraisals, furniture refinishing and restoration, upholstery, and fabric selections. Upon request, they can ship your purchases anywhere in the U.S. or abroad.

**Midwest Quilt Exchange**
495 S. 3rd St.
614/221-8400

**Joseph M Hayes Antiques**
491 City Park Ave.
614/221-8200

**Church On The Lane Antiques Inc.**
1245 Grandview Ave.
614/488-3606

**Maggie's Place-Buy & Sell**
682 E Hudson St.
614/268-4167

**Gene's Furniture**
1100 N. High St.
614/299-8162

**Alexandra Pengwyn Books Ltd.**
2500 N. High St.
614/267-6711

**Uncle Sams Antiques**
3169 N. High St.
614/261-0078

**Antiques Etc. Mall**
3265 N. High St.
614/447-2242

**All Things Considered**
179 E. Arcadia Ave.
614/261-6633

**Minerva Park Furn Gallery**
5200 Cleveland Ave.
614/890-5235

**Findley-Kohler Interiors Inc.**
57 Granville St.
614/478-9500

**Biashara**
780 N. High St.
614/297-7367

**Downstairs Attic**
2348 N. High St.
614/262-4240

**Echoes of Americana**
3165 N. High St.
614/263-9600

**Clintonville Antiques**
3244 N. High St.
614/262-0676

**Euro Classics**
3317 N. High St.
614/447-8108

**Unique Treasures**
3514 N. High St.
614/262-5428

**Antique Etc.**
3521 N. High St.
614/262-7211

**Second Thoughts Antiques**
3525 N. High St.
614/262-0834

**Reserve Fine Area Rugs**
4784 N. High St.
614/447-9955

**Antique Mall on South High**
1045 S. High St.
614/443-7858

**Greater Columbus Antique Mall**
1045 S. High St.
614/443-7858

**Pritts Antiques and Collectibles**
3745 Karl Road
614/261-8187

**David Franklin Ltd.**
2216 E. Main St.
614/338-0833

**Powell Antique Mart**
26 W. Olentangy St.
614/841-9808

**German Village Furniture Co**
960 Parsons
614/444-1901

**Vintage Jewels**
65 E. State St.
614/464-0921

**Thompson's Haus of Antiques**
499 S. 3rd St.
614/224-1740

**G B Antique Guns**
1421 Union Ave.
614/274-4121

**Myra's Antiques & Collectibles Inc.**
2799 Winchester Pike
614/238-0520

**Antiques & Uniques**
247 W. 5th Ave.
614/294-9663

### *Interesting Side Trips*

Travel U.S. Route 23 (High St.) to just north of downtown Columbus. The Short North Gallery District, bridging downtown and The Ohio State University, is Columbus's Bohemia. Here galleries sell everything from fine art to folk art to kitsch. As you explore, you'll find vintage clothing stores, coffee houses and restaurants of every description. Don't miss the Gallery Hop, the first Saturday each month, when galleries and shops hold parties and open houses.

## 27 CONNEAUT

**Papa's Antiques & Military Collectibles**
1000 Buffalo St.
440/593-3582

**Studio Antiques**
242 W. Main Road
440/599-7614

**Ferguson Antique Shop**
282 E. Main Road, Route 20
440/599-7162

**The Furniture Doctor**
314 W. Main Road
440/593-4121

## 28 COSHOCTON

### C & M Collectibles
603 S. Second St.
740/622-6776
Mon.-Thurs. 12-5:30, by chance or appointment Fri.-Sun.
*Directions: I-77 (N&S) Exit 65 (between Cleveland and Marietta), travel west approximately 20 miles, cross bridge, turn right on Second Street.*

C & M Collectibles is a small Ma and Pa operation located within 1200 square feet and a basement area. Customers often comment on how they are pleasantly surprised to find such excellent collectibles at this shop. The owners are very cautious not to mislead their customers; therefore, they make every effort to offer good smalls, glassware, toys, pottery pieces, small furniture pieces and more. Additionally, they purchase items from a variety of styles and periods in hopes that they will have something to offer each and every one of their customers.

**Coshocton Antique Malls**
315 Main St.
740/622-7792

## 29 CUYAHOGA FALLS

**House For Collectors**
2128 Front St.
330/928-2844

**Accent Antiques Gifts**
2204 Front St.
330/922-5411

**Hidden Pearl**
2206 Front St.
330/928-8230

**River Walk Antiques**
2237 Front St.
330/945-6898

**Bill Holland & Assoc.**
2353 N. Haven Blvd.
330/923-5300

**Silver Eagle Antiques**
2215 Front St.
330/929-0066

**Oakwood Antiques & Collectibles**
3265 Oakwood Dr.
330/923-7745

**Consignment Cottage**
2080 State Road
330/929-2080

**Signature Gifts & Antiques**
2208 Front St.
330/922-4528

## 30 DAYTON

Dayton has an extraordinary heritage of industry and invention. Daytonians devised the cash register and the automobile self-starter, which spawned the strong local presence of General Motors and NCR. The city's most clever sons were Orville and Wilbur Wright, the bicycle makers who elevated their skills to invent the airplane.

**Ginger Jar Antiques**
7521 Brandt Pike
937/236-6390

**Taylor & Mahan Emporium**
100 S. Clinton St.
937513/222-0999

**Then And Now**
436 E. 5th St.
937/461-5859

**Feathers Vintage Clothing**
440 E. 5th St.
937/228-2940

**Dorothys Vintage Boutique**
521 E. 5th St.
937/461-7722

**Accents Antiques Etc.**
635 Kling Dr. & Patterson
937/298-7666

**Old World Antiques & Est Jwlry**
4017 N. Main St.
937/275-4488

**Springhouse Antiques**
49 S. Main St.
937/433-2822

**Treasure Barn Antique Mall**
1043 S. Main St.
937/222-4400

**Purple Pig**
23 Park Ave.
937/294-8197

**Park Avenue Antiques**
51 Park Ave.
937/293-5691

**Ann's Furniture**
1917 E. 3rd St.
937/254-7214

**House of Marks**
2025 Wayne Ave.
937/253-5100

**Good Ole Stuf**
621 Watervliet Ave.
937/254-9144

**Arms Depot Gun Shop**
746 Watervliet Ave.
937/253-4843

**Barn Antiques Gallery**
29 W. Whipp Road
937/438-1080

## 31 DELAWARE

**J & D Furniture**
206 London Road
740/363-7575

**Delaware Antiques Ltd.**
27 Troy Road
740/363-3165

**Corner Filling Station**
3770 U.S. Hwy. 42 S.
740/369-0499

**Crabtree Cottage**
4 W. Winter St.
740/369-0898

**Katie's Gifts & Antiques**
2210 U.S. Hwy. 23 N.
740/363-5566

## 32 FINDLAY

Findlay was an active Underground Railroad center. In 1860, the local newspaper editor began publishing outrageously satirical letters signed by the fictitious Southern sympathizer, Petroleum V. Nasby. These humorous Nasby Papers became so widely read that they helped sway national public opinion against slavery.

**Jeffreys Antique Gallery**
11326 Allen Twp. Road #99
419/423-7500

**Antiques Establishments**
3143 Crosshill Dr.
419/424-3699

**Blue House Antiques**
200 W. Lima St.
419/425-1507

**Kate's Korner**
540 S. Main St.
419/423-2653

**Bowman's Antiques**
303 E. Sandusky St.
419/422-3858

**Am-Dia Inc.**
16960 N. State Route 12 E.
419/424-1722

**Old Mill Antique Shop**
10111 W. U.S. Route 224
419/424-4012

## 33 GENEVA

**Geneva Antiques**
28 N. Broadway
440/466-0880

**Broadway Antiques & Collectibles**
71 N. Broadway
440/466-7754

**Martha's Attic**
5501 Lake Road (Route 531)
440/466-8650

## 34 GRANVILLE

**Lynne Windley Antiques**
226 Broadway E.
740/587-3242

**Wee Antique Gallery**
1630 Columbus Road
740/587-2270

**Greystone Country House Antiques**
128 S. Main St.
740/587-2243

**Cream Station Antiques**
1444 Newark Granville Road
740/587-4814

**Our Place Antiques**
121 S. Prospect St.
740/587-4601

### *Great Places To Stay*

### The Porch House
241 Maple St.
740/587-1995; 1-800-587-1995
Open year round; reservations recommended. Please do not call after 9 p.m.
*Directions: From I-70, go north on Route 37, nine miles to Granville. Turn right on Broadway. At the second light, turn right on South Pearl. The Porch House is on the corner of East Maple and South Pearl.*

The Porch House, a turn-of-the-century home in historic Granville, offers charming guest rooms with private baths. The home is adjacent to one of Ohio's most visited bike paths and within short walking distance of village shops. A full country breakfast is served.

## 35 HAMILTON

**Grand Antiques**
1749 Grand Blvd.
513/895-5751

**Augspurgers Antiques**
315 Ludlow St.
513/893-1015

**Dennys Antiques**
119 Main St.
513/887-6341

**The Brass Pineapple**
159 Millville Oxford Road
513/863-6166

**Garden Cottage**
8977 Princeton Glendale Road
513/942-1110

## 36 HARTVILLE

**Hartville Antiques**
Ediston St. N.W.
330/877-8577

**Harville Coin Exchange**
1015 Edison St. N.W.
330/877-2949

**Past Memories**
751 Edison St. N.W.
330/877-4141

**Bennett's Antiques**
128 Erie Ave.
330/877-4336

**Bennett's Country Store**
106 E. Maple St.
330/877-6044

**Hartville Square Antiques**
107 W. Maple St.
330/877-3317

## 37 HIGGINSPORT

### *Great Places To Stay*

**J. Dugan Ohio River House Bed & Breakfast and Antiques**
4 Brown St.
513/375-4395
B&B is open year round; call for reservations
Antique shop is open most days 9-7 or by appointment
*Directions: 35 miles east of Cincinnati, 7 miles west of Ripley, just 1/4 mile off Hwy. 52. In Higginsport, turn south off Hwy. 52 onto Brown St. in the center of town.*

Situated high on a hill in the scenic River Hills area of Brown County, Ohio, and set back from town by the expansive grounds, J. Dugan Ohio River House escorts its visitors to a quiet, secluded and exceptional river view.

J. Dugan Ohio House B & B was originally the home of J. Dugan, a merchant and river trader. The "four-brick-thick" tin-roofed house was built in 1830 from bricks handmade in the town. The adjacent all-brick warehouse which now houses the apartments and antique business once served as a coal unloading station and meat-packing house during its years of service in the river trade. The Dugan house was one of only a few houses in Higginsport that survived the "great flood of 1937." After passing through many hands, not all of which treated this grand old house with the love and care it deserved, the Dugan home was purchased by Pat and Bob Costa in 1970, at which time, to use Bob's words, "there was only one pane of glass in any of the windows." After years of hard work by the Costas, the house was restored to its original splendor. The current owners, the Lloyds, purchased the property from the Costas and are continuing the restoration.

The Lloyds encourage travelers to "stop on by" for a visit in the antique shop and a tour of the house with its antique-furnished spacious rooms and several extensive collections of turn-of-the-century glassware. A seat on the terrace to watch the river traffic or moon rise grants you the escape and vision of what life was like in a quieter time.

Bed and breakfast accommodations include outdoor riverside terrace, lovely grounds and antique-filled common and guest rooms. The J. Dugan Ohio River House also has two furnished apartments with full kitchen available for overnight or longer stays. All overnight guests savor the complimentary full country breakfast.

The area surrounding the bed & breakfast offers public boat docks, great sightseeing outings, in addition to a multitude of antique shops within an hour's drive.

## 38 HILLSBORO

**Memory Lane Mall**
116 S. High St.
937/393-8202

**Fields Framing Antiques Art Gift**
921 N. High St.
937/393-5357

**Ayres Antiques**
114 E. Main St.
937/393-1629

**Old Pants Factory Mall**
135 N. West St.
937/393-9934

## 39 HUBBARD

**Liberty Bell Antiques**
142 N. Main St.
330/534-3639

**Hubbard-Liberty Antique Mall**
5959 W. Liberty St.
330/534-9855

**Antiques & Things**
6138 W. Liberty St.
330/534-0880

## 40 KENT

**Hughes Antiques**
100 W. Crain Ave.
330/677-4489

**Dolphin Antiques**
135 Gougler Ave.
330/678-9595

**City Bank Antiques**
115 S. Water St.
330/677-1479

**Brown & Brown**
134 N. Willow St.
330/673-4396

## 41 KINSMAN

**The Hickory Tree**
8426 State St.
440/876-3178

**Antiques of Kinsman**
8374 Main St.
440/876-3511

## 42 KIRTLAND

**Yesteryear Shop**
7603 Chardon Road
440/256-8293

**Canterbury Station**
9081 Chillicothe Road
440/257-0321

## 43 LANCASTER

**Po Folks Antiques**
1016 Sugar Grove Road. S.E.
740/681-9099

**Guthrie Place Antiques**
118 N. Columbus St.
740/654-2611

**Uniquely Yours Antiques**
139 W. 5th Ave.
740/654-8444

**Emporium-Downtown**
154 W. Main St.
740/653-5717

**Priscilla's**
156 W. Main St.
740/653-1355

**Lancaster Antique Emporium**
201 W. Main St.
740/653-1973

## 44 LEBANON

Brick sidewalks and broad avenues of fine old homes characterize this handsome southwestern Ohio town. Once a site of a Shaker settlement, Lebanon now has numerous antique and specialty shops featuring Shaker items. Collectors come from far and wide for Lebanon's January antique show and the annual holiday festival, which features a wonderful candlelight parade of horse-drawn antique carriages. (Warren County Convention & Visitors Bureau, 1-800-617-6446)

At the Warren County Historical Museum, several rooms of fascinating antiques make its Shaker collection one of the world's largest and best known. Also popular is a collection of nineteenth century storefronts assembled around a village green.

**A Gentler Thyme**
7 N. Broadway St.
513/933-9997

**Charles Gerhardt Antiques**
33 N. Broadway St.
513/932-9946

**Treasurer's Dust Antiques**
135 N. Broadway St.
513/932-3877

**Signs of our Times**
2 S. Broadway St.
513/932-4435

**Broadway Antique Mall**
15 S. Broadway St.
513/932-1410

**Oh Suzanna**
16 S. Broadway St.
513/932-8246

**Garden Gate**
34 S. Broadway St.
513/932-8620

**The Cottage**
114 S. Broadway St.
513/933-9711

**Miller's Antique Market**
201 S. Broadway St.
513/932-8710

**Sycamore Tree Antiques**
3 S. Sycamore St.
513/932-4567

**Linda Castiglione Antiques**
15 E. Main St.
513/933-8344

**Hunter's Horn**
35 E. Main St.
513/932-5688

**Captain Jack's**
35 E. Mulberry St.
513/932-2500

**Vice's Antiques**
519 Mound Court
513/932-7918

**Main Antiques**
31 E. Mulberry St.
513/932-0387

**Shoe Factory Antique Mall**
120 E. South St.
513/932-8300

## 45 LIMA

**Larry's Books**
1033 N. McClure Road
419/649-3420

**Uptown Antiques**
218 E. High St.
419/227-1814

## 46 LISBON

**Kiewall's Florist**
7735 State Route 45
330/424-0854

**Treasure Chest**
119 W. Lincoln Way
330/424-3016

**Treasures of Yesteryear**
343 W. Lincoln N. Ave.
330/424-0102

**New Lisbon Antiques**
120 S. Lincoln Ave.
330/424-1288

**Ye Olde Oaken Bucket Antiques**
38279 Adams Road
330/424-9914

## 47 LITHOPOLIS

**Lithopolis Antique Mart**
9 E. Columbus St.
614/837-9683

## 48 LOVELAND

**Hole In The Wall Antiques**
110 Broadway St.
513/683-7319

**Antique Market of Branch Hill**
392 Bridge St.
513/683-8754

**Path Through The Attic**
122 W. Loveland Ave.
513/683-5022

**Bike Trail Antiques**
124 W. Loveland Ave.
513/677-1224

**Loveland Antiques**
204 W. Loveland Ave.
513/677-0328

## 49 MADISON

**Colonel Lees Antiques**
120 N. Lake St.
440/428-7933

**The Red Geranium**
120 N. Lake St.
440/428-7933

**Little Mountain Antiques**
7757 S. Ridge Road
440/428-4264

**Unionville Antiques**
7918 S. Ridge Road
440/428-4334

**Collector's Delight**
5813 N. Ridge Road
440/428-3563

## 50 MANSFIELD

**Cranberry Heart Inc.**
1461 Ashland Road
419/589-0340

**Mid-Ohio Antiques Mall**
155 Cline Ave.
419/756-5852

**Mansfield Antique Mall**
1095 Koogle Road
419/589-5558

**The Antique Gallery**
1700 S. Main St.
419/756-6364

**Brantina's**
335 Park Ave. E.
419/524-5282

**Little Journeys Bookshop**
376 Park Ave. W.
419/522-2389

**Cricket House**
825 Park Ave. W.
419/524-7100

**Yesteryear Mart**
1237 Park Ave. W.
419/529-6212

## 51 MARIETTA

**Riverview Antiques**
102 Front St.
740/373-4068

**Fort Harmar Antiques**
154 Front St.
740/374-3538

**Stanley & Grass Vintage Furniture**
166 Front St.
740/373-1556

**Dollie Maude's Country Store**
176 Front St.
740/374-2710

**Tin Rabbit Antiques**
204 Front St.
740/373-1152

**Old Tool Shop**
208 Front St.
740/373-9973

**Dads Advertising Collectibles**
118 Maple St.
740/376-2653

**Looking Glass**
187 Front St.
740/376-0113

## 52 MASON

**Dupriest Antiques**
207 W. Main St.
513/459-8805

**Route 42 Antique Mall**
1110 Reading Road
513/398-4003

**Something Old Something New**
4064 State Route 42
513/398-6036

## 53 MEDINA

**Moon & Star Antiques**
217 N. Court St.
330/723-9917

**Gramercy Gallery**
221 S. Court St.
330/725-6626

**Heirloom Cupboard**
239 S. Court St.
330/723-1010

**Unique Antiques & Collectibles**
602 W. Liberty St.
330/722-6666

**1894 Gift Co.**
1342 Medina Road
330/239-1311

**Country Collectibles**
2768 Pearl Road
330/723-1416

**Cnsnmt.Shop in Granny's Attic**
4184 Pearl Road
330/725-2277

**Creations of the Past**
44 Public Square
330/725-6979

**Chuck's Antiques**
7530 Tower Road
330/723-4406

**Brothers Antique Mall**
6132 Wooster Pike
330/723-7580

**Medina Antique Mall**
2797 Medina Road
330/722-0017

## 54 MENTOR

**Gold Coin & Card Outlet**
7292 Lakeshore Blvd.
440/946-0222

**Antique Center**
8435 Mentor Ave.
440/255-3315

**Garage Sale Store**
8510 Mentor Ave.
440/255-6296

**Mentor Village Antiques**
8619 Mentor Ave.
440/255-1438

**Maggie McGiggles Antiques**
8627 Mentor Ave.
440/255-1623

**Yesterday's**
8627 Mentor Ave.
440/255-7930

**Antique Dolls**
8920 Mentor Ave.
440/974-8600

## 55 MESOPOTAMIA

**Coffee Corners Antiques**
8715 Parkman-Mesopotamia Road
440/693-4376

**Beverly Tiffany Antiques**
7594 S. R 534
440/693-4322

**Fannie Mae Emporium**
8809 State Route 534
440/693-4482

## 56 MIAMITOWN

**Camille's Antiques**
State Route 128
513/353-9323

**Miamitown Antiques**
6655 State Route 128
513/353-4598

**An Added Touch**
6661 State Route 128
513/353-4144

**Vintage Antiques & Accents**
6737 State Route 128
513/353-2945

**Antiques & Things**
6755 State Route 128
513/353-1442

**Werts & Bledsoe Antique Mall**
6818 State Route 128
513/353-2689

**Merry's Go Round**
6828 State Route 128
513/353-1119

**Sweet Annie's Antiques & Accents**
6849 State Route 128
513/353-3099

**House of Antiques & Collectibles**
6850 State Route 128
513/353-9776

**Cades Crossing Antiques**
6868 State Route 128
513/353-2232

## 57 MIDDLEFIELD

**Antiques of Middlefield**
14449 Old State Road (Route 600)
440/632-5221

**Country Collection Antiques**
15848 Nauvoo Road
440/632-1919

## 58 MIDDLETOWN

**Beauverre Studios**
4473 Marie Dr.
513/425-7312

**Dailey's Antiques**
32 S. Clinton St.
512/422-7277

**Fisher Antiques & Design**
1316 Central Ave.
513/422-0850

**Middletown Antique Mall**
1607 Central Ave.
513/422-9970

## 59 MILAN

**Kelly's Antiques**
32 Park
419/499-4570

**Crosby's Antiques**
4 Main St. N.
419/499-4001

**Sights & Sounds of Edison**
21 Main St. N.
419/499-3093

**Samaha Antiques**
28 Park
419/499-4044

**Betty Dorow Antiques**
29 Park
419/499-4102

**Milan Antique Quarters**
29 Park
419/499-4646

## 60 MILFORD

**Seiberts Antique Barn**
5737 Deerfield Road
513/575-1311

**Picket Fence Antiques**
5 Main St.
513/821-1500

**Village Mouse Antiques**
32 Main St.
513/831-0815

**Earlys Antiques Shop**
123 Main St.
513/831-4833

**Backroom Antiques**
129 Main St.
513/831-5825

**Remember When Antiques & Cllbls.**
413 Main St.
513/831-6609

## 61 MILLERSBURG

Ever see a McDonald's drive-through window designed for buggies? You'll find one in Millersburg, in the heart of Amish Country. Ohio is proud to be home to the largest population of Amish people in the world. The Amish foreswear modern conveniences, such as automobiles and electricity, in favor of a simpler way of life. In Amish Country, women wear crisp white bonnets and long-sleeved dresses. Men wear simple black clothes and broad-brimmed hats. A few too many black buggies, and you have a traffic jam.

Most Amish in Ohio live in Geauga, Holmes, Trumbull, Tuscarawas and Wayne Counties. When you visit, keep an eye out for slow-moving buggies on the road. And be respectful of the privacy of these "plain people"—don't take close-up pictures.

For a look at Amish life firsthand, visit the Amish Farm and Home in Berlin, where you can see daily life among the Amish. Or head to Walnut Creek and Yoder's Amish Farm, an authentic working farm where you can enjoy such seasonal events as the making of apple butter. Guides at Yoder's explain the history and customs of the Amish religion, and lead you on a tour of two houses and a barn. One house is typical of an Amish home from the late 1800s, with exposed wooden floors, simple furniture and such appliances as a pump sewing machine. The other is similar to a present-day Amish home, with running water and gas floor lamps.

Kidron's Amish and Mennonite communities join together for the annual Mennonite Relief Sale the first Sunday of August. Hundreds of collectors bid for the quilts, tools and folk art presented by members of more than 100 congregations. And while you're in Kidron, don't miss Lehman's hardware store. There you'll find crockery, washboards, grist mills, copper and cast-iron kettles, water pumps—more than an acre's worth of non-electric tools and appliances. Like quilts? Head next door to the Hearthside Quilt Shoppe.

Hungry? The Amish take as much pride in their food as in their crafts. Troyer's Genuine Trail Bologna, in Trails, sells the famous bologna in a country store near the factory where it's made. Try the out-of-this-world green moon cheese at Heini's Cheese Chalet in Berlin. Heini's sells more than 50 varieties of cheeses. At Guggisberg Cheese, near Charm, you can watch as Alfred Guggisberg's famous Baby Swiss Cheese is prepared each day from a secret recipe, in a factory that resembles a Swiss Chalet. Across the road, at the Chalet in the Valley restaurant, you can sit down to a meal of Wiener schnitzel, bratwurst, freshly baked pies and Black Forest cake. As you eat, you'll be serenaded by yodelers and accordion players. If you prefer losing yourself in a nationally known peanut butter pie, try the Homestead Restaurant, where the menu of entrees also includes fried chicken and roast beef with mashed potatoes.

To soothe your sweet tooth, head for Burton and the sugar camp. You can buy candy and maple syrup from the camp at Burton Log Cabin. While you're in town, tour Century Village, a collection of historic buildings.

If you've never witnessed the Amish way of life, you may travel to Amish Country for the first time out of curiosity about a lifestyle unaffected by constantly changing surroundings. Once you've been there, you'll want to go back, again and again.

**Antique Emporium**
113 W. Jackson St.
330/674-0510

### *Great Places To Stay*

**Fields of Home Guest House Bed & Breakfast**
7278 County Road 201
330/674-7152
Web site: www.bbonline.com/oh/fieldsofhome/
Open year round; Sundays by reservations only.
Owned & Operated by the Mervin Yoder Family
Rates $75-125
*Directions: From Berlin, take SR 39 west 1/2 mile to CR 201; turn right onto CR 201 at the Dutch Harvest Restaurant. Go north on 201 for 3.8 miles.*

Talk about a room with a view! Fields of Home Guest House overlooks the beautiful Amish countryside near Millersburg, Ohio. Return to a simpler time...rolling hills, spring-fed ponds, the smell of freshly plowed soil, crickets singing, the clippity-clop of horses pulling black buggies...relax and enjoy an unhurried world of gentle people, where home is a quiet retreat, peaceful and cozy, and you're secure in the trust that tomorrow will be like today. This log cabin guest house offers all the accommodations of home and more; private baths with whirlpool tubs, fireplaces, kitchenettes, a large front porch with rocking chairs and beautiful views. A wonderful place to experience the simple pleasures of life.

## 62 MONTGOMERY

### Drackett Designs & Antiques
9441 Main St. (Montgomery)
513/791-3868
Tues.-Sat. 10-5 and by appointment
*Directions: Interstate 71 north of Cincinnati to Cross County Parkway Exit. After exiting, move to left lane and go north on Montgomery Road to Remmington Road. Turn right and they are on the corner of Remmington & Main St. Parking lot behind house (also behind Montgomery Inn and across from Pomodori's Pizza).*

Located in an historic home built in 1846, Drackett Designs & Antiques specializes in 18th & 19th Century English antiques and accessories. The shop also offers interior design services.

## 63 MOUNT VICTORY

**Newland's Antiques**
11262-11266 Lake View
937/842-3021

**Attic Treasures**
101 N. Main St.
937/354-5430

**Corbin Cottage**
111 S. Main St.
937/354-4330

**House of Yesteryear Antique Mall**
125 S. Main St.
937/354-2020

**Victory Corner Antiques**
305 Taylor St. E.
937/354-5475

## 64 NEW PHILADELPHIA

### Riverfront Antique Mall
1203 Front St.
1-800-926-9806
Mon.-Sat., 10-8; Sun., 10-6
*Directions: From I-77, take Exit 81. Go east on Route 39 to first light; right on Bluebell Drive, and follow to Riverfront Antique Mall.*

Situated near the heart of Amish country, this mammoth antique mall proclaims itself to be "The Greatest Show in Ohio Seven Days a Week." Boasting 84,000 square feet and 350 dealers on one floor, the mall offers a 6,400-square-foot furniture showroom with another 6,000 square feet allotted to a "Rough Room," featuring unrestored and "as-is" finds.

Some of the finest dealers in the Midwest exhibit their wares in room settings or in showcases at Riverfront Antique Mall. Early advertising memorabilia, old dolls, telephones, cash registers, and toys are just a few of the collectibles offered. Elegant glassware, pottery, lighting and lots of the unusual can always be found.

## 65 NEW RICHMOND

**A Loving Remembrance**
204 Front St.
513/553-9756

***Great Places To Stay***

### Quigley House Bed & Breakfast
100 Market St.
513/553-6318
Open year round
Rates $85
*Directions: Take 275 E. to Exit 17, New Richmond (U.S.-52). Go 11 miles to New Richmond. Then go through 2 traffic lights. The next street to the right is Walnut St. Make a right to the stop sign, then a left onto Market St. Go 1 block, and the bed & breakfast is on the corner.*

Quietly situated in the heart of historic New Richmond is the village's first bed and breakfast. Unique defines this lovely turn-of-the-century home which offers four spacious guest rooms with private baths, queen size beds and decorative fireplaces. Guests will awaken to the aroma of freshly brewed coffee, served in the elegant dining room along with a deluxe continental breakfast. A lovely, large front porch invites you to reminisce and capture the nostalgia of this small river town.

Interests in the area include boating on the beautiful Ohio River with overnight mooring accommodations, restaurants, shops and golfing. Located just minutes away from River Downs Racetrack, River Bend Concert Center, Old Coney Island, Sunlight Pool, Riverfront Stadium and downtown Cincinnati.

## 66 NEWARK

**Arcade Korner Mall**
20 N. 4th St.
740/345-9176

**Loewendick's**
4248 Linnville Road S.E.
740/323-3127

**Park Place Antiques & Collectibles**
14 N. Park Place
740/349-7424

**American Antiques**
39 N. 3rd St.
740/345-0588

## 67 NORWICH

**White Pillars Antique Mall**
7525 E. Pike Road
740/872-3720

**Olde Trail Antiques**
7650 E. Pike Road
740/872-4001

**Kemble's Antiques**
55 N. Sundale Road
740/872-3507

**Antique Mall-Bogarts**
7527 East Pike
740/872-3514

## 68 PAINESVILLE

**Treasure Shop**
213 High St.
440/354-3552

**Ye Olde Oaken Bucket**
776 Mentor Ave.
440/354-0007

**My Country Place**
2200 Mentor Ave.
440/354-8811

**Windsor Antiques**
2200 Mentor Ave.
440/357-5792

**A-1 Antique Buyers & Sellers**
1581 N. Ridge Road
440/352-3038

**Miscellaneous Barn**
240 Mantle Road
216/354-5289

## 69 PENINSULA

**Antique Roost**
1455 Whines Hill Road
440/657-2687

**Innocent Age Antiques**
6084 N. Locust St.
440/657-2915

**Downtown Emporium**
1595 Main St.
440/657-2778

**Olde Players Barn**
1039 W. Streetsboro Road
440/657-2886

## 70 PERRY

**Main Street Antiques**
4179 Main St. (Narrows Road)
440/428-6016

**Dad's Old Store**
4184 Main St. (Narrows Road)
440/259-5547

## 71 PERRYSBURG

**Specks Antique Furniture**
23248 Dunbridge Road
419/874-4272

**Jones & Jones Ltd. Antiques**
114 W. Indiana Ave.
419/874-2867

**Perrysburg Antiques Market**
116 Louisiana Ave.
419/872-0231

**Stony Ridge Antiques**
5535 Fremont Pike
419/837-5164

## 72 PICKERINGTON

**Olde Time Antiques**
12954 Stonecreek Dr. N.W.
614/759-7660

## 73 PIQUA

**Avenue & Alley Antiques**
312 E. Ash St.
937/778-1110

**Cheries Antiques & Fine Jewelry**
317 E. Ash St.
937/773-0779

**World Of Oz**
325 E. Ash St.
937/773-2130

**Memory Lane Antiques**
9277 N. County Road 25 A
937/778-0942

**Apple Tree Gallery**
427 N. Main St.
937/773-1801

## 74 PORTSMOUTH

**Leading Lady Company**
620 Chillicothe St.
740/353-0700

**Mr. Binn's Antique Shop**
604 2nd St.
740/353-2856

**Oakery**
225 Harding Ave.
740/776-7481

**Ratliffs Relics**
1608 Gallia St.
740/353-7409

**River Bend Antiques & Gifts**
440 2nd St.
740/354-3759

**Shope Country**
537 2nd St.
740/353-4880

**Olde Towne Antique Mall**
541 2nd St.
740/353-7555

**Gay 90s Antiques**
543 2nd St.
740/353-6111

## 75 POWELL

**Depot Street Antiques**
41 Depot St.
614/885-6034

**Windsor Ltd. Antiques**
9280 Dublin Road
614/761-7900

**Powell Antiques Center**
26 W. Olentangy St.
614/888-6447

**Seasons Past Antiques**
38 W. Olentangy St.
614/431-1265

**Lane Interiors Ltd.**
84 W. Olentangy St.
614/846-1007

**Country Reflections**
87 W. Olentangy St.
614/848-3835

**Manor At Catalpa Grove**
147 W. Olentangy St.
614/798-1471

## 76 RAVENNA

*Directions: Take Ohio Turnpike Exit 13A to Route 44S. Follow Route 44S into Ravenna. From I-76, use Exit 38B, Route 44N, and follow Route 44 north into Ravenna.*

Ravenna, Ohio is a town chock-full of antique shops, bed and breakfasts, and restaurants.

For specific information see review at the beginning of this section.

**AAA I-76 Antique Mall**
4284 Lynn Road
1-888-476-8976
*Directions: Convenience and accessibility make the AAA I-76 Antique Mall at Ravenna, Ohio, one of "Ohio's Best". Excellent visibility from I-76 at exit 38B (St. Route. 44) make it a stopping point for many east-west cross-country travelers.*

For specific information see review at the beginning of this section.

## 77 READING

**Every Now & Then Antique. Mall**
430 W. Benson St.
513/821-1497

**Millcreek Antiques**
100 Mill St. (Lockland)
513/761-1512

**The Furniture Craftsman**
17 Pike St. (Rear)
513/554-0095

**Casablanca Vintage**
9001 Reading Road
513/733-8811

**Talk of the Town**
9019 Reading Road
513/563-8844

**Grand Antique Mall**
9701 Reading Road
513/554-1919

**Amazing Grace Antiques**
149 W. Benson St.
513/761-8300

## 78 SANDUSKY

**Judee Hill Antiques & Appraisals**
809 Hayes Ave.
419/625-4442

**Bay Window**
223 E. Market St.
419/625-1825

**Now & Then Shoppe**
333 W. Market St.
419/625-1918

**Hobson's Choice Tiques-M-Porium**
135 Columbus Ave.
419/624-1591

**Lake Erie Arts, Crafts & Gifts**
1521 Cleveland Road
419/627-0015

## 79 SHANDON

**General Store & More**
4751 Cinti Brookvl Road
513/738-1881

**Bruce Metzger Antiques**
4807 Cinti Brookvl Road
513/738-7256

**Red Door Antiques**
4843 Cinti Brookvl Road
513/738-0618

## 80 SHARON CENTER

**Country Trader**
6324 Ridge Road
330/239-2104

## 81 SPRINGFIELD

### AAA I-70 Antique Mall
4700 S. Charleston Pike (State Route 41)
937/324-8448
*Directions: Convenience and accessibility make the AAA I-70 Antique Mall at Springfield one of "Ohio's Best." Adjacent to the I-70 east bound off-ramp at Exit #59 (State Route 41).*

For specific information see review at the beginning of this section.

**Old Canterbury Antiques**
4655 E. National Road
937/323-1418

**Knight's Antiques**
4750 E. National Road
937/325-1412

**Central Ohio Antique Center**
1735 Titus Road
937/322-8868

**American Antiquities**
126 E. High St.
937/322-6281

**Deborah's Attic**
719 S. Limestone St.
937/322-8842

**Mary's Variety Store**
42 W. High St.
937/324-5372

## 82 STEUBENVILLE

**Pottery City Antiques**
4th & Market
1-800-380-6933

**Yesterday Antiques & Collectibles**
159 N. 4th St.
740/283-2445

**Antique Emporium**
2523 Sunset Blvd.
740/264-7806

**Oldies But Goodies**
1939 Majestic Circle #250
740/282/3926

## 83 STRASBURG

Strasburg provides a convenient stop for antiquing travelers. Four antique shops, one mall, and one indoor Sunday Flea Market are all within one mile of Interstate 77, Exit #87 on Hwy. 250.

### Strasburg 77 Antiques & Collectibles
780 South Wooster
330/878-7726
Tues.-Sun. 11-5, and by chance or appointment
*Directions: ¼ mile west of I-77 at Exit 87, State Route 250.*

Strasburg 77 Antiques & Collectibles is a treasure chest for those seeking interesting and unusual collectibles. The shop is packed with advertising memorabilia, old books and toys, bottles, tins, and those ever-popular Disney collectibles.

### Carol's Collection
840 South Wooster
330/878-7898
Tues.-Sun., 11-5
Directions: ¼ mile west of I-77 at Exit 87, State Route 250

Another great place to go for collectibles in Strasburg, Carol's Collection offers the usual in the way of collectibles such as bottles, advertising, books, etc. However, she loves to seek out and buy for her customers the unusual such as Indian arrowheads and relics, marbles and painted beer and soda bottles.

**Yesterdays Memories Antiques**
116 N. Wooster Ave.
330/878-7021

**Kandle Antiques**
1180 N. Woodster Ave.
330/878-5775

## 84 SUNBURY

**Pieces of the Past**
74 E. Cherry St.
614/965-1231

**Coffee Antiques**
25 E. Granvill St.
614/965-1113

**Sunberry Antique Mall**
20 S. Vernon
614/965-2279

**Village Antiques**
5 S. Columbus St.
614/965-4343

**Weidner's Village Square Antq. Mall**
31 E. Granvill St.
614/965-4377

**Cherry St. Antiques Center**
34 W. Cherry St.
614/888-6447

## 85 TIFFIN

**Deerfield Station**
60 Clay St.
419/448-0342

**That Old Log House Antiques**
1443 W. Seneca Ave.
419/447-0381

**Tiffin Town Antiques**
368 N. Washington St.
419/447-5364

**The Gallery**
215 Riverside Dr.
419/447-1568

**Shumway Antiques**
94 N. Washington St.
491/447-8746

**Knic-Knac's Treasures**
22 S. Washington St.
419/447-5922

## 86 TIPP CITY

**Kim's Furniture Store**
7505 S. County Road 25 A
937/667-3316

**Angels Antiques**
27 E. Main St.
937/667-8861

**Venkin Antique Gallery**
14 E. Main St.
937/667-5526

**Benkin & Company**
14 E. Main St.
937/667-5975

**Jezebel's Vintage Clothing**
15 N. 2nd St.
937/667-7566

## 87 TOLEDO

**Cobblestone Antiques Mall**
2635 W. Central Ave.
419/475-4561

**Leffler's Antiques**
2646 W. Central Ave.
419/473-3373

**The Station Shop**
130 W. Dudley
419/893-5674

**Custer Antiques & Investment Co.**
534 W. Laskey Road
419/478-4221

**Colour Your World**
414 Main St.
419/693-5283

**Keta's Antiques & Oriental Rugs**
2640 W. Central Ave.
419/474-1616

**Gold & Silver Lady**
5650 W. Central Ave.
419/537-9009

**Hymans Red Barn**
922 Lagrange St.
419/243-9409

**The Gift Horse**
520 Madison Ave.
419/241-8547

**Frogtown Books Inc.**
2131 N. Reynolds Road
419/531-8101

**Cottage Antiques**
2423 N. Reynolds Road
419/536-3888

**Ancestor House Antiques**
3148 Tremainsville Road
419/474-0735

**Antique Barn**
1598 W Sylvania Ave.
419/470-0118

## 88 UNIONTOWN

**Wayside Antiques**
12921 Cleveland Ave. N.W.
330/699-2992

**Antique Mall Uniontown**
13443 Cleveland Ave. N.W.
330/699-6235

**Ashley's**
12980 Cleveland Ave. N.W.
330/699-5370

**Colonial Antique Arts & Crafts**
13075 Cleveland Ave. N.W.
330/699-9878

**Antiques of Yesteryears**
13501 Cleveland Ave. N.W.
330/699-2090

## 89 UNIONVILLE

**The Green Door & Red Button**
6819 S. Ridge E. Route 84
440/428-5747

**Unionville Antiques**
Route 84
440/428-4334

**Little Mountain Antiques**
7757 S. Ridge E. Route 84
440/428-4264

## 90 URBANA

**Charlie Brown's Antiques**
4815 Cedar Creek Road
937/484-3535

**Upper Valley Antiques**
3345 W. U.S. Hwy. 36
937/653-6600

**Kaleidoscope**
117 N. Main St.
937/653-8010

## 91 VAN WERT

**Williman's Antiques**
115 S. Market St.
419/238-2282

**Heritage Coin & Antique Shop**
119 N. Washington St.
419/238-1671

**Years Ago Antique Mall**
108 W. Main St.
419/238-3362

## 92 WADSWORTH

**Wadsworth Antique Mall**
941 Broad St.
330/336-8620

**Antique Design**
112 Main St.
330/334-6530

**Lady Sodbuster Antiques**
121 E. Prospect St.
330/336-5239

**Country Trader**
6324 Ridge Road
330/239-2104

**William Hromy Antiques**
5958 Ridge Road
330/239-1409

## 93 WAPAKONETA

**Take It From The Top**
24 E. Auglaize St.
419/738-2421

**Antique Vault**
36 E. Auglaize St.
419/738-8711

**Antiques Etc.**
215 E. Auglaize St.
419/739-9382

**Rapunzel's**
115 W. Auglaize St.
419/738-3331

**Auglaize Antique Mall**
116 W. Auglaize St.
419/738-8004

**Brick Place**
202 W. Auglaize St.
419/738-5555

**Ivy Haus**
1321 Bellefontaine St.
419/739-9489

**Log Cabin**
408 S. Blackhoof St.
419/738-7578

**Purple Goose**
11539 Glynwood Road
419/738-7952

## 94 WASHINGTON COURT HOUSE

**Past & Present Memorabilias**
109 E. Court St.
740/333-3222

**This Old House**
427 E. East St.
740/335-8102

**Storage House**
153 S. Hinde St.
740/335-9267

**B & D Collectibles**
143 N. Main St.
740/335-8417

**Midland Mall**
153 S. Main St.
740/636-1071

## 95 WATERVILLE

**American Heritage Antiques. Waterville**
17 N. 3rd St.
419/878-8355

**Waterville Antique Center**
19 N. 3rd St.
419/878-3006

**K & G Antiques & Etc.**
36 N. 3rd St.
419/878-7778

**Mill Race Antiques**
217 Mechanic St.
419/878-8762

## 96 WAYNESVILLE

Off I-71at Exit 45, take Route 73 west to Waynesville, then U.S. Route 42 south to Lebanon. Waynesville is known for its antique shops. It is also know for its ghosts; the town's Main St. has been dubbed: "America's Most Haunted." If you visit in October, take the Not-So-Dearly-Departed Tour. One stop will be the Hammel House Inn, where antiques and apparitions converge. If there are ghosts in nearby Lebanon, it's a safe bet they'll be at Pioneer Cemetery, eternal home of Sarah, Elizabeth, Mary, and Ann Harner. According to Ripley's "Believe It Or Not", the four sisters were simultaneously killed by a ball of lightning that came down the chimney of their farmhouse and struck them all, though each was in a different room.

**Highlander House**
22 S. Main St.
513/897-7900

**Remember When Antiques**
43 S. Main St.
513/897-2438

**Miscellany Collection**
49 S. Main St.
513/897-1070

**Bittersweet Antiques**
57 S. Main St.
513/897-4580

**Velvet Bear Antiques**
61 S. Main St.
513/897-0709

**Waynesville Antique Mall**
69 S. Main St.
513/897-6937

**My Wife's Antiques**
77 S. Main St.
513/897-7455

**Little Red Shed Antiques**
85 S. Main St.
513/897-6326

**Olde Curiosity Shoppe**
88 S. Main St.
513/897-1755

**Cranberry Corner Antiques**
93 S. Main St.
513/897-6919

**Baker's Antiques**
98 S. Main St.
513/897-0746

**Brass Lantern Antiques**
100 S. Main St.
513/897-9686

**Golden Pomegranate Antique Mall**
140 S. Main St.
513/897-7400

**Crazy Quilt Antiques**
211 S. Main St.
513/897-8181

**Back In The Barn**
239 S. Main St.
513/897-7999

**The Rose Cottage**
258 S. Main St.
513/897-1010

**Tiffany's Treasures**
273 S. Main St.
513/897-0116

**Spencer's Antiques**
274 S. Main St.
513/897-7775

**Silver City Mercantile Antiques**
1555 E. State Route 73
513/897-9000

## 97 WEST CHESTER

### Hidden Treasures Antiques
8825 Cincinnati Dayton Road
513/779-9908
Tues.-Sat. 11-6, Sun. 1-5
*Directions: I-75 Exit 21 to Cincinnati-Dayton Road. South approximately 1/2 mile to 8825 Cincinnati-Dayton Road.*

For specific information see review at the beginning of this section.

**Van Skaiks Antiques**
9355 Cincinnati-Columbus Road
513/777-6481

**Memory Lane Antiques & Repair**
8872 Cincinnati-Dayton Road
513/777-8565

## 98 WESTERVILLE

**Springhouse Antique Mall**
2 N. State St.
614/882-2354

**Heart's Content Antique Mall**
9 N. State St.
614/891-6050

**Allen's Jewelry**
399 S. State St.
614/882-3937

**Nestor's Antiques**
8999 Robinhood Circle
614/882-1939

**Mills Antique**
3790 E. Powell Road
614/890-7020

## 99 WILLOUGHBY

**Somewhere In Time Antiques**
4117 Erie St.
440/975-9409

**Friends Antiques**
4119 Erie St.
440/946-1595

**Tiffany Rose Antiques**
4075 Erie St.
440/942-2065

**Mr. Willoughby's Antiques**
14 Public Square
440/951-5464

**Market Square Antiques**
24 Public Square
440/975-1776

## 100 WOOSTER

### Norton's Antiques, Etc.
9423 Ashland Road
330/262-6439
Daily by chance or by appointment
*Directions: Halfway (10 miles) between Wooster and Ashland on State Route 250 in the village of New Pittsburg.*

Inside Norton's Antiques, etc., there are a host of small possibilities. In fact, Mr. Norton refers to the majority of his stock as a collection of "smalls." From "primitives to depression," his selections are worthy of your attention. He offers pottery, china, figurines, and glassware of all varieties. A wide selection of costume jewelry is also available. Norton's Antiques, etc., located near Amish country in the village of New Pittsburgh, is an excellent reminder that, very often, good things do come in small packages.

**Uptown/Downtown Antique Mall**
215 W. Liberty St.
330/262-9735

**Green Room II Antiques**
1357 Old Columbus Road
330/264-7071

## 101 YOUNGSTOWN

**Kozak's Antiques & Appraisals**
1328 Elm St.
330/747-2775

**Thomas E Marsh Antiques Inc.**
914 Franklin Ave.
330/743-8600

**The Joshua Tree**
4059 Hillman Way
330/782-1993

**Home Classics**
15 W. McKinley Way
330/757-0423

**Now & Then Shoppe**
2618 Mahoning Ave.
330/799-8643

**Twice-Loved Books**
19 E. Midlothian Blvd.
330/783-2016

**Antique Alley**
104 E. Midlothian Blvd.
330/783-1140

## 102 ZANESVILLE

**Log Hollow**
2825 Chandlersville Road
740/453-2318

**Corner Cupboard Antiques**
1032 Linden Ave.
740/453-3246

**Allies Antiques**
524 Main St.
740/452-2280

**Olde Towne Antique Mall**
525 Main St.
740/452-1527

**Elaine's Antique & Collectibles Mart**
531 Main St.
740/452-3627

**Market St. Gallery**
822 Market St.
740/455-2787

**A Le Clara Belle**
4868 E. Pike Road
740/454-2884

**Seven Gables Antiques**
1570 S. River Road
740/454-1596

**Christines Unique Antique Mall**
28 N. 7th St.
614/455-2393

# Oklahoma

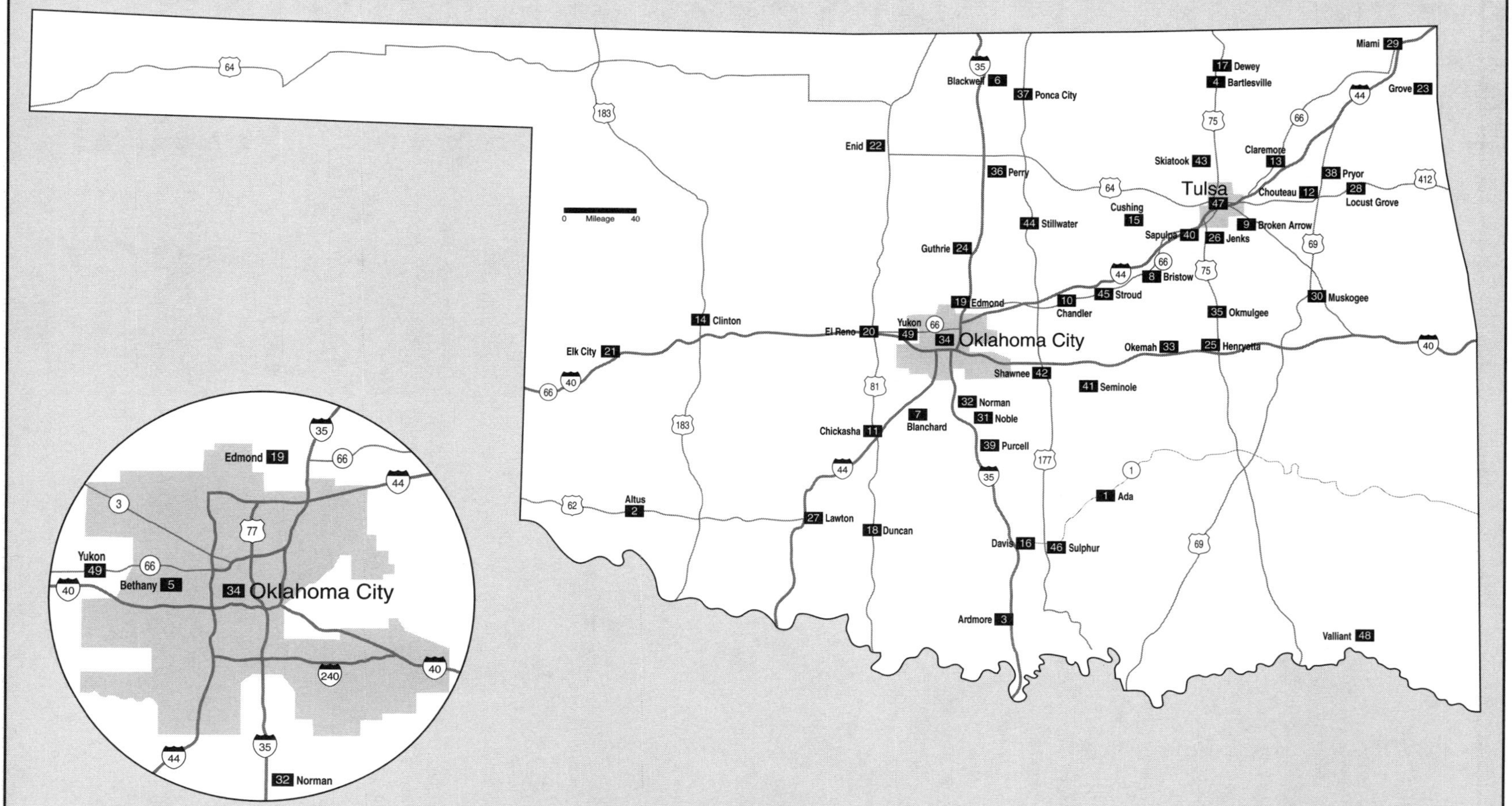

Miami 29
Grove 23
17 Dewey
4 Bartlesville
Blackwell 6
37 Ponca City
Enid 22
36 Perry
Claremore 13
Skiatook 43
38 Pryor
Tulsa 47
Chouteau 12
28 Locust Grove
Cushing 15
9 Broken Arrow
44 Stillwater
Sapulpa 40
26 Jenks
Guthrie 24
8 Bristow
19 Edmond
45 Stroud
10 Chandler
30 Muskogee
35 Okmulgee
14 Clinton
El Reno 20
Yukon 49
34 Oklahoma City
Elk City 21
Okemah 33
25 Henryetta
Shawnee 42
41 Seminole
32 Norman
31 Noble
7 Blanchard
Chickasha 11
39 Purcell
1 Ada
Altus 2
27 Lawton
18 Duncan
Davis 16
46 Sulphur
Ardmore 3
Valliant 48
0 Mileage 40
Edmond 19
Yukon 49
Bethany 5
34 Oklahoma City
32 Norman

## ROUTE 66

From its official beginning in 1926 through the heyday of auto travel in the '50s and '60s, Route 66 was the road for dreamers. It exemplifies the open road, beckoning adventure with the promise of freedom. It carried families, vagabonds, and untold others through bustling cities and into neon-lit small towns in the heart of America.

During the depression of the '30s, it was the road of hope for "Okies": poor Oklahoma farm families who abandoned their drought-ravaged homes and headed west for a better way of life. Their plight was made famous by John Steinbeck's novel *The Grapes of Wrath*.

Route 66 is "still the place to get your kicks" thanks to dozens of Route 66 cities who have kept their downtowns vibrant. Many today boast a diverse assemblage of shops featuring antiques, collectibles and Route 66 memorabilia. Movie theaters and building facades are being restored to the splendor of time past. Businesses are returning to their downtown districts, and those who remember the Mother Road during its heyday are proudly embracing their heritage. Route 66 is rich in Oklahoma, and it looks like the Main Street of America is here to stay.

## 1 ADA

**Alford Warehouse Sales**
217 S. Johnston St.
580/332-1026

**Treasures In Time**
211 E. Main St.
580/436-1200

**Ada Antique Mall**
222 E. Main St.
580/332-9927

**Granny's Attic**
715 E. Main St.
580/436-4241

## 2 ALTUS

### The Enchanted Door
111 W. Commerce St.
580/477-0004

The Enchanted Door offers an "enchanting" shopping experience. Here you'll find antiques, crystals, decorative accessories as well as gift baskets and specialty toys.

**Granny's Antiques**
905 E. Broadway St.
580/477-1565

**Designs For The Goodtimes**
Bunker Hill Shopping Center
580/477-0298

**Yesterdaze Treasures**
113 E. Commerce St.
580/482-1229

**Remember When**
103 N. Hudson St.
580/482-3773

**Sue's Collectibles & Antiques**
110 Falcon Road
580/482-4461

**North Main Antique Mall**
601 N. Main St.
580/477-1991

**Catch All**
1500 S. Main St.
580/482-6950

**Al's Antiques**
720 S. Spurgeon St.
580/482-2022

## 3 ARDMORE

**Surrell's**
318 Lake Murray Dr. E.
580/223-3799

**Ardmore Furniture**
15 Sam Noble Pkwy.
580/226-2090

**Antique Sampler**
15 Sam Noble Pkwy.
580-226-7643

**Portico**
21 N. Washington St.
580/223-4033

**Honey Creek Emporium**
212 E. Main St.
580/369-3524

**Main Antique Mall**
1 W. Main St.
580/226-4395

**Peddlers Square Mall**
15 N. Washington St.
580/223-6255

**Watermark Antiques & Interiors**
19 N. Washington St.
580/223-7900

## 4 BARTLESVILLE

**Lace & Such**
502 S. Cherokee Ave.
918/336-8000

**Apple Tree Mall**
3900 E. Frank Phillips Blvd.
918/335-2485

**Piper Furniture**
110 S.W. Frank Phillips Blvd.
918/336-1300

**Victorian Memories**
310 S.W. Frank Phillips Blvd.
918/336-2952

**Gans Mall**
3801 S.E. Kentucky St.
918/335-1046

**Hog Shooter Antiques Etc.**
3922 Nowata Road
918/333-3333

**Good Earth**
101 E. Frank Phillips Blvd.
918/336-6633

**Country Store**
Route 3 Box 8970
918/336-0351

**Depot Corner Antiques**
127 S.W. 2nd St.
918/336-9313

**Alayne's Doll Boutique**
1609 Oklahoma
918/337-0366

**Aunt Lou's Collectibles**
1205 S.W. Frank Phillips Blvd.
918/337-0033

**Keepsake Candles Factory**
Route 3, Box 8970
918/336-0351

**Media Futures Bookstore**
Road 2400
918/333-3695

**Normandy Antiques**
117 S.E. Frank Phillips Blvd.
918/338-0818

**Vineyard's Vintages**
615 Delaware
918/336-4165

**Yocham's Custom Leather**
Nowata Road (4 mi. E. of Hwy. 75)
918/335-2277

## 5 BETHANY

Before travelers even realize they've left Oklahoma City, 39th St. suddenly looks like a small- town Main St. again. It courses past old gas stations, the Route 66 Trading Post (boasting the "best collection in the nation" of memorabilia) and Oklahoma Southern Nazarene University. A stretch of the old highway curves by the north edge of Lake Overholser and along a rusty steel truss bridge. The old route can be followed around to the west to Yukon, where State Hwy. 66 takes over.

**Judy's Antiques Collectibles & Gifts**
6722 N.W. 39th Expressway
405/787-2366

**Ewok Shop**
6632 N.W. 36th St.
405/495-8565

**Ancient Tastes & Treasures**
3921 N. College Ave.
405/495-3239

**Antique Garden**
3926 N. College Ave.
405/495-9117

**Bethany Antiques Mall**
3901 N. College Ave.
405/495-7091

**Cobblestone Gifts & Interiors**
6716 N.W. 39th Expressway
405/495-7446

## 6 BLACKWELL

**Ashby's Antique Mall**
110 N. Main St.
580/363-4410

**Rowe's Antique Mall**
116 N. Main St.
580/363-2233

**Larkin Gallery**
201 N. Main St.
580/363-0645

**Time Worn Antiques Mall**
112 S. Main St.
580/363-3262

## 7 BLANCHARD

**Janet's Eats & Sweets**
100 N. Main St.
405/485-2638

**Yesterdays Best Antique Mall**
109 N. Main St.
405/485-2550

**Merctl Antiques & Collectibles**
113 N. Main St.
405/485-3131

**Main St Antiques**
114 N. Main St.
405/485-3688

**Shade Tree Antiques**
115 N. Main St.
405/485-9600

**Aged To Perfection**
114 2nd St.
405/485-3449

## 8 BRISTOW

**Trash & Treasures**
112 N. Main St.
918-367-6201

**Joe Mounce Antiques**
9th & Main St.
918/367-6492

## 9 BROKEN ARROW

**Picket Fence**
1000 N. Elm Place
918/258-2969

**Medicine Man Mercantile**
222 S. Main St.
918/251-1229

**Antique Centre**
412 S. Main St.
918/251-7092

**Nailbenders**
1819 S. Main St.
918/258-4644

**Riverhill Antiques**
19285 E. 131st St.
918/455-7530

**Memory Lane Antique Mall**
211 S. Main St.
918/251-9060

## 10 CHANDLER

Chandler is headquarters for the Oklahoma Route 66 Association. Delightful styles of vintage gas station architecture and twelve buildings on the National Historic Register survived citywide destruction after an 1897 tornado. The Museum of Pioneer History tells the story of Chandler's early days. Three miles west of town is the often-photographed metal barn advertising Meramac Caverns in Stanton, Missouri.

**Treasure Barn**
1112 W. 15th St.
405/258-3115

**Brown Furniture**
920 Manvel Ave.
405/258-1717

**Fine Things on the Corner**
923 Manvel Ave.
405/258-5101

**Days of Yesteryear**
1214 Manvel Ave.
405/258-2217

**Outskirts**
1909 E. 1st St.
405/258-2902

## 11 CHICKASHA

**Artistic Expressions Mall**
309 W. Chicasha Ave.
405/224-9199

**Yellow Rose Antique Mall**
516 W. Chickasha Ave.
405/222-2112

**Dangie's Antiques**
524 W. Chickasha Ave.
405/224-9019

**Rockys Ole Time Shoppe**
1002 S. 4th St.
405/224-6945

**Ersland Antiques**
1124 S. 17th St.
405/224-2049

**Collectors Corner**
2001 S. 6th St.
405/224-3819

## 12 CHOUTEAU

### Black Star Antiques
702 S. Chouteau Ave. (Hwy. 69 S.)
918/476-6188
Mon.-Sat. 10-6, Sun. 12-6
*Directions: Traveling Hwy. 412 take Chouteau Exit. Go north 1 mile. Chouteau Avenue is Hwy. 69 S.*

Space galore and jam-packed with items, this 14,000-square-foot shop houses antique clocks, tobacco tins, grocery store memorabilia, carnival chalkware (Kewpie dolls, Betty Boop, various figures). In addition, antique furniture, primitives, art and advertising collectibles are also available.

**Frailey's Antiques**
Hwy. 69 S.
918/476-6581

## 13 CLAREMORE

Claremore is home of the world-famous Will Rogers Memorial and Roger's burial site. Visitors can drive by the boarded-up Will Rogers Hotel, once resplendent with radium water baths on its top floor and a street level cafe. On the Rogers State College campus is the Lyon Riggs Memorial honoring the playwright for Green Grows Like the Lilacs, from which came the beloved Rogers and Hammerstein musical *Oklahoma*! Great antique browsing in dozens of shops, many of which are within expansive malls. J. M. Davis Gun Museum features more than 20,000 guns and related items, plus steins, swords, musical instruments and more.

**Wardens Antique Clock Shop**
105 N. Boling St.
918/341-1770

**Chamwood Antique Mall**
2409 N. Hwy. 20
918/341-7817

**Milk Barn Antiques**
220 N. Missouri Ave.
918/342-1116

**Custom Frames & Collectibles**
101 S. Seminole Ave.
918/341-2900

**Frontier General Store & Antique Mall**
318 W. Will Rogers Blvd.
918/341-3442

**Shadows of Time**
404 W. Will Rogers Blvd.
918/342-2633

**Peachtree Antiquary**
409 W. Will Rogers Blvd.
918/341-1360

**Sanbear Antique Mall**
508 W. Will Rogers Blvd.
918/341-6227

**Hoover's Have All Mall**
714 W. Will Rogers Blvd.
918/341-7878

**A Place In Time Antiques & Cllbls.**
1215 W. Will Rogers Blvd.
918/343-9800

**Antique Peddlers Mall**
422 W. Will Rogers Blvd.
918/341-8615

## 14 CLINTON

In 1899, two men, waiting for a train at a station house, climbed on a box car to look over the countryside. Their eyes traveled over the Washita River Valley, and one of them said, "There's the place to build a town." The men were J. L. Avant and E. E. Blake. They were looking at the site where the town of Washita Junction would spring up, almost overnight, some four years later. However, before the dream could become a reality, there was a political fight that reached as far as the United States Congress, and the start of a feud between Arapaho and Washita Junction. The postal department refused to accept the name Washita Junction for the new town. Therefore, "Clinton" was chosen in honor of the late Judge Clinton Irwin.

**Antique Mall of Clinton**
815 Frisco
580/323-2486

**Mohawk Lodge Indian Store**
1 mi. E. on Old 66 Hwy.
580/323-2360

## 15 CUSHING

**Friday Store**
112 W. Broadway St.
918/225-3936

**The Full Moon**
120 W. Broadway St.
918/225-3936

## 16 DAVIS

**Nelson's Cottonwood Corner**
Hwy. 77 S.
580/369-3836

**D & D**
206 E. Main St.
580/369-2398

**Miss Sarah's**
201 E. Main St.
580/369-2092

**Honey Creek Emporium**
212 E. Main St.
580/369-3524

**The New Dusty Steamer Mall**
222 E. Main St.
580/369-2959

**Somethin Old Somethin New**
503 E. Main St.
580/369-3418

**Bric-A-Brac House**
509 E. Main St.
580/369-3916

**Country General**
1 mi E. of 1/2 Mile Road N.
580/369-3954

**Davis General Store**
112 N. Third St.
580/369-3409

## 17 DEWEY

### Dewey Antique Mall
202 N. Osage Hwy. 75
918/534-2660
Mon.-Sat. 10:30-5:30, Sun. 1-5

A collector's paradise! Thirty dealers offer an amazing array of old Ertle banks, Western memorabilia, primitives, glassware and much, much more.

**Treasures Are We**
306 E. Don Tyler Ave.
918/534-3878

**Something Different**
319 E. Don Tyler Ave.
918/534-3645

**Campbell's Antiques**
418 Don Tyler Ave.
918/534-3068

**Bar-Dew Antiques**
Hwy. 75 N.
918/534-0222

**Lighthouse**
115 S. Osage
918/534-0662

**Forget Me Not**
305 S. Osage
918/534-3737

**Linger Longer Antiques**
814 N. Shawnee Ave.
918/534-0610

**Chancellor Antiques**
400 E. Don Tyler
918/534-3338

**Susie's Miniature Mansion**
623 E. Don Tyler
918/534-2003

**The Right Place**
810 N. Wyandotte
No Phone # Listed

**The Right Place Too**
301 S. Osage - Hwy. 75
No Phone # Listed

## 18 DUNCAN

**Company's Comin**
9 N. 8th St.
580/252-1844

**Duncan Antique Mall**
920 Main St.
580/255-2552

**The Ginger Jar Antiques**
1609 N. Hwy. 81
580/252-2329

**Decors of Duncan**
1898 N. Hwy. 81
580/252-9090

**Brass Rail Antiques**
5051 N. Hwy. 81
580/252-7277

**Red Rose**
5051 N. Hwy. 81
580/225-4925

**Nancy's Antiques**
Hwy. 70 (Waurika)
580/228-2575

**Ace High Pawn**
112 E. Main St.
580/252-7296

**Antique Market Place & Tea Room**
726 W. Main St.
580/255-2499

**2 Bs Closet**
806 W. Main St.
580/255-2211

**K-Rider Co.**
806 W. Main St.
580/255-2211

**Pat's Corner Mall**
809 W. Main St.
580/255-4988

**Aunti Msl**
832 W. Main St.
580/252-3945

## 19 EDMOND

The city actually began in 1887 when the Santa Fe Railroad built a watering station at the highest point between the Cimarron and North Canadian rivers. The town sprang to life as homesteaders staked their claims around the station during the great Land Run on April 22, 1889.

The founders embodied the true spirit of pioneers—they were trailblazers who worked hard to ensure the best for their families and their futures. This is evident in the "firsts" they accomplished. Edmond was the first town in Oklahoma Territory to have a public school house as well as the first church. The territory's first library was organized in Edmond and the "Normal School" for teachers was established here. The Normal School is now the University of Central Oklahoma.

**Country Collectibles**
15 N. Littler Ave.
405/359-7210

**Broadway Antique Mall**
114 S. Broadway St.
405/340-8215

**Edmond Antique Mall**
907 S. Broadway St.
405/359-1234

**Courtyard Antique Market**
3314 S. Broadway St.
405/359-2719

## 20 EL RENO

Motorists may notice something odd about the aged-looking broken neon sign in front of the Big Eight Motel; it boastfully proclaims the place as "Amarillo's Finest." Looks can be deceiving though—the sign is a leftover prop from the movie Rain Man, which was filmed in part in Oklahoma, and Dustin Hoffman and Tom Cruise really slept here. El Reno was a major rail center for the Rock Island years ago, but a ghostly rail yard is all that remains today. Carnegie Library has archived photos of the famed Bunion Derby and paving of Route 66. On the west edge of town is old Fort Reno, where World War II German prisoners are among those buried in its windswept cemetery.

### The Old Opera House
110 N. Bickford
405/422-3232
Mon.-Sat. 10-5, Sun. 1-5

This renovated opera house features antiques and crafts. Furniture and accessories, collectibles, art and rugs offer a sampling of the items presented within the charming elegance of this massive and historic structure.

### Route 66 Antique Mall
1629 E. State Hwy. 66
405/262-9366
Tues.-Sat. 10-6, Thur. 10-8, Sun. 1-5, closed Mondays

On the west end of the city, 120 booths display varied and interesting pieces. Primitives are well represented. Other booths offer all types and descriptions of glassware and Americana.

## 21 ELK CITY

**Old 66 Antique Mall**
401 E. 3rd St.
580/225-9695

**Kandie's Kreations & Kollectibles**
2424 W. Third (Old Route 66)
580/225-6900

**Country Creations Craft & Antique Mall**
114 S. Main St.
580/225-7312

## 22 ENID

**Mini-Mall**
129 E. Broadway Ave.
580/233-5521

**The Trolley Shop**
910 W. Broadway Ave.
580/242-3123

**Down Memory Lane Antiques**
101 S. Grand St.
580/242-2100

**Olden Daze Antique Mall**
117 N. Grand St.
580/242-5633

**Tommy's This N That**
104 N. Independence
580/233-5642

**Cherokee Strip Antiques**
124 S. Independence
580/234-7878

**Ben's Antiques**
1205 S. Van Buren
580/237-5968

**Enid Flea Market**
S. Van Buren
580/237-5352

**Cher-Dans**
827 W. Maine Ave.
580/237-6880

## 23 GROVE

**Flour Sack**
307 S. Grant St.
918/786-4075

**Precious Things**
311 S. Grand St.
918/786-7044

**Crystal's Antiques**
Hwy. 59
918/786-9220

**TBN Antiques & Uniques**
3650 Hwy. 59 N.
918/786-7721

**Donna's Antiques And Collectibles**
2124 Hwy. 59 N.
918/786-3534

**Old Homestead**
6 W. 3rd St.
918/786-8668

**Sister's Trading Co.**
Hwy. 59
918/786-9511

**Don's Swap Shop**
5525 Hwy. 59 N.
918/786-9590

**Village Barn Antiques**
Main St.
918/786-6132

## 24 GUTHRIE

On a single day in April, 1889, a city was born...a new capital for a new territory. Overnight, 10,000 pioneers turned an open prairie into a sprawling array of crude tents, wagon beds, and rough-hewn wooden buildings. From that first day of chaos, an elegant Victorian city evolved with remarkable architecture and expressive character to become the capital of the 46th state, Oklahoma.

When the capital was moved south, this majesty of the plains fell by the wayside. Today, through careful restoration, this rich architectural legacy has been preserved in all its grandeur. Visitors can shop the numerous boutiques, antique malls and specialty shops downtown and also see the homes of governors, editors, law men, and outlaws in Guthrie's residential district.

Historic walking and trolley tours, jubilant festivals, cowpunching rodeos, live professional theatre, captivating museums, exquisite dining and a charming community make Guthrie a turn-of-the-century destination.

**Elk's Alley**
210 W. Harrison
405/282-6100

**Antiques Etc.**
113 W. Oklahoma Ave.
405/282-9610

**Recollections Antique Mall**
124 N. First
405/260-0101

**Vic's Place**
124 N. 2nd St.
405/282-5586

**King's Antiques**
107 W. Oklahoma Ave.
405/282-0534

**Aunt Bea's Attic**
114 W. Oklahoma Ave.
405/282-4548

**89er Antique Mall**
119 W. Oklahoma Ave.
405/282-2661

**Red Earth Antiques**
103 S. 2nd St.
405/260-1030

## 25 HENRYETTA

**B & Jays Antiques**
214 W. Main St.
918/652-7552

**Country Violet Antiques**
1202 W. Main St.
918/652-4211

**Attic Treasures Mall**
115 N. 2nd St.
918/652-2484

## 26 JENKS

Jenks, like many other towns in Indian Territory originated around a railroad. It started as a Midland Valley Railroad Depot along a route between Tulsa and Muskogee.

Adhering to the provisions of the treaty concluded on February 14, 1833, between the Creek Indians and the United States of America, the final Roll of Citizens and Freedmen of the Five Civilized Tribes in Indian Territory had been completed. Those Indian citizens and Freedmen (formerly slaves) received allotments. (In 1904, the land that became the townsite of Jenks, Indian Territory was on the allotment of three Freedmen.) The Midland Valley Railroad Company purchased about 130 acres for the town. In 1907, Jenks became a town with 150 people. The city of Jenks, OK, now consists of nearly 8,800 people.

There are various stories as to the origin of the town name. Some report that it honored a Midland Valley Railroad engineer or conductor; others say the name was that of a carpenter named Jenks who built the depot. Still others believe the town was named for Dr. Jenks who was an early day resident. The agent for the Midland Townsite Company says the name "Jenks" came from a director in the Philadelphia corporation that built the Midland Valley Railroad.

**Cornerstone Memories**
102 S. 1st St.
918/298-6255

**Linda's Things**
105 N. 5th St.
918/299-5350

**Abbey Road Antiques**
107 E. Main St.
918/299-4696

**Paradise Found Antiques**
109 E. Main St.
918/299-2691

**Miss McGillicutty's**
203 E. Main St.
918/298-4287

**Jenks House**
410 E. Main St.
918/299-9100

**Ancestors Antiques**
610 W. Main St.
918/298-3080

**Niche In Tyme/Radio City Mus. Hall**
112 S. 1st St.
918/298-1957

**Main Street Antique Mall**
105 E. Main St.
918/299-2806

**Bittersweet Antiques**
108 E. Main St.
918/298-9408

**Kracker Box**
116 E. Main St.
918/299-5353

**Serendipity**
207 E. Main St.
918/298-5628

**Auntie Em's Victorian Village**
101 W. Main St.
918/299-7231

**Jenkins Guild Shops**
Main St.-General Info
918/299-5005

## 27 LAWTON

**Johnson's Furniture Repair**
915 S.W. A Ave.
580/357-7307

**Pickering Antiques**
2 S.E. B Ave.
580/357-3276

**Yesterdays Antique Mall**
423 S.W. C Ave.
580/353-6005

**Okies Antiques**
1706 N.W. Cache Road
580/355-4104

**Wooden Windmill**
5224 N.W. Cache Road
580/357-9697

**Pickles Antique Mall**
620 S.W. D Ave.
580/353-5050

**Antiques by Helen**
1002 S.W. D Ave.
580/357-1375

**Another Time Antiques**
709 S.W. E Ave.
580/353-0639

**Antiques & Crafts by Cathy**
404 S.W. 10th St.
580/355-0710

## 28 LOCUST GROVE

**Pap's Country Market**
607 N. Hwy. 82
918/479-5541

**McFarland's Unique Antiques**
111 E. Harold Andrews Blvd.
918/479-6311

### *Favorite Places To Eat*

**Country Cottage**
608 N. Hwy. 82
918/479-6439

Buffet style or changing menu. The specialty is fried chicken.

## 29 MIAMI

Wind along Main Street to the grand old Coleman Theater, a 1929 Spanish Mission-style structure built with profits from the Turkey Fat Mine in Commerce. The Coleman, once a regular stop on the vaudeville circuit, is now undergoing a $1.5 million renovation project. Visitors may stop by the Chamber office to arrange a tour. Miami's downtown features retail shops and a cafe, and a block away is the Dobson Museum, which houses pioneer and mining artifacts.

**Ole Shoppe**
301 B St. S.E.
918/540-2961

**Gramma's Antique Mall**
417 D St. N.E.
918/542-1585

**Classy Brass Antiques**
31 S. Main St.
918/542-2203

**Box Office Antiques**
105 N. Main St.
918/540-0557

**Magnolia Manor**
107 N. Main St.
918/542-2046

**Antiques & Uniques**
113 N. Main St.
No Phone # Listed

**Charlotte's C & T Bargain Center**
123 S. Main St.
918/540-0543

## 30 MUSKOGEE

**Collectible Corner & Antique Mall**
30 W. Broadway St.
918/682-4335

**Beavers Antiques**
540 Court St.
918/682-5503

**Mr. Haney's Treasures**
210 N. Edmond St.
918/687-6276

**Yellow Brick Road**
120 S. Main St.
918/686-8704

**You Never Know**
120 S. Main St.
918/682-8506

**Old America Antique Mall**
Hwy. 69 S.
918/687-8600

**Antiques Galore**
2225 W. Shawnee St.
918/683-3281

**Mid-American Antique Mall**
2251 S. 32nd St. W.
918/683-2922

**Main Street USA Antique Mall**
2426 N. 32nd St. W.
918/687-4334

## 31 NOBLE

**Remember When**
119 S. Main St.
405/872-8484

**Vintage Village Antiques**
1722 N. Main St.
405/872-7062

## 32 NORMAN

**The Company Store Antique Mall**
300 E. Main St.
405/360-5959
Mon.-Fri. 10-6, Sat. 10-5, Sun. 1-5
*Directions: From I-35, take the Main St. exit east. Go 2 miles. Shop located on the corner of Main and Crawford St.*

When you reach the old green and red buckboard overflowing with colorful flowers, you've found The Company Store. This 7,000 square foot building is a local landmark (the old Palace Garage) built c. 1900. Inside, 60 dealers present an outstanding variety of distinctive antiques including Flow Blue, Roseville and Rookwood along with exceptional stained glass pieces. Superb furnishings, unusual collectibles and elegant costume jewelry are also available.

**Kensington Market Antique Mall**
208 W. Gray St.
405/364-8840

**Olde Town Market Place**
219 E. Gray St.
405/447-8846

**Whispering Pines Antiques**
Hwy. 9
405/447-8297

**Gallery Nouveau**
1630 W. Lindsey St.
405/321-8687

**Hope Chest Antiques & Collectibles**
1714 W. Lindsey St.
405/321-8059

**Peddlers Shop**
209 W. Main St.
405/360-1015

**Hoover Antique Galleries**
210 36th Ave. S.W.
405/360-4488

**Lorri Ann's Antiques**
3417 Sooner Fashion Mall
405/321-8633

**Theo's Marketplace**
3720 W. Robinson St.
405/364-0728

## 33 OKEMAH

**Pioneer Mall**
215 W. Broadway St.
918/623-9124

## 34 OKLAHOMA CITY

The old route is sometimes hard to follow as it jogs down Lincoln Boulevard, past the State Capitol (note the oil wells on the Capitol grounds), then west along Northwest 23rd and 39th Streets. Look for a retro-style McDonald's restaurant at 23rd and Pennsylvania. Not far from the National Cowboy Hall of Fame and the Western Heritage Center on the city's northeast side, an old speakeasy once known as the Kentucky Club now welcomes all as a barbecue restaurant called the Oklahoma County Line. The eclectic Route 66 store at 50 Penn Place Mall injects local flavor into modern folk art, books and other symbols of the Main Street America. West on 39th Street, past Portland is Route 66 Bowl, the oldest still-operating bowling alley in Oklahoma City. A cool purple and green sign outside Meike's Route 66 Restaurant at Meridian Ave. hints of the nostalgic decor inside. A Texaco clock, old gas pump, and an assortment of metal toys give customers a feast for their eyes while they enjoy hearty home style Italian food.

**Carolyn's Keepsakes**
1116 N.W. 51st St.
405/842-1296

**Pat & Barb's Antiques**
1120 N.W. 51st St.
405/840-1220

**My Daughter's Place**
2648 S.W. 44th St.
405/685-5784

**Abalache Book & Antique Shop**
311 S. Klein Ave.
405/235-3288

**Star Antiques**
311 S. Klein Ave.
405/232-5901

**Top of the Mart**
311 S. Klein Ave.
405/239-8325

**Colonies**
1120 N.W. 51st St.
405/842-1279

**What-Not Shelf Antiques**
1120 N.W. 51st St.
405/842-7176

**Michael's Antique Clocks**
5920 W. Hefner Road
405/722-3300

**Raggedy Anne's Market Antiques**
311 S. Klein Ave.
405/239-2273

**Trader Jean**
311 S. Klein Ave.
405/232-8044

**Country Temptations**
4801 N. Macarthur Blvd.
405/789-8876

**Bricktown Antique Shop**
100 E. Main St.
405/235-2803

**Antique Co-Op**
1227 N. May Ave.
405/942-1214

**23rd Street Antique Mall**
3023 N.W. 23rd St.
405/947-3800

**Spivey's Antiques**
2500 N. May Ave.
405/947-5454

**Return Engagement**
7423 N. May Ave.
405/843-6363

**Antique House**
4409 N. Meridian Ave.
405/495-2221

**Antique Centre Inc.**
1433 N.W. Expressway
405/842-0070

**Architectural Antiques**
By Appointment
405/232-0759

**Crow's Nest**
2800 N.W. 10th St.
405/947-6655

**Apple Orchard**
2921 N.W. 10th St.
405/946-3015

**English Tea Co.**
4405 S.E. 28th St.
405/672-0484

**Oodles & Aah's**
7622 N. Western
405/848-7099

**Etta's Gift Gallery**
6017 N.W. 23rd St.
405/495-1048

**Antiques & Design**
4512 N. Western
405/524-1969

**Scranton Uniques**
7512 N. Western
405/521-8715

**Jody Kerr Antiques**
7908 N. Western
405/842-5951

**Mike's Antiques**
1008 N. May Ave.
405/949-0707

**Buckboard Antiques & Quilts**
1411 N. May Ave.
405/943-7020

**Unique Antiques & Collectibles**
2125 N. May Ave.
405/943-0404

**Villa Antique Mall**
3132 N. May Ave.
405/949-1185

**Apple Tree Antique Mall**
1111 N. Meridian Ave.
405/947-8999

**Pine Shop**
12020 N.E. Expressway (I-35)
405/478-0220

**Southern Antq. Mall/Treas. House**
2196 S. Service Road
405/794-9898

**Coca-Nuts Antiques**
3234 E. I-240 Service Road
405/672-5600

**Bare Necessities Mall**
2842 N.W. 10th St.
405/943-2238

**Apple Barrel Antique Mall**
4619 N.W. 10th St.
405/947-7732

**Easleys Touch of Class Antiques**
4633 S.E. 29th St.
405/672-9010

**Collectibles Etc.**
1516 N.W. 23rd St.
405/524-1700

**Top Hat Antiques**
4411 N. Western
405/557-1732

**Covington Antique Market**
6900 N. Western
405/842-3030

**Discoveries**
7612 N. Western
405/842-9555

**Painted Door Gallery Ltd.**
8601 S. Western
405/632-4410

**Langhorne Place Antiques**
9115 N. Western
405/848-3192

**Sampler Antiques & Wood Works**
9201 N. Western
405/848-7007

**Nothing But The Best**
By Appointment Only
405/842-2545

**Antique Hardware**
1920 Linwood Blvd.
405/236-5662

**A Family Tree Antique Mall**
2422 S. Agnew Ave.
405/634-1159

## 35 OKMULGEE

**Kate's Antiques**
107 S. Grand Ave.
No Phone

**Ye Olde Lamp Post**
113 S. Grand Ave.
918/756-4539

**Starr Collectibles**
100 S. Morton Ave.
918/756-0736

**Legacy Antiques**
218 E. 6th St.
918/756-0567

## 36 PERRY

**Georgias Fine Furniture**
611 Delaware St.
405/336-4501

**Antiques on the Square**
615 Delaware St.
405/336-3327

**Cherokee Strip Antique Mall**
645 Delaware St.
405/336-4598

**The Antique Spot**
902 11th St.
405/336-5290

**Memories Of Yesteryear**
317 N. 7th St.
405/336-5650

**The Antique Station**
625 6th St.
405/336-5743

**Hazel's Antiques**
817 Wakefield
405/336-4794

## 37 PONCA CITY

**Terri's Toys & Nostalgia**
419 S. 1st St.
580/762-8697

**Early Attic**
510 N. 1st St.
580/762-5142

**Christy's**
3005 N. 14th St.
580/765-3800

**Granary**
218 W. Grand Ave.
580/762-5118

**Grand Avenue Antique Mall**
206 E. Grand Ave.
580/762-5221

**West End Interiors**
223 W. Grand Ave.
580/765-8864

## 38 PRYOR

**Wacky Jackie**
118 S. Adair St.
918/825-6125

**Heritage Antique Mall**
122 S. Adair St.
918/825-5714

**Rustiques**
207 S. Adair St.
918/825-6151

**Mary's Whatnots**
103 E. Graham Ave.
918/825-3757

## 39 PURCELL

**T's Antiques Mall**
116 W. Main St.
405/527-2766

**Auntie Mae's Antiques**
127 W. Main St.
405/527-5214

**Butler Antiques**
202 W. Main St.
405/527-9592

## 40 SAPULPA

Home of Frankoma Pottery, Sapulpa is a popular stopping-off place for travelers seeking diversion. Tours are offered weekdays, and the gift shop is open all week. In town, the Sapulpa Historical Museum is open afternoons except Sunday. Since the 1950s, locals have gathered at Norma's Diamond Cafe, and the Hickory House Restaurant serves up great barbeque and the only live music in town. A three-mile stretch of original Route 66 signed as the Ozark Trail can be found west of town, where venturesome motorists will cross the steel-and-brick Ozark bridge, under an old concrete Frisco railroad bridge, and go by the Teepee Drive In, which still operates in summer.

**Antiques N Stuff**
15 E. Dewey Ave.
918/224-8049

**Homespun Treasures**
209 E. Dewey Ave.
918/227-4508

**A Moment in Time**
205 E. Dewey Ave.
918/224-7158

**Neat Stuff**
1115 E. Dewey Ave.
918/224-6097

**Foote & Son Antique Investment Co.**
15 N. Elm St.
918/227-0250

**Sara's Country Corner**
1 S. Main St.
918/224-6544

**Schwickerath Furniture**
Main St.
918/224-5396

### *Favorite Places To Eat*

**Freddie's**
1425 Sapulpa Road
918/224-4301

For more than 30 years, loyal Freddie's customers have been enjoying its famous barbecue, perfect steaks and super seafood selections, served with Freddie's special tabouli, hummus and cabbage rolls.

This full-service restaurant is a favorite for a friendly, comfortable atmosphere, generous portions and reasonable prices.

## 41 SEMINOLE

**Country Road Antique Market**
Exit 200 I-40
405/382-1133

**Memory Lane**
217 N. Main St.
405/382-8200

**Lil's**
State Hwy. 3 – 1 ½ mi. N. of Seminole College
405/382-7716

**Another Mans Treasures**
300 W. Broadway Ave.
405/382-0651

## 42 SHAWNEE

### Crafters Showplace
115 E. Main St.
405/273-7985
Mon.-Sat. 10-5:30, Jan.- March, closed Mon.

In historic Downtown Shawnee, antiques such as furniture and collectibles will catch your attention. But, the shop's main focus is smaller bric-a-brac pieces and kitchen accessories. In addition, crafts persons will enjoy the array of supplies and completed craft projects for sale.

### Antiques of Distinction
111 N. Broadway
405/878-9839
Mon.-Sat.10-5 , closed Sun.

Fine antiques with an elegant air line your stroll through this shop. Furniture stripping and refinishing are an added specialty.

### Legends
124 N. Beard
405/878-0066

With the name hinting fine, quality pieces, antiques and collectibles serve as the basis of the selection. Furniture and accessories are in large part responsible for the singular style of this shop.

**Kickapoo Korner**
1025 N. Kickapoo St.
405/275-6511

**Groves**
602 E. Highland St.
405/878-9919

**Oliver-Hardin Antiques**
313 Macarthur St.
405/273-5060

**Main St. Gifts**
16 E. Main St.
405/275-1088

**OK Territory Antiques Ltd. Co.**
214 E. Main St.
405/878-0214

**Sante Fe Trading Post**
524 E. Main St.
405/275-5900

**Green's Corner**
723 E. Main St.
405/273-2021

**Grandma Had It Antiques**
36700 W. Old High #270
405/275-7766

## 43 SKIATOOK

**Ford's Antiques & Collectibles**
100 E. Rogers Blvd.
918/396-4268

**Christi's Unlimited**
112 E. Rogers Blvd.
918/396-0248

**Third Time Around**
120 E. Rogers Blvd.
918/396-3144

**Rogers Blvd. Antiques**
101 W. Rogers Blvd.
918/396-0065

**Antique Mall of Skiatook**
2200 W. Rogers Blvd.
918/396-1279

## 44 STILLWATER

**Jeanne's Antiques**
520 S. Knoblock St.
405/372-8567

**Delores Antiques**
4224 N. Washington St.
405/372-1455

**Antique Mall of Stillwater**
116 & 122 E. 9th Ave.
405/372-2322

**The Myriad**
119 E. 9th Ave.
405/372-6181

**Mrs. Brown's Attic**
211 N. Perkins Road
405/624-0844

**Rock Barn Relics**
1623 S. Perkins Road
405/372-2276

## 45 STROUD

City streets are bustling these days, thanks to the Tanger Outlet Mall that opened just a few years ago. Good restaurants are open throughout town, but the Rock Cafe is a truly Route 66 relic. Open since 1939, the eatery was once billed as the busiest truck stop along the old road. Its original owner paid $5 for the stones dug up during the construction of Old 66, and those stones were used to build the cafe. Tasty smoked meats, buffalo, and delectable Swiss/German cuisine are the bill o' fare, and the owner speaks German, Italian, French, English, and Swiss.

**Antique Alley Mall**
309 W. Main St.
918/968-3761

**Memory Lane**
405 W. Main St.
918/968-3491

**Friends Arts & Antiques**
404 W. Main St.
918/968-2568

***Great Places To Stay***

### Stroud House Bed and Breakfast
110 E. Second St.
918/968-2978 or 1-800-259-2978
Rates: $65-100

When you need a break from the hassles of life (which I do after writing this book), visit the Stroud House Bed and Breakfast, a nationally recognized historic Victorian home. The Stroud House was constructed by J.W. Stroud in 1900 and renovated by the hosts in 1992. Four beautifully decorated guest rooms offer rest and relaxation. Each guest gets a "famous" Stroud House cookie. (I need a care package sent to me now!)

## 46 SULPHUR

### Memory Lane Antiques & Collectibles
820 W. 12th St.
580/622-2090
Mon.-Sat. 10-5, Sun. 12-5
*Directions: Traveling I-35 south, take Hwy. 7 east approximately 12 miles. In Sulphur, turn right 1/2 block at the traffic light on 12th St. (If going I-35 North, take Exit 51.)*

A stroll among pieces from yesteryear inside this 2-building, 4,000-square-foot collector's treasure chest reveals fine porcelains such as Haviland, Limoges, Old Ivory and R.S. Prussia. Antique furniture, wall pockets, kitchen collectibles plus collector plates add to the harvest of goods.

**Gettin Place**
100 W. Muskogee St.
580/622-3796

**Quail Hollow Depot**
20 Quail Hollow Road
580/622-4081

***Favorite Places To Eat***

### Bricks Restaurant
2112 W. Broadway
580/622-3125
Sun.-Thurs. 11-9, Fr. & Sat. 11-9:30

Specialties are barbecue and home cooking.

## 47 TULSA

### Heart of Tulsa
Exposition Center at Expo Square
1-800-755-5488
Call for dates

Over 600 exhibitors from Oklahoma and the Midwest gather to display antiques, collectibles, arts and crafts.

**Great American Antique Mall**
9216 E. Admiral Place
918/834-6363

**Browsery**
3311 E. 11th St.
918/836-4479

**White Bear Antiques & Teddy Bears**
1301 E. 15th St.
918/592-1914

**Spectrum**
1307 E. 15th St.
918/582-6480

**Antiquary**
1325 E. 15th St.
918/582-2897

**Colonial Antiques**
1329 E. 15th St.
918/585-3865

**Charles Faudree**
1345 E. 15th St.
918/747-9706

**Sophronia's**
1515 E. 15th St.
918/592-2887

**Lampost Silver Co.**
13012 E. 21st St.
918/438-3636

**Jared's Inc.**
1602 E. 15th St.
918/582-3018

**Zoller Iqbal Designs & Antiques**
1603 E 15th St.
918/583-1966

**Cisar-Holt Inc.**
1605 E. 15th St.
918/582-3080

**Amir's Persian Imports**
2204 E. 15th St.
918/744-6464

**Tulsa Antique Mall**
2235 E. 51st St.
918/742-4466

**Kay's Antiques**
2814 E. 15th St.
918/743-5653

**Paula's Antiques & Estate Furniture**
2816 E. 15th St.
918/742-6191

**Deco To Disco**
3213 E. 15th St.
918/749-3620

**Glasstique**
1341 E. 41st St.
918/742-3434

**Sam Spacek's Antiques**
8212 E. 41st St.
918/627-3021

**Brass Buff**
1124 S. Harvard Ave.
918/592-1717

**Estate Furniture**
1531 S. Harvard Ave.
918/743-3231

**Side Door Antiques**
1547 S. Harvard Ave.
918/742-5912

**Centrum**
8130 S. Lewis Ave.
918/299-3400

**Snow's Consignment Store**
909 S. Memorial Dr.
918/266-7446

**And Then**
4717 S. Mingo Road
918/622-9447

**Flowers, Interiors, Antqs. by Phillip**
3740 S. Peoria Ave.
918/748-9450

**Consignment Treasures**
3807 S. Peoria Ave.
918/742-8550

**Zelda's Antiques**
1701 E. 7th St.
918/583-5599

**Tulsa Card Co.**
4423 E. 31st St.
918/744-8020

**Country Charm Antiques & Gifts**
3316 E. 32nd St.
918/743-3656

## 48 VALLIANT

**Vicki's Antiques, Collectibles & Crafts**
Hwy. 70
405/933-5220

## 49 YUKON

**Eagle Crest Antiques**
430 W. Main St.
405/350-7474

**Grandma's Treasures**
453 W. Main St.
405/350-1415

**Yukon's Yunique Antique**
456 Main St.
405/354-2511

# Oregon

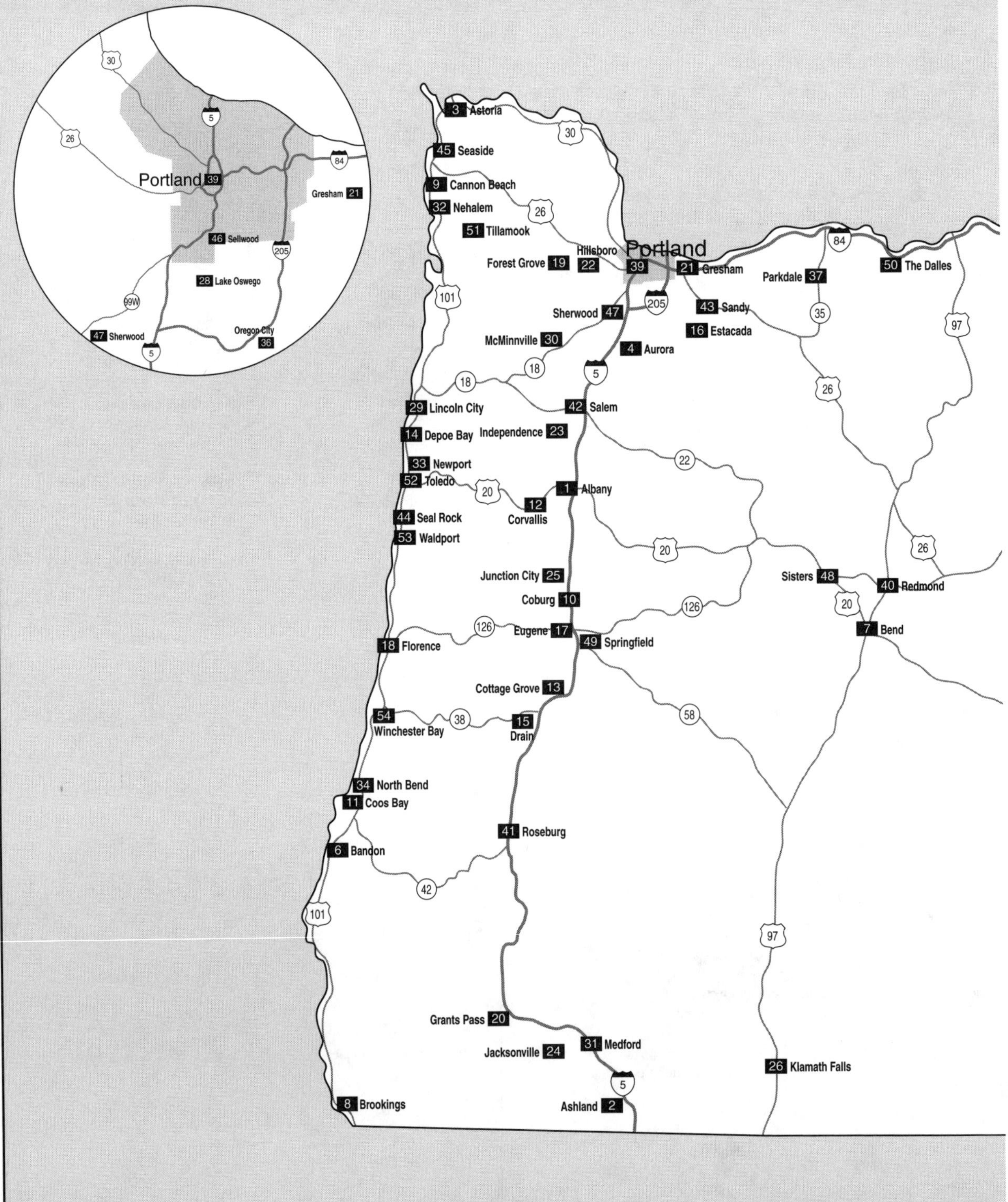

Portland 39
Gresham 21
46 Sellwood
28 Lake Oswego
47 Sherwood
Oregon City 36
3 Astoria
45 Seaside
9 Cannon Beach
32 Nehalem
51 Tillamook
Forest Grove 19
Hillsboro 22
Portland
39
21 Gresham
Parkdale 37
50 The Dalles
43 Sandy
16 Estacada
Sherwood 47
McMinnville 30
4 Aurora
29 Lincoln City
42 Salem
14 Depoe Bay
Independence 23
33 Newport
52 Toledo
1 Albany
12 Corvallis
44 Seal Rock
53 Waldport
Junction City 25
Coburg 10
Sisters 48
40 Redmond
7 Bend
Eugene 17
49 Springfield
18 Florence
Cottage Grove 13
54 Winchester Bay
15 Drain
34 North Bend
11 Coos Bay
41 Roseburg
6 Bandon
Grants Pass 20
31 Medford
Jacksonville 24
26 Klamath Falls
8 Brookings
Ashland 2

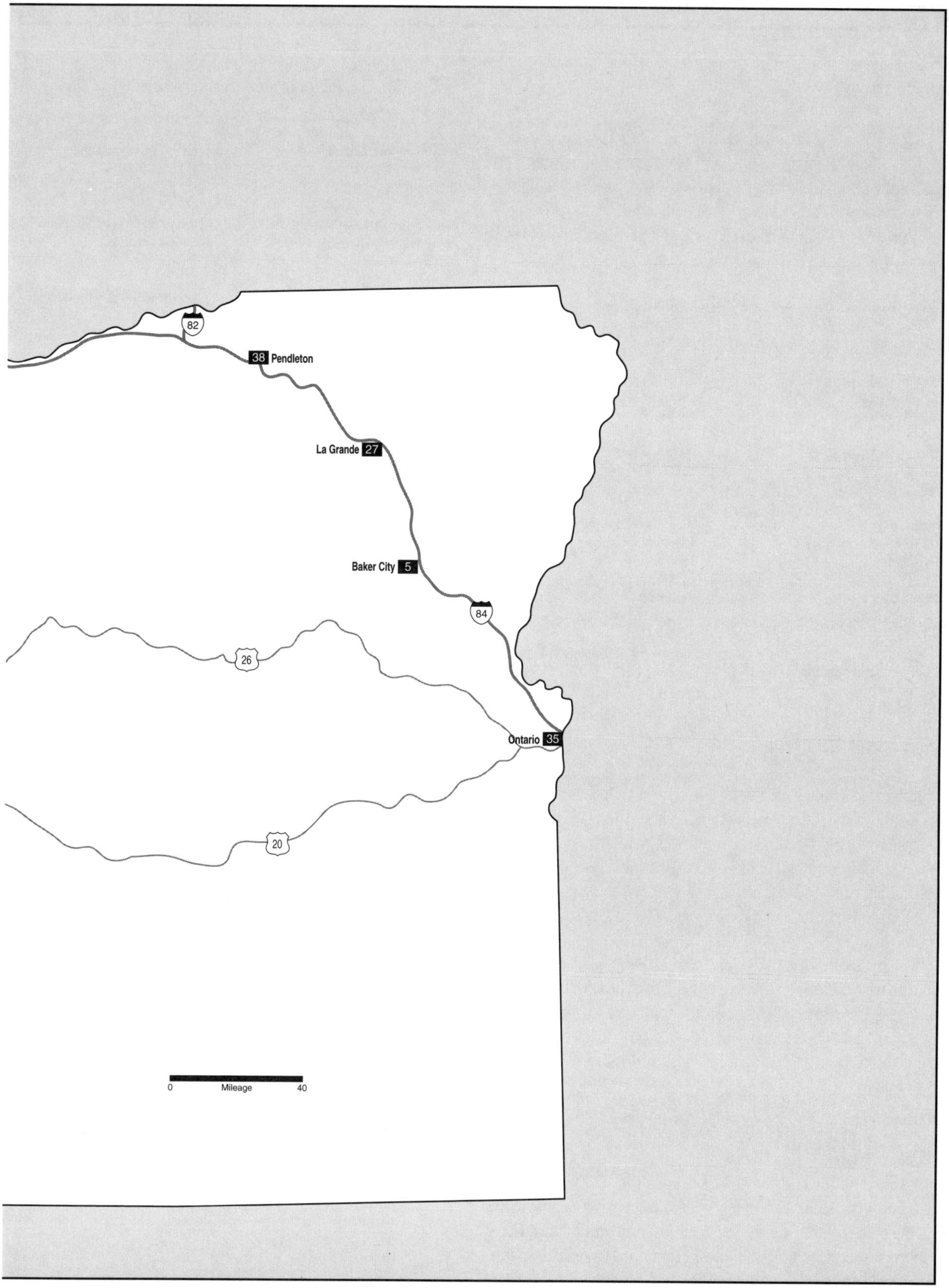

82
38 Pendleton
La Grande 27
Baker City 5
84
26
Ontario 35
20
0 Mileage 40

# Oregon

## 1 ALBANY

A drive east along the Wilamette River on Hwy. 20 takes you back in time to Albany. Here, historic charm is evident in more than 700 beautifully preserved buildings, churches and homes, including the Monteith House, Albany's oldest frame-built home. While you're here discover antique shops, Victorian gardens and a farmers' market via a downtown trolley or horse-drawn wagon tour.

**Feather Tree**
121 Broadalbin St. S.W.
541/967-9381

**Mitsch's Antiques**
131 Broadalbin St. S.W.
541/926-724

**Antique Traditions**
122 Ferry St. S.W.
541/926-0380

**Peabody's Antiques-Gifts**
238 1st Ave. W.
541/926-3654

**Arlene's Victorian Rose**
244 1st Ave. S.W.
541/928-4203

**Byers Antiques**
305 1st Ave. W.
541/928-3195

**Pastimes Antiques**
317 1st Ave. W.
541/926-0303

**First and Ferry Antiques**
343 1st Ave. W.
541/928-8774

**Albany Book Co.**
1425 Pacific Blvd. S.E.
541/926-2612

**Clockwise**
211 2nd Ave. S.W.
541/926-8507

**B and E Antiques and More**
223 2nd Ave. S.W.
541/928-2174

## 2 ASHLAND

As the southernmost town in the I-5 corridor, Ashland is the gateway for many Oregon visitors. The main attraction is the Tony Award-winning Oregon Shakespeare Festival. From mid-February through October, it presents 11 plays on three unique stages. Tickets and bed and breakfast reservations can be hard to come by on weekends and in the summer months, so plan in advance if you can. Better yet, schedule your visit for spring or fall.

While in town, take the Backstage Tour. Visit the Exhibit Center, where you can try on old costumes, then explore some of the other features that play a leading role in the character of Ashland such as antique shops, boutiques, and unusual art galleries.

**Rita's Relics**
93 Oak St.
541/482-0777

**Perry S. Prince Asian Antiques**
349 E. Main St.
541/488-1989

## 3 ASTORIA

Named after John Jacob Astor, the North Coast city of Astoria, at the mouth of the Columbia, is the site of the first permanent United States settlement west of the Rockies. Its historic charm and Victorian ambiance have provided the settings for movies such as Free Willy and Kindergarten Cop.

**Phog Bounder's Antique Mall**
1052 Commercial St.
503/325-9722

**River's Edge Decorators**
1145 Commercial St.
503/325-7040

**Fort George Trading Co.**
1174 Commercial St.
503/325-1690

**Commercial Street Collectibles**
1227 Commercial St.
503/325-5838

**Marine Drive Antiques**
2093 Marine Dr.
503/325-8723

**Uppertown Antiques & Gallery**
2911 Marine Dr.
503/325-5000

**Persona Vintage Clothing**
100 10th St.
503/325-3837

## 4 AURORA

**Impressions of Aurora**
Hwy. 99 E. & Main St.
503/678-5312

**Old Miller Place**
21358 Hwy. 99 E.
503/678-1128

**Aurora Crossing Antiques**
21368 Hwy. 99 E.
503/678-1630

**Aurora Antique Mall**
21418 Hwy. 99 E.
503/678-2139

**Gary's Antiques**
21627 Hwy. 99 E.
503/678-2616

**Antique Colony**
21581 Main St. N.E.
503/678-1010

**Main Street Mercantile**
21610 Main St. N.E.
503/678-1044

**Time After Time**
21611 Main St. N.E.
503/678-5463

**Cottage Antiques**
21631 Main St. N.E.
503/678-5911

**Jacobs House**
21641 Main St. N.E.
503/678-3078

**Aurora State Bank Antiques**
21690 Main St. N.E.
503/678-3060

**Craig's Four Seasons Antiques**
14979 2nd St.
503/678-2266

## 5 BAKER CITY

**Mr. G's**
2175 Broadway St.
541/523-2376

**Windfall Antiques**
2306 Broadway St.
541/523-7531

**Baker City Collectibles**
2332 Broadway St.
541/523-3592

**Francis Memory House Antiques**
1780 Main St.
541/523-6227

**Do Overs Antiques**
2658 10th St.
541/523-5717

## 6 BANDON

**Country Cottage Antiques.**
Morrison Road & Hwy. 42 S.
541/347-3800

**Angle's Nest**
735 3rd St. S.E.
541/347-1414

**Big Wheel General Store**
130 Baltimore Ave. S.
541/347-3719

**Wild Angel Wholesale Antiques**
735 3rd St. S.E.
541/347-1717

## 7 BEND

**Buffet Flat**
64990 Deschutes Market Road
541/389-9797
Daily 10-6 except Christmas Day
*Directions: Situated halfway between Bend and Redmond at Deschutes Junction. From Hwy. 97, travel approximately 500 feet to the northeast corner of Deschutes Junction, turn at the "Big White Wagon." Ask for further directions upon arrival as a new overpass is being constructed in 1997.*

Featured in *Self Magazine*, on PBS' The Collectors and The Learning Channel's Neat Stuff, Buffet Flat houses a remarkable antique, souvenir and "re-use it" store. Among the extraordinary collection of wares are pieces from the 1800s to 1950s including Victoriana, Art Nouveau, Art Deco, Moderene and Atomic. The shop serves as the jumping off point for The Funny Farm, a private park and playground which is open to the public, no admission. Mind-boggling adventure awaits as you gaze upon such sights as the Bowling Ball Garden, The Love Pond and Cupid's Arrow, or the rare Punk Flamingo to name a very few.

**Icehouse Trading Post**
20410 N.E. Bend River Mall Dr.
541/383-3713

**Farm Antiques**
838 N.W. Bond St.
541/382-8565

**Homespun Antiques**
856 N.W. Bond St.
541/385-3344

**Enchantments Fine Antiques**
1002 N.W. Bond St.
541/388-7324

**Bond Street Antiques**
1008 N.W. Bond St.
541/383-3386

**Deja Vu Experienced Furniture**
225 S.W. Century Dr.
541/317-9169

**Iron Horse Second Hand Store**
210 N.W. Congress St.
541/382-5175

**Sally's Antiques & Collectibles**
61360 S. Hwy. 97
541/385-6237

**Trivia Antiques**
106 N.W. Minnesota Ave.
541/389-4166

**605 Antiques**
604 N.W. Newport Ave.
541/389-6552

**Cottage Collectibles**
210 S.E. Urania Lane
541/389-2075

## 8 BROOKINGS

**Old Town Collectibles & Misc.**
547-Chetco Ave.
541/469-0756

**Van's Antiques**
15714 Hwy. 101 S.
541/469-3719

## 9 CANNON BEACH

**Tolovana Antiques**
3116 S. Hemlock
503/436-0261

**Pat & Mike's Antiques**
148 S. Monro Road
503/436-1843

**Blue Door**
Sandpiper Square
503/436-9542

## 10 COBURG

**Coburg Inn Antique Shops**
91108 N. Willamette St.
541/343-4550

**Iron Kettle Antiques**
1359 Goodpasture Island Road
541/683-1267

**Dotson's Coburg Antiques**
91109 Willamette St.
541/342-2732

**Joseph's Antiques**
32697 E. Pearl St.
541/345-0092

**Jolene's Antiques**
32697 E. Pearl St.
541/302-3310

**Ages Ago**
90999 S. Willamette St.
541/343-6363

**Mathew House Antiques**
32702 Pearl St.
541/343-3876

**Ollie's Oldies**
90559 Coburg Road
541/343-9989

**Big Wheel Antiques**
1091 Coburg Road
541/344-7300

**Schram's Antiques**
3699 Coburg Road
541/683-4965

**Willow Tree Antique Mall**
Coburg Road
541/465-4817

**Cara's Antiques**
155 N. Willamette St.
541/345-2142

**Coburg Road Antiques**
90934 Coburg Road
541/683-3310

## 11 COOS BAY

**Auction Company of Southern Oregon**
Call ahead for Auction Dates
541/267-5361

When an auction bills itself as a "full service" country auction, you never know what to expect. Anything from antiques to the family farm could be up for grabs. That's what makes it so interesting, Granny could have stuffed a lot of things away in the old barn.

# Oregon

**Marshfield Mercantile Annex**
145 S. Broadway
541/267-7706

**Marshfield Mercantile Antq. Emp.**
145 Central Ave.
541/267-4636

**Maddie's Antiques & Collectibles**
1161 Cape Arago Hwy.
541/888-9214

**Charleston Mall**
8073 Cape Arago Hwy.
541-888-8083

**Apple Blossom Consignments**
285 S. Broadway
541/269-0153

**Boat Basin Plaza Antiques**
5005 Boat Basin Dr.
541/888-8024

## 12 CORVALLIS

**Finders Keepers**
5820 N.W. Hwy. 99
541/745-5848

**Gold Dust**
1413 N.W. 9th St.
541/758-7427

**Beekman Place**
635 S.W. Western Blvd.
541/753-8250

**Corvallis Antiques Co.**
3207 N.W. Polk Ave.
541/752-8004

## 13 COTTAGE GROVE

**Rose Garden Mall Antiques & Gifts**
501 E. Main St.
541/942-5064

**Mike & Bev's Antiques**
637 E. Main St.
541/942-3664

**Apple Pie Antiques**
811 E. Main St.
541/942-0057

**Petersen's Antiques**
818 E. Main St.
541/942-0370

**Preston's Treasure Hunt**
820 W. Main St.
541/942-3763

## 14 DEPOE BAY

**What Not Shop**
362 S.E. Hwy. 101
541/765-2626

**Recollections**
Hwy. 101
541/765-2221

## 15 DRAIN

**Nana's Oldies and Goodies**
301 N. 1st
541/836-7363

## 16 ESTACADA

**Petals N Treasures**
398 N. Broadway St.
503/630-4411

**Tole Barn**
22597 S. Day Hill Road
503/630-4680

## 17 EUGENE

**Fifthpearl Antiques**
207 E. 5th Ave.
541/342-2733

**The Antique Heart**
409 High St.
541/465-1158

**Antique Clock Shop**
888 Pearl St.
541/683-1349

**Brian's Furniture Farm Antiques**
115 N. Seneca Road
541/689-3358

**Nostalgia Collectibles**
527 Willamette St.
541/484-9202

**Goodness Gracious**
767 Willamette St.
541/345-4517

**Copper Penny Antiques**
1215 Willamette St.
541/686-2104

## 18 FLORENCE

**Bay Window**
1308 Bay St.
541/997-2002

**Collectors Corner**
1623 15th St.
541/902-8077

**Divine Decadence**
129 Maple St.
541/997-7200

**Old Town Treasures**
299 Maple St.
541/997-1364

**Fine Timed Collectibles**
513 Hwy. 101
541/997-6430

## 19 FOREST GROVE

**Sentimental Journey Antiques**
2004 Main St.
503/357-2091

**Acanthus Antiques**
2011 Main St.
503/357-3213

**Collections In The Attic**
2020 Main St.
503/357-0316

**Rachel's**
1930 Pacific Ave.
503/357-2356

**Days Past Antiques & Collectibles**
1937 Pacific Ave.
503/357-5405

**Verboort Village Antiques**
39690 N.W. Verboort Road
503/359-0454

## 20 GRANTS PASS

**Black Swann**
100 Lewis Ave.
541/474-2477

**Danill Boone's Trading Post**
470 Redwood Hwy.
541/474-2992

**Blue Moon Antiques Gifts**
220 S.W. 6th St.
541/474-6666

**Elegance**
321 S.E. 6th St.
541/476-0570

**6th Street Antique Mall**
328 S.W. 6th St.
541/479-6491

**Grandma's Attic**
122 S.E. H St.
541/479-7363

**Grant's Pass Antique Mall**
224 S.W. 6th St.
541/474-5547

## 21 GRESHAM

**Antiques by Renee**
17 N.W. 1st St.
503/665-4091

**By Request**
101 N. Main Ave.
503/661-4994

**Nostalgia Antiques & Collectibles**
19 N.E. Roberts Ave.
503/661-0123

## 22 HILLSBORO

**Q's Shoppe**
2437 S.E. Brookwood Ave.
503/648-4785

**Heinrich's Antiques & Collectibles**
136 E. Main St.
503/693-7457

**Lestuff & Floral Too**
230 E. Main St.
503/640-9197

**Old Library Antiques**
263 E. Main St.
503/693-7324

**Country Crossroads Antiques**
8750 N.W. Old Cornelius Passroad
503/645-9025

**Jill's Cottage**
23483 S.W. Rosedale Road
503/591-8970

**Sniders Hill Theatre Antique Mall**
127 N.E. 3rd Ave.
503/693-1686

**Snider's Main Street Antique**
247 E. Main St.
503/693-0417

**Stratford House**
207 E. Main St.
503/648-7139

## 23 INDEPENDENCE

**Main Street Antiques**
144 S. Main St.
503/838-2595

**River Bend Antiques & Used Goods**
184 S. Main St.
503/838-4555

**Joni's Antiques**
194 S. Main St.
503/838-5944

**Mostly Quilts Vintage**
235 Main St.
503/838-5261

## 24 JACKSONVILLE

**J Bailey's Antiques**
120 W. C St.
541/899-1766

**Trash Pile Antiques & Collectibles**
650 N. 5th St.
541/899-1209

**Three Gables Antiques**
305 S. Oregon
541/899-1891

**Abigail's Corner**
160 W. C St.
541/899-7537

**L & K Antiques**
660 N. 5th St.
541/899-7143

**Pickety Place**
130 N. 4th St.
541/899-1912

## 25 JUNCTION CITY

Offering a number of excellent antique shops through which to roam, modern Junction City began with a western flavor. In 1871, the railroad had reached the settlement drawing many citizens from nearby Lancaster to relocate to Junction City. The town's name was conceived along with the notion that a west railroad line would join the main line at this point. Due to finances, no west line was constructed until 1910. Even so, the railroad town grew.

Railroad crew members found Junction City a suitable second home with its numerous rooming and boarding houses and, of course, saloons. Travelers had money to spend, and a boom time with its accompanying businesses and reputation thrived. Unfortunately, fires ravaged the business section between 1878 and 1882 with the last of the great fires burning out in 1915. The town physically changed direction after this fire as its expansion began to the west.

Today travelers return to Junction City in mid-August as the Scandinavian Festival sprinkles downtown with the appearance of a Scandinavian village while citizens outfit themselves accordingly. Tasty Scandinavian foods are the feature of this event.

**Brimhall's Antiques**
595 Ivy St.
541/998-2770

**Roberta's Collectibles**
1480 Ivy St.
541/998-8782

**Lingo's Sheepbarn Antiques**
27579 High Pass Road
541-998-2018

## 26 KLAMATH FALLS

**Country Mercantile**
1833 Avalon St.
541/882-8808

**Ant Mini Antiques & Mini Barns**
1633 Division St.
541/882-9429

**Linkville Antique Co.**
1243 Kane St.
541/883-1285

**Cat's Meow**
825 Main St.
541/885-3933

**Assistance League Findables**
1330 E. Main St.
541/883-1721

**Petri's Interiors of Yesterday**
125 N. 9th St.
541/882-8543

**Carson's Old West**
1835 Oregon Ave.
541/882-4188

**Always Antiques & Art Gallery**
915 Pine St.
541/882-8700

**White Pelican Antique Mall**
229 S. 6th St.
541/883-7224

**Armour Antiques & Collectibles**
7341 S. 6th St.
541/882-0263

**Shades of the Past**
417 N. Spring St.
541/884-1188

**Crafters Market**
3040 Washburn Way
541/882-5270

## 27 LA GRANDE

**Ten Twelve Adams Antiques**
1012 Adams Ave.
541/962-7171

**Jefferson Antiques**
1114 Jefferson Ave.
541/963-9358

**Hills Antiques & Refinishing**
1529 Jefferson Ave.
541/963-4223

**Wooden Nickel**
2212 E. Penn Ave.
541/963-7507

## 28 LAKE OSWEGO

**Frederick E. Squire III**
24 A Ave.
503/697-5924

**Uncle Albert's Antiques**
15964 Boones Ferry Road
503/635-5535

**Marquess of Granby**
16524 Boones Ferry Road
503/635-3544

## 29 LINCOLN CITY

**Portals of the Past**
4250 N. Hwy. 101
541/996-2254

**Rocking Horse Mall**
1542 N.E. Hwy. 101
541/994-4647

**Toby Torrances Pastime**
545 N.W. Hwy. 101
541/994-9003

**Jade Stone Gallery**
3200 S.E. Hwy. 101
541/996-2580

**Mouse House**
6334 S.E. Hwy. 101
541/996-4127

**Herself's**
1439 S.W. Hwy. 101
541/994-9566

**Beachtime Antiques**
5053 S.W. Hwy. 101
541/994-4001

**Ron's Relics**
1512 S.E. Hwy. 101
541/994-6788

**Vintage Corner**
1520 N.E. Hwy. 101
541/994-7797

**Little Antique Store**
2826 N.E. Hwy. 101
541/994-8572

**Curio Cabinet Mall**
1631 N.W. Hwy. 101
541/994-9001

**Snug Harbor Antiques**
5030 S.E. Hwy. 101
541/996-4021

**Streetcar Village**
6334 S.E. Hwy. 101
541/996-4480

**Bush's Antiques**
5021 S.W. Hwy. 101
541/994-7363

**Judith Anne's Antiques**
412 S. Hwy 101
541/993-9912

**A Change of Seasons**
304 Southeast Hwy. 101
541/994-3765

## 30 McMINNVILLE

**Blue Angel Antique Shoppe**
228 N.E. 3rd St.
503/434-5784

**Out of the Blue N.W. Ltd.**
620 N.E. 3rd St.
503/650-8665

**Old Salon Antique Shop**
238 N.E. 3rd St.
503/472-8209

## 31 MEDFORD

**Downtown Merchants Mall**
117 S. Central Ave.
541/779-6640

**Brass Horseshoe**
2581 Jacksonville Hwy.
541/772-8466

**Jueden's Furniture**
220 E. Main St.
541/772-3260

**Micellany**
220 N. Fir St.
541/770-9097

**Mary's Dream**
125 W. Main St.
541/857-1132

**Crafters Blend**
2308 Poplar Dr.
541/770-5052

**L C Antiques**
2312 Poplar Dr.
541/779-1115

**Jane's Antiques**
308 W. 2nd St.
541/535-1315

**Main Antique Mall**
30 N. Riverside Ave.
541/779-9490

**Medford Antique Mall**
1 W. 6th St.
541/773-4983

## 32 NEHALEM

**Nehalem Antique Mall**
Hwy. 101
503/368-7190

**Three Village Gallery Inc.**
35995 Hwy. 101
503/368-6924

**Pete's Antiques**
Hwy. 101
503/368-6018

**Robin's Reliques**
36025 7th St.
503/368-4114

## 33 NEWPORT

About halfway down the coast, the picturesque Yaquina Head Lighthouse welcomes you to Newport, a town known for its Dungeness crab and glorious harbor under the graceful Yaquina Bay Bridge. The historic Bay Front offers a mixture of shops, galleries, canneries and restaurants that serve fresh clam chowder, shrimp, oysters, crab and salmon.

### *Great Places To Stay*

**Oar House**
520 S.W. Second St.
541/265-9571

Formerly a boarding house, bordello, and most recently a bed and breakfast, Oar House has been serving guests since the early 1900s. This Lincoln County historic landmark situated in the beautiful Nye Beach area of Newport delights guests with its history, ghost and nautical theme. Each guest room provides a queen-size bed in addition to a view of the ocean. Be amazed by the 360 degree view of the coast area from the lighthouse.

## 34 NORTH BEND

**Granny's Hutch**
1964 Sherman Ave.
541/756-1222

**Wagon Wheel Antiques & Collectibles**
1984 Sherman Ave.
541/756-7023

**Treasures**
1997 Sherman Ave.
541/756-4678

**Old World Antiques**
2072 Sherman Ave.
541/756-2121

**Fran Carter**
1966 Sherman Ave.
541/756-4333

**Echoes of Time**
1993 Sherman Ave.
541/756-4072

**Bric Brac Shack**
2048 Sherman Ave.
541/756-2329

**Beauty & The Beast Antiques**
615 Virginia Ave.
541/756-3670

## 35 ONTARIO

**Back At The Ranch**
2390 S.W. 4th Ave.
541/889-8850

**Maria's Antiques**
364 S. Oregon St.
541/889-3684

**Grandma's Cellar Antiques & Furniture**
715 Sunset Dr.
541/889-8591

**Collectibles Etcetera**
166 S. Oregon St.
541/889-4585

**Good Ole Days Antique Mall**
2601 N.W. 4th Ave.
541/889-3416

## 36 OREGON CITY

**McLoughlin Antique Mall**
502 7th St.
503/655-0393

**Maijas Antiques and Collectibles**
402 S. McLoughlin Blvd.
503/656-9610

**Oregon City Antique Co.**
502 7th St.
503/657-6527

## 37 PARKDALE

### Parkdale Plain & Fancy

Baseline at 3rd Ave.
541/352-7875
Tues.-Fri. 10:30-4:30 and Sat. & Sun. 10:30-5:30, closed Jan. & Feb.
*Directions: Traveling I-84, take Exit 64 at Hood River; travel south on Hwy. 35 for 15 miles to Cooper Spur Road. Take a right on Cooper Spur Road going 2 miles to Baseline. Turn right from Baseline to 3rd. OR Traveling north on Hwy. 35, turn left at Parkdale, then exit onto Baseline. Follow Baseline into downtown Parkdale to 3rd Ave.*

For a leisurely browse through the finer and everyday items of yesterday, the former 1930s drugstore, now, Parkdale Plain and Fancy offers its eclectic collection. Among the items overflowing in this shop are antique furniture, books, as well as glassware such as Carnival, Depression and crystal. Primitive items (plates, vases, jugs, churns) enliven the selection. Linger over the house specialty—antique bottles.

## 38 PENDLETON

**Pendleton Antique Co.**
104 S.E. Court Ave.
541/276-8172

**Georgianna's**
207 S.E. Court Ave.
541/276-4094

**Collectors Gallery**
223 S.E. Court Ave.
541/276-6697

**Vintage Court Antiques**
224 S.E. Court Ave.
541/276-0747

**Picket Fences**
239 S.E. Court Ave.
541/276-9515

**Twice Nice Antiques & Collectibles**
815 S.E. Court Ave.
541/278-1407

**Frieda N Friends Antique Mall**
1400 S.W. Court Ave.
541/276-7172

**Lee's Antiques**
813 S.E. Frazer Ave.
541/276-4158

## 39 PORTLAND

### Mother Goose Antiques

1219 S.W. 19th
503/223-4493
Mon.-Sat. Afternoons - Best to Call First
*Directions: Call for specific directions.*

Owner, Sigrid Clark has been in the antiques business over twenty years. Wandering through her shop you will find a wonderland of vintage smalls: garment buttons, collectible holiday items, kitchen collectibles including patented items, dollhouse minatures (50s & older), cookbooks, an impressive array of sewing items, costume jewelry, salt & pepper shakers, silver trinkets, advertising items, spice tins, matchboxes, postcards, and children's toys. As the owner puts it, "this is a fun place to shop."

**Embry & Co Antiques & Gifts**
4709 S.W. Beaverton Hillsdale Hwy.
503/244-1646

**Quintana Galleries**
501 S.W. Broadway
503/223-1729

**Abacus**
1224 S.W. Broadway
503/790-9303

**Partners In Time**
1313 W. Burnside St.
503/228-6299

**Enterprises Antiques**
2955 E. Burnside St.
503/223-8866

**J K Hills Antiques**
7807 S.W. Capitol Hwy.
503/244-2708

**Le Meitour Gallery**
7814 S.W. Capitol Hwy.
503/246-3631

**Laurie's and Casey's Antiques**
7840 S.W. Capitol Hwy.
503/244-6775

**Pagenwood Restoring**
7783 S.W. Capitol Hwy.
503/246-6777

**Toby's Antiques & Collectibles**
7871 S.W. Capitol Hwy.
503/977-2546

**Really Good Stuff**
3121 S.E. Division St.
503/238-1838

**Family Ties**
12659 S.E. Division St.
503-761-7047

**Old Town Antique Market**
32 N.W. 1st Ave.
503/228-3386

**New Antique Village Mall Inc.**
1969 N.E. 42nd Ave.
503/288-1051

**Antique Alley**
2000 N.E. 42nd Ave.
503/287-9848

**Foster Road Collectibles**
4932 S.E. Foster Road
503/788-9474

**Goods Antique Mall & Emporium**
5339 S.E. Foster Road
503/777-9919

**Alameda Floral Antqs. & Interiors**
5701 N.E. Fremont St.
503/288-6149

# Oregon

**At The Rainbow End**
5723 S.E. Foster Road
503/788-1934

**Bucks Stove Palace & Antiques**
6803 S.E. Foster Road.
503/771-3374

**Antiques By The Wishing Corner**
9201 S.E. Foster Road
503/771-1549

**Mill Creek Crossing**
9209 S.E. Foster Road
503/775-3141

**Tony's Antiques and Collectibles**
3709 S.E. Gladstone St.
503/788-1223

**Maxine Cozzetto's**
2228 N.E. Glisan St.
503/232-4656

**Glass Works Gifts & Collectibles**
10105 S.W. Hall Blvd.
503/246-9897

**Ruby's Antiques, Fine Gifts & Interiors**
3590 S.E. Hawthorne Blvd.
503/239-9867

**Store II**
1004 N. Killingsworth St.
503/285-0747

**Leighton House Antiques**
1226 Lexington
503/233-4248

**Noce Antiques**
8332 N. Lombard St.
503/286-3560

**Tyrell's Antiques**
6429 S.W. Macadam Ave.
503/293-1759

**Fanno Creek Mercantile**
12285 S.W. Main St.
503/639-6963

**Stars Antique Malls**
7027 S.E. Milwaukie Ave.
503/239-0346

**Stars Antique Malls**
7030 S.E. Milwaukie Ave.
503/235-5990

**Handwerk Shop**
8317 S.E. 13th Ave.
503/236-7870

**Amy's Antiques**
5851 S.E. Foster Road
503/777-1497

**Handwerk Shop**
8317 S.E. 13th Ave.
503/236-7870

**Wishing Corner**
9201 S.E. Foster Road
503/771-1549

**Amsterdam Trading Co.**
536 N.W. 14th Ave.
503/229-0737

**Portland Antique Co.**
1211 N.W. Glisan St.
503/223-0999

**End of the Trail Collectibles**
5937 N. Greeley Ave.
503/283-0419

**Uncommon Treasures**
3530 S.E. Hawthorne Blvd
503/234-4813

**Antiques Plus**
6403 N. Interstate
503/289-8788

**Classic Antiques**
1805 S.E. M. L. King Blvd.
503/231-8689

**Slot Closet Antiques**
5223 N. Lombard St.
503/286-3597

**Milwaukie Antique Mall**
10875 S.E. McLoughlin Blvd.
503/786-9950

**Tigard Antique Mall**
12271 S.W. Main St.
503/684-9550

**A Child at Heart Antiques**
6802 S.E. Milwaukie Ave.
503/234-3807

**Old Friends**
3384 S.E. Milwaukie Ave.
503/231-0301

**Timeless Memories Antiques**
7048 Milwaukie Ave.
503/234-3807

**David H Palmrose Antiques**
1435 N.W. 19th Ave.
503/220-8253

**Habromania**
203 S.W. 9th Ave.
503/223-0767

**Avalon Antiques**
318 S.W. 9th Ave.
503/224-7156

**Abundant Life Antiques**
1130 S.E. 182nd Ave.
503/665-4301

**Vintage Corner Antique Mall**
13565 S.W. Pacific Hwy.
503/684-7024

**George's Antiques**
640 S.E. Stark St.
503/233-7787

**Plaid Rabbit Button Exchange**
111 N.W. 2nd Ave.
503/224-0678

**Polished Image**
122 N.W. 10th Ave.
503/228-8347

**Renaissance Galleries & Interiors**
414 S.W. 10th Ave.
503/226-1982

**Richard Rife French Antique**
300 N.W. 13th Ave.
503/294-0276

**Gold Door Antiques & Art**
1434 S.E. 37 th Ave
503/232-6069

**Andrew's Antiques**
916 S.E. 20th Ave.
503/234-9378

**Classic Woods**
1108 N.W. 21st Ave.
503/242-1849

**Jack Heath Antiques**
1700 N.W. 23rd Ave.
503/222-4663

**N.W. Collectibles & Antique Paper**
7901 S.E. 13th St.
503/234-6061

**White Parrot Antiques & Collectibles**
7919 S.E. 13th Ave.
503/236-5366

**Corner House Antiques**
8003 S.E. 13th Ave.
503/235-3749

**Palookaville**
211 S.W. 9th Ave.
503/241-4751

**Stone Fox Gallery**
506 N.W. 9th Ave.
503/228-7949

**Phone Company**
135 S.E. 102nd Ave.
503/253-1124

**L L Trading Post**
12115 S.E. Powell Blvd.
503/761-5960

**Antique Slot Machines Inc.**
12037 S.E. Stark St.
503/253-3773

**Arthur W. Erickson Inc.**
1030 S.W. Taylor St.
503/227-4710

**Jerry Lamb Interiors & Antiques**
416 N.W. 10th Ave.
503/227-6077

**Retrospection**
619 S.W. 10th Ave.
503/223-5538

**Cubby Hole Antiques**
7824 S.W. 35th Ave.
503/246-8307

**Geraldine's**
2772 N.W. Thurman St
503/295-5911

**Star's N.W. Antique Mall**
305 N.W. 21st Ave.
503/220-8180

**Shogun's Gallery**
206 N.W. 23rd Ave.
503/224-0328

**Peter M. Sargent Antiques**
2430 S.W. Vista Ave.
503/223-3395

**Kathryn's Antiques & Collectibles**
7907 S.E. 13th Ave.
503/236-7120

**General Store**
7987 S.E. 13th Ave.
503/233-1321

**Den of Antiquity**
8012 S.E. 13th Ave.
503/233-7334

**Treasure Chest Antiques**
8015 S.E. 13th Ave.
503/235-6897

**Gilt Vintage Jewelry & Antiques**
8017 S.E. 13th Ave.
503/231-6395

**The Sellwood Collective**
8027 S.E. 13th Ave.
503/736-1399

**Farmhouse Antiques**
8028 S.E. 13th Ave.
503/232-6757

**Royal Antiques**
8035 S.E. 13th Ave.
503/231-9064

**Sellwood Peddler Attic**
8065 S.E. 13th Ave.
503/235-0946

**Spencer's Antiques**
8130 S.E. 13th Ave.
503/238-1737

**Sellwood Antiques Mall**
7875 S.E. 13th Ave.
503/232-3755

**Consignment Gallery**
8133 S.E. 13th Ave.
503/234-6606

**Anomaly**
8235 S.E. 13th Ave.
503/230-0734

**American Country Antiques**
8235 S.E. 13th Ave.
503/234-8551

**Lily White**
8235 13th Ave.
503/234-1630

**The Green Door**
8235 S.E. 13th Ave., #11
503/231-2520

**Ragtime Antiques & Repairs**
8301 S.E. 13th Ave.
503/231-4023

**The Blue Hen & Company**
8309 S.E. 13th Ave.
503/234-3197

**Wood Pile Antiques**
8315 13th Ave.
503/231-1145

### *Great Places To Stay*

**General Hooker's Bed and Breakfast**
125 S.W. Hooker
541/222-4435 or 1-800-745-4135
Fax: 503/295-6410
Rates: $70-115

As the early morning's misty fog clears from town, General Hooker's bed and breakfast sits in the midst of its tranquil historic district. The Victorian townhouse, a stroll from downtown, displays a restrained Victorian ornamentation. Much of the casually comfortable atmosphere grows out of the 19th century family heirloom furnishings. Furniture is tasteful and cozy. In addition, Northwestern art provides an interesting flare to the decor. Throughout the house, guests move to the music of Bach and Vivaldi. Guest accommodations include four rooms, two with private baths.

## 40 REDMOND

**Old Farmer's Co-op Antiques**
106 S.E. Evergreen Ave.
541/548-7975

**Country Pleasures**
502 S.W. Evergreen Ave.
541/548-1021

**Route 97 Trading Post**
2424 N. Hwy. 97
541/923-4660

**The Gilbert House**
203 S. 6th St.
541/548-1342

**World of Treasures**
215 S.W. 6th St.
541/923-0226

**Past & Presents**
418 S.W. 6th St.
541/923-0147

**Memory Shoppe**
422 S.W. 6th St.
541/923-6748

**Country by Design Antiques**
453 S.W. 6th St.
541/923-3350

**The Keeping Room**
528 S.W. 6th St.
541/548-7888

## 41 ROSEBURG

**Majestic Antiques**
715 S.E. Cass Ave.
541/672-1387

**Woodtique**
2660 N.E. Stephens St.
541/673-8385

**From Days Gone By**
630 S.E. Rose St.
541/673-7325

**Antique Mall & Marketplace**
1212 S.E. Stephens St.
541/672-8259

**Angles in the Attic**
400 S.E. Jackson St.
541/673-7101

## 42 SALEM

**Antique Village**
211 Commercial St. N.E.
503/581-0318

**Earle Antique Co.**
223 Commercial St. N.E.
503/370-9666

**A Part of the Past Antique Mall**
241 Commercial St. N.E.
503/581-1004

**A Touch of Nostalgia**
255 Court St. N.E.
503/588-9123

**Best Dressed Doll**
385 Howell Prairie Road S.E.
503/362-6583

**Gingerbread Haus Antiques**
145 Liberty St. N.E.
503/588-2213

**Engelberg Antiks II**
148 Liberty St. N.E.
503/363-8155

**Icons & Keepsakes**
148 Liberty St. N.E.
503/370-8979

**Nancy Van Zandt Antiques**
1313 Mill St. S.E.
503/371-8612

**Reid's Antiques**
2625 Salem Dallas Hwy. N.W.
503/581-1455

**Et Cetera Antiques**
3295 Triangle Dr. S.E.
503-581-9850

**Every Bloomin Thing**
615 Wallace Road N.W.
503-378-1821

## 43 SANDY

**Sandy Traders**
38905 Proctor Blvd.
503/668-5749

**Something Old Something New**
38922 Pioneer Blvd.
503/668-0808

**Treasures Antique Mall Inc.**
39065 Pioneer Blvd.
503/668-9042

## 44 SEAL ROCK

**Antiques Etc.**
Hwy. 101
541/563-2242

**Granny's Country Store**
10261 N.W. Pacific Coast Hwy.
541/563-4899

**A Part of the Past**
10841 N.W. Pacific Coast Hwy.
541/563-5071

**Purple Pelican Antique Mall**
10641 N.E. Pacific Coast Hwy.
541/563-4166

## 45 SEASIDE

What was once "The End of Lewis & Clark Trail" is now Oregon's largest beach resort community. Seaside's legacy of hospitality dates back to 1873, when railroad baron Ben Holladay built the luxurious Seaside Hotel.

**Wesrose's Antiques**
3300 Hwy. 101 N.
503/738-8732

**Ike & Debbie's Red Barn Antiques**
3765 Hwy. 101 N.
503/738-0272

**Yankee Trader**
4197 Hwy. 101 N.
503/738-6633

**Cottage and Castle**
501 S. Holladay Dr.
503/738-2195

**Cynthia Anderson Antiques**
567 Pacific Way
503/738-8484

## 46 SELLWOOD

**Sellwood Bazaar Antiques**
7733 S.E. 13th Ave.
503/236-9110

**The Raven Antiques & Military**
7805 S.E. 13th Ave.
503/233-8075

**Golden Girls' Antiques**
7834 S.E. 13th Ave.
503/233-2160

**Misty's Antiques**
7825 S.E. 13th Ave.
503/233-9564

**Sellwood Antique Mall**
7875 S.E. 13th Ave.
503/232-3755

**Leighton House Antiques, LTD.**
1226 Lexinton
503/233-4248

**N.W. Collectibles & Antique Paper**
7901 S.E. 13th Ave.
503/234-4248

**Kathryn's Antiques & Collectibles**
7907 S.E. 13th Ave.
503/236-7120

**The General Store**
7987 S.E. 13th Ave.
503/232-1321

**Corner House/Queen Anne's Lace**
8003 S.E. 13th Ave.
503/235-3749

**Den of Antiquity**
8012 S.E. 13th Ave.
503/233-7334

**The Treasure Chest**
8015 S.E. 13th Ave.
503/235-6897

**Gilt Antiques**
8017 S.E. 13th Ave.
503/231-6395

**Farmhouse Antiques**
8028 S.E. 13th Ave.
503/232-6757

**The Sellwood Collective**
8027 S.E. 13th Ave.
503/736-1399

**Royal Antiques**
8035 S.E. 13th Ave.
503/231-9064

**1874 House**
8070 S.E. 13th Ave.
503/233-1874

**Sellwood Pedler, Attic Goodies**
8065 S.E. 13th Ave.
503/235-0946

**Sellwood Antiques & Cllbls. Market, Inc.**
8132 S.E. 13th Ave.
503/236-9650

**R. Soencer Antiques, Inc.**
8130 S.E. 13th Ave.
503/238-1737

**The Anomaly, Parlor of Eclectic Art**
8235 S.E. 13th Ave.
503/230-0734

**American Country Antiques**
8235 S.E. 13th Ave.
503/234-8551

**Ragtime Antiques**
8301 S.E. 13th Ave.
503/231-4023

**The Blue Hen and Co.**
8309 S.E. 13th Ave.
503/234-3197

**Woodpile Antiques**
8315 S.E. 13th Ave.
No Phone Listed

**The Handwerk Shop**
8317 S.E. 13th Ave.
503/236-7870

## 47 SHERWOOD

**Smockville Station Antiques**
170 N.W. 1st St.
603/625-5866

**Main Street Crossing**
5 N.W. Main St.
503/625-5434

**Manhattan Trade Post Antique Mall**
22275 S.W. Pacific Hwy.
503/625-7834

**Bare Pockets**
230 N.W. Railroad Ave.
503/625-5491

**Railroad Street Antique Mall**
260 N.W. Railroad Ave.
503/625-2246

**Whistle Stop Antique Mall**
130 N.W. Railroad Ave.
503/625-5744

### *Great Places To Stay*

**Inn of the Oregon Trail**
416 S. McLoughlin
503/656-2089

A stone's throw from the end of the Oregon Trail waits an 1867 Gothic Revival-style home built by E.B. Fellow, Inn of the Oregon Trail. Overlooking the landscaped gardens are three delightfully outfitted guest rooms on the third floor. The ground floor provides another room which offers a private entrance, bath, fireplace and wet bar. Fellows House Restaurant occupies the main floor and is open to the public weekdays, but private dinners for inn guests can be arranged with advance notice. Explore the inn and the surrounding historic Oregon City.

## 48 SISTERS

**Lonesome Water Books**
255 W. Cascade
541/549-2203

**Treasure Trove Craft & Antiques**
160 S. Hood St.
541/549-2142

**Country Collections**
351 W. Hood St.
541/549-7888

## 49 SPRINGFIELD

**Antique Peddlers I & II**
612 Main St.
541/747-1259

**Rolla's Relics & Reusables**
868 Main St.
541/741-0838

**Pretty Things For You**
2142 Main St.
541/747-7718

**Rose Moss**
214 Pioneer Pkwy. W.
541/741-2411

**Country Rose**
3000 Gateway St.
541/746-4605

**Glory Days Antique Mall**
2020 Main St.
541/744-1112

**Mare's Place**
448 Main St.
541/744-2021

**Paramount Antique Center**
143 21st St.
541/747-3881

## 50 THE DALLES

**Klindt's Used Books & Collectibles**
319 E. 2nd St.
541/296-4342

**2nd Street Place**
402 E. 2nd St.
541/296-8500

**Bishop's Antiques Gifts & Collectibles**
422 W. 2nd St.
541/298-1804

**Old Mill Bargain Center**
2917 E. 2nd St.
541/296-6706

**Clem's Attic**
2937 E. 2nd St.
541/296-4448

## 51 TILLAHOOK

### *Great Places To Stay*

### Blue Haven Inn Over Flow Shop

3025 Gienger Road
503/842-2265
Rates $60-75
The inn never closes.
*Directions: Turn west off Hwy. 101 at Gienger Road. The Inn is located 2 miles south of Tillamook, Oregon.*

Sitting in the midst of two-acres surrounded by tall evergreens, Blue Haven affords guests country serenity and seclusion. Built in 1916, the country home has been skillfully restored featuring charming antiques and limited edition collectibles throughout. Each of the 3 guest bedrooms provides a unique decor. Tara, overlooking the garden, presents a *Gone With the Wind* theme highlighted by its four poster bed, Civil War chess set and memorabilia from the movie. The queen-size brass bed in La Femme hearkens to the "feminine and frilly" ladies boudoir of earlier days. A nautical atmosphere engulfs Of The Sea, a most comfortable room, with wingback chair and ottoman in addition to a view of the garden. Enjoy a relaxing pause on the country porch to swing. Listen to music from an old radio or antique gramophone in the library/game room. In the mornings, sit down to the complimentary gourmet breakfast served in the formal dining room on fine bone china and crystal. (Dietary preferences are carefully catered to.) Step around to the "Overflow Shop" adjacent to the inn offering antiques, glassware, limited edition plates, dolls, sewing machines, as well as clawfoot bathtubs.

**Smokehouse Antiques Mall**
116 Main St.
503/842-3399

**Dekunsam's Second Hand Store**
1910 2nd St.
503/842-2299

## 52 TOLEDO

**Sherwood Antiques**
112 W. Graham St.
541/336-2315

**Adas Gifts & Collectibles**
123 N. Main St.
541/336-2524

**Antiques N More**
199 S. Main St.
541/336-4210

**Main Street Antique Mall**
305 N. Main St.
541/336-3477

**Cedric & Christy Brown Antiques**
404 N. Main St.
541/336-3668

## 53 WALDPORT

**Waldport Mercantile**
145 S.W. Arrow St.
541/563-4052

**Old Maid New**
255 S.W. Maple St.
541/563-6411

**Doug and Mims**
340 N.W. Hemlock Hwy. #-34
541/563-2454

**Family Tree Collectibles**
1265 S.W. Range Dr.
541/563-2099

**Glass Treats & Antqs. Prcln. & Restoration**
332 N. Deer Hill Dr.
541/563-6282

**Mim's Whims**
340 N.W. Hemlock (Hwy. 34)
541/563-2454

**Antiques & Reference Books**
Hwy. 101
541/563-2318

## 54 WINCHESTER BAY

Winchester Bay offers over 300 camp sites on the Pacific Ocean, Umpqua River or on beautiful Lake Marie. The area provides great fishing opportunities for the guys and kids while mom antiques.

### Winchester Bay Trading Company

Corner of Broadway & 8th St.
1 block from Hwy. 101
541/271-9466
Fax: 541/271-6947
Daily 10-4
*Directions: Hwy. 101, 2 miles south of Reedsport or 25 miles north of Coos Bay.*

The personal touch thrives at Winchester Bay Trading Company. This husband and wife team hand select the shop's merchandise from regional estate sales. Because of their nearness to the bay, a large supply of nautical items can always be found amongst the rare books, Fitz and Floyd pieces, exquisite glassware and unique items such as an old tin bath tub.

# Pennsylvania

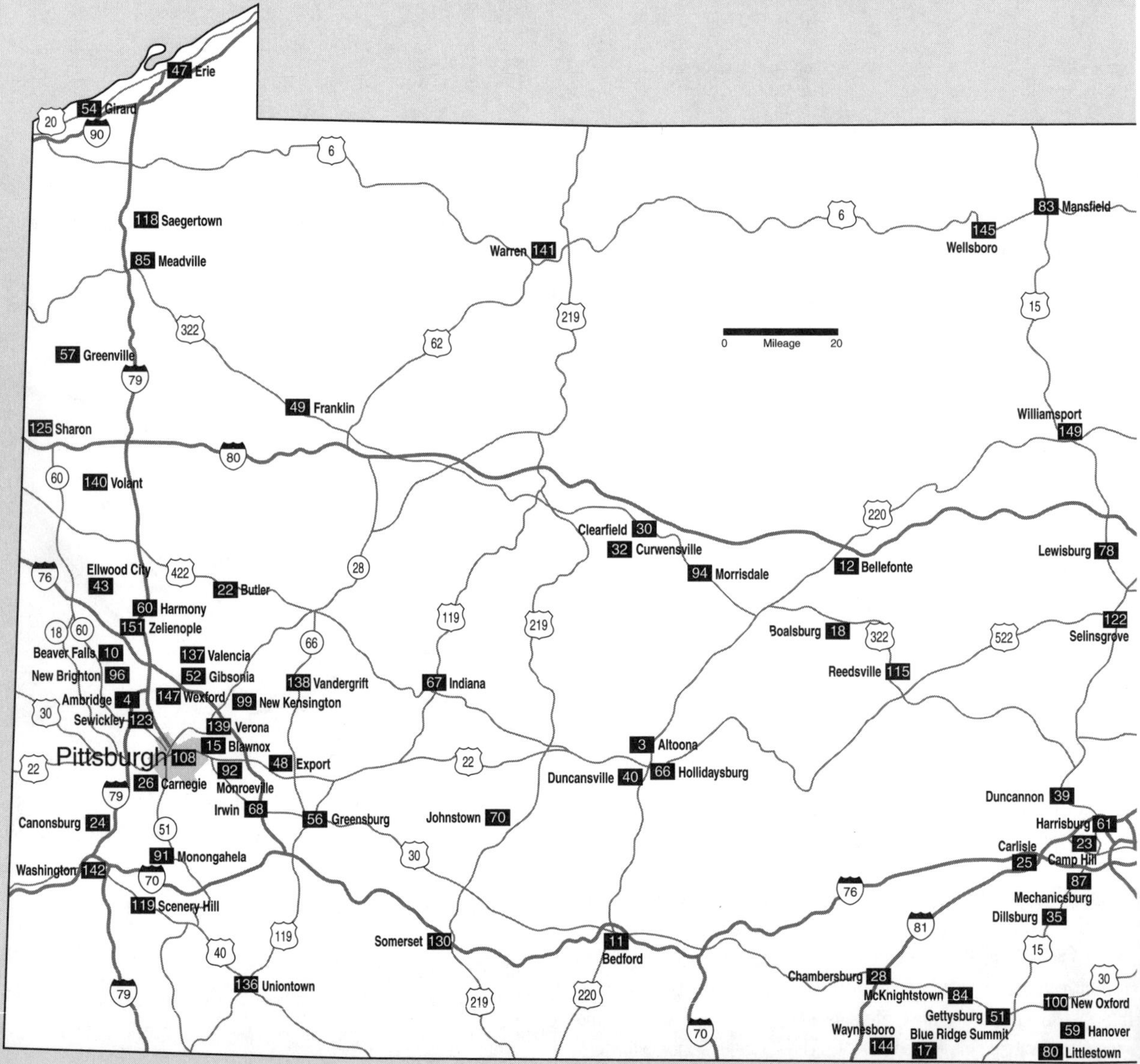

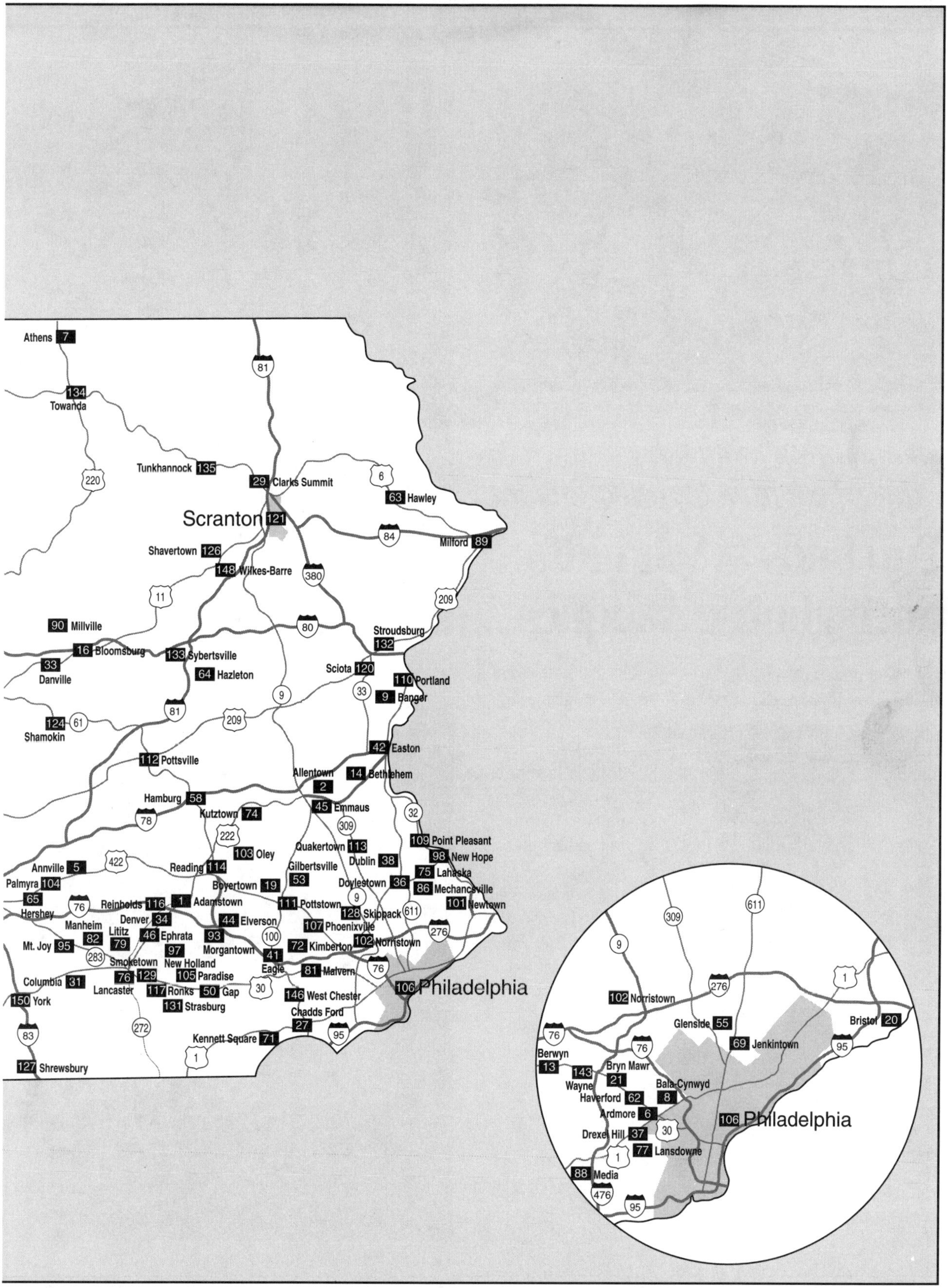
Athens 7
81
134 Towanda
220
Tunkhannock 135
29 Clarks Summit
6
63 Hawley
Scranton 121
84
Milford 89
Shavertown 126
148 Wilkes-Barre
380
11
209
90 Millville
80
Stroudsburg 132
16 Bloomsburg
133 Sybertsville
33 Danville
64 Hazleton
Sciota 120
110 Portland
33
9 Bangor
9
81
124 61
Shamokin
209
42 Easton
112 Pottsville
Allentown 2
14 Bethlehem
Hamburg 58
Kutztown 74
45 Emmaus
32
78
309
222
103 Oley
Quakertown 113
109 Point Pleasant
98 New Hope
Annville 5
422
Reading 114
Gilbertsville 53
Dublin 38
75 Lahaska
Palmyra 104
Boyertown 19
Doylestown 36
86 Mechanicsville
65
76
Reinholds 116
1 Adamstown
111 Pottstown
9
128 Skippack
611
101 Newtown
Hershey
Denver 34
44 Elverson
Manheim 82
Lititz 79
46 Ephrata
93
100
107 Phoenixville
276
Mt. Joy 95
283
97
Morgantown
41
72 Kimberton
102 Norristown
Smoketown
76 129
New Holland
105 Paradise
Eagle
81 Malvern
76
Columbia 31
Lancaster
117 Ronks
50 Gap
30
106 Philadelphia
150 York
131 Strasburg
146 West Chester
Chadds Ford
27
83
272
Kennett Square 71
95
1
127 Shrewsbury
309
611
9
276
1
102 Norristown
Glenside 55
Bristol 20
76
69 Jenkintown
Berwyn
13
76
95
143
Bryn Mawr
21
Wayne
Bala-Cynwyd
8
Haverford 62
Ardmore 6
106 Philadelphia
Drexel Hill 37
30
1
77 Lansdowne
88 Media
476
95

*Pennsylvania tables and cupboards are favorites at Schmidt's.*

*Charming spinning wheel is ready to spin out skeins of yarn as it has in bygone days.*

## *An Antiquing moment: A quick peek from the antiquing trail*

# Fun finds at Schmidt's Springhouse Antiques

A true Pennsylvania antiquing experience, Schmidt's Springhouse Antiques, owned by Betty & Ed Schmidt, is dedicated to providing a large variety of ready to display quality antique furniture, country, primitives, Empire, Victorian, oak and depression. Open since 1993, the shop provides 6,000 square feet and will expand to over 10,000 square feet in 1999.

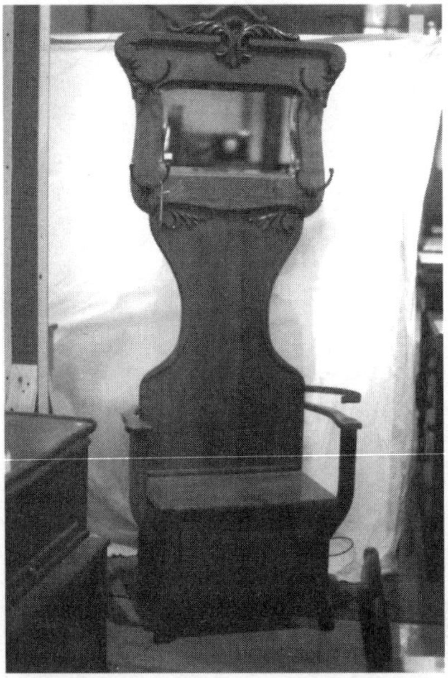

*Ornately carved hall tree with mirror and seat discovered at Schmidt's Springhouse Antiques.*

*Schmidt's Springhouse Antiques is located at Route 66 at Pfeffer Road in Export. For additional information see listing #48 (Export).*

*A mammoth selection of quality antiques abound at Schmidt's.*

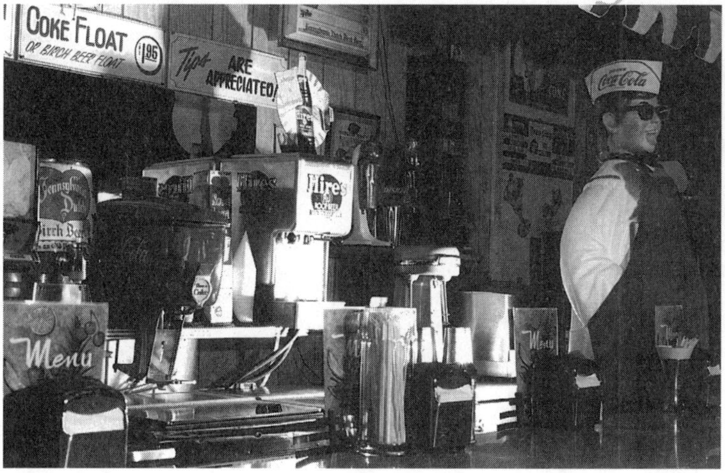

*Not your average antique mall, the Old Sled Works features exhibits documenting the history of the factory.*

*One of the big attractions for families at the Old Sled Works is the '50s soda fountain, complete with soda jerk. On the weekends crowds gather for the creamy treats.*

# Time stands still for all at the Old Sled Works

Tradition and good family memories can often be the motivating factors in our lives as we ponder the age-old question of "what do I want to do when I grow up?" These factors were precisely the motivation behind Jimmy Rosen's Old Sled Works, an enormous, old family-owned factory building in Duncannon, Pennsylvania that now houses an antique mall, crafts center, sled museum, penny arcade, and soda fountain.

Flash back, if you will, to Jimmy's childhood (he's in his early 30s now). He grew up around the old factory, which his father owned, only then it was Standard Novelty Works. The factory produced not only wooden novelties like porch gates and swings, now scooters, and sink protectors, but it also housed the Lightning Guider Sled Factory, which manufactured sleds - hundreds of thousands of sleds - from 1904 to 1988. In its heyday, the factory was one of the busiest and best-known makers of children's sleds in the country, turning out 1,600 to 1,800 sleds a day during the 1920s and 1930s, but the whole factory closed in 1990, a victim of high-tech toys and shopping malls.

So the Rosen family was left with an empty factory, but Jimmy could not accept its demise. As his drive, ambition and memories went into high gear, an idea began to emerge. Duncannan had lots of traffic - it's near Routes 11, 15 and 322 - but it was no tourist mecca, and it didn't have an established market for anything. Rosen had to create a draw for his town, and he chose antiques. But not just any antiques store or mall would do; this is where childhood memories kicked in.

In Jimmy's words, "I wanted to distinguish this (business) from most other antique malls in central Pennsylvania. Even though I'm set up in a historic old sled factory with over 125 great antique and craft vendors, I wanted something more for my customers. As a kid, I fondly remember playing in the arcades during my family's vacations in Miami Beach. Also, we lived close to Hershey Park, which I frequented. I would dream about having my own arcade and how great it would be to have a key to each machine so you could collect all the coins or play for free as many times as you wanted. Guys would think you were cool, and the girls would swoon, I suppose. Obviously, it was just a dream back then. However, when I opened the Old Sled Works, I had some extra space so I thought, "This is the time and place for my arcade. 'I wanted only electro-mechanical machines, like those I remember, and since most of my customers are roughly 35 to 64, I knew many would remember these older machines, too, and would be thrilled to relive their childhoods."

The old soda fountain isn't a museum, at least not in the 'look but don't touch or use' sense. Everything works just fine, and on weekends everyone crowds the fountain to get some old-fashioned ice cream goodies, like fountain drinks, banana splits, malts, and milk shakes - oh yes, and to listen to the 1950s music from the old juke box.

The complete soda fountain runs along the wall facing the games: counter, stools, freezers, ice cream dispensers, a life-sized soda jerk in full costume, signs, adverting. Everything was lifted straight from the original setup. A small seating area forms an alcove at the end of the fountain counter complete with vintage 1950s furniture of chrome, vinyl and glass table tops.

The old sled museum is a link between this time past and time present. Jimmy wanted folks to know the history of the old factory building, which was a town landmark for nearly a century, so he put together exhibits covering the factory's 85 years. He has sleds displayed from each decade of operation, old catalogs and other advertising pieces, patent and trademark papers, tools, early printing and stenciling equipment and the original sled factory time clock. Many of the museum pieces are owned by the Old Sled Works, but several local collectors have donated or loaned items to the museum, including a valuable watch fob, sled advertising thermometer, and miscellaneous paper advertising. In 1992, the building became a registered historic site in Pennsylvania and now boasts a blue and gold marker on the grounds.

*Old Sled Works Antique and Craft Market is located at 722 North Market St. Call for more information at 717/834-9333.*

## 1 ADAMSTOWN

What began as a temporary, stop-gap solution to a vacancy problem in a farmer's market has turned into the largest antique destination in the northeast. Adamstown, Pa., began its reign as "Antiques Capital USA" in the early 1960s when Charles Weik, an antique dealer in the area, began holding flea markets in a place called Shupp's Grove on Sundays.

Shupp's Grove had long been a favorite spot for reunions, picnics, gospel singing, get-togethers and country western music shows. The antiques offered at that time were excellent examples of Pennsylvania Dutch primitives, and there was already an established tradition of antiques shops in the area that were frequented by the Rockefellers, DuPonts, Barneses and Weygandts.

In the mid 1960s, Terry Heilman, resident manager of the former Renninger's Farmers' Market and himself an antiques collector, spent many of his Sundays at Shupp's. His farmers' market had a serious vacancy problem, so in the fall, when Shupp's Grove usually closed, Heilman began offering inside space at Renninger's to the antique dealers at Shupp's, which was all outdoors. They liked it, and by spring, the dealers wanted to stay. So Renninger's began the transformation from farmers' market to antique mall. Other ideas and things were added, and the idea grew – and grew – and grew.

Literally everything is for sale in what has become the northeast's leading year-round antiques destination that pours hundreds of thousands of shoppers and visitors into this tiny town of 3,300. The range of objects runs from 18th to 20th century, sold by a true mixed-bag of dealers; big firms, little dealers, co-ops, mom-and-pop operations, beginners, pros, you name it - indoor shops, outdoor groves, malls, farms, any and everywhere.

The anchor stores here are the original Renninger's, now called Renninger's Antique and Collector's Market, and the Black Angus Antiques Mall, both having been started over 25 years ago.

Renninger's has several hundred dealers. The Black Angus has 500. Both are open only on Sundays, and both have national reputations and followings.

Then there are the cooperatives, the fairly recent development in the antique world that has brought antiquing from its original "Sundays only" market to a daily retail-like level.

Antiques Alley in Adamstown has some of the best cooperatives on the East Coast, including South Pointe Antiques, General Heath's Antiques, Antiques Showcase at the Black Horse, and Adams Antique Market. Adamstown also has three yearly "Antiques Extravaganza" weekends that draw several thousand more dealers from all over the country. These special events are the last weekend in April, June and September.

**South Pointe Antiques**
Route 272 and Denver Road
717/484-1026

**General Heath's Antiques**
Route 272
717/484-1300

**Adamstown Antique Mall**
94 Lancaster Ave.
717/484-0464

**Oley Valley Architectural Antiques**
2453 N. Reading Road at Route 272
717/484-2191

**Greenwood Antique Center**
2455 N. Reading Road
717/335-3377

**Friedman & Timmons Antiques**
Route 272
717/484-0949

**Heritage Antique Center**
Route 272
717/484-4646

**Country French Collection**
Route 272
717/484-0200

**Renninger's Antique Market**
Penn. Turnpike, Exit 21, Route 272
717/385-0104

**Schupps Grove**
Route 897 at Willow St.
717/484-4115

**Stoudt's Black Angus**
Penn. Turnpike, Exit 21, Route 272
717/484-4385

### *Great Places To Stay*

**Adamstown Inn Bed & Breakfast**
62 W. Main St.
1-800-594-4808

Experience the simple elegance of The Adamstown Inn, a Victorian bed and breakfast resplendent with leaded glass windows and door, magnificent chestnut woodwork, and oriental rugs. All four guest rooms are decorated with family heirlooms, handmade quilts, lace curtains, fresh flowers and many distinctive touches which make your stay special.

## 2 ALLENTOWN

**Cottage Crafters**
4636 Broadway
610/366-9222

**Golden Eagle Antiques**
1425 E. Gordon St.
610/432-1223

**Burick's Antiques**
880 N. Graham St.
610/432-8966

**Toonerville Junction Antiques**
522 W. Maple St.
610/435-8697

**Pete's Used Furniture & Antiques**
231 N. 7th St.
610/433-4481

**Abe Ark Antiques**
1115 N. 22nd St.
610/770-1454

**Camelot Collectibles & Antiques**
1518 W. Walnut St.
610/433-7744

## 3 ALTOONA

**Johnny's Used Furniture & Antiques**
501 4th St.
814/944-3423

**Michelle's Antiques**
1546 Pleasant Valley Blvd.
814/943-6111

**T & L's Antiques**
3958 5th Ave.
814/946-5266

## 4 AMBRIDGE

**Toms Old Country Store**
511 Merchant St.
724/266-7215

**Attic Attractions**
576 Merchant St.
724/266-3020

**Nello's Taj Mahal**
1415 Merchant St.
724/266-5656

## 5 ANNVILLE

**Chris Machmer Antiques**
146 W. Main St.
717/867-4244

**Meadow View Antiques**
Route 322
717/838-9443

## 6 ARDMORE

**En Garde Antiques & Collectibles**
24 W. Lancaster Ave.
610/645-5785

**Ardmore Antiques & Oriental Rugs**
321 W. Lancaster Ave.
610/649-4432

**Daniel Wilson Antiques**
24 E. Lancaster Ave.
610/645-9533

## 7 ATHENS

**J & M Antiques**
122 N. Elmira St.
717/888-0650

### *Great Places To Stay*

### Failte Inn B&B and Antique Shop
Route 2, Box 323
717/358-3899
Rates: $65-70 per room, per night
*Directions: Hwy. 220 to the blinking light in the village of Uster, PA. Cross over the Susquehanna River bridge and turn left at end of bridge on SR 1043. Three miles to inn on right. From Towanda: turn left on SR 1043 after crossing James St. bridge. From Athens: turn right on SR 1043 after crossing Susquehanna River bridge in downtown Athens.*

Failte Inn is nestled in the Susquehanna Valley surrounded by the beautiful Endless Mountains of rural Pennsylvania. You can relax in the country atmosphere of rolling farmland, away from the noise of city traffic and the stress of busy lifestyles.

Enjoy the unhurried charm of yesterday in a turn of the century farmhouse decorated in the graceful elegance of the Victorian era. Escape to a quiet, well-stocked library, listen to fine music or play and enjoy the antique baby grand piano. Relax in front of warm fires in the library or parlor on a cold winter's day. Feel the cool mountain breezes beneath the paddle fans on the wide verandahs during the lazy days of summer.

Enjoy a full country breakfast served in the elegantly appointed formal dining room or on the screened wraparound verandahs overlooking 3 acres of green lawns, apple orchards and beautiful flower gardens. (Served 8 a.m. to 10 a.m.)

Join the innkeepers for a complimentary wine or brandy, coffee or tea accompanied by cheeses or homemade pastries in the historically, restored Speak-Easy dating form the days of prohibition.

Failte Inn offers 5 beautifully decorated guest rooms - each with its own private bath; Susan's Room on the ground floor, Catherine's Suite with sitting room, Mama's Room with Jacuzzi tub, Chelsea's Room with king size bed, and Jennifer's Room, their most selected room.

"The Failte Inn antique shop specializes in glass and furnishings from the Victorian period."

## 8 BALA-CYNWYD

**General Ecletic**
159 Bala Ave.
610/667-6677

**Pieces of Tyme**
323 Montgomery Ave.
610/664-2050

**Something Beautiful To Buy**
333 Montgomery Ave.
610/667-2969

## 9 BANGOR

**Tolerico's Antiques & Baseball Cards**
53 Broadway
610/588-5510

**Tolerico's Past Present Future**
13 N. Main St.
610/588-6981

**Hartzell's Auction Gallery**
521 Richmond Road
610/588-5831

**Expressions Thur Glass-More**
2242 Ridge Road
610/588-1490

## 10 BEAVER FALLS

### Leonard's Antiques & Uniques Mega Mall
2586 Constitution Blvd.
724/847-2304 or 1-800-443-5052
Web site: leonards.antiqueshopper.com
Email: leonards@timesnet.net
Mon.-Sat., 10-8; Sun., 10-6 (Open 362 days a year, closed Thanksgiving Day, Christmas Day and Easter Sunday, but open until midnight on New Year's Eve!)
*Directions: Leonard's is located in the Chippewa Mall at the junction of Route 51 and Route 60, approximately 12 miles from the Ohio state line. From the Penn. Turnpike, take Exit #1A onto Route 60. Take Exit #15 off of Route 60 onto Route 51 at the Chippewa Mall.*

Leonard's is the largest antiques mall in western Pennsylvania, with more than 300 dealers all under one roof, covering approximately 68,000 square feet! Inside this enormous mall, there are over a million-and-a-half items! It certainly lives up to its billing as a mega mall! Of course, as you would expect in a space this large, they carry everything from pottery to china, primitives to paper, furniture to fine and costume jewelry. And what a great idea - staying open until midnight on New Year's Eve!

**Peggy Smith's Collections**
621 7th Ave.
724/843-2622

**Antique Emporium**
818 7th Ave.
724/847-1919

**American & European Antiques**
601 Darlington Road
724/846-1002

**Memory Lane Antiques**
456 Constitution R 51
724/847-9910

## 11 BEDFORD

**Founders Crossing**
100 S. Juliana St.
814/623-9120

**Graystone Galleria**
203 E. Pitt St.
814/623-1768

**Lins Touch of Elegance**
238 E. Pitt St.
814/623-2673

**Thomas Antiques**
Road 6 Box 21 Cumberland Road
814/623-5574

**Doug's Antiques**
112 N. Richard St.
814/623-7858

## 12 BELLEFONTE

**Times Past Antiques & Collectibles**
141 S. Allegheny St.
814/353-1750

**Hayloft Antiques**
660 Benner Pike
814/355-7588

## 13 BERWYN

**Circa Antiques & Decor**
712 Lancaster Ave.
610/651-8151

**McCoy**
722 W. Lancaster Ave.
610/640-0433

**Deja Vu**
11 Waterloo Ave.
610/296-2737

**And Antiques**
19 Waterloo Ave.
610/644-3659

**Anything & Everything Shop**
36 Waterloo Ave.
610/647-8186

## 14 BETHLEHEM

**C & D Guns Coins & Antiques**
121 E. Broad St.
610/865-4355

**Sir Pack Rat**
99 W. Broad St.
610/974-8855

**Valley Antiques Gifts & Imports**
729 W. Broad St.
610/865-3880

**Yesterdays Ltd.**
2311 Center St.
610/691-8889

## 15 BLAWNOX

**Cottage Antiques**
231 Freeport Road
724/828-9201

**The Marlene Harris Collection**
238 1/2 Freeport Road
724/828-1245

**Mulberry Antiques**
262 1/2 Freeport Road
724/828-0144

**China Shop**
266 Freeport Road
724/826-8075

**Lotus Gallery**
309 Freeport Road
724/828-7588

**A Child's Heart**
334 Freeport Road
724/826-9192

**Blawnox Antiques**
340 Freeport Road
724/828-2224

**The Building Arts**
340 Freeport Road
724/828-6876

**Maple Hill Antiques & Lighting**
340 Freeport Road
724/826-9226

**Kirk's Antiques**
352 Freeport Road
724/828-7470

**Velvet Swing Antiques**
407 Freeport Road
724/828-4943

**B Merry Interior Design**
1144 Freeport Road
724/781-6556

## 16 BLOOMSBURG

**Meckley's Books & Collectibles**
36 W. Main St.
717/784-3765

**Red Mill Antiques**
44 Red Mill Road
717/784-7146

**Hoffman's Antiques**
RR 4
717/784-9534

**Liberty Antiques**
RR 4
717/683-5419

## 17 BLUE RIDGE SUMMIT

### Wooden Horse Antiques

717/794-2717 (bus. day phone)
301/241-3460 (evening phone)
Open by appointment only
*Directions: If traveling on I-81, take Exit #3 (Greencastle, Penn./ Route 16 East). Proceed east through Waynesboro (8 miles) and then to Blue Ridge Summit (6 miles). Go to the bottom of the mountain after Blue Ridge Summit. Wooden Horse is the third place on the right - there's a sign out front. If traveling Route 15, take the Emmetsburg/Route 140 West Exit and proceed into Pennsylvania, where Route 140 West becomes Route 16 West. The shop is approximately 4 miles into Pennsylvania on the left - look for the sign out front.*

The folks at Wooden Horse Antiques have been wholesaling to the antique trade for 25 years. They specialize in fancy oak and Victorian furniture and accessories; also country and period furniture and estate contents. Everything is sold in "as is" condition, but these folks look for and offer the "finer" pieces. In a recent conversation with Randy Sutton (the owner), he told me that he has been doing "quite a lot" with the finer circa 1900-1930s mahogany dining room and bedroom furniture. "Mostly ball and claw," he says. "I've also been fortunate to grab some outstanding estates lately." Dealers take note - you never know what might pop up in an estate. My suggestion is to make sure you stop to see Randy when traveling through Pennsylvania.

## 18 BOALSBURG

**Gates Antiques**
805 Boalsburg Pike
814/466-6333

**Serendipity Valley Farms**
122 E. Main St.
814/466-7282

## 19 BOYERTOWN

**Bashful Barn**
1 E. Philadelphia Ave.
610/367-2631

**Castle Hall Antiques**
5 E. Philadelphia Ave.
610/367-6506

**Homestead Antiques**
Route 73
610/367-6502

**Greshville Antiques**
Route 562
610/367-0076

**Boyertown Antiques**
1283 Weisstown Road
610/367-2452

## 20 BRISTOL

**Wilhelmina's**
369 Main St.
215/945-8606

**Another Time Antiques**
307 Mill St.
215/788-3131

**Place**
5 Pond St.
215/785-1494

## 21 BRYN MAWR

**Greentree Antiques**
825 W. Lancaster Ave.
610/526-1841

**Susan P Vitale Antiques**
835 W. Lancaster Ave.
610/527-5653

**Sandy Demaio Antique Jewelry**
860 W. Lancaster Ave.
610/525-1717

## 22 BUTLER

**Bergbigler New & Used Furniture**
321 Center Ave.
724/287-0865

**Fox's Antiques**
160 Church Road
724/352-4500

**Thomas Antiques Shoppe**
424 S. Jackson St.
724/287-6839

**Ken's Antiques**
1251 Lake Vue Dr.
724/586-7271

**Antiques**
102 N. Main St.
724/282-2899

**William Smith Antiques**
102 N. Main St.
724/282-2899

**Arthurs Gift Shop**
126 N. Main St.
724/282-4000

**Store on Main**
108 S. Main St.
724/283-9923

**Alley Antiques**
125 S. Main St. (Rear)
724/283-6366

**Butler Antiques & Collectibles**
119 E. Wayne St.
724/282-7195

**Step Back in Time**
224 N. Washington St.
724/283-7509

## 23 CAMP HILL

**Rose Marie's Antiques**
2136 Market St.
717/763-8998

**Cordier Antiques**
307 N. 25th St.
717/731-8662

**Collector's World**
6 W. Main St.
717/763-8288

## 24 CANONSBURG

**Canonsburg Antique Mall I**
145 Adams Ave.
724/745-1333

**Treasure Lane**
24 W. Pike St.
724/745-7414

**Where The Toys Are**
45 W. Pike St.
724/745-4599

**Tri-State Antique Center**
47 W. Pike St.
724/745-9116

**Annabelles Antiques**
51 W. Pike St.
724/746-5950

**Antique Junction**
2475 Washington Road
724/746-5119

**Route 19 Antique Mall**
2597 Washington Road
724/746-3277

**Canonsburg Antique Mall II**
99 Weavertown Road
724/745-1050

**Whiskey Run Antiques**
849 S. Washington Road
412/745-5808

**Thomas Brown Antiques**
710 Waterdam Road
412/941-7143

## 25 CARLISLE

**Antiques by James L Price**
831 Alexander Spring Road
717/243-0501

**Antiques on Hanover**
17 N. Hanover St.
717/249-6285

**Country Heritage**
24 N. Hanover St.
717/249-2600

**H & R Jewelry & Antiques**
33 N. Hanover St.
717/258-4024

**Baker's Antiques**
34 N. Hanover St.
717/258-1383

**Downtown Antiques**
152 N. Hanover St.
717/249-0395

**Northgate Antique Mall**
725th Hanover Manor #726N
717/243-5802

**Old Stone Tavern Antiques**
2408 Walnut Bottom Road
717/243-6304

**The Antique Quilt Source**
385 Springview Road #D
717/245-2054

**Hillcrest Antiques**
31 E. Slate Hill Road
717/249-1987

**Linden Hall Antiques**
211 Old Stonehouse Road
717/249-1978

## 26 CARNEGIE

**Heidelberg Antiques**
1451 Collier Ave.
724/429-9223

**Heidelberg Antiques**
1550 Collier Ave.
724/429-9222

**Black Swan Art & Frame Gallery**
301 E. Main St.
724/276-3337

## 27 CHADDS FORD

### Olde Ridge Village Antique Shoppes
Route 202 & Ridge Road
610/459-0960
Daily 10-5, 10-8 Thurs.
*Directions: Route 202 & Ridge Road One mile south of Route 1. Traveling on Interstate 95 in the Wilmington, DE. area, take the Wilmington/West Chester Exit 8 north on Route 202. After crossing the PA border, travel 2 miles to the shop on the left. Coming from the PA Turnpike, take Exton Exit 23 south on Route 100. Exit onto Route 202 south and cross Route 1 (the shop is on the right 1 mile down).*

"Olde Ridge" is a cooperative antique shop which is part of a twenty-store village of individually owned small shops and restaurants. Located in Pennsylvania's Historic Chadds Ford, the shop is a twelve room, turn of the century farm house filled with two floors of antiques and collectibles from about a dozen dealers. Displayed in room settings with country, Victorian and 30s-40s furnishings, the shop also offers a number of showcases holding incredible antiques and collectibles. China, glassware, advertising and children's items are just a few of the specialities.

**Village Peddler**
Baltimore Pike
610/388-2828

**Antique Reflections**
170 Fairville Road
610/388-0645

**Diane's Antiques**
RR 1
610/388-3956

**Jane's Antiques**
RR 1
610/388-6730

**Pennsbury Chadds Ford Antique**
RR 1
610/388-6480

**Aaron Goebel's Antiques**
Route 202 & Pyle Road
610/459-8555

**Frances Lantz Antique Shop**
Route 202 & State Line Road
610/459-4080

**Wendy's Corner Antiques**
210 Wilmington W.
610/358-4077

**Joanne Rollins Antiques**
Pennsbury Chadds Ford
610/388-0959

**Brandywine River Antiques**
878 Baltimore Pike
610/388-2000

**Antique Mall**
640 Baltimore Pike
610/388-1620

## 28 CHAMBERSBURG

**House of the Gabler**
71 N. Main St.
717/263-2202

**Gateway Gallery**
643 Kriner Road
717/263-6512

## 29 CLARKS SUMMIT

**Carriage Barn Antiques**
1550 Fairview Road
717/587-5405

**Heritage House Shoppes**
402 N. State St.
717/586-8575

## 30 CLEARFIELD

***Great Places To Stay***

### Christopher Kratzer House Bed & Breakfast
101 E. Cherry St.
814/765-5024 or 1-888-252-2632
Open year round
Rates $55-70
*Directions: Traveling I-80: Take Exit #19 and follow the signs to Clearfield (322W.). Turn left at the light before the Nichol St. bridge onto Front St. (Route 153 South). Continue along the river past Pine, Locust and Market St. to the corner of Front and Cherry, across from the park and church.*

This old (pre-1840) Greek Revival house is decorated with an eclectic mix of contemporary and antique pieces, artistically intermingled by innkeepers, Bruce and Ginny Baggett. Bruce is a musician and Ginny is a printmaker, and the interior of the house reflects not only their interest in preserving history, but also their interests in art and music. Bruce has a collection of musical instruments and memorabilia of his more than 30 years in show business; he even entertains guests with songs at the piano in the music room! Ginny has filled the house with original art work for sale and has installed an art gallery on the second floor.

This is the oldest house in Clearfield, built by Christopher Kratzer, a noted lumberman, carpenter, architect, politician, and owner of the county's first newspaper. It is located in the Old Town Historic District and predates the Victorian era in which most of the other homes were built. The home overlooks the Susquehanna River and Witmer Park, and is within easy walking distance of shops, the public library, restaurants, a movie theater and the Clearfield County Historical Museum.

Guests have a choice of four rooms, two with views of the river and park, one with mahogany twin beds, the other with an antique queen-size spool bed. There is an upstairs sitting room that converts to a bedroom, and an additional bedroom with a private bath.

**Carousel Antiques**
404 W. 7th Ave.
814/765-8518

**Winter Barn Antiques**
Susquehanna Bridge Road
814/765-5248

## 31 COLUMBIA

**Restorations Etc.**
125 Bank Ave.
717/684-5454

**C A Herr Annex**
35 N. 3rd St.
717/684-7850

**Partners Antique Center**
403 N. 3rd St.
717/684-5364

## 32 CURWENSVILLE

**Errigo's**
848 State St.
814/236-3403

## 33 DANVILLE

**Cloverleaf Barn Antiques**
120 McCracken Road
717/275-8838

**Rising Sun Antiques**
6 Mill St.
717/275-1776

**Wispy Willows**
419 Mill St.
717/275-1658

**Fleming Antiques & Lamps**
1609 Montour Blvd.
717/275-2081

## 34 DENVER

**Antique Showcase @ Black Horse**
2222 N. Reading Road
717/336-3864

**Adams Antique & Collectibles Mkt.**
Route 272/2400 N. Reading Road
717/335-3116

**Heritage II**
Route 272
717/336-0888

**Covered Bridge Antiques**
Route 272
717/336-4480

**Lancaster County Antiques & Collectibles**
Route 272
717/336-2701

**Exit 21 Antiques & Collectibles**
Route 272
717/336-7482

**Adamstown Antique Gallery**
2000 N. Reading Road
717/335-3435

**J. S. Maxwell Jr./Virginia Caputo**
2350 N. Reading Road (Route 272)
717/336-2185

**Renningers Antique Market**
Route 272
717/336-2177

**Barr's Auction & Antique World**
2152 N. Reading Road
717/336-2861

**Lancaster County Antique Market**
2255 N. Reading Road
717/336-2701

**Shupps Grove**
1686 Dry Tavern Road
717/484-4115

## 35 DILLSBURG

**B & J Antique Mall**
14 Franklin Church Road
717/432-7353

## 36 DOYLESTOWN

**New Britain Antiques**
326 W. Butler Ave.
215/345-7282

**Consignment Galleries**
470 Clemens Town Center
215/348-5244

**Nejad Gallery Fine Oriental Rugs**
1 N. Main St.
215/348-1255

**Dragons Den of Antiques**
135 S. Main St.
215/345-8666

**Y-Knot Shop**
New Galena Road & Route 313
215/249-9120

**Frog Pond**
128 W. State St.
215/348-3425

**Doylestown Antique Center**
3687 Old Easton Road
215/345-9277

**Orchard Hill Collection**
4445 Lois Lane
215/230-7771

**Renaissance Furnishings**
635 N. Main St.
215/348-3455

## 37 DREXEL HILL

**Brandywine House Antiques**
1201 Cornell Ave.
610/449-5208

**Fields Antique Jewelers**
Landsdowne & Windsor Ave.
610/853-2740

**Spring House Antiques**
4213 Woodland Ave.
610/623-8898

**Ardmart Antique Village**
802 N. Lansdowne Ave.
610/789-6622

## 38 DUBLIN

**Kramer's Rainbow Rooms**
104 Middle Road
215/249-1916

## 39 DUNCANNON

**Old Sled Works**
722 N. Market St.
717/834-9333
Wed.-Sun., 10-5
*Directions: Old Sled Works is located 1 mile off Route 11 and 15 or off Routes 22 and 322. The Works is approximately 15 miles northwest of Harrisburg.*

See Collector Interview at the beginning of this section.

**Cove Barn**
10 Kinsey Road
717/834-4088

**Leonard's Antique Co-op**
1631 State Road
717/957-3536

**Peggy's Antique Shop**
2205 State Road
717/834-9379

## 40 DUNCANSVILLE

**Duncansville Antique Depot**
1401 2nd Ave.
814/696-4000

**Dodson's Antique Shop**
614 3rd Ave.
814/695-1901

**Creekside Antiques**
1031 3rd Ave.
814/695-5520

**Black Kermit**
1032 3rd Ave.
814/695-5909

**David Donnelly Antiques**
1224 3rd Ave.
814/695-5942

**Don's Antiques**
1324 3rd Ave.
814/696-0807

## 41 EAGLE

**Little Bit Country**
Route 100
(across from Historic Eagle Tavern)
610/458-0363
Mon.-Fri. 10-5; Sat., 11-7; Sun., 12-6
*Directions: Little Bit Country is located just north, approximately 1 1/2 miles of the Pennsylvania Turnpike Exit 23, along Route 100 North.*

This interesting shop, with a name that sounds suspiciously like a country hit song, carries a selection of antiques and primitives that varies. They also handle fabrics and gifts.

## 42 EASTON

**Dylan Spencer Antiques**
200 Northampton St.
610/252-6766

**Barry's New & Used Furniture**
500 Northampton St.
610/250-0220

**Brick House Antiques**
1116 Northampton St.
610/515-8010

**Eagle's Nest Antiques**
1717 Butler St.
610/258-4092

## 43 ELLWOOD CITY

**Marketplace on Main**
402 Lawrence Ave.
724/752-1201

**Into Antiques**
RR 1
724/758-5127

**Gramma's House**
326 6th St.
724/758-4262

## 44 ELVERSON

**Rosalind Lee's Antiques**
S. Chestnut St.
610/286-9869

**Tom E. Fisher**
11 E. Main St.
610/286-6618

**Chamberlain Antiques**
3601 Saint Peters Road
610/469-0894

## 45 EMMAUS

**Twin Jugs Consignments**
4033 Chestnut St.
610/967-4010

**Sweet Memories & Tea Room**
180 Main St.
610/967-0296

**The Tin Shop**
161 E. Main St. (Macungie)
No Phone # Listed

## 46 EPHRATA

Located in the picturesque and well-known Lancaster County, home of the Pennsylvania Dutch, Mennonite and Amish communities, Ephrata was actually settled in 1732, by a German religious society under the leadership of Johann Beissel. The men and women formed the Society of the Solitary Brethren, a semi-monastic order advocating celibacy and favoring common ownership of property, although neither marriage nor private ownership was prohibited. By 1740 the self-sufficient community consisted of 36 brethren and 35 sisters housed in a single building known as the Cloisters. At the height of its prosperity, the community numbered about 300 members. The hymns and experimental melodies of founder Johann Beissel that were published here were a major influence on American hymnology.

After Beissel's death in 1768, John Miller became the head of the community and was commissioned by the U.S. Congress to translate the Declaration of Independence into several European languages. In 1745 the second printing press in Pennsylvania was set up in Ephrata, and Continental money was printed in Ephrata during the British occupation of Philadelphia. After the battle of Brandywine in 1777, the community buildings were used as hospitals. The Society of the Solitary Brethren declined after Miller's death, and today the Cloisters are maintained as a museum by the Pennsylvania Historical and Museum Commission.

Also today, the Route 272 corridor between Ephrata and Adamstown (in the vicinity of Exit #21 on the Pennsylvania Turnpike) is widely known as a flea market haven. Actually called "The Adamstown Antique Mile," it began as a strip of restaurants and motels easily accessible to the turnpike. This area is also the home of Pepperidge Farms, Inc.

**Summer House Antiques**
1156 W. Main St., Route 322
717/733-8989

**Olde Carriage House**
2425 W. Main St.
717/738-2033

**Goods Collectibles**
2460 W. Main St.
717/738-2033

**Mother Tucker's Antiques**
566 N. Reading Road
717/738-1297

**Grandma's Attic**
1862 W. Main St.
717/733-7158

**Three T's Antiques**
Route 272 South @ 322
717/733-6572

**Antiques at Ephrata**
1749 W. Main St.
717/738-4818

**Clay House**
2465 W. Main St.
717/721-9400

### *Great Places To Stay*

**The Inns at Doneckers**
318-324 N. State St.
717/738-9502
Open year round except Christmas
Rates $59-185
*Directions: From the Penn. Turnpike, take Exit #21 and take Route 222 S. to the Ephrata exit. Turn right onto Route 322, which becomes Main St. in Ephrata. Go to the 4th traffic light and turn right onto State St. The inns are about 4 blocks on the left.*

There are four individual inn properties surrounding the Doneckers community here in Ephrata, each within walking distance of Doneckers Fashion Stores for the family and home, and a gourmet restaurant. Also within walking distance in the community is an Artworks Complex of more than 30 studios and galleries of fine art, quilts and designer crafts, and a farmer's markets. If that is not enough for you, the inns are just minutes from Adamstown's antique markets, a short scenic drive from Lancaster County's Amish Farmland and attractions, and are convenient for a day trip to historic Gettysburg.

The four inns together offer 40 rooms (38 with private baths), each one furnished in antiques and hand-stenciled walls, and some rooms have fireplaces and Jacuzzis. Guests get to choose among the Guesthouse, the Historic 1777 House, the Homestead, and the Gerhart House.

### *A sampling of what you'll find at The Inns at Doneckers*

**1777 House at Doneckers**
This late Georgian-style home, which takes its name from the year of its construction, was built by Jacob Gorgas, a clockmaker in the religious Ephrata Cloister community located in Lancaster County in 1777. Later, the house served as a tavern for travelers in Conestoga wagons on their way from Philadelphia to Pittsburgh. The house has been carefully restored, and the original stone masonry, tile flooring and many other authentic architectural details have been saved.

There are 12 guest rooms in this inn (some with fireplaces), all named for brothers and sisters of the Cloister. The adjacent Carriage House offers an additional two suites with lofts.

**The Guesthouse at Doneckers**
Three turn-of-the-century Victorian homes have been artfully joined together to create The Guesthouse at Doneckers, offering 19 uniquely appointed rooms and suites. Fine antiques from Mr. Donecker's personal collection are used throughout the Guesthouse, as well as hand-stenciled walls and antique hooked rugs as art. A cheerful sunroom for relaxing has been added to complement the exisiting parlor, which is centrally located and used for games, reading and television viewing. Suites include a fireplace and/or oversized whirlpool bath for added luxury. Each room includes a private phone and air conditioning. Original Victorian features of the home have been retained, including inlaid wood floors and stained glass windows.

**The Homestead at Doneckers**
Once the residence of the senior Mr. & Mrs. Donecker, this stately home has been restored to four charming suites and rooms, each with mini-refrigerator, remote control cable color television, a fireplace and/or oversized whirlpool bath. Family antiques and local textiles have been used throughout the inn. The Homestead is a non-smoking inn.

**The Gerhart House**
Built in 1926 by local builder Alexander Gerhart, the home features the superior construction methods for which Gerhart was know: inlaid pine floors, frosted, beveled or stained glass and native chestnut doors and trim. The five rooms are perfect for a group to share, with a cozy living room as a shared common area. Many family reunions, getaways among friends, and small retreats have been hosted at The Gerhart House.

## 47 ERIE

**Antique Attractions**
202 E. 10th St.
814/459-0277

**Folly Antique Mall & Guns**
654 W. 26th St.
814/459-2503

**Dempsey & Baxter**
1009 E. 38th St.
814/825-6381

**Erie Antique Store**
1015 State St.
814/454-6256

**A Toy Collector**
1041 W. 31st St.
814/868-0592

**Antiques by Walker House**
1945 W. 26th St.
814/459-0880

**B. T. Antique Gallery**
400 Mill Creek Mall
814/866-8892

**Drumm's Toys & Antiques**
1012 Holland St.
814/455-5257

**Lee's Antiques**
601 W. 17th St.
814/455-9461

**Rage**
613 W. 26th St.
814/456-9931

**Antique Interiors by Dennis Pistone**
1209 State St.
814/455-6992

**Sherifs Imported Rugs**
3854 Peach St.
814/864-6460

**Dennis Pistone Antiques**
1207 State St.
814/454-1510

**Antique Buyer's Gallery**
411 E. 10th St.
814/898-1671

**Collector's Choice**
3421 W. Lake Road
814/838-6833

**Collector's Corner**
3020 Buffalo Road
814/899-5102

**Fine Antiques & Art by Linda**
1648 W. 8th St.
814/459-5927

**Tregler Gallery**
301 Cascade St.
814/454-0315

## 48 EXPORT

**Schmidt's Springhouse Antiques**
Route 66 at Pfeffer Road
724/325-2577, 1-800-771-2684
Tue.-Sat. 10-5, Sun. 1-5, closed Christmas, Thanksgiving, Easter.
*Directions: Located on the west side of Route 66, 5 miles north of Route 22 and 1 1/2 miles south of Route 366.*

For specific information see review at the beginning of this section.

## 49 FRANKLIN

**Franklin Antique Mall & Auction**
1280 Franklin Ave.
814/432-8577

**Haylett's**
338 Grant St.
814/432-5686

**Every Thing**
1335 Liberty St.
814/432-4460

**Angus Antiques**
1581 Pittsburgh Road
814/432-3325

**Knotty Pine Antiques**
304 2nd Ave.
814/432-4193

**Debence Downstairs Mall**
1261 Liberty St.
814/437-6550

**Buttermilk Hill Antiques**
Buttermilk Hill
814/432-5691

## 50 GAP

**Mechanical Musical Memories**
5281 Lincoln Hwy.
717/442-8508

**Gap Village Store**
5403 Lincoln Hwy.
717/442-5263

## 51 GETTYSBURG

Don't ever accuse Southerners of being obsessive about the War Between the States, because there are probably not any folks more immersed in that era than the residents of Gettysburg, Penn.!

There are probably only a handful of Americans who don't know something about this landmark battle of the American Civil War. It took place in July of 1863, and was the turning point of the war and the beginning of the end for the Confederacy. Here, General Robert E. Lee's Confederate army of 75,000 men and the 97,000-man Northern army of General George G. Meade met - by chance - when a Confederate brigade, sent to the area for supplies, observed a forward column of Meade's cavalry.

Of the more than 2,000 land engagements of the Civil War, Gettysburg remains the single great battle of the war. It left us with names forever connected to battle: Seminary Ridge, Cemetery Ridge, Pickett's Charge. After the battle 51,000 casualties were counted, making Gettysburg the bloodiest battle of American history. Although the war raged for another two terrible and savage years, the Confederacy never recovered from the losses at Gettysburg, and Lee never again attempted an offensive operation of such proportions. The tide had turned at Gettysburg.

**T. T. & G.'s Antique Collectible Co-op**
2031 York Road
717/334-0361
Mon.-Sat. 9-4:30; Sun. 12-4:30
*Directions: Located on U.S. 30, 7 miles west of New Oxford Square and 3 miles east of Gettysburg Square, south of the highway.*

T. T. & G.'s is 6,500 square feet of space in an old barn with 25 or more regular dealers. They carry everything from late 18th century Victorian pieces (like Eastlake) to modern. They no longer operate an upholstery shop, but are opening a reproduction room for accessories and furniture. The wood types they handle include oak, mahogany, walnut and pine.

**Time Travel Antiques**
312 Baltimore St.
717/337-0011

**Farnsworth House Inn**
401 Baltimore St.
717/334-8838

**Antique & Collectibles & Curio Shop**
22 Carlise St.
No Phone

**Mel's Antiques & Collectibles**
103 Carlisle St.
717/334-9387

**Arrow Horse**
51 Chambersburg St.
717/337-2899

**Maggie's Another Place & Time**
52 Chambersburg St.
717/334-0325

**Gettysburg Antiques & Collectibles**
54 Chambersburg St.
717/337-0432

**School House Antiques**
2523 Emmitsburg Road
717/334-4564

**Keystone Country Furniture**
2904 Emmitsburg Road
717/337-3952

**Antique Center of Gettysburg**
7 Lincoln Square
717/337-3669

**Hope Springs Antiques**
2540 Mummasburg Road
717/677-4695

**Great Stuff**
45-47 Stienwehr Ave.
717/337-0442

**Magic Town**
49 Steinwehr Ave.
717/337-0492

**Fields of Glory**
55 York St.
717/337-2837

**Antiques & Collectibles Curio Shop**
22 Carlisle St.
No Phone Listed

### *Great Places To Stay*

**The Brafferton Inn**
44 York St.
717/337-3423
Web site: www.bbhost.com/braffertoninn

In the town of historic Gettysburg the Brafferton Inn is one of its gracious landmarks. The elegant 1786 fieldstone home, listed on the National Registry of historic places, has been fully restored to include a private bath for each of the ten guestrooms. Featured in *Country Living*, the inn has exquisite antiques and original artistry throughout.

**Brickhouse Inn**
452 Baltimore St.
1-800-864-3464
Web site: www.brickhouseinn.com

Located in Gettysburg's downtown historic district, guest of The Brickhouse Inn enjoy the comforts of today's living in a style reminiscent of the turn of the century. Throughout the 1898 brick home, family heirlooms and selected antiques combine Victorian grace with modern amenities. Superb hospitality, bountiful breakfasts, exceptional guest comfort and attention to detail are only the beginning of an unforgettable visit to this historic town.

**James Gettys Hotel**
27 Chambersburg St.
717/337-1334

In 1787, the founder of Gettysburg, James Gettys, sold his first piece of land to John Troxell, Sr. In 1804, a tavern "Sing of the Buck" was opened to accomodate those traveling to the western frontier of Pennsylvania and beyond. This structure has served as an inn, tavern or hotel for almost 200 years, and was used as a hospital for the wounded soldiers during the Battle of Gettysburg. In 1888, the third and fourth floors were added to accomodate the veterans as they returned to Gettysburg for the 25th Anniversary of the Battle. From 1888 to the late 1930s, the hotel could accommodate 250 guests a night. The hotel was later used as an apartment building and also a youth hostel. In 1995, the building changed ownership to reopen as the James Gettys Hotel in September, 1996. The building has had nine different names during its 193 years of existence and today each suite is named after a previous business or person who played a significant role in the hotel's history. The James Gettys Hotel offers eleven tastefully appointed suites each with sitting area, kitchenette, bedroom, private bath, and all the comforts of home.

## 52 GIBSONIA

**Atlantic Crossing Antiques**
3748 Gibsonia Road
724/443-5858

**Allagheny Hrtg. Antiques**
5500 Molnar Dr.
724/443-6425

**Jim's Antiques**
Route 8
724/443-4866

**Richland Antiques**
RR 8
724/443-8090

## 53 GILBERTSVILLE

**Shafer's Antiques**
1573 E. Philadelphia
610/369-1999

**Sutterby's Oak Furniture**
Zern's Market - Route 73
610/369-1777

## 54 GIRARD

**What Not Shop**
18 Main St.
814/774-4413

**Westaway's Antiques**
21 Myrtle St.
814/774-2829

**Heartland Antiques & Gifts**
10100 Old Ridge Road
814/774-0344

## 55 GLENSIDE

**Ludwigs Scattered Treasures**
221 W. Glenside Ave.
215/887-0512

**Kirkland & Kirkland**
Keswick Ave.
215/576-7771

**Yesterday and Today**
280 Keswick Ave.
215/572-6926

## 56 GREENSBURG

**J A Henderson Blacksmith, Inc.**
509 S. Main St.
724/838-7656

**Antique Treasures**
Route 22
724/837-4474

## 57 GREENVILLE

**Iron Bridge Shoppe**
108 Main St.
724/588-2455

**Country Store**
220 W. Methodist Road
724/588-9692

**Country Store**
133 Orangeville Road
724/588-5820

**J-Net Antiques & Gifts**
42 Shenango St.
724/588-6361

## 58 HAMBURG

**F & F Shop**
1 N. 4th St.
610/562-7687

## 59 HANOVER

**Nagengast Antiques**
37 Frederick St.
717/633-1148

## 60 HARMONY

**In Harmony**
250 Mercer St.
724/452-0203

**Into Antiques**
280 Perry Hwy.
724/452-3210

**Olde Country House**
575 Perry Hwy.
724/452-0100

**Finders Keepers**
657 Perry Hwy.
724/452-9960

**Bee Four Collectibles**
Route 19 N.
724/452-0922

**Bear Bottom Antiques**
Main St.
724/452-5270

**J. Fox Antiques**
333 Perry Hwy.
724/452-4323

## 61 HARRISBURG

**Antiques at Towne House Gallery**
242 North St.
717/238-4199

**Doehnes Ox Box Shop**
N. Progress Ave.
717/545-7930

**Crafty Generations**
Strawberry Square
717/234-5521

**Medina**
901 N. 2nd St.
717/233-0115

## 62 HAVERFORD

**Mock Fox**
15 Haverford Station Road
610/642-4990

**French Corner Antiques Ltd.**
16 Haverford Station Road
610/642-6867

**Chelsea House Ltd.**
45 Haverford Station Road
610/896-5554

**McClees Galleries**
343 W. Lancaster
610/642-1661

## 63 HAWLEY

Natural resources have played an important part in the history of Hawley. The community was first inhabited in the late 18th century by pioneers who liked the potential of this area where three creeks converged. They settled, built a sawmill, and began sending lumber down the rivers to Philadelphia. The first child of the settlement was born in 1812; the first store opened in 1827; the Delaware & Hudson Canal, running from Honesdale to New York, was completed in 1828, and anthracite coal began moving on barges along towpaths through Hawley to the New York markets.

The area around Hawley saw great prosperity from the 1840s to the 1860s, with the economy continuing to be based around the coal industry to support businesses. In the 1920s, industries began to supplant Hawley's coal and lumber base, including fine cut glass, and silk and textile mills.

Another growth cycle began in 1925 with the introduction of hydroelectric power. The Pennsylvania Power & Light Company dammed the Wallenpaupack Creek and created the state's largest man-made lake, thus changing the focus of the area's industry. The Hawley region became an area of recreational and related business opportunities and continues in this field today.

### Timely Treasures

475 Welwood Ave. (Route 6)
717/226-2838, Fax 717/226-3943
Web site: www.timelytreasures.com
Thurs.-Mon. 10-5, closed Tues. and Wed.

During the late 1800s, the building which now houses Timely Treasures was the town power plant. From this building power was made available to the residents of Hawley who chose to have electricity in their homes. An appropriate site for housing wonderful antiques, the shop has six rooms of antiques from the turn of the century through the 1950s. Their speciality is furniture (1850-1950s) but, the owners also provide a nice selection of cut glass from the brilliant period, china, lamps, pottery (Roseville) and more.

### Castle Antiques & Reproductions

515 Welwood Ave.
1-800-345-1667
Mon.-Sat. 8:30-5
*Directions: Hawley is located between Scranton and Milford, about 45 minutes from Scranton and about 30 minutes from Milford. From Scranton: Take 84E to Exit 6, go left onto Route 507. Go to the end, make a left onto Route 6, and go 1 1/2 miles. Castle Antiques is on the right. From New York state or Milford, Penn.: Take 84W to Penn. Exit 8 (Blooming Grove). Make a right onto Route 402. Go 5 miles to the end, make a left onto Route 6, and go 5 miles. Castle Antiques is on the right.*

You really cannot miss this shop - it looks like a castle! Very appropriately named, Castle Antiques & Reproductions is housed in the historic landmark known as Sherman Mill. It was constructed in 1880 and is the largest bluestone granite building in North America.

The original water-powered mill sits in the picturesque Pocono Mountains, and the unusual stone architecture gives it the appearance of a castle. It was last purchased in 1989 and has undergone extensive renovations to return it to its original beauty. Now it offers 35,000 square feet of showroom space filled with treasures from around the world.

Some of the merchandise shoppers will find at the "Castle" includes American and imported furniture, lighting fixtures, statuary, bronzes, Tiffany style lamps, and general merchandise, both old and new.

**Barbara's Books & Antiques**
730 Hudson St.
717/226-9021

**Antiques & Collectibles**
202 Main Ave.
717/226-9524

**Hawley Antique Center**
318 Main Ave.
717/226-8990

**Decorators Den & Resale**
RR 6
717/226-0440

**Loft Antiques**
RR 590
717/685-4267

## 64 HAZLETON

**Remember When**
2 E. Broad St.
717/454-8465

**Mariano's Furniture & Gifts**
1042 N. Church St.
717/455-0397

**AAA Antiques**
163 Edgerock Dr.
717/455-8331

## 65 HERSHEY

**Canal Collectibles**
22 W. Canal St.
717/566-6940

**Cocoa Curio Historical Militaria**
546 W. Chocolate Ave.
717/533-1167

**Ziegler's Antique Mall**
825 Cocoa Ave.
717/533-7990

### *Great Places To Stay*

**The Hen-Apple Bed & Breakfast**
409 S. Lingle Ave.
717/838-8282
Open year round
Rates $55-65
*Directions: For specific directions to The Hen-Apple Bed & Breakfast, please call ahead. The innkeepers will provide excellent directions from your location.*

A visit to the Hen-Apple is a chance to really enjoy the simple pleasures of country living. This bed and breakfast is a circa 1825 Georgian-style farmhouse situated on an acre of land on the edge of town. A "down home" atmosphere prevails, from the antique and reproduction furnishings to the full country breakfast. There are six guest rooms, all with private baths, plus three common rooms, a screened-in back porch, a front porch and a Wicker Room for guests to enjoy. Or take a stroll among the stand of old fruit trees, or snooze in the hammock or lawn chairs and play with the resident cat. And if and when you feel like exerting yourself, you'll be only minutes away from Hershey, Harrisburg, Gettysburg, Ephrata, Reading, antiques galore, auctions, crafts shops, Amish country, the Mt. Hope Winery, and so on and so on.

## 66 HOLLIDAYSBURG

**Remember When**
1414 Allegheny St.
814/696-4638

**Burkholders Antique Shop**
Route 22
814/695-1030

## 67 INDIANA

**Kemp's Old Mill Antique Shop**
Route 286 N. Box 170
724/463-0644

**Denise's Log Cabin Antique Mall**
Old Route 119 N. & 110
724/349-4001

## 68 IRWIN

**Antiques Odds & Ends**
508 Lincoln Hwy. E., Route 30
724/863-9769
Daily 11-5:30
*Directions: Antiques Odds & Ends is located ½ mile off Pennsylvania Turnpike Exit #7 on Route 30 East.*

Antiques Odds & Ends is a husband-and-wife business. Vince and his wife have been partners for 26 years and were the "first in the State to open up an all-in-one antique shop." (I'm quoting Vince here, so figure this one out on your own.)

I've never personally met Vince, but he and I had a rather nice long chat (over the phone) about the antiques business. When he told me he had been in the "biz" for 26 years, I just had to pick his brain for some tips. This man has an incredible knowledge of antiques! We went on to discuss how sometimes it's very difficult to locate antique shops since most do not advertise. With a chuckle, Vince offered this very clever piece of advice, "A Place Of Business With No Sign, Is A Sign Of No Business."

Vince, Thanks and Here's Your Sign!



**Mays Antiques**
624 Main St.
724/863-1840

**Victoria's Looking Glass**
624 Main St.
724/863-1868

**Attic Treasures**
Route 993
724/863-0338

## 69 JENKINTOWN

**Hidden Treasure**
400 Leedom St.
215/887-4150

**Jeffrey Caesar Antiques**
214 Old York Road
215/572-6040

**Jenkintown Antique Guild**
208 York Road
215/576-5044

## 70 JOHNSTOWN

**Seven Gables Gifts & Antiques**
1404 Dwight Dr.
814/266-7117

**Curiosity Corner**
570 Grove Ave.
814/535-5210

**Greenwood's Antiques & Gifts**
3549 Menoher Blvd.
814/255-5057

**Always Antiques**
125 Truman Blvd.
814/539-0543

**Aardvark Antiques**
7 Bond St.
814/539-0185

## 71 KENNETT SQUARE

**Garrett Longwood**
864 S Baltimore Pike Road
610/444-5257

**McLiman's**
806 W. Cypress St.
610/444-3876

**Clifton Mill Shoppes**
162 Old Kennett Road
610/444-5234

**Antiquus**
120 W. State St.
610/444-9892

**Kennett Square Jewelers**
123 W. State St.
610/444-5595

## 72 KIMBERTON

**Kimber Hall**
Hares Hill Road
610/933-8100

**Corner Cupboard Antiques**
Kimberton Road
610/933-9700

**Thorum's Antiques**
Prizer Road
610/935-3351

## 73 KINZER

### Old Kinzer Firehouse Antiques
3576 Lincoln Hwy. E. (U.S. Route 30)
717/442-1977, 410/323-0445
Email: OKFrhsANTQ@aol.com

2,000-square-foot shop specializing in Mission and Victorian furnishings.

## 74 KUTZTOWN

### Greenwich Mills Antiques
1097 Krumsville Road
610/683-7866
Open: Weekends and by appointment
*Directions: 2 1/2 miles north of Kutztown along Route 737. Between Kutztown and I-78 (exit 12).*

Greenwich Mills Antiques, located in an old 1860s stone grist mill, is filled with local country furniture, primitives, textiles, art and collectibles. (One of my favorite places to shop).

**Renninger's Antiques & Collectibles**
Noble St.
610/683-6848

**Louise's Old Things**
163 W. Main St.
610/683-8370

**Baver's Antiques**
232 W. Main St.
610/683-5045

**Bruce M Moyer & Karen**
276 W. Main St.
610/683-9212

**Colonial Shop**
224 W. Main St.
610/683-3744

## 75 LAHASKA

**Oaklawn Metalcraft Shop**
5752 Route 202
215/794-7387

**Pickets Post**
5761 Route 202
215/794-7350

**Darby-Barrett Antiques**
5799 Route 202
215/794-8277

**Choate & Von Z**
Route 202
215/794-8695

**Lahaska Antique Courte**
5788 York Road
215/794-7884

**Pfeifer Antiques**
5806 Route 202 York Road
215/794-7333

## 76 LANCASTER

### The Antique Market-Place
2856 Lincoln Hwy. E.
717/687-6345
Daily 10-5
*Directions: The Antique Market-Place is located 5 miles east of Lancaster in Soudersburg, across from Dutch Haven, and 2 miles west of Paradise! From the Pennsylvania Turnpike, go south on Route 222 about 18 miles to Route 30. Go east on Route 30 about 8 miles. The mall is about 5 miles east on Lancaster on Route 30.*

This is an interesting shop, full of great pieces and knowledgeable dealers, who operate the store themselves. There are 35 dealers in this large yellow building, all of whom have been there since 1981. In fact, The Antique Market-Place was one of the first full-time antique cooperatives in the area. In the mall's 7,000 square feet you will find country and primitive furniture, glassware, linens, old tools, salts, old games, toys, miniatures, quilts, silver, lamps, china, collectibles, and antique jewelry, among other things.

**Chris' Buy & Sell**
201 W. King St.
717/291-9133

**Book Haven**
146 N. Prince St.
717/393-0920

**Pondoras Antiques**
2014 Old Philadelphia Pike
717/299-5305

**Olde Towne Interiors Inc.**
224 W. Orange St.
717/394-6482

## 77 LANSDOWNE

**Good Old Days Antiques**
201 E. Plumstead Ave.
610/622-2688

**Clock Services**
2255 Garret Road
610/284-2600

**Ye Olde Thrift Shoppe**
213 W. Baltimore Ave.
610/623-3179

**Before Our Time Antiques**
54 W. Marshall Road
610/259-6370

**Ardmart Antique Mall**
State & Landsdowne
610/789-6622

**Henry Gerlach Jewelers**
414 S. State Road
610/449-7600

**Attic Door**
8904 W. Chester Pike
610/446-6690

**Spring House Antiques**
4213 Woodland Ave.
610/623-8898

**Ann's Antiques & Curios**
213 W. Baltimore Pike
610/623-3179

## 78 LEWISBURG

**Lewis Keister Antiques**
209 Market St.
717/523-3945

**Route 15 Flea Market**
Route 15
717/568-8080

**Brookpark Farms Antiques**
RR 45 W.
717/523-6555

**Victorian Lady**
RR 45 W.
717/523-8090

**Lewisburg Roller Mills Marketplace**
517 Saint Mary St.
717/524-5733

**Thomas K Peper Antiques**
Stein Lane
717/523-8080

## 79 LITITZ

**The Workshop**
945 Disston View Dr.
717/626-6031

**Hardican Antiques**
34 E. Main St.
717/627-4603

**House of Unusuals**
55 E. Main St.
717/626-7474

**Garthoeffner Antiques**
122 E. Main St.
717/627-7998

**Sylvan B Brandt**
651 E. Main St.
717/626-4520

**1857 Barn**
Route 322 & Route 501
717/626-5115

**Brickerville Antiques & Decoys**
117 N.E. 28th Divisi Dr.
717/627-2464

**Heritage Map Museum**
55 N. Water St.
717/626-5002

## 80 LITTLESTOWN

**Second Chance Antqs. & Yesterday's Stuff**
4895 Baltimore Pike
717/359-4038

**Betty & Jack's Antiques**
31 W. King St.
717/359-4809

**Grandma Whitman's Country Cupboard**
40 N. Queen St.
717/359-4527

**King and Queen Antiques**
1 S. Queen St.
717/359-7953

## 81 MALVERN

**Conestoga Antiques**
30 Conestoga Road
610/647-6627

**King Street Traders**
16 E. King St.
610/296-8818

**Nesting Feathers**
218 E. King St.
610/408-9377

**Station House Antiques Ltd.**
1 W. King St.
610/647-5193

**Steven's Antiques**
627 Lancaster Ave.
610/644-8282

## 82 MANHEIM

**Noll's Antiques**
1047 S. Colebrook Road
717/898-8677

**Conestoga Auction Co. Inc.**
768 Graystone Road
717/898-7284

**Exit 20 Antiques**
3091 Lebanon Road
717/665-5008

**Country Store Antiques & Museum**
60 W. Main St.
717/664-0022

## 83 MANSFIELD

**Country Trader**
9 N. Main St.
717/662-2309

**Main St. Antiques Co-op**
17 N. Main St.
717/662-2444

**Mansfield Antique Shop**
763 S. Main St.
717/662-3624

**Times Remembered**
Route 6 W.
717/662-3474

**Tin Goose Gift Shop**
14 S. Main St.
717/662-3950

## 84 McKNIGHTSTOWN

### *Great Places To Stay*

**Country Escape Bed & Breakfast**
275 Old Route 30
717/338-0611
Open year round
Rates $65-80
*Directions: From the square in Gettysburg, drive west on Route 30. When you are 5.4 miles from the square, turn left at the small McKnightstown sign onto Old Route 30. Country Escape is the last house on the right in McKnightstown, just past the old post office.*

As innkeeper, Merry Bush, describes it, this is a "laid back" bed and breakfast. Her idea is to get people to relax and enjoy themselves and the beautiful surroundings, but she does offer desktop publishing and faxing services for you "type A" personalities who just can't unwind!

Country Escape offers queen sized beds and all the comforts of home "amid the bucolic setting complete with mountain vistas and flower gardens." After you've refreshed yourself with a good night's sleep and a hearty breakfast, you can browse through the eclectic gift shop at the inn, soak in the hot tub, or explore the many battle sites all around the inn. The inn is located on the road where Confederate forces marched to the battle of Gettysburg.

## 85 MEADVILLE

**Troyer's Antiques**
Baldwin St. Extension
814/724-4036

**Artists Gallery**
245 Chestnut St.
814/336-2792

**Marcia's Mercantile**
9006 Mercer Pike
814/724-8131

**Pine Antique Shop**
988 Park Ave.
814/336-2466

**Unger's Antique Shop**
1197 Pennsylvania
814/336-4262

**Tamarack Treasures**
Springs Road
814/333-2927

# Pennsylvania

## 86 MECHANICSVILLE

**Buck House Antiques**
3336 Durham Road
215/794-8054

**Howard Szmolko Antique Shop**
5728 Mechanicsville Road
215/794-8115

## 87 MECHANICSBURG

**Alexander's Antiques**
6620 Carlisle Pike
717/766-5165

**Rose's Odds & Ends**
123 E. Main St.
717/766-5017

**Veronique's Antiques**
124 S. Market St.
717/697-4924

**Mitrani & Company**
6 State St.
717/766-8367

**White Barn Antiques**
973 W. Trindle Road
717/766-8727

**Country Gifts N Such**
5145 E. Trindle Road
717/697-3555

**Dave & Annie Brown Antiques**
24 Hogestown Road
717/697-6880

## 88 MEDIA

**Hometown Collection**
212 W. Baltimore Pike
610/565-9627

**Fitzgerald Group**
220 W. Baltimore Ave.
610/566-0703

**Remember When Antiques**
21 W. State St.
610/566-7411

**Antique Exchange of Media**
23 W. State St.
610/891-9992

**Atelier**
36 W. State St.
610/566-6909

## 89 MILFORD

**Ann East Gallery**
109 E. Ann St.
717/296-5166

**AAA Quality Antiques**
100 Bennett Ave.
717/296-6243

**Schouppe's Antiques**
100 Bennet Ave.
717/296-6243

**Forrest Hall Antique Center**
Broad & Hartford
717/296-4893

**Antiques of Milford**
216 Broad St.
717/296-4258

**Judy's Antiques**
220 Broad St.
717/296-8626

**Pear Alley Antiques**
220 Broad St.
717/296-8919

**Elizabeth Restucci's Antiques**
214 Broad St.
717/296-2118

**Clockworks**
319 Broad St.
717/296-5236

**110 East Catharine St.**
110 E. Catharine St.
717/296-4288

**Pieces of Time**
Route 663 & Allentown Road
215/536-3135

**Milford Antiques**
Route 663
215/536-9115

## 90 MILLVILLE

**Down on the Farm**
RR 1
717/458-4956

**Cat's Pajamas Vintage Clothing**
Route 42
717/458-5233

**Gay Fisk Ann Antiques**
RR 42
717/458-5131

## 91 MONONGAHELA

**Longwell House**
711 W. Main St.
724/258-3536

**Main Street Antiques**
800 W. Main St.
724/258-3560

**Collectiques**
808 W. Main St.
724/258-4773

## 92 MONROEVILLE

**Flowers in the Attic**
4713 Northern Pike
724/856-7001

## 93 MORGANTOWN

**Cinnamon Stick**
W. Main St.
610/286-7763

**Treasure Hill**
W. Main St. Route 23
610/286-7119

**Antique Collection**
238 W. Main St.
610/286-5244

**Morgantown Antique Center**
325 W. Main St.
610/286-8981

## 94 MORRISDALE

**Chris' Collectibles**
Allport Cut-off Road 1
814/342-3482

## 95 MOUNT JOY

**White Horses Antique Market**
973 W. Main St.
717/653-6338

### *Great Places To Stay*

**Hillside Farm Bed & Breakfast**
607 Eby Chiques Road
717/653-6697
Email: hillside3@juno.com
Web site: www2.epix.net/~bblanco/hillside.htm/
Open year round
Rates $60-75
*Directions: Traveling Route 283 (westbound), take Salunga Exit; (eastbound) take the Salunga Exit. If eastbound, turn right onto Spooky Nook Road. Either way go 1 1/4 miles to Eby Chiques Road.*

*Turn right and go 1/4 mile to Hillside. Hillside Farm is the first place on the right.*

Everything about this charming bed and breakfast is a tribute to the farming area and all the bed and breakfast's immediate neighbors - dairy farms! Hillside Farm B&B is housed in an old (circa 1863) farmhouse, surrounded by an old barn and outbuildings; however, today's owners do not farm and have no farm animals except the barn cats. But they are surrounded by one of the largest areas of farmland left in Lancaster County, which is why it is so peaceful here. Just a half mile down the road is one of the many Amish farms that dot the area, and a one-room schoolhouse. Innkeepers Deb and Gary Lintner can even arrange for guests to eat dinner with an Amish family (with advance reservations) and to see a modern milking at one of the other neighboring farms.

The B&B's "bottle theme" evolved from this dairy history and by an accidental discovery some few years ago. While Gary was cleaning some brush off a bank behind the barn, he noticed something shiny in the ground. Looking closer he discovered 21 unbroken antique milk bottles from different local dairies, most of which stopped operating in the late 1940s. These bottles are now displayed in the dining room.

Along with the bottles, Hillside is furnished with traditional furniture and other dairy antiques. The farmhouse is a two and a half story brick home featuring a standard design of four main rooms on each floor; although over the years, that design has been modified. Now the second floor features bedrooms, each with a view of the surrounding farmland. There are five guest rooms, three with private baths, and a hot tub for six on the porch. Guests get a full breakfast, afternoon snacks, recommendations for dinner, and directions to all the antique shops and malls in the area! Then they can come back to the inn and relax on the balcony that overlooks Chiques Creek with a view of the mill dam and an old generator house. They can listen to the owls, bullfrogs and cows and watch rabbits, squirrels and woodchucks play in the yard and drift off to sleep with the sounds of nature and the country singing their own special lullaby.

## 96 NEW BRIGHTON

**Todd Antiques Plus**
920 3rd Ave.
724/847-0840

**Capo Furniture**
928 3rd Ave.
724/846-0721

**Pennypackers**
1010 3rd Ave.
724/843-3336

**Past and Presents**
1301 3rd Ave.
724/847-3006

**Our Barn Shoppe**
539 Harmony Road
724/847-9100

## 97 NEW HOLLAND

**Frank Cabanas Antiques**
1453 Division Hwy.
717/354-6564

**School House Antiques**
Main St. Route 23
717/455-7384

**Stew Country**
Route 322
717/354-7343

## 98 NEW HOPE

**Pink House**
W. Bridge St.
215/862-5947

**Hobensack & Keller**
57 W. Bridge St.
215/862-2406

**Bridge Street Old Books**
129 W. Bridge St.
215/862-0615

**Ferry Hill**
15 W. Ferry St.
215/862-5335

**Katy Kane Inc.**
34 W. Ferry St.
215/862-5873

**Don Roberts Antiques**
38 W. Ferry St.
215/862-2702

**Kennedy Antiques**
6154 Lower York Road
215/794-8840

**Lehmann Antiques**
6154 Lower York Road
215/794-7724

**James Raymond & Co.**
6319 Lower York Road
215/862-9751

**Francis J Purcell II**
88 N. Main St.
215/862-9100

**Crown & Eagle Antiques Inc.**
Route 202
215/794-7972

**Gardners Antiques**
Route 202
215/794-8616

**Ingham Springs Antique Center**
Route 202
215/862-0818

**Olde Hope Antiques**
Route 202
215/862-5055

**Hall and Winter**
429 York Road
215/862-0831

**Cockamamie's**
9A W. Bridge St.
215/862-5454

### *Great Places To Stay*

**Pineapple Hill Bed & Breakfast**
1324 River Road
215/862-1790, 215/862-5273
Email: www.pineapplehill.com
*Directions: For specific directions from your location, please call the Innkeepers.*

Enjoy the charm of a beautifully restored colonial manor house built in 1790. Set on almost 6 acres, this Bucks County bed and breakfast rests between New Hope's center and Washington Crossing Park.

In the 1700s it was customary to place a pineapple on your front porch as a way of letting friends and neighbors know you were welcoming guests. Pineapple Hill continues this tradition by offering the same hospitality to their guests.

The eighteen inch walls and original woodwork at the historically registered Pineapple Hill exemplify a craftsmanship long forgotten. On the grounds, the ruins of a stone barn enclose a beautiful hand tiled pool.

Breakfast at Pineapple Hill is always the treat. A full gourmet breakfast is skillfully prepared and served in the common room each morning. Breakfast is served from 8a.m. until 10a.m. at individual candle-lit tables. This room is available to use at your leisure - to watch a movie, read a book, or just curl up on a chilly evening in front of the fireplace.

Each of the spacious guestrooms is individually furnished with locally obtained antiques, collectibles, and original artwork. For your reading pleasure, all rooms are well stocked with books and magazines. Three of the guestrooms are accompanied by a separate living room with comfortable furnishings and cable televisions. Located on the second and third floors of the inn, all guestrooms at Pineapple Hill feature private baths for your comfort and convenience.

Pineapple Hill is located deep in the heart of antiquing territory, where treasure hunting at the local shops, auctions and flea markets is readily available. There are also art galleries, theatre and speciality shops all nearby.

## 99 NEW KENSINGTON

**Jolar Inc.**
879 5th Ave.
724/339-4766

**Gifts International**
2517 Leechburg Road
724/339-7075

**Bill's Antiques**
1152 7th St.
412/339-0559

**Howard F. Gordon Antiques**
3049 Bair Road
412/335-7164

## 100 NEW OXFORD

**Hart's Country Antiques**
2 Carlisle St.
717/624-7842

**Sarah's Antiques**
109 Carlisle St.
717/624-9664

**Rife Antiques**
4415 York Road
717/624-2546

**Fountainview Antiques N' Things**
10 Center Square
717/624-9394

**Center Square Antiques**
16 Center Square
717/624-3444

**New Oxford Antique Mall**
214 W. Golden Lane
717/624-3703

**Collectors Choice Antique Gallery**
330 W. Golden Lane
717/624-3440

**Willow Way Enterprises**
390 Gun Club
717/624-4920

**Storms Antiques & Collectibles**
1030 Kohler Mill Road
717/624-8112

**Adam's Apple**
3 Lincoln Way
717/624-3488

**Bill's Old Toys**
19 Lincoln Way E.
717/624-4069

**KEH'R Corner Cupboard**
20 Lincoln Way E.
717/624-3054

**Stonehouse**
100 Lincoln Way E
717/624-3755

**Heartland Antiques & Gifts**
111 Lincoln Way E.
717/624-9686

**Lau's Antiques**
112 Lincoln Way E.
717/624-4972

**Americas Past Antiques**
114 Lincoln Way E.
717/624-7830

**Remember When Shop**
4 Lincoln Way W.
717/624-2426

**Oxford Hall Irish Too**
106 Lincoln Way W.
717/624-2337

**Betty & Gene's Antiques**
110 Lincoln Way W.
717/624-4437

**Oxford Barn**
330 Lincoln Way W.
717/624-4160

**New Oxford Antique Center**
333 Lincoln Way W.
717/624-7787

**Barry Click Antiques**
145 Newchester Road
717/624-3185

**Conewago Creek Forks**
1255 Oxford Road
717/624-4786

**Golden Lane Antique Gallery**
11 N. Water St.
717/624-3800

**Black Shutter Shoppes**
4335 York Road
717/624-8766

**Corner Cupboard**
4335 York Road
717/624-4242

**Week's Antiques**
4335 York Road
717/624-7979

## 101 NEWTOWN

**Nostalgia Nook**
591 Durham Road
215/598-8837

**Hanging Lamp Antiques**
140 N. State St.
215/968-2015

**Temora Farm Antiques**
372 Swamp Road
215/860-2742

**Miller & Co.**
15 S. State St.
215/968-8880

## 102 NORRISTOWN

**Auntie Q's**
403 W. Marshall St.
610/279-8002

**Stephen Arena Antiques**
2118 W. Main St.
610/631-9100

## 103 OLEY

**Shadow Brook Farm Antiques**
Road 2 Box 17C
610/987-3349

**Oley Valley General Store**
Route 73
610/987-9858

## 104 PALMYRA

**Lenny's Antiques & Collectibles**
31 N. Railroad St.
717/838-4660

## 105 PARADISE

**Spring Hollow Antiques**
121 Mount Pleasant Road
717/687-6171

### *Great Places To Stay*

**Creekside Inn B&B**
44 Leacock Road
717/687-0333, Fax 717/687-8200
Web site: www.thecreeksideinn.com

This 1781 stone house is centrally located in the heart of Lancaster County and "Amish Country," peacefully situated on 2 acres along the Pequea Creek. From the porch, you can listen to the sound of horse and buggy passing by as you retire from a busy day of antique shopping and sightseeing. A wide variety of dining choices are nearby, and the innkeepers can also arrange for you to have dinner in an Amish home.

The inn offers relaxing air-conditioned guest quarters appointed with antiques and Amish quilts. There are four second floor rooms and a first floor suite all with private in-room baths. Two of the bedrooms have working stone fireplaces. The warm and welcoming living room with its stone fireplace, or the lattice enclosed porch with rockers, offer guests a chance to socialize and enjoy this countryside inn.

A full country breakfast, featuring home baked treats, local Amish dishes, Lancaster County meats and farm fresh eggs and milk, is served each morning at 8:30 in the two dining rooms. After breakfast the innkeepers can help you plan your day and offer advice on how to see the "Undiscovered Lancaster County."

This is a non-smoking inn. Visa, MasterCard, Discover and personal checks are accepted. They can only accommodate children over 12 and they cannot accommodate pets.

Other nearby attractions include: Adamstown ("Antiques Capital of the USA") - 10 miles, Longwood Gardens - 30 miles, Hershey - 40 miles and Gettysburg - 55 miles.

## 106 PHILADELPHIA

**Stoneman of The Delaware**
Box 15309
215/322-1470

Stoneman of The Delaware is located in the Lambertville Antique Market in Lambertville, N.J. See listing under Lambertville, N.J., #37. When traveling in Philadelphia, you may reach Michael Barnes at the above number.

**Garden Gate Antiques**
8139 Germantown Ave.
215/248-5190

**Watson 20th Century Antiques**
307 Arch St.
215/923-2565

**Blum Chestnut Hill Antiques**
45 E. Chestnut Hill Ave.
215/242-8877

**Antiques at the Secred Garden**
12 East Hartwell Lane
215/247-8550

**Castor Furniture**
6441 Castor Ave.
215/535-1500

**Washington Square Gallery**
221 Chestnut St.
215/923-8873

**Schwarz Gallery**
1806 Chestnut St.
215/563-4887

**David David Gallery**
260 S. 18th St.
215/735-2922

**Tyler's Antiques**
5249 Germantown Ave.
215/844-9272

**Porch Cellar**
7928 Germantown Ave.
215/247-1952

**Antique Gallery**
8523 Germantown Ave.
215/248-1700

**Philadelphia Antique Center**
126 Leverington Ave.
215/487-3467

**Antique Marketplace Manayunk**
3797 Main St.
215/482-4499

**Bob Berman Mission Oak**
4456 Main St.
215/482-8667

**Calderwood Gallery**
4111 Pechin St.
215/509-6644

**Classic Antiques**
922 Pine St.
215/629-0211

**M. Finkel & Daughter**
936 Pine St.
215/627-7797

**G B Schaffer Antiques**
1014 Pine St.
215/923-2263

**Belle Epoque Antiques**
1029 Pine St.
215/351-5383

**Schaffer Antiques Since 1906**
1032 Pine St.
215/923-2949

**Sorger & Schwartz Antiques**
1108 Pine St.
215/627-5259

**Southwood House**
1732 Pine St.
215/545-4076

**Stuart's Stamps**
1103 Cottman Ave.
215/335-0950

**McCarty Antiques**
7101 Emlen St.
215/247-5220

**Chandlee & Bewick**
7811 Germantown Ave.
215/242-0375

**Small's Antique Market**
7928 Germantown Ave.
215/247-1953

**Harvey Wedeen Antiques**
8720 Germantown Ave.
215/242-1155

**Niederkorn Antique Silver**
2005 Locust St.
215/567-2606

**Ida's Treasures & Gifts**
4388 Main St.
215/482-7060

**Philadelphia Trading Post**
4025-35 Market St.
215/222-1680

**Ad Lib Antiques & Interiors**
918 Pine St.
215/627-5358

**Reese's Antiques**
930 Pine St.
215/922-0796

**Antiques & Interiors**
1010 Pine St.
215/925-8600

**Antique Design**
1016 Pine St.
215/629-1812

**Jeffrey L Biber**
1030 Pine St.
215/574-3633

**First Loyalty**
1036 Pine St.
215/592-1670

**Kohn & Kohn**
1112 Pine St.
215/627-3909

**Keith's Antiques Ltd.**
7979 Rockwell Ave.
215/342-6556

**Lock's Philadelphia Gun Exchange**
6700 Roland Ave.
215/332-6225

**Classic Lighting Emporium**
62 N. 2nd St.
215/625-9552

**Architectural Antiques Exchange**
715 N. 2nd St.
215/922-3669

**Scarlet's Closet**
261 S. 17th St.
215/546-4020

**Hampton Court**
6th St. @ Lombard
215/925-5321

**Antiquarian's Delight**
615 S. 6th St.
215/592-0256

**Den of Antiquities**
618 S. 6th St.
215/592-8610

**Bob's Old Attic**
6916 Torresdale Ave.
215/624-6382

**Charles Neri**
313 South St.
215/923-6669

**Celebration Antiques**
416 South St.
215/627-0962

**Mode Moderne**
111 N. 3rd St.
215/923-8536

**Moderne Gallery**
159 N. 3rd St.
215/627-0299

**Calderwood Gallery**
1427 Walnut St.
215/568-7475

**Eberhardt's Antiques**
2010 Walnut St.
215/568-1877

**Urban Artifacts**
4700 Wissachickon Ave.
215/844-8330

**Lumiere**
112 N. Third St.
215/922-6908

### *Great Places To Stay*

**Ten Eleven Clinton**
1011 Clinton St.
215/923-8144
Email: 1011@concentric.net
Rates $115-175

Ten Eleven Clinton is an all-apartment bed and breakfast housed in an 1836 Federal period townhouse in the heart of Philadelphia's historic, cultural and business districts. All the apartments have private baths and queen sized beds, and most have working fireplaces. Breakfast is served to each room and there is a flower-lined courtyard for guests to relax in the summer.

Although the inn is located on a quiet residential street, guests will find themselves only a five-minute walk from the Historic District and Independence Hall, the antique and jewelry districts, Chinatown, the Italian Market, South Street and the Academy of Music, just to name a few. Just a 10 to 15-minute walk brings guests to Penn's Landing Waterfront, the ferry to the New Jersey State Aquarium and Sony Entertainment Center, Rittenhouse Square, Center City shopping district and major department stores. Other area sites and attractions are only a short cab ride away.

## 107 PHOENIXVILLE

**Scioli's Antiques**
235 Bridge St.
610/935-0118

**Somogyi Antiques**
129 Route 113
610/933-5717

**Karl's Korner**
843 Valley Forge Road
610/935-1251

**Bridge Antiques Shop**
234 Bridge St.
610/917-9898

## 108 PITTSBURGH

**Dargate Galleries**
5607 Baum Blvd.
724/362-3558

**Jess This N That**
139 Brownsville Road
724/381-1140

**Etna Antiques**
343 Butler St.
724/782-0102

**Lawrenceville Antiques**
3533 Butler St.
724/683-4471

**Arsenal Antiques**
3803 Butler St.
724/681-3002

**Antiques on North Canal**
1202 N. Canal St.
724/781-2710

**Yesterdays News**
1405 E Carson St.
724/431-1712

**Antique Parlor**
1406 E Carson St.
724/381-1412

**Antique Gallery**
1713 E. Carson St.
724/481-9999

**Andtiques**
1829 E. Carson St.
724/381-2250

**Make Mine Country**
190 Castle Shannon Blvd.
724/344-4141

**Pittsburgh Antique Mall**
1116 Castle Shannon Blvd.
724/561-6331

**Mark Evers Antiques**
4951 Centre Ave.
724/633-9990

**East End Galleries**
600 Clyde St.
724/682-6331

**Caliban Book Shop**
410 S. Craig St.
724/681-9111

**B's South Park Antique Mall**
5710 Curry Road
724/653-9919

**Antiques on Ellsworth**
5817 Ellsworth Ave.
724/363-7188

**Eons**
5850 Ellsworth Ave.
724/361-3368

**Merryvale Antiques**
5865 Ellsworth Ave.
724/661-3200

**Kozloff & Meaders**
5883 Ellsworth Ave.
724/661-9339

**Crown Antiques & Collectibles**
1018 5th Ave.
724/422-7995

**Crimes of Fashion**
4628 Forbes Ave.
724/682-7010

**Cottage Antiques**
231 Freeport Road
724/828-9201

**Avenue Furniture Exchange**
6600 Hamilton Ave.
724/441-8538

**Four Winds Gallery, Inc.**
1 Oxford Center (Level 3)
724/355-0998

**Joys Antique & Estate Jewelry**
Clark Bldg./717 Liberty Ave.
724/261-5697

**Demetrius**
1420 W. Liberty Ave.
724/341-9768

**Antique Exchange**
2938 W. Liberty Ave.
724/341-7107

**Southbery Antiques**
5179 Library Road
724/835-4750

**North Hills Antiques**
1039 McKnight Road
724/367-9975

**Tucker's Books**
2236 Murray Ave.
724/521-0249

**Aunt Nettie's Attic**
2010 Noble St.
724/351-2688

**Classiques**
6014 Penn Circle S.
724/361-5885

**Interior Accents**
6015 Penn Circle S.
724/362-4511

**So Rare Galleries**
701 Smithfield St.
724/281-5150

**Old Steuben Village**
6181 Steubenville Pike
724/787-8585

**Edgewood Station Antiques**
101 E. Swissvale Ave.
724/242-6603

**Antiques Plus**
104 Swissvale Ave.
724/247-1016

**Antique Prints**
5413B Walnut St.
724/682-6681

**Four Winds Gallery Inc.**
5512 Walnut St.
724/682-5092

**Antiques of Shadyside**
5529 Walnut St.
724/621-4455

**Angie's Antique Center**
701 Washington Road
724/343-5503

**Mastracci's Antiques**
802 Wenzell Ave.
724/561-8855

**Allegheny City Stalls**
940 Western Ave.
724/323-8830

## 109 POINT PLEASANT

**Jacques M Cornillon**
56 Byram Road
215/297-5854

**River Run Antiques**
River Road (166)
215/297-5303

**1807 House**
4962 River Road
215/297-0599

## 110 PORTLAND

**Long Ago Antiques**
Delaware Ave.
717/897-0407

**Portland Antiques & Collectibles**
Delaware Ave.
717/897-0129

**Graystone Collectiques**
511 Deleware Ave.
717/897-7170

## 111 POTTSTOWN

**Shaner's Antiques & Collectibles**
403 N. Charlotte St.
610/326-0165

**Bill's Carpet Shop**
1359 Farmington Ave.
610/323-9210

**St. Peter's General Store**
Saint Peters Road
610/469-1000

## 112 POTTSVILLE

**Dave & Julie's Then & Now**
16 N. Centre St.
717/628-2838

**Curious Goods**
556 N. Centre St.
717/622-2173

**Bernie's Antiques**
313 W. Market St.
717/622-7747

## 113 QUAKERTOWN

### Quakertown Heirlooms
141 E. Broad St.
215/536-9088
Jim & Linda Roth, Owners
Daily 10-5, Fri. until 7, closed Sun.
*Directions: From the PA Turnpike: Quakertown Exit Route 663 north to 313 east about 1 1/2 miles. One block after railroad tracks on left corner. From I-78: Route 309 south to 313 east. Same as above.*

Quakertown Heirlooms is an eclectic antique consortium featuring antiques, classic furniture, elegant glass, primitives, collectibles, treasured tomes, and nostalgia. Visa/MasterCard/Personal Checks accepted.

**Trolley House Emporium**
108 E. Broad St.
215/538-7733

**Grandpa's Treasures**
137 E. Broad St.
215/536-5066

**Curio Corner**
200 E. Broad St.
215/536-4547

**Pat & Louis Curiosity Shop**
513 W. End Blvd.
215/536-8248

**Quaker Antique Mall**
70 Tollgate Road
215/538-9445

## 114 READING

**Ray's Antiques & Refinishing**
401 N. 5th St.
610/373-2907

**Weavers Antique Mall**
3730 Lancaster Pike
610/777-8535

**Search Ends Here Antiques**
RR 6
610/777-2442

**Berk's County Antique Center**
Route 222
610/777-5355

**Alternative Furnishing Antiques**
3728 Lancaster Pike
610/796-2990

**Memories**
622 Penn Ave.
610/374-4480

**White's Store Front**
304 N. 5th St.
610/374-8128

## 115 REEDSVILLE

**Old Woolen Mill Antiques**
RR 1
717/667-2173

**Dairy Land Antique Center**
Route 665
717/667-9093

## 116 REINHOLDS

**General Heath's Antiques**
Route 272/Seoudeburg Road
717/484-1300

**Clock Tower Antiques**
Cocalico Road
717/484-2757

### *Great Places To Stay*

**Brownstone Corner B&B**
590 Galen Hall Road
717/484-4460
1-800-239-9902
*Directions: For specific directions from your location, please call the innkeepers.*

Located in northeastern Lancaster County, Brownstone Corner is situated on seven acres amid the farms and old German towns of the "Pennsylvania Dutch." The so-called "Pennsylvania Dutch" are not Dutch at all, but are the descendants of German (Deutsch) Mennonite and Amish settlers who emigrated here in the 1700s. It was one of these descendants who, between 1759 and 1790, built the present three-story brownstone structure.

Today, this unique house still maintains its original colonial charm. Inside, the wide plank wooden floors, lofty windows, and family antique furnishings create a warm, cozy feeling.

The house is sheltered by large, age-old sycamore trees, and the property is surrounded by mature blue spruce and fir trees which afford the guests the privacy they deserve.

Guests are invited to relax in the comfortable setting of the living room where one can read literature about the Old Order Amish, find information on local attractions and activities, or sit back and watch TV or videos.

Start your day with a full, family style breakfast in the large country kitchen with the ambiance of colonial America. Fresh fruit, juice, freshly baked quiche or souffles, home-baked breads and cakes, homemade jellies, and fresh brewed coffee and assorted teas are just an example of the country fare that awaits you after a restful night in this tranquil setting.

Lancaster and Berks Counties offer numerous diverse popular attractions. Among the many reasons people come to this area are to visit Amish farms, antique hunting, shopping at nearby discount factory outlets, or to simply get away from the hectic city life.

## 117 RONKS

**Ja-Bar Enterprises**
2812 Lincoln Hwy. E.
717/393-0098 (business office)
717/687-6208 (shop)
Days and hours of operation vary according to the season!
*Directions: Traveling U.S. Route 30 East out of Lancaster, Penn., cross Penn. Route 896. Continue 1 1/2 miles east to Ronks Road. The shop is located 200 feet east of the intersection, directly across from the Miller's Smorgasbord in the heart of Pennsylvania Dutch Country.0*

The personalities of owners, Jack and Barbara Wolf (especially Jack's), make these shops what they are - fun! Jack is known as Mr. Fun in Lancaster County, also as Mr. Tree - he's been a top tree surgeon for almost 50 years, while Barbara keeps things climbing smoothly in the office of the tree-cutting business.

Together they now have Ja-Bar Enterprises, an eclectic place they bill as "fun shops." They divide their stock into Jack's Junque and Barb's Bric-a-brac and have it scattered about in a collection of small shops that has something for everyone: collectibles, military items, farm items, toys, household items, plus the mainstay of hats and canes. Seems like Jack started collecting hats and canes some 30 years ago and kept his collection on display in the basement of their home. When Barbara gently suggested one day that Jack sell his collection at a public sale, he decided right then that he would open an antique shop. Now he collects and sells his favorites. "I love wood," Jack says, in explanation of his passion for canes and walking sticks. "And hats always have fascinated me." When you catch Jack at the shop, you never know which hat he'll be wearing. He's been known to dress up as a clown and hand out balloons to kids of all ages; on some days he may be decked out in his chef's hat, dishing up some edible treats from the Dutch Hutch outdoor kitchenette that serves fried sweet bologna sandwiches, pork roll sandwiches, hot dogs and drinks.

**The Antique Market-Place**
2856 Lincoln Hwy. E.
717/687-6345
Daily 10-5
*Directions: The Antique Market-Place is located 5 miles east of Lancaster in Soudersburg, across from Dutch Haven, and 2 miles west of Paradise! From the Pennsylvania Turnpike, go south on Route 222 about 18 miles to Route 30. Go east on Route 30 about 8 miles. The mall is about 5 miles east on Lancaster on Route 30.*

This is an interesting shop, full of great pieces and knowledgeable dealers, who operate the store themselves. There are 35 dealers in this large yellow building, all of whom have been there since 1981. In fact, The Antique Market-Place was one of the first full-time antique cooperatives in the area. In the mall's 7,000 square feet you will find country and primitive furniture, glassware, linens, old tools, salts, old games, toys, miniatures, quilts, silver, lamps, china, collectibles, and antique jewelry, among other things.

**Dutch Barn Antiques**
3272 W. Newport Road
717/768-3067

**Country Antiques**
2845A Lincoln Hwy. E.
717/687-7088

## 118 SAEGERTOWN

**Memory Lane Antiques & Collectibles**
211 Grant
814/763-4916

**McQuiston's Main St. Antiques**
440 Main St.
814/763-2274

**Richard J Sheakley**
RR 1
814/763-3399

## 119 SCENERY HILL

**Heart of Country Antiques**
Route 40
724/945-6687

**Little Journeys**
Route 40
724/945-5160

**Pepper Mill**
Route 40
724/945-5155

## 120 SCIOTA

### Halloran's Antiques
Fenner Ave.
717/992-4651
Sat. 12-4, Sun. 9-5, open weekends year round, open daily 11-4 during July and August, also open by chance or by appointment.
*Directions: Traveling I-80, take Exit #46A. Travel south approximately 9 miles and take the exit marked "Route 209 South Lehighton." Take the first exit (Sciota). At the bottom of the exit ramp, make a right turn, then take the second left onto Fenner Ave. Go one block to Halloran's Antiques. Look for the two red barns on the right.*

Hallroan's has two barns full...sort of like "three bags full," only larger! These folks specialize in the purchase of complete local estates and have a great selection of "the unusual" in antiques. They also offer an excellent selection of antique American brass and copper, old holiday items and kitchen gadgets. Halloran's is a family-run business that has been in its same location for over 18 years, so you know that they know what they're doing.

**Collectors Cove Ltd.**
Route 33
717/421-7439

**Yestertiques Antique Center**
Route 209 & Bossardsville
717/992-6576

**Whispers In Time Antiques**
Fenner Ave.
717/992-9387

## 121 SCRANTON

**Sacchetti Enterprises**
1602 Capouse Ave.
717/969-1779

**Originally Yours**
1614 Luzerne St.
717/341-7600

**Alma's Antiques**
921 S. Webster Ave.
717/344-5945

**N B Levy's Jewelers**
120 Wyoming Ave.
717/344-6187

**Garth T Watkins Antiques**
409 Prospect Ave.
717/343-1741

**Wildflower Antiques**
1365 Wyoming Ave.
717/341-0511

## 122 SELINSGROVE

**Dutch Country Store**
6B S. Hwy. 11 #15
717/743-4407

**Gaskins Antiques**
300 S. Market St.
717/374-9275

**Kinney's Antiques**
412 W. Pine St.
717/374-1395

## 123 SEWICKLEY

**Nickelodeon Antiques**
433 Beaver St.
724/749-0525

**Antiquarian Shop**
506 Beaver St.
724/741-1969

**Natasha's**
551 Beaver St.
724/741-9484

**Sewickley Traditions**
555 Beaver St.
724/741-4051

## 124 SHAMOKIN

From a space carved out of rugged, raw wilderness, Shamokin went from a wilderness settlement to the "home" of coal in America. The current town of Shamokin encompasses 400 acres of what used to be mountain forests surrounding a narrow river valley of almost impenetrable swamp, densely covered with pine, hemlock, laurel and rocks, where a tortuously winding river flowed.

The first settlers came in the mid 1700s, with the Old Reading Road that opened in 1770, running through what is now Shamokin in its route between Sunbury and Reading. The town was laid out in 1835, but didn't start growing until 1838, when the western section of the Danville and Pottsville Railroad was completed. By 1839 Shamokin actually looked like a small village, and by 1890 its population was just over 14,000.

Coal was first discovered in Shamokin in 1790, when Isaac Tomlinson picked some pieces out of the earth and took them into a neighboring county for a blacksmith to try. But the ore was not put to practical use until 1810. From this small beginning coal emerged as an industrial weapon, and played a big part in the Industrial Revolution and in the industrial development of Shamokin. By 1889 more than 2.5 million tons of the black rock were being mined by 12,085 men and boys in Shamokin. At the peak of the industrial movement based on coal, Shamokin's population had grown to 16,879. But as the coal industry declined, so did the town's populace, and by the 1990 census there were only 9,184 residents in the town.

### Odds & Ends Store

415 N. Shamokin St.
717/648-2013
Mon.-Sat. 10-5 or by appointment, closed Sun. except by appointment
*Directions: From Harrisburg, Penn., go east on I-78 to I-81. Go north on I-81 to Exit #35/Route 901/Mt. Carmel. Go north on Route 901 to Shamokin, Penn. (approx. 16 miles). At the second traffic light in Shamokin City, turn left onto Shamokin St.*

This shop has over 8,000 square feet of show space and display area in which they offer shoppers everything from primitive and country pieces to items of the 1960s. An enormous selection of antique glassware, pottery and other various collectibles can also be found here.

## 125 SHARON

**Honey House Antiques**
71 N. Sharpsville Ave.
724/981-2208

**Treasure Chest**
110 S. Sharpsville Ave.
724/981-1730

**Tannie's Antiques**
141 E. State St.
724/347-4438

## 126 SHAVERTOWN

**Quilt Racque**
183 N. Main St.
717/675-0914

**The Bay Window Shops**
100 E. Overbrook Road
717/675-6400

## 127 SHREWSBURY

**Shrewsbury Antique Center**
65 N. Highland Dr.
717/235-6637

**Antiques on Shrewsbury Square**
2 N. Main St.
717/235-1056

**Olde Towne Antiques Shrewsbury**
10 N. Main St.
717/227-0988

**Sixteen N. Main Antiques**
16 N. Main St.
717/235-3448

**Full Country Antiques & Collectibles**
21 N. Main St.
717/235-4200

**Antique Sounds**
4 S. Main St.
717/235-3360

**Another Time**
49 N. Main St.
717/235-0664

**Village Studio Antiques**
13 N. Main St.
717/227-9428

## 128 SKIPPACK

**Remains To Be Seen**
4022 Skippack Pike
610/584-5770

**Thorpe Antiques**
4027 Skippack Pike
610/584-1177

**Nostalgia**
4034 Skippack Pike
610/584-4112

**Snyder Antiques**
4006 Skippack Pike
610/584-6454

## 129 SMOKETOWN

### *Great Places To Stay*

### Homestead Lodging

184 E. Brook Road (Route 896)
717/393-6927
Open all year
Tour buses available daily; children welcome; MasterCard/Visa accepted/No pets allowed.
*Directions: Take Route 30 to Route 896 N. The Homestead is located one mile on the left. From the Pennsylvania Turnpike, take Exit #21 to Route 222 South to Route 30 East to Route 896 North. Go one mile and the inn is on the left.*

Here's a place in the country where guests can enjoy clean country air, good country cooking, and interesting country company. Located in the heart of Lancaster County, the Homestead is right in the middle of Amish country. As a matter of fact, guests can hear the clippity-clop of Amish buggies as they go by. There is even an Amish farm down the lane from the inn. But that's not all that's nearby. The inn is located within walking distance of restaurants, and is minutes from farmer's markets, quilt, antique and craft shops, outlets, auctions and museums. All rooms have private baths, color TV, refrigerator, queen & double beds, individually controlled heating and cooling. Complimentary continental breakfast served each morning.

## 130 SOMERSET

**Somerset Antique Mall**
113 E. Main St.
814/445-9690

**Somerset Galleries**
152 W. Main St.
814/443-1369

**Shoemaker's Antiques**
398 W. Patroit St.
814/443-2942

**Bryner's Antiques & Clock Repair**
RR 6
814/445-3352

**Exit 10 Antiques**
RR 7
814/445-7856

## 131 STRASBURG

**William Wood & Son Old Mill**
215 Georgetown Road
717/687-6978

**Iron Star Antiques**
53 W. Main St.
717/392-5175

**James W. Frey Jr.**
209 W. Main St.
717/687-6722

**Sugarbush Antiques**
832 May Post Office Road
717/687-7179

**Spring Hollow Antiques**
121 Mt. Pleasant Road
717/687-6171

**Antiques & Uniques**
1545 Oregon Pike
717/397-9119

**Beech Tree Antiques**
1249 Penn Grant Road
717/687-6881

**Strasburg Antique Market**
207 Georgetown Road
717/687-5624

## 132 STROUDSBURG

**Eleanor's Antiques**
809 Ann St.
717/424-7724

**Lavender and Lace**
350 Main St.
717/424-7087

**Ibi's Antiques**
517 Main St.
717/424-8721

**Olde Engine Works Market Place**
62 N. 3rd St.
717/421-4340

**Log Cabin Antiques**
Route 940 (Pocono Summit)
717/895-1001

### Pocono Bazaar Flea Market

Sat.-Sun. 9-5

*1 mile north of Marshall's Creek on Route 209. Take Route 80, Exit 52.*

One of Pennsylvania's largest and best antiques markets. Open every weekend. Highly recommended.

## 133 SYBERTSVILLE

**Angie's Antiques & Collectibles**
Main St.
717/788-4461

**A Country Place**
Route 93
717/788-2457

## 134 TOWANDA

**Martin's Antiques**
Bailey Road
717/265-8782

**Foster Hall Antiques & Gifts**
512 Main St.
717/265-3572

**Jac's Antiques & Collectibles**
417 State St.
717/265-6107

## 135 TUNKHANNOCK

**Harry's Wood Shop**
RR 6
717/836-2346

**La Torres Antiques**
RR 6
717/836-2021

**Old Store**
RR 6
717/836-6088

**Village Antique Mall**
RR 6
717/836-8713

**Country Classics Gift Shoppe**
19 E. Tioga St.
717/836-2030

**Bygones Antiques & Collectibles**
8 W. Tioga St.
717/836-5815

**Marcy A. Rau Antiques**
11 E. Tioga St. (Route 6)
717/836-3052

## 136 UNIONTOWN

**Country Stroll Antiques & Collectibles**
RR 119 S.
724/438-2700

## 137 VALENCIA

**Larry Fox Antiques**
124 Mekis Road
724/898-1114

**Wagon Wheel Antiques**
Route 8
724/898-9974

## 138 VANDERGRIFT

**Odyssey Gallery Antiques**
110 Grant Ave.
724/568-2373

**Grant Ave. Express Antiques**
124 Grant Ave.
724/568-2111

**Vantiques**
140 Lincoln Ave.
724/567-5937

## 139 VERONA

**Allegheny River Arsenal Inc.**
614 Allegheny River Blvd.
724/826-9699

**Ages Ago Antiques**
722 Allegheny River Blvd.
724/828-9800

**Three Antiques**
760 Allegheny River Blvd.
724/828-8140

## 140 VOLANT

**Volant Mills**
Main St.
724/533-5611

**Leesburg Station Antiques**
1753 Perry Hwy.
724/748-3040

**Something Different**
RR 19
724/748-4134

**Wayne's World**
RR 19
724/748-3072

## 141 WARREN

**McIntyre's Antiques**
334 Pennsylvania Ave. W.
814/726-7011

**Steppin Back Antiques**
1208 Pennsylvania Ave. E.
814/726-9653

**Antiques Kinzua Country**
102 Pennsylvania Ave. W.
814/726-0298

## 142 WASHINGTON

**Antiques Downtown**
88 S. Main St.
724/222-6800

**Old Pike Antique Center**
438 E. National Pike
724/228-6006

**Krause's**
97 W. Wheeling St.
724/228-5034

## 143 WAYNE

**Wilson's Main Line Antiques**
329 E. Constoga
610/687-5500

**Golden Eagle Antiques**
201 E. Lancaster Ave.
610/293-9290

**Old Store**
238 E. Lancaster Ave.
610/688-3344

**Pembroke Shop**
167 W. Lancaster Ave.
610/688-8185

**Knightsbridge Antiques Ltd.**
121 N. Wayne Ave.
610/971-9551

## 144 WAYNESBORO

**Andy Zeger Antiques**
32 E. Main St.
717/762-6595

**Antique Market**
86 W. Main St.
717/762-4711

## 145 WELLSBORO

**Etc. Antiques Station**
5 East Ave.
717/724-2733

**Country Owl Florist**
15 Queen St.
717/724-6355

**Stefanko's Has Good Stuff**
RR 6
717/724-2096

## 146 WEST CHESTER

**Woman's Exchange**
10 S. Church St.
610/696-3058

**My Best Junk**
622 E. Gay St.
610/429-3388

**Sunset Hill Jewelers**
23 N. High St.
610/692-0374

**Baldwin's Book Barn**
865 Lenape Road
610/696-0816

**T. Newsome & Morris Antiques**
106 W. Market St.
610/344-0657

**Herbert Schiffer Antiques Inc.**
1469 Morstein Road
610/696-1521

**Fleury Olivier Inc.**
708 Oakbourne Road
610/692-0445

**Palma J Antiques**
1144 Old Wilmington Pike
610/399-1210

**R M Worth Antiques**
1388 Old Wilmington Pike
610/388-2121

**H L Chalfant Antiques**
1352 Paoli Pike
610/696-1862

**My Best Junk**
500 N. Pottstown Pike
610/524-1116

**Coldren Monroe Antiques**
723 E. Virginia Ave.
610/692-5651

### *Great Places To Stay*

**The Bankhouse Bed & Breakfast**
875 Hillsdale Road
610/344-7388

The Bankhouse B&B is an 18th century "bankhouse" nestled in a quiet country setting overlooking a field and pond. The rooms are charmingly decorated with country antiques, stenciling, folk art and handmade quilted wall hangings. The Bankhouse is ideally located; you can reach either Philadelphia (downtown or airport) and Lancaster within 45 minutes.

## 147 WEXFORD

**Wexford General Store Antique Center**
150 Church Road
724/935-9959

**North Hills Antique Gallery**
251 Church Road
724/935-9804

**Ruth Arnold Antiques**
End of Baur Road off English
724/935-3217

**Antique Treasures of Wexford**
10326 Perry Hwy. Route 19
724/934-8360

**Scharf's Antiques**
511 Wallace Road
724/935-3197

**Red Chimney Antiques & Millies**
Warrendale Bakerstown Road
724/935-1990

**Foster's Antique Shop**
181 Route 910
724/935-2206

## 148 WILKES-BARRE

**A A G International**
1266B Sans Souci Pkwy.
717/822-5300

**Penn Floral & Antiques**
235 Scott St.
717/821-1770

## 149 WILLIAMSPORT

**Cillo Antiques & Coins**
11 W. 4th St.
717/327-9272

**Harrar House**
915 W. 4th St.
717/322-2900

**Canterbury House Antiques**
315 S. Market St.
717/322-2097

**Do Fisher Antiques & Books**
345 Pine St.
717/323-3573

**Lycoming Creek Trading Co.**
RR 4
717/322-7155

**D. Keller Merchant**
152 W. 4th St.
717/322-7001

**Edmonston's Old Style Furniture**
2705 Euclid Ave.
717/323-1940

## 150 YORK

**The York Antiques Fair**
Jim Burk Antique Shows
3012 Miller Road
Washington Boro, Pa. 17582
717/397-7209
For information on show dates
call the number listed above

**Antique Center of York**
190 Arsenal Road
717/846-1994

**Pantry Antiques**
314 Chestnut St.
717/843-5383

**Leon Ness Jewelry Barn**
2695 S. George St.
717/741-1113

**Paul L. Ettline**
3790 E. Market St.
717/755-3927

**Dec-Art Antiques**
1419 W. Market St.
717/854-6192

**Kennedy's Antiques**
4290 W. Market St.
717/792-1920

**J & J Plitt Furniture. & Antiques**
2406 N. Sherman St.
717/755-4535

**York Tailgate Antiques Show**
Barry Cohen, Manager
P.O. Box 9095
Alexandria, Va. 22304
703/914-1268
For information on show dates
call the number listed above

**Bernie's What-Nots**
7129 Carlisle Pike
717/528-4271

**Antique Fishing Tackle Shoppe**
133 N. Duke St.
717/845-4422

**Almost Anything**
500 Hanover Road
717/792-4386

**Thee Almost Anything Store**
324 W. Market St.
717/846-7926

**Dennis' Antiques**
1779 W. Market St.
717/845-2418

**Wish-N-Want Antiques**
4230 N. Susquehanna Trail
717/266-5961

**Olde Factory Antique Market**
204 S. Sumner St.
717/843-2467

***Great Places To Stay***

### Friendship House Bed and Breakfast

728 E. Philadelphia St.
717/843-8299

Although the house was built in 1897, it wasn't until June of 1992 that it was opened to the public as Friendship House Bed and Breakfast. The master room or Philadelphia Room is of country decor with a private bath connected. The Rose Room has a taste of Victorian with black, pinks, and white. Finally, the Young at Heart Room is decorated with toys, a school desk, and a single, metal bed. Just off this room is the original bath, complete with the original tub and wainscoting. Breakfast is served in the spacious and bright country kitchen, or outside in the private yard. A perfect place to stay while attending the York Antiques Shows.

## 151 ZELIENOPLE

**Andrea's**
110 N. Main St.
724/452-4144

**Thru Time**
107 E. New Castle St.
724/452-2270

**Main Street Antiques**
204 S. Main St.
724/452-8620

**Vanwhy's Antiques**
300 S. Main St.
724/452-0854

# Rhode Island

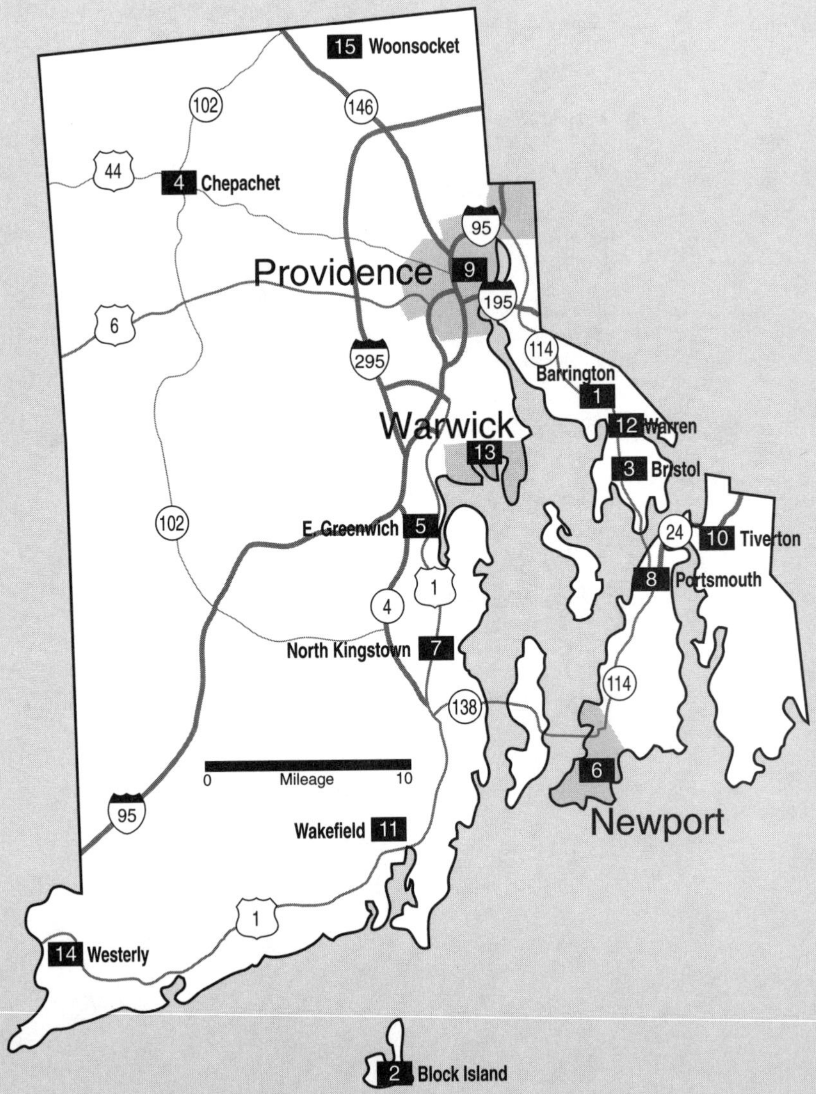
15 Woonsocket
102
146
44
4 Chepachet
95
Providence
9
195
6
114
295
Barrington
1
Warwick
12 Warren
13
3 Bristol
102
E. Greenwich
5
24
10 Tiverton
8 Portsmouth
1
4
North Kingstown
7
114
138
0
Mileage
10
6
95
Newport
Wakefield
11
1
14 Westerly
2 Block Island

*Collectable crockery remains on the shelves for only a short time at The Island Exchange. Mixing bowls are a special favorite of the customers.*

*Pine, maple, cherry and oak furniture is stocked by Dodie Sorenson, along with the treasures of over 300 consignors.*

# Sail in to The Island Exchange for collectors' bounty

This uniquely located shop brings to its customers furniture, china, glassware, collectibles and housewares. Items may be antique or merely second-hand, according to Dodie Sorensen the store owner. However, the selection is varied with new pieces arriving daily.

*Tasteful groupings enhance display*

At any one time, there are items belonging to 300-350 consignors in addition to store-owned specialties such as pine, maple, cherry and oak furniture, white ironstone and wonderful old utilitarian crockery (mixing bowls are the favorite). Turnover is fast and the shop changes noticeably from week to week especially in the spring, fall and summer.

Dodie relates a charming story of determination regarding the shop. "Even though The Island Exchange is on an island at sea, there is always a way to get that special item home. A few years ago, a couple bought a huge spinning wheel and the matching yarn winder, but they were traveling on their sailboat. The resourceful husband had a taxi bring the items to the marina dock where he loaded them into a borrowed dinghy and then towed it behind his own dinghy out to the sailboat at its mooring in the harbor. Safely stowed away, the spinning wheel sailed away to its new home, leaving a harbor full of astonished spectators behind."

*The Island Exchange is located at Ocean Ave. on Block Island. For additional information see listing #2 (Block Island).*

*From split oak baskets and utilitarian crockery, to accents such as decorative mirrors and the perfect side chair, The Island Exchange is filled with tempting wares.*

## 1 BARRINGTON

**The Stock Exchange & The Annex**
57 Maple Ave. & 232 Wascca Ave.
401/245-4170
Tues.-Sat. 10-4, Thurs. open until 7 p.m., Sun. 12-4, closed Mon.
*Directions: From Route 95 north or south - Take 195 east to Barrington exit - Route 114 south. Follow Route 114 for 8 miles. Coming into the center of Barrington, the Town Hall will be on your left. Take a right at the light onto Maple Ave. The Stock Exchange is the 5th building on the right. From Newport - Cross the Mt. Hope Bridge into Bristol, bear left after the bridge onto Route 114 N., pass through the center of Bristol, then the center of Warren and over two small bridges into Barrington. At the 4th light turn left onto Maple Ave. The Stock Exchange is the 5th building on the right. The Annex is two blocks away; just continue past The Stock Exchange on Maple Ave., at the corner of West St. take the first left at Vienna Bakery. Then two blocks down turn left onto Wascca Ave.*

The proprietor, Jennifer LaFrance, has developed The Stock Exchange, established in 1977, into Rhode Island's premiere consignment store for fine home furnishings and antiques. Enjoying another successful year, The Stock Exchange found itself bursting at the seams. With no room to expand at the original location, Jennifer opted to open a second location within the same town. The Annex, just two blocks away, offers a larger selection of fine furniture and features a cozy reading nook with an ever changing variety of pre-owned books. The perfect place to spend a rainy afternoon.

The Stock Exchange & Annex continues to consign and sell countless household items, including but not limited to: furniture, lamps, linens, china, silver, crystal, glassware, pictures, rugs, tools, pots and pans. Jennifer loves to keep the store interesting and diverse, so they welcome a wide range of consignable items at affordable prices. Attorneys, estate planners, trust officers and realtors have come to realize what a valuable asset the store can be. The Stock Exchange & Annex specializes in buying and removing entire households and estates. Jennifer and her staff invite you to visit and wander through five floors and two locations of fine home furnishings and antiques. Jennifer guarantees you will be planning your next visit before you leave.

**Hearts & Flowers Antiques**
270 County Road
401/247-0770

**Antique Depot**
40 Maple Ave.
401/247-2006

**House of Windsor**
233 Waseca Ave.
401/245-7540

**Barrington Place Antiques**
70 Maple Ave.
401/245-4510

## 2 BLOCK ISLAND

Block Island is one of Rhode Island's scenic wonders. This rustic and pristine island was rated one of the twelve best unspoiled areas in the Western Hemisphere. A short ferry ride brings you to a place where you can enjoy spectacular vistas from awe-inspiring bluffs. It is ideal for visitors seeking lighthouses, delightful inns, and peace and quiet.

**The Island Exchange**
Ocean Ave.
401/466-2093
June 15-Labor Day, 7 days a week, 1-5; Labor Day-June 15, open most Sat., Sun., and Mon. holidays, 1-5
*Directions: To reach Block Island by ferry—From Route 95 N., take Exit 92; turn right on Route 2, and proceed to Route 78 (westerly bypass). Follow Route 78 to end; go left on Route 1, and travel east to Narragausett. Exit at sign for Block Island Ferry, turn right, then right again onto Route 108, then right to Galilee. From 95 S., Exit 9 onto Route 4 south, to 1 S., to Narragausett and to Route 108 south, to Galilee.*

For specific information see review at the beginning of this section.

### *Great Places To Stay*

**The 1661 Inn & Hotel Manisses**
One Spring St.
1-800-MAN-ISSE
Email: biresorts@aol.com

The Hotel Manisses was built in 1872 as the ideal holiday destination and today still retains its stature as a premier hotel on the island. The hotel's seventeen rooms and parlors have been furnished with Victorian antiques. All of the rooms provide private baths, and in addition, a number of rooms feature a luxurious whirlpool tub. A Victorian landmark, the hotel boasts of an elegant dining room, known as one of the finest places to dine on the island. The Top Shelf Bar, located in the parlor, is celebrated for its tableside flaming coffees.

## 3 BRISTOL

**Stickney & Stickney Antiques**
295 Hope St.
401/254-0179

**Alfred's Annex**
331 Hope St.
401/253-3465

**Gift Unique**
458 Hope St.
401/254-1114

**Dantiques**
676 Hope St.
401/253-1122

**Center Chimney**
39 State St.
401/253-8010

**Jesee-James Antiques**
44 State St.
401/253-2240

### *Great Places To Stay*

**Williams Grant Inn**
154 High St.
1-800-596-4222

Just two blocks from Bristol's unspoiled harbor you'll find the Sea Captain's House that Deputy Governor William Bradford granted to his grandson in 1808. Mary and Mike Rose restored and remodeled the five-bay colonial/federal house, turning it into a gracious, beautifully appointed inn decorated with traditional and folk art. Breakfasts are always a treat, with home-baked goodies, fresh fruit and perhaps Mike's Huevos Rancheros or Mary's Pesto Omelets.

## 4 CHEPACHET

**Harold's Antique Shop**
1191 Main St.
401/568-6030

**Stone Mill Antique Center**
Main St.
401/568-6662

## 5 EAST GREENWICH

**Hill & Harbour Antiques**
187 Main St.
401/885-4990

**Shadow of Yesteryear**
307 Main St.
401/885-3666

**Gallery 500**
500 Main St.
401/885-6711

**Antique Boutique**
527 Main St.
401/884-3800

**Country Squire Antiques**
Main St.
401/885-1044

## 6 NEWPORT

**What Not Shop**
16 Franklin St.
401/847-4262

**Newport Book Store**
116 Bellevue Ave.
401/847-3400

**Exotic Treasures**
622 Thames St.
401/842-0040

**Bellevue Antiques**
121 Bellevue Ave.
401/846-7898

**Courtyard Antiques**
142 Bellevue Ave.
401/849-4554

**Newport China Trade**
8 Franklin St.
401/841-5267

**Patina**
26 Franklin St.
401/846-4666

**J. B. Antiques**
33 Franklin St.
401/849-0450

**Ramson House Antiques**
36 Franklin St.
401/847-0555

**A & A Gaines**
40 Franklin St.
401/849-6844

**Alice Simpson Antiques**
40 ½ Franklin St.
401/849-4252

**Smith Marble, Ltd.**
44 Franklin St.
401/846-7689

**Lee's Wharf Eclectics**
5 Lees Wharf
401/849-8786

**Lamp Lighter Antiques**
42 Spring St., #5
401/849-4179

**Renaissance Antiques**
42 Spring St., #7
401/849-8515

**New England Antiques**
60 Spring St.
401/849-6646

**Nautical Nook**
86 Spring St.
401/846-6810

**Harbor Antiques**
134 Spring St.
401/848-9711

**Michael Westman**
135 Spring St.
401/847-3091

**Drawing Room**
152 Spring St.
401/841-5060

**Forever Yours**
220 Spring St.
401/841-5290

**Armory Antique Center**
365 Thames St.
401/848-2398

**Prince Albert's Victorian**
431 Thames St.
401/848-5372

**AArdvark Antiques**
475 ½ Thames St.
401/849-7233

### *Great Places To Stay*

**Castle Hill Inn & Resort**
590 Ocean Dr.
401/849-3800
Web site: www.castlehillinn.com

Castle Hill is located on a forty-acre peninsula at the west end of Newport's world-renowned Ocean Dr. The inn offers guests the romance, seclusion, and extraordinary beauty of a private oceanfront resort. An elegantly restored Victorian mansion overlooking Narragansett Bay and quaint beach cottages nestled along the coastline provide an enchanting escape from the outside world.

**Inn at Shadow Lawn**
120 Miantonomi Ave.
1-800-352-3750
Web site: www.bbhost.com/innatshadowlawn

From the moment you step through the door you know there's something special about The Inn at Shadow Lawn. A quiet place, yet convenient to Newport's attractions, the Inn at Shadow Lawn reflects the grace and style of Newport's yesterday while providing the modern comforts of today.

## 7 NORTH KINGSTOWN

**Lavender & Lace**
4 Brown St.
401/295-0313

**Wickford Antique Center II**
93 Brown St.
401/295-2966

**Apple Antiques**
11 Burnt Cedar Dr.
401/295-8840

**Lillian's Antiques**
7442 Post Road
401/885-2512

**Lafayette Antiques**
814 Ten Rod Road
401/295-2504

**Antique Center**
1121 Ten Rod Road
401/294-9958

**Mentor Antiques**
7512 Post Road
401/294-9412

## 8 PORTSMOUTH

**Stock & Trade**
2771 E. Main Road
401/683-4700

**Caron & Co. Antiques & Decor**
980 E. Main Road
401/683-4560

**Eagle's Nest Antique Center**
3101 E. Main Road
401/683-3500

## 9 PROVIDENCE

In Providence, scores of 18th century homes line Benefit Street's "Mile of History." The most famous are the palatial Gilded Age Newport mansions that were once the summer "cottages" of New York's wealthiest families

**Benefit Street Gallery**
140 Wickenden St. FL l
401/751-9109

**Providence Antique Center**
442 Wickenden St.
401/274-5820

**Alaimo Gallery**
301 Wickenden St.
401/421-5360

**Eastwick Antiques**
434 Wickenden St.
No Phone # Listed (new business)

**Angell Street Curiosities**
183 Angell St.
401/455-0450

**Lee Hartwell**
141 Elmgrove Ave.
401/273-7433

**Carole's Antiques**
219 Lenox Ave.
401/941-8680

**Boulevard Antiques**
773 Blackstone Blvd.
401/273-4934

**Doyle's Antiques**
197 Wickenden St.
401/272-3202

**This & That Shoppe**
236 Wickenden St.
401/861-1394

**Antiques at India Point**
409 Wickenden St.
401/273-5550

**Antiques & Artifacts**
436 Wickenden St.
401/421-8334

**Robert's Gallery**
777 Westminister St.
401/453-1270

**Forgotten Garden**
60 Gano St.
401/453-3650

**Jerry's Gallery**
5 Traverse St.
401/331-0558

**Philip Zexter Antiques**
460 Wickenden St.
401/272-6905

**Providence Antique Center**
442 Wickenden St.
401/274-5820

### *Great Places To Stay*

**Charles Hodges House**
19 Pratt St.
401/861-7244

In the heart of Providence's east side, the Charles Hodges House is an impressive Federal home built by a coal merchant in 1850. Wide pine floors set off the extensive decor of the 19th century antique furnishings and memorabilia. Two rooms accommodate guests in cozy comfort. Breakfast is served on a huge oak table that came from the state capitol, or, in good weather, on the flower laden porch under a spreading ash tree. Visitors are one block from Benefit St., which features some of America's finest colonial architecture.

## 10 TIVERTON

**Past & Presents Tearoom**
2753 Main Road
401/624-2890

**Country Cabin**
3964 Main Road
401/624-2279

**Peter's Attic**
3879 Main Road
401/625-5912

## 11 WAKEFIELD

**Olde Friends Antiques**
355 Main St.
401/789-1470

**Dove & Distaff Antiques**
365 Main St.
401/783-5714

## 12 WARREN

**Fortier's Antiques**
Route #136
401/247-2788

**Country Antique Shop**
382 Market St.
401/247-4878

**Water Street Antiques**
149 Water St.
401/245-6440

**Crosstown Antiques**
309 Market St.
401/245-9176

**Warren Antique Center**
5 Miller St.
401/245-5461

**Tony Cellar**
23 Market St.
401/245-2020

## 13 WARWICK

**Clock Shop**
667 Bald Hill Road
401/826-1212

**Antique Haven**
30 Post Road
401/785-0327

**Pontiac Mill Antiques**
334 Knight St.
401/732-3969

**Pre-Amble Consignments**
2457 Post Road
401/739-8886

**Apponaug Village Antiques**
3159 Post Road
401/739-7466

**Antique & Decorating Warehouse**
626 Warwick Ave.
401/461-0008

**Golden Heart Antiques**
1627 Warwick Ave.
401/738-2243

**Brown Dog Antiques**
334 Knight St.
402/826-1007

**Riklyn Collectibles**
2260 W. Shore Road
401/738-3939

**Golden Era Antiques**
858 W. Shore Road
401/738-2518

**Aable Antiques**
1615 Warwick Ave.
401/738-6099

**Emporium**
1629 Warwick Ave.
401/738-8824

**Treasure Barn Antiques**
334 Knight St.
401/736-9773

## 14 WESTERLY

**Mary D's Antiques & Collectibles**
3 Commerce St.
401/596-5653

**Riverside Antiques**
8 Broad St.
401/596-0266

**Frink's Collectables**
271 Post Road
401/322-4055

**Buried Treasures**
12 Canal St.
401/596-6633

## 15 WOONSOCKET

**The Corner Curiosity Shoppe**
279 Greene St.
401/766-2628

**Main Street Antiques & Collectibles**
32 Main St.
401/762-0805

**L'Antiques & Decoys**
489 Diamond Hill Road Route 114
401/767-3336

**Vazinan's Antique Marketplace**
101 Main St.
401/762-9661

# South Carolina

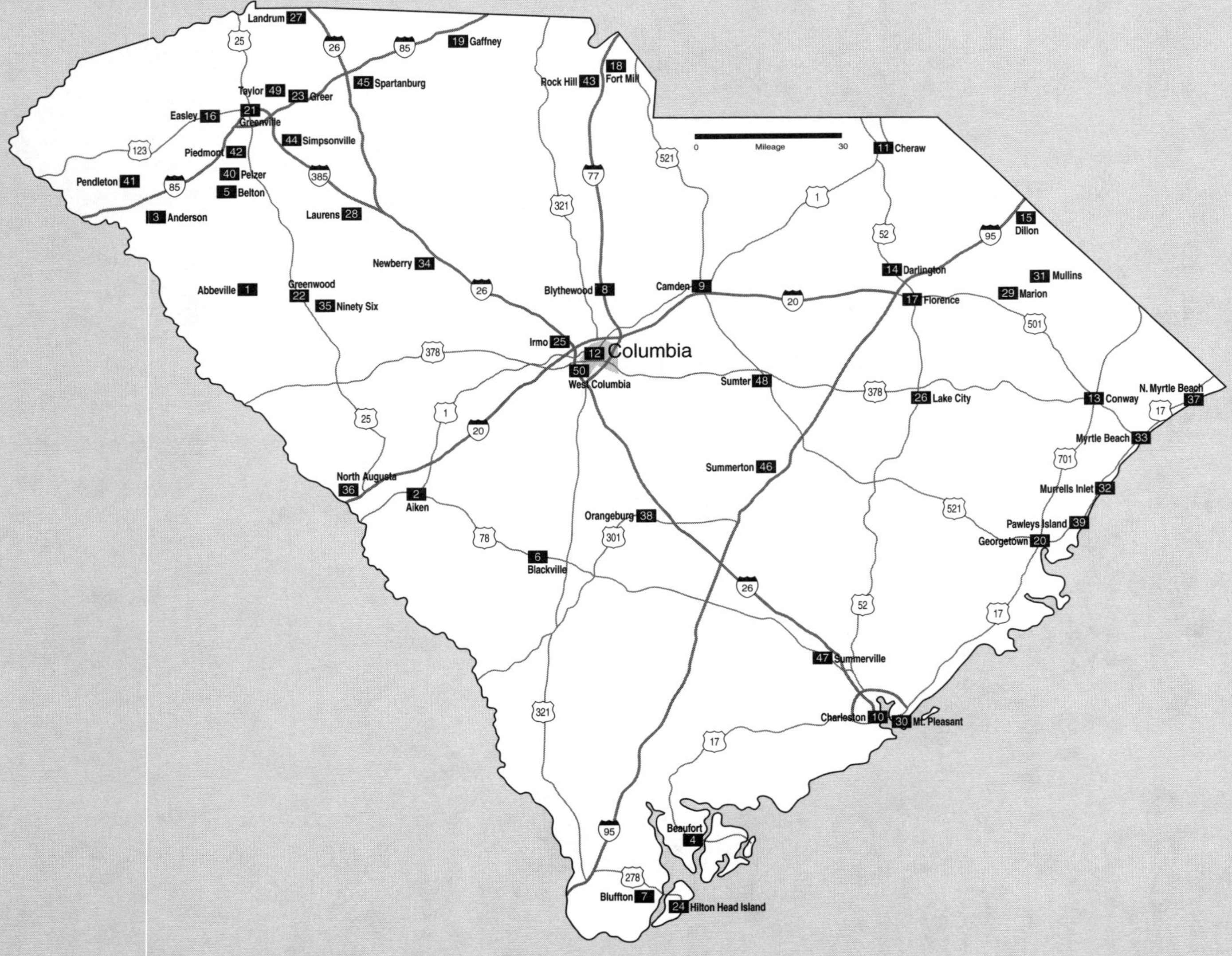

## 1 ABBEVILLE

**Edith's Decor House & Attic Antiques**
Court Square
864/459-5222

**Emporium**
115 Trinity St.
864/459-5388

**Bagwell's Furniture Warehouse**
130 Trinity St.
864/459-5861

**Collectors Antique Mall Abbeville**
300 S. Main St.
864/459-5935

**Miriam's Southern Accents**
128 Trinity St.
864/459-5995

## 2 AIKEN

### Aiken Antique Mall

112-114 Laurens St. S.W.
803/648-6700
Mon.-Sat. 10-6, Sun. 1-6
*Directions: Two doors from the intersection of State Hwys. 1 and 78.*

Fifty dealers fill 13,000 square feet in this old department store building. A variety of antiques such as kitchen items, period furniture, cut glass, art glass, crystal, silver, primitives, painted furniture, vintage books and Civil War relics may be found here. One dealer specializes in old hunting and fishing collectibles with a large quantity of old fishing lures. Another dealer is a local artist and historian, displaying prints and paintings that are historically correct.

### Swan Antique Mall

3557 Richland Ave. W.
803/643-9922
Mon.-Sat. 10-5:30, closed Sun.
*Directions: From I-20, exit onto Hwy. 1 and go 4 miles into Aiken.*

With 35 dealers and 20,000 square feet, this easily accessible mall carries all types of antiques and collectibles. They offer their customers very good prices, friendly service, and a huge parking area.

**York Cottage Antiques**
809 Hayne Ave. S.W.
803/642-9524

**Sanford Oaks Ltd.**
Laurens St. S.W.
803/641-1168

**Antique Mall-Market Place**
343 Park Ave. S.W.
803/648-9696

**Memory Lane Antiques**
2483 Williston Road
803/652-3096

## 3 ANDERSON

**Brookgreen Courts**
311 N. Main St.
864/225-3126

**Bee Hive**
510 N. Main St.
864/225-2377

**Belinda's Antique Mall & Jewelry**
711 S. Main St.
864/224-0938

**Highland House Interiors**
1307 North Blvd.
864/226-4626

**Eason's Antiques & Linens**
2711 Whitehall Ave.
864/226-0415

**Avenue of Oaks Antiques**
2409 S. Main St.
864/225-8530

**McDowell's Emporium**
104 Oak Dr.
864/231-8896

## 4 BEAUFORT

**Rhett Gallery**
901 Bay St.
843/524-3339

**Michael Rainey Antiques**
702 Craven St.
843/521-4532

**Consignors Antique Mall**
913 Port Republic St.
843/521-0660

**Bellavista Antiques & Interior**
206 Carteret St.
843/521-0687

**Chitty & Co.**
208 Carteret St.
843/524-7889

**Sturdy Beggar**
900 Port Republic St.
843/521-9006

**Past Time**
205 Scott St.
843/522-8881

**Den of Antiquity**
330 Hwy. 170 W.
843/521-9990

## 5 BELTON

**Ox Yoke Antiques**
3023 Hwy. 29 N.
864/261-3275

## 6 BLACKVILLE

**Parrott's Antiques & Gifts**
108 Lartigue St.
803/284-3670

### *Great Places To Stay*

### Floyd Manor Inn

111 Dexter St., Hwy. 78
803/284-3736
Open year round
*Directions: Located on Hwy. 78 between Charleston, S.C. and Atlanta, Ga.*

A stay at Floyd Manor Inn is a true step back into the luxurious "Old South" of movies and books. Located on the edge of South Carolina's famous Thoroughbred Country, Floyd Manor was built around 1886 as the manor house of an 8,000 acre plantation in the west central section of the state.

As you approach the impressive front of the mansion, you see multi-faceted reflections of leaded glass fan lights as you pass between the massive, Masonic Gothic pillars that frame the front of the house. The hallway is an amazing example of the beautiful pressed metal ceilings so popular before the turn of the century in the southern homes of South Carolina. The public rooms of the house showcase inlaid oak floors, and spacious decks overlook the back gardens and outdoor pool.

The inn offers guests a choice of five luxurious guests rooms, three with private bath. The Francis Scott Key Room is on the corner of the ground floor, directly off the main hall, with a view of the garden. It is named after Key, who was related to the original owners. The Eleanor Room has a magnificent copper tub with brass dolphin feet set in a beautiful alcove. The bedroom is rich in color and furnishings, with plush burgundy carpets and a queen size rice bed, with balloon back chairs by the fireplace.The Henry Floyd Room is named in honor of the great, great grandfather of the present lady of the house. Henry escaped religious persecution in Wales and fled to England, where he raised two sons, who were later Knighted by Queen Elizabeth. The Queen Victoria Room is named for the ruling monarch of England at the time the house was built. It holds an awesome display of Victorian pieces, with a high back bed accented with English lace and matching drapes, a high marble top dresser, and pale lime green walls that are the perfect background for the color portrait of the Queen herself. The Sam Still Room was named for Sam Still I and II. Sam I built the house and Sam II, a Citadel graduate, became an attorney and worked with President Roosevelt in Washington, and then as a Librarian of Congress.

## 7 BLUFFTON

**Barrett L. Antiques**
Hayward St.
843/757-6630

**Stock Farm Antiques**
Hwy. 46
843/757-2511

## 8 BLYTHEWOOD

### Blythewood Antiques
206 Blythewood Road
803/754-1116
Tues.-Sat. 10-6, closed Sun.-Mon.
*Directions: Take Exit #27 off I-77*

Blythewood Antiques is located in a house with rooms set up for show of antique furniture, glassware, collectibles, linens and more.

### The Root Cellar
10500 Wilson Blvd.
803/754-7578
Tues.-Sat. 10-6, closed Sun.-Mon.
*Directions: The Root Cellar is located at Exit #24, just 1 mile off I-77 on Hwy. 21/Wilson Road.*

The Root Cellar holds 3,000 square feet of antique and collectible consignments, including furniture, dolls, china, lamps, old toys, linens, fine art, handpainted furniture and crystal.

### Heart's Desire
162 Langford
803/691-8833
Tues.-Fri., 10-5:30; Wed., 10-1:30, Sat. 10-5, closed Sun.-Mon.
*Directions: Take Exit #24 off I-77. Heart's Desire is located 3 miles from I-77 at Hwy. 21 and Langford Road.*

Heart's Desire is a delightful, magical gift and antique shop housed in a spacious home built in 1875. Their antiques range from dolls to jewelry to furniture and more, while their gifts include baskets, florals and gifts for home and garden.

## 9 CAMDEN

Established in 1732, Camden is the oldest inland city in South Carolina and was the major British garrison of Lord Cornwallis. The Battles of Hobkirk Hill and Camden were fought in the vicinity and twelve other Revolutionary War battles took place nearby. The Camden area is also known for the fine horses trained and bred here and for its beautiful homes. The world-famous "Colonial Cup," a day of steeplechase and flat racing, takes place around Easter.

### Wartime Collectibles
539 Dekalb St.
803/424-5273
Tues.-Fri. 10:30-6, Mon. and Sat. by chance
*Directions: From I-20, take Exit 92 or 98, at the intersection of U.S. Hwy. 1 and State Route 521.*

This shop specializes in military memorabilia, both foreign and domestic from World Wars I and II, as well as the Civil War. All items are authentic and guaranteed. You will also find included in the inventory many old toys.

**Camden Antiques Exchange**
818 Broad St.
803/424-1700

**Camden Antique Mall**
830 Broad St.
803/432-0818

**Granary Antiques**
830 Broad St.
803/432-8811

**Timley Treasures**
845 Broad St.
803/424-0171

**Antiques on Broad**
2513 Broad St.
803/424-1338

**Dusty Bin Antiques**
2606 Broad St.
803/432-3676

**South's Treasures**
538 Dekalb St.
803/432-7709

**Fancy That Antiques**
914 Market St.
803/425-5111

**Boykin Furniture Co.**
922 Broad St.
803/432-4386

**Pine Burr Antiques**
1004 Tickle Hill Road
803/432-4636

## 10 CHARLESTON

Her charm and beauty have long proven to be irrestible. You'll see it in the lacy trim of her breezy piazzas and feel it in the spirit of her rich heritage. A port city steeped in history, barely changed since its founding in 1670.

Here you'll find the very best of the South. A genteel nature, so inviting, so gracious and an indomitable strength that has proudly withstood great fires, earthquakes, pirate rouges, a Civil War and hurricanes with little more than a bat of an eye.

Indeed, the Charleston area is a place that visitors rarely want to leave. In 1995, *Glamour* magazine rated the area one of the top ten travel destinations in the U.S., and *Conde Nast* readers rated it fourth as a destination in a list of its top ten cities. With a metro population of over 500,000, this aristocratic colonial port boasts 73 pre-Revolutionary buildings, 136 from the late 18th century and more than 600 others built prior to the 1840s. Come wander along cobblestone streets, smell the sea breezes, explore antique shops and boutiques and treat yourself to the delicious fresh seafood. Come experience the Charleston area—her streets, her homes, her people.

### Period Antiques

194 King St.
843/723-2724
Mon.-Sat. 10-5
*Directions: Take I-26 to its end in Charleston and take the King St. Exit. Turn right onto King St. and continue about a mile to the heart of downtown Charleston. Period Antiques is at 194 King St. on the left.*

An interesting, unusual and changing selection of choice American and European antiques can be found at Period Antiques, including furniture, paintings, mirrors and decorative accessories - a small shop full of treasures.

**Zinn Rug Gallery**
269 E. Bay St.
843/577-0300

**Acquisitions**
273 E. Bay St.
843/577-8004

**Charleston Rare Book Co.**
66 Church St.
843/723-3330

**Century House Antiques**
85 Church St.
843/722-6248

**Church Street Galleries**
100 Church St.
843/937-0808

**Trio Ltd.**
175 Church St.
843/853-9966

**Second Fling Antiques**
7440 Cross Country Road
843/552-6604

**Nazan**
4501 Dorsey Ave.
843/745-0005

**Goat Cart**
18 E. Elliott St.
843/722-1128

**Chicora Antiques Inc.**
154 King St.
843/723-1711

**152 A.D. Antiques**
152 King St.
843/577-7042

**Estate Antiques**
155 King St.
843/723-2362

**Ginkgo Leaf**
159 King St.
843/722-0640

**Moore House Antiques**
161 1/2 King St.
843/722-8065

**Livingston and Sons**
163 King St.
843/723-9697

**Helen Martin Antiques**
169 King St.
843/577-6533

**Decorator's Alley**
177 1/2 King St
843/722-2707

**Poppe House Inc.**
177 King St.
843/853-9559

**D Bigda Antiques**
178 King St.
843/722-0248

**English Patina Inc.**
179 King St.
843/853-0380

**Jack Patla Co.**
181 King St.
843/723-2314

**John Gibson Antiques**
183 King St.
843/722-0909

**Joint Ventures Estate Jewelry**
185 King St.
843/722-6730

**Carolina Prints**
188 King St.
843/723-2266

**George C Birlant & Co.**
191 King St.
843/722-3842

**D & D Antiques**
192 King St.
843/853-5266

**Architrave Antiques**
193 King St.
843/577-2860

**The Silver Vault**
195 King St.
843/722-0631

**Jean Keegan**
196 King St.
843/723-3953

**Verdi Antiques & Accessories**
196 King St.
843/723-3953

**Elysia Antiques**
200 King St.
843/853-8502

**Petterson Antiques**
201 King St.
843/723-5714

**A Zola**
202 King St.
843/723-3175

**A'Riga IV**
204 King St.
843/577-3075

**Riddler Page Rare Maps**
205 E. King St., Suite 102
843/723-1734

**Golden & Associate Antiques**
206 King St.
843/723-8886

**Granny's Goodies**
301 King St.
843/577-6200

**Croghan's Jewel Box**
308 King St.
843/723-6589

**James Island Antiques**
2028 Maybank Hwy.
843/762-1415

**Terrace Oaks Antique Mall**
2037 Maybank Hwy.
843/795-9689

**Antiquities Historical Galleries**
199 Meeting St.
843/720-8771

**Seymour Antique Center**
1066 E. Montague Ave.
843/554-5005

# South Carolina

**Flynn's**
Old Market 188 Meeting
843/577-7229

**D & M Antiques**
4923 Rivers Ave.
843/744-6777

**Architectural Elements**
1011 Saint Andrews Blvd.
843/571-3389

**Tanner's Collectibles**
1024 Savannah Hwy.
843/763-0199

**Antique Mall**
2241 Savannah Hwy.
843/766-8899

**Shalimar Antiques**
2418 Savannah Hwy.
843/766-1529

**Carpenter's Antiques**
1106 Chuck Dawley Blvd. (Mt. Pleasant)
843/884-3411

**Goat Cart**
18 E. Elliott St.
843/722-1128

**Peacock Alley Antiques**
9 Princess St.
843/722-6056

**Brass & Silver Workshop**
758 Saint Andrews Blvd.
843/571-4302

**Grey Goose Antique Mall**
1011 Saint Andrews Blvd.
843/763-9131

**Livingston & Sons Antiques Inc.**
2137 Savannah Hwy.
843/556-6162

**Roumilliat's Antique Mall**
2241 Savannah Hwy.
843/766-8899

**Attic Treasures**
2024 Wappoo Dr.
843/762-0418

**Architrave Antiques**
153 King St.
843/577-2860

**Red Torii Oriental Antiques**
197 King St.
843/723-0443

## 11 CHERAW

**Antique Imports Inc.**
92 Powe St
843/537-5762

**L & M Antiques**
RR 1
843/623-7307

**Cheraw Furniture Refinishing**
133 Second St.
843/379-3562

**Thomas Antique Co.**
92 Powe St
843/537-3422

**Sentimental Journey**
242 2nd St.
843/537-0461

**Expressions**
129 Main St. (12 mi. W.)
843/623-6668

## 12 COLUMBIA

**Ole Towne Antique Mall**
2956 Broad River Road
803/798-2078

**Amicks Bottles & Collectibles**
6420 Garners Ferry Road
803/783-0300

**Past & Present Inc.**
8105 Garners Ferry Road
803/776-6807

**Mais Oui Ltd.**
929 Gervais St.
803/733-1704

**Heirloom Antiques & Collectibles**
6000 Garners Ferry Road
803/776-3955

**Ole Towne Antique Mall**
7748 Garners Ferry Road
803/695-1992

**City Market Antiques Mall**
701 Gervais St.
803/799-7722

**Mary Clowney Antiques & Interiors**
1009 Gervias St.
803/765-1280

**Chic Antiques**
602 Huger St.
803/765-1584

**B & M Enterprises Inc.**
3510 Phillips St.
803/799-6153

**Balloonyville USA**
141 S. Shandon St.
803/771-4555

**Ole Towne Antique Mall Inc.**
8724 Two Notch Road
803/736-7575

**Non E Such**
2754 Devine St.
803/254-0772

**Wolfe's Antiques**
7001 Patricia Dr.
803/783-6327

**Columbia Antique Mall**
602 Huger St.
803/765-1584

**Antique Mall**
1215 Pulaski St.
803/256-1420

**BC Treasure Barn**
2515 Two Notch Road
803/799-7366

**Charlton Hall Galleries, Inc.**
912 Gervais St.
803/779-5678

**Olde Towne Antique Mall**
2918 Broad River Road
803/772-5057

## 13 CONWAY

**Hidden Attic Antiques Mall**
1014 4th Ave.
843/248-6262

**Kingston Antiques**
326 Main St.
843/248-0212

**Trader John Antiques**
2197 Hwy. 501 E.
843/248-9077

## 14 DARLINGTON

Built around a courthouse square, the mural on the side of the courthouse is a graphic reminder of the country's colorful past. The town really comes alive on Labor Day weekend when the "Granddaddy of them all," the Mountain Dew Southern 500 stock car race is held.

**Scarlett's Antiques**
500 E. Broad St.
843/393-4952

**H & M Plunder Shop**
512 S. Main St.
843/393-4888

## 15 DILLON

**Chris' Pack House**
Hwy. 9
843/774-6144

**House of Willow Antiques**
2806 Hwy. 9 W.
843/841-3040

**Breeden's Old Stuff**
201 Harrison St.
843/774-6321

## 16 EASLEY

**Main Street Market**
203 W. Main St.
864/855-8658

**Adam's Attic Antiques**
223 W. Main St.
864/859-4996

**King's Things Antiques**
1001 Pelzer Hwy.
864/859-0313

**Wilma's Antiques**
4225 Calhoun Memorial Hwy.
864/220-1055

## 17 FLORENCE

### Red Brick House
1005 S. Cashua Dr.
843/669-4860
Thurs.-Sat. or by chance
*Directions: From I-95, take Exit #157 and travel east to the first red light. Turn right on Cashua and the shop is three miles further on the left.*

Owner David Robinson can help shoppers in several ways. He can sell you something from his 7,000-square-feet of antiques (mostly furniture). He can refinish a piece for you in his shop on the premises. He can help you pick out a gift from the line of gift items he carries. Is that what they mean by one-stop shopping?

**Ann's Patchwork Palette**
105 S. Franklin Dr.
843/665-1944

**Hodge's Furniture Shop**
Hwy. 52 N.
843/669-7391

**Grapevine Antiques Collectibles Etc.**
2138 3rd Loop
843/629-9745

**Hamilton House Antiques**
549 W. Evans St.
843/665-7161

**Antique Market & Etc.**
1356 James Jones Ave.
843/665-1812

**Trading Post**
217 N. Irby St.
843/673-0332

## 18 FORT MILL

**Antique Mall of the Carolinas**
3700 Ave. of The Carolinas
803/548-6255

**Antique & Garden Shop**
229 Main St.
803/547-7822

**Antiques on Main**
233 Main St.
803/802-2242

## 19 GAFFNEY

**Vassey's Antiques**
1084 N. Green River Road
864/461-8111

**Pieces from the Past**
2105 Cherokee Ave.
864/489-4668

**Vassey's Antiques**
1084 N. Green River Road
864/461-8111

**Pieces From the Past**
2105 Cherokee Ave.
864/489-4668

## 20 GEORGETOWN

### Tosh Antiques
802 Church St.
843/527-8537
Mon.-Sat. 10-5, Sunday by chance
*Directions: Located on Hwy. 17 in downtown Georgetown.*

Everything is of fine quality here. You'll find Victorian furniture, pieces from Occupied Japan, primitives, as well as Roseville, sterling silver, and brilliant cut glass.

**Hill's Used Furniture & Antiques**
4161 Andrews Hwy.
843/546-6610

**Clement's Carolina**
803 Front St.
843/545-9000

**Grandma's Attic**
2106 Highmarket
843/546-2607

## 21 GREENVILLE

### The Corner Antique Mall
700 N. Main St.
864/232-9337
Mon.-Sat. 10-5, closed Sun.
*Directions: The Corner Antique Mall is located on U.S. Hwy. 276, where it intersects with Main St. However, traveling I-85, take Exit #51 and travel north on I-385 to Exit #42, which is Stone Ave. Turn right and go to the "corner" at Stone and Main.*

This 5,000 square foot "corner" of the antique world is packed with treasures, including advertising collectibles, books and magazines, art, china, glassware, pottery, jewelry, dolls and figurines, vintage clothing, some furniture and accessories, and many more collectibles and antiques.

**Little Stores of West End**
315 Augusta St.
864/467-1770

**Brown Street Antiques Inc.**
115 N. Brown St.
864/232-5304

**Penny Farthing Antiques**
93 Cleveland St.
864/271-9370

**Reedy River Antiques**
220 Howe St.
864/242-0310

**Antiques Associates**
633 S. Main St.
864/235-3503

**Accents Unlimited Inc.**
520 Mills Ave.
864/235-4825

**Greenville Furniture Exchance Inc.**
113 Poinsett Hwy.
864/233-3702

**Bedding World Antiques**
236 Wade Hampton Blvd.
864/242-0908

**William Key Interiors**
909 E. Washington St.
864/233-4329

**Gallery at Park & Main**
605 N. Main St.
864/235-8866

**Greystone Antiques**
1501 Augusta St.
864/242-2486

**All That Jazz**
1547 Wade Hampton Blvd.
864/292-3900

**Southern Estate Antiques**
415 Mauldin Road
864/299-8981

**Robbin's Rarities Inc.**
2038 Laurens Road #C
864/297-7948

**North Country Treasures**
110 Poinsett Hwy.
864/271-4030

## 22 GREENWOOD

**Brewington Antiques**
1215 Montague Ave.
864/229-3086

**Bud's Antiques**
803 Ninety Six Hwy.
864/227-8999

**Rainbo Antiques**
2720 Hwy. 25 S.
864/227-1921

**Mackey's**
1728 Montague Ave.
864/223-3400

**Memories Antique Shop**
626 Lowell Ave.
864/229-6353

## 23 GREER

**Pot Luck Antiques**
2013 Hwy. 101 S.
864/877-1818

**Cooper Furniture Co.**
214 Trade St.
864/877-2761

**Mercantile on Trade**
230 Trade St.
864/801-1300

**Coach House Antiques**
401 Johnson Road
864/879-2616

**West Gerald Interiors**
711 W. Wade Hampton Blvd.
864/879-2148

**Ralph's Antiques & Auctions**
116 Bright Road
864/879-3073

## 24 HILTON HEAD ISLAND

**Decorator's Wholesale Antiques**
1 Cardinal Road #5
843/681-7463

**Low Country Collectibles**
32 Palmetto Bay Road
843/842-8543

**Bargains & Treasures**
4 Archer Road, #E
843/785-7929

**Michael & Co. Antiques**
26 Arrow Road
843/686-3222

**Ruth Edward's Antiques**
8 Beach Lagoon Road
843/671-2223

**Interiors-Kay Buck A Rare Find**
Village at Wexford, #E6
843/686-6606

**Annie's Attic of Consigned**
20 Palmetto Bay Road
843/686-6970

**Guggenheim's**
20 Dunnigans Alley
843/785-9580

**Nearly New**
27 Arrow Road
843/785-7911

**Swan House Antiques Gallery**
7 Bow Circle
843/785-7926

## 25 IRMO

**Broad River Antiques**
7232 Broad River Road
803/749-6909

**Farmhouse Antiques**
1300 Old Dutch Fork Road
803/732-6287

**Dutch Fork Antiques**
1000 Dutch Fork Road
803/781-7174

## 26 LAKE CITY

Established in 1732, tobacco was introduced in the late 1800s. The market was established in 1889 and has grown to become one of the largest in the state. The crop is saluted every September during the town's Tobacco Festival. Dr. Ronald E. McNair, one of the astronauts aboard the Space Shuttle Challenger, was born and buried here.

**Gloria's Antiques & Gifts**
116 E. Main St.
843/394-8360

**Oakdale Antiques**
3831 W. Turbeville
843/659-2210

## 27 LANDRUM

### Landrum Antique Mall
221 Rutherford Road
864/457-4000
Mon.-Sat. 10-5, closed Sundays
*Directions: From I-26, take Exit #1 and the shop is located 1 mile off of the interstate.*

There's lots in a relatively small space here, so browse slowly and don't miss a thing! Fifty dealers have filled 10,000 square feet with early 1900s furniture, collectibles, silver, chandeliers, rugs, china and estate jewelry.

**My Favorite Shop**
203 E. Rutherford St.
864/457-4840

**Lasting Impressions**
227 E. Rutherford St.
864/457-4697

**Bloomsbury Cottage Antqs. & Ints.**
204 E. Rutherford St.
864/457-3111

## 28 LAURENS

This town is named for Revolutionary War statesman Henry Laurens, who was imprisoned in the Tower of London for his patriotism. The courthouse square was purchased in 1792 for two guineas (about $21). It was in this vicinity that Andrew Johnson, 17th President of the United States, once operated a tailor shop.

**Treasure House Antiques**
Dial Place Road
864/682-5915

**Hall Antiques**
Hwy. 221
864/984-0315

**Jeff's Antiques & Furniture**
Hwy. 221 S.
864/682-8079

**Palmetto Antiques & Auction**
106 E. Main St.
864/984-3011

**Harper House**
101 Wayside Dr.
864/984-7945

## 29 MARION

**Antiques Dujour**
231 N. Main St.
843/423-3366

**Swamp Fox Antiques & Books**
326 Main St.
843/423-0819

**Judy's Antiques**
329 N. Main St.
843/423-5227

**Cuckoo's Nest**
403 N. Main St.
843/423-1636

**Theodosia's**
724 N. Main St.
843/423-7693

## 30 MOUNT PLEASANT

**Linda Page's Thieves Market**
1460 Ben Sawyer Blvd.
843/884-9672

**Carpentiers Antiques & Restoration**
1106 Chuck Dawley Blvd.
843/884-3411

**Pleasant Antiques**
616 Coleman Blvd.
843/849-7005

**Lowcountry Antique Mall**
630 Coleman Blvd.
843/849-8850

**Victoria & Thomas Trading Co.**
803 Coleman Blvd.
843/849-7230

**Sweet Magnolias**
976 Houston Northcutt Blvd.
843/856-9131

**Mike's Antiques Inc.**
401 Johnnie Dodds Blvd.
843/849-1744

**Tomorrow's Treasures & Antiques**
113 Pitt St.
843/881-2072

## 31 MULLINS

**Southern Treasures**
155 S. Main St.
843/464-6425

**Patsy's Antiques**
302 S. Main St.
843/464-2066

## 32 MURRELLS INLET

**Wachesaw Row Antique Mall**
4650 Hwy. 17 S.
843/651-7719
Mon.-Sat. 10-5
*Directions: Located between Georgetown and Myrtle Beach on Hwy. 17 Bypass.*

This seven-dealer mall carries a little bit of everything including American, French, and English furniture and accessories, primitives, paintings, prints, china and glassware. They also offer a selection of coins, guns, and sports memorabilia.

**Golden Image Game Room**
2761 Hwy. 17
843/651-0338

**Legacy Antique Mall**
3420 Hwy. 17
843/651-0884

**Tillie's Attic**
3692 Hwy. 17
843/651-1900

**A & G Furniture**
3974 Hwy. 17
843/651-3777

**Memories Antiques**
4763 Hwy. 17 Bypass
843/651-7888

**Long Bay Trading Co.**
4771 Hwy. 17 Bypass
843/357-1252

## 33 MYRTLE BEACH

**Peggy's Antiques & Collectibles**
1040 Hwy. 17 S.
843/238-1442

**Myrtle Beach Antiques Mall**
1014 Hwy. 501
843/448-4762

**Collectibles Mall**
4011 Hwy. 501
843/236-1029

**Fox & Hounds Antiques Mall**
4015 Hwy. 501
843/236-1027

**Socastee Trading Post**
8569 Hwy. 544
843/236-2244

**Joseph Bridger Fine Antiques**
5311 N. Kings Hwy.
843/449-4171

**Noah & Friends**
1307 Celebrity Circle
843/448-8105

## 34 NEWBERRY

**Leslie's Main Street Antiques & Auctions**
934 Main St.
803/276-8600

**Antiques and SoForths**
1213 Main St.
803/276-1073

**Trader John's**
11213 S.C. Hwy. 121
803/276-0432

## 35 NINETY SIX

**Burnett House**
118 Main St. N.W.
864/543-3236

**Mainly Antiques**
101 Main St. N.E.
864/543-3636

## 36 NORTH AUGUSTA

In 1833, the Charleston-Hamburg Railroad ended its 138-mile rail line, then the longest steam-operated railroad in the world, at the small town of Hamburg, near the present-day town of North Augusta. Chartered by the state in 1906, North Augusta was once a foremost winter resort frequented by the very wealthy. Magnificent old Victorian cottages and imposing churches are reminders of the city's past.

**Plunder Valley Antiques**
207 Belvedere Clearwater Road
803/279-1200

**Peddlers Way**
4631 Jefferson Davis Hwy.
803/593-4447

## 37 NORTH MYRTLE BEACH

**Junktique**
204 Hwy. 17 N.
843/249-7443

**B & B Antiques**
1604 Hwy. 17 S.
843/361-0101

**Cottage Antiques of Cherry Grove**
621 Sea Mountain Hwy.
843/249-7563

**Curious Mermaid**
1669 Old Hwy. 17 N.
843/280-0050

## 38 ORANGEBURG

**Browsabout Antiques & Accents**
1036 Broughton St.
803/536-2182

**Something Different**
1041 Broughton St.
803/536-0710

## 39 PAWLEYS ISLAND

**Elizabeth Taylor Satterfield**
42 N. Causeway
843/237-8701

**Mary Frances Miller Antiques**
Hammock Shop/Hwy. 17
843/237-2466

**Traddrock Antiques & Design**
2176 S. Kings Hwy.
843/237-9232

**Harrington Altman Limited**
10729 Ocean Hwy.
843/237-2056

**McElveen Design, Antiques & Furniture**
13302 Ocean Hwy.
843/237-3326

**Classic Consignments, Inc.**
11195 Ocean Hwy.
843/237-8355

## 40 PELZER

**Pelzer Antique Market**
19 Main St.
864/947-5558

**Sue's Antiques & Collectibles**
6633 Hwy. 29 N.
864/947-2039

## 41 PENDLETON

**Pendleton Antique Co.**
134 E. Main St.
864/646-7725

**Pendleton Place Antiques**
651 S. Mechanic St.
864/646-7673

## 42 PIEDMONT

**P & N Antiques International**
100 Piedmont Road
864/295-3134

**Papa's Book Haven Antiques**
2510 River Road
864/269-5700

## 43 ROCK HILL

**Antique & Garden Shoppe**
609 Cherry Road
803/327-4858

**Upcountry Antiques & Handcraft**
1449 Ebenezer Road
803/324-5503

**Reid Antiques**
2641 India Hook Road
803/366-4949

**Collectibles on Main**
427 E. Main St.
803/366-8337

**Antique Mall**
104 S. Oakland Ave.
803/324-1855

**Pix Designer Warehouse**
147 W. Oakland Ave.
803/325-1116

## 44 SIMPSONVILLE

### Cudds Zoo Antiques
101 E. Curtis St.
864/963-2375
Mon.-Sat. 10-5, and by appointment
*Directions: Located three miles off I-385 on Main St.*

This shop carries mostly glass: Depression, pressed, cameo, and art. There is also a small quantity of quality furniture. The owner does chair recaning.

**Hunter House Antiques & B&B**
201 E. College St.
864/967-2827

**Satterfield's Antiques**
106 W. Curtis St.
864/967-0955

## 45 SPARTANBURG

### John Morton Antiques
160 E. Broad St.
864/583-0427
*Directions: Follow the Spartanburg exits off either I-26 or I-85. John Morton Antiques is located in downtown Spartanburg.*

This shop specializes in period, regional and country furniture and accessories, and has a furniture restoration service attached.

### South Pine Antique Mall
856 S. Pine St.
864/542-2975
Mon.-Sat. 10-6; closed Sun.
*Directions: Take Exit #585 off Interstate 85. Located five miles south of Interstate on Pine St.*

This 6,000-square-foot mall encompasses a variety of furniture, glassware, lamps, mirrors, pictures and collectibles. Several quality period pieces as well as '40s mahoganys may also be found here.

**Old Southern Trading Co.**
1926 Boiling Springs Road
864/578-1025

**Town & Country Antiques & Cllbls.**
2929 Boiling Springs Road
864/578-0970

**Yesterdays Treasures**
2306 Chesnee Hwy.
864/542-9888

**Chestnut Galleries Antiques**
144 Chestnut St.
864/585-9576

**C W Trantham Trading Co.**
360 Dogwood Club Road
864/542-2311

**Ballard's Sales Co.**
8521 Fairforest Road
864/582-4852

**Bye-Gone Treasures**
169 E. Main St.
864/542-1590

**Nan's Antiques & Collectibles**
330 E. Main St.
864/585-6039

**Shades of the Past Antique Mall**
512 E. Main St.
864/585-1172

**Prissy's Antique Mall**
914 E. Main St.
864/582-1032

**Treasures of Time**
155 W. Main St.
864/573-7178

**Jeanne Harley Antiques**
910 S. Pine St.
864/585-0386

**Rickinghall Antiques Warehouse**
400 Westbrook Court
864/583-7221

## 46 SUMMERTON

**Antiques Etc.**
103 Main St.
803/485-8714

**Antique Mall**
123 Main St.
803/485-2205

## 47 SUMMERVILLE

### Country Store & Antiques
1106 Main St.
843/871-7548
Mon.-Sat. 10-5:30, Sun. 1-5 in Oct., Nov., and Dec.
*Directions: Country Store is located 1/2 mile from I-26 at Exit 199A.*

These folks have been in business for 13 years, and their motto is "Where Customers Are Friends." The shop's 2,000-square-feet are filled with primitives, oak furniture and pottery. They also carry a line of gifts including All God's Children by Martha Holcomb.

**Missy's Memories Antiques**
127 S. Main St.
843/871-5334

**Carriage House Collectables**
1213 S. Main St.
843/873-5704

**Early Traditions**
100 W. Richardson Ave.
843/851-1627

**Antiques N Stuff**
128 E. Richardson Ave.
843/875-4155

**People Places & Quilts**
129 W. Richardson Ave.
843/871-8872

**Town Fair Antiques**
131 E. Richardson Ave.
843/873-3462

**Granny's Attic**
71 Trolley Road
843/871-6838

**Remember When**
301 Trolley Road
843/821-1018

**Adell's**
211 W. Richardson Ave.
843/871-8249

**Antiques N Stuff**
128 E. Richardson Ave.
843/875-4155

**North & South Gun Shop**
113 S. Main St.
843/821-7524

## 48 SUMTER

**T. J. Player**
202 Broad St.
803/778-1173

**Why-Not Antiques**
202 Broad St.
803/778-1173

**Broadstone Manor Antiques**
204 Broad St.
803/778-1890

**Estate Antiques Gifts and Clocks**
210 Broad St.
803/773-4214

**Keepsakes and Collectibles**
408 Broad St.
803/773-2235

**Sumter Antique Mall**
719 Broad St.
803/778-0269

## 49 TAYLOR

**Spinning Wheel Antiques**
3228 Wade Hampton Blvd.
864/244-3195

**Danny's Antique Mall**
4949 Wade Hampton Blvd.
864/848-7316

**Buncombe Antiques Mall**
5000 Wade Hampton Blvd.
864/268-4498

**Way Back When Antique Mall**
5111 Wade Hampton Blvd.
864/848-9839

## 50 WEST COLUMBIA

### 378 Antique Mall
620 Sunset Blvd.
803/791-3132
Mon.-Sat. 10-5; Sun. 1:30-5:30
*Directions: From I-26, take the Hwy. 378 exit, go 2.8 miles (Hwy. 378 and Sunset Blvd. are one and the same).*

With more than fifty dealers in 20,000 square feet of space, and 10 years in business, visitors can expect to find just about everything they are looking for at the 378 Antique Mall. They feature furniture from the 1800s to the early 1900s, glassware, lamps, framed art, military items, vintage jewelry, country collectables, dolls, porcelains, chandeliers, silver, art glass and cameo glass.

**Harvest Moon**
351 Meeting St.
803/739-0637

**Rudy's Upper Deck**
511 Meeting St.
803/739-9191

**De Ja Vu Antiques**
615 Meeting St.
803/926-0021

**Boltinhouse Jewelers**
3015 Platt Springs Road
803/794-1466

**Westbank Antique Mall**
118 State St.
803/796-9764

**State Street Antiques**
131 State St.
803/791-0008

**Old Mill Antique Mall**
310 State St.
803/796-4229

**Treasure Aisles Bazaar**
1217 Sunset Blvd.
803/791-5777

**Park's Furniture Antiques**
3131 Sunset Blvd.
803/791-4071

**Dewey's Antiques**
3740 Sunset Blvd.
803/794-9075

**Eau Gallie Interiors**
3937 Sunset Blvd.
803/926-9370

**Attic Treasures**
620 Sunset Blvd.
803/796-1882

# South Dakota

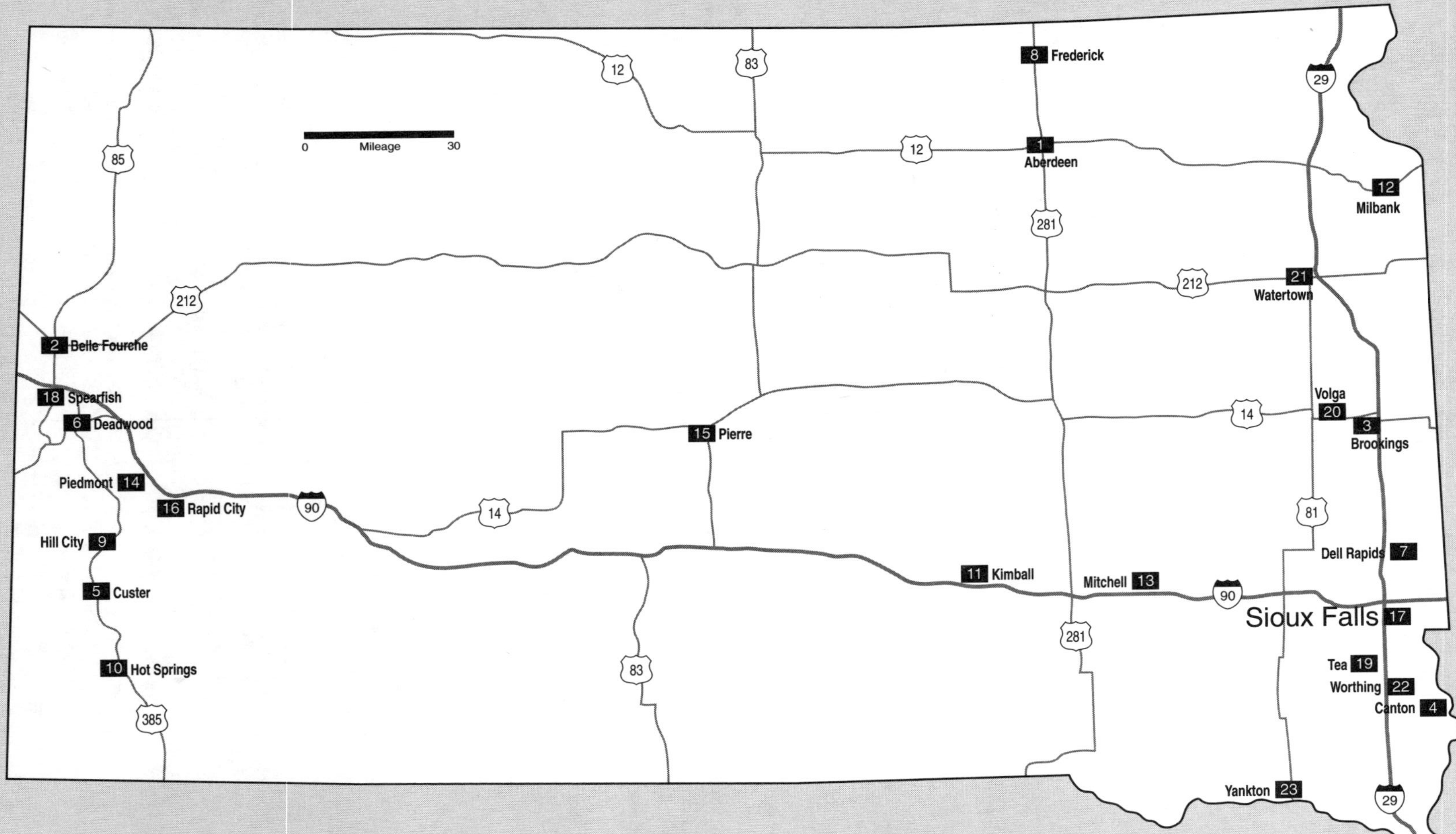

*Shops here follow the theme of businesses on an old-fashioned street. Mannequins dressed as ladies of the evening parade around the perimeter of The Brothel, where vintage clothing is the specialty.*

# Second Impression Palace has award-winning display

This unique antique mall is a fascinating layout of old storefronts built from reassembled antique wood, glass, metal and tin. The award-winning display has been acclaimed from New York to San Francisco, and is a museum in itself.

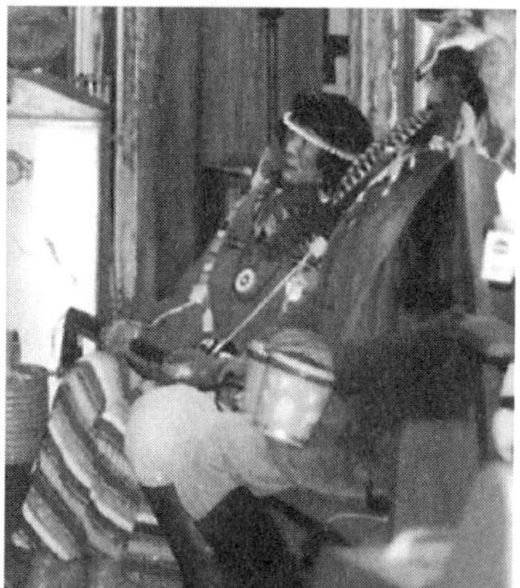

*Dressed up figures are a touch of whimsy.*

Behind the doors of this indoor "Main Street" are more than 40 dealers and 50 consignors with enough selection to satisfy everyone.

Walk down the boardwalk of time to the General Store and find trunks, dressers and Hoosier cabinets. For a more elegant variety of furniture try the Undertaker's. If vintage clothing and accessories are what you seek, you'll want to check into the Brothel. At the Sheriff's Office/ Jailhouse, you'll find old tools, car accessories, and horse gear.

*Second Impression Palace is located at 412 N. Main St. in Mitchell. For additional information see listing #13 (Mitchell).*

*Architectural details add to the fun of the theme: An old-time barbershop may be stocked with collectibles, or a bank vault holds stacks of books instead of cash. Here, a stuffed pigeon roosts on the eaves of the old bank building.*

## 1 ABERDEEN

Aberdeen was once the home of Frank Baum, an 1890s Aberdeen newspaper editor who later wrote the all-time favorite children's story *The Wonderful Wizard of Oz*.

**Mother's Antique Mall**
117 S. Main St.
605/225-8992

**Bourdon's Furniture Antiques**
38497 133rd St.
605/226-0604

**Heirlooms Etc. at the Depot**
1100 S. Main St.
605/226-3660

**Lauinger's Country Store**
305 6th Ave. S.W.
605/225-0910

**Remember When Antiques**
504 S. State St.
605/226-3612

**Court Street Lighting**
123 Railroad Ave. S.E.
605/229-0359

**Hitch'n Post Antiques & Collectibles**
2601 6th Ave. S.E.
605/229-1655

**Meier Antiques**
524 State St. & Railroad Ave.
605/229-5453 or 605/225-9592

## 2 BELLE FOURCHE

Belle Fourche (beautiful fork) had its beginnings during the days of the dusty cattle drives when the wealth of the region attracted people such as Butch Cassidy and the Sundance Kid. The arrival of the railroad in 1890 led to the establishment of the city and the beginning of a wealthy, rowdy cattle baron dominated era. In the very early 1900s Belle Fourche became known as the largest cattle-shipping point in the world. Belle Fourche is also the center of the largest concentration of sheep in the United States, which makes it natural that it also ships more wool from its two warehouses than any other city. Belle Fourche remains to this day a "Cowtown" and its residents are proud of its history.

### Love That Shoppe
515 State St.
605/892-4006
Mon.-Sat. 9-8, Sun. 1-4
*Directions: The shop sits in Downtown Belle Fourche at Hwys. 85 and 212.*

Located in an historic 9,000-square-foot building, Love That Shoppe's 50 plus dealers' mix of Victorian, primitives, depression glass, heirloom jewelry, crockery and period furniture combine to make an enjoyable day for shopping. And when you tire of shopping, The Rocking '50s Soda Fountain located in the shop will take you back to the old drug store soda fountain days with their menu of bottled cokes, root beer floats, hot dogs, soft pretzels, ice cream sodas, sundaes and banana splits.

### Tri-State Bakery Studio
705 State St.
605/892-2684
Tues.-Sat 9:30-5:30, Mon. 9:30-2
*Directions: Downtown Belle Fourche at Hwys. 85 and 212*

The old Tri-State Bakery Building, dating back to 1927, is on the National and State Historical Registers and is truly representative of its early days. All the old equipment once used in creating the delicious confections, pastries and breads is still housed in the building and is available for viewing by interested customers.

Today, it has been converted to the Tri-State Bakery Studio offering a large selection of vintage advertising papers and tins and a limited amount of furniture. Also located here is the town's only Espresso Bar which features mochas and Italian sodas.

### The Old Grizz Trading Post
2207 Fifth Ave. and 512 State St.
605/892-6668
Daily 10-5

This 6,800-square-foot shop specializes in cowboy and western memorabilia, as well as a large variety of antiques and collectibles. The furniture selection mainly consists of, but is not limited to, pieces from the 1870s up through the '30s and '40s.

The Agers live on the premises at the Fifth Street location, a stately old home, dating back to 1892. They are currently in the process of restoring it to its original condition. The house still has 80% of its original wallpaper and an original 50-foot mural in the dining room.

The Agers encourage you to stop in anytime; if they're home; they're open.

**Robb House Antiques**
By Appointment Only
605/892-2846

## 3 BROOKINGS

**Threads of Memories Antique Mall**
309 4th St.
605/697-7377

**Country Peddler**
320 Main Ave.
605/697-6292

## 4 CANTON

### Canton Square Antique Emporium
121 E. Fifth St.
605/987-3152
Mon.-Fri. 9-8, Sat. & Sun. 9-5
*Directions: Exit 62 from I-29, then 9 miles east.*

Antique shop in the atmosphere of an old variety store, now a historical building. The owner says they have anything you want or ever hoped for in the way of antiques and collectibles.

**Lincoln County Antique Center**
123 W. 5th St.
605/987-4114
Mon.-Sat. 10-5, closed Sun.
*Directions: Exit Hwy. 18 off I-29. Travel east 8 miles to Canton.*

Presenting 10,000 square feet of quality Victorian furniture, art and books.

**Norma's This N That Shop**
109 N. Main St.
605/987-5816
Thurs.-Sat. 10-5 or by appointment (call 605/987-2269 for appointment)
*Directions: Located 8 miles off I-29. Take Hwy. 18 east to Canton.*

A general line of antiques and collectibles are featured.

## 5 CUSTER

**Mountain Valley Antiques**
3 miles W. on Route 16
605/673-5559

**Wild Bill's Antq. Mall & Rock Shop**
2 miles W. of Custer on Hwy. 16
605/673-4186

## 6 DEADWOOD

**Aunt Sophia's**
By Appointment Only
800/377-1516

## 7 DELL RAPIDS

**S & L Antiques & More**
416/418 4th St.
605/428-4457

## 8 FREDERICK

**Worthy Treasures Antiques**
39147 105th St.
605/329-2143

**Adeline Antiques**
1149 300 91st Ave.
605/329-2112

## 9 HILL CITY

**Orloske Antiques**
Deerfield Road (Hwys. 16 & 385)
605/574-2181
Daily 9-5, and by appointment
*Directions: 1 1/2 miles west of Hill City on Deerfield Road and also at the intersection of Highways 16 and 385.*

The total combined shopping area of these two shops is 10,000 square feet. 1800s furniture, primitives, glassware, toys, western items (saddles, tack, etc.) and Redwing Pottery are offered throughout the shop.

**Big 45 Frontier Gun Shop**
23850 Hwy. 385
605/574-4702

## 10 HOT SPRINGS

**Fargo Mercantile**
321 N. River St. (Across from foot bridge)
605/745-5189

**Pioneer Trading Co.**
143 S. Chicago
605/745-5252

## 11 KIMBALL

**Mentzer Antiques**
Main St.
605/778-6688

### *Great Places To Stay*

**Red Barn Inn**
Rural Route 2, Box 102
605/778-6332
Open year round
Rates: $32.50 and up
*Directions: From I-90 eastbound traffic: Take Exit 272; then travel 1/2 mile south, 7 1/2 miles east, and 3 miles south on a gravel road. From I-90 westbound traffic: Take Exit 284; then go 4 miles west and 3 miles south on a gravel road.*

American know-how triumphs again in this 70-year-old horse barn. No longer do steel bits, leather harnesses or hay decorate the interior. Today, a rustic decor outfitted with antique furniture and accessories celebrates the barn's reincarnation. Four rooms with separate baths serve as accommodations. Complimentary breakfast is served.

## 12 MILBANK

**5th Street Antiques**
902 S. 5th St.
605/432-5326

**Bleser House Bed & Breakfast**
311 S. 4th St.
605/432-4871

**Reflections In Time**
W. Hwy. 12
605/432-9495

## 13 MITCHELL

**Second Impression Palace**
412 N. Main St.
605/996-1948
Spring-Summer: Mon.-Sat. 8:30-6:30, Sun. 11-4; Fall-Winter: Mon.-Sat. 9-6, Sun. Closed
*Directions: Located only 1-1/2 blocks south of the World's Only Corn Palace! Eastbound on I-90: Take Exit 330 north to Havens, east to Sanborn, north to 1st Ave., east to Main St., north to 412*

# South Dakota

*North Main St. Westbound on I-90: From Exit 332, go north to 1st Avenue, west to Main Street, north to 412 North Main St.*

For specific information see review at the beginning of this section.

**Cellar**
400 N. Main St.
605/996-0515

## 14 PIEDMONT

**James O Aplan Antiques & Arts**
I 90 Exit 40 Tilford Road
605/347-5016

## 15 PIERRE

**Capital City Antiques**
819 N. Euclid Ave.
605/224-4971

## 16 RAPID CITY

**Traders Corner**
3501 Canyon Lake Dr.
605/341-4242

**Country Estates Heritage House**
2255 N. Haines Ave.
605/348-5994

**Antique & Furniture Mart**
1112 W. Main St.
605/341-3345

**Gaslight Antiques**
13490 Main St.
605/343-9276

**Hidden Treasures**
1208 E. North St.
605/342-7286

**Big K**
805 E. Denver St.
605/343-1221

**Coach House Antiques**
Hwy. 79
605/399-3838

**Country Lane Furniture Brian Peck**
2332 W. Main St.
605/343-9401

**St. Joe Antique Mall & Gifts**
615 Saint Joseph St.
605/341-1073

**Antiques & Collectibles**
225 Omaha St.
605/342-8199

### *Great Places To Stay*

**das Abend Haus Cottages & Audrie's Bed and Breakfast**
23029 Thunderhead Falls Road
605/342-7788
Open year round
*Directions: From I-90: Take Exit 57 to light (Omaha St. and Hwy. 44). Turn right; follow Hwy. 44 west. Hwy. 44 will turn left at the next light. 7 miles west of Rapid City in the National Forest. One half mile past the Fireside Inn Restaurant, turn left onto Thunderhead Falls Road for 1/4 mile. From Hwy. 385: Turn at Junction 44; go east for 7 miles; turn right onto Thunderhead Falls Road for 1/4 miles.*

Old World hospitality is thriving in the Black Hills at this enchanting retreat for couples only. Rich in the Abend Haus tradition, the spacious suites and log cottages are furnished with the largest collection of European antiques anywhere in the state.

## 17 SIOUX FALLS

**Architectural Elements**
818 E. 8th St.
605/339-9646

**Kolbe's Clock & Repair Shoppe**
1301 S. Duluth Ave.
605/332-9662

**Eight St. Treasure Chest**
1002 E. 8th St.
605/338-6878

**Maxwell House Antiques Inc.**
612 W. 4th St.
605/334-3640

**Recycled Treasures**
801 N. Main Ave.
605/330-9473

**Chopping Block Antiques Ltd.**
207 S. Phillips Ave.
605/334-1469

**Cliff Ave. – Flea Vendors**
3515 N. Cliff Ave.
605/338-8975

**The Patina**
26th & Western Park Ridge Mall
605/357-8884

**The Book Shop**
223 S. Phillips Ave.
605/336-8384

**D&J Glass & Art Clinic**
26707 466th Ave.
605/361-7524

**Koenig's Antiques**
1103 N. Main Ave.
605/338-0297

**Exchange**
1512 E. 10th St.
605/338-9155

**Emporium**
923 S. Grange Ave.
605/334-8813

**Midwest Antiques Gallery**
1502 W. 10th St.
605/334-3051

**Antiques Gallery Midwest**
1502 W. 10th St.
605/334-3051

**Old House Stuff**
818 E. 8th St.
605/339-9646

**Irish's Garage Antiques**
618 S. 5th Ave.
605/334-6540

**The Curiosity Shoppe**
725 N. Main Ave.
605/334-1412

**Antique Mall**
828 N. Main Ave.
605/335-7134

**Cedar Acres Antiques**
"Sebbo's" 3721 N. Cliff
605/334-8689

**Off The Hook Phone Service**
"Phone First"
605/334-3151

**Prairie Home Antiques**
5900 E. 10th
605/338-2042

**Dakota Weaver**
5016 E. 16th St.
605/336-7336

**Packaging Store**
1404 W. 41st St.
605/332-4789

**Antique Furniture Co.**
27102 Elbers Ave.
605/368-2112

**Dakota Collectibles**
101 N. Fairfax Ave.
605/338-8797

**Exchange West**
1005 W. 11th St.
605/333-0049

## 18 SPEARFISH

### Snowy Creek Antiques
112 W. Illinois St.
605/642-2660
Mon.-Fri. 8-5
*Directions: Take the Spearfish exit from I-90. Shop is located in downtown Spearfish off Main St. on Illinois St.*

Oak furniture, old oak file cabinets, African art, western collectibles, primitives, toys, china, glassware are just a few of the many items offered here.

### Old Mill Antiques
222 W. Illinois St.
605/642-4704
Mon.-Sat. 10-5 (Winter), Mon.-Sat. 9-6 (Summer)
*Directions: Exit I-90. Shop is located in downtown Spearfish off Main St.*

15 dealers – a good general line of antiques and collectibles including late 1800s to '40s furniture, kitchenware, depression glass, pottery and mining and railroad collectibles.

**The Browser Bin**
206 Colorado
605/642-7434

**Key Antiques**
344 N. 5th St.
605/642-7087

**Seifert's Country House**
RR 1 Box 143K
605/642-4930

**Kiefer Consignments**
513 Spearfish Canyon Road
605/642-7436

## 19 TEA

### I-29 Antiques & Collectibles Mall
46990 271st St.
605/368-5810
Mon. 9-9, Tues.-Sat. 9-5, Sun. 12-5
*Directions: From I-29, take Exit 73, and go 1/4 mile west.*

Featuring McCoy, Fiesta, Hall pottery and Red Wing stoneware, all 10,000-square-feet of this mall have been put to good use by the 75 dealers. The curious antiquer can also find old toys, antique furniture, pictures, jewelry, glassware, and "tokens." More unusual items such as old signs plus well pumps add a touch of rustic to the collection.

## 20 VOLGA

**Red Barn Antiques**
46080 U.S. Hwy. 14
605/627-5394

## 21 WATERTOWN

**Main Street Antiques**
6 E. Kemp Ave., uptown Watertown
605/886-1919

**Yellowed Pages Used Books Vol. II**
10 E. Kemp Ave.
605/886-3640

**Westgate**
125 E. Kemp Ave.
605/882-1361

## 22 WORTHING

**Antiques & Things**
112 Main St.
605/372-4853

## 23 YANKTON

### Kollectible Kingdom
317 W. 5th St.
605/668-9353
Daily (closed Tue.) May-Nov. 9-6, Dec.-April 11-5:30 (some Sun. 12-5)
*Directions: Traveling Hwy. 81 (easily accessible from I-29 or I-90). Turn east on 5th St. which is located between Coastal convenience store and Super Lube. Shop is located behind Super Lube.*

Red Wing stoneware and Depression glass are the most popular and are featured pieces in this intimate and jam-packed shop. Also notable among the diverse and plentiful selections are unusual glassware and china. For those seeking a delightful challenge, a rummage sale section allows for sifting and digging.

**Dakota Antiques & Cllbls**
408 W. 11th & Broadway
605/665-7230

**Gingerbread Shack**
515 E 4th St.
605/665-9924

**Wright's Antique Shop**
313 Mulberry St.
605/665-2003

**Lewis & Clark Gallery**
221 W. 3rd St.
605/665-0129

# Tennessee

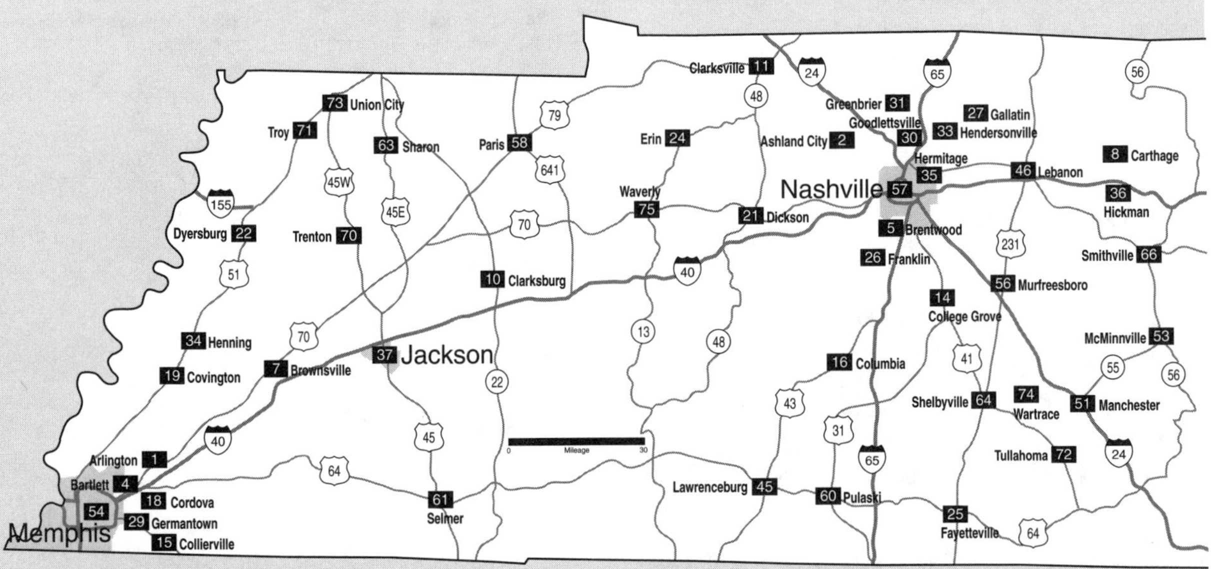

Clarksville 11
Greenbrier 31
Goodlettsville 30
27 Gallatin
33 Hendersonville
Union City 73
Troy 71
63 Sharon
Paris 58
Erin 24
Ashland City 2
Hermitage 35
46 Lebanon
8 Carthage
Nashville 57
36 Hickman
Waverly 75
21 Dickson
5 Brentwood
Dyersburg 22
Trenton 70
26 Franklin
Smithville 66
10 Clarksburg
56 Murfreesboro
14 College Grove
34 Henning
McMinnville 53
37 Jackson
16 Columbia
19 Covington
7 Brownsville
Shelbyville 64
74 Wartrace
51 Manchester
Mileage
0
30
Tullahoma 72
Arlington 1
Bartlett 4
18 Cordova
Lawrenceburg 45
60 Pulaski
54
61 Selmer
25 Fayetteville
29 Germantown
Memphis
15 Collierville


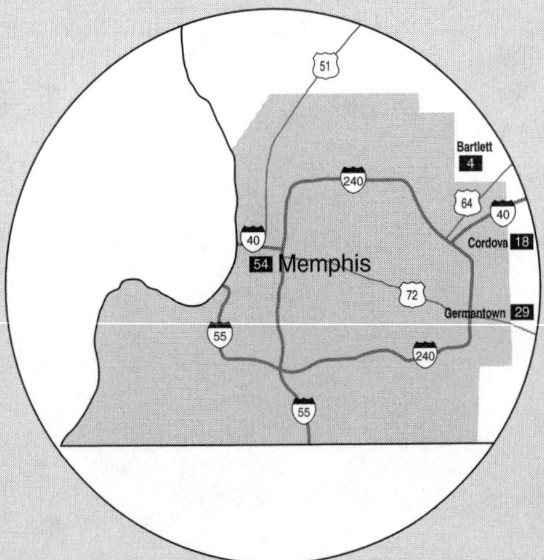

Bartlett 4
Cordova 18
54 Memphis
Germantown 29


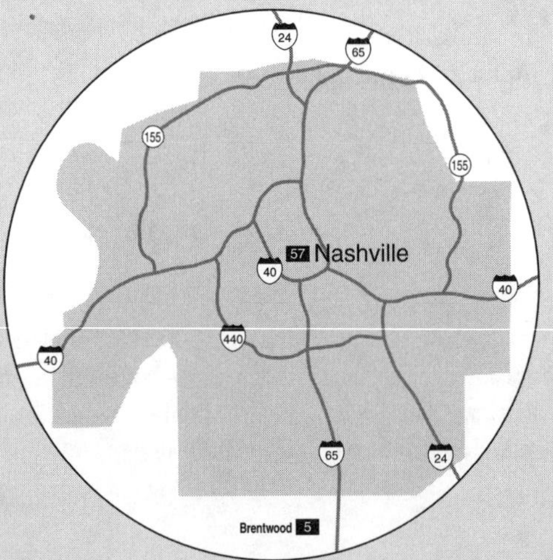

57 Nashville
Brentwood 5

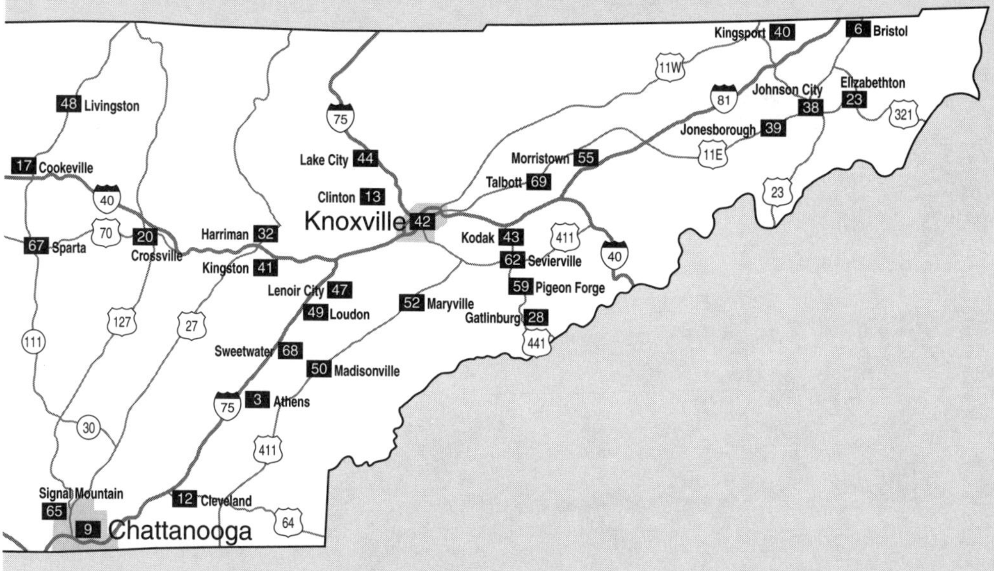
Kingsport 40
6 Bristol
11W
81
Johnson City
Elizabethton
38
23
321
Jonesborough 39
11E
48 Livingston
75
Lake City 44
Morristown 55
Talbott 69
23
17 Cookeville
40
Clinton 13
Knoxville 42
Harriman 32
67 Sparta
70
20 Crossville
Kodak 43
411
40
62 Sevierville
Kingston 41
Lenoir City 47
59 Pigeon Forge
52 Maryville
49 Loudon
Gatlinburg 28
127
27
111
441
Sweetwater 68
50 Madisonville
75
3 Athens
30
411
Signal Mountain
65
12 Cleveland
64
9 Chattanooga

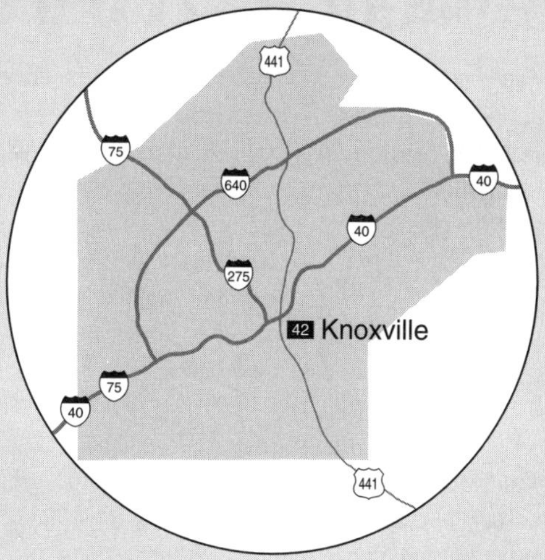
441
75
640
40
40
275
42 Knoxville
75
40
441

# Tennessee

*Although the 35,000-square-foot mall has a lot to offer for the man in your life, women will enjoy it, also. They have a huge handmade basket section, a great area featuring advertising memorabilia, and a very nice country candy counter for stocking up on snacks for the road.*

# Your first adventure in the Smokies begins at Riverside Antique and Collectors Mall

I once spent four hours in this mall looking for nothing but blue and white dishes. The selection was great. One dealer had an entire wall filled with every imaginable pattern and maker. The great thing about this mall is its diverse selection. While I was looking for dishes, David was pre-occupied with the "man things." This mall has a lot to offer for the man in your life; matchbox cars, fishing equipment, old tool boxes, sports memorabilia, Indian Relics and collectible knives.

Riverside Antique Mall encompasses 35,000 square feet so, I could burn up a lot of paper mentioning the usual hodge podge of items most malls of this size offer. Instead I think I'll tell you about some of the unusual things you'll find here. For starters, they stock over 400 reference book titles, including Leggetts' Antiques Atlas, (so if you've borrowed the one you're reading, stop by and get your own). They have a huge handmade basket section, row after row of showcases housing many rare items and a nice country candy counter with all sorts of varieties of candies and dried fruits (recommended for snacking on down the road). The mall is decorated with hundreds of advertising signs which really sets the mood for shopping the minute you walk in the door. And, since I've mentioned advertising signs, I probably should tell you they have much to offer in that section as well.

Even after spending over four hours at Riverside, I still don't think we saw everything. It is one of the most interesting and clean (especially the bathrooms) antiques malls I have ever been in. On our next trip to the Great Smoky Mountains, I am going to allow more time for Riverside Antique and Collectors Mall.

*Highly recommended.*

*Riverside Antique and Collectors Mall is located at 1442 Winfield Dunn Pkwy. (Hwy. 66) in Sevierville, just minutes from the Great Smoky Mountains National Park. The mall is open daily 9-6, with extended summer hours.*

*Directions: From I-40, take Exit 407 (Gatlinburg, Sevierville, Hwy. 66). Go south five miles and the mall is located on the right side of the highway. For more information, call the Mall at 423/429-0100.*

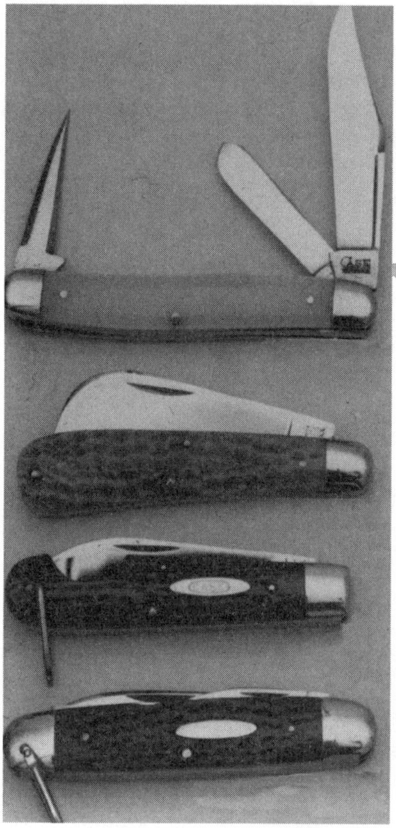

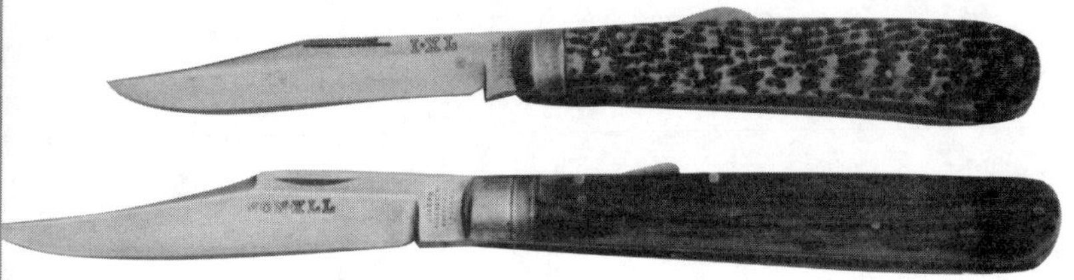

*Case, Boker, Remington, limited editions and commemorative knives, Indian artifacts, firearms and so much more await shoppers at the Riverside Cutlery Co., located inside the Riverside Antiques and Collectors Mall.*

# Riverside Cutlery Co. is more than a husband recovery area

Grudgingly, but with a smile I wheeled into the parking lot of another antique mall, but this one was the largest of any we had already been to. As we entered the building I was immediately struck with a sense of amazement, this one was different. The first thing to catch my eye was a nice display of Indian Artifacts and Remington bronzes. As I looked over the gigantic selection of reference book titles, I saw out of the corner of my eye, a huge antique and collectible knife department. I was truly on a mission now. I had to see these knives, touch them, hear the "walk and talk" of precision steel. As I peered deep into these well lit, neatly arranged showcases, I heard someone say, "May I show you something?" Yes, all of them..I thought. There were knives of all kinds...Case, Boker, Remington, Ka-Bar, Winchester, Queen, bargain knives, limited editions, commemoratives, and so much more. I told this nice young man about my personal collection of knives, a story I am sure he has heard many times before from others. He told me about this great catalog called appropriately, Riverside Cutlery Co., which was just recently mailed out free to over 700 avid collectors like myself. He had me put my name on the mailing list right there so I could be sure to get the next mailing. I was really amazed at the quality of antique and collectible knives that I found hidden within the pages. The next thing that caught my eye was a wall full of fine antique firearms, Winchesters, Colts, Remingtons, Military and Western firearms, I couldn't believe the amount of great items. I was really impressed with the amount of fine merchandise there was to choose from in this knife department as well as the entire mall. As I decided what to buy, (my wife was waiting on me for a change!!), this fine Riverside employee told me if I ever decided to sell my collection to give him a call. He said they also buy collections, large or small!! I left Riverside knowing that on my next trip to the Smoky Mountains, I would bring some of my knives and maybe do some trading!!

***Riverside Cutlery is located inside the Riverside Antiques and Collectors Mall*** *at 1442 Winfield Dunn Pkwy. in Sevierville. For catalog and other information, the address is P.O. Box 278, Kodak, TN 37764. The phone number is 423/453-9558.*

*Fine porcelains such as flow blue, Dresden and Limoges are offered.*

# Rare books among the many finds at Campbell Station Antiques

Established in 1983, this 35-dealer mall has several specialties to tempt shoppers. In its 10,000 square feet of space you'll find vintage linens and clothing from the Victorian era through the 1960s, sterling serving pieces, fine porcelains such as flow blue, Dresden and Limoges. Dealers in the mall specialize in period furniture (American, Country and French) and one dealer travels to Europe to buy.

*10,000 square feet of antique-filled space welcomes you at Campbell Station Antiques.*

*A hundred years of clocks are offered, from 1820s to 1920s models. This dignified grandfather clock is just one selection.*

A large selection of clocks from the 1820s-1920s are offered at Campbell Station in addition to architectural accents such as mantles, columns, stained glass and garden accents. The shop specializes in rare and hard to find books and offers a search service to its many customers from around the U.S.

*Campbell Station Antiques is located at 620 Campbell Station Road in Knoxville. For additional information see listing #42 (Knoxville).*

*Amish clothing from Pennsylvania — broad-brimmed hats of both straw and wool, hang on wooden pegs with handmade shirts, trousers and overgarments.*

# Country collectors open home to fellow antiquers

Kitty and Tony Ables have been personal friends of mine for a long time. We talk almost daily about this crazy antiques business and offer opinions to each other as to why something does or does not sell. Of course we have all the answers to this perplexity, so one would think we should be wealthy just for offering all this advice. But, until the world learns that we have the answers to all their problems, we probably should keep doing what we hope is best — selling antiques.

Kitty and Tony have a knack for finding some of the best early authentic pieces. Their eye for style and detail have enabled them to swoon the attention of some very influential people. They travel the U.S. to attend the finest antiques shows such as Heart of Country in Nashville and Marilyn Gould's Shows. Several times a year, Kitty and Tony open their home to unloading sales. People come from ten states just to attend these sales, mostly because the Ables' have gained a reputation for selling quality, authentic antiques. If you are traveling through Tennessee near Memphis, you can call anytime to let Kitty know you're in the area and would like to stop by. Her home is always open to fellow antiquers.

*Kitty and Tony specialize in upscale country furnishings and accessories. Their home is in Henning, Tennessee and they are open by appointment, or, you can catch up with them at finer antique shows nationwide. Call for show schedules or more information 901/738-2381.*

*An oak country cupboard from the 1800s glows with the patina of age.*

*1820s French Canadian cupboard shows loads of personality.*

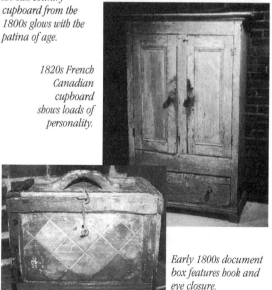

*Early 1800s document box features hook and eye closure.*

*Though no more than shells of their former selves, the personality of these buildings was irresistable to their new owners, who have completely renovated the two. In their new incarnation, they house vintage collectibles and antiques. Fine art is a specialty.*

# Trek along Tennessee back roads charms California travelers

Historical downtown Hickman was once a bustling 23 store metropolis. Because the railroad ran through town, it was almost chosen as the county seat. Unfortunately, the Cumberland River ran through the nearby town of Carthage and due to ever increasing commercial boat traffic, Carthage won the bid for county seat. This doomed Hickman's commercial growth. The tomato cannery finally closed, the once internationally famous mule trading went to the wayside, the infamous 'hotel on the hill' closed or burned, the grainery closed and one by one, all the businesses ceased to exist. Only the Bank of Hickman remained until it surrendered to the 1930s crash, along with the town's general store which survived well into the 1980s.

By 1996, only the bank and general store complex remained in its original state, the last remaining evidence of a once thriving business center. In May of 1996, Larry and Penny Bartlett while visiting the area, chanced upon these two historic buildings. The picture above represents what they say they fell in love with and bought on that visit. Windows broken out and/or boarded up, no electricity in the bank, no floors or ceilings, in other words, a shell. The general store was in better condition, but still needed extensive restoration. Penny asked Larry, "How long will it take to get it open for our antique mall?" Larry responded, "About three months." Two years later, the store was finally opened. The Bartlett's were not in a position to hire the work done, so Larry quit his job in California and began the restoration himself. Seven days a week, ten to twelve hours a day, definitely a labor of love, the results of this painstaking work is evidenced by the now completely restored complex.

The mall consists of many collectibles of various types, as well as antique furniture and artifacts in the more upscaled range. No new items, and reproductions are consistently purged. The second floor of the bank is dedicated to art, from signed limited editions to fine oils, once again, of the vintage type. The art gallery also consists of various unique objects d'art and statuary. They have commissioned a famous artist in Venice, Italy to create an exclusive masterpiece for display. Truly, one of the best examples of revitalization in the area.

*Antique Malls of Tennessee is located at 2 Sykes Road (at Gordonsville Hwy.) For additional information see listing #36 (Hickman).*

*An elegant pair of velvet upholstered armchairs with bold carved accents sit at a graceful accent table upon which a china tea service is displayed at the Antique Gallery.*

# Antique Gallery offers shopping and tea for two

Dealer space of 35,000 square feet may seem imposing, but the only overwhelming thing about the Antique Gallery is the positive response of its visitors. From abounding friendliness to the pride expressed in the displays of the 150 dealers, shoppers delight in taking part in this group shop. Although extremely spacious, the gallery is always full, but never overcrowded, as owner Robert Bowden and manager Eric Triche strive to maintain an "airy" feeling. Booths are inviting with excellent dealer presentation of the merchandise.

Boasts Mr. Bowden, "The prices offered in the Gallery are fantastic, the best in the area, and because of the fairness in pricing, collectors are drawn here from all regions of the country." Dealers are offered even better pricing through discounts.

Within such immenseness you would not expect the diversity the Antique Gallery provides. Offerings include most any familiar name: Nippon, Hummel, Dresden, Wedgwood, Roseville, Hull, McCoy, Royal Doulton, Limoges - to name a few - and also an array of categories like depression glass, carnival glass, crystal, silver, and flow blue. The selection in furniture is equally diverse. Many other collectibles are also part of the inventory. Showcases highlight the small and often rare items.

Include the family in this stop and dine in the Serendipity Tea Room any day, except Sunday, from 11 a.m. to 2 p.m. Menu items are freshly made and include soups, salads, sandwiches, and deliciously-different biscuits. Twenty-eight specialty teas are also offered. Private parties and receptions can be held in the Serendipity Teas Room after 6 p.m. If you find any of the furnishings inviting, they too, are offered for sale.

*The Antique Gallery is located at 6044 Stage Road in Bartlett. For additional information see listing #4 (Bartlett).*

*The stylish inlaid headboard of this poster bed with matching vanity table and nightstand is sure to grasp the attention of customers of the Antique Gallery.*

*Formal dining room service displayed with tasteful flair.*

*Offerings at the mall include, clockwise from left: A grouping of advertising memorabilia, finely carved sideboard, and collectable fishing gear.*

# Quality is first priority at East Town Antique Mall

This upscale mall, opened 10 years ago by John and Carol Hudson, allows antiques and collectibles only - no reproductions. "We stress quality," says Carol, "and we discourage damaged merchandise." With more than 300 booths and showcases, you can imagine the diversity of items you will find here. An abbreviated list includes the area's largest selection of American art pottery, two dealers who specialize in advertising memorabilia, several depression and elegant glass dealers, one dealer who carries R.S. Prussia and art glass, one dealer who has specialized in pressed glass for more than 25 years, two dealers who carry American, German, Russian and Japanese military collectibles (all authentic), several dealers whose display of American and English dinnerware includes many hard-to-find patterns, one dealer who offers a huge array of signed case iron, including a complete set of Griswold skillets from the smallest to the largest, another dealer who specializes in Torquay and who is past president of the collector's club, several toy and cowboy memorabilia dealers, one dealer who specializes in Nippon, another who carries many hard to find primitive items. The mall is also home to many retired modern collectibles such as Department 56, David Winter, Lladro, Royal Doulton, Wedgwood, Hummel, Disney Classics and others.

They keep a 'Want List' for customers looking for special items, and with their new expansion of 12,000 square feet, the Hudson's have added a large selection of fine furniture in all styles. There are several motels and restaurants at East Town's Exit, so plan to spend the night to explore all that Chattanooga has to offer.

*East Town Antique Mall is located at 6503 Slater Road in Chattanooga. For additional information see listing #9 (Chattanooga).*

*Row upon row of antiques and collectibles fill the little church where Jane Carson was wed and worshipped.*

# The little church that was 'saved'

*Dumplin Valley Antiques and Collectibles' church was built in 1839.*

Most of us save the top of our wedding cake, the dress, or flowers as a memento of our wedding day. But Jane Carson saved the entire church! The little church in which Jane and her husband, William, were married was built in 1839. Over the past 158 years it has sheltered many members of the faith (including Jane herself) and hosted hundreds of weddings. So, when Jane heard that her little church was being torn down to build a new one, she bought it, had it moved, and opened an antique shop in it.

Today, instead of preachers and pews, you'll find depression glassware, china, pottery, lamps, late 1800s and early 1900s furniture and more. Two dealers specialize in Fostoria, china and wood and tin advertising items.

*Dumplin Valley Antiques & Collectibles is located at 340 W. Dumplin Valley Road in Kodak. See listing #43 (Kodak) for additional information.*

*Inside, stained glass can be found, along with other unique collectibles and furnishings from kerosene lamps to centerpiece vases, accent tables, antique desks and more.*

*From finely wrought decorative porcelain, to exotic display pieces or functional tableware, Brooks' Auction always offers a fine selection.*

# Brooks' Auction has lots of action when antiques cross the auction block

Brooks' Auction, located on the Court Square in Covington, has been a monthly outing for us since 1994. Brad Brooks, the auctioneer, was raised in the auction business and schooled by his father from a very young age. The auctions are held the third Saturday night of each month at 6:30 sharp. The merchandise ranges from top of the line, fine quality, home or showroom ready, to some interesting fixer-uppers. You just need to be there to see what crosses the auction block.

Tip For Glass Collectors: Brad always has some very nice glassware; depression, Roseville, etc. I would say he has an excellent picker.

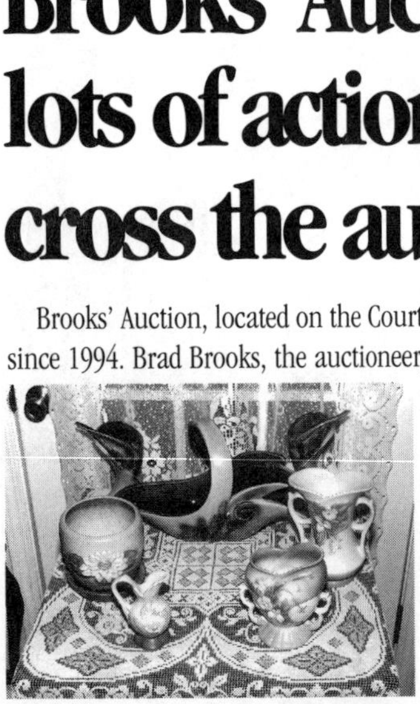

*Delightful small vases share delicate floral motifs.*

*Brooks' Auction is located on the Court Square in Covington. To get on his mailing list call 901/475-1744.*

*The luck of the lot determines whether or not a piece as handsome as this carved oak display case with shelves and mirror will cross the auction block.*

*George and Charlien McGlothin spent 4 1/2 years completing the restoration of Historic Falcon Manor.*

Photo by Dennis Klein

# White elephant transforms into elegant Victorian lady

In the year 1896, wealthy entrepreneur Clay Faulkner constructed the solid brick mansion now known as Falcon Manor. He promised to build his wife "the finest home in the county" if she would move next to the mill outside McMinnville where he made Gorilla Jeans.

But the building looked more like the victim of a terrorist bombing than the finest house in the county when George McGlothin bought it at an auction in 1989. Faulkner's mansion had been converted into a hospital and nursing home in the middle part of this century.

George and Charlien McGlothin spent 4 1/2 years completing the restoration, doing about 95 percent of the work themselves. With both the mansion's decor and their extensive collection of Victorian antiques, the McGlothins have authentically recreated Clay Faulkner's 1890s. Local octogenarians who remember the mansion in its heyday, say Falcon Manor is even more beautiful than it was in Faulkner's time.

Historic Falcon Manor took first prize in the bed and breakfast category of the 1997 Great American Home Awards. The National Trust added the B&B category just to pay tribute to "a type of establishment that has not only supported countless building rescues but also introduced their many visitors to the pleasures of living, if only temporarily, in old houses."

"George decided we'd would just work on restoring it as we had time and then retire there," remembers Charlien."It didn't take us long, though, to realize that this place has a friendly elegance and warmth that draws people to it. Even when we were just beginning the restoration, folks were stopping to ask for tours. We concluded this would always be a public place, whatever our intentions, so we made it official by opening Historic Falcon Manor as a bed and breakfast in 1993."

In addition to giving B&B guests an opportunity to "relive the peaceful romance of the 1890s," the mansion is open for tours each day at l p.m. "This is a favorite getaway for honeymooners, couples celebrating birthdays and anniversaries, and folks who just want to escape the stress of modern life," George observed. "History buffs, antique collectors, and people who've been involved in home restoration projects themselves take a special delight in experiencing the place. Of course, with the Victorian theme being so popular, we play host to lots of weddings as well."

The spacious guest rooms boast rich colors and museum-quality antiques. A sweeping staircase beckons guests to explore the mansion, while the 100-foot-long, wraparound gingerbread veranda invites them to rock in the shade of century-old trees and sip Falcon Manor's signature pink lemonade. McMinnville's location halfway between Nashville and Chattanooga makes it an ideal base for a Tennessee vacation.

In 1995, the McGlothins opened a Victorian Gift Shop in the original smokehouse. Their latest project, a 200-seat Victorian Carriage House dining room, is the site for elegant weekend meals by reservation.

The mansion was listed on the National Register of Historic Places in 1992, and it was designated as a historic site on Tennessee's Heritage Trail in 1996.

*Historic Falcon Manor is located at 2645 Faulkner Springs Road in McMinnville. For additional information see listing #53 (McMinnville) or visit their Web site at www.FalconManor.com.*

## 1 ARLINGTON AREA

**Lamb Crossing Antiques**
11022 Hwy. 70
901/867-0404
Fax: 901/867-0929
Mon.-Fri. 10-4; Sat. 10-2:30; Sun. 1-5 (closed last Sun. of the month)
*Directions: Traveling I-40, take Exit 20. Go north on Canada Road for 2 miles to Hwy. 70. Turn right and continue 3 miles. The store is on the left just after the Arlington city limits sign.*

This store opened in March of 1997. It's a quaint little shop, located in an old store, and filled with an eclectic blend of country and unusual items. Make sure you stop by on your way to Memphis.

### *Favorite Places to Eat*

**Bozo's**
Hwy. 70 (approximately 20 miles from Memphis)
901/294-3400

Bozo's menu becomes apparent about a half-mile away - barbecue! About the time you see the cloud of hickory smoke hovering over the restaurant, you start smelling all that sizzling pork. Bozo's is one of west Tennessee's landmarks, having been open every day except Sundays since 1923!

There is absolutely nothing about the decor to inspire a sense of elegance or upscale atmosphere - tired wood paneling, formica-topped tables, wooden chairs, a well-scuffed linoleum floor, pale green stools line up at gray counters, a Chevrolet-time clock on the wall. The only reason you go to Bozo's is for some of the best food you'll ever eat. They serve shrimp, chicken, salads, and steak, but the house specialty is pork, especially something called a "white and brown pulled pig plate." It's succulent white meat from the inside of the shoulder, and crustier brown meat from the outside, pulled into shreds and hunks and heaped on a plate along with saucy barbecue beans and sweet cold slaw. You can also get chopped plates and barbecue sandwiches, and sauce on the side. Nobody does it better!

## 2 ASHLAND CITY

**B J's Attic**
108 N. Main St.
615/792-7208

**Saint Elsewhere Antiques**
110 N. Main St.
615/792-9337

**Ruth Ellen's Antiques**
202 N. Main St.
615/792-1915

## 3 ATHENS

**Ourloom**
804 S. White St.
423/745-6055

**Antiques Unique**
Hwy. 30 W.
423/745-5941

**Gene's Olde Country Shoppe**
813 S. White St.
423/745-2254

**Cottage Antiques & Gifts**
15 W. Washington Ave.
423/745-8528

**Piedmont Antique & Inteiror Design**
104 N. White St.
423/745-2731

**Hughes Furniture Company**
316 N. White St.
423/745-2183

## 4 BARTLETT

**Upstage Antiques**
6214 Stage Road
901/385-0035
Mon.-Wed. 10-6; Thurs.-Sat. 10-8; Sun. 12-6

**The Antique Gallery**
6044 Stage Road
901/385-2544
Mon.-Sat. 10-6, Sun. 1-5
*Directions: On I-40, Exit 12 and travel north on Sycamore View to Stage Road. Turn right onto Stage Road and left at the first light between McDonald's and KFC.*

For specific information see review at the beginning of this section.

## 5 BRENTWOOD

**Ivy Crest Gallery**
1501 Franklin Road
615/377-0676

**Alcove Antiques**
9825 Concord Road
615/776-5152

**Gallery of Cool Springs**
7104 Crossroads Blvd., #115
615/661-5435

## 6 BRISTOL

**Oak Door Antiques**
1258 Hwy. 126
423/968-7177

**States Alternative Antiques**
105 17th St.
423/764-3188

**Ruth King Antiques**
618 State St.
423/968-9062

**Antiques Unlimited**
620 State St.
423/764-4211

**Mary Ann Stone Antiques**
610 State St
423/968-5181

### *Great Places To Stay*

**New Hope Bed & Breakfast**
822 Georgia Ave.
423/989-3343 or 1-888-989-3343
Open daily
Rates $70-130
*Directions: From I-81, take Exit 3 onto Commonwealth Ave. Turn left onto State St. (downtown Bristol) and pass under the large sign. At the second light after the sign turn right onto Georgia Ave. and go five blocks. The inn is on the right, on the corner of Georgia and Pine.*

The New Hope B&B is an 1892 Victorian that wraps its guests in a cloud of turn-of-the-century memories. The house exudes an atmosphere of Victorian elegance, complete with furnishings that are a mixture of antique and period. Located in an historic neighborhood, guests can stroll the streets on guided walking tours. The large wrap-around porch is the setting not only for morning or afternoon relaxation, but where breakfast is served in good weather. The private baths are large and inviting, with robes provided for after-bath enjoyment.

## 7 BROWNSVILLE

**Mid-Town Auction**
230 S. Church St.
901/772-3382
Auction Dates: First Sun. of the month at 10 a.m.
*Directions: Off I-40*

This little country auction has some surprising results. They always manage to have something that I want. The merchandise varies from sale to sale; sometimes early primitive pieces; sometimes rough; sometimes depression. You just never know so, you have to be there. They usually have lots of glass and advertising items, Roseville and other potteries and old prints can almost always be found. A great dealer auction!

## 8 CARTHAGE

**The Specialty Shop**
209 3rd Ave. W.
615/735-8441

**Creekside Collectibles**
115 Water St.
615/735-3190

**Shirley's Antiques**
47 Cookeville Hwy.
615/735-9887

**Massey's Country Antiques**
336 Defeated Creek Hwy.
615/774-3146

**Windy Hill Antiques**
Hwy. 70 N.
615/735-2561

## 9 CHATTANOOGA

**East Town Antique Mall**
6503 Slater Road
423/899-5498 or 423/490-0121
Daily 10-6 and Sat. 9-8 during daylight savings.
*Directions: From I-75: Take Exit 1 or 1B one half mile south of the junction of I-24 and I-75 (one mile north of the Georgia state line). Traveling south, take Exit 1, turn right, then turn right at the first red light. Traveling north, take Exit 1B, turn right at the second red light. The mall is behind Cracker Barrel.*

For specific information see review at the beginning of this section.

**Coates Antiques**
520 Ashland Terrace
423/870-1880

**Chase Dacus Collection**
3214 Brainerd Road
423/622-1715

**Temple & Co. Antiques**
1816 Broad St.
423/265-9339

**McCracken Bros.**
2622 Broad St.
423/266-0027

**Davis' Trading Post**
3627 Cummings Hwy.
423/821-0061

**Norma Jean's Antiques**
3829 Hixson Pike
423/877-5719

**Furniture Barn**
39 E. Main St.
423/265-1406

**Lambs & Ivy Antiques**
249 Northgate Mall
423/877-6871

**Junque Nique Shop**
6009 Ringgold Road
423/894-7817

**Antiques on the Southside**
Corner of 14th & Williams
423/265-3003

**Antiques on the Southside**
1401 Williams St., #C
423/265-3003

**Dacus Antiques**
3214 Brainerd Road
423/622-1717

**Cooper's Antiques & Decor**
3210 Brainerd Road
423/629-7411

**Marie's Antiques**
6503 Slater Road
423/899-4607

**Chattanooga Antique Mall**
1901 Broad St.
423/266-9910

**High Point Antiques**
1704 Cummings Hwy.
423/756-9566

**Dacus Antiques & Fine Furniture**
2422 S. Hickory
423/622-2220

**Barnyard Antiques Etc.**
7160 Lee Hwy.
423/899-3913

**Berning House Antiques & Dolls**
605 Marlboro Ave.
423/624-4436

**Lowe's Antiques**
4000 Ringgold Road
423/633-2902

**Cross The Years**
6503 Slater Road
423/892-4193

**Antiques & Country Decor**
3813 Dayton Blvd.
423/870-3687

**Clement's Carnahan Inc.**
2420 S. Hickory St.
423/698-2800

**Fanny's Antiques & Fancies**
3202 Brainerd Road
423/624-6421

**Galleries at Southside**
1404 Cowart St.
423/267-8101

**Status Symbol**
1707 Cummings Hwy.
423/267-3001

### *Great Places To Stay*

**Adams Hilborne**
801 Vine St.
423/265-5000

Located at the cornerstone of the Fort Hood Historic District, this majestic Romanesque Victorian mansion is built in castle-like proportions of native mountain stone. The Adams Hilborne is lavished with fine antiques, original artwork, and exquisite fabrics in all the oversized guest suites.

## 10 CLARKSBURG

**Oma's Antik Haus**
3375 Hwy. 22
901/986-3018

## 11 CLARKSVILLE

**East Gate Antiques**
321 Drinkard Dr.
931/551-9572

**Traditions**
131 Franklin St.
931/551-9800

**High Street Antique Mall**
40 High St.
931/553-4040

**Cherry Station Antiques & More**
212 Warfield Blvd.
931/648-4830

**Ragin Cajun Antiques**
210 Kraft St.
931/552-0545

**The Emporium**
739 Madison St.
931/645-1607

**Madison Street Antiques**
1461 Madison St.
931/553-0420

**Granny's Antiques**
924 Providence Blvd.
931/648-0077

**Alcock's Heritage Hill Antiques**
416 N. 2nd St.
931/648-3989

**D R Marable Sales Antiques**
1303 Tylertown Road
931/551-3259

**Saint John's Antiques**
128 University
931/503-1515

**Salem Place Antiques**
1761 Hwy. 48
931/645-3943

## 12 CLEVELAND

**Carousel**
80 Church St. N.E.
423/339-3934

**Lace Emporium**
2065 Collins Dr. N.W.
423/476-5836

**Antiques Parlour**
208 Grove Ave. N.W.
423/476-6921

**Westside Shop**
2910 Harrison Pike
423/339-9838

**Treasures Forever**
151 Inman St. S.E.
423/478-2711

**Cleveland Furniture Sales**
220 Inman St. S.W.
423/472-0099

**Boardwalk Uniques & Antiques**
251 Inman St. N.E.
423/478-1010

**Reflections**
94 Mikel St. N.W.
423/559-0140

**Presswood's Vintage Antiques**
3350 Ocoee St. N.
423/479-4460

**Lamps & Things**
702 17th St. N.W.
423/339-3963

**Carolyn's Antiques & Oriental**
464 1st St. N.W.
423/472-5000

**Yesterday's Treasures**
2101 Dalton Pike S.E.
423/476-1808

## 13 CLINTON

**Clinton Antique Mall**
317 N. Main St.
423/457-3110

**Market Place Antiques**
333 Market St.
423/463-8635

## 14 COLLEGE GROVE

**Leon Tywater & Sons Auction Company**
Hwy. 31 A
615/790-7145, 615/368-7772
Call for auction dates
*Directions: 30 miles South of Nashville on 31A*

There are lots of reasons to attend Leon & Andy's (that's Leon's son) auction. One being, that for an auction to be located so far out in the sticks, they sure have some "good stuff." I honestly don't know where they get their merchandise, but I can tell you this, it is exceptional. If you are into early American (as I am), then this is the sale for you. The last time I attended the auction I purchased an 1800s plantation desk, a cannonball rope bed, a cherry sideboard (pegged), a mantle with original mustard paint and I let a fabulous sugar chest get away. But, if this isn't reason enough to encourage you, then this most assuredly will. Leon's wife is a wonderful cook! Leon too! They start cooking about a week in advance of the sale. Leon smokes the barbecue, and his wife makes homemade sandwiches, pies (several kinds), cakes and fried pies. But, my favorite is the chocolate cake, "it's to die for." The last time I talked to Leon he told me to call first and he would have her bake me a whole one. Well, get ready Leon, as soon as this book goes to print I'm on my way, so preheat the oven.

## 15 COLLIERVILLE

Collierville has over thirteen shops and malls, all within a short distance of each other. Most of the shops are located on the Historic Town Square however, two wonderful malls can be found as you enter Collierville on Poplar Ave. These two malls are listed below.

*Directions to Collierville: From I-240, take the Poplar Ave. exit for Germantown. Continue on Poplar through Germantown. Collierville is located approximately 10 minutes from Germantown.*

*To reach the Town Square, continue on Poplar to the third light past Abbington Antique Mall. Turn right on Main St. A Historical Town Square marker is located in front of the bank on your right to indicate the location of the Town Square.*

### Sheffield Antiques Mall
708 W. Poplar Ave.
901/853-7822
Mon.-Thurs. 10-5; Fri.-Sat. 10-8; Sun. 12-6
*Directions: Located behind Wendy's on the left.*

Sheffield Antiques Mall is Collierville's largest antique haven. With over 150 quality dealers you are sure to find many treasures here. The mall is represented by some of the best dealers in the Memphis area, offering a wonderful selection of French, English and American antiques.

Lunch in The Garden Room Cafe located within the mall. Open for lunch 11-2, Tue.-Sat., the Cafe features gourmet soups, salads, sandwiches and desserts. A sampling of the sumptuous menu includes; Hot Ham Delights, Crab Toasties Florentine, Faccacia Rueben, Napa Valley Chicken Salad, Shrimp and Crab Louis, Caribbean Tuna Salad and Gorgonzola Potato Salad. The dessert menu includes Sweet German Chocolate Pie (the best), Cream Cheese Clouds and Fruit Cobbler.

### Abbington Antiques Mall
575 W. Poplar Ave.
901/854-3568
Mon.-Sat. 10-6, Sun. 12-6
*Directions: Located across the street from Wal-Mart on Poplar Ave.*

Abbington Antiques, since its very beginning, has been known for exceptional antiques. Presenting distinctive pieces for the discerning customer is the desire of the dealers who make Abbington what it is today. With a focus on decorating for the home or office, an unusual offering of architectural iron, sewing collectibles, Regina music boxes, phonographs, radios, lamps, mirrors, statuary, candles, antique tools and more is available. The furnishings offered by the shop are of excellent style and quality and are often sought after by decorators from the Memphis area.

**DeSheilds Lighting, Inc.**
451 Hwy. 72
901/854-8691

**White Church Antiques & Tea Room**
196 N. Main St.
901/854-6433

**Old Towne Antiques & Gifts**
521 W. Poplar Ave.
901/854-7063

**Past & Presents**
307 W. Poplar Ave.
901/853-6454

**Roseview Antique Mall**
112 U.S. Hwy. 72 E.
901/854-1462

**Unique Antiques & Auction**
449 U.S. Hwy. 72 W. #3
901/854-1141

Listed below are the shops located around the Historic Town Square.

### Center Street Antiques
198 S. Center St.
901/861-3711
Mon.-Sat. 10-5, Sun. & evenings by appointment
*Directions: From I-240, take Poplar Ave. exit for Germantown. Continue on Poplar through Germantown to Collierville, take a right (east) on Hwy. 72. At the first traffic light, turn left on Center St.*

Located one block south (across the railroad tracks) of Collierville's Historic Town Square, Center Street Antiques is the newest addition to the town's growing collection of antique shops. Filled with a unique assortment of English, Continental, American, primitive and Victorian furniture, there's something for everyone. The great selection of architectural pieces, gardenware, vintage lighting, china, antique toys and collectibles is sure to inspire the decorator in you. With each new dealer, the list of fabulous finds continues to grow.

**Town Square Antique Mall**
118 E. Mulberry St.
901/854-9839

**Not Forgotten**
94 N. Main St.
901/854-8859

**Sentimental Journey Antiques**
118 N. Main St.
901/853-9019

**Liberty Tree Antiques**
120 N Main St.
901/854-4364

**English Country Antiques**
102 E. Mulberry St.
901/853-3170

**Remember When Antiques**
110 E. Mulberry St.
901/853-5470

**Shepherd's Store**
122 E. Mulberry St.
901/853-8415

**Antique Marketplace of Collierville**
88 N. Main St.
901/854-8859

## 16 COLUMBIA

### Accents and Antiques of Columbia
Northway Shopping Center, Suite 123
119 Nashville Hwy. - Hwy. 31
931/380-8975
Fax: 931/388-5353
Mon.-Sat. 10-5, Sun. 1-5
*Directions: From I-65: Take Exit 46, then turn left onto Hwy. 412. At the end of the highway, take a left onto Hwy. 31. Follow the road until the 2nd light. Accents and Antiques is on the right.*

Owner Debbie Harris has been in business three years and has over 7,000 square feet of general antiques and collectibles. She offers the very needed service of lamp repair, so when your lighting treasures burn out, you know where to go.

**Sewell's Antiques**
217 Bear Creek Pike/Hwy. 412
931/388-3973

**Memory Shop Antiques**
1564 Bear Creek Pike/Hwy. 412
931/388-4131

**High Attic Antiques**
216 W. 8th St.
931/381-2819

**Uptown Antiques**
220 W. 8th St.
931/388-4061

**Moore's Antiques & Etc.**
910 S. Garden St.
931/388-6926

**Steely's Corner**
201 E. 9th St.
931/388-7101

## 17 COOKEVILLE

**A-l Clock Shop & Antiques**
8 S. Washington
931/526-1496

**Broadway Antiques**
247 W. Broad St.
931/520-1978

**Cookeville Antique Mall**
1095 Bunker Hill Road
931/526-8223

**Attic Window**
1281 Bunker Hill Road
931/528-7273

**Cedar Street Antiques**
44 S. Cedar Ave.
931/528-9129

**Cherry Creek Antiques**
5589 Cherry Creek Road
931/526-7834

**Fiesta Plus**
380 Hawkins Crawford Road
931/372-8333

**City Square Antiques**
8 S. Washington
931/526-6939

**Antique Vault**
26 W. Broad St.
931/528-3388

## 18 CORDOVA

### Antique Market of Cordova
1740 Germantown Pkwy.
901/759-0414
Mon.-Sat. 10-6, Sun. 1-5
*Directions: Traveling I-40 just east of Memphis, take the Germantown exit which will be Germantown Parkway. Turn south and stay on Germantown Parkway through two red lights. The market is located at the third red light on the southeast corner, where Dexter Road intersects with Germantown Parkway. Look for the big red ANTIQUES sign. Turn left on Dexter Road and make an immediate right into the Dexter Ridge Shopping Center parking lot. Located in the corner of the center. You can't miss it. Only about 1 mile from I-40.*

Within this quality upscale market you'll find pieces from Victorian to Primitive to Deco. A charming shop to explore, the shop is known for its quality glassware and pristine furnishings. One dealer specializes in old radios and lamps. Garden accessories are a favorite among locals so you are sure to find wonderful pieces available at all times.

### Sign of the Goose
9155 Rocky Cannon
901/756-0726
Open by appointment only

The Sign of the Goose is a "must see" for anyone who likes antiques, old homes, history, or just a good story.

The shop itself is located at the unique, two-story log house where Bill and Sylvia Cochran live. Sylvia actually uses her entire house as an informal showroom - but call first, because this is a by-appointment-only arrangement.

The house/shop began as an 1810 log home in Kentucky. In the 1970s a man had disassembled, tagged, numbered and hauled the logs to Tennessee, where he planned to rebuild it. But he decided not to finish the project, and that's how Sylvia first saw her family's future home: as a skeletal framework and a pile of old logs. She knew she could turn it into a wonderful home, and after much discussion with her family, Sylvia realized she would get her chance when husband Bill gave her a box of Lincoln Logs for their 16th anniversary!

The Cochrans moved the entire home - as it was - to their 20-acre homesite in Cordova near Memphis. The house was already atypical of log homes of its period, with its original 2,000 square feet and full second floor with high ceilings. And it was ideal for raising five children, who not only had a big, tough home, but acres of woods and ponds and outdoor delights to explore and enjoy. After reconstructing it, bringing it up to modern standards, adding a new porch and balcony across the front, and a kitchen addition to the back, the Cochrans had their dream house.

The rough, strikingly colored walls and plank flooring are an ideal and authentic setting for Sylvia's collection of American country furniture. She's been antiquing for 20 years, and has amassed an enormous wealth of pieces, accessories, and knowledge to share with customers.

An interesting note: During the Cochran's building process, they discovered a secret hidey-hole where an early 19th century deed of sale was found. It had been stuffed into a chink in one of the giant timbers. Now it hangs, carefully framed, on one of the log walls. Be sure to look for it as you browse through the country American antiques and architectural pieces.

### *Great Places To Stay*

**The Bridgewater House Bed & Breakfast**
7015 Raleigh LaGrange Road
901/384-0080

A romantic step back into history awaits you when you walk into this Greek Revival home which has been magnificently converted from a school house into a lovely, elegant dwelling filled with remembrances of travels, antiques, family heirlooms and Oriental rugs. The living room has 12 foot bookcases flanking a 200-250 year old Adams mantel with an ornate three sectional mirror reminiscent of a figure head on a ship's bow. The Bridgewater House has the original hardwood floors cut from five different trees on the property. There are enormous rooms, high ceilings, leaded glass windows and deep hand marbled moldings.

## 19 COVINGTON

**Brooks' Auction**
Court Square
901/475-1744

For specific information see review at the beginning of this section.

**That Certain Touch**
1702 Hwy. 51 S.
901/475-9100
Mon.-Sat. 9-5, closed Sun.

**Main Street Antiques**
650 U.S. Hwy. 51 S.
901/475-6181

**Six Oaks Antiques Inc.**
4095 Hwy. 59 E.
901/476-3135

## 20 CROSSVILLE

**Stonehaus Winery, Inc.**
2444 Genesis Road
Exit 320, I-40
931/484-WINE (9463)
Fax: 931/484-9425
Mon.-Sat. 9-6, Sun. 12-5 (Reduced hours during the winter months)
*Directions: Stonehaus Winery is located at I-40 Exit 320 (Genesis Road), just across the interstate from Vanity Fair Shopping Mall.*

Grapes, vineyards, and award-winning wines are not the things that one generally thinks of when the state of Tennessee is mentioned, but the Stonehaus Winery in Crossville, Tennessee will be producing from 80,000 to 100,000 bottles of wine this year. A wide selection of premium wines are available, including Reds, Whites, Rose and Blushes to suit the most discriminating palates.

The entire wine process is accomplished at Stonehaus, from the crushing and pressing of grapes to the fermentation, aging and bottling.

A gift shop situated in the adjoining building features many fine items from which to choose. Stroll through the shop and sample the homemade fudge. From there you can enter the cheese pantry where over 40 varieties of domestic and imported cheese, homemade bread and gourmet foods are available. From the winery you can visit the Stonehaus Antiques Shop located on the property, featuring eleven rooms of quality antiques such as quilts, glassware, furniture and more.

**Antique Village Mall**
I-40 Exit 320 Genesis Road
931/484-8664

**Rose of Sharon**
2238 Peavine Road
931/484-5221

**Crossville Collectibles**
314 Old Homestead Hwy.
931/456-7641

**Cumberland Mt. General Store**
6807 South York Hwy.
931/863-3880

**Crossville Antique Mall**
Hwy. 127 N.
931/456-8768

**Finders Keepers Treasures**
100 West Ave. S.
931/456-5533

**Page's Furniture**
302 Rockwood Ave.
931/456-0849

**Grandma's Attic**
371 Hwy. 68
931/456-5699

**Stonehaus Antique Shop**
2444 Genesis Road (located on the winery property)
931/456-5540

## 21 DICKSON

Dickson can probably best be compared to some type of rubber ball or toy that keeps bouncing back every time after being flattened! The town wasn't actually chartered until 1873, although there were settlers in the immediate area long before then. In 1883, just ten years later, the town charter was revoked over some kind of argument about whiskey, and they didn't get it back until 1899. In the meantime, the town burned down! Then there was another fire in 1893 that destroyed all but three of the downtown buildings. Another fire in 1905 wiped everything out again! That's why there is very little 19th century architecture in the town today. On the other hand, Dickson is almost a perfect personification of mid-century America - the 1950s, with nighttime cruising down the main streets in 50s hot rods and classics, even down to the drive-in theater that's been open since 1950!

They also have an Old Timers Day, held the first Saturday in May since its beginning in 1958! It starts with a parade and goes on to lots of crafts, a flea market, plenty of food and entertainment that includes a liars contest and a seniors talent contest that's wide open to whatever kind of talent the old timers want to show off.

**Ox-Yoke Antique & Gift**
1901 Hwy. 46 S.
615/446-6979
Mon.-Sat. 10-5 and by appointment
*Directions: Take I-40 to Exit 172 onto Hwy. 46. The red brick store is about 1 3/4 miles north at the red light.*

Mr. and Mrs. Yates have been very busy and inventive over the last 30 years. Their building has housed four very different types of businesses - and they have owned and operated all of them! First they opened a service station in 1967; years later it became a fabric store. Then it was a steak house for the next 13 years, and in 1991, they transformed it into an antique store. Mrs. Yates, with her eye for display, carries a lot of oak, walnut and pine furniture, all kinds of collectibles including glassware, pottery, some 1950s ware, silverplate, lamps, and a nice array of jewelry.

**Hamilton Place**
202-210 N. Mulberry St.
615/446-5255
Mon.-Sat. 9-5

Within nearly 9,000 square feet of space filled with forty-eight booths, Hamilton Place antique mall is simply packed with wonderfully unique items. Owners Jim and Ruby Reynolds remodeled and air-conditioned the historic old Roger L. Hamilton Super Market, owned by her parents, which covers half a block.

Hamilton Place is filled with booths offering mostly antiques and collectibles (including "David Winter Cottages," "Hamilton Collection Dolls," and "Boyds Bears") woodcrafts, silk and dried floral items, linens, lace, brass, home accessories, "Tennessee and English" gift baskets, books, ceramics, porcelain dolls, framed prints, custom curtains and accessories and more. There is a bridal registry, layaway and an item locator service, plus all credit cards are accepted. The Reynolds also have a bed and breakfast (See below). If you like to shop, you'll love Hamilton Place.

**Nana's Attic**
208 W. College St.
615/441-6032

**Reeder House Gallery**
705 W. College St.
615/446-2603

**Haynie's Corner**
101 S. Main St.
615/446-2993

**Hamilton Place**
202 N. Mulberry St.
615/446-5255

**Collectors Corner**
206 Sylvis St.
615/446-0552

**Main St. Antiques Mall**
131 N. Main St.
615/441-3633

**Behind Times Antiques**
105 W. Railroad St.
615/441-1864

### *Great Places To Stay*

**Deerfield Country Inn**
170 Woodycrest Close
615/446-3325
*Directions: From Nashville, travel west on I-40 approximately 35 miles to Exit 172. Exit right onto Hwy. 46. Go about two miles to the first red light. Turn left onto Pomona Road and drive to its end (about two miles) then turn left onto West Grab Creek Road. Go 1/4 mile to Woodycrest Road (first road on your right). Turn right and go to the end of the road (about 1/2 mile). Turn left onto Woodycrest Close. The inn is on your right amidst a grove of trees. From Memphis, travel east on I-40 to Exit 172 - then refer to the directions above.*

The Deerfield Country Inn is a newly constructed, stately, six-columnar Georgian colonial home that blends Old South charm with modern-day amenities.

Fancy yourself as Scarlet or Rhett as you saunter to the spacious front porch and enter a foyer spotlighting a grand circular staircase. Impressive antiques, oriental rugs and chandeliers augment your sense of opulence as you ramble through the main rooms. An open, airy kitchen accented with Quimper pottery and Longaberger baskets engenders a warm, welcoming ambiance.

The large first and second-story verandahs in front and two sizeable decks on the lower level at the rear entice enjoyment of a serene, rustic setting. Savor bountiful breakfasts or succumb to decadent desserts. You can always burn the calories by exploring 57 acres of shady paths and rolling hills, go bicycling or play a game of croquet.

Guest Room 1 is The Susie Lucille Room. Named for the late mother of Jim Reynolds, this cozy room overlooks the field of dreams from the upstairs verandah facing southeast - the front of the house. The room is decorated with Laura Ashley wallcovering and accessories. Of special interest is the ornate double-iron bed and a dresser acquired from the estate of former Tennessee Governor Frank Clement. Guest Room 2 is The Pearl Margaret Room. This generous-sized room - named in honor of the late mother of Ruby Hamilton Reynolds - faces northwest and boasts an antique twin-bedded suite and doll collection. Guest Room 3 is The Mulberry Room. Stretch out and unwind on the carved bed in this roomy space. Sit in one of the antique chairs by the large bay window facing northwest and listen to birds singing in the trees. This room is decorated with Eastlake antiques, old-fashioned purses and a compelling collection of books, pictures and memorabilia of the Royal family - acquired during the years your hosts lived in England. This is a great get-away for those who want to experience Southern hospitality and peaceful seclusion.

Deerfield Country Inn is conveniently located just minutes from I-40 and downtown Dickson. Stroll along historic Main Street and exchange hearty greetings with the locals. Hunt for treasures at many area antique shops. Tap your toes to a live country music show downtown on Saturday night. Take afternoon tea and nibble on tarts at a charming area tea room. Enjoy a Southern-cooked meal or a fine dinner at one of several restaurants.

Your gracious hosts at Deerfield Country Inn are well traveled and have lived abroad periodically. Since they're familiar with many cultures, you'll find them easy to talk to. As owners of an antique mall, they're happy to share their collectibles savvy. And because Jim's an accomplished carpenter and Ruby's an interior decorator, things aren't always the same at the inn!

## 22 DYERSBURG

**Memphis Antiques & Interiors**
575 Mall Blvd.
901/285-0049

Owned by Kim and David Leggett, authors of *Leggetts' Antiques Atlas*.

**Walton's Antique Mall**
2470 Lake Road
901/287-7086
Mon.-Sat. 10-5, Sun. 1-5
*Directions: Exit 13 off I-155. Located behind McDonald's.*

This 12,000 square foot mall of 25 dealers, offers the antiquer an eclectic selection of antique furnishings and accessories including garden and architectural pieces, Victorian, primitive, old toys, pottery, nice glassware, linens and old books, just to name a few. But, if you miss this mall you'll be passing up on the opportunity to purchase some of the best and most unusual early collectibles around. Bill Walton, the owner, has a "nose" for finding the rare; old grape crushers, trunks and boxes, great advertising pieces (much to choose from), early toys, quilts, old coffee grinders, tools, farm tables and more. You never know what he'll find next! (I highly recommend a stop at Walton's Antique Mall)

**Dyersburg Antique Gallery**
2004 E. Court St.
901/285-0999

**Days Gone By**
913 Forrest St.
901/285-2704

**Antiques & Things**
Court Square
901/285-7923

**Babe's**
Court Square
New business

## 23 ELIZABETHTON

**Antique & Curio Corner**
441 E. Elk Ave.
423/542-0603

**Antiques on Elk**
509 E. Elk Ave.
423/542-3355

**Duck Crossing Antique Mall**
515 E. Elk Ave.
423/542-3055

**Sycamore Shoals Antiques**
1788 W. Elk Ave.
423/542-5423

**Rasnick's Antiques**
Hwy. 19 E. Bypass
423/543-2494

**Antique Mall**
Hwy. 19 E.
423/542-6366

**Maude's Antiques**
Hwy. 19 E Bypass
423/543-1979

## 24 ERIN

**Carousel Antiques & Gifts**
106 Arlington St.
931/289-3057

**Irish Sales**
Hwy. 49 E.
931/289-4400

**Old Homeplace**
Hwy. 13 N.
931/289-5336

**Shamrock Gallery**
13 Spring St.
931/289-4117

## 25 FAYETTEVILLE

**Fayetteville Antique Mall**
112 College St. E.
931/433-1231

**Cobblestone Collectibles**
209 College St. E.
931/433-4778

**Wyatt Antiques**
301 Elk Ave. N.
931/433-4241

**Clark Antique & Collectibles**
3011 Huntsville Hwy.
931/438-0377

**Magnolia Mall Antiques & Gifts**
121 Main Ave. S.
931/433-9987

**Tennessee Antiques Collectible**
2939 Huntsville Hwy.
931/433-6084

## 26 FRANKLIN

The town of Franklin was officially established in 1799 in Williamson County, which was one of the wealthiest counties in the state by the mid-1800s, and still is today. The town itself, as well as the surrounding area, is full of historic homes and antebellum plantations, most of which have been restored. Two in particular are often mentioned in connection with Franklin, the Carter House and Lotz House.

The Carter House had the great misfortune to be caught exactly in the middle of the battlefield of one of the worst battles of the Civil War - the Battle of Franklin. The Carter family huddled in the cellar of their house while 35,000 soldiers fought in an area roughly two miles long by one mile wide...all centered around the house. According to area historians, there were more generals (12 total) either killed or wounded here than in any other battle in the history of warfare, and the Carter House is the most battle-damaged site in the country, with evidence of over 600 cannonball and bullet holes, 203 in one structure alone! All of this damage was done in the space of a five-hour battle, two-thirds of which was fought in total darkness.

Ironically, just across the street from this amazing relic is the Lotz House. During the same battle, the Lotz family hid in the basement of the Carter house with the Carter family, but the Lotz House has no battle scars! Presumably, Mr. Lotz, who was an extraordinarily skilled woodworker, repaired the damages to his home. The house is now a museum containing the South's largest privately-owned collection of Civil War memorabilia for public display.

**Franklin Antique Mall**
Winner of Tennessean's Reader's Choice Award and former nominee of The Commerical Historical Preservation Award
251 Second Ave. S.
615/790-8593

In 1980, Joan and Archie Glenn opened the Franklin Antique Mall as their dream. Little did they know how successful the activity at the old "Icehouse" would become, as what started out as 35 booths, grew through three expansions to more than 100 dealers and 14,000 square feet. Located twenty miles south of Nashville, in a huge, handmade brick structure, the multi-level building, constructed in 1870, originally became a flour mill and was more widely known as Williamson County's Icehouse at the turn of the century. It has now become home to one of the area's most charming malls. Inside amongst the wood and brick decor, collectors will find one of the South's biggest collections of furniture, from Early American to Victorian and turn of the century pieces in solid cherry, walnut, mahogany and oak. There is an ample supply of chests, tables, desks, beds, bookcase, sets of chairs and even a Jackson Press or two. There is a wide array of glassware from all periods, pottery, china, books, quilts, linens, clocks and pictures, and a booth of old lamps and replacement parts. Each booth is a treasure chest of nostalgia that collectively is an antique buff's bonanza.

The Franklin Antique Mall, multiple past winner of the Tennessean's Reader's Choice Award and former nominee of the Commericial Historical Preservation Award, just celebrated its 19th anniversary last year. The mall is now owned and operated by Amanda Glenn Pitts and Shawn Glenn with the death of their mother Joan last February.

"The Mall With It All" dubbed by Nashville Magazine is located at the corner of Second Avenue South and South Margin Street in Franklin and is open 10:00 a.m. to 5:00 p.m., Monday through Saturday and 1:00 p.m. to 5:00 p.m. on Sunday.

**Doris & Daughter**
108 E. Fowlkes St.
DORRISDAU@aol.com

**Winchester Antique Mall**
113 Bridge St.
615/791-5846

**Country Charm Mall**
301 Lewisburg Ave.
615/790-8908

**J. J. Ashley's**
119 S. Margin St.
615/791-0011

**Harpeth Antique Mall**
529 Alexander Plaza
615/790-7965

**Heritage Antique Gallery**
527 Alexander Plaza
615/790-8115

**Antiques of Second Avenue**
236 2nd Ave. S.
615/794-6159

**Battleground Antique Mall**
232 Franklin Road
615/794-9444

**First Avenue Antiques**
210 2nd Ave. S.
615/791-8866

**Heirloom Antiques**
125 S. Margin St.
615/791-0847

**Hood's Retreat Antiques**
117 1st Ave. N.
615/591-7819

**Legacy Antiques**
420 Main St.
615/791-5770

**Leipers Fork Antiques**
4149 Old Hillsboro Road
615/790-9963

**Magic Memories, Inc.**
345 Main St.
615/794-2848

**Patchwork Palace**
304 Main St.
615/790-1382

**Rustic House Antiques**
111 Bridge St.
615/794-7779

**Woodland Antiques**
5180 Fire Tower Road
615/794-7791

## 27 GALLATIN

**Mick's Antiques & Flea Market**
803 S. Water Ave.
615/451-0878

**Gallatin Antiques**
913 S. Water Ave.
615/452-4373

**Antiques on Main**
117 W. Main St.
615/451-0426

## 28 GATLINBURG

**Morton's Antiques**
409 Parkway
423/436-5504

See Sevierville for additional antique shop listings.

### *Great Places To Stay*

**Butcher House in the Mountains**
1520 Garrett Lane
423/436-9457

Nestled within the pristine beauty of the Smoky Mountains, and secluded from any commercial area is Butcher House in the Mountains. A favorite hideout for artists, photographers, hikers, and guests with a palate for uniquely different cuisine. Hugh, a former executive, is now the "Muffin Man", creating fresh delicacies every morning. Gloria, is an Italian "Yankee" from the North, and Hugh being a "Southerner" can create riotous conversations in the morning. Breakfast time is party time!

Italian hospitality is found here in abundance just like the European Gourmet meal. The indescribable view of a 6,000 ft. mountain range as far as the eye can see will greet you each morning. AAA calls the view "spectacular".

## 29 GERMANTOWN

**Anderson Mulkins Antiques**
9336 Poplar Ave. (Hwy. 72)
901/754-7909
Tues.-Sat. 10-5
*Directions: From Memphis: Take I-240 and exit at Germantown. Go 8 miles to 9336 Poplar Ave. (Poplar is also Hwy. 72 and Hwy. 57) and the shop is on the left side, at the corner of Johnson Road and Poplar Ave. The address is on the mailbox. The shop is between Germantown and Collierville, 4 miles either way.*

The Mulkins and family really know antiques. They have been in the retail business (antiques) since 1906 -90 years!...and the business is still family owned and operated. Shoppers at Anderson's will find furniture and accessories, but they specialize in dining room chairs. Over the past 90 years they have forgotten more than most people ever know! It's worth a stop just to talk to them and hear what they have to say, not only about antiques, but about the life and times they have experienced first-hand - a life that most of us would call "antique" itself!

## 30 GOODLETTSVILLE

**Fanny's Sugar Barrell**
112 Old Brick Church Pike
615/859-7319

**Antique Corner Mall**
128 N. Main St.
615/859-7673

**Sweet Memories**
400 N. Main St.
615/851-9922

**Main Street Antique Mall**
120 N. Main St.
615/851-1704

**Goodlettsville Antique Mall**
213 N. Main St.
615/859-7002

**Rare Bird Antique Mall**
212 S. Main St.
615/851-2635

## 31 GREENBRIER

**Ox Yoke**
2141 Hwy. 41 S.
615/643-0843

**Little Bit of Everything**
2616 Hwy. 41 S.
615/643-8029

**Sanders Antiques & Restoration**
2606 Hwy. 41
615/329-1017

## 32 HARRIMAN

**Wright's Antiques**
2120 S. Roane St.
423/882-6060

**Out of the Past Antiques**
1310 S. Roane St.
423/882-9756

## 33 HENDERSONVILLE

**Antique Gallery/Treasure Hut Antiques**
115 Dunn St.
615/824-0930

**Hendersonville Antique Mall**
339 Rockland Road
615/824-5850

**Tuttle Bros. Antiques**
691 W. Main/Hwy. 31 E.
615/824-7222

## 34 HENNING

A great many people know about Henning, Tenn., because of one man, his book, and the epic TV mini-series. The man of course is Alex Haley, and the book and epic TV mini-series is 'Roots.' But there is more to Henning than Alex Haley. It is a town of interesting history and homes, a community intermingled with black and white people, and a town that is now striving to preserve its' heritage and become a source for future generations.

Although unknown to a lot of people in the West Tennessee area, Henning is the home of a Choctaw Indian Reservation. Each fall and summer the reservation sponsors an Indian Festival. Thousands of people from across the country flock to this tiny town to participate in the celebration and to learn more about the Choctaw culture. (For information on the Choctaw Indian Festivals call Cubert Bell at 901/738-2951.)

**J & A Antiques & Collectibles**
236 Graves St., Hwy. 87 E. (1/2 mile off Hwy. 51)
901/738-5367

John and Aliene Richards handle the general spread of collectibles, particularly smalls, glassware and costume jewelry, but they also specialize in one item you don't find often - old marbles! They also know how to make-do in a pinch, as this funny story shows: "We loaded up to do a flea market in Arkansas and went over the evening before," say Aliene. "The van was full to within 12 inches of the ceiling. When we arrived, there were no motels available and we had to set up at daybreak, so we slept on top of the tables in the van. When we got up at daybreak to start setting up, John had lost his glasses somewhere in the van during the night, and couldn't see to begin setting up! After much searching, we finally found his glasses, but we haven't had to sleep on tables since that show, and don't plan to do so again!"

**Kitty & Tony Ables**
140 N. Main St.
901/738-2381

For specific information see review at the beginning of this section.

**Scoggins Collectibles**
114 S. Main St.
901/738-5405

**Peas-n-Pod**
105 Moorer
901/738-2959

## 35 HERMITAGE

**Spring Valley Antiques**
4348 Lebanon Road/Hwy. 70
615/889-0267

**Hermitage Antique Mall**
4144 Lebanon Road #B
615/883-5789

## 36 HICKMAN

### Antique Malls of Tennessee
2 Sykes Road (at Gordonsville Hwy.)
615/683-6066
Fax: 615/683-6067
Call ahead for hours
*Directions: Approximately 45 miles east of Nashville on I-40. From I-40 take exit #258 (Carthage - Gordonsville exit). Go south (right) 2 miles to Hickman.*

For specific information see review at the beginning of this section.

## 37 JACKSON

### Yarbro's Antique Mall
350 Carriage House Dr.
901/664-6600
Mon.-Sat. 10-5, Sun. 1-5
*Directions: Visible from I-40. Call for directions.*

With its recent relocation, this mall promises even more dealers with more selections than every before. They carry a general line of antiques including Victorian furniture and accessories and many flow blue pieces. One dealer specializes in country furniture.

### Brooks Shaw's Old Country Store and Casey Jones Village
Casey Jones Village
901/668-1223 or 1-800-748-9588
Fax: 901/664-TOUR
Station Inn reservations 1-800-628-2812
Summer 6-10, Winter 6-9
*Directions: Casey Jones Village is located nearly mid-point between Nashville and Memphis on I-40 and Hwy. 45 By-Pass, exit 80A, in Jackson, just 90 seconds off the interstate. Look for the original 50-foot caboose sign.*

At the Old Country Store and Casey Jones Village, visitors can shop, eat, sleep and get a dose of history all at the same time. An extremely popular tourist stop, the entire place is perfectly suited for little folks and big people alike, especially if they are into trains. At the Old Country Store, visitors can eat in an enormous restaurant/buffet setting, then stroll through 6,000 square feet of gifts, confections, collectibles and souvenirs, then dive into the 1890s ice cream parlor for dessert while gazing at 15,000 Southern antiques on display. If that's not enough, the historic home of Casey Jones is right next door, along with a railroad museum and train store, complete with a Lionel dealer on the premises. You can climb aboard Engine #382, then take a mini train ride and then play miniature golf. At this point you should be ready to fall asleep, and the Casey Jones Station Inn is conveniently right there, offering 50 train-themed rooms. You can choose to sleep in a rail car suite or a caboose. Kids of all ages will love it!

**Trading Post**
116 W. Chester St.
901/424-9511

**Yesterdays Antiques**
212 N. Liberty St.
901/427-2690

**Tara Antiques**
205 S. Shannon St.
901/422-3935

**I-40 Antique Mall**
2150 U.S. Hwy. 70 E.
901/423-4448

**Old South Antique Mall**
1155 Rushmeade Road
901/664-9692

***Great Places To Stay***

### Highland Place Bed & Breakfast
519 N. Highland Ave.
901/427-1472
Fax: 901/422-7994
Open year round, 7-10 (Office hours)
*Directions: From I-40 traveling either from Memphis or Nashville, take Exit #82A onto Highland Ave. (also Hwy. 45 South). The inn is just 3.3 miles south of I-40 on Highland Ave., between Arlington St. and West King St. in the North Highland Historical District, five blocks from downtown Jackson.*

There's plenty to do and see in and around Jackson, but the layout of this particular B&B suggests you carefully choose your traveling companion - it is a romantic delight and should be especially considered for those intimate little getaways you occasionally indulge in!

Highland Place has four guest rooms, with an arrangement flexible enough to have one's own multiple-room suite. The Louis Room has a sitting area, antique vanity and king size bed, with an authentic claw foot bath tub with solid brass plumbing and hand-held shower. The Butler Suite boasts a queen size cherry bed with feather mattress and a sitting area with working table (great for corporate travelers) and private bath. The Hamilton Suite offers an antique walnut dresser and a custom-built walnut queen size canopy bed, a working fireplace (very nice for romance), and just across your own private hall, a bath with a tub large enough for two. The newest addition (as of yet unnamed) is a suite with skylight, feather mattress on a queen size bed, and a private bath with a waterfall shower for two!

## 38 JOHNSON CITY

**Granny's Attic**
200 N. Commerce St.
423/929-2205

**Curiosity Shop**
206 E. 8th Ave.
423/928-3322

**Antiques & Heirlooms**
126 W. Main St.
423/928-8220

**American Pastimes Antique Market**
217 E. Main St.
423/928-1611

**Antique Village**
228 E. Main St.
423/926-6996

**Town Square Antiques**
234 E. Main St.
423/929-3373

**Memory Lane Antiques & Mall**
324 E. Main St.
423/929-3998

**Antiques Antiques Antiques**
125 W. Market St.
423/928-8697

**Youngdale Antiques**
214 Mountcastle Dr.
423/282-1164

**Finishing Touch**
158 Austin Springs Road
423/915-0395

**Country Peddler**
1121 N. Roan St.
423/975-0935

## 39 JONESBOROUGH

This is Tennessee's oldest town, chartered in 1779. Its history has been colorful and exciting, and today the town is a perfect window to the past. Among the many things to do and see in Jonesborough is a stop at the Visitor's Center, where you can become acquainted with the town and its history; a visit to the Washington County History Museum; shopping in the numerous antique and specialty stores in the historic districts; and visits to the annual festivals held in July (Historic Jonesborough Days), August (Quilt Fest, with classes and exhibits), November and December (holiday arts and crafts and celebrations), and the big event in Jonesborough - the National Storytelling Festival in October. The National Storytelling Association, based in Jonesborough, has been holding this festival every year since 1973. Visitors can hear tall tales, Jack tales, Grandfather tales, anecdotes, legends, myths and more, while getting a glimpse of the oral tradition that has entertained and informed Americans for more than 200 years!

**Mauks of Jonesborough**
101 W. Main St.
423/753-4648

**Jonesborough Antique Mart**
115 E. Main St.
423/753-8301

**Old Town Hall**
144 E. Main St.
423/753-2095

**Trading Post Antiques**
1200 W. Main St.
423/753-3661

### *Favorite Places To Eat*

**The Parson's Table**
102 Woodrow Ave.
615/753-8002
Open for lunch and dinner weekdays
Sunday buffet 11:30-2
*Directions: From Knoxville, take I-81 to Exit 23 (Hwy. 11-E). Traveling south, take 181 to the Jonesborough exit. The restaurant is behind the courthouse off Main St.*

This lovely Gothic structure that was once the First Christian Church in Jonesborough, has been a temperance hall, lecture room, and woodworking shop.

Carefully preserving its history while enhancing its Victorian origin, Chef Jeff Myron and his wife Debra have converted the architectural landmark into a soul-satisfying restaurant. The fare is Continental, or as they say, "refined Southern, with a little bit of French, and a whole lot of love."

The heavenly selections include crepes, Rack of Lamb Dijoinaise, Roast Duckling a l'orange, with a choice of sinful desserts such as "Parson's Passion" and "Devilish Chocolate Ecstasy."

## 40 KINGSPORT

**The Antique Mall**
9951 Airport Pkwy.
423/323-2990

**Smith Sholals Antiques**
315 Beulah Church Dr.
423/239-6280

**Antiques I-81**
9959 Airport Pkwy.
423/323-0808

**Amanda's Antiques**
115 Broad St.
423/245-1423

**Anchor Antiques**
137 Broad St.
423/378-3188

**Haggle Shop Antique Mall**
147 Broad St.
423/246-6588

**Adams Company & Friends**
231 Broad St.
423/247-9775

**Colonial Antique Mall**
245 Broad St.
423/246-5559

**Country Square Antiques**
635 Fairview Ave.
423/378-4130

**Pittypat's Country Interiors**
2633 Fort Henry Dr.
423/247-2244

**Village Antiques**
4993 Hwy. 11 W.
423/323-2287

**Toy Train Antiques**
214 E. Market St.
423/245-8451

## 41 KINGSTON

**Cottage**
411 Gallaher Road
423/376-1926

## 42 KNOXVILLE

### Campbell Station Antiques
620 Campbell Station Road
423/966-4348
Mon.-Sat. 10-6, Sun. 1-6
*Directions: From I-40 and I-75, take Exit 373. Turn south and go 200 yards. The shop is on the left in Station West Center next to Cracker Barrel.*

For specific information see review at the beginning of this section.

**Farragut Antique Mall**
101 Campbell Station Road
423/671-3630

**B E L Antiques**
5520 Brier Cliff Road
423/688-2664

**Broadway Bargain Barn**
1305 N. Broadway St.
423/524-5221

**Marty's Antiques & Collectibles**
1313 N. Broadway St.
423/522-6466

**South Fork Furniture**
712 N. Central St.
423/525-0513

**French Market Shops**
4900 Chambliss Ave.
423/558-6065

**The Bottom Antiques & Collectibles**
3701 Chapman Hwy.
423/579-4202

**Gateway Antiques**
5925 Chapman Hwy.
423/573-2663

**Chapman Hwy. Antique Mall**
7624 Chapman Hwy.
423/573-7022

**Fever**
133 S. Gay St.
423/525-4771

**Sullivan Street Market**
118 E. Jackson Ave.
423/522-2231

**Kingston Pike Antique Mall**
4612 Kingston Pike
423/588-2889

**Antiques Plus**
4500 Walker Blvd.
423/687-6536

**Time Trader**
720 Broadway St.
423/521-9660

**Attic Antiques on Broadway**
1313 N. Broadway St.
423/524-2514

**Key Antiques**
133 S. Central St.
423/546-2739

**Chance's Antiques**
1509 N. Central St.
423/522-0311

**South Knox Collectibles Mall**
3615 Chapman Hwy.
423/577-6252

**Colonial Antique Mall**
4939 Chapman Hwy.
423/573-6660

**Crossroads Antiques**
7100 Commercial Park Dr.
423/922-9595

**Blair House Antiques**
210 Forest Park Blvd.
423/584-8119

**Jackson Ave. Antique Market Place**
111 E. Jackson Ave.
423/521-6704

**Carpenter Clock & Watch Repair**
4612 Kingston Pike
423/584-2570

**Antiques and Accents**
5002 Kingston Pike
423/584-5918

**Dominick's Antique Galleries**
5119 Kingston Pike
423/584-1513

**Antiques Inc.**
5121 Kingston Pike
423/588-5063

**West End Antique Market**
5613 Kingston Pike
423/588-1388

**Incurable Collector**
5805 Kingston Pike
423/584-4371

**Northern Friends**
1507 9th Ave.
423/546-5400

**Wildwood Gallery & Frames**
2924 Sutherland Ave.
423/546-3811

**Homespun Craft & Antique Mall**
11523 Kingston Pike
423/671-3444

**Broadway Antiques**
2310 N. Broadway St.
423/546-3303

**Vieux Carre Antiques**
1204 N. Central St.
423/544-7700

**Garrison Collection**
5130 Kingston Pike
423/558-0906

**Sequoyah Antiques Exchange**
5305 Kingston Pike
423/588-9490

**Calloway's Lamps Shades & Gifts**
5714 Kingston Pike
423/588-0684

**Bearden Antique Mall**
310 Mohican St.
423/584-1521

**Appalachian Antiques**
11312 Station West Dr.
423/675-5690

**A True North Inc.**
611 Worcester Road
423/675-7772

**Bill Moore Silver Matching**
310 Mohican St.
423/584-7642

**ESA US Antique Market**
1549 Coleman Road
423/588-1233

## 43 KODAK

### Dumplin Valley Antiques & Collectibles
340 W. Dumplin Valley Road
423/932-7713
Fri. 10-6, Sat. & Sun. 9-6
*Directions: Traveling I-40, Exit 407. Turn south on Hwy. 66 toward Gatlinburg. Turn right on the first road which is Dumplin Valley Road Continue 1 mile. Shop is on the right.*

For specific information see review at the beginning of this section.

## 44 LAKE CITY

**Valley Antiques**
808 N. Main St.
423/426-9445

## 45 LAWRENCEBURG

**Lawrenceburg Antique & Auction**
266 N. Military Ave.
931/762-6695

**Carriage House II**
34 & 38 Public Square
931/766-0428

**Flea Market Shop**
46 Public Square
931/762-6963

**Clover Leaf Antiques**
4449 Waynesboro Hwy./Hwy. 64
931/762-5658

**Gibb's Antiques & Collectibles**
2310 Pulaski Hwy./Hwy. 64
931/762-1441

**Market Place Antique Mall**
34 Public Square
931/762-1619

## 46 LEBANON

*Directions: Take I-40 to the Lebanon Exit #238, go north on Hwy. 231 to find the town square area and south to find everything else.*

It's difficult to picture the now bustling public square in Lebanon as once vacant, but that was the scene before its transformation. Originally, Lebanon was an active town, with business held inside its buildings and outside in the square. Time, as in many small towns, took its toll as movement to the perimeter of town, rather than the center, became the trend. Lebanon was fortunate in that, one by one, its wonderful structures in the public square area were purchased or leased and revived to become the center of activity once again. As crafters and antiquers occupied the old buildings, public interest grew, and so did that of professionals who also wanted to become a part of the newly-created, active center of town. Now the town, built in 1819, has experienced a re-birth and has undergone a facelift so that passersby, too, can share their proud heritage.

**Tennessee Treasures**
109 S. Cumberland
615/443-2136
Mon.-Sat. 10-5

There's no telling what you'll encounter at Tennessee Treasures, but you can be reasonably assured that if grandma had one, this shop does too! Although their specialty is kitchen items, you'll find a unique garden section with old plows, wheelbarrows, garden utensils, and gifts related to gardening. Also a part of the offerings are upscale furniture, unusual vintage clothing, and handmade Country American Christmas ornaments. There's even a birthing chair that breaks down to be carried in a bag by a mid-wife. Stop in, you never know when you'll catch a sale in progress!

**In Cahoots!**
123 Public Square
615/444-8037
Tues.-Sat. 10-6, Sun.-Mon. by chance

If you're searching for old drug store or five-and-dime store merchandise visit In Cahoots!. They also carry antique and vintage furniture, or for something a little different see their hand-painted children's furniture. As an added surprise, In Cahoots! Includes a full-service doll shop that performs minor repairs or redresses and cleans dolls. Madam Alexander, Lee Middleton, Susan Wakeen, and antique and vintage dolls are just part of their line.

**Rainbow Relics**
27 Public Square
615/449-6777
Mon.-Sat. 9-6, Sun. 1-6

Originally a bank that was torn down then rebuilt around its old vaults in 1977, it become home to Rainbow Relics and now houses antiques, including furniture - especially oak, primitives, linens, and glassware. Also offered are collectibles of art glass by Boyd and Marble Mountain Creations, which are limited edition pieces made from Georgia marble in the shape of, for example, cars, tractors, and trains.

**Cuz's Antique Center**
140 Public Square
615/444-8070
Mon.-Sat. 9-5, Sun. 11-5

Dubbed a "center" because it spans three buildings, Cuz's is the largest collection of merchandise in the area. Inventory includes not only fine examples of American, English, and French antiques, but also wonderful reproductions of such pieces. Cuz's also carries furniture, glassware, and bronzes. As you would expect, their selection includes oil paintings, stained glass windows, and a tremendous selection of jewelry, both estate and modern. For the pocket knife collector, Cuz's is also the home of the Fightin' Rooster Cutlery Company.

**Off The Square Cafe**
109 S. Cumberland St.
615/444-6217

If all of your searching for treasures has created an appetite, stop at the Off The Square Cafe, located inside the Tennessee Treasures Antique Mall. Try one of their specialty sandwiches like the homemade apple and grape chicken salad or the Cajun roasted beef. If a sandwich is a little heavy, try one of the thick and hearty homemade soups prepared daily, or have half a sandwich and a cup of soup. Whatever you choose, just save room for one of their homemade desserts!

**Coach House Antiques**
Public Square
615/443-1905

In the early days, Coach House Antiques was the town lawyer's office. It would be interesting to know the kinds of legal problems the town's folk had back in the 1800s. But, today throughout this historic building, the only decisions to be made are those of a "selective" nature. The shop carries a general line of antiques - everything from antique furnishings to collectibles.

**Bonnie Blue Antiques**
107 S. Cumberland
615/453-1158

What once was the men's store of Lebanon has now transformed into a chapter from Gone With The Wind collectibles and memorabilia. Victorian furnishings and accessories, vintage clothing and exquisite glassware are also offered at Bonnie Blue.

**Downtown Antique Mall**
112 Public Square
615/444-4966

Downtown Antique Mall once sparkled with diamonds and jewels as the town jewelry shop. Today it's no different. For the past 15 to 20 years, this shop has furnished its' customers with jewels of a different nature. This 2-story building houses some of the best American furnishings in the area as well as outstanding glassware.

**Denise's Timeless Treasures**
146 Public Square
615/443-4996

For the past seventy years this store has been a favorite with women. It began life as a shoe store and now houses fine antiques, particularly from the Victorian period. In addition, the shop stocks accessories to compliment the furnishings as well as pretty stationery for your writing table.

**Southern Rose Antiques**
105 Public Square
615/444-3308

Isn't it amazing how some things were just meant to be? Southern Rose was once a furniture warehouse and it still is today. This shop is filled to the brim with furniture from all styles and periods. Most likely you can spot pieces which appeared there over 100 years ago when they were sold as new.

**Ophelia's Antiques**
107 Public Square
615/443-0783

A hodge-podge, fun place to shop, Ophelia's carries antiques and collectibles covering many periods. Glassware, china, furniture, linens, prints, and more can be found at this antique "stop".

## 47 LENOIR CITY

**Buttermilk Road Antiques**
144 Antique Lane
423/376-5912

**Allen's Antiques**
103 E. Broadway
423/986-2724

**John Farmer Sales**
105 W. Broadway
423/986-5144

**Victoria's Antique Mall**
1200 W. Broadway
423/988-7957

**Valley Antiques**
I-75, Exit 76, 11020 Hotchkiss Valley Road
423/986-6636

**Twin Lakes Antiques**
11827 Hwy. 321 S.
423/986-8082

**"Good" win's Antiques**
9900 White Wing Road/Hwy. 321
423/986-3396

## 48 LIVINGSTON

**A Different Drummer**
106 E. Broad St.
No Phone # Available

**Zpast Antique Warehouse**
313 S. Church St.
931/823-8888

**Court Square Emporium**
108 N. Court Square
931/823-6741

**Antique Market**
116 N. Court Square
931/823-4943

**Livingston Trade Center**
203 S. Goodposture St.
931/823-2898

**Helen's Now And Then**
521 E. Main St.
931/823-1626

## 49 LOUDON

**Shirley's Charm Shop**
407 Grove St.
No Phone # Listed

**Sisters**
Mulberry St.
423/458-8027

**Brick Box**
400 Mulberry St.
423/458-0850

**General Store**
411 Mulberry St.
423/458-6433

**Carroll's Bargain Box**
854 Mulberry St.
423/458-6320

**Sweet Memories Antique Mall**
930 Mulberry St., Suite 104
423/458-2331

**Warehouse Antiques Collectibles & Gifts**
1034 Mulberry St.
423/458-3412

**Judy's Antiques**
100 Steekee Creek Road
423/458-4211

## 50 MADISONVILLE

**Ye Ole Towne Antiques & Collectibles**
203 Tellico St.
423/442-5509

**Two Ps in a Pod**
266 Warren St.
423/442-6607

## 51 MANCHESTER

**Top of the Hill Antiques**
5751 Cathey Ridge Road
931/728-2610

**Lester's Antiques**
707 Gowen Road
931/728-2669

**Antiques-A-Rama**
626 Hillsboro Blvd.
931/723-4209

**North Side Clocks**
2032 MacArthur/Hwy. 55
931/728-4307

**Somewhere In Time**
324 Ragsdale Road
931/728-8987

## 52 MARYVILLE

**Boone's Barn Antiques Collectibles**
2408 N.W. Lamar Alexander
423/681-0877

**Back In Time Antiques**
504 Odell
423/983-7055

**Law's Interiors Inc.**
306 S. Washington St.
423/982-0321

**Memories of the Past Antiques**
931 E. Broadway Ave.
423/982-2810

## 53 McMINNVILLE

This is one of the strangest and most fun places to visit that you're likely to run across! McMinnville is the "Nursery Capital of the World," has the second largest cavern system in the country, has a bed and breakfast in a fabulous old Victorian mansion. And on top of all this, it has antiques. Is this a combination or what!

There really are between 400 and 500 nursery growers (trees, plants, that kind of nursery) in the area. This is evidently the only place in the world that has such a perfect combination of climate and soil. This industry began in the 1800s when the area was widely known for its apples and especially for the apple brandy that was produced. The apple tree business grew and evolved into this enormous industry that is now world famous.

Cumberland Caverns are open to the public May through October. They were discovered in 1810 and are now a national landmark.

### McMinnville Antique Mall, Inc.

2419 Smithville Hwy.
931/668-4735
Mon.-Sat. 9-5, Sun. 1-5
*Directions: Take Exit 111 (Manchester) off I-24, Hwy. 55, or take Silver Point exit off of I-40, Hwy. 56. The shop is one mile past McDonald's on Hwy. 56 North off of Hwy. 70 South.*

Pay close attention, because this gets confusing. Barbara Oliver owns the mall, and Susan is Barbara's daughter and Charlotte is Barbara's daughter-in-law. Susan went to work at this mall, and she and Charlotte decided they wanted to own it. So they asked Barbara to buy it so they could run it. Barbara agreed, bought the mall, Susan and Charlotte manage it, and Barbara has her own shop elsewhere. Susan and Charlotte have 28 dealers in the McMinnville Antique Mall, offering a variety of furniture, Depression and other glassware, as well as pottery and a multitude of other items. It's not confusing if you're just going there to shop...

**Antiques on High**
301 S. High St.
931/473-0922

**B & P Lamp Supply**
843 Old Morrison Hwy. 55
931/473-3016

***Great Places To Stay***

### Historic Falcon Manor

"Winner of the 1997 Great American Home Award for outstanding home restoration by the National Trust For Historic Preservation"
2645 Faulkner Springs Road
931/668-4444
Web site: www.Falconmanor.com
Email: FalconManor@FalconManor.com
*Directions: From I-24: Take Manchester Exit 111 east to McMinnville. DO NOT go into the business district. Keep going straight on Hwy. 70 S. Bypass. At the fifth traffic light, turn left onto Faulkner Springs Road. The mansion is at the end of the road, 1 3/10 miles from the Bypass. From I-40: Take exit 273 S. And go straight through Smithville. In McMinnville, turn left onto Hwy. 70 S. Bypass, then left at the second light onto Faulkner Springs Road.*

For specific information see review at the beginning of this section.

## 54 MEMPHIS

### Satterfield's Home Accessories

2847 Poplar Ave., Suite 102
901/324-7312
*Directions: From I-40: Take I-40 to Sam Cooper Blvd. And turn left on Tillman. Take a right on Poplar Ave., then a left on Humes. From I-240: Exit at Poplar Ave. and then head toward downtown, west.*

Satterfield's is a distinctive decorator shop filled with treasures from around the world. Some of its wares include Majolica, Spelter, porcelain and crystal. They also have a large selection of oil paintings, mirrors and bronzes.

**Pinch Antique Mall**
430 N. Front St.
901/525-0929

**Cottage Antiques & Gifts**
2330 S. Germantown Road
901/754-5975

**David's Antiques**
3397 Lamar Ave.
901/566-0953

**Crump-Padgett Antique Gallery**
645 Marshall Ave.
901/522-1155

**Springer's Antiques**
5050 Park Ave.
901/681-0025

**Cottage House Mall**
4701 Summer Ave.
901/761-5588

**Broken Spoke Collectiques**
6445 Summer Ave.
901/377-7974

**Savannah's Fine Antiques**
2847 Poplar Ave., Suite 104
901/452-7799

**Chip N' Dale's**
3475 Summer Ave.
901/452-8366

**Chip N' Dale's**
3457 Summer Ave.
901/452-5620

**PALLADIO Antique & Interior Marketplace**
2169 Central Ave.
901/276-3808

**Antique Mall of Midtown**
2151 Central Ave.
901/274-8563

**Antique Warehouse**
2563 Summer Ave.
901/323-0600

**Bill Rick's Antiques**
733 S. Cooper St.
901/725-9635

**Bo-Jo's Antique Mall**
3400 Summer Ave.
901/323-2050

**Buckley's Antiques**
1965 Madison Ave.
901/726-5358

**Common Market, Inc.**
364 S. Front St.
901/526-4501

**Consignments**
2300 Central Ave.
901/278-5909

**Crocker Galleria**
2281 Central Ave.
901/274-1515

**Flashback Inc.**
2304 Central Ave.
901/272-2304

**House of Yesteryear**
1692 Madison Ave.
901/276-0416

**Idlewild House**
149 Union Ave.
901/527-9855

**Madison Antiques**
1964 Madison Ave.
901/728-5520

**Market Central**
2215 Central Ave.
901/278-0888

**Second Hand Rose**
2129 Central Ave.
901/276-4600

**Union Avenue Antique Mall**
1652 Union Ave.
901/276-0089

**Vance Boyd Antiques & Collectibles**
171 S. Cooper St.
901/726-4652

## 55 MORRISTOWN

**A-Z Repeat N More**
5968 W. Andrew Johnson Hwy.
423/581-2623

**Yesterday-Antiques & Uniques**
128 E. Morris Blvd.
423/586-9273

**Dianne's Place Antiques**
1040 Buffalo Trail
423/318-0700

**Johnny's Antiques**
415 E. Converse Ave.
423/587-4750

**Bacon's Antiques & Collectibles**
413 N. Cumberland St.
423/581-7420

**Radio Center Antiques**
1225 S. Cumberland St.
423/586-4337

**Farm House Antiques**
148 W. Main St.
423/581-1527

**Olde Towne Antique Mall**
181 W. Main St.
423/581-6423

## 56 MURFREESBORO

Located in the "Heart of Tennessee", Murfreesboro's location is the geographical center of the State. Home to Middle Tennessee State University and the Stones River National Battlefield. The location of the Nissan USA Motor Manufacturing plant and its close proximity to Nashville has made Rutherford County one of the fastest growing in the State.

### Antique Centers I & II
2213-2219 S. Church St.
615/896-5188 (I) and 615/890-4252 (II)
Mon.-Sat. 9-5, Sun. 10-5
*Directions: From I-24 (25 miles southeast of Nashville) take exit 81-B at U.S. 231 Murfreesboro. Turn onto the access road in front of Burger King. The Centers are next to Cracker Barrel.*

The Antique Center has been at the same location since its beginning in 1973. The 30,000 square foot building was divided into two shops at that time and has continued as such, therefore, giving it the name "I & II". Antique Center I has 40 dealers, three of whom have been with the center since 1973. Antique Center II has 30 dealers. Both shops carry a wide selection of furniture to meet the needs of both decorator and first-time buyers. Several dealers specialize in depression glass, elegant glassware such as Fostoria, Cambridge, Tiffin, Heisey, carnival and art glass. Showcases highlight pottery such as Roseville, Hull, Weller, Watt, sterling silver, holiday collectibles, black memorabilia, toys and dolls. Antique Center II specializes in chandeliers. The chandeliers have been refurbished and are ready to go into the home. They range in size from 18" to 6 ft., and from one bulb to 12 or more as well as gas light fixtures. Delivery and shipping is available.

**Chick's Antique Shop**
516 S. Church St.
615/893-2459

**Antiques Unlimited**
2303 S. Church St.
615/895-3183

**Keepsakes Antiques**
2349 S. Church St.
615/890-4125

**Ed's Antiques**
7497 Hwy. 231
615/893-6719

**Yesteryear Civil War Relics**
3511 Old Nashville Hwy.
615/893-3470

**Magnolias**
229 River Rock Blvd.
615/848-2905

## 57 NASHVILLE

### Antique Merchants Mall

2015 8th Ave. S.
615/292-7811
Mon.-Sat. 10-5, Sun. 1-5
*Directions: The Antique Merchants Mall is located in the heart of Nashville's "Antique District." It is five minutes south of downtown Nashville. Traveling from Memphis: follow I-40 to I-65 south, then take Exit 81 (Wedgewood). Take a right and go to the traffic light and take a left at 8th Ave. S. The mall is the third business on the right. From the Opryland/Airport area, take I-40 west to I-440 W. to I-65 north toward Nashville, Exit 81 (Wedgewood). Take a left at the exit and go to the traffic light, which is at 8th Ave. S. At 8th Ave. S. take a left, and the mall is the third business on the right.*

For 20 years The Antique Merchants Mall has been Nashville's premier source for antiques and collectibles. It has been in business since 1977, making it one of the oldest antique malls in the Middle Tennessee area. It has over 40 dealers in about 6,000 square feet of space, with some dealers specializing in American, French, and English furniture. Shoppers will also find porcelains, china and crystal, as well as booths filled with pottery, silver, furniture, paintings, depression glass, and one dealer with over 12,000 out-of-print, rare and collectible books.

**Oriental Shop**
2121 Bandywood Dr.
615/297-0945

**Antique & Flea Gallery**
4606 Charlotte Pike
615/385-1055

**Curiosity Shop**
996 Davidson Dr.
615/352-3840

**Downtown Antique Mall**
612 8th Ave. S.
615/256-6616

**Art-Deco Shoppe & Antique Mall**
2110 8th Ave. S.
615/386-9373

**American Classical II Antiques**
2116 8th Ave. S.
615/297-5514

**Van-Garde Alternative Clothing**
2204 Elliston Place
615/321-5326

**Ted Leland Inc.**
3301 W. End Ave.
615/383-2421

**The Gallery of Belle Meade**
Belle Meade Shopping Center
615/298-5825

**Crystal Dragon Antiques & Cllbls.**
4900 Charlotte Pike
615/383-2189

**White Way Antique Mall**
Edgehill & Villa Place
615/327-1098

**Pia's Antique Gallery**
1800 8th Ave. S.
615/251-4721

**Cane Ery Antique Mall**
2112 8th Ave. S.
615/269-4780

**Elders Book Store**
2115 Elliston Place
615/327-1867

**Made In France Inc.**
3001 W. End Ave.
615/329-9300

**Germantown Antiques**
1205 4th Ave. N.
615/242-7555

**Temptation Gallery**
2301 Franklin Road
615/297-7412

**Little Antique Shop**
6017 Hwy. 100
615/352-5190

**Marymont Plantation Antique Shop**
6035 Hwy. 100
615/352-4902

**Streater Spencer**
6045 Hwy. 100
615/356-1992

**Calvert Antiques**
6518 Hwy. 100
615/353-2879

**Cinnamon Hill Antiques & Interiors**
6608 Hwy. 100
615/352-6608

**Polk Place Antiques**
6614 Hwy. 100
615/353-1324

**Green Hills Antique Mall**
4108 Hillsboro Road
615/383-4999

**Tennessee Antique Mall**
654 Wedgewood Ave.
615/259-4077

**Forsyth's Antiques**
2120 Crestmoor Road
615/298-5107

**Belmont Antiques**
3112 Belmont Blvd.
615/383-5994

**Dealer's Choice Auction**
2109 8th Ave. S.
615/383-7030

**Fairbank's Antique & Furniture**
7330 Charlotte Pike
615/352-4986

**Glenn's Antiques Gallery**
2919 Nolensville Road
615/832-5277

**Courtyard Gate Antiques**
2504 Franklin Road
615/383-0530

**Tony Brown Antiques**
6027 Hwy. 100
615/356-7772

**Evelyn Anderson Galleries**
6043 Hwy. 100
615/352-6770

**Spaulding Antiques**
6608 Hwy. 100
615/352-1272

**Ro's Oriental Rugs Inc.**
6602 Hwy. 100
615/352-9055

**Pembroke Antiques**
6610 Hwy. 100
615/353-0889

**Harpeth Gallery**
4102 Hillsboro Road
615/297-4300

**Cinemonde**
138 2nd Ave. N.
615/742-3048

**Wedgewood Station Antique Mall**
657 Wedgewood Ave.
615/259-0939

**Always Antiques**
505 Gallatin Road
615/860-3400

**Davishire Interiors**
2106 21st Ave. S.
615/298-2670

**Ejvind's Antiques**
2108 8th Ave. S.
615/383-2012

**Gatti's Antiques**
6264 Nolensville Road
615/834-4582

## 58 PARIS

**Old Depot Antique Mall**
203 N. Fentress St.
901/642-0222

**Grapevine Mall**
114 W. Washington St.
901/642-7850

**Market Street Antique Mall**
414 N. Market St.
901/642-6996

## 59 PIGEON FORGE

See Sevierville #62 for antiquing in Pigeon Forge.

### *Great Places To Stay*

**Hiltons Bluff Bed and Breakfast**
2654 Valley Heights Dr.
1-800-441-4188

This romantic hilltop hideaway is a beautiful two-story cedar inn with covered decks, oak rockers and nature's ever-changing mountain views. Decorated with country quilts and lace, the ten guestrooms-honeymoon suites feature deluxe king beds, waterbeds and heart-shaped Jacuzzi. Elegant country living minutes from the heart of Pigeon Forge and the Great Smoky Mountains National Park.

## 60 PULASKI

**Harmony Farms Gifts & Antiques**
211 N. 1st St.
931/424-5937

**Bee-Line This & That**
705 N. 1st St.
931/424-5120

**Mama's Cedar Chest**
Hwy. 64
No Phone Available

**Kevin Walker Antiques**
110 N. 2nd St.
931/424-1825

**Bunker Hill Antiques**
145 Bunker Hill/Bryson Road
931/732-4500

## 61 SELMER

**Kennedy's Antique World**
160 W. Court Ave.
901/645-6357

**King's Antiques**
Hwy. 45 S.
901/645-5581

**Memory Lane**
124 W. Court Ave.
901/645-7734

## 62 SEVIERVILLE

**Riverside Antique and Collectors Mall**
1442 Winfield Dunn Pkwy. (Hwy. 66)
423/429-0100
Fax: 423/428-5221
Daily 9-6, with extended summer hours
*Directions: From I-40, take Exit 407 (Gatlinburg, Sevierville, Hwy. 66). Go south five miles and the mall is located on the right side of the highway. Look for the huge light gray building with a dark red roof.*

For specific information see review at the beginning of this section.

**Memory Lane Antique Mall**
1838 Winfield Dunn Pkwy.
423/428-0536
Daily 9-5:30 March-October; 9-5 November-February
*Directions: From I-40, take Exit 407. The mall is 4 1/2 miles off I-40 on the right off 66 or Winfield Dunn Parkway.*

The outside of this place is deceiving. It looks much smaller than it really is and in fact even though it's larger when you get inside I still can't figure out how that much glassware could fit into that size space. (That's almost a tongue twister.) Memory Lane's unusually large glass selection consists of Tiffany, Daum, Loetz, French Cameo, along with Austria and German pieces. If you are looking to add to your depression glass collection you'll probably find it here. The various dealers who display in the shop carry a huge offering of such pieces. The furniture, though limited, is in excellent condition.

**Wagon Wheel Antiques**
131 Bruce St.
423/429-4007

**Family Antiques**
2093 Chapman Hwy.
423/428-6669

**Antiques of Chapman Hwy.**
2121 Chapman Hwy.
423/428-3609

**Wears Valley Antique Gallery**
3234 Wears Valley Road
423/453-5294

**Tudor House Antiques & Collectibles**
1417 Winfield Dunn Pkwy.
423/428-4400

**Heartland Antiques & Collectibles**
1441 Winfield Dunn Pkwy.
423/429-1791

**Olden Days Antiques & Collectibles**
1846 Winfield Dunn Pkwy.
423/453-7318

**Action Antique Mall**
2189 Winfield Dunn Pkwy.
423/453-0052

## 63 SHARON

**Willow Creek Collectibles**
5117 Hwy. 45 S.
901/456-2433

## 64 SHELBYVILLE

*Directions: Take I-24 to the Beech Grove Road/Shelbyville Exit #97, go west on Hwy. 64, then turn right at Hwy. 41-A/Madison St. Hwy. 231, which intersects with Hwy. 41-A, leads to the town square.*

Shelbyville is known for three things: one well-known, two almost unheard of. The first thing is its international designation as the "Walking Horse Capital of the World." The second thing is its almost unknown title of Pencil City, because the town is the center of the American pencil-making industry! The third thing is that the Shelbyville town square, laid out in 1809, was used as a prototype for town squares all over the South and Midwest.

Synonymous with Shelbyville, in most people's minds, is "The Celebration," the largest and most renowned walking horse show in the world. The show is held each year in late summer for the 10 days ending on the Saturday night before Labor Day.

Other area attractions that will be familiar to visitors are the towns of Wartrace and Bell Buckle, the Jack Daniel and George Dickel Distilleries, and perhaps unknown but worth a stop, the family-owned and operated Tri-Star Vineyards and Winery just north of Shelbyville.

**Judy's Jewels Antiques & Collectibles**
730 N. Main St.
931/685-4200
Open Daily

Judy's Jewels are found within her wonderful collection of antiques, a love that grew out of an affection for her mother's beautiful, old things. Among her treasures are Persian rugs, bronzes, pictures, glassware, and a fabulous collection of fine porcelain that include R.S. Prussia, Nippon, Royal Bayreuth, and Beleek. An exquisite selection of furnishings are available as well.

**The Antique Marketplace**
208 Elm St.
931/684-8493

The Antique Marketplace is the largest antique mall and auction house in Shelbyville. Over 100 quality dealers occupy what once was the old Coca-Cola Bottling Plant. Come take a step back in time with Cavigny and Mike House and enjoy an old fashion bottled coke and a sample of homemade fudge. The mall offers an eclectic array of wonderful antiques from which to choose; furniture, excellent depression glassware, costume jewelry, pottery, Blue Ridge, primitives and garden accessories. Special services are also offered such as furniture stripping, sandblasting, framing, chair caning and lamp repair. A monthly auction is held on the second Friday of each month. Call to be added to their list.

## 65 SIGNAL MOUNTAIN

**Antique Stations**
1906 Taft Hwy.
423/886-7291

**The Log Cabin Herbs & Antiques**
4111 Taft Hwy.
423/886-2663

**Church's Antique & Access**
1819 Taft Hwy.
423/886-9636

**Aunt Polly's Parlor**
3500 Taft Hwy.
423/886-4705

**Woody's Goodies**
4702 Taft Hwy.
423/886-4095

## 66 SMITHVILLE

**Fuston's Antiques**
123 W. Market St.
615/597-5232
Mon.-Sat. 9-5
*Directions: Traveling I-40 east from Nashville or west from Knoxville, take Exit 273 and travel south on Hwy. 56 approximately 12 miles to the first red light. At the light turn right and go two blocks to the courthouse square. Go halfway around the courthouse and turn right onto Main St. Go to the red light and turn left onto College St. Go one block. The shop is located on the corner of Walnut St. and South College St.*

Fuston's is a breath-taking, awe-inspiring, ocular odyssey of 25 years of accumulation. The store holds the most amazing collection of antique and collectible glassware, antique clocks and music boxes, china and lamps - both oil and electric. But the "shop" is in reality a total of five buildings all crammed with loads of furniture and everything else. Mr. Fuston has over 25,000 square feet of merchandise to choose from. Two of the buildings were, until fairly recently, the 1930s era Fuston's Five and Dime (his since the 1950s). An amazing place and an owner to match - don't miss it!

## 67 SPARTA

**Country Treasures**
447 W. Brockman Way
931/836-3572

**Liberty Square Antiques**
1 Maple St.
931/836-3997

**Jonger's Antiques & Gifts**
137 S. Young St.
931/836-2822

## 68 SWEETWATER

**Bottle Shop**
121 County Road 308
423/337-0512

**Country Store**
121 County Road 308
423/337-6540

## 69 TALBOTT

**Alpha Antique Mall**
6205 W. Andrew Johnson Hwy.
423/581-2371

## 70 TRENTON

**Carol's Antique Mall**
148 Davy Crockett
901/855-0783

**Bill Hamilton's Antiques**
203 W. Huntingdon St.
901/855-9641

**Virginia's Antiques**
209 W. Eaton St.
901/855-0261

## 71 TROY

**Apple Square**
107 W. Westbrook St.
901/536-6479

**Troy Antique Mall**
1104 N. U.S. Hwy. 51 S.
901/536-4211

## 72 TULLAHOMA

**Keepsake Antiques & Collectibles**
310 S. Anderson St.
931/455-8612

**Ole World Antiques**
321 S. Anderson St.
931/455-7666

**Memories Antique & Mall**
117 W. Lincoln St.
931/455-3992

**Lincoln Street Antiques**
212 E. Lincoln St.
931/454-9391

**Davicki House**
407 S. Jackson St.
931/393-4549

**Good Ole Days Antiques**
803 E. Lincoln St.
931/455-2026

**Tullahoma Art & Antiques**
114 N. Collins St.
931/455-0777

## 73 UNION CITY

**Keeping Room**
202 S. 1st St.
901/885-2554

**Faye's Antiques**
516 S. 1st St.
901/885-9507

## 74 WARTRACE

*Directions: Take I-24 to the Beech Grove Road/Shelbyville Exit 97. Take Hwy. 64 directly to Wartrace.*

This antique hamlet is known as the "Cradle of the Tennessee Walking Horse," because walking horses were first bred here in the 1930s. The town gets its name from the Native American trail that passed through the town and was used as a war path or war "trace" (the designation of wilderness roads - "traces" - during the 1600s and 1700s).

### *Great Places To Stay*

**Walking Horse Hotel and Shops**
101 Spring St.
931/389-7050, 1-800-513-8876
Open Daily

While we were in Wartrace visiting Emily, we happened upon a magnificent structure that immediately drew us in. It came as no surprise that we weren't the only ones mystified by the Walking Horse Hotel. New owner, John Garland, was inside, steadily working on the Hotel's renovation. He, too, had happened upon the Hotel, which was in desperate need of repair, but, captivated by its history and charm, decided to purchase it and move to Wartrace from his home in Oregon. We understood his enthusiasm. The Walking Horse was, in its day, a first class hotel. In the 1930s Middle Tennessee was fast becoming "The Walking Horse Capital of the World". The Hotel's "claim to fame" was accredited to the breeding and boarding of "Strolling Jim", a high-stepping horse who won the first World Grand Championship Title in 1939. The champion trainer was Floyd Caruthers who owned both the Hotel and the stables. "Strolling Jim" is still at home as his final resting place is in the backyard of the Hotel.

Today, the Walking Horse Hotel has been restored to its grandeur with seven guest rooms, six occupying the third floor. Specialty shops adorn the second floor level offering a barber shop, candy shop, and framing studio, along with several gift shops. The restaurant located on the main floor serves delicious Southern cuisine.

**Ledford Mill Bed & Breakfast**
Route 2
931/455-2546 or 454-9228
Open Daily

This is another story of someone who came to visit and decided to stay. In December, 1995, Dennis and Kathleen Depert bought the mill and moved from their home on an Island in Puget Sound off the coast of Washington State to the tiny town of Wartrace. The Deperts have converted the mill into a wonderful bed and breakfast inn with three special accommodations all having access to the gardens, waterfall and creek. The Mill's original machinery is highlighted in each room, where early 1900s furnishings are arranged within a spacious old factory setting. Visitors to the gift shop on the main floor are quite taken with the floor to ceiling mural in sepia tones, depicting an old mill delivery wagon. Kathleen drew her inspiration for this from an old photograph. The main floor also includes a lobby, old time kitchen and breakfast room overlooking the falls.

Ledford Mill is still one of the best kept secrets on the Tennessee backroads. It is not unusual that a Nashville, Chattanooga or Huntsville traveler, taking a different turn, will discover the mill tucked in its secluded hollow and decide to stay the night. One guest was heard to say recently, "this is not your daily grind." *Highly recommended.*

**The Log Cabin Bed & Breakfast**
171 Loop Road
931/389-6713
Open Daily

Emily Pomrenke is kinda (that's Southern for kind of) special to us. She was one of the early supporters of The Antique Atlas. Shortly after our commitment to this huge undertaking Emily called to express her interest and excitement in a three hour phone conversation. The conversations continued to the point that we decided to go meet her in person. The Log Cabin is out in the country on a small paved road where everybody waves when they pass. It was easy to spot - the marker on the road led us up the driveway to the cabin on the hill. It was just as I had pictured it - a wonderful get-a-way with an informal atmosphere. Each of the three guest rooms has its own theme. The Heart of Texas Room, the one most requested by horse enthusiast who stay with Emily while competing in the nearby Shelbyville Horse Shows, is decorated in Texas memorabilia. The Swing By The Window (there really is one) has a springtime appeal. The family room, synonymous with its intent - to welcome a family - has plenty of sleeping space.

## 75 WAVERLY

You could spend a day or two here in Waverly just poking around in the various museums and odd places in town. The town was founded in 1838 and named for one of the founding families. There is a barely-changed 1948 movie house that's still operating on the square and a 1960s drive-in theater just down the highway, owned by the same family. There's Mr. Pilkington's World-O-Tools Museum just past the Farmers Co-op, be sure and call first to make sure Mr. Pilkington is there. Collecting tools was just a hobby for Mr. P in the 1950s, but now he has about 25,000 old and unique tools, primarily from the 20th century, but lots from the 1800s and even earlier. Also on the square is the Humphreys County Museum, open whenever the Chamber of Commerce is open, because they're both in the same building.

**Nolan House**
375 Hwy. 13 N.
931/296-2511
Open March-December 9-7
Rates $50-75
*Directions: From I-40: Take Exit 143 (Hwy. 13 North) past Loretta Lynn's Dude Ranch, approximately 14 miles. At the Waverly town center, follow Hwy. 13 North across the viaduct. At the top of the viaduct turn left at the first house. From U.S. 70 East or West: Follow the Hwy. 13 North signs across the viaduct. At the top of the viaduct run left at the first house.*

The Nolan House offers a little bit o' Ireland in the rural Tennessee countryside. This National Register home was built after the Civil War by Irishman James Nicholas Nolan, who stayed in Waverly after the war and became a very successful businessman. It remained in the Nolan family for 109 years, until the last family member died in 1979. The current owners, Linda and Patrick O'Lee, are keeping the Irish legacy alive by offering spacious guests rooms, decorated with antiques. The warm ambiance of the spacious Great Room is the setting for breakfast served on fine china. Country living at its most gracious includes day trips to Nashville, Memphis, state parks with hiking, canoeing, swimming, golfing, visiting historic Civil War sites, and, of course, antique shopping. Legend has it Jesse James hitched his horse in front of the Nolan House.

# Texas *Western*

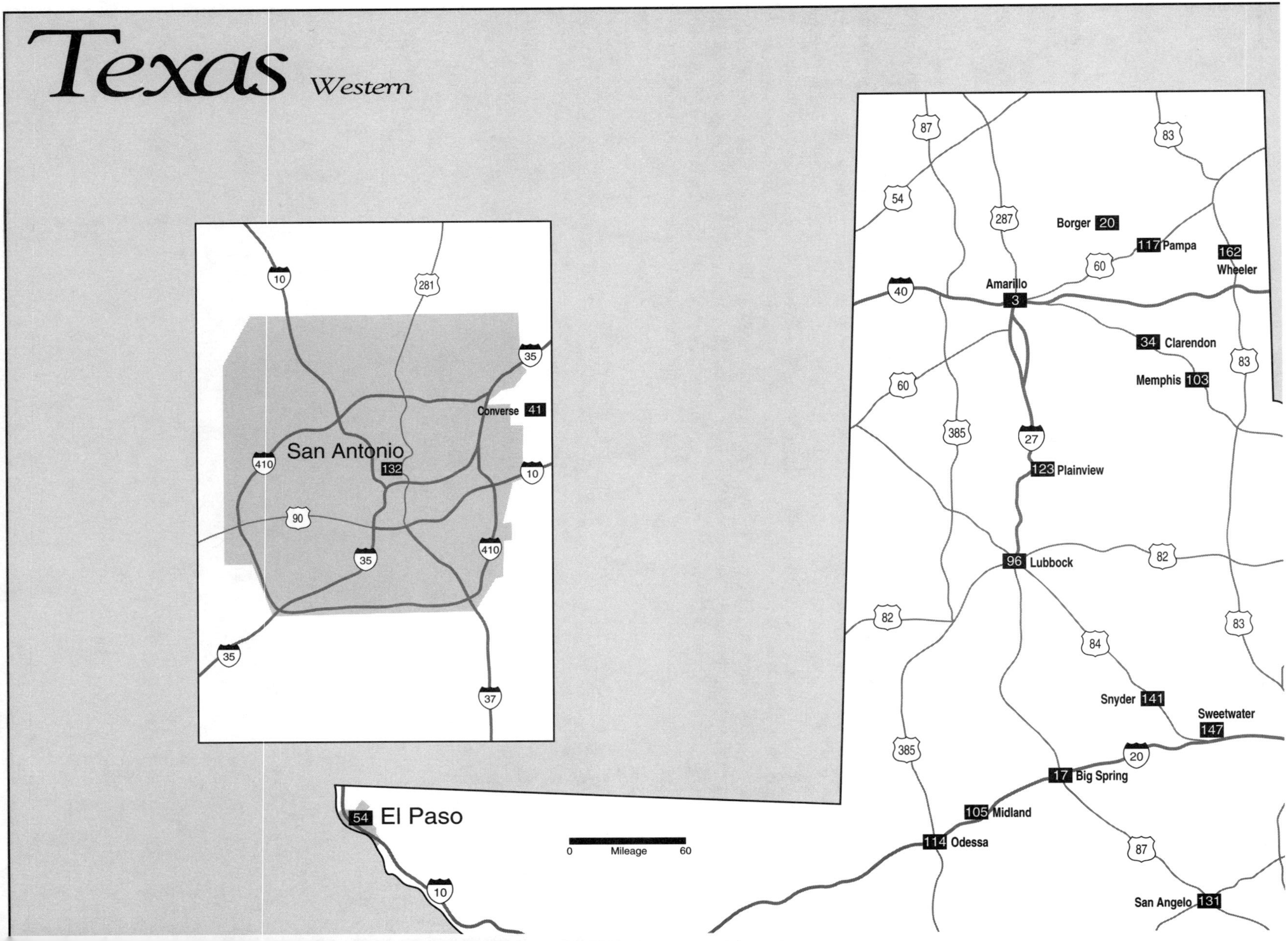

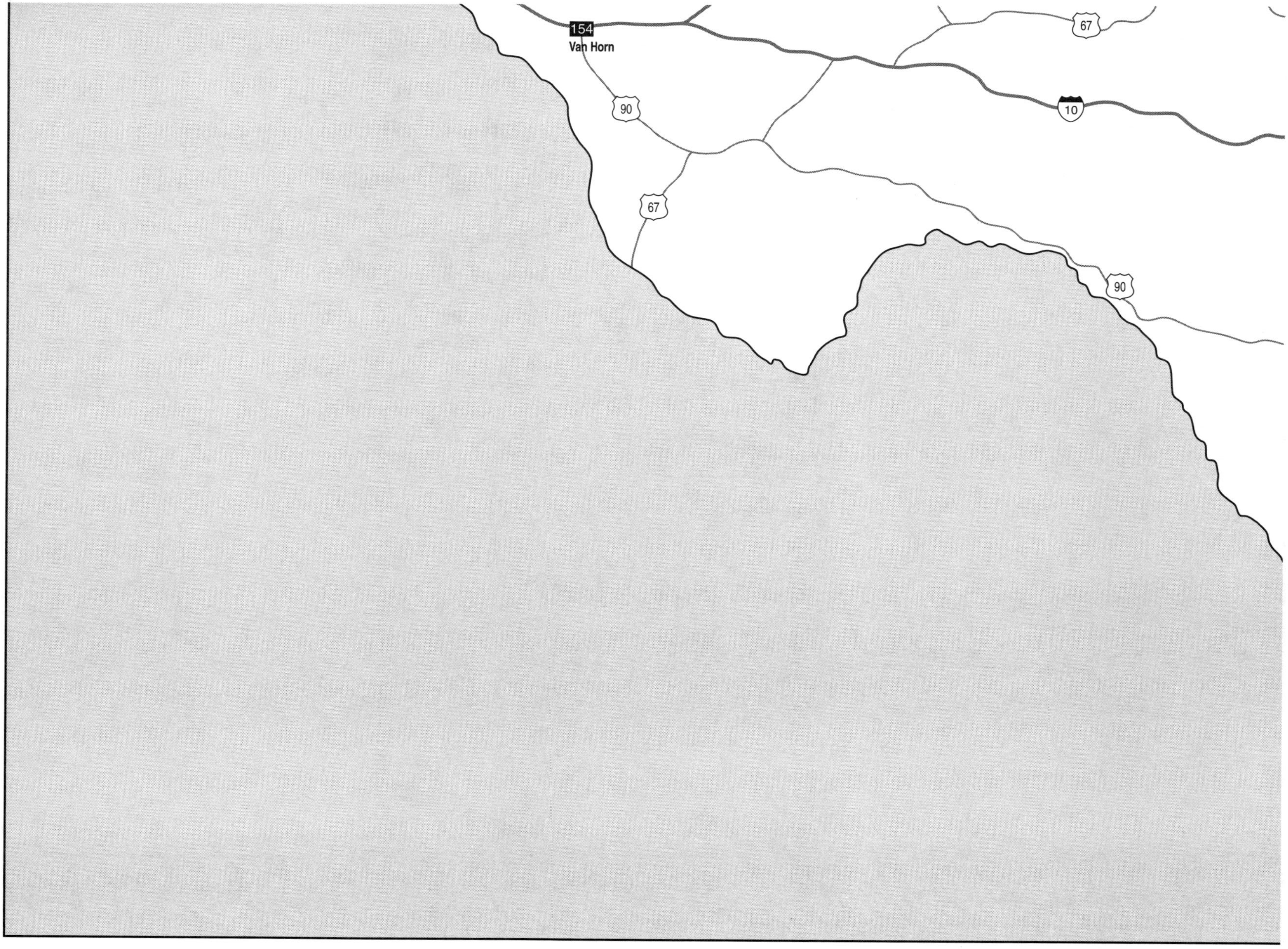

154
Van Horn
67
10
90
67
90

# Texas *Eastern*

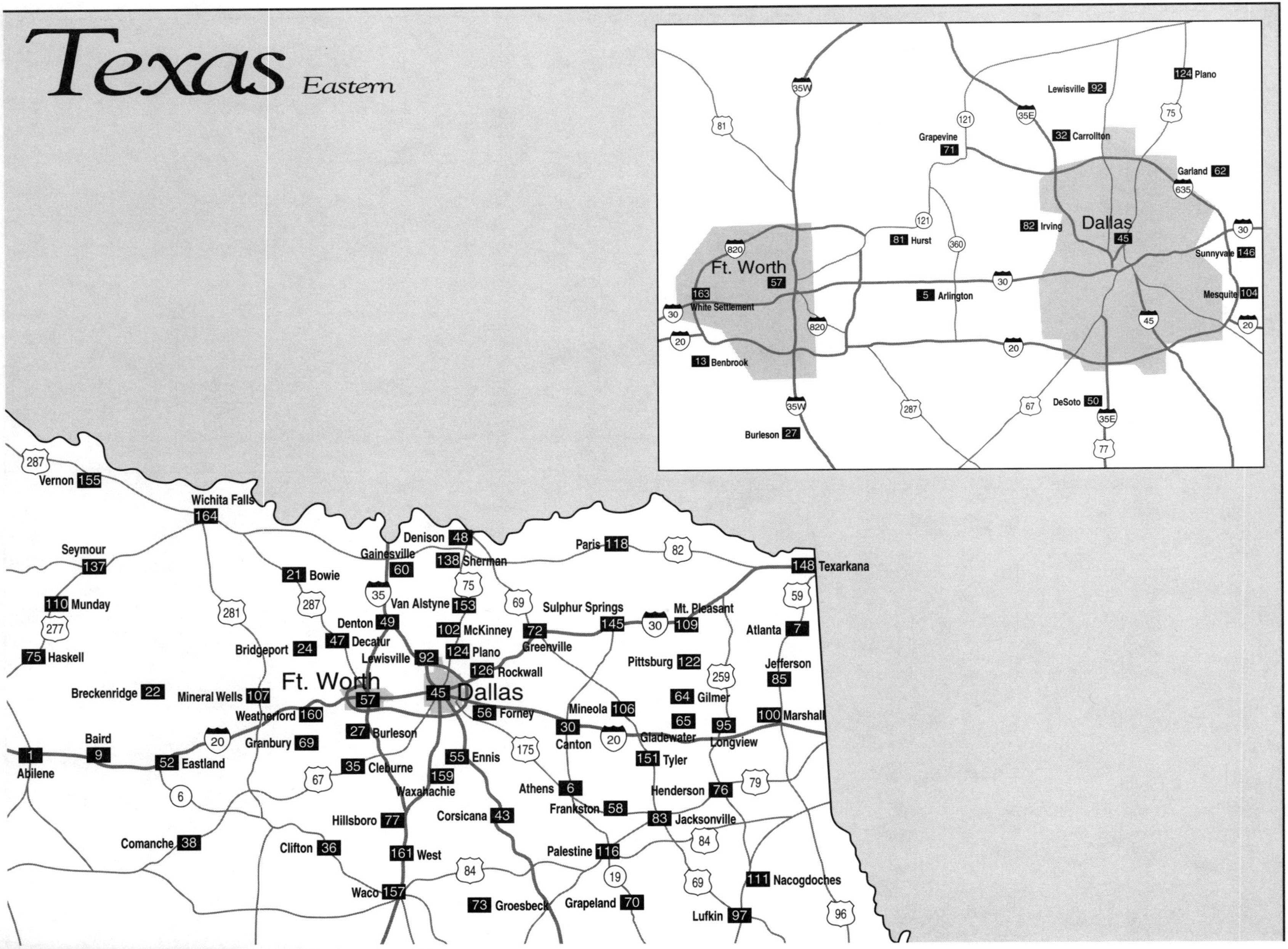

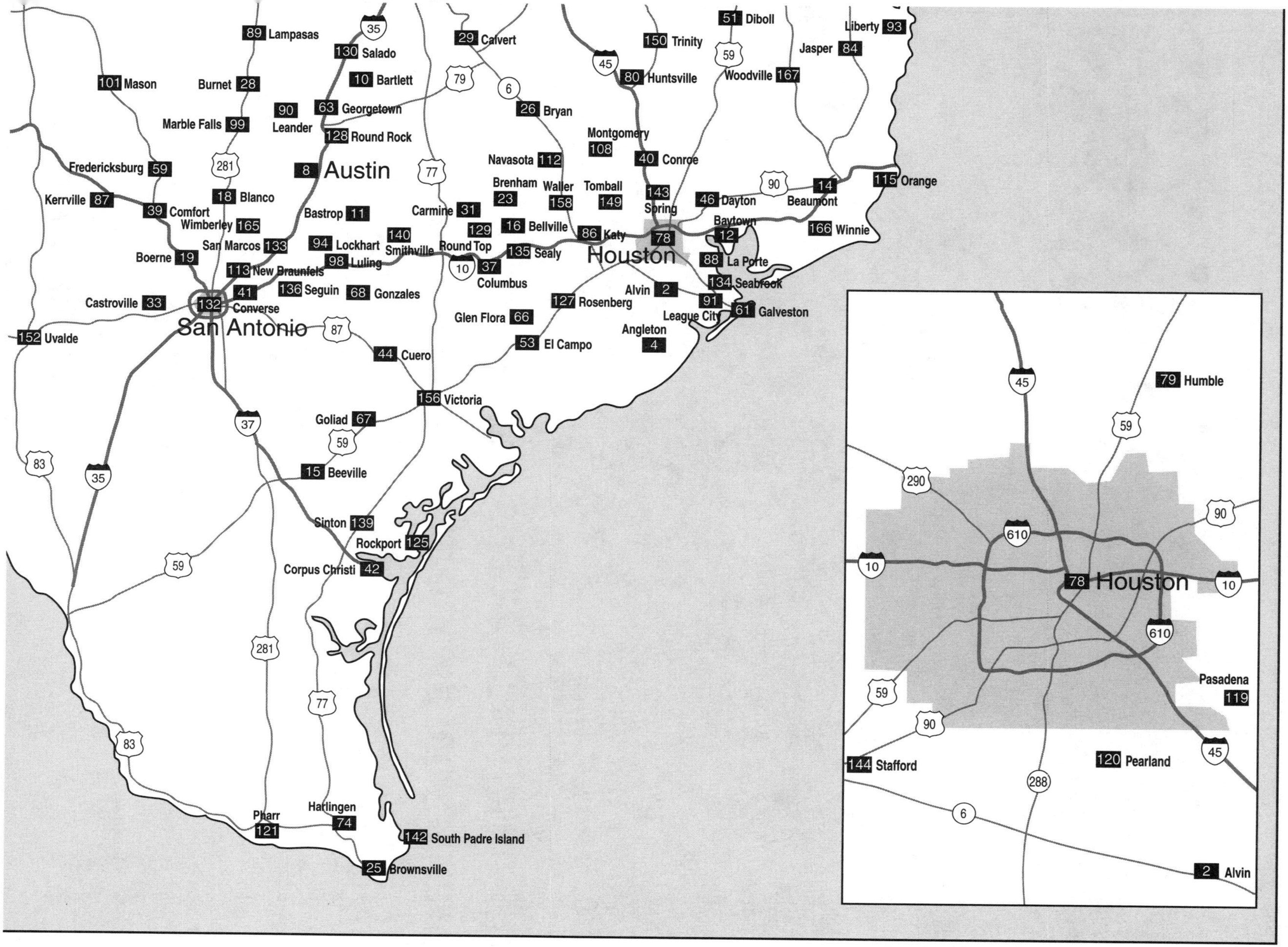

89 Lampasas
130 Salado
10 Bartlett
29 Calvert
150 Trinity
51 Diboll
Liberty 93
Jasper 84
101 Mason
Burnet 28
Woodville 167
80 Huntsville
26 Bryan
Marble Falls 99
90 Leander
63 Georgetown
128 Round Rock
Montgomery 108
40 Conroe
Navasota 112
8 Austin
Fredericksburg 59
Brenham 23
Waller 158
Tomball 149
143 Spring
46 Dayton
14 Beaumont
115 Orange
Kerrville 87
18 Blanco
39 Comfort
Wimberley 165
Bastrop 11
Carmine 31
129
16 Bellville
86 Katy
78
Baytown 12
166 Winnie
San Marcos 133
94 Lockhart
140 Smithville
Round Top
135 Sealy
Houston
88 La Porte
Boerne 19
113 New Braunfels
98 Luling
37 Columbus
134 Seabrook
Alvin 2
136 Seguin
68 Gonzales
41
Castroville 33
132 Converse
San Antonio
127 Rosenberg
91 League City
61 Galveston
Glen Flora 66
Angleton 4
152 Uvalde
53 El Campo
44 Cuero
156 Victoria
Goliad 67
15 Beeville
Sinton 139
Rockport 125
Corpus Christi 42
Pharr 121
Harlingen 74
142 South Padre Island
25 Brownsville
79 Humble
Houston 78
Pasadena 119
144 Stafford
120 Pearland
2 Alvin

*A Touch of Class Antique Mall is located in a historic furniture store, which was the pride of the Red River Valley for over 100 years.*

# Historic Touch of Class Antique Mall offers wares from the top dealers in the Southwest

A Touch of Class Antique Mall offers fine antique furniture, quality glassware, and a large variety of collectibles and primitives in this historic furniture store which was the pride of the Red River Valley for over 100 years.

From the top dealers in the Southwest, you will find a large selection of tin toys, fire department, railroad, fishing and golf memorabilia. Imported antiquities from China, England, France and more, complete the exquisite offering at A Touch of Class Antique Mall.

Take exit 58 off Highway 75. Go 3 blocks east on Lamar St. to downtown Sherman - across from the Courthouse.

*A Touch of Class Antique Mall is located at 118 W. Lamar St. in Sherman. For additional information call the store at 903/891-9379 or 902-868-3153*

*Find the perfect accent for your home in the large selection offered at the Touch of Class Antique Mall. From antiquities imported from around the world to fishing and golf memorabilia, you'll find it here.*

# Get your kicks in the one mile stretch of the Historic Route 66 District in Amarillo

Amarillo is the pride of West Texas, and the pride of Amarillo is the Historic Route 66 District! This one mile stretch of history was once a trolley car suburb of Amarillo, which has become a regional center for many activities on the hottest stretch of the "Mother Road."

With its quaint shops, galleries, eateries, and historic attractions, Sixth Street has something for everyone.

"The Summer Festival," an annual event, takes place on the third weekend in June. Activities include shopping, eating, street dancing to live music, art displays, and other functions. The towns host other special events throughout the year. Nightly entertainment is offered at many of the restaurants.

*For more information, contact Historic Route 66 Association, P. O. Box 4117, Amarillo, Texas 79116 or call 806/372-US66. For a complete listing of shops and eateries in Amarillo see listing #3 (Amarillo).*

*Baird is enjoying a boom in its antiques business, with travelers from all over the country flocking to town to discover the unique historic setting and unique shops.*

# Hankering for antiques? It's Baird or bust!

Baird, the official "Antique Capital of West Texas" extends to you a warm, "West Texas Welcome!" As a progressive town with a cooperative spirit, it has blossomed within the past 7 years and is now enjoying the strongest economic growth since the railroad boom of the late 1800's. The decline in railroad activity forced many businesses to close, and Baird was left virtually deserted.

*Antique shops are housed in the historic buildings of Baird.*

The majority of the old, historic buildings left vacant in the downtown area have been renovated and beautifully restored to house the various antique shops, antique and collectible malls, gift and craft shops, restaurants and soda fountain, candy factory, hardware stores, bank, and other retail and professional businesses. These buildings once served as boarding houses for weary travelers and railroad employees, mercantile and grocery stores, furniture and casket stores, a hatchery, banks, livery stable, hardware and dry goods stores, drug and soda shops, lodge halls, theaters, and even a hospital. These wonderful old structures are situated up and down Market Street between the Callahan County Courthouse and the old Texas and Pacific Railroad Depot. Others are located within a block of Market Street. Two well appointed Bed and Breakfasts provide comfort and convenience for groups and individuals visiting and shopping in Baird. An RV Park located a short distance from the downtown area offers amenities for motor homes and travel trailers and a 28-room Baird Motor Inn with RV campground is available on I-20.

*Baird is the colorful setting for special events such as the "Trades Festival" with a rodeo in June and a "Cowboy Gathering" in late August.*

Several special events are held throughout the year, including an "Art Show" in March, a "Trades Festival" with Rodeo in June, and a "Cowboy Gathering" in late August. New events planned for the future will provide additional pleasure and entertainment.

*Contact the Baird Chamber of Commerce at 915/854-2003 for a schedule of events, map, and other information about Baird. Directions: Exits 306, 307, or 308 off I-20 approximately 120 miles west of Ft. Worth or 20 miles east of Abilene.*

*Highly sought after matching suites for the formal dining or living room are available at Henson's Antiques, along with fine quality accessories.*

# Henson's Antiques is jewel of tiny west Texas town

If you are an advanced collector of fine quality American antique furniture and accessories or if you are a designer whose clients demand only the best, then you'll be delighted with the personally selected inventory available at Henson's Antiques. The shop specializes in American Victorian period furniture, both walnut and rosewood, ranging from gorgeous matched suites for bedroom, parlor and dining room to striking single pieces such as armoires, secretaries, marble top tables, pier mirrors and hall trees. With no intention of excluding any collectors, Henson's inventory offers styles from other periods including top of the line oak, carved front china cabinets, roll-top desks, bedroom suites and bookcases for home or office.

*Clients flock from as far away as Ney Work to Henson's for the quality merchandise.*

The shop most recently attracted the attention of *Southern Living Magazine*. An unusual tambour roll filing cabinet was featured in an article entitled "Ticket to Yesterday in Baird." It is not unusual for the elite members of the press or customers for that matter to be drawn to Henson's Antiques. Clients from as far away as New York, California, Florida and Washington flock to Henson's for the outstanding offering of quality merchandise. What is unusual, however, is that the shop is located in a tiny West Texas town.

A few years back, Baird was a railroad town but when the Texas & Pacific Railroad closed shop, the town felt its tomorrow had left the station. For years, only the rustle of leaves and whistle of wind rambled along Baird's Market Street. Then, in 1993 the tiny town of Baird received State recognition when the Texas Legislature declared it the "Antique Capital of West Texas" due to the revitalization efforts and the numerous antique shops.

Betty Henson, owner of Henson's Antiques, was a leader in the town's revitalization. She and her husband, Weldon, have been avid collectors of formal American antiques for more than 25 years. Betty first became interested in antiques while studying interior design in the late 60s. The antiques found in Betty's shop are selected using the same criteria as is used in the selection of pieces for her own home; excellent quality, condition, uniqueness, function, design, style and age are all considered.

You will often find pieces from well known American cabinet makers who took great pride in the pieces they produced. In addition to the many fine furnishings available, you'll find decorative accessories including clocks, mirrors, lamps, prints, paintings, china, glass, porcelain, silver and silverplate.

*Henson's Antiques is located at 230 Market St. in Baird. The shop is open Mon.-Sat. 10-5:30. For additional information call 915/854-1756.*

# Find outstanding quality antiques at Carolyn Thompson's Antique Center

*Carolyn Thompson's Antique Center of Texas is Houston's largest and finest antiques market. Over 200 dealers present their wares in this 35,000-square-foot building complete with Texas Tea Room.*

No trip to, or near, Houston would be complete without a visit to Carolyn Thompson's Antique Center. David and I recently spent an entire day browsing throughout the store. Fortunately for us the Center has a Texas Tea Room (David is not a happy shopper when he's hungry). The food was wonderful. Our choice was the special of the day offered from a menu of soups, salads, sandwiches or hot entree (the special) along with desserts and cookies for munching as you shop.

The Antique Center is the kind of store every antique shop or mall should be. The inventory is very diverse offering something for everyone. For me this makes for a very pleasant shopping experience. My selections are usually primitive, early American painted pieces and I was thrilled to find a nice offering of such pieces amongst the exquisite formal furnishings found throughout the store. If your decor requires massive, finely crated, artfully detailed furnishings, then look no further than Carolyn Thompson's where you'll find the absolute best in the nation. Accessories of comparable quality are also available to complete an outstanding room-setting. Below is a partial listing of the items available from over 200 dealers at Carolyn Thompson's Antique Center of Texas: rugs, clocks, china, bronze, cabinets, chandeliers, art glass, French, Italian, American furnishings, stained glass, porcelain (one dealer specializes in Haviland), flow blue, silver, lace, paintings, architectural pieces, religious items, vintage hunting and fishing equipment, jewelry, dolls, and a large selection of collectibles.

*Carolyn Thompson's Antique Center of Texas is located at 1001 West Loop North in Houston. The Center is open daily 10-6. For more information call 713/688-4211 or see listing #78 (Houston). You can reach the shop on the web at www.txantiquemall.com.*

*The Trade Mart of Houston is 70,000 square feet filled with the finest of antique furniture and decorative items and memorabilia.*

# Browse through antiques from around the world at the 'Antique Lover's Paradise': The Trade Mart

This 70,000 sq. ft. building is an Antique Lover's Paradise. Consisting of over 100 unique shops, you can find anything from exceptional antique furniture and unique collectibles to unusual gift items. Each shop is staffed with helpful and knowledgeable dealers to assist you with your questions and purchases. When it's time to take a break, you can relax at the cafe for a delicious meal or snack.

*Knowledgeable dealers will help you with your antiques purchase.*

Fine antiques and collectibles from England, Europe, Asia, China, and America are available in mahogany, walnut, pine, oak, cherry, and other woods. Custom furniture makers can help you design and will construct a piece of furniture to your specifications. Persian rugs, old coins, stamps, books, Civil War and western memorabilia are just a few of the specialty shops in the market. China, depression glass, stemware, silverware, paintings, and decorative items for the home and office are in great supply at The Trade Mart. Many of Houston's finest interior decorators stop by The Trade Mart for unusual items for their clients.

The Trade Mart has a vast selection of gift shops to visit. There are specialty shops featuring estate and designer jewelry, Goebel figurines, chandeliers, light fixtures, tools and tapestries.

*Houston's most savvy interior designers know that they can find unusual items for their clients at The Trade Mart.*

*The Trade Mart is open Friday, Saturday, and Sunday from 10 to 6 and is located between Highway 290 and I-10 on the west side of Sam Houston Parkway at Hammerly Exit. Just 2 miles north of I-10. For additional information call 713/467-2506.*

# For those who seek the best European antiques of superior craftsmanship, look to LR Antiques

Since 1987, LR Antiques has been known in Houston, Texas for offering the finest in European antiques of the best craftsmanship, design, and beauty.

The owners of LR Antiques travel all over Europe to personally select an exceptional assortment of investment quality 18th, 19th and 20th century furnishings and accents. Their goal is to bring the discriminating collector beautiful one-of-a-kind pieces that they will enjoy and cherish throughout the ages.

LR Antiques brings four or five, 40 foot containers a year from France, Belgium, Holland, Ireland, and England. All items are unique in a variety of styles from Art Deco to Renaissance, Art Nuevo to Louis III-VI.

These and other items are always available for viewing and sale at 2230 Bissonnet St.

*LR Antiques is located at 2230 Bissonnet St. in Houston (between Greenbrair and Shepherd). The store hours are Monday through Saturday, 10 a.m. - 6 p.m. or call them at 713/524-3272.*

*Stunning pieces from Europe fill LR Antiques, from beautiful furniture of many important periods in fine woods, to silver tea sets or unique vases. The goal of the owner is to offer heirloom quality items that can be cherished throughout a lifetime.*

*Container loads of antique furniture pieces and smalls arrive from a different country monthly at the Antiques Showroom in Dennison.*

# "Tag It Sold" at The Antique Showroom of Denison

Would you like to buy antique furniture and small goods direct from ʼurope at dealer prices? If so, you should make a special effort to attend he monthly "Tag Sale" held in Denison, Texas the third Thursday of ach month. The Antique Showroom imports 40 foot containers of antique urniture to the United States and every month a full container load of urniture and small goods arrives from a different country; England, cotland, Northern Ireland, France and Italy are some of the countries hat are represented at the sale. The sale is conducted as a "Tag Sale," neaning that each and every item is individually priced and marked ith a two-part perforated price tag. The pricing is based on "Cost Plus" usually 20-25%), this helps keep the sale a no-hassle event, which can rovide everyone with great bargains. The Antique Showroom is entering s third year of presenting full container loads of antiques for sale. The oncept of the "Tag Sale" has been extremely successful and received ry well by the general public and antique dealers alike. It allows everyone browse through the entire load being offered and make buying decisions ithout the pressure and confusion associated with auctions.

The Antique Showroom also offers full containers for sale to dividuals, antique malls or auction houses seeking to buy in volume in large quantities. A full container load can have as many as 200 rniture pieces and up to 50 or 60 lots of small goods. Auctioneers have found container loads to be very profitable and a great way to build a regular following of customers.

Group buying trips are another service offered by the Antique Showroom. Every April, August and December you have the opportunity to travel with the buyers from the Antique Showroom to purchase antiques in any one of five countries throughout the United Kingdom and Europe. A buying trip can be a great way to find that special piece of furniture you have been searching for and have the opportunity to visit some of the most interesting and beautiful cities in the world.

*Buying trips to Europe are arranged.*

*The Antique Showroom is located in Historic Downtown Denison, Texas at 421 W. Main. For more detailed information about the "Tag Sale," purchasing a full container load of antiques or the buying trips, call 903/465-2253 or 903-465-2211, or fax your messages to 903/465-2241. Their email address is antiqueshwrm@texoma.net. The store is open Mon.-Sun. 10-5:30.*

*Trails End Bed and Breakfast is host to many antiquers who take a break from the hunt to refresh and replenish their energy at this scenic location.*

# It's a happy trail's end for antiquers at this unique B&B

*Trails End Bed & Breakfast provides the perfect getaway vacation.*

*Enjoy the afternoon breeze and the garden's fragrance as you swim, or gather to relax around the outdoor pool.*

## Enjoy the wide porches, sitting in the gazebo or exploring the Texas hill country surrounding this haven

This is the perfect place to go for a getaway weekend or vacation. Trails End is a country retreat located in the unique central Texas hill country. As innkeepers JoAnn and Tom Patty say, "There is nothing immediate you have to do at Trails End Bed & Breakfast." That means guests get to kick back and enjoy the porches, decks, the gazebo, the refreshing pool, walking in the woods or riding bikes.

Make it a family vacation-there's a private guesthouse for six-and bring the boat or water toys for a splashing good time on nearby Lake Travis. For golfing guests, a number of golf courses are convenient. When the urge to explore hits, downtown Austin is just 35 minutes away, and Georgetown, Round Rock, Cedar Park, Lago Vista, Leander, Burnet and Salado are an easy drive.

*Trails End Bed & Breakfast is located at 12223 Trails End Road in Leander. For specific information and directions see listing #90*

*Left: Courthouse Antiques is named for the 102-year-old courthouse of this Victorian town which has been featured in numerous movies.*

*Courthouse Antiques offers Haviland china, chocolate pots and tea sets, Wedgwood, Noritake, Johnson Bros. and various European china and more.*

*Vintage clothing and decorative items add to the quaint atmosphere.*

# The verdict: Courthouse Antiques wins shoppers

Courthouse Antiques, Collectibles, and Gifts is situated in the very shadow of the beautiful and famous Ellis County Courthouse located in Waxahachie, TX. The 102-year-old courthouse and this charming Victorian town have been featured in numerous movies, and located right on the historic courthouse square you'll find the store. In keeping with the surroundings, they offer vintage clothing; Haviland china, including chocolate pots and tea sets; Wedgwood, Noritake, Johnson Bros. and various European china; vintage baby items such as wicker strollers and baby scales and ceramic baby feeders; furniture dating back to the early 19th century, some in its original condition and some beautifully and faithfully restored; toys and dolls, some dating back to the '20s and '30s and some highly collectible like Madame Alexander dolls, Gund plush toys, Ideal and Matchbox cars and planes; stained glass and other architectural pieces; books; linens and lace; jewelry and watches; clocks; glassware, atomizers, decanters and bottles; bedroom and dining suites; trunks and luggage. They also buy antiques and are especially interested in buying Haviland, vintage clothing, children's items and toys.

*Courthouse Antiques, Collectibles, and Gifts is located at 200 S. Rogers in Waxahachie. For additional information see listing #159 (Waxahachie).*

*Teddie Bear's Antiques is a true country market with 2 acre grounds packed with all kinds of interesting items. Outdoors is the junk galore and indoors are the collectible items.*

# Junk galore and more at Teddie Bear's Antiques

A true country market, Teddie Bear's may just very well be the most intriguing and most fun place to visit that we've discovered! Two acres of antiques and uniques to browse through is only part of the reason everybody should stop in if you are in the area. The variety of items stuffed onto these two acres range from neat "stuff" on outside sales tables to indoor highly collectible treasures. Dealers can ask for a private tour of the huge barn full of early American primitives on the Garrison's farm just four miles away.

Ted "the Teddy Bear" and Victoria Garrison are always available to greet old and new friends alike. Ted will gladly help load things in your car or even make a free delivery if you live in the vicinity. One of the reasons people keep coming back to visit Teddie Bear's is for the genuine friendliness they find there. Victoria explains it this way: "We always have something new to surprise our customers. We're a two-acre mini-flea market that keeps expanding with a life of its own! One stops leads to another, if for nothing else than to see what we've started next at Teddie Bear's!"

*Teddie Bear's Antiques and Collectibles is located on Hwy. 19 in Trinity.* *For additional information see listing #150 (Trinity).*

*Shelves and shelves of fascinating items are arranged for your perusal at Teddie Bear's Antiques and Collectibles, where looking is half the fun.*

## 1 ABILENE

**Poppy's Antique Mall & Museum**
126 S. Access Road
915/692-7755

**Antique Gallery**
2544 Barrow St.
915/692-2422

**Antique & Almost**
3146 S. 11th St.
915/695-2423

**Barnard's Antiques**
501 Hickory St.
915/677-9076

**Sharon Specialties**
721 Hickory St.
915/672-1793

**Yesterdaze Mall**
2626 E. Hwy. 80
915/676-9030

**Gizzmotique**
641 Pecan St.
915/677-0041

**McCloskey's**
1646 N. 6th St.
915/672-6277

**One Horse Sleigh Antiques**
1009 S. Treadaway Blvd.
915/676-1429

**Olde Abilene Treasures**
2102 N. 1st St.
915/672-6493

**R. Honeys**
3301 S. 14th St.
915/698-9696

**Twin Mill Antiques**
350 S. U.S. Hwy. 83
915/692-9578

## 2 ALVIN

**Village Antiques & Shoppes**
1200 FM 1462
281/585-1959

**Once Upon A Time**
1004 W. Hwy. 6
281/331-7676

**Finders Keepers**
312 E. House St.
281/585-0806

**Country Notions**
217 W. South St.
281/585-6582

**Dixieland Antiques**
1255 W. Hwy. 6.
281/585-4085

**Sarah's ByPass Antiques**
820 N. Hwy. 35 Bypass
281/585-2909

## 3 AMARILLO

### Historical Route 66 at Amarillo, Texas

For a look at Historical Route 66 Amarillo see review at the beginning of this section.

### Town and Country Antiques Mall
2811 W. Sixth St.
806/373-3607
Mon.-Sat. 10-5:30, Sun. 1-5

A wonderful place for an eclectic assortment of collectibles and antiques. Town and Country specializes in great furniture.

### Alex's 66 Antique Mall
2912 W. Sixth St.
806/376-1166
Mon.-Sat. 10-5, Sun. 1-5

Eighteenth and Nineteenth Century antiques plus collectibles.

### Country Co-op Mall
2807 W. Sixth St.
806/372-4472
Mon.-Sat. 10-5:30, Sun. 1-5

This 12,000-square-foot mall of 50+ antique dealers is filled with antiques, collectibles and gift items.

### Webb Galleries Amarillo
2816 W. Sixth St.
806/342-4044
Wed.-Sat. 11-5

Regional and Contemporary Art.

### Worldwide Antiques
3218 W. Sixth St.
806/372-5288

European and American antiques. Unique antiques and gifts.

### No Boundaries Antiques, Gifts and Collectibles
602 S. Carolina St.
806/371-7270
Mon.-Sat. 10-5

A charming house filled with treasures.

### This Olde House
3901 W. Sixth St.
806/372-3901
IN TOUCH INFO LINE 806/376-1000 #6153
Weekdays 10-5:30, Sun. 1-5, Closed Tues.

An old craftsman style house filled with antiques, collectibles and gifts.

### Red Door Antiques
3211 W. Sixth St.
806/373-0316
IN TOUCH INFO LINE 806/376-1000 #6150
Mon.-Sat. 10-5:30

A complete line of American and European furniture, as well as glassware: including Fiesta and American Fostoria.

**Adobe Walls Woodworks**
2904 W. Sixth St.
Web site: www.adobewalls.com

Handcrafted Southwest furniture, artworks and home accents.

**Puckett Antiques**
2706 W. Sixth St.
806/372-3075
Mon.-Sat. 10-5:30

Gifts for everyone, small and large - old and new. From fine china, crystal, furniture to barbed-wire.

**The Mustard Seed**
3323 W. Sixth St.
806/376-9209
Mon.-Sat. 10-5:30

Specializing in Primitives, both large and small. A great selection of linens and gift items.

**Clay and Company**
604 S. Maryland
806/376-7866

Antiques, collectibles and ladies fine clothing.

**Buffalo Gals**
2812 W. Sixth St.
806/374-6773
Mon.-Sat. 10-6

Antiques, collectibles and gifts. An assortment of homemade fudge.

***Favorite Places to Eat on Route 66 Amarillo***

**Golden Light Cafe**
2908 W. Sixth St.
806/374-9237
IN TOUCH INFO LINE 806/376-1000 #6158
Serving food 10-10, beverage service until 2 a.m.

The longest continuously-operated restaurant on Historic Route 66. The menu features burgers, fries, chili, sandwiches and many varied beverages.

**The Park on Sixth**
3315 W. Sixth St.
806/374-7275
Mon. 10-4, Tues.-Sat. 10-10
Dinner Menu: Thurs., Fri., and Sat.

**Norman Antiques & Art**
1006 S. Adams St.
806/376-7115

**Depot Antiques**
500 W. Amarillo Blvd.
806/376-6352

**Slesick Studio & Gallery**
6666 W. Amarillo Blvd.
806/352-8823

**Hobbs Street Mall**
3218 Hobbs Road
806/356-6552

**Phoenix & Co.**
3701 Plains Blvd., Suite 83
806/355-4264

**Sixth Street Antique Mall**
2715 W. 6th Ave.
806/374-0459

**Carousel Antiques & Collectibles**
2806 W. 6th Ave.
806/373-9142

**Timeless Accents**
3020 W. 6th Ave.
806/373-5473

**D & N Collectibles**
3208 W. 6th Ave.
806/371-8400

**Victorianna**
3300 W. 6th Ave.
806/374-6568

**Don R Reid Inc.**
2717 Stanley St.
806/356-0903

**Minka's Garden**
3615 W. 6th Ave.
806/372-1199

**Beauford Hill Antiques**
500 W. Amarillo Blvd.
806/376-6352

**English Rose**
6203 W. Amarillo Blvd.
806/359-7905

**Cornerstone Consignments**
3218 Hobbs Road.
806/356-0225

**Amarillo Antique Mall**
3701 Plains Blvd.
806/355-4264

**Galaxy Toys**
2461 I-40 W.
806/352-0800

**Clockworks**
2725 W. 6th Ave.
806/371-7121

**Scent and Fantasy Two**
2818 W. 6th Ave.
806/371-0773

**Antiques Plus**
3119 W. 6th Ave.
806/372-3137

**Delightful Treasures**
3304 W. 6th Ave.
806/379-7107

**Rusty and Dusty Antique Shop**
3302 W. 6th Ave.
806/374-6568

**Antique Amarillo**
2700 W. 6th Ave.
806/374-1066

**The Nat Antiques & French Bakery**
2705 W. 6th Ave.
806/372-8685

***Great Places To Stay***

**Maryland House Bed & Breakfast**
600 S. Maryland St.
806/376-7866

## 4 ANGLETON

**Jeters Old World Antiques**
Hospital Dr.
409/849-5452

**Yesterdaze**
517 E. Mulberry St.
409/849-8834

**Kellys Crossroads Antiques**
112 W. Mulberry St.
409/849-0308

**The Magnolia Tree**
724 W. Mulberry St.
409/848-8044

**Bargain Palace**
200 S. Velasco St.
409/849-4711

**Gallery Antiques & Collectibles**
212 N. Velasco St.
409/849-9336

**County Seat Antiques**
227 N. Velasco St.
409/848-1810

**Attic Treasures**
125 E. Cedar
409/849-7307

## 5 ARLINGTON

### Antiques by Ellis

1906 W. Park Row
817/275-6761
817/274-6879 for special appointments
Tues.-Sat. 11-5:30 or by appointment Sun.-Mon.
Shop is closed when on buying trips or when attending shows. Please call in advance if you are traveling.
*Directions: From I-30 take Fielder Exit, south 4 miles, right on Park Row, 2 blocks on the left. From I-20 take Cooper Exit, north 5 miles, left on Park Row past Fielder, 2 blocks on the left.*

Located in the same spot for the past 20 years, Sue and Asa Ellis specialize in fine American antiques from 1840-1910. If you are searching for true antique furniture, accessories and lighting, then this is one antique "stop" you shouldn't pass up (no reproductions). Their speciality is furniture with an emphasis on quality and the unusual. The inventory is evenly divided between formal Victorian and fancy oak with approximately 200 exceptional pieces available at all times.

**Antique Marketplace Arlington**
3500 S. Cooper St.
817/468-0689

**Smith's Antiques & Refinishing**
3650 Garner Blvd.
817/265-7048

**Antique Sampler Mall & Tearoom**
1715 E. Lamar Blvd.
817/861-4747

**D Militaria & Collectibles Shop**
823 Oram St.
817/274-3515

**Moth Ball**
401 E. Randol Mill Road
817/459-2553

**Helen's Antiques & Used Furniture**
2307 Medlin
817/275-2064

**Design Center**
138 S. Bowen
817/265-0549

**Antiques, Etc.**
404 E. First St.
817/543-1567

**Al's Antiques**
1543 S. Bowen
817/548-8151

**Abram Street Antiques**
500 E. Abram
817/460-7250

**Antiques & Moore Mall & Tearoom**
3708 W. Pioneer Pkwy.
817/548-5931

## 6 ATHENS

**Olga Antiques**
312 S. Carroll St.
903/677-1733

**Waldenwood Country Antiques**
504 E. Corsicana St.
903/675-2561

**Eden Antiques**
400 N. Prairieville St.
903/677-1560

**Goode's Imporium**
109 E. Tyler St.
903/675-9425

**Alley Antiques & Collectibles**
400 N. Prairieville St.
903/675-9292

**Serendipity**
412 N. Prairieville St.
903/675-8335

**Wooden Nickel Mall**
2001 S. Palestine St.
903/677-9496

## 7 ATLANTA

**Yesterdays Antique Mall**
212 N. East St.
903/796-9742

**Atlanta Antiques**
113 E. Hiram St.
903/796-4942

**Hiram St. Antique Mall**
117 E. Hiram St.
903/796-9474

**Memory Lane Mall**
110 E. Main St.
903/796-0485

## 8 AUSTIN

**Lelysee Antiques**
5603 Adams Ave.
512/459-1727

**Mona and Dons Antiques**
5617 Adams Ave.
512/458-1661

**Chantal's Antique & Design Center**
2525 W. Anderson Lane
512/451-5705

**Antique Outlet**
10401 Anderson Mill Road
512/257-1020

**Antique Marketplace**
5350 Burnet Road
512/452-1000

**Halbert Antiques**
5453 Burnet Road
512/451-8037

**The Market**
701 Capital of Tx. Hwy.
512/327-8866

**Now & Always Antiques**
1413 S. Congress Ave.
512/707-2692

**Rue's Antiques**
1500 S. Congress Ave.
512/442-1775

**Antigua**
1508 S. Congress Ave.
512/912-1475

**Uncommon Objects**
1512 S. Congress Ave.
512/442-4000

**Off The Wall**
1704 S. Congress Ave.
512/445-4701

**Armadillo Antiques & Jewelry**
1712 S. Congress Ave.
512/443-7552

**Turn of the Century Antiques**
1703 N. Cuernavaca Dr.
512/263-5460

**Tipler's Lamp Shop**
1204 W. 5th St.
512/472-5007

**Antiques by Grace Homan**
3303 Glenview Ave.
512/472-7366

**Log Cabin Antiques**
9600 W. Hwy. 290
512/288-4037

**House of Harriette & John**
12719 W. Hwy. 71
512/263-5103

**Craftown Gallery**
13945 Hwy. 183
512/331-4252

**Capitol Used Furniture & Antiques**
11115C N. Lamar Blvd.
512/836-1472

**Accent Antiques**
2200 S. Lamar Blvd.
512/441-6656

**Lamar Antiques**
2058 S. Lamar Blvd.
512/448-3184

**Danforths Antiques & Gifts**
1612 Lavaca St.
512/478-7808

**Austin Antique Mall**
8822 McCann Dr.
512/459-5900

**Eradeco Antiques & Collectibles**
110 E. North Loop Blvd.
512/450-0861

**Robert Gage Antiques**
1304 Rio Grande St.
512/472-4760

**Jean's Antiques and Gifts**
2 Miles south of Wimberly
512/282-1541

**Radio Ranch**
1610 W. 35th St.
512/459-6855

**Architects and Heroes Antiques**
1809 W. 35th St.
512/467-9393

**Attal's Galleries**
3310 Red River St.
512/476-3634

**Austin House Antiques**
2041 S. Lamar Blvd.
512/445-2599

**James Powell Antiques**
715 West Ave.
512/477-9939

**Amelias Retro Vogue and Relics**
2024 S. Lamar Blvd.
512/442-4446

**Corner Collectors**
6539 N. Lamar Blvd.
512/453-4556

**Garner & Smith Antiques Etc.**
1013 W. Lynn St.
512/474-1518

**Hog Wild Vintage Toys**
100A E. North Loop Blvd.
512/467-9453

**Hurt's Hunting Grounds**
712 Red River St.
512/472-7680

**Dreyfus Antiques**
719 E. 6th St.
512/473-2191

**Fancy Finds**
1009 W. 6th St.
512/472-7550

**Bradys of Austin**
1807 W. 35th St.
512/459-8929

**Antiques Warehouse**
5530 Burnet Road
512/453-6355

**Austin Antique Glassware**
13107 FM 969
512/276-7793

**Durham Trading & Design Co.**
1009 W. 6th St.
512/476-1216

### *Great Places To Stay*

**Trails End Bed & Breakfast**
The B & B Store (gift shop)
12223 Trails End Road #7
512/267-2901 or 1-800-850-2901
B&B open year round
Rates $55-170
Gift shop open year round 1-5 pm - call for appt.
*Directions: From IH 35 two miles out of Georgetown, take RM 1431 and go 11.85 miles to Trails End Road. Turn left onto Trails End and go 7/10 of a mile to the gravel road. There will be several mail boxes next to the gravel road. Turn left and go to where the road curves to the right. Keep on going around the curve and the B&B is a large gray house trimmed in white on the left. An appointment is needed. The inn is located on the north side of Lake Travis between Cedar Park, Jonestown, Austin and Leander.*

For specific information see review at the beginning of this section.

## 9 BAIRD

The town of Baird, Texas is a great comeback story. The downtown district is only three blocks long, but has five antique malls and over a dozen individual shops with either antiques or collectibles. All of the shops are located either on Market St. (the main street) or within a half block on an intersecting street.

There are several good places to eat and two bed and breakfasts, with a third in progress. More buildings are being restored all the time on the three block historic downtown strip, and the town hopes to eventually have all of them filled with shops that are either antiques or related businesses. In 1993 Baird received the designation of "Antique Capital of West Texas" from the Texas Legislature due to their revitalization efforts and the numerous antique businesses, none of which existed prior to 1991.

Before they began their revitalization program, there were only two hardware stores and a drug store in the downtown area. It's quite different now, and they draw large numbers of antique shoppers from all over.

Baird is located 20 miles east of Abilene and 120 miles west of Fort Worth.

For a look at the charming town of Baird see review at the beginning of this section.

**Henson's Antiques**
230 Market St.
915/854-1756
Mon.-Sat. 10-5:30
*Directions: Take Exits 306, 307 or 308 off Hwy. 20. Located 20 miles east of Abilene and 120 miles west of Ft. Worth.*

For specific information see review at the beginning of this section.

**Market Street Mall**
212 Market St.
915/854-1408
Tue.-Sat., 10-5:30; Sun., 1:30-5:30, closed Mon.
*Directions: Take Business 20 to downtown Baird. Market St. intersects.*

Market Street Mall is a multi-dealer mall located in a historic building in downtown Baird. With new items arriving weekly, this unique shop offers a wide array of antiques and collectibles. From Victorian through '50s; furniture and a wide variety of smalls, Market Street Mall is an antiquer's delight with wide aisles, good lighting, climate control, and handicap accessibility.

**The Antique Market**
334 Market St.
915/854-1997

**Creations by Collene**
331 Market St.
915/854-5980

**Em's Sweets, Eats, & Antiques**
140 Market St.
915/854-5956

**Flashback**
234 Market St.
915/854-1410

**Hughes Trading Co. & Antiques**
743 W. 4th St.
915/854-1714

**Konczak Pawn**
219 Market St.
915/854-1293

**Antique Memories**
304 Market St.
915/854-2021

**Barbara's Country Tyme Antiques**
300 Market St.
915/854-2424

**Cowboy Merc. & Lonesome Dove Saddlery**
124 E. 2nd St.
915/854-1265

**AAA Antqs., Appraisal & Auc. Assoc.**
P.O. Box 777
915/893-2705

**Callahan County Collectibles**
209 W. 3rd St.
915/854-1782

**Cha Waken Indian Crossing**
201 Market St.
915/854-2575

**The Corn Stalk**
205 Market St.
915/854-2501

**Plaza Corner**
245 Market St.
915/854-5972

**Primrose Lane**
203 Market St.
915/854-5936

**Trail's End Antiques**
223 Market St.
No Phone

**Wanda's Good Stuff**
341 Stella St.
915/854-1973

**The Old Shoppe**
312 Market St.
915/854-1911

### *Bed & Breakfasts/Motel/RV Parks*

**Four Seasons Guest House**
425 Market St.
915/854-1565

**The Old Conner House B&B**
348 Vine St.
915/854-1898

**Robbins RV Park**
318 E. 2nd St.
915/854-2456

**Baird Motor Inn**
& RV Campground
I-20

## 10 BARTLETT

**Clark St. Antique Shop**
Clark St.
254/527-3933

**Mary Jane's II**
Clark St.
254/527-4445

**Crumbley's Antiques**
Clark St.
254/527-3141

**The Trellis**
Clark St.
254/527-4300

**Bartlett Antique Mall**
10 E. Clark St.
254/527-3251

**Village Antique Mall**
16 E. Clark St.
254/527-3234

**Rooms with a View**
135 E. Clark St.
254/527-4460

**Major Roome's Emporium**
221 Clark
254/527-3111

## 11 BASTROP

**Wyldwood Antique Mall**
Hwy. 71 W.
512/321-3280

**Old Town Emporium**
918 Main St.
512/321-3635

**Texas Mercantile**
921 Main St.
512/303-1843

**Apothecary's Hall Antiques**
505 Main St.
512/321-3022

**Ritz**
1005 Main St.
512/321-4326

## 12 BAYTOWN

**Burns Antiques & Trading Emporium**
600 N. Alexander Dr.
281/422-7321

**The Consignment**
2312 N. Alexander Dr.
281/837-1061

**Buford's Antiques**
3716 Decker Dr.
281/424-4081

**Decker Drive Antiques**
3716 Decker Dr.
281/424-5211

**Temptations**
207 W. De Fee St.
281/422-5693

**Goose Creek Emporium**
219 W. De Fee St.
281/427-6690

**Bea's Treasure Chest**
2 N. Main St.
281/420-3494

**Town & Country Sales**
5215 Sjolander Road
281/421-1904

**Schoolmarm's Attic**
1504 E. Texas Ave.
281/427-3914

**Trash & Treasures**
1106 Largo St.
281/422-0618

**Baytown Country Shop & Gifts**
723 E. Texas Ave.
281/427-0749

## 13 BENBROOK

### *Favorite Places To Eat*

**Cracker Barrel Old Country Store**
I-20 & Winscott, Exit 429B
817/249-3360

## 14 BEAUMONT

**McCoy's Antiques**
1455 Calder St.
409/835-1764

**Finders Fayre Quality Antiques**
1485 Calder St.
409/833-7000

**Calder House**
1905 Calder St.
409/832-1955

**Select Antiques & Furnishings**
2694 Hazel St.
409/833-7610

**Time After Time Antiques**
2481 Calder St.
409/832-0016

**Old Store Antiques**
8370 College St.
409/866-2205

**The Cottage**
2391 Calder St.
409/832-3447

**Old Store Antiques**
8319 College St.
409/866-6280

**Collage**
2470 N. 11th St.
409/899-3545

**Old Crockett Street Market**
881 Crockett St.
409/832-3209

## 15 BEEVILLE

**Final Touch**
207 W. Carter St.
512/358-5808

**McKitchens Antiques & Tea Room**
401 E. Houston St.
512/358-1442

**Delphine's**
114 W. Hefferman St.
513/362-2144

**The Antique Place**
1101 N. Washington St.
512/358-2908

## 16 BELLVILLE

**Bellville Antique Mall**
11 N. Bell St.
409/865-9620

**Julia's Antiques**
410 Centerhill Road
409/865-5285

**Rafters Antiques**
467 Hwy. 36 N.
409/865-3316

**Cottonwood Cottage**
8 N. Holland St.
409/865-8411

**Antiques Etc. Emporium**
14 N. Holland St.
409/865-8087

**The Country Shop**
20 E. Main St.
409/865-9639

**Nothing Ordinary Antiques**
123 E. Main St.
409/865-8033

**Andy's Candys**
11 N. Bell St.
409/865-9620

**Barn & Bell**
854 FM 529 (Burleigh)
409/865-9648

**On The Square**
4 S. Holland St.
409/865-2230

**Square Trader**
12 N. Holland St.
409/865-9305

**Frog Hollow**
22 N. Holland St.
409/865-3007

**Front Porch on the Park**
145 N. Holland St.
409/865-8833

## 17 BIG SPRING

**Aunt Bea's Antiques**
1711 N. FM 700
915/263-6923

**Antique Mall of Big Spring**
110 Main St.
915/267-2631

**Antique Korner**
217 Main St.
915/268-9580

**The Country Store**
Lamesa Hwy. 1/2 Mile N. Hwy. 20
915/267-8840

**Main Street Emporium**
113 Main St.
915/263-1212

**The Country Store**
209 Runnels
915/263-3093

**Alamo Antiques**
114 E. 2nd St.
915/264-9334

**Dahmer's Antiques**
204 S. Main St.
915/267-5223

**Dahmer's Antiques**
7309 N. Service Road
915/393-5537

## 18 BLANCO

### Unique Antiques
315 Main St.
210/833-2201 or 1-800-460-1733
Thurs.-Tues. 10-5, closed Wed.
*Directions: Unique Antiques is located on Hwy. 281, which is Main St., on the west side of the old Blanco County Courthouse Square.*

Although Unique Antiques handles antiques and collectibles, glassware and gifts in general, they particularly carry American oak furniture and a large selection of depression glass. They also carry the largest collection of flow blue in Texas hill country. All their items are top quality and shoppers can buy just one piece or a whole estate!

**Blanco Flea Market**
5th & Pecan St.
210/833-5640

**A Step Back**
Hwy. 281 S.
210/833-4270

**Merchantile**
313 Main St.
210/833-2225

**Classic Antiques**
317 Main St.
210/833-2216

**Blanco Trash & Treasures**
313 4th St.
No Phone # Listed

**Nannie's Antiques**
303 Main St.
210/833-9001

**Cranberry Antiques**
400 3rd St.
210/833-5596

## 19 BOERNE

**Antiques N Things**
106 S. Main St.
210/249-2313

**Antiques & Old Lace**
146 S. Main St.
210/816-2530

**The Rusty Bucket**
195 S. Main St.
210/249-2288

**Boerne Clock Co.**
233 S. Main St.
210/249-6080

**Iron Pigtail**
470 S. Main St.
210/249-8877

**Carousel Antiques & Pickles**
118 S. Main St.
210/249-9306

**Boerne Emporium**
179 S. Main St.
210/249-3390

**St. George & The Dragon**
210 S. Main St.
210/249-2207

**Landmark**
404 S. Main St.
210/249-6002

**Heyday**
615 S. Main St.
210/249-4951

## 20 BORGER

### House of Coffee & Gifts
100 West Grand St.
806/274-7375

While antiquing in Borger, Texas, plan to visit the "House of Coffee" located at the corner of South Main and Grand St. in one of the first hotels built in 1926, in the original town of Isom, Texas. Isom was part of the heritage of the Texas Panhandle and the pioneering spirit that changed the Panhandle from a habitat of buffalo and cattle to a land of people.

Housed in this building is a wonderful gift shop featuring a blend of gifts: crystal, handkerchiefs, pewter frames, flower wreaths, all set in a Victorian flair with consignment antiques from Timeless Treasures.

Plan to stay for a cup of espresso coffee, a spot of tea from 15 varieties or one of many cocoa flavors. The summer months offer frozen latte, along with 14 varieties of bagels and cream cheese toppings. If you visit in the fall or winter months, you could be served soup on Tuesday or Thursday at noon.

It took six months to transform the bottom area of the old hotel into this unique coffee house. The owner, Michele Nelson is a Borger native and has fond memories of when this part of the building was Barney's Pharmacy. The soda equipment in the pharmacy was taken out for the Youth Building at First Methodist Church, however, Michele still has the counter bar, with the names carved, on display as well as other memorabilia. Future plans for the 24 hotel rooms upstairs with original sink, heaters and transom windowed doors is undecided.

The building began as the "Isom Hotel" and was the center of Isom before it became Borger. When leased to John and Pearl Mulkey, the hotel sign read "Mulkey Hotel". They claimed it as their homestead in 1929 even though according to records, it belonged to Agnes Howe. The next owners, Light James and his family named it "St. James". The James brothers lived there until 1940.

The bottom south end of the building was sub-leased to the Hatcher Drug Co., in 1929. In the 1934 phone book it was listed "West Grand". In 1936 Byron Andress leased the space and the building housed Dr. J. R. Walker's office and a barber shop and the Hotel Isom lobby. Later the entire north end was used by Drs. W. G. & M. M. Stephens and Dr. Harvey Hayes. Mrs. Viola Stephens sold the building to Michele and she then opened for business in October 1996. You are welcome to come by and browse awhile, have a cup, and experience Isom, Texas, now known as Borger.

**Season's Antiques**
120 5th St.
806/274-6130

**Four Sisters**
416 N. Main St.
806/274-5220

**Timeless Treasures**
700 W. Wilson St.
806/273-6802

## 21 BOWIE

**Nostalgia Antiques**
200 N. Mason St.
940/872-6272

**Days Gone By**
204 N. Mason St.
940/872-2033

**Antique Express**
210 N. Mason St.
940/872-4717

**Market Place**
216 N. Mason St.
940/872-5011

**Texas Pride Cards & Collectibles**
Newport Hwy.
940/872-5114

**Martha's Attic**
206 Smythe St.
940/872-4705

**Treasure House**
303 W. Wise St.
940/872-1899

**Chisolm Trail Antique Mall**
202 N. Mason St.
940/872-4450

## 22 BRECKENRIDGE

**Antique Shoppe**
105 W. Walker St.
254/559-1639

**The Pat Rogers Collection**
201 W. Walker St.
254/559-6653

**Antique Depot**
500 E. Walker St.
254/559-9724

## 23 BRENHAM

Brenham holds a special place in the hearts of romantics because of a colorful piece of history and artwork that is in the town. Brenham is home to one of only 12 antique carousels in Texas, and this particular one is the only example of a C. W. Parker Carousel with Hersehill-Spillman horses. Manufactured prior to 1910, this piece of Americana is at Fireman's Park in Brenham and visitors can ride it anytime.

Brenham is also home to Blue Bell Creameries, said to produce the best ice cream in the country. They ought to know how to do it - they've been making ice cream since 1911.

**Country Co-Op**
101 E. Alamo St.
409/830-0679

**Today & Yesterday**
101 W. Alamo St.
409/830-0707

**J. H. Faske Company**
114 E. Alamo St.
409/836-9282

**Seek & Find Antiques**
115 W. Alamo St.
409/830-1930

**Somewhere In Time**
204 W. Alamo St.
409/277-9511

**Brenham Antique Mall**
213 W. Alamo St.
409/836-7231

**K & S Collectibles**
Houston Hwy.
409/836-3575

**Nancy's Antiques**
1700 Key St.
409/836-7520

**Catherine Newton's Antiques**
1302 W. Main St.
409/836-2898

## 24 BRIDGEPORT

**Serendipity House**
1003 Halsell St.
940/683-3999

**T & L Antique Shop**
1004 Halsell St.
940/683-5545

**Granny's Antiques**
1010 Halsell St.
940/683-4043

**Hidden Away Memories**
1016 Halsell St.
940/683-8050

**Our Antiques & Collectibles**
1018 Halsell St.
940/683-3959

**Once Again Antique Mall**
1020 Halsell St.
940/683-6717

**Once Again Antiques**
1105 Halsell St.
940/683-6455

## 25 BROWNSVILLE

**Pilar's Antiques & Tea Room**
302 E. Adams St.
210/541-7450

**Second Thought**
2265 Boca Chica Blvd.
210/541-7423

## 26 BRYAN

**Attic Antiques**
118 S. Bryan Ave.
409/822-7830

**Old Bryan**
202 S. Bryan Ave.
409/779-3245

**Gazebo Antiques**
3828 S. College Ave.
409/846-0249

**By Jacs**
701 E. Villa Maria Road
409/822-2662

**Plantation Shop**
2024 S. Texas Ave.
409/822-6220

**Tin Barn Antiques & Collectibles**
3218 S. Texas Ave.
409/779-6573

**By-Mac Collections**
202 W. 26th St.
409/775-7875

**Brazos Trader Antiques**
210 W. 26th St.
409/775-2984

**Amity of Bryan**
300 W. 26th St.
409/822-7717

## 27 BURLESON

**Burleson Old Town Collectibles**
108 S. Main St.
817/295-3301

**Burleson Antique Mall**
2395 S.W. Wilshire Blvd.
817/295-7890

## 28 BURNET

**Cobblestone Cottage**
212 E. Jackson St.
512/756-7407

**Burnet Antique Mall**
206 S. Main St.
512/756-7783

**A Taile of Two Antiques**
212 S. Main St.
512/756-9806

**Treasures on the Square**
216 S. Main St.
512/756-8514

**Shoppee**
206 E. Polk St.
512/756-7984

## 29 CALVERT

**Front Porch**
505 S. Main St.
409/364-2933

**Boll Weevil Antiques**
508 S. Main St.
409/364-2835

**Farmer's Wife Antiques**
515 S. Main St.
409/364-2489

**S & S Antiques**
517 S. Main St.
409/364-2634

**Calvert Antique Mall**
509 N. Main St.
409/364-2089

## 30 CANTON

The saying that everything is bigger and grander in Texas must have started in Canton. This town, with its regular population of just about 3,000, is the undisputed home of the granddaddy of all trade days!

Canton's First Monday Trade Days are world famous. This unbelievable happening dates back at least 150 years, with records existing back to the mid-1800s; most likely it's much older. First Monday Trade Days developed around the circuit court held on the first Monday of each month. In the pioneer days of East Texas, this was a time to set aside work and go into town to the county seat to hear court, buy needed supplies and sell produce and farm animals. In the mid-1960s a progressive-thinking Canton city council saw the monthly market as a potential gold mine and began purchasing land to form the First Monday Park. The park currently encompasses over 300 acres.

Through the years this gathering evolved into today's multi-acre grounds with over 6,000 booths offering literally everything: antiques, arts and crafts, clothing, toys, tools, junk, even animals from dogs to zebras! Weather is not a factor, even though a lot of the area is still outdoors. Many of the booths are now inside 14 pavilions, with an additional 35,000 square feet of building devoted strictly to antiques.

Any one of four exits off I-20 will bring you to downtown Canton.

**Buffalo Village**
202 N. Buffalo St.
903/567-2434

**Recollections & Vintage Quilts**
138 E. Dallas St.
903/567-6945

**Times Past**
114 E. Dallas St.
903/567-5709

**Stone's Antiques**
Hwy. 120
903/567-6620

**Timeless Treasures**
111 S. Hwy. 19
903/567-6762

**Marcella's Antiques**
150 E. Terrell St.
903/567-6936

## 31 CARMINE

**Antiques & Stuff**
Hwy. 290
409/278-3866

**Hoppe Store Antiques**
Hwy. 290
409/278-3713

## 32 CARROLLTON

**T L C Treasures**
1013 S. Broadway St.
972/245-7729

**Dolls of Yesterday & Today**
1014 S. Broadway St.
972/242-8281

**Mary Lou's**
1015 S. Broadway St.
972/466-1460

**Ten of Arts**
1019 S. Broadway St.
972/242-3357

**Pleasures Past**
1105 S. Broadway St.
972/242-2084

**Finishing Touch Antique Mall**
1109 S. Broadway St.
972/446-3038

**Classic Militaria**
1810 N. Interstate 35
972/242-1957

**Old Craft Store**
1110 W. Main St.
214/242-9111

## 33 CASTROVILLE

**Alice's Antiques**
1213 Fiorella St.
210/931-9318

**Market Place Antiques**
1215 Fiorella St.
210/538-3350

**Cottage**
413 Lafayette St.
210/538-9713

**Castroville Emporium Antiques**
515 Madrid St.
210/538-3115

**Attic**
1105 Fiorella St.
210/931-9602

## 34 CLARENDON

**Curiosity Shop**
Hwy. E. 287
806/874-2409

**Poor Boys Antiques**
206 S. Kearney
806/874-2233

**Petty's Antiques & Collectibles**
222 S. Kearney
806/874-3875

**My Playhouse**
300 S. Kearney
No Phone # Listed

**S & S Gallery**
317 S. Kearney
806/874-5096

## 35 CLEBURNE

**Butch's Treasures Chest**
207 E. Henderson
No Phone # Listed

**A Taste of Time**
216 E. Henderson
817/558-2288

**Randy's Antiques & More**
204 S. Main St.
817/645-1985

**Cleburne Antique Mall**
215 S. Main St.
817/641-5550

**Bettie's Antiques & Mall**
216 S. Main St.
817/645-2723

## 36 CLIFTON

**Clifton Antique Mall**
206 W. 5th St.
254/675-2300

**Hobbyhorse Gifts & Antiques**
114 Main St.
254/675-7723

**Bosque County Emporium**
121 Main St.
254/675-8133

**Yankee Clipper Antiques**
325 W. 5th St.
254/675-1722

## 37 COLUMBUS

**Hometown Hall**
1120 Milam St.
409/732-5425

**Double Tree & English Ivy**
1237 Bowie St.
409/732-8802

**Little of This - Little of That**
1004 Milam St.
409/732-6034

**Lasting Impressions**
1124 Milam St.
409/732-9700

## 38 COMANCHE

Comanche is named for the Comanche Indians who once ruled the Southwest Plains. Nestled in the hills of Central Texas, Comanche has friendly people who will help make your visit memorable. There are antique shops, restaurants and over eighty motels and bed and breakfast rooms. See the historic "Fleming Oak" and "Old Cora Courthouse" on the square. Great fishing, camping, water sports and golf can be found at nearby Lake Proctor.

**Furniture Barn**
300 N. Austin
915/356-2787

**Comanche Trading Post**
300 W. Central Ave.
915/356-5022

**Antique Country**
400 E. Central Ave.
915/356-2248

**Sybil's Antiques**
410 E. Central Ave.
915/356-3338

**Old Tyme Antiques**
508 E. Central Ave.
915/356-3550

**Quilts & Tops**
605 E. Central Ave.
915/356-2047

**Red Top Antiques**
605 W. Central Ave.
915/356-2173

**This Ole House Antiques**
706 W. Central Ave.
915/356-2441

**Martin's Antiques**
804 E. Central Ave.
915/356-5711

**Dee Dee's Corner**
807 E. Central Ave.
915/356-2118

**Culbertson's Custom Quilting**
201 W. Grand
915/356-3901

**Selections on the Square**
127 N. Houston St.
915/356-3153

## 39 COMFORT

**Antiquities Etc.**
702 High St.
210/995-4190

**Comfort Common**
717 High St.
210/995-3030

**Bygone Days Antiques**
815 High St.
210/995-3003

**Faltin & Company**
Main St. & 7th St.
210/995-3279

**Southwestern Elegance**
509 7th St.
210/995-2297

**Comfort Emporium**
607 Hwy. 27
210/995-4000

**Marketplatz Antique Center**
405 7th St.
210/995-2000

## 40 CONROE

**Russ Clanton Antiques**
711 W. Dallas St
409/756-8816

**Ah Collectables**
920 W. Lewis St.
409/539-5122

**Paulines Antiques**
915 Cable St.
409/756-4762

**Pamela's Antique Parlor**
FM 2854
409/441-6895

**Heintz Furniture & Antiques**
701 N. Frazier St.
409/756-3024

**Golden Eagle Traders**
1908 N. Frazier St.
409/441-7355

**Antique Mall of Conroe**
725 W. Davis St.
409/788-8222

**Edith's Antiques & Gift Shop**
910 Cable St.
409/756-3711

**Attic Antiques**
1304 FM 2854
409/539-9116

**Stock Exchange Antique Mall**
302 N. Frazier St.
409/760-3800

**Tizzies Antiques & Collectibles**
916 W. Lewis St.
409/788-2344

## 41 CONVERSE

**De's Oldies N Goodies**
209 S. Seguin Road
210/658-2083

**Chism Trail Antiques**
616 S. Seguin Road
210/659-2104

## 42 CORPUS CHRISTI

### Sand Dollar Hospitality
3605 Mendenhall Dr.
1-800-528-7782

If you are searching for that perfect getaway vacation or just an exceptional place to spend the night, then I suggest contacting Sandy at Sand Dollar Hospitality. The service represents a wide variety of bed and breakfast and guest cottages in Corpus Christi and the surrounding areas.

**Lee-Cunningham**
3100 S. Alameda St.
512/882-4482

**Betty's Trash To Treasures Too**
4315 S. Alameda St.
512/993-1027

**Emma's Arbor**
4309 S. Alameda St.
512/985-8309

**Gene's Antiques**
4331 S. Alameda St.
512/994-0440

**Home Sweet Home Antique Market**
4333 S. Alameda St.
512/991-4001

**Sister Sue's**
4323 S. Alameda St.
512/992-5300

**Betty's Trash To Treasures**
3301 Ayers St.
512/882-9144

**Antiques Downtown**
312 N. Chaparral St.
512/882-8865

**Country Peddlers Downtown**
317 N. Chaparral St.
512/887-6618

**Rucker & Rucker Inc.**
451 Everhart Road
512/994-1231

**Irene's Antique Flea Market**
3906 Leopard St.
512/884-4467

**McLaughlin Furniture Shop**
1227 12th St.
512/882-3991

**Odds & Ends**
9841 E. Padre Island Dr.
512/937-8944

**Dragonfly Antiques**
821 S. Staples St.
512/888-5442

**Wild Good Chase**
3509 S. Staples St.
512/851-9535

**Second Hand Rose Antiques**
4343 S. Alameda St.
512/993-9626

**Lea's Glass Nook**
1911 Ayers St.
512/884-3036

**Country Peddlers**
4337 S. Alameda St.
512/993-7237

**Victorian Lady**
315 N. Chaparral St.
512/883-1051

**Antiquity Inc.**
318 N. Chaparral St.
512/882-2424

**Two J's Antiques**
613 Everhart Road
512/994-0788

**Yesterday Peddler**
3131 McArdle Road
512/851-2141

**Objets D'Art II**
5858 S. Padre Island Dr.
512/993-2126

**Quaint Shop**
811 S. Staples St.
512/884-9541

**W. Gardner**
821 S. Staples St.
512/887-9351

## 43 CORSICANA

**This & That Antiques**
101 S. Beaton St.
903/874-6941

**Carousel Crafts & Antiques**
118 S. Beaton St.
903/872-4141

**Jim's Clock Shop**
127 W. Collin St.
903/874-5141

**CSL Antiques & Collectibles**
106 W. 6th Ave.
903/874-8333

**Home Town Antiques**
110 N. Beaton St.
903/874-8158

**Merchant's**
320 N. Beaton St.
903/872-6445

**Traders Outpost**
105 W. 7th Ave.
903/872-5392

## 44 CUERO

**Gallery of Memories**
121 N. Esplanade St.
512/275-9226

**Country Collectables**
Hwy. 87
512/275-2011

## 45 DALLAS

**The Boulevard Emporium**
1010 N. Industrial Blvd.
214/748-1860
Mon.-Sat. 10-5

Quality Antiques and Design Accessories.

**Clements Antiques and Auction Gallery**
1333 Oak Lawn Ave.
214/747-7700
Mon.-Fri. 9-5

Specializing in 18th and 19th Century Antiques.

**Country Garden Antiques**
147 Parkhouse
214/741-9331
Daily 11-5 or by appt.

Furnishings for Home and Garden.

**The Estate Warehouse**
905 Slocum St.
214/760-2424
Mon.-Sat. 9-6 or by appt.

Monthly Estate Liquidations.

**Farzin Designs**
1515 Turtle Creek Blvd. (at The Gathering)
214/747-1511
Mon.-Sat. 10-6 or by appt.

Decorative Antiques, Rugs, and Accessories.

**The Gathering**
1515 Turtle Creek Blvd.
214/741-4888
Mon.-Sat. 10-6 or by appt.

Over 100 International Quality Antiques, Art, and Design Dealers.

**Jaime Leather and Fabric Upholstery**
1100 N. Industrial Blvd.
214/742-8700
Mon.-Fri. 8-6, Sat. 9-3

Specializing in the Upholstery of Antique Furniture.

**Liberty and Son Designs**
1506 Market Center Blvd.
214/748-3329
Mon.-Sat. 10-6, Sun. by appointment

Extensive Selection of Antique and Decorator Furnishings.

**Lots of Furniture**
910 N. Industrial Blvd.
214/761-1575
Mon.-Sat. 10-5, Sun. 12-5

12,000 square feet of antique Furniture and Exotics.

**Mama's Daughters' Diner**
2014 Irving Blvd.
214/742-8646
Mon.-Fri. 6-3, Sat. 7-3

Homemade Breakfast and Lunch.

**Parkhouse Antiques**
114 Parkhouse
214/741-1199
Wed.-Sun. 11-6

For Home and Garden.

**The Rocket Restaurant**
1838 Irving Blvd.
214/741-1324
Mon.-Sat. 5-2:30

Full Breakfast and Lunch.

**Sandaga Market African Imports**
1325 Levee
214/747-8431
Mon.-Fri. 9-6 or by appointment

Selection of Ceremonial & Decorative Art.

### Silver Eagle
1933 Levee
214/741-2390
Tues.-Sat. 10:30-5

Unusual and Affordable Antiques.

### Special Consideration by Pettigrew & Associates, Inc.
1715 Market Center Blvd.
214/475-1351
Mon.-Fri. 9-5

New-Old-Odd Lot Furniture & Decorative Items.

### White Elephant Antiques Warehouse
1026 N. Industrial Blvd.
214/871-7966
Mon.-Sat. 10-5

18,000 square feet, 75 Dealers, & 90 Vignettes.

### The Wrecking Barn
1421 N. Industrial Blvd., Ste. 102 at Glass St.
214/747-2777
Mon.-Fri. 9-5, Sat. 10-3

Architectural Salvage.

**Designing Men**
4209 Avondale, Suite 308
214/599-0029

**Antiques Antiques**
5100 Belt Line Road, Suite 218
972/239-6124

**The Emporium At Big Town**
Big Town Mall (Mesquite)
214/320-2222

**Sample House**
122 Casa Linda Plaza
214/327-0486

**Kornye Gallery**
2200 Cedar Springs Road
214/871-3434

**Love Field Antique Mall**
6500 Cedar Springs Road
214/357-6500

**Ken Riney Antiques**
500 Crescent Court
214/871-3640

**Beckie's Antiques & Gifts**
1005 W. Davis St.
214/942-8626

**Atrium**
3404 Belt Line Road
972/243-2406

**Consignment Store**
5290 Belt Line Road
972/991-6268

**Mary Cates & Co.**
2700 Boll St.
214/855-5006

**Ornaments & Heirlooms**
2512 Matton St.
214/871-2020

**Roxy**
3826 Cedar Springs Road
214/827-8593

**Cathy's Antiques**
500 Crescent Court, Suite 140
214/871-3737

**Sample House & Candle Shop**
9825 N. Central Expressway
214/369-6521

**Corner Shop**
Decorative Center
214/741-1780

**Gregor's Studios**
1413 Dragon St.
214/744-3385

**Heritage Collection Ltd.**
2521 Fairmount St.
214/871-0012

**Three Graces Antiques**
2603 Fairmount St.
214/969-1922

**Eagles Antiques**
2711 Fairmount St.
214/871-9301

**Sam's Antique Rugs**
5333 Forest Lane
972/233-9777

**Trinkets & Treasures**
10244 Garland Road
214/320-3794

**Antique Bahr**
1801 Greenville Ave.
214/826-1064

**House of Prokay Antiques**
1807 Greenville Ave.
214/824-7618

**Lula B's Antique Mall**
2004 Greenville Ave.
214/824-2185

**Allison Daughtry Antiques**
2804 Greenville Ave.
214/823-8910

**Anna's Etc.**
3424 Greenville Ave.
214/828-9393

**Nicole's Antiques**
3611 Greenville Ave.
214/821-3740

**Ivy House**
5500 Greenville Ave.
214/369-2411

**Connie Williamson Antiques**
2815 N. Henderson Ave.
214/821-4134

**Nick Brock Antiques**
2909 N. Henderson Ave.
214/828-0624

**Canterbury Antiques**
2923A N. Henderson Ave.
214/821-5265

**Joe Cooner Gallery**
1605 Dragon St.
214/747-3603

**Les Antiques Inc.**
2600 Fairmount St.
214/720-0099

**Uncommon Market Inc.**
2701 Fairmount St.
214/871-2775

**Forestwood Antique Mall**
5333 Forest Lane
972/661-0001

**Curiosity Corner**
8920 Garland Road
214/320-1752

**Lone Star Bazaar**
10724 Garland Road
214/324-1484

**A S C Deco**
1805 Greenville Ave.
214/821-8288

**Linda's Treasures & Tea Room**
1929 Greenville Ave.
214/824-7915

**Lower Greenville Antique Mall**
2010 Greenville Ave.
214/824-4136

**Chique & Shabby**
2915 Greenville Ave.
214/828-0500

**Waterbird Traders**
3420 Greenville Ave.
214/821-4606

**Copper Lamp**
5500 Greenville Ave.
214/521-3711

**Albert Copeland Continental**
11117 Harry Hines Blvd.
214/241-9686

**Brant Laird Antiques**
2901 N. Henderson Ave.
214/823-4100

**Kent-Stone Antiques**
2819 N. Henderson Ave.
214/826-7553

**Richard Alan Antiques**
2923 N. Henderson Ave.
214/826-1588

**Whimsey Shoppe**
2923 N. Henderson Ave.
214/824-6300

**Beaux-Arts**
1505 Hi Line Dr.
214/741-5555

**Gameroom Express**
141 Howell St.
214/747-3232

**Garrett Galleries**
1800 Irving Blvd.
214/742-4343

**Knox Street Antiques**
3319 Knox St.
214/521-8888

**The British Trading Co./Pine Shoppe**
4518 Lovers Lane
214/373-9071

**Lovers Lane Antique Market**
5001 W. Lovers Lane
214/351-5656

**Market Antiques**
5470 W. Lovers Lane, Suite 335
214/352-1220

**Silver Vault**
5655 W. Lovers Lane
214/357-7115

**Antique Galleries**
2533 McKinney Ave.
214/871-1516

**El Paso Import Co.**
4524 McKinney Ave.
214/559-0907

**Mews**
1708 Market Center Blvd.
214/748-9070

**Unlimited Ltd.-The Antique Mall**
15201 Midway Road
972/490-4085

**Antique Shop**
5616 E. Mockingbird Lane
214/823-7718

**Millennium**
3601 Parry Ave.
214/824-7325

**507 Antiques**
10755 Preston Road
214/368-1100

**On Consignment Inc.**
2927 N. Henderson Ave.
214/827-3600

**Del Saxon Fine Arts & Antiques**
1525B Hi Line Dr.
214/742-6921

**Market Antiques**
430 N. Park Center
214/369-7161

**Notable Accents**
8204 Kate St.
214/369-5525

**William Little Antiques**
7227 Lakehurst Ave.
214/368-8230

**Park Cities Antique Mall**
4908 W. Lovers Lane
214/350-5983

**Le Passe**
5450 W. Lovers Lane, Suite 227
214/956-9320

**Consignment Galleries**
5627 W. Lovers Lane
214/357-3925

**Windsor Antique Mall**
6126 Luther Lane-Preston Center
214/750-8787

**McKinney Ave. Antique Market**
2710 McKinney Ave.
214/871-1904

**Loyd-Paxton**
3636 Maple Ave.
214/521-1521

**Trains & Toys**
109 Medallion Center
214/373-9469

**Englishman's Antiques**
15304 Midway Road
972/980-0107

**Antique Angie**
603 Munger Ave.
214/954-1864

**China Cupboard**
718 N. Paulus Ave.
214/528-6250

**HMI Architectural**
1811 Rock Island St.
214/428-7774

**Saint John's Silver**
2603 Routh St.
214/871-2020

**Pearle Dorrace Antiques**
2736 Routh St.
214/855-0008

**Adam & Eve Antiques**
3121 Routh St.
214/871-0225

**Modern & Antique Clock Repair**
10435 Springhaven Dr.
972/216-9514

**Maison De France**
1007 Slocum St.
214/742-1222

**East & Orient Company**
1123 Slocum St.
214/741-1191

**Pittet Co.**
1215 Slocum St.
214/651-7033

**Oriental Rugs Inc.**
1404 Slocum St.
214/748-8891

**Louis Rosenbach Antiques Inc.**
1518 Slocum St.
214/748-0906

**Old Wicker Garden**
6606 Snider Plaza
214/373-8241

**Rosedale House**
6928 Snider Plaza
214/369-6646

**Remember When Shop**
2431 Valwood Pkwy.
972/243-3439

**Odds and Ends Shop**
210 W. Yarmouth St.
214/942-9326

**Shalanes Antique Gallery**
5811 S R L Thornton Freeway
214/374-7455

**Drew Ltd. Antique Gallery**
2722 Routh St.
214/880-0009

**Collage 20th Century Classics**
3017 Routh St.
214/880-0020

**Antiques Unique**
180 Spring Creek Village
972/386-5477

**Southwest Gallery**
4500 Sigma @ Welch
972-960-8935

**Gary Elam & Associates**
1025 Slocum St.
214/747-4767

**Somerset Galleries**
1205 Slocum St.
214/760-7065

**Oriental Treasures**
1322 Slocum St.
214/760-8888

**Le Louvre French Antiques**
1313 Slocum St.
214/742-2605

**Y C King & Sons**
1528 Slocum St.
214/698-1977

**Samplers**
6817 Snider Plaza
214/363-0045

**Snider Plaza Antiques**
6929 Snider Plaza
214/373-0822

**Days of Olde**
2901 Valley View Lane
972/247-2417

**Bettyann & Jimbo's Antq. Mktplc.**
4402 W. Lovers Lane
214/350-5755

## 46 DAYTON

### The Old School
111 W. Houston
409/258-9342 or 1-800-491-9342
Wed.-Sat. 9:30-5:30, Mon.-Tues. by appointment
*Directions: Dayton is midway between Houston and Beaumont on Hwy. 90. Houston St. is one block south of Hwy. 90. The shop is directly behind the Sonic Drive-in.*

Anyone care to guess why Ann Westmoreland's shop is called The Old School? I'll give you a hint: it used to house teachers and students and was a place of learning for the community. The building was constructed somewhere in the late 1800s, and was last used as a school in 1908. Ann carries furniture, glassware, primitives, jewelry, coins, some Southwestern artifacts along with other antiques and collectibles.

**Charlette's Web**
FM 1960
409/258-5933

**Main Street Bazaar**
312 N. Main St.
409/258-4049

**General Store**
212 N. Main St.
409/258-8928

## 47 DECATUR

**Sisters Four Collectibles**
115 W. Main St.
940/627-3177

**Charles Antiques**
408 W. Main St.
940/627-2485

**Red Pepper Trading Post**
121 N. State St.
940/627-7959

**Memory Lane Antiques**
104 N. Trinity St.
940/627-1121

**Crossroads Antiques Mall**
301 S. Washburn St.
940/627-7047

## 48 DENISON

### Antique Showroom
421 W. Main St.
903/465-2253 or 903/465-2211
Fax: 903/465-2241
email: antiqueshwrm@texoma.net
Mon.-Sat. 10-5:30

For specific information see review at the beginning of this section.

**Antiques & Cars by Bob Taylor**
213 W. Heron St.
903/463-9924

**Castaway Furniture**
1500 W. Johnson St.
903/463-9855

**Katy Antique Station**
104 E. Main St.
903/465-7352

**Tucker Furniture**
422 W. Main St.
903/465-3630

**Hart Place Mall**
500 W. Main St.
903/463-1230

**Manor House Antiques & Cllbls.**
611 W. Main St.
903/465-2601

**Wright's Antiques**
1030 W. Main St.
903/465-9392

**Blue Moon Antique Mall**
410 W. Main St.
903/463-7505

## 49 DENTON

**Memories So Special**
105 Hickory St.
940/484-8560

**Courthouse Collection**
111 W. Hickory St.
940/381-1956

**Downtown Mini Mall**
108 N. Locust St.
940/387-0024

**Cooks Red Barn Antiques**
212 E. Hickory St.
940/382-5004

**Antique Warehouse**
809 N. Locust St.
940/565-0666

**Carriage Hill Collectables**
105 W. Hickory St.
940/484-6194

## 50 DESOTO

***Favorite Places To Eat***

### Cracker Barrel Old Country Store
I-35 E. & Wintergreen Blvd., Exit 416
972/224-3004

## 51 DIBOLL

**Quaint Shop**
Route 3, Box 601
409/829-3466

**Village Antiques**
Hwy. 59 S.
409/829-4500

**The Dusty Attic**
910 N. Temple Dr.
409/829-2743

**Live Oak Antiques & Collectibles**
1443 N. Temple Dr.
409/829-3554

## 52 EASTLAND

**House of Antiques**
908 S. Bassett
254/629-1124

**Hogs N Clover Antiques Gifts**
109 E. Commerce St.
254/629-2755

**Antiques & Uniques**
114 W. Commerce St.
254/629-2143

**I-20 Antiques**
Exit 343
254/629-8682

**Kountry Korner**
112 S. Seaman St.
254/629-2214

## 53 EL CAMPO

**Rose Garden**
123 S. Mechanic St.
409/543-1097

**Pararie Antiques & Collectibles**
708 N. Mechanic St.
409/543-9511

## 54 EL PASO

**Posada San Miguel**
9618 Socorro Road
915/858-1993

**Ye Olde Antiques**
5024 Doniphan Dr.
915/584-7630

**Raquel's**
5372 Doniphan Dr.
915/584-7861

**Rosebud Antiques & Gifts**
6016 Doniphan Dr.
915/584-7227

**Stephen's Antiques**
6016 Doniphan Dr.
915/585-0028

**A J's**
6022 Doniphan Dr.
915/833-3432

**Swan's Antiques**
6022 Doniphan Dr.
915/585-7358

**Stars & Stripes Antiques**
6458 Doniphan Dr.
915/833-6228

**Caldarella's Furniture Inc.**
5660 El Paso
915/859-4777

**Rings Antiques & Collectibles**
7924 Gateway Blvd. E.
915/594-0673

**Wooden Horse Antiques**
132 W. Redd Road
915/581-1976

**Mesa Street Antique Mall**
7410 Remcon Circle
915/584-0868

**Grapevine Antiques & Collectibles**
5024 Doniphan Dr.
951/584-3981

**Marketplace at Placita Sante Fe**
5034 Doniphan Dr.
915/585-9296

**Another Man's Treasure**
6016 Doniphan Dr.
915/581-0077

**Ruby's**
6016 Doniphan Dr.
915/581-0077

**P & L Trading Post**
6020 Doniphan Dr.
915/581-0287

**Mary McNellis Antiques**
6022 Doniphan Dr.
915/584-6878

**C R V Enterprises**
6184 Doniphan Dr.
915/581-6416

**Antique Borderland**
6465 Doniphan Dr.
915/584-3230

**Eastside Antique Mall**
7924 Gateway Blvd. E.
915/594-0673

**Antiques Etcetera**
8022 N. Mesa St.
915/833-4712

**Eagles Nest**
7410 Remcon Circle
915/584-0868

**Nana's Treasures**
7410 Remcon Circle
915/585-0940

## 55 ENNIS

**On The Corner**
101 S. Dallas St.
972/875-8825

**Deedees Antiques Collectibles & More**
808 E. Ennis Ave.
972/875-2011

**Magnolia Station Antiques**
201 S. Dallas St.
972/875-7360

**Good Time Charlies Antiques**
114 W. Knox St.
972/875-9737

## 56 FORNEY

**Pavillion Antiques**
4 Forney Industrial Park
972/222-8902

**Wholesale Antiques**
5 Forney Industrial Park
972/564-4433

**Snooper's Paradise**
6 Forney Industrial Park
972/564-4214

**Star Antique Mall**
Forney Industrial Park
972/564-1055

**Philbeck's Antiques**
119 E. Hwy. 80
972/564-9842

**Bowling Antiques**
10512 W. Hwy. 80
972/564-1433

**Cotton Gin Mall**
210 Hwy. 688
972/564-1220

**Deridder Antiques Corp.**
Forney Industrial Park
972/226-8407

**Doc's Antiques**
107 Hwy. 80
972/552-4305

**Clement's Antiques of Texas Inc.**
121 E. Hwy. 80
972/564-1520

**Little Red's Antiques**
Hwy. 80
972/226-2304

**Aires Limited**
E. 125 Hwy. 80
972/564-4913

## 57 FORT WORTH

### Cowtown Antiques The Trading Post
2400 N. Main St.
817/626-4565
Tues.-Thurs., 10-5, Fri.-Sat., 11-6, Sun., 12-5, closed Mon.

Cowtown Antiques and The Trading Post are two different shops located almost together and owned by the same folks. Both are open the same hours (listed above) so you can get double your shopping time in here. The shops are in the historic Fort Worth Stockyards..."Where the West Begins," and shoppers can experience the old time atmosphere and rich heritage of this Fort Worth landmark.

With the sounds of cowboy music filling the background, shop for Western collectibles and memorabilia, pocket watches, Western wear, mounts, and hides. In addition, there is furniture, stained glass and advertising memorabilia.

### Harris Antiques & Imports
7600 Scott St.
817/246-8400 or 817/246-5852
Fax: 817/246-6859
*Directions: Harris Antiques & Imports is located in West Fort Worth, in a suburb called White Settlement. The shop is at I-30 W., Cherry Lane Exit (north), then right on Scott St.*

Carolyn Harris and company sells both wholesale and retail, with about 95% of their sales being to dealers, auctioneers and designers. Anyone who loves antiques should go to the showroom just to look and be impressed. Their new location is an air-conditioned mall that is the length of three football fields - a total of 440,000 square feet of antiques and accessories! Harris Antiques & Imports has been in business in Fort Worth for over 35 years, and offers merchandise to shoppers world-wide. Besides all the furniture, they offer bronzes, oil paintings, cut glass and porcelain. It's no wonder they hold the title of "the world's largest home furnishings, accessories and antiques store."

**Black Orchid**
3801 Camp Bowie Blvd.
817/731-8611

**Leigh-Boyd**
4632 Camp Bowie Blvd.
817/738-3705

**Antique Colony Inc.**
7200 Camp Bowie Blvd.
817/731-7252

**Antique Shop**
5401 Jacksboro Hwy.
817/740-9966

**Yabba Dabba Doo Antiques**
6517 E. Lancaster Ave.
817/654-4100

**Antique Connection**
7429 E. Lancaster Ave.
817/429-0922

**Lake Worth Bazaar**
4024 Merrett Dr.
817/237-8064

**Cornish Antiques & Collectibles**
320 S. Oakland Blvd.
817/536-9975

**Lemon Tree Antiques Art & Books**
804 Pennsylvania Ave.
817/332-5519

**Harris' Antiques**
7600 Scott St.
817/246-5852

**Norma Baker Antiques**
3311 W. 7th St.
817/335-1152

**Butler's Antiques & Uniques**
514 W. Seminary Dr.
817/921-3403

**Quilter's Emporium**
3526 W. Vickery Blvd.
817/377-3993

**Hidden Treasures Antiques**
8906 White Settlement Road
817/246-8864

**Florie's Antiques**
3915 Camp Bowie Blvd.
817/763-5380

**Fort Worth Antiques**
4909 Camp Bowie Blvd.
871/731-4220

**From The Hide**
117 W. Exchange Ave.
817/624-8302

**Doll House**
1815 E. Lancaster Ave.
817/332-8674

**Drew's Antiques & Primitives**
7113 E. Lancaster Ave.
817/451-8822

**Stockyard Antiques**
1332 N. Main St.
817/624-2311

**Montgomery St. Antique Mall**
2601 Montgomery St.
817/735-9685

**Choices on Park Hill**
2978 Park Hill
817/927-1854

**Nicks Frame & Antique Shop**
2616 Scott Ave.
817/534-3601

**Sample House**
1540 S. University Dr.
817/429-7857

**Market**
3433 W. 7th St.
817/334-0330

**Lambert Antiques**
2812 Stanley Ave.
817/926-3450

**Newtons Antiques**
5216 White Settlement Road
817/737-7009

### *Great Places To Stay*

**Azalea Plantation Bed and Breakfast**
1400 Robinwood Dr.
1-800-68R-ELAX

Azalea Plantation is a stately plantation style home reminiscent of Tara, nestled in a quiet residential neighborhood near downtown's restored Sundance Square and only ten minutes from the Stockyards Historic District. The bed and breakfast sits amidst one and a half acres of oak trees highlighted with rock terracing, gazebo and fountains. Guest rooms and cottages are spacious, furnished with antiques and very private with private baths. The Magnolia Cottage/Suite is the perfect honeymoon/ anniversary romantic getaway spot, with its Texas size whirlpool for two, cozy bedroom and charming parlor.

## 58 FRANKSTON

**Pandora's Box**
102 W. Main St.
903/876-5056
Mon.-Sat. 9-5:30, closed Sun.
*Directions: Pandora's Box is located on the square in Frankston, one block west of Hwy. 155 and one block south of Hwy. 175.*

Here's a true junque store that's not afraid to say so! That's their description of themselves: a 4,000 square foot true junque store with architectural antiques and a garden shop, all housed in an old automobile dealership building.

## 59 FREDERICKSBURG

**Watkins Hill**
608 E. Creek
210/997-6739 or 1-800-899-1672
Year round, business hours Mon.-Fri. 8-5, Sat.-Sun. 8-2

Watkins Hill Guest House is so perfectly suited for the scenic area in which it is located. Visitors are attracted to the European atmosphere, historic landmarks and the bread and pastries for which Fredericksburg is famous. Watkins Hill is conveniently accessible from Austin, San Antonio, Houston and Dallas/Fort Worth. Mr. Edgar Watkins, the innkeeper, will provide excellent directions to the Guest House from your location.

Watkins Hill, is an unusual - and unusually elegant - bed and breakfast complex in Fredericksburg, Texas.

Dreamchild of native Texan Edgar Watkins, Watkins Hill began life just a few years ago when Watkins gave up a career in product design and public relations to return to his home state and buy the 1855 Basse House, now the centerpiece of his inn. He knew he wanted something out of the ordinary for his bed and breakfast, and he knew what he didn't like about other B&Bs, so he designed Watkins Hill with these things in mind. One of his pet peeves is sitting down to breakfast with a group of strangers in the custom of traditional B&Bs. So he decided to serve his guests with breakfast by room service at the guest's requested time. He also doesn't like the term "bed and breakfast," instead preferring to call his accommodation a "guest house."

Another concept from the start was not to fill the inn with Texas farm furniture. Instead Watkins created an imaginary scenario, and went from there, "I fantasized that a stylish bachelor had moved here in the 1850s from the East, and had brought his family's furniture with him." Following that fantasy, the Basse House is furnished with upscale antiques from the mid-18th century to the mid-19th century, including a rare little steel bathtub from a Paris hotel.

The entire complex currently spans two acres, with seven buildings, four of which are historic 19th century structures (1835, 1840, 1855 and 1890). Twelve guest rooms are available, with a total sleeping capacity of about 40 guests. All of this is located just two blocks from Fredericksburg's Main St. and its shops, yet longhorn cattle graze across the way on the opposite side of the street and along the creek that runs beside it.

All but two rooms have fireplaces and porches or balconies. Every room has a butler's pantry with a refrigerator stocked with complimentary wine, two kinds of coffee and several kinds of tea, distilled water, fruit juice and apples. Guests also get four kinds of snacks, current magazines, and recommendations of places to dine.

There are so many little touches of elegance, luxury and whimsey that guests could spend all their time just wandering around looking for these surprises. Beeswax tapers and potted candles glow beside a mid-19th century faux bamboo French daybed. One living room wall is covered floor to ceiling with a circa 1870 theatrical backdrop. It's a scarred canvas painting of a forest, but the creases and nicks in it fit beautifully with the combination of primitive and elegant decors that swirl throughout the house. The frayed edges of the canvas are disguised at the top behind a pressed tin valance dipped in brass, and along both sides by a pair of 19th century pilasters from New York state. Doors at either end open onto the porches, with the open front door offering a view of a Victorian cast-cement fountain and an expansive meadow. Luxury and style with the unusual make wonderful weekend or week-long companions for guests who like to be pampered and intrigued.

**'exas Trading Co.**
09 N. Adams St.
10/997-1840

**Room No. 5**
239A W. Blvd. #5
210/997-1090

**merican Hiddledy Piggledy**
11 S. Lincoln St.
10/997-5551

**Homestead Warehouse Store**
411 S. Lincoln St.
210/997-0954

**lle Hours**
1 S. Lincoln St.
10/997-2908

**Wild Goose Chase Antiques**
105 S. Llano St.
210/997-4321

**Antique Haus**
107 S. Llano St.
210/997-2011

**Showcase Antiques Shop**
119 E. Main St.
210/997-5505

**Cornerstone Market**
201 E. Main St.
210/997-3204

**Remember Me**
203 E. Main St.
210/997-6932

**Jabberwocky Antiques**
207 E. Main St.
210/997-7071

**Red Baron's Antiques**
215 E. Main St.
210/997-6368

**Lauren Bade Antiques**
229 E. Main St.
210/997-9570

**Main St. Antiques**
234 W. Main St.
210/997-8913

**Der Alte Fritz Antiques**
409 E. Main St.
210/997-8249

**Rustic Styles**
414 E. Main St.
210/997-6219

**Three Horse Trader**
609 W. Main St.
210/997-6499

## 60 GAINESVILLE

**Recollection Antiques**
105 W. California St.
940/668-2170

**Old West Traditions**
107 W. California St.
940/665-7503

**Miss Pitty Pat's Antique Porch**
111 W. California St.
940/665-6540

**Shady Oak Gallery**
111 S. Commerce St.
940/665-0275

**Lindsay House**
318 E. California St.
940/665-7171

**Naughty Lady Antiques**
108 N. Chestnut St.
940/668-1767

**Carousel Antique Mall**
112 S. Dixon St.
940/665-6444

**Gainesville Antique Mall Main**
1808 N. IH-35
940/668-7798

## 61 GALVESTON

**Madame Dyer's Bed & Breakfast**
1720 Postoffice St.
409/765-5692
Open year round
*Directions: Take I-45 south from Houston to Galveston. When you cross over the Causeway onto the island, the interstate highway becomes Broadway. Travel about 50 blocks to 18th St. Make a left turn onto 18th St. and go 5 blocks to Postoffice St. Turn right onto this one-way street. Madame Dyer's is the second house on the left. Park in front.*

This elegant 1889 Victorian mansion is located in the East End Historic Homes District, which is one of the most beautiful and best preserved areas of Victorian homes in the country. It is within walking distance of The Strand Historic District, where restored vintage buildings house specialty shops, galleries, museums, restaurants, outlet shops and antique malls; and is two blocks away from Gallery Row, where upscale antique and gallery shops abound. In other words, its location is perfect! Guests can even have a horse drawn carriage pick them up at the B&B's front door, or they can catch the historic trolley just two blocks away.

The ornate, two-store mansion has been faithfully restored to its turn-of-the-century glory, with two wrap-around porches, high airy ceilings, wooden floors and lace curtains. Each room is furnished with antiques, including the three guest rooms. Ashten's Room, with private bath, is furnished with a queen size bed of carved oak and antique accent pieces. Blake's Room, with a queen size bed set in a bay window, is decorated in English antiques and antique rug beaters, shoe lasts and sewing memorabilia. The private bath just down the hall holds a claw-foot tub. Corbin's Room holds a king size bed, a tiled fireplace with an oak mirrored mantel, antique dolls, whimsical old hats, and a pedestal sink and claw-foot tub in the adjoining bath.

There is a coffee/tea buffet provided each morning upstairs for early risers, a full breakfast every morning in the dining room, homemade cookies in the dining room at all times, and complimentary snacks and beverages available in the kitchen round the clock.

**Jewels & Junque**
2715 Broadway St.
409/762-3243

**B. J.'s Antiques**
2111 Postoffice St.
409/763-6075

**Collectors Gallery**
2222 Postoffice St.
409/765-6443

**Hendley Market**
2010 Strand
409/762-2610

**Old Peanut Butter Warehouse**
100 20th St.
409/762-8358

**Yesterday's Best**
120 20th St.
409/765-1419

**Somewhere In Time Antiques**
124 20th St.
409/762-1094

**La Maison Rouge**
418 22nd St.
409/763-0717

**Off The Wall Antiques**
1811 23rd St.
409/765-9414

## 62 GARLAND

**Chase & James Furniture**
1817 S. Garland Ave.
942/864-0092

**The Cabbage Patch**
901 Jupiter
942/272-8928

**Old South Antiques & Auction**
1413 N. I Hwy. 30
942/240-4477

**The Ritz**
Main St.
942/494-0083

**Treasure Chest of Antiques**
115 N. 6th St.
942/276-6075

**Farm House Antiques**
509 W. State St.
942/487-8262

**Old Garland Antique Mall**
108 N. 6th St.
942/494-029

## 63 GEORGETOWN

**Cobblestone**
708 S. Austin Ave.
512/863-9607

**On The Square**
712 S. Austin Ave.
512/869-0448

**Rust & Dust**
113 E. 7th St.
512/863-6463

**Georgetown Emporium**
114 E. 7th St.
512/863-6845

**Georgetown Antique Mall**
713 S. Main St.
512/869-2088

**Texas Sampler**
101 River Hills Dr.
512/863-7694

**Poppy Hill Marketplace**
820 S. Austin Ave.
512/863-8445

## 64 GILMER

**Old Town Mall**
201 Henderson St.
903/843-2359

**Corner Store Antiques**
203 W. Tyler St.
903/843-2466

## 65 GLADEWATER

**Gladewater Antique Mall**
100 E. Commerce Ave.
903/845-4440

**Jade Junction**
106 E. Commerce Ave.
903/845-3876

**Now & Then Antique Mall**
109 W. Commerce Ave.
903/845-5765

**Bygone Tymes Mall**
109 N. Main St.
903/845-2603

**B & B Bygones Antiques**
111 S. Main St.
903/845-2655

**Old Tyme Antiques & Collectibles**
111 S. Main St.
903/845-4708

**Antiques**
112 S. Main St.
903/845-6493

**Carlyne's Collectables**
112 N. Main St.
903/845-3923

**Main Street Treasures**
113 N. Main St.
903/845-6671

**Good Old Stuff**
114 S. Main St.
903/845-8316

**K D Wayside Shop**
119 S. Main St.
903/845-4093

**Mel's Country Classics**
120 S. Main St.
903/845-2519

**The Loft**
121 S. Main St.
903/845-4429

**Country Girl Collection**
124 S. Main St.
903/845-6143

**Dru's Knick Knacks**
125 S. Main St.
903/845-5635

**Country Carousel Mall**
201 S. Main St.
903/845-4531

**Studio**
201 N. Main St.
903/845-6910

**Bishop's Antique Mall**
202 S. Main St.
903/845-7247

**Saint Clair Antique Emporium**
104 W. Pacific Ave.
903/845-4079

**Heritage Antiques & Collectibles**
112 W. Pacific Ave.
903/845-3021

## 66 GLEN FLORA

**Glen Flora Emporium**
103 S. Bridge St.
409/677-3249
Wed.-Sun. 10-6
*Directions: Glen Flora is five miles north of U.S. Hwy. 59 at Wharton, Texas. Take the Eagle Lake Exit and travel north on FM 102 until you reach the small town of Glen Flora. Bridge St. is FM 960, which intersects with FM 102. The shop is at the intersection of FM 102 and FM 960. Turn left into the parking lot. You can't miss the emporium - it's the largest building for miles.*

The town of Glen Flora was founded in 1900 and is currently undergoing restoration and reconstruction. The building that houses the emporium was built in 1912. This 20 plus dealer mall handles furniture, glassware, pottery, jewelry, vintage clothing and so on.

## 67 GOLIAD

Goliad is one of the three oldest municipalities in Texas and was the site of the Aranama Indian village name Santa Dorotea. In 1749 the Spanish government transferred The Royal Presidio (fort) of Nuestra Senora De Loreto De La Bahia De Expiritu Santo to this location along with the Mission Nuestra Senora Del Espiritu Santo De Zuniga. A small villa grew up around the walls of the fort and was called La Bahia. This area was occupied by the Spanish until 1821 when Mexico became an independent nation. In 1829 the name "Goliad" was officially adopted. It is an anagram of the name "Hidalgo" in honor of the patriot priest of the Mexican Revolution.

In what was termed the first offensive action of the Texas Revolution, local colonists captured Goliad on October 9, 1845. The First Declaration of Texas Independence was signed here on December 20. Along with it was raised the "Bloody Arm Flag", the first flag of Texas independence. During the 1836 campaign, Col. James Fannin's Texans were defeated at the Battle Of Coleto and were massacred one week later on March 27, 1836 at the Presidio La Bahia. The Goliad Massacre represents the largest single loss of life (352) in the cause of Texas independence and inspired the battle cry "Remember The Alamo - Remember Goliad."

**The Honeycomb Antiques**
122 N. Courthouse Square
512/645-2331

**The Christmas Goose**
136 N. Courthouse Square
512/645-8087

## 68 GONZALES

**Catty Corner Antiques**
501 N. Saint Joseph St.
210/672-2975

**Dubs Antique Mall**
517 N. Saint Joseph St.
210/672-7917

**Bowdens Antiques**
620 N. Saint Joseph St.
210/672-7770

**Violet's Treasures**
712 N. Saint Joseph St.
210/672-9744

**Laurel Ridge Antiques**
827 N. Saint Joseph St.
210/672-2484

**Polly's House Flowers & Antiques**
830 Saint Paul St.
210/672-2013

## 69 GRANBURY

**Brazos River Trading Co.**
115 E. Bridge St.
817/573-5191

**Sugar & Spice Antiques**
117 W. Bridge St.
817/579-1224

**Antique Emporium**
116 1/2 N. Crockett St.
817/573-1939

**Wagon Yard Antiques**
213 N. Crockett St.
817/573-5321

**Scarlet Thread**
3018 Fall Creek Hwy.
817/326-3430

**Antique Mall Of Granbury**
4303 N. Hwy. 37
817/279-1645

**Classic Antiques**
4316 Hwy. 377
817/579-5658

**The Bazaar**
4318 E. Hwy. 377
817/579-9295

**Trading Company**
109 N. Houston St.
817/573-3800

**Hightower Antiques & Uniques**
130 N. Houston St.
817/573-4488

**Pearl St Antiques & Treasures**
503 E. Pearl St.
817/279-1270

**Witherspoon's Antiques**
600 E. Pearl St.
817/573-5254

## 70 GRAPELAND

**Bobbye's**
315 S. Market St.
409/687-4979

**Echoes of Texas**
924 N. Market St.
409/687-2070

**Flo's Antiques**
210 Main St.
409/687-4778

## 71 GRAPEVINE

**Guests Main Street Antiques**
201 E. Franklin St.
817/488-3647

**Julia's Antiques & Tearoom**
210 N. Main St.
817/329-0622

**Air Nostalgia**
420 S. Main St.
817/481-9005

**Collectors Exchange**
415 N. Northwest Hwy.
817/329-6946

**Grapevine Antique Mall**
415 N. Northwest Hwy.
817/329-6946

## 72 GREENVILLE

**Better Days Antiques**
2402 Lee St.
903/455-3035

**Courthouse Square Antiques**
2512 Lee St.
903/455-0557

**Downtown Tradin Days**
2801 Lee St.
903/454-9908

**Billie Taggart's 1800 Shop**
2417 Oneal St.
903/455-4151

**Country Craft Mall**
2814 Terrell Road
903/455-7736

**Greenville Village**
2316 Johnson St.
903/455-1887

**Greenville Antiques**
2605 Halifax St.
903/454-2488

**Texan Antiques & Gifts**
2712 Lee St.
903/455-6246

## 73 GROESBECK

**Groesbeck Antiques Mall**
105 N. Ellis St.
254/729-3443

**Bonds Store & Gallery**
217 W. Navasota St.
254/729-5511

## 74 HARLINGEN

### Tejas Finders

Paul C. Moon Jr.
Route 1, Box 695 Wilson Road
210/423-6870

He's only 20 years old, but already well on his way to establishing a solid professional name for himself in the antique trade. "He" is Paul C. Moon, Jr., and he is what's known as a "picker" in the antique world.

"I search for whatever the buyer is looking for," says Moon. "When I locate the piece, I send the buyer photographs of the piece, if possible, and, if he is completely satisfied, we come to an agreement and I expedite the deal."

Moon began his interest in antiques when he was managing an antique shop in the Harlingen, Texas area. He was fascinated by the Victorian style and era, and now specializes in Victorian pieces; however, he will search for whatever style and pieces a buyer wants to find. He's been a picker for two years, and business is good.

Working out of his home in Harlingen, Moon generally limits his travels and searches to the valley area around Harlingen. Situated in the very southeastern tip of Texas, Harlingen is conveniently located in the coastal region of east Texas, where the Victorian style abounds, left over from the influence of the steamboat and paddlewheeler days, plus the influence of changing styles that were easily accessible by water routes.

The next time you need a certain piece and style, call Moon. If it's Victorian in Texas, he probably knows right where to look.

**Hilites**
107 E. Jackson St.
210/412-7573

**Frank's Collectables & Antiques**
123 E. Jackson St.
210/423-4041

**Antique Furniture Warehouse**
2710 S. F St.
210/425-3131

**Somewhere In Time Antiques**
111 E. Jackson St.
210/412-2577

**Youngblood Interiors & Antiques**
302 E. Jackson St.
210/412-1155

## 75 HASKELL

Hub of the rolling plains, Haskell was named after Charles Ready Haskell, a Revolutionary soldier who fell with Fannin at Goliad. Haskell was incorporated in 1885 and known in pioneer days as "Willow Pond Springs" and later as "Rice Springs." Today Haskell offers a beautiful city park, overnight RV parking, fishing, hunting and, of course, antiquing.

### Nemir's Antiques

510 N. 2nd St.
940/864-2258
Fax: 817/864-3124
Mon.-Fri., 10-5
*Directions: Nemir's is located at the corner of 2nd St. and N. Avenue F. From Hwy. 380, turn north 1 block west of the main red light, which is Avenue F. Go 1 block to 2nd St. and turn east. The shop is right on the corner. From Hwy. 277, turn west 1 block north of the main red light. This will be 2nd St. and the shop is on the corner.*

Nemir's Antiques is a large, family-owned store with a grand selection of quality antiques and collectibles. The 5,000-square-foot store offers something for everyone including, but by no means limited to, a variety of old toys and pottery.

**Peddlers Village**
304 S. 1st St.
940/864-2878

**Old Stuff Antiques & Gifts**
300 S. Ave. E.
940/864-2430

## 76 HENDERSON

**Ms Patty's Attic**
501 Kilgore Dr.
Hwy. 259 N.
903/655-1146

**Trunks & Treasures**
123 E. Main St.
903/657-8879

**Nelda's Nook**
112 N. Marshall St.
903/657-2332

**Sweet Lorraine's**
501 1/2 Kilgore Dr.
Hwy. 259 N.
903/657-1163

**Emporium on the Square**
102 N. Marshall St.
903/657-3854

**Four Oaks Gallery**
709 State Hwy. 43 E.
903/657-8207

## 77 HILLSBORO

**Veranda's Interiors & Antiques**
114 S. Covington St.
254/582-9995

**Dee Dee's Gifts & Tiques**
106 E. Elm St.
254/582-0355

**Old Citizens Emporium**
50 W. Elm St.
254/582-1995

**Arnold's Country Charm**
110 W. Elm St.
254/582-5201

**ranklin St. Antiques**
5 W. Franklin St.
54/582-0055

**Antique Village Inc.**
116 E. Franklin St.
254/582-8632

**ainbow Gems Jewelers & Antique Mall**
5 N. Waco St.
54/582-8430

**Hillsboro Antique Mall**
114 S. Waco St.
254/582-8330

## 78 HOUSTON

### arolyn Thompson's Antique Center of Texas
001 W. Loop N.
13/688-4211
aily 10-6
*irections: 1001 W. Loop N., just 2 miles north of The Galleria.*

For specific information see review at the beginning of this section.

### rade Mart Antiques
am Houston Tollway @ Hammerly
13/467-2506
ri, Sat. & Sun. 10-6
*irections: Located at Sam Houston Tollway @ Hammerly, 2 miles orth of I-10.*

For specific information see review at the beginning of this section.

### R Antiques
230 Bissonnet St.
13/524-3272
on.-Sat. 10-6
*irections: Located between Greenbriar and Shepherd off Hwy. 59.*

For specific information see review at the beginning of this section.

### allery Auctions, Inc.
43 Blue Bell
31/931-0100 or 1-800-764-8423

Auction each Monday morning at 10 a.m. and Tuesday night at 7 m. Call for special auction schedules.

### herry Kelley's Antiques
323 Woodhead St.
3/520-7575
x: 713/520-6362
on.-Sat., 10-6
*irections: From Hwy. 59, the Southwest Freeway, exit Shepherd d go north on Shepherd to Fairview. Turn east (right) on irview and go to the first stop sign, which is Woodhead. Sherry lley's Antiques is at the corner of Fairview and Woodhead. From 10, exit Shepherd and go south to West Gray and turn left. Go east Woodhead and turn right. Proceed south to 2323 Woodhead and Fairview. The shop is two blocks north of Westheimer and 7 blocks east of Fairview.*

Sherry Kelley is a direct importer of European antiques, making up to five trips a year to Europe, hand picking each item. Sherry specializes in mahogany Georgian style furniture, prints, books, crystal and decorative items.

**Knight's Gallery**
1320 W. Alabama St.
713/521-2785

**Lynette Proler Antique Jewelers**
2622 W. Alabama St.
713/521-1827

**Dorothy Mostert Antiques**
404 Avondale St.
713/523-9165

**Warren Antique Collection**
2121 N. West Belt
713/465-2985

**Carl Moore Antiques**
1610 Bissonnet St.
713/524-2502

**Gilded Monkey**
2314 Bissonnet St.
713/526-8661

**Silver Shop**
2348 Bissonnet St.
713/526-7256

**R & S Antiques**
2402 Bissonnet St.
713/524-9178

**Southwest Antiques & Collectibles**
6735 Bissonnet St.
713/981-6773

**H Karl Scharold Antiques Inc**
5243 Buffalo Speedway
713/661-3466

**Back Porch Antiques**
17715 Clay Road
713/345-9238

**Cleary's Antiques**
10817 Craigheard Dr.
713/664-6643

**Odeon Gallery**
2117 Dunlavy St.
713/521-1111

**Inside Outside**
510 W. 18th St.
713/869-6911

**Brian Stringer Antiques**
2031 W. Alabama St.
713/526-7380

**Almeda Antique Mall**
9827 Almeda Genoa Road
713/941-7744

**Barziza's Antiques**
2121 N.W. Belt Dr.
713/467-0628

**Simone Antique & More II**
11723 W. Bellfort
713/561-7403

**Madison Alley Antiques**
1720 Bissonnett St.
713/526-6146

**Britannia Antiques**
2338 Bissonnet St.
713/529-3779

**Antiques Antiques**
14546 Carol Crest St.
713/527-0841

**Southwest Antiques Too**
6727 Bissonnet St.
713/981-6633

**Simpson's Galleries**
4001 Main St.
713/524-6751

**Gabriel Galleries of Houston**
7600 Burgoyne
713/528-2647

**Crescent Enterprises Antiques**
9229 Clay Road
713/462-4880

**Antiques Houston**
3200 W. Dallas Ave.
713/523-4705

**J Silver Antiques**
3845 Dunlave St.
713/526-2988

**Candlelight Cottage**
7979 N. Eldridge Pkwy.
713/469-4210

**Four Roses Antiques**
7979 N. Eldridge Pkwy.
713/897-0507

**Adkins Architectural Antiques**
3515 Fannin St.
713/522-6547

**Made In France**
2912 Ferndale St.
713/529-7949

**Ferndale Gallery & Antiques**
2935 Ferndale St.
713/527-8358

**The Market-Champion Village**
5419 W. FM 1960
713/440-8281

**French Antique Exchange**
3301 Fondren Road
713/785-0785

**Carriage House**
10609 Grant Road
713/469-4840

**T's Antiques**
10609 Grant Road
713/890-8899

**Cobblestone Antiques**
7623 Louetta
713/251-0660

**Campbell & Co. Antiques**
3110 Houston Ave.
713/880-8178

**Picket Fence**
3010 Hwy. 146
713/474-4845

**Woodlands Antique Mall**
26710 N. IH 45
713/364-8111

**Timely Treasures Antiques**
11503 Jones Road
713/897-9577

**Bediko Antiques & Refinishing**
3402 Laura Koppe Road
713/692-3008

**Gillespie's Antiques**
4113 Leeland St.
713/247-9604

**Richard's Antiquites Inc.**
3500 Main St.
713/528-5651

**Sander's Antiques**
315 Fairview St.
713/522-0539

**James A Gundry Inc.**
2910 Ferndale St.
713/524-6622

**Phyllis Tucker Antiques**
2919 Ferndale St.
713/524-0165

**McLaren's Antiques & Gifts**
3225 FM 1960
713/893-0432

**White & Day Antiques**
6711 FM 1960
713/444-3836

**Ann's Creative Framing &Antiques**
1928 Fountain View Dr.
713/781-7772

**Look**
5110 Griggs Road
713/748-6641

**Burton's Antiques**
9333 Harwin Dr.
713/977-5885

**Silvi's Antiques Etc.**
2223 Hwy. 6 S.
713/597-8557

**Once Upon A time**
1004 W. Hwy. 6
713/331-7676

**Gypsy Savage**
1509 Indiana St.
713/528-0897

**Meg's Cottage Inc.**
2819 W T C Jester Blvd.
713/956-2229

**Nelly's Porch**
16300 Kuykendahl Road
713/893-4659

**Stevens Antique Furniture**
5301 Laura Koppe Road
713/631-3196

**Annie's Art & Antiques**
1415 Murray Bay St.
713/973-6659

**Norbert Antiques**
3617 Main St.
713/524-4334

**Once in a Life Time**
12454 Memorial Dr.
713/465-8828

**Thistle Antiques**
12472 Memorial Dr.
713/984-2329

**Happenings**
4203 Montrose Blvd.
713/524-1507

**Old Katy Road Antiques**
9198 Old Katy Road #B
713/461-8124

**Market Place Antiques**
10910 Old Katy Road
713/464-8023

**Sitting Room**
2402 Quenby
713/523-1932

**Baca Antique**
2121 W. Sam Houston Pkwy. N.
713/984-0228

**Hurta's Historics**
2121 W. Sam Houston Pkwy. N.
713/468-1680

**Antique Panache**
9137 Spring Branch Dr.
713/464-2022

**Country Home Antiques**
14916 Stuebner Airline Road
713/440-1186

**Reeves Antiques**
2415 Taft St.
713/523-5577

**Flashbacks Funtiques**
1626 Westheimer Road
713/522-7900

**Rosen Kavalieriques**
1715 Westheimer Road
713/527-0660

**Pride And Joy Antiques**
1727 Westheimer Road
713/522-8435

**The Emporium Architectural Antiques**
1800 Westheimer Road
713/528-3808

**Howard Graetz Antiques**
1844 Westheimer Road
713/522-5908

**Darby's Off-Memorial**
12460 Memorial Dr.
713/465-0245

**Antiques at Rummel Creek**
13190 Memorial Dr.
713/461-9110

**Antiques on Nineteenth**
345 W. 19th St.
713/869-5030

**C & H Antiques**
10910 Old Katy Road
713/465-1120

**Max Miller Antiques**
10910 Old Katy Road
713/467-0450

**Norman**
2425 Ralph St.
713/521-1811

**British Emporium**
2121 W. Sam Houston Pkwy. N.
713/467-3455

**General Mothers Antiques**
2121 W. Sam Houston Pkwy. N.
713/984-9461

**Cabin Creek Lodge**
1703 Spring Cypress Road
713/350-5559

**Mattye's This And That Antiques**
14916 Stuebner Airline Road
713/580-4222

**Abelar Antiques**
6008 W. 34th St.
713/683-8055

**Antique Warehaus/Trash & Treasures**
1714 Westheimer Road
713/522-6858

**Old Blue House Antiques**
1719 Westheimer Road
713/521-2515

**Westheimer Antique Center**
1738 Westheimer Road
713/529-8585

**Past Era Antique Jewelry**
2311 Westheimer Road
713/524-7110

**Hillingham Antiques**
1848 Westheimer Road
713/523-4335

**Kay O'Toole Antiques**
1921 Westheimer Road
713/523-1921

**Antique Pavilion**
2311 Westheimer Road
713/520-9755

**David Lackey Antiques & China**
2311 Westheimer Road
713/942-7171

**Margaret K. Reese Antiques**
2233 Westheimer Road
713/523-8889

**Wicket Antique**
2233 Westheimer Road
713/522-0779

**Brownstone Gallery**
2803 Westheimer Road
713/523-8171

**The Market**
4060 Westheimer Road
713/960-9084

**Joyce Horn Antiques**
1008 Wirt Road
713/688-0507

**Carol Gibbins Antiques**
1817 Woodhead St.
713/524-9011

**John Holt Antiques & Primitives**
2416 Woodhead St.
713/528-5065

**House of Glass**
3319 Louisiana St.
713/528-5289

**River Oaks Antiques Center**
2119 Westheimer Road
713/520-8238

**Crow & Company**
2311 Westheimer Road
713/524-6055

**M. J. Fine Things**
2311 Westheimer Road
713/529-6960

**Florian Fine Art**
2323 Westheimer Road
713/942-9919

**R.N. Wakefield & Co.**
2702 Westheimer Road
713/528-4677

**Lewis & Maese Arts Antiques**
3738 Westheimer Road
713/960-1454

**Belgravia Antiques**
11195 Westheimer Road
713/785-4797

**Cottage Antiques**
2233 Westheimer Road
713/523-8889

**Golden Eye**
2121 Woodhead St.
713/528-3379

**Las Cruces Antiques**
2422 Woodhead St.
713/524-2422

**Studio**
3951 San Felipe St.
713/961-7540

### *Historical Houston Heights*

Whether you are seeking affordable antiques, an outstanding playground for the kids, or turn-of-the-century showplace homes, Houston Heights is the place to go. Founded in 1887, this planned streetcar community, designed to be a rural sanctuary from Houston, is located just four miles from downtown. A landmark for over a century, its main thoroughfare, Heights Boulevard, was modeled after Boston's Commonwealth Avenue and has been designated by the City of Houston as a "Scenic Right-of-Way." Victorian and early 20th century homes, churches, and a public library still line the Boulevard, and today an excellent walking trail exists along the esplanade where the trolley once ran. The spectacular new Heights Playground, a Robert Leathers design, complete with a depot and Victorian castle, plus Marmion Park with its majestic gazebo, and the Victorian Rose Garden are all on the Boulevard. All three are maintained by Heights' neighborhood organization, the Houston Heights Association. In addition to the beauty and historical attractions of this area, the Heights also provides shoppers with a wealth of antique stores, clothing stores, folk art shops, and casual eateries.

### Old Fashioned Things

811 Yale St.
713/880-8393
Fax 713/868-7464
Email: harelec@swbell.net
*Directions: Exit off I-10 West or 610 North Loop West - From I-10W take the Yale/Heights Blvd. Exit and go north. From 610 N. Loop, take the Yale St. Exit and go south.*

Located in a cottage built in 1906, in the heart of the Historic Houston Heights, Old Fashioned Things is just four blocks north of Interstate 10, between downtown Houston and the Galleria area. Old Fashioned Things offers a truly unique shopping experience. Upon entering, you'll be greeted by the wonderful aromas of scented candles, potpourri, sachets, and oils that grace the tops and shelves of vintage curio cabinets, linen presses, and washstands from the turn of the century. The shop also features collectible furniture, lighting fixtures, textiles, French lace, frocks, glassware, and costume jewelry. A special section is reserved for infants and children, which includes garments, furniture, books, and toys. You'll find romantic gift items that compliment the historic atmosphere, such as English friendship balls and Forever soaps.

Note from the proprietors:

*Laura and Dennis Virgadamo, invite you stop by and visit Monday through Saturday 10 a.m. to 6 p.m. or Sunday by appointment. They accept Mastercard, Visa, Discover and personal checks with proper identification. Lay-aways are welcome.*

### R & F Antiques

Specializing in American Antiques
912 Yale St.
713/861-7750
Sun.-Tues. by chance or appt., Wed.-Sat. 10-5:30
*Directions: Located approximately 7 blocks north of I-10 at the Heights and Yale exit.*

In this "barn" red building, you will find seven rooms brimming with American furniture. For more than 25 years, Gary & Jennifer Baroski have brought the finest quality antiques to the Houston area. The shop features curved glass china cabinets, tables, chairs, secretaries, beds, chests and an outstanding selection of fireplace mantels. **Note: I personally have not visited this shop, but I have been told by several serious collectors that it is one of the best shops in the country.*

**11th Street Antiques**
720 W. 11th St.
713/802-2719

**Alabama Furniture & Accessories**
2200 Yale St.
713/862-3035

**Chippendale Eastlake in Heights**
250 W. 19th St.
713/869-8633

**Byers Original Finishes**
115 W. 13th St.
713/868-5937

**Heights Antique Co-op**
321 W. 19th St.
713/864-7237

**Homestyle Resale**
215 E. 11th St.
713/868-3400

**John's Flowers & Antiques**
373 W. 19th St.
713/862-8717

**Sugar's Collectables**
249 W. 19th St.
713/868-7006

**Twenty Second Second**
611 W. 22nd St.
713/864-0261

**Past Connections & Collectibles**
235 West 19th St.
713/802-1992

**Heights Country Store**
801 Heights Blvd.
713/862-4161

**Heights Collection**
3617 White Oak Dr.
713/880-8203

**On The Corner**
837 Studewood St.
713/863-9143

**Heights Antiques on Yale**
2110 Yale
No Phone # Listed

**Antiques on Nineteenth**
345 W. 19th St.
713/869-5030

**Charm of Yesteryear Antiques**
355 W. 19th St.
713/868-1141

**Historic Heights Antiques & Intrs.**
249 W. 19th St.
713/868-2600

**Inside Outside**
510 W. 18th St.
713/869-6911

**Laroy Antiques & Refinishing, Inc.**
632 W. 19th St.
713/862-5051

**Stardust Antique**
1129 E. 11th St.
713/868-1600

**William & Mary's Antiques**
605 W. 19th St.
713/864-7605

**August Antiques**
803 Heights Blvd.
713/880-3353

**Everything Special**
1906 Ashland
713/869-6906

**Heights Station Antiques**
121 Heights Blvd.
713/868-3175

**Jubilee**
242 W. 19th St.
713/869-5885

**Edie's Sales, Unlimited**
701 E. 20th St.
No Phone # Listed

### *Great Places To Stay*

**Angel Arbor Bed and Breakfast Inn**
848 Heights Blvd.
1-800-722-8788
Web site: www.angelarbor.com

Located on a tree-lined boulevard with jogging trails, this elegant Georgian-style inn is a local historic landmark. To visit Angel Arbor is to be magically returned to the early 1920s, to the stately brick residence built originally for John and Katherine McTighe. The first floor of the inn boasts an antique filled parlor, reading room, formal dining room, and a sunroom for games or casual dining. A wicker furnished solarium overlooks the backyard garden, and artfully placed angel statue. Upstairs, three spacious bedrooms each contain queen bed and private bath. Also, a separate outside suite provides seclusion with a sitting room and deck.

## 79 HUMBLE

**Spruce Goose Shoppes**
620 2nd St.
281/540-7766

**Granny Jean's Antiques**
212 Charles St.
281/548-3020

## 80 HUNTSVILLE

**Bluebonnet Square Antique Mall**
1110 11th St.
409/291-2800

**Victorian House Antiques**
Hwy. 19
409/295-3904

**Fisher's Antiques**
Hwy. 190
409/295-7661

**Good Old Days**
604 S. Sam Houston Ave.
409/291-8407

**Scottie's**
1110 Sam Houston Ave.
409/291-9414

**Stone Wall Antiques**
1202 Sam Houston Ave.
409/291-3422

**The Raven Antiques & Gallery**
1204 Sam Houston Ave.
409/291-2723

**Sam Houston Antique Mall**
1210 Sam Houston Ave.
409/295-7716

**Avalon Antiques**
1215 Sam Houston Ave.
409/291-6097

## 81 HURST

**Antiques Et Al**
208 W. Bedford Euless Road
817/282-8197

**Country Express**
245 W. Bedford Euless Road
817/282-9335

**Hurst Antique Mall**
416 W. Bedford Euless Road
817/282-2224

**Antique Flea**
431 W. Bedford Euless Road
817/285-8859

**Whistle Stop**
1350 Brookside
817/282-3224

**Antique Homestead**
750 W. Pipeline Road
817/268-1527

## 82 IRVING

**Antiques On Main Street**
105 S. Main St.
972-259-1093

**Ken's Discount Antiques & Gifts**
108 W. 6th St.
972/259-5505

**Timeless Treasures**
111 S. Main St.
972/254-9007

**Irving Antique Mall**
129 S. Main St.
972/254-0339

**Oliver's Used Books & Things**
130 S. Main St.
972/253-1299

**Ye Olde Shoppe**
135 S. Main St.
972/254-0615

**Patsy B**
136 S. Main St.
972/254-1086

**Yesterdaze Collectibles**
304 W. Pioneer Dr.
972/253-6473

**Kimberleys Antiques**
247 Plymouth Park
972/986-5733

**Moss Rose**
510 E. 2nd St.
972/579-7491

**Nostalgia Etc**
1120 Senter Road, Suite 102
972/554-6781

**B & E Ventures**
410 E. 6th St.
972/253-7615

**Debby's Emporium**
929 E. 6th St.
972/438-5895

## 83 JACKSONVILLE

### Treasure Cove Mall
2027 N. Jackson (Hwy. 69 N.)
903/586-6140
Mon., Thurs., Fri., Sat., 10-6; Sun. 12-5, closed Tues. & Wed.
*Directions: Located on Hwy. 69 north approximately 2 miles from the intersection of Hwys. 69 & 79.*

Treasure Cove Mall is an exceptional shop in the wares that it presents and for one very unique service. For 6 years the mall has specialized in refinishing and restoring grand pianos! Three staff refinishers complete the "huge" task of turning your 1800s grand into a true masterpiece. Additionally, the shop provides caning and wicker repair. For those of you just wanting to shop, the mall offers an outstanding selection of quality antiques within its 10,000 square feet; Roseville, Weller, glassware, quilts, clocks, Coke collectibles, Blue Ridge, old tools and furnishings from formal to primitive are just a few of the items available from the mall's 50 dealers.

**Smith Barret Antiques**
31 N. Bolton St.
03/586-5123

**Ruffles**
114 E. Commerce St.
903/586-0141

**Jackson Street Merchantile**
201 S. Jackson St.
03/586-0282

## 84 JASPER

**The Cottage**
57 College
09/384-7862

**Nancy Jane's**
403 College
409/384-4781

**ast Time Antiques**
wy. 96 S.
9/384-6440

**Hwy. 63 Antiques**
Hwy. 63
409/384-7324

**earts & Flowers**
9 E. Houston
9/384-2462

**The Heart Of Things**
126 E. Lamar
409/384-9374

**ancock Drug Store**
5 N. Main St.
9/384-2541

**S.E. Texas Antique Mall**
2034 S. Wheeler St.
409/384-7078

**Treasures of Old**
2573 N. Wheeler St.
409/384-9580

## 85 JEFFERSON

***Great Places To Stay***

### Maison-Bayou Bed & Breakfast Plantation
300 Bayou St.
903/665-7600
Fax: 903/665-7100
Web site: www.maisonbayou.com
Open year round
Rates $59-135
*This place is so wonderful we decided to use more text than usual - so therefore we opted to omit the directions. For specific directions from your location, please call Jan or Pete.*

On the surface of your mind, it's sort of hard to connect Texas with Louisiana swamps and bayous — unless you live in east Texas — but if you think about it, or if you look at a map, you realize that east Texas butts right up to Louisiana and the two states sort of blur the lines between them for quite a ways into Texas. That's why you end up with such an anomaly like Maison-Bayou in Jefferson, Texas. Just over the Texas/Louisiana state line and northwest a bit from Shreveport, Jefferson itself sits on a river beside the Big Cypress Bayou.

Maison-Bayou, a Creole plantation, is located on the ancient river bed of the Big Cypress, in the middle of 55 wooded acres, yet it is only a short walk or a very short drive to the center of historic downtown Jefferson. The main house is an authentic reproduction of an 1850s Plantation Overseer's House, which features heart of pine floors, pine walls and ceilings, natural gas burning lanterns in each room, and period antiques and fabrics. A full breakfast is served in the dining room. The cabins are architecturally styled after authentic slave quarter cabins, with modern amenities carefully mixed in. All cabins have private baths, and yes, they all have indoor plumbing - although the toilets are the old fashioned pullchain variety - and individually controlled heat and air conditioning. Each cabin is located on the cypress alligator pond with a full view. Alligators are often spotted during the summer, while beaver and otters cavort in the pond during the winter.

Cabin One is the most authentically reproduced example of a slave cabin on the plantation, with cypress shake shingle roof, high pitched ceiling, wood walls and heart of pine floors. The hand-made four poster bed is full size and features a hand-made quilt. The cabin also provides a wood burning fireplace and a pier with a canoe.

Cabin Two features whitewashed walls, heart of pine floors and old-style tin roof. The Mission style full size wooden bed dates to the turn of the century and is adorned with a traditional quilt. Youth size bunk beds are included in the cabin as well. Relax in the rocking chair and watch the beaver pond from the cabin.

Cabins Three and Four are built in the "dog trot" architectural style: two independent cabins having a common roofline, sharing a full-length front and back porch, separated by a six-foot wide breezeway that runs the entire width between both cabins. Each cabin holds a primitive four poster wooden bed, rocking chairs and tables with reading lamps.

Next choice for guests is the Robert E. Lee replica steamboat paddlewheeler, moored along the bank of the cypress pond. Guests sleep in a queen size sleigh bed, and relax downstairs on the bow under a cooling ceiling fan. Or, they can climb the spiral staircase to the pilots' house and go outside for a view of the cypress pond, then stretch out for a sunbath on the deck!

Don't feel quite comfortable sleeping with the 'gators'? For all you landlubbers, there are two railroad cars and three bunkhouses still available. First is the authentic private rail car. Here guests are surrounded by beautifully varnished wood walls and ceiling, accented by 20 windows and 2 skylights, giving a panoramic view of the woods and Big Cypress Bayou.

The riverfront caboose sits directly on the banks of Big Cypress Bayou. This old Frisco line caboose offers a full size iron bed and a view of the river from the bed or from the observation windows.

The three bunkhouses are built on the old Jefferson to Marshall stagecoach road and, appropriately, overlook the corral where horses, a burrow and a llama make their homes. Buck, doe and fawns graze in nearby pastures.

As if these unusual accommodations aren't enough to hold your interest, there are a multitude of activities for guests to enjoy. On-site events and catering include pig roasts, crawfish boils, barbecues, trail rides and hayrides, weddings and receptions, company outings, family gatherings, camp and church groups and birthday parties. Wonderful nature trails and excellent fishing holes are a favorite with guest.

Maison-Bayou is a one-stop pleasure destination in a setting that's like a page out of history or a good novel. Don't miss it!

**Pride House**
409 Broadway
1-800-894-3526
Rates $85-110

Mythic America lives in this former steamboat port of 2,200; in antique houses, behind picket fences, along brick streets and on Cypress Bayou. Step into 19th century small-town America as you walk through the doors of the finest homes in town, chug through the lilypads on the paddlewheel steamer, cheer the newlyweds leaving the church, listen to the gossip over catfish at the cafe, and find things at the hardware you haven't seen in years.

Located in the 19th century antique capital of Texas, Pride House Bed & Breakfast invites you to shop in dozens of antique shops by day and sleep in one at night!

Guests will find 10 rooms with private baths in this turn-of-the-century home with its 12-foot ceilings, stained glass windows, family steamboat memorabilia, antiques and heirlooms, original art, footed bathtubs and fireplaces. Their enticements include some statements that anyone would be hard-pressed to ignore: "Come on the weekend – we'll bake you a cake. Weekdays, we'll cut your rate. Every day we'll treat you like family – with hot or cold drinks whenever you like and breakfasts you'll never forget." These legendary breakfasts include things like their own Jefferson Pecan Coffee, Pears Praline, Not Eggsactly Benedict, Texas Bluebonnet Muffins and Strawberry Butter.

**River City Mercantile**
111 Austin St.
903/665-8270

**Jefferson General Store**
113 E. Austin St.
903/665-8481

**Old Mill Antiques**
210 E. Austin St.
903/665-8601

**Liz-Beths Antiques**
216 W. Austin St.
903/665-8781

**Country Corner**
Hwy. 59 S.
903/665-8344

**Granny Had It**
114 N. Polk St.
903/665-3148

**Jefferson Bottling Works**
203 Polk St.
903/665-3736

**Old Store II**
226 N. Polk St.
903/665-2422

**Three Rivers Antiques**
116 N. Walnut St.
903/665-8721

**Walnut Street Market**
121 N. Walnut St.
903/665-8864

**The Old Store I & Jefferson Fudge Co.**
123 N. Walnut St.
903/665-3562

**Old House Antiques**
304 N. Walnut St.
903/665-8852

**Golden Oldies**
203A N. Polk St.
No Phone # Listed

**Jefferson Arts**
607 E. Broadway
903/665-3174

**Petticoat Junktion**
120 Polk St.
903/935-7322

**Robbie's Music Machines**
215 Polk St.
903/665-8533

**Sweet Memories**
Corner Walnut & Hwy. 49 E.
903/665-3533

**Turner's Place**
Hwy. 59 N.
903/665-2282

**Choices Antiques Mall**
215 Polk St.
903/665-8504

**Cypress Cargo**
120 W. Lafayette
903/665-1414

**Gold Leaf**
207 N. Polk St.
903/665-2882

## 86 KATY

**From Rags to Riches**
5714 1st St.
281/391-8200

**Classic Home Furnishings**
5305 Hwy. Blvd.
281/391-7515

**Country Village**
5809 Hwy. Blvd.
281/391-2040

**Decorative Treasures**
5626 2nd St.
281/391-2299

**Limited Editions**
2nd St.
281/391-1994

## 87 KERRVILLE

**Corner Post**
1518 Broadway
830/792-3377

**Five Points Antiques**
607 E. Lane
830/257-8424

**Grandma's House**
200 S. Sidney Baker
830/896-8668

**Pampell's Antiques**
701 Water St.
830/257-8484

**Water Street Antique Co.**
820 Water St.
830/257-5044

## 88 LA PORTE

**A Unique Store**
300 W. Main St.
281/471-5551

**Roelof's Antiques**
301 W. Main St.
281/471-3807

**Through The Ages**
324 W. Main St.
281/470-6614

**L & B Antiques**
312 W. Main St.
281/470-8533

## 89 LAMPASAS

**Country Collectables**
1900 S. Hwy. 281
512/556-5686

**Antique Emporium**
406 S. Live Oak St.
512/556-6843

**Ashley's Antiques & Collectibles**
523 E. 3rd St.
512/556-6555

## 90 LEANDER

### *Great Places To Stay*

**Trails End Bed & Breakfast**
The B & B Store (gift shop)
12223 Trails End Road #7
512-267-2901 or 1-800-850-2901
B & B open year round
Rates $55-170
Gift shop open year round 1-5, Call for appointment
*Directions: From IH 35 two miles out of Georgetown, take RM 1431 and go 11.85 miles to Trails End Road. Turn left onto Trails End and go 7/10 of a mile to the gravel road. There will be several mail boxes next to the gravel road. Turn left and go to where the road curves to the right. Keep on going around the curve and the B&B is a large gray house trimmed in white on the left. An appointment is needed. The inn is located on the north side of Lake Travis between Cedar Park, Jonestown, Austin and Leander.*

For specific information see review at the beginning of this section.

**Hitching Post**
18643 FM 1431
512/267-9125

## 91 LEAGUE CITY

**Hole in the Wall Antiques**
447 Hwy. 3 S.
281/332-3953

**Past & Presents**
809 E. Main St.
281/332-1517

**Lee Holley's Antiques**
1824 E. Main St.
281/332-5823

## 92 LEWISVILLE

**After Glow Antiques**
417 E. Church St.
972/221-6907

**Buttermilk Flats Antiques**
565 E. Church St.
972/221-1993

**Rare Bits Antiques**
310 Lake Haven
972/420-4222

**Antiques Etc.**
180 Lewisville Plaza
972/436-5904

**Corner Home Antique & Gallery**
101 W. Main St.
972/219-0887

**Victorian Rose Antiques**
102 W. Main St.
972/221-7266

**String of Pearls**
104 W. Main St.
972/436-9337

**Old Red Tractor Antiques**
109 W. Main St.
972/221-4022

**Pepper Tree**
112 W. Main St.
972/221-6345

**Looking Glass Antique Mall**
788 S. Mill
972/221-4022

**Sample House**
2403 S. Stemmons Freeway
972/315-0212

## 93 LIBERTY

**Trinity River Trading Post**
818 Commerce St.
409/336-3652

**Beverly's Then & Now**
1806 Sam Houston St.
409/336-9005

**Liberty Bell Antique Co-Op**
2040 Trinity St.
409/336-5222

## 94 LOCKHART

**Royals Antiques**
401 S. Commerce St.
512/398-6849

**Archway Antiques**
113 N. Main St.
512/398-7001

**Lockhart Antique Emporium**
119 W. San Antonio St.
512/398-4322

## 95 LONGVIEW

**Blue Door Antiques**
1311 Alphine St.
903/758-7592

**Petticoat Lane Antiques**
208 N. Center St.
903/757-8988

**Betty's Antiques**
414 E. Cotton St.
903/753-8204

**Jean's Antiques**
2111 S.E. Man Road
903/234-9011

**Classic Collections**
409 W. Loop #281
903/663-1028

**Jean's Antiques**
1809 E. Marshall Ave.
903/234-9010

**Alice's Wonderland**
3712 W. Marshall Ave.
903/295-1295

**Link To The Past**
100 W. Tyler St.
903/758-6363

**Christie's Collectibles**
113 W. Tyler St.
903/234-0816

**George Preston's Antiques**
205 N. Center St.
903/753-8041

**Turner Antiques**
211 E. College St.
903/758-2562

**Antiques Traders**
207 N. Court St.
903/758-9707

**Frederick-Nila Jewelers**
306 N. 4th St.
903/753-2902

**Consignments by Carolyn**
1003 E. Marshall Ave.
903/758-7211

**Linda's Best of Both Words**
2713 W. Marshall Ave.
903/759-4422

**Gifts of Distinction**
4005 W. Marshall Ave.
903/759-6055

**Treasures at Uptown Mall**
106 W. Tyler St.
903/757-4425

## 96 LUBBOCK

### Antique Mall of Lubbock

7907 W. 19th St.
806/796-2166
Fax 806/796-2164
*Directions: From I-27 take Loop 289 to West 19th St. (Levelland Hwy. 114W). Continue west on 19th St. 3 miles and look for the Big Yellow Awning on the south side of the highway.*
*General Information: "The Source For Dealers" open 7 days a week from 10 to 6 with over 24,000 sq. ft. with 150 quality showcases and 80 fabulous booths specializing in "Hard to Find" Americana antiques and collectibles.*

If you're an Antique Lover, this is one antique mall you truly don't want to miss! No brag, but they are told almost daily by dealers who travel the country that the Antique Mall of Lubbock is the BEST MALL they have ever been to. In addition, the Lubbock area has exploded with 5 malls and over 40 shops in the immediate area. Here are some of the collectibles you will find at the Antique Mall of Lubbock.

*Booth 7 - "Jennie Lee's Red Wing Shop" specializing in all types of pottery and stoneware especially some of the most fantastic pieces of Red Wing you will ever find!

*Booth 8 - "Dick Tarr's Treasures" specializes in a general line of furniture and collectibles including fine porcelain, carnival glass and one of the largest selections of Ertl banks in the Southwest!

*Booth 14 - Emma Ward's "Collectors Corner" specializes in all types of glass and dinnerware, including depression and Elegant glassware, Franciscan, Fiesta and Coors Rosebud.

*Booth 29 - Joyce Cheatham's "Bagladi's" booth has 1000s of small collectibles of every description imaginable.

*Booth 36 - "Chris' Collectibles" booth includes dolls of every description plus hundreds of toys and figures from the baby boom era.

*Booth 28 - "Ray Summer's Western Booth" has anything western related plus tools, farm and ranch related items.

*Booth 55 - "DR & Co. Collectibles" carries a general line of all types of furniture, toy trains, fountain pens, tins, toys, books, sports memorabilia, black memorabilia and much more.

*Booth 59 - "RB's General Store" specializing in quality advertising, old store stock and anything unusual and hard to find. Expect to be impressed with quality and quantity! Catering to Quantity Buyers!!

*Booth 99 - "Nina's Treasures" has a HUGE quantity of general line antiques and collectibles of every description from small to large that are fabulous!

The booths listed above are just a few mentioned, but you can't miss "Papa's Pharmacy" which includes old drug store merchandise in pristine condition, "Shane's General Store" that has thousands of old store stock merchandise that are unbelievable - A MUST TO SEE, "Clay's Cowboy Hideaway", "Cory's Sport Booth", "Nina's Elegant Booth", "Kristy's Kitchen", "Logan's Blue Room", "Matt's Oil Booth", "Timmy's Coke Collectibles", and many more.

The Antique Mall has been voted by the people of Lubbock and the Lubbock area as the BEST ANTIQUE MALL four years in a row! This speaks volumes - so don't miss out!

**Garden Patch**
1311 Alcove Ave.
806/793-0982

**Mandrells Antiques & Collectibles**
5628 Brownfield Hwy.
806/799-0172

**Carey Me Away Antiques**
2309 E. 50th St.
806/765-0160

**Antiques and More**
3407 50th St.
806/791-1691

**Flea Market**
2323 K Ave.
806/747-8281

**Bobo's Treasures**
202 S Ave.
806/744-6449

**Treasure Chest Antiques**
2226 Buddy Holly
806/744-0383

**Katz In The Alley**
2712 50th St.
806/795-9252

**Finishing Touch**
1401 N. Gary Ave.
806/762-2754

**Train Station Antiques**
6105 19th St.
860/788-0603

**Glass Hut**
7323 W. 19th St.
806/791-1260

**Lucky's World Antique Market**
3612 P Ave.
806/744-2524

**Clark's Collectibles**
2610 Salem Ave.
806/799-4747

**Vintage Rose**
2610 Salem Ave
806/793-7673

**Antiques Galleria**
1001 E. Slaton Road
806/745-3336

**Antiques Lubbock**
2217 34th St.
806/763-5177

**Pat's Antiques**
2257 34th St.
806/747-4798

**As Time Goes By**
4426 34th St.
806/795-0840

**Chaparral Antique Mall**
2202 Q Ave.
806/747-5431

**Old Time Clock Shop**
2610 Salem Ave.
806/797-8203

**Ruth Little Art & Antiques**
3402 73rd St.
806/792-0485

**J Patricks Antiques & Collectibles**
2206 34th St.
806/747-6731

**The Cottage**
2247 34th St.
806/744-3927

**Antique Marketplace**
2801 26th St.
806/785-1531

## 97 LUFKIN

**Lufkin Antique Mall**
118 N. 1st St.
409/634-9119

**Paul Nerren's Junk Barn**
4500 U.S. Hwy. 59 N.
409/632-2580

**Warehouse Antiques**
Hwy. 59 N.
409/632-5177

**Carousel Antiques**
302 N. Raguet & Frank St.
409/639-4025

**Angelina Antique Gallery**
205 Herndon St.
409/634-4272

**Kinards Antiques & Collectibles**
5151 U.S. Hwy. 59 N.
409/634-6933

**Wishing Well Antiques & Gifts**
901 S. John Redditt Dr.
409/632-4707

## 98 LULING

**Cripple Creek Mine**
17 E. Davis St.
10/875-5062

**Welcome Back Antiques**
11 E. Davis St.
10/875-3738

**Trinkets Treasures & Trash**
519 E. Davis St.
210/875-9100

**Nature's Nest-Unique Gift Shop**
946 E. Pierce St.
210/875-2383

## 99 MARBLE FALLS

**ntiques Plus**
00 W. Hwy. 1431
30/693-3301

**Wise Owl**
3409 Hwy. 281
830/693-3844

**Main Street Emporium**
204 Main St.
830/693-7037

**Carol's Cottage**
108 Main St.
830/693-7668

**Past & Presents**
700 Main St.
830/693-8877

## 100 MARSHALL

**La Trouvaille**
203 W. Austin St.
903/938-2006

**Antiques N Things**
214 S. Lafayette St.
903/935-3339

## 101 MASON

**Country Collectibles**
Hwy. 87 N.
915/347-5249

**Antique Emporium**
106 S. Live Oak
915/347-5330

**Underwoods Antique Mall**
100 N. Live Oak
915/347-5258

**P.V. Antiques**
Ft. McKevett
915/347-5496

## 102 McKINNEY

**Iron Kettle Antiques**
Hwy. 5
972/542-4903

**Affordable Antiques & More**
719 N. Kentucky St.
972/562-5551

**Antique House**
212 E. Louisiana St.
972/562-0642

**Remember This Antiques**
210 N. Tennessee St.
972/542-8011

**Pat Parker's Art Antiques**
108 W. Virginia St.
972/562-6571

**Treasures From The Past**
115 E. Virginia St.
972/548-0032

**The McAllister Collection**
101 N. Kentucky St.
972/562-9497

**One of a Kind**
214 N. Kentucky St.
972/542-7977

**Duffy's Antiques**
202 E. Louisiana St.
972/542-5980

**McKinney Antiques**
112 N. Tennessee St.
972/548-8044

**Victorian Corner**
100 W. Virginia St.
972/548-9898

**Town Square Antiques**
113 E. Virginia St.
972/542-4113

**Antique Company Mall**
213 E. Virginia St.
972/548-2929

## 103 MEMPHIS

**Grandmaw's Attic**
5th & Main St.
806/259-2575

**Crafts & Collectibles**
315 Hwy. 287 N.
806/259-3817

**Ivy Cottage**
121 N. 5th St.
806/259-3520

## 104 MESQUITE

**Antique Plus**
2611 N. Belt Line Road
972/226-6300

**Emporium @ Big Town**
950 Big Town Shopping Center
214/690/6996

**The Dusty Attic**
3330 N. Galloway Ave.
972/613-5093

**Missing Pieces**
109 W. Main St.
972/288-3513

**Sharon's Main St. Antiques**
120 E. Main St.
972/329-3147

## 105 MIDLAND

**ABC Antiques**
110 Andrews Hwy.
915/682-4595

**Cat's Meow**
408 Andrews Hwy.
915/687-2004

**Geri's Antiques & Fine Linens**
307 Dodson St.
915/687-2660

**Antiques by Josephs**
325 Dodson St.
915/687-3040

**Old Town Antiques**
329 Dodson St.
915/570-0588

**Judy Jacksons Bargain Barn**
2420 W. Front St.
915/682-0227

**Antiques Etc.**
2101 W. Wadley Ave.
915/682-9257

**Laura's Things Finer**
2101 W. Wadley Ave.
915/683-4422

**Motif**
2101 W. Wadley Ave.
915/683-4331

**Yesterdays News Antique Mall**
3712 W. Wall St.
915/689-6373

**Craft's Bazaar**
3712 W. Wall St.
915/689-8852

## 106 MINEOLA

**Places In The Heart**
111 E. Broad St.
903/569-9096

**Broad Street Mall**
118 E. Broad St.
903/569-0806

**Unique Mall**
124 E. Broad St.
903/569-9321

**Beckham Hotel Antique Mall**
115 E. Commerce St.
903/569-0835

**Heirloom Shoppe**
119 E. Commerce St.
903/569-0835

**Main Street Emporium**
102 S. Johnson St.
903/569-0490

**Country Girls Antiques**
110 S. Johnson St.
903/569-6007

**Roses and Relics**
219 N. Newsom St.
903/569-9890

**The Brownstone Mall**
408 S. Pacific St.
903/569-6890

**Durham Antiques**
1823 N. Pacific St.
903/569-2916

## 107 MINERAL WELLS

**Wynnwood Village Antiques Mall**
2502 U.S. Hwy. 180 E.
940/325-9791

**Thurmon's Bargain Barn**
3703 N. Hwy. 281
940/325-1695

**Down Memory Lane**
201 E. Hubbard St.
940/328-0609

**Mama Jo's Treasures**
800 E. Hubbard St.
940/328-0043

**Richey's Antiques & Uniques**
1201 E. Hubbard St.
940/325-5940

**Sarah Jane's Antiques & Crafts**
115 N. Oak Ave.
940/325-3005

**Wild Rose Antiques**
213 N. Oak Ave.
940/325-9502

**Century Corner Antiques**
225 N. Oak Ave.
940/325-2525

**Anita's Antiques**
307 N. Oak Ave.
940/325-1455

## 108 MONTGOMERY

**Antique Emporium**
404 Eva
409/597-6903

**Westlake Antqs. & Old Book Shop**
25400 Hwy. 105 W.
409/582-6829

**Liberty Bell Antiques**
207 Liberty
409/597-4606

**Olde Towne Montgomery**
208 Liberty
409/597-5922

**The Old Post Office & Drugstore Antiques**
210 Liberty
409/597-4400

## 109 MOUNT PLEASANT

**Odds and Ends Shop**
100 W. Alabama St.
903/572-2802

**Browns Country Attic**
1705 W. Ferguson Road
903/577-9240

**Classic Place**
2000 W. Ferguson Road
903/572-6667

**Antiques & Uniques**
109 N. Madison Ave.
903/572-1545

**Grand Nanny's Attic II Antiques**
115 N. Madison Ave.
903/572-7081

**A Little Bit Of Country**
Union Hill Road
903/572-3173

**Jo's Antiques**
Union Hill Road
903/572-3173

## 110 MUNDAY

### Memories of Munday Mall
110 E. Main St.
940/422-5400
Open Mon.-Sat. 10-6, Sun., 1-5
*Directions: Memories of Munday is located at the intersection of Hwy. 277 and Hwy. 222 in downtown Munday, Texas, which is*

*approximately midway between Abilene and Wichita Falls (75 miles).*

Located in the early 1900s community of Munday, the Memories of Munday Mall offers a varied selection of items from ten area dealers. Furniture, glassware, costume jewelry, and collectibles as well as a nice selection of vintage linens are displayed for your appeal.

News Alert: The shop features Ty Beanie Babies and will ship to you anywhere in the world!

**Schoolmarm Antiques**
210 W. Main St.
940/422-4474

## 111 NACOGDOCHES

**Bremond Doll Shoppe**
416 Bremond St.
409/569-9676

**K H Newman Antiques**
7144 Center Road
409/564-0820

**Sparks Antiques**
276 Community Road
409/564-4838

**Nannys Antiques**
Hwy. 259
409/564-2433

**Aubrey's Main Shoppe**
1523 E. Main St.
409/569-7962

**Squash Blossom Colony Mall**
209 E. Main St.
409/560-1788

**Antique Market**
412 E. Main St.
409/564-8294

**Sloane's Antiques**
413 E. Main St.
409/559-0013

**Moth Nest Vintage Clothing**
2012 E. Main St.
409/560-5114

**Pineapple Post**
102 North St.
409/564-8285

**Laurel's Antiques**
4705 North St.
409/569-6290

**Xavier Sanders Antiques**
116 N. Pecan St.
409/560-3131

**Old Pillar St. Antiques**
108 E. Pillar St.
409/564-6888

## 112 NAVASOTA

**Past & Present**
119 E. Washington Ave.
409/825-7545

**Downtown Antique Mall**
207 E. Washington Ave.
409/825-8588

**Twin Oaks Antique Mall**
716 E. Washington Ave.
409/825-1837

## 113 NEW BRAUNFELS

**Hope's Carousel**
47 E. Faust St.
830/629-8113

**Palace Heights Antiques Mall**
1175 Hwy. 81 E.
830/625-0612

**Lee's Antiques**
125 Hwy. 81 W.
830/629-7919

**Second Time Around**
870 S. State Hwy. 46
830/629-6542

**Gruene Antique Company**
1607 Hunter Road
830/629-7781

**Gruene General Store**
1610 Hunter Road
830/629-6021

**Hampe House**
1640 Hunter Road
830/620-1325

**Cactus Jacks Antiques Etc.**
1706 Hunter Road
830/620-9602

**New Braunfels Log Haus Antiques**
469 IH 35 S.
830/629-3774

**Front Porch Antiques & Gifts**
471 Main Plaza
830/629-0660

**New Braunfels Emporium Nostalgia**
209 W. San Antonio St.
830/608-9733

**Good Pickins**
219 E. San Antonio St.
830/625-9330

**Downtowner Antique Mall**
223 W. San Antonio St.
830/629-3947

**Voigt House Antiques**
308 E. San Antonio St.
830/625-7072

**Vicky's Antiques**
719 W. San Antonio St.
830/625-2837

**Headrick Country Home Antiques**
697 S. Seguin Ave.
830/625-1624

**Dan's Collectables**
921 S. Seguin Ave.
830/629-3267

**Be-Bops**
1077 S. Seguin Ave.
830/625-6056

## 114 ODESSA

**A Antique Shoppe**
402 E. 8th St.
915/333-1718

**D & D Antiques**
2210 W. 416 46th St.
915/367-9427

**Chez La Nae Fine Furnishings**
5701 Austin Ave.
915/550-3106

**Country Mercantile**
6108 Ector Ave.
915/363-8909

**The Brass Lamp/Antique Auto Museum**
709 S. Grandview
915/332-9875

**Wagon Wheel Antiques**
6070 W. University Blvd.
915/381-6638

## 115 ORANGE

**Nana & Poppie's Antiques**
3834 W. Park Ave.
409/883-6941

**Antiques & Uniques**
2207 Macarthur Dr.
409/883-7989

**Pats This & That**
2490 Martin Luther King Jr. Dr.
409/883-7215

**This Ol House Co-Op**
3433 Martin St.
409/883-3991

**Country Porch**
521 S. Hwy. 87
409/883-6503

**Parlours**
902 10th St.
409/886-0146

# Texas

## 116 PALESTINE

**Linda's Antiques**
3913 W. Oak St.
903/729-1448

**Barbara Harden's Antiques**
Hwy. 84 E.
903/729-6604

**Vintage House**
616 W. Palestine Ave.
903/729-7133

**J's Music & Antiques**
400 N. Queen St.
903/729-3144

**Shelton Gin Antiques & Sandwich Shop**
310 E. Crawford St.
903/729-7530

## 117 PAMPA

**L & P Interiors**
110 S. Cuyler
806/665-3243

**Yesterdays Treasures**
618 W. Francis Ave.
806/665-9449

**Call Antiques**
620 W. Francis Ave.
806/665-1391

**J & B Antiques & Used Books**
302 W. Foster Ave.
806/665-8415

**Trash & Treasure Shop**
1425 N. Hobart St.
806/669-6601

**Collectors Corner**
2216 N. Hobart St.
806/665-3246

**Cottage Collection**
922 W. 23rd Ave.
806/665-4398

## 118 PARIS

**Kaufman Korner Mall**
134 1st St. S.W.
903/784-6012

**Antiques by Winona**
138 Clarksville St.
903/784-4862

**Curiosity**
101 Grand Ave.
903/739-2716

**Paris Antique Mall**
Hwy. 19/Hwy. 24
903/785-0872

**Blackburns Antiques**
Hwy. 82 E.
903/785-0862

**Great Expectations**
7 Lamar Ave.
903/784-4499

**Reflections of Ducharme**
6335 Lamar Ave.
903/784-3823

**Reno Antique Mall**
6720 Lamar Ave.
903/737-9904

**Junk Lady Antiques**
286 N.E. Loop #286
903/785-2513

**Saffle Antique Mall**
20 N. Plaza
903/785-8446

## 119 PASADENA

**Heritage Collectables & Antiques**
3207 Preston Road
281/998-2775

**Collectors Corner**
701 Houston Ave.
281/473-9345

**Stuff and Such**
1615 Richey
281/473-6144

**A-l Antiques**
1905 Shaver St.
281/472-3777

**Country Roads Antiques**
1415 Southmore Ave.
281/473-2092

**Antique Junction**
111 W. Southmore Ave.
281/473-9824

**Stephanies Antique Furniture**
5220 Spencer Hwy.
281/487-3900

## 120 PEARLAND

**Cole's Antique Village**
1014 N. Main St.
281/485-2277

**A Dream Come True**
2316 N. Main St.
281/997-6468

**Country Merchant Antiques**
14602 Suburban Garden Road
281/997-1319

## 121 PHARR

**Eva's Antiques**
508 N. Cage Blvd.
210/787-6457

**Bygones by Guy Antiques**
119 W. Park St.
210/702-4661

**Socorros Antiques**
620 W. Ferguson St.
210/702-0494

**Memories Antiques & Mall**
1311 W. Hwy. 495
210/781-4881

## 122 PITTSBURG

**Charlotte's Market St. Antiques**
1 Market St.
903/856-2577

**Rick's Antiques Safari**
121 Quitman St.
903/856-6929

**All Occasions Mall**
122 & 128 Quitman St.
903/856-3285

## 123 PLAINVIEW

**Old World Antiques**
431 Broadway St.
806/293-3118

**Horton Antiques & Collectibles**
607 Broadway St.
806/293-7054

**Antiques by Billie**
609 Broadway St.
806/293-9407

**Uniques and Antiques**
615 Broadway St.
806/293-7826

**Shoppe**
707 Broadway St.
806/296-2201

**Harman-Y House Antiques**
815 Columbia St.
806/296-2505

**Moore's Lantern Antiques**
1406 Joliet St.
806/296-6270

**Second Story Antqs. & Collectibles**
403 Yonkers St.
806/296-5444

## 124 PLANO

**Antiqueland**
1300 Custer Road
972/509-7878

**English Pine Co**
3000 Custer Road, Suite 220
972/596-4096

**Blue Goose**
1007 E. 15th St.
972/881-9295

**Main Street Gifts & Antiques**
1024 E. 15th St.
972/578-0486

**Sherwood House**
3100 Independence Pkwy.
972/519-0194

**History House Antiques**
1408 J Ave.
972/423-2757

**The Market**
4709 W. Parker
972/596-2699

**Blue Goose**
3308 Preston Road, Suite 315
972/985-5579

**Simple Country Pleasures**
1013 E. 15th St.
972/422-0642

**Ann's Place**
1025 E. 15th St.
972/422-5306

**Cobwebs Antiques Mall**
1400 J Ave.
972/423-8697

**Nanny Granny's Antique Museum**
1408 J Ave.
972/423-3552

**Sample House**
1900 Preston Road
972/985-1616

## 125 ROCKPORT

**Bent Tree Galleries**
504 S. Austin St.
512/729-4822

**Moore Than Feed**
902 W. Market St.
512/729-4909

**Harcrows**
S. Hwy. 188
512/729-1724

**Mary Ann's Antiques**
1005 E. Main St.
512/729-1945

## 126 ROCKWALL

**Lakeview Lodge Antiques**
706 S. Goliad St.
972/722-0219

**Rockwall Antiques**
212 E. Rusk St.
972/722-1280

**Bountiful**
708 S. Goliad St.
972/722-1313

**Past Times Antiques & Collectibles**
214 E. Rusk St.
972/771-8100

## 127 ROSENBERG

**ack When Antiques**
615 Ave. H
81/342-0601

**algers Cottage**
030 Lawrence
81/232-6421

**emory Shoppe**
31 3rd St.
81/232-7353

**Bakers Woods & Wares**
3117 Ave. I
281/232-7733

**Old Town Antiques**
828 3rd St.
281/232-2125

## 28 ROUND ROCK

**ntique Mall Of Texas**
01 S. I-35
2/218-4290

**Wooten & Son**
1401 Sam Bass Road
512/255-1447

## 129 ROUND TOP

**Emma Lee Turney's Antiques Productions**
P. O. Box 821289
Houston, TX 77282-1289
281/493-5501
281/293-0320
e-mail: turnyshows@aol.com

Twice each year Emma Lee Turney brings outstanding antiques shows to the Round Top area. Billed as one of the largest antiques fairs in the nation, the show attracts dealers and buyers from across the United States and abroad. Emma Lee has recently written a book on her antiquing adventures.

***Favorite Places To Eat***

**Royers Round Top Cafe**
"On the Square"
1-800-624-PIES

Cut through the backroads between Houston and Austin to find the tiny town of Round Top and one of the smallest town squares in America. Here you'll find three antique shops and Royers' Cafe which serves some of the best "sophisticated" food in the country.

My favorite—the ribs, along with buttermilk pie (the best I've ever eaten). The cafe also offers fresh salmon, grilled quail, chicken and a variety of pasta dishes.

## 130 SALADO

**Antique Jewelry & Collectables**
N. Main St.
254/947-9161

**Fletcher's Books & Antiques**
Main St.
254/947-5414

**Hutchens House**
369 N. Main St.
254/947-8177

**Recollection Antiques**
Royal & Center
254/947-0067

**Red Barn Antique Center**
90050 B Royal
254/947-1050

**Main Street Place**
3 Salado Square
254/947-9908

**Classic Antiques**
N. Main St.
254/947-0604

**Salado Country Antiques**
Main St.
254/947-8363

**Salado Antique Mall**
550 N. Main St.
254/947-1010

**Royal Emporium**
Royal & Main St.
254/947-5718

**Spring House Antiques**
Royal
254/947-0747

## 131 SAN ANGELO

**Consignments Etc.**
109 S. Chadbourne St.
915/658-6480

**June's Folly**
202 S. Chadbourne St.
915/655-9459

**Hard Time Post**
915 N. Chadbourne St.
915/657-0905

**Jewel of the Concho**
10 E. Concho Ave.
915/653-8782

**Sassy Fox**
34 E. Concho Ave.
915/658-8083

**Cactus Patch**
108 E. Concho Ave.
915/655-1456

**Hodgepodge Antiques**
114 Hardeman Pass
915/655-5148

**Centerpiece Antiques**
Municipal Airport Lobby
915/949-9078

**Treasure Trunk**
37 W. Twohig Ave.
915/658-6697

**Grammy's Corner**
117 S. Chadbourne St.
915/655-8400

**Arclight Antiques**
230 S. Chadbourne St.
915/653-8832

**S & R Trading Post**
4736 N. Chadbourne St.
915/655-5087

**J Wilde**
15 E. Concho Ave.
915/655-0878

**Confetti Antique Mall**
42 E. Concho Ave.
915/655-3962

**Traders Mall**
79 E. 14th St.
915/655-9617

**American British Antiques**
746 U.S. Hwy. 87 S.
915/651-4873

**Vi's Country Village**
5270 Old Christoval Road
915/651-9088

**Washington Square**
230 W. Washington
915/658-5765

## 132 SAN ANTONIO

**Plantiques**
1319 Austin Hwy.
210/824-2634

**Pristine Peacock Estate Jwlry**
555 W. Bitters Road
210/494-6230

**Halfmoon Antique Mall Inc.**
112 Broadway St.
210/212-4401

**Land of Was**
3119 Broadway St.
210/822-5265

**Pat Pritchard Antiques & Folkware**
5405 Broadway St.
210/829-5511

**Hugh Lackey Antiques**
3505 Broadway St.
210/829-5048

**Charlott's Antiques & Clocks**
2015 Austin Hwy.
210/653-3672

**Blanco Fulton Antiques**
1701 Blanco Road
210/737-7208

**Alamo Antique Mall**
125 Broadway St.
210/224-4354

**Lion & Eagle**
3511 Broadway St.
210/826-3483

**Christo's**
5921 Broadway St.
210/820-0424

**J. Adelman Antiques & Art**
7601 Broadway St.
210/822-5226

**Marshalls Brocante**
8505 Broadway St.
210/804-6320

**Chicago Connection**
8505 Broadway St.
210/804-6322

**Affordable Antiques**
8934 Broadway St.
210/822-9600

**Lasting Impressions**
600 & 606 W. Hildebrand Ave.
210/737-9130

**Abbey's Antiques**
1503 W. Hildebrand Ave.
210/732-5266

**Antiques Downtown Mall**
515 E. Houston St.
210/224-8845

**Antique Connection**
4119 McCullough Ave.
210/822-4119

**J. Adelman Antiques & Estate Jewelry**
Mengu Hotel at Alamo Plaza
210/225-5914

**Gas Light Antique Shoppe**
208 E. Park Ave.
210/227-4803

**Dear Things**
8324 Pat Booker Road
210/590-3003

**River Square Antiques, Gifts & Collectibles**
514 River Walk St.
210/224-0900

**Accents Antiques & Design**
119 W. Sunset Road
210/826-4500

**Different Drummer**
1020 Townsend Ave.
210/826-3764

**Center For Antiques**
8505 Broadway St.
210/804-6300

**San Antonio's Center for Antiques**
8505 Broadway St.
210/804-6300

**Bobs Gifts & Antiques**
3461 Fredericksburg Road
210/734-9007

**Antiques on Hildebrand**
521 W. Hildebrand Ave.
210/734-9337

**Barn Haus**
26610 U.S. Hwy. 281 N.
210/980-7678

**Echoes from the Past**
517 E. Houston St.
210/225-3714

**Timeless Treasures Inc.**
4343 McCullough Ave.
210/829-7861

**Main Place For Antiques**
102 W. Mistletoe Ave.
210/736-4900

**York's Furniture Annex**
306 E. Park Ave.
210/226-1248

**Greenlight Antiques**
13316 O'Connor Road
210/590-6107

**Moran Antiques & Appraisals**
2119 San Pedro Ave.
210/734-5668

**Treasures & Trifles Inc.**
210 W. Sunset Road
210/824-9381

**Ivy Cottage Antiques & Collectibles**
407 8th St.
210/224-2597

### Great Places To Stay

**The Columns on Alamo**
1037 S. Alamo St.
210/271-3245 (phone and fax) or 1-800-233-3364
Open daily 8-9
*Directions: From I-37, take Exit #140B (Durango St.) at the Alamodome, and go 2 blocks from the freeway westbound on Durango to Alamo St. Turn right and go south on Alamo five blocks to the corner of Sheridan St. and Alamo.*

Innkeepers Ellenor and Art Link decided to open their elegant and stunning home as a bed and breakfast in 1994. The massive house is an 1892 Greek Revival home and they also use the adjacent 1901 guesthouse as part of the inn. Located in the historic King William District near the trolley, the inn offers 11 guest rooms, all with private baths, furnished with Victorian antiques and period reproductions. Guests can share the common areas in both houses and on the landscaped grounds.

The Links are resident innkeepers and are always ready and able to suggest excursion itineraries, dining and shopping forays for guests, and to help in planning which cultural and seasonal events to attend. They prepare their guests for the day's adventures with a full breakfast served in the main house.

When staying at The Columns, guests will be within easy walking distance to the River Walk, the Alamo, the Convention center, Southtown restaurants and shops, La Villita, German Heritage Park and Rivercenter Mall. It's only a short drive from The Columns to the Spanish Mission Trail, San Antonio Alamodome, Sea World, Fiesta Texas and the Lone Star Brewery and Hall of Horns.

**Falling Pines Inn**
300 W. French Place
210/733-1998
Rates $100-150

This is an interesting place in an already interesting city - a purely luxurious bed and breakfast in an historic home that caters to the upscale crowd. Construction of Falling Pines began in 1911, under the plans and directions of famed architect Atlee Ayeres. Pine trees, not native to San Antonio, tower over the mansion on a one-acre, park-like setting in the Monte Vista Historic District, one mile north of downtown San Antonio.

The house itself is a combination of brick and limestone, with a green tiled roof, shuttered windows, and a magnificent limestone archway entrance and veranda on the front facade. The entry level has six rooms with quarter-cut oak paneling, wood floors, oriental carpets, fireplaces and a tiled solarium where breakfast is served. The large and elegantly appointed guest rooms are on the second level. The third level is entirely one suite, the 2,000 square foot Persian Suite that commands a grand view of downtown San Antonio and the nearby Koehler Mansion, home of a beer baron. The Persian Suite has two large, private balconies and a luxurious private bath, and is draped in miles and miles of material, reminiscent of exotic Persian tents.

## 133 SAN MARCOS

**Ashleys Attic**
2201 Hunter Road
512/754-0165

**Centerpoint Station**
3946 IH 35 S.
512/392-1103

**Antique Outlet Mall**
4200 IH 35 S.
512/392-5600

**Maudie's Antiques**
202 N. LBJ Dr.
512/396-8999

**Paper Bear Heartworks Co.**
214 N. LBJ Dr.
512/396-2283

**Anchor Antqs. & Hndcrftr. Iron Beds**
360 S. LBJ Dr.
512/353-3995

**Partin's Second Tyme Furniture**
2108 RR 12
512/396-4684

**Partin's II**
2300 RR 12
512/396-2777

### Great Places To Stay

**Crystal River Inn**
326 W. Hopkins
512/396-3739
Fax: 512/353-3248
Open year round
*Directions: Crystal River Inn is located in San Marcos, off I-35 at Exit #205. Exit #205 is Hopkins St.*

With 13 guest rooms to choose from, visitors will enjoy this Texas inn that has garnered three stars in the Mobil Travel Guide. The inn itself is a romantic, luxurious Victorian mansion set in the middle of Texas hill country. It's close to the headwaters of the crystal clear San Marcos River - hence the name - and is filled with antiques, fireplaces and fresh flowers. There are gardens and fountains, a wicker-strewn veranda, and the beautiful outdoors. Gourmet breakfasts and brunches include such delectable items as stuffed French toast and bananas Foster crepes. Mystery weekends, river trips and romantic getaways are the hosts' specialty.

## 134 SEABROOK

**Glory To God Antiques**
1417 Bayport Blvd.
281/474-3639

**Victorian Rose**
909 Hall Ave.
281/474-1214

**Another Era**
909 Hardesty Ave.
281/474-7208

**Town & Country Antiques**
913 Hardesty Ave.
281/474-2779

**Picket Fence**
3010 Hwy. 146
281/474-4845

**Carousel Antiques**
1002 Meyer Road
281/474-4451

**Old Seabrook Antique Mall**
1002 Meyer Road..
281/474-4451

**Marilyn's Antiques**
1402 2nd St.
281/474-4359

## 135 SEALY

**Sealy Sampler Antiques**
419 Hardeman St.
409/885-3349

**Classic Collections**
223 Fowlkes St.
409/885-7930

**Country Antiques**
121 Meyer Road..
409/885-7976

**Antique Shop**
413 Meyer St.
409/885-0285

**Sealy Antique Center**
663 Hwy.. 90 E.
409/885-6556

**Lillys Antiques**
502 N. Meyer St.
409/885-4040

## 136 SEGUIN

**Art-Iques by Ken Miller**
106 N. Austin St.
210/379-3209

**A Wild Hare**
112 W. Court St.
210/372-4822

**Antique Trading Post**
1530 N. State Hwy. 46
210/303-2037

**Affordable Antiques**
6771 N. State Hwy. 123
210/303-3135

**Blue Hills Antique Mall**
6832 N. State Hwy. 123
210/379-2059

## 137 SEYMOUR

**Granny's Stuff**
101 S. Main St.
940/888-2213

**Hogues**
300 S. Main St.
940/888-2511

**See More Antiques & Collectibles**
910 N. Main St.
940/888-2689

**Classics**
1620 Main St.
940/552-0672

## 138 SHERMAN

### A Touch of Class Antique Mall
118 W. Lamar St.
903/891-9379 or 972/529-5206
Fax: 903-868-3153
Open: Mon.-Sat., 9:30-5:30; Sun. 12:30-5:00
*Directions: From Hwy. 75, take Exit #58 (Lamar St.). Go to the second stoplight on the southwest corner of the downtown square, across from the Courthouse.*

For specific information see review at the beginning of this section.

**Elm House Antiques**
710 N. Elm St.
903/892-4418

**Donna's Corner**
308 E. Houston St.
903/813-0044

**Bobby Denes Antiques & Vintage**
333 W. Jones St.
903/892-4272

**Sherman Antique Mall**
221 S. Travis
903/892-1225

**Kelly Square Antiques**
115 S. Travis
903/868-1771

**Pieces of the Past**
901-B E. Lamar
903/868-2253

**Ray Bob Antiques**
220 W. Houston
903/892-8745

## 139 SINTON

**Country Cornerstone Co-Op**
207 W. Sinton St.
512/364-5756

**Gwen's Antiques**
223 E. Sinton St.
512/364-1165

## 140 SMITHVILLE

**Alum Creek Antique Center**
W. Hwy. 71
512/237-3817

**Cedar Chest Antiques**
W. Hwy. 71
512/237-3817

**Silver Fox Antiques**
W. Hwy. 71
512/237-4825

**House of Antiques**
116 Main St.
512/237-4393

**Century House**
119 Main St.
512/237-5549

**Crystal's Corner**
204 Main St.
512/237-3939

**Main St. Village**
216 Main St.
512/237-2323

**Simply Country**
106 N.E. 2nd
512/237-2038

**Wild Rose Antiques**
108 N.E. 2nd St.
512/237-5122

## 141 SNYDER

Known as the "Land of the White Buffalo," Snyder is where buffalo hunter J. Wright Mooar, killed one of only seven white buffalo ever seen in the U.S. The original hide is on display at the ranch home of Mooar's granddaughter Judy Hays, who hosts the huge White Buffalo Festival annually in October. Another favorite for visitors to Snyder is the "Legends of Western Swing Festival" in June at the Scurry County Coliseum with the biggest names in western swing music. Sites in Scurry County include fields of snow white cotton, herds of Texas cattle, miles of bobbing pump jacks bowing to past and present, oil rigs highlighting the terrain like magnificent monuments, rustic canyons full of the plants and animals that add to the beauty and mystery of West Texas and the most beautiful sunsets and starry nights your mind can imagine.

**Timber and Threads**
1801 25th St.
915/573-4018

**Nathalie's**
1803 25th St.
915/573-9680

**House of Antieks**
4008 College Ave.
915/573-4422

## 142 SOUTH PADRE ISLAND

**Padre Antiques & Collectibles**
104 E. Hibiscus St.
956/761-7440

**Peddlers Co-Op**
5813 Padre Blvd.
956/761-7585

**Island Emporium**
1900 Padre Blvd.
956/761-4529

## 143 SPRING

**Keepsakes & Kollectables**
219 A Gentry St.
281/353-9233

**The Doll Company**
315 Gentry St.
281/350-4904

**A Place in Time**
315 Gentry St., Suite A
281/353-6323

**Diane's Spring Emporium**
324 Gentry St.
281/288-9202

**Gentry Square Galleries**
315 Gentry St.
281/353-5568

**The Doll Hospital**
419 Gentry St.
281/350-6722

**Cobblestone Antiques**
7623 Louetta Road, Suite 121
281/251-0660

**Brenda's Attic**
134 Main St.
281/288-0223

**The Spotted Pony**
202 Main St.
281/355-1880

**Buffalo Spirit**
215 Main St.
281/355-8100

**Antiques & More on Main**
302 Main St.
281/350-1214

**The Wild Goose Chase**
118 B Midway
281/288-9501

**Friends**
214 Midway St.
281/353-2255

**Robyn's Nest Antiques**
200-1 Noble St.
281/288-7252

**Southern Charm**
26303 Preston E.
281/288-4933

**Lana Williams Gallery**
26407 Preston
281/288-4043

**Krystal Lain Antiques Etc.**
130 Spring Cypress Road
281/353-7442

**Granny's Odds & Engs**
219 B Spring Cypress Road
281/288-6530

**Pete & Sue's Antique Clocks**
1408 Sue Ann Lane
281/288-7188

**Spring Antique Mall**
1426 Spring Cypress Road
281/355-1110

**Cabin Creek Lodge Antique Mall**
1703 Spring Cypress Road
281/350-5559

**Antique Mall**
21127 Spring Town Dr.
281/350-4557

## 144 STAFFORD

**Simone Antiques & More**
1723 W. Bellfort St.
81/561-7403

**Elegant Junk**
Main St. (Hwy. 90)
281/242-3424

**Antiques Etc.**
3202 S. Main St.
281/499-9669

## 145 SULPHUR SPRINGS

**Bright Star Antique Mall**
102 College St.
903/885-4584

**Grannys Attic**
105 N. Davis St.
903/885-5042

**Burrows Antiques**
725 Davis St. N.
903/885-5173

**Old Town Antique Mall**
101 Gilmer St. N.
903/885-5646

**Sanderson Antique Mall**
109 Linda Dr.
903/439-0259

**Victorian Rose**
206 Main St.
903/885-2482

## 146 SUNNYVALE

**East Fork Mall Antiques**
613 E. Hwy. 80
972/226-2704

**Jot Um Down Store**
613 E. Hwy. 80
972/226-0974

**Accent Antiques**
616 E. Hwy. 80
972/226-9830

**Fischers Antiques**
536 Long Creek
972/226-1445

## 147 SWEETWATER

Sweet-Water, established in the 1870s, was a trading post with the name derived from "Mobeetie", the Kiowa word for "sweet water" to describe the water in a nearby creek. Today, Sweetwater is a very modern small city. Annual events include the famous Rattlesnake Round-up and the AJRA National Finals Rodeo.

**Rat Rows Antiques**
113 Oak St.
915/235-8651

**Second Hand Rose**
122 Oak St.
915/235-1504

**Arlene's Book House**
124 Oak St.
915/235-1504

**Raspberry Corner Antique Mall**
301 Oak St.
915/235-3885

**Lone Star Antiques Mall**
318 Oak St.
915/235-8177

**Vernon's Antiques**
401 Oak St.
No Phone # listed

## 148 TEXARKANA

**Oak Tree**
123 E. Broad
501/773-1588

**M & M Antiques Mall**
401 E. Broad
501/773-1871

**Dun Sailin Oldes**
611 Burma Road
903/838-9430

**Jennie's Antique Mall**
1901 College Dr.
903/792-2333

**Red Wagon Antiques**
Hwy. 59
903/832-6841

**Nick's Antiques**
213 Wood St.
501/772-6194

**Pot Luck Antique Shop**
I-30 W. Exit #218
903/832-1151

**State Line Antique Mall**
1104 State Line Road
501/772-8414

**J Brown Antiques**
817 Walnut
903/793-4114

**Garden Gate Antiques**
603 E. 9th
501/773-1147

**Green Country**
1216 Trexler Road
903/671-2521

## 149 TOMBALL

**Whistle Stop Tearoom**
107 Commerce St.
281/255-2455

**Precious Temptations**
115 Commerce St.
281/351-2119

**Antique Station**
119 Commerce St. & Walnut
281/351-7887

**Blue Caboose**
104 N. Elm St.
281/255-8788

**Patchwork Blue**
605 Mason
281/351-5301

**Tomball Haus**
216 W. Main St.
281/255-8282

**Faye's Antiques**
315 W. Main St.
281/255-3844

**The Owl's Nest**
408 W. Main St.
281/351-1103

**J T Texas Co**
611 W. Main St.
281/351-2202

**Past & Present**
701 W. Main St.
281/255-8855

**Victoria Station Antiques**
111 Commerce St.
281/357-0555

**Tender Touch**
115 Commerce St.
281/351-2119

**Maggie Mae's**
121 Commerce St.
281/255-8814

**Country Harbor**
106 N. Elm St.
281/255-2330

**Tomball Antique Co-Op**
208 W. Main St.
281/351-4160

**314 East Main Antiques**
314 E. Main St.
281/351-9488

**Three Sisters Antiques**
330 W. Main St.
281/351-4725

**Just Passin' Time**
418 W. Main St.
281/255-2999

**Antique Press**
701 W. Main St.
281/255-8855

## 150 TRINITY

### Teddie Bear's Antiques and Collectibles
Hwy. 19 S.
(four miles south of Trinity at Bridge)
409/594-6321 or 1-888-TED-DY88
Open 365 days a year, 9-dark @ 7 pm
e-mail: www.teddiebears.com
*Directions: Teddie Bear's is located 19 miles east of Huntsville, Texas (I-45) on Hwy. 19, just across the Trinity River Bridge, or 4 miles south of Trinity, Texas on Hwy. 19.*

For specific information see review at the beginning of this section.

## 151 TYLER

### Antiques & Uniques
433 S. Vine
903/593-2779
Tues.-Sat. 10-5, Sun.-Mon. By chance or appointment
*Directions: Traveling I-20, take the exit to Hwy. 69 and follow to downtown Tyler.*

This is another shop that is very important to know. If you are into lamps, these folks can help you in every way. Not only do they buy and sell antiques, handle appraisals and estate sales, carry gift items and reproductions, they also custom build, rewire and repair lamps, and sell lampshades. They keep over 500 lampshades in stock at all times!

**John R Saul's Antiques**
108 S. Broadway Ave.
903/593-4668

**Rose Tyler Antiques**
202 S. Broadway Ave.
903/592-6711

**Barham's Antiques**
308 S. Broadway Ave.
903/593-3863

**Brass Lion Antiques**
5935 S. Broadway Ave.
903/561-1111

**Front Street Antiques**
202 W. Front St.
903/531-0008

**Old City Antique Mall**
302 E. Locust St.
903/533-1110

**Crossroads Gallery Antiques**
114 W. 6th St.
903/597-3021

**Tyler Square Antiques & Tearoom**
117 S. Broadway Ave.
903/535-9994

**V Js Antique Mall**
236 S. Broadway Ave.
903/595-3289

**Hudson House Interiors**
2301 S. Broadway Ave.
903/593-2611

**Mary's Attic**
417 S. College Ave.
903/592-5181

**Latifs Antiques**
13819 U.S. Hwy. 69 N.
903/882-6031

**Special Effects**
4517 Old Bullard Road
903/509-0020

**Grey Pony**
12663 State Hwy. 31 W.
903/593-8905

**Glass Owl Antiques**
428 S. Vine Ave.
903/595-0251

## 152 UVALDE

**Loessbergs**
524 E. Pecos St.
830/278-3958

**Open House Antiques**
100 W. North St.
830/278-9380

**Market Square Antiques**
103 N. West St.
830/278-1294

**Way Out West Antiques**
103 N. West St.
830/278-3648

## 153 VAN ALSTYNE

**Yellow Rose Drug Store Antique Mall**
210 E. Marshal St.
903/482-6167

### *Great Places To Stay*

**The Durning House Bed & Breakfast and Restaurant**
205 W. Stephens
903/482-5188
Bed & Breakfast open daily, restaurant open for lunch Wed.-Fri., 11:30-2, dinner (Fri.-Sat.only) 6-9, antiques by appointment or during restaurant hours.
*Directions: From Hwy. 75, take Exit #51. After exiting toward town (east), go 6 blocks and the B&B is on the right at 205 West Stephens. If you come to a red light (the only one in town), you've gone a block too far. Van Alstyne is 50 miles north of Dallas, 15 miles north of McKinney and 15 miles south of Sherman, Texas.*

When the Hixes purchased this wonderful little Victorian home, it housed their antique shop called "Elderly Things Antiques." The house is totally decorated in antiques, and some of the pieces scattered throughout the B&B and restaurant are for sale.

Guests are first greeted by three concrete pigs lolling in the front garden area, sporting hats befitting the seasons and holidays.

Diners have enjoyed the food so much that many of the recipes offered here have been included in a cookbook called Hog Heaven - Recipes from the Durning House. As an added incentive, if you mention The Antique Atlas, you will receive a 10% discount!

## 154 VAN HORN

### *Great Places To Stay*

**Los Nopales**
1106 W. Broadway
915/283-7125
Daily 2-6
*Directions: Traveling I-10 East, take Exit #138 and continue 1.3 miles on Business Loop 10. Traveling I-10 West, take Exit #140B and continue 1.5 miles on Business Loop 10. From the intersection of U.S. 90, U.S. 54 and Business Loop 10, travel .8 miles west. Los Nopales is located next to Chuy's Mexican Food Restaurant*

Los Nopales is, indeed, different! They carry antiques and collectibles, art and rare books, including Texana, and there is a refinishing and upholstery shop adjoining the antique shop. They also sell Southwest native plants, and that's also connected to the name of the shop, as owner Joy Scott explains: "When I purchased a commercial lot with an abandoned building on it here in Van Horn, I was searching for an unusual business name that might truly represent our uniqueness. As we set about cleaning up the place, we discovered a prickly pear - in Spanish a "nopal" - growing on the roof amid all the debris that had accumulated there for years. There were prickly pear plants already growing in front of a fence on one part of the property. It seemed like destiny to name the business Los Nopales. For a multi-faceted business like ours, with a Southwestern flair, there just couldn't be a more appropriate name."

## 155 VERNON

**Jailhouse Village**
1826 Cumberland
940/553-4004

**Hall H/Ware & Furniture**
1512 Fannin St.
940/552-5391

**Yellow Rose Antique Mall**
1516 Main St.
940/553-1511

**Yesterdaze Antiques & Collectibles**
1519 Main St.
940/552-6727

**PMH Enterprises**
1601 Main St.
940/552-1660

## 156 VICTORIA

**Victoria Antique Shop**
804 Berkman Dr.
512/575-2203

**Antique Attic**
1401 S. Laurent St.
512/575-5043

**Laurent Street Antique Mall**
1602 N. Laurent St.
512/578-0813

**Victoria's House of Lamps**
1042 N. Main St.
512/575-6200

**Homestead**
106 W. Rio Grande St.
512/572-9666

**Mundine Antiques**
601 E. Rio Grande St.
512/576-9445

**Blue Moon Antique Mall**
1520 E. Rio Grande St. (Hwy. 59)
512/575-3233

## 157 WACO

**Crystal Palace Antiques**
618 Austin Ave.
254/756-7662

**Cottage Shop**
708 Austin Ave.
254/756-0988

**Antiques on Austin**
1525 Austin Ave.
254/753-1795

**Courtyard Classic Antiques**
4700 Bosque Blvd.
254/751-7077

**Laverty's**
600 N. 18th St.
254/754-3238

**Saint Charles Shops**
600 Austin Ave.
254/753-5531

**Show & Tell Antiques**
1525 Morrow Ave.
254/752-5372

**Goodie Mill**
2300 Washington Ave.
254/753-9616

**Victoriana Antiques & Gifts**
561 Westview Village
254/772-7704

## 158 WALLER

**Autumn's Morn**
40142 Hempstead Hwy.
409/372-5415

**Clark's Collectables & Antiques**
3106 Taylor
409/921-2960

**Queenie's Antiques & Co-Op**
2611 Washington St.
409/372-9346

**Bluebonnet Antiques**
2510 Hempstead Hwy.
409/931-2951

## 159 WAXAHACHIE

### Courthouse Antiques
200 S. Rogers
972/938-2777, 1-888-983-5144
Mon.-Fri. 10-5:30, Sat. 10-6, Sun. 12:30-5:30
*Directions: Located in Historic Downtown Waxahachie*

For specific information see review at the beginning of this section.

**Gingerbread Antique Mall**
310 S. College
972/937-0968

**Links to the Past**
512 N. College
972/937-1421

**Briarpatch**
404 W. Main St.
972/937-7717

**Grans Antiques**
208A S. Rogers St.
972/923-2207

**Old Town Village Antiques**
307 S. Rogers St.
972/938-9515

**Waxahachie Crafters & Antiques**
315 S. Rogers St.
972/938-1222

**Barbara's Antiques**
113 N. College
972/935-9338

## 160 WEATHERFORD

**Wanda's Antiques**
2206 E. Bankhead Dr.
817/594-6222

**On The Level Antique Mall**
1716 Blair Dr.
817/594-8991

**Horton House**
1103 Ft. Worth Hwy.
817/599-8945

**Dresser Drawer Antiques**
118 S. Main St.
817/594-1191

**Age Before Beauty**
209 N. Main St.
817/596-8550

**Patty's Country Memories**
219 N. Main St.
817/594-9303

**Sparks Antiques & Collectibles**
220 Main St.
817/598-0089

**Miss B's**
311 N. Main St.
817/596-0902

**The Land of Aah's**
315 E. Oak
817/598-0101

**Wanda's Antiques**
1116 Pala Pinto St.
817/599-4112

**Texas Treasures**
1124 Palo Pinto St.
817/599-9505

**Granny's Attic**
127 York
817/613-9011

## 161 WEST

**Molly B's Antiques**
415 S. George Kacir Dr.
254/826-3052

**Rasberry's Consignor Antiques**
2481 IH 40 W.
254/355-5181

**Huaco Antiques**
20818 N. I-35
254/826-7262

**Heritage Antiques**
I-35
254/826-3042

**West Mercantile**
126 N. Main St.
254/826-4461

**Olde Czech Corner Antiques**
130 N. Main St.
254/826-4094

**Way Out West**
105 E. Oak St.
254/826-3924

## 162 WHEELER

### Antique Cupboard
103 W. Texas St.
806/826-3741
Open Mon.-Sat., 9:30-5, Sun. by appointment
*Directions: From I-40 at Shamrock, Texas, take Hwy. 83 north for 16 miles to downtown Wheeler.*

Here's a shop that lists itself as having "a little bit of everything" including a large selection of depression glass, elegant glass, kitchen collectibles, quilts and primitives.

## 163 WHITE SETTLEMENT

**Harris Antiques & Imports**
7600 Scott St.
817/246-8400 or 817/246-5852
Fax: 817/246-6859
Mon.-Sat. 8:30-5:30
*Directions: Harris Antiques & Imports is located in West Fort Worth, in a suburb called White Settlement. The shop is at I-30 West, Cherry Lane Exit (north), then right on Scott St.*

This store gets my vote for being the largest antique shop in America. Carolyn Harris and company sells both wholesale and retail, with about 95% of their sales being to dealers, auctioneers and designers. But anyone who loves antiques should go to the showroom just to look and be impressed. Their new location is an air-conditioned mall that is the length of three football fields - a total of 440,000 square feet of antiques and accessories! Harris Antiques & Imports has been in business in Fort Worth for over 35 years, and offers merchandise to shoppers world-wide. Besides all the furniture, they offer bronzes, oil paintings, cut glass and porcelain. It's no wonder they hold the title of "the world's largest home furnishings, accessories and antiques store."

## 164 WICHITA FALLS

**Sue's Antique Mall**
609 7th St.
940/322-9552
Tues.-Sat. 10-5
*Directions: From I-44 and Hwy. 287, take 8th St. east to Ohio St., turn left one block to 7th St., then turn left again and go 1/2 block to the shop.*

Few antique shops are fortunate enough to be able to display their goods in an antique building. Sue's Antique Mall occupies a 100+ year old building that is still being researched. You won't have to research the items you find here however, as there is something for everyone who has a love for antiques and collectibles.

**The Hand Place**
4304 Call Field Road
940/691-4563

**Depression Glass by Bonnie**
1032 Covington St.
940/855-1591

**Colonial House Antiques I & II**
1510 Monroe St.
940/761-2280

**The Market on Monroe**
1512 Monroe St.
940/723-4997

**Johnson's Junction**
1514 Monroe St.
940/723-5332

**Village Antique Mall**
1516 Monroe St.
940/322-6255

**Corner Cupboard Antiques**
1518 Monroe St.
940/767-6583

**Monroe St. Antique Mall**
1523 Monroe St.
940/761-4151

**King Alberts Antiques & Interiors**
1827 Pearl Ave.
940/761-4226

**Griffis Antiques**
5521 Northwest Freeway
940/855-7711

**Depot Square Antiques**
620 Ohio Ave.
940/766-6321

**Potts Antique Shop**
1310 10th St.
940/322-3488

## 165 WIMBERLEY

**O'Neals Antiques**
100 Lange Road
512/847-3148

**Jeans Antiques, Gifts & Boutique**
11552 Ranch Road 12 S.
512/487-2307

**Old Mill Store**
Wimberley Square
512/847-3068

## 166 WINNIE

**Just What You Need**
344 Broadway
409/296-3099

**Old Time Trade Days**
I-10 & 1663
409/296-3300

**Winnie Antique Mall**
Hwy. 124 & Cedar St.
409/296-2701

## 167 WOODVILLE

**Family Tree**
304 W. Bluff St.
409/283-2116

**Pine Country Antiques**
511 W. Bluff St.
409/283-3183

**Another Time**
104 Charlton St.
409/283-8222

**Yvonne's Antiques**
112 S. Charlton St.
409/283-2119

**Family Affair Antiques**
Hwy. 190 W.
409/283-5685

# Utah

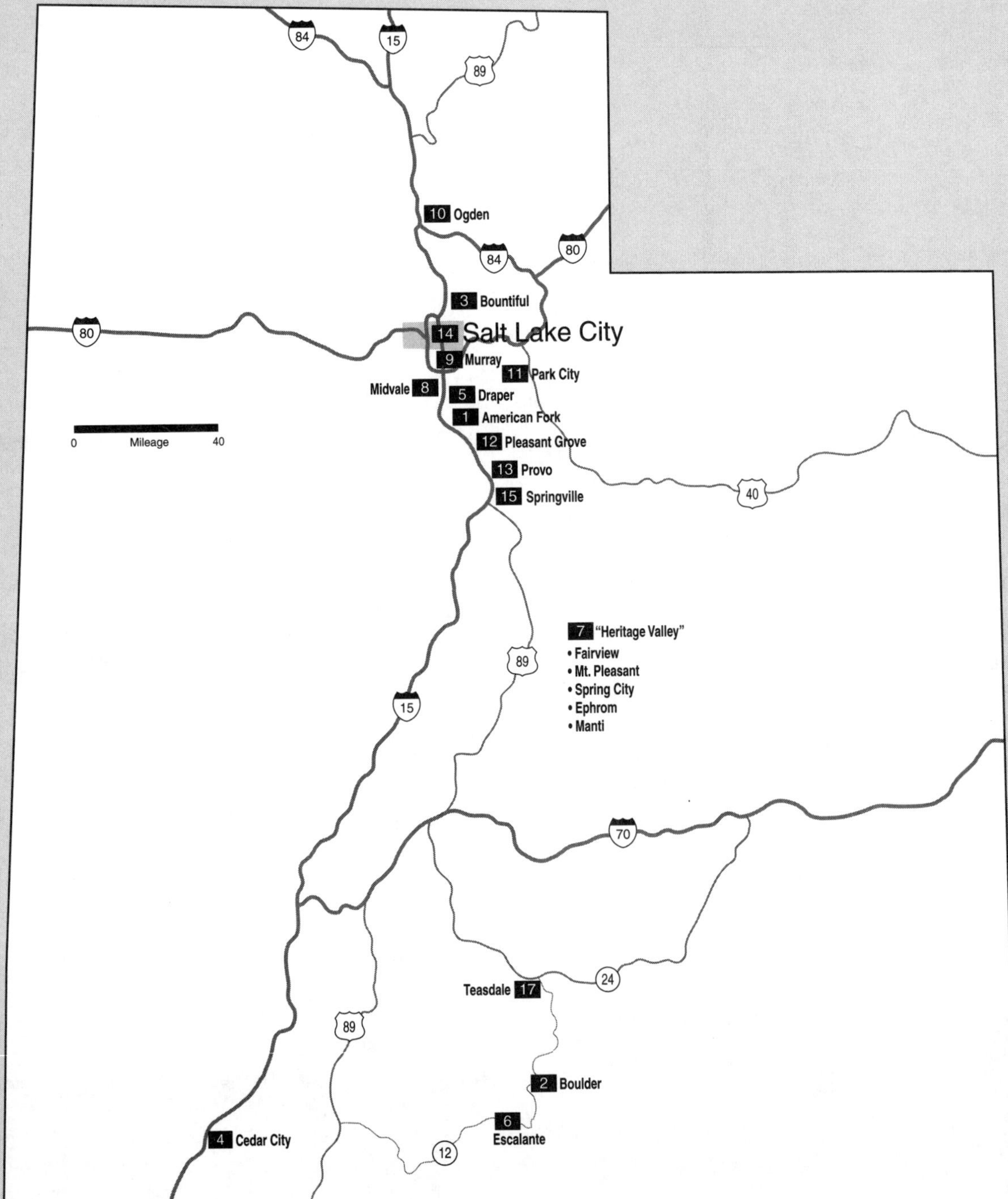

84
15
89
10 Ogden
84
80
3 Bountiful
80
14 Salt Lake City
9 Murray
11 Park City
Midvale 8
5 Draper
1 American Fork
0 Mileage 40
12 Pleasant Grove
13 Provo
15 Springville
40
7 "Heritage Valley"
• Fairview
• Mt. Pleasant
• Spring City
• Ephrom
• Manti
89
15
70
24
Teasdale 17
89
2 Boulder
6 Escalante
4 Cedar City
12
15
St. George 16
9
89

## 1 AMERICAN FORK

**Lake City Antiques**
143 N. 200 W.
801/756-9149

**Flamingo Road**
35 North Barratt Ave.
801/763-8142

## 2 BOULDER

### *Great Places To Stay*

**Boulder Mountain Ranch and Bed & Breakfast**
Hells Back Bone Road
801/335-7480
Open at all time
*Directions: Located 3 1/2 miles off Scenic Byway 12. Just seven miles from rural Boulder.*

This working cattle ranch offers the urban cowboy an opportunity to participate in the "western experience." One to six day excursions are available offering horseback riding along with other adventures for a taste of the true west. Set out on a five day ride from Bryce Canyon to the ranch along the Great Western Trail or if you're a "true cowboy" try trail riding and cattle working. For relaxation, fish in the nearby streams. Lodge rooms or cabins are available. Breakfast is available each morning.

## 3 BOUNTIFUL

**Newman's Antiques & Art**
44 S. 400 RR 2
801/298-2884

**Bountiful Antiques**
399 N. Main St.
801/295-7227

## 4 CEDAR CITY

**Grey Wolf's Antiques & Collectibles**
223 N. 100 W.
801/865-1973

**Betty's Antiques & Collectibles**
1181 S. Main St.
801/586-7221

## 5 DRAPER

**Treasures Unlimited**
132 81 S. Minuteman Road
801/576-8626

## 6 ESCALANTE

Situated in the heart of Scenic Byway 12, Escalante and its environs were among the last frontiers to be explored in the continental United States. In the 1700s, two Spanish priests, along with their expedition, came through the area looking for a passable trail to Los Angeles. The town was eventually named for one of these priests. In 1876, Mormon pioneers settled here because of its mild climate, good grazing land, and abundance of minerals and water.

One of the few places that can still boast clean air, Escalante is surrounded by the mysteries of the past. Little is known about the civilization that lived here centuries ago, and visitors will want to explore the cliff-dwellings and artifacts left by the ancients who once occupied the mountains and canyons.The wildlife is plentiful for hunters and fishermen, and the sweeping vistas are ideal for photographers.The town itself offers modern accommodations, as well as a variety of gift and specialty shops in which to roam. The restaurant and cafes promise anything from sandwiches to steaks to satisfy even the hungriest explorer.

**Serenidad Gallery - Fine Art and Antiques**
360 W. Main St.
801/826-4810
Mon.-Sat. 8-9, Sun. 1-8
*Directions: Go 60 miles from Hwy. 89 to the west, and 65 miles from Hwy. 24 to the northeast. The town is in the heart of Scenic Hwy.12.*

With an eye for quality, this shop carries a fine selection of art and antiques with a Western theme.

### *Great Places To Stay*

**Rainbow Country Tours and Bed & Breakfast**
586 E. 300 S.
1-800-252-8824; 801/826-4567
Fax: 801/826-4557
*Directions: Located on the east end of Escalante. Turn behind the Chevron Station, go 1/4 mile to the first house on the right.*

This bed and breakfast offers you an idyllic place to unwind. Comfortable and peaceful, it provides all the amenities of a traditional bed and breakfast - private rooms and hearty food - plus hot tub and wrap-around sun deck with sweeping vistas of mountain and desert.

For your entertainment, they provide off-the-beaten-path jeep and/or hiking tours, as well as overnight camping. Owner Gene Windle can also take you safely and comfortably in his 8-passenger wagon to see "some of the most beautiful, remote places in the American West." Ask him to show you the petrified forests and the 3000-year-old Indian rock art.

## 7 HERITAGE VALLEY

By the time Utah became a state in 1896, the population had comfortably settled in nearly every corner of its boundaries. In fact, settlers had been colonizing likely townsites for nearly fifty years.

Such is the case with the historic towns of, Spring City, Fairview, Mt. Pleasant, Ephraim, and Manti. This string of communities was settled during the 1850's by industrious and determined Mormons from the United States and Europe.

Today, these towns form Utah's "Heritage Valley". In a state where history is preserved with pride, these central Utah towns stand out for their uncommon devotion to preserving their 19th century origins with architectural integrity and continuing pioneer spirit.

Spring City is one of Utah's finest examples of preservation. Laid out using the strict grid design considered ideal by early Mormons, the entire town of Spring City is on the National Historic Register. Spring City is architecturally eclectic. Some homes are styled with the Scandinavian designs favored by early settlers, and other structures are built in Greek and Romanesque Revival and classic Victorian styles. Heritage Days, a celebration held each spring, includes tours of historic homes, and artists' studios, wagon rides, a turkey barbecue, and much more. A self-guided walking tour is available year-round.

Fairview was settled in 1859, and many of the buildings from this era remain. The Fairview Museum of History and Art offers an excellent collection of items evocative of pioneer days including hand-crafted household implements. The museum also exhibits the remnants of ancient Pueblo cultures common to the area, and modern-day paintings and sculpture.

Mt. Pleasant was also settled permanently in 1859. Its colorful Main Street is a model of community pride and hard work. The majority of the streets' structures were built between 1880 and 1905. Mt. Pleasant's rich history includes the signing of the treaty between central Utah settlers and the Ute Indians. Mt. Pleasant hosts a pioneer pageant each summer.

Settled by a few determined families in the 1850s, Ephraim's quiet streets are lined today with carefully preserved buildings and homes, both common and ornate. The renovated "Ephraim Cooperative Mercantile Association" building is one Main Street example. Guided tours of historic sites are available. Ephraim is the home of Snow College, founded in the 1880s. Today's enrollment is about 2,500 students. A Scandinavian Festival held each Memorial Day weekend pays homage to the Mormon convert settlers.

Manti was one of the first five towns incorporated into the "State of Deseret", as early Mormons hoped their territory would someday be known. The town's most famous structure is the Mormon Temple constructed between 1877 and 1888, and still in use today. The grounds of the cream-colored oolite limestone edifice are the location of the Mormon Miracle Pageant each July. Drawing thousands of spectators nightly, it tells the story of the founding of the LDS Church, and of the early pioneers who settled this area.

For more information about ways to enjoy Utah's Heritage Valley, Contact: Sanpete Economic Development, P. O. Box 59, Ephraim, Utah 84627, 801-283-4321.

### *Antique Shops*

**Antiques Etc.**
58 N. Main St.
Manti
801/835-1122

**Pherson House Antiques & Bed and Breakfast**
244 S. Main St.
Ephraim
801/283-4197

### *Bed & Breakfast*

**Ephraim Homestead**
135 W. 100 N.
Ephraim
801/283-6367

**Heritage House**
498 N. 400 W.
Manti
801/835-5050

**Larsen House**
298 S. State St.
Mt. Pleasant
801/462-9337

**Legacy Inn**
337 N. 100 E.
Manti
801/835-8352

**Mainti House Inn**
401 N. Main St.
Manti
801/835-0161

**Yardley Inn**
190 S. 200 W.
Manti
801/835-1861

### *Museums*

Mon.-Sat. 10-5, Summer 10-6, Sun. 2-6

**Fairview Museum**
86 N. 100 E.
Fairview
801/427-9216

**Mt. Pleasant Museum**
150 S. State
Mt. Pleasant
801/462-2456

## 8 MIDVALE

**Bingham Junction Antiques**
23 N. Main St.
801/255-0330

**Antiques Emporium**
32 N. Main St.
801/565-0242

**First Class Antiques & Collectibles**
7615 State St.
801/568-7878

**Amusement Sales**
127 N. Main St.
801/255-4731

## 9 MURRAY

### Lyn Annes Collectables
4844 S. State St.
801/263-2293
Mon.-Fri. 11-5:30, Sat. 11-5

This is a unique shop that specializes in vintage wearables, including accessories. They also carry a selection of costume jewelry and glassware.

### After Glow
4844 S. State St.
801/263-2293
Mon.-Fri. 11-5:30, Sat. 11-5
*Directions: From I-15 take the 53rd South Exit #303. Go east to State St.*

Offering the largest selection of glassware in the area, this shop also features a variety of fine china, primitives, costume jewelry, and paper.

The shop gladly offers dealer discounts and appraisal services.

**Sherry's Antiques**
4859 S. State St.
801/266-3145

**Notions**
4838 S. State St.
801/263-7733

**Rare Necessities**
4967 S. State St.
801/288-0518

## 10 OGDEN

**Boom Town Antiques**
406 Canyon Road
801/621-6778

**Young's General Store**
109 Historic 25th St.
801/392-1473

**Painted Lady**
115 Historic 25th St.
801/393-4445

**Lilt of Yesteryear**
3638 Jackson Ave.
801/394-1896

**Country Way Gifts & Antiques**
460 Second St.
801/392-0332

**Abbys Antique Mall**
134 31st St.
801/394-9035

**Curio Shop**
241 25th St.
801/393-0926

**Erika Martin Antiques**
3480 Washington Blvd.
801/393-5963

**Cowboy Trading Post**
268 25th St.
801/399-9511

**Country Antiques**
118 24th St.
801/394-4934

**Ginger Jar Antiques**
424 29th St.
801/399-4901

**Reflections Antiques & Collectibles**
2386 Wall Ave.
801/392-4904

## 11 PARK CITY

**Southwest Indian Traders**
550 Main St.
801/645-9177

***Great Places To Stay***

### Angel House Inn
713 Norfolk Ave.
1-800-ANGEL-01; 801/647-0338
Open year round
*Directions: From Salt Lake City, take I-80 to Route 224. This becomes Park Ave. At town lift, turn right on 8th St.; go two blocks, then left onto Norfolk.*

Set in historic Park City, with the rugged Wasatch Mountains as a backdrop, an exquisite Victorian mansion has been transformed into the Angel House Inn. Built in 1889, during an era of elegance and service, proprietors Joe and Jan Fisher Rush have restored this historical house to its former grandeur and welcome you to experience one of its 9 romantically designed and themed rooms. Highlights of its amenities include its immediate access to Park City resorts for world class skiing in the winter and adventurous hiking and mountain biking in the summer.

Each of its 9 designer appointed rooms are named after angels who represent and embody the essence of romance and pleasure of the natural world. The inn also features an elegant sitting and breakfast area that ensures your stay is one reminiscent of the Victorian era.

### Old Miners' Lodge-A Bed and Breakfast Inn
615 Woodside Ave.
1-800-648-8068; 801/645-8068
Fax: 801/645-7420
Open year round

Situated in the Historic District, this 1889 lodge was once a boarding house for fortune seeking miners. Besides the three suites and ten antique-filled guest rooms (complete with down comforters and pillows) there is a large fireplace in the living room and an outdoor hot tub available to guests all year round. Other amenities include terry cloth robes in all guest baths and a full breakfast each morning.

With the Park City ski area just a stone's throw away, this inn can easily accommodate groups or family gatherings.

## 12 PLEASANT GROVE

**Collector's Cottage**
100 E. State Road
801/785-6782

**Rosebud Antiques**
15 S. Main St.
801/796-0108

## 13 PROVO

**Kristi & Joseph Antiques**
260 N. University Ave.
801/375-1211

**This N That Antiques**
1585 W. Center St.
801/375-3133

## 14 SALT LAKE CITY

**Brass Key Antiques**
43 W. Broadway
801/532-2844

**Beehive Collectors Gallery**
368 E. Broadway
801/533-0119

**Trolley Antique & Unique**
602 S. 500 Ave. (Trolley Square)
801/575-8060

**Temptations Plus**
3922 Highland Dr.
801/272-6222

**Antique Shoppe**
2016 S. 1100 E.
801/466-2171

**Jitter Bug-Toy Dealers**
243 E. 300 S.
801/537-7038

**Wasatch Furniture Co.**
623 S. State St.
801/521-8845

**Bearcat Antiques**
43 W. 300 S.
801/532-2844

**Kennard Antiques**
65 W. 300 S.
801/328-9796

**Antiques Gallery**
217 E. 300 S.
801/521-7055

**Copper Cowboy Antiques**
268 S. 300 E.
801/328-4401

**Due Time**
279 E. 300 S.
801/521-4356

**Cobwebs**
1054 S. 2100 S.
801/485-9295

**Generations Antiques**
2085 S. 900 E.
801/466-0456

**Ec-Lec-Tic**
380 Pierpont Ave.
801/322-4804

**Sugar House**
2144 Highland Dr., Suite 130
801/487-5084

**Ken Sanders Rare Books**
268 S. 200 E.
801/521-3819

**Elemente**
353 Pierpont Ave.
801/355-7400

**Squires Antiques**
357 W. 200 S.
801/363-1191

**Briar Patch Antiques**
407 E. 300 S.
801/322-5234

**Gary Thompson Antiques & Art**
43 W. 300 S.
801/532-2844

**Olympus Cove Antiques**
179 E. 300 S.
801/532-1070

**Antoinette's**
247 E. 300 S.
801/359-2192

**Carmen Miranda's**
270 S. 300 E.
801/359-7741

**Thomson & Burrows Antiques**
280 S. 300 E.
801/521-0650

**Honest Jon's Hills House**
126 S. 200 W.
801/359-4852

### *Great Places To Stay*

**Wildflowers Bed & Breakfast**
936 E. 1700 S.
801/466-0600

Built in 1891, this beautiful Victorian home is surrounded by an array of wonderful colors, one of which is evident in the blue spruce trees which surround the grounds, and more so in the wildflowers of all different shades of the rainbow. Listed on the National Register of Historic Places, the Wildflowers Bed & Breakfast is gorgeously enhanced with original chandeliers, stained glass windows, Oriental rugs, antiques, and an astonishing hand carved staircase.

A gourmet breakfast is served to the guest, making the stay at Wildflowers a complete and enjoyable one.

## 15 SPRINGVILLE

**P J's Antiques**
211 N. Main St.
801/489-9137

**Pioneer Antiques**
391 N. Main St.
801/489-6853

**T C Antique Barn**
2310 S. State St.
801/489-9623

## 16 ST. GEORGE

**Holland House**
70 N. 500 E.
801/628-0176

**Bentley's House of Antiques**
46 N. 100 W.
801/674-1812

**Dixie Trading Post**
111 W. Saint George Blvd.
801/628-7333

**Butterfield's Antiques**
248 E. Saint George Blvd.
801/673-8333

**General Store Antiques**
640 E. Saint George Blvd.
801/628-8858

## 17 TEASDALE

**The Old House**
417 S. 500 W. (Loa) 20 mi. from Teasdale
801/836-2382

### *Great Places To Stay*

**Cockscomb Inn Bed & Breakfast**
97 S. State St.
801/425-3511
Open seven days a week, year round.

This quaint inn is only minutes from Capitol Reef National Park. The charming rooms all have private baths. Hiking and biking information is available. Excellent full breakfast is served.

# Vermont

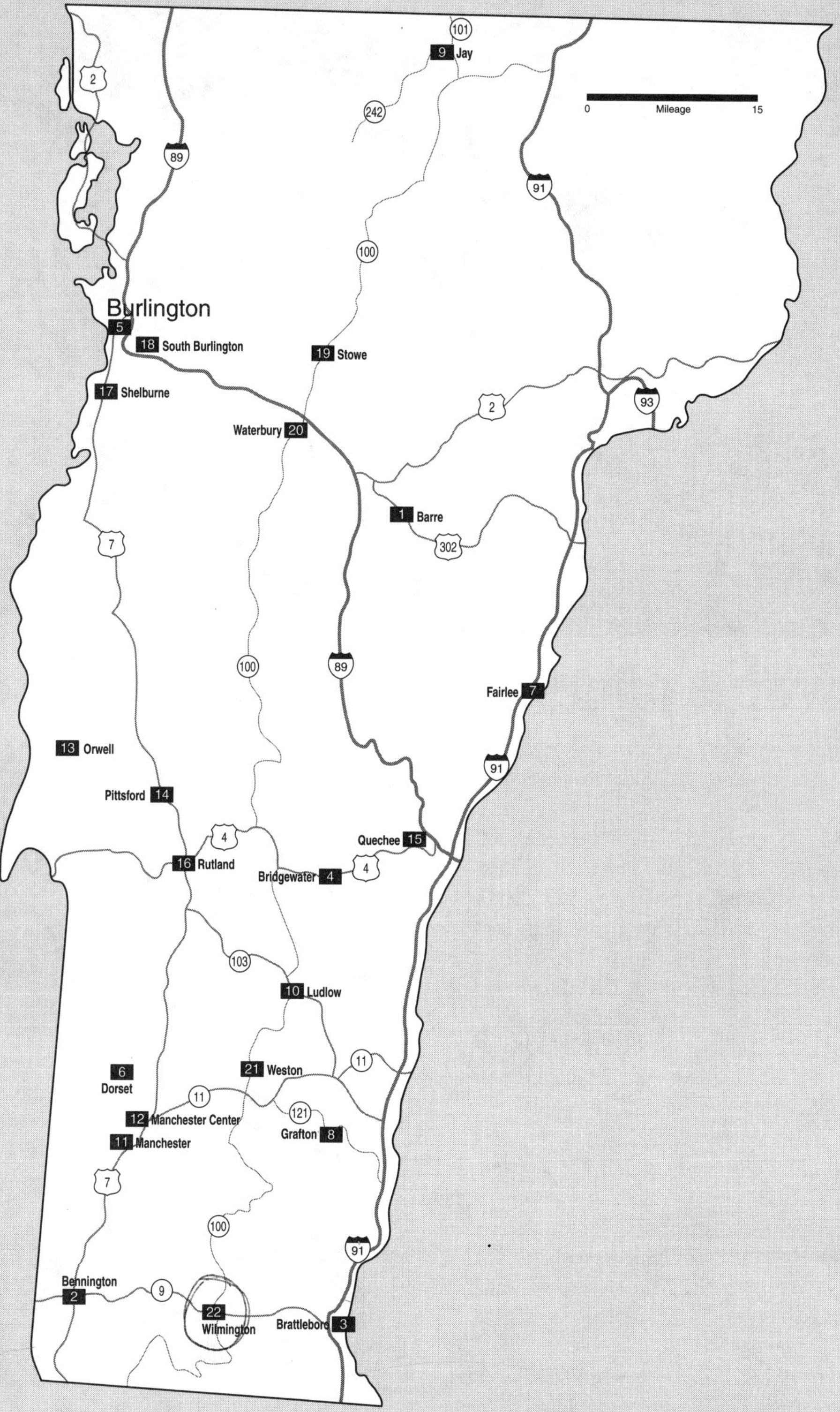

0 Mileage 15
9 Jay
Burlington
5
18 South Burlington
19 Stowe
17 Shelburne
Waterbury 20
1 Barre
Fairlee 7
13 Orwell
Pittsford 14
Quechee 15
16 Rutland
Bridgewater 4
10 Ludlow
6 Dorset
21 Weston
12 Manchester Center
11 Manchester
Grafton 8
Bennington 2
22 Wilmington
Brattleboro 3
101
242
2
89
91
100
93
7
302
4
103
11
121
9

Vermont

*Brandywine is a spacious village inn on the National Register of Historic Places. A relaxing place to visit in an area featuring many opportunities for sightseeing and sport.*

# Brandywine offers bed, breakfast and antiques

Located in the center of Vermont's most charming village, Brandywine wraps you in the peace of enjoying gorgeous surroundings in a country-formal atmosphere.

It's a wonderful place to relax, or if you are looking for activity, you can enjoy many sports and hobbies right in town. The surrounding area offers many miles of fabulous hiking trails, biking, tennis, and beautiful streams for fishing. Guests can take a horse drawn carriage ride through the charming village or enjoy a picnic lunch on one of the beautiful covered bridges located on the property. For those who enjoy golf, there are several outstanding courses in the immediate area.

Built in the 1830s, this spacious village inn is on the National Historic Register. It is beautifully furnished with period antiques, and is as comfortable as it is elegant.

For those in love with the sport of antiquing, there is a 25 x 50-foot post and beam barn filled with a fabulous array of antiques for sale. The two floors of treasures are sure to please those who enjoy finding a bargain. From primitive through refined, you will discover one of Vermont's most interesting and eclectic antique shops.

Brandywine is always delighted to have families with children and offers accommodations for your cat, dog or horse.

*Enjoy a carriage ride tour of the village.*

*The pastoral setting will delight vacationers who love a view.*

*Brandywine Bed & Breakfast and Antiques is located on Main St. in Grafton. For additional information see listing #8 (Grafton).*

## 1 BARRE

**East Barre Antique Mall**
133 Mill St.
(East Barre)
802/479-5190
Daily 10-5
*Directions: Located just off the junction of U.S. Route 302 E. & Route 110 on Mill St. in the heart of East Barre. Bear right at the fork and up the hill.*

East Barre Antique Mall is a group shop located in the center of East Barre, Vermont. Besides a general line of antiques, they offer the largest selection of antique furniture in the area, antique silver, glassware, framed prints, sports items, primitives and collectibles. The largest and cleanest shop in Central Vermont, over 12,000 square feet, the items are tastefully displayed throughout making it easy to spot your favorite pieces.

**Red Wagon Antiques**
1079 S. Barre Road
802/479-3611

**Everything Under The Sun**
Barre Road
802/479-2563

## 2 BENNINGTON

**Four Corners East**
307 North St.
802/442-2612

**Antique Center at Camelot Village**
60 West Road
802/447-0039

**Molly Stark Antiques**
Route 9 E.
802/442-2129

**Pentimento**
359 Main St.
802/442-8550

## 3 BRATTLEBORO

**Village Farm Antiques**
Green River Village
802/254-7366

**Richter Gallery**
111 Main St.
802/254-1110

**Black Mountain Antique Center**
Route 30
802/254-3848

**Kit Barry Antiques**
109 Main St.
802/254-3634

## 2 BRIDGEWATER

**Bridgewater Mill Antique Centre**
**Old Mill Marketplace**
Route 4
802/672-3049
Daily 10-6
*Directions: Take I-91 north to Exit 9 (Hartland). Take Route 12 north to Route 4 west, which goes to Bridgewater. The Old Mill Marketplace is situated on the left side of Route 4. Bridgewater is 10 miles west of Woodstock and 15 miles east of Killington.*

The Bridgewater Antique Centre is located on the third floor in The Old Mill Marketplace, a 150 year old woolen mill turned antique shop. With over 100 quality dealers in 8,000 square feet, the Centre features a large assortment of antique furniture, glassware, and collectibles. They also have an impressive selection of Victorian furniture, oak dressers and tables, reconstructed pie safes, jelly and corner cupboards, dry sinks, harvest tables, and armoires.

Shipping arrangements can be made in-house for delivery of large furniture anywhere in the United States. United Parcel Service (UPS) shipping is available for smaller pieces.

**Red Horse**
Route 4
802/672-3220

## 5 BURLINGTON

**Underground Antiques**
96 Church St.
802/864-5183

**Architectural Salvage Warehouse**
212 Battery St.
802/658-5011

**Bygone Books**
31 Main St.
802/862-4397

**Calliope Music**
202 Main St.
802/863-4613

**Miss Pickle's Attic**
151 Battery St.
802/865-4788

## 6 DORSET

**Marie Miller American Quilts**
Main St.
802/867-5969

**Carlson Antiques**
On The Village Green/Route 30
802/867-4510

## 7 FAIRLEE

**Vollbrecht Antiques**
Main St.
802/333-4223

**Paper Americana**
Main St.
802/333-4784

## 8 GRAFTON

### *Great Places To Stay*

**Brandywine Bed and Breakfast and Antiques**
Main St.
802/843-2250
Open 7 days a week
*Directions: Located 8 miles off of Route 91 N. Exit 5. Brandywine is 25 minutes from Manchester University and 30 minutes from Mount Salow as well as Straton Mountain; 45 minutes south of Ludlow, Vt., and 1 hour south of Ruthana.*

For specific information see review at the beginning of this section.

## 9 JAY

**The Tickle Trunk**
Jay Village
Box 132
802/988-4731
Thurs.-Sun., 11-5 (7 days a week at holiday times)
*Directions: One mile from Jay Peak Ski Resort. At main intersection in Jay Village on Route 242 and Crossroads. From I-19, Exit 27 to Newport. 30 minute drive to Jay via Route 105 to Route 101 to Route 242.*

The Tickle Trunk, as the name implies, is noted for trunks. They also specialize in clocks, primitives, Victorian furniture, vintage clothing, costume jewelry from the '40s up, and numerous other wonderful antiques and collectibles.

## 10 LUDLOW

**Village Barn**
126 Main St.
802/228-3275

**Cool-Edge Collection**
Route 100 N.
802/228-4168

**Needham House**
Route 100 N.
802/228-2255

## 11 MANCHESTER

**Clarke Comollo Antiques**
Route 7 A
802/362-7188

## 12 MANCHESTER CENTER

**Center Hill Past & Present**
Center Hill
802/362-3211

**Cachet**
Route 11
802/362-0058

**Carriage Trade Antique Center**
Route 7 A N.
802/362-1125

**Brewster Antiques**
Route 30
802/362-1579

**Maiden Lane**
Elm St.
802/362-2004

**Judy Pascal Antiques**
Elm St.
802/362-2004

**Equinox Antiques**
29 Historic Main
802/362-3540

## 13 ORWELL

**Brookside Farms Country Inn and Antique Shop**
Hwy. 22 A
802/948-2727

Listed on the National Register of Historic Places, this restored 1789 farmhouse and the 1843 Greek Revival mansion is located on a 300 acre estate. Both the farmhouse and the Mansion are decorated in 18th and 19th century furnishings. An antique shop is located on the property as well.

## 14 PITTSFORD

**Tuffy Antiques**
Route 7
802/483-6610

**Rutland Antiques**
Route 7
802/483-6434

## 15 QUECHEE

**Quechee Gorge Village**
Route 4
802/295-1550

**Antiques Collaborative, Inc.**
Waterman Place/Route 4
802/296-5858

## 16 RUTLAND

**Park Antiques, Inc.**
75 Woodstock Ave.
802/775-4184
Daily 10-5, except Mon.
*Directions: Located 1/4 mile east on Route 4 from Route 7.*

Park Antiques, Inc. is the home of an ever-changing stock of furniture (Victorian and oak), primitives, collectibles, jewelry, stoneware, paintings, china, glassware and more.

**Conway's Antiques & Decor**
90 Center St.
802/775-5153

**The Gallery of Antiques & Cllbls.**
Route 4
802/773-4940

**Trader Ricks**
407 West St.
802/775-4455

**Treasure Chest**
Route 4 E. (Shops at Mendon W.)
802/775-0310

## 17 17 SHELBURNE

**Vincent Fernandez Oriental Rugs and Antiques**
Route 7
802/985-2275
Mon.-Sat. 10-5
*Directions: On Interstate 89 take Shelburne Exit, travel south on Route 7, shop is six miles on the left across from the Shelburne Museum.*

Rugs have been used in homes in America since the 17th century. Oriental rugs during the early periods were sometimes used on a table rather than on the floor. At Vincent Fernandez Oriental Rugs and Antiques the offerings are spectacular. You're sure to find something to enhance any decor. This shop always carries an excellent selection of antiques.

**Shelburne Village Antiques**
Route 7-On The Green
802/985-1447
Mon.-Sat. 10-5; also most Sun.
*Directions: Located on Route 7, six miles from I-89 in the heart of Shelburne Village. Within walking distance of Shelburne Museum.*

A unique collection of New England furniture and decorative accessories, along with a complete line of Americana, Folk Art and primitives invitingly beckons the traveler to stop and shop.

**Black Hawk**
2131 Route 7-On The Green
802/985-8049
Mon.-Sun. 10-5
*Directions: Traveling I-89, south to Shelburne Village. Black Hawk is a 5 minute walk from The Shelburne Museum.*

Black Hawk, located in an Historic 19th century store front, is known for its American antiques and accessories.

**Somewear In Time**
2131 Route 7
802/985-3816

**Burlington Center For Antiques**
1966 Shelburne Road
802/985-4911

**Champlain Valley Antique Center**
1991 Shelburne Road
802/985-8116

**Its About Time Ltd.**
3 Webster Road
802/985-5772

### *Interesting Side Trips*

**Shelburne Museum**
Route 7
802/985-3346
From late May to late Oct.: Daily 10-5
From late Oct. to late May: Daily 1 p.m. guided tour
*Directions: From I-89, take Exit 13 to Route 7 south to Shelburne.*

Described as New England's Smithsonian, Shelburne Museum is located in the heart of Vermont's scenic Champlain Valley. It was founded in 1947 by Electra Havemeyer Webb, a pioneer collector of American folk art. Mrs. Webb became captivated by the sometimes unexpected beauty of utilitarian objects that exemplified "the ingenuity and craftsmanship of the pre-industrial era".

The 37 exhibit buildings, situated on 45 scenic acres, house 80,000 objects of art, artifacts, and architecture spanning 3 centuries of American culture.

At first glance the museum looks like a well-preserved historic village, but look again, the Adirondack-style hunting lodge sits near a turn-of-the-century paddle wheel steamboat, which in turn borders a collection of community buildings and historic houses that date back to the 18th and 19th century.

The contents in some of these architectural treasures document the era of the particular building, but others serve as galleries for diverse collections to be enjoyed in a friendly and informal way.

The Shelburne Museum is a lively and intriguing combination of art and history that promises visitors a veritable patchwork of America's past.

## 18 SOUTH BURLINGTON

**Ethan Allen Antique Shop**
32 Beacon St.
802/863-3764

**New England Import Rug Gallery**
930 Shelburne Road
802/865-0503

## 19 STOWE

**Rosebud Antiques at Houston Farm**
2850 Mountain Road
802/253-2333
Wed.-Sun. 9-5; closed Mon. & Tues.
*Directions: Exit 10 (Stowe) off I-89. Take 100 north. At the crossroads in the village take Mountain Road (108) 2 miles. Shop is on the right.*

Visiting with this shop owner by phone was quite a treat. This quaint little shop, attached to an 1850s home, is ten minutes from a ski resort. As you might surmise, they specialize in sports antiquities: skiing, fishing, snow shoes, etc. They also have a wonderful collection of children's antique sleds.

Old chocolate and ice cream molds are another hard-to-find item from the past featured in this shop.

**Belle Maison**
1799 Mountain Road
802/253-8248

**Stowe Antiques Center**
51 S. Main St.
802/253-9875

### *Great Places To Stay*

**Bittersweet Inn**
692 S. Main St. (Route 100)
802/253-7787

The 18th century brick farmhouse and converted carriage house provides comfortable lodging, private baths, a friendly warm atmosphere, and courteous service by your host and hostess. Bittersweet Inn is located on the south edge of Stowe Village, just a half-mile walk from the center of town, and just minutes away from the ski lifts and cross-country touring centers. Hiking and bike trails abound.

**Brass Lantern Inn**
717 Maple St.
1-800-729-2980
Web site: www.stoweinfo.com/saa/brasslantern

Warm your hearts at the Brass Lantern Inn in picturesque Stowe, Vermont. From the cozy fireplaces and soothing whirlpool tubs to the handmade quilts and spectacular mountain views, this charming restored farmhouse and carriage barn defines romance. Exquisite cuisine, glorious shopping and outdoor recreation nearby. Hearty country breakfast prepared with local Vermont products and produce. The inn is AAA - Three Diamond approved.

## 20 WATERBURY

**Early Vermont Antiques**
Route 100 N.
802/244-5373
Daily 10-5 daily
*Directions: From I-89, take Exit 10, onto Route 100. The shop is directly across from Ben and Jerry's Ice Cream Store.*

This shop is the perfect place to stop if you're "hot" because they are located directly across the street from Ben & Jerry's Ice Cream Store. Once you cool off with all that ice cream (it's absolutely wonderful, you know) then cross the street to visit Barbara at Early Vermont. This fabulous group shop offers the finest in early American antiques. Tastefully displayed throughout the shop you will find early furnishings, glass, collectibles, and accessories often native to the Vermont area.

**Sugar Hill Antiques**
Route 100
802/244-7707

## 21 WESTON

**Weston Antiques Barn**
Route 100
802/824-4097
Mon.-Fri. 10-5, Sun. 11-4 during Nov.-May; Mon.-Sat. 10-5, Sun. 11-4 during June- Oct.
*Directions: The Weston Antiques Barn is located on Route 100, 1 mile north of "Historic" Weston Village.*

This twenty-five dealer shop offers a wide array of furniture, pottery, glass, paintings, books, metals and textiles. A great source for collectors, decorators, and anyone looking for something unique to treasure.

**The Vermont County Store**
Route 100
802/362-2400
Open Mon.-Sat. 9-5; closed Sundays

Known in all 50 states through The Voice of the Mountains mail order catalogue, here you will rediscover products you thought had long disappeared such as penny candy, Vermont Common Crackers, and floursack towels, as well as many other useful and practical items. Interspersed with the merchandise are hundreds of artifacts from the past - its like shopping in a museum. A visit you'll remember long after you get home.

## 22 WILMINGTON

**Left Bank Antiques**
Route 9 and 100
802/464-3224
Open Thurs.-Mon. 11-5, closed Tues. and Wed.
*Directions: Located at the Junction of Routes 9 and 100 (at the light).*

Roseville pottery, chandeliers and lighting, early 1900's furniture, old trunks and a multitude of glassware are only a few of the examples of fine antiques you will find in this eight dealer shop.

**Royles Bazaar**
W. Main St.
802/464-8093

**Etcetera Shop**
Route 9 W.
802/464-5394

**Yankee Pickers**
Route 100
802/464-3884

**Pine Tree Hill Antiques**
21 Warnock Road
802/464-2922

**Sugar House Antique Center**
W. Main St.
802/464-8948

### *Great Places To Stay*

**The Inn at Quail Run**
106 Smith Road
1-800-343-7227
Web site: www.sover.net/~dvalnews/quailrun.html

Off the beaten track and nestled in the woods - yet only three and a half miles from Mt. Snow, Quail Run is located on fifteen pristine wooded acres and offers a spectacular view of the Mt. Snow Valley. As a family oriented inn, children of all ages and well behaved pets are welcome. The inn has eleven recently renovated guest rooms, all with private bath and several with gas fireplaces. There is a two-room suite as well as a four room, four bath cottage complete with kitchen and living room. A full country breakfast is served each morning.

# Virginia

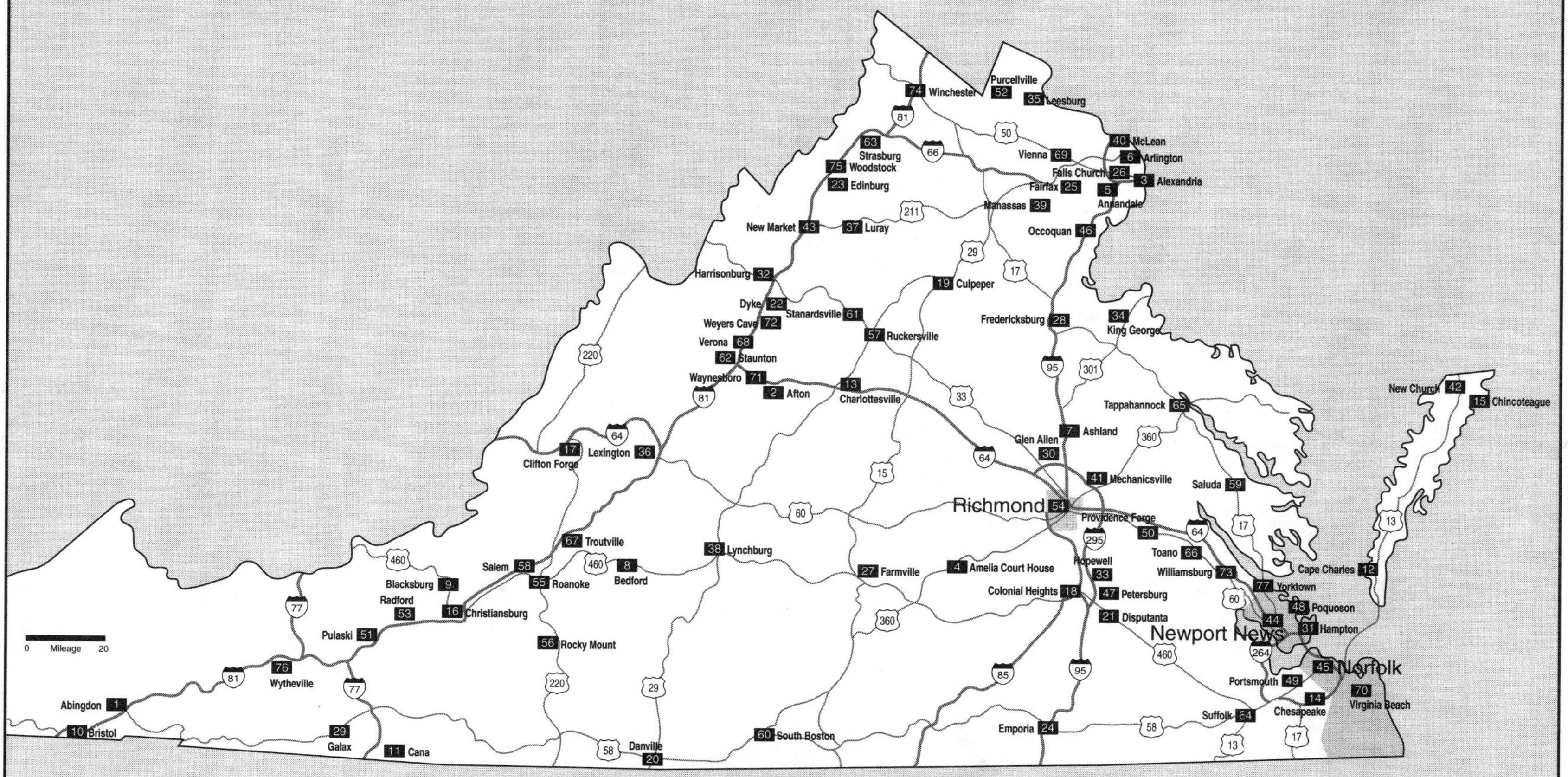

74 Winchester
52 Purcellville
35 Leesburg
40 McLean
6 Arlington
3 Alexandria
26 Falls Church
69 Vienna
25 Fairfax
5 Annandale
39 Manassas
46 Occoquan
63 Strasburg
75 Woodstock
23 Edinburg
43 New Market
37 Luray
32 Harrisonburg
19 Culpeper
22 Dyke
61 Stanardsville
72 Weyers Cave
68 Verona
57 Ruckersville
62 Staunton
28 Fredericksburg
34 King George
71 Waynesboro
2 Afton
13 Charlottesville
65 Tappahannock
42 New Church
15 Chincoteague
7 Ashland
30 Glen Allen
17 Clifton Forge
36 Lexington
41 Mechanicsville
59 Saluda
54 Richmond
50 Providence Forge
67 Troutville
38 Lynchburg
66 Toano
73 Williamsburg
58 Salem
8 Bedford
27 Farmville
4 Amelia Court House
33 Hopewell
12 Cape Charles
9 Blacksburg
55 Roanoke
18 Colonial Heights
47 Petersburg
77 Yorktown
53 Radford
16 Christiansburg
21 Disputanta
48 Poquoson
44 Newport News
31 Hampton
51 Pulaski
56 Rocky Mount
45 Norfolk
76 Wytheville
49 Portsmouth
70 Virginia Beach
1 Abingdon
14 Chesapeake
64 Suffolk
10 Bristol
29 Galax
11 Cana
20 Danville
60 South Boston
24 Emporia
0 Mileage 20

# The Oaks: A proud Victorian in a class by itself

Situated atop the highest hill in town, The Oaks is the focal point of the East Main Street Historic District in Christiansburg, Va. The home was designed by a New York architect. Construction began in 1889 and was completed in 1893 for Major W. L. Pierce, who built the magnificent Queen Anne Victorian for his wife and seven children. It remained in the Pierce family for 90 years, then was purchased by the Hardies in 1982. Preserving the original floor plan and elegant interior, the home was extensively restored and renovated, including the addition of modern bathrooms and other amenities. Tom and Margaret Ray bought the home on September 21, 1989, and converted it to one of the premier bed and breakfast facilities in the nation.

The Oaks is a relaxing place – in perfect harmony with an elegant, gracious atmosphere. Guests awake to the aroma of freshly ground, perked coffee and a newspaper. All rooms have a queen or king size bed, and private bathrooms - modern and stocked with plush towels, fluffy terry robes and toiletries.

The garden gazebo houses a new hydro jet hot tub. Breakfast is always generous. Each day, the menu varies with delightful specialties such as curried eggs served in white wine sauce with Shitake mushrooms, raisin, Granny Smith apple or broccoli/lemon quiche, shirred eggs in spinach nests, rum raisin French toast or whole wheat buttermilk pancakes in praline syrup with toasted pecans and maple cream, and fluffy omelets with surprise fillings and sauces. Oven-fresh breads accompany the entrees: spicy pear, French apple and banana muffins, cranberry and pumpkin teabreads and Southern buttermilk biscuits. Sausage, bacon and ginger braised chicken breast are favorites.

*The Oaks Victorian Inn is located at 311 Main Street in Christiansburg. For additional information see listing #16 (Christiansburg)*

*Designer linens on the four poster bed, complete with VIB Bears are a testament to Evergreen The Bell-Capozzi House's attention to comfort.*

# Sweet dreams at the Evergreen The Bell-Capozzi House

Fully called Evergreen The Bell-Capozzi House, this Southwestern Virginia bed and breakfast graces the hills of Christiansburg. Guest will be surprised that the house's lavish facade hides an inground heated pool in the backyard, replete with lounge chairs, gazebo, rose garden, and fish pond.

After a good workout in the pool, you can settle into comfort in a poster bed of one of the large bedrooms, each individually decorated with captivating works of talented, local artists.

Yes, there is a "Gone with the Wind" bedroom in this Victorian mansion. It features a king-size, four-poster bed along with a desk and comfortable chairs. Scarlett O'Beara and Rhett Bearler complete the makeup. Among the home's 17 rooms are five guest quarters, all with heart pine floors, original light fixtures, and private baths.

Fireplaces warm the two parlors. The formal library converts easily into a conference room that can accommodate 12 people. Innkeepers, Rocco, transplanted from Corning, NY, and Barbara, a native of Virginia whose great-grandfathers fought in the Civil War, restored and decorated "for comfort" the house without altering it. Guests call it a "relaxed elegance."

Your hosts cook up a traditional southern breakfast with homemade biscuits, country ham, cheese grits, silver dollar pancakes, fresh fruit, locally-made jams and jellies, and apple butter, and growing-in-fame, Mill Mountain coffee and tea.

Tea time arrives in style at 5:00 p.m. in the library during winter months with scones, cookies, cake, and small sandwiches. Summer guests are served on the porches, humming with rockers and swings.

*Evergreen The Bell-Capozzi House is a fine example of a southern Victorian mansion.*

Two blocks away are the Montgomery Museum and Lewis Miller Regional Art Center. The 204-year-old city of Christiansburg is the county seat for Montgomery County. Nearby Virginia Tech is a premier depository of American Civil War history and home base for noted Civil War historian James I. Robertson, Jr.

When you're finished scouting out the Civil War archives, you can canoe or raft the Little and New Rivers, play bocce ball on Evergreen's lawn, fish Claytor Lake and the rivers, golf at Round Meadow or Virginia Tech, hike the Appalachian Trail and George Washington-Jefferson National Forest, horseback ride at Mountain Lake, or play tennis at several convenient sites. At Evergreen, when you aren't swimming, you can try your hand at puzzles, bridge, or the 1887 Bechstein concert grand piano.

*Evergreen The Bell-Capozzi House is located at 201 E. Main Street in Christiansburg. For additional information see listing #16 (Christiansburg).*

## 1 ABINGDON

**Court Street Collectibles**
104 Court St. N.E.
540/628-3500

**Storyteller's Antiques**
173 E. Main St.
540/628-8669

**Highland Antique Mall**
246 W. Main St.
540/676-4438

**Garden Artifacts**
272 W. Main St.
540/628-9686

**Brandy Wine Antiques**
477 W. Main St.
540/676-3944

**J & R Furniture & Design**
108 W. Main St.
540/628-2369

**Abingdon Mercantile & Frames**
130 S. Wall St.
540/628-2788

### *Great Places To Stay*

**River Garden Bed and Breakfast**
19080 N. Fork River Road
1-800-952-4296; 540/676-0335
7 days a week, year round
Rates: $60-65
*Directions: Exit 17 off I-81 in Virginia following signs to Abingdon, and the road becomes Cumings St. Continue on Cumings St. to Valley St. (dead end), and take a left on Valley St. At Russell Road (dead end) turn right. Go to Highway 19 N. Turn right on 19 north (Porterfield Hwy.). At Route 611 (North Fork River Road) turn right. River Garden is 2 1/2 miles on the right.*

The River Garden Bed and Breakfast, located on the bank of the Holston River, and seated at the base of Clinch Mountain, provides a beautiful welcome sight for travelers. Each room has its own private bath. Rooms are furnished with antique and period furniture, complete with full, queen, or king beds. To make the stay feel more homey, guests are welcome to share the kitchen area, living room, den, and dining room. Enjoy the deck from each room, which overlooks the Holston River. With private entrances, guests are invited to come and go as they please.

Full breakfast is served each morning by the delightful hosts Carol and Bill Crump.

**Maplewood Farm B&B**
20004 Cleveland Road
540/628-2640

Maplewood Farm is truly a naturalist's haven. The 66-acre horse farm, originally part of a King's grant, has high wooded land with hiking trails and a lake stocked with bass and sunfish. The home, circa 1880, is a beautifully renovated farmhouse shaded by old maple trees, hence the name Maplewood Farm. Two guest rooms and a two-bedroom suite all include private baths. Full breakfasts are served in the Garden Room or on an outside deck overlooking the lake and meadow.

## 2 AFTON

**Whitehouse Antiques**
2621 Greenfield Road
540/942-1194
Mon.-Sun. 10-5
*Directions: Exit 99 from I-64 (Waynesboro/Afton exit). Exit 107 from I-64 (Crozet Exit). U.S. Route 250 to State Route 6 on the east side of Afton Mountain*

With a building over 100 years old as home and Virginia's famous Blue Ridge Mountains as landscape, Whitehouse Antiques presents fine American antiques in room settings. Specializing in furniture from country to formal, many pieces are local antiques selected from area estates. Decorative and accessory "smalls," also available, provide distinctive touches to any decor.

**Antiques @ Afton**
State Route 6
540/456-6515

## 3 ALEXANDRIA

**Belgravia Fine Art**
411 Cameron St.
703/548-7702

**Reunions**
1719 Centre Plaza
703/931-8161

**Bird-In-The-Cage Antiques**
110 King St.
703/549-5114

**Antiques on King Street**
917 King St.
703/739-9750

**French Country Antiques**
1000 King St.
703/548-8563

**Iron Gate Antiques**
1007 King St.
703/549-7429

**King Street Antiques**
1015 King St.
703/549-0883

**Random Harvest**
1117 King St.
703/548-8820

**Banana Tree**
1223 King St.
703/836-4317

**Odds & Ends Antique Shop**
1325 King St.
703/836-6722

**Michelines Antiques**
1600 King St.
703/836-1893

**Cambridge Classics**
210 N. Lee St.
703/739-2877

**Old Town Antiques**
210 N. Lee St.
703/519-0009

**Teacher's Pet Antiques**
210 N. Lee St.
703/549-9766

**Times Juggler**
210 N. Lee St.
703/836-3594

**Trojan Antiques**
210 N. Lee St.
703/549-9766

**Trojan Antiques Too**
216 N. Lee St.
703/836-5410

**Reflections Antiques**
222 N. Lee St.
703/683-6808

**Alexandria Coin Sales**
6550 Little River Turnpike
703/354-3700

**Trojan Three**
320 Prince St.
703/548-8558

**Thieves Market Antiques Center**
8101 Richmond Hwy.
703/360-4200

**Lenore & Daughters Antiques**
130 S. Royal St.
703/836-3356

**James Wilholt Antiques**
150 N. Saint Asaph St.
703/683-6595

**Old Colony Shop**
222 S. Washington St.
703/548-8008

**Donna Lee's Cllbls. & Rare Book Shop**
419 S. Washington St.
703/548-5830

**Sumpter Priddy III Inc.**
601 S. Washington St.
703/299-0800

**Antiques of Essence**
5801 Duke St.
703/642-8831

**Alexandria's House of Antiques**
124 S. West St.
703/836-3912

**Boxwood Antiques & Fine Art**
603 Cameron St.
703/518-4444

**uropean Concepts**
009 King St.
03/739-8885

**loyd's Row**
19 S. Henry St.
03/684-1711

**Presidential Coin & Antique Co.**
6550 Little River Turnpike
703/354-5454

**Cavalier Antiques**
400 Prince St.
703/836-2539

**Jane's Antiques**
8853 Richmond Hwy.
703/360-1428

**Seaport Traders Arts & Antiques**
1201 N. Royal St.
703/684-2901

**Icon Gallery**
101 N. Union
703/739-0700

**Brockett's Row Antiques & Fine Art**
303 N. Washington St.
703/684-0464

**Studio Antiques & Fine Art**
524 N. Washington St.
703/548-5188

**Frances Simmons Antiques**
619 S. Washington St.
703/549-1291

**Alan Marschke's Gallery**
687 S. Washington St.
703/548-0909

**Antique Warehouse**
8123 Richmond Hwy.
703/360-4700

**Curzon Hill Antiques**
108 S. Columbus St.
703/684-0667

**Hulda's Antiques**
1518 Belle View Blvd.
703/765-5159

**Washington Square Antiques**
689 S. Washington St.
703/836-3214

## 4 AMELIA COURT HOUSE

**melia Antique Mall**
hurch St.
4/561-2511

**denes Antiques**
710 Patrick Henry Hwy.
4/561-3333

**rry's Now & Then**
urt St.
4/561-5075

**Cindy Garrett Antiques**
13241 Mount Olive Lane
804/561-3999

**Emerson Antique Mall & Cllbls.**
19720 Patrick Henry Hwy.
804/561-5276

## 5 ANNANDALE

**Heart's Desire**
7120 Little River Turnpike
703/916-0361

**Antique Medley**
7120 Little River Turnpike
703/354-6279

**Chris' Collectibles**
7120 Little River Turnpike
703/941-0361

**Chrystal Mint**
7120 Little River Turnpike
703/256-6688

**The Cottage**
7120 Little River Turnpike
703/256-6688

**Dlove's Antiques**
7120 Little River Turnpike
703/256-6688

**French Connection**
7120 Little River Turnpike
703/256-6688

**Guinevere's Journey**
7120 Little River Turnpike
703/941-0130

**Joan's**
7120 Little Rive Turnpike
703/256-6688

**Kabul Antiques & Jewelry**
7120 Little River Turnpike
703/642-8260

**Lady Randolph's**
7120 Little River Turnpike
703/750-1609

**Misty Memories**
7120 Little River Turnpike
703/642-1052

**Osbourne House**
7120 Little River Turnpike
703/256-6688

**Peggotly Antiques & Collectibles**
7120 Little River Turnpike
703/642-5750

**Shamma's Antiques**
7120 Little River Turnpike
703/750-6439

**Southerland**
7120 Little River Turnpike
703/256-6688

**Krueger's Antique Plus**
7129 Little River Turnpike
703/941-3644

**Bill Siaz**
7120 Little River Turnpike
703/256-6688

**Christian Deschamps**
7120 Little River Turnpike
703/256-6688

**The Clock Works**
7120 Little River Turnpike
703/256-6688

**David's Place**
7120 Little River Turnpike
703/256-6688

**Figaro Gallery**
7120 Little River Turnpike
703/354-3200

**Gene's Antiques**
7120 Little River Turnpike
703/256-6688

**Henrys Antiques**
7120 Little River Turnpike
703/256-6688

**JR's**
7120 Little River Turnpike
703/256-6688

**Kim's Country House**
7120 Little River Turnpike
703/256-6688

**Mary's Antiques**
7120 Little River Turnpike
703/256-6688

**The Old Crank**
7120 Little River Turnpike
703/256-6688

**Past Pleasure Antiques**
7120 Little River Turnpike
703/256-6688

**Rags To Riches**
7120 Little River Turnpike
703/941-0130

**Showcase Antiques**
7120 Little River Turnpike
703/941-0130

**Vintage Radio**
7120 Little Rive Turnpike
703/256-6688

**Virgilian Fine Arts, Antiques & Collectibles**
7120 Little River Turnpike
703/256-6688

**And Antiques**
7129 Little River Turnpike
703/941-7360

**Grammies Collectibles**
7129 Little River Turnpike
703/642-3999

**Ken's Antiques**
7129 Little River Turnpike
703/750-5453

## 6 ARLINGTON

**Granny's Attic**
3911 Lee Hwy.
703/812-0389

**Consignments Unlimited**
2645 N. Pershing Dr.
703/276-0051

**Corner Cupboard**
2649 N. Pershing Dr.
703/276-0060

**Something Unique**
933 N. Quincy St.
703/807-2432

**Book Ends**
2710 Washington Blvd.
703/524-4976

**Home Artifacts**
2836 Wilson Blvd.
703/812-8348

## 7 ASHLAND

**Billy's Collectibles**
12083 Washington Hwy.
804-798-9414

**Brumble's Antiques**
10449 Design Road
804/752-5871

### *Great Places To Stay*

**Henry Clay Inn**
114 N. Railroad Ave.
1-800-343-4565

Enjoy the small town atmosphere of Ashland and take advantage of its central location to the historic areas of Richmond, Williamsburg, Charlottesville and Fredericksburg. This fifteen room Georgian Revival inn is furnished in antique reproductions with private baths and other amenities.

## 8 BEDFORD

**Elizabeth N Gladwell & Associates**
124 S. Bridge St.
540/586-4567

**Bridge Street Antiques**
201 N. Bridge St.
540/586-6611

**Hamilton's**
155 W. Main St.
540/586-5592

**Granny's Antiques & Etc.**
Route 460 E.
540/586-6861

**Stoney Creek Antiques**
Route 460 W.
540/586-0166

**Olde Liberty Antique Mall**
802 E. Washington St.
540/586-3804

**Bedford Antique Mall**
109 S. Bridge St.
540/587-9322

## 9 BLACKSBURG

**Other Times Ltd.**
891 Kabrich St.
540/552-1615

**Grady's Antiques**
208 N. Main St.
540/951-0623

**Heirlooms Originals**
609 N. Main St.
540/552-9241

**Whitaker's Antiques**
1102 Progress St.
540/552-1186

## 10 BRISTOL

**Antiques on Commonwealth**
57 Commonwealth Ave.
540/669-1886

**Bristol Antique Mall**
403 Commonwealth Ave.
540/466-4064

**Abe's Antiques**
411 Commonwealth Ave.
540/466-6895

**Frank's Antiques**
413 Commonwealth Ave.
540/669-4138

**Art History & Antiques**
42 Piedmont Ave.
540/669-6491

**Heritage Antiques**
625 State St.
540/669-9774

**Pete Moore Antiques**
1615 W. State St.
540/669-2333

## 11 CANA

**Thelma Lou's Antiques & Collectibles Inc.**
Route. 1, Box 43-A
Hwy. 52 N.
540/755-2858
*Directions: Located in Cana, Va., between Mt. Airy, N.C., Andy Griffith's hometown, and the Blue Ridge Parkway at Fancy Gap, Va., on Scenic Hwy. 52. From I-77 south in Virginia, Exit #8, turn left go 1/2 mile to Hwy. 52. Turn right, go approximately 7 miles. On your right next to Nance Interiors.*
*From I-77 north in North Carolina, Exit #100 onto Route 89. Turn right. Go 7 1/4 miles to Hwy. 52 By-Pass North. Go 6 1/2 miles. On left next to Nance Interiors.*

Thelma Lou's is a wonderful collectibles shop offering Gone With the Wind, Wizard of Oz and Mayberry collectibles, plus a large selection of Madame Alexander, Seymour Mann and other dolls. In addition to the collectibles, there are thirty quality dealers with a nice variety of furniture, glassware, cookie jars, carnival glass, bottles, old paints and more.

**Antique House**
Hwy. 52
540/755-4700

**Mountain Side Antiques**
Hwy. 52
540/755-3875

**Van Noppen T P Antiques**
Hwy. 52
540/755-4382

## 12 CAPE CHARLES

**Charmer's Antique**
211 Mason Ave.
757/331-1488

### *Great Places To Stay*

**Bay Avenue's Sunset Bed & Breakfast**
108 Bay Ave.
757/331-2424
Rates: $75-85
*Directions: From Route 13 traffic light, go west 2 miles on Route 184 to Chesapeake Bay. Turn right, 4th house.*

Unwind under the spell of a by-gone era in a 1915 Victorian home nestled directly on Chesapeake Bay. This recipient of AAA's 3 diamond rating and American Bed and Breakfast Association's 3 crown "Excellent" Award offers accommodations with individual decor including the Victorian Room (period wallpaper, window seat, pedestal sink, old claw foot tub), Sheena Room (extra large contemporary with a touch of the rain forest), the Courtney Room (white wicker furniture, bay view), and the Abigail Room (colonial in decor). The common area provides a view of the bay from 3 windows. Sitting back in a rocker on the west-facing front porch is a delightful way to soak in the sunset. The nearby historic district is host to several quaint antique and specialty shops.

## 13 CHARLOTTESVILLE

**Aaron's Attic**
1700 Allied St.
804/295-5760

**First Street Antiques**
107 N. 1st St.
804/295-7650

**Stedman House**
201 E. High St.
804/295-0671

**1740 House Antiques & Fine Art**
3449 Ivy Road (Route 250 W.)
804/977-1740

**Consignment House Unlimited**
21 W. Main St.
04/977-5527

**yster House Antiques**
19 E. Main St.
04/295-4757

**eloach Antiques**
211 W. Main St.
4/979-7209

**Heartwood Books**
59 Elliewood Ave.
804/295-7083

**Court Square Antiques**
216 4th St.
804/295-6244

**Eternal Attic**
2125 Ivy Road
804/977-2667

**Ming-Quing Antiques**
111 Main St.
804/979-8426

**20th Century Art & Antiques**
201 E. Main St.
804/296-6818

**Daniel Chenn Gallery**
619 W. Main St.
804/977-8890

**1817 Antique Inn**
1211 W. Main St.
804/979-7353

**Jefferson Coin Shop**
301 E. Market St.
804/295-1765

**The Antiquers Mall**
Route 29 N.
804/973-3478

**Kenny Ball Antiques**
Ivy Commons
804/293-1361

**Second Wind**
1117 E. Market St.
804/296-1413

**Renaissance Gallery**
By Appointment Only
804/296-9208

### *Great Places To Stay*

**The Inn at Monticello**
Hwy. 20 S.
1188 Scottsville Road
804/979-3593

The Inn at Monticello is a charming country manor house built circa 1850. The property has the quiet atmosphere of a lovely classic getaway spot, enhanced by a bubbling brook, flowers and trees, with lovely mountain views. Guest rooms, each with private bath, are uniquely decorated in period antiques and fine reproductions, all coordinated with the elegance and comforts befitting a romantic country inn. Gourmet breakfasts are outstanding.

**The Inn at the Crossroads**
P.O. Box 6519
804/979-6452
Web site: www.crossroadsinn.com

Registered as a Virginia historic landmark, the inn has been welcoming travelers since 1820. Located on four-acres in the foothills of the Blue Ridge Mountains, it is a charming four-story brick building with timber framing and an English kitchen on the lower level. Its' simple Federal style is characteristic of the public houses of that period. Separate from the main building, a two room cottage offers guests that honeymoon-like escape.

## 14 CHESAPEAKE

**American Antiques at Blue Ridge**
1505 Blue Ridge Road
757/482-7330

**Cal's Antiques**
928 Canal Dr.
757/485-1895

**Maria's Antiques & Collectibles**
3021 S. Military Hwy.
757/485-1799

**Way Back Yonder Antiques**
916 Canal Dr.
757/487-8459

**Fran's Antiques**
3017 S. Military Hwy.
757/485-1656

**Chesapeake House Antiques**
3040 S. Military Hwy.
757/487-2219

**T-N-T Treasures**
3044 S. Military Hwy.
757/485-3927

**Now & Then Shop**
3112 S. Military Hwy.
757/485-1383

**Quiet Shoppe Saddlery**
3935 Poplar Hill Road
757/483-9358

## 15 CHINCOTEAGUE

### *Great Places To Stay*

**Island Manor House**
4160 Main St.
757-336-5436

The Island Manor House, built in 1848, was the grand home of Nathaniel Smith, the island's first doctor, who tended troops during the Civil War. Beautifully restored in Federal style, the inn offers eight lovely guestrooms, six with private baths, furnished with antiques to provide a warm and comfortable ambiance. Noteworthy are the Garden Room where guests relax by the fireplace amid collections of antiques, fine art, and rare books.

## 16 CHRISTIANSBURG

**Cambria Emporium**
596 Depot St. N.E.
540/381-0949

### *Great Places To Stay*

**The Oaks Victorian Inn**
311 E. Main St.
540/381-1500
Open year round
*Directions: From I-81, take Exit 114. At the bottom of the ramp, turn left if approaching from the south, and right if approaching from the north. You are on Main St., so is the Oaks. Continue for approximately 2 miles to fork at Park and Main St., bear right on Park, then left into the Oaks' driveway. From the Blue Ridge Parkway take Route 8 (MP 165) through Floyd to Christiansburg. Route 8 becomes Main St. Follow earlier directions.*

For specific information see review at the beginning of this section.

**Evergreen The Bell-Capozzi House**
201 E. Main St.
1-800-905-7372 or 540/382-7372
Web site: www.bnt.com/evergreen
Email: evegrninn@aol
*Directions: For specific directions, please call the Innkeepers.*

For specific information see review at the beginning of this section.

## 17 CLIFTON FORGE

**Mary's Antiques & Collectibles**
608 Main St.
540/863-8577

**Always Roxie's**
622 Main St.
540/862-2999

**Dews Etc.**
420 E. Ridgeway
No phone

## 18 COLONIAL HEIGHTS

**Blue and Gray Relic Shop**
2012 Boulevard
804/526-6863

**T J's Corner**
17100 Jefferson Davis Hwy.
804/526-3074

**Friendly Hearth Antiques**
17002 Jefferson Davis Hwy.
804/526-1900

## 19 CULPEPER

**Country Shoppes Of Culpeper**
10046 James Monroe Hwy. (U.S. 29 N.)
540/547-4000
Mon.-Sat. 9-6, and Sun. 12-5
*Directions: Located on U.S. Hwy. 29 (James Monroe Hwy.) 2 mi. south of Culpeper, Va., and 35 miles west of I-95/Route 3 Fredericksburg exit.*

One hundred dealers have stuffed this 15,000-square-foot mall full of antique furniture, accessories, collectibles, glassware, jewelry, and so much more. Unique gifts and gourmet foods enhance the selection. Daily additions to vendor's wares increase possibilities and variety.

**ACE Books & Antiques**
120 W. Culpeper St.
540/825-8973

**Barter Post at Davis Street**
179 E. Davis St.
540/829-6814

**Minute Man Mini Mall**
746 Germanna Hwy.
540/825-3133

**Leonard's Antiques & Collectibles**
10042 James Monroe Hwy.
540/547-4104

## 20 DANVILLE

**Pikes End Antiques**
103 Franklin Turnpike
804/836-2449

**Judy Adkins Antiques**
230 Lamberth Dr.
804/822-2257

**John's Antiques**
2011 N. Main St.
804/793-7961

**Finders Antique House**
1169 Piney Forest Road
804/836-6782

**Majestic Interiors**
127 Tunstall Road
804/792-2521

**Antiques Cellar English Imports**
643 Tunstall Road
804/792-1966

**Westover Antiques**
2720 Westover Dr.
804/822-0443

## 21 DISPUTANTA

**Antiques Junction**
10020 County Dr.
804/991-2463

**Mule Shed**
10026 County Dr.
804/991-2115

**Kathy's Hideway Antiques**
10032 County Dr.
804/991-2061

**Yesterdays Treasure**
9909 County Dr.
804/991-3013

## 22 DYKE

### *Great Places To Stay*

**Cottages at Chesley Creek Farm**
P.O. Box 52
804/985-7129

Chesley Creek Farm is situated on 200 acres in the Blue Ridge Mountains, twenty eight miles northwest of Charlottesville. There are two cottages on the property, Creek House and LaurelWood. All dishes and utensils necessary for preparing meals are provided with gas BBQ grills on the deck. All towels and linens are furnished.

## 23 EDINBURG

**Richard's Antiques**
14211 Old Valley Pike
540/984-4502

## 24 EMPORIA

**Dutchman's Treasures**
135 E. Atlantic St.
804/634-2267

**Reid's of Emporia**
408 S. Main St.
804/634-6536

## 25 FAIRFAX

**Culpeper Shoppe**
1821 Lee Hwy.
703/631-0405

**My Home Shop**
12501 Lee Hwy.
703/631-0554

**Fairfax Antique Mall**
10334 Main St.
703/591-8883

## 26 FALLS CHURCH

**Falls Church Antique Co. Ltd.**
[illegible]0 W. Broad St.
703/241-7074

**Old Market Antiques**
442 S. Washington St.
703/241-1722

**Place Where Louie Dwells**
[illegible]1 N. Maple Ave.
703/237-5312

## 27 FARMVILLE

**Granny's Attic**
Hwy. 15 N.
804/392-8699

**Suzi's Antiques**
235 N. Main St.
804/392-4655

**Poplar Hall Antiques**
308 N. Main St.
804/392-1658

**Mottley Emporium**
518 N. Main St.
804/392-4698

## 28 FREDERICKSBURG

Long before Union and Confederate cannons fired across the rolling hills, Fredericksburg was already rich in Colonial and Revolutionary history. George Washington grew up at Ferry Farm, where legend has it that he swung an axe against a cherry tree. Patriots like Thomas Jefferson and James Monroe knew Fredericksburg well. In four of the Civil War's bloodiest battles, armies under Lee and Grant fought to decide the course of our nation.

History is still alive today in more than 350 original 18th and 19th century buildings all contained within a 40-block National Historic District. The buildings house antique and gift shops as well as many fine restaurants.

**Caroline Square**
910-916 Caroline St.
540/371-4454
Mon.-Sat. 10-5, Sun. 12-5
*Directions: From I-95, take the Fredericksburg-Culpeper Exit to Route 3 which becomes William St. in Fredericksburg. Turn right at Caroline St. Or from I-95, take the Massaponax-Fredericksburg Exit onto Route 1 which jogs to the left to become Jefferson Davis Hwy., then left onto Caroline St.*

A rich collection of the past awaits you in this court of shops featuring fifty dealers. Choose from antique furniture and collectibles, quilts, dolls, as well as Shaker furniture. Most shops welcome special orders.

**Neat Stuff**
109 Amelia St.
540/373-7115

**Picket Post**
602 Caroline St.
540/371-7703

**Bonannos Antiques Inc.**
619 Caroline St.
540/373-3331

**Beck's Antiques & Books**
708 Caroline St.
540/371-1766

**Morland House Antiques**
714 Caroline St.
540/373-6144

**Blockade Runner**
719 Caroline St.
540/374-9346

**Pavilion Inc.**
723 Caroline St.
540/371-0850

**Future Antiques**
820 Caroline St.
540/899-6229

**Busy B's Treasures**
822 Caroline St .
540/899-9185

**Antique Corner Fredericksburg**
900 Caroline St.
540373-0826

**Upstairs Downstairs Antiques**
922 Caroline St.
540/373-0370

**Antique Court of Shoppes**
1001 Caroline St.
540/371-0685

**Willow Hill Antiques**
1001 Caroline St.
540/371-0685

**Fredericksburg Antique Gallery**
1023 Caroline St.
540/373-2961

**Past And Present**
5099 Jefferson Davis Hwy.
540/891-8977

**Consignment Junction Ltd.**
2012 Lafayette Blvd.
540/898-2344

**Gold Rooster Consignment**
4010 Lafayette Blvd.
540/898-4349

**Antique Village**
4800 Plank Road
540/786-9648

**Amore Antiques Collectibles & Gifts**
1011 Princess Anne St.
540/372-3740

**Virginians Antiques Inc.**
2217 Princess Anne St.
540/371-2288

**Sophia Street Antiques**
915 Sophia St.
540/899-3881

**She-Kees Antique Gallery**
919 Sophia St.
540/899-3808

**Gary L Johnson Antiques**
1005 Sophia St.
540/371-7141

**Country Crossing**
106 William St.
540/371-4588

**Liberty Park Antiques**
208 William St.
540/371-5309

**Fredericksburg Antique Mall**
211 William St.
540/372-6894

**Century Shop**
202 Wolfe St.
540/371-7734

**Southern Heritage Antiques**
107 William St.
540/371-0200

***Great Places To Stay***

**Richard Johnston Inn**
711 Caroline St.
504/899-7606

This elegant bed and breakfast was constructed in the mid to late 1700s and served as the home of Richard Johnston, Mayor of Fredericksburg from 1809 to 1810. The inn still reflects all the grace and charm of a past era, while providing all the amenities necessary for the traveler of today. The seven bedrooms and two suites have been decorated with antiques and reproductions and all have private baths.

## 29 GALAX

**Vernon's Antiques**
Hwy. 58
540/236-6390

**Antique Apple**
118 S. Main St.
540/236-0881

**L & H Antiques**
Main St.
No phone

**Robert's Gift Gallery**
203 S. Main St.
540/238-8877

## 30 GLEN ALLEN

**Dixie Trading Co.**
9911 Brook Road
804/266-6733

**Treasures Inc.**
9915 Greenwood Road
804/264-8478

**Dick & Jeanette's Antiques**
10770 Staples Mill Road
804/672-6138

**Wigwam Reservation Shops**
10412 Washington Hwy.-Route # 1
804/550-9698

**Singletree Antiques**
10717 Staples Mill Road
804/672-3795

## 31 HAMPTON

**Odessey Village & Old Village Books**
26 S. King St.
757/727-0028

**Poquoson Antique Shop**
969 N. King St.
757/723-0501

**Victorian Station**
36 N. Mallory St.
757/723-5663

**Return Engagements**
18 E. Mellen St.
757/722-0617

**Free City Traders**
22 Mellen St.
757/722-3899

**The Way We Were Antiques**
33 E. Mellen St.
757/726-2300

**CC & Co.**
1729 W. Pembroke Ave.
757/727-0766

**Chuck's Anything Shop**
3927 Kecoughtan Road
757/727-0740

## 32 HARRISONBURG

**Bea's Bears & Variety Shop**
Hwy. 724
540/434-3337

**Rolling Hills Antique Mall**
779 E. Market St.
540/433-8988

**Villager Antiques**
673 N. Main St.
540/433-7226

For a great place to stay while visiting in the Harrisonburg area see New Market #43.

## 33 HOPEWELL

**Bargain Bazaar**
201 E. Broadway Ave.
804/458-1122

**Hamilton's Civil War Relic**
257 E. Broadway Ave.
804/458-6504

**Curio Shop**
501 N. 7th Ave.
804/458-7990

**AAA Antiques**
2602 Oaklawn Blvd.
804/452-0967

**Junk Shop**
3305 Oaklawn Blvd.
804/458-3473

## 34 KING GEORGE

**End-Of-Lane Antiques**
9553 James Madison Pkwy.
540/755-9838

**Shadyview Antiques**
9294 Lambs Creek Church
540/775-0506

**Swamp Fox Antiques**
9553 James Madison Pkwy.
540/775-5534

## 35 LEESBURG

Travel south on U.S. 15 to Leesburg, described by the National Register as "one of the best preserved, most picturesque communities in Virginia."

The Loudoun Museum in downtown Leesburg displays artifacts chronicling the area's colorful history from the Colonial era to the 20th century. Take a walking tour past more than fifty historic structures, and enjoy summer Sunday evenings with the music from the Bluemont Concert Series on the Courthouse lawn.

**Loudoun Antiques Marketplace**
850 Davis St. S.E. (Route. 15 South)
703/777-5358

**Leesburg Antq. "Court of Shoppes"**
Route 15, 2.5 Miles
703/777-7799

**Leesburg Downtown Antique Center**
27 S. King St.
703/779-8130

**Leesburg Antique Gallery**
7 Wirt St. S.W.
703/777-2366

**Leesburg Antique Emporium**
32 S. King St.
703/777-3553

**Spurgeon-Lewis Antiques**
219 W. Market St.
703/777-6606

**Loudoun Street Antiques**
3 Loudoun St. S.W.
703/779-4009

**Crafters Gallery**
9 W. Market St.
703/771-9017

**K & L Market St. Antiques**
5 E. Market St.
703/443-1827

**Preston's Antiques**
1 Loudoun St. S.W.
703/777-6055

**Catheran C. Johnston Antiques**
101 S. King St.
703/777-3337

**My Wit's End**
12810 James Monroe Hwy.
703/777-1561

**Uncle Sam's Attic Antiques**
Loudoun St. S.W., #B
703/777-5588

## 36 LEXINGTON

**Lexington Antique & Craft Mall**
Hwy. 11
540/463-9511

**A. Fairfax Antiques**
13 W. Nelson
540/463-9885

**Lexington Antiques**
5 W. Washington St.
540/463-9519

### *Great Places To Stay*

**Inn at Union Run**
325 Union Run Road
1-800-528-6466
Web site: www.virtualcities.com/ons/va/r/var1602.htm

This 1883 manor house is located on a creekfront mountainside three miles from historic Lexington and is situated on ten picturesque acres with views of the Allegheny and Blue Ridge mountain ranges. Located along the Union Run Creek, where the Union Army camped during and after the Battle of Lexington, the inn's name is derived from the Civil War event. The inn offers eight spacious guestrooms, all with private baths, and six with Jacuzzis. The common area and the guestrooms are filled with authentic period antiques, including Meissen porcelain, Venetian glass and furniture collections. Many of these antiques are from the estate of S. S. Kresege, Helena Rubenstein, Henry Wadsworth Longfellow and Winston Churchill.

## 37 LURAY

**Woods Antiques**
Hwy. 211 E.
540/743-4406

**Wanda's Wonders**
Hwy. 340 S.
540/743-4197

**Mama's Treasures**
22 E. Main St.
540/743-1352

**James McHone Antiques**
24 E. Main St.
540/743-9001

**Zib's Country Connection**
24 E. Main St.
540/743-7394

**Luray Antique Depot**
49 E. Main St.
540/743-1298

**P Buckley Moss Gallery**
Mimslyn Inn-Main St.
540/743-5105

## 38 LYNCHBURG

**James River Antiques Lynchburg**
503 Clay St.
804/528-1960

**Dee's Antiques**
1724 Lakeside Dr.
804/385-4008

**Scarlett's Treasures Antique Mall**
1026 Main St.
804/528-0488

**Sweeneys Curious Goods**
1220 Main St.
804/846-7839

**Langhorne-Stokes Antiques**
1421 Main St.
804/846-7452

**Redcoat Gallery & Antiques**
1421 Main St.
804/528-3182

**Saks Ally**
172 Norfolk Ave.
804/846-4712

**Jackson's Antiques**
2627 Old Forest Road
804/384-6411

**Time & Again Antiques**
2909 Old Forest Road
804/384-4807

**Lynchburg Florist & Antiques Inc.**
3224 Old Forest Road
804/385-6566

**Wildwood Antique Market**
195 Old Timberlake Road
804/525-0207

### *Great Places To Stay*

**1880s Madison House Bed and Breakfast**
413 Madison St.
1-800-828-6422
Web site: www.bbhost.com/1880s-madison

The 1880s Madison House is an elegantly restored Victorian bed and breakfast whose nine-colored painted exterior testifies to something wonderful within. The bed and breakfast opened in Lynchburg in 1990 and is located in the Garland Hill Historic District, one of five historic districts in the city. The home retains its authentic Victorian appeal throughout the house, and offers many amenities including warm, soft robes.

## 39 MANASSAS

Travel east on U.S. 50, west on U.S. 15 and east on I-66 to Manassas, an important Civil War site.

Step back in time at Rohr's, an old-time variety store and museum with tin ceilings, penny candy and displays of antique toys, household and business items.

Take the walking trail at Manassas National Battlefield Park — scene of two Civil War battles known in the South as First and Second Manassas — that leads to Henry Hill with a panoramic view of the battlefield where Confederate Gen. Thomas "Stonewall" Jackson earned his nickname. The driving tour will take you to key points of interest in the fields. The visitor center of the 5,000 acre battlefield park features exhibits, a slide presentation and a map program explaining movements of the opposing armies on an intricate scale model of the battlefield.

**Delisle Antiques**
9115 Center St.
703/330-1160

**Laws Antique Complex**
7209 Centreville Road
703/631-0590

**Roger's Antiques**
7217 Centreville Road
703/368-3366

**Silk Purse**
7217 Centreville Road
703/369-7817

**Wicker Place Antiques**
7305 Centreville Road
703/361-8622

**Cunningham Antiques**
7217 Centreville Road
703/335-6534

**Don Mattingly Antiques**
7217 Centreville Road
703/368-2252

**First Impressions**
8388 Centreville Road
703/369-5696

**Law's Antique Center**
7208 Centreville Road
703/330-9282

**Lilian's Antiques**
7217 Centreville Road
703/361-7712

**Manassas Treasures**
9023 Centreville Road
703/368-8222

**Sam's Coins & Decoys**
7208 Centreville Road
703/361-3199

**Traditions**
7618 Centreville Road
703/361-4303

**Yorkshire Furniture Co.**
7312 Centreville Road
703/361-4697

## 40 McLEAN

**Lilly Parker Antiques Inc.**
1317 A Chain Bridge Road
703/893-5298

**Solovey Jewelers Inc.**
1475 Chain Bridge Road
703/356-0138

**East And Beyond Ltd.**
6727 Curran St.
703/448-8200

**Folk Art Gallery**
6216 Old Dominion Drive
703/532-6923

**Abbott Gallery & Framing**
6673 Old Dominion Dr.
703/893-2010

**Lights Fantastic**
6825 Tennyson
703/356-2285

## 41 MECHANICSVILLE

**Mechanicsville Antique Mall**
7508 Mechanicsville Turnpike
804/730-5091
Daily 10-5
*Directions: Once on 295 take Exit 37B; from the Main 360 take first right. (Business 360)*

In August, 1997, Mechanicsville Antique Mall was voted the 2nd Best Antique Mall in Richmond by *Richmond Magazine*. This comes as no surprise since this 30,000 square foot mall is jammed packed with over 100 booths and 25 showcase galleries featuring the best in early American, Victorian, golden oak, art pottery, art glass, toys and clocks. The mall even offers clock repair. Be sure to check out Hanover Auction House - adjacent to the antique mall. For information on fine quality estate auctions, call 1-800-694-0759.

**Antique Village**
10203 Chamberlayne Road
804/746-8914

**Governor's Antiques Ltd.**
Polegrain Road
804/746-1030

**Maplewood Farm Antiques**
10203 Chamberlayne Road
804/730-0698

**Whitings Old Paper at Village**
6700 Chamberlayne Road
804/746-4710

## 42 NEW CHURCH

**Bluewater Trading Co.**
6180 Lankford Hwy.
757/824-3124

**Worchester House**
Lankford Hwy.
757/824-3847

## 43 NEW MARKET

**New Mkt. Btlfld. Civil War Military Mus.**
9500 Collins Dr.
540/740-8065

**B & B Valley Antiques**
9294 N. Congress St.
540/740-8700

**Elliot's Vly Shenandoah Antiques**
9298 N. Congree St.
540/740-3827

**Benny Long's Antiques**
9386 N. Congress St.
540/740-3512

**Paper Treasures**
9595 S. Congress St.
540/740-3135

**Antiques by Burt Long**
345 Old Valley Pike
540/740-3777

### *Great Places To Stay*

### Cross Roads Inn Bed and Breakfast

9222 John Sevier Road
540/740-4157
Offering year round accommodations
Rates: $55-100
*Directions: Take Exit 264 (New Market) off I-81. Go east on Route 211 through town 3/4 mile.*

Cross Roads Inn features bedrooms with English floral wallpapers and tasteful antiques, including four-poster and canopy beds with cozy down comforters. Each bedroom has a private bath.

Gourmet breakfast, included with your room, is served in the sunny breakfast room, or on the terrace. Served with your breakfast are home baked European breads and muffins as well as gourmet Austrian coffee.

Their Austrian tradition of hospitality includes your first cup of coffee in your room if you desire, and afternoon coffee/tea with Mary-Lloyd's famous strudel.

## 44 NEWPORT NEWS

**Lorraine's**
758 J Clyde Morris Blvd.
757/596-1886

**Brill's Antiques**
10527 Jefferson Ave.
757/596-5333

**ine Arts Shop**
0178 Warwick Blvd.
57/595-7754

**Another Mans Treasure**
10239 Warwick Blvd.
757/596-3739

**hameleon**
0363 Warwick Blvd.
57/596-9324

**Plantiques Hilton Village**
10377 Warwick Blvd.
757/595-1545

**enbigh Antique & Collectible Mall**
3811 Warwick Blvd.
57/875-5221

**Debs Antiques & Collectibles**
13595 Warwick Blvd.
757/886-0883

## 45 NORFOLK

**nne Spencer Antiques**
5 Botetourt St.
7/624-9156

**Gale Goss Country French Antiques**
1607 Colley Ave.
757/625-1211

**ros Antiques & Appraisals**
01 Colonial Ave.
7/627-1111

**Nick Nack's Collectibles & Antiques**
1905 Colonial Ave.
757/533-9545

**llingsworth Antiques**
9 Granby St.
7/625-6525

**Fran's Fantasies Granby St. Antique**
1022 Granby St.
757/622-6996

**Nineteenth Century Antiques**
1804 Granby St.
757/622-0905

**Grey Horse Antiques**
1904 Granby St.
757/626-3152

**Country Boy's Antiques**
1912 Granby St.
757/627-3630

**David's Antiques**
2410 Granby St.
757/627-6376

**A Touch of Mystery**
2412 Granby St.
757/622-7907

**Decades Art & Antiques**
2608 Granby St.
757/627-0785

**A Niche In Tyme**
9631 Granby St.
757/588-1684

**Wooden Things II**
2715 Monticello Ave.
757/624-1273

**Merlo's**
131 W. Olney Road
757/622-2699

**G Carr Ltd. Art & Antiques**
522 W. 20th St.
757/624-1289

**Carriage House Antiques**
110 W. 21st St.
757/625-4504

**Fairfax Shop**
120 W. 21st St.
757/625-5539

**Grapevine of Ghent**
122 W. 21st St.
757/627-0519

**Richard Levins Garfields**
122 W. 21st St.
757/622-0414

**Intrntl Antiques Importers Co.**
240 W. 21st St.
757/624-9658

**Morgan House Antiques Gallery**
242 W. 21st St.
757/627-2486

**Palace Antiques Gallery**
300 W. 21st St.
757/622-2733

**Primrose**
400 W. 21st St.
757/624-8473

**Ghent Antique & Consignment Emporium**
517 W. 21st St.
757/627-1900

**Norfolk Antique Co.**
537 W. 21st St.
757/627-6199

**Scott & Company**
537 W. 21st St.
757/640-1319

**Monticello Antique Shop**
227 W. York St.
757/622-4124

**Di-Antiques**
5901 E. Virginia Beach Blvd.
757/466-1717

**Nautical Antiques & Ntcl Furniture**
6150 E. Virginia Beach Blvd.
757/461-2465

**A Touch of Mystery**
333 Waterside Dr.
757/627-9684

## 46 OCCOQUAN

**Country Hollow**
210 A Commerce St.
703/490-1877

**Commerce Street Gallery**
204 Commerce St.
703/491-9020

**Heart of Occoquan**
305 Mill St.
703/492-9158

**Sisters**
308 Mill St.
703/497-3131

**Future Antiques**
407 Mill St.
703/491-5192

**Sloan's Antique Gallery**
407 Mill St.
703/494-5231

**Victoria's Past Tyme**
308 A Poplar Alley
703/494-6134

## 47 PETERSBURG

**Hall's Antiques**
12 W. Bank St.
804/861-6060

**White Oak Antique & Gift Shop**
24118 Cox Road
804/861-9127

**Woody's Antiques**
3 W. Old St.
804/861-9642

**John Reads Row**
102 W. Old St.
804/732-5690

**Cockade Antiques**
1 W. Old St.
804/861-2417

**Village Jaile Shoppe**
20829 Chesterfield Ave.
804/526-7073

**America Hurrah Antiques**
406 N. Market St.
804/861-9659

**Estate Treasures & Antiques**
9 W. Old St.
804/732-3032

**Coin Exchange**
104 W. Old St.
804/861-6449

## 48 POQUOSON

**Joanne's This That & The Other**
798 Poquoson Ave.
757/868-4770

**Antiques East**
476 Wythe Creek Road
757/868-9976

**Shoppe on Wythe Creek**
501 Wythe Creek Road.
757/868-9751

**Martin-Wilson House**
326 Wythe Creek Road
757/868-7070

**Candlelight Antiques & Designs**
499 Wythe Creek Road
757/868-8898

## 49 PORTSMOUTH

**Prison Square Antiques**
440 High St.
757/399-4174

**Mount Vernon Antique Shop**
258 Mount Vernon Ave.
757/399-6550

**Old Schoolhouse Antiques**
4903 Portsmouth Blvd.
757/465-3145

**Olde Towne Sales**
719 High St.
757/399-4009

**Jems From Jennie**
Poplar Hill Shopping Center
757/484-9581

**Prison Square Antiques**
327 High St.
757/399-4174

## 50 PROVIDENCE FORGE

### *Great Places To Stay*

**Jasmine Plantation Bed and Breakfast Inn**
4500 North Courthouse Road
804/966-9836 or 1-800-NEW-KENT
Open 7 days a week, 52 weeks a year
*Directions: Halfway between Williamsburg and Richmond, the inn is located 2.4 miles south of I-64 at Exit 214. OR from Route 60, go north on State Route 155 for 1 4/10 miles.*

A great place to relax between antiquing days is this 1750s farmhouse offering 6 rooms with antique decor. Enjoy the afternoons sitting on the front porch or enjoying nature along the 47 acres of walking trails. Don't pass up the complimentary full "skip lunch" country breakfast.

## 51 PULASKI

**Upstairs Downstairs**
27 Main St. W.
540/980-4809

**Around the World Antiques**
86 W. Main St.
540/980-8389

**Colony of Virginia Ltd.**
61 W. Main St.
540/980-8932

## 52 PURCELLVILLE

**Noni's Attic**
148 N. 21st St.
540/338-3489

**Swanson & Ball Antiques & Collectibles**
142 N. 21st St.
540/338-7077

**Mary Ellen Stover**
120 N. 21st St.
540/338-3823

**Where the Attic Bird Sings**
21st & Main St.
540/338-5474

**The Petite Emporium**
105 E. Main St.
540/338-2298

**Ray E. Fields III**
120 Main St.
540/338-3829

**Iron Gate Antiques**
151 W. Main St.
540/338-6636

**Carousel/Finders Keepers**
144 N. 21st St.
540/338-9075

**Nick Greer Antique Restoration**
Route 711
540/338-6607

**Clark & Palmer**
108 N. 21st St.
540/338-7229

**Irene Mary Antiques & Collectibles**
Corner 21st & Main St.
540/338-1999

**End of the Rainbow**
121 E. Main St.
540/338-5913

**Preservation Hall**
111 N. 21st St.
540/338-4233

**Samuel S. Case Antiques**
120 W. Main St.
540/338-2725

## 53 RADFORD

**Once Upon A Time**
221 1st St.
540/633-3987

**Grandma's Memories Antqs. Shop**
237 1st St.
540/639-0054

**Uncle Bill's Treasures**
1103 Norwood St.
540/633-0589

## 54 RICHMOND

### Mechanicsville Antique Mall
7508 Mechanicsville Turnpike
804/730-5091
Daily 10-5
*Directions: Once on 295 take Exit 37B; from the Main 360 take first right. (Business 360)*

In August, 1997, Mechanicsville Antique Mall was voted the 2nd Best Antique Mall in Richmond by *Richmond Magazine*. This comes as no surprise since this 30,000 square foot mall is jammed packed with over 100 booths and 25 showcase galleries featuring the best in early American, Victorian, golden oak, art pottery, art glass, toys and clocks. The mall even offers clock repair. Be sure to check out Hanover Auction House - adjacent to the antique mall. For information on fine quality estate auctions, call 1-800-694-0759.

### Midlothian Antiques Center
Coolfield Road
804/897-4913
and
### West End Antiques Mall
6504 Horsepen Road
804/285-1916
Both locations: Mon.-Sat. 10-6, Sun. 12-6

Antiques Centers, Inc., with its two locations, makes finding your treasure even easier. These centers have a combined 160 dealers and 36,000 square feet of merchandise. Choose from a huge selection of country, formal, or vintage wicker furniture, quilts, linens, glassware and books. You may also want to check their framed collectibles, woodblock prints and pewter.

**erry's Antiques**
18 W. Broad St.
04/643-1044

**ntique Boutique & Delectable Cllbls.**
310 E. Cary St.
04/775-2525

**orld of Mirth**
25 W. Cary St.
4/353-8991

**Shamburger's Antiques**
5208 Brook Road
804/266-8457

**Bygones Vintage Clothing**
2916 W. Cary St.
804/353-1919

**Distinctive Consignments Ltd.**
3422 W. Cary St.
804/359-3778

**Johnson's Antiques**
5033 Forest Hill Ave.
804/231-9727

**Antique Exchange**
6800 Forest Hill Ave.
804/272-2990

**Kim Faison Antiques**
5608 Grove Ave.
804/282-3736

**Hampton House**
5720 Grove Ave.
804/285-3479

**Glass Lady**
7501 Iron Bridge Road
804/743-9811

**Robin's Nest**
6925 Lakeside Ave.
804/553-1061

**Civil War Antiques**
7605 Midlothian Turnpike
804/272-4570

**Tudor Gallery Estate Jewelry & Antiques**
113 S. 12th St.
804/780-0020

**Barbara L. Gordon Antiques**
8211 Bevlynn Way
804/288-5155

**Vintage Antique & Art Co.**
5047 Forest Hill Ave.
804/233-1808

**Exile**
822 W. Grace St.
804/358-3348

**Robert Blair Antiques**
5612 Grove Ave.
804/285-9441

**Chadwick Antiques**
5805 Grove Ave.
804/285-3355

**Jahnke Road Antique Center**
6207 Jahnke Road
804/231-5838

**Bradley's Antiques**
101 E. Main St.
804/644-7305

**Halcyon-Vintage Clothing**
117 N. Robinson St.
804/358-1311

**Antiques Warehouse**
1310 E. Cary St.
804/643-1310

**Kaleidoscope**
7501 Iron Bridge Road
804/743-9811

## 55 ROANOKE

**12 E Campbell Antiques**
12 Campbell Ave. S.W.
540/343-7946

**Continental Antiques**
1809 Franklin Road S.W.
540/982-5476

**White House Galleries**
4347 Franklin Road S.W.
540/774-3529

**Carriage House**
5999 Franklin Road S.W.
540/776-0499

**Howard R McManus**
11 S. Jefferson St.
540/344-2302

**BoLily Antiques**
124 Kirk Ave. S.W.
540/343-0100

**Bargain Corner Antique Shop**
3804 Melrose Ave. N.W.
540/366-1278

**Sandra's Cellar**
109 Campbell Ave. S.W.
540/342-8123

**John Davis Antiques**
4347 Franklin Road S.W.
540/772-7378

**Home Place Antiques**
5348 Franklin Road S.W.
540/774-0774

**Sissy's Antiques**
2914 Jae Valley Road
540/427-1712

**Bob Anderson Antiques**
617 S. Jefferson St.
540/343-7008

**Bob Beard Antiques**
105 Market Square S.E.
540/981-1757

**Olde Window Glass Co.**
4026 Melrose Ave. N.W.
540/362-3386

**Webb's Antiques**
3906 Old Garst Mill Road
540/774-3790

**Kirk's**
312 2nd St. S.W.
540/344-8161

**Now & Then Shop**
3133 Williamson Road N.W.
540/366-1905

**Russell's Yesteryear**
117 Campbell Ave. S.E.
540/342-1750

**Roanoke Antique Mall**
2302 Orange Ave. N.E.
540/344-0264

**Trudy's Antiques**
2205 Williamson Road N.E.
540/366-7898

**Happy's**
5411 Williamson Road N.W.
540/563-4473

## 56 ROCKY MOUNT

**Spinning Wheel Antiques**
Route 220
540/489-5355

**Blue Ridge Antique Center**
Route 220-20100 Virgil H Goode Hwy.
540/483-2362

## 57 RUCKERSVILLE

**Archangel Antiques & Fine Art**
Route 29 S.
804/985-7456

**Early-Time Antiques & Fine Art**
Route 29 N.
804/985-3602

**Red Fox Antiques**
Route 29 N.
804/985-2080

**Lawson's Antiques-Collectibles**
Route 33 E.
804/985-1070

**Country Store Antique Mall**
Route 29
804/985-3649

**Green House Shops**
Route 29 N. & 33
804/985-6053

**Antique Collectors**
Route 29 N. & 33
804/985-8966

## 58 SALEM

### Wright Place Antique Mall
27 W. Main St.
540/389-8507
Mon.-Sat. 10-6, Sunday 12:30-6

Step back in time at Wright Place Antique Mall located in the middle of downtown antique Salem. Enjoy a cup of coffee or a cold drink while you browse.

The mall offers a distinctive collection of beautiful furniture including: oak, walnut, mahogany, cherry & primitive. Tables, chairs, beds, kitchen cabinets, rockers, bookcases and secretaries, railroad items: dishes, lanterns, nails, locks, paper items, etc., advertising: Coke items, signs, neons, smoking items, bottles, etc, books on history, novels, civil war, science novels, books for all ages, quilts, rugs, linens, license plates, crocks, toys, dolls, clocks, cookie jars, McCoy, Hull, Watt pottery, Weller, Roseville, art, pictures, statues, jewelry, iron items, lamps: glass chandeliers, hurricane, etc., glassware: cut glass, depression, Fenton, china, carnival glass, etc.

Antique in one of the nation's most beautiful settings, and take home memories to last a lifetime. Experience a sunrise from the Blue Ridge Parkway or the Appalachian Trail, two of America's most-revered scenic byways, both winding their way through the Roanoke Valley. Enjoy the sights, sounds and smells of the farmers' markets in Roanoke, Salem and Vinton as they come to life almost every morning with their offerings of produce, flowers, baked goods and handmade items.

No visit would be complete without exploring all the shopping options which one will find at every turn. From antiques to outlets, and million-square-foot malls to boutiques in historic settings, there is something to satisfy every taste and need.

After indulging in the areas many attractions and shops, tempt your taste buds by enjoying a sumptuous meal in one of the many area restaurants. The valley has long held an excellent reputation for its wide variety of outstanding dining facilities. Delight in old-fashioned, down-home Southern cooking or a romantic candlelit dinner for two.

There's history, architecture, whimsy and excitement all over the valley. You'll meet some of the friendliest, most hospitable people in the world, who welcome the opportunity to share the area with you.

*Note: Plenty of lodging is available for over-nighters who need to spend just one more day in beautiful, historic Salem.

**Christopher Gladden Bookseller**
211 S. College Ave.
540/389-4892

**Salem Market Antiques**
1 W. Main St.
540/389-8920

**Green Market-Antique Mall**
8 E. Main St.
540/387-3879

**Olde Curiosity Shoppe Antique Mall**
27/29 E. Main St.
540/387-2007

**Auntie Em's Antiques & More**
514 W. Main St.
540/389-2294

**Red Barn Antiques**
4506 W. Main St.
540/380-4307

**Antique Mall 50 Plus Shops**
27 W. Main St.
540/389-2484

**Eddy Street Antiques**
1502 Eddy St.
540/389-9411

**Virginia Showcase Antiques**
4 E. Main St.
540/387-5842

**Elite Antique & Consignments**
17 W. Main St.
540/389-9222

**Olde Salem Stained Glass Art**
120 E. Main St.
540/389-9968

**Antique Lamp Shop**
1800 W. Main St.
540/389-3163

**Guthrie's Antiques**
221 E. 6th St.
540/389-3621

### *Great Places To Stay*

**The Inn at Burwell Place**
601 W. Main St.
1-800-891-0250 or 540/387-0250
Rates include full breakfast and private bath. $70-110
*Directions: From I-81 southbound, take Exit 140 (Route 311) south 1 1/4 miles to East Main St; turn right on East Main St. and go through downtown Salem, 1 mile. The inn is on the right.*

This spacious mansion was built in 1907 by Samuel H. McVitty, a local industrialist, on a summit overlooking Salem and the Southwest Roanoke Valley. Mr. McVitty built the mansion on land purchased from Mr. Nathaniel Burwell (pronounced Burr-ell) a prominent Salem landowner, civic leader, State Assemblyman and gentleman justice of the County Court.

In 1915, McVitty sold the mansion to Lewis E. Dawson, whose family lived there until 1971. The Dawsons made major renovations and an addition to the house in 1925. The house was home to six Dawson children and their families during this period. It was the site of many parties, weddings, and family gatherings.

During the 1970s and the 1980s the mansion was used as an architect's office and the YWCA.

Each guest-room has its own bathroom with vintage 1920s fixtures and a queen-size 4-poster bed. A wide hallway connects the second floor bedrooms. Antique walnut and cherry furnishings adorn each room.

Downstairs, the expansive common area consists of a living room, sun porch (complete with 6 x 8 foot antique carousel), two dining rooms and a massive wraparound front porch, an ideal place for reading and watching television. The common area has been the scene of many weddings, receptions, parties and business meetings reminiscent of yesteryear. Within a short walk from the inn is a restored park and duck pond (circa 1890); historic downtown Salem, with numerous antique shops, gift boutiques, restaurants and coffee shops.

The inn serves a full breakfast consisting of the Chef's choice of Eggs Benedict, hash browns, fruit compote, a special fruit juice blend, fresh baked muffins or fruit breads, coffee and teas. Another popular entree is French Toast prepared with fresh apple-cinnamon bread.

## 59 SALUDA

**The Shops At Saluda Market**
Route 17 & 33
804/758-2888

**Trimble's Antiques**
Hwy. 17
804/758-5732

**Urbanna Antique Gallery**
24 Rappahannock Ave.
804/758-2000

**Courthouse Antiques**
S-17 Bypass
804/758-4861

## 60 SOUTH BOSTON

**Z's Antiques**
Hwy. 58 W.
804/572-6741

**Van's Barnyard Antiques**
Hwy. 716 Airport Road
804/572-4754

**Miss W. & Sis Art All Nations**
206 Main St.
804/575-0858

**My Brother's Place Antique Mall**
234 S. Main St.
804/572-8888

**Crystal Hill Antiques**
1902 Seymour Dr.
804/575-8810

## 61 STANARDSVILLE

**Towne Shops**
121 W. Main St.
804/985-8222

**Trader Mike's Antiques**
313 E. Main St.
804/985-6440

**J & T Antiques**
317 Main St.
804/985-7299

## 62 STAUNTON

**Turtle Lane**
10 E. Beverly St.
540/886-8591

**Once Upon A Time Clock Shop**
25 W. Beverly St.
540/885-6064

**Warehouse Antiques & Collectibles**
26 W. Beverly St.
540/885-0891

**Honeysuckle Hill**
100 E. Beverly St.
540/885-8261

**Memory Makers**
15 Middlebrook Ave.
540/886-5341

**Jolly Roger Haggle Shop**
27 Middlebrook Ave.
540/886-9527

## 63 STRASBURG

**Sullivan's Country House Antiques**
Hwy. 55 & I 81 Exit #296
540/465-5192

**River Gallery**
208 W. King St.
540/465-3527

**Heritage Antiques**
102 Massanutten Manor Circle
540/465-5000

**Wayside of Virginia Inc.**
108 N. Massanutten St.
540/465-4650

**Strasburg Emporium**
110 N. Massanutten St.
540/465-3711

**Vilnis and Company Antiques**
305 N. Massanutten St.
540/465-4405

**Tiques**
114 Orchard St.
540/465-4115

**Emmart's Antiques Classics**
28814 Old Valley Pike
540/465-5040

## 64 SUFFOLK

**Holly Bluff Antiques**
2697 Bridge Road
757/484-4246

**Once Upon A Time Antiques**
2948 Bridge Road
757/483-1344

**Judy's Treasures**
723 Carolina Road
757/934-7624

**Southern Gun Works**
109 Cherry St.
757/934-1423

**Carolyn's Country Charm**
3093 Godwin Blvd.
757/934-2868

**Attic Trunk**
167 S. Main St.
757/934-0882

**Nansemond Antique Shop**
3537 Pruden Blvd.
757/539-6269

**Willow's**
800 W. Washington St.
757/934-2411

**Now & Then Antiques**
6140 Whaleyville Blvd.
757/986-2429

## 65 TAPPAHANNOCK

**A To Z Antiques**
608 Church Lane
804/443-4585

**Antiques Place**
804 Church Lane
804/443-6549

**Hoskin's Creek Table Co.**
1014 Church Lane
804/443-6500

**Mayhew's Antiques**
205 Queen
804/443-2961

**Queen Street Mall 2**
227 Queen
804/443-2424

**Nadji Nook Antiques**
Queen & Cross St. Route 360
804/443-3298

## 66 TOANO

**Charlie's Antiques**
7766 Richmond Road
757/566-8300

**Pocahonta's Trail Antiques**
7778 Richmond Road
757/566-8050

**Colonial Antique Center**
7828 Richmond Road
757/566-8720

**J & L Treasure Chest**
7880 Richmond Road
757/566-1878

**King William Antiques**
7880 Richmond Road
757/566-2270

## 67 TROUTVILLE

**Buffalo Creek Antiques**
941 Lee Hwy. S.
540/992-5288

**Troutville Antique Mart**
941 Lee Hwy. S.
540/992-4249

**Kelly's Real Deal**
1411 Lee Hwy. S.
540/992-5096

**Harris Antiques**
2240 Roanoke Road
540/992-5225

## 68 VERONA

**Factory**
I-81 Exit 227
540/248-1110

**Pat's Antique Mall**
5505 Lee Hwy.
540/248-7287

**Verona Flea Market**
Hwy. 11
540/248-3532

**Wilson Gallery**
4719 Lee Hwy.
540/248-4292

**Village Antique**
Route 11 (Mount Sidney)
540/248-7807

**Dusty's Antique Market**
Route 11 (Mount Sidney)
540/248-2018

## 69 VIENNA

**Finders Keepers**
131 N.W. Church St.
703/319-9318

**Now And Then**
131 N.W. Church St.
703/242-3959

**Village Antiques**
120 Lawyers Road N.W.
703/938-0084

**Vienna Bargains**
128 Maple Ave. E.
703/255-6119

**Twig House**
132 Maple Ave. E.
703/255-4985

**Cameo Coins & Collectibles**
444 Maple Ave. E.
703/281-7053

**Cabbage Rose**
213 Mill St.
703/242-2051

**Pleasant Street Antiques**
115 Pleasant St. N.W.
703/938-0003

**Furniture Center**
126 Maple Ave. E.
703/938-1714

## 70 VIRGINIA BEACH

**Colonial Cottage Antiques**
3900 Bonney Road
804/498-0600

**Mary's Attic**
3900 Bonney Road
804/498-0600

**Pat's Antiques**
3900 Bonney Road
804/463-1252

**Pelican Bay**
3900 Bonney Road
804/481-4445

**Hard Timz & Sunshine**
244 London Bridge Shop
804/463-7335

**Something Unique**
1600 Independence Blvd.
804/363-9512

**Echoes of Time Antiques**
320 Laskin Road
804/428-2332

**Shutter Door Antiques**
968 Laskin Road
804/422-6999

**La Galleria Inc.**
993 Laskin Road
804/428-5909

**Garden Gallery**
1860 Laskin Road
804/428-8427

**Chesapeake Antiques & Collectibles**
210 24th St.
804/425-6530

**Rudy's Antiques**
3324 Virginia Beach Blvd.
804/340-2079

**Eddie's Antique Mall**
4801 A Virginia Beach Blvd.
804/497-0537

**Barrett Street Antique Center**
2645 Dean Dr.
757/463-8600

**Christy's Antiques**
6353 Indian River Road
757/424-8770

## 71 WAYNESBORO

**Annetteque's Antiques**
305 12th St.
540/949-7670

**Apple Acres Antiques**
1432 Lyndhurst Road
540/949-8522

**Ladd Framing Shop**
Route 340 S.
540/943-6287

**Unique Andteek**
Hwy. 340 N.
540/949-4983

**Village Showcase**
601 Shenandoah Village Dr.
540/932-7599

**Tommy's Olde Town Used**
208 Arch Ave.
540/949-5559

**Someplace Else**
430 N. Commerce Ave.
540/942-9888

**The Silent Woman Antiques**
139 N. Wayne Ave.
540/949-4483

**Treasures 'N' Things**
141 N. Wayne Ave.
540/942-3223

**Stuart's Draft Antique Mall**
Route 340 S. (4 mi. S. of Waynesboro)
540/946-8488

## 72 WEYERS CAVE

**Rocky's Antique Mall**
Hwy. 11
540/234-9900

**Ace Antiques**
Hwy. 11
540/234-9079

**Blue Ridge Antiques**
Hwy. 11
540/234-0112

## 73 WILLIAMSBURG

**London Shop**
1206 Jamestown Road
757/229-8754

**Old Chickahominy House**
1211 Jamestown Road
757/229-4689

**Shaia Oriental Rugs Williamsburg**
1325 Jamestown Road
757/220-0400

**TK Oriental Antiques**
1654 Jamestown Road
757/220-8590

**Hamilton's Book Store**
1784 Jamestown Road
757/220-3000

**Quilts Unlimited**
Merchants Square
757/253-0222

**J L McCandlish Antiques Art**
1915 Pocahontas Trail
757/259-0472

**Peacock Hill**
445 Prince George St.
757/220-0429

**Attic Collections**
2229 Richmond Road
757/229-0032

**R & M Antiques**
5435 Richmond Road
757/565-3344

**Lamplighter Shoppe Ltd.**
5502 Richmond Road
757/565-4676

**Things Unique**
6506 Richmond Road
757/564-1140

**Oriental Textile Arts**
Village Shop
757/220-3736

**Williamsburg Antique Mall**
500 Lightfoot Road
757/565-2587

### *Great Places To Stay*

**Applewood Colonial B&B**
605 Richmond Road
1-800-899-2753

"An 'Applewood' a day, for a memorable stay," says innkeeper Fred Strout. This Flemish bond brick home was built in 1929 by the construction manager for the Colonial Williamsburg restoration and features many finely crafted Colonial details of the 18th century. Antiques and twentieth century comfort throughout the house are accented by the owner's unique apple collection. Guest enjoy a full breakfast served by candlelight in the elegant dining room.

**Williamsburg Sampler B&B**
922 Jamestown Road
1-800-722-1169

The Sampler is the finest 18th-century plantation-style Colonial located in the Architectural Corridor Protection Distric of Williamsburg. Proclaimed by Virginia's Governor as the 1995 Inn Of The Year ('I call its significance to the attention of all our citizens.') Guests rooms have king or queen size four-poster beds, TV and private bath. Additionally, suites have wetbar/refrigerator, fireplace and TV.

## 74 WINCHESTER

**Betty's Antiques**
127 Morgan Mill Road
540/667-8558
Wed.-Sat. 12 until 5, Sun.-Tues. by chance or appointment
*Directions: Take Exit 315 from I-81 onto Route 7. The shop is east of Winchester.*

Established in 1973, the shop specializes in refinished American oak furniture. Pieces such as bedroom suites, dressers, and round tables are just a few of the many quality antiques available here.

**Past And Present**
1121 Berryville Ave.
540/678-8766

**Boscawen Gold & Silver**
41 W. Boscawen St.
540/667-6065

**Kimberly's Antiques & Linens**
135 N. Braddock St.
540/662-2195

**Glover's Antiques**
422 S. Cameron St.
540/662-3737

**Stone Soup Gallery/Old Downtown Mall**
107 N. Loudoun St.
540/722-3976

**Winchester Antiques & Collectibles**
1815 S. Loudoun St.
540/667-7411

**Clay Hill Antiques**
2869 Middle Road
540/662-3623

**Millwood Crossing Shops**
381 Millwood Ave.
540/662-5157

**Doll House Antiques**
618 S. Cameron St./By Appointment
540/665-0964

**50 West Antiques**
2480 Northwestern Pike
540/662-7624

**Wrenwood Antique Gallery**
39 W. Piccadilly St.
540/665-3055

**Cecil Antiques**
522 N. Sunnyside St.
540/667-0787

**Applegate Antiques & Art**
1844 Valley Ave.
540/665-1933

## 75 WOODSTOCK

**Valley Treasures**
660 N. Main St.
540/459-2334

**Spring Hollow Antiques**
322 S. Main St.
540/459-3946

### *Great Places To Stay*

**River'd Inn**
1972 Artz Road
540/459-5369
1-800-637-4561
Lodging available seven days a week, $150-325/night includes full breakfast.
Restaurant open Wednesday-Sunday 5-9pm, Sunday Brunch served 11am-2pm.
*Directions: I-81 to Route 11, just north of Woodstock take SR 663 2 1/10 miles.*

The River'd Inn offers luxurious accommodations nestled in the heart of Virginia's Shenandoah Valley. Spacious bedrooms feature antique furnishings, fireplaces and private baths with whirlpool tubs. Beautiful views from decks and porches. Gourmet restaurant, open to the public, features French-based cuisine. Fine selection of beer, wine, and spirits available. Outdoor pool with hot tub. Situated on 25 forested acres with gardens, mountain views, and paths to the Shenandoah River. Numerous attractions including Civil War sites, antique and gift shops, wineries, golf, skiing, hiking, canoeing, picnicking, and more nearby. Easy access from Interstate 81. Handicapped accessible dining and lodging.

## 76 WYTHEVILLE

**Old Fort Antique Mall**
I-81 Exit # 80
540/228-4438

**Snoopers Inc.**
I-81 Exit # 80
540/637-6441

## 77 YORKTOWN

**High Cotton Ltd.**
3630 George Washington Mem Hwy.
757/867-7132

**Scott's Corner Antiques**
4827 George Washington Mem Hwy.
757/898-1404

**Galleria Antique Mall**
7628 George Washington Mem Hwy.
757/890-2950

**Swan Tavern Antiques**
300 Main St.
757/898-3033

# Washington

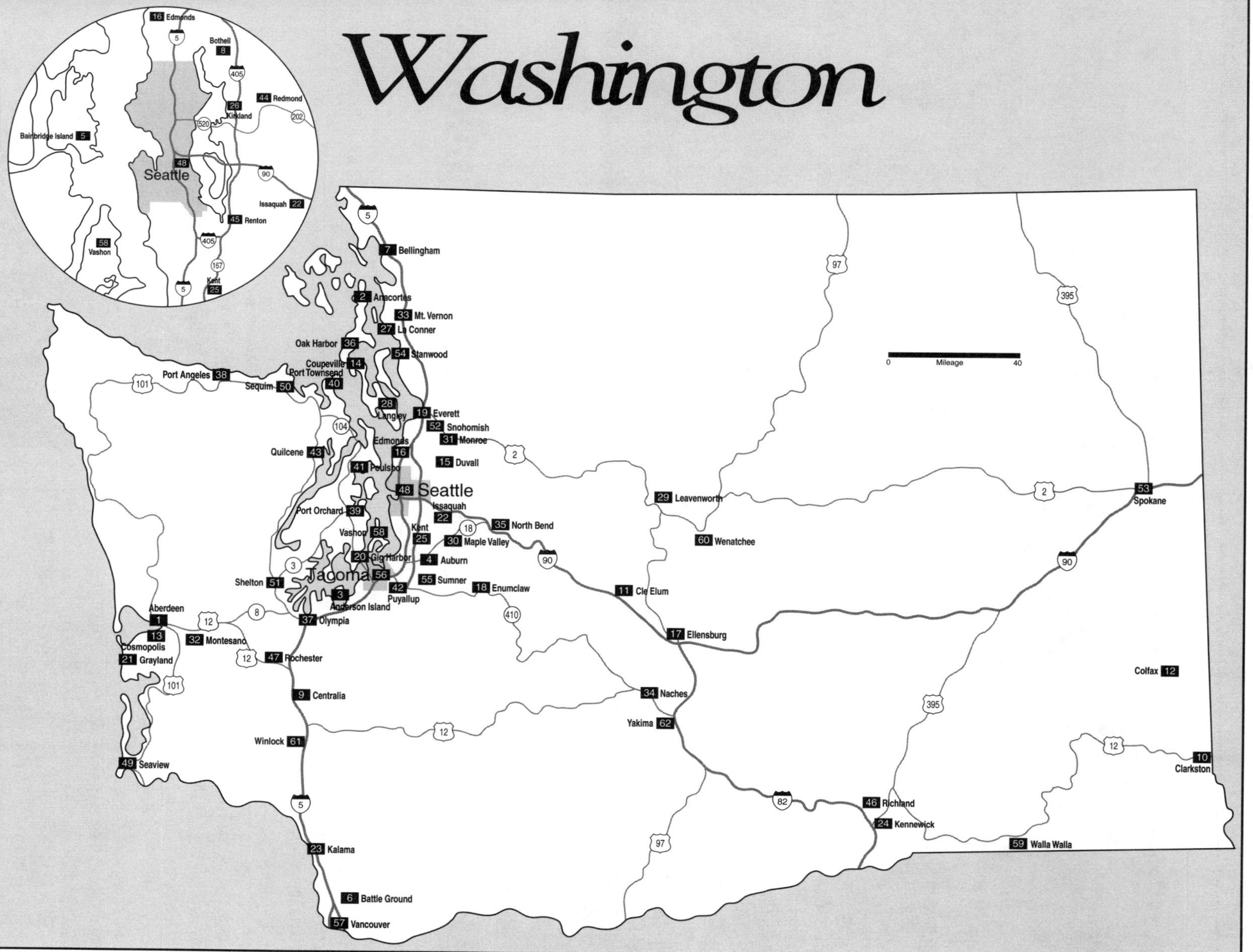
16 Edmonds
Bothell 8
26 Kirkland
44 Redmond
Bainbridge Island 5
48 Seattle
Issaquah 22
45 Renton
58 Vashon
Kent 25
7 Bellingham
2 Anacortes
33 Mt. Vernon
27 La Conner
Oak Harbor 36
54 Stanwood
Coupeville 14
Port Townsend 40
Port Angeles 38
Sequim 50
28 Langley
19 Everett
52 Snohomish
31 Monroe
Edmonds 16
15 Duvall
Quilcene 43
41 Poulsbo
48 Seattle
Issaquah 22
Port Orchard 39
35 North Bend
Kent 25
Vashon 58
30 Maple Valley
20 Gig Harbor
4 Auburn
Tacoma 56
55 Sumner
Shelton 51
42 Puyallup
3 Anderson Island
18 Enumclaw
Aberdeen 1
37 Olympia
13 Cosmopolis
32 Montesano
21 Grayland
47 Rochester
9 Centralia
Winlock 61
49 Seaview
23 Kalama
6 Battle Ground
57 Vancouver
0 Mileage 40
29 Leavenworth
60 Wenatchee
53 Spokane
11 Cle Elum
17 Ellensburg
34 Naches
Yakima 62
Colfax 12
10 Clarkston
46 Richland
24 Kennewick
59 Walla Walla

*Left: The Aster's antique shop was a school, a saloon, and a grocery store in its former lives.*

*Theresa Starbird, 92, is the matriarch of the family. She entertains customers with fascinating yarns about the history of the area.*

# History is firsthand at Aster Inn and Antiques

A visit to Aster Inn & Antiques is a chance to experience firsthand some living history and hear about life early in the century in the Washington area from people who have literally experienced it. There are two interconnected parts of this living history saga; Aster Inn and Aster Antiques.

The antique store, which is attached to the inn, sells everything from collectibles to primitives, mostly in "as is" condition. This is a family-owned business, established at the turn of the century and now running continuously for more than 90 years. Innkeeper and third generation family member Patrecia Starbird says, "We can almost guarantee every shopper will be entertained by stories of the local bordellos (now extinct), coal mines, early one-room school houses, arranged brides, etc. The stories aren't even secondhand, but are the experiences of the two proprietors!"

These two proprietors are still working at the store and in the inn's office every summer—Theresa, age 92 and the matriarch of the family, and her bother, Dominic, age 87. The 1885 "store" has been at various times a school house, saloon, grocery store, gift shop, and for the last thirty years, an antique shop.

Aster Inn was built in 1934 and has been remodeled recently, retaining and maintaining a 1930s atmosphere with some "thoroughly Modern Millie" rooms! Jacuzzi, clawfoot tubs and mini-stocked kitchens are favorites.

*Aster Inn & Antiques is located at 521 East 1st St. in Cle Elum. See listing #11 (Cle Elum) for additional information.*

*Aster Inn is a family-owned business, built in 1934 and recently remodeled.*

## 1 ABERDEEN

**Clevenger's Antique Mall**
201 S. Broadway St.
360/533-1317

**Grand Heron**
200 E. Heron St.
360/532-5561

**Judy's Antiques & Collectibles**
401 W. Market St.
360/532-4359

**Central Park Antiques**
6617 Olympic Hwy.
360/538-1173

**Karrie's Furnishings**
110 W. Wishkah St.
360/533-7330

**Antique Co-Op**
112 W. Wishkah St.
360/533-6516

## 2 ANACORTES

**The Business**
1717 Commerical Ave.
360/293-9788

**Left Bank Antiques**
1904 Commercial Ave.
360/293-3022

**Home Sweet Home Antiques**
2701 Commercial Ave.
360/293-1991

**Days Gone By**
3015 Commercial Ave.
360/299-2222

**15th St. Antiques & Gallery**
1012 15th St.
360/299-3120

**Anacortes Junk Co.**
202 Commercial Ave.
360/293-4014

## 3 ANDERSON ISLAND

**Oro Bay Merchantile**
12312 Eckenstam Johnson Road
253/884-1700

### *Great Places To Stay*

**Hideaway House Bed and Breakfast**
11422 Leschi Circle
253/884-4179
Fax: 253/884-2083
Daily around the clock
Rates: $55-75
*Directions: From I-5 either north or south: Take Exit 119 and follow the signs to Steilacoom. After about 3 1/2 miles the road leads to the ferry, with parking on the left. It is a beautiful 20 minute ferry ride to Anderson Island. Proceed west off the ferry and veer to the left at the "Y" in the road. Pass the store on the right, turn left onto West Josephine Blvd.. Go one mile, turn right onto Leschi Circle, and go to the blue house.*

This description of Hideaway House and innkeepers Hank and Faye Lynn Hollenbaugh makes you appreciate that old-fashioned common courtesy and genuine desire to help others, is not entirely dead.

The Hollenbaughs started their B&B unintentionally. The ferry schedule to the island is often confusing to tourists, which used to result in frequently stranded travelers. They often came to the Island General Store, where Hank works, looking for a solution. Many of them were without funds, and things only got worse when they discovered they were stranded on the island until the next morning's ferry at 6:30 a.m. Out of compassion, Hank and Faye Lynn found themselves saying, "Well, we have a room...things will look better in the morning."

And things did look better, after a good night's sleep, hot shower, hearty breakfast and directions back to the ferry dock. Unfortunately, accepting this freely given gift of hospitality from strangers was a source of embarrassment to some guests. Eventually, Hank and Faye Lynn decided to accept donations, if the guests insisted.

This happened often enough that they decided to do some major remodeling. Under the canopy of giant fir trees that surround the house, they added a large, open deck that opens into a suite decorated in garden/sunflower motif (the Sunflower Room). The focal point of the suite is a bright sunflower quilt created by Hank's 82-year-old mother in Pennsylvania. The suite includes a kitchenette and private bath, and children are welcome.

The deck also leads into the Angel Room. This suite holds a tulip quilt, created by the late, well-known islander Lois Scholl and offers a double spa tub. Both suites have access to the upstairs of the main house and to the dining area, where guest are graciously and amply fed wonderful, home-cooked meals.

## 4 AUBURN

**Maw's Antiques and Collectibles**
121 E. Main St.
253/939-3740

**Auburn Main Street Antiques**
124 E. Main St.
253/804-8041

**Lynn's Antiques & Refinishing**
130 W. Main St.
253/939-6799

**Back by Popular Demand**
33620 135th Ave. S.E.
253/939-1239

**Cedar Chest**
119 E. Main St.
253/833-4165

## 5 BAINBRIDGE ISLAND

**Rose Gulch Antiques**
11042 Forest Lane N.E.
206/842-5002

**Now And Then Shoppe**
901 S.W. 152nd St.
206/242-8238

**Bad Blanche Antiques**
133 Winslow Way E.
206/842-1807

**Discoveries Downstairs**
155 Winslow Way E.
206/842-5873

**Sow's Ear & Friends**
554 Winslow Way E.
206/842-1203

## 6 BATTLE GROUND

**Rock Creek Antiques**
31902 N.E. Lewisville Hwy.
360/687-1892

**Jo's Antiques**
612 E. Main St.
360/687-0251

**Main Street Antiques**
706 E. Main St.
360/687-2365

**Old Post Office Antique Mall**
718 E. Main St.
360/687-1805

### 7 BELLINGHAM

**Secret Treasures**
186 E. Bakerview Road
360/734-5057

**American Antiques**
2330 Elm St.
360/650-9037

**Fairhaven Antiques & Art**
1200 Harris Ave.
360/734-7179

**Urban Archeologist Antique Mall**
214 W. Holly St.
360/676-0695

**Bristol Antiques & Books**
310 W. Holly St.
360/733-7809

**Bellingham Bay Collectibles**
314 W. Holly St.
360/676-9201

**Pink Flamingo**
407 W. Holly St.
360/671-2789

**Aladdin's Lamp Antique Mall**
427 W. Holly St.
360/647-0066

**Old Town Antique Mall**
427 W. Holly St.
360/671-3301

**Jack's By The Tracks**
705 W. Holly St.
360/647-9422

**Cheryl Leaf Antiques & Gifts**
2828 Northwest Ave.
360/734-2880

**Glass Affair**
4392 Northwest Dr.
360/734-0382

**I-5 Antique Mall**
4744 Pacific Hwy.
360/384-5955

**Wynne Associates**
4744 Pacific Hwy.
360/384-5955

### 8 BOTHELL

**Farmhouse Antiques**
23710 Bothell Everett Hwy.
425/483-3354

**White House Antique Mall**
23712 Bothell Everett Hwy.
425/483-0676

**Town Hall Antique Mall**
23716 Bothell Everett Hwy.
425/487-8979

**Red Barn Antique Cllbls. & Gifts**
23929 Bothell Everett Hwy.
425/486-7309

**Red Barn Loft**
23929 Bothell Everett Hwy.
425/485-6582

**Wrecking Bar Ranch Antiques**
24323 Lockwood Road
425/486-3203

### 9 CENTRALIA

**Common Folk Company**
125 E. High St.
360/736-8066

**Q's Country Shoppe**
Centralia Square – 202 W. Locust St.
360/330-2844

**Elderly Things Antiques**
918 W. Locust St.
360/736-8927

**Cranberry Bog**
920 W. Locust St.
360/330-0594

**Centralia Square Antique Mall**
201 S. Pearl St.
360/736-6406

**Collector's Showcase**
201 S. Pearl St.
360/736-6026

**Maxine's Antiques**
201 S. Pearl St.
360/736-1699

**Rose Blue**
111 N. Tower Ave.
360/736-0370

**Irresistibles**
113 N. Tower Ave.
360/330-0338

**Hidden Treasures**
302 N. Tower Ave.
360/736-7572

**Rob Duffy's Antiques**
310 N. Tower Ave.
360/736-1282

**Timeless Treasures & Co.**
314 N. Tower Ave.
360/736-3898

**A & D Antique Mall**
405 N. Tower Ave.
360/330-5240

**American Antique Furniture Market**
120 S. Tower Ave.
360/330-0427

**Centralia Antique Furniture Market**
120 S. Tower Ave.
360/736-4079

**Rick's Wholesale Antiques**
120 S. Tower Ave.
360/736-2529

### 10 CLARKSTON

**Hangar Old Tyme Photos**
935 Port Way
509/758-0604

**Bric-A-Brac Mall**
834 6th St.
509/758-7772

**Dan's Antiques**
823 6th St.
509/758-6223

### 11 CLE ELUM

**Many Visions**
113 E. First St.
509/674-2568

***Great Places To Stay***

**Aster Inn & Antiques**
521 E. 1st St.
509/674-2551
Fax: 509/674-1866
Daily 10-10 except Christmas, New Years and Thanksgiving
*Directions: From the west, from I-90: Take Exit 84 straight for approximately 10 blocks (five blocks east at the only stoplight). The inn is on the left at the opposite end of the block from Cle Elum's Gourmet Bakery and Meat Market. From the east, from I-90: Take Exit 85. Turn left on Hwy. 903 and follow the signs to Cle Elum. It is exactly 1 7/10 miles from the freeway exit on the right.*

For specific information see review at the beginning of this section.

### 12 COLFAX

**Bryans Antiques**
Hwy. 195
509/397-3259

**Whitman Mall**
121 S. Main St.
509/397-2522

**Quail Crossing**
707 N. Main St.
509/397-6026

## 13 COSMOPOLIS

**Cooney Mansion**
1705 Fifth St.
360/533-0602

## 14 COUPEVILLE

**Front Street Antiques**
7 N.W. Front St.
360/678-7514

**Country & Victorian Treasures**
2531 W. Libbey Road
No Phone # Listed

**Salmagundi Farms**
185 S. State Hwy. 20
360/678-5888

**San De Fuca Old Store**
694 N. State Hwy. 20
360/678-3626

**Elkhorn Trading Co.**
15 N.W. Front St.
360/678-2250

## 15 DUVALL

**McCoy's Mercantile**
15515 Main St. N.E.
425/788-7920

**Country Collections**
15525 Main St. N.E.
425/788-2939

**Liberty's Lighthouse**
15720 Main St. N.E.
425/788-8683

**Tuxedo's Junction**
15904 Main St. N.E.
425/788-9678

**Duvall's Trading Post**
15906 Main St. N.E.
425/788-9455

**Old Memories**
15925 Main St. N.E.
425/788-7508

## 16 EDMONDS

**E & E Collectibles At Beeson Hse**
116 4th Ave. N.
425/774-3431

**Heaton House Gallery**
122 5th Ave. S.
425/771-7855

**Edmonds Antique Mall**
201 5th Ave. S.
425/771-9466

**Old General Store**
201 5th Ave. S., #12
425/771-2561

**Added Touch Antiques & Collectibles**
23428 7th Ave. W.
425/778-3108

**Amaryllis Antiques**
18606 7th Ave. W.
425/775-2252

**Country Cove Antiques**
27 Dayton St.
25/672-9277

**Aurora Antique Pavilion Inc.**
24111 Hwy. 99
425/744-0566

**Rosa Mundi's Antiques**
18 Main St.
25/771-6598

**Edmonds Sports Collectibles**
508 Main St.
425/672-7892

**alhalla Antiques & Collectibles**
08 Main St.
25/771-1242

**Glorious Treasures Antique Shop**
518 Main St.
425/775-5753

**Wally's World**
519 Main St.
425/774-0040

**Mam's Vintage Linens & Things**
537 Main St.
425/771-5310

**Waterfront Antique Mall**
190 Sunset Ave. S.
425/670-0770

**Mainly Antiques**
519 Main St.
425/774-0040

## 17 ELLENSBURG

**Etcetera Shoppe**
115 E. 4th Ave.
509/962-2578

**Edsel Antiques**
213 W. 4th Ave.
509/962-5295

**Main Street Market Antique Mall**
308 N. Main St.
509/925-1762

**Anchor In Time**
310 N. Main St.
509/925-7067

**Meadowlark Farm**
606 N. Main St.
509/962-3706

**Hub Antiques & Estate Sales**
307 N. Pearl St.
509/925-6581

**Showplace Antique Mall**
103 E. 3rd Ave.
509/962-9331

**Fogarty's Antiques**
107 E. 3rd Ave.
509/962-3476

**Attic**
109 E. 3rd Ave.
509/925-7467

## 18 ENUMCLAW

**Enumclaw Antique Mall**
1501 Cole St.
360/825-4546

**Delees Antiques & Accents**
1717 Cole St.
360/825-9112

**Country Peddler**
19428 S.E. 400th St.
360/825-8313

## 19 EVERETT

**Simply Victorian**
1911 Hewitt Ave.
425/303-0760

**Irene's Archives**
1917 Hewitt Ave.
425/258-1881

**Timeless Antiques**
1922 Hewitt Ave.
425/258-9350

**Country Peddler**
2114 Hewitt Ave.
425/258-1557

**Maxine's Antiquities & Curios**
2715 Hewitt Ave.
425/252-7812

**Grand Central Antique Mall**
2804 Grand Ave.
425/252-1089

## 20 GIG HARBOR

**Barber Shop Antiques**
1617 Stone Dr. N.W.
253/858-2922

**Hide & Sea**
3306 Harborview Dr.
253/858-8971

**Pandora's Inc.**
3801 Harborview Dr.
253/851-5164

**Key Center Trading Post**
15510 92nd St. KPN
253/884-2220

## 21 GRAYLAND

**Dittos Antiques & Gifts**
1634 State Route 105
360/267-4644

**Olde Merchantile**
1820 State Route 105
360/267-0121

**Pregnant Onion Antiques**
2399 Tokland Road
360/267-6914

**Grandma's Treasure Chest Antiques**
2190 State Route 105
360/267-1616

## 22 ISSAQUAH

**Haus of Antiques**
157 1/2 Front St. N.
425/392-3424

**Gillman Antiques Gallery**
625 N.W. Gilman Blvd.
425/391-6640

**Washington Antiques & Restorations**
685 N.W. Gilman Blvd.
425/391-7947

## 23 KALAMA

**River Town Antique Mall**
155 Elm St.
360/673-2263

**Heritage Square**
176 N. 1st St.
360/673-3980

**Drew & Davis Antiques**
222 N.E. 1st St.
360/673-4029

**Columbia Antiques & Collectibles**
364 N. 1st St.
360/673-5400

**Memory Lane Antique Mall**
413 N. 1st St.
360/673-3663

## 24 KENNEWICK

**Sloping M Antiques Collectibles**
W. Kennewick Ave.
509/582-1631

**Nostalgia Revisted**
323 W. Kennewick Ave.
509/586-7250

**Carmichaels Antiques**
3900 S. Oak St.
509/582-8216

**Appleseed Gallery & Shops**
108 Vista Way
509/735-2874

**Lea's Last Place Antiques**
302 N. Union St.
509/735-4305

**Crown Collectibles**
109 N. Washington St.
509/586-6501

## 25 KENT

**Robin's Antique Mall**
201 1st Ave. S.
253/854-6543

**Lace Legacy Etc.**
220 1st Ave. S.
253/852-0052

**The Shop**
223 1st Ave. S.
253/852-5892

**Fanny Jean's Antiques & Things**
213 W. Meeker St.
253/852-2053

**Now N Then**
218 W. Meeker St.
253/852-5890

**Joy's Collectables**
304 W. Meeker St.
253/854-6403

**Stagg's Coins Baseball Cards**
317 W. Meeker St.
253/854-6340

**Mad Hatter Antiques**
25748 101st Ave. S.E.
253/859-9293

**Accrete Antiques**
24526 104th Ave. S.E.
253/854-8916

**Anniebelle Countryside Antiques**
218 1st Ave. S.
253-852-6094

## 26 KIRKLAND

**Mambo**
205 Kirkland Ave.
425/889-8787

**Danish-Swedish Antiques**
207 Kirkland Ave.
425/822-7899

**Alexander McCallum Toppin**
215 Lake St. S.E.
425/827-6593

**Woodshed Antiques**
5918 Lake Washington Blvd. N.E.
425/822-8600

**Antiques at Park Lane**
128 Park Lane
425/803-0136

**Bettina's**
128 Park Lane
425/889-0234

**Kirkland Antique Gallery**
151 3rd St.
425/828-4993

## 27 LA CONNER

**Nasty Jack's Antiques**
103 E. Morris St.
360/466-3209

**Morris Street Antiques**
503 E. Morris St.
360/466-4212

**Cameo Antique Mall**
511 E. Morris St.
360/466-3472

### *Great Places To Stay*

**Katy's Inn-A Victorian Bed and Breakfast**
503 S. Third St.
360/466-3366 or 1-800-914-7767
Rates: $69-99
*Directions: From I-5 going north from Seattle: Take Exit 221. Go west (left) over the freeway and take the first right to Conway/La Conner. Travel a country road for 10 minutes that leads to La Conner (signs are posted). Enter La Conner on Morris St. Go left (south) on Second 1 block, then left up the hill on Washington St. 1 block. Katy's Inn is on the corner of Third and Washington St.— 1 1/4 hours drive from Seattle; 1 1/2 hours from Vancouver, B.C.*

Katy's Inn is first in several things: first-rate in location-within walkin distance of everything in town, the first house in La Conner (built i 1876), and the first bed and breakfast in town (begun in 1984). Thi 1876 Victorian sits on a hillside two blocks above historic La Conne which is filled with shops, galleries, antique stores, and waterfront cafe Captain John Peck built this charming country Victorian for his wife an four daughters. It is filled with antiques, and the gardens are a blaze

Victorian glory. The inn offers five guest rooms: four upstairs (two with private baths), with French doors that open onto a wraparound porch with a beautiful view of the town and the Swinomish Channel, and a suite with private bath downstairs and a private entrance that opens into the garden.

If guests want a little activity before hot-tubbing or rocking and reading at the inn, they can feed the sea gulls on the waterfront; sail, raft or canoe down the Swinomish Channel; fish from the pier; take a cruise on the San Juan Islands ferry; ride a bike through the world-famous tulip fields of the Skagit Valley; or take a bird watching/whale watching cruise.

## 28 LANGLEY

**Whidbey Island Antiques**
Anthes Ave. @ 2nd Ave.
360/221-2393

**Lowry-James Fine Antiques**
101 Anthes
360/221-0477

**Virginia's Antiques & Gifts**
206 1st St.
360/221-7797

**Saratoga Antiques**
221 1st St.
360/221-4363

## 29 LEAVENWORTH

**Cabin Fever Rustics**
923 Commercial St.
509/548-4238

**Country Things Antiques & Gifts**
221 8th St.
509/548-7807

**Happy Wanderer**
833 Front St.
509/548-6584

## 30 MAPLE VALLEY

**Maple Valley Trading Post**
12400 Renton Maple Valley Road S.
425/413-0277

**Antique Loft**
25531 S.E. 240th St.
425/432-0669

### *Great Places To Stay*

### Maple Valley Bed and Breakfast

20020 S.E. 228th
425/432-1409
Fax: 425/413-1459
Open daily-reservations required
*For specific directions, please call the innkeeper who will be happy to direct you from your location.*

If you have a hankering to be in the woods, in the quiet of the Pacific Northwest, this is your place. Innkeepers Clarke and Jane Hurlbut have turned their rustic cedar cottage into the Maple Valley Bed and Breakfast, complete with turret and especially built second floor suites. The hand-hewn cottage offers cedar walled guest rooms, one of which was actually built around its special bed! The bed, a handcrafted cedar piece created by Clarke out of logs cut from a nearby woods, is a prized family possession. French doors lead from each guest room onto a spacious balcony. Mint laced jugs of water and chocolate cookies await guests in each suite, and "hot babies" are quietly slipped between the sheets at night. Sounds intriguing, doesn't it? In fact, these "hot babies" have, on more than one occasion, given many guests an unexpected thrill as toes make contact with the warm, shifting lump tucked discreetly between the covers. According to the Hurlbuts, more than one person has sprung from the bed wondering if they had gotten closer to nature than they had ever intended! (Just for the record: "hot babies" are sand-filled bed warmers placed at the foot of the beds at night.)

Breakfast at the inn features Jayne's house specialty hootenanny oven pancakes, an old family recipe; or she might serve any of a number of her other specialties, like omelets, eggs benedict, or waffles. The rustic inn is not only a bed and breakfast, but an almost mythical destination for cyclists, foreign visitors and neighbors, and bed and breakfast guests mingle freely with whomever comes to share the Hurlbuts special kind of hospitality.

## 31 MONROE

**Antique Boutique**
119 W. Main St.
360/805-0325

**Cobweb Antiques**
21928 Yeager
360/794-4256

**Antiques**
110 E. Main St.
No Phone # Listed

### *Great Places To Stay*

### The Frog Crossing Antiques & Collectables, Bed & Breakfast

306 S. Lewis
206/881-7089, 360/794-7622
Directions: 1/4 mile south from Hwy. 2 and directly on State Route 203 (Lewis St.)

The home of The Frog Crossing Antiques & Collectables, Bed & Breakfast was built in 1913 and sets on 3/4 of an acre near old Main Street in Monroe. Monstrous old maple trees and gorgeous rhododendrons surround the house giving it the feel of walking through a park. Carriage tracks from the wagon trains which crossed its path in the olden days can still be see in the front yard.

Romantic rooms with fireplaces set the stage for the perfect get-away vacation. A beautiful Victorian bed with appropriate accessories from the same time period complete the decor.

The bed and breakfast houses an antique shop offering wonderful pieces from which to choose as a momento of your stay at The Frog Crossing. For those of you wanting to explore, The Frog Crossing is only a hop, skip and jump away from Snohomish - The Antique Capital of the Northwest.

## 32 MONTESANO

**Fox's Den**
124 Brumfield Ave.
360/249-5850

### *Great Places To Stay*

**The Abel House Bed and Breakfast**
117 Fleet St. S.
360/249-6002
Rates begin at $55
*Directions: Montesana is at the intersection of State Highways 12 and 107, about 40 miles west of Olympia and 10 miles east of Aberdeen. In-town signs direct you to the Abel House Bed and Breakfast.*

People should visit the Abel House just to see it! You don't often see houses (this one built in 1908) with nine bedrooms on three of the four floors! The main floor is conveniently a common area, with the living room and library boasting "box beamed" ceilings and unique fireplaces. The entry, staircase, and dining room feature the original natural wood with a genuine Tiffany chandelier in the dining room. As the inn's brochure says, "Alas, as with many vintage homes, one bathroom per floor was considered "quite adequate". Fortunately for guests, the Abel House has recently added an addition that has eased the situation somewhat and provided some private baths. There is a game room on the upper floor, and the three lower floors are serviced by an elevator. The mansion's grounds have been lovingly and meticulously maintained and are open for guests' strolling pleasures. Breakfast and tea are served in the garden, the country English dining room, or in the privacy of the guest's room, whichever is preferred. As innkeeper Victor Reynolds says, "Eight years of repeat business indicates the house and staff are first-rate for even the most discriminating B&B goer!"

## 33 MOUNT VERNON

**Old Movie House Antique Mall**
520 Main St.
360/336-8919

**D B's General Store**
1670 Old High #99 S.
360/424-5908

**Posh**
312 Pine St.
360/336-2728

## 34 NACHES

**Bales Antiques**
81 Locust Lane
509/653-2090

**Country Kitchen Antiques**
224 Naches Ave.
509/653-2008

**Hobbit Shop Antiques**
2450 S. Naches Road
509/965-0768

**Wayside Antiques**
10000 U.S. Hwy. 12
509/653-2120

## 35 NORTH BEND

**Bad Girls Antiques**
42901 S.E. North Bend Way
425/888-1902
Wed.-Sat. 11-5, Sun. 12-5
*Directions: From eastbound I-90: Take Exit 27, take a left off the exit, and stay on the road straight through the town of North Bend. Bad Girls is on the right, 4+ miles from the exit and 1 mile from the stoplight in town. From westbound I-90: Take Exit 32, take a right off the exit, and follow the road until you must turn. Turn left. The shop is about 1/2 mile on the left.*

These "bad girls" offer a 4,000 square foot building filled to the brim for your shopping pleasure! Browsers and buyers can take their pick from quality furniture, antique and not-so-old items, unique collectibles, art pottery, fine glass, and 1940s dinnerware.

As is common with most antique dealers, their customers often create some very funny moments. Such is the case in this story as told by Jeanne Marie Klein. "A customer came into the store one day with a lamp that she wanted to know more about. She showed it to my partner," says Jeanne Marie Klein, a Bad Girl owner, "claiming it was made (and signed) by someone named 'Art Newvoo.' 'Who was this man?' she wanted to know. My partner was quizzically examining the lamp when I entered the room. She was very puzzled and asked if I recognized the name as a designer. Frowning, I thought 'Art Newvoo??' The light dawned, and I exclaimed, "You mean Art Nouveau-that's not a person, it's a style!" The poor lady was mystified until we explained further. After she left, we had a good laugh and decided that 'Art Newvoo' must have a sister called 'Arlene Deco!'"

**Zara's Collectables**
401 Ballarat Ave. N.
425/888-0271

**Jaclyn Rose Antiques**
107 W. North Bend Way
425/831-5403

**Snoqualmie Valley Antique Co.**
116 W. North Bend Way
425/888-5900

## 36 OAK HARBOR

**Joseph's Antiques**
28 E. Fakkema Road
360/679-3242

**Lorenzo's Lighting & Antiques**
770 W. Pioneer Way
360/675-7619

**Aladdin's Antiques/DB's General Store**
780 S.E. Pioneer Way #101
360/679-4744

**Oak Harbor Antique Mall**
1079 W. Pioneer Way
360/679-1902

## 37 OLYMPIA

**Mike Cook Antiques & Collectibles**
106 1/2 4th Ave.
360/943-5025

**Hexen Glass**
1015 4th Ave. E.
360/705-8758

**Lamplight Antiques**
2906 Capitol Blvd. S.
360/943-9841

**Once Upon A Time**
7141 Old High #101 N.
360/866-4050

**Summit Lake Antiques & Restorations**
10724 Summit Lake Road N.W.
360/866-0580

**Second Hand Rose**
9243 Yelm Hwy. S.E.
360/459-0954

**Homespun Craft & Antique Mall**
5729 Little Rock Road S.W.
360/943-5194

**R Vernon's**
2724 Pacific Ave. S.E.
360/705-0108

**Old Bank**
404 Washington St. S.E.
360/786-9234

**Sherburne Antiques & Fine Art Inc.**
100 E. 4th Ave.
360/357-9177

## 38 PORT ANGELES

**Marion's Port Angeles Antiques**
220 W. 8th St.
360/452-5411

**Corps Shop**
222 N. Lincoln St.
360/457-7041

**Waterfront Antique Mall**
124 W. Railroad Ave.
360/452-3350

**Mouse Trap Antiques & Gifts**
128 W. 1st St.
360/457-1223

**Springtime Robins & Rainbows**
719 S. Lincoln St.
360/452-4019

**Retro-Ville Antiques & Collectibles**
118 W. 1st St.
360/452-1429

## 39 PORT ORCHARD

**Side Door Mall**
701 Bay St.
360/876-8631

**Harbor Antique Mall**
802 Bay St.
360/895-1898

**Owl In The Attic Antiques**
5637 S.E. Mile Hill Dr.
360/871-0382

**Olde Central Antique Mall**
801 Bay St.
360/895-1902

**Great Prospects Variety Mall**
1039 Bethel Road
360/895-1359

## 40 PORT TOWNSEND

**Port Townsend Antique Mall**
02 Washington St.
60/385-2590

**ncestral Sell**
30 Water St.
60/385-1475

**pril Fool & Penny Too**
25 Water St.
0/385-3438

**Starrett House Antiques**
802 Washington St.
360/385-2590

**Undertown**
211 Taylor St.
360/379-8069

**Antique Company**
1133 Water St.
360/385-9522

## 41 POULSBO

**igails Attic Antiques**
00 N.W. Vinland
0/697-7077

**Hiding Place Antiques**
18830 Front St. N.E.
360/779-7811

**Bad Blanche**
18890 Front St.
360/779-7788

**Cat's Meow**
18940 Front St. N.E.
360/697-1902

**Granny & Papa's Antique Mall**
19669 7th Ave. N.E.
360/697-2221

**Front Street Antiques**
18901 Front St. N.E.
360/697-1899

**Antique Junction**
122 N.E. Moe St.
360/779-1890

### *Great Places To Stay*

### Edgewater Beach Bed & Breakfast

26818 Edgewater Blvd.
1-800-641-0955
*Directions: For specific directions from your location, please call the innkeepers.*

The Edgewater Beach Bed & Breakfast is a charming and peaceful retreat ideally suited for those who want to get away from the hustle and bustle of everyday life and commune with nature. The unassuming front of this two-story cottage-style home conceals a large 4,800 square foot structure of which 3,000 square feet are dedicated to the guests.

The house was built in 1929 by Dr. Mayme MacLafferty, a Seattle physician and surgeon who selected the beautiful land to be the site of her weekend home in the country.

The guest area includes a warm, 670 square foot Great Room which surrounds an impressive, two-sided granite fireplace. Off of the Great Room is a large, bright Sun Room that opens onto an immense 2,800 square foot deck overlooking Puget Sound's fjord, (Hood Canal), an inlet of the ocean that flows in a channel carved by a glacier. The views from the Sun Room and the deck are awe inspiring. From the deck or Sun Room, the vast panoramic vista of the Olympic Mountains behind the fjord is simply breath-taking.

A family of Great American Bald Eagles lives on the edge of the fjord, and their flights are beautiful to watch. Many birds including crows and herons make their homes here; and sometimes the guests are visited by otters, sea lions and deer. On rare occasions, a whale has been spotted swimming in the fjord.

The Edgewater Beach Bed & Breakfast has accommodations for three parties. In addition to the Great Room and Sun Room, guests have access to a glass-enclosed dining room and a spacious, old-fashioned kitchen. The home is furnished in a relaxed, eclectic and sometimes whimsical manner that puts guests at ease while lightening their spirits. Many antiques and treasures from all over the United States create a delightful melange of beauty and playfulness.

Guests are treated to a bountiful breakfast basket that includes: smoked salmon, smoked turkey, cheeses, fresh fruit, pastries, cereal and sparkling beverage and juice.

# Washington

## 42 PUYALLUP

**Heier Echelon**
107 W. Meeker
253/841-3187

**Real Oldies Of Yesteryears**
110 S. Meridian
253/845-4471

**Traditions Antiques**
202 S. Meridian
253/840-8732

**Carnaby Antique Mall**
8424 River Road
253/840-3844

**Antique City**
103 S. Meridian
253/840-4324

**Pioneer Antique Mall**
113 S. Meridian
253/770-0981

**Anderson's Edgewood Mall**
10215 24th St. E.
253/952-5295

**Puyallup Antique Mall**
201 3rd St. S.E.
253/848-9488

## 43 QUILCENE

**Grannys House of Glass**
Hwy. 101 N.
360/765-3230

**Ju Ju Junque**
11 Old Church Road
360/765-3500

**Gay Lees Bowser Beads**
11 Old Church Road
360/765-3545

**Quilcene Art & Antiques**
11 Old Church Road
360/765-4447

## 44 REDMOND

**Olde Stuff Antiques**
16545 N.E. 80th St.
425/869-1697

**Golden Days**
8058 161st Ave. N.E.
425/883-0778

**Valley Furniture & Interiors**
8200 164th Ave. N.E.
425/885-4222

**Edwardian Antiques Inc**
7979 Leary Way N.E.
425/885-4433

**Washington Antiques**
8309 165th Ave. N.E.
425/881-7627

## 45 RENTON

**Park Avenue Antiques**
101 Park Ave. N.
425/255-4255

**Relics Antiques**
229 Wells Ave. S.
425/227/6557

**Antique Palace Too**
807 S. 3rd St.
425/235-9171

**Antique Country Station**
926 S. 3rd St.
425/235-6449

**Downtown Renton Antique Mall**
210 Wells Ave. S.
425/271-0511

**St. Charles Place Antiques**
230 Wells Ave. S.
425/226-8429

**Cedar River Antique Mall**
900 S. 3rd St.
425/255-4900

## 46 RICHLAND

**Carel's Antiques**
1119 S.E. Columbia Dr.
509/783-1775

**Richland Antiques Mall**
1331 George Washington Way
509/943-6762

**Collector's Emporium**
1315 George Washington Way
509/943-2841

**Uptown Antiques Mall**
1340 Jadwin Ave.
509/943-1866

## 47 ROCHESTER

**Up The Creek Antiques**
474 Ingalls Road
360/736-3529

**Honest Don's Antiques**
19225 Joselyn Road S.W.
360/273-8114

## 48 SEATTLE

### Eileen of China
624 S. Dearborn St.
206/624-0816
Daily 10-6

This 30,000-square-foot showroom is filled with exquisite, elegant and unique Asian Antiques and Arts. Enhance your home with traditional Chinese furniture; Zitan, Haunghwali, Hardwood and Rosewood. Simplicity of workmanship.

### G. C. C. Gallery
408 Occidental Ave.
206/344-5244

G. C. C. Gallery is a family opened business which has been producing top of the line replica antique furnishings in Seoul Korea since 1976. The Gallery specializes in authentic oriental styles in such finishes as oyster oliver, burr elm, zelkova, paulownia as well as veneers.

### Lyon's Antique Mall
4516 California S.W.
206/935-9774
WebSite: www.lyonsam.com
Mon.-Sat. 10-6, Sun. 11-5
*Directions: Located in the old JC Penney, one block north of Alaska Junction in West Seattle*

This large antique mall offers a wide variety of antiques an collectibles, including Art Deco, books, crystal, pottery, dolls and Barbie furniture, jewelry, primitives, silver, toys, records and porcelain.

**Antique Importers**
640 Alaskan Way
206/628-8905

**Seattle Antique Market Inc.**
1400 Alaskan Way
206/623-6115

**Antique Warehouse**
1400 Alaskan Way
206/624-4683

**Dragers Classic Toys**
4905 Aurora Ave. N.
206/545-4400

**Cascade Mall**
9530 Aurora Ave. N.
206/524-9626

**Rhinestone Rosie**
606 W. Crockett St.
206/283-4605

**Hunter's Antiques**
106 Denny Way
206/285-9172

**Bogart Bremmer & Bradley Antiques**
8000 15th Ave. N.W.
206/783-7333

**M. Maslan Hist. Photos, Pstcds. & Ephm.**
214 1st Ave. S.
206/587-0187

**Flury & Company Ltd.**
322 1st Ave. S.
206/587-0260

**Kagedo Japanese Antiques**
520 1st Ave. S.
206/467-9077

**Azuma Fine Art & Gallery**
530 1st Ave S.
206/622-5599

**Legacy Ltd.**
1003 1st Ave.
206/624-6350

**Asia Gallery**
1220 1st Ave.
206/622-0516

**Isadora's Antique Clothing**
1915 1st Ave.
206/441-7711

**Village Manor**
17651 1st Ave. S.
206/439-8842

**The Junk Shop**
1404 14th Ave.
206/329-4148

**Fremont Antique Mall**
3419 Fremond Place N.
206/548-9140

**Johnson & Johnson Antiques**
820 Greenwood Ave.
206/789-6489

**Hobby Horse Antiques**
421 Greenwood Ave.
206/789-1574

**Japanense Antiquities Gallery**
200 E. Boston St.
206/324-3322

**Greg Davidson Antiques**
1307 First Ave.
206/625-0406

**Campbell Antiques & Collectibles**
13027 Des Moines Memorial Dr.
206/243-6807

**Mandrake's**
8300 15th Ave. N.W.
206/781-2623

**Carolyn Staley Fine Prints**
313 1st Ave. S.
206/621-1888

**Antiquarius**
514 1st Ave. N.
206/282-5489

**Clarke and Clarke**
524 1st Ave. S.
206/447-7017

**Pioneer Square Mall**
602 1st Ave.
206/624-1164

**Antique Elegance**
1113 1st Ave.
206/467-8550

**Rudy's Vtg. Clthng. & Antq. Watches**
1424 1st. Ave.
206/682-6586

**Jukebox City**
1950 1st Ave. S.
206/625-1950

**David Weatherford Antiques**
133 14th Ave. E.
206/329-6533

**Chelsea Antiques**
3622 N.E. 45th St.
206/525-2727

**Private Screening**
3504 Fremont Place N.
206/548-0751

**Goode Things**
7114 Greenwood Ave.
206/784-7572

**Pelayo Antiques**
7601 Greenwood Ave.
206/789-1999

**Pelayo Antiques**
8421 Greenwood Ave.
206/789-1333

**Jean Williams Antiques**
115 S. Jackson St.
206/622-1110

**Daily Planet**
11046 Lake City Way
206/633-0895

**Antique Galleria**
17171 Lake Forest Park N.E.
206/362-6845

**First Hill Collectibles**
1004 Madison St.
206/624-3207

**Apogee**
4224 E. Madison St.
206/325-2848

**Stuteville Antiques**
1518 E. Olive Way
206/329-5666

**Auntie Shrew's Antiques**
816 S.W. 152nd St.
206/242-0727

**Antique Junktion Mall**
23609 Pacific Hwy. S.
206/878-3069

**Raven's Nest Treasure**
85 B Pike St.
206/343-0890

**Wrinkled Bohemia**
1125 Pike St.
206/464-0850

**Great Western Trading Co.**
1501 Pike Place
206/622-6376

**Old Friends Antiques**
1501 Pike Place
206/625-1997

**N B Nichols & Son**
1924 Post Alley
206/448-8906

**Curbside Collectables**
7011 Roosevelt Way N.E.
206/522-0882

**Kobo**
814 E. Roy St.
206/726-0704

**Hurd's Antiques Etc.**
8554 Greenwood Ave.
206/782-2405

**Honeychurch Antiques**
1008 James St.
206/622-1225

**Gen's Antiques & Dolls**
12518 Lake City Way N.E.
206/365-5440

**Hotel Lobby Antiques**
4105 Leary Way N.W.
206/784-5340

**Veritables**
2816 E. Madison St.
206/726-8047

**Michael Reed Black Antiques**
125 W. Mercer St.
206/284-9581

**Antiques of Burien**
209 152nd St. S.W.
206/431-0550

**My Granny's Attic**
901 S.W. 152nd St.
206/243-3300

**Spindrifters**
Pike Place Market #321
206/623-6432

**B & W Antiques**
311 E. Pike St.
206/325-6775

**Antique Touch**
1501 Pike Place Market, #318
206/622-6499

**Mugs Antiques**
1501 Pike Place
206/623-3212

**Inside Out**
Westlake Center/400 Pine St.
206/292-8874

**Broadway Clock Shop**
2214 Queen Anne Ave. N.
206/285-3130

**Vintage Costumers**
7011 Roosevelt Way N.E.
206/522-5234

**Shahlimar**
217 2nd Ave. S.
206/447-2570

**Ruby Montana's Pinto Pony Ltd.**
603 2nd Ave.
206/621-7669

**Partners In Time**
1332 6th Ave.
206/623-4218

**Silhouette Antiques & Gifts**
1516 N.E. 65th St.
206/525-2499

**Craniums Cool Collectibles**
12331 32nd Ave. N.E.
206/364-8734

**Carriage House Galleries**
5611 University Way N.E.
206/523-4960

**Fairlook Antiques**
81 1/2 Washington
206/622-5130

**Reba's Classic Ceramics**
222 Westlake Ave. N.
206/622-2459

**Antique Liquidators**
503 Westlake Ave. N.
206/623-2740

**Turner Helton Antiques**
2600 Western Ave.
206/322-1994

**The Antlers**
15214 9th Ave. S.W.
206/242-3304

**Laguana Vintage Pottery**
609 2nd Ave.
206/682-6162

**Ageing Fancies**
308 N.E. 65th St.
206/523-4556

**Pacific Galleries**
2121 3rd Ave.
206/441-9990

**Porter Davis Antiques**
103 University St.
206/622-5310

**Oasis Antique Oriental Rugs**
5655 University Way N.E.
206/525-2060

**Downtown Antique Market**
2218 Western Ave.
206/448-6307

**222 Westlake Antique Mall**
222 Westlake Ave. N.
206/628-3117

**Antique Distributors**
507 Westlake Ave. N.
206/622-0555

**Madame & Co. Vintage Fashions**
117 Yesler Way
206/621-1728

## *Great Places To Stay*

### Beech Tree Manor

1405 Queen Anne Ave. N.
206/281-7037
Fax: 206/284-2350
Year round 9-8

*Directions; Beech Tree Manor is located at the northwest corner of the intersection of Queen Anne Ave. N. and Lee St. It has on-street parking. Electric trolleys link the Manor to downtown Seattle and, by transfer, to the entire Metro area.*

Nestled on historic Queen Anne Hill, adjacent to downtown Seattle, this turn-of-the-century mansion has been beautifully restored. Its name comes from the rare and massive Copper Beech tree on the property that has, so far, withstood nature, man, and progress. This bed and breakfast has been described as "an excellent bed and breakfast" by the *New York Times*, and "stunning" by *Seattle's Best Places*. Winning such praises as these comes from the inn's attitude about itself, which is described in its brochure as "organized for the enjoyment of those who require a genteel atmosphere for their temporary housing and special celebrations". To achieve this "genteel atmosphere", the inn offers a very proper English decor, with seven guest rooms (some with private bath). The mansion is filled with a lifetime collection of antiques and offers "all the modern amenities a seasoned traveler expects," plus a few extras, like pure white cotton sheets and a shady porch with wicker rockers. So if proper English is your style, we suggest a stay at the Beech Tree.

## 49 SEAVIEW

**Dory's Antiques & Collectibles**
48th @ Pacific Hwy.
360/642-3005

**Stagecoach Antiques**
4005 Pacific Hwy., #103
360/642-4565

**Sea-Tryst Antiques**
48th Place
360/642-4888

**Gollywobbler Antiques**
4809 Pacific Hwy. S.
360/642-8685

## 50 SEQUIM

**Bramble Cottage Antiques Ltd.**
305 W. Bell St.
360/683-1724

**Lighthouse Antique**
261321 Hwy. 101
360/681-7346

**Gardiner Antiques**
10417 Hwy. 101
360/797-7728

**Queen's Cabinet Antiques**
157 W. Cedar St.
360/681-2778

**Anne's Sequim Antiques**
253 W. Washington St.
360/683-8287

## 51 SHELTON

**Frontier Antiques**
317 S. 1st St.
360/426-7795

**Second Floor Antiques**
107 S. 4th St.
360/427-9310

**Carole's Jewelry**
221 W. Railroad Ave.
360/426-7847

**Olympic Gateway Coins & Cllbls.**
106 S. 4th St.
360/426-0304

**Red Rose Antiques**
1209 Olympic Hwy. S.
360/426-1290

## 52 SNOHOMISH

**Ranee-Paul Antiques**
900 1st St.
360/568-6284

**Rick's Antiques**
916 1st St.
360/568-4646

**Black Cat Antique Mall**
923 1st St.
360/568-8144

**Remember When Antique Mall**
908 1st St.
360/568-0757

**Old Store Antiques**
922 1st St.
360/568-1919

**Another Antique Shop**
924 1st St.
360/568-3629

**River City Antique Mall**
1007 1st St.
360/568-1155

**First Bank Antiques**
1015 1st St.
360/568-7609

**Snohomish Antiques Company**
1019 1st St.
360/563-0343

**Antique Station**
1108 1st St.
360/568-5034

**Victoria Village**
1108 1st St.
360/568-4913

**Antique Palace**
1116 1st St.
360/568-2644

**Michaels 1st Street Antique Mall**
1202 1st St.
360/568-9735

**Egelstads Clock Shop**
809 2nd St.
360/568-3444

**Collectors Book Store**
829 2nd St.
360/568-9455

**Star Center Mall Antiques**
829 2nd St.
206/402-1870

**Casablanca Antiques**
104 C Ave.
360/568-0308

**Faded Glory Ltd.**
113 C Ave.
360/568-5344

**Sharons Antique Mall**
111 Glen Ave.
360/568-9854

**Antique Gallery Mall**
117 Glen Ave.
360/568-7644

**Brenda's Antiques & Collectibles**
118 Glen Ave.
360/568-2322

**Collector's Showcase**
118 Glen Ave.
360/568-1339

**Star Center Mall**
123 Glen Ave.
360/402-1870

**Louis C Wein Antiques & Art**
102 Union St.
360/568-8594

### *Great Places To Stay*

**Redmond House Bed and Breakfast**
317 Glen Ave.
360/568-2042
Rates: $85-100
*Directions: Snohomish is located on Hwy. 9, just east of Everett, Washington. Traveling from I-5 either north or south: use the Wenatchee-Stevens Pass Exit to Hwy. 2. Cross the "Trestle" and stay to the right. The first exit will take you right into town and onto Avenue D. Turn east on 4th Street and right on Glen.*

The Redmond House is another "must" for dyed-in-the-wool antique junkies. It's located in the Victorian era town of Snohomish, within easy walking distance of the "Antique Capital of the Northwest"- 400 antique dealers, gift shops, and restaurants. For the better halves who don't want to spend every minute poking through "old stuff," there are all types of outdoorsy things to do, like exploring the Centennial Trail and the walking tour of Snohomish, plus other hiking, boating, golfing, skiing, hot air ballooning, parachuting, and visits to wineries and sports events all right here in town or within easy driving distance.

The inn greets guests with wonderful gardens and a wraparound porch complete with wicker furniture and a porch swing. The house itself is furnished with period antiques and quilts for everyone's comfort. There's a sunroom with games and a hot tub, a ballroom with big band music, bedrooms with featherbeds, and some even with clawfoot tubs for soaking, plus complimentary tea or sherry at the end of a hard day.

## 53 SPOKANE

**Persnickey's Antiques & Collectibles**
408 N. Argonne Road
509/891-7858

**Duprie's Antiques**
920 W. Cora Ave.
509/327-2449

**B J' Books N Brew**
1320 W. Francis Ave.
509/327-2988

**Vintage Post Cards & Stamps**
1908 N. Hamilton St.
509/487-5677

**Luminaria & La Tierra**
154 S. Madison St.
509/747-9198

**Cloke & Dagger Antiques**
4912 N. Market St.
509/482-2066

**Aunt Bea's Antiques**
5005 N. Market St.
509/487-9278

**Hillyard Variety Consnmt Store**
5009 N. Market St.
509/482-3433

**United Hillyard Mall**
5016 N. Market St.
509/483-2647

**Collectors Showcase Antique Mall**
5201 N. Market St.
509/482-7112

**Benson's Antiques**
5215 N. Market St.
509/487-3528

**Monroe St. Bridge Antique Market**
604 N. Monroe St.
509/327-6398

**Antique Gallery**
620 N. Monroe St.
509/325-3864

**Spokane Book Center**
626 N. Monroe St.
509/328-2332

**Worthington Discontinued China**
2217 N. Monroe St.
509/328-7072

**Vintage Rabbit Antique Mall**
2317 N. Monroe St.
509/326-1884

**Wooden Rail**
818 N. Pines Road
509/922-3443

**Spokane Valley Antique Mall**
23 S. Pines Road
509/928-9648

**Ben's Antiques**
2130 E. Sprague Ave.
509/535-4368

**N.W. Collector Arms**
12021 E. Sprague Ave.
509/891-0990

**Spokane Antique Mall**
12 W. Sprague Ave.
509/747-1466

**Larsen's Antique Clock Shop**
953 E. 3rd Ave.
509/534-4994

**Antiquex**
28 W. 3rd Ave.
509/624-6826

**Timeless Treasures Antiques**
10309 E. Trent Ave.
509/928-0819

**Schade Brewery Antique Mall**
528 E. Trent Ave.
509/624-0272

**No Place Like Home**
13409 E. Wellesley Ave.
509/922-4246

## 54 STANWOOD

**Apple Barrell Antiques**
1415 Pioneer Hwy., #530
360/652-9671

**Yo Mama's Attic Antiques**
8617 271 St. N.W.
360/629-3995

## 55 SUMNER

**The Blue Lantern**
1003 Main St.
253/863-5935

**Whistle-Stop Antique Mall**
1109 Main St.
253/863-3309

**Cobwebs Removed Inc.**
1008 Main St.
253/863-1924

## 56 TACOMA

**Abigail's Antiques**
8825 Bridgeport Way S.W.
253/588-9712

**Victoria's**
702 Broadway
253/272-5983

**Freighthouse Antiques Empor**
728 Broadway
253/627-8019

**Memory Mall**
744 Broadway
253/272-6476

**Lily The Pad**
756 Broadway
253/627-6858

**Collectors Nook**
213 N. I St.
253/272-9828

**European Antique Imports**
1930 Pacific Ave.
253/272-8763

**Pacific Run Antique Mall**
10228 Pacific Ave. S.
253/539-0117

**Aries Antiques**
16120 Pacific Ave.
253/582-9029

**Claudia Smith's Antiques**
5101 N. Pearl St.
253/759-6052

**Anchor Antiques Co.**
5129 N. Pearl St.
253/752-1134

**Treasure Chest**
11605 Bridgeport Way S.W.
253/581-2454

**Mimi's Antique Furniture**
3813 N. 26th St.
253/759-0506

**Sanford & Son Antiques**
743 Broadway
253/272-0334

**Time Machine**
746 Broadway
253/272-7254

**Woodward's Antiques**
12146 C St.
253/531-1005

**Bellocchio Antiques & Bistro**
1926 Pacific Ave.
253/383-3834

**Ramlawn Antiques**
1936 Pacific Ave.
253/272-5244

**Parkland Parish Antique Mall**
12152 Pacific Ave. S.
253/537-0978

**Valentino's Antiques & Books**
4931 N. Pearl St.
253/759-3917

**Ruston Antique Galleries**
5101 N. Pearl St.
253/759-2624

**Curtright & Son Gallery**
759 Saint Helens Ave.
253/383-2969

**Teri's Curiosity Shop**
760 Saint Helens Ave.
253/383-3211

**Museum Antiques**
5928 Steilacoom Blvd. S.W.
253/584-3930

**Katy's Antiques & Collectibles Mall**
602 E. 25th St.
253/305-0203

**Key Antiques**
5485 Steilacoom Blvd S.W.
253/588-0569

**Mandarin Oriental Antiques**
5935 Steilacoom Blvd. S.W.
253/582-6655

### *Great Places To Stay*

### The DeVoe Mansion Bed & Breakfast

208 E. 133rd St.
206/539-3991
Fax: 253/539-8539
Daily 8-9
Rates: $80-90
Email: devoe wolfenet.com
Web site: www.wolfenet.com/~devoe/
*Directions: From Seattle or Tacoma: Take I-5 south (from Olympia take I-5 north) to Exit 127. Go east on Hwy. 512 approximately two miles to the Pacific Ave. exit (signs also say Mt. Rainier, State Route 7, Parkland, Pacific Lutheran University). Go south on Pacific Ave. approximately 2 miles, and turn left on 133rd St. South. Continue two blocks and the DeVoe Mansion is on the corner of 133rd St. and B Ave.*

Ladies, this one's for you! The 1911 DeVoe Mansion was named to the National Historic Register in 1993 in honor of a tireless pioneer in the women's suffrage movement. The home was built for John and Emma Smith DeVoe, who moved into the mansion one year after Emma had successfully helped the women of Washington State achieve the right to vote. It would be another 10 years before all women in the United States were granted that same right. Emma's home was named to the National Historic Register as a tribute to her devoted efforts to the suffrage cause on both national and state levels.

To understand and appreciate the mansion's history and decor, guests need to know a little about Emma, because Emma's life's work in the suffrage movement is the decorating basis for each of the mansion's guest rooms. Emma's dedication to the suffrage cause began when she was eight years old, when she and her sister attended a rally featuring Susan B. Anthony. When Emma came to Washington State in 1906, she found a very disorganized, unmotivated suffrage association. Her first winter on the West Coast saw her elected as president of the Washington State Equ[al] Suffrage Association, and she spent the next four years traveling the state rejuvenating and revitalizing the association. On November 8, 191[0] Washington became the fifth state in the union to pass women's suffrag[e]

Each of the guest rooms is named for someone who was significant [in] Emma's life. The Susan B. Anthony Room features an 1880's hand-carv[ed] oak bedroom set, private sitting area and private bath. The Carrie Chapman Catt Room is highlighted by a queen-sized, four poster mahogany rice bed with an old growth Alaskan cedar tree just outside the window. The John Henry DeVoe Room is named for Emma's most devoted supporter-her husband. It holds an antique queen-size 1860s pine bedroom set. Guests are also treated to two porches for rocking and relaxing, a hot tub on the deck, landscaped grounds for strolling, and breakfast.

## 57 VANCOUVER

**Yesterdays Treasures**
707 Grand Blvd.
360/695-2330

**Downtown Main Antique Mall**
1108 Main St.
360/696-2253

**Something Nice Antiques & Collectibles**
2310 Main St.
360/694-2948

**Henkers**
14013 S.E. Mill Plain Blvd.
360/256-5620

**Vendors Outlet Mall**
7907 N.E. Hwy. 99
360/574-6674

**Main Street Trader**
1916 Main St.
360/695-0295

**Country Peddler**
2315 Main St.
360/695-6792

**Jadestone Gallery**
10922 N.E. St. Johns Road
360-573-2580

## 58 VASHON

**Lawing's Antiques & Textiles**
16619 Westside Hwy. S.W.
206/463-2402

**Owens Antiques & Decorative Arts**
19605 Vashon Hwy. S.W.
206/463-5193

**Sandy's Antiques & Jewelry**
17607 Vashon Hwy. S.W.
206/463-5807

## 59 WALLA WALLA

**onnie's Antiques**
815 E. Isaacs Ave.
09/529-2009

**ountry Collectors**
26 E. Main St.
9/529-6034

**hady Lawn Antiques & Espresso**
1 N. Rose St.
9/529-2123

**General Store**
211 W. Main St.
509/522-8663

**Antique Mall at Vintage Square**
315 S. 9th Ave.
509/525-5100

## 60 WENATCHEE

**Pretentious Antique Co.**
328 N. Chelan Ave.
509/663-8221

**Village Mall Antiques**
611 S. Mission St.
509/662-9171

**Antique Mall of Wenatchee**
11 N. Wenatchee Ave.
509/662-3671

**Collectors Gallerie**
928 N. Wenatchee Ave.
509/663-5203

**Adams Supply Co.**
509 S. Mission St.
509/662-2210

**Early American Light Lamps**
1206 Okanogan Ave.
509/662-0386

**Dimitri's Antiques & Seconds**
810 S. Wenatchee Ave.
509/662-2920

**Treasures of the Heart**
20 S. Wenatchee Ave.
509/663-8112

## 61 WINLOCK

**Kattywampus Antique Mall**
405 1st St. N.E.
360/785-4427

**Old Hatchery**
707 N.E. 1st St.
No Phone

## 62 YAKIMA

**Somewhere In Time**
3911 S. 1st St.
509/248-7352

**Shopkeeper**
807 W. Yakima Ave.
509/452-6646

**Mt. Mommie's General Store**
225 Naches Ave.
509/653-2556

**Churchill's Books & Antiques**
125 S. 2nd St.
509/453-8207

**Antiques Etc.**
5703 Tieton Dr.
509/966-2513

**Yesterday's Village**
15 W. Yakima Ave.
509/457-4981

**Depot**
32 N. Front St.
509/576-6220

**Antique Alley Mini-Mall**
1302 W. Lincoln Ave.
509/575-1499

**Calico Barn Antiques**
1471 S. Naches Road
509/966-1462

**Antiques & Decor Ltd.**
108 S. 3rd Ave.
509/457-6949

**Lantern Antiques**
8507 Tieton Dr.
509/966-1396

**Green Gables**
302 E. Yakima Ave.
509/577-0744

# West Virginia

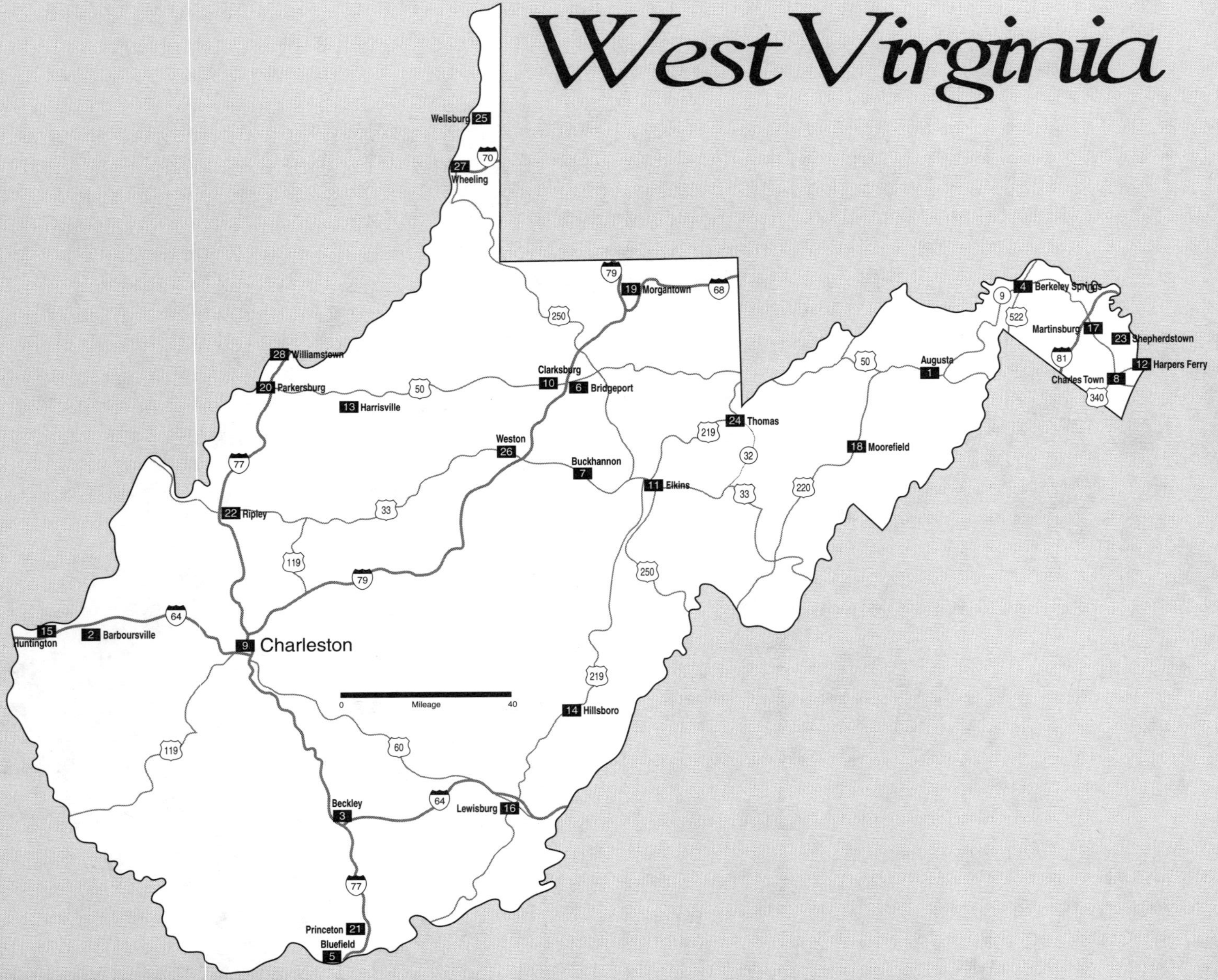

## 1 AUGUSTA

**Dan's Antiques**
Route 50
304/496-8187

**Smith's Antiques**
Route 50
304/496-9474

## 2 BARBOURSVILLE

### Miller House Antiques

1112 Main St.
304/736-0845 or 304/523-6064
Tue.-Sat. 10-5, Sun.-Mon. by appointment
*Directions: From I-64, take the Barboursville exit. Continue for 2 miles into downtown Barboursville. The shop is located on Main St. in the historic Downtown area.*

The William Clendenim Miller home was built in 1852 out of "Barboursville brick," made on site. It served as the town post office from 1840 to 1860, and W.C. Miller, who was postmaster, would read letters to the townspeople from his porch or the parlor. On July 14, 1861, the Civil War's first skirmish of Barboursville took place within sight of the home, and Miller's son, John William, took a little double-barreled pistol and joined the Confederate forces. During the second skirmish the 2nd Virginia Cavalry (Union) was ordered to attack the house on rumors that it was the headquarters of Confederate Brig. A.S. Jenkins. Union Duty Sergeant, Braxton P. Reeves, was killed and his body placed on the porch of the Miller House until it could be retrieved by the Union.

In the early 1900s the home was purchased from the Miller family and used as a college boarding house. In 1914 John W. Miller, son of the original owner, bought back his birthplace for obvious sentimental reasons.

Today, the house is an antique shop and is decorated with period furniture, china, paintings, quilts, etc. All are for sale. There are 11 rooms, each with a fireplace. The house is on a daily scheduled walking tour of historic Barboursville.

## 3 BECKLEY

**ckley Antique Mall**
8 George St.
4/255-6825

## 4 BERKELEY SPRINGS

### rkeley Springs Antique Mall

0 Fairfax St.
4/258-5676
ur.-Tues. 10-5, closed Wed.
*rections: From Route 70, take Hwy. 522 south and follow it aight for 7 miles to the heart of downtown Berkeley Springs.*

Berkeley Springs offers visitors a general line of antiques from 30 lers in 6,500 square feet of space housed in a 1910 building.

**Curiosity Shop**
101 N. Washington St.
304/258-1634

**Antique House**
312 N. Washington St.
304/258-9420

## 5 BLUEFIELD

If a taste of coal culture piques your interest, head for West Virginia's southern-most border. Bluefield, off I-77, is the scene of much coal history, both past and present. The downtown overlooks an extensive network of railroad tracks, often loaded with car after car of glittering black rock. The Eastern Regional Coal Archives are housed in the Craft Memorial Library and include coal company records, diaries, oral histories and displays of miners' tools and industry artifacts.

**Second Time Around**
1715 Bluefield Ave.
304/325-9855

**Landmark Mini Mall**
200 Federal St.
304/327-9686

**Antiques at the Old Trade Post**
1204 Augusta St.
304/325-2554

### *Interesting Side Trip*

A few miles northwest of Bluefield on U.S. 52 is Bramwell, once considered the richest town in the United States. As many as 14 millionaires resided there in the early 20th century during the height of the coal boom. Tours, available in May and December, or can be arranged anytime. The town's late 19th century fairy-tale architecture of turrets, gables, slate and tile roofs, leaded and stained glass, ornate woodwork and wide porches are a well-preserved reminder of West Virginia's Gilded Age.

## 6 BRIDGEPORT

### Shahadys Antiques

214 E. Main St.
304/842-6691 or 1-800-252-0766
Tues.-Sat. 10-5
*Directions: Traveling I-79, take Exit 119 (Bridgeport/Clarksburg West Virginia) to Route 50 east 1.5 miles to downtown Bridgeport.*

Shahady's carries the largest diversified inventory in the tri-state area, with 500 pieces of furniture in stock, ranging from the 1800s to the 20th century. They also handle stoneware, lighting fixtures and glassware, plus architectural antiques, both retail and wholesale to the trade.

### Grey Fox Farm Antiques

RR 1, #39 A
304/842-4219
Mon.-Sat. 11-3
*Directions: From I-79, take Exit 119. Turn left and go east on Route 50 for several miles. Turn right onto Route 58 and go a half-mile to the stop sign. Turn left on Route 26. The shop is located 2 9/10 miles farther on the right.*

The shop is actually located in the barn of Grey Fox Farm. They specialize in carefully selected 18th and 19th century furniture, as well as offering a wide selection of decorative accessories and gifts.

## 7 BUCKHANNON

**Buckhannon Antique Mall**
Clarksburg Road
304/472-9605

**Franklin Trash & Treasury Antiques**
Clarksburg Road
304/472-8738

**Antiques Etc.**
4 E. Main St.
304/472-1120

### *Great Places To Stay*

**Post Mansion Inn B&B**
8 Island Ave.
1-800-301-9309

The Post Mansion, one of the oldest bed and breakfasts in Upshur County, was constructed in 1860 and remodeled of prison cut stone in 1892 for Senator William Post. Being the largest example of a native cut stone house in Upshur County, the home has fondly been called the mansion or castle. The house contains thirty rooms, five of which are guest rooms, five baths, old wood staircases, stained glass windows, and porches. The inn is located on six acres of land with the Buckhannon River bordering both the front and rear.

## 8 CHARLES TOWN

**Wooden Shoe**
222 W. Washington St.
304/725-1673

**Grandma's Treasures**
615 E. Washington St.
304/728-2199

## 9 CHARLESTON

**Hale St. Antiques & Collectibles Mall**
213 Hale St.
304/345-6040
Tues.-Sun. 11-5
*Directions: From I-64 east, take the Lee St. Exit and turn right onto Hale St.*

This antique mall is located in a historic hardware and paint store, and is the largest antiques shop in Charleston. Its three floors are filled with a variety of furniture, glassware and collectibles.

**Alex Franklin Ltd.**
1007 Bridge Road
304/342-8333

**Attic Antiques**
313 D St.
304/744-8975

**South Charleston Antique Mall**
4800 MacCorkle Ave. S.W.
304/766-6761

**Tiny Tim's**
5206 MacCorkle Ave. S.E.
304/768-8111

**Trophy Design**
418 Virginia St. W.
304/346-3907

**Tiki's Antique Gallery**
1312 Watts St.
304/346-6160

**Belle's Antiques**
4270 Woodrums Lane
304/744-5435

**Kanawha Coin/Antiques**
707/712 Fife
304/342-8081

**Split Rail Antiques**
2580 Benson Dr.
304/342-6084

## 10 CLARKSBURG

Clarksburg, the birthplace of General Thomas "Stonewall" Jackson, was the adopted home of thousands of immigrant laborers after the Civil War and, thanks to the discovery of gas and oil, a manufacturing center for glass, tin and zinc.

Two monuments mark the town's heritage. A likeness of "Stonewall" sits astride a bronze horse on the courthouse plaza and nearby, a heroic sculpture represents the Belgian, Czech, Greek, Hungarian, Irish, Italian, Romanian and Spanish immigrants who flocked to the region beginning in the 1880s.

**Kollage**
1625 Buckhannon Pike
304/622-8137

**West End Antiques**
97 Milford St.
304/624-7600

**Red Wheel Antiques**
600 Southern Ave.
304/622-2192

**Carneys Fine Antiques**
315 Spring Ave.
304/622-1317

**Briar Patch Antiques**
Route 20 S.
304/623-1213

## 11 ELKINS

**Bittersweet Books & Antiques**
212 Davis Ave.
304/636-6338 or 1-800-417-6338
Mon.-Sat. 10-5, Sundays by appointment or chance
*Directions: Bittersweet is accessible from Highways 250, 33 and 219, all of which lead to historic downtown Elkins.*

Bittersweet Books and Antiques specializes in paper, as well as carryi[ng] a general line of antiques. Their paper goods include sheet musi[c,] postcards, magazines, trade cards, and old and rare books.

**S and S Company**
204 Findley St.
304/636-2366

**Grannys Attic**
427 Kerens Ave.
304/636-4121

**Justines Antiques Etc.**
Old Seneca Road
304/636-2891

**Mrs. McGillicuddy's Antiques**
203 4th St.
304/636-9356

### *Great Places To Stay*

**The Warfield House Bed & Breakfast**
318 Buffalo St.
1-888-636-4555
Open all year
Rates: $65-75 includes a complimentary full breakfast. Children 12 and older welcome. Absolutely smoke free residence
*For specific directions to The Warfield House Bed and Breakfast call the innkeepers.*

The Warfield House Bed & Breakfast provides the traveler with comfort, warm hospitality, and good food all in an elegant turn-of-the-century setting. Whether you're looking for a mountain retreat or an activity-packed vacation you will find it in the beautiful mountains of West Virginia. The quaint town of Elkins is the perfect central location for year-round outdoor recreation and The Warfield House is the perfect "home base" from which to explore.

Built in 1901 by a local bank executive, Harry Ridgely Warfield and his wife Susan Stadtler, the grand shingle and brick house was listed on the National Register of Historic Places in 1997. The spacious rooms display an abundance of woodwork, beautiful stained glass, and period fixtures. The foyer opens to an interior vestibule where an oak staircase, bathed in rich hues from the two-story stained glass window on the landing, rises to four large guest rooms on the second floor. Two of these four rooms currently have private baths but a planned renovation to the rear porch will allow another bath to be added, thus equipping all the guest rooms with private baths in the near future. The fifth bedroom, over the kitchen wing, is accessed by its own private staircase and has a private bath.

Guests are welcome to make use of the parlor, library, and dining room on the first floor to relax, read, eat, or plan their next excursion. After a full breakfast of fresh fruit, home baked breads and pastries, and hot entree served family style at the massive oak table you may choose a day trip to Blackwater Falls State Park, Canaan Valley Resort, Cass Scenic Railroad, Spruce Knob/Seneca Rocks Recreation Area, the historic Swiss Village of Helvetia or Rich Mountain Battlefield.

If you choose instead to stay close to home, a five minute walk to downtown Elkins will bring you to cozy restaurants, an artists gallery, and of course, several terrific antique shops. Among our favorites is Bittersweet Books and Antiques, specializing in old and rare books, ephemera, and a general line of antiques.

The bed and breakfast cannot accommodate your pets but their dog, "Boo" and cat, "Red" welcome your attention.

## 12 HARPERS FERRY

The town of Harpers Ferry is perhaps livelier today than it was in 1859, when abolitionist John Brown staged his raid on the United States Arsenal there, setting off a chain of events that resulted in the Civil War. Undoubtedly more beautiful than ever, its historic section is polished and maintained as a national historic park, and is part of the Civil War Discovery Trail.

**Hodge Podge**
144 High St.
304/535-6917
Mon.-Fri. 10-5, Sat.-Sun. 10-6
*Directions: Located on Hwy. 340 in downtown historic Harpers Ferry.*

Hodge Podge handles small antiques, gifts, collectibles, and Civil War items—a true "hodgepodge" of merchandise!

**Stone House Antiques**
108 Potomac St.
304/535-6688

**Washington St. Antiques**
1080 Washington St.
304/535-2411

### *Great Places To Stay*

**Ranson Armory House Bed & Breakfast**
690 Washington St.
304/535-2142

Ranson Armory House Bed & Breakfast is located in Historic Harper's Ferry at the confluence of the Potomac and Shenandoah Rivers. The original dwelling, dating from the 1830s, was built by the Federal government to house U.S. Armory staff. It was enlarged in the 1890s with Victorian architectural features. The spacious rooms are furnished with antiques and family heirlooms and have mountain views.

### *Interesting Side Trip*

Wind along the cobblestone streets of Harpers Ferry to the town of Bolivar, where shops feature a remarkable collection of antiques including Civil War memorabilia and local crafts.

## 13 HARRISVILLE

A short detour off Hwy. 50 south on West Virginia Route 16 takes you to quaint Harrisville, where Berdine's 5 & Dime, the nation's oldest five and dime, still operates after 80 years on Court St. Its solid oak cabinets and glass bins offer penny candy, small toys and practical household items.

**The Upper Room**
201 A E. Main St.
304/643-2599

**Barb & Ben's Antique Shop**
1012 E. Main St.
304/643-2977

## 14 HILLSBORO

On the literary front, Hillsboro is the birthplace of Pearl S. Buck, one of the world's best loved authors. Her family home, the Stulting House, is open for tours, and contains original furnishings and memorabilia. Among its annual events is Author's Day in August, dedicated to keeping the Nobel and Pulitzer Prize writer's spirit alive.

While in Hillsboro, step back in time at the Hillsboro General Store, and stop for a bite to eat at the popular little Country Roads Cafe.

**Hillsboro General Store**
Route 219
304/653-4414

### *Favorite Places To Eat*

**Country Roads Cafe**
Route 219
304/653-8595
Tues.-Fri.11-9, Sat. & Sun. 8-9

The modern occupation of Country Roads Cafe is serving up home-cooked meals with fresh-baked desserts. Breakfast, lunch and dinner specials are regular features. This 100-year-old establishment still possesses a ladder from its earliest years as a general store. Furnishings are antique, and visitors can buy antique wire-made frames, mirrors, and numerous other small delights.

## 15 HUNTINGTON

**Antique Center, Inc.**
610 14th St. W.
304/523-7887

**Adams Avenue Antique Mall**
1460 Adams Ave.
304/523-7231

**Collectors Store Antique Mall**
1660 Adams Ave.
304/429-3900

**Stouffer's Shady Business**
845 8th Ave.
304/697-8905

**Bus Barn Antiques Mall**
402 18th St. W.
304/429-3485

**Hattie and Nan's Antique Mkt. Place**
521 14th St. W..
304/523-8844

**Mark's Antiques**
600 14th St. W.
304/525-3275

**Pieces of the Past**
606 14th St. W.
304/522-7892

**Bob's Second Hand**
619 14th St. W.
304/523-6854

**Lucky Penny**
1404 Washington Ave.
304/522-1777

**Lewis' Antiques & Collectibles**
720 14th St. W.
304/522-0444

**Memories of the Heart**
1408 Adams Ave.
304/697-5301

**A Touch of Country**
418 9th St.
304/525-2808

**Mimmi's Collectors Dolls**
544 6th Ave.
304/522-4841

**Central City Antique Mall**
611 14th St. W.
304/523-0311

**Classics Antiques & Interiors**
1337 5th Ave. W.
304/697-3416

**Adell's Antiques**
444 W. 14th St.
304/529-1177

## 16 LEWISBURG

**Antiques**
120 E. Washington St.
304/647-3404

**Peddlar's Alley Antiques**
123 E. Washington St.
304/645-4082

### *Great Places To Stay*

**Lynn's Inn Bed & Breakfast**
Route 4, Box 40
1-800-304-2003
Open year round
Seasonal rates
*Directions: Lynn's is located 1 1/2 miles north of I-64 (Exit 169) on U.S. Hwy. 219.*

This is a switch from the majority of bed and breakfasts because, instead of being a former farm, this is a working farm—they actually raise beef cattle. The inn itself is a former tourist home built in 1935 and furnished with original antiques. There are four guest rooms, all with private baths and two sitting rooms. Guests are served a full country breakfast, and there is a large porch with rockers and ferns to help folks enjoy a true country weekend.

**General Lewis Inn**
301 E. Washington St.
1-800-628-4454

The General Lewis is a unique blend of the old and the new, created and operated by the Hock family since 1928. The eastern end of the building, including the dining room, the kitchen and a suite of rooms on the first floor plus two bedrooms and a suite on the second floor, was a brick residence built in the early 1800s by John H. Withrow. Mr. and Mrs. Randolph Hock purchased it from Withrow's daughter. Walter Martens, a well-known West Virginia architect who designed the Governor's Mansion in Charleston, designed the main section and the west wing according to their plans. The Hock family spent many years gathering antiques from Greenbrier and adjourning counties to furnish the inn. Spool and canopy beds, chests of drawers, china, glass, old prints and other memorabilia are throughout the home.

## 17 MARTINSBURG

Incorporated in 1778, Martinsburg later flourished as a railroad town home to the B & O Railroad engine shop. Coveted by both sides in the Civil War, the Union army held it for 32 months, the Confederate for 1

Old Town Martinsburg offers a variety of antique shops specializing in primitives, Victorian, dolls, linens and unusual accessories.

**Manor House Antiques**
242 S. Queen St
304/263-5950

**Affordable Antiques & Furniture**
556 N. Queen St.
304/263-9024

**Little Shop Antiques**
563 N. Queen St.
304/267-1603

**Blue Ridge Country Antqs. & Ints.**
204 S. Queen St.
304/263-4275

### *Favorite Places To Eat*

**Market House Grill**
100 N. Queen St.
304/263-7615

To dine at the historic Market House Grill is considered an "eating adventure," with both Continental and Cajun fare their specialty—quite out of the ordinary for the location.

### *Interesting Side Trips*

**The Apollo Civic Theatre**
128 E. Martin St., P.O. Box 519
304/263-6766

The Apollo Civic Theatre has the distinction of being the oldest live performance stage in West Virginia. Call for a complete listing of shows, times and ticket prices.

## 18 MOOREFIELD

### *Great Places To Stay*

**McMechen House Inn**
109 N. Main St.
1-800-298-2466

Innkeepers, Bob and Linda Curtis, invite you to return to the mid-1800s. Imagine a time of delicate antebellum grace backdropped against soaring political activity. The McMechen House is a splendid romantic home built in 1853 by Samuel A. McMechen, a local merchant and political activist. The three-story brick home features Greek Revival style and is located in the center of Moorefield Historic District. During the Civil War the house served as headquarters to both the Union and Confederate forces as military control of the valley changed hands.

Here you will find excellent food, spacious rooms, friendship, and generous hospitality. Tour local wineries or shop the antique and gift shops. Catch a community play or ride the Potomac Eagle (seasonal) or just simply relax on one of the inn's spacious porches. Cradled in the historic South Branch Valley and surrounded by the majestic mountains of the Potomac Highlands, you can enjoy a myriad of river sports - fishing, canoeing, or kayaking.

## 19 MORGANTOWN

**Bittersweet Antiques**
Beechurst
304/296-4602

**Dale's Oldtiques**
Stewartstown Road
304/599-9074

**Sally's Alley**
1389 University Ave.
304/292-9230

## 20 PARKERSBURG

Antique shops in the region frequently carry a broad selection of vintage regional glass. Maher's Antiques in Parkersburg offers glass, plus a selection of crocks with A.P. Donagho's Excelsior Pottery signature, recalling the days when homes throughout the Midwest stored food in the Parkersburg Company's pots.

**Maher's Antiques**
1619 Saint Mary's Ave.
304/485-1331

**Pure & Simple Antiques & Cllbls.**
60 Schultz St.
304/422-3117

## 21 PRINCETON

**Hobby Shop Antiques**
305 Mercer St.
304/487-1990

**Olde Towne Shoppe**
929 Mercer St.
304/425-3677

**A-Z Trading Center**
509 Roger St.
304/425-4365

## 22 RIPLEY

**Blue Ribbon Antiques**
Route 33
304/372-5006
Tues.-Sat. 9-4, closed Sun.-Mon.
*Directions: Take Exit 138 off I-77. The shop is 2 miles west of the Ripley Exit on Route 33.*

Here's one for a rainy day or for the serious browser. Housed in a 200-year-old seven-room farmhouse, the shopkeeper describes Blue Ribbon Antiques as being "floor to ceiling, wall to wall; the old house is literally bulging with antiques and glassware."

**Country Place**
111 Court St. S.
304/372-5048

**Millie's Antiques**
1 Starcher Place
304/372-1859

## 23 SHEPHERDSTOWN

Just a few miles northeast of Martinsburg lies Shepherdstown, one of the oldest towns in West Virginia, established in the 1730s as Mechlenberg. Today, it's a quaint town of wooden storefronts and tree-lined streets, where specialty shops, charming restaurants, small inns and cultural programs of Shepherd College fill the town with visitors.

The eclectic 1930s Yellow Brick Bank, The Olde Pharmacy Cafe, complete with original pharmaceutical trappings, and Ye Olde Sweet Shoppe offer historic settings and good food.

**Matthews & Shank Antiques**
139 W. German
304/876-6550

***Great Places To Stay***

**Stonebrake Cottage**
P.O. Box 1612
304/876-6607

Stonebrake Cottage is a darling Victorian country home located at the edge of the owner's 145 acre farm. It is unique because the guests occupying the cottage have the exclusive use of the entire cottage for their stay. The cottage will sleep up to six people in one part and is decorated throughout with early American antiques.

## 24 THOMAS

**Eagle's Nest I & II**
Route 32
304/463-4186 or 304/463-4113
Daily 10-5
*Directions: Both Eagle's Nests are located on Route 32 in Thomas.*

These two stores carry collectibles, antiques and good junque. They also claim to have the best selection of handmade dolls and crafts in West Virginia. After you're through admiring the familiar, the strange and the remarkable, have a refreshment at their coffee bar while you decide what to take home from the shop.

## 25 WELLSBURG

True to its beginnings as a late 18th century port, Wellsburg's Downtown Wharf still welcomes vintage river boats such as the Mississippi Queen in July and the Delta Queen in October. For each visit, the town puts on a party, with bands, food, artisans and boat tours.

Wellsburg's downtown National Historic District features specialty shops, riverside greens and restaurants. A short drive from downtown you'll find Drover's Inn, an authentic 1848 country inn with handcrafted furnishings, an Old English-style pub and a restaurant famous for its home-cooked buffet.

**Wellsburg Flower Shop, Inc.**
600 Charles St.
304/737-3380

**Raggedy Ann's Country Store**
740 Charles St.
304/737-1518

**Watzman's Old Place**
709 Charles St.
304/737-0711

## 26 WESTON

**Ethel's Antiques & Collectibles**
107 Main Ave.
304/269-7690

**A Penny Saved Antique & Cllbls.**
230 Main Ave.
304/269-3258

## 27 WHEELING

Wheeling is the historical and commercial hub of the Northern Panhandle. From its earliest days as a pre-Revolutionary outpost and stop along the National Road's path to the western frontier, to its 18th and 19th century role as a port of entry, through its boom and bust Victorian Era as the center of glass, steel and textiles, Wheeling has preserved and persevered.

Independence Hall in downtown Wheeling has served as an 18th and 19th century customs house, as the capitol of the Restored Government of West Virginia, and later as the state capital for the new state of West Virginia. Today, it serves as a center for art and a showcase for the state's history, and is part of the Civil War Discovery Trail.

The city's most distinctive historic landmark, the 1849 Wheeling Suspension Bridge, dazzles visitors at night with its brilliant necklace of decorative lights. The oldest major long span suspension bridge in the world, the bridge is a designated National Historic Landmark.

Just blocks from downtown, Wheeling's Centre Market district is listed on the National Register of Historic Places. It's also high on the list for shoppers seeking antiques, traditional crafts, gourmet and specialty food items and unique gifts. Restaurants and a Victorian-style confectionery will rejuvenate the weary shopper.

The Old Town neighborhood on Main St. in north Wheeling also offers shoppers the opportunity to visit another era. Shops located in historic townhouses and mansions offer fine works of art, antiques and Victorian decorations and accents. Unique restaurants provide a relaxing respite.

**Northgate Antiques & Interiors, Inc.**
735 Main St.
304/232-1475

**Outdoor Store**
1065 Main St.
304/233-1080

**Downtown Wheeling Antiques**
1120 Main St.
304/232-8951

**Antiques on the Market**
2265 Market St.
304/232-1665

## 28 WILLIAMSTOWN

Since 1905, Williamstown's Fenton Art Glass Company has bee[n] producing the finest in original art glass. On a free plant tour, you'll s[ee] molten glass born in fiery hot furnaces begin its unique journey on t[heir] way to becoming tomorrow's heirlooms. Under the persuasion of mas[ter] craftsmen using century-old tools and techniques, beautiful Fent[on] glassware takes shape amidst a constant, roaring baptism of fire. Fo[r a] nominal fee, visit the company's glass museum to view one-of-a-ki[nd] glass pieces, including Fenton's original carnival glass, and to watc[h a] video on the history of Fenton Glass.

**Williamstown Antique Mall**
439 Highland Ave.
304/375-6315

# Wisconsin

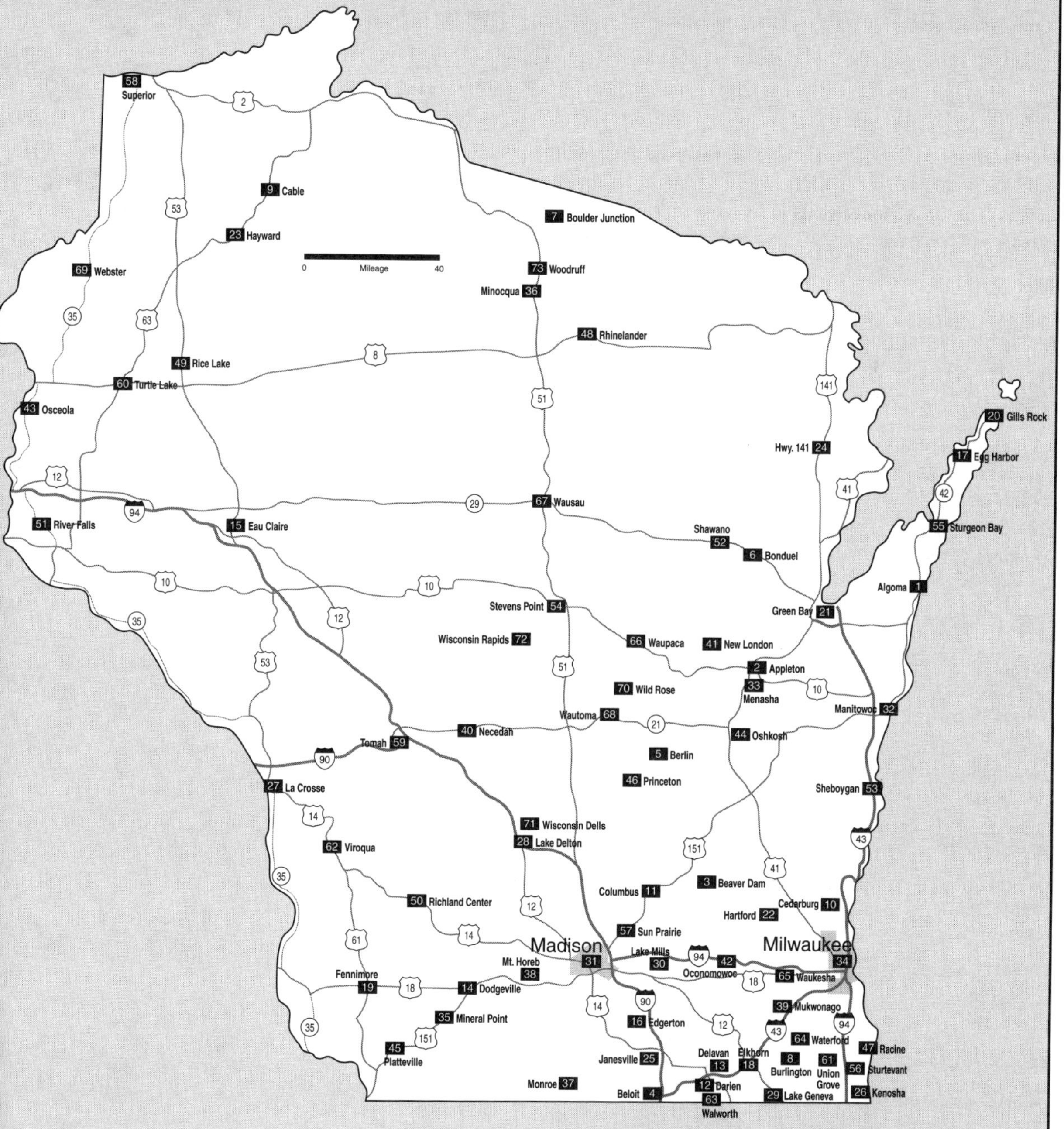

58 Superior
2
9 Cable
53
7 Boulder Junction
23 Hayward
0 Mileage 40
69 Webster
73 Woodruff
Minocqua 36
35
63
48 Rhinelander
8
49 Rice Lake
60 Turtle Lake
141
51
43 Osceola
20 Gills Rock
Hwy. 141 24
17 Egg Harbor
12
41
42
67 Wausau
29
94
51 River Falls
15 Eau Claire
55 Sturgeon Bay
Shawano
52
6 Bonduel
10
10
Algoma 1
Stevens Point 54
Green Bay 21
35
12
Wisconsin Rapids 72
66 Waupaca
41 New London
53
51
2 Appleton
70 Wild Rose
33
Menasha
10
Wautoma 68
Manitowoc 32
21
40 Necedah
44 Oshkosh
Tomah 59
90
5 Berlin
27 La Crosse
46 Princeton
Sheboygan 53
14
71 Wisconsin Dells
62 Viroqua
28 Lake Delton
43
151
35
41
3 Beaver Dam
Columbus 11
50 Richland Center
12
Cedarburg 10
Hartford 22
57 Sun Prairie
14
61
Madison
Milwaukee
Lake Mills
94
Mt. Horeb
31
30
42
34
38
Oconomowoc
18
65 Waukesha
Fennimore
19
18
14 Dodgeville
90
14
39 Mukwonago
35 Mineral Point
16 Edgerton
12
94
35
151
43
64 Waterford
47 Racine
45
Platteville
Janesville 25
Delavan
13
Elkhorn
18
8
Burlington
61
Union
Grove
56 Sturtevant
Monroe 37
Beloit 4
12 Darien
63
Walworth
29 Lake Geneva
26 Kenosha

# Wisconsin

## 1 ALGOMA

**Algoma Antique Mall**
300 4th St.
920/487-3221

**Granny's Attic Antiques**
1009 Jefferson St.
920/487-3226

**Gaslight Antiques**
1000 Freemont
920/487-5705

**White Pine Antiques**
720 3rd St.
920/487-7217

## 2 APPLETON

**Audios Antiques**
1426 N. Ballard Road
920/734-2856

**Avenue Coins & Jewelry**
303 E. College Ave.
920/731-4740

**Memories Antique Mall**
400 Randolph Dr.
920/788-5553

**Am. Heritage Antique & Appraisale**
6197 W. City Tk. Kk
920/734-8200

**Harp Gallery Antiques & Furniture**
2495 Northern Road
920/733-7115

**Fox River Antique Mall**
1074 S. Van Dyke Road
920/731-9699

## 3 BEAVER DAM

**Added Touch**
108 Front St.
920/887-2436

**Crosswalk Antiques**
124 Front St.
920/887-9586

**Tree City Antiques**
114 Front St.
920/885-5593

**General Store Antique Mall Inc.**
150 Front St.
920/887-1116

## 4 BELOIT

**Nest Egg Ltd.**
816 E. Grand Ave.
608/365-0700

**Caple Country Antiques**
309 State St.
608/362-5688

**Riverfront Antiques Mall**
306 State St.
608/362-7368

## 5 BERLIN

**Abe Old Antiques**
166 Huron St.
920/361-0889

**Picture That Antiques Mall**
107 W. Huron St.
920/361-0255

**Picture That**
102 E. Huron St.
920/361-0255

## 6 BONDUEL

**Hearthside Antique Mall**
129 S. Cecil St.
715/758-6200

## 7 BOULDER JUNCTION

**Joan's Antiques**
10377 Main St.
715/385-2600

**Fisherman's Wife**
10382 Main St.
715/385-9205

## 8 BURLINGTON

**Gingham Dog Antiques**
109 E. Chestnut St.
414/763-4759

**Antique Alley Mall**
481 Milwaukee Ave.
414/763-5257

**Hemenway House Antiques**
N5503 State Road 120
414/723-2249

**Gingham Dog Antiques**
120 E. Chestnut St.
414/763-2348

**Alby's Antiques & Amusements**
216 N. Pine St.
414/767-1191

## 9 CABLE

**Cottage Shop**
Box #-113
715/798-3077

**Honey Creek Antiques**
RR 1 #-73
715/798-3958

**Nordik Sleigh Antiques**
Hwy. M
715/798-3967

## 10 CEDARBURG

**Creekside Antiques**
N69 W6334 Bridge Road
414/377-6131

**Robin's Nest Antiques & Gifts**
N70 W6340 Bridge Road
414/377-3444

**Antiquenet**
6920 Kingswood Dr.
414/375-0756

**Antique Loft**
576 62 Ave.
414/377-9007

**American Country Antiques**
W61 N506 Washington Ave.
414/375-4140

**Nouveau Antique & Jewelry Parlor**
W62 N594 Washington Ave.
414/375-4568

**Stonehouse Antiques**
2088 Washington Ave.
414/675-2931

**Cedar Creek Antiques**
N70 W6340 Bridge Road
414/377-2204

**Spool N Spindle Antiques**
N70 W6340 Bridge Road
414/377-4200

**Don's Resale & Antique Shop**
N57 W6170 Portland Road
414/377-6868

**Crow's Nest**
6404 66 St.
414/377-3039

**Heritage Lighting**
W62 N572 Washington Ave.
414/377-9033

**Patricia Frances Interiors**
W62 N634 Washington Ave.
414/377-7710

## 11 COLUMBUS

**Antique Shoppes of Columbus Mall**
141 W. James St.
920/623-2669

**Antique Shops of Columbus**
902 Park Ave.
920/623-3930

**Columbus Antique Mall & Museum**
239 Whitney St.
920/623-1992

## 12 DARIEN

**Ice Cream Shoppe**
18 S. Beloi St.
414/724-5060

## 13 DELAVAN

**Geneva Lakes Imports & Antiques**
2460 N. County Tk. O S.
414/728-8887

**Treasure Hut Florist**
6551 State Road 11
414/728-2020

**Antiques of Delavan**
229 E. Walworth Ave.
414/728-9977

**Beall Jewelers**
305 E. Walworth Ave.
414/728-8577

**Remember When**
313 E. Walworth Ave.
414/728-8670

**Beall Jewelers Clock Gallery**
306 E. Walworth Ave.
414/728-8577

**Buttons & Bows**
312 E. Walworth Ave.
414/728-6813

**Delavan Antique & Art Center**
230 E. Walworth Ave.
414/740-1400

## 14 DODGEVILLE

### Carousel Collectibles & Antiques
121 N. Iowa St.
608/935-5196
May-Dec. 7 days a week, Jan.-Apr., Mon.-Sat. Call ahead to be sure shop is open, Hours vary.
*Directions: * Traveling north from Dubuque on Hwy. 151, exit to Hwy. 23 North into downtown Dodgeville. * Traveling west from Madison on 151-18, take Exit 60 (18 W.) to Hwy. 23. At stoplight turn left to downtown Dodgeville. * From Spring Green, stay on Hwy. 23 South to downtown Dodgeville.*

Carousel Horses have been a big part of the Reynolds family's lives for the past 20 years. Virginia Reynolds began painting carousel horses at the House On The Rock. She learned a very unique method of painting, and after five years passed this knowledge on to her daughter Cherie. During the next 15 years, the two worked together painting hundreds of carousel horses in all sizes. The painting of each horse is one-of-a-kind. In 1985 Carousel Collectibles and Antiques was opened. Through her creativity and artistic talents, Virginia passed on her love of carousels to many people who came to the shop. Virginia died unexpectedly in January 1995, which was a great loss to all those who knew her and admired her work. Cherie continues the painting of carousel horses with the hopes of carrying on her mother's memory and her love of carousels.

In addition to beautifully handpainted carousel horses, the shop carries a wide variety of collectibles - stunning glassware, handpainted dishes, pottery, primitives, furniture, paper collectibles, pictures, books and more. The shop also carries many carousel gift items including the handpainted carousel horses ranging from 12 to 60 inches in size.

**Rustic Floweral Antiques**
101 W. Leffler St.
608/935-5564

**Woodshed**
RR 1
608/935-3896

## 15 EAU CLAIRE

**Rice's Antiques**
202 S. Barslow St.
715/835-5351

**Piney Hills Antiques**
5260 Deerfield Road
715/832-8766

**Antique Emporium**
306 Main St.
715/832-2494

**Molly's Mercantile**
2807 E. Hamilton Ave.
715/839-8535

## 16 EDGERTON

**Mildred's Antiques**
4 Burdick St.
608/884-3031

**Antiques & Art Gallery**
104 W. Fulton St.
608/884-6787

**Sisters Act**
114 W. Fulton St.
608/884-6092

**Edgerton Resale Mall**
204 W. Fulton St.
608/884-8148

## 17 EGG HARBOR

**Basil Sweet Ltd.**
7813 Egg Harbor Road
920/868-2300

**Country Bumpkin**
6228 State Hwy. 432
920/743-8704

**Door County Antiques**
7150 State Hwy. 42
920/868-2121

**Bay Trading Co.**
7367 State Hwy. 42
920/868-2648

**Olde Orchard Antique Mall**
7381 State Hwy. 42
920/868-3685

**CJ's Antiques Etc. & CJ's Too**
7899 State Hwy. 42
920/868-2271

**Shades of the Past**
8010 State Road 42
920/868-3800

**Cupola House**
7836 Egg Harbor Road
920/868-3941

## 18 ELKHORN

**Powell's Antique Shop**
14 W. Geneva St.
414/723-2952

**Front Parlor Antiques**
6696 Millard Road
414/742-3489

**Twin Pines Antique Mall**
5438 State Road 11
414/723-4492

**Bits of the Past & Present**
5691 State Road 11
414/723-4763

**Loveless Antiques**
7091 U.S. Hwy. 12
414/742-2619

**Heirlooms**
12 S. Wisconsin St.
414/723-4070

**Dave's Antiques**
W6610 N. Lakeshore Dr.
414/742-2416

**Van Dyke's Apple Basket**
20 S. Wisconsin St.
414/723-4909

## 19 FENNIMORE

**Tuckwood House**
1280 10th St.
608/822-3164

## 20 GILLS ROCK

### *Great Places To Stay*

**Harbor House Inn**
12666 Hwy. 42
920/854-5196

This 1904 Victorian bed and breakfast is located in Gills Rock, a fishing village on the northern tip of beautiful Door County. The original home has been in the Weborg family since its inception, and has recently been restored to its original elegance. A Scandanavian wing has been added with large rooms, each with kitchenettes and decks overlooking the harbor. Cottages are also available (one with a woodburning fireplace). A thirty-five foot lighthouse has recently been erected, providing a romantic luxury accomodation with fireplace and Jacuzzi. All rooms feature private baths. Enjoy a continental-plus breakfast each morning.

## 21 GREEN BAY

**American Antiques and Jewelry**
1049 W. Mason St.
920/498-0111

**Meadow Suite**
630 E. Walnut St.
920/432-1733

**Towne Trader Antiques & Auction Service**
914 Main St.
920/435-8070

**Red's-Shirley Antiques**
1344 Main St.
920/437-3596

**Yesteryears Antique Mall**
611 9th St.
920/435-4900

**Packer City Antiques**
712 Redwood Dr.
920/490-1095

**Ginny's Antiques & Collectable**
3808 Riverside Dr.
920/336-3666

**Sue's Antiques & Collectibles**
1231 S. Military Ave.
920/497-2033

**Antique Collectors Corner**
898 Elmore St.
920/497-7141

**J & S Antique Mall**
3110 Kewaunee Road
920/863-3203

## 22 HARTFORD

**Sharron's Antiques**
135 N. Main St.
414/673-2751

**Hartford Antique Mall**
147 N. Rural
414/673-2311

**Erin Antiques**
1691 State Road (Hwy. 835)
414/673-4680

### *Great Places To Stay*

**Jordan House Bed and Breakfast**
81 S. Main St.
414/673-5643
Open year round. Reservations required
Rates: $65 Private Bath, $55 Shared bath
*Directions; From Hwy. 41, take Hwy. 60 exit west 7 miles to downtown Hartford (intersection of Highways 60 and 83). Turn left on Main St., go 1 1/2 blocks.*

Built at the turn-of-the-century the Jordan House was designed by Mr. Jacob Jacoby, a noted Milwaukee architect. The original building plans are still intact and reflect the care and substance of construction. Four spacious guest rooms decorated with period furniture await your arrival. A hearty country breakfast is served each morning.

Convenient to all major highways in southeastern Wisconsin, antique malls and shops abound in the area. Hartford is also the home of the Kissel automobile. Built from 1906 until the Depression in 1931, the Kissel was a high caliber custom built car. The Hartford Heritage Auto Museum, within walking distance of the Jordan House, provides a rare opportunity to see the largest assembled group of these rare luxury cars as well as over ninety other vintage cars and other automobile memorabilia.

## 23 HAYWARD

**Red Shed Antiques**
County Road, #B
715/634-6088

**Remember When**
114 N. Dakota Ave.
715/634-5282

**Hill's Antiques**
RR 2
715/634-2037

**Nelson Bay Antiques**
RR 3
715/634-2177

**Main Street Curiosity Shop**
214 Main St.
715/634-1465

### *Great Places To Stay*

**Edgewater Inn B&B**
Route 1, Box 1293
715/462-9412

The fieldstone foundation and fireplace offer a hint of history fr this turn-of-the-century home. Records show Arthur White and his w

Lillian purchased 147 acres in the township of Spider Lake on August 15, 1905. They later added more tracts of land totaling 300 acres. On this lakefront property, Art, a lumberman and entrepreneur, built one of the area's largest farms.

## 24 HWY. 141

These shops are located within a few miles of each other throughout the small towns of Lena, Coleman, Middle Inlet, Wausaukee, Amberg, Pembine and Niagra along Hwy. 141.

**The White Rabbit Collector's Mall**
135 N. Rosera (Hwy. 141)
(Lena)
920/892-6290

**Up Nort Antiques**
202 N. Hwy. 141
(Coleman)
920/897-4900

**Collector's Paradise Antique Mall**
N9205 Hwy. 141
(Middle Inlet)
715/854-3187

**McNeely's Old Store**
723 Main St. (Hwy. 141)
(Wausaukee)
715/856-5831

**Amberg Antiques & Sweets**
N15450 Hwy. 141
(Amberg)
715/759-5343

**Serendipity Shop**
W7510 County Z (1 mi. east on Z)
(Pembine)
715/324-5556

**Woodsong Gallery**
N18360 Hwy. 141
(Pembine)
715/324-6482

**Niagra Emporium**
1049 Main St. (Hwy. 141)
(Niagra)
715/251-4190

## 25 JANESVILLE

**Carousel Consignments**
31 S. Main St.
608/758-0553

**Foster Lee Antiques**
218 W. Milwaukee St.
608/752-5188

**Pipsqueak & Me**
220 W. Milwaukee St.
508/756-1752

**Franklin Stove Antiques**
301 W. Milwaukee St.
608/756-5792

**ieneral Antique Store**
301 N. U.S. Hwy. 1 St.
08/756-1812

**Yesterdays Memories Antique Mall**
4904 S. U.S. Hwy. 51
608/754-2906

**nother Antique Shop**
19 W. Milwaukee St.
08/754-5711

**Just Between Friends**
904 Rockport Road
608/758-4783

## 26 KENOSHA

**ara Jane's Antiques & Collectibles**
7 58th St.
4/657-5588

**A Miracle on 58th Street**
706 58th St.
414/652-3132

**press Tree**
2 50th St.
4/652-6999

**Country Cove Antiques**
710 57th St.
414/654-0738

**iry Land Antiques**
20 120th St.
4/857-6802

**Greta's**
4906 7th Ave.
414/658-1077

**Laura's Resale & Collectibles**
6013 Sheridan Road
414/657-1810

**Red Barn Antique**
12000 Sheridan Road
414/694-0424

**Hyden Seec Antiques**
5623 6th Ave.
414/654-8111

**Helen's Remember When Antiques**
5801 6th Ave.
414/652-2280

**Memory Lane Antiques**
1942 22nd Ave.
414/551-8452

**Apple Lane Antiques**
5730 Burlington Road
414/859-2017

## 27 LA CROSSE

**Caledonia Street Antique Mall**
1213 Caledonia St.
608/782-8443

**Plantique**
115 7th St. S.
608/784-4053

**Hornet's Nest Antiques**
1507 Caledonia St.
608/785-2998

**Wild Rose**
1507 Caledonia St.
608/785-2998

**4th St. Antique Gallery**
119 4th St.
608/782-7278

**Manon's Vintage Shop**
535 Main St.
608/784-2240

**Antique Center-La Crosse Ltd.**
110 3rd St. S.
608/782-6533

**Vintage Vogue**
115 5th Ave. S.
608/782-3722

## 28 LAKE DELTON

**Old Academy Antiques & Gift Mall**
Hwy. 12
608/254-4948

**Our Gang Antique Mall**
Hwy. 23
608/254-4401

**Braun's Happy Landing Antique Shop**
30 N. Judson
608/253-4613

## 29 LAKE GENEVA

**Sign of the Unicorn**
233 Center St.
414/248-1141

**Antiques International**
611 W. Main St.
414/248-1800

**Steffen Collection**
611 W. Main St.
414/248-1800

**Cedar Fields**
755 W. Main St.
414/248-8086

**Lake Geneva Antique Mall**
829 Williams St.
414/248-6345

### *Great Places To Stay*

**T. C. Smith Historic Inn B&B**
865 Main St.
1-800-423-0233

This stunning 1845 mansion features 19th century light fixtures, converted from gas lights. Parquet floors, magnificent hand tooled black walnut balustrades and staircase, and the hand painted walls with miniature oil paints and original trompe oeil, all by famed Chicago artist John Bullock, are just a hint of what you'll experience at this historic inn.

## 30 LAKE MILLS

### Old Mills Market
109 N. Main St.
920/648-3030
Winter: Sun.-Sat. 10-5, Tues. by chance; Summer: Daily 10-5
*Directions: Located 24 miles east of Madison on I-94 OR 64 miles west of Milwaukee on I-94. From I-94, exit onto Hwy. 89 South; go 3/4 mile. In Lake Mills, shop is located across from the Commons Park.*

Tucked inside the turn-of-the-century historic Luetzow Meat Market building, the eclectic selection of antiques and collectibles includes furniture, vintage clothing, jewelry, heirloom gifts, linens and one-of-a-kind jackets fashioned from vintage materials. Appraisals, by on-staff qualified appraiser, and estate services are provided. A treat for the tummy while shopping comes in the shop's "special" hand-dipped chocolates.

**Opera Hall Antique**
211 N. Main St.
920/648-5026

**Gwen's Antiques**
102 Church St.
920/648-6183

## 31 MADISON

**Broadway Antiques Mall**
115 E. Broadway
608/222-2241

**Bethel Parish Shoppe**
315 N. Carroll St.
608/255-9183

**Antiques Mall of Madison**
4748 Cottage Grove Road
608/222-2049

**Janet's Antiques**
815 Fern Dr.
608/238-4474

**Hopkins & Crocker, Inc.**
807 E. Johnson St.
608/255-6222

**Florilegium**
823 E. Johnson St.
608/256-7310

**Vintage Interiors**
2615 E. Johnson St.
608/244-3000

**Antique Gallery**
6608 Mineral Point Road
608/833-4321

**Chris Kerwin Antiques & Interiors**
1839 Monroe St.
608/256-7363

**Mapletree Antique Mall**
1293 N. Sherman Ave.
608/241-2599

**Kappel's Clock Shop**
2250 Sherman Ave.
608/244-6165

**Rick's Olde Gold**
1314 Williamson St.
608/257-7280

**Stony Hill Antiques**
2140 Regent St.
608/231-1247

### *Great Places To Stay*

### Mansion Hill Inn
424 N. Pinckney St.
608/255-3999
Web site: www.mansionhillinn.com

Mansion Hill Inn is an 1858 Romanesque Revival home that was lovingly restored by the Alexander Company in 1985. Eleven exquisite guest rooms are filled with period antiques, hand carved Italian marble fireplaces, and floor to ceiling arched windows. All guest rooms have private baths, many with whirlpool tubs.

## 32 MANITOWOC

**Ebert's Antiques**
5712 Country Trunk JJ
920/682-0687

**Washington St. Antique Mall**
910 Washington St.
920/684-2954

**Antique Mall of Manitowoc**
301 N. 8th St.
920/682-8680

**Viking Antiques**
314 N. 8th St.
920/682-0100

**Pine River Antiques**
7430 Hwy. Cr.
920/726-4440

**Larco Resale & Antiques**
2204 N. Rapids Road.
920/682-9066

**Medley Resale & Antiques**
1114 S. 10th St.
920/682-8400

**Wheeler on the River Antiques**
436 N. 10th St.
920/682-3069

**Timeless Treasures**
112 N. 8th St.
920/682-6566

## 33 MENASHA

### About Time/Red Barn/Menasha Jack's Antiques
68 Racine
920/725-4880
Tues.-Sat. 10-4:30 March-January, Sat. 10-4:30 only in February
*Directions: Take Hwy. 441 to Menasha, exit at Racine St. Go south approximately 1 mile.*

Three stores in one offer not only a wide variety, but also a large quantity of antiques such as furniture, fixtures, lamps, jewelry, primitives, graniteware, stoneware and pottery. In addition to great selections, the shops buy and appraise antique pieces.

**Anderson Resale Shop**
922 Appleton Road
920/725-5599

**Country Goose My**
1018 Appleton Road
920/722-1661

**Not New Now**
212 Main St.
920/725-5545

**Wood-Shed**
746 3rd St.
920/725-3347

## 34 MILWAUKEE

**Wishful Things**
207 E. Buffalo St.
414/765-1117

**Noah's Ark**
7153 W. Burleigh St.
414/442-1588

**Capital City Comics**
2565 N. Downer Ave.
414/332-8199

**Fifth Avenue Antiques**
422 N. 5th St.
414/271-3355

**Antique Center-Walkers Point**
1134 1st St.
414/383-0655

**Architectural Antiques**
804 W. Greenfield Ave.
414/389-1965

**Past Presence Collectibles**
7123 W. Greenfield Ave.
414/774-7585

**Peter Bentz Antiques & Appraisals**
771 N. Jefferson St.
414/271-8866

**Milwaukee Antique Center**
341 N. Milwaukee St.
414/276-0605

**chols Antiques & Gifts**
230 W. North Ave.
14/774-5556

**ileen's Warehouse Antiques**
25 N. Plankinton Ave.
14/276-0114

**own & Country Shop Inc.**
322 N. Port Washington Road
4/352-6570

**ny's Resale**
9 N. 27th St.
4/931-0949

**hts of Olde**
3 N. Water St.
/223-1130

**nturies Antiques**
N. Water St.
/278-1111

**ique Cupboard Sterling Matching**
2 N. 92nd St.
/464-0556

**Time Traveler Book Store**
7143 W. Burleigh St.
414/442-0203

**Chattel Changers Inc.**
2520 E. Capitol Dr.
414/961-7085

**Village Bazaar**
2201 N. Farwell Ave.
414/224-9675

**Brass Light Gallery**
131 S. 1st St.
414/271-8300

**Carter's on Delaware**
2466 Graham St.
414/482-0014

**Collectors Toystop**
6026 W. Greenfield Ave.
414/771-7622

**Celebrity Coin & Stamp**
4161 S. Howell Ave.
414/747-1888

**American Estates**
2131 S. Kinnickinnic Ave.
414/483-2110

**D & H Antiques Toys & Trains**
501 W. Mitchell St.
414/643-5340

**Military Relics Shop**
6910 W. North Ave.
414/771-4014

**Legacies Ltd.**
7922 N. Port Washington Road
414/352-8114

**Colonel's Choice**
2918 S. 13th St.
414/383-8180

**American Victorian**
203 N. Water St.
414/223-1130

**Water St. Antiques**
318 N. Water St.
414/278-7008

**D & R International Antiques Ltd.**
137 E. Wells St.
414/276-9395

**Elizabeth Bradley Antiques**
1115 W. Greentree Road
414/352-1521

**Shorewood Coin Shop**
4495 N. Oakland Ave.
414/961-0999

## 35 MINERAL POINT

**Livery Antiques**
303 Commerce St.
608/987-3833

**Green Lantern Antiques**
261 High St.
608/987-2312

## 36 MINOCQUA

**Island City Antique Market**
8661 Hwy. 51 N.
715/356-7003

**Finders Keepers**
7 Hwy. W.
715/356-7208

**Hildebrand's Antiques**
7537 U.S. Hwy. 51 S.
715/356-1971

## 37 MONROE

**New Moon Antiques**
1606 11th St.
608/325-9100

**Bevs Attic Treasures**
1018 17th Ave.
608/325-6200

**Ii's A Bunch of Crock Antiques**
1027 16th Ave.
608/328-1444

**Log Cabin Antiques**
W5848 County Road B
608/325-7795

**Garden Gate Floral & Antiques**
1717 11th St.
608/329-4900

**Breezy Acres Li Antiques**
1027 16th Ave.
608/325-1201

**Luecke's Diamond Center Inc.**
1029 16th Ave.
608/325-2600

## 38 MOUNT HOREB

**First Street Antiques**
111 S. 1st St.
608/437-6767

**Main Street Antiques**
126 E. Main St.
608/437-3233

**Lucy's Attic**
520 Springdale St.
608/437-6140

**Hoff Mall Antique Center**
101 E. Main St.
608/437-4580

**Isaac's Antiques**
132 E. Main St.
608/437-6151

**Yapp's Antique Corner**
504 E. Main St.
608/437-8100

## 39 MUKWONAGO

**Country Junction**
101 N. Rochester St.
414/363-9474

**Indian Creek Antiques**
214 S. Rochester St.
414/363-7015

## 40 NECEDAH

### Northland Collectors Mart
211 S. Main St.
608/565-3730
Spring/Summer 10-5 Mon.-Sat., 10-4 Sun.; Nov. & Dec. 10-4, 7 days; Jan.-Mar., Thurs.-Sun. 10-4
*Directions: Necedah is situated at the intersection of Highways 21 and 80.*

Across from the town gazebo sits a collector's haven crammed with antiques and collectibles. Among the extraordinary array of styles, periods, textures, and functions, antiquers roam among furniture, glassware, figurines, pottery, jewelry and artifacts.

## 41 NEW LONDON

**Studio Antiques**
1776 Division St.
920/982-4366

## 42 OCONOMOWOC

**Mapleton Antiques**
W360 8755 Brown St.
920/474-4514

**Old Homestead Lighting**
514 Silver Lake St.
920/567-6543

**Marsh Hill Ltd.**
456 N. Waterville Road
920/646-2560

**Ye Old Antiques-Rural**
N880 W38726 McMahon Road
920/474-4380

**Gathering Place**
5780 359 St.
920/567-5123

## 43 OSCEOLA

### Osceola Antiques
117 Cascade St.
715/294-2886
Mon.-Sat. 10-5, Sun. Noon-5
*Directions: Downtown Osceola is on Wisconsin Hwy. 35. From I-94, go north at Hudson on Hwy. 35.*

Osceola Antiques is Northwest Wisconsin's largest antique shop. With over 11,000 square feet for prime antique hunting you're sure to find just what you're looking for here. The shop displays furniture of all eras, linens to accent, art, jewelry, loads of glassware and more. For collectors and the curious, over 800 antique reference books are available. Enjoy ice cream, homemade candy or cappuccino while you shop.

**Old Mill Stream Antiques**
105 Cascade St.
715/755-2344

## 44 OSHKOSH

**A Blend of the Past Antiques**
738 N. Oakwood Road
920/235-0969

**Wagon Wheel Antiques**
2326 Oregon St.
920/233-8518

**Impressions-Antiques Etc.**
1773 S. Washburn St.
920/235-3899

**Cat's Meow Antiques & Collectibles**
807 Ohio St.
920/231-6369

**Originals Mall of Antiques**
1475 S. Washburn St.
920/235-0495

**Treasure Shop**
2968 Jackson St.
414/231-5551

## 45 PLATTEVILLE

**Marilee's Main Street Mall**
70 E. Main St.
608/348-6995

**Milly McDonnell's**
5946 U.S. Hwy. 151
608/348-8500

**Platteville Antiques**
5924 State Road 80 #-81
608/348-4533

## 46 PRINCETON

**River City Antique Mall**
328 S. Fulton St.
920/295-3475

**Melcherts Antiques**
605 S. Fulton St.
920/295-4243

**Victorian House Antiques**
330 W. Water St.
920/295-4700

**Parkside Antique Mall**
501 S. Fulton St.
920/295-0112

**Merry's Little Toy Shop**
615 W. Water St.
920/295-6746

**Princeton Antique Mall**
101 Wisconsin St.
920/295-6515

## 47 RACINE

**Fair Trader**
1801 Douglas Ave.
414/637-2222

**Travel Through Time Antiques**
1859 Taylor Ave.
414/637-7721

**Now & Then Gifts & Antiques**
1408 Washington Ave.
414/634-8883

**Avenue Antiques**
1436 Washington Ave.
414/637-6613

**Antique Mall of Racine**
310 S. Main St.
414/633-9229

**Ace & Bubba Treasure Hunters**
218 6th St.
414/633-3308

**Another Man's Treasure**
1354 Washington Ave.
414/633-6869

**D & J's Junque**
1428 Washington Ave.
414/633-9884

**Americana Antique Shop**
2330 Airline Road
414/886-0416

**Midwest Antiques**
2504 Douglas Ave.
414/637-6562

## 48 RHINELANDER

**Jane's Country Cottage**
3961 Indian Lake Road
715/272-1444

**Demitra Lane Antiques & Gifts**
432 Lincoln St.
715/362-2206

**Second Hand Rose Antiques**
1309 Lincoln St.
715/369-2626

## 49 RICE LAKE

**Country Antique Shop**
1505 Fencil Ave.
715/234-4589

**Bits of Yesteryear Antiques**
2237 Lakeshore Dr.
715/234-4641

**Victorian Cottage**
601 N. Main St.
715/234-3482

**Portals To The Past**
613 N. Main St.
715/234-7530

## 50 RICHLAND CENTER

**Valley Antiques**
186 S. Central Ave.
608/647-3793

**Antiques & Etc.**
194 E. Court St.
608/647-4732

**Memory Lane Antique Mall**
177 E. Haseltine St.
608/647-8286

**Ray's Trading Post**
RR 1
608/536-3803

## 51 RIVER FALLS

**Chicken Coop Antiques**
7086 N. 820th St.
715/425-5716

**Little River Antiques**
363 Cemetery Road
715/425-5522

**Homestead Antiques**
208 N. Main St.
715/425-9522

**County Line Antiques**
RR 3 #-148A
715/425-9118

## 52 SHAWANO

**Zurko's Midwest Promotions**
:11 W. Green Bay St.
'15/526-9769

**Yesterdays Antique Mall**
712 E. Green Bay St.
715/524-6050

**-C Antiques**
:oute 2
15/524-5254

## 53 SHEBOYGAN

**raftmaster Antiques & Restoration**
)34 N. 15th St.
20/452-2524
on.-Sat. 10-4, closed Sun.
*irections: Take Hwy. 23, exit east to 14th St. Make a left turn on 4th St., Make a right turn on 15th St. or exit Hwy. 42 into eboygan. Make a left turn on Geele Ave., make right turn on 5th St.*

Enjoy an old mill setting and browse on three floors full of antiques and collectibles. Discover fine furniture, primitives, china, glassware, stoneware, light fixtures, collectibles and a little bit of everything for everyone. The shop holds true to its slogan: Variety at a reasonable "take home" price!

**Sheboygan Antiques**
336 Superior Ave.
920/452-6757

**Treasure Gardens**
1327 N. 14th St.
920/458-8232

**Sheridan Park General Store**
632 S. 14th St.
920/458-5833

**Three Barns Full-Two**
7377 State Road 42
920/565-3050

**Hiding Place**
1219 Michigan Ave.
414/452-4566

## 54 STEVENS POINT

**Downtown Antiques Shops**
1100 Main St.
715/342-1442

**Memory Market**
2224 Patch St.
715/344-2026

**Second Street Antiques**
900 2nd St.
715/341-8611

**Kurtzweil Antiques**
1652 Burgundy Lane
715/344-0874

**Sweet Briar**
1157 Main St.
715/341-8869

## 55 STURGEON BAY

**Westside Antiques**
22 S. Madison Ave.
920/746-9038

**Antiques of Institute**
4530 State Hwy. 57
920/743-1511

**Cottage Antiques and Quiltry**
820 Egg Harbor Road
920/746-0944

### *Great Places To Stay*

**Whitefish Bay Farm B&B**
3831 Clark Lake Road
920/743-1560
Web site: www.whitefishbayfarm.com

Enjoy the quiet rural atmosphere of this restored 1908 farmhouse and eighty acre farm. Light filled, spacious guest rooms are decorated in contemporary country furnishings, handmade quilts, handwoven wool rugs and throws, and original artwork. An abundant homemade breakfast is served at the dining room table where guests meet to share conversation and experiences.

**Scofield House B&B**
908 Michigan St.
1-888-463-0204

A stay at the Scofield House is a true bed and breakfast experience. Afternoon "sweet treats" on the buffet, with complimentary gourmet drinks, has become a Scofield House ritual. Oven fresh cookies and baked goods are something to come home to after a long day of "recreational shopping" or enjoying other more natural pursuits the county has to offer.

## 56 STURTEVANT

**Revival**
9410 Durand Ave.
414/886-3666

**Carridge House Antiques**
9525 Durand Ave.
414/886-6678

**School Days Mall**
9500 Durand Ave.
414/886-1069

**Antique Castle Mall**
1701 S.E. Frontage Road
414/886-6001

**Tree of Life**
2810 Wisconsin St.
414/886-1601

## 57 SUN PRAIRIE

**Circa Victoriana**
104 E. Main St.
608/837-4115

**Coffee Mill Antique Mall**
3472 Hoepker Road.
608/837-7099

## 58 SUPERIOR

**Superior Collectible Inv.**
1709 Belknap St.
715/394-4315

**Port of Call Superior Marketplace**
4101 E. 2nd St.
715/398-5030

**Berger Hardware & Antiques**
525 Tower Ave.
715/394-3873

**Curious Goods**
1717 Winter St.
715/392-7550

**Doherty's Antiques**
207 39th Ave. E.
715/398-7661

## 59 TOMAH

### Antique Mall of Tomah
I-94 and Hwy. 21 East
608/372-7853
Apr.-Dec., Mon.-Sat. 8-8, Sun. 9-5; Jan.-Mar. 9-5 daily
*Directions: From I-94 and Hwy. 21 East, take Exit 143 to Tomah.*

The 60 plus dealers of quality antiques and collectibles specialize in "smalls." Primitives, jewelry, glassware, plates and dishware, in addition to a large assortment of lamps make up the pleasing selection. The stock of furniture is limited but offers fine workmanship and good condition.

**Oakdale Antique Mall**
Route 3
608/374-4700

**Esther's Antiques**
RR 4
608/372-6690

## 60 TURTLE LAKE

**Memories Antiques and Collectibles**
231 W. U.S. Hwy. 8
715/986-4950

**Country Side Antiques**
12 W. U.S. Hwy. 8
715/986-2737

## 61 UNION GROVE

**Storm Hall Antique Mall**
835 15th Ave.
414/878-1644

**House on Main**
1121 Main St.
414/878-1045

**Ye Olde Red Barn Antiques**
20816 Durand Ave.
414/878-2044

## 62 VIROQUA

**Golden Comb & Etc.**
124 W. Court St.
608/637-7835

**Main Street Antique Mall**
207 N. Main St.
608/637-8655

**Etc. Antiques & Collectibles**
124 W. Court St.
608/637-6429

**Antiques Cellar**
205 N. Main St.
608/634-2749

**Lam's Ear Country Gifts**
608/637-2099

**Small Ventures**
608/637-8880

## 63 WALWORTH

**On The Square Antique Mall**
109 Madison
414/275-9858

**Bittersweet Farm**
114 Madison
414/275-3062

**Van's Antiques**
1937 U.S. Hwy. 14
414/275-2773

**Raggedy An-Tiques**
216 S. Main St.
414/275-5866

## 64 WATERFORD

**Freddy Bear's Antique Mall**
2819 Beck Dr.
414/534-2327

**Heavenly Haven Antique Mall**
318 W. Main St.
414/534-4400

**Afternoon Tea Antiques & Furniture**
411 E. Main St.
414/534-3664

**Dover Pond Antiques**
28016 Washington Ave.
414/534-6543

## 65 WAUKESHA

**Just A Little Bit of Country**
N4 W22496 Bluemont Road
414/542-8050

**Babbling Brook**
416 E. Broadway
414/544-4739

**Store**
301 N. Grand Ave.
414/547-2740

**James K Beier Antique Maps**
2312 N. Grandview Blvd
414/549-5985

**Susan H. Kruger Antiques**
401 Madison St.
414/542-7722

**Gift Sampler**
275 W. Main St.
414/544-1343

**Bix Stripping & Refinishing**
850 Martin St.
414/542-3185

**Fortunate Finds**
124 E. Saint Paul Ave.
414/542-8110

**A Dickens of a Place**
521 Wisconsin Ave.
414/542-0702

### *Great Places To Stay*

**Mill Creek Farm Bed and Breakfast**
S47 W22099 Lawnsdale Road
414/542-4311
Office hours: 7-11, 7 days.
Rates: $65-75
*Directions: From I-43 going west, take Racine Ave. (Exit 54) north 2 miles to County 1 (Lawnsdale Road). Turn left on County 1, go 1.6 miles. The farm is on the left. Located 7 miles southeast of Waukesha, 20 miles southwest of Milwaukee.*

Located on 160 acres in Waukesha County, you'll find one of the area's loveliest, private retreats. Mill Creek Farm offers two special rooms adorned with fine linens and all the amenities to make your stay a pleasant one. Guests share a fully renovated, skylit bath, elegantly decorated for comfort and convenience right down to the heated towel rack! The reading/ television room offers a subdued atmosphere for curling up with a good book or watching a romantic movie.

This wooded Shangri-la offers a variety of outdoor activities to help you escape. You can head out on a paddle boat and absorb the serenity of Mill Creek Pond, or fish for bass and bluegills in this one-acre spring fed pond.

For the more active relaxer, there are 3 miles of groomed trails to hike, jog, or cross country ski.

This amusing anecdote was submitted by the Mill Creek Farm Bed and Breakfast: "Last summer we had as our guests a young family from the Chicago area. Mother, father, and two sons came for a three-day period planning to enjoy the Milwaukee Zoo, Wisconsin State Fair, Old World Wisconsin, and several other attractions in the area. However, when they got here they discovered our pond for which we provided them with fishing poles and paddle boat. The boys began to catch fish, frogs, and all manner of pond life. As the first day progressed, they decided to stay on the farm and not venture out for other sights. The second day, the same decision. Third day, same decision. So it turned out, they never left the farm for the whole three-day stay! And as they were leaving on the morning of the fourth day, Noah, who is 7, turned to his father and said, 'Dad, how much would it cost to buy this place?' We concluded that Noah was the youngest sale prospect we've ever had!"

## 66 WAUPACA

**Grey Dove Antiques & Resale**
118 S. Main St.
715/258-0777

**Danes Home**
301 N. Main St.
715/256-0693

## 67 WAUSAU

**Kimberly's Old House Gallery**
1600 Jonquil Lane
715/359-5077
Thurs., Fri. & Sat. 10-5, and by chance or appointment

Roam 10,000 square feet packed with antique architectural pieces. Fireplaces, lighting, plumbing, and millwork represent some of the finds. Building salvage, cross-country delivery and locating services also available.

**Kasens Bittersweet Antique Furniture**
8705 Bittersweet Road
715/359-2777

**Rib Mt. Antique Mall**
3300 Eagle Ave.
715/848-5564

**Stoney Creek Antiques & Jewelry Shop**
4307 State Hwy. 52
715/842-8354

**Ginny's Antiques & Consignments**
416 3rd St.
715/848-1912

## 68 WAUTOMA

**Coach's Corner Antiques**
2192 Hwy. 152
920/787-3845

**Silver Lake Antique Mall**
W. 7853 State Road 21
920/787-1325

**Finishing Touch Antiques**
502 W. Main St.
920/787-2525

## 69 WEBSTER

**Lake Country Mall**
Hwy. 35
715/866-7670

**Old House Antiques**
7419 Airport Road
715/349-7289

## 70 WILD ROSE

**Finders Keepers Antiques**
526 Front
920/622-3077

**Sampler**
N6571 State Road 22
920/622-4499

**Oakwood Farm Antiques & Crafts**
Alp Road
920/622-3165

## 71 WISCONSIN DELLS

**Antique Mall of Wisconsin Dells**
720 Oak St.
608/254-2422

**Days Gone By Antique Mall**
729 Oak St.
608/254-6788

## 72 WISCONSIN RAPIDS

**Kellner Pioneer Shop**
8620 County Trunk W.
715/424-2507

**Whetstones Antiques**
322 State Hwy. 73 S.
715/325-5139

**Hi Button Shoe**
9420 State Hwy. 13 S.
715/325-2444

**Antique Heaven**
3620 8th St.
715/423-3599

**Aunt Nancy's Antiques Collectibles**
6421 State Hwy. 13 S.
715/325-2800

## 73 WOODRUFF

**Mill**
1405 1st Ave.
715/356-5468

**Town N Travel Antique Shop**
237 U.S. Hwy. 51 N.
715/358-2535

**Roxane's Antiques & Gifts**
189 U.S. Hwy. 51 N.
715/356-7718

# Wyoming

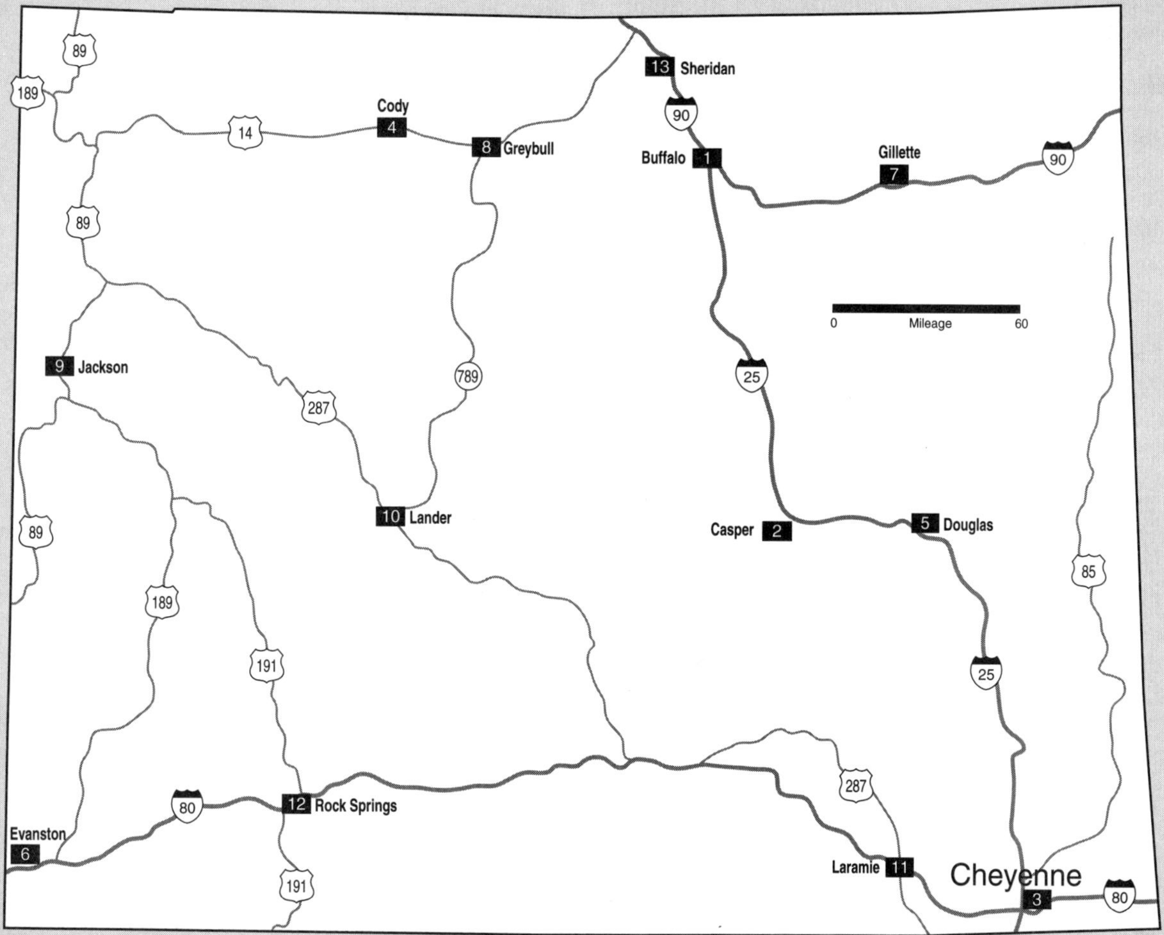

13 Sheridan
Cody
4
8 Greybull
Buffalo 1
Gillette
7
9 Jackson
10 Lander
Casper 2
5 Douglas
12 Rock Springs
Evanston
6
Laramie 11
Cheyenne
3
0 Mileage 60
89
189
14
90
25
789
287
85
191
80

# Wyoming

## 1 BUFFALO

**Yesterdays Treasures**
100 E. Hart St.
307/684-7318

**Rock Bottom Country Store**
29448 Hwy. 196
307/684-2364

**Heritage Antiques**
22 S. Main St.
307/684-2326

## 2 CASPER

### Doubletree Antiques & More
146 S. Elk
307/472-4858
Tues.-Sat., 10-5, closed Sun. and Mon.
*Directions: Exit off I-25 at McKinley St. Go south on McKinley to First St. Turn east on First then south on Elk.*

This shop has a constantly changing inventory, which means business is good. On a regular basis, they stock 1800s through Art Deco furniture, a wide selection of oak furniture, glassware such as Depression, carnival and much more. An additional bonus; there is a furniture refinisher on site who gives free estimates. What more can you ask for?

### Carriage House Antiques
830 W. 15th St.
307/266-2987
Tues.-Sat., 10-5; Fri. 11-5; closed Sun. and Mon.
*Directions: Take Poplar St. Exit off I-25. Travel south on Poplar to CY Ave. Turn left on CY then immediately right on 15th St.*

Carriage House has a complete line of antiques including glassware, pottery, jewelry, toys, Cowboy and Indian collectibles.

**Mary's**
341 W. Yellowstone Hwy.
307/577-5206

**What's In Store**
211 W. Collins Dr.
307/237-8137

**Antique Lighting Inc.**
1514 S. Kenwood St.
307/265-4614

**Accents**
227 E. 1st St.
307/473-1781

**Lotsa Stuff**
1023 E. 2nd St.
307/473-2212

**Yellow Horse Antiques**
107 Jonquil St.
307/235-1457

***Great Places To Stay***

### Durbin Street Inn Bed & Breakfast
843 S. Durbin St.
307/577-5774

Combine the comfort and friendliness of a bed and breakfast with the excitement of the Old West. The Durbin Street Inn was built in 1917 and is a comfortable two-story American Foursquare. Located in what is now an historical residential area known as the 'big tree' area, it is within blocks of downtown shopping, good restaurants, museums, and just minutes from Casper Mountain. The area offers about everything you could desire in cultural events, the nearby historical sites of Old Ft. Casper and Independence Rock.

## 3 CHEYENNE

### Sidekick Antique Mart
1408 S. Greeley Hwy.
307/635-3136
Daily 10-6
*Directions: Exit south on Greeley Hwy. off I-80. Located one to two miles on the right.*

This multi-dealer market (70-80 dealers) with its 10,000 square foot of space is filled with primitives, old tools, barnwood furniture, 1800s to 1950s oak, walnut and mahogany furniture, Fenton, Cambridge and Imperial glassware, porcelains, black powder guns, brewery, Coke, sports and Indian memorabilia and Persian rugs. The inventory is limitless. If you can't find it here, you'll probably have a hard time finding it anywhere.

**Old Gold Antiques**
1309 W. 8th St.
307/632-8557

**Tee Pee**
3208 S. Greeley Hwy.
307/635-8535

**Tomorrow's Treasures Antiques**
903 W. Lincoln Ave.
307/634-1900

**Bart's Flea Market**
Lincolnway & Evans
307/632-0063

**Collectibles Corner**
2622 Pioneer Ave.
307/634-7706

**Antiques Central**
2311 Reed Ave.
307/638-6181

**Grandma's Attic**
113 W. 17th St.
307/638-6126

**Frontier Antiques**
1715 Carey Ave.
307/635-5573

**Downtown Flea Market**
312 W. 17th St.
307/638-3751

**The Avenue Flea Market**
315 1/2 E. 7th Ave.
307/635-5600

**Treasures From The Heart**
1024 E. Pershing Blvd.
307/638-6736

**Bart's Flea Market**
Lincolnway & Tomes
307/632-0004

**Collectables Corner**
2622 Pioneer Ave.
307/634-7706

**Old Gold Antiques**
1309 W. 18th St.
307/632-8557

***Great Places To Stay***

### Porch Swing Bed and Breakfast
712 E. 20th St.
307/778-7182
Rates: $43-66

The Porch Swing Bed and Breakfast in its charming authentical restored 1907 two-story cottage is filled with antiques. Handmade quilts are on every bed. Summer gardens are fragrant with flowers and herbs. Edible flowers are served as well as a full breakfast by the fire in the winter and on the back porch in the summer. Located within walking distance is downtown Cheyenne where you may enjoy museums and restaurants as well as other forms of entertainment. Not far from the bed and breakfast, mountain parks for hiking, bicycling, and cross-country or downhill skiing are available.

## 4 CODY

### Olde General Store

1323 Sheridan Ave.
307/587-5500
Summer 9-9 (7 days a week), June-August; Winter 9-6, Mon.-Sat., 12-4 Sun.
*Directions: Hwy. 14 is the main street in Cody. Shop is located on Hwy. 14 which is also Sheridan Ave.*

The two floors of this shop specialize in mostly oak furniture including a few pieces of Mission Oak. They also have added a line of handmade Wyoming log furniture. Throughout the store, you'll find primitives, collectibles, western memorabilia as well as gifts and decorative accessories.

**Old West Antiques**
1215 Sheridan Ave.
307/587-9014

**The Wiley House**
913 Sheridan Ave.
307/587-6030

**Cottage Antiques**
1327 Rumsey Ave.
307/527-4650

**Bear Tooth Floral & Gifts**
1316 Beck Ave.
307/587-4984

***Great Places To Stay***

### Parson's Pillow Bed & Breakfast

1202 14th St.
307/587-2382
1-800-377-2348
*Directions: Located just off Hwys. 14, 16, 20 and 120. For specific directions from your location please call the Innkeepers, Lee & Elly Larabee.*

Put on your boots and amble down "Main Street" Cody, visiting fine restaurants, shops, and galleries. After a hard day on the antique trail, have an old fashioned ice cream soda...or saddle up old tin lizzy and head out to the Cody Nite Rodeo, Old West Trail Town or visit the Buffalo Bill Museum.

Then, after a short ride out of town watching the buffalo roam and the antelope play, knock the dust off your boots at Parson's Pillow Bed and Breakfast, a wood framed church dedicated in 1902 as a Methodist Episcopal Church. Prior to that, Mr. Beck, one of William F. Cody's closet friends who helped Buffalo Bill in the founding and building of Cody, was involved in a poker game one evening. The pot grew to a whopping $500!!! At that point, Mr. Beck and his opponent agreed that the winner would use the money to build Cody's first church building. Mr. Beck won and built an Episcopal Church. However, even in losing, the Methodists built their own church at the corner of 14th and Beck Avenue! The former bell tower with its magnificent bell, which was donated by a cousin of Buffalo Bill's (herself an Episcopalian), was the envy of Mr. Beck and all the Episcopalians!

Today, comfort, elegance and the sense of coming home are yours to enjoy as a guest of Parson's Pillow B & B. Filled with antiques and turn of the century lace, this 1902 former church has been caringly restored so that all who enter it might experience western homestyle hospitality. Choose from four themed guest rooms; the Rose - filled with Barbara Cartland novels to enhance your romantic fantasies; the Garden - provides a private vintage pedestal tub; the Western - rustic simplicity with an private oak framed prairie tub; and the Memories - featuring an antique bed with fluffly feather pillows. Breakfast is served in the dining room.

## 5 DOUGLAS

**Antiques Etc.**
404 S. 4th St.
307/358-2253

**Country Touch**
421 S. 4th St.
307/358-3641

**Briar Patch**
115 N. 3rd St.
307/358-4437

## 6 EVANSTON

The story of Evanston is largely a story of the Union Pacific Railroad, which was, at that time laying track through the country at a rate of seven miles per day. One November, the graders had reached Bear River City, about 90 miles west of Green River.

The Bear River City Riot of November 21, 1868 was instigated by the rough element which preyed on the railroad workers. The riot has served as the prototype for nearly every Western movie ever made, the good guys against the bad guys. Soldiers from Fort Bridger were called to quell the disorder, but the good guys had things well in hand by the time they arrived.

Bear River City eventually grew into Evanston, which was named for the surveyor who platted the town, and Evanston became the commercial and shipping center of the area.

### Sheila's Memories Antiques and Collectibles

900 Main St.
307/789-0638
Mon.-Sat., 10-5
*Directions: Take Front St. Exit off I-80. Go 3 blocks; turn left at 9th St. Go one block to Main St. Located at the corner of 9th and Main. An alternative: Exit I-80 at Harrison Drive. Go to Main St.; turn left and store is at the corner of 9th and Main.*

Collectors listen up! Inside this 7,200 square foot shop, boasting to have a large selection of everything, sit two rare and in good condition 1950s pinball machines. Hummel figurines grace tabletops as well. Grandeur and beauty increase with prints from Parrish, Fox and Thompson. Additional pieces include Victorian furniture and accessories, old dolls and toys, as well as vintage jewelry. Appraisal services are offered.

**Eliza Doolittle's**
944 Main St.
307/789-5656

**Blue Moon Collectibles**
221 10th St., #101
307/789-6268

## 7 GILLETTE

**Doc's Swap Shop Antiques**
950 Chandler Lane
307/682-1801

**Flower Boutique**
1001 S. Douglas Hwy.
307/682-4569

**Collectors**
1612 E. U.S. Hwy. 1416
307/682-8929

## 8 GREYBULL

Established in 1909 as a railroad town, Greybull is named for the Greybull River which itself was derived from a legendary grey bison bull said to be sacred to the Indians. Currently a center for bentonite mining, Greybull is also a region rich in Indian relics, fossils and semiprecious stones. The Greybull Museum (Free admission) is just one block east of the Post Office on Greybull Ave. Displayed are Indian apparel and artifacts, old weapons and pioneer utensils. There are outstanding agate collections dating back millions of years. Don't miss the largest fossil ammonite in the world.

## 9 JACKSON

### Samuel's Continental Imports

745 W. Broadway
307/733-4794
Mon.-Sat. 10-9, Sun. by appointment only
*Directions: Jackson Hole is considered the kickoff point when approaching the Grand Tetons and Yellowstone National Park from the south, Samuel's is easy to find. Just follow the signs on I-80 or I-15 and you will arrive at the doorsteps at 745 West Broadway as you enter the town of Jackson, Wyo., Samuel's is the large green building just opposite the Virginia Lodge. You can't miss it. The American and Italian flags are always flying outside the door.*

Samuel's Continental Imports had its beginning in 1993, when two people, Sam Galano and Molly Morgan, with a love for fine old European and American furniture felt that there was a lack of the same in the ever increasing number of antiques and designer stores in Jackson Hole, Wy., and the surrounding areas. So they decided to bring "the stuff" they loved to this western town through overseas buyers in addition to their own finds in barns, estate sales, auction houses, and private homes. They imported the graceful lines of many eras and styles and rejoiced in the warm patinas of the quality wood that European and American craftsmen have used to create decorative and practical furniture for generations. They even have an "in house doctor" for the pieces. Sam Galano, part owner of the business, has a highly trained eye and years of knowledge and expertise in restoration. Samuel's Continental Imports also offers custom framing and uses only conservation materials to preserve the quality of each piece being framed. Sam is responsible for this work and takes an artistic approach to insure the art work is complemented, not overwhelmed. They haven't ignored the smalls, offering everything from art glass and fine china to nail kegs and horseshoes. The store carries an extensive line of antique lighting fixtures and showcases the original artwork of wonderful artists.

**Showcase Antiques**
115 W. Broadway Ave.
307/733-4848

**Bear Print**
140 N. Cache
307/733-1558

**Fighting Bear Antiques**
35 E. Simpson
307/733-2669

**Beyond Necessities Antiques**
335 S. Millward
307/733-7492

**Back Porch**
145 E. Pearl Ave.
307/733-0030

**Cheap Thrills**
250 W. Pearl Ave.
307/739-9266

**Antiques of Jackson Hole**
745 W. Broadway St.
307/733-0311

**Cottage Antiques**
155 W. Pearl Ave.
307/733-0849

## 10 LANDER

**Village Store**
23 Shrine Club Road
307/332-2801

**Annie's Attic**
523 Garfield
307/332-2279

***Great Places To Stay***

### Blue Spruce Inn

677 S. 3rd St.
1-888-503-3311
Web site: rmisp.com/bluespruce

Built in 1920, the Blue Spruce Inn is surrounded by giant blue spruc trees and flower gardens. Throughout the inn, magnificent oak crow molding and woodwork prevail as outstanding examples of the Arts ar Crafts period of the early 20th Century.

**Piece of Cake B&B**
P.O. Box 866
307/332-7608

Butch Cassidy never had such luxury! Lodge with two rooms and three cabins-all private large baths, Egyptian cotton linens. Breathtaking views-10,000 plus open acres, yet five minutes to Main St. Free loop tour package and picnic lunch with two night or longer stay. Miss the 'other world'? Come into the lodge great room and view the projection screen television with all major networks at three different time zones or relax with your selection of videos or books.

### 11 LARAMIE

The city of Laramie is noted as playing a definite role in the testing of many of Wyoming's unique laws. Reporters flocked to the Gem City of the Plains to witness the first woman in the world to serve on a jury in March, 1870. In the fall of 1871, another first occurred in Laramie when "Grandma" Louiza Swain went to the polls and was the first woman in the world to vote in a general election.

**Golden Flea Gallery**
725 Skyline Road
307/745-7055
Daily 10-6
*Directions: On the south side of Laramie near the Holiday Inn and Motel 6. Once on Skyline Road, go 4/10 mile as it bends to the left, Golden Flea is on the left side of the street. Getting to Skyline Road: From I-80 heading east: take Exit 313 (Third St.). Turn left onto Skyline Road (at Holiday Inn). From I-80 heading west: take Exit 313 (Third St.). Turn left onto Third St. Go 2/10 miles then turn left as though to get on I-80 E., but then immediately turn right onto service road (Skyline Road) by Holiday Inn. From Hwy. 287 N. from Fort Collins, Colorado: turn right as if to get on I-80 E., then immediately turn right onto service (Skyline) road.*

The "great wide open" of Wyoming has come indoors at this 20,000 square foot gallery. Inside, among the wares of over 140 dealers, you can wander among antique furnishings and accessories, collectibles, old records and books. An interesting and surprising assortment of gift items adds to the greatness of this showcase named after such a small creature (the flea).

**ountry Antiques The 2nd Story**
5 E. Ivinson Ave.
7/745-4423

**Curiosity Shoppe**
206 S. 2nd St.
307/745-4760

**nder One Roof**
02 S. 3rd St.
7/742-8469

**Granny's Attic**
1311 S. 3rd St.
307/721-9664

**Victoria's Treasures**
408 S. 2nd St.
307/742-6062

### 12 ROCK SPRINGS

**Olde Towne Antiques**
426 S. Main St.
307/382-3207
Mon.-Sat. 10 to 5
*Directions: Exit I-80 at Elk St. Travel south to old downtown Rock Springs.*

This eight dealer shop offers a large selection of depression glass, pottery, kitchen collectibles, advertising and railroad items, 1920s and '30s furniture, stoneware and toys. Big selection, great prices!

**Antique Mall**
411 N. Front St.
307/362-9611

**Tynsky's Rock Shop**
706 Dewar Dr.
307/362-5031

### 13 SHERIDAN

**Raven's Nest Antiques**
1617 N. Main St.
307/672-8171
Mon.-Sat. 10-5, closed Sun.
*Directions: Traveling east on I-90 exit Sheridan Main St. Downtown. Shop is about eight blocks from I-90 across from Kentucky Fried Chicken.*

This five dealer, 3,000 square foot shop features high boys, oak and pine Hoosiers as well as other fine pieces of furniture. From days of yore you will find elegant glassware, fiesta, sheet music, vintage clothing, costume jewelry and Western memorabilia.

**Pack Rat**
157 W. Brundage St.
307/672-0539

**Interior Images**
200 W. Brundage St.
307/674-7604

**Best Out West Antiques & Collectibles**
109 N. Main St.
307/674-5003

**Q Man Music & Antiques**
528 N. Main St.
307/672-9636

**North Main Antiques**
1135 N. Main St.
307/672-3838

# Largest Malls

## ALABAMA

### Birmingham
**Riverchase Antique Gallery**
3454 Lorna Road
205/823-6433
146 dealers - 36,000 sq. ft.

### Chelsea
**Chelsea Antique Mall**
14569 Hwy. 280
205/678-2151
100 dealers

### Dothan
**Alabama Antq. Mall & Auction Ctr.**
U.S. 231 S.
1-800-922-0720
75 dealers

### Foley
**Gas Works Antique Mall**
818 N. McKenzie St. (Hwy. 59 N.)
334/943-5555
70 dealers - 45 showcases

### Harpersville
**Hen/Son's Antique Mall**
917 U.S. Hwy. 280 W.
205/672-7071
9,000 sq. ft. - 40 dealers

### Heflin
**The Willoughby St. Mall**
91-A Willoughby St.
205/463-5409
35,000 sq. ft.

### Huntsville
**HartLex Antique Mall**
1030 Old Monrovia Road
205/830-4278
60,000 sq. ft. - 300 dealers

### Jasper
**The Antique Market**
5077 Hwy. 78 E.
205/384-6997
10,000 sq. ft.

### Millbrook
**Sisters Antique Mall**
1951 Market St.
334/285-5571
10,200 sq. ft. - 28 dealers

### Mobile
**Mobile Antique Gallery**
1616 S. Beltline Hwy.
334/666-6677
21,000 sq. ft.

### Montgomery
**Montgomery Antique Galleries**
1955 Eastern Blvd.
334/277-2490
20,000 sq. ft. - 50 dealers

**SouthEast Antiques & Collectibles**
2530 E. South Blvd.
334/284-5711
15,000 sq. ft. - 40 dealers

### Northport
**Anne Marie's Antique Emporium**
5925 Hwy. 43
1-888-333-1398
30,000 sq. ft.

### Vernon
**Falkner Antique Mall**
Courtsquare
205/695-9841
14,000 sq. ft. - 60 dealers

### Winfield
**Between A Rock & A Hard Place**
Hwy. 78 W.
205/487-2924
72,000 sq. ft. plus monthly auctions

## ARIZONA

### Bisbee
**On Consignment In Bisbee**
100 Lowell Traffic Circle
520/432-4002

### Glendale
**The Town of Glendale**
80 antique and speciality shops

### Mesa
**Antique Plaza**
114 W. Main St.
602/833-4844
20,000 sq. ft. - 100 dealers

**Mesa Antique Mart**
1455 S. Stapley Ste. 12
602/813-1909
84 dealers

**Treasures From The Past**
106 E. McKellips Road
602/655-0090
80 dealers

### Phoenix
**Antique Gallery**
5037 N. Central Ave.
602/241-1174
80 dealers

**Brass Armadillo**
12419 N. 28th Dr.
1-888-942-0030
700 dealers

### Scottsdale
**Antiques Super-Mall**
1900 N. Scottsdale Road
602/874-2900
60,000 sq. ft. - 250 dealers

**Antique Trove**
2020 N. Scottsdale Road
602/947-6074
125 dealers

**Antique Centre**
2012 N. Scottsdale Road
602/675-9500
125 dealers

### Tucson
**Antique Mall**
3130 E. Grant Road
520/326-3070
100 dealers

## ARKANSAS

### Alma
**Days Gone By**
400 Heather Lane
501/632-0829
27,000 sq. ft. - 175 dealers

**Sisters 2 Too Antique Mall**
702 Hwy. 71 N.
501/632-2292
130 dealers

### Benton
**Jerry Van Dyke's Den & Attic Antiques**
117 S. Market St.
501/860-5600
25 rooms in historic downtown building

### Camden
**Downtown Antique Mall**
131 South Adams St. S.E.
870/836-4244
18,000 sq. ft.

### Clinton
**Antique Warehouse of Arkansas**
Hwy. 65 N. & 110
501/745-5842
5 buildings full of antiques

### Eureka Springs
Yesteryears Antique Mall
Hwy. 62/412 @ Rock House Road
501/253-5100
125 dealers

### Keo
**Morris Antiques**
306 Hwy. 232 W.
501/842-3531
50,000 sq. ft. - 8 large buildings

### Little Rock
**Fabulous Finds Antiques**
1521 Merrill Drive, Ste. D175
501/224-6622
17,000 sq. ft. - 80 dealers

### North Little Rock
**Crystal Hill Antique Mall**
I-40 & Crystal Hill Road
501/753-3777
12,000 sq. ft. - 60 dealers

**I-40 Antique Mall**
13021 Longfisher Road
501/851-0039
10,000 sq. ft. - 42 dealers

### Pine Bluff
**Sissy's Log Cabin**
2319 Camden Road
870/879-3040
3 buildings full

### Rogers
**Shelby Lane**
719 W. Walnut
501/621-0111
300 booths

### Searcy
**Frances Antiques**
701 W. Race Ave.
501/268-2154
3 buildings full

**Room Service Antiques**
2904 E. Race
501/279-0933
95 dealers

### Texarkana
**M & M Antique Mall**
401 E. Broad St.
870/773-1871
100 dealers

### Van Buren
**Antique Warehouse of Arkansas**
402 Main St.
501/474-4808

## CALIFORNIA

### Aptos
**Village Fair Antiques**
417 Trout Gulch Road
408/688-9883
17,000 sq. ft. - 20 shops

### Bakersfield
**5 & Dime Antq. Mall & Luncheonette**
1400 19th St.
805/323-8048
22,000 sq. ft. - 70 dealers

# Largest Malls

## Beaumont
**Nelson's Giant Antique Showcase & Booth Mall**
630 California Ave.
909/769-1934

## Carlsbad
**Carlsbad Antique District**
Three Blocks of Shops
9 shops

## Carmicheal
**Antiques Unlimited**
6328 Fair Oaks Blvd.
916/482-6533
96 dealers

## Carson
**Memory Lane Antique Mall**
20740 S. Figueroa St.
301/538-4130
20,000 sq. ft. - 250 dealers

## Chico
**Eighth & Main Antique Center**
745 Main St.
916/893-5534
25,000 sq. ft.

## Clovis
**Clovis Antique Mall**
530 & 532 Fifth St.
209/298-1090
00 dealers

## Dana Point
**he Landmark Antiques**
4241 Coast Hwy.
14/489-1793
00 dealers

## El Cajon
**agnolia Antique Mall**
56 N. Magnolia Ave.
9/444-0628
,000 sq. ft. - 85 dealers

## Fresno
**lton's Folly Antique Mall**
0 E. Olive Ave.
9/268-3856
dealers

## Glendora
**e Orange Tree Antique Mall**
5 N. Glendora Ave.
/335-3376
shops in a quaint village

## Grass Valley
**e Palace Antiques & Collectibles**
E. Main St.
/273-6043
00 sq. ft.

## Healdsburg
**Vintage Plaza Antiques**
44 Mill St.
707/433-8409
19,000 sq. ft.

## Jackson
**Sisters**
5 Main St.
209/223-2930
10,000 sq. ft.

## Loma Linda
**Loma Linda Antique Mall**
24997 Redlands Blvd.
909/796-4776
55 air conditioned shops

## Long Beach
**Julie's Antique Mall**
1133 East Wardlow Road
562/989-7799
17,000 sq. ft. - 120 dealers

**Sleepy Hollow Antique Mall**
5689 Paramount Blvd.
562/634-8370
17,000 sq. ft. - 180 dealers

## Los Angeles
**The Antique Guild**
3225 Helms Ave.
310/838-3131
130 showcases and booths

**Westchester Faire**
8655 S. Sepulveda Blvd.
310/670-4000
30,000 sq. ft. - 75 dealers - 3 cafes

## Modesto
**Antique Emporium**
1511 J. St.
209/759-9730
1208 Ninth St.
209/527-6004
17,500 sq. ft. - 70 dealers

## Napa
**Red Hen Antiques**
5091 St. Helena Hwy.
707/257-0822
70 dealers

**Riverfront Antique Centre**
705 Soscol Ave.
707/253-1966
24,000 sq. ft. - 100 dealers

## Ontario
Treasures 'N' Junk Antique Mall
215 S. San Antonio
909/983-3300
15,000 sq. ft. - 70 dealers

## Orange
**Antique Annex**
109 S. Glassell
714/997-4320
40 shops

**Country Roads Antiques & Gardens**
204 W. Chapman
714/532-3041
15,000 sq. ft. - 5,000 sq. ft. garden

**Orange Circle Antique Mall**
118 S. Glassell
714/538-8160
125 dealers

## Orinda
**The Family Jewels**
572 Tahos Road
510/254-4422
Over 100,000 pieces of vintage jewelry

## Pasadena
**Novotny's Antique Gallery**
60 N. Lake
818/577-9660
70 dealers

**The Pasadena Antq. Center & Annex**
444-480 S. Fair Oaks
626/449-7706
33,000 sq. ft. - 130 dealers

## Paso Robles
**Heritage House Antique Gallery**
1345 Park St.
805/239-1386
12,000 sq. ft.

**The Antique Emporium Mall**
1307 Park St.
805/238-1078
12,000 sq. ft. - 55 dealers

## Petaluma
**Vintage Bank Antiques**
101 Petaluma Blvd.
707/769-3097
3 floors

## Pleasanton
**Main St. Antiques & Collectibles**
641 Main St.
510/426-0279
11,000 sq. ft.

## Pomona
**Pomona's Antique Row**
100-200 block of E. 2nd St.
400 dealers - 20 stores

**Robbins Antique Mart**
200 E. 2nd St.
909/623-9835
27,000 sq. ft. - 110 dealers

## Porterville
**Cotton Center Trading Post**
15366 Rd. 192
209/784-4012
90 dealers

## Rancho Cordova
**Antique Plaza**
11395 Folsom Blvd.
916/852-8517
75,000 sq. ft. - 250 dealers

## Redlands
**Emma's Trunk Antique Mall**
1701 Orange Tree Lane
909/79-TRUNK
100 dealers

**Illa's Antiques & Collectibles and The Packing House Mall**
215 East Redlands Blvd.
909/793-8898
30,000 sq. ft. - 80 dealers

**Precious Times Antique Mall of Redlands**
1740 Redlands Blvd.
909/792-7768
150 dealers

## Sacramento
**River City Antique Mall**
10117 Mills Station Rd.
916/362-7778
20,000 sq. ft. - 70 dealers

**57th St. Antique Mall**
875 57th St. (Off H St.)
916/451-3110
10,000 sq. ft.

## San Bernardino
**The Heritage Gallery**
1520-A S. E St.
909/888-3377
25,000 sq. ft.

**Treasure Mart Antique Mall**
293 E. Redlands Blvd.
909/825-7264
90 dealers

## San Carlos
**Laurel St. Antiques**
671 Laurel St.
650/593-1152
10,000 sq. ft.

**The Antique Trove**
1119 Industrial Way
650/593-1300
30,000 sq. ft.

# Largest Malls

### San Diego
**T & R Antiques Warehouse**
4630 Santa Fe St.
619/272-2500
15,000 sq. ft.

### San Francisco
**San Francisco Antique Design Mall**
701 Bayshore Blvd.
415/656-3530
36,000 sq. ft.

### San Jose
**West San Carlos St.**
Over 200 dealers in a one mile strip

### San Juan Capistrano
**Yesterday's Paper**
31815 Camino Capistrano
714/248-0945
3 large showrooms

### San Marcos
**San Marcos Antique Village**
983 Grand Ave.
760/744-8718
12,000 sq. ft. - 65 dealers

### Santa Monica
**Santa Monica Antique Market**
1607 Lincoln Blvd.
310/314-4899
20,000 sq. ft. - 150 dealers

### Sebastopol
**The Antique Society**
2661 Gravenstein Hwy. S.
707/829-1733
20,000 sq. ft. - 100 dealers

### Sherman Oaks
**Sherman Oaks Antique Mall**
14034 Ventura Blvd.
818/906-0338
95 shops

### Simi Valley
**Penny Pinchers**
4265 Valley Fair
805/527-0056
72 dealers

### Solvang
**Solvang Antique Center**
486 First St.
805/686-2322
100 plus galleries & showcases

### Soquel
**Historic Soquel Village**
Soquel Drive
5 multi-dealer shops - 9 single shops

### Studio City
**The Cranberry House**
12318 Ventura Blvd.
818/506-8945
15,000 sq. ft.

### Sutter Creek
**Water St. Antiques**
78 Main St.
209/267-0585
35,000 sq. ft.

### Vallejo
**Yesteryear's Marketplace**
433 Georgia St.
707/557-4671
10,000 sq. ft.

### Ventura
**35 shops within a 1 mile radius**
Visitor's Information: 800/333-2989

### Visalia
**Antiques at The Works Showcase Mall**
26644 S. Mooney
209/685-1125
16,000 sq. ft. - 100 dealers

### Whittier
**King Richard's Antique Center**
12301 Whittier Blvd.
562/698-5974
100,000 sq. ft.

### Woodland
**Tinker's Antiques & Collectibles**
338 Main St.
916/662-3204
11,000 sq. ft.

## *COLORADO*

### Denver
**Antique Market**
1212 S. Broadway
303/744-0281

**Architectural Salvage, Inc.**
1215 Delaware St.
303/615-5432

**The Gallagher Collection @ the Antique Guild**
1298 S. Broadway
303/756-5821
Located on Denver's Antique Row

### Englewood
**Van Dyke's Antiques**
3663 S. Broadway
303/789-3743

### Littleton
**Colorado Antique Gallery**
5501 S. Broadway
303/794-8100

## *CONNECTICUT*

### Clinton
**Clinton Antique Center**
78 E. Main St. (Rt. 1)
860/669-3839
75 dealers

### Collinsville
**The Collinsville Antiques Co.**
Rt. 179
860/693-1011
17,000 sq. ft. - 2 floors

### Coventry
**Memory Lane Countryside Antiques**
2224 Boston Turnpike, Rt. 44 & 31 N.
860/742-0346
3 buildings - 50 dealers

### East Hampton
**Old Bank Antiques**
66 Main St.
860/267-0790
3 floors - 6,000 sq. ft.

### Glastonbury
**Tobacco Shed Antiques**
119 Griswold St.
860/657-2885
10,000 sq. ft. - 2 buildings

### Old Saybrook
**The Antiques Depot**
455 Boston Post Rd.
860/395-0595
10,000 sq. ft.

**Essex Saybrook Antiques Village**
345 Middlesex Turnpike (Rt. 154)
860/388-0689
120 dealers

**Essex Town Line Antiques Village**
985 Middlesex Turnpike (Rt. 154)
860/388-5000
10,000 sq. ft.

**Old Saybrook Antiques Center**
756 Middlesex Turnpike (Rt. 154)
860/388-1600
125 dealers

### Putnam
**The Antiques Marketplace**
109 Main St. & Rt. 44
860/928-0442
22,000 sq. ft. - 300 dealers

### Stamford
**Antique & Artisan Center**
69 Jefferson
203/327-6022
22,000 sq. ft. - 100 dealers

**Stamford Antiques Center**
735 Canal St.
1-888-329-3546
135 dealers

### Stratford
**Stratford Antique Center**
400 Honeyspot Road
203/378-7754
200 dealers

## *DELAWARE*

### Dover
**Dover Antique Mart**
4621 N. Dupont Hwy.
302/734-7844
6,000 sq. ft. - 35 dealers

### Georgetown
**Passwaters Antiques**
6 Primrose Lane
302/856-6667
31 dealers

### Lewes
**Heritage Antique Market**
130 Hwy. One
302/645-2309
10,500 sq. ft.

### Rehoboth Beach
**Antiques Village Mall**
221 Hwy. One
302/369-1160
3 buildings

## *FLORIDA*

### Chipley
**Historic Chipley Antique Mall**
1368 N. Railroad Ave.
850/638-2535
10,000 sq. ft. - 50 dealers

### Deerfield
**Hillsboro Antique Mall & Tea Room**
1025 E. Hillsboro Blvd.
954/571-9988
32,000 sq. ft. - 200 dealers

### Ft. Lauderdale
**Nostalgia Mall**
2097 Wilton Drive
1-888-394-7233
9,000 sq. ft.

# Largest Malls

### Havana
**Havana's Cannery**
115 E. 8th Ave.
850/539-3800
16 shops - over 125 dealers

### High Springs
**High Springs Antique District**
From I-75 Exits 78, 79, 80 or Hwy. 441
1-888-454-7655 Visitor Info

### Jacksonville
**Avonlea Antique Center**
11000 Beach Blvd.
904/645-0806
100,000 sq. ft. - 180 dealers

### Lake City
**Britannia Antiques**
U.S. 90, 1/2 mile W. Of I-75
904/755-0120
15,000 sq. ft.

**Webb's**
I-75 @ Exit 80
904/758-9280
150,000 sq. ft. - 1000 booths

### Micanopy
**Smiley's**
I-75 @ Exit 73, Rd. 234
342/466-0707

### Mount Dora
**Renninger's**
20651 U.S. Hwy. 441
352/383-8393
200 dealers

### Panama City
**ntique Mall**
wy. 77
50/271-9810
0,000 sq. ft.

### Pensacola
**urch Antiques**
401 N. T St.
50/433-5153
cond Location: 3160 N. T St.

### St. Augustine
**vejoy's Antique Mall**
02 N. Ponce de Leon Blvd. (U.S. 1)
4/826-0200
4 dealers

### St. Petersburg
**tique Exchange**
35 Central Ave.
3/321-6621
) dealers

**Patty & Friends**
1225 & 1241 9th St. N.
813/821-2106
80 dealers

### Tampa
**Gaslight Antiques**
3616 Henderson Blvd.
813/870-0934
Half a city block - 3 huge stores

### Winter Park
**Orange Tree Antiques Mall**
853 S. Orlando Ave.
407/644-4547
85 dealers

## GEORGIA

### Atlanta
**Cheshire Antiques**
1859 Cheshire Bridge Road
404/733-5599
7,000 sq. ft. - 35 dealers

### Byron
**The Big Peach Antiques & Collectible Mall**
119 Peachtree Road
912/956-6256
40,000 sq. ft. - 200 dealers

### Calhoun
**Calhoun Antique Mall**
1503 Red Bud Road N.E.
706/625-2767
10,000 sq. ft. - 80 dealers

### Chamblee
**Broad Street Antique Mall**
3550 Broad St.
770/458-6316
20,000 sq. ft.

**Moose Breath Trading Company**
5461 Peachtree Road
770/458-7210
20,000 sq. ft.

### Gainesville
**Gainesville Antique Gallery**
131 Bradford St.
770/532-4950
25,000 sq. ft.

### Kennesaw
**Big Shanty Antique Mall**
1720 N. Roberts Road
770/795-1704
50,000 sq. ft. - 150+ dealers

### Macon
**Old Mill Antique Mall**
155 Coliseum Dr.
912/743-1948
35,000 sq. ft.

### Marietta
**Dupre's Antique Market**
17 Whitelock Ave. N.W.
770/428-2667
Over 17,000 sq. ft.

### Perry
**Perry's Antiques & Cllbl. Mall**
351 General Courtney Hodges Blvd.
912/987-4001
100+ dealers

### Ringgold
**Gateway Antiques Center**
4103 Cloud Springs Road
706/858-9685
40,000 sq. ft. - 300 dealers

### Rome
**Heritage Antiques**
174 Chatillon Road
706/291-4589
10,000 sq. ft. - 37 dealers

### Roswell
**Roswell Antique Gallery**
10930 Crabapple Road
770/594-8484
30,000 sq. ft. - 245 dealer spaces

### Savannah
**Jere's Antiques**
9 N. Jefferson St.
912/236-2815
30,000 sq. ft.

### Tifton
**Sue's Antique Mall**
I-75 @ Exit 23
912/388-1856
10,000 sq. ft. - No reproductions

## IDAHO

### Boise
**Collectors Choice I & II**
5284 Franklin Road
208/336-2489
5150 Franklin Road
208/336-3170
Two large locations - 75+ dealers

### Coeur D'Alene
**Coeur D'Alene Antique Mall**
3650 N. Government Way
408 W. Haycraft Ave. #11
208/667-0246
125+ dealers - 2 large locations

## ILLINOIS

### Chicago
**Armitage Antique Gallery**
1529 W. Armitage
773/227-7727
40 dealers

**Lincoln Antique Mall**
3141 N. Lincoln Ave.
773/244-1440
11,000 sq. ft.

**Wrigleyville Antique Mall**
3336 N. Clark St.
773/868-0285
10,000 sq. ft.

### Coal Valley
**Country Fair Mall**
504 W. 1st Ave. (Hwy. 6)
309/799-3670
20,000 sq. ft.

### Divernon
**Lisa's I & II Antique Malls**
I-55 & Route 104
217/628-1111
40,000 sq. ft.

### East Peoria
**Pleasant Hill Antique Mall**
315 S. Pleasant Hill Road
309/694-4040
30,000 sq. ft. - over 200 dealers

### El Paso
**El Paso Antique Mall**
I-39 & Rt. 24
309/527-3705
16,000 sq. ft. - 200 dealers

### Grayslake
**Antique Warehouse**
2 S. Lake St.
708/223-9554
65 dealers - No Reproductions

### Greenup
**Historic Western Style Town Antq. Mall**
113 E. Kentucky St.
217/923-3514
14,000 sq. ft.

# Largest Malls

### Kankakee
**Indian Oaks Antique Mall**
N. Route 50 & Larry Power Road
815/933-9998
18,000 sq. ft. - 170 dealers

### Orland Park
**Beacon Avenue Antique Row**
708/460-8433
Five shops on one block.

**Station House Antique Mall**
12305 W. 159th St.
708/301-9400
10,000 sq. ft.

### Princeton
**Sherwood Antique Mall**
1661 N. Main, I-80, Exit 56 S.
815/872-2580
40,000 sq. ft.

### Sandwich
**Sandwich Antiques Market**
U.S. 34 Fairgrounds
773/227-4464
550 quality dealers

### Springfield
**The Barrel Antique Mall**
5850 S. 6th St.
217/585-1438
27,000 sq. ft. - 138 dealers

### Warrenville
**Route 59 Antique Mall**
3 S. 450 Route 59
630/393-0100
10,500 sq. ft. - 60 dealers

### Wheeling
**Antiques Center of Illinois**
1920 S. Wolf Road
847/215-9418
50 shops under one roof

## INDIANA

### Anderson
**Anderson Antique Mall**
1407 Main St.
765/622-9517
30,000 sq. ft. - four floors

### Bloomington
**Bloomington Antique Mall**
311 W. 7th St.
812/332-2290
120+ dealers

### Centerville
**Webb's Antique Malls**
200 W. Union St.
765/855-5542
100,000 sq. ft. - 600+ dealers

### Chesterton
**Yesterday's Treasures Antique Mall**
700 Broadway
219/926-2268
30,000 sq. ft. - 100+ dealers

### Decatur
**Yvonne Marie's Antique Mall**
152 S. 2nd St.
219/724-2001
76 dealers - three full floors

### Evansville
**Franklin St. Antique Mall**
2123 W. Franklin St.
812/428-0988
21,000 sq. ft.- Historic Building

### Ft. Wayne
**Karen's Antique Mall**
1510 Fairfield
219/422-4030
18,000 sq. ft. - 65+ dealers

### Indianapolis
**Fountain Square Antique Mall**
1056 Virginia Ave.
317/636-1056
14,000 sq. ft. - 70+ dealers

**Manor House Antique Mall**
5454 U.S. 31 S.
317/782-1358
20,000 sq. ft. - 140 dealers

**Southport Antique Mall**
2028 E. Southport Road
317/786-8246
29,000 sq. ft. - 210 dealers

### Knightstown
**Knightstown Antique Mall**
136 W. Carey St.
765/345-5665
city block of merchandise

### LaPorte
**Coachman Antique Mall**
500 Lincolnway
219/326-5933
23,000 sq. ft. - 100 dealers

### Madison
**Lumbermill Antique Mall**
721 W. First St.
812/273-3040
Madison's Largest - 3 floors

### Muncie
**Off Broadway Antique Mall**
2404 N. Broadway
765/747-5000
½ acre under one roof! - 70+ dealers

### Nappanee
**Borkholder Dutch Village**
CR 101
219/773-2828
Noblesville

**Lazy Acres Antiques**
77 Metsker Lane
317/773-7387
10,000 sq. ft.

### Plainfield
**Gilley's Antique Mall**
5789 E. U.S. Hwy. 40
317/839-8779
7 buildings - 400+ booths

### Scottsburg
**Scottsburg Antique Mall**
4 Main St.
812/752-4645
10,000 sq. ft.

### Terre Haute
**Shady Lane Antique Mall**
9247 S. U.S. Hwy. 41
812/299-1625
10,000 sq. ft. - 50 dealers

### Westfield
**R. Beauchamp Antiques**
16405 Westfield Blvd.
217/867-3327
15,000 sq. ft.

**Westfield Antique Mall**
800 E. Main St., Hwy. 232
317/867-3327
17,000 sq. ft.

## IOWA

### Ames
**Memories on Main**
203 Main St.
515/233-2519
11,000 sq. ft. - 80+ dealers

### Cedar Rapids
**Wellington Square Antique Mall**
1200 2nd Ave. S.E.
319/368-6640
17,000 sq. ft. - 118 dealers

### Davenport
**Antique America Mall**
702 W. 76th St.
319/386-3430
23,000 sq. ft. - 150 dealers

### Des Moines
**Brass Armadillo Inc.**
701 N.E. 50th Ave.
515/282-0082
36,000 sq. ft. - 450 dealers

## KANSAS

### Augusta
**White Eagle Antique Mall**
10187 S.W. U.S. Hwy. 54
316/775-2812
100 dealers

### Emporia
**Wild Rose Antique Mall**
1505 E. Road 175
316/343-8862
60 dealers

### Lawrence
**Quantrill's Antq. Mall & Flea Market**
811 New Hampshire St.
913/842-6616
20,000 sq. ft. - 150 dealers

### Leavenworth
**Caffee's Leavenworth Antique Mall & Tea Room**
505 Delaware
913/758-0193
3 floors

### Ottawa
**Ottawa Antique Mall & Restaurant**
202 S. Walnut St.
785/242-1078
17,000 sq. ft. - 100 dealers

### Prairie Village
**Mission Road Antique Mall**
4101 W. 83rd St.
913/341-7577
40,000 sq. ft. - 2 floors - 250 dealers

### Salina
**Auld Lang Syne**
101 N. Santa Fe
913/825-0020
90 dealers

### Topeka
**Antique Plaza of Topeka**
2935 S.W. Topeka Blvd.
913/267-7411
18,000 sq. ft.

### Valley Falls
**Valley Falls Antiques**
423 Broadway
913/945-3666

### Wichita
**White Eagle Antique Mall**
10187 S.W. U.S. Hwy. 54
316/775-2812
100 dealers

**Wooden Heart Antiques**
141 S. Rock Island St.
316/267-1475
Large two story warehouse

## *KENTUCKY*

### Corbin
**Past Times Antique Mall**
135 W. Cumberland Gap Pkwy.
606/528-8818
14,000 sq. ft. - 95 dealers

### Franklin
**Franklin Kentucky Antiques**
300 booths
4 private shops

### Georgetown
**Central Kentucky Antique Mall**
114 E. Main St.
502/863-4018
9,000 sq. ft.

**Georgetown Antique Mall**
124 W. Main St.
502/863-1275
100+ dealers-4 buildings-6 floors

### Harrodsburg
**The Antique Mall of Harrodsburg**
540 N. College St. (Hwy. 127)
606/734-5191
Over 130 dealers

**North Main Center Antique Mall**
520 N. Main St.
506/734-2200
22,000 sq. ft.

### Lexington
**Boone's Antiques of Kentucky**
996 Old Versailles Road
06/254-5335
7,000 sq. ft.

**Country Antique Mall Inc.**
455 Leestown Road
Meadowthorpe Shopping Center
06/233-0075
4,000 sq. ft. - 60 dealers

### Louisville
**Louisville Antique Mall**
0 Goss Ave.
2/635-2852
,000 sq. ft.

**wan Street Antique Mall**
7 E. Breckinridge St.
2/584-6255
000 sq. ft. - 125 dealers

### Mt. Sterling
**Monarch Mill Antiques**
101 S. Maysville St.
606/498-3744
Over 13,000 sq. ft.

### Newport
**471 Antique Mall**
901 E. 6th St.
606/431-4753
20,000 sq. ft. - 2 floors

### Nicholasville
**Coach Light Antique Mall**
213 N. Main St.
606/887-4223
75 dealers

## *LOUISIANA*

### Baton Rouge
**AAA Antiques**
9800 Florida Blvd.
504/925-1644
80,000 sq. ft. - 75 dealers

**Landmark Antique Plaza Inc.**
832 St. Phillip St.
504/383-4867
55,000 sq. ft.

**Westmoreland Antique Gallery**
3374 Government St.
504/383-7777
55,000 sq. ft.

### Covington
**Past Restored**
2380 W. 21st Ave.
504/892-7475
10,000 sq. ft.

### Denham Springs
**Benton Brothers Antique Mall**
115 N. Range Ave.
504/665-5146
12,000 sq. ft.

### New Orleans
**New Orleans Antique District**
"Magazine St."
Over 80 shops

### Shreveport
**Heirloom Antiques**
3004 Highland Ave.
318/226-0146
10,000 sq. ft.

**Nigel's Heirloom Antique Gallery**
421 Texas St.
318/226-0146
22,000 sq. ft. - 5 floors

### Washington
**O'Conner's Antiques**
210 S. Church St.
318/826-3580
15,000 sq. ft.

### West Monroe
**Antique Alley**
Located Downtown
Trenton St.
14 shops

## *MAINE*

### Auburn
**Orphan Annie's Antiques**
96 Court St.
207/782-0638
3 warehouses

### Brewer
**Center Mall**
39 Center St.
207/989-9842
12,000 sq. ft. - 55 dealers

### Kennebunkport
**Antiques USA**
RR 1
207/985-7766
Over 200 dealers - One of largest in state

### Searsport
**Searsport Antique Mall**
RR 1
207/548-2640
8,000 sq. ft. - 80 dealers

### Wells
**Wells Union Antique Center**
1755 Post Road
207/646-6996
9 buildings

### York
**York Antiques Gallery**
Rte. 1
207/363-5002
4 floors - 80 dealers

## *MARYLAND*

### Baltimore
**"Howard Street" Antique District**
Over 20 shops

**Antique Amusements**
**A-1 Jukebox & Nostalgia Co.**
208 South Pulaski St.
410/945-8900
5,000 sq. ft. In a 5 story building

**Antique Warehouse at 1300**
1300 Jackson St.
410/659-0662
15,000 sq. ft. - 35 dealers

### Bethesda
**Grapevine of Bethesda**
7806 Old Georgetown Road
301/654-8690

### Cambridge
**Packing House Antique Mall**
411 Dorchester
410/221-8544
60,000 sq. ft. - 140 dealers

### Easton
**Sullivan's Antique Warehouse**
28272 St. Michaels Road
410/822-4723
4 large buildings

### Ellicott
**Shops at Ellicott Mills**
8307 Main St.
410/461-8700
100 dealers

### Frederick
**Antique Station**
194 Thomas Johnson Dr.
301/695-0888
New section "mile long"

### Hanover
**AAA Antiques Mall**
2659 Annapolis Road
410/551-4101
58,000 sq. ft.

## *MASSACHUSETTS*

### Andover
**Andover Antiques, Inc.**
89 N. Main St.
978/475-4242
40 dealers

### Boston
"Charles St." Antique District
Over 20 shops.

### Cambridge
**Antiques on Cambridge Street**
1076 Cambridge St.
617/234-0001
100 dealers

**Cambridge Antique Market**
201 Monsignor O'Brien Hwy.
617/868-9600
150 dealers, 5 floors

### Dennis
**Antiques Center Warehouse**
243 Main St., Route 6A
508/385-5133
235 dealers, 2 buildings

# Largest Malls

### Framingham
**Framingham Centre Antiques**
931 Worchester Road (Route 9)
508/620-6252
2 floors, 40 dealers

### Georgetown
**Sedler's Antique Village**
51 W. Main St.
978/352-8282
10,000 square feet, 30 shops

### Old Deerfield
**5 & 10 Antique Gallery**
Routes 5 & 10
413/773-3620
Two levels

### Sandwich
**Sandwich Antiques Center**
131 Route 6A
508/833-3600
Over 150 dealers

### Southampton
**Southampton Antiques**
172 College Hwy. (Route 10)
413/527-1022
3 large barns with five floors

### Sturbridge
**Showcase Antique Center, Inc.**
Entrance to Old Sturbridge Village
508/347-7190
160 dealers

### West Townsend
**Hobart Village Antique Mall**
445 Main St.
978/597-0332
80 plus dealers

## MICHIGAN

### Allen
**Antique Capital**
260 dealers
120,000 sq. ft. of shopping on Hwy. 12

**Allen Antique Mall**
9011 W. Chicago St.
517/869-2788
260+ dealers - "Michigan's Largest"

### Bay City
**Bay City Antiques Center**
1010 N. Water St. @ Third
517/893-1116 - 888/893-0251
53,000 sq. ft. - 3 floors

### Blissfield
**J & B Antiques Mall**
109 W. Adrian St. (U.S. 223)
517/486-3544
Over 75 dealers

### Clinton
**First Class Antique Mall**
112 E. Michigan Ave.
517/456-6410
15,000 sq. ft.

### Flint
**Reminisce Antiques & Collectibles**
3124 S. Dort Hwy.
810/744-1090
15,000 sq. ft. - 50 dealers

### Grand Haven
**West Michigan Antique Mall**
13279 168th Ave.
616/842-0370
12,000 sq. ft. - 75 dealers

### Grand Rapids
**Antiques by the Bridge**
445 Bridge St. N.W.
616/451-3430
9,000 sq. ft.

**Plaza Antique Mall**
1410 28th St.
616/243-2465
9,000 sq. ft. - 68 dealers

### Holland
**Tulip City Antique Mall**
3500 U.S. Hwy. 31
616/786-4424
30,000 sq. ft. - 200 dealers

### Lansing
**Mid Michigan Mega Mall**
15487 U.S. Hwy. 27
517/487-3275
230 dealers

### Lowell
**Flat River Antique Mall**
212 W. Main St.
616/897-5360
40,000 sq. ft. - 5 floors

### Muskegon
**Downtown Muskegon Antique Mall**
1321 Division St.
616/728-0305
12,000 sq. ft.

### Niles
**Niles Michigan**
4 malls - 300 shops
80,000 sq. ft.

### Saginaw
**The Antique Warehouse**
1910 N. Michigan @ Genesee
517/755-4343
30,000 sq. ft. - 70 dealers - lunchroom

### Schoolcraft
**Norma's Antiques & Collectibles**
231 Grand (U.S. Hwy. 131)
616/679-4030
Over 10,000 sq. ft. - 3 floors

### Union Pier
**Antique Mall & Village Inc.**
9300 Union Pier Road
616/469-2555
15,000 sq. ft. - 4 buildings

### Williamston
**Antiques Market of Williamston**
2991 Williamston Road
517/655-1350
75+ dealers

## MINNESOTA

### Hopkins
**Hopkins Antique Mall**
1008 Main St.
612/931-9748
68 dealers

### Maple Plain
**Country School House Shops**
5300 U.S. Hwy. 31
612/479-6353
3 story schoolhouse - 100 plus dealers

### Stillwater
**Mid Town Antique Mall**
301 S. Main St.
612/430-0808
11,000 square feet - 75 dealers

**More Antiques**
312 N. Main St.
612/439-1110
11,000 square feet

**Stillwater Antiques Mall**
101 S. Main St.
612/439-6281
60 plus dealers

**The Mill Antiques**
410 N. Main St.
612/430-1816
20,000 square feet - 80 plus dealers

## MISSISSIPPI

### Biloxi
**Beauvoir Antique Mall**
190 Beauvoir Road
601/388-5506
Huge building - 50 plus dealers

### Greenwood
**Warehouse Antiques**
229 Carrollton Ave.
601/453-0785
10,000 square feet

### Hattiesburg
**Old High School Antiques**
846 N. Main St.
601/544-6644
4 stories - 50 plus dealers

**The Antique Mall**
2103 W. Pine St.
601/268-2511
2 full stories

### Natchez
**Natchez Antique District**
Located on Franklin St.
12 plus shops

### Ridgeland
**Antique Mall of the South**
367 Hwy. 51
601/853-4000
50 dealer mall

## MISSOURI

### Bonne Terre
**Bonne Terre Antiques**
1467 State Hwy. 47
573/358-2235
3 large buildings

### Branson
**Antique City**
Hwy. 76 W.
417/338-2673
12,000 square feet - 100 plus dealers

### Columbia
**Ice Chalet Antique Mall**
3411 Old Hwy. 63 S.
573/442-6893
28,000 square feet - 200 plus dealers

### Eureka
**Ice House Antiques**
19 Dreyer
314/938-6355
14 shops on 4 floors

**Wallach House Antiques**
510 West Ave.
314/938-6633
3 levels of quality shopping

### Greenwood
**Greenwood Antiques & Country Tea Room**
5th & Main St.
816/537-7172
15,000 square feet - 70 shops

### Independence
**Country Meadows**
4621 Shrank Dr.
816/373-0410
40,000 square feet - 400 dealers

# Largest Malls

## Monett

**V B Hall**
201 W. Main St.
417/235-1110
12,000 square feet, 75 dealers

## Ozark

**Antique Emporium**
1702 W. Boat St.
417/581-5555
12,000 square feet - 100+ dealers

**Finley River Heirlooms**
105 N. 20th St.
417/581-3253
18,000 square feet - 300 dealers

**Maine Streete Mall**
1994 Evangel St.
417/581-2575
27,000 square feet

**Ozark Antiques & Collectibles**
200 S. 20th St.
417/581-5233
17,000 square feet - 100 plus dealers

**Riverview Antique Center**
909 W. Jackson
417/581-4426
20,000 square feet - over 100 dealers

## Platte City

**I-29 Antique Mall**
unction I-29
16/858-2921
2,000 square feet - 80 plus dealers

## St. Charles

**t. Charles Antique Mall**
1 Charlestowne Plaza
14/939-4178
0,000 square feet - 450 dealers

## St. Louis

**outh County Antique Mall**
3208 Tesson Ferry Road
14/842-5566
acre - 650 dealers

**arson Woods Antique Mall**
091 Manchester Road
4/909-0123
,000 square feet - over 350 dealers

## MONTANA

## Anaconda

**ewery Antiques**
5 W. Commercial St.
6/563-7926

**rk St. Antique Mall**
3 E. Park St.
/563-3150

## Billings

**Depot Antique Mall**
2223 Montana Ave.
406/245-5955
60 plus dealers

## Bozeman

**Country Mall Antiques**
8350 Huffine Lane
406/587-7688
65 plus dealers

## Helena

**MT Antique Mall**
4528 U.S. Hwy. 12 W.
406/449-3334
30 plus dealers in an historic hotel

## St. Regis

**The Place of Antiques**
Downtown St. Regis
406/649-2397
70 plus dealers

## NEBRASKA

## Grand Island

**Great Exchange Flea Market**
N.E. Corner of Hwy. 34 & Locust St.
308/381-4075
12,000 square feet - 60 dealers

## Kearney

Kaufmans Antiques & Cllbl. Emporium
2200 Central Ave.
308/237-4972
8,000 square feet - 65 dealers

## Lincoln

**Aardvark Antique Mall**
5800 Arbor Road
402/464-5100
25,000 square feet

**Q Street Mall**
1835 Q St.
402/435-8422
80 plus dealers

## Omaha

**Meadowlark Antique Mall**
10700 Sapp Brothers Dr.
1-800-730-2135
Over 400 dealers

## Waterloo

**Venice Antiques**
26250 W. Center Road
402/359-5782
10,000 square feet

## NEVADA

## Las Vegas

**Red Rooster Antiques**
1109 Western Ave.
702/382-5253
25,000 square feet

**Sampler Shoppes Antiques**
6115 W. Tropicana @ Jones
702/368-1170
40,000 square feet - 200 dealers

## Reno

**Antique Mall I**
1215 S. Virginia St.
702/324-1003
12,000 square feet - 60 dealers

## NEW HAMPSHIRE

## Amherst

**101-A Antiques & Collectibles Center**
141 State Route 101A
603/880-8422
175 plus dealers

**Antiques @ Mayfair**
119-121 State Route 101A
603/595-7531
2 large buildings

**Needful Things/Antiques & Cllbls.**
112 State Route 101A
603/889-1232
185 dealers

## Meredith

**Burlwood Antique Center**
Route 3
603/279-6387
170 dealers

## Milford

**New Hampshire Antique Co-op**
Elm St. - Route 101A
603/673-8499
280 dealers

## West Swanzey

**Knotty Pine Antique Market**
Route 10
603/352-5252
300 antique shops under one roof.

## Wilton

**Noah's Ark**
Route 101
603/654-2595
234 dealers

## NEW JERSEY

## Andover

**Great Andover Antique Company**
124 Main St.
973/786-6384
2 huge buildings

## Burlington

**H. G. Sharkey Antq. & Coffee House**
306 High St.
609/239-0200
Historical building

## Dover

**The Iron Carriage Antique Center**
1 W. Blackwell
973/366-1440
100 dealers - 30,000 sq. ft.

## Haddonfield

**Haddonfield Antique District**
Kingo Hwy. E.
7 shops within 2 blocks

## Hopewell

**Tomato Factory Antique Center**
Hamilton Ave.
609/466-9860
Shops in old two story canning factory

## Lambertville

**Lambertville Antique & Auction Ctr.**
333 N. Main St.
609/397-9374

## Lebanon

**Lebanon Antique Center**
U. S. Hwy. 22 E.
908/236-2851
5 acres

## Manahawkin

**The Shoppes @ Rosewood**
182 N. Main St.
609/597-7331
Group in Victorian neighborhood

## Midland Park

**Brownstone Mill Antique Center**
11 Paterson Ave.
201/445-3074
Twenty-five shops under one roof

## Mount Holly/Hainsport

**Country Antique Center**
1925 Route 38
609/261-1924
8,000 sq. ft. - 100 dealers

## Mullica Hill

**The Warehouse**
2 S. Main St.
609/478-4500
Large multi-dealer

# Largest Malls

### Somerville
**Somerville Center Antiques**
17 Division St.
908/526-3446

## NEW MEXICO

### Albuquerque
**Antique Connection**
12815 Central N.E.
505/296-2300
70 plus dealers

**Classic Century Square**
4616 Central S.E.
505/265-3161
40,000 sq. ft.

**I-40 Antique Mall**
2035 12th St. N.W.
505/243-8011
50 plus dealers

### Roswell
**Monterey Antique Mall**
1400 W. 2nd St.
505/623-3347

### Silver City
**Silver City Trading Co.**
205 W. Broadway
505/388-8989
12,500 sq. ft.

## NEW YORK

### Bouckville
**The Depot Antique Gallery**
Route 20
315/893-7676
7,000 sq. ft.

**The Gallery Co-op**
Route 20
315/893-7752

### Brooklyn
**Brooklyn Antique District**
Atlantic Ave.
12 shops

### Clarence
**Downtown Clarence**
Main St.
14 plus shops

### Hudson
**5 historic walking blocks of antique shops**

### Port Washington
**Port Washington Antique Center**
289 Main St.
516/767-3313
Multi dealer

## NORTH CAROLINA

### Aberdeen
**Cameron's Antique Station**
Hwy. 211 E. - Ashley Heights
910/944-2022

**Town & Country Antique Mall**
1369 Sandhills Blvd. N.
910/944-3359

### Asheville
**Fireside Antiques**
30 All Souls Crescent
704/274-5977
Four galleries of antiques

### Boone
**Boone Antique Mall**
631 W. King St.
704/262-0521

**Wilcox Emporium**
161 Howard St.
704/262-1221
60,000 sq. ft. plus 3 new large showrooms

### Charlotte
**Black Lion Furniture**
**Gift & Design Showcases**
10605 Park Road
704/541-1148

### Farmville
**The Hub Mall**
104 S. Main St.
919/753-8560

### Gastonia
**J & W Antiques**
181 W. Main St.
704/867-0097
28,000 sq. ft.

### Hendersonville
**Hendersonville Antique District**
Downtown Main St.
Multiple shops - all within blocks

### Raleigh
**Oakwood Antiques Mall**
1526 Wake Forrest Road
919/834-5155
10,000 sq. ft. - 43 plus dealers

### Statesville
**Riverfront Antique Mall**
1441 Wilkesboro Hiwy.
800/856-2182
60,000 sq. ft.

### Wilson
**Fulford's Antique Warehouse**
320 Barnes St. S.
919/243-7727
67,000 sq. ft.

## NORTH DAKOTA

### Bismark
**Antique Interiors**
200 W. Main Ave.
701/224-9551

### Jamestown
**Antique Attic**
219 1st Ave. S.
701/252-6733
42 dealers

**Treasure Chest**
213 1st Ave. S.
701/251-2891
Located in 1900s early bank

### Valley City
**E & S Antiques**
148 E. Main St.
701/845-0369
Located in 1890s opera house

## OHIO

### Ashville
**South Bloomfield Antique Mall**
5004 Walnut St. N. (Hwy. 23)
614/983-4300
50 dealers

### Bellaire
**Imperial Plaza**
29th & Belmont St.
614/676-8300
40,000 sq. ft.

### Findlay
**Jeffrey's Antique Gallery**
11326 Township Road 99
419/423-7500
40,000 sq. ft.

### Medina
**Medina Antique Mall**
2797 Medina Road
330/722-0017
52,000 sq. ft.

### New Philadelphia
**Riverfront Antique Mall**
1203 Front St.
1-800-926-9806
96,400 sq. ft. - 350 dealers

### Ravenna
**AAA I-76 Antique Mall**
4284 Lynn Road
1-888-476-8976
50,000 sq. ft. - 450 dealers

**Ravenna Antique District**
The entire town of Ravenna offers many antiquing possibilities

**Springfield**
***AAA I-10 Antique Mall***
4700 S. Charleston Pike
(State Route 41)
513/324-8448
150,000 sq. ft. - 250 dealers

## OKLAHOMA

### Ada
**Alford Warehouse Sales**
217 S. Johnston St.
580/332-1026
2 large buildings

### Ardmore
**Peddler's Square Mall**
15 N. Washington St.
580/223-6255

**Black Star Antiques**
702 S. Chouteau Ave.
918/476-6188
14,000 sq. ft.

### El Reno
**Rt. 66 Antique Mall**
1629 E. State Hwy. 66
405/262-9366
120 booths

### Muskogee
**Old America Antique Mall**
Hwy. 69 S.
918/687-8600
27,000 sq. ft.

### Oklahoma City
**Oklahoma City Antique District**
"Over 400 dealers"

## OREGON

### Lincoln
**Lincoln City Antique District**
16+ shops on Highway 101

### North Bend
**Sherman Avenue Antique Shops**

### Portland
Antique Capital of Oregon
Over 100 shops

# Largest Malls

### Sellwood
**Sellwood Antique District**
13th St.
26+ shops

## *PENNSYLVANIA*

### Adamstown
**Renninger's Antique Market**
PA Turnpike, Exit 21, Route 272
717/385-0104
Several hundred booths

**South Pointe Antiques**
Route 272 & Denver Road
717/484-1026
135 dealers

**Stoudt's Black Angus**
PA Turnpike, Exit 21, Route 272
717/484-4385
Over 500 booths

### Beaver Falls
**Leonard's Antqs. Uniques Mega Mall**
2586 Constitution
704/847-2304
58,000 sq. ft. - 300 dealers

### Denver
**Denver Antique District**
Numerous shops and markets located
n Route 272

### Export
**chmidt's Springhouse Antiques**
oute 66 at Pfeffer Road
24/325-2577
,000 sq. ft.

### Gettysburg
**T. & G's Antique Collectible Co-op**
31 York Road
7/334-0361
500 sq. ft.

### Hawley
**stle Antiques & Reproductions**
5 Welwood Ave.
300-345-1667
cated in 1880s granite castle

### Irwin
**tiques Odds & Ends**
Lincoln Hwy. E. (Route 30)
/863-9769
rge buildings - 8,000 sq. ft.

### Ronks
**Antique Market-Place**
5 Lincoln Hwy. E.
'687-6345
0 sq. ft.

### Sciota
**Halloran's Antiques**
Fenner Ave.
717/992-4651
3 barns full

### Shamokin
**Odds & Ends Store**
415 N. Shamokin St.
717/648-2013
8,000 sq. ft.

## *RHODE ISLAND*

### Barrington
**The Stock Exchange & The Annex**
57 Maple Ave. & 232 Wascca Ave.
401/245-4170

### Newport
Aardvark Antiques
475 1/2 Thames
401/849-7233
65,000 sq. ft.

**Armory Antique Center**
365 Thames St.
401/848-2398
125 dealers - 8,000 sq. ft.

### Portsmouth
**Eagles Nest Antique Center**
3101 E. Main Road
401/683-3500
124 dealers

### Providence
**"Wickeden Street Antique District"**
Numerous shops within walking distance.

### Warren
**Warren Antique Center**
5 Miller St.
401/245-5461
Located in old theatre - 4 levels - 100+ dealers

## *SOUTH CAROLINA*

### Aiken
**Aiken Antique Mall**
112-114 Laurens St. S.W.
803/648-6700
13,000 sq. ft. - 50 dealers

**Swan Antique Mall**
3557 Richland Ave. W.
803/643-9922
20,000 sq. ft.

### Landrum
**Landrum Antique Mall**
221 Rutherford Road
864/457-4000
10,000 sq. ft.

### West Columbia
**378 Antique Mall**
620 Sunset Blvd.
803/791-3132
20,000 sq. ft.

## *SOUTH DAKOTA*

### Belle Fourche
**Love That Shoppe**
515 State St.
605/892-4006
9,000 sq. ft. - 50 plus dealers

**Old Grizz Trading Post**
2207 Fifth Ave.
605/892-6668
6,800 sq. ft.

### Canton
**Canton Square Emporium**
121 E. Fifth St.
605/987-3152

**Lincoln County Antique Center**
123 W. 5th St.
605/987-4114
10,000 sq. ft.

### Hill City
**Orloske Antiques**
Deerfield Road
605/574-2181
10,000 sq. ft.

### Mitchell
**Second Impression Palace**
412 N. Main St.
605/996-1948
2 full floors

### Tea
**I-29 Antiques & Collectibles**
46990 271st St.
605/368-5810
10,000 sq. ft. - 75 dealers

## *TENNESSEE*

### Bartlett
**Antique Gallery**
6044 Stage Road
901/385-2544
35,000 sq. ft. - 150 dealers

**Upstage Antiques**
6214 Stage Road
901/385-0035
Large selection of quality antiques

### Chattanooga
**East Town Antique Mall**
6503 Slater Road
423/899-5498
30,000 sq. ft. - over 300 booths and showcases

### Collierville
**Sheffield Antiques**
708 W. Poplar Ave.
901/853-7822
150 dealers

### Columbia
**Accents & Antiques of Columbia**
Northway Shopping Center, Suite 123
119 Nashville Hwy. - Hwy. 31
931/380-8975
7,000 sq. ft.

### Cordova
**Antique Market of Cordova**
1740 N. Germantown Pkwy., Suite 18
901/759-0414
8,500 sq. ft. - 30+ dealers

### Dickson
**Hamilton Place**
202-210 N. Mulberry St.
615/446-5255
9,000 sq. ft. - 48 booths

### Dyersburg
**Walton's Antique**
2470 Lake Road
901/287-7086
12,000 sq. ft.

### Franklin
**Franklin Antique Mall**
251 Second Ave. S.
615/790-8593
14,000 sq. ft. - 100 dealers

### Hickman
Antique Malls of Tennessee
2 Sykes Road
Gordonsville Highway
615/683-6066

### Jackson
**Brook Shaw's Old Country Store**
Casey Jones Village
901/668-1223
6,000 sq. ft.

### Knoxville
**Antiques Plus**
4500 Walker Blvd.
423/687-6536
12,000 sq. ft.

**Campbell Station Antiques**
620 Campbell Station Road
423/966-4348
10,000 sq. ft.

**Homespun Craft & Antique Mall**
Village Green Shopping Center
11523 Kingston Pike
423/671-3444
9,000 sq. ft. - 180 dealers

# Largest Malls

### Lebanon
**Lebanon Antique District**
Downtown Lebanon
"Public Square"

### Morristown
**Olde Town Antique Mall**
181 W. Main St.
423/581-6423
15,000 sq. ft.

### Murfreesboro
**Antique Centers I & II**
2213-2219 S. Church St.
615/896-5188
30,000 sq. ft.

### Nashville
**Antique Merchants Mall**
2015 8th Ave. S.
615/292-7811
6,000 sq. ft.

### Sevierville
**Riverside Antique & Collectible Mall**
1442 Winfield Dunn Pkwy.
423/429-0100
35,000 sq. ft.

**Volunteer Showcase Mall**
1436 Winfield Dunn Pkwy., Suite 2
423/429-7666
85 Showcases

### Shelbyville
**The Antique Marketplace**
208 Elm St.
931/684-8493
100 plus dealers

### Smithville
**Fuston's Antiques**
123 W. Market St.
615/597-5232
25,000 sq. ft.

## TEXAS

### Abilene
**Poppy's Antique Mall**
126 S. Access Road
915/692-7755
10,000 sq. ft.

### Amarillo
**Historical Route 66**
Sixth Street
806/372-3901
Numerous shops located between Western and Georgia on Sixth Street on Historical Route 66.

### Baird
More than 20 antique shops and related businesses.

### Dallas
**Unlimited Ltd.**
The Antique Mall & Tea Room
15201 Midway Road
972/490-4085
175 antique and collectible shops

**White Elephant Antiques Warehouse**
1026 N. Industrial Blvd.
214/871-7966
18,000 sq. ft. - 75 dealers

### Fort Worth
**Harris Antiques & Imports**
7600 Scott St.
817/246-8400
440,000 sq. ft.

### Houston
**Almeda Antique Mall**
9837 Almeda Genoa
713/941-7744
100 shops and showcases

**Carolyn Thompson's Antique Center of Texas**
1001 W. Loop N.
713/688-4211
200 plus dealers

**Trade Mart**
Sam Houston Tollway @ Hammerly
713/467-2506
70,000 sq. ft.

### Lubbock
**Antique Mall of Lubbock**
7907 W. 19th St.
806/796-2166
24,000 sq. ft. - 150 booths

### Trinity
**Teddie Bears Antiques & Collectibles**
Hwy. 19 S., Route 4
409/594-6321
Two acres of antiques and junque to browse

## VERMONT

### Barre
**East Barre Antique Mall**
133 Mill St.
802/479-5190
12,000 sq. ft.

### Quechee
**Quechee Gorge Village**
Route 4
1-800-438-5565
450 dealers

## VIRGINIA

### Culpeper
**Country Shoppes of Culpeper**
10046 James Monroe Hwy.
540/547-4000
15,000 sq. ft. - 100+ dealers

### Fredericksburg
**Caroline Square**
910-916 Caroline St.
540/371-4454
50 dealers

### Mechanicsville
**Mechanicsville Antique Mall**
7508 Mechanicsville Turnpike
804/730-5091
30,000 sq. ft. - 100 booths

### Richmond
**West End Antiques Mall**
6504 Horsepen Road
804/285-1916
Combined 36,000 sq. ft. - 160 dealers

### Salem
**Wright Place Antique Mall**
27 W. Main St.
540/389-8507

## WASHINGTON

### Centralia
**Centralia Square Antique Mall**
201 S. Pearl St.
360/736-6406
2 large buildings - 90 dealers

### Kalama
**Kalama Antique District**
1st St.
150 dealers

### Walla Walla
**Shady Lawn Antiques & Expresso**
711 N. Rose St.
509/529-2123
10,000 sq. ft.

## WEST VIRGINIA

### Bridgeport
**Shahady's Antiques**
214 E. Main St.
304/842-6691
Over 500 pieces of furniture

### Charleston
**Hale Street Antiques**
213 Hale St.
304/345-6040
3 full floors

## WISCONSIN

### Appleton
**Fox River Antique Mall**
1074 S. Van Dyke Road
920/731-9699
20,000 sq. ft. - 165 dealers

### Bonduel
**Heathside Antique Mall**
129 S. Cecil St.
715/758-6200

### Lake Mills
**Old Mills Market**
109 N. Main St.
920/648-3030

### Osceola
**Osceola Antiques**
117 Cascade St.
715/294-2886
11,000 sq. ft.

### Sheboygan
**Craftmasters Antiques & Restorations**
2034 N. 15th St.
920/452-2524
Three full floors of merchandise

### Tomah
**Antique Mall of Tomah**
I-94 & Hwy. 21 E.
608/372-7853
60 dealers

### Wausau
**Kimberly's Old House Gallery**
1600 Jonquil Lane
715/359-5077
10,000 sq. ft.

## WYOMING

### Cheyenne
**Antiques Central**
2311 Reed Ave.
307/638-6181
7500 sq. ft.

**Sidekick Antique Mart**
1408 S. Greeley Hwy.
307/635-3136

### Laramie
**Golden Flea Gallery**
725 Skyline Road
307/745-7055
140 dealers